6·2·98

Giant of the *Grand Siècle*

Giant of the *Grand Siècle*

THE FRENCH ARMY, 1610–1715

John A. Lynn

University of Illinois at Urbana-Champaign

CAMBRIDGE
UNIVERSITY PRESS

PUBLISHED BY THE PRESS SYNDICATE OF THE UNIVERSITY OF CAMBRIDGE
The Pitt Building, Trumpington Street, Cambridge CB2 1RP, United Kingdom

CAMBRIDGE UNIVERSITY PRESS
The Edinburgh Building, Cambridge CB2 2RU, United Kingdom
40 West 20th Street, New York, NY 10011–4211, USA
10 Stamford Road, Oakleigh, Melbourne 3166, Australia

© John A. Lynn 1997

First published 1997

Printed in the United States of America

Typeset in ITC Galliard

Library of Congress Cataloging-in-Publication Data
Lynn, John A. (John Albert), 1943–
Giant of the grand siècle : the French Army, 1610–1715 / John A. Lynn.
p. cm.
Includes bibliographical references.
ISBN 0–521–57273–8 (hardbound)
1. France. Armée – History – 17th century. 2. France. Armée – History –
18th century. 3. France – History, Military – 1610–1643. 4. France – History,
Military – 1643–1715. I. Title.
UA702.L9523 1997
355'.00944' 09032 – dc20
96–22239
CIP

*A catalogue record for this book is available from
the British Library.*

ISBN 0 521 57273 8 hardback

To the memory of my parents,
Judd Benjamin Lynn (1903–1958)
Adelle Savage Lynn (1908–1985)

Contents

PART FIVE: THE PRACTICE OF WAR

Preface

I keep safe the memory of an invisible giant. The son of kings, this armed colossus once towered above his foes to bestride a continent. He ate a mountain of bread and drank a river of wine at each meal. Yet historians renowned for being the most forward looking and sophisticated in skill and interpretation, fail to see him; they write as if he never existed. He must be invisible. Otherwise, how could something so big, so costly, and so powerful remain so long unnoticed? This book is a portrait of that giant, the French army of the *grand siècle*, made visible again.

THE GREAT UNKNOWN

As a subject for historical inquiry, the army of the *grand siècle* has attracted the attention of only a few diligent scholars and talented amateurs, but it has never been at center stage, in the spotlight. Such neglect seems all the more bizarre given the self-evident importance of the subject. The army of the *grand siècle* was the largest institution created by the monarchy; in the 1690s its paper strength climbed to 420,000 men, over six times larger that it had been a century before. The wars of Louis XIII and Louis XIV defined the borders of the state, and the needs of the army that fought those wars shaped its government. Supporting such a gargantuan force also exhausted France and in one fashion or another imposed upon the lives of most of her population. Certainly such an army deserves to be cast in a central role. Yet it remains but dimly perceived.

It is easier to prove that few have seen the giant than to explain why. An understanding of this disregard, such selective blindness, must account for, first, those with a predisposition to regard the history of war as something of inherent interest or practical value and, second and more importantly, those with a broader view of the past for its own sake.

French authors who turned to history to satisfy an audience excited by tales of martial glory, a popular audience that has always seemed to be there, extolled French Imperial conquests, not the *grand siècle*. The glare of Napoleonic brilliance outshone the radiance of the Sun King. The Napoleonic wars have probably attracted more attention from nineteenth and twentieth century readers than any other period of French military history. Library shelves groan under the weight of works on the campaigns of Napoleon, yet to my knowledge the only complete history of the campaigns of Louis XIV was written in the first half of the eighteenth century – the seven-volume study by the marquis de Quincy, *Histoire militaire de Louis le Grand roi de France* (1727).

Soldier historians who studied military history for what it might teach them about the conduct of future wars also shunned Louis XIV in favor of Napoleon I. The Section historique of the French general staff, which operated between 1899 and 1914, provides one measure of the military's interests; it published eighty volumes on the Revolutionary and Napoleonic wars but only six specialized studies dealing with the reign of Louis XIV.[1] After all, the emperor had marched his armies across Europe, from Lisbon to Moscow, while Louis's forces ventured less far from home. Napoleon's wars were short and decisive, brought to a head in climactic battles, at least until the debacle of 1812, while Louis's conflicts dragged on as long, indecisive, and costly wars of attrition. In short, there seemed to be more to be learned from a study of Napoleon's military genius. To this day, war colleges dissect the Ulm-Austerlitz and Jena-Auerstadt campaigns, but they have little interest in the siege-dominated wars fought by Louis's great generals.

It is harder to explain why historians of a more general cast of mind have not discussed the military institutions of the seventeenth century to any great degree. Only in the nineteenth century did Europeans turn seriously to writing history as something other than a means of memorializing the past, mining it for moral examples, or employing it to abstract rules and principles. The professional historians living in that period studied the *grand siècle* and produced major biographies, histories, and collections of documents. One such collection assembled by Jean Pelet and François Vault, *Mémoires militaires relatifs à la succession d'Espagne* (1835–62), dealt with military matters extensively, but it was the exception. Pelet was, in fact, a general with the staff and the director of the military archives. While Richelieu, Louis XIV, Colbert, and other dominant figures received their biographers, the army remained in the shadows. Perhaps the most obvious answer for this neglect is that French scholars left the discussion of military phenomena to military enthusiasts and specialists, who, as we have seen, had other things on their minds.

The lack of interest in seventeenth-century warfare among French scholars in the decades after World War I is more easy to comprehend. The great war became the focus of professional military studies, pushing aside the

---

[1] John A. Lynn, "The Publications of the *Section historique*, 1899–1915," *Military Affairs* (April 1973), 56–59. The count of volumes given here is a count of volumes not of titles, so multivolume works are added in by the number of volumes in the work.

Napoleonic fixation, while the long casualty lists horrified the intellectuals. How could those who witnessed the massacre of Verdun speak of war without revulsion? As a consequence, the modern intellectual's inherent distaste for the study of war only grew. But the historical community harbored additional motives for turning a blind eye to the military past. Shock at the human cost of World War I was amplified by fashions in professional historical studies in France as they turned decidedly to the left. Warfare seemed a far less important subject for study than did society and economics, which, it was claimed, explained the existence of armed conflict in the first place. The most notable historical work on the wars of Louis XIV that appeared between the world wars centered on Vauban, the great fortress builder, perhaps as a reflection of the Maginot Line psychology. Certainly, having just endured a monstrous war of attrition, the French had no desire to relive the endless wars fought by the Sun King.

After World War II, the giant remained unseen. Historiographical trends in France and elsewhere continued to drift to the left. All too often, enthusiasm for social history was coupled with contempt for political history. Many French scholars became fascinated with history "from below" and emphasized the life of the lower classes; others stressed the need to study the "*longue durée*," rejecting political events, most notably wars, as mere surface phenomena. Particularly in America, the historical community has most often paid attention to military institutions only to condemn them and has mistakenly censured those who concentrate on the military past as individuals who must idealize war. Adding to this sense of revulsion is the notion that while the exploration of other phenomena is uplifting and part of a positive social or political program, the study of military history possesses no social value. The American intelligentsia's natural and abiding distaste for military history became even deeper during the Vietnam war. Today, the "cutting edge" of scholarship welcomes gender and cultural studies to form a blessed trinity with social themes and condemns the history of war and military institutions with what seems to be growing self-righteous conviction.

There have been some recent attempts, however, to ascertain what has been invisible for so long. André Corvisier, in his social examination, *L'armée française de la fin du XVIIe siècle au ministère du Choiseul: Le soldat* (1964), translated the study of the military into a mode acceptable to dominant currents of interpretation. Corvisier has been a key mover in the effort to read military institutions back into their social context, an effort solemnized in numerous books written in a "war and society" vein. While war and society studies may have opened the door to the profession at large, the price of grudging and partial approval has been the acceptance of an agenda dictated by those with little interest in the military per se. A related trend that has won ground for military history of the *ancien régime* is the debate over a Military Revolution in early modern Europe. This began with the publication of an inaugural lecture by Michael Roberts in 1956 and accelerated with the publication in 1988 of Geoffrey Parker's *The Military Revolution:*

Military innovation and the rise of the West, 1500–1800. While this historiographical discussion has stimulated a great deal of new work, it has hurried
on to sweeping conclusions before mastering the details. In their rush, scholars have again passed by the army of the *grand siècle* without giving it much
of a second glance. Clearly the theory of the Military Revolution cries out for
a study of the greatest of the seventeenth-century armies, but it has yet to
appear.

HISTORIOGRAPHICAL LIMITATIONS

This account of why the army of the *grand siècle* has remained largely invisible does not mean that it received no attention. But the treatments devoted
to it have been brief or narrowly conceived, and they have fragmented the
subject by time and focus. Sections of major surveys describe the hidden
form. In Hanoteau's massive *Histoire de la nation française* (1925), François
Reboul spent 130 pages on "les armées du *grand siècle*," and in the first tome
of the new *Histoire militaire de France* (1991), André Corvisier and Anne
Blanchard between them wrote 180 pages on the period from 1598 to 1715.
Both of these general coverages are typical of their eras, the first emphasizing
the nuts and bolts of military technology and organization while detailing
specific campaigns, and the second more driven by the modern French preoccupation with the social details of military institutions. But while they
differ profoundly, they share the same brevity.

    To these overviews must be added a few rare and dated classic studies
with narrower focuses. Here, biographies have dominated, and those of
Louvois and Le Tellier say a great deal about the state of scholarship on the
army. Camille Rousset's four-volume *Histoire de Louvois* provides a detailed
account of that famous war minister, an account unequaled by any subsequent work; Corvisier's more recent *Louvois* (1983) can be best regarded as a
readable abridgment of Rousset. Scholars still must use the *Histoire de Louvois*
as their best source, yet it was published in 1862–64. What other field of
history would attract so little modern work that historians must still constantly appeal to a study well over a century old? Much the same is true for
Louis André, *Michel Le Tellier et l'organisation de l'armée monarchique*, a crucial piece of scholarship that appeared in 1906. To these biographies must be
added lives of major military commanders, such as Condé, Turenne, Vauban,
and Villars. Two brief descriptions of the French army at particular moments
also provide points of reference, the short volume by Victor Belhomme,
L'armée française en 1690, and H. Pichat's article, "Les Armées de Louis XIV
en 1674," but again, regardless of their merits, these efforts, both by professional military officers, date back to 1895 and 1910, respectively. The dates tell
the story; the historiography of the army has grown weak with old age. With
few exceptions, modern "war and society" additions have been too narrow,
esoteric, or tangential to reinvigorate the subject as a whole.

    If scholarship on the army suffers from being both sparse and aged, it is also disjointed. The seventeenth-century brought constant and important evolution in military institutions and practices, but attempts to study this change only through examinations that deal with it during a short time span distort its coherent and often gradual nature. Perhaps such distortion comes as a nearly unavoidable byproduct of the emphasis on biographies, since such works try to encompass a major subject within the decades of an individual's active life. Biography not only encapsulates history; the biographer tends to champion his or her subject. This is certainly the case for studies of Le Tellier and Louvois, and the same can be said for treatments of French affairs under the Richelieu administration. Such segmented approaches, instead of dealing with the military in a more continuous fashion, worry too much about which minister deserves the prize as the most important innovator.

Recently, a few historians have turned to the army as a subject of study once again, yet while they have supplied more pieces to the puzzle, they have yet to assemble the whole. David Parrott's dissertation, "The Administration of the French Army During the Ministry of Cardinal Richelieu," while superb, only covers the years 1635–37 in detail. A conference held in 1985, "La présence de la guerre au XVIIe siècle," and a two-volume set, *Guerre et paix dans l'Europe du XVIIe siècle* (1991), may mark something of a renaissance in the subject. Doubtless, the efforts of Corvisier, Blanchard, and others have been admirable, but they are limited by a desire to deal with the military past in a way acceptable to current fashions in historical scholarship. Attempts to deal with the army within the parameters of contemporary historiographical themes most often stress the army exclusively as a social institution and neglect or even deny its essence. Ultimately, armies are for fighting, and they define themselves in combat and in preparation for combat. But in his discussion of French military history between 1598 and 1715, in *Histoire militaire de France*, André Corvisier devotes only 5 of his 140 pages to weapons and tactics, a subject that will take up several chapters here. He and other current historians seem fascinated by such questions as the Invalides and prisoners of war, topics that are marvelously off the point most of the time, since pensioners and prisoners have ceased to be involved in the primary combat duties of the army. It may be part of the soldier's life, but it is not the "military experience" but the military itself that most needs attention. There is no question that old-line military historians gave too little concern to the common soldier, and if the field is to heed John Keegan's challenge to paint the true face of battle, it must become more inclusive. But modern treatments of military institutions seem to err in the other direction.

Another problem associated with current studies of the army is that they stress the impact of war – both the human cost of conflict and the influence of war on state formation – without coming to grips with the institutions of warfare. As always, dealing immediately with consequence without adequate knowledge of process can result in error. This is particularly obvious in discussions of state formation, the most exciting and promising line of inquiry intertwined with the history of war and armies. Studies with this focus too

often base their conclusions about the origins and nature of Bourbon absolutism on an imperfect understanding of the army of the *grand siècle*. In a
typical example, the generally fine book Bruce D. Porter's, *War and the rise
of the state* (1994), is at its weakest when discussing the France of Louis XIV.
In this case, the fault lies not so much with the author, who tried to use the
best available scholarship, as with that scholarship itself, which is outdated
and limited. It is hard not to agree with David Kaiser, another student of
state formation, who complains, "we lack any really systematic studies of
[Louis XIV's] armies."[2]

THE APPROACH AND GOALS OF THIS VOLUME

In *Giant of the Grand Siècle*, I hope to provide that needed systematic study.
This volume accepts the army of the *grand siècle* as the main player of the
piece, not as a minor character hovering in the background. Placing the army
in the preeminent role does not reflect a moral judgment, for the army will
be alternately hero and villain; instead it results from a recognition of the
military's great importance.

In order to reveal the army's outline and character as never before, this
volume examines a broad range of material over an extended period of time.
Only a comprehensive method that explores the subject in both its breadth
and depth can expose interrelationships and trace developments – the classic
issues of continuity and change. While this is the fundamental goal, it feeds
into other purposes. Once achieved, an understanding of interrelationships
and developments redefines the part played by the army in grander historical
dramas.

Failure to consider different levels of military institutions in a single study
has led to misconceptions even by the finest scholars. For example, historians
and political scientists who concern themselves with state formation posit a
direct one-to-one relationship between military expansion and bureaucratization and centralization; it seems reasonable because larger armies must have
required that the central government collect and disburse more resources to
support those forces. But this fundamental assumption fares badly in these
pages, where it will be demonstrated that the army was not financed and administered from the center of power alone. The army also drew heavily upon
provincial sources of funding and, consequently, answered to institutions
and personnel based in the provinces, not in Paris. In addition, individual
field armies provided their own logistical systems, usually through private
contractors, and collected money and goods for their own needs on campaign. Furthermore, at the lowest level, regimental officers, notably colonels
and captains, contributed their own wealth and credit to the maintenance of
their units and carried out many supply and support functions that today

---

[2] David Kaiser, *Politics and War* (Cambridge, MA: 1990), 153.

would fall to a central administration. With four different levels of finance and control, the relationship between army growth and state formation is far more complex and diffuse than current scholarship realizes.

Seeing things over too short a time period can be as damaging as trying to limit the range of institutions and practices considered. In his classic, and generally excellent, study of Le Tellier as secretary of state for war, Louis André credits Le Tellier with turning away from private contractors for logistical support and providing instead "direct service by the state."[3] But André could only claim this because he did not look further than the career of Le Tellier. Later, under Louis XIV, supply by private contractors, *munitionnaires*, again became the rule. What André described as a forward-looking innovation was, it will be seen, only a catch-as-catch-can response to a financial breakdown that forced contractors to abandon the army. Only in taking the long view can the contribution of each minister be set in its proper place. More careful examination reveals not an administrative revolution at any one point, but a steady evolution in administrative practice and power from the early seventeenth century into the 1690s at least.

Weighing change and continuity in the army of the *grand siècle* interjects this book into the historiographical discussion of the Military Revolution. At times, this theoretical debate turns into a search for some magic technology that transformed war and armies. For Geoffrey Parker, it is the *trace italienne* fortress, while Jeremy Black emphasizes the introduction of the bayonet that relegated the pike to the status of an historical relic. This volume rejects both assertions and others in favor of an evolutionary path not driven by technological innovation but by conceptual and institutional development.

By covering so much territory through an inclusive and integrated approach, this book not only describes the army of the *grand siècle* and contributes to present-day scholarly dialogue, but it can provide a starting point for other studies. Perhaps it can serve as both an encyclopedia of detail and as a baseline of interpretation. If so, these pages could be of value for investigations yet to be conceived and debates yet to be joined.

To fulfill its promise of revealing the features of the giant to all, this volume must serve a variety of readers, from French historians knowledgeable about the chronology, personalities, and institutions of the *grand siècle*, to military specialists less well informed about these matters but steeped in the details of military technology, tactics, and practices. To explain the subject to one audience requires supplying information already familiar to another. Each individual reader ought to bear in mind this need to cover what he or she may regard as assumed. By the same token, an expert in a particular field of study may desire more discussion on that area than this volume presents, but because the volume takes on a wide spectrum of time and material,

---

[3] Louis André, *Michel Le Tellier et l'organisation de l'armée monarchique* (Paris: 1906), 434. In a later work, *Michel Le Tellier et Louvois* (Paris: 1942), André did consider a broader time span, but his first book is still the classic.

it cannot examine each topic in all its complexity. The importance of the subject requires that this work reach out to different audiences and that it be cast in broad terms, and the benefits of this approach more than compensate for any shortcomings it entails.

SKETCHING THE IMAGE

Before beginning the long and complicated task of painting a full portrait of the giant, a brief sketch of his features can serve as a guide. Begin with the four most prominent features of the subject: the transition in army style from aggregate contract to state commission, the tremendous growth of the army, the limitations put on performance and policy by financial constraints, and the evolutionary character of military change other than army expansion. The French army, particularly its infantry, had once been an aggregate of temporary mercenary units and private forces raised by grandees, but by the mid-1600s, it had become the province of the king alone, a royal instrument with a large permanent establishment directly commanded by the monarch. This new style of army then expanded to unprecedented size. When France entered the Thirty Years' War, the army swelled to proportions too large for the state to support and control, and troops became predatory on French society. Later growth during the personal reign of Louis XIV did not cause such turmoil, but in a financial sense, the Bourbon state never grew into its army. As a consequence, administration and supply were conducted in ways that most conveniently, though often inefficiently, mobilized credit. The need to turn to financial expedients hamstrung administrative reform. Lack of adequate funding and the multi-tiered form of administration explains the evolutionary pace of administrative reform while army growth made revolutionary leaps. Even in this environment, however, military administration made great strides in regularizing the supply of food, clothing, equipment, and armament as never before.

The officer corps reflected a unique culture of command based upon aristocratic values that attracted young nobles to the service but limited the professionalization of the army. On the regimental and company level, Louvois encouraged practices and institutions designed to increase the competence of officers, but his efforts ran afoul of the need to commission rich men because their wealth and credit were required for the proper maintenance of their units. Once again the financial straits of the government set limits to the extent of reform. However, Louis XIV was able to curb the arrogant independence of his generals through such measures as the *ordre de tableau*, which established seniority as the principle.

Men from the lower reaches of society supplied the rank and file, who shared little in common with their aristocratic officers. Common soldiers were not expected to display great commitment or initiative, although the promise of better care for the wounded and veterans was designed to bind the soldier more to the state and to encourage enlistments. Ostensibly voluntary enlistment provided most of the recruits; however, recruiters often employed deceit and violence to fill their quotas. The need for manpower in the last two of Louis's wars inspired the creation of a provincial militia system to conscript men into the ranks. This device was not meant and did not operate as a replacement for voluntary enlistment; instead it was an expedient required to build an army larger than could have been assembled through traditional means.

Tactically, the French did not experience a radical Military Revolution during the *grand siècle*. To a large degree, tactics changed only incrementally because they rested upon unaltering assumptions concerning the limited reliability of the rank and file. Infantry armament and tactics altered as the French integrated Dutch and Swedish advances and, most importantly, adopted drill. Fusils gradually replaced muskets, while pikes gave ground before firearms until the bayonet eliminated the pike altogether. Cavalry weapons and practices remained remarkably stable throughout the century. Artillery also changed surprisingly little, although it had the chance to benefit from important improvements in cannon design. At midcentury, the French represented the highest levels of tactical competence, but by the War of the Spanish Succession, they had probably slipped behind the English and the Dutch.

Operationally, the French came to avoid battle and embrace siege warfare. The seventeenth century brought a conception of battle as a test of will and order, in which it seemed more important to absorb casualties without breaking than it was to inflict losses on the enemy. This style of forbearance in combat emphasized the costly nature of battle, and this, combined with the indecisive character of most combat in the field, led Louis, his advisors, and his generals to prefer siege operations. Thanks to the genius and energy of Vauban, the French mastered fortress construction and siege warfare as did no other power in Europe. Fortifications and siege warfare also became so important because fortresses controlled territory that could be exploited for money and material while fortifications denied these resources to the enemy. Thus, the fact that the state never mastered the ability to pay for its own army underlay operational and strategic decisions. The state's own flaws tethered the giant.

In one sense, it is surprising that a volume like this has taken so long to appear, yet in another, this may be a book too soon. The effort is both necessary and necessarily incomplete: necessary because the topic is too important to remain without a general overview, and necessarily incomplete because so few detailed studies exist to supply the basis for synthesis. The highest goal of such an undertaking is not simply to spread knowledge, but rather to convince others of the value of the topic and the need for further work. Ultimately, if this book is successful, it will stimulate the studies that will make it obsolete in the future. It is scholarship on a suicide mission.

Acknowledgments

O VER the several years that this project has consumed, many organizations and individuals have aided me in my work. Research for this
project was made possible by a N.E.H. Summer Stipend, a Hewlett Summer
Research Stipend, and grants from the Program in Arms Control, Disarma-
ment, and International Security, the College of Liberal Arts and Sciences,
and the Research Board at the University of Illinois at Urbana-Champaign.
I am also indebted to my colleagues for a one-year appointment to the
Center for Advanced Study at the University of Illinois, which allowed me
an all-important unobstructed year to pursue research and writing on this
volume. Publication of *Giant of the Grand Siècle* has been aided by a subven-
tion to the press granted by the Research Board of my university.

Parts of this volume have appeared as journal articles or as chapters. Much
of Chapter 2 appeared in *French Historical Studies* as "Recalculating French
Army Growth During the *Grand siècle*, 1610–1715," and the majority of Chap-
ter 6 first saw light in the *Journal of Modern History* as "How War Fed War:
The Tax of Violence and Contributions During the *grand siècle*." Chapters 14
and 15 make use of material and text that first appeared in "Tactical Evolution
in the French Army, 1560–1660," published in *French Historical Studies*.
Important sections of Chapter 16 come from "The *trace italienne* and the
Growth of Armies: the French Case," from the *Journal of Military History* and
"Food, Funds, and Fortresses: Resource Mobilization and Positional Warfare
in the Campaigns of Louis XIV," an essay in my *Feeding Mars: Logistics in
Western Warfare from the Middle Ages to the Present*.

Clinton Grubbs, Jeff McKeage, George Satterfield, Brian Sandberg, David
Stewart, and Ed Tenace ably served as my research assistants. Other of my
graduate students at Illinois and at my second campus, The Ohio State
University, have helped me with their comments and questions; I thank
them all, most importantly Roy McCullough and William Reger. I owe
thanks to Douglas Baxter, Ron Martin, and James B. Wood for providing
me with valuable research materials and to Charles Tilly and Paul Sonnino

for reading drafts of various chapters. My very dear friend Frederic C. Jaher has put in hours of labor editing this entire volume, sacrifice well beyond the call of duty. He has saved me from myself time and again. Geoffrey Parker, once my colleague at the University of Illinois, served as friend and foil to my ideas and plans. While we have not always agreed on details or interpretations, he both encouraged my efforts and helped me secure funding for them. And I must thank the readers for Cambridge University Press, Jeremy Black and, especially, Frank Tallett, for their comments and suggestions, which have made this a better volume.

Lastly, once again I am in debt to my wife, Andrea E. Lynn, who has supported me and my work with her usual blend of personal grace and editorial talent.

PART ONE

CONTEXT AND PARAMETERS

I

Contexts of Military Change
in the Grand Siècle

THE classical façade of Versailles faces the gardens decorated with statues and fountains, traversed by gravel paths. Walking through those gardens, watching the fountains play – if you are lucky enough to be there when they do – and glancing back at the palace, it is hard not to think of Racine and Molière, Le Vau and Le Nôtre, or Lully and Charpentier – hard not to be impressed with the glory of the *grand siècle*. But at the same time, Versailles is too massive, too overwhelming to be graceful. Versailles symbolizes something other than the culture of the *grand siècle*; it is more about power than about art. Carved trophies of arms with helmets and weapons stand at attention along the roof line, as if to announce that Versailles arose as much from the victories of armies as from the inspiration of architects.

The *grand siècle,* for all its glittering accomplishments, was, at base, a century of war. Considering only the major conflicts that afflicted France, over half of the calendar years from 1610 through 1715 witnessed either interstate or civil war; and if minor conflicts are added in, the proportion rises to three quarters. The primary force of the Bourbons was their army, since except for brief periods the French proved unable or unwilling to maintain a great fleet. The army grew to overshadow all other institutions of the monarchy in size and in appetite. So the record of the seventeenth century remains incomplete without the history of the army; few who walked the paths at Versailles 300 years ago would have disputed that fact.

In order to be understood properly, this description of the giant of the *grand siècle* should be considered in at least four contexts. The first is most theoretical and places French military development on a scale of army evolution for over a millennium. Changes within the army during the seventeenth century ought not to be seen as isolated developments but as part of an important military evolution that affected both France and the rest of Europe. The second context concerns the evolution not of military institutions, but of internal and international conflict during the early modern era, 1495–1815. The *grand siècle* witnessed a transition in the intensity of warfare;

3

Europe endured a horribly destructive series of wars before 1660, but after 1660 the character of warfare moderated to a degree. This moderation both reflected and influenced the evolution of armies.

The third necessary context is the narrative of French wars, 1610–1715, that provides the background for all that is discussed in this volume. An account of those conflicts must precede materials presented in the following chapters, for it provides the factual framework of issues, events, and personalities. The fact that French monarchs were unable to pay for this long series of wars not only hamstrung strategy but warped institutional reform; so the fourth context must be fiscal. An understanding of the financial limitations of the Bourbon monarchy is absolutely fundamental to any intelligent discussion of military development during the *grand siécle*. The army related to financial restrictions both as effect and as cause – effect in that inadequate resource mobilization shaped the army, and cause in that the appetite of war defined the financial needs of the state.

THE EVOLUTION OF ARMIES, 800–2000

The army of the *grand siècle* should not be portrayed as static; on the contrary, it carried out one of the fundamental transitions of military history. To appreciate the significance of that transition, the army's institutional development is best considered as part of a long-term evolution in army style across Europe. Unfortunately, there is a tendency to talk of the army of the *ancien régime* as if it were of one mold from Louis XIII, or at least from Louis XIV, through Louis XVI, changing little more than did the name of the king – the army of the Louis's. However, the army evolved a great deal over the course of the *grand siècle*, and this volume concerns itself, more than anything else, with that change. Once the new French pattern emerged, its influence extended beyond the borders of France, for when victory crowned the Bourbon army as the preeminent force on the continent, it became a new model of military organization and administration throughout Europe.

Recently the nature of military change in early modern Europe has attracted a great deal of attention from historians. Their efforts usually center around some attempt to define a Military Revolution, commonly placing all or part of it in the seventeenth century. Michael Roberts began this quest with a provocative essay forty years ago, and the debate has picked up in recent years, thanks largely to the work of Geoffrey Parker, who recasts the span of his Military Revolution to include three centuries, 1500–1800.[1]

---

[1] Important works on the Military Revolution include the following: Michael Roberts, *The Military Revolution, 1560–1660* (Belfast: 1956); George Clark, *War and Society in the Seventeenth Century* (Cambridge: 1958); Geoffrey Parker, "The 'Military Revolution' 1560–1660 – a Myth?" *Journal of Modern History* 48 (June 1976) and *The Military Revolution: Military Innovation and the Rise of the West, 1500–1800* (Cambridge: 1988). For criticisms of the Roberts and Parker formulations of the theory, see Jeremy Black, *A Military Revolution? Military Change and European Society, 1550–1800* (Atlantic Highlands, NJ: 1991) and *European Warfare, 1660–1815*

Theories of a Military Revolution posit a radical change, or a series of radical changes, driven by innovations in weapons technology and tactics, although other factors are also given emphasis from time to time. Parker, for example, lays great stress on sixteenth-century artillery and advances in fortification that yielded a new style, the *trace italienne*, designed to counter cannon in siege warfare.

For a number of reasons, the existing theories of a single or multiple revolutions leave something to be desired. They seem to assume that military development works by great sea changes rather than by more incremental innovations. In addition, the emphasis on technology stresses hardware over conceptions of warfare and other less tangible factors that probably exerted stronger influences over early modern military institutions. Lastly, current theories tend to isolate the early modern experience from the rest of military history.

Without entirely rejecting Roberts's or Parker's visions of change, this volume accepts an alternative theory of the evolution of armies.[2] It separates the flow of European military history into seven periods defined not by military technology, periods of warfare, or great military personalities but by army style. Sketched in only its most basic outlines, the theory hypothesizes that European armies, and, for the purposes of this work specifically the French, experienced seven stages of evolution since the eighth century A.D. The breaks between one period and the next were neither instant nor absolute. Each stage retained something of the earlier style, and the key elements of the next type of army appeared in rudimentary form before they prevailed; therefore, the process was more evolutionary than revolutionary. Essential elements of army style include recruitment, remuneration, motivation, organization, command, and relationship to society and government. Technology, tactics, and training are also involved, but more as secondary factors. Judged by these criteria, Western armies have passed through seven evolutionary stages since about A.D. 800: feudal, medieval stipendiary, aggregate contract, state commission, popular conscript, mass reserve, and volunteer technical.

Feudal armies were raised by calling up aristocratic landowners who held their property in exchange for a defined term of annual military service, while towns also supported their lords by assembling urban militia. Peasants could also be summoned in accord with older practices that levied all able-bodied men, although the peasantry rarely possessed formidable military skill. Feudalism in France dates from the mid–eighth century, and it spread slowly in France and throughout western Europe. England was not feudalized until

---

(New Haven, CT: 1994), and John A. Lynn, "The *trace italienne* and the Growth of Armies: the French Case," *Journal of Military History*, July 1991, 297–330. For a collection of essays on the subject, see Cliff Rogers, ed., *The Military Revolution Debate: Readings on the Military Transformation of Early Modern Europe* (Boulder, CO: 1995).

[2] See John A. Lynn, "The Evolution of Army Style in the Modern West, 800–2000," *International History Review* 18, no. 3 (August 1996), for a discussion of this evolutionary taxonomy.

the conquest by William, and some areas such as the forests and mountains of Switzerland were never thoroughly feudalized. Since warriors could return home after fulfilling a set obligation, often forty days, an army assembled from feudal contingents had the drawback that it could only undertake limited campaigns. Staggering the call-up of feudal levies could mitigate this problem, but it also limited the number of combatants that were in the field at any one time. In addition, the political independence of major lords and even of their lesser vassals made it advantageous to seek an alternative kind of military force.

As early as the twelfth century, a burgeoning money economy, the willingness of feudal contingents to pay money in lieu of actual service, and increased resources in the hands of princes allowed them to hire soldiers either as the core of their armies or as entire forces. Thus, the English during the Hundred Years' War raised professional, paid armies to fight in France. Such medieval stipendiary armies often contained the same kind of men who would have served the king in the older feudal forces, for example, nobles who fought now for pay, booty, and out of a sense of adventure. Many of the older loyalties for the king or other war leader still held, but the commitment to service rested on money payment. At this time, infantry became a more important contingent of European armies as English longbowmen, Gascon crossbowmen, Flemish pikemen, and others hired on. Medieval stipendiary armies could still contain large feudal contingents, particularly when a prince fought on his own lands where he could summon his nobility at the height of a campaign, as did the French during the Hundred Years' War.

The difficulty of using feudal levies far from home, the excellence of paid professional troops, and the growing wealth of European monarchs encouraged them to rely even more on professional mercenaries. In the case of the French monarchy, such mercenaries were not usually subjects of the king, but Swiss, German, Italian, and others. The tendency for French monarchs to rely most heavily upon infantry hired abroad began no later than the reign of Louis XI, who showed a taste for Swiss infantry that would last for centuries. Although the French generally favored their own cavalry, in the Wars of Religion they also hired German horsemen. Armies during the late fifteenth, sixteenth, and early seventeenth centuries were assembled for particular campaigns from a combination of native French units, foreign mercenary bands, and the private armies of major nobles who offered their services in exchange for money or favor. Thus, armies were aggregate in character and built around a core of troops raised by contract, hence the term *aggregate contract army*.

Princes concluded the contracts in question not with individual soldiers but with the leaders of soldier bands, epitomized by the military entrepreneurs who supplied foreign troops. Units hired in this fashion were "off the shelf," arriving already armed, trained, and organized for battle, with their own officers. When the princely paymaster had no need of them any more, they were simply paid off and put back on the shelf until needed again. There was little need to maintain such expensive troops over the winter, in lulls during wartime, and certainly not between wars. As a result, armies regularly hit peak size, fought a major engagement, and quickly shrank to much smaller proportions. There was little need to maintain a large peacetime force, since the major occupation of that force was simply to garrison a few key fortresses and police the roads. Consider, for example, François I's use of an aggregate contract army in the war that began in 1542. After a series of inconclusive campaigns, the struggle climaxed in a double invasion of France in 1544; an English army under Henry VIII besieged and took Boulogne but did little else, while the main threat came from Charles V, who led an army into eastern France in the late spring. François reacted by contracting for as many as 16,000 Swiss in July, what seems like the last moment, and yet they arrived in time to form the heart of his main army at the camp de Jalons in late August.[3] The desire to create French units that mobilized as rapidly as did hired Swiss and Germans may explain François's attempts to create native infantry "legions" with the same off-the-shelf character. However, the quality of the foreign mercenaries was much higher than the far less professional French, and the reliance on foreign infantry remained throughout the sixteenth century.

The next stage in army evolution, labeled as the *state commission army*, emerged in the seventeenth century. Henri IV's plans for mobilization in 1610 still relied heavily upon German and Swiss mercenary units, and during the minor wars of the period 1611–34, Louis XIII repeatedly enlisted the support of private armies raised by trusted aristocratic supporters, such as the duke d'Epernon, eager to gain royal favor. The rationale behind such aggregate practices remained the need to create a field army quickly without maintaining a large and expensive peacetime force in being. But at the start of the war with Spain in 1635, Louis XIII decided not to turn to private French forces anymore, and the days of contract armies drew to an end, with one important exception. Richelieu purchased the services of the entire army led by Bernard of Saxe-Weimar in 1635; the French renewed the agreement with his remaining officers in 1639 after Bernard's death and simply appointed a Frenchman to command in his stead. Aggregate contract armies had produced forces with good technical skill but suspect loyalty. The requirement for even higher levels of technical expertise, the need for far larger armies, and the desire of monarchs to maintain peacetime forces for military and political reasons led to the state commission army.

The transition from aggregate contract to state commission armies required a change in attitudes and expectations concerning mobilization for war. The former could be assembled very rapidly; the latter took some time to come on line and essentially required a larger standing army to provide the core around which to build the wartime force. The king now issued

---

[3] See the discussion of the 1544 campaign in Ferdinand Lot, *Recherches sur les effectifs des armées françaises des Guerres d'Italie aux Guerres de Religion, 1494–1562* (Paris: 1962), 87–114.

commissions to officers, primarily French officers, to raise and train regiments in the king's name in accord with royal ordonnances. Unlike the independent contractors of before, the new units were to be the king's troops, loyal only to him. The regiments that the king commissioned remained in being for extended periods, either throughout a war or even during peacetime. Long-term army expenses probably increased, but the military and political benefits were worth it. The political advantages of this system were at least threefold: the greater loyalty of the army, liberation from dependency on private armies raised by nobles, and the creation of a standing army.[4]

At this time, the French army expanded immensely. An army that hit a theoretical, or paper, high of 80,000 in the sixteenth century reached about 200,000 in the 1630s and expanded even further to about 280,000 in the Dutch War and 420,000 in the Nine Years' War, again as paper strengths. The state commission army also entailed a large peacetime standing army, which grew even more dramatically than wartime forces over the course of the seventeenth century, hitting 165,000 in the 1680s.

Jean Meyer, who has touched on this evolution, characterizes the sixteenth-century form of what I call here the *aggregate contract army* as one in which the actual field force had to be assembled from scratch at the start of each war, because the very small peacetime contingent was completely subsumed by the wartime entity. The state commission army, which Meyer terms an *armée royalisé*, was only made possible by a tremendous growth of the peacetime army that could then serve as a basis for expansion once a conflict had begun. This peacetime force was *royalisé* because it was ingrained with discipline and commanded by an officer corps loyal to the king. For Meyer, this also required the nationalization of the army through recruiting the king's own subjects and the "renobilization" of the officer corps by relying upon the royalty's own aristocracy rather than upon foreign entrepreneurs.[5]

While providing the state with a base for wartime force expansion and a tool for internal coercion, the standing army also stimulated rudimentary military planning. States now needed to make intelligent decisions as to where to station peacetime military forces, and this implied evaluating that state's internal security, its potential enemies, and its future international goals.

To attain the large proportions that the army reached in the seventeenth century required mobilizing every available source of reliable manpower. This explains why foreign units still served in the French army, but they were recruited and trained in the same manner as French units, rather than arriving off-the-shelf. Under Louvois's direction, the French also began to conscript their own peasantry for service in the royal army in 1688, and this practice was resurrected in a somewhat different form in 1701. Conscription never provided the bulk of the army under the *ancien régime*, but it topped

---

[4] I must thank my graduate student Brian Sandberg for his contributions through our many discussions on the nature of aggregate contract and state commission armies.

[5] Jean Meyer, "'De la guerre' au XVIIe siècle," *XVII siècle*, 37 (1985), 278–79.

off the volunteer recruitment that supplied most new soldiers. The expanded officer corps provided many posts for a nobility willing, even anxious, to serve in the new army. The monarchy required that these new commissioned officers perform as disciplined servants of the king and established a strict hierarchy even for its general officers. This subordination can be credited to Louvois above all, but it was not simply his work.

This volume mainly tells the story of the way in which the French created the archetypal state commission army, which then became the paradigm for other European land forces. It is not a static story, but one of transition. Nor is it a story of continual French military preeminence, because once the French created the form, they became too set in their ways, and other European forces first met and then surpassed the French in certain important respects.

Looking past the death of Louis XIV, the state commission army remained the pattern until the French Revolution ushered in the form termed here the *popular conscript army*. Conscription which had appeared in the seventeenth century as an ancillary form of recruitment became the norm, first in the *levée en masse* of 1793, but more lastingly through the Jourdan Law of 1798, which set up a regular system of yearly conscription that set the pattern for Europe west of Russia. All soldiers were expected to be loyal to the nation, whereas only personal loyalty to the king was expected before. As it evolved after 1815, the popular conscript army did not place primary emphasis upon reserves, although the Prussians did better with their reserves than did any other power in Europe.

The late nineteenth century brought still a different kind of force, the *mass reserve army*, which relied heavily upon reserve components. No longer the *armée de métier* of the period 1815–70, the peacetime army became a training institution meant to produce numerous reserves that could be mobilized in the first weeks of a major war. While defeat in the Franco-Prussian War drove the French to military reform, they did not adopt the mass reserve army until the 1880s. Huge mass reserve armies of Europe squared off against one another at the start of World War I and World War II.

The postwar world has seen the mass reserve army give way to a final form, the *volunteer technical army*, for both political and military reasons. While European states, most notably France and Germany, supplied the paradigms for the previous army styles, the United States serves as the model for this last stage. Politically, the use of conscript armies in postcolonial wars has proven too costly, as it did for the United States in Vietnam. To American problems in South East Asia should be added the American preference for high-tech weaponry, which though very lethal requires an advanced level of competence to maintain and employ. The result is that a smaller number of self-selected, highly motivated, and highly trained volunteers form a politically more useful and militarily more effective force. With the end of the Cold War, the expenses of maintaining large forces that no longer seem to be necessary will in all likelihood drive other major powers to follow the U.S. example. But this is getting far beyond the story of the *grand siècle*.

TRANSITIONS IN THE INTENSITY OF
EUROPEAN WARS, 1495–1815

If the French army evolved over the course of the *grand siècle*, so did the intensity of warfare that abated somewhat midway through the seventeenth century. Generations of military historians have claimed that an age of limited warfare lay between the Thirty Years' War and the Wars of the French Revolution, and no historian laid more emphasis on this notion than did John U. Nef in his classic *War and Human Progress.* "For Western Europe as a whole, years of war were still the rule, years of peace the exception. Yet there was more or less continuous moderation in the fierceness of the fighting."[6] The contention is that after a period of warfare typified by irrational, primarily religious, motivations and fought with little constraint against enemy soldiers and unfortunate civilians alike, war became more rational in its goals and more humane in its conduct. As religion ceased to be a primary motivation, war became more a question of dynastic politics, and regimes fought not to destroy one another but simply for limited territorial or economic gain. At the same time, better military administration relieved the pressures that drove soldiers to prey on towns and villages just to survive, and laws of war regulated the conduct of armies toward civilians. Of course, there were exceptions to the rule, and from time to time armies committed terrible excesses, but in the main, wars became more reasonable in their goals and conduct.

From its earliest formulations, this concept has been attacked. In the European context, critics point to the assault on Prussia during the Seven Years' War, 1756–63, as one designed to eliminate Prussia, not simply to defeat it. And certainly Frederick the Great had to respond by mobilizing his state as completely as he could to fight off the Austrians and the Russians. In addition, warfare along the southern frontier of Hapsburg lands retained its religious dimension and victimized civilians on both sides.

Here it is less important to render a verdict for all of Europe than simply to judge if the period 1610–1715 witnessed a significant shift in the nature and intensity of warfare for France. The historian Jean Meyer goes so far as to talk about a transformation from *guerre totale* during the Thirty Years' War and the war with Spain to *guerre contrôlée* during the wars of Louis XIV.[7] For Meyer and also for André Corvisier, when Louis XIV seized the reins of government in 1661, he ushered in an era of limited warfare that stretched until the French Revolution again redefined warfare at the close of the eighteenth century. This characterization of warfare in the *grand siècle* cannot be accepted without comment and qualification.

French wars changed in intensity but not in some simple sense of moving

---

[6] John U. Nef, *War and Human Progress* (Cambridge, MA: 1950), 155. The period he is discussing is 1640–1740 in a chapter entitled, "Less Blood and More Money."
[7] Meyer, "'De la guerre' au XVIIe siècle," 278.

Table 1.1. *France at war, 1495–1815.*[a]

Period	Total years	War years	Interstate war years	Internal war years
1495–1559	65	50 (76.9%)	48 (73.8%)	3 (4.6%)
1560–1610	51	33 (64.7%)	17 (33.3%)	28 (54.9%)
1611–60	50	41 (82.0%)	30 (60.0%)	21 (42.0%)
1661–1715	55	36 (65.5%)	36 (65.5%)	6 (10.9%)
1716–88	73	31 (42.5%)	31 (42.5%)	0 (0%)
1789–1815	27	23 (85.2%)	23 (85.2%)	4 (14.8%)

[a]In this table, if a war consumed any part of a given year, it is counted as a war year; thus, the Nine Years' War, 1688–97, is calculated here as involving ten years.

from "total war" to "controlled war." In order to judge a transformation in warfare during the *grand siècle*, the periods that preceded and followed it need to be included in the picture; this means considering certain parameters of war from 1495 to 1815, an era that can be subdivided into six different periods of conflict from the French perspective. The parameters of war deserving of note include the number of years that knew war, the extent to which France had to fight its interstate wars on its own territory, and the degree of internal or civil conflict that afflicted the state.

Table 1.1 presents the six periods of warfare, 1495–1815, and the percentages of war years and the percentage of internal or civil war years in each.

The most cursory examination suggests that measured by the number of calendar years in which interstate war occurred, the period 1661–1715 had more in common with the eras that preceded it than it did with the remaining years of the *ancien régime*, but more needs to be said.

During the Italian Wars, 1495–1559, the Valois kings undertook wars against foreign enemies during three quarters of the years involved, and while the years after 1542 witnessed several incursions into French territory, the lion's share of the wars were fought outside France in Italy. In addition, the Valois were bothered by little internal rebellion. The era 1560–1610 encompassed the French Wars of Religion; while interstate conflicts were significant, internal and civil war dominated, as over half the calendar years involved such conflicts, and virtually all French warfare was visited upon French territory itself, with the attendant political, economic, and human costs. The major fighting in the first half of the *grand siècle* shared some important similarities with the Wars of Religion. First, internal conflict still played a very great role, since 42 percent of the years witnessed some form of internal war. Second, even during the great interstate conflict with the Empire and Spain, a great many of the campaigns took place on French soil. This internal mayhem climaxed in the years of the Fronde, which combined interstate and civil war in a deadly mixture.

In comparison to the periods 1560–1610 and 1611–60, the wars of Louis XIV were less disastrous. First, while Louis engaged in long interstate conflicts, these wars were primarily fought across French frontiers or right at the borders. Certainly some invasions did occur, particularly those that Alsace suffered during the Dutch War, but they never penetrated far and never threatened the heart of France. Second, the forces of the French king, which had behaved so rapaciously toward his own subjects during the long struggle with Spain, now showed much greater discipline when on French soil. Third and last, little internal rebellion threatened Louis; the most obvious cases came in Bordeaux and Brittany, 1675, and in the Cévennes, 1702–4, but they struck only the peripheries of France, and the first involved little fighting. Jean Meyer concludes, "This war however, was no longer, after 1660, total war: it was war harnessed [*aménagée*], rendered supportable for states, for participants, and populations."[8] But he goes too far. Calculating the extent, intensity, and expense of interstate war changes the picture. Louis spent 65.5 percent of the years after 1661 at war, and late in his reign, 1688–1715, only a few years did not know armed struggles. Moreover, his wars were great conflicts, mobilizing huge armies for long periods of time. These characteristics make his wars look much less limited, since they resembled those that preceded them more than those that followed.

After one considers the martial character of Louis XIV's reign, the period 1716–88 looks quite peaceful. The French engaged in interstate wars on the more modest scale of 42.5 percent of the calendar years. And if two quite minor wars – first, with Spain, 1718–20, and second, the War of the Polish Succession, 1733–38 – are excluded, then the percentage falls to 31.5, less than half that under Louis XIV. In addition, Bourbon dedication to warfare in Europe seemed less than complete, and French borders were never seriously threatened. Certainly the French suffered humiliation during the Seven Years' War, initially at the hands of the Prussians in Germany and then at the hands of the British across the seas in North America and India. However, after 1757, the French failed to mobilize on the scale that they had under Louis XIV. With France never fundamentally at risk, and with the periods between major wars long enough to allow the state and people to recover, war never matched the intensity of the years before 1715. This era truly deserves the title of an age of limited war, since for the French, armed conflict did not really come to them; they literally had to journey from home to find it. André Corvisier even suggests that the lessened intensity of warfare, at least, as viewed from the perspective of Paris, fostered the optimism of the Enlightenment.[9] That limited quality stands out all the more because it was followed by the Revolutionary and Napoleonic Wars, which afflicted France with desperate and sometimes glorious conflict continuously from 1792 to 1815, with only two pauses, the first, for a year after the Treaty of Amiens, 1802,

---

[8] Meyer, "'De la guerre' au XVIIe siècle," 286.
[9] André Corvisier, "Guerre et mentalités au XVIIe siècle," *XVII siècle*, 37 (1985), 231.

and the second following Napoleon's abdication in 1814. Then the issues at stake were fundamental, from survival of the new republic to Napoleonic hegemony over Europe. Enemies invaded French territory at the start of the Revolutionary and at the end of the Napoleonic eras, toppling the French government on two occasions. The armed turmoil of the Revolution spawned one of the most costly civil wars of French history in the Vendée, as well as bringing armed revolt to Lyon, Bordeaux, and Toulon. The period 1789–1815 truly deserves Meyer's categorization as "total war."

Seen in this perspective, the *grand siècle* witnessed a transformation in the intensity of warfare, at least for France, but not of the kind usually described. Warfare of the period 1610–60 shared much in common with the century that preceded it in terms of the many years afflicted with war, the rapacious character of the conflicts, the prevalence of campaigns within French borders, and the propensity to major civil war. The period 1661–1715 saw diminished violence within the borders of France because better-paid and better-disciplined soldiers did not prey on Louis's own subjects, because the success of French arms meant that wars were fought primarily outside his realm, and because France was largely spared internal rebellions. Yet the percentage of years consumed by interstate wars remained relatively the same – 60.0 percent for 1611–60 and 65.5 percent for 1661–1715 – and the burdens of the latter wars were very great indeed. In the next era, 1716–88, the proportion of years spent in interstate warfare declined sharply to only 42.5 percent or less, and the remote sites of those wars, plus the absence of any significant internal rebellion, made it seem a very benign age. In fact, then, it is reasonable to see the *grand siècle* as part of a movement toward more moderate levels of warfare, from the great internal troubles and terrors of the second half of the sixteenth century, through the very difficult years of the first half of the seventeenth century, followed by the period 1661–1715 with its decreased internal conflict but continued major interstate wars, finally to the internal tranquillity and lessened levels of interstate war of the era after the great king's death. The half-century between 1661 and 1715 did not bring "controlled war," but it constituted an important step in that direction.

THE NARRATIVE OF FRENCH WARS,
1610–1715

Moderation of war's fury was not accompanied by any decline in number of years consumed by international conflict, at least from the French perspective. The era 1610–1715 was an age of warfare throughout. Richelieu classed war as "an inevitable evil" but "absolutely necessary"; it was, in short, a fact of life.[10] If war was inevitable, it was also omnipresent for generation after generation. Warfare did not simply take place on the periphery of life; it shaped French existence during the *grand siècle*. Of course, this influence was

[10] Philippe Contamine, ed., *Histoire militaire de la France*, vol. 1 (Paris: 1992), 336.

felt most strongly within the army itself; therefore, the story of Bourbon wars provides context for the institutional development discussed in this volume.

The Bourbon monarchy of Louis XIII and Louis XIV confronted a changing constellation of international opponents in a series of wars; during the first half of the *grand siècle*, Spain posed the most serious threat to France, but during the second half, an isolated France fought against the maritime powers and the Austrian Hapsburgs. When Louis XIII succeeded his father in 1610, he did not sit securely on his throne. His mother, Marie de Medici, and her corrupt cronies actually held the power for the nine-year-old boy king. Rebellious aristocrats, most notably the prince de Condé, opposed the regent, even taking to arms, and Marie bought them off with money and concessions. Finally, in 1617, Louis seized power from his own mother and her entourage. His accession to real authority did not end internal strife, as a series of "Princes' Wars" and other rebellions continued to plague France. Beyond these troubles, Louis XIII also inherited the long struggle with the Hapsburgs that had consumed the sixteenth century. Although Europe's most enduring war at the time, the Eighty Years' War between the Spanish and the Dutch, enjoyed a truce at the time that Louis took the throne, the horribly destructive Thirty Years' War soon broke out in Germany in 1618, and when the truce expired in the Low Countries, they too ignited.

Louis XIII alone, though a conscientious king and a competent soldier, was not equal to the challenges that faced him, but he possessed a characteristic essential to a successful monarch, the ability to choose extremely able state servants. In 1624, Louis elevated the great Armand du Pléssis, Cardinal Richelieu, to the powerful position of first minister. Richelieu harbored a strong and lasting desire to increase French prestige by toppling the Spanish. He saw France encircled on her land borders by Hapsburg holdings: Spain to the south, the Spanish Netherlands to the north, and a string of territories belonging to Spain and her allies running from the Netherlands down through Italy, what was known at the time as the Spanish Road, by which reinforcements and funds reached the Spanish armies fighting in the north. In 1625, French troops, in alliance with Venice and Savoy, cut the "road" at the Val Telline pass over the Alps, but Protestant rebellion at home forced the French to retire.

The French Protestants, or Huguenots, won the status of a virtual state within a state through the Edict of Nantes in 1598, a compromise peace that awarded the Huguenots certain fortresses and the right to retain military forces of their own. Richelieu understandably believed that the monarchy could not tolerate such independent power within French borders, and the revolt of the Huguenots in 1625 confirmed his worst fears. Louis and Richelieu now conducted a war against Protestant power, a war that culminated in the siege of La Rochelle, 1627–28, which fell despite English aid. Immediately after taking La Rochelle, Louis and Richelieu marched their army to settle affairs in Italy by humbling the duke of Savoy in a brief campaign early in

1629. Later in the spring of that year, royal arms defeated the Protestants led by the duke de Rohan and imposed the Grace of Alais on the Huguenots. It took from them the right to hold towns, to appoint their own magistrates, and, in short, to function as a separate political authority, but it did guarantee their religious rights, which the Huguenots greeted as an unexpected blessing after such a sound defeat.

Richelieu could again focus his attention on the Hapsburg threat and the Thirty Years' War. By paying subsidies to the Protestant champion Gustavus Adolphus, he attempted to fight the Hapsburgs by proxy, 1630–35; however, that great warrior-king died at the battle of Lützen in 1632, and although his forces were ably led after his death, a Swedish defeat at Nördlingen in 1634 forced the French to enter the war outright. Louis, Richelieu, and the secretaries of state for war – Abel Servien to 1636 and then Sublet de Noyers – fielded the largest armies that the French had employed to date. Despite an initial victory, the war soon went badly for France; a Spanish invasion in 1636 threatened Paris and called forth a great French resistance, probably Louis XIII's finest hour as a soldier. Years of indecisive campaigns followed.

Richelieu died in 1642, long before the outcome of the contest was clear. He was succeeded as first minister by the Italian, Guilio, Cardinal Mazarin. Louis XIII did not long survive Richelieu; the king died in 1643, passing the throne to his four-year-old son, Louis XIV. Obviously, this small boy could not rule, and his mother Anne of Austria assumed the regency aided by Cardinal Mazarin. A few days after the death of the old king, the French won a victory of major proportions at Rocroi, where the young duke d'Enghien defeated the Spanish under Melo. Upon the death of his father in 1646, Enghien assumed the title of Louis II, prince of Condé, to go down in history as the Great Condé. Although Rocroi did not settle the issue, Condé and the second great French commander of the day, Henri de la Tour d'Auvergne, viscount Turenne, helped to drive the Austrians and Bavarians out of the war by 1648, when the Treaties of Westphalia ended the Thirty Years' War.

These treaties did not conclude the French struggle against Spain or bring internal peace to France. The Fronde rebellion, which struck in 1648 just as war in Germany subsided, weakened the French and thus prolonged the fight with their traditional enemy. What began as a revolt of legal elites composed of aristocratic judges and magistrates centered on the highest courts of France, the *parlements*, ended as an affair of the great princes, most notably Condé, who challenged the authority of the queen regent and Mazarin. The antics of the princes and their co-conspirators at times gave the Fronde the air of a bad opera, but the Fronde was a bitter civil war, fought viciously over very real issues of state authority. Rival French armies exposed the heart of France to the kind of ravages that afflicted Germany during the Thirty Years' War. By the end of the Fronde, the unreconciled Condé, whose talent in the field was only exceeded by his pride, served the Spanish.

From 1643, Michel Le Tellier held office as secretary of state for war, and he would remain in power for a generation. A man of high administrative ability, he could not make order out of chaos until the Fronde died down and French armies defeated the Spanish. Final victory came at the battle of the Dunes in 1658, when Turenne, now Louis's premier general, defeated an army under don Juan of Austria, then viceroy of the Spanish Netherlands, and Condé. In 1659, the Peace of the Pyrenees ended this war in French triumph, realized by the addition of Alsace to France and symbolized by Louis's marriage to a Spanish princess. The conflict that began in 1635 and ended with the Peace of the Pyrenees was France's longest war of the century, yet it has no simple title, since although it was part of the Thirty Years' War at the outset, it outlasted that struggle. For convenience here, the war of 1635–59 will simply be called the war with Spain.

The return of peace following so many years of conflict brought a new era in French history. Mazarin, after guiding the young king and forming French policy for nearly two decades, died in 1661. At this point, Louis XIV declared that unlike his father he would now be his own first minister. At age 22, Louis truly assumed the royal authority; although he had been king since boyhood, only now did he begin his personal reign, which lasted until his death. Louis XIII's reign and the minority of Louis XIV had been afflicted with civil war and rebellions, but the personal reign of Louis XIV would see only limited internal turmoil; the pattern of great international contests would continue.

Louis enjoyed a great military inheritance as he began his personal reign. Even after demobilization, his army remained large and skilled; in Turenne and Condé, now back in French service, he probably had the best field commanders in Europe; and the able Le Tellier directed his war department. Soon Le Tellier would share his office with his equally able but brutal son, the marquis de Louvois, who eventually succeeded his father and held the post of secretary of war until his death in 1691.

A young king with a lust for glory would not let such a fine military instrument grow dull from disuse. Louis continually eyed the Spanish inheritance that he believed his wife brought with her. When his father-in-law, King Philip IV of Spain, died in 1665, Louis maneuvered to gain territory from the Spanish Netherlands. The outcome of his machinations was the War of Devolution, 1667–68. Louis entered the war expecting that France's long-time ally against Spain, the United Provinces, would support him. But the Dutch, concluding that a weak Spain was now a safer neighbor than a strong France, formed an alliance with the English and the Swedes and threatened to intervene unless the French withdrew. For this act, Louis never forgave the Dutch. Still, the Treaty of Aix-la-Chapelle, which ended the War of Devolution, added some important towns to France, notably Lille, so Louis enjoyed limited success. But this would not be enough for him.

Louis plotted to chastise the Dutch and continue his acquisition of Spanish lands. He carefully isolated the Dutch from their allies and struck in 1672. This Dutch War, 1672–78, began with an invasion, masterfully supported and supplied by Louvois, which came up through the Bishopric of Liège and succeeded in occupying much of the United Provinces south of the Zeidersee. Louis intended to defeat and humble the Dutch so as to force them to give him a free hand in the Spanish Netherlands, but he failed.[11] William III of Orange assumed the office of stadthalter and forged alliances with the Spanish, the Austrian Hapsburgs, and several German princes to resist French aggression, so in 1674, Louis reluctantly withdrew his forces from Dutch soil and continued the war in the Spanish Netherlands and along his eastern border. The year 1675 brought a change of guard and a change of policy. While leading an army to defend the borders of Alsace that year, Turenne died when struck by a cannonball, and at the end of the campaign, Condé retired, prematurely aged by decades of campaigning. In the field, Louis relied on less glorious commanders like Humières, Créqui, Schomberg, and the young duke of Luxembourg. However, he turned to his war minister, Louvois, for primary counsel and to that minister's protégé, Sébastien le Prestre de Vauban, the master of the siege warfare that became ever more important as the years passed. From this point on, Louis, though ready to seize whatever opportunities for gain presented themselves, seemed more intent on constructing defensible frontiers for his beloved lands than on conquering new ones. The Treaty of Nymwegen brought the Dutch War to a close; it awarded Louis the province of Franche-Comté and additional territory along his northern border. Now Louis enjoyed the adulation of his subjects; he was Louis le Grand, the Sun King.

The gains at Nymwegen satisfied neither Louis's appetite for territory nor his desire to buttress his frontier. With the encouragement of Louvois, and even with the backing of the usually unaggressive Vauban, Louis claimed valuable defensive positions along his northeast frontier, on the basis that the places claimed were dependencies of lands granted him in past treaties. Although these land-grabs went by the benign name of "Reunions," coercion and violence attended them. In 1681, the French army seized Strasbourg in an impressive and mercifully bloodless operation. But the fortress of Luxembourg would not be taken so peacefully; a blockade of several years culminated in a siege of 1684. The fall of Luxembourg merged into a brief War of the Reunions, 1683–84. The Spanish had been so bullied by France that when Louis's armies came to take more, the Spanish declared war on France in hopes of forcing the Hapsburg emperor to come to their aid. The emperor, however, had his hands full with the Turks, who had nearly taken Vienna in 1683 and had only just been driven away. Isolated, Spain proved unable to parry the French forces that conducted a particularly brutal campaign in the Spanish Netherlands. At the same time, Louis ordered a bombardment of Genoa and threatened an overland attack to punish that city for its support of the Spanish.

Brutality paid, but it also lured Louis into further harsh acts that ultimately resulted in a war he really did not want. His short and successful War

---

[11] See Paul Sonnino, *Louis XIV and the Origins of the Dutch War* (Cambridge: 1989).

of the Reunions ended in the Truce of Ratisbon, which recognized his Reunions, including Strasbourg and Luxembourg, for a period of twenty years. However, as Louis witnessed the success of the Austrian Hapsburgs against the Ottoman Turks, he feared that once the Hapsburgs triumphed they would turn against France, and in this fear he seems to have been correct. In addition, Louis had long enjoyed the support of Cologne, a bishopric that served as an outpost on the Rhine, but when the bishop died and Louis's attempts to put his own candidate in power were blocked, the Sun King resolved upon a short war to win German compliance with his wishes and to see the concessions of Ratisbon recognized as permanent. In September 1688, the French besieged the fortress of Philippsburg, a key fortress on the Rhine frontier of Alsace. Louvois and Louis expected a rapid victory in three or four months, but their actions set off the Nine Years' War, 1688–97.

When the German princes did not accede to his demands as he had expected, the French devastated the Palatinate, Baden, and parts of Würtemburg in an attempt to make their own frontier more secure from invasion by laying waste the country north and east of it. This act scandalized Europe and aided William III, who had taken the opportunity to seize the English throne while French forces were tied up along the Rhine. Soon he formed the Grand Alliance, including the United Provinces, England, Spain, Savoy, and important German princes, including the emperor. By winning battles at Fleurus, Steinkirke, and Neerwinden, Marshal Luxembourg soon established himself as a field commander on a par with Condé and Turenne. So successful was he in capturing enemy battle flags, which then hung as trophies in Paris, that he became known as the *tapisier* of Notre Dame. But Luxembourg died early in 1695, and no one stepped up to replace him. Although the French did well in the field during the Nine Years' War, the effort ruined them. Louis mobilized an army that reached 420,000 men on paper, and this gargantuan force proved beyond his means to maintain without risking bankruptcy. The war ended in a peace of exhaustion, the Treaty of Ryswick, by which Louis lost much that he had gained since Nymwegen, including the fortress of Luxembourg, although he retained Strasbourg.

Louvois administered the army into the Nine Years' War and helped to form the plans for that conflict; however, he died suddenly in 1691. Just as Louvois had succeeded his father, now his son, the marquis de Barbézieux, assumed Louvois's office of secretary of state for war. But while Barbézieux held the office, Louis XIV relied more on personal military advisors, notably the marquis de Chamlay, in policy matters. When Barbézieux went to an early grave in 1701, he was followed in office first by Chamillart, and then in 1709 by Voysin. It is generally conceded that those who served as secretaries of state for war after Louvois did not match his competence and energy, and the army suffered accordingly.

The Nine Years' War chastened the proud Sun King, and he made a real effort to avert another armed struggle over the next great crisis, a crisis that all Europe knew was approaching. The ailing and childless king Charles II of Spain could not survive much longer, and at his passing, the worldwide inheritance of Spain must pass to one of three rival claimants. The first was archduke Charles, son and heir of the Hapsburg emperor; the second was the heir to the French throne, the dauphin; and the third was a Bavarian prince, then only a boy aged seven. In order to avoid war over the succession, Louis agreed to a partition treaty in 1698 that gave most to the Bavarian candidate and little more than Naples and Sicily to the French candidate. But in 1699, the former died. In reaction, Louis pushed for a new partition treaty that would award Spain and the Indies to the Hapsburg claimant, while giving only Naples, Sicily, and Lorraine to the dauphin. But Carlos II, adamant that his realm not be subdivided, drafted a will giving everything to Philippe d'Anjou, second son of the dauphin and thus unlikely to ever claim the French throne. But if Philippe declined, then everything would be offered to the Hapsburg candidate. When Carlos died in 1700, Louis decided, quite reasonably, to accept the will of Carlos II since the Hapsburgs had never agreed to the second partition treaty in any case. Had Louis moderated at this point, he might have averted a general European war, although a fight with the Hapsburgs seemed inevitable. Unfortunately, Louis reverted to his proud ways by seizing the Spanish Netherlands to secure it for his grandson, demanding special trading privileges for the French in Spanish America, and refusing to give assurances that the French and Spanish realms would never be united under a single monarch. A furious William III assembled another coalition against France, although this time the Spanish under their new Bourbon king, recognized as Philip V, stood with France.

The War of the Spanish Succession, 1701–14, proved to be the longest and most exhausting war of Louis's personal reign. The duke of Marlborough, perhaps England's greatest general, led British forces, while prince Eugene of Savoy, an excellent general in his own right, commanded the main Imperial armies. For years, the French could not find a winning commander, and disaster followed disaster. At the battle of Blenheim, 1704, the allied team of generals so devastated the French army before them that the French would not again venture deep into Germany. At the battle of Turin in 1706, Eugene essentially drove the French out of Italy, while Marlborough and Eugene won battles at Ramillies, 1706, and Oudenarde, 1708, that secured the Spanish Netherlands for the Allies. The year 1709 brought with it the greatest famine of the century, but during that year of horrors, Louis finally found a commander who could hold the field against his enemies, Marshal Claude Louis Hector, duke de Villars. In September of that year at the battle of Malplaquet, Villars confronted Marlborough and Eugene. Although the French lost that battle, they retired in good order and inflicted such great casualties that Marlborough would not again face the French in the open field. In fact, Malplaquet remained the bloodiest European battle until the great Napoleonic clashes exceeded its butcher's bill a century later. In 1711, Marlborough lost his command following the fall of the Whigs in England, and the French made a great deal of headway in the last years of the war.

Villars defeated allied forces at Denain in 1712 and captured a number of cities in the Spanish Netherlands and along the Rhine. In 1713, the French concluded the Treaty of Utrecht with their enemies, except the Empire, which continued the fight until the Treaties of Rastatt and Baden finally ended all fighting in 1714. Louis at last achieved his goal of securing Spain and the Indies for his grandson, although Louis promised that the crowns of France and Spain would never be united. For France proper, the status quo antebellum was restored. Therefore, Louis finally won the War of the Spanish Succession, since Philip sat on the Spanish throne, but the cost for France was unacceptably high.

Thus, in brief, runs the history of French wars during the *grand siècle*.

FRENCH FINANCE

This long series of wars multiplied state expenses far beyond Bourbon ability to pay for them; the result was repeated financial crisis and eventual collapse. Richelieu commented, "It is always said that finances are the sinews of the state, and it is true that they constitute the fulcrum of Archimedes, which being firmly established provides the means of moving the entire world."[12] In no case was that fulcrum more essential than in the pursuit of war, the costliest of all state ventures, but when conducting major struggles, Bourbon absolutism never found secure purchase for its financial levers. So great was the importance and so crippling the consequences of French state financial weakness that it has attracted a great deal of scholarly attention. This section does not attempt to rival the body of financial histories already available but rather to reflect them briefly in order to establish that the question of money was indeed one of the most fundamental parameters of military development.

The financial demands of maintaining a major conflict always surpassed the resources of the Bourbon treasury. War became vastly more expensive in the seventeenth century. In 1558–59, Henry II spent the equivalent of 210 tons of silver, whereas in 1639, this sum had reached the equivalent of 1,000 tons of silver, a fivefold increase in real terms, not simply the produce of inflated currency.[13] Clearly, warfare constituted the major explanation for the rise in state expenses. After 1598, Henri IV may have balanced the books, and his chief financial officer, the *surintendant des finances* Effiat, insisted that through the 1620s, the French ran only modest annual deficits of 5 million livres. But this shortfall multiplied tenfold in the 1630s.[14] Louis XIII thought that he could support war in 1635 by spending only 1 million livres more than it had cost him to subsidize his allies in the conflict, but he was very wrong.[15] Although average total government expenses for the six years 1628–33 had

---

[12] Richelieu, *Testament politique*, ed. Louis André (Paris, 1947), 427–48.
[13] Contamine, *Histoire militaire*, 1:370.
[14] Julian Dent, *Crisis in Finance* (New York, 1973), 42–43.
[15] Richard Bonney, *The King's Debts* (Oxford: 1981), 169, 307.

run 51 million livres per year, war nearly doubled them, as annual expenses of the period 1635–40 soared to 90 million.[16] Richelieu would have to admit that no state could pay two or three armies at the same time, and once the French committed to war in 1635, they did exactly that.[17] Under Louis XIV, the difference in wartime and peacetime expenses were equally great. Annual expenses for the peacetime period 1662–66 reached 63 million, whereas they ran 103 million during the war years 1672–76. Corvisier, looking at military expenses alone, estimates a 92 percent increase from 1683 to 1691, as the French entered the Nine Years' War.[18] French fiscal resources could not keep up with the demands of warfare, and the result was bankruptcy.

Wartime expenses led not only to fiscal crisis but to social turmoil. A frustrated *surintendant des finances*, Bullion warned Richelieu in 1639, "Expenditure in cash is up to at least 40 millions, the [creditors] are now abandoning us, and the masses will not pay either the new or the old taxes. We are now at the bottom of the pot . . . and I fear that our foreign war is degenerating into a civil war."[19] His fear was justified. The French suffered a series of tax revolts, particularly before the personal reign of Louis XIV. The rising of the Nu-Pieds in 1639 was particularly notable, and the Fronde itself rated as a rebellion against royal financial exactions.

Historians have proposed differing explanations for French fiscal failure. For Julian Dent, it lay in the nature and extent of short-term borrowing at illegally high rates, while for Richard Bonney, the key was the failure to raise revenues effectively.[20] But all intelligent explanations put it down more to politics and society than to sheer economics, for France was a rich country. In any case, the way of raising money for state purposes left the monarchy dependent on a financial community that produced capital only at the price of high interest and fiscal corruption.

Taxes and Other Revenues

The French monarchy raised funds in a variety of manners, involving everything from taxation to the sale of offices to borrowing. Some of these methods seem at first glance to approximate modern, regular, methods, but on closer examination, they were generally inefficient and inadequate.

Direct taxation most closely approximated modern state revenue. The most important direct tax was the *taille*, which varied from region to region

---

[16] Figures taken from Jean Roland de Mallet, *Comptes rendus de l'administration des finances du royaume de France* (London: 1789), 222–23. Mallet corresponds very well with AN, KK 355, "État par abrégé des recettes et dépenses, 1662–1700."

[17] David Parrott, "The Administration of the French Army During the Ministry of Cardinal Richelieu," Ph.D. dissertation, Oxford University, 1985, 39.

[18] André Corvisier, *Louvois* (Paris: 1983), 330.

[19] 25 October 1639, Bullion to Richelieu, Richelieu, *Lettres*, 6:608 in Orest Ranum, *Richelieu and the Councillors of Louis XIII* (Oxford: 1963), 145.

[20] Bonney, *The King's Debts*, 272.

and took two forms: a tax on real property, the *taille réelle*, or on all personal wealth, the *taille personnelle*. *Pays d'états* and more recently acquired territories generally enjoyed the more moderate and equitable *taille réelle*. The Estates General granted the monarchy the right to levy the *taille* pretty much at its own discretion in 1439 as a form of war tax to maintain forces meant to bring security back to France late in the Hundred Years' War. In certain important aspects, granting the *taille* proved a fatal blow to whatever hope the Estates General might have had to bridle the monarchy, since with this permanent tax the king could raise military forces without turning to the Estates General for support.

In provinces under direct administration of the monarchy, the *pays d'élection*, officers of the crown "elected," in the sense that they chose, what amount localities were to pay. *Pays d'élection* comprised roughly two thirds of France. In other provinces that still guarded their medieval assemblies, the *pays d'états*, these assemblies, or estates, bargained with the monarchy to set the tax rate. In the bargaining process, the *pays d'états* fared better than the *pays d'élection*.

Other direct taxes that went directly to support the army included the *taillon*, *étapes*, *subsistances*, and *ustensile*. Henri II created the *taillon* in 1549 to supplement the pay of his troops. *Étapes* were a further augmentation of the *taille* meant to pay for the food and housing of troops on the march. The *subsistances*, started in 1638, and *ustensile* were both taxes paid to defray the cost of maintaining troops in winter quarters.

Indirect taxes were levied on the sale of goods rather than on the wealth or property of individuals. The most infamous of the indirect taxes was that on salt, the *gabelle*. The monarchy used its royal monopoly on salt to extract great sums from the populace, but the *gabelle* varied so much as to be viewed as a great inequity. In general, *pays d'état* paid considerably less than did *pays d'élection*. Variation in the price of salt encouraged smuggling across internal borders. Other indirect taxes included the hated *aides*, which taxed wine. Whereas direct taxes were imposed and collected by agents of governmental institutions, indirect taxes were farmed out to financiers, who bid for the right to collect these sums for the king. They promised a fixed return, and anything they raised over this and the necessary costs of collection amounted to profit. Thus, private individuals or consortiums of private individuals carried out the basic state function of revenue collection.

A third form of revenue was the *deniers extraordinaires*, or extraordinary levies, such as the sale of offices or of annuities [*rentes*]. These revenues were also raised through financiers who became *traiteurs*; that is, they entered into a contract, or *traité*. Again they sought to turn a profit, meaning necessarily that those who raised the money had everything to gain by ensuring that all that was raised did not end up in state coffers. In some ways, *deniers extraordinaires* were the archetypal war tax, because they could be created rapidly and sold off to *traiteurs*, even though the very institution of *traiteurs* made for financial inefficiencies and abuses. Come emergencies, the monarchy was always ready to create new offices and titles for the sake of their purchase prices. For example, *deniers extraordinaires* soared from 5.6 million livres in 1630 to an annual average of 51.8 in the period 1633–40.[21]

The Church provided a fourth source of revenue in lieu of direct taxation. Formally tax exempt, the *Assemblée générale du clergé* bargained with the monarchy and agreed to make certain interest payments for the crown and to allot it periodic free gifts, or *dons gratuit*. These negotiations could turn into battles, but the spoils were worth the fight; in 1635–36, the Church finally agreed to hand over an unusual bounty of 3.7 million livres, and a nasty confrontation of 1640–41 yielded 5.5 million livres.[22] As in most things, the situation became both calmer and more regular during the personal reign of Louis XIV, when the Church increased its contribution to an annual average of more than 3 million livres, in comparison to 2 million under Louis XIII.[23] As welcome as these amounts were, they did not represent a fair payment by the Church, so in a sense, the *don gratuit* can be seen as money spent to buy off the monarchy and preserve the Church's tax-exempt status.

The French system produced revenues, but without equity or efficiency. Historians now recognize that the nobility of France enjoyed only partial, not total, tax exemption, but aristocratic status was a great financial advantage nonetheless. In fact, one of the reasons that led individuals to try to buy their way into the nobility through the purchase of offices was to gain that exemption. The system worked to the advantage of those with power and those who controlled institutions that could bargain with the monarchy. They used their leverage to lessen the burdens that they had to bear. Bargaining institutions included the aristocracy itself, the Church, the provincial estates, and even the cities of France. Fiscal privileges won or maintained by this leverage meant that those without bargaining power had to make proportionally higher payments. While the Bourbon monarchy chipped away at traditional privileges, it never purged them in the name of justice or necessity. Therefore, to an important degree, the mounting costs of war were paid by those segments of the population least able to afford them.

The burden of taxation mounted steadily from 1600 to 1661. According to the historian Jean Meyer, French taxes quadrupled between 1630 and 1640.[24] The bitterness of tax revolts reflected the perceived lack of equity in this spiraling taxation. Once he began his personal reign, Louis XIV turned away from further great tax increases. But he also failed to carry out any great tax reform either; therefore, he relied more on borrowing at high interest. As a result, he may have won France temporary social peace but only by preserving an inefficient and inequitable system of tapping French resources.

---

[21] Bonney, *The King's Debts*, 175.

[22] Frank Tallett, "Church, State, War and Finance in Early-Modern France," *Renaissance and Modern Studies* 36 (1993), 26–27. Tallett provides a fine brief account of the Church's role in war finance.

[23] Talett, "Church, State, War and Finance," 29.

[24] Meyer, "'De la guerre' au XVIIe siècle," 272.

At the same time that much was paid through taxation and *deniers extra-ordinaires*, a great deal never reached the royal treasury. As the Venetian ambassador to the French court observed in 1647, "Such are the methods in practice in the confused state of financial administration that the king never has a penny in his purse."[25] The same ambassador also said that waste was so great that the king thought himself well served that if out of 100 *écus* spent, 40 actually went to the good of his service.[26] This failing had to do with the extensive use of financiers in the system, men whose incentives were to keep as much as they could and pay the state as little as possible. Although financiers could be corrupt, they were still necessary to the system because they were sources not only of revenue but credit as well. So, perhaps, the monarchy's reliance on credit made the reform of its revenue system difficult, if not impossible.

Credit

The Bourbon monarchy depended on credit to finance its wars. The scale of borrowing escalated during conflicts. During the period 1630–35, it amounted to only 4.2 million livres, when annual revenues stood at 20.5 million, but during the period 1640–45, borrowing soared to 57.2 million livres, exceeding state revenues, which only reached 56.4 million.[27] The monarchy turned to credit due to the inability of revenue to cover the entire costs of conflict and because revenues arrived slowly and on an uncertain schedule, whereas armies needed to be paid promptly at set times to maintain the condition and discipline of the troops.

On a certain level, it is hard to separate borrowing from revenue raising. Tax farming and *traités* were, in a sense, credit devices, since in both cases, financiers promised and paid (one could say loaned) the monarchy sums in the expectation of being repaid, with interest, by revenues that they were authorized to collect. It is also important to recognize that the same financiers who bought the farms and *traités* were those who also loaned money to the monarchy in more direct forms. Profits made from tax farming and *traités* would find their way back to the monarchy as loans.

In particular, short-term credit proved essential to finance the wars of France. To a large degree, this situation was common to other major European states. Even as late as the Nine Years' War, long-term borrowing only accounted for 10 percent of British war expenses.[28] Credit cost the French dearly; between 1656 and 1661, they paid an average of about 15 percent on

---

[25] Venetian ambassador, in Georges Livet, "International Relations and the Role of France, 1648–60," *New Cambridge Modern History*, vol. 4 (Cambridge: 1971), 415.

[26] Angelo Correr in Louis André, *Michel Le Tellier et l'organisation de l'armée monarchique* (Paris: 1906), 25–26.

[27] Bonney, *The King's Debts*, appendix two, table 8, 317; Mallet, *Comptes rendus*, 226, 248.

[28] John Brewer, *The Sinews of Power* (London: 1989), 153.

loans, while the Dutch paid only 4 percent in 1655.[29] French interest rates for short-term credit were set by regulation, but these limits were mainly honored in the breach. To win over new creditors, government financiers awarded them illegally high interest and slipped them illicit payments. "By 1661, the royal finances had been almost entirely subverted by the search for short term credit," writes Dent.[30]

Certainly Colbert had the power, energy, and talent to put back some sense in French financial practices. Yet even he could not and did not end the reliance on short-term credit. Perhaps he could have managed without it in peacetime, but when a major war broke out in 1672, he could not avoid the old expedients. Louis XIV also resorted to "anticipations"; money would be loaned on the government's promise to repay the loan with certain future tax income stipulated in advance. Such a method compromised future revenues and thus made borrowing a necessity in years to come, since further loans were needed to cover the shortfall of revenues already promised to pay past debts.

Expenses for debt service soared as war continued. In 1694, 78.72 percent of government expenses went to direct military costs and only 8.07 percent to debt service, but by 1697, these percentages changed to 63.61 percent and 23.03 percent, respectively. In 1698, military outlays fell to 49.93 of total expenses, and debt service climbed to 50.00 percent.[31] Debt service amounted to as much of a cost of war as did the money spent on gunpowder.

No one could rebuild the foundations of French finance as long as French society operated as a strict social hierarchy with great privileges, including tax exemptions, for those at the top. The tax privileges that so favored the Church and the aristocracy insulated much of their wealth from the state. Colbert could not end them; neither could he abolish the purchase of titles of nobility and offices that extended them to greater numbers of the well-to-do.

One nagging question is why, since the Dutch and the English founded successful state banks during this period, were the French unable to create such an institution, which would have allowed them rationally to exploit long-term credit at reasonable rates. Colbert established a more regular credit fund, the *Caisse d'emprunt*, which performed some of the functions of a deposit bank in 1674, but it closed in 1683, and the first true French state bank created under John Law in 1716 failed in a few years.[32] The absolutism of Louis XIV may itself have made a strong state bank impossible. National banks thrived among the maritime powers, because their forms of government by assembly put power into the hands of the very men willing and able

[29] Bonney, *The King's Debts*, 318; Frank Tallett, *War and Society in Early Modern Europe, 1495–1715* (London: 1992), 212–14.

[30] Dent, *Crisis in Finance*, 232.

[31] Contamine, *Histoire militaire*, 1:429. See the table on French expenses on p. 428.

[32] Tallett, *War and Society*, 214.

to invest in government securities. Dutch and English national banks were monitored or controlled by the same creditors whose confidence was essential to ensure low rates. Such men could trust in repayment because they could trust themselves. In contrast, Louis demonstrated more inclination to borrow than to repay. Fundamentally, he could not hold the reins of government as firmly as he wished if he abdicated fiscal power to the moneyed segments of society, nor would the aristocracy have permitted him to do so. It was out of the question. In any case, the fact is that under Louis XIV, the absolutist state never effectively mobilized credit through a state bank, and the first attempt at a French national bank, under Law in 1716, failed. The French would not really have a national bank until 1800, and it required a revolution to make such an institution possible.

Financiers and Fraud

Dependence on credit meant dependence on financiers. Richelieu said "financiers . . . make up a separate party, prejudicial to the state but, however, necessary."[33] Dent estimates that by 1660 there were about 4,000 men of finance in France.[34] While some individuals who were important in French military finance operated outside Paris, that city had become the undisputed hub of the money market after Lyon slipped, never having recovered from its mistake of backing the Catholic League in the sixteenth century.

There was an ongoing belief that financiers were nonentities who became rich overnight by rapacious dealings with the government.[35] As one contemporary manuscript complained, "For a long time the financiers [*participants*] insult the misery of the poor people that they ruin by the display of their sumptuous carriages [*équipages*] and the luxury of their wives. The majority of them did not have five sols at the beginning of the war. . . . Their great wealth acquired in so little time is sufficient proof that they have stolen from the king and the public."[36] But if there were great fortunes to be won in funding the government, there were also great risks. In fact, many financiers ended their days in ruin. Even if they survived, they were expected to put their private fortunes at the service of the state.

The state financial system operated by principles that would at best be condemned as conflicts of interest today and at worst would qualify as outright fraud. The major officers within the French fiscal bureaucracy often owed their positions to their personal contacts with the world of the financiers,

---

[33] Richelieu, *Testament politique*, 250.

[34] Julian Dent, "An Aspect of the Crisis of the Seventeenth Century: The Collapse of the Financial Administration of the French Monarchy, 1653–61," *Economic History Review* (August 1967), 256.

[35] See hate of financiers as getting quick profits in AG, Arch. hist., feuille 2, undated, probably ca. 1700; and financier nonentities who then became rich, Jean-Baptiste Primi Visconti, *Mémoires sur la cour de Louis XIV, 1673–1681*, François Solnon, ed. (Paris: 1988), 131.

[36] AG, Arch. hist. 78, feuille 2.

contacts that allowed them to draw upon its resources. At times, this even required financial officers to borrow on their own credit in order to transfer that money into state accounts. Also, the need to tap the private resources of financiers for the public purposes of the state, even when that state suffered from very shaky credit, led to a complexity of fraud that is only partially understood. Without questionable deals and illegal payments, it would have been impossible to coax money from creditors who had every reason to doubt that the state would honor its commitments.

The French state suffered virtual bankruptcy in 1598 and actually declared bankruptcy in 1648; there was also much talk of threatened collapse in the 1630s and 1650s. Another collapse came in 1661, when Colbert estimated the state debt at 451 million livres and the young Louis despaired that finances were "entirely exhausted."[37] Louis XIV subsequently staved off bankruptcy, but the state finances collapsed again in 1715–16 when he died, leaving a staggering debt of 2.5 billion livres.[38]

In addition to the total collapse of state finance, periodic *chambres de justice* could spell ruin for individual financiers.[39] *Chambres de justice* were special courts created to expose financial fraud and misconduct. They were staffed by eighteen to thirty of the king's men holding commissions that could be revoked at any minute. Therefore, the *chambres* could be used to pursue the monarch's political as well as his fiscal goals. For Mousnier, *chambres* served to assuage public opinion that detested financiers. In 1624 and 1661, *chambres* were also used to remove particular *surintendants des finances*: La Vieuville and Fouquet respectively, and their coterie of *traitants*. Under the early Bourbons, *chambres de justice* were fairly common, occurring in 1597, 1601, 1605–7, 1607, 1624, 1635, 1643, 1645, 1648, 1656–57, and 1661–65. In fact, the last Estates General held before the French Revolution, that convened in 1614, asked that *chambres de justice* be convened regularly every ten years. After Louis XIV's great *chambre* of 1661–65, the next one came only in 1716, after his death. The sentences handed down by *chambres de justice* ranged from contributions to charity, fines, and prison terms, to banishment, condemnation to the galleys, and death. Since *chambres* allowed the king to seize financier's profits and write off part of his debt, they amounted to a form of limited bankruptcy.

To an important degree, recourse to bankruptcy and *chambres de justice* functioned as an extraordinary requisition of wealth from the business and financial community. But the benefits gained from mobilizing such assets for state use were undermined by the fact that such financial conduct drove up interest rates to exorbitant levels.

---

[37] Colbert in Dent, *Crisis in Finance*, 43; Louis XIV, *Mémoires de Louis XIV*, Charles Dreyss, ed., 2 vols. (Paris, 1860), 2:376.

[38] Fernand Braudel and Ernest Labrousse, eds., *Histoire économique et sociale de la France*, vol. 2 (Paris: 1970), 277.

[39] On *chambres de justice*, see Mousnier, *The Institutions of France*, 2:485–90.

In such a situation, finance ministers and their agents, such as *intendants des finances*, called on their personal connections and a good deal of fraud to convince the financial community to lend money to the crown. For example, the government set official limits to the amount of interest that could be paid, with legal caps at 8.33 percent during the period 1594–1601, at 6.25 percent during 1601–34, and at 5.55 percent during 1634–65.[40] However, the risk involved could not justify such low returns, so to win over new creditors, government officials awarded creditors, often their friends or relatives, illegally high interest and slipped them illicit payments.

Before 1661, when things were at their worst, official accounts had to hide where the money was really going rather than render an exact report of transactions. Much of what the government paid came by way of *ordonnances de comptant*. These ordonnances, sent out over the king's signature, were not subject to verification or inspection and were not even listed under specific budget lines that would reveal their purpose. The huge extent of *ordonnances de comptant* during the war years 1635–59 made it, and makes it, impossible to figure the actual cost of the war. For example, consider the period 1635–40, when annual expenses listed in the royal budget, the *état au vrai*, ran about 42.5 million livres.[41] During the same time, Bonney argues that the secret expenses by *ordonnances de comptant* ran at an additional 37.7 to 39 million per year.[42]

One of the great values of the *ordonnances de comptant* is that they threw a false scent across the path of that other financial bloodhound of the monarchy, the *Chambre des comptes*. Whereas *chambres de justice* were held infrequently, the *chambre des comptes* was a permanent auditing body. However, the monarchy kept its mandate limited to verifying accounts in the narrowest sense so that it could not stall the already complicated machinery of state credit. In any case, auditing of accounts was subject to long delays, running ten years and more. Military accounts were no exception; in one case, correspondence of 1705 was still concerned with payments filed in 1677.[43] The financial historian Marcel Marion described the *chambre des comptes* as an "archaic institution, almost without any utility for the good order of public accounts, and even less for the good order of finances."[44]

Financiers kept their dealings secret to avoid retrospective taxation by a *chambre de justice* or examination by the less threatening *chambre des comptes*; consequently, the official financial records, the *états*, were designed to disguise transactions.[45] This is why Dent talks of the "cloud cuckoo land of the *états au vrai*," insisting on the unreliability of official budgets from the period

---

[40] Bonney, *The King's Debts*, 19.   [41] Mallet, *Compts rendus*, 224–25.

[42] See Bonney, *The King's Debts*, appendix 2, table 3.

[43] AN, G^{7}1777, #75–76. For other cases of delay see, AN, G^{7}1774, # 86, G^{7}1775, #82–84, and G^{7}1774, 16 February 1684.

[44] Marcel Marion, *Dictionnaire des institutions de la France aux XVIIe et XVIIIe siècles* (Paris: 1923), 82.

[45] Bonney, *The King's Debts*, 278.

before 1661.[46] Manipulation of state finances made many a fortune; even Mazarin used his special position to play the game, as did Fouquet and even Colbert. In a more self-righteous moment, Colbert condemned the system, which he claimed "the cleverest men in the realm, concerned in it for forty years, had so complicated in order to make themselves needed [since] they alone understood it."[47] The fact is that without corruption and fraud, the system could not have functioned. "It is clear," concludes Dent, "that the whole central financial administration was involved on a permanent basis in conspiracy to commit fraud."[48]

While Colbert brought some reform after 1661, he did not transform the system. Certainly, the fact that Louis XIV functioned not only as his own first minister but also as his own *surintendant des finances* improved the situation. However, the most important factor allowing more regular financial practice was the return of peace. Reform was unthinkable during wartime, since it would threaten the flow of credit. For all Colbert's accomplishments, when the French forced a major war in 1672, much of his work went for nothing. Colbert tried to resist the war because of its inevitable effect on finances, and he protested that the expense would be impossible. Louis threatened his *contrôleur général*, "Think about it. If you can't do it, there will always be someone who can."[49] And Colbert capitulated. Renewed war brought renewed reliance upon the same old varieties of "obfuscation and deceit."[50] Once again the government turned to traditional abuses – sale of offices, bloated short-term bills of credit, alienation of future revenues, and so on.

Other Sources of Finance

The military expenses borne directly by the monarch were great, and the means employed to raise funds to meet them were both demanding and complicated, but the full amount spent to maintain the army exceeded the treasure lavished on it by the central government. Towns, provinces, and field armies themselves contributed money and other resources to maintain the troops. Even military officers and state bureaucrats tapped their private wealth to meet military needs.

In support of the army, local governmental units appropriated funds in excess of taxation passed on to the central government. Towns, for example, contributed to the expense of lodging troops within their walls. Provinces shouldered expenses for *étapes* and for sustaining the *milice*, particularly during the Nine Years' War.[51] Special situations brought additional demands.

---

[46] Dent, *Crisis in Finance*, 85.
[47] Colbert in Dickson and Sterling, "War Finance, 1689–1714," 298.
[48] Dent, *Crisis in Finance*, 83.
[49] Paul Sonnino, *Louis XIV and the origins of the Dutch War* (Cambridge: 1989), 172.
[50] Dent, *Crisis in Finance*, 23.
[51] Victor Belhomme, *L'armée française en 1690* (Paris: 1895), 142–43.

The estates of Hainault supplied 1,500 carts for the siege of Namur in 1692, and the Languedoc estates contributed over 3.5 million livres to support the war effort in 1693–94, including 345,000 livres for mules to transport the troops' baggage.[52] Corvisier estimates that as much as 20 percent of military expenses were charged to such local sources.[53]

War finance drew upon further resources in two other manners: through requisition and by tapping the personal wealth and credit of its officer corps. Before 1659, the most common form of requisition amounted to little better than pillage, and the most common victims of this were the French population itself. As the *grand siècle* wore on, the more regular, but still violent, practice of levying contributions spread. Contributions were requisitions of money laid upon territories outside France occupied by French troops. In their form, they mimicked taxation, except that the alternative to payment was the burning of offending towns by Bourbon troops. The huge expense of maintaining an army in the field and the potential of supporting troops by levying demands on the enemy's population, resulted in the strategic advisability of sending your armies to fight on enemy territory.

As a matter of course, the state required that colonels and captains foot many of the bills for their units. It was common for colonels to create entire new regiments in wartime largely at their own expense. In addition, the state made use of the credit of other officers, reimbursing them only later, if at all, for authorized outlays. The nature of the expenses imposed on officers were such that it will never be possible to arrive at exact figures for their losses, but they were substantial, contributing to the financial decline of the aristocracy.

As the preceding discussion demonstrates, French financial structures and practices constituted a complicated, inefficient, and archaic but necessary aspect of the French military administration in the *grand siècle*. Although it is tempting to conclude that nothing improved, even under the mighty Louis XIV, this would not be fair, for the financial system was not plagued by the same high level of chaos under the Sun King that had afflicted it under his father – witness the lack of bankruptcies and *chambres de justice* between 1665 and 1715. Nevertheless, problems in war finance continued to cripple the Bourbons, because ultimately the king could not have solved his financial problems without entirely redefining French society, a task that was too imposing for even Louis XIV.

CONCLUSION

This opening discussion has dealt with four contexts for the story that follows, but it should also signal a fifth. The army of the *grand siècle* was not simply a product of its age; it helped to form that era as well. In particular,

---

[52] André Corvisier, *Les Français et l'armée sous Louis XIV* (Vincennes: 1975), 188; William Beik, *Absolutism and Society in Seventeenth-Century France* (Cambridge: 1985), 137.
[53] Contamine, *Histoire militaire*, 1:429.

war and military institutions were central factors in state formation, a key topic that has drawn scholars to look again at military details once regarded as unimportant.

Intertwined with Bourbon absolutism, the army both drove and exemplified the increased power of the monarchy. Whereas it has lately become a mark of historical sophistication to shy away from the term *absolutism* – or at least to redefine it extensively – this volume embraces a fairly time-honored version of the concept. Traditionally, absolutism signified a notable rise in the authority of the king, often at the expense of the aristocracy, with increased centralization and bureaucratization of government, packaged in baroque grandeur. Where once seventeenth-century absolutism was thought to mark a sharp break with the past, today there is greater emphasis on continuity with a feudal past. Doubtless, the inability of the monarchy to reform its financial house adds credence to such a view. Although this study accepts important continuities and limitations, it also argues strongly for significant change in military institutions, which along with the monarchy itself constituted the very essence of the state. Change may have been firmly rooted in the past, but it was change nonetheless, and it clearly prefigured the future. Movement, although often frustrated or modified by financial restraints and social privileges, proceeded in the direction of control, centralization, and bureaucratization – classic absolutism. Given the centrality of military institutions to the state, the transition from an aggregate contract to a state commission army, as outlined in these pages, may best establish the reality of absolutism in the *grand siècle*.

To examine state formation at this point would be premature, for that examination must rely on information yet to be presented in the succeeding chapters. It is best to wait until the end of the journey just begun. But from the start, bear in mind that if the army shaped the state and society, as well as fought their wars, then it is a subject of note for its own sake. It stands as the foundation for the decorative façade of Versailles, the hard substance behind the elegant display.

2

Army Growth

BY the end of the seventeenth century, European warfare pitted collosal armies against one another – armies that dwarfed those of the past. France boasted the greatest of these Goliaths, a force that totaled as many as 420,000 soldiers, at least on paper. It was the largest and hungriest institution maintained by the state. Yet as important as this giant was, the pattern and timing of its growth and its final dimensions remain matters of debate. This chapter presents a new and more rigorous calculation of French army expansion between 1610 and 1715.

Of all the developments summed up in the theory of a Military Revolution in early modern Europe, none matters more in the strictly European context than the growth of armies. Across the seas, as Westerners took their first steps toward global domination, numbers mattered less. On foreign shores, they imposed their presence and overcame resistance through superior military technology, discipline, and organization. But on the continent of Europe, contending powers shared the same or similar levels of technology and organization. Victory rested as much on quantity as on quality. French efforts to marshal military forces of ever greater proportions exerted influences far beyond the battlefield. To a large extent, the stress of mobilizing resources to support the new armies reshaped government, redefining basic issues of power and altering methods of finance and administration. The social impact of increased army expansion rivaled the political. The lower strata of the population filled the ranks through massive recruitment and, after 1688, through conscription, while those who remained at home could not escape the oppressive taxation required by the costs of war. Elites defined and were defined by their role in a large officer corps. Beyond this, horrendous abuses of civilian communities by troops supposedly loyal to the Bourbons, repeated rebellions spurred by spiraling impositions, and the potential for intimidation and repression threatened by a huge army, all demand that historians give significant weight to the phenomenon of French army growth during the seventeenth century. At the base of any such study must be an accurate picture of the pattern and proportions of that growth.

For over a century, historians divided French military expansion into two stages. First, in order to challenge Spain, Richelieu and Louis XIII assembled an army of unprecedented size in 1635. Totaling 150,000 or more, this force was at least twice as large as any previous wartime military maintained by the French monarchy. A second phase of growth followed the military and administrative reform associated with the first decades of the personal reign of Louis XIV. Troop strength reached 280,000 during the Dutch War and attained 400,000 in the Nine Years' War, continuing at that level for the War of the Spanish Succession.

Since the mid-1950s, proponents of a Military Revolution in early modern Europe, most notably Michael Roberts and Geoffrey Parker, have insisted that the need to raise and support armies larger than ever before dictated administrative, fiscal, and governmental reforms. This side of the Military Revolution has attracted historians and social scientists concerned with state formation, most notably Charles Tilly, who writes, "As they fashioned an organization for making war, the king's servants inadvertently created a centralized state. First the framework of an army, then a government built around that framework – and in its shape."[1] Of course, reason dictates that in order for military necessity to have brought on government reform, the growth of the army must have predated that reform, not the other way around.

Recently published revisionist scholarship jettisons this longstanding portrayal. The most serious attack denies military growth prior to 1659, while asserting that growth after that date came as a byproduct of social stability under Louis XIV. David Parrott, a young English scholar, has played a key role in questioning substantial military expansion before the Peace of the Pyrenees.[2] While not the first, he has been the most effective in arguing that very little actual reform occurred during the war years of the Richelieu era.[3] Parrott states that the historical thesis that Richelieu instituted a virtual administrative revolution is "underpinned by an assumption that the size of the army increased massively from 1635. But this assumption proves equally

---

[1] Charles Tilly, *The Contentious French* (Cambridge, MA: 1986), 128. See as well, Tilly, *Coercion, Capital, and European States, AD 990–1990* (Oxford: 1990); Brian M. Downing, *The Military Revolution and Political Change in Early Modern Europe* (Princeton: 1992); and Karen A. Rasler and William R. Thompson, *War and State Making: The Shaping of the Global Powers* (Boston: 1989).

[2] David Parrott, "The Administration of the French Army During the Ministry of Cardinal Richelieu," Ph.D. dissertation, Oxford University, 1985, and "Strategy and Tactics in the Thirty Years' War: The 'Military Revolution,'" *Militärgeschichtliche Mitteilungen*, XVIII, 2 (1985).

[3] Other works that detail the ineffectiveness of reform before 1659 include Patrick Landier, "Guerre, Violences, et Société en France, 1635–1659," doctorat de troisième cycle, Université de Paris IV, 1978; Jonathan Berger, "Military and Financial Government in France, 1648–1661," Ph.D. dissertation, University of Chicago, 1979; and Bernard Kroener, *Les routes et les étapes. Die Bersorgung der franzoschichen Armeen in Nordostfrankreich (1635–1661)*, 2 vols. (Munster: 1980).

untenable."[4] In his recent *A Military Revolution?*, Black embraces Parrott's arguments, putting them in even stronger terms than Parrott intended. Black disputes the concept of a Military Revolution, particularly as originally proposed by Michael Roberts, who assigned it to the century 1560–1660.[5] Crucially, Black ascribes all French military growth to Louis XIV's personal reign. The fact that he shifts the time period away from Roberts's original dates is of little consequence in itself, since others, including Parker, had done that before. More critically, Black insists that the military expansion occurring after 1660 came only as the consequence of increased government capacity made possible by social and political compromises hammered out under Louis XIV. Therefore, Black dismisses the army and war as *causes* of political change and instead reduces them to mere *effects*.

While controversy over the Military Revolution draws attention to military expansion during the first half of the seventeenth century, André Corvisier requires historians to look again at the army that fought the last war of the Sun King. Historians have long featured the War of the Spanish Succession as Louis's greatest war effort, one which, in the words of the most recent book on the subject, saw "armies inflated to reach unprecedented size."[6] Corvisier goes even further, insisting that the forces mobilized to fight the War of the Spanish Succession approached in size those raised by revolutionary France nearly a century later. Recently he restated this thesis in the first volume of the new *Histoire militaire de la France*.[7] There he adds new contingents to the forces of Louis XIV to boost their numbers until it compares favorably with the *levée en masse*. To the 300,000 French troops that he claims for the regular army circa 1709–10, Corvisier would add naval forces, local militias, and other forces to yield a grand total of 600,000.

His debatable mathematics seem to flow from a resolution to demonstrate that a patriotic wave à la 1792 engulfed the France of the Sun King. Here he follows Emile G. Léonard, who posited this view in the 1950s.[8] The larger the forces raised during the War of the Spanish Succession, the more they justify Corvisier's notion of a nationalistic effort predating the fall of the Bastille. While Corvisier's thesis is neither so new nor so important as those of Parrott and Black, its restatement in a work that promises to become a standard reference for a generation or more requires some response.

Revisionist challenges to traditional conceptions of army growth as they relate to the Military Revolution, state formation, and a "patriotic" effort

---

[4] Parrott, "The Administration of the French Army," iv.

[5] Black presents his most strident case in *A Military Revolution?* (Atlantic Highlands, NJ: 1991), but his *European Warfare, 1660–1815* (New Haven, CT: 1994) uses figures generated in John A. Lynn, "Recalculating French Army Growth During the *Grand siècle*, 1610–1715," *French Historical Studies*, vol. 18, no. 4 (Fall 1994), so it is more in accord with this chapter.

[6] Frank Tallett, *War and Society in Early-Modern Europe, 1495–1715* (London: 1992), 80.

[7] Corvisier section in Philippe Contamine, ed., *Histoire militaire de la France*, vol. 1 (Paris: 1992), 531.

[8] Emile G. Léonard, *L'armée et ses problèmes au XVIIIe siècle* (Paris: 1958).

under Louis XIV make a recalculation of military expansion necessary. Until the last few years, it was acceptable to speak of army size by appealing to official financial and military statements, *états*, but today an evaluation of army size demands a new methodology employing a wider range of source material.

METHODOLOGY: DISTINCTIONS AND SOURCES

An effort to set the record straight must be very careful concerning exactly what is to be counted and the kinds of sources to be employed. Trying to fix army size involves numerous technical points, but many of them come down to being certain that one is not comparing apples with oranges. The first and the most basic difference to bear in mind is that between a field force and a state's entire army. A single field force, usually assembled in one location under one commander, only constitutes part of the total armed might of the state, which may have more than one army on campaign at the same time, while committing still other troops to garrison duty. As strange as it may seem, historians are forever muddying the distinction between the troops marshaled for a single battle and the army as a whole. This chapter concerns itself with total army size; the number of troops committed to particular campaigns and battles is dealt with later.

This leads to the question of who should be counted as part of an army. Obviously, field armies and garrison forces composed of regular troops must be included, but who else? Local and provincial units who stayed at home to guard their towns and man their walls but were not supported by the monarchy and did not necessarily serve full time ought not to be tallied as royal troops. However, militiamen who after 1688 served the king at the front in their own or regular battalions belong in the totals presented here. Noncombatants traveling with the army pose another problem. Often discussions of early modern armies calculate the numbers of traders, women, and children who accompanied the troops; however, such camp followers will not be considered here. Nor do valets, pages, grooms, or other personal servants qualify.[9]

In counting troop numbers, it is also important to differentiate when units are tallied. Above all, one must contrast peacetime with wartime forces, because they differed in size and composition. Obviously, peacetime figures were much smaller than wartime numbers, with few exceptions. By 1670, wartime tallies generally stood three times higher than the number of troops maintained between conflicts. At the end of each war, the government demobilized, or "reformed," individual soldiers, surplus companies, and entire regiments. The fact that armies were much smaller during peacetime years under Louis XIV meant that when conflicts began these forces had to expand,

---

[9] According to Oudard Coquault, during the Fronde, an army of 20,000 men had 10,000 valets. Albert Babeau, *La vie militaire sous l'ancien regime*, 2 vols. (Paris: 1890), 1:198–99.

and, understandably, this took some time. Beyond these dramatic shifts, more subtle rhythms determined army size during times of conflict. The combat strength of military units normally fluctuated over the course of the year. Established regiments enjoyed their most complete complement just as they entered the campaign season in May or June, but battle casualties and losses from disease and desertion eroded numbers over the summer months. Winter quarters provided time for rest, refitting, and recruitment. New levies arrived in late winter or early spring to flesh out units, so that they grew until they went off on campaign to repeat the cycle.

Not only does a careful accounting of army size need to bear in mind the nature of forces to be compared and the times when those forces are to be examined, but it must also take into account the different types of sources that provide the basis for such a study. In general, this includes four varieties of records: (1) military ordinances; (2) financial *contrôles* and *états*; (3) review reports and *routes*; and (4) miscellaneous correspondence. A minute study of the first, military ordinances, promises to reveal the decrees altering army size. In the nineteenth century, Victor Belhomme made the most thorough attempt to undertake this laborious feat. He charted the number of French regiments year by year, sometimes month by month, for the entire seventeenth century.[10] However, the problem with employing military ordinances is that, as in other aspects of government as well, official ordinances may bear little relation to reality. In fact, Belhomme's figures are suspect, because they greatly exceed the levels generated by more reliable sources until he deals with the period after 1670, by which time Louis and Louvois had imposed greater regularity on the system.

Administrators also left behind a number of contemporary *états* that supply numbers of troops for the army as a whole. Such *états* come in several forms. A small collection known as the "Tiroirs de Louis XIV" were reports and planning documents in the king's own possession.[11] In the majority of cases, however, official records stating the size of the entire army are financial documents generated as aids in estimating the cost of supporting the army in the present or coming year. Such financial *contrôles* provide a consistent, and convenient, source for the study of army size; therefore, generations of historians have uncritically appealed to them when judging army size. Yet the *contrôles* have recently come under attack. David Parrott questions their value, making the important and valid point that they were only financial documents designed to predict the amount of money that would be paid out

---

[10] Victor Belhomme, *Histoire de l'infanterie en France*, 5 vols. (Paris: 1893–1902). Actually, his lack of theoretical discussion and footnotes hide his exact sources, but it seems virtually certain that he based his work on the military ordinances collected at the ministry of war and the Bibliothèque Nationale.

[11] Louis was probably referring to these when he confidently stated that "What makes me more certain of my enterprises is that I have an accurate *état* of my troops, their quartering, and their number." Louis's journal for April 1667, Louis XIV, *Mémoires de Louis XIV*, Charles Dreyss, ed., 2 vols. (Paris: 1860), 2:167.

by the monarchy for salaries and sustenance. Troop sizes drawn from them are entirely theoretical, so Parrott would completely discard them.[12] But this goes too far. True, *contrôles* were statements of anticipated expenditures rather than head counts; however, the expenditures in question were figured as a given number of payments to a given number of troops, and therefore they reflected projections of army size.

Financial *contrôles* retain important value as theoretical maximums that can then be discounted to approximate real numbers. A basic method used to set army size in financial documents and other estimates of total army size involved calculating the number of companies or battalions and squadrons present, and then multiplying that number by the regulation complement of men set for that unit by ordinance. While this method of calculation is not always explicitly employed, it is so common that it can be assumed as underlying virtually all gross statements of army size. Working within the parameters of this seventeenth-century technique, other documents, review reports and *étapes routes,* allow the raw data supplied in *états* and *contrôles* to be refashioned into more realistic estimates of actual army size.

Review reports and *étapes routes* provide actual head counts of troops. Review reports were prepared by military bureaucrats for administrative reasons, as when distributing pay and rations to soldiers. Troops on the road traveling from place to place carried *routes,* documents that stipulated their route and the stops that they were allowed to make along the way. At each stop, they were entitled to rations and lodging, so the *routes* stated exactly how many men of what ranks were to be fed and housed. By their nature, review reports and *routes* dealt only with individual units or small groups of units rather than with an entire army, but they will be put to a broader use here. Because the actual sizes of units can be calculated from reviews and *routes*, these numbers can be used to estimate the percentage of regulation strength actually present under arms. Gross statements of army size can then be discounted by this percentage to yield a reasonable estimate of real troop numbers.

The last category of sources covers a varied range of documents that, while not systematic, can be very useful. In particular, when government officials discuss the king's forces in their letters and memoranda, they provide valuable corroboration of other sorts of documents, notably those financial *contrôles* that have come under attack. The use of sources in this manner underlines the fact that the best estimates of army size emerge from combining different sources and cross-checking whenever possible.

A NECESSARY BASELINE: ARMY FIGURES, 1300–1610

No matter how careful the selection and calculation of figures, a study of military expansion can still go awry should it fail to establish a proper baseline

---

[12] Parrott, "The Administration of the French Army," 135.

against which to measure growth after 1610. In the interest of creating reasonable grounds for comparison, a careful study must go back before the start of the century, even extending the search to the medieval era.

Philippe Contamine supplies a series of estimates for the size of royal forces during the late Middle Ages. He believes that the medieval French monarchy mustered its largest force in 1340, when it assembled 60,000 troops in two theaters at the start of the Hundred Years' War, although this number included feudal levies.[13] Over the course of the next century, the ravages of the Black Death precluded putting as many men in the field again.[14] Under Louis XI (1461–83), wartime highs began to approach the proportions of the pre-plague past. Taking the entire second half of the fifteenth century into consideration, Contamine pegs wartime forces as generally between 40,000 and 45,000 combatants.[15]

During the fifteenth century, peacetime forces also grew. Charles V (1364–80) kept garrison forces that reached only 5,200.[16] Charles VII (1422–61) created the first permanent standard units, the *compagnies d'ordonnance*, in 1445. These fifteen companies each contained 100 lances at a time when a lance included six mounted men, of whom only four qualified as combatants. Therefore, 1,500 lances produced 6,000 combatants, not the 9,000 often cited. Adding in garrison infantry, the *mortes payes*, Contamine estimates the average peacetime level of the army, 1445–75, as about 14,000.[17] During the last three years of his reign, Louis XI maintained a huge force of 47,500–24,000 of which assembled in his "camp de guerre."[18] This costly military establishment did not survive Louis's death, and by 1490, the army contained only about 12,800 cavalry, 3,500 *mortes payes*, and 800 household guards.[19]

As the focus changes to the sixteenth century, Ferdinand Lot, *Recherches sur les effectifs des armées françaises des Guerres d'Italie aux Guerres de Religion, 1494–1562*, provides the best guide to the study of French army size. However, two caveats must be borne in mind when using Lot's work. First, it is not always clear whether his figures should be taken as theoretical or real totals. Second, he emphasizes field forces for particular campaigns rather than estimates of total army size; therefore, his figures often need to be supplemented by the research of other historians.

---

[13] Contamine, *Histoire militaire*, 1:137–38.

[14] After 1340, numbers fell off rapidly; in 1342, the king could claim only 9,500, and in 1383, he sent off but 16,000 to the relief of Ypres, although this was only a single field army. Contamine, *Histoire militaire*, 1:137, 172.

[15] Philippe Contamine, *Guerre, état et société à la fin du moyen âge. Études sure les armées des rois de France, 1337–1494* (Paris: 1972), 316–17.

[16] During the months of bad weather, this declined to 3,400. Contamine, *Histoire militaire*, 1:145.

[17] Contamine, *Guerre, état et société*, 278–83, 286.

[18] According to Philippe de Commynes in Contamine, *Histoire militaire*, 1:229–30, 232.

[19] 3,200 lances figured at four combatants each. Contamine, *Histoire militaire*, 1:219–21. See total figure of 18,400 in Contamine, *Guerre, état et société*, 317.

Lot deflates traditional, overblown statements of French army size. He rejects exaggerated notions of the army that Charles VIII led on his first invasion of Italy. Excluding Italian units not in the pay of France, Lot arrives at a figure of 22,000 to 27,200.[20] The French staged the invasion of 1499 in much the same proportions, with 23,000 to 29,000 troops.[21] He argues that this second figure represented the entire force of the French army, since Louis XII left only "a simple escort" back in France. Lot estimates that 41,000 troops served François I at the time of Marignano, 1515, including troops left north of the Alps to protect the provinces.[22] Putting his faith in the Bourgeois de Paris, a source Lot rejects, Henry Lemonnier gives the number of troops at 57,750 in 1523, which again includes 10,200 left to garrison France.[23] Lot speculates that the field army size during the first half of the century may have reached an apogee of 50,000–60,000 late in 1536, but even Lot regards his sources here as "naturally doubtful."[24]

In fact, 1544 seems a better candidate for peak total army size. In April, French forces won the battle of Ceresoles in Piedmont, but summer brought invasions by both Henry VIII and Charles V in the north of France. François scurried to assemble forces to meet them, withdrawing as many as 12,000 troops from Italy and hiring thousands of Swiss and Germans. Counting François's main army around Jalons, Brissac's force that confronted the Imperialists at Saint-Dizier, Biez's army that threw itself into Montreuil, the garrison of Boulogne, Vendôme's army around Hesdin, and troops remaining in Italy, as well as providing for miscellaneous garrisons, the total of French forces probably added up to 69,000 to 77,000 troops.[25] This was an extraordinary and short-lived strain on French resources, since the army only existed at this level briefly during the late summer. It is worth noting that François I wrote that at best, his subjects could support 50,000 troops.[26]

There is little reason to believe that the French topped this figure during 1552, the year that witnessed both the French "Voyage d'Allemagne" and the siege of Metz by Charles V. Lot's analysis reveals that Henri II conducted only 36,650 paid troops on his "voyage," while another 11,450 remained to

---

[20] Ferdinand Lot, *Recherches sur les effectifs des armées françaises des Guerres d'Italie aux Guerres de Religion, 1494–1562* (Paris: 1962), 21. He devotes his entire first chapter to conflicting claims.

[21] Lot, *Recherches sur les effectifs*, 27. This represents something of a discounted figure, since on page 26 Lot also suggests a less critical figure of 26,000 to 38,000 as presented by Léon Pélissier, *Louis XII et Ludovic Sforza*, 2 vols. (Paris: 1896), 1:384–86.

[22] Lot, *Recherches sur les effectifs*, 41.

[23] Lemonnier's figures for cavalry exceed Lot's, since the former counts the entire lance and the latter counts only the combatants within it. Henry Lemonnier, *Histoire de France*, ed. Ernest Lavisse, vol. 5, part 2, *La lutte contre la maison d'Autriche, 1519–1559* (Paris: 1904), 84fn.

[24] Lot, *Recherches sur les effectifs*, 65.

[25] Lot, *Recherches sur les effectifs*, 95, 104; Charles Oman, *History of the Art of War in the Sixteenth Century* (London: 1937), 340, 343; Lemonnier, *La lutte contre la maison d'Autriche*, 114; Contamine, *Histoire militaire*, 1:242.

[26] Contamine, *Histoire militaire*, 1:305.

defend France.[27] Even if an additional 10,000 troops garrisoned Piedmont and certain French outposts, the total still only reached 60,000. Henri again led field forces of similar proportions in 1558, when he assembled 40,150 to 40,550 at Pierrepont.[28] Winding up his discussion of the Italian Wars, Lot credits Charles IX with an army of 36,720 in 1562, after the Peace of Cateau-Cambrésis, but it seems best to reject this exaggerated estimate, because it rests on very questionable sources.[29]

Unfortunately, Lot did not devote his considerable skills to the study of the Wars of Religion (1562–98). To be sure, the confusion of the Wars of Religion daunts the boldest of scholars. In his treatment of them, Corvisier provides only a few generalizations for the second half of the sixteenth century. He concludes that owing to demographic, fiscal, and military limitations, the kings of France could support no more than 50,000 men at any one time.[30]

Recently, James B. Wood has presented more impressive estimates for the maximum size of the royal army during the months of December 1567 and January 1568. He calculates that the monarchy claimed a paper force of 72,388 troops in the theater of combat.[31] To this substantial force should be added 12,000 troops stationed elsewhere in France and Italy as well as an unknown number of small garrisons, raising the theoretical total to at least 84,000, the largest force mustered by the French monarchy during the Wars of Religion.[32] However, the manner in which Wood calculated his estimate requires that it be shaved down to an absolute paper maximum of less than 80,000.[33] Even allowing for this, Wood demonstrates that the government intended to maintain wartime forces that equaled those marshaled by François I and Henri II. Of course, the rebel armies arrayed against the king are not counted, even though they too were French forces maintained by French resources. The Royal army's peacetime numbers were understandably much smaller. Wood documents the average peacetime strength of the *gendarmerie* at 6,500

---

[27] "Estat de l'armée," Bibliothèque Nationale, hereafter cited as BN, f. fr. 2965, fol. 2–4, in Lot, *Recherches sur les effectifs*, 129–30, 133, with corrections and additions for garrison troops. Lot makes a mistake in his addition, sending the figure 1,000 men higher than shown here.

[28] Review of Pierrepont and Rambutin in Lot, *Recherches sur les effectifs*, 179–86. In addition, Henri would also have reinforcements of 8,400 and surviving cavalry from Gravelines, p. 186.

[29] "Abrégé de l'État militaire de la France," a financial document, in Lot, *Recherches sur les effectifs*, 190–92. James Wood dismisses his documentation as "very poor" for this figure. Personal letter of 3 September 1992.

[30] Contamine, *Histoire militaire*, 1:305.

[31] Figures based on a series of *états* presented in table form by James B. Wood, "The Royal Army During the Early Wars of Religion, 1559–1576," in Mack P. Holt, ed. *Society & Institutions in Early Modern France* (Athens, GA: 1991), 10–11.

[32] In a letter of 3 September 1992, Wood states that the 72,000 was only a theater estimate and that there were other infantry and gendarmes elsewhere. He believes that "the second war [of religion] represents a maximum for the royal forces."

[33] Wood combined the maximum sizes for all units, even if particular units might be cited as smaller in other documents.

horsemen between 1559 and 1576.[34] Adding this to the 6,229 infantry garrison troops listed for January 1572 generates a total of approximately 12,700 standing troops that year.[35]

In the final stage of the Wars of Religion, after Henri IV ascended to the throne in 1589, the best estimates put his army in the neighborhood of 50,000 to 60,000 based on multiplying the number of companies by their theoretical strengths.[36] The return of peace at the close of the sixteenth century brought a thorough demobilization of French forces under the thrifty and efficient direction of Sully. Soon after the Treaty of Vervins, 1598, the army shrank to a strength of 7,200 to 8,500.[37] After the brief Savoyard War (1600), the figure seems to have hovered about 10,000 during the first decade of the seventeenth century.[38] When Henri IV decided to challenge Spain in 1610, he and Sully drew up plans for wartime forces on the scale of the previous century, totaling about 55,000 men in two major armies, a mobile reserve, and garrison troops.[39] Assassination put an end to both the monarch and his plans.

This examination of the period from the late Middle Ages through 1610 reveals less military growth than might be expected. Wartime highs ranged from 40,000 to 45,000 in the late fifteenth century and reached 50,000 to 80,000 in the sixteenth. Peacetime levels varied more, but considering the period as a whole, peacetime highs of 10,000 to 20,000 were common; Louis XI's attempt to maintain permanent forces far in excess of that figure was simply a brief aberration.

THEORETICAL MAXIMUM TROOP FIGURES, 1610–1715

Bearing this benchmark in mind, consider the theoretical paper totals raised and maintained by the French after 1610. The minor wars and rebellions that

---

[34] Wood claims that during peacetime lulls, 1559–76, the monarchy supported on average sixty-four to sixty-nine companies of gendarmes, totaling about 6,500 horsemen. Wood, "The Royal Army During the Early Wars of Religion," 3.

[35] Wood, "The Royal Army During the Early Wars of Religion," 5–6.

[36] For 1588–89, see BN, Chatre de Cangé, vol. 18, #393, "Estat des compagnies de gens de guerre à pied." See, as well, Nicolas Edouard Delabarre-Duparcq, *L'art militaire pendant les guerres de religion, 1562–1598* (Paris: 1863), 24. For 1597 see BN, Chatre de Cangé, vol. 20, #33, "État des regiments et des capitaines ayant charge de compagnies de gens de pied pour le service du Roy tant en son armée que aux garnisons de Picardie, Champagne, Bourgoyne et Bresse en janvier 1597."

[37] Sully, *Mémoires de Maximillien de Béthune duc de Sully*, 3 vols. (London: 1747), 2:26. Joseph Servan, *Recherches sur la force de l'armée française, depuis Henri IV jusqu'à la fin de 1806* (Paris: 1806), 2, uses the same figures.

[38] Infantry regiments stood at 4,100, cavalry at 2,637, and garrison infantry at 3,000 for a total of 9,737, according to Servan, *Recherches*, 2–4.

[39] Sully, *Mémoires des sages et royales oeconomies d'estat de Henry le grand*, vols. 8 and 9 in Petitot, ed., *Collection des Mémoires relatifs à l'histoire de France*, 2nd ser.(Paris: 1821), 8:351, 9:65–68. Different editions and translations of Sully's *Mémoires* give different figures.

broke out during the regency and extended into the 1630s sent the size of the French army above the 10,000 peacetime level.[40] As early as 1615, there may have been 30,000 men assembled in royal field forces to fight against internal revolt.[41] At the Assembly of Notables held in 1626, marshal Schomberg announced the monarchy's intention to maintain an army of 30,000.[42] However, a "Projet de dépense" for 1627 indicates a strength of only about 18,000 men.[43] Renewed war with the Huguenots made such a force inadequate; the siege of La Rochelle, 1627–28, alone required 28,000 troops.[44] David Parrott believes that by 1630 the official strength of the army, with forces in Champagne and Italy, stood at 39,000.[45]

Full-scale war would send these figures soaring in the next five years. Direct French participation in the Thirty Years' War began in 1635, and the struggle continued long after the Treaties of Westphalia were signed in 1648; not until the Peace of the Pyrenees in 1659 would peace return. This war with Spain created armies of unprecedented size, according to official documents. Since so much of the current historiographical debate rests on the timing and level of increases between 1635 and 1659, they demand special attention.

Several sources point to important increases in 1634 as the French mobilized to enter the war with Spain. An "Estat des gens de guerre qui sont sur pied à la fin d'Aoust 1634" shows 100,368 soldiers in service at that time.[46] A letter from Richelieu to the king on 13 September supports this figure, mentioning 89,000 men in French service, out of an intended 95,000, with more on the way.[47] In October, an additional "Estat des troupes faict en

---

[40] Deageant stated that Louis's council advised him to levy "an hundred thousand Men," but there is no indication that such a force was ever actually raised before 1635. Guichard Deageant de Saint-Martin, *Memoirs of Monsieur Deageant* (London: 1690), 135. I thank Brian Sandberg for supplying this material. Belhomme would have us believe that the French mustered 97,000 infantry in 1622 and 64,000 in 1624, figures which as usual seem far to high. Belhomme, *Infanterie*, 1:331, 337.

[41] Jacques Humbert, *Le Maréchal de Crequy: Gendre de Lesdiguières, 1573–1638* (Paris: 1962), 71–72. *Mercure français*, vol. 6, 323–33. Again, thanks to Brian Sandberg for this material.

[42] Figures in Nicolas Edouard Delabarre-Duparcq, *Histoire de l'art de la guerre*, vol. 2 (Paris: 1864), 159, and detailed in Belhomme, *Infanterie*, 1:337.

[43] BN, Chatre de Cangé, vol. 22, #64, "Projet de dépense de l'extraordinaire des guerres pour l'année 1627." This source actually counts 12,572 men, but it gives the financial upkeep for "garnisons ordinaires," and figured at the same rate as line infantry, this would yield another 5,500 troops. See as well, BN, Chatre de Cangé, vol. 22, #63, which gives a count of 11,810 without garrisons.

[44] F. de Vaux de Folletier, *Le siège de la Rochelle* (Paris: 1931), 237–38.

[45] Table of projected and real troop strength in Parrott, "The Administration of the French Army," 142.

[46] BN, f. fr. 6385.

[47] Armand du Plesis, duc de Richelieu, *Lettres, instructions diplomatiques et papiers d'état du cardinal de Richelieu*, ed. Avenel, 8 vols. (Paris: 1853–77), 4:601. Discussing this letter, Parrott accepts a figure of 45,000 infantry, 8,000 cavalry, and an additional 30,000 garrison troops, a total of 83,000 troops in service. Parrott, "The Administration of the French Army," 106.

octobre 1634," boosts the number to 124,500.[48] Building from such an expanding base, the financial documents for 1635 seem reasonable. A projection for 1635 drafted in November 1634 set the number of troops slightly higher at 125,000.[49] Again correspondence confirms this financial document as more than merely a statement of funds to be spent. Servien, the Secretary of State for war, outlined the use of 115,000 men for 1635 in a document written in January of that year; even in Parrott's opinion, this letter is "an indication of actual intentions."[50] Servien's total falls short of 125,000 by a mere 8 percent. It seems reasonable to surmise that as war approached and tensions grew, so did the desire for more troops, and this may explain the higher projections made by mid-1635. A *contrôle* from April sets troop size at 142,000 to 144,000.[51] The well-known and much misused *contrôle* for May 1635, prominently reprinted in Avenel's collection, is usually employed to justify claims that the French planned to mobilize 150,000 troops; however, if its numbers are calculated with care, they actually project a force of as many as 168,100.[52] With such documentation as a basis, it seems entirely reasonable, even modest, to adopt the traditional estimate of French intentions: 150,000 troops for the campaign season of 1635.

The year 1636 brought even higher projections. A "Contrôle général des armées du Roy pour l'année 1636" dated December 1635 and contained in the collection of military ordinances at the Archives de Guerre, breaks the year into three periods with the following troop strengths: 157,979 to 15 April; 179,900 from 15 April to the end of July; and 164,260 from the end of July to the point when the troops would enter winter quarters.[53] Since this particularly interesting document takes into account the natural growth and

---

[48] BN, f. fr. 6385.

[49] AAE, 811, fol. 120, 7 November 1634 plans for 1635, in Parrott, "The Administration of the French Army," 19. AAE, France 811, fol. 129, 7 November 1634 in Richard Bonney, *The King's Debts* (Oxford: 1981), 173, arrives at 124,500.

[50] AAE, France, 813, fol. 15, letter of 10 January 1635, Servien to Richelieu, in Parrott, "The Administration of the French Army," 107.

[51] AAE, France 813, fol. 301, 23 April 1635, in Bonney, *The King's Debts*, 173.

[52] AAE, 70, fol. 37, *Contrôle* for 1635, in Richelieu, *Lettres*, 5:3–6. The confusion arises from the complicated way that totals are shown. First there are two different columns for infantry with a difference of 1,500 between them, 134,000 or 135,500. Cavalry is then shown as 16,680, though it would appear that it should have been 16,480. Some take this as the full count, giving a total of 150,680. However, it misses three points. Sandwiched in the cavalry is a notation for 6,000 "chevaux" not counted as cavalry because they might have been some other form of "horse." Next to the cavalry is a column for 4,200 "dragons"; these should be counted too, giving a corrected total for all mounted arms of 26,680 (with corrected addition), not 16,680. Moreover, a notation on the infantry says "Garrisons, 36,000, who at the most will be paid only as 30,000," and since the document is fundamentally a financial one, garrisons are counted only at the lower figure; however, the infantry total with the larger garrison figure should be 140,000 to 141,500. This plus the corrected cavalry total gives 166,680 to 168,180.

[53] SHAT, Bib., Collection des ordonnances militaires, vol. 14, #87, "Contrôle general des armées du Roy pour l'année 1636," dated December 1635.

decline in numbers over the course of the year, it seems to reflect military reality more than simply to serve as a financial convenience. Other *contrôles*, apparently put together later, gave markedly higher estimates. Both David Parrott and Richard Bonney cite *contrôles* that projected 172,000 infantry, 21,400 cavalry, and 12,000 additional cavalry, for a total of 205,000 troops, which included the small army under Bernard of Saxe Weimar, which received French pay.[54]

Numbers dropped in 1637 – a *contrôle* for that year reduced the troop total to 134,720 – however, numbers mounted again in 1638–39.[55] An "État des troupes devant servir en 1638," which dealt with forces in the spring, listed 160,010 troops.[56] Another "Etat des troupes pour 1639," describing winter quarters in 1638–39, brought the number down to 148,180.[57] But a July 1639 *état* presents a much higher total, perhaps the highest for the war, 211,950.[58] This again includes troops under Bernard. One last source worth mentioning provides the basis for an estimate of troop strength in 1642. This "Estat des armées du roy en 1642" lists only the numbers of infantry and cavalry companies, but figuring these at their full strengths produces a total of at least 164,000 troops.[59] So the Richelieu ministry recorded paper numbers that varied from 135,000 to 211,000 and commonly hovered around 150,000 to 160,000. Lest these grand sums seem entirely out of line, it is worth noting that Richelieu reconciled Louis XIII to the expense of the war by reminding him that by sustaining 180,000 troops the king had provided "posterity an immortal argument of the power of this crown."[60]

It seems that *contrôles* and *états* listing the entire army are rare or nonexistent during the Mazarin regime. Still, Belhomme's study of the ordinances may aid in tracing the pattern of army size after 1642. While his numbers are not acceptable as literal reality, their rise and fall probably reflect official

[54] AAE, France 820, fol. 200, Contrôle générale, 15 April 1636, in Parrott, "The Administration of the French Army," 91, 99. Bonney, *The King's Debts*, 173fn, seems to err slighting, counting the total as 199,400. He also gives an additional citation to AAE, France 823, fol. 255.

[55] AAE, France 828, fols. 311–23, 330–51, 1637, in Parrott, "The Administration of the French Army," 115.

[56] AAE, France 832, fol. 1, in Bernard Kroener, "Die Entwicklung der Truppenstärken in den französischen Armeen zwischen 1635 und 1661," in Konrad Repgen, ed., *Forschungen und Quellen zur Geschichte des Dreissigjährigen Krieges* (Munster: 1981), 201. Using other documents in the same carton, AAE, France 832, fols. 1–19, 1638, Parrott, "The Administration of the French Army," 117, calculated a total of 164,000.

[57] AAE, France 832, fols. 288–293, in Kroener, "Die Entwicklung der Truppenstärken," 201. This is apparently the "État au vrais des effectifs et de la solde" for 1639 cited by Ernest Lavisse, *Histoire de France*, ed. Ernest Lavisse, vol. 6, part 2 (Paris: 1911), 318, since it lists the same total.

[58] BN, f. fr. 17555, fol. 1, "État des troupes tant d'infanterie que de cavalerie dont seront composées les armees du roy durant l'année 1639," in Kroener, "Die Entwicklung der Truppenstärken," 203.

[59] BN, Collection Dupuy, #590, #244.

[60] Richelieu, "Succincte narration des grandes actions du roi," in Petitot, ed., *Collection des mémoires relatifs à l'histoire de France*, 2nd ser. (Paris: 1821), 11:317.

intentions to alter army size by changing company strengths and adding or subtracting entire regiments. His calculations indicate two high points in the curve of army size, one in 1636 and a second somewhat higher level from 1644 until the partial demobilization that followed the Treaties of Westphalia.[61] After 1649, the army never again matched the levels it had attained during 1635–48.[62]

At the victorious conclusion of the long and exhausting struggle with Spain, the French "reformed" the army by cutting the number of companies drastically and the number of troops decidedly less. Belhomme's purely speculative figures for infantry alone show a drop from 156,000 infantry in 1658 to a post-demobilization figure of 67,000 in 1659, rising to 75,000 in 1660.[63] Given his methods, he really demonstrates only an abolition of units after the war. In fact, Louis apparently kept a large percentage of the actual troops. Mazarin informed Turenne late in 1659, "It is therefore necessary to eliminate [*reformer*] a good number of companies . . . [but] it is the King's intention not to discharge a single cavalryman or infantryman, but to fortify well the companies that remain, by incorporating into them the soldiers from those [companies] that are eliminated."[64] Review reports collected by Kroener reveal the practical effect of the pruning and filling that followed the war. Companies that presented only fifteen men in 1659, or 50 percent of their regulation strength of thirty, mustered fully fifty men or more, 100 percent of their new increased official complement, in 1660.[65]

Louis XIV himself boasted of having nearly 72,000 troops in 1660, after demobilization, clearly the largest peacetime force the French had ever supported.[66] The army continued to shrink for the next several years, declining sometime before early 1665, when a tally of units pegs the army at about 50,000 just before the build up for the War of Devolution sent totals upward again.[67] The number of troops began to increase late in 1665, probably passing 60,000.[68] Referring to a letter of March 1666, Rousset concludes that the king's troops reached 72,000 then, whereas Louis André, citing other documents, argues that the army topped 97,515 later in the year, a figure that

[61] See Belhomme, *Infanterie*, vols. 1 and 2.

[62] Corvisier's statement that the army numbered 250,000 in 1658 should not be accepted; it seems to be based on Belhomme's inflated figures. Corvisier, *Louvois*, 83.

[63] Belhomme, *Infanterie*, 2:88, 92.

[64] Jules Mazarin, *Lettres du cardinal Mazarin pendant son Ministère*, Chéruel and Avenel, eds., vols. 6–9 (Paris: 1890–1906), 9:378, letter of 19 October 1659.

[65] Bernard Kroener, *Les routes et les étapes*, 177. This finding receives additional support in Mazarin, *Lettres*, 9:412–13, 9 November 1659, to duke de Navailles.

[66] Louis XIV, *Oeuvres de Louis XIV*, Grimoard and Grouvelle, eds., 6 vols. (Paris: 1806), 3:32. An editorial comment criticizes *Recherches* as employing a document designed to exaggerate the size of the army. Servan, *Recherches*, 53–54, gives the figure as 125,000.

[67] AG, Arch. hist. 78, feuille 165.

[68] AG, Arch. hist. 78, feuille 165, states that early in 1665 there were 805 companies of infantry (45,216 men) and 103 companies of cavalry (5,850 troopers). The army expanded over 1665 by 270 companies of infantry at fifty men each, making a total of 64,566.

seems high.[69] During the first year of the War of Devolution, Louis's personal information set the strength at about 82,000, but this may not include all garrisons.[70] The careful historian Paul Sonnino estimates the size of Louis's army at 85,000 by the end of the 1667 campaign.[71] The year 1668 brought even larger armies totaling 134,000.[72] The return to peace again caused the French to demobilize to only 70,000.[73]

Louis next began to gear up for the Dutch War. In 1670, he expanded his army once again by raising 20,000 new men to bring his forces up to 90,000.[74] In 1671, additional soldiers were hired, so that in early 1672 the army reached about 120,000.[75] This figure grew over the course of the year, as Louis issued orders to recruit enough troops to raise the number to 144,000.[76] The Dutch War high attained 279,610, as indicated by a key document from January 1678.[77] This combined 219,250 infantry with 60,360 cavalry, while 116,370 of the total served in garrisons. The inevitable "reform" of the army after the Treaty of Nymwegen reduced forces to 146,980 men, officers not included, in 1679.[78] This seems to have fallen to about 125,000 in 1681.[79] Numbers

[69] AG, A¹198, 5 March 1666, letter from Louvois to Pradel in Camille Rousset, *Histoire de Louvois*, 4 vols. (Paris: 1862–64), 1:97. BN 4255 folios 5–8, 9–13, 177 in Louis André, *Michel Le Tellier et l'organisation de l'armée monarchique* (Paris: 1906), 294, and *Michel Le Tellier et Louvois* (Paris: 1942), 314n.

[70] AG, Bibliothèque du Ministère de Guerre, hereafter cited as BMG, Tiroirs de Louis XIV, page 36, "États des regiments de cavalerie en 1667"; page 37, "États des troupes destinées pour la garde de S. M. et pour servir dans les armées"; and pages 39–40, "État des troupes d'infanterie estants sur pied en l'année 1667."

[71] Paul Sonnino, *Louis XIV and the Origins of the Dutch War* (Cambridge: 1988), 17. As usual, Belhomme's overestimate of 178,500 infantry in December 1667 cannot be taken seriously. Belhomme, *Infanterie*, 2:134.

[72] AG, BMG, Tiroirs de Louis XIV, pages 46–48, "Estat des trouppes d'infanterie que le Roy a sur pied en mars 1668"; pages 50–64, "Estat des trouppes de cavalerie que le Roy a sur pied en mars 1668."

[73] Sonnino, *Origins of the Dutch War*, 127–28fn.

[74] Sonnino, *Origins of the Dutch War*, 127. Servan, *Recherches*, 54, putting it at 131,265, allows for virtually no demobilization at all.

[75] For 1671 levies see Sonnino, *Origins of the Dutch War*, 155. AG, BMG, Tiroirs de Louis XIV, pages 76–77, 4 February 1672, puts the French infantry in 1,287 companies with 446 companies of cavalry, and 2,950 additional troops in the royal household, but it may not take garrisons into account. Rousset, *Louvois*, 1:346–47, refers to this document and figures the total at 120,000.

[76] Orders issued January–March 1672 to raise another 400 companies of infantry and 120 companies of cavalry, 26,000 men, that would make the total size of army 144,000 in Sonnino, *Origins of the Dutch War*, 177, 162. Servan, *Recherches*, 54, put the invading army at 176,087; clearly this is too high.

[77] AG, BMG, Tiroirs de Louis XIV, page 110, "Troupes que le Roy auvis sur pied le premier janvier 1678." Interestingly, it is at this point that Belhomme's figures and archival sources become close; he lists 229,970 infantry for May 1667. Belhomme, *Infanterie*, 2:206–7.

[78] AN, G⁷1774, #52, AN, G⁷1774, #52, "État des troupes que le Roy a eu sur pied," this interesting financial document details troop strength for 1679, 1684, 1696, and 1699.

[79] AG, A¹687, 20 September 1681, letter from Le Pelletier to Louvois, in Rousset, *Louvois*, 3:216.

increased again for the brief contest with Spain that broke out in 1683, with demobilization back to 165,000 after the Truce of Ratisbon.[80]

During the Nine Years' War, the French army reached and exceeded 400,000 for the first time, at least on paper. At the start of the conflict, Louvois believed that he could field about 207,000 by late 1688, with the levies he anticipated.[81] In his *L'Armée française en 1690*, Belhomme argues that forces reached 381,819 men and 23,138 officers, for a total of 404,957 that year.[82] It should be remembered that in 1688 Louvois instituted the royal *milice*, which allowed the monarchy to conscript men to serve at the front in new provincial battalions. Here Belhomme's figures do not appear to be excessive, since other sources ascribe even greater numbers to the French army. No less an authority than Louis's great engineer, Sébastien le Prestre de Vauban, a man quite given to calculations and statistics, estimated royal forces in 1693 at the generous figure of 438,000.[83] A financial *état* dating from the 1690s gives a detailed accounting of 343,323 infantry and 67,334 cavalry, a total of 410,657 troops, not including officers, for the year 1696.[84] Adding officers to the numbers in the *état* would produce a total equal to that supplied by Vauban. These sources, then, exceed the traditional figure of 400,000 French troops for the Nine Years' War; in fact, an estimate of 420,000 officers and men would not be out of place.[85] According to the aforementioned *état*, by early 1699 the army had fallen to about 185,716 enlisted men, after regiments had been disbanded.[86] Then, with a reduction of company strength in December 1699, the size of the army fell by about 40,000, contracting it further to 140,000 to 145,000.[87]

The return of fighting in 1701 sent army size spiraling upward again. In

---

[80] AN, G⁷1774, #52, sets the number at 165,807 troops, without officers. AG, A¹772, #267, in Rousset, *Louvois*, 3:287, puts the number at 161,995.

[81] AG, A¹808, 8 September 1688, letter from Louvois to Asfeld, in Rousset, *Louvois*, 4:88.

[82] Victor Belhomme, *L'armée française en 1690* (Paris: 1895). This includes the royal army at 363,154 (p. 104), the provincial militia at 24,930 (p. 119), and the local Protestant militia of Languedoc and Dauphiné as 14,600 (p.119). The total does not include the local militias, as they are omitted in government totals, as AN, G⁷1774, #52.

[83] Sébastien le Prestre de Vauban, *Oisivetés de M. de Vauban*, 3 vols. (Paris: 1842–46), 2:237, 252–60.

[84] AN, G⁷1774, #52. Such a force would have required over 20,000 officers. The total presented here does not include 1,500 for the Hôtel des Invalides and 3,080 for the arrière ban. It might also be best to cut 15,000 militia shown. If this is done, the total with officers still approaches 420,000.

[85] Servan, *Recherches*, 58, credits Louis with 395,865.

[86] AN, G⁷1774, #52. See Georges Girard, *Le service militaire en France à la fin du règne de Louis XIV: Racolage et milice (1701–1715)* (Paris: 1915), 4, concerning the cut in cavalry company size from thirty-five to twenty troopers.

[87] For reduction of 40,000, see Girard, *Racolage et milice*, 4. Compare figures in Belhomme for February and December. Belhomme, *Infanterie*, 2:342–43. This gives a good indication of declining numbers. Servan, *Recherches*, 58, gives the interwar low as 140,216.

1702, it reached 220,502.[88] Servan's study set the wartime high at 392,223.[89] However, original sources set the number as smaller than Servan's figures. A detailed financial *état* listing troops to be employed in 1707 supports an estimate of army size at 318,000 infantry, 39,000 cavalry, and 16,000 dragoons, for a total of 373,000 officers and men.[90] This document, which does not appear to have been used by military historians before now, corroborates another much-used *état* dating from 1710. It lists 319,541 infantry, including detached companies, 41,073 cavalry, and 16,491 dragoons, adding up to a total of only 377,105 troops, of whom 21,062 were officers.[91] Once again, the monarchy called upon the *milice*, although its conscripts no longer stayed in their own battalions at the front, but simply filled the gaps in regular regiments. These numbers fall short of justifying the traditionally accepted paper figure of 400,000 soldiers engaged as full-time troops in garrison or with the field armies; in fact, 380,000 would seem more in line with archival sources. After peace returned, the army fell back to a peacetime strength of about 133,000.[92] Over the remaining decades of the *ancien régime*, the army typically echoed the figures that it had reached under Louis XIV in war and peace.[93]

Such is the tally of theoretical numbers; however, revisionist scholarship rightly demands that historians probe for a firmer core of reality within the inflated paper totals.

DISCOUNTING THE PAPER FIGURES

By establishing the difference between the official dimensions and the actual size of units, review reports and *routes* provide the data necessary to discount official statements of army size. Bernard Kroener supplies the foundation of

---

[88] AG, A[1]1579, "Mémoire des trouppes que le roy à sur pied, janvier, 1702" in Girard, *Racolage et milice*, pp. 5–7.

[89] Servan, *Recherches*, 58–59.

[90] AN, G[7]1780, #212, "État des régiments d'infanterie, cavalerie et dragons, companies d'infanteries separées, companies de fusilliers des officers majors des places et des partisans et autres troupes qui seront au service du Roy pendant la campagne 1707." This valuable document lists companies and regiments, not men. The figure of 373,000 resulted from: (1) multiplying listed units by their official size; (2) using AG, MR 1701, #13, to supply figures for certain regiments that were not included, most notably the Swiss line infantry and the regiments of guards; and (3) also using AG, MR 1701, #13, to provide a basis for calculating the number of officers.

[91] AG, MR 1701, #13, "Estat contenant le nombre des officers, des soldats, des cavaliers, et des dragons dont les regimens etoient sur pied en 1710." It lists 336,918 men and 21,062 officers, plus 425 detached companies of 45 men each, totaling 19,125 men. If an additional 1,275 officers are added to the total to account for the detached companies, the total would reach 378,380.

[92] Servan, *Recherches*, 60.

[93] See the discussion of army size from 1715 to 1789 in John A. Lynn, "The Pattern of Army Growth, 1445–1945," in John A. Lynn, ed., *The Tools of War: Ideas, Instruments, and Institutions of Warfare, 1445–1871* (Urbana, IL: 1990), 3–4.

this effort by compiling review reports that establish the average number of men actually present under arms in French infantry and cavalry companies during 1635–60.[94] A second data set compiled from archival sources for this chapter covers the remainder of the *grand siècle*.

Since the most crucial figures for the first half of the seventeenth century, and those best documented in the *contrôles*, come from the period 1635–39, these five years deserve the most attention. Unfortunately, Kroener's treatments of 1635 and 1636 are somewhat in error. On average, the infantry companies that he studied for 1635 claimed 43 men present; however, he mistakenly assumes that regulation company strength for French foot in both 1635 and 1636 was 50 men when it was, in fact, 100.[95] Thus, while he put the infantry at a suspiciously high 86 percent of regulation strength, they actually stood at only 43 percent. This lower figure tallies much better with the percentage for cavalry companies, which only reached 46 percent of official strength. Pursuing this line even further, in 1636, usually accepted as a high point for the army as it massed to repel a Spanish invasion, Kroener's sample suggests an infantry company strength of only 35 percent with cavalry at 38 percent.

Combining the corrected version of Kroener's numbers with theoretical highs taken from financial *contrôles* results in some unexpected findings. The discounted size of the army in 1635 falls to about 72,000 troops. This seems a small figure, particularly in light of the fact that Richelieu already believed that 89,000 men had been massed before the end of 1634.[96] If Kroener's sample can be trusted, not only was the army of 1635 small, but it was not exceeded by the forces assembled in 1636. The situation changed greatly during 1638–39, years for which Kroener's methods seem both clear and correct. For these two years, the infantry complement rose to 60 percent and 72 percent, and cavalry stood at 45 percent and 70 percent. Such full ranks make 1639 the year of highest troop strength, with a very substantial 152,000 men.[97] It should be noted that André Corvisier also employed Kroener's work to calculate actual numbers, but Corvisier erred by accepting Belhomme's inflated estimates as the raw data to be discounted. As a result, Corvisier credits infantry alone with a discounted size of 166,320 soldiers for 1639; the addition of similarly elevated cavalry figures would drive the estimate for the total army above 200,000.[98]

---

[94] Kroener, *Les routes et les étapes*, 177–78.

[95] He seems to arrive at this incorrect official size by reading backward from winter-quarters regulations for 1637. Kroener, "Die Entwicklung der Truppenstärken," 169. On 100-man companies, see Richelieu, *Testament politique*, ed. Louis André (Paris: 1947), 478; AG, A^{1}32, #250, 1636; and AG, A^{1}29, fol. 219, 13 September 1636. I thank David Parrott for supplying these last two archival references.

[96] Avenel, *Lettres*, 4:601, 13 September 1634, Richelieu to the king.

[97] BN, f. fr. 17555, fol. 1, "État des troupes tant d'infanterie que de cavalerie dont seron composées les armees du roy durant l'année 1639," in Kroener, "Die Entwicklung der Truppenstärken," 203.

[98] Contamine, *Histoire militaire*, 1:364.

Given the great variety between the lows and highs generated by Kroener's percentages, perhaps a safer course might be not to accept his exact estimates year by year but to take them as a basis to arrive at a general discount rate to cover the first critical five years of the war. A straight mathematical average of Kroener's corrected estimates results in a discount rate of 57 percent. At one point in his own work, David Parrott proposes an estimate built upon Kroener's original figures and his own examination of reports from field armies: "The forces maintained by France were probably 50 percent smaller than the sweeping estimates of 130–150,000 soldiers that have been proposed."[99] Here Parrott echoes Richelieu, who commented, "[I]f one wants to have fifty thousand effectives, it is necessary to levy one hundred, counting a regiment of twenty companies that ought to have 2,000 men as only 1,000."[100] Parrott then further reduces the actual number by assuming a 25 percent error caused by officers padding their companies with phony soldiers, *passe volants*, to make their companies look bigger at reviews. With all these deductions, he pulls down the traditional figure of 150,000 for 1635 to 50,000–55,000.[101] But Parrott cites varying figures in somewhat different contexts in such a way that they can be read, and cited, to support conflicting theses. At another point, he credits the real force with about 70,000 troops, at least for the first half of the campaign.[102] And both figures need to be put in the context of his overall estimate: "Aside from the exceptional, by definition, temporary, peaks in troop strength, such as that of summer 1636, the French army was rarely of more than 60–70,000 infantry and 15–20,000 cavalry during the 1630s."[103] Accepting this last, and most authoritative, set of figures produces a total of 75,000 to 90,000 troops, which he would peg even higher in 1636.[104]

While there is no simple mechanical method to manufacture a discount rate from the foregoing findings and claims, an overview of the best research suggests that a rate of 60 percent provides the most reasonable guide. This is the discount rate that Corvisier accepts, and even Parrott gives it credence as the contemporary principle of "*douze pour vingt*," the belief that to secure twelve men in the ranks, it was necessary to issue commissions to recruit twenty.[105] Multiplying official tallies for 1636 and 1639 by this discount yields

[99] Parrott, "The Administration of the French Army," 135.

[100] Richelieu, *Testament politique*, 478.

[101] Parrott, "The Administration of the French Army," 135. Here he states that this is the possible maximum maintained "consistently" through 1635.

[102] Parrott, "The Administration of the French Army," 110–111.

[103] Parrott, "The Administration of the French Army," iv.

[104] In a letter of 2 August 1992, he stated that his 70,000 estimate for 1635 was "well on the way to the 80–100,000 that I suggest is the size of force which the government is striving to maintain from 1636."

[105] Corvisier, *Louvois*, 82 and Corvisier in Lucien Bély et al., *Guerre et paix dans l'Europe du XVIIe siècle*, 2 vols., *Regards sur l'histoire*, vols. 77–78 (Paris, 1991), 1:14. AAE, France, 814, fol. 262, 14 July 1635 and AAE, France, 828, fols. 265–862, *état* of troops for 1637, in Parrott, "The Administration of the French Army," 111. Mazarin's correspondence also seems to justify the

a high point for the war of about 125,000 men. Such an estimate falls between the extremes generated by Kroener's modified numbers. Moreover, it even approaches Parrott's second estimate of 75,000 to 90,000, when adjusted for extreme wartime peaks, such as occurred in 1636 and 1639. Adopting 125,000 as a wartime peak for the war with Spain might even be credited as an act of moderation, since a case could be made for a top figure of 152,000 in 1639.

Turning to the data collected for this chapter, the next discounted wartime high dates from the Dutch War, since data for the War of Devolution is very thin.[106] According to a sample of 155 companies, in 1676–77, when a French infantry company was supposed to number 50 men, actual companies mustered a surprisingly high average of 44.4 men, or 89 percent of full strength.[107] As strange as this may seem, it accords with Louis's own evaluation, since he argued in 1667 for a discount of 85 percent.[108] Cavalry companies were even more likely to fill up, mounting 96 percent of their full complement of 50.[109] This very high percentage of cavaliers in a unit was typical of the personal reign of Louis XIV. Three factors explain this phenomenon: (1) the much greater prestige of service in the cavalry, (2) the larger recruitment bounties paid to cavalrymen, and (3) the higher salaries they earned. As a result of these three factors, cavalry regiments had their pick of men, meeting their goals before infantry units did.

Using these percentages in conjunction with paper figures for peak size during the Dutch War leads to an estimate of 253,000 actual troops. This figure certainly seems high; it may result from the fact that the sample dates from the end of winter quarters, when recruits had just been added and units enjoyed their maximum strength of the year. In any case, the numbers show units far closer to their theoretical strength than they had been before 1659. With the return of peace, reviews of 171 companies in garrison in Italy in 1682 suggest that companies approached full strength during the period of half war/half peace that was the 1680s.[110] With such high percentages, the official

---

douze pour vingt rule. Mazarin, Lettres, 6:151, Mazarin to Besmaux, 17 April 1654 and 6:186, 22 June 1654, to Talon.

[106] See the numerous routes preserved in Amiens, EE 392, March 1676, plus the following: Nord, C 2321, 6 October 1672; SHAT, Bib., A^{1b}1628, vol. 2, 5–7, 9–10, 13–15, 17–19, 21–23, 25–27, 33–35, 65–67, 69–71; AG, A^{1}295, #86; and AN, G^{7}1774, #10, #11.

[107] See AG, MR 1972, for the figure of 50 men per infantry company. Puységur and Belhomme also use the figure of 50.

[108] "I counted always on a real strength [pied] much less than the declared one [effectif], because I knew how a fall in numbers always occurs when troops have been on campaign a while. So that in place of the 40,000 men that I can comfortably send [faire marcher] [on campaign], I count only on 35,000." Louis XIV, Mémoires, 2:306. Supplement for 1667.

[109] François Sicard, Histoire des institutions militaires des français, vol. 2 (Paris: 1834), 433.

[110] In 1682, the infantry companies in question boasted at least 84 percent of a full complement, while mounted companies reached 77 percent for regular cavalry and 98 percent for dragoons. AN, Z^{1c}414, August 1682, December 1682. The fact that all the mounted units were reviewed in December, the depths of winter quarters, may explain their weaker numbers. On company sizes, see AN, G^{7}1774, #2 and AG, Arch. hist., 78, fol. 166–68.

figure of about 150,000 men in the peacetime army need be pared down only to roughly 120,000 in real terms.

The Nine Years' War provides some of the most interesting discoveries. Early in the war, 1689–92, company strengths ran fairly high once again. A sample of 226 companies, all of which passed through Amiens and left *routes* in their wake, reveals an average infantry company of 42.2 men and sergeants, or 84 percent of the official full strength of 50.[111] A small sample from Burgundy and a very large one that marched through in Alsace, 1691–92, correspond with the Amiens numbers. The 40 companies from Burgundy stood at an average of only 33.5, but this low figure results from the inclusion of one particularly understrength regiment; without it, the average rises to 39.0.[112] The massive sample of units receiving *étapes* in Alsace must be handled with great care, since the accountants listed several regiments as full that were not. Using only the most solid listings, the Alsace sample still consists of 416 companies, and these records suggest an average of about 41 men per company, or 82 percent.[113] The 57 cavalry companies from six different regiments listed on Amiens *routes* averaged 34.9 men, or 87 percent of official strength of 40; dragoons had essentially full complements of 40.[114] A sample of 90 cavalry companies that rode through Alsace during the first half of 1691 numbered 36.3 men per company, or 90.1 percent full strength; 47 dragoon companies averaged out at 37.4, or 93.5 percent.[115]

Later, in 1695–96, the percentages had not changed much, according to a sample of 523 companies all from Amiens *routes*. French infantry battalions, which had included 16 companies in 1690, now claimed only 13 companies, but they were a bit larger at 55 men per company.[116] These, in fact, stood at

---

[111] Amiens, EE 394, EE 395, EE 396. On infantry company size ca. 1690 see Belhomme, *L'armée française en 1690*, 11–12, and AG, MR 1972.

[112] Dijon, H 228, 8 February 1692; Dijon, H 228, 8 February 1692; and Côte d'Or, C 3675, 23 January 1693. The Manlevine (?) regiment passing through Dijon had a company strength of only 22.1.

[113] BN, f. fr. 4565–4567, three "estat et compte . . . de la fourniture des estappes" presented to la Grange, conseiller du roi, covering the months from April 1691 to March 1692. These formal accounts listing over 1,200 companies seem to follow an administrative convenience of showing as completely full, battalions that almost certainly were not. This is unmistakably the case in some instances that listed a regiment at partial strength on one day and full on the next, at a time when replacements would not have been arriving at the front. It would appear that allowances were awarded at full strength to compensate officers for building up their companies. So to make use of the Alsace account books without skewing the sample, I have excluded from my count any infantry companies listed as 48 through 50. This reduces the sample to only 416 companies, which averaged 40.9 men. My thanks to Dr. David Stewart of Hillsdale College, who acted as my research assistant to run down these figures.

[114] On cavalry company size during 1688–97, see Belhomme, *L'armée française en 1690*, 86, 100; and AN, G⁷1774, #52, seems to count normal cavalry and dragoon companies at 45 men in 1696. Puységur is not reliable on shifting company size in Louis's last two wars.

[115] BN, f. fr. 4566. These mounted units had to be treated much as had the accounts of infantry, so only 137 companies were used in the sample.

[116] Col. des ord., vol. 28, #38, 1 December 1692; AN, G⁷1774, #52, "Etat des troupes que le Roy a eu sur pied"; AG Bib Aⁱh 638 tome II.

43.8, or 80 percent of capacity.[117] *Milice* companies, theoretically at 60, had 50.2, or 83.7 percent;[118] cavalry and dragoons claimed 35.5 and 35.3, respectively, or 88.8 and 88.3 percent of a full complement each, if the regulation size remained 40 men per company.[119]

The *étapes* documents employed for the Nine Years' War do not simply date from the spring, when regiments had just incorporated recruits, but from the fall as well, when regiments would be at a relatively weak point. The balance seems reasonable. Therefore, if one accepts that theoretical size stood as high as 420,000 in 1696, a sixth of which would have been cavalry, the real count could have reached 340,000.

During the few years between the Nine Years' War and the War of the Spanish Succession, the official number of men in French companies fell somewhat, but the percentage at full strength rose. In 1700, French line infantry companies, which were then set at 35 by regulation, averaged out at 35.1 men per company in the 39 companies of the sample.[120] Cavalry companies, which in December 1699 were officially reduced to only 20 troopers each, showed 20.3 men present, so their numbers topped 100 percent of full strength.[121] Putting all this together fully justifies the estimate of total troop strength at about 140,000 men.

With the return of war, an exhausted France mobilized once again, but it did not reach the level of forces that it had attained in the previous contest. A sample of 240 infantry companies that passed though Amiens and Lille puts the size of the average company at only 32.3 in 1702–4.[122] This, at a time when regulation size was 45, meant real companies were only 72 percent of full size.[123] A much smaller sample of only 16 cavalry companies again shows them at very near their regulation strength of 35. With 34.1 men per company, they mounted 97 percent of theoretical size.[124]

---

[117] Amiens, EE 403, EE 405.

[118] An ordinance of 12 December 1691 raised the size of *milice* companies from 50 to 60. Léon Hennet, *Les milices et les troupes provinciales* (Paris: 1884), 32.

[119] AN, G^{7}1774, #52, suggests that the regulation size of a cavalry company had dropped to 35 in 1696. Four companies per squadron seemed to stay the rule throughout the war. Belhomme, *L'armée française en 1690*, 86, 100; Amiens, EE 405. If figured on a theoretical company strength of 35, the cavalry would have been essentially complete, and estimates of total army size thus would be even higher. I have again adopted the conservative course and opted for the larger company size, although this may be an error.

[120] Lille, 11,113, 10 & 24 October, 7 & 8 November, and 2, 12 & 26 December 1700. For regulation company size, see AG, MR 1972, #7.

[121] For changes in company size in 1699, see Girard, *Racolage et milice*, 4.

[122] Amiens, EE 411, EE 412; Lille, 11,113, 5 & 26 March, 4 April 1702; see, as well, Girard, Georges, ed., "Un soldat de Malplaquet: Lettres du capitaine de Saint-Mayme," *Carnet de Sabretache* (1922), 515. David Chandler, *The Art of Warfare in the Age of Marlborough* (New York: 1976), 97, refers to a British document that assumed that French companies included 42 men, but this seems to be an overestimate.

[123] Infantry company size stood at 45 until the regulation of 20 September 1710 raised it to 50. Girard, *Racolage et milice*, 11.

[124] Chandler, *The Art of Warfare*, 45, cites a British report of 1706 that states that a French squadron ran about 140 on campaign, or four companies of 32 men and 3 officers each.

By late in the war, 1709–11, infantry and cavalry companies had declined somewhat. The large and varied sample of companies used here includes 1,284 French companies listed in *routes* from Amiens, review reports from Dijon, and tallies of front-line units reported in military correspondence.[125] French infantry companies changed in size during the war; until 1710, they stood at 45 men, but a regulation of that year raised their size to 50 soldiers.[126] The average company strength of 31.2 means that infantry was 62 to 69 percent complete. Cavalry and dragoons were again organized in companies of 35 men; but in reality, cavalry companies stood at 30.5, or 87 percent, and dragoons at 31.1, or 89 percent. The sources that generate these estimates deserve some discussion, since they lead to important conclusions.

Documents from Amiens, Dijon, and the front showed roughly similar company sizes. The average number of men in infantry companies moving through Amiens was 29.9, whereas it rose to 34.0 in Dijon reports.[127] This is a significant difference, to be sure, but it only amounts to 8 percent in a company of 50 men. Another key document is the "Etat de la force de quarante-deux battalions et de ce qu'on leur donne de recrues," dated 17 September 1709, but it requires some interpretation, since the battalions listed had just suffered casualties at the bloody battle of Malplaquet. Approximate battalion size before the battle can be reconstructed by allowing for the casualty rates of these battalions. This method yields an average company of 31.9 men.[128] Interpreting the document in another fashion, one can add in the number of replacements assigned to each battalion to arrive at a new company strength

---

[125] Amiens, EE 421, EE 423, EE 424, EE 427, EE 432; Dijon, H 243, H 244; AG, A^{1}2152, #208, 17 September 1709, "État de la force de quarante-deux battalions et de ce qu'on leur donne de recrues," in Vault and Pelet, ed., *Mémoires militaires relatifs à la succession d'Espagne sous Louis XIV*, vol. 9 (Paris: 1855), 383; AG, A^{1}2214, 10 April 1710, letter from d'Alborgessy, review of troops being sent to Douai.

[126] Regulation of 20 September 1710, Girard, *Racolage et milice*, 10–11.

[127] The larger Dijon figure is explained by the passage through Dijon of one large and probably new regiment enjoying a nearly full complement. Dijon, H244, 6–7 May 1710.

[128] In early August, the army of Flanders claimed 128 battalions of infantry. See AG, A^{1}2152, #31, "Disposition de l'infanterie," in Vault and Pelet, *Mémoires militaires*, 333–34. Detailed casualty reports for officers at Malplaquet suggest that the battalions of the 17 September review suffered average casualties on the same level as the other battalions in the army. (There was no detailed accounting of casualties among enlisted ranks.) See AG, A^{1}2152, #225, "État des officiers tués, blessés et prisonniers à la bataille de Malplaquet," in Vault and Pelet, *Mémoires militaires*, 378–81. The average battalion in the army suffered 9.8 officers killed and wounded, while these 37 suffered 10.3. Consequently, it is reasonable to argue that the battalions suffered no more than an average number of casualties in the ranks. If 11,000 is a reasonable estimate for French casualties at Malplaquet, the infantry alone would perhaps have lost two thirds of these men. Gaston Bodart, *Militär-historisches Kriegs-Lexikon, 1618–1905* (Vienna and Leipzig: 1908), 160; Claude G. Sturgill, *Marshal Villars and the War of the Spanish Succession* (Lexington, KY: 1965), 98. (It should be remembered that there was very heavy cavalry fighting and great losses at Malplaquet.) So infantry losses can be roughly estimated at 7,330; and each battalion lost on average about 57 men (7330/120). This would mean that the sample that claimed an average company strength of 27.2 after Malplaquet probably was up to 31.9 before the action.

Table 2.1. *The growth of the French Army, 1445–1750.*

Time period or war	Theoretical peace high	Theoretical war high	Discounted war high
1445–75	14,000		
Second half of the 15th Century		40–45,000	
1490	17,100		
1540s & 1550s		70–80,000	60–70,000?
1567–68		80,000	70,000?
Early 1570s	12,700		
Wars of Religion, 1589–98		50–60,000	
1600–10	10,000		
1610, as planned		55,000	
1610–15	10,000		
Thirty Years' War, 1635–48		200,000	125,000
1660–66	72,000		
War of Devolution, 1667–68		134,000	
Dutch War, 1672–78		279,600	253,000
1678–88	165,000		
Nine Years' War, 1688–97		420,000	340,000
1698–1700	140–145,000		
War of the Spanish Succession, 1701–14		380,000	255,000
1715–25	130–160,000		
War of the Austrian Succession, 1740–48		390,000	
1749–56	160,000		

of 30.9. A second battlefield report listing units to be sent to Douai in April 1710 shows company strength down to 28.2.[129]

Using the sample collected for this study to discount army size stated in 1707 and 1710 yields a figure of about 255,000 troops. This is much smaller than the 340,000 estimated for the Nine Years' War. Remember, both figures are only estimates and discount the army on the basis of percentages for only French regiments; therefore, they may understate the totals somewhat, since foreign regiments in French service tended to be closer to their full complements than were native units.

COMPARING RESULTS: REVISIONISM REVISED

With the discounted figures in hand, it is possible to make certain judgments concerning the pattern of military expansion during the *grand siècle*. [See Table 2.1 and Figure 2.1.] Most importantly, the data presented here demonstrate

[129] AG, A¹2214, #107, 10 April 1710, letter from d'Alborgessy, review of troops being sent to Douai. Claude Sturgill overstates the weakness of battalions under Villars, saying that they declined to 250 men. The documents that he cites to support this conclusion do not justify it. Sturgill, *Marshal Villars*, 101–2.

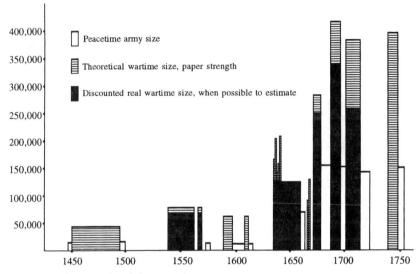

Figure 2.1. The growth of the French army, 1445–1750.

that with the onset of war in 1635, royal forces increased significantly over previous levels. Their expansion ought to be measured against a baseline of wartime highs, 1495–1610, which repeatedly reached 50,000 and peaked at 80,000 on occasion before 1570. If such levels are compared with theoretical maximums of 205,000 to 211,000 soldiers during the period 1635–48, the increase ranges from 250 percent to 400 percent. But this would not be a fair comparison, since the key figures for the earlier period presented here are closer to actual than theoretical maximums. The discounted totals for 1635–42 arrived at earlier reduce the peak size of the army to 125,000. Consequently, even if the 50,000–80,000 total for the period before 1610 is taken without discount, the army raised under Richelieu was still at least 60 percent larger than anything that preceded it, and if the earlier tallies are discounted by as little as 10 percent, which seems reasonable, even modest, then one has to conclude that the army of 1635–42 exceeded sixteenth-century highs by at least 75 percent. In addition, the army created in 1635 doubled the size of any royal French force mobilized since 1570. Such increases may not equal the extreme estimates of some historians, but they still constitute a quantum leap upward. The contrast between the 55,000 troops that Henri IV intended to raise for his struggle with Spain in 1610 and the 150,000 that Louis XIII tried to mobilize against the same enemy in 1635 highlights the military expansion of the first half of the seventeenth century.

In his dissertation, David Parrott makes a strong case that the Richelieu ministry clumsily improvised its way through the daunting task of supporting its army without engaging in substantial reform. Parrott believes that the army did not grow enough to impose reform upon the government; moreover, he seems to assume that if the army existed at a given size, it had to be supported by the government at that size. Yet the French monarchy fielded armies larger than it could maintain from its own resources. At this critical juncture, the army relied upon its own methods to make ends meet. For one thing, the monarchy called upon the personal financial resources of the officers, who contributed to the maintenance of their own commands, as will be established in Chapter 7. For another, despite official protests, soldiers took for themselves what the state failed to supply; in short, they pillaged, as discussed in Chapter 6. The chaos and horrors typical of the war between France and Spain came precisely because the army grew substantially, not because it did not grow enough to precipitate reform.

Jeremy Black would uncouple the reforms that occurred after 1659 from the strains exerted by army growth before that date. Yet while the expansion of the army during 1635–59 may have been less impressive than that which came later in sheer numerical terms, the earlier growth clearly caused greater institutional and social crisis. Without the turmoil that France suffered as a consequence of war and military expansion before the Peace of the Pyrenees or, to be more specific, without the desire to avoid similar disasters in the future, her later stability seems unaccountable. Tumult was as important a spur to institutional change in France as was the abuse of Brandenburg during the Thirty Years' War to the creation of the state and army of the Great Elector after 1648.

While military expansion before 1659 rates as substantial, that occurring after 1659 was staggering. Theoretical maximums reached 420,000 during the Nine Years' War, while discounted figures for the same war set the number of troops under arms as about 340,000. Measured by either scale, this was unparalleled. By the end of the century, theoretical wartime levels had increased 500 to 800 percent over the peaks of the sixteenth century. Discounted tallies rose 400 to 700 percent. Peacetime levels rose by even greater percentages; if theoretical peacetime figures before 1610 were normally between 10,000 and 20,000, the peacetime strength after 1679 hovered between 130,000 and 150,000, an increase of 650 percent to 1,500 percent!

The expansion of the army during the War of the Spanish Succession (when discounted regular army strength only reached 255,000) did not match that attained during the Nine Years' War. This happened despite the fact that the paper figures for both wars hovered in the range of 400,000. On reflection, this makes sense. The number of troops that the state could support depended directly upon the amount of wealth that the monarchy could mobilize for its army, and Louis XIV had run out of resources. First, the Nine Years' War had exhausted government finance. Second, the potential to raise "contributions," or war taxes, on occupied territory decreased as repeated defeats drove French forces back to their own borders in the northeast. And third, the traditional recourse of relying upon aristocratic officers to maintain their units out of pocket had already overtaxed noble fortunes in the previous war, so that particular well was going dry.

The numbers do not support Corvisier's thesis that the forces raised under Louis XIV matched those levied in 1794, the height of Republican defense. To his count of 300,000 troops in regular French regiments, Corvisier adds naval forces, bourgeois militias, and coast guards to yield a grand total of 600,000. If the point that Corvisier wishes to make is that far more men bore arms than a simple tally of soldiers would indicate, he makes his point admirably. Yet it is another matter to compare this to the national defense mounted by the Revolutionary regime. If one adds together numbers in this fashion for Louis XIV, one must do it for the Revolution, and the sum of the army, navy, National Guard, and *armées révolutionaires* in 1793–94 would greatly surpass anything under Louis XIV.[130] Returning the focus to front-line troops only, once the *levée en masse* had raked in its bounty of recruits, the French had mobilized 1,169,000 men by the late summer of 1794, and it has become almost traditional to discount this to 750,000 men actually under arms.[131] This far exceeds the 255,000 army troops credited here to Louis XIV for 1709–11.

If calculated as percentages of French population, the forces marshaled by the Republic are also far more impressive than those that served Louis XIV. If the population of France stood at 21,500,000 in 1700, then the amount of troops maintained for each 1,000 of population was 15.8 in 1696 and 13.4 in 1710.[132] Since the French population rose to about 28,600,000 by 1790, an army of 750,000 meant that the French fielded 26.2 soldiers per thousand of population. And if one took into account only *Frenchmen* mobilized to fight for their king during the *ancien régime*, the disparity would be even greater, since Louis XIV recruited many soldiers from outside France.

A CAVEAT: BEYOND THE NUMBERS

All the attention given here to figures should not obscure the point that the contrast between the seventeenth-century army and its predecessor was more than just a matter of how many more soldiers served Louis XIV than fought for François I. Beyond the simple question of size, the army changed in character over time, evolving from an aggregate contract to a state commission force, and it could be argued that this evolution mattered as much or more than did numbers alone. "Off-the-shelf" units raised by contract with their captains relinquished pride of place to regiments recruited by officers carrying the king's commission. In the state commission army, new recruits fleshed out established French regiments or stood to colors in entirely new

---

[130] The National Guard alone was supposed to provide a reserve of 1,200,000 men in 1789. Jacques Godechot, *Institutions de la France sous la Révolution et l'Empire* (Paris: 1968), 133.

[131] Godechot, *Institutions de la France*, 362. Both Godechot and Jean-Paul Bertaud, *La Révolution armée* (Paris: 1979), 137–39, work with the 750,000-man figure.

[132] J. Dupaquier, ed. *Histoire de la population française*, vol. 2 (Paris: 1988), 64–65. Dupaquier's figures somewhat overstate the French population in 1700, since they are based on the modern borders of France.

units when war came. The government equipped, fed, and paid the common soldier while he learned his profession, and it characteristically took many months before such an army was ready to go into action at full force. Moreover, regiments served summer and winter, as long as the war lasted. Thus, as opposed to assembling an army from "spare parts" for a particular campaign, the Bourbon state created and maintained an army in being that put a consequently greater burden on finance and administration in the long run. Over and above the great increase in numbers, saying that François I mustered 80,000 troops in the late summer of 1544 means something very different from saying that Louis XIV commanded 420,000 in 1696.

HYPOTHESIS ON WARTIME FORCES: RESOURCES AND AMBITIOUS POLICY

While the growth of the French army over the course of the *grand siècle* is both undeniable and obvious, the reasons that explain that growth are far less obvious, and they probably lie outside the scope of this volume of institutional military history. However, since some historians have attempted to explain that growth in simple and sufficient military terms, this study cannot entirely sidestep the challenge of explaining the army's expansion.

Over the past two decades, Geoffrey Parker has repeatedly accounted for the growth of early modern European armies by reference to the creation and spread of a style of fortress created in Italy during the late fourteenth and early fifteenth centuries. This *trace italienne* employed the bastion to render fortifications far less vulnerable to armies equipped with the more plentiful and much improved artillery of the age. He first stated his thesis in a 1976 article, "The 'Military Revolution' 1560–1660 – a Myth?," and more recently updated it in *The Military Revolution*. When he rhetorically asks why the Military Revolution came to different parts of Europe at different times, he replies: "The key variable appears to have been the presence or absence of the *trace italienne* in a given area, for where no bastions existed, wars of maneuver with smaller armies were still feasible."[133] He insists that fortresses drove up army size in two manners. In his earlier article, Parker stresses the huge numbers of troops required to besiege a fortress.[134] In his later book, he emphasizes the need to garrison great lines of fortresses more than the need to starve out or storm individual works.[135]

In fact, an examination of the size of forces required by siege warfare reveals that the amount of troops devoted to the actual work of a siege did not increase.[136] According to a data base including 135 sieges, from the

[133] Parker, *Military Revolution*, 24.   [134] Parker, "The 'Military Revolution,'" 208.
[135] Parker, *Military Revolution*, 39–40.
[136] For a more complete critique of the Parker thesis on the *trace italienne*, see John A. Lynn, "The *trace italienne* and the Growth of Armies: The French Case," *Journal of Military History*, July 1991, 297–330. This article is reprinted in a somewhat expanded form in Cliff Rogers,

middle of the fifteenth century, the attacking armies in sieges involving French troops most commonly numbered 20,000 to 40,000.[137] Vauban believed that the minimum reasonable force required to hold even short lines of circumvallation was about 20,000, and in most cases this rough estimate held true.[138] All in all, there is little evidence that offensive siege operations account for army growth, at least in the case of the French army.

Perhaps the best explanation for the rapid expansion of the seventeenth century combines a number of factors. France had increased in population and wealth by the *grand siècle*. It is interesting to note that the French army only expanded modestly from 1445 to 1635, yet during those two centuries, Europe restored the population lost to the plague in the late Middle Ages. Demographic growth created the potential for eventual military expansion, like a great wound spring awaiting a release. Population increase also created the economic base to sustain larger armies. This is particularly true of agriculture, for with a greater number of productive peasants at work, the surplus that could be extracted in taxes, requisition, or pillage increased. In addition, the mercantile wealth of Europe expanded, through fulfilling the needs of a greater European population and exploiting the riches of world trade and imperialism. This produced wealth, credit institutions that mobilized that wealth, and urban development.

Parker's assertion that large armies and fortresses occurred in the same places at the same time could be explained by insisting that the two were results of a similar economic-political-strategic complex. For fortifications to lie thick on the ground, the area in question must be populated by the cities, or at least large towns, that required fortifications. And the walled cities had to be rich enough to contribute substantially to the construction of their modern defenses. Even then, it would be foolish to invest in fortifications were the area not strategically open to repeated attack. Now an area that was urbanized, wealthy, and in danger might well spawn both fortifications and large armies.

The search for the trigger that activated the potential created by demography and economics leads to French international ambition. Richelieu and Mazarin adopted international goals designed first to forestall Spain and later to bring her down. This involved taking on the greatest power in Europe on battlefields from Italy to the Netherlands, and to do so required the mobilization of armies and resources on a far greater level than ever before. Richelieu resolved to raise an army whose size matched his goals: "Many princes have lost their countries and ruined their subjects by failing to

ed., *The Military Revolution Debate: Readings on the Military Transformation of Early Modern Europe* (Boulder, CO: 1995), 169–99.

[137] Lynn, "The *trace italienne* and the Growth of Armies," 324–28.

[138] Vauban, *Oeuvres*, 1:33. St. Rémy, an artillery authority of the late seventeenth century, stated that 40,000 troops were sufficient for most siege operations. Chandler, *The Art of Warfare*, 241. So perhaps 20,000 to 40,000 should be the range. This certainly fits the figures.

maintain sufficient military forces for their protection, fearing to tax them too heavily."[139]

Louis XIV pursued a foreign policy even more ambitious than those of the strong first ministers who manipulated the international scene before 1661. Richelieu and Mazarin had succeeded to a large degree in isolating their enemies and gaining allies. In contrast, Louis's brutal methods and obsession with the absolute security of France eventually isolated France and united the Grand Alliance to oppose him. Gone was the standing of France as the guarantor of German liberties, the natural ally of the Dutch, and the occasional friend of England. As early as the Dutch War, Louis confronted a combination of enemies greater than he had anticipated; consequently, the forces he committed to the war at first proved to be insufficient. At the close of 1672, Condé urged Louvois to put more troops in the field, because the French had to contend with not only the Dutch but the German states and the Spanish as well.[140] The pressures only became worse. In his final two conflicts, Louis XIV pursued military operations in four separate theaters in order to fight off his many enemies.

On this point, Vauban makes a good witness. Repeatedly he expressed concern that more troops had to be marshaled in field armies to match the foes of Louis XIV. As is shown later, he argued that the number of fortifications be limited so that garrison forces could be liberated for field duty: "However great the forces of the kingdom, one ought not to imagine that it alone can furnish troops to guard and maintain so many fortresses and at the same time put armies in the field as great as those of Spain, Italy, England, Holland and the Empire joined together."[141]

In a sense, Louis took heed of Vauban's logic, if not of his conclusions. The Sun King did not sacrifice his fortresses and their garrisons as Vauban proposed, but instead created the 400,000-man army to ensure his *gloire*. At that level, the army was at the breaking point of the resource base that the monarchy could tap; not until the French Revolution would the French put more troops in the field. The fact that Louis could not match his armies of the Nine Years' War during the War of the Spanish Succession because he had already expended the resources to do so simply adds to the power of this argument.

HYPOTHESIS ON PEACETIME FORCES: THE DEMANDS OF GARRISONS

If the preceding assertions are true, then the increasing wartime strength of the French army during the *grand siècle* did not result from the intricacies

---

[139] Cardinal Richelieu in Bruce D. Porter, *War and the Rise of the State* (New York: 1994), 63.

[140] 12 December 1672 letter from Condé to Louvois in Griffet, *Recueil des lettres pour servir d'eclaircissement à l'histoire militaire du règne de Louis XIV*, vol. 2 (Paris: 1760), 143–50.

[141] SHAT, Bib., Gen. 11 (fol.), Vauban, "Les places fortifiées du Royaume," fol. 12 ver.

of the *trace italienne* and the demands of siege warfare. However, this leaves
open the stronger possibility that peacetime army size might still have been
driven up by the need to garrison France's fortified frontier.

The number of troops committed to garrison duty multiplied during the
grand siècle. As France entered its war with Spain in 1635–36, frontier garrisons consumed only about 30,000 soldiers.[142] Figures from the era of the
War of Devolution echo this level. Louvois reported in 1666 that 25,000 men
garrisoned the frontier fortresses at a time when he counted total troop
strength at 72,000.[143] Later, both the number and percentage of troops devoted to garrison duty climbed. An *état* dated 1 January 1678 lists 279,610
troops under arms, of which 116,370 stood behind walls.[144] In a highly detailed memoir drawn up early in the Nine Years' War, Vauban claimed that
fortresses and fortified posts throughout France swallowed up 166,000
troops.[145] A second report drafted in 1705 increased the total to 173,000
infantry and cavalry.[146] Vauban thus put garrison forces at 40 to 45 percent
of total theoretical wartime strength.

By the 1670s, military opinion insisted that it was unacceptable to maintain a fortress without a suitable garrison, and from this assumption it followed that the number and size of fortifications dictated a minimum size for
the army. Not to staff a fortress on the frontier was to offer a defensive
position to the enemy, who could take the works with a small force that,
once ensconced, could do infinitely more damage than its modest numbers
might imply.[147] If a fortress existed, it demanded a garrison, but this tied up
troops that might be used in field armies. In 1644, Turenne feared that, "in
putting the infantry necessary in the fortresses there will not remain any for
the campaign."[148] Consequently, there was pressure to limit the number of
forts in order to free up troops. More than one authority argued for the
abandonment and dismantling of unnecessary strongholds. As early as 1675,

---

[142] Documents cited in Parrott, "The Administration of the French Army," 94.

[143] AG, A¹198, 5 March 1666, letter from Louvois to Pradel.

[144] SHAT, Bib., Tiroirs de Louis XIV, état of 1 January 1678.

[145] SHAT, Bib., Gen. 11 (fol.), Vauban, "Les places fortifiées du Royaume avec les garnisons
necessaires à leur garde ordinaire en temps de guerre." This document is without date, but
marginal notes, apparently by an archivist, date the document as ca. 1690 based on the
fortresses mentioned. Gaya in 1692 produces a list of "villes, citadelles, forts, & reduits où
le Roy entretient garnisons," and if citadels are counted, the garrisons listed number 203,
which corroberates Vauban. Louis de Gaya, *Le nouvel art de la guerre et la manière dont on
la fait aujourd'huy en France* (Paris: 1692), 249–61.

[146] SHAT, Bib., Génie 11 (fol.), Vauban memoirs, "Etat général des places forts du royaume,"
dated November 1705.

[147] Derek Croxton discusses the fate of fortresses in 1644 and 1645 that fell quickly because they
were defended by small garrisons or by none at all. Charles Derek Croxton, "Peacemaking
in Early Modern Europe: Cardinal Mazarin and the Congress of Westphalia, 1643–1648,"
Ph.D. dissertation, University of Illinois at Urbana-Champaign, 1995, 73, 108.

[148] Letter from Turenne to Mazarin, 3 September 1644, in Croxton, "Peacemaking in Early
Modern Europe," 164.

Vauban urged elimination of forts to save manpower: "It seems to me that the King has only too many advanced places; if he had fewer, five or six that I know well, it would be stronger by 12–14,000 men and the enemy weaker by at least 6–7,000."[149] He later drafted the memoirs cited earlier to drive home his point that the French had too many forts demanding costly garrisons.

The numbers presented by Vauban do not account for the 400,000-man wartime forces of the Nine Years' War and the War of the Spanish Succession, but they probably explain the peacetime size of the army. His two memoirs accord well with a third piece he wrote concerning French infantry. In it he asserted that about 132,000 French foot, assisted by 30,000 foreign and household troops, could effectively garrison French fortresses "in time of peace and war."[150] The usual assertion that peacetime armies were garrison armies can be a bit of a tautology, since they had no other place to go. But Vauban's memoirs demonstrate that this was not just a matter of convenience, of using fortresses as handy containers for the army between wars. With authority, he argued that the numbers of men maintained in peacetime were the minimum needed to provide garrisons at sufficient strength when war made its inevitable return. Any less, and fortresses would become prey to enemy action at the outset of the next conflict. Therefore, the French peacetime army, which hovered around 150,000 troops, was defined by garrison duty.

To some extent, this conclusion may justify Parker's later claims that fortresses propelled military expansion through garrison requirements, but even here there are two qualifications. First, Parker concerned himself with wartime levels, whereas the greatest influence of garrison forces was on peacetime strengths, at least for the French. Second, the mere physical existence of fortresses did not in itself set the number of troops. As late as midcentury, fortresses might stand unguarded. In 1653, Turenne reported that there was "no infantry at all in the fortresses" in the war zone because the king was so short of troops.[151] The need for garrisons was never simply a matter of technological determinacy but a matter of policy and strategy.

Decisions made by the Bourbons gave fortresses their leverage over military institutions. Ironically, France probably bristled with more fortresses early in the *grand siècle* than existed by its close, but many had no appreciable royal garrisons. Instead, they were often held by the personal retainers of great lords or by urban militias. But these garrisons might resist the king's forces during rebellions, and this was a political risk that the Bourbons were unwilling to accept. Therefore, Louis XIII and Louis XIV acted from political as well as military motives when they destroyed some fortifications and garrisoned the remainder with royal troops. Strategic conceptions also played

---

[149] Vauban to Louvois, 4 October 1675, Rochas d'Aiglun, *Vauban, sa famille et ses écrits*, 2 vols. (Paris: 1910), 2:131–32.
[150] Memoir on infantry, undated, in Rochas d'Aiglun, *Vauban*, 1:287.
[151] Turenne, *Mémoires de Turenne* (Paris: 1872), 187.

a role. The maintenance of large garrison forces resulted from the Sun King's resolve to secure his territory with a great fortress line. Louis XIV chose to build barriers, whereas earlier and later military men – Turenne and Napoleon, for example – preferred mobile forces. Only after these fundamental choices had been made, did judgments as to the size and composition of garrisons rest on the state of the art in siege warfare.

Since the standing army was synonymous with the peacetime army, it is reasonable to argue that the standing army was a product of the military need to hold fortresses against foreign enemies and the political necessity to guarantee them against internal rebels. This argument stands in opposition to assertions that the standing army was created as a device to subjugate the French population as a whole.

CONCLUSION

This chapter has charted the dimensions and development of one of those giants that dominated warfare by 1700: the army of France. On the whole, earlier, traditional notions of French army growth have fared well in these pages, even though particular figures have been questioned or redefined. The two-step concept of French military expansion, first substantial under Richelieu and later spectacular under Louis XIV, emerges in a modified form but still intact. Louis XIII nearly doubled previous troop levels when he and his able first minister entered the lists against Spain. Later, the Sun King commanded wartime forces five to eight times greater than those that had fought for his Valois predecessors, and perhaps even more impressive was the standing army that remained in peacetime to support the monarchy. Yet this recognition of dramatic army expansion under Louis XIV is qualified by the knowledge that the aging monarch's forces during the War of the Spanish Succession did not reach the proportions of those he had marshaled for the Nine Years' War.

French army growth through the reigns of Louis XIII and Louis XIV surpassed in importance all other military phenomena of the age: Military expansion was truly revolutionary in character. Both product and tool of dynastic and internal warfare, greater forces were integral to the transformation in army style and essential to the creation of absolutism. In addition, fundamental social questions involving the elites and the masses revolved around the fact of expansion. Therefore, an understanding of the history of French military institutions in the *grand siècle* begins with a knowledge of army growth. After beginning with this step, the journey of understanding can continue.

PART TWO

ADMINISTRATION AND SUPPLY

3

The Military Administration

A S the army loomed ever larger, it became more powerful and more
dangerous – a towering brute with the strength to serve or to cripple
the state. If handled well, this giant might dutifully overwhelm the enemies
of France, but if mishandled, it might cause more harm to France itself than
to her foes. Turning the army's potential to the purposes of the state required both the mobilization of resources demanded by the new giant and
effective military administration to feed and control it. Field commanders
would be helpless to lead their forces if military administration failed in its
less glorious but still essential tasks.

No other aspect of the military has received as much attention from historians of the seventeenth century as has administration. Its involvement
with great historical figures and its obvious links to emerging absolutism –
as well as its remoteness from the battlefield, a venue that academic historians
have tried to avoid – explain its popularity. Most attention has been given
to the work of Le Tellier and his son, Louvois, whose years in office span
nearly half the *grand siècle*, 1643–91. Louis André and Camille Rousset contributed the classic studies, and André Corvisier has recently added to their
impressive works. Coming from very different perspectives, Jules Caillet and,
now, David Parrott, have studied military administration during Richelieu's
regime. Only the era that extended from the death of Louvois to that of his
master, Louis XIV, has failed to attract considerable attention, although it
should.

The extensive bibliography on military administration provides the abundant detail on hierarchy and control presented in this chapter, so one goal
here is simply to combine the available material together into a coherent
whole that covers the entire *grand siècle*. As a consequence of this reliance
upon existent works, the resultant outline of French absolutist government,
central military administration, and the individuals who directed it may be
of less immediate interest to readers who already possess an understanding
of seventeenth-century France than to those whose background leaves them

less informed as to the operation of Bourbon absolutism. Nonetheless, by reviewing governmental and bureaucratic growth over the course of the entire century here, instead of focusing on the administration of only one or another individual, a picture emerges that is more original to this volume and not simply a transcription of what has already been written. That picture is one of surprising continuity in a period of change typified by important, but incremental, innovations rather than one of radical and total transformation – this despite the fact that the army underwent rapid and unprecedented growth.

Discussion of military administration runs the danger of emphasizing the rational procedures found in ordinances over the catch-as-catch-can practices actually employed. To some degree, the pressures of time and space select for the former over the latter in this chapter. Other sections of this volume will emphasize the difference between regulation and reality in greater detail. That difference was always present and often very great, and the history of that gap is perhaps more interesting, and certainly more revealing, than a simple list of official offices and directives.

In general, military bureaucracy grew and paperwork multiplied over the course of the seventeenth century. The effectiveness of that bureaucracy is, however, open to debate. A period of stagnation followed the death of Henri IV in 1610. When Richelieu assumed the position of minister in chief to the young Louis XIII, he instituted important changes in the formal administration of the army. The war with Spain, 1635–59, witnessed continued paper reforms, as the monarchy struggled to create the institutions to maintain an expanded army. These plans for change met with limited success, often foundering on the chaotic fiscal condition of the government. During the rebellion of the Fronde, conditions sank to a nadir of indiscipline, pillage, and mutiny caused largely by a breakdown in administration and supply.

The day-to-day challenges of the war frustrated Le Tellier's reform plans, but the horrors of warfare also gave those plans a greater urgency, an urgency that eventually assisted him in constructing a better system once peace returned. If his goals had not been realized prior to the personal reign of Louis XIV, they set the direction for what would come later. The return of peace in 1659 allowed serious financial and military reforms to take hold. The first decade of Louis XIV's personal reign witnessed a series of practical innovations carried out by LeTellier and Louvois. While the Dutch War led to a return of fiscal abuses, the army ran well. With Louvois at the top of the military administration, French military preeminence continued into the Nine Years' War. Whether the level of effectiveness slipped after his death in 1691 is open to dispute. The military successes of the previous decades may have eluded the French, but the challenges that they faced were much greater, since the army swelled to its greatest size of the century even though the French never solved the key problem of state, and thus military, finance.

POWER AT THE CENTER

The Monarchs, Their First Ministers, and Their Councils

France of the *grand siècle* lay somewhere between medieval and modern. It operated by logic and values different from today's. True enough, authority was becoming increasingly bureaucratic, yet the monarch still dominated, still set military policy, so that power within the government flowed from the top down. And at the top stood very few individuals.

Only two kings, Louis XIII and Louis XIV, ruled over the *grand siècle*, and although both were noteworthy monarchs, father and son possessed different characters and styles. Louis XIII ranks as one of France's least understood kings. Perhaps his more modest image is bound to be obscured by the glaring brilliance of his son. Louis XIII was effective but in a manner not associated with history's outstanding monarchs. As a private person he stuttered, sank frequently into melancholy, and tortured himself with suspicions of others and doubts about himself. Poor health dogged him throughout his life, and he died at age forty-two. But as a king, although Louis may have lacked a commanding personality, he was every inch a sovereign, with a firm sense of his role and duty. Intelligent and hard working, he never relinquished his ultimate authority. Louis was also a true soldier-king, who commanded his troops at the front. Roland Mousnier has gone so far as to say, "This suffering and anguished individual was a leader and a great king."[1]

At the death of his father, Henri IV, Louis was only a boy, and his mother, Marie de Medici, served as regent. Weak and corrupt, she fell under the influence of unscrupulous and self-seeking servants, the Concinis. Conniving at the murder of Concini, Louis seized power himself in 1617 and banished his mother to Blois. But the young and uncertain man of sixteen could neither govern effectively himself nor locate an outstanding minister to operate as his agent until 1624, when Cardinal Richelieu entered his government to guide affairs for eighteen years as first minister. Once Louis recognized Richelieu's ability, the monarch backed him with wisdom and courage, even in Richelieu's least popular decisions.

Richelieu's authority always rested on the favor of the king. The cardinal never dictated to Louis, but the minister managed his master as best he could. Louis was prone to moods, and the cardinal monitored these personally or through his agents. Richelieu staffed the government with his own relatives, friends, and supporters – his clients, his creatures.[2] Old family contacts rose to high positions, such as the Bouthilliers who became secretaries of state. By making sure that those government servants with the ear of the

---

[1] Roland E. Mousnier, *The Institutions of France under the Absolute Monarchy, 1598–1789*, vol. 2, *The Organs of State and Society* (Chicago: 1984), 17.

[2] See Orest Ranum, *Richelieu and the Councillors of Louis XIII* (Oxford: 1963) for a discussion of Richelieu and his creatures.

king were all his creatures, Richelieu insulated the king from rivals and rival opinions. Richelieu himself served as an intermediary and clearinghouse between the king and other levels of administration.

Besides the all-important first minister, Louis governed through his councils. The most exclusive council, the *conseil secrète* included only the king, Richelieu, and the chancellor. However, the council that became the most important of the *grand siècle* was the *conseil des affaires*, which after 1643 was known as the *conseil d'en haut*. In 1633, this council included Louis, Richelieu, the chancellor, the *surintendant des finances*, and the secretary of state for war.[3] Richelieu sought influence through unanimity, so he chose and advanced men who worked together well under his leadership. He did his best to reconcile opinions before he ever proposed actions or policies to the king. After all, dissension in the *conseil d'en haut* would by its very nature threaten Richelieu, since a strong clash of opinion there meant that Richelieu's favored plans had encountered opposition. The king concerned himself with the councils, but he had little taste for the mundane business of administration. While bureaucracy grew under Louis XIII, he never became a *roi bureaucrat* as did his son. Louis was more prone to action than to consideration.

Richelieu died in 1642, and six months later, Louis XIII followed him to the grave. Before the monarch died, he chose a new first minister, Mazarin, Italian by birth and a protégé of Cardinal Richelieu. The new king, Louis XIV, was only four years old; this meant that a regent would again exercise real power. Louis XIII, ever distrustful of his wife, had excluded the queen, Anne of Austria, from the council of regency. Mazarin, however, aided Anne in overturning the late king's will and in establishing a new council of regency with her at its head. Mazarin, a man of brilliance and skill, ingratiated himself with Anne, who rewarded him with loyalty and affection and left policy in his able hands. The cardinal also became the tutor and surrogate father of the boy-king. While Mazarin enjoyed the regent's and the king's confidence, he met resistance from other quarters. This resistance, the pressures of an ongoing war, and the inherent weakness of a regency government made most of his regime a time of troubles. Vicious pamphlets attacked his reputation, and assassination plots threatened his life. Not until after the defeat of the Fronde and the majority of Louis XIV did Mazarin's position become truly strong.

Mazarin devoted himself to resisting attempts to undermine royal authority within France while at the same time securing victory over Spain. Mazarin could never be as direct and brutal as Richelieu; rather, the Italian dealt in the more subtle arts of compromise and deception. Anne was willing to let Mazarin take charge, since she was confident that he would put the interest of her son first. This he did, though he also became immensely rich in the process. The conciliar form of government remained, and Mazarin made use of a special Council of War, organized shortly after Richelieu's death by

---

[3] Mousnier, *The Institutions of France*, 2:131.

Gaston d'Orléans, but it seems to have had only a short career.[4] Mazarin chose able men for high office; it was under his regime that Le Tellier rose to secretary of state for war. Considering the turmoil of the period, it seems amazing that as much was accomplished as actually was. Still, solid reforms would have to await the coming of peace in 1659 and the personal reign of Louis XIV.

Louis XIV acted as an apprentice until the death of Mazarin in 1661, when the king actually took the reins of government in his own hands. From then until his own death in 1715, Louis ruled France directly and actively. He had come to the throne after a quarter century of exhausting warfare, complicated by the Fronde. The young monarch resolved that his authority would not again be challenged by the great nobles or privileged law courts that had threatened it in the Fronde, nor would he ever have recourse to a first minister after the death of Mazarin.

In substance and style, Louis XIV defined the pattern of absolutism. An absolute monarch in Louis's mold was not a dictator; to cast him as such would be anachronistic, since his power knew limits set by tradition and necessity. However, in those matters over which he claimed authority, he brooked no interference, and paramount among the king's lifelong concerns were diplomacy and military affairs; there he set and managed policy on a daily basis. He successfully overwhelmed potential competitors for his authority during his lifetime. France's medieval representative assembly, the Estates General, met last in 1614 and would not assemble again until 1789. The great sovereign law courts of France, confusingly known as *parlements*, had attempted to assert their authority during the Fronde but failed, and under Louis XIV, they remained relatively docile. Although the Catholic Church in France might have become a factor in foreign policy when Louis squared off against the Vatican, it did not exert great influence. Louis also brought his own government servants to heel, both those at the center and those in the provinces. To a great degree, he suppressed independent action, even among his military commanders on campaign. More and more authority concentrated at court, under the direct supervision of the king.

Louis could not expect to master every detail of government; rather, he saw his role as making decisions based on common sense, balancing expert advice offered by the chief figures of his government. Louis, like his father, regularized the decision-making process in a series of councils. By chairing the meetings, he kept his finger on the pulse of government affairs. Again the most important of these councils, the *conseil d'en haut*, dealt with the most critical matters, including war and peace issues. Those who sat on it could call themselves "ministers" of state. Louis refused to set the membership of this council by ordinance, leaving himself free to choose the three, four, or

---

[4] Charles Derek Croxton, "Peacemaking in Early Modern Europe: Cardinal Mazarin and the Congress of Westphalia, 1643–1648," Ph.D. dissertation, University of Illinois at Urbana-Champaign, 1995, 80. Croxton doubts that the Council of War met after 1643.

five who regularly attended its meetings. Louis kept its size small to ensure secrecy. The most common members included the secretaries of state for foreign affairs, war, and navy, and the *contrôleur général des finances*. However, the post of secretary of state did not necessarily carry with it automatic entrée into the *conseil*. One secretary of state for war, the marquis de Barbézieux, did not receive an invitation to the *conseil d'en haut*, since Louis preferred the opinions of the marquis de Chamlay, his personal military advisor of long standing.[5] Louis kept control over this council in other ways as well and expressly forbade his ministers to meet if he were not present.[6]

The members of the *conseil* vied for influence amongst themselves, a situation that Louis exploited by playing his advisors off against each other so as to give himself leverage and leeway. Such conflicts most commonly saw the two major ministerial families – the Le Telliers and the Colberts – contend over policy, power, and preference. As the observer, Primi Visconti, wrote, "Le Tellier and Colbert are not very good friends, the one wants to surpass the other; but the king holds them in equilibrium, the better to do his business."[7] Here was a great contrast with government under Louis XIII and Richelieu. Richelieu had to present a common front to the monarch to guarantee control, but Louis XIV as monarch fostered dissension in order to maintain his authority.

The *conseil d'en haut* met on no regular schedule; its sessions were entirely at the king's pleasure. Louis used his *conseil* as he saw fit; however, at times, he seems to have viewed it as an annoyance, since there his elevated civil servants might try to temper or oppose the king's designs. Inside the council, members discarded the formalities of court and discussed issues openly and in strict confidence; ministers criticized the king's positions, though in public they dared not. After an issue was discussed and the ministers made their opinions known, Louis usually decided with the majority; however, sometimes he would oppose it for no other reason than to demonstrate his power.

For this system to function under the monarch's real, as well as theoretical, control, the king had to possess a great appetite for work – and Louis XIV did. He wrote, "I imposed upon myself the rule of working regularly twice a day two or three hours each time with divers persons of government, not counting the hours I spend myself or the time required for extraordinary affairs."[8] Outside this council, he discussed matters of foreign policy, strategy, and operations with his secretaries of state and other experts, one on one. Even lesser officials conferred directly with the king on a regular basis.

---

[5] Martin, Ronald. "The Marquis de Chamlay, Friend and Confidential Advisor to Louis XIV: The Early Years, 1650–1691," Ph.D. dissertation, University of California at Santa Barbara, 1972, argues that Chamlay won Louis's confidence from the Dutch War on.

[6] John C. Rule, "Colbert de Torcy, an Emergent Bureaucracy, and the Formulation of French Foreign Policy, 1698–1715," in Ragnhild Hatton, ed., *Louis XIV and Europe* (Columbus, Ohio: 1976), 281.

[7] Primi Visconti, *Mémoires*, 130.

[8] Louis in John B. Wolf, *Louis XIV* (New York: 1968), 168.

The Great Bureaucrats

Immediately after the king, and first ministers in the case of Richelieu and Mazarin, came the *surintendant* or *contrôleur général des finances* and the secretaries of state, who headed the growing bureaucracy of royal government. Until 1661, the *surintendant des finances* directed financial administration, but Louis XIV abolished the office that year and replaced it with a new and more restricted post, the *contrôleur général des finances*. This was a less grand title, since a *"contrôleur"* was technically only an accountant, but the *contrôleur général* was an important figure, indeed, with direct access to the king. Though not directly a military official, the chief financial officer of the monarchy and his agents were central to maintaining the army.

Four secretaries of state also enjoyed direct access to the king and sat in the most powerful councils. While the office of secretary of state was not a creation of the *grand siècle*, it was during this era that the functions of the secretaries were regularized and defined.[9] These offices evolved over time from the clerks who maintained the kings' correspondence. A single secretary already held sway over matters dealing with war under François II (1559–60). Henri III (1574–89) both elevated four secretaries and tried to exert greater control over these four when he gave them the title secretaries of state, and he made their position, or *charge*, revocable.[10] By the late sixteenth century, the four secretaries divided the provincial correspondence between them, each having a particular geographic authority in addition to whatever aspect of government he might be charged with. A *règlement* of 1619 defined the responsibilities of the secretary of state for war. It gave him the right to write commissions and orders only for the "first and principal army," while garrisons and other armies fell to the secretaries who held the responsibility for the provinces in which the armies or garrisons were located. When an army crossed the geographic lines separating the jurisdictions of two secretaries, it was up to the secretaries to decide who would write the orders for the army. Obviously, such a situation gave rise to dispute.

The famous *règlement* of 11 March 1626 defined the four secretaries in more complete form, and, thus, Richelieu often receives credit for creating the office of secretary of state. Yet the secretaries of state had begun the process of specialization well before Richelieu, and the *règlements* of 1619 and 1626 simply recognized this existing differentiation and then further clarified its lines. According to the 1626 act, each of the four received responsibility for certain provinces plus a further administrative department, most notably, war, foreign affairs, and the royal household. Eventually one secretary of state was put in charge of naval affairs. According to the 1626 regulation, Beauclerc received the provinces of Lyonnais, Dauphiné, Provence, Saintonge,

[9] See, in particular, Ranum, *Richelieu and the Councillors of Louis XIII* on the evolution of the secretaries of state.
[10] Ranum, *Richelieu and the Councillors of Louis XIII*, 48.

La Marche, Angoumois, Limousin, and Poitou in addition to the department of war.[11] Along with provincial authority came certain military duties
for each of the other three secretaries of state; for example, they controlled
fortifications in their territories, at least until 1661.

While the differentiation of the positions of the secretaries of state were
legitimized in regulations, the tendency to split or combine secretaryships
complicated the actual jurisdictions. These positions were not defined by
concrete-hard lines of authority. At important junctures, one individual could
hold more than one major office; for example, Colbert was *contrôleur général*
during 1661–83, to which he joined secretary of state for the navy in 1669–
83 and secretary of state for the royal household in 1668–83. During the same
period, Le Tellier, secretary of state for war since 1643, shared the office with
his son Louvois, from 1662. Also, in contrast to modern practice, son often
followed father, or uncle, in office, and ministerial dynasties tended to dominate offices – the most obvious cases being the Le Telliers and the Colberts.
Louvois succeed his father, Michel Le Tellier, and was in turn succeeded by
his own son, Barbézieux. Colbert's son Seignelay followed his father as both
secretary for the navy and the household; and Demaretz, nephew of Colbert,
later held the post of *contrôleur général*. The Bouthilliers under Louis XIII
and the Phélypeaux under Louis XIII and Louis XIV constituted lesser examples of such dynasties. Family succession was bolstered by the fact that the
right to succeed in these positions could be bought, though only with the
king's accord. They essentially became family possessions, which demanded
a high price, as when Chamillart paid the family of Barbézieux 300,000 livres
to succeed him as secretary of state for war in 1701.[12]

The authority wielded by the small knot of advisors and administrative
heads around Louis derived not from their own birth and wealth but from
the fact that Louis called upon them to serve. He scrupulously kept powerful
nobles of old families, the peers of France, from high bureaucratic posts and
from the councils. He once explained that "it was not in my interest to seek
men of a more eminent birth because having need above all to establish my
own reputation, it was important that the public know by the rank of those
whom I choose to serve me, that I had no intention of sharing my authority
with them . . . ."[13] The men he placed in power possessed legal and administrative backgrounds, and they sprang from families only recently ennobled.
Court grandees looked down on government ministers. During a procession
of the knights of the Order of the Holy Spirit, an order to which Louvois
belonged, the wife of Philippe d'Orléans yelled, "See how Louvois has the air
of a bourgeois! . . . No Order can hide his condition."[14] There were only rare

[11] Mousnier, *The Institutions of France*, 2:143–44. In 1626, Beauclerc also received responsibility
for the Mediterranean fleet.
[12] Marcel Marion, *Dictionnaire des institutions de la France aux XVIIe et XVIIIe siècles* (Paris:
1923), 503.
[13] Louis in André Corvisier, *Louvois* (Paris: 1983), 278.
[14] Primi Visconti, *Mémoires sur la cour de Louis XIV, 1673–81*, Jean-François Solnon, ed. (Paris:
1988), 27.

breaks in Louis's exclusion of the well-born: Marshal Turenne, for example, enjoyed great influence over the king in the 1660s, and he was from the princely family La Tour d'Auvergne.

Since the secretaries and the *contrôleur général* controlled considerable patronage, they accumulated networks of clients, men who depended on their good will and who in turn acted as their supporters. This gave Louis's major servants something of an independent power base, yet while such a network might aid a secretary in rising to power, maintaining himself in office, or in fending off his rivals, it was not a tool to assert independence against the will of the king.

Over the course of the century, the departments of state and the office of the *surintendant/contrôleur général* became more and more bureaucratized. This was particularly the case for the departments of war and foreign affairs. As a consequence, Louis XIV played the role of chief administrator, the *roi bureaucrat*, more than had his father. But even under the Sun King, the bureaucracy did not rule, for Louis XIV crafted it not to govern in his stead but to ensure that he alone governed. The fact that French bureaucracy later developed into a perpetual-motion machine, as bureaucracies tend to do, is beside the point.

The Surintendant des finances, *the* Contrôleur général, *and Their Agents*

As money constitutes the sinews of war, the financial administration played a vital role in supporting the French army, and agents of that administration went to the field with the troops. Before Louis abolished the office, the *surintendant des finances* was the state's top financial officer.[15] Actually, *surintendants* is a better term, because often two individuals jointly held the post. The position of *surintendant* fluctuated between what Mousnier calls personal and collegial approaches. Henri IV tried to replace the *surintendant* with a commission of eight upon the death of François d'O, who had been *surintendant* during 1578–94. When this failed, Rosny, soon to become duke de Sully, operated as *surintendant* effectively from 1598 and in title from 1601, but with Henri IV's death, Sully was driven from office in 1611.[16]

Under Louis XIII, the most important *surintendants* were *fidèles* of Richelieu. Today, no commission for the major financial official dates before 1619, and it seems none was issued before then. Regulations of 1624 and 1630 gave the *surintendant*, first, a seat on the *conseil d'en haut*, and, second, title of minister of state. The next major individual to occupy this post during the first half

---

[15] For a short discussion of the *surintendant des finances*, see Mousnier, *The Institutions of France*, 2:180–214; and for the *surintendant* under Richelieu, see Ranum, *Richelieu and the Councillors of Louis XIII*, 120–80. Richard Bonney, *The King's Debts* (Oxford: 1981), in his Appendix one, table one, 285–87, lists all *surintendants*, 1578–1661.

[16] Bonney, *The King's Debts*, 285.

of the *grand siècle* was the very able Antoine Coiffier de Ruzé, marquis d'Effiat, 1626–32, a man loyal to Richelieu. After Effiat died, Claude de Bullion and Claude le Bouthillier held the post jointly, although Bullion was clearly the senior partner until his death in 1640, when Bouthillier carried on alone until 1643.[17] Richelieu dominated financial concerns more under his client Bouthillier than he had under Bullion.

The position was held by ten different persons, individually or in pairs, from 1643 to 1653, when it came into the hands of Abel Servien and Nicolas Fouquet. Fouquet, the more ambitious and driving of the two became increasingly dominant but only held the title alone after Servien died in 1659. Like others before and after him, Fouquet was himself a financier, who loaned his own money to the government when necessary, as when he advanced the crown 3 million livres in 1656–57.[18] Fouquet's ambition destroyed both himself and his office, as Louis XIV abolished the surintendancy in 1661, deciding "to take to himself the care of administering his own finances, in order to eliminate all the abuses that have slipped in to this date."[19]

Louis supervised financial policy and administration through a special council, the *conseil royal des finances*, created by the *règlement* of 15 September 1661.[20] Actually, one form or another of such a council predated his personal reign. Henri IV had tried to use a commission to run finances (1594–98) and thereafter, commissions and councils played a role. A *règlement* of 1630 even stipulated particular days of the week for meetings of a *conseil des finances*; however, the *conseil* did not take on permanent form and function until 1661. Generally, Louis presided over this important council twice each week.[21]

Below the *surintendant des finances* before 1661, and later in its stead, stood the *contrôleur général des finances*. This post began as a rather modest office, employed to audit, really to certify, royal accounts. Before Colbert, it was not a strong position, and often there were as many as four *contrôleurs générals* serving at the same time.[22] However, Louis XIV raised the post to the status of finance minister when he turned it into a commission in 1665 and appointed Colbert as the first new *contrôleur général*. Recourse to a new style of finance minister signified that the task of daily financial administration proved too much for Louis, but it did not mean that he abdicated his control. The *contrôleur général* enjoyed less independence than had the *surintendant*. Louis used his *conseil des finances* to keep on top of things and to ensure that it was his will that was done. The elevation of Colbert also marked the triumph of the personal, as opposed to collegial, financial administration of finance. From that time on, there would be only one *contrôleur général* at a

---

[17] Ranum, *Richelieu and the Councillors of Louis XIII*, 166–80.
[18] Peter Jonathan Berger, "Military and Financial Government in France, 1648–1661," Ph.D. dissertation, University of Chicago, 1979, 245–46.
[19] *Règlement* of 15 September 1661 in Marion, *Dictionnaire*, 523.
[20] Marion, *Dictionnaire*, 134–35.   [21] Mousnier, *The Institutions of France*, 2:18.
[22] Bonney, *The King's Debts*, in his Appendix one, table two, 288, lists *contrôleurs généraux*, 1594–1665.

time. Colbert held the commission until his death in 1683, when Le Pelletier de Morfontaine succeeded him. Louis Phélypeaux, count de Pontchartrain, occupied the post from 1689 to 1699. He was followed by Michel de Chamilliart (1699–1708) and Nicolas Demaretz, a nephew of Colbert (1708–15).

A number of *intendants des finances* served both the *surintendant* and, later, the *contrôleur général*. They varied in number from era to era. Under François I, there were two; Sully employed two or three; from 1615 to 1649, eight served at a time; this number was increased to twelve in 1654.[23] Since these offices were up for sale, the temptation was to create more in times of need. The housecleaning that followed the war with Spain brought the number back down to two in 1660, but the number increased to four in 1690. The duties of these *intendants* varied; if serving with an army, as Sublet de Noyers did in the 1630s, they performed much as army *intendants*.

Other financial officers who played roles in war finance included the *trésoriers* and *receveurs*. *Trésoriers* supervised the various funds of the monarch. The most important were the *trésoriers d'épargne*. In order to ensure a degree of honesty and accountability, this post, and that of other major treasurers, changed hands each year. But upon inspection, the list of names of *trésoriers* reveals that this post tended to oscillate back and forth between two or three individuals.[24] So at the start of the *grand siècle*, Etienne Puget, Vincent Bouhier, and Raymond Phélypeaux alternated in the job in neat succession from 1598 to 1624, with the substitution of Thomas Morant for Puget after 1616. At midcentury, Guénégaud, Jeanin, and Macé II Bertrand played musical chairs with the post. *Receveurs* supervised the collection and accounts of funds for the monarchy, and they existed on a number of levels for a great variety of taxes and funds. *Receveurs des tailles* monitored the collection of that tax in each taxing district. Higher on the scale were the *receveurs générals*, one in each *généralité*. There were also *receveurs* for special war taxes, including contributions levied on occupied territory.

As discussed in Chapter 1, *surintendants*, *contrôleurs générals*, and *intendants des finances*, and other financial officers were important less for their executive talent than for their connections with wealth and their own personal credit, which the state repeatedly called upon.

Trésoriers *of the Military Accounts*

Imbedded in the nearly unaccountable system of French finance, military finance had its own administrative complexities. It made use of several budget lines that increased in number during the *grand siècle*. The oldest was the *ordinaire des guerres*, which by the seventeenth century covered the pay of

---

[23] Bonney, *The King's Debts*, 6; Marion, *Dictionnaire*, 299.
[24] Bonney, *The King's Debts*, in his Appendix one, table four, 290–92, lists *trésoriers de l'épargne*, 1589–1661.

Table 3.1. *Military expenses for 1692.*

Budget item	Expenses in livres tournois
Extraordinaire et ordinaire des guerres	72,622,840
Pain de munition	12,658,546
Garnisons ordinaires	2,523,374
Étapes	10,075,617
Fortifications	6,424,951
Pensions et gratifications aux troupes	2,070,539
Artillerie	1,816,942
Maréchaux de France	552,754
Gardes du corps etc.	184,523

household and guard troops but little else. It had shrunk to a minor amount by the seventeenth century. The primary military account was the *extraordinaire des guerres*. The *extraordinaire* was so much larger than the *ordinaire* that in most existent accounts it simply subsumes the *ordinaire*.[25]

As a gauge of the relative importance of the several military budget lines carried in contemporary *états*, consider Table 3.1, which lists annual outlays in 1692 at the peak year of the Nine Years' War.[26]

Not only were the *ordinaire* and *extraordinaire des guerres* administered separately, but both were divided into two departments, Picardy and Piedmont, the first dealing with the twelve provinces north of the Loire, and the second with the rest of France. Two or three *trésoriers généraux* headed each department and rotated in office.[27] It would appear that the only major military accounts handled by other treasurers were artillery and fortifications.[28]

From a strictly military point of view, the *trésoriers* of the *extraordinaire*

---

[25] Victor Belhomme, *L'armée française en 1690* (Paris: 1895), 142–43, gives a useful breakdown of just what the *ordinaire* and *extraordinaire* covered. Items under the *ordinaire* included: general officers, troops of the *maison*, guards regiments, *gendarmerie* and *maréchaussée*, and the *ordinaire* shares of artillery and maintenance of fortresses. The *extraordinaire* covered the following: pay of other troops, *vivres*, hospitals, lodging, and the *extraordinaire* share of artillery and the construction of new fortifications.

When *ordinaire* accounts are found, they are quite small. BN, f. fr. 7749, Monteil, "État des finances de la France depuis 1600 jusqu'à l'année 1786," lists *ordinaire* in 1675 as only 4,000 livres, at a time when Mallet lists *"Extraordinaire et ordinaire"* as 48,391,000 livres. AN, KK 355 does not even carry a budget line for the *ordinaire des guerres*, and Mallet, *Compts rendus* shows the same number that KK 355 shows as *extraordinaire* as *extraordinaire et ordinaire*.

[26] Data in table from Mallet, *Compts rendus*, 399.

[27] Contamine, *Histoire militaire*, 1:344.

[28] Accounts for 1692 from the treasurer for the *extraordinaire* seem to cover everything with two exceptions: (1) a line of payment to the *trésorier de l'artillerie* roughly equivalent to the budget for artillery indicates that this budget though it may have passed through the extraordinaires was managed by its own treasurer; and (2) there is no mention of expenses for fortifications, which were run through its own *surintendant*, Le Pelletier de Souzy.

de guerres were particularly important officials. Just as particular *trésoriers d'épargne* served for only one year at a time, so also did the *trésoriers généraux de l'extraordinaire des guerres*. At times, however, two to five *trésoriers* officially served jointly, as throughout much of the period 1688–1715. Claudine Fages argues, however, that while the royal almanac might list several names of treasurers, the actual signatures on official documents reveal that usually only one individual exercised the actual functions of the post.[29] Other *trésoriers* and *commis* served below the *trésoriers généraux*, and again rotation of these commissions was also supposed to make for more honest accounts. Permission was denied when exceptions were proposed, as in 1696. "You propose to keep on Devicourt during the present year as *commis* of the *trésoriers de l'extraordinaire de la guerre* d'Ambrun et des Vallèes. As it is customary to change this post every year, in order that they render their accounts more clearly, it is not possible to keep him in this position."[30] Armies and even units, such as the Gardes suisses, had their own treasurers as well, so the term *trésorier* existed on a wide range of levels. Additional financial agents, such as *contrôleurs*, *receveurs*, and *payeurs*, staffed the financial administration with the field armies.

Secretary of State for War

The secretary of state for war directed military administration during the seventeenth century, and over the course of the century, his position evolved considerably. This constant evolution has given rise to considerable debate over who actually founded modern military administration. Audouin gives the palm to Henri IV and his minister Sully, Caillet believes that Richelieu deserves credit, Wolf applauds Sublet, André praises Le Tellier, and Rousset insists it was Louvois. To a degree, this is only a marginally productive effort to establish at what point on a steadily rising curve the line crossed the threshold from old to modern.

Lay Audouin's claims aside, since he seems isolated in this insistence and since the chaos of the 1630s discounts the lasting impact of Sully's reforms. Without doubt, some key moves were made under Richelieu, before he brought Sublet de Noyers on the scene. Then Sublet and his more important successor, Le Tellier, outlined a system on paper, and adopted what they could of it in practice, but financial chaos, army growth, military crisis, and civil rebellion greatly hampered what they could accomplish under Richelieu and Mazarin during the war with Spain. However, after 1661, the return of peace, the improvement in royal finance, and the strong hand of a young and unchallenged monarch allowed first Le Tellier and then his son Louvois to

[29] Claudine Fages, "Le service de la guerre sous Louis XIV de 1699 à 1715" (1974), manuscript catalogue of documents in AN, G⁷1774–88, which contain the correspondence and records of the *trésoriers généraux de l'extraordinaire des guerres*, 1695–1715.

[30] AG, A¹1339, p. 96, letter of 11 January 1796.

construct a new edifice based upon the blueprint drafted by Le Tellier. By the death of Louvois in 1691, the patterns of *ancien régime* military administration were largely set until the French Revolution. Administrators seem to have done little to change them in the remaining years of Louis's reign, which has led some to claim that the system became ossified.

As already mentioned, war had been the primary responsibility of a single secretary of state since the mid–sixteenth century, but other secretaries held authority over troops stationed in the provinces for which they were responsible. Caillet argues that before Richelieu, virtual anarchy reigned in French military administration.[31] While this exaggerates the situation, certainly conflicting lines of authority and inadequate administrative practices and personnel frustrated the reforms that would be necessary for the far larger armies that fought after 1635.

Richelieu deserves credit even if, as already mentioned, the 1626 act formally differentiating the functions of the secretaries represented an evolution more than a revolution. The 1626 *règlement* increased the jurisdiction of the secretary of state for war and gave him responsibility for all correspondence with armies outside the realm.[32] Real-world developments continued to add power and bureaucratic staff to the secretaries and to validate their authority with time and habit. As is detailed later, the abolition of the constable in 1627 was probably the most important move that Richelieu made.

Beauclerc held the post of secretary of state for war during 1626–30, immediately after Richelieu's *règlement*; Corvisier thus identifies him as the first French minister of war.[33] Able Servien, the next to hold the post, 1630–35, performed with ability under the aegis of Richelieu; however, it was Sublet de Noyers, 1635–43, who devised the means to muster a great army for a full-scale war in the era of absolutism; this may explain why John B. Wolf calls Sublet de Noyers the first true administrator of the "new army."[34] Beauclerc, Servien, and Sublet have failed to attract major biographers in the same way as Le Tellier and Louvois, so their briefs before the historical court remain thin.

Probably Orest Ranum provides the best account of Sublet de Noyers.[35] Sublet served as an *intendant* of finance and a military *intendant* before rising to secretary of state. Sublet was a creature of Richelieu and would not have been granted the post were he not. While never free from the tutelage of the cardinal, who sent him military memoranda and instructions, the first minister's limitations of time and health left Sublet considerable autonomy to act in the name of the minister and the king. In Ranum's judgment, the

[31] Jules Caillet, *De l'adminstration en France sous le ministère du Cardinal de Richelieu* (Paris: 1857), 362–63.

[32] Corvisier sees the 1626 act as the first major step in an evolution. Corvisier, *Louvois*, 82.

[33] Philippe Contamine, ed., *Histoire militaire de la France*, vol. 1 (Paris: 1992), 340.

[34] Wolf, *Louis XIV*, 148.

[35] Ranum, *Richelieu and the Councilors of Louis XIII*, devotes an entire chapter to Sublet de Noyers.

importance and goals of the secretary of state for war were defined under Sublet: "the essential elements for a new order were determined: the secretary spoke and wrote in the name of the king, and the goal, the unification of the entire military administration, was already established."[36] Without doubt, a good many new regulations and ordinances date from Noyer's administration, but the practical effect of particular decrees has been challenged. David Parrott and Peter Berger doubt the reality of military reform under Richelieu, since the army suffered such administrative collapse during the first decade of the war with Spain. So if Sublet set a direction, he made little substantive progress along it. In any case, when Richelieu died, Sublet bid to replace the cardinal as first minister and compromised himself in the process. Sublet had to go in 1643, making way for Michel Le Tellier.

Like his predecessor, Le Tellier worked as an army *intendant* before assuming the secretaryship. From 1640 to 1643, he served as *intendant* with the Army of Italy. Since Sublet actually owned the post of secretary, for two years Le Tellier held a provisional title and only received title in full when Sublet died in 1645. While Le Tellier busied himself with the tasks of military administration, he seems to have had little part in shaping French strategy, which remained firmly in the hands of Mazarin.[37]

Le Tellier's career in office might usefully be divided into two periods. During the first period, from his accession to office in 1643 until the beginning of the personal reign of Louis XIV in 1661, Le Tellier produced a great many ordinances and regulations. In fact, by André's count, the years of the seventeenth century most filled with his legislative activity were 1643, 1645, 1647, 1649, 1651, 1653–55, 1661–63, and 1665–66, so the great majority of Le Tellier's work of drafting a new military system occurred early.[38] Yet because of the ongoing war with its attendant military crisis and financial collapse, Le Tellier proved unable to apply these ordinances in a consistent and effective manner. War raged, campaigns often went badly, France was periodically occupied by enemy troops, and rebellion challenged the authority of the monarch. Still, the historian Louis André asserts that Le Tellier brought "the progressive and methodical transformation of the army of France."[39] But David Parrott casts doubts upon this evaluation by making the immensely valid point that there was a great difference between the neat prescriptions set out in regulations and the confused expedients encountered in real life. He charges that André relied too much upon official ordinances rather than basing his conclusions upon correspondence coming in from the field, which reported the actual collapse of administration during the 1640s. To a degree, this complaint is valid, but a close reading of André reveals that he repeatedly states that Le Tellier had to await the defeat of the Fronde in 1653, the return

---

[36] Ranum, *Richelieu and the Councillors of Louis XIII*, 119.
[37] Croxton, "Peacemaking in Early Modern Europe," 81.
[38] Louis André, *Michel Le Tellier et Louvois* (Paris: 1942), 314.
[39] Louis André, *Michel Le Tellier et l'organisation de l'armée monarchique* (Paris: 1906), 113.

of peace in 1659, and, most importantly, the fiscal reforms of Colbert after 1661 before he could turn his paper systems into reality. So André was not quite so gullible as to mistake intentions for accomplishments, the de jure for the de facto.

From 1662 until his retirement from the secretaryship in 1677, Le Tellier shared the office with his son Louvois. Consequently, there is considerable debate as to whether the accomplishments of this later period ought to be credited to father or son. Since practically the entire legislative basis for French military administration had been laid down by this point, André sees Le Tellier as the architect of that system, and Corvisier concurs: "It must be stated that in the administration of the army nothing had changed fundamentally from what Le Tellier had put in order."[40] Yet the plans of the father required the efforts of the son.

Louvois was slated to follow his father from an early age. Le Tellier obtained for his son the right to succeed to office in December 1655, when Louvois was only fifteen.[41] On his marriage in 1662, the twenty-two-year-old Louvois received the right to sign as secretary of state for war as a wedding gift from the king. André attacks Louvois's greatest biographer, Camille Rousset, for saying that Louvois deserves credit for running the show from that date on, although he clearly began as an apprentice.[42] In any case, by 1670, Louvois exerted the major force in the department.[43] Officially, Le Tellier resigned the post of secretary of state only to accept that of chancellor in 1677.

It should be said that for a time early in Louvois's career, Turenne virtually played the role of minister of war without running the administration of secretary of state. In the late 1660s, as Louis sought to learn the art of war from its greatest French master, Turenne enjoyed considerable influence with the monarch, attending the *conseil d'en haut*. However, by the Dutch War, Turenne's star had slipped somewhat, and Louvois had gained preponderance.[44]

As he matured, Louvois dominated the army though sheer force of personality, or as Rousset put it, "The genius of Louvois was will."[45] Le Tellier was an innovative systematizer, and before Louis's personal reign, Le Tellier needed also to be the modest and flexible man of compromise. Thus, the father was more in the mode of Mazarin than in the style of the imperious Sun King. In contrast, Louvois fitted the personality of the Sun King, enforcing the regime of that Apollo who must be obeyed. Saint-Simon described Louvois as "haughty, brutal, coarse," while to Primi Visconti he had a "hard and violent character."[46] Sensitivity would have been no asset for the

---

[40] Corvisier, *Louvois*, 179.
[41] Camille Rousset, *Histoire de Louvois*, 4 vols. (Paris: 1862–64), 1:14.
[42] André, *Le Tellier et Louvois*, 307.   [43] Corvisier, *Louvois*, 176.
[44] Rousset, *Louvois*, 1:320.   [45] Rousset, *Louvois*, 1:176.
[46] Saint-Simon and Primi Visconti in Corvisier, *Louvois*, 151–52.

Louvois who operated as the king's enforcer, as a minister who could write to a subordinate, "The king desires that you put in prison or lock up the first who does not obey you or who gives you the least difficulty."[47] Along with his will came great energy. Louvois traveled constantly; during the Dutch War, he spent more than 25 percent of his time away from court.[48]

Much of the rest of this chapter is devoted to the work of Le Tellier and Louvois. Le Tellier appreciated the problems posed by larger armies in an era of absolutism and was able to devise important solutions; Louvois possessed the secure royal backing and the force of character to apply those solutions with vigor. The arguments over who was the greater seem to miss the point; in the long run, they complemented each other and owed their accomplishments to one another.

Our knowledge of the secretaries of state for war after Louvois declines sharply. None have found the biographers they deserve, and administrative histories tend to leave a gap from the death of Louvois in 1691 until the passing of his master in 1715. Rousset condemns Louvois's successors as mediocre.[49] Louvois, like his father before him, secured the succession for a son. In 1681, Louvois purchased this right for his oldest son, but he proved to be ill suited to the task, so in 1685, the father obtained permission to transfer the succession to his youngest son, the marquis de Barbézieux, a youth of seventeen who showed better aptitude for work. In March 1687, he began to function in the *charge*, with the right to enter the conseil but without the right to express his opinions there.

But Barbézieux fell short of Louvois, and Louis XIV realized this, so when the father died, Louis turned to an experienced military administrator and a colleague of Louvois, Chamlay, recalling him from Germany. Louis may have actually offered the office of secretary of state to Chamlay, but in any case, Barbézieux maintained the post while Chamlay became the king's personal military advisor.[50] In fact, Barbézieux was not at first up to the task before him, and the king considered dismissing him. Barbézieux did not retain the right to attend the *conseil d'en haut*, so while secretary of state, he cannot be termed a minister.[51] A libertine, he died at the age of thirty-three in 1701.

Under Barbézieux, the main work of the department of war fell to Chamlay and Saint-Pouenges. Critics claim that from this point on, the French did not innovate but simply carried on the practices of Louvois, though without his ruthless efficiency. Stephen Baxter goes as far as to say that even before his death, the French army had become a flabby giant.[52] The logic of the argument comes from comparing the administration of the army during the

---

[47] 22 August 1673, Corvisier, *Louvois*, 179.   [48] Contamine, *Histoire militaire*, 1:391.

[49] Rousset, *Louvois*, 3:323.   [50] Wolf, *Louis XIV*, 464; Corvisier, *Louvois*, 480.

[51] Xavier Audouin, *Histoire de l'administration de la guerre*, 4 vols. (Paris: 1811), 2:371.

[52] Stephen Baxter, *William III and the Defense of European Liberty, 1650–1702* (New York: 1966), 282.

Dutch War with that during the Nine Years' War, but this may be unfair and is certainly simplistic. The French army only hit its peak size about the time of Louvois's death, and it is impossible to know how successfully he could have maintained it at those proportions. What are seen as the failings of his successors may, indeed, have stemmed from inferior talent, but to this must be added the fact that those successors had to shoulder a far greater burden than Louvois had been forced to carry.

Barbézieux's death ended the Le Tellier family's sixty-year hold on the office of secretary of state for war. Louis next awarded the office to his *contrôleur général des finances*, Michel Chamillart. It will be seen that the conduct of war always involved both the secretary of state and the *contrôleur général*, who each maintained his own agents with the armies in the field. By combining both chains of administrative command, some benefits might have accrued. But the weight of office wore down Chamillart and turned him defeatist. He surrendered the post of *contrôleur général* in 1708 and that of secretary of state for war in 1709. Daniel Voysin replaced him in the war department. Wolf describes Voysin as "an able and vigorous administrator," but we have no study of his conduct during the crisis years of the War of the Spanish Succession.[53] But by 1709, French resources were nearly exhausted, and the task at hand was survival. Voysin held his thankless post until Louis died.

Department of War

Historians seem a bit confused as to what is the best title for the bureaucracy headed by the secretary of state for war, since it bore no official title. Corvisier refers to it as a *secretariat*; other historians have labeled it a *ministry* from time to time.[54] The most convenient choice is the term *département* used in its *ancien régime* sense, meaning an area of administrative responsibility, as when an *intendant* referred to the *généralité* that he ran as his department.[55] A contemporary, Spanheim, used precisely this word in this sense when he praised the efficient conduct of the secretariat serving Louvois, stating that Louvois "found himself particularly aided by the great order that he brought in the review and expedition of business in his *département*."[56]

At its inception, the embryonic department amounted only to a few clerks who maintained the correspondence of the secretary of state. Clerks assisted the royal secretary charged with the primary tasks of military administration before that officer ever received the official title of secretary of state for war.[57]

---

[53] Wolf, *Louis XIV*, 561; Claude C. Sturgill, *Marshall Villars and the War of the Spanish Succession* (Lexington, KY: 1965), 87.

[54] Corvisier, *Louvois*, 327.   [55] See Marion, *Dictionnaire*, 168.

[56] Spanheim in André, *Le Tellier*, 645.

[57] For a short description of the secretariat that served a secretary of state, see Mousnier, *The Institutions of France*, 2:144–45.

They appeared as regular functionaries in 1567. A regulation of 1588 permitted each secretary to employ a chief clerk, a *commis*, and six lesser clerks. In 1599, another regulation awarded the original *commis* the title of *premier commis* or *principal commis* and termed all the subordinate clerks *commis*. The role of *premier commis* could be substantial; *premier commis* in foreign affairs had access to the king. Important *commis* earned considerable salaries and rated more as administrators than head clerks. The actual supervision of the regular *commis* could fall to the personal secretary of the secretary of state or to a special *commis*.

The department grew immensely and differentiated itself into bureaus over the course of the *grand siècle*. Mousnier sees the demise of the constable as accelerating the expansion of the secretary's bureaucracy, while war on an unprecedented scale after 1635 also drove on the growth.[58] By the mid-seventeenth century, Le Tellier had divided his office into at least five bureaus. At the close of the war with Spain, these were headed by Le Roy, Saint-Pouenges, Carpatry, Charpentier, and Le Boistel, all men who were clients of Le Tellier, trained by him, and passed on to his son.[59] André insists that Louvois simply inherited the organization and the personnel, just adding to the number of bureaus when need arose. By 1680, the department contained seven bureaus as follows.[60]

Saint-Pouenges – officers' commissions, reviews, hospitals, tents, sand bags;
Bellou – secretariat, letters and secret instructions, fortifications, cadets, *rôles des mois*;
Dufresnoy – sending of patents, powers, regulations, ordinances, and commissions;
Charpentier – establishing routes, ordinances, and regulations concerning the movement of troops;
Tourmont – statements [*états*] of money, foodstuffs, and pensions;
Bourdon – petitions, information on the disputes of the troops;
Le Renaudière – rolls of benefices, correspondence dealing with general petitions to the king for the months when this was the responsibility of the secretary of state for war (this was one of the duties that rotated among the four secretaries of state).

The bureaus at first worked in the hotel Louvois in Paris, but when the court settled down in Versailles, the primary secretariat moved there. It first resided in a commandeered town house and then transferred to the hôtel de la Surintendance after Colbert died in 1683. When the court traveled, the main personnel of the department followed it. At all times, much of the basic staff remained in Paris.[61]

In 1688, Louvois assigned Bellou an additional duty, the creation of a formal archive, the *Dépôt de la guerre*. The documents gathered there had

---

[58] Mousnier, *The Institutions of France*, 2:142.   [59] André, *Le Tellier*, 645.
[60] Corvisier, *Louvois*, 327–28.   [61] Contamine, *Histoire militaire*, 1:391.

been collected since 1637, when Richelieu instructed Sublet de Noyers to have his clerks make copies of all instructions, orders, and dispatches, "which can serve historical memory in order that they be added to my journals."[62] André insists that Le Tellier was the first to save minutes and copies conscientiously and thus was the real founder of the *Dépôt*.[63] The documents assembled in the *Dépôt* constitute the invaluable A¹ series now held by the Service historique de l'armée de terre in the Archives de guerre at the Chateau de Vincennes.

Corvisier has tallied the amount of correspondence produced by the various secretaries of war as a rough measure of the amount of work they performed. The correspondence also indicates the size of the department of war. The mean number of letters preserved in the war archives written annually during the Servien years amounted to only 830, rose to 1,100 for Sublet's administration, and totaled 2,400 for Le Tellier, 1643–66.[64] Looking at the minutes, or the hurriedly written notes for letters to be sent out, the annual number peaked at about 4,500 during the shared ministry of Le Tellier and Louvois, climbed to over 10,000 under Louvois, but fell sharply under Barbézieux, sinking as low as 2,500 in 1700.[65] The reason for the decline under Barbézieux relates to the fact that he did not hold the full range of responsibilities that his father possessed; Louvois had been *surintendant des postes* and *surintendant des bâtiments, arts et manufactures*, as well as chief administrator of French fortifications in addition to his job as secretary of state. The number of minutes escalated again with the return of war. With Chamillart at the helm, it passed 13,000 in 1706, far more than at any time under Louvois, and the number exceeded 10,000 per year again under Voysin; such were the strains of administration during Louis's last and most trying war.[66]

CIVIL ADMINISTRATORS IN THE PROVINCES AND WITH THE ARMIES

The central administration headed by the secretary of state for war controlled both the conduct of field operations and the administration of French forces, but it did so through two different chains of command. In the case of military operations, the secretary of state for war dealt directly with army commanders, but in the case of administration, the secretary worked through civilian officials dispatched to the provinces and to the armies in the field. Many administrative duties that today fall to uniformed soldiers were performed by men who held no military rank in the seventeenth century. Thus, the French maintained a curious split command; military officers led troops, while civilian bureaucrats paid and supplied them.

[62] Richelieu in Corvisier, *Louvois*, 328.   [63] André, *Le Tellier*, 651.
[64] Contamine, *Histoire militaire*, 1:361.   [65] Contamine, *Histoire militaire*, 1:392.
[66] Contamine, *Histoire militaire*, 1:536.

Not only did these two hierarchies differ in function; they differed in the kind of individuals that staffed them. In the main, seventeenth-century military officers identified themselves as the old nobility that traced its claims of elite status back to feudal service in arms; they were "sword" nobility. Administrative posts were held either by bourgeois non-nobles (*roturiers*) or by individuals whose families had only recently been elevated to the nobility through legal and administrative service; this newer type of aristocracy were "robe" nobility. Since administrative and judicial positions that bestowed aristocratic status on their holders could be purchased, buying such offices served as an entrée into the nobility for bourgeois traders, lawyers, and civil servants.

In his classic but now dated study, Franklin Ford drew a sharp line between the two nobilities in the seventeenth century and described the sword as bearing considerable animosity toward the robe, but more recent research, most notably by William Beik, portrays nobles of differing origins uniting in the provinces for their shared benefit.[67] This volume on military institutions does not contradict the revisionist view in regard to class interests and provincial power, but nonetheless these pages argue that within the more restricted environment of the aristocratic officer corps, differences in origin and length of lineage mattered a great deal. The army was, after all, the defining arena for the sword nobility. Proud officers continually condemned men lacking proper lineages, rich men of "little birth" who used their money to rise to positions beyond their appropriate station. To the disdainful sword, men sprung from the middle class who purchased offices to gain aristocratic status, by nature robe nobles, were no more than jumped-up commoners. Diatribes against men with thin bloodlines condemn such recently ennobled individuals, or *annoblis*, with *roturiers* in the same breath.[68] Therefore, while the sword–robe contrast may be a flawed analytical tool in many cases, it still retains substantial relevance within the army.

Other complexities made seventeenth-century military administration different in practice and personnel from its modern descendent. Problems arose from the fact that, as mentioned earlier, many positions carried a price tag – in other words, an individual had to buy the right to exercise authority. This was true for both certain military commanders and for many civil administrators; venality was the general rule. Some positions became the personal, and inheritable, property of the holder. Men who owned such positions, or *charges*, tended to be independent of royal control to a disturbing degree, at least to a degree disturbing to absolutists. Reformers struggled to centralize the government by replacing offices owned outright with new administrators

---

[67] Franklin Ford, *Robe and Sword* (Cambridge, MA: 1953); William Beik, *Absolutism and Society in Seventeenth-Century France* (Cambridge: 1985).

[68] See David Bien, "La réaction aristocratique avant 1789: l'exemple de l'armée," *Annales: économies sociétés, civilizations*, 29 (1974) for the best discussion of noble-*roturier-annobli* tensions in the army late in the eighteenth century.

who only held a commission – that is, a revocable royal authorization to act in the king's behalf. Since venal offices produced money for the crown that sold them, there was pressure to increase the number of these offices particularly before 1659. This brought considerable and confusing duplication of function, as administrators multiplied without relation to efficiency. This tendency to create more officeholders was further exaggerated by the French tendency in civil and military administration to solve a problem by adding new levels of functionaries without eliminating the old, so that layer was imposed upon layer.

This section concentrates upon the two most important of the civil administrators with the army, the *commissaires des guerres* and the *intendants d'armée*. Other officials receive mention when they help to place the main players into context. Together the *commissaires* and *intendants* provided the most essential services, so to understand their powers and problems is to understand much of military administration in general.

Commissaires des guerres

The origins of the *commissaires* stretch back into the fifteenth century.[69] Charles VII created *commissaires députés à faire les montres des gens de guerre*, empowered, as their name stated, to carry out reviews of troops, in this case the *compagnies d'ordonnance*. Later, these individuals, known by the time of Louis XI as *commissaires des guerres*, were joined by *commissaires à la conduite*, disciplinary officials attached to particular military units. In the late sixteenth century, both positions became venal. A third layer of these *commissaires* appeared in the *commissaires provinciaux*, who exercised the authority of a *commissaire à la conduite* over an area, not over a specific regiment. The *commissaires des guerres* had financial authority concerning reviews and pay; the *commissaires à la conduite* had none. The latter became quite numerous because they were temporarily attached to each regiment, where their judicial authority conflicted with the provosts in the field.[70] A large part of the rationale behind this multiplication of *commissaires* had to do with the profits to be gained by selling the posts as opposed to any real gain in efficiency.

In addition to the confusing assortment of *commissaires*, the late sixteenth century saw the creation of *contrôleurs des guerres*, who would become linked with *commissaires*. These officers did not answer to the secretary of state but to the *contrôleur général des finances*. While the different chain of command might suggest that they held financial authority at reviews, Parrott's research suggests that they performed essentially the same duties as *commissaires des*

---

[69] This discussion of the evolution of *commissaires* from their creation through the 1640s is borrowed from Parrott's detailed, documented, and intelligent discussion of the *commissaires*. David Parrott, "The Administration of the French Army During the Ministry of Cardinal Richelieu," Ph.D. dissertation, Oxford University, 1985, 222–82.

[70] André, *Le Tellier*, 615.

guerres. André claimed that *contrôleurs* were not venal offices, but Parrott demonstrates that they too were up for sale. In fact, the rationale for their creation again had more to do with greed than need. Regulations stated that both *commissaires des guerres* and *contrôleurs des guerres* were to attend reviews, but the *contrôleurs* seemed to have had little to do. Parrott interprets the regulations and correspondence as giving them the role of assistants to *commissaires*. Parrott's detailed analysis of administration comes to the conclusion that "the systems of both financial and judicial administration as they existed in 1635 were confused and ineffective – all too obviously the product of innumerable, quite separate, initiatives taken by different departments of the central government over a long period."[71]

In the early years of the war with Spain, the *commissaires des guerres* seemed to hold the promise of becoming the dominant figures in military administration in the field. As the war began, the first impulse of the government was to expand the authority of the *commissaires* to meet the challenge. In addition to duties at reviews, they received judicial functions plus authority to recruit soldiers, discharge units, quarter troops, and inspect fortifications. Local authorities appealed to *commissaires*, as well as *intendants*, for redress when troops got out of hand.[72]

The growing power and number of *commissaires des guerres* led the government to create *charges* of *commissaires généraux des guerres* to supervise *commissaires* in a given army.[73] There were precedents for this before the war with Spain, but it escalated then. A chosen *commissaire général* had a voice in the Council of War under Mazarin, but the main responsibilities of this post remained with individual armies. Perhaps the most notable *commissaire général* was Alexandre de Prouville, Marquis de Tracy, who served as *commissaire général* with the Army of Germany, first under Guébriant and later under Turenne. Eventually, as we shall see, the rise of another method of control, the use of *intendants d'armée*, undercut the *commissaires générals* and relegated them to obscurity.

Parrott argues that senior positions such as *commissaire* were prestigious and analogous to *maîtres des requêtes*, a high post in the civil/legal administration. An ordinance of 1623 ordered that *commissaires* march at the left hand of the commanders in the field, a position of honor.[74] And from at least 1634 on, *commissaires* and *contrôleurs des guerres* enjoyed an exemption from the *taille*, the burdensome land tax.[75]

At the same time that *commissaires* extended their authority, the government muddied waters by giving in to financial temptation and creating more

---

[71] Parrott, "The Administration of the French Army," 246.

[72] Patrick Landier, "Guerre, Violences, et Société en France, 1635–1659," doctorat de troisième cycle, dissertation, Université de Paris IV, 1978), 20.

[73] For details on *commissaires généraux*, see André, *Le Tellier*, 449–55, and Bernard Kroener, *Les routes et les étapes. Die bersorgung der franzoschichen Armeen in Nordostfrankreich (1635–1661)*, 2 vols. (Munster: 1980), 28–32.

[74] AG, MR 1881, #19.   [75] André, *Le Tellier*, 624.

and more positions of *commissaires*, *contrôleurs*, and related offices. On top of confusion, corruption afflicted the system, since venal officeholders attempted to make up some of their investment by raking in money illegally.

The attempt to administer the army primarily through the *commissaires des guerres* failed, and the *intendants* rose to a dominant administrative position in their stead. It was a classic victory of commission-holder over office-owner. Since *intendants* held revocable commissions without a price tag, there was little pressure to multiply their *charges*, and they remained few in number and responsive to royal authority.

With the rise of the *intendants*, the position of the *commissaires des guerres* regularized as subordinate agents of the *intendants* and their immediate assist-ants, the subdelegates. The *commissaires* broke down into two main groups, the sedentary *commissaires provinciaux des guerres*, whose authority knew specific geographic bounds, and the *commissaires des guerres*, who functioned as their agents and as the agents of the *intendants*.

Le Tellier wanted to "eliminate the multiplicity of useless individuals," but he had to wait until the return of peace.[76] In 1661, he had his chance, cutting the number of *commissaires* and *contrôleurs* to twenty of each office.[77] This pruning of unnecessary *commissaires* and *contrôleurs* with conflicting authorities could not but help to clear up some of the administrative muddle and allowed Le Tellier to retain only the most able men. By 1666, there were twenty-two areas with *commissaires provinciaux* in France.[78] It would seem at this point that during peacetime, *commissaires provinciaux* sufficed, since there were no field armies in being. With the approach of war in 1667, the number of *commissaires* and *contrôleurs* rose to forty of each.[79] If anything, the cut in the number of *commissaires* raised their prestige. André spoke of them as a corps d'elite.[80]

Commissaires des guerres now carried a wide variety of powers not re-stricted to reviews. The commission granting authority to Person as *commis-saire des guerres* at the fortress of Rosas in November 1654 provides an excellent example of these powers.[81] As detailed in the commission, they included the following long list: to hold reviews, to certify rolls, to punish *passe volants*, to inspect the quartering rolls, to inspect the quality and weight of bread fed to the troops, to make sure that food and material stored in the fortress were of proper quality and quantity, to make sure stored items were used only in case of siege, to make sure the fortress was in good repair, to find out about disorders and to turn the culprits over to justice, to maintain discipline and

---

[76] Le Tellier in André, *Le Tellier*, 626.   [77] André, *Le Tellier*, 627.

[78] André gives a table of areas and *commissaires*. André, *Le Tellier*, 615.

[79] André, *Le Tellier*, 627.

[80] They still occupied a position of honor at the left of the commander of a unit on the march. 4 April 1664 ordinance in AG, MR 1881, #40.

[81] Commission to le sieur Person 20 November 1654 as reproduced in Chennevières, *Détails militaires* (Paris: 1750) in Claude C. Sturgill, *Les commissaires des guerres et l'administration de l'armée française, 1715–1730* (Vincennes, France: 1985), 10–12.

punish those who infringed against it, to admit no officer not known by him or the fortress governor, to receive the letters of commission of new replacement officers, and "to cause the military ordinances and regulations to be kept and observed."

The role of the *commissaires des guerres* seems to have stabilized early in Louis's personal reign, changing little as the years went by. The military writer Gaya listed as the functions of *commissaires*: holding fortnightly reviews, maintaining police and discipline, and taking oaths of new officers.[82] In 1698, the *intendant* Turgot described *commissaires* in his jurisdiction: "There are *commissaires des guerres* in each fortress there to carry out reviews of troops and examine their number; in joint with mayors and alderman, to provide lodging for the troops; and in accord with the *intendant*, to supply even food for them."[83] Despite his wide range of authority, there were things a *commissaire* might not do. *Commissaires* seem to have had no direct control over funds; rather, this seems to have been left to the *contrôleurs* and their agents. Also, as Louvois insisted in a strong letter written to the commissaire Pérou in 1665, "A *commissaire des guerres* has no right to claim any command over troops or over the inhabitants of the towns in his jurisdiction."[84]

In the last years of Louis's life, the corps of *commissaires* reorganized slightly. An edict and a declaration of 1704 divided France into districts, each headed by a "*commissaire ordinaire des provinciaux des guerres de conduite, police et discipline.*" He was assisted by several *commissaires des guerres*.[85] Sturgill traces the organization of the *commissaires* at the close of Louis's rule and the beginning of the reign of his great-grandson, another boy-king, Louis XV.[86] From a provincial *commissaire*, the line of authority ran both to the secretary of state for war and to the *intendant* and his subdelegates. The *intendant* answered to the secretary of state and the *contrôleur général des finances*, as well as to the king. Another line of authority ran down from the *contrôleur général* through the *trésoriers royaux* and *trésoriers de l'extraordinaire des guerres* to the *contrôleurs des guerres*. As with the *commissaires*, the *contrôleurs des guerres* also obeyed the *intendants*. Below the *contrôleurs des guerres* ran the financial administration of a military district, the *trésoriers principaux des troupes, trésoriers des troupes, payeurs des troupes*, and *receveurs*.

The position of *commissaires* held the potential for considerable abuse. They were essentially inspectors charged with guarding against cheating by officers and civilian suppliers. Although they did not directly pay captains or contractors, their approval was required before payments could be made. Thus, there were ill-gotten gains to be made by falsifying reports, particularly

---

[82] Louis de Gaya, *Le nouvel art de la guerre et la manière dont on la fait aujourd'huy en France* (Paris, 1692), 41.

[83] Turgot memoir in 1697–98 memoirs for the education of the dauphin, AN, F fs 2210, fol. 110, in André Corvisier, *Les Français et l'armée sous Louis XIV* (Vincennes: 1975), 129.

[84] Letter of 7 May 1665 from Louvois to Pérou in Rousset, *Louvois*, 1:77.

[85] Sturgill, *Commissaires*, 13.   [86] Sturgill, *Commissaires*, 15.

in collusion with military officers. As with all other abuses, this probably reached its height before 1659. Since these men had bought their offices, they were understandably anxious to make good on their investments by fair means or foul. Parrott reveals that they either conspired with officers to pad review musters, in order to pick up the extra allowances, or they were overly severe at reviews, in order to take the money saved by not paying men who were present. In any case, complaints about corrupt *commissaires* were rampant.

Later Feuquières complained that "The greed for gain and the ease of conspiring with the *commissaires des guerres* caused the reviews to be inaccurate."[87] Corvisier goes so far as to argue that because of the financial confusion and exhaustion of the period before 1659, the irregularities of the *commissaires* were "almost the only way of sustaining [*faire vivre*] the royal army,"[88] since inflated reviews were the only means to coax money out of the beleaguered administration.

Records demonstrate that at least some commissaires who committed abuses were still maintained in office. Servien complained about *commissaire* Le Vacher in 1635; he was arrested for corruption in 1638; yet he still remained in 1664, when Louvois criticized him as a man of low capacity.[89] Le Tellier and Louvois did what they could to limit abuses. In 1671, Louvois went to great pains to catch the *commissaire* Aubert for falsifying reviews. A cornered captain admitted that for six years he had paid Aubert three soldiers' wages to be warned forty-eight hours in advance of any review, so that the captain could arrange to pad his unit with *passe volants*.[90]

The Evolution of Intendants

Seventeenth-century French administration is practically defined by the rise of *intendants*. The word *intendant* could be used for several *charges*; that which matters here is the *intendant de la justice, police et finances*. There were two types of these *intendants*, those assigned to permanent geographical areas, known as *intendants des provinces*, or provincial *intendants*, and those assigned to field forces, known as *intendants d'armée*, or army *intendants*.[91] Whereas discussions on military administration usually focus only or primarily on the second, both had substantial military responsibilities.

The origins of the office of the provincial *intendant* are less than crystal clear. They seem to lie in the inspection tours carried out by *maîtres des requêtes* in the sixteenth century. These were important magistrates who handled complaints and requests to the king, served as judges, and provided

---

[87] Feuquières in André, *Le Tellier*, 625.   [88] Corvisier, *Louvois*, 81–82.

[89] Parrott, "The Administration of the French Army," 281.

[90] Rousset, *Louvois*, 1:199–200.

[91] For a brief and authoritative account of the origins and duties of provincial *intendants*, see Mousnier, *The Institutions of France*, 2:502–63. The best work on the military *intendants* is Douglas Baxter, *Servants of the Sword, French Intendants of the Army, 1630–70* (Urbana: 1976). My discussion owes much to these two sources.

administrative services to the king at a high level. As part of their duties, they periodically toured the provinces, inspecting the conduct of the king's legal and administrative affairs. They were appointed by specific commissions, issued for a specified place for a limited time. Some of them took the title of *intendant* in the late sixteenth century, but the term fell out of use after 1600. It reappeared under the regency of Marie de Medici with the return of internal disorder, and thus the need to empower new individuals for extra-ordinary duties, and they began to take the title *intendant* again. France was divided into financial districts, called *généralités*, and these new *intendants* became the king's representatives there. In the period 1624–31, *intendants* served in fourteen of seventeen *généralités*. Often Richelieu receives credit for creating the office of *intendant*, particularly by the edict of May 1635, when in fact he simply placed greater reliance upon an already existing type of functionary who was more responsive to royal authority, being a commission-holder instead of an office-owner. From the early 1630s through the 1640s, the institution of *intendants* evolved into something new by collecting more authority over justice, finance, and administration.[92] In a real sense, the *intendants* proved an ally to the monarchy in lieu of the traditional office of governor, a provincial official of high birth and considerable power that had proven contentious in the past. The provincial *intendants* played a key role in the extension of royal absolutism, although the importance of *intendants* varied over time. They were royal inspectors by origin and nature, and they could become a nuisance or danger to independent-minded local authorities. One of the demands of the Fronde was the elimination of provincial *intendants*, and an edict of July 1648 revoked most of their commissions. However, they returned with the defeat of the Fronde. Early in the personal reign of Louis XIV, virtually all of France was administered by *intendants* supervising their *généralités*, with Brittany being the last area of old France to receive a provincial *intendant* in 1689. By that point, provincial administration worked best when *intendants* and governors worked in tandem rather than pulling against one another.

Army *intendants* evolved out of a centuries-old practice of sending royal commissioners to watch over the use of the king's funds in his armies. Such commissions date back to the late Middle Ages, and over time, the responsibilities of these commissioners grew. The historian Douglas Baxter suggests that the title *intendant* had its base in two separate commissions for "the charge and intendance of our finances" and for "the charge and intendance of justice" with royal armies, as shown in commissions issued under Henri IV.[93] He sees the first *intendants* not as those with that exact title but with individuals empowered with *intendance* of the king's affairs. Arguing in this way, the first sort of "*intendant*" answered to the *surintendant des finances* and

---

[92] Mousnier, *The Institutions of France*, 2:512. See, as well, the description of *intendants* in Andrew Lossky, *Louis XIV and the French Monarchy* (New Brunswick, NJ: 1994).

[93] Baxter, *Servants of the Sword*, 14.

the other to the chancellor. Neither was a functionary of the secretary of state charged with the conduct of war, and by this logic, an army required at least two *intendants*.

No later than 1630, army *intendants* existed in name and fact. Each royal army had one or more. Commissions at this point varied; some stipulated only finance, some only justice, and some, as that for Charles Le Roy and Dreux d'Aubray in 1630, included the "intendance de la justice et finances."[94] This last commission displays another characteristic of the institution at this early stage, as two *intendants* were appointed to the same army. Multiple *intendants* seemed to be needed at first because, as a letter of 1635 insisted, to do the work right in Condé's army would require "one *intendant des finances* and two *intendants de la justice* at the same time."[95] In contrast, the commission granted solely to Le Tellier to serve as *intendant* with the army of Italy in 1640 was quite complete in its delegation of authority over finance, supply, and discipline.[96]

Parrott provides the best account of army *intendants* during the first years of the war with Spain. Parrott argues that their power grew owing to the pressure of events during the war, so that reading back the full-blown institution of the 1670s into the 1630s and 1640s distorts reality, committing "the fallacy of inexorable development."[97] He argues that at least before the Fronde, the *intendant*'s authority was shaky enough that his success depended upon his relations with the military commander of the army to which he was posted. Should the two clash, the ministry would not support the *intendant*. Kroener has shown that at the same time, the *intendants* collided with the authority of the *trésoriers de France*, but the *intendants* eventually held the upper hand in that ongoing clash of authorities.[98] After the Fronde, *intendants* became more secure and enjoyed the support of the secretary of state for war. Le Tellier regarded *intendants* as his personal supporters; in fact, his *intendants* were often his clients, relatives, and friends.[99] But the secretary could not always impose his choice; as late as 1673, Turenne vetoed the appointment of Charuel as his *intendant*, and Louvois backed down.[100]

The personal reign of Louis XIV commenced in peace. Without armies in the field, there was no need for army *intendants*. This, Baxter argues, brought something of a resurgence of the authority of *commissaires des guerres*.[101] During this quiet period, according to Baxter, Le Tellier groomed a small number of select individuals to play this role whenever war began – men like Jacques Chareul, Etienne Carlie, and Louis Robert.[102] They received a series of lesser commissions to give them the experience that a later *charge* as

[94] Baxter provides a list of *intendants* and their commissions, 1630–91. Baxter, *Servants of the Sword*, 209–27.

[95] AG, A¹24, fo. 349, 30 May 1635.   [96] André, *Le Tellier*, 49–51fn.

[97] Parrott, "The Administration of the French Army," 284.

[98] Kroener, *Les routes et les étapes*, 12–23.   [99] André, *Le Tellier*, 635–37.

[100] Rousset, *Louvois*, 1:492–93.   [101] Baxter, *Servants of the Sword*, 139–40.

[102] Baxter, *Servants of the Sword*, 143.

intendant would require. When war began again in 1667, one army *intendant* served with each of the three major forces. The evolution of the *intendant* was not yet complete, but by 1670, Baxter asserts, it was well along the way toward completion.

Provincial and Army Intendants

As these institutions took full form early in the personal reign of Louis XIV, provincial and army *intendants* shared key military responsibilities, a point not made clear enough in many accounts of these institutions. During wartime, the authority of the two kinds of *intendants* and their agents could overlap. Since an army *intendant* held sway in a particular army, while a provincial *intendant* administered a *généralité*, if a field army marched over French territory, there was the possibility of conflict between authorities. But during intervals of peace, without forces assembled along the frontiers, the king issued no commissions to army *intendants*, except for unusual expeditions outside France, such as those the French sent to aid the Hapsburgs or the Venetians against the Ottomans. So in peacetime, the provincial *intendants* ranked as the highest military administrators below the secretary of state for war. The concern of military historians with campaign history, and thus with army *intendants*, has obscured this fact.

The regular duties of provincial *intendants*, peacetime and wartime, covered a broad range. Primarily, the *intendant* concerned himself with financial matters, such as the collection of taxes, most notably the *taille*, and the supervision of the tax farms. He also carried out numerous general administrative tasks, from regulating the royal post to arresting beggars. The *intendant* bore the responsibility for maintaining public order. His duties toward the military forces in his *généralité* included supervising recruitment, arranging for the feeding and housing of troops in transit, and maintaining discipline among officers and the rank and file. In wartime, a large percentage of the troops served in garrisons throughout the year; this proportion can be reasonably estimated at 40 percent. Such troops remained the responsibility of provincial *intendants*, who also bore virtually all the other provincial duties concerned with maintaining the war effort. The variety of tasks proved to be such a burden that eventually *intendants* required a series of assistants, or subdelegates. As late as 1682, the king sought to limit the number and functions of subdelegates, but necessity drove the *intendants* to multiply the subdelegates, most notably after 1688. For example, by 1700 there were thirty subdelegates in the *généralité* of Moulins, fifteen each in Châlons and Besançon, and sixty in Brittany.[103] An edict of 1704 created offices of subdelegate in the major city of each election; subdelegates had become so useful that they became compulsory.[104] Also, Baxter argues that the provincial *intendants* were so overburdened with their other duties that they, in fact, delegated much of

---

[103] Mousnier, *The Institutions of France*, 2:529.   [104] Marion, *Dictionnaire*, 519.

their military authority to the *commissaires provinciaux des guerres* in their jurisdictions.

When the French armies occupied enemy territory, the king appointed *intendants* of conquered regions. While their commissions were less permanent than provincial *intendants*, they too were assigned a particular area and exercised authority over it in ways very similar to provincial *intendants*. *Intendants* of conquered areas also supervised the collection of "contributions," or war taxes, imposed on occupied populations. So concerned were they with military affairs that there was "a hazy borderline between an army *intendant* and that of a newly conquered area," writes Baxter. In fact, army *intendants* might also have received the responsibility of administering the territory occupied by that army.[105]

An army *intendant* carried a commission to administer a particular field army on campaign. His responsibilities included the critical tasks of feeding, paying, clothing, and arming the king's troops. He also stood at the top of that army's disciplinary system. The nature of the army *intendant*'s duties allowed him to concentrate on military affairs alone, freeing him from the need for a corps of subdelegates working directly under his direction; instead, his most important assistants were the ubiquitous *commissaires des guerres* serving that particular army. In addition, the *intendant* directed those officials appointed by the *contrôleur général des finances* – that is, the *trésoriers*, *payeurs*, and *receveurs*. Although an *intendant* attended the meetings of war councils held by the marshal or general commanding the army, he, of course, did not have a command voice beyond advising on matters of supply.

To eliminate conflicting lines of authority, an army *intendant* might on occasion be the *intendant* of the *généralité* that bordered the area of the army's operations. Feuquières argued that this was the best solution because a provincial *intendant* could use his territorial authority to make sure that his army had what it needed.[106] In 1630, Le Roy and d'Aubray held responsibility for both the province of Provence and the military forces there. Much later, in 1683, Chauvelin was both *intendant* of Franche-Comté and *intendant* of the army formed under Boufflers, while in 1689 and 1690, Bouchu was the *intendant* of Dauphiné and the *intendant* of the French army of Piedmont.[107]

Both provincial and army *intendants* were robe nobles. Provincial *intendants* generally served as *maîtres de requêtes* before rising to an intendance. Army *intendants* had more varied origins, often as *maîtres des requêtes*, but also as *commissaires des guerres*, legal officials, or even provincial *intendants*. All were wealthy men. Some complained that *intendants* were making money on war,

---

[105] For example, this was the case with Louis Robert in Holland in 1672. Baxter, *Servants of the Sword*, 223.

[106] Feuquières, *Mémoires du marquis de Feuquières* (Londres: 1736), 160.

[107] Baxter, *Servants of the Sword*, 225–26. Belhomme, *L'armée française en 1690*, 147, stated "When one formed an army on a frontier, the provincial intendant was named intendant of the army." This did occur, but it was not universal.

as Villars grumbled in his "Traité," but this seems not to have been the case.[108] As mentioned earlier, secretaries of state appointed army *intendants* as part of their patronage, so the *intendants* were clients, *fidèles*, of the secretaries. As such, secretaries wanted their own men in office; Sublet de Noyers kept only one of fifteen *intendants* employed by Servien, and Le Tellier kept only five of twenty employed by Sublet. Between 1644 and 1691, forty-two of 131, or 32 percent, of commissions issued for army *intendants* went to relatives of Michel Le Tellier, a trend that peaked during the Dutch War when sixteen of twenty-three commissions, or 70 percent, went to the Le Tellier clan.[109]

The personnel of military administration, represented best in the positions of secretary of state for war, the army *intendant*, and the *commissaire des guerres* was in place at the onset of the Dutch War. There is no reason to believe that it would not be adequate to the task as long as it had the resources to do the job. However, if French military administration suffered from a weakness, that weakness lay precisely in resource mobilization, a key issue that remained outside the power of the secretary of state for war and entirely enmeshed with French society and politics.

THE TRADITIONAL MILITARY OFFICES

A handful of honored military offices stood in potential conflict with the secretary of state for war and his *commissaires* and *intendants*. These were the constable, grand master of artillery, colonel general of infantry, and colonel general of cavalry; all four were elevated to the level of "crown offices," a status that gave them the highest prestige and implied special access to the king. Historians have often discussed the decline of these offices as an indicator of the greater centralization of military administration in the *grand siècle*. They seemed to represent an older tradition in which the great sword nobles of France ran the military establishment, often in lieu of direct royal authority and certainly in contrast to a system in which the army was maintained by high placed, but only recently ennobled, robe civilians who faithfully served the secretary of state for war and the monarch.

Traditional historical interpretations by such deservedly respected historians as Caillet, Rousset, Avenel, André, Corvisier, and even Mousnier have viewed the crown offices as roadblocks to centralized administration, as obstacles that had to be removed before the rational and modern systems of the secretaries of state for war could operate effectively. Much may be said for their arguments, but the most authoritative recent commentary on these offices under the Richelieu regime stands in contrast to their views. David

---

[108] BN, f. fr. 6257, Claude Louis Hector Villars, "Traité de la guerre de campagne," 29–30.

[109] André Corvisier, "Clientèles et fidélités dans l'armées française aux 17e et 18e siècles," in Y. Durand, ed. *Hommage à Roland Mousnier. Clientèles et fidélités en Europes à l'époque moderne* (Paris: 1981), 216.

Parrott disagrees fundamentally with traditional descriptions of these offices during the first half of the seventeenth century and, consequently, casts the movement for reform in a different light. Historians need to take into account the analyses put forth both by past luminaries and by the revisionist Parrott.

Constable

Writing during the nineteenth century, Caillet described the abolition of the constable in 1627 as the most important military reform made by Richelieu, and this judgment is repeated in more modern works.[110] To Caillet and others, the constable, an office with medieval origins, was a pretender to supreme commander of the army. Consequently, the elimination of the office by Richelieu represented a quantum leap in the cardinal's drive to increase and centralize royal authority.

Legally, the constable commanded the army in the king's absence – no small claim to power.[111] Richelieu himself referred to the office as dangerous "by the absolute authority that it gave to the holder."[112] The constable did have control of the *ordinaire des guerres*, although this, Parrott points out, amounted to only 0.5 percent of expenditure.[113] The constable also stood at the peak of the army's legal system, directing its highest court. By the most extreme interpretation, it would have been difficult for the king to command or control his army without the concurrence of the constable. Moreover, the constable possessed a number of lucrative rights. He could claim as his own all the goods within a town that had fallen to siege, except gold, prisoners, and the copper and bronze claimed by the grand master of artillery. Also, the constable received one day's pay from all officers, save from princes of the blood and their households.

In reality, however, the constable had been in "obvious decline" for some time, according to Parrott.[114] In addition, except for his leverage on the *ordinaire des guerres* and his legal role, the constable had no direct administrative responsibility in the army. Thus, the post was rich but expendable by the early seventeenth century.

When constable Lesdiguières died in 1627, Richelieu let the office die with him, transferring the legal authority to the marshals. Although this act may have eliminated a major office that could have frustrated the rise of the secretary of state for war, the rationale for abolishing the office had more to do with court politics than with a drive to centralize military authority. After

---

[110] Caillet, *De l'administration en France*, 363.

[111] For accounts of the constable, see François Sicard, *Histoire des institutions militaires des français*, 4 vols. (1834), 1:156–60; Marion, *Dictionnaire*, 129–30; Parrott, "The Administration of the French Army," 312–14.

[112] Richelieu in Parrott, "The Administration of the French Army," 312.

[113] Parrott, "The Administration of the French Army," 313.

[114] Parrott, "The Administration of the French Army," 314.

Lesdiguières died, the obvious candidate for the office was Montmorency. Richelieu had just driven Montmorency from the office of admiral, albeit with a substantial cash settlement, and Montmorency clearly was not among Richelieu's *fidèles*. Therefore, the strongest rationale to eliminate the office was Richelieu's desire to keep such a lucrative and prestigious post out of Montmorency's hands. Parrott suggests that had Richelieu been able to put forward one of his *fidèles* as constable, he would not have abolished the office.[115] In fact, the 1627 abolition was apparently not regarded as permanent, since it was repeated in April 1643.[116]

The Grand Master of Artillery

The grand master of artillery exercised an authority as ancient and independent as that held by the constable before 1627. There were masters of artillery in France even before there were cannon. This apparent oxymoron is explained by the fact that large siege engines before the age of gunpowder also went by the name "artillery."[117] So Guillaume de Dourdan took the title of master of the artillery of the Louvre in 1291, and the grand masters evolved from this office. For a time, the actual artillery officers served under the grand master of *arbelétiers*, but this post was abolished. François I created the actual post of grand master of artillery in 1515 to control all the equipment and personnel of the royal artillery train, and in 1599, Henri IV elevated the post to considerable dignity and awarded it to Sully.[118]

Sully organized the office into one of great independence, directly under the king, and complete with its own budget lines in the royal accounts, the *ordinaires* and *extraordinaires de l'artillerie*. In theory, the grand master exercised control over every aspect of the arm, from the founding of the cannon and shot to the naming of artillery officers. He also was colonel of the royal artillery regiment, which first appeared as the Fusiliers du Roi in 1671, to become rechristened the Regiment Royal Artillerie in 1693. When in the field, he directed sieges and received all bells and copper utensils from towns that had fallen to siege. The grand master even ran his own judicial system to judge those under his authority and crimes committed near the artillery park.[119]

The grand master headed a group of administrators who discharged his numerous duties. He was assisted by a *bailli*, a lieutenant general, a *procureur du roi*, and a *greffier*. Under these officers served a *lieutenant*, a *surintendant des poudres et salpêtres*, a *commissaire général*, and several *lieutenants provinciaux*.

---

[115] Parrott, "The Administration of the French Army," 313.

[116] Parrott, "The Administration of the French Army," 314.

[117] See Sicard, *Histoire des institutions militaires*, 1:164–70 and André, *Le Tellier*, 500–2 for short discussions of the office of grand master.

[118] David Buisseret, *Sully and the growth of centralized government in France, 1598–1610* (London: 1968), 140–69.

[119] Parrott, "The Administration of the French Army," 228–29.

Richelieu maneuvered to reduce the power of the grand master by placing his own man in the office. Henri IV had done this by appointing the faithful and effective Sully, who was then succeeded by his less effective son (1618–21). When the cardinal could, he passed the post on to his cousin, the compliant duke de La Meilleraye, in 1634. Under La Meilleraye, Richelieu took over many of the functions of the grand master for himself, eroding the authority of the office.[120] By this point, Parrott argues, the grand master concerned himself with little more than the purchase and distribution of ammunition.[121]

Richelieu's successors continued the method of controlling this lucrative *charge* by granting it only to those loyal to the court, often men closely bound to the king or his first minister. In 1648, the amiable duke de La Meilleraye was replaced by his son, who was so linked to the ministry that he married one of the nieces of cardinal Mazarin and took the Mazarin name himself as the duke de Mazarin. After holding the *charge* until 1669, the duke sold it to a protégé of Louvois, the count de Lude, who occupied the office until 1685. The duke du Maine, illegitimate son of Louis XIV, took the post in 1694, passing it on to his son in 1710, who held it until it was abolished in 1755.

So while the office of grand master remained, it did not possess its original powers, and it did not have to be abolished because it had become allied to the king and his ministers.

Colonel General of Infantry

After that of constable, the colonel general of infantry was the most important, and valuable, of all military *charges*.[122] François I created the post in 1542 as a royal commission, but it became a venal office under Henry II in 1547. In 1582, Henri III appointed the son of one of his favorites, the duke d'Epernon, to the office, and in 1584, the king further elevated the post by making it a crown office. The duke held the post for sixty years, until his death in 1642. Then his son, the new duke d'Epernon, rose to this office and occupied it until he died in 1661, but at this point, Louis XIV abolished the office.

Most historical accounts claim that the influence and power of the colonel general was great. As the title implies, he was the chief officer of French infantry, but beyond this he was also the colonel of all French infantry regiments. Consequently, the colonel general was the only true infantry colonel among all the French regiments, with the right to nominate or appoint all

---

[120] Parrott, "The Administration of the French Army," 321–22.

[121] Parrott, "The Administration of the French Army," 323.

[122] For brief treatments of the colonel general, see Sicard, *Histoire des institutions militaires*, 1:198–203; Rousset, *Louvois*, 1:175; and André, *Le Tellier*, 158–65; Parrott, "The Administration of the French Army," 314–20.

their officers. Patronage possibilities from this right could be colossal. In addition, the first company of each permanent regiment, the colonel's company, belonged to him. The captain of this company, who thus took the place of the colonel general, bore the rank of lieutenant colonel. As a sign of the honor due the colonel general, the lieutenant colonel marched ahead of the actual regimental commander, styled the *mestre de camp*. Only with the demise of the colonel general, Rousset insisted, would "all the infantry officers . . . be named or agreed upon by the king, all the brevets prepared and signed by the secretary of state for war."[123]

Here Parrott diverges from standard accounts insofar as they deal with the history of the office under the two dukes d'Epernon. Henri III raised the office of colonel general to the status of a court office in 1584 to strengthen Epernon so that he could better support the king in a troubled court. This elevation led to a brief apogee of the colonel general, during which Epernon exercised the de facto power to appoint all officers of infantry. But, Parrott argues, this power did not exist before 1584 and would not exist after 1588, when court intrigues achieved the disgrace of Epernon, who was temporarily suspended from office. The assassination of his patron Henri III the next year meant that Epernon would never again regain his position of influence. Most importantly, while the colonel general continued to nominate officers for commissions, Henri IV and his successors refused to accept these nominations as binding. Two things are to be noted here. First, the definition and power of office had more to do with court politics than with any concern for military efficiency. Second, the colonel general only briefly enjoyed a level of authority that historians define as the standard perquisites of the office.

Epernon's decline did not end in 1588, since he remained an active player in a losing game of court intrigue. Henri IV imposed new restrictions on Epernon, forcing him to give up the general right to make nominations and left him only the right to nominate every other captain in the guards and captains for the permanent regiments. In addition, he retained the right to appoint officers in the colonel's companies and, on the regimental level, sergeant majors, their aides, surgeons, and chaplains. By the 1630s, Epernon retained control over only the colonel's companies and certain regimental staff posts. But his troubles continued, because as punishment for his role in the loss of the battle of Fuentarrabia in 1638, Richelieu stripped him of the office. After Epernon died in 1642, an ordinance denied his son the right of succession, and the office was abolished in 1643. However, Louis XIII died that year, and the regency government restored the colonel general and awarded the office to the new duke Epernon, probably because the weak regency sought to gain support and pacify the great nobles. Although the colonel general still commanded wealth and patronage, this restored office obviously possessed nothing like the power it had held during the period 1584–88. In 1649, the duke secured the right of succession for his own son,

---

[123] Rousset, *Louvois*, 1:175.

but the far more secure situation of Louis XIV in 1661 permitted him to abolish the office altogether. By pointing to this earlier fall from grace, Parrott argues that the later elimination of the colonel general was less impressive an act than most works would contend.[124] Perhaps it might be correct to interpret the elimination of the colonel general of infantry in the same light as the fall of Fouquet; it announced Louis's intentions to take charge.

The Colonel General of Cavalry

The last court office was the colonel general of cavalry, which goes back in one form or another to the fifteenth century but was only raised to an office in title by Charles IX in 1565, as *colonel général de la cavalerie légère*.[125] Unlike the colonel general of infantry, that for cavalry survived throughout the *ancien régime*, only to be suppressed in 1790. In the first half of the seventeenth century, the powers of the colonel general of cavalry were similar to those of the colonel general of infantry. Even as Louvois worked to erode some of the power of the office, it retained great monetary value. Bérenger estimates the value of the post during Turenne's tenure as 600,000 livres, which approached the worth of all his lands, valued at 800,000.[126]

If abolition of the colonel general of infantry marked an assertion of Louis XIV's independence of the old military officers, why was not the colonel general of cavalry abolished as well? Louis André explains this apparent diversion from the course set by Sublet, Le Tellier, and Louvois as being quite the opposite of what it seems, since for André preservation of the cavalry position aided royal authority.[127] At midcentury, 1622–57, the colonels general were three nonentities: the duke of Angoulême, the count of Alais, and the duke de Joyeuse. This may have equaled a de facto elimination of the office, and since such men were no threat, Richelieu, Mazarin, and Le Tellier saw no need to attack their position. In addition, during the war with Spain, the king issued commissions for subsidiary colonels general of cavalry to manage disciplinary problems better in the field, thus aiding, not challenging, the will of monarch and ministers.[128] When the post became vacant in 1657, rather than let it die, Louis awarded it to Turenne, as a reward for his faithful service in the latter stages of the Fronde and as a counter to influence that Condé might exert. Of course, once awarded to Turenne, the grandeur of that individual made abolition of the office inconceivable. Since a colonel general continued in the cavalry, the highest regimental officer remained a *mestre de camp*, rather than a colonel.

---

[124] Parrott, "The Administration of the French Army," 317–18.
[125] For details on the colonel general of cavalry, see Sicard, *Histoire des institutions militaires*, 1:206–10; André, *Le Tellier*, 149–50; Rousset, *Louvois*, 1:175–76.
[126] Bérenger, *Turenne*, 483. The figure of 600,000 livres also equals the value of the office of secretary of state, which Berenger puts at 600,000 to 900,000 livres.
[127] This is the interpretation offered by André, *Le Tellier*, 149–50.
[128] Parrott, "The Administration of the French Army," 320–21.

Even under the influential Turenne and his nephew, who assumed the office at Turenne's death in 1675, the colonel general of cavalry did not challenge the secretary of state for war. Rousset argues that the authority of the colonels general declined, "slowly, but constantly, invaded by continual usurpation by Louvois, denied their essential rights, reduced to their exterior and honorific privileges."[129]

The staff of the colonel general included other high-ranking and prestigious posts. *Mestre de camp général* of cavalry was the greatest plum. One of its occupants, the contentious Bussy-Rambutin, who continually quarreled with his master, Turenne, called it "one of the best [*plus belles*] *charges* of war."[130] When the colonel general of cavalry decided which field army he would serve with, the *mestre de camp* would go to another to exercise his command. As a move to reduce the power of the colonel general, Le Tellier created a third major officer to share the authority. Whereas the colonel general and the *mestre de camp général* were venal offices, this new position came only by revocable commission and thus went by the title of *commissaire général* of cavalry. He functioned much as an inspector.[131]

Other Colonels General

Several other colonels general existed for short or long periods during the *grand siècle*, but they were not crown offices. Most prestigious among them was the *colonel général des Suisses et Grisons*, created by Charles IX in 1571. This officer possessed certain honors, including the first company of the Gardes suisses; however, his authority was not extensive. In addition, a series of colonels general led various other foreign troops in French service and operated primarily as go-betweens for the troops with the secretary of state for war. Such were colonels general for Italians, Corsicans, Polish, English, and Scottish soldiers. As with the troops concerned, these colonels general seemed to serve for relatively brief periods. The colonel general of lansquenets, created in 1544, passed from the scene only in 1632; the colonel general of Polish troops disappeared in 1654; and that for English units was eliminated in 1660. Beyond the colonels general for foreign infantry, Louis XIV created a new colonel general for mounted troops when in 1668 he instituted the colonel general of dragoons to head this new category of regiment, which multiplied late in his reign.

The foregoing survey of the fate of the crown officers discourages any assertion that some single great act, or a few great acts, snatched the army away from chaos, or away from the control of the great nobility, and returned it to the king and his secretary of state for war. Neither the elimination of the

---

[129] Rousset, *Louvois*, 1:176.   [130] Bussy-Rambutin in André, *Le Tellier*, 151.
[131] For details on the *mestre de camp général* and the *commissaire général*, see André, *Le Tellier*, 150–54.

constable in 1627 nor the abolition of the colonel general of infantry in 1661
rate as such. An overview demonstrates that the great offices declined in
authority incrementally over decades. In the case of the colonel general of
infantry at least, this decline began in the sixteenth century and simply continued in the seventeenth. When offices were abolished, it was not because
the monarch or his ministers had finally struck down a powerful source of
opposition and seized its power for themselves but that the office was already
a weak and hollow position that the monarch could eliminate with relative
impunity.

INSPECTORS: THE LIMITATIONS OF CIVILIAN CONTROL

The decline and elimination of the court offices discussed earlier increased
the relative power of the civilian secretary of state for war and his robe
agents, although perhaps not as much as usually believed. But however strong
the secretary of state and his immediate agents became, it is important to
realize that the military administration could not function solely through
civilian officials. One of the duties of the old court offices had been to maintain and survey the combat competence of units. In a sense, the inspectors
general created under Louis XIV inherited these functions that only an actual
soldier could perform.

The inspectors represented a different kind of military administrator, precisely because they were first and foremost soldiers. Contrary to most accounts, the idea of sending an inspector out to French troops predated Louis
XIV's famous actions. Mazarin wrote to Turenne in 1657: "Orders have been
sent to marshal d'Aumont to have the general inspection of all the troops
who remain in the Boulonnais and on the frontier there."[132] It is not clear,
however, if this commission to inspect troops involved the same duties that
would later be given to the inspectors general. In any case, as part of the
effort to improve the level of tactical performance in the French army, Louis
XIV created the Regiment du Roi in 1662 as a special training ground for
officers and as an example of the standards to which Louis hoped his entire
army would ascribe. In 1667, its lieutenant colonel Martinet (the colonel was
no less than the Sun King himself) became the first inspector general of
infantry. Of course, the name Martinet became a synonym for meticulous
attention to military detail and strict discipline.

It is clear from the start that part of the goal in creating the inspector
general was to apply high and uniform standards to the army and thus to
regularize the quality and ability of French infantry. Louvois wrote to his
father in 1669: "If all that I will see of the troops, from this point on until
my return, is in as fine a state as that which I have seen up to now, the King
has reason to be entirely satisfied and to persuade himself that if the visits of

---

[132] Mazarin to Turenne, 1 December 1657, Mazarin, *Lettres*, 8:227.

Monsieur Martinet continue, in three months there will be no difference between all the rest of the infantry and his Regiment du Roi."[133] A prime method in this quest was for Martinet to shake up the officer corps, or in the words of Louvois, "to wake up a little the officers who are sleeping."[134] This would also require an enhanced sense of hierarchy and obedience. "You ought to make understood by all officers who command units that the intention of the king is that they reestablish obedience without reply with regard to the officers who are their subalterns, and that, to achieve this effect, the first who happens to disobey will be broken."[135] In relation to this directive, Corvisier concludes "Never had a discipline this strict been imposed on the officers."[136] The initiative with infantry led to one with cavalry as well, and in 1669, Louis named Fourilles to the new post of inspector general of cavalry.

One might wonder why Louis needed officer inspectors when the civilian *intendants* and *commissaires des guerres* were already on the scene. After all, when the inspectors concerned themselves with numbers and equipment, their duties overlapped with civil *commissaires*. The inspectors were there, however, to judge what only a commissioned officer dare judge – the fighting quality of the unit. To a degree, this involved counts of men, arms, and clothing, but it also required them to enforce standards of tactical competence, something outside the range of the civilians. Perhaps the need for inspectors was dictated by professional and social differences between officers and civil administrators. An experienced soldier could command the respect of another when the business of soldiering was the subject, and a noble of the sword could pretend to speak of such matters with both military and social authority, whereas a robe administrator could not. Robe nobles, *annoblis*, or even bourgeois might be fine for running the business of war, but the fighting ought to be left to the sword. Therefore, the need for inspectors as an integral part of military administration signifies the limits of civil administration in the French army of the *grand siècle*.

As the army expanded, so did the corps of inspectors and inspector generals. In 1689, as the army geared up for the Nine Years' War, the number of inspectors general of infantry rose to four, each a general officer responsible for a particular region: (1) Flanders and Hainault, (2) the northeast provinces, (3) the Lyonnais, Dauphiné, and Provence, and (4) Languedoc, Roussillon, and Guyenne. Below these inspector generals served inspectors, who carried the rank of brigadier.[137] Later in that conflict, Louis established sixteen inspectors for the army.[138] These inspectors surveyed the number and condition of troops and in addition signed the authorizations for military payment presented to the *extraordinaire des guerres*. In other words, some of their duties overlapped with those of the *intendants* and *commissaires des guerres*.

---

[133] AG, A¹241, 19 May 1669, letter from Louvois to Le Tellier, in Rousset, *Louvois*, 1:210.
[134] AG, A¹241, 19 May 1669, letter from Louvois to Le Tellier, in Rousset, *Louvois*, 1:210.
[135] AG, A¹232, 18 March 1669, letter from Louvois to Martinet, in Rousset, *Louvois*, 1:211.
[136] Corvisier, *Louvois*, 189.   [137] Corvisier, *Louvois*, 349–50.   [138] Marion, *Dictionnaire*, 292.

CONCLUSION

This overview of French military administration reveals no single administrative revolution, not under Richelieu, Le Tellier, or Louvois; instead, the pattern was one of incremental change. Because of the current state of knowledge, it is tempting to conclude that administrative reform ended with Louvois, but detailed studies of administration from 1691 to 1715 may demonstrate that it continued to adjust and change to the demands of even larger armies. In any case, what some historians have portrayed as great leaps were more like small steps, the product of long evolution and a fortuitous opportunity to realize plans long laid. The character of that administrative change did not seem to have matched the dramatic increase in the size of the army and the consequent growth in the demands that it made upon the state. Still, obviously, military and state administration responded to the military challenge, as witnessed by the fact that army expansion did not produce in the Dutch War the chaos that attended the war with Spain. Perhaps the apparent paradox of more moderate administrative development in the face of radical military growth was made possible by the way in which services were delivered. Central French military administration did not so much provide services directly to the troops as it supervised the work of others charged with feeding, clothing, equipping, and housing the army. In a sense, then, all these officials of the French military administration were inspectors, meant to examine and certify the work of contractors and officers. The next four chapters explore that system in greater detail.

✦

4

Food and Fodder

FOR an army to fight, it must eat; victory is seldom the companion of
starvation. Hence, logistics form the basis of military action, and the fate
of empires can depend on bread. The giant of the *grand siècle* was no exception to this rule.

Food for men and fodder for horses were both essential, but they posed
very different problems for administrators and generals. Building upon the
experience of the previous century, Diderot's *Encylopédie* put it clearly, "There
are two sorts of subsistence: the first which are found in the field, like forage,
and often grains for distributions. The others are found at a distance, like
bread, wine, meat, and the variety of *fournitures* for the army."[1] In general,
fodder could be gathered in the field, although this was no easy task, and it
brought its own risks. But food had to be brought to the army, often from
magazines and army ovens. Around this second chore, an expensive, complicated, but absolutely necessary, system grew up, or to be exact systems, since
practices differed depending on whether troops were in the field, in garrison,
or on the road.

The seventeenth century, particularly the administrations of Le Tellier and
Louvois, garners praise as an era in which the state took upon itself more and
more responsibility for the care of its soldiers. No service could be more vital
than the dependable supply of food and fodder for the king's forces, and
Louis XIV was well aware of that fact. For the Sun King, the proper care
of his troops stood as a solemn moral obligation: "just as the soldier owes
obedience and submission to those who command him, the commander
owes his troops care for their subsistence."[2] It was a matter of honor: "The
clever general never undertakes an affair that requires time without examining all the things necessary to sustain his men. . . . [I]t is inhuman to put

---

[1] Denis Diderot, et al., *Encyclopédie*. 17 vols. text, 12 vols. plates (Paris: 1751–65), 15:582.
[2] Louis XIV, *Mémoires de Louis XIV*, Charles Dreyss, ed., 2 vols. (Paris: 1860), 2:250.

brave men in danger of losing their lives under conditions in which valor will not guarantee success."[3]

The growth of the army implies that French military administration under Louis created a new capacity to feed such large forces in the field, a task that could be enormous. Villars reported that his army in 1709 required 1,200 sacks of grain each day, enough to make as many as 216,000 rations of bread.[4] Logic and history concur that French administration developed sufficiently to meet the logistic challenge, but questions remain. Did this change occur in a revolutionary or evolutionary manner? To what extent were men and animals fed through the regular efforts of supply services, and to what extent did armies feed themselves by living off the country? Only a detailed examination of French logistics can answer these queries.

FOOD

Bread: The Basic Food

"The necessity for foodstuffs is the first thing that a prince ought to think about."[5] So Louis XIV stated his concern to feed his armies, for even in the *ancien régime*, armies marched on their stomachs, and French stomachs must be filled with bread. His marshal Villars put it another way, "We can go some time without money, but without bread it is impossible."[6] Bread was essential; even though French armies could also eat biscuit, it was less palatable and took far more fuel to cook, making it too expensive. Supplying the staff of life endlessly challenged seventeenth-century military administration, for should it be lacking, armies dissolved, campaigns withered, and strategy went begging, begging for a crust of bread.

The methods and personnel that supplied this vital need in the *grand siècle* had roots in the previous century. In the early sixteenth century, captains took personal responsibility for their companies, purchasing bread directly from the population around them. Troops were also supplied by requisitions carried out by local officials and set off against taxes. Furthermore, the monarchy turned to contractors during the wars of midcentury, but this method suffered when the state failed to pay the contractors.[7]

In response to problems, Henri II (1547–59) began what the historian Audouin claimed was "a revolution in the administration of food supplies," although it seems clear Audouin exaggerated.[8] Without abolishing older practices, Henri II instituted new ones. Troops in garrisons continued to receive their rations through the older system of purchase and local requisition; however, troops on campaign got their bread directly from royal

---

[3] Louis XIV in John B. Wolf, *Louis XIV* (New York: 1968), 203.
[4] Claude Louis Hector Villars, *Mémoires du maréchal de Villars*, ed. Vogüé, 5 vols. (Paris: 1884–95), 3:42.
[5] Louis XIV, *Mémoires de Louis XIV*, 2:170.   [6] Villars, *Mémoires*, 3:47.
[7] Xavier Audouin, *Histoire de l'administration de la guerre*, 4 vols. (Paris: 1811), 2:39–45.
[8] Audouin, *Histoire de l'administration de la guerre*, 2:43–50.

administrators. Such a contrast between the method used to supply garrison forces and that used in the field would remain throughout the *ancien régime*. On campaign, officials now bought grain, had it stored and processed into bread, and, finally, supervised its direct distribution to the soldiers. The ordinances of the 1550s created two *commissaires général des vivres* to supervise this system, while other major *commissaires* served under the orders of these top officials; those actually with the army bore the title of *commis des vivres*, and *commissaires des vivres* served in every province of France.[9] All agents justified their accounts before the *chambre des comptes*.

But this system of direct state supply could break down, and Henri III let out what the historian Audouin considered to be the first modern contracts, *marchés* or *traités*, to private entrepreneurs when the foregoing methods failed. Audouin found what he believed to be the first *marchés* granted in 1575, when the general commanding the siege of Lusignan had exhausted local requisition purchases by *commissaires*.[10] However, James Wood discusses a 1572 contract with merchants from Niort to supply the camp at La Rochelle in 1572 with 30,000 twelve-ounce loaves each day, 10,800 pints of wine, and 20,000 pounds of beef.[11] Such *marchés* stipulated the exact weight and price of rations and set the pattern for later agreements with *munitionnaires*, entrepreneurs who contracted to supply *pain de munition* and other foodstuffs. The reliance upon private suppliers at Lusignan also demonstrated that recourse to *munitionnaires* amounted to an appeal to credit. Royal agents had to have the money up front to buy grain, but at Lusignan, they ran out of funds. *Munitionnaires* put up their own assets in return for installment payments over the life of the contract; thus they provided food immediately in expectation of future payment. Appeals to *munitionnaires* from this point onward marked the fact that the government could not marshal all the cash it needed for war.

To feed its troops during the first half of the seventeenth century, the government adopted and refined several methods that grew out of earlier precedent. Troops in garrison, in winter quarters, or on the road from place to place, might receive their bread from local requisition, with or without compensation, or from contractors. During the war with Spain, soldiers might simply be expected to purchase their food with their pay, in which case, government *commissaires* published price ceilings on basic items to protect the soldiers from gouging.[12] In winter quarters, when infantry received bread directly, cavalry were required to buy their own food.

[9] Audouin, *Histoire de l'administration de la guerre*, 2:167; Philippe Contamine, ed., *Histoire militaire de la France*, vol. 1 (Paris: 1992), 316.

[10] Audouin, *Histoire de l'administration*, 2:51.

[11] James B. Wood, "The Royal Army During the Early Wars of Religion, 1559–1576," in Mack P. Holt, ed., *Society & Institutions in Early Modern France* (Athens, GA: 1991), 20.

[12] For example, AG, MR 1881, #19, 20 Mars 1623, at the arrival of the troops, *commissaires* were to set a price list, and troops were to pay according to these prices for food. However, it is not always true that prices rose around the troops, because troops might seize all the grain and sell it below market price. Bernard Kroener, *Les routes et les étapes. Die bersorgung der franzoschichen Armeen in Nordostfrankreich (1635–1661)*, (Munster: 1980), 135.

Of much greater interest is the manner in which the monarchy supplied its armies on campaign. Here the primary contrast during the seventeenth century was that between direct state supply through royal agents, on the one hand, and employment of *munitionnaires*, on the other. The system of direct supply, as inherited by Louis XIII, proved incapable of meeting the needs of an expanded army after 1635, even though Richelieu increased the number of officials involved in the supply administration and appointed himself *grand maitre des vivres*. The *commissaires généraux* remained, and by an edict of June 1627, Richelieu added four new positions to join the two existing *commissaires généraux* and christened the lot *surintendants et commissaires généraux des vivres*.[13] The six *surintendants* were to receive annual wages of 3,000 livres plus 4 percent of all money paid for supplies of foodstuffs in the armies, in addition to other financial privileges. On top of this, they enjoyed entrée to the king. In 1631, the crown added *conseillers commissaires des vivres* in each *élection*, and, about the same time, six *trésoriers généraux des vivres* to handle the funds used by *surintendants des vivres* to purchase foodstuffs.[14] André reads these creations as a step toward direct state supply, and certainly these were offices connected with these functions. Audouin sees them as simply complicating affairs.[15] In any case, these were also offices for sale, so efficiency may have played second fiddle to avarice in creating them. The positions of *surintendant* carried a stiff price tag, valued at 100,000 livres, so a strong possibility exists that the creation of the offices was primarily a way of raising a quick 400,000 livres. In any case, the *surintendant* and *commissaires des vivres* slipped in real authority, as the secretary of state for war, *intendants*, and *munitionnaires* ran the system under Louis XIV.[16]

Whatever the multiplication of officers charged with direct supply, when an expanded army marched off to fight a great war in 1635, the monarchy again turned to *munitionnaires*. In 1635, the French relied on a single contractor to supply their troops, but when this proved disastrous, the number of contractors was increased, and in 1636, the hard-pressed ministry assigned a greater role for its agents in amassing magazines of grain between campaigns.[17]

Since the government lacked the funds to supply its troops directly, it had to employ *munitionnaires*, but since it also often lacked the funds even to pay the installments owed to *munitionnaires*, these entrepreneurs committed abuses, or at the worst, the system simply broke down. When Le Tellier came to office in 1643, money was scarce, and the troops suffered, but Le

---

[13] This ordinance is given in full in François Nodot, *Le munitionnaire des armées de France* (Paris: 1697), 609–12.

[14] The 1631 ordinance is in Nodot, *Le munitionnaire*, 612–15; Audouin, *Histoire de l'administration*, 2:167, 221.

[15] Audouin, *Histoire de l'administration*, 2:168.

[16] See Kroener, *Les routes et les étapes*, 6–56, on the administration of *vivres* during the long war with Spain.

[17] David Parrott, "The Administration of the French Army During the Ministry of Cardinal Richelieu," Ph.D. dissertation, Oxford University, 1985, 44.

Tellier was unable to jettison the old system or revamp it fundamentally. Still, Louis André praises Le Tellier's administration of *vivres* as a turn toward modernity. "The period during which he was the only one to direct military administration is in this regard a period of transition between a system of individual enterprise and that of direct service by the state" – by this, he meant the replacement of *munitionnaires* by *intendants* and other government agents.[18] It is hard to understand why André would say this, since it is clear that the personal reign of Louis XIV brought not direct supply but rather the complete triumph of *munitionnaires*. In fact, what André sees as a new use of government agents was evidence of a breakdown in the *munitionnaire* system, not its reform. For example, in 1648, Falcombel, the contractor responsible for French forces in Lombardy, refused to continue on. Backed into an impossible situation, Le Tellier sent an official from the household of Mazarin to get the job done under the authority of the *intendant*.[19]

While Le Tellier's agents built up magazines of foodstuffs, this practice goes back to Sublet de Noyers at least, and probably back to the *commissaires des vivres* of the sixteenth century. Audouin was closer to the truth than was André, because the former read this period as one that ended the system of direct supply furnished through *commissaires* and *surintendants des vivres*. In its stead came the dominance of the private *munitionnaire*, since the monarchy proved unable to shoulder full responsibility for managing supply when finance remained precarious.[20]

The period 1643–61 makes more sense as one of expedients and responses than one during which France forged new military institutions. French military administration repeatedly broke down. Vauban said of the latter stages of the war with Spain, "I remember that in the old war, when we were in enemy country, we went three whole weeks sometimes without getting a ration of bread."[21] Logistic failure inspired a variety of suggestions. In 1644, Turenne even urged a complete reversion to the practice of paying the men and letting them purchase their own food at controlled prices; at other times, he would have left the captain of each company to feed his own men.[22]

In all of this, the *commissaires généraux des vivres* became not agents of direct supply but inspectors, supervisors of a system of supply by private entrepreneurs. The *commissaires* and the *intendants* shared in these duties by regulating the movement of troops and arranging for support of those troops

[18] Louis André, *Michel Le Tellier et l'organisation de l'armée monarchique* (Paris: 1906), 434.

[19] André, *Le Tellier*, 447–48.

[20] Audouin, *Histoire de l'administration*, 2:221–23. Interestingly enough, Nodot also defines the old system as one based on requisitions from the people, saying that this lasted through Louis XIII, but that since then, *munitionnaires* have become the rule. Nodot, *Le munitionnaire*, 564.

[21] Vauban to Louvois, 13 September 1677, AG, A¹556 in Camille Rousset, *Histoire de Louvois*, 4 vols. (Paris: 1862–64), 1:248.

[22] Jean Bérenger, *Turenne* (Paris: 1987), 197; Nodot, *Le munitionnaire*, 585.

while on the march, and these officials also collected grain and ensured its storage.[23] However, when it came to actually supplying troops in the field, their roles were restricted to supervising those who had taken on the task for a fee.

Louvois built upon a given set of regulations, many drafted by his father and some that dated back to the 1620s. His powerful personality and the strong support of Louis XIV produced a workable, though far from perfect, system that supplied bread to larger armies than France had ever fielded before and that won him the sobriquet of *grand vivier*. In fact, Louvois was still learning his craft during the War of Devolution (1667–68), when Colbert cut the deals with *munitionnaires* and other contractors.[24] That war and the Lorraine campaign of 1670 functioned as dry runs. Of the latter, Louvois wrote "The manner in which the king has made his troops live on campaign presently is that which his majesty would like should they have war."[25]

Louvois deserves particular credit for his use of magazines, although it is not correct to say that he created them in the sense that most historians claim. For Rousset, Louvois ranks as the great innovator here.[26] Yet state agents had built up caches of grain during wartime since the sixteenth century. Richelieu and Le Tellier had employed officials, most notably *intendants* and *commissaires des vivres*, to collect foodstuffs for the next campaign. This is why André insists that Louvois must share credit with Le Tellier, without recognizing that what Le Tellier did, others had done before. Yet Europe had probably never seen anything like the magazines that supported the French advance of 1672.

While deserving praise as an innovator in provisioning, Louvois probably attained his greatest successes by making an existing system work to peak efficiency. In doing so, he may have institutionalized a system that in many ways was quite "unmodern." Audouin, while calling the period 1661–83 "the most memorable in the history of the administration of the armies," still condemns Louvois for "abandoning administration to the avarice of entrepreneurs."[27] Direct supply by *intendants* and *commissaires* was limited to their part in building up magazines and in their care for troops on the march in the *étapes* system. Audouin argues that the monarchy's poor financial practices and the growing size of armies compelled bad choices.

Louvois generally did well at the logistical game because he held some high cards. He enjoyed the full support of Louis XIV, a king who exerted a degree of considerable authority within traditional limits. In addition, Louvois could build upon the administrative foundations laid by his father and Richelieu. Beyond these advantages there are some that, although less commonly noted, deserve attention. He won the title of *grand vivier* in a war

[23] 12 May 1651 ordinance, by Le Tellier, in André, *Le Tellier*, 451; Louis André, *Michel Le Tellier et Louvois* (Paris: 1942), 374.

[24] Rousset, *Louvois*, 1:118–19.   [25] Rousset, *Louvois*, 1:300.   [26] Rousset, *Louvois*, 1:249.

[27] Audouin, *Histoire de l'administration*, 2:207, 222.

that followed thirteen years of economic and fiscal recovery. His successors would not be so lucky. Not only was he an able man, but he could call upon some extremely able administrators in his department, like Saint-Pouenges and Chamlay, who played particularly notable roles in provisioning the armies.[28] The field armies that this team fed during the Dutch War were still fairly modest in size when compared to those that fought the battles of the last two wars of Louis XIV. And while Louvois did see three years of the Nine Years' War, he did not have to maintain its 340,000-man force over the long haul. Lastly, he may have benefited from an especially talented group of *munitionnaires* who learned their profession under Le Tellier. Such men would not be so readily available to his successors after 1688. Without going so far as to agree with Saint-Simon's charge that Louvois was slipping from royal favor at the time of his death, it is interesting to speculate whether Louvois's reputation would have survived the Nine Year's War.

After the death of Louvois, succeeding secretaries of state for war did not feed the army as reliably or speedily. This may be, as so many charge, because they were mediocre men or because the system crafted by Louvois ossified. It can be debated whether or not their abilities declined, but it cannot be denied that the challenges they faced mounted. In the Nine Years' War, army size towered far above what it had been in the previous conflict. This put a much greater burden on the supply system, which survived the challenge, although with many a creak and groan. The French exhausted themselves in that conflict, and with only a few years of peace, they launched into another great war even longer than the last. Supply broke down in the War of the Spanish Succession even before the disastrous winter of 1708–9, but after that catastrophe, the situation went from dim to desperate. How could this be blamed solely on poor administration or corrupt *munitionnaires*?

Although the system of providing rations changed, the amount of food, particularly bread, prescribed for men on campaign remained essentially constant. Military ordinances repeatedly defined the ration in the 1620s and 1630s, and those amounts remained standard for the *grand siècle*. The Code Michau of 1629 set the daily allowance at 24 ounces of bread, 1 pound of meat, and a pint of wine.[29] The 1636 regulation on *étapes* confirmed the amounts provided in 1629.[30] From this point on, the daily ration of 24 ounces of bread remained constant for troops on campaign or on the march. Regulations for winter quarters follow similar patterns; that for 1651 prescribed the same 24 ounces of bread, a mixture of wheat and rye, "cooked and firm [*rassi*], between brown and white."[31] The greatest difference in the

---

[28] Rousset, *Louvois*, 1:250.

[29] Albert Babeau, *La vie militaire sous l'ancien regime*, 2 vols (Paris: 1890), 1:127–28.

[30] SHAT, Bib., Col. des ord., vol. 14, #94, 26 March 1636.

[31] Article 8 of the 4 November 1651 *règlement* for winter quarters in André, *Le Tellier*, 672. "Rassi" today means "stale," the point then was that the bread had to be firm enough to be carried in pack or caisson, so it had to be long enough out of the oven to be reasonably solid.

regulations concerning bread rations contrasted supply for infantry to that for cavalry. Throughout the century, infantrymen received bread both on campaign and in winter quarters, while cavalrymen did not receive bread directly but had to purchase it out of their pay.[32] Yet by the last two great wars of Louis XIV, troopers also received bread on campaign in addition to their pay.[33] The actual weight of loaves varied, so a ration might require two loaves while at times a single loaf was so large that it amounted to two rations.[34] A change in weights causes some confusion among historians. Earlier regulations speak of a pound of only 12 ounces, whereas by the end of the century, the ordinances dealt in a 16-ounce pound. Therefore a 2-pound ration in 1629 contained the same number of ounces as a 1.5-pound ration by 1700.

The soldier washed down his bread with wine or other alcoholic beverages. The 1629 code set the drink ration at a pint of wine, and while this varied, reaching as much as three pints of wine, it tended to hover at the pint mark. In most regulations, a pot of beer or cider could replace the pint of wine if it was not the local drink.[35]

Neither did the system of *vivres* alter much late in the reign of Louis XIV. By 1691, it was securely in place, for good or ill. *Munitionnaires* financed and supplied the bread that fueled Louis's armies, but the funds to pay them fell short, and perhaps the men themselves were not as good at their demanding tasks. Having mentioned *munitionnaires* tangentially so many times, it is best now to examine their work directly.

Munitionnaires

As mentioned earlier, the use of entrepreneurs in supply predated the *grand siècle*. Under Richelieu, negotiations for these contracts involved contentious consultations between the *munitionnaire*, the *surintendant des finances*, and the secretary of state for war.[36] In the late 1640s, when Le Tellier served as secretary of state, the *conseil du roi* publicly posted the basic terms of the contract that it wished to conclude and then entertained offers. Such details included the need to provide a specific number of bread rations at a set price per ration and the transport to carry the bread to the front. The *munitionnaire* chosen would be paid in advance month by month.[37] Different *munitionnaires*

---

[32] Parrott, "The Administration of the French Army," 85–86; André chapter on *vivres*, André, *Le Tellier*, 415–68.

[33] See the charts of campaign pay during the War of the Spanish Succession in Jean Roland de Mallet, *Compts Rendus de l'administration des finances du royaume de France*. (London: 1789), 169–70.

[34] Victor Belhomme, *L'armée française en 1690* (Paris: 1895), 150; Louis de Gaya, *Le nouvel art de la guerre et la manière dont on la fait aujourd'huy en France* (Paris: 1692), 46.

[35] Babeau, *La vie militaire*, 1: 127–28; see, for example, SHAT, Bib., Col. des ord., vol. 14, #94, 26 March 1636.

[36] Parrott, "The Administration of the French Army," 86.

[37] André, *Le Tellier*, 441. In addition, see the 1646 *règlement* for the *munitionnaire général*, p. 445n.

contracted for different tasks; Kroener, in his historical study of supply, argued that there were three different kinds of *munitionnaires* during the period 1635–61 – those that supplied a particular field army wherever it might be, those that supplied all troops in a particular area, and those that supplied only garrisons.[38]

In his long treatise on the profession of the *munitionnaire*, Nodot, a contractor himself at the end of the 1600s, provides the text of a *traité* concluded with Alexandre de l'Espine to supply bread to troops in Savoy, Piedmont, Catalonia, and Roussillon during the six months of the campaign season, 1 May to 31 October 1694.[39] It set the rations at 10,000 for Savoy, 80,000 for Piedmont, and 26,000 for Catalonia and Roussillon. The bread was to be made of a fifty-fifty mixture of wheat and rye, and to weigh 28 ounces as dough and 24 ounces in the final cooked form. It also stipulated where he was to establish his magazines of grain and how many sacks each should contain. He was to arrange for milling and baking, as well as providing 2,800 mules with pack frames or horses with caissons in Piedmont and Savoy, and 400 in Rousillon and Catalonia. The government agreed to supply the *munitionnaire* with 70,000 200-pound sacks of wheat at Marseilles at 18 livres per sack. This cache was apparently one that the government had built up in its own magazines. The *traité* promised to provide l'Espine with "all the escorts necessary for the security" of his grain, bread, and equipment by land or waterways. If the enemy should take or destroy his gear or animals, the government agreed to pay for his losses at a set rate – 150 livres for mules and horses, 50 livres for wagons. It also allowed for ransom to be paid for captured teamsters and muleteers. For these services, the *munitionnaire* was to receive 67 deniers a ration for troops in Savoy and Piedmont but only 36 deniers for Catalonia and Rousillon. Espines would get a total of 7,470,977 livres to be paid one sixth in each of the months of February, March, and April, with the remaining to be paid in equal portions during the six months of the campaign.

Contracts like that with de l'Espine covered only a single campaign season, and with the end of that season in November, the *munitionnaire* dismantled the supply apparatus. If the hired captains who commanded the wagons and teamsters were subcontractors with their own staff, animals, and equipment, the *munitionnaire* dismissed them. If the *munitionnaire* owned the wagons and horses, he stored the wagons in the care of craftsmen, who made necessary repairs, as the horses plodded off to winter away from the front. His employees dispersed, to be reassembled when the *munitionnaire* won the contract for the next year. The strategic implications of this practice were great, for even if a general wanted to conduct a winter campaign, he lacked the logistic apparatus to take the field. Only in extraordinary situations was this rule broken – the most famous example being Turenne's winter campaign of 1674, which concluded in early January 1675.

---

[38] Kroener, *Les routes et les étapes*, 121.   [39] Nodot, *Le munitionnaire*, 531–50.

It is not surprising that the official definition of the campaign season late in the *grand siècle* matches well with reality. In his study of the War of the Spanish Succession, Jamel Ostwald charts allied campaign seasons in the Spanish Netherlands.[40] Only twice did troops take the field before May, and then they operated in late April. Likewise, only three times did actual campaigning last into November, and it continued through November but once.

Munitionnaires might also contract to supply bread for garrison troops during the year. In general, the state offered less per ration for garrison troops than for units in the field. Louvois habitually offered 2 sous per ration to *munitionnaires* for field units and 10 deniers less per ration for garrison troops.[41]

A *munitionnaire* took on a complicated, expensive, and risky business. The 600-odd pages of Nodot's handbook suggest the great variety of talent, knowledge, and resources required. To perform these duties, a *munitionnaire* had not only to amass grain in magazines; he also had to buy sacks for grain, hire animals, construct wagons, produce baking tools, and acquire materials to build field ovens. Moreover, he had to hire workers, drivers, officers, clerks, and supervisors. A *général des vivres* headed the *munitionnaires* staff and served as the *munitionnaire's* lieutenant if the contractor himself was not with the army, as was often the case. This general, who stood at the right hand of the army *intendant*, was assisted by two treasurers, two *commis-généraux*, and a number of clerks. A *capitaine général* bore responsibility for the wagon train and had his own staff as well. The train was divided into *équipages* of 100 horses and 25 wagons and drivers, commanded by a captain.[42] The captains might be subcontractors who supplied one or more *équipages*. Thus, a great deal of skilled personnel backed up the *munitionnaire*.

While knowledge about *munitionnaires* remains incomplete, there seems to be universal agreement that some particularly talented individuals worked with Louvois, most notably François Jacquier. Early in the Fronde, Jacquier contracted to supply fortified places in Flanders. He soon received the office of *commissaire général des vivres aux campes et aux armées du Roy*, combining authority of both contractor and *commissaire*.[43] Nodot portrays him as the greatest *munitionnaire* and ascribes the successes of 1672–78 in part to the abilities of skilled entrepreneurs like him.[44]

A shortage of talent and experience posed a great problem for French supply later in Louis's reign, and the thinning of talent began right at the

---

[40] Jamel Ostwald, "The Failure of 'Strategy of Annihilation': Battle and Fortresses in the War of the Spanish Succession," M. A. thesis, Ohio State University, 1995, 82–84.

[41] Nodot, *Le munitionnaire*, 565.

[42] Nodot, *Le munitionnaire*, 20–21, provides a chart of men in the supply train under the rank of captain and their wages.

[43] Kroener, *Les routes et les étapes*, 31, on Jacquier.

[44] Rousset, *Louvois*, 1:250, 338, also mentions great *munitionnaires* as Jacquier and Berthelot. Berthelot was instrumental in the buildup for 1672; charged with buying grain, he was a *fournisseur* but practically a government agent.

top. Nodot reports a shift in the practice of concluding *traités*. In the Dutch War, the monarchy tended to rely on a single *munitionnaire* to supply a particular army, but with the Nine Years' War, the French turned to companies of *munitionnaires* composed of several individuals who shared the work and the risks.[45] It is true that some combinations of *munitionnaires* functioned very well; Nodot provides the example of one composed of six contractors in 1672 that served as a model of how such a company should apportion duty.[46] Yet he charges that the companies at the end of the century were formed by financiers who did not know the business. While he lived, Louvois did what he could to solve this problem by imposing experienced *commis* on inexperienced *munitionnaires*.[47] However, even before Louvois's death, there were not enough experienced men to run the business in the field as *généraux des vivres* and their *commis*, and incompetent companies of *munitionnaires* hired mere "adventurers" to head their operations and were defrauded by their *commis*.

Nodot blames this lack of talent on two primary factors. First, the French lacked a regular training program to prepare new men to work as *commis*. In the past, some *munitionnaires* had taught the ropes to a sufficient body of men who learned by doing in wartime. Nodot singles out Jacquier as leaving a particularly rich legacy of trainees. Yet by 1688, few of these remained, and men who knew the job were scarce. Second, the great expansion of armies required more skilled personnel than could be provided by the small pool of truly qualified *munitionnaires* and top staff. At midcentury, there were many accomplished entrepreneurs and fewer troops, but by the end of the century, it had gone the other way.[48]

Munitionnaires did not enjoy a high reputation. Richelieu called military suppliers "those colossal cheats."[49] Marshal Villars, no fan of theirs either, commented concerning one: "He merited being hanged one hundred times; [but] I do not know how this can be done."[50] When things got hard for Villars's troops in 1709, he broke into the warehouses of *munitionnaires* and seized their grain. They shared some of the hate visited on financiers and received blame for the sufferings of poorly fed troops. Audouin refers to the use of *munitionnaires* under Louis XIV as "this horrible system" and again blames it on the government's financial straits.[51] Still there were *munitionnaires* who earned a good reputation, men like Falcombel, Jacquier, and Raffi. And *munitionnaires*, as men of wealth in state service, might be expected to use their own funds for the army's needs. In 1693, the *munitionnaire* for the army in Piedmont, whom the treasury still owed 2 million livres for 1692, could not

[45] Nodot, *Le munitionnaire*, 251.   [46] Nodot, *Le munitionnaire*, 552.
[47] Nodot, *Le munitionnaire*, 566–68.   [48] Nodot, *Le munitionnaire*, 566.
[49] Richelieu, *Lettres*, 3:133 in Michael Duffy, ed., *The Military Revolution and the State* (Exeter: 1980), 38.
[50] Villars in Audouin, *Histoire de l'administration*, 2:389.
[51] Audouin, *Histoire de l'administration*, 2:236–37.

get adequate funds from the government and had to advance his own money to buy necessary supplies.[52]

Details of Bread and Equipages

In order to carry out the tasks of transporting grain, flour, and bread, the army and government employed two distinct methods. In periods of extreme pressure on supply – for example, during sieges – military and government agents requisitioned animals, carts, and drivers from local government or the population. Such requisitions could involve a large number of pack animals, teams, and wagons for short periods of time.[53] The French monarchy exploited this right of requisition throughout the seventeenth century, although Le Tellier tried to discourage it, since it led to incompetence and delays.[54]

More important than recourse to local cartage was the second basic form of transport – the train belonging to military contractors. Le Tellier generally receives credit for organizing the *équipage*, but despite the praise he has received, Le Tellier did not create the use of *équipages*, which seem to have existed before him.[55] For example, he did not originate the use of special caissons or coffers to carry the bread, for as early as 1622, du Praissac described in detail coffers that held 1,500 ten-ounce loaves for transport.[56] In fact, du Praissac's work leads one to question Louis André's enthusiasm for Le Tellier's originality. Du Praissac bears witness to considerable continuity in the seventeenth-century commissary, since he was clearly describing *équipages* of a pattern similar to that which the French employed even late in the *grand siècle*. In fact, the term *équipage des vivres* appears in military correspondence in the 1630s.[57] It may well be the case, however, that the use of formal *équipages* was hit or miss before Le Tellier and that too great a reliance was placed upon local requisition of less than competent locals. Otherwise, why would Richelieu have felt the need to write in 1640, "give orders, if you please, to have them fasten down a cover to hold [the bread]; otherwise, all will go wrong, as the least rain would spoil it."[58] The later professionals of the supply train would have needed no such counseling. It seems fairest,

---

[52] Belhomme, *L'armée française en 1690*, 154.

[53] André Corvisier, *Les Français et l'armée sous Louis XIV* (Vincennes: 1975), 188; William Beik, *Absolutism and Society in Seventeenth-Century France* (Cambridge: 1985), 137.

[54] André, *Le Tellier*, 453, argues that Le Tellier relied less on requisition of transport. André also gives the terms for requisition when it was used.

[55] Nodot, *Le munitionnaire*, 573; Audouin, *Histoire de l'administration*, 2:208; André, *Le Tellier*, 452–53.

[56] Praissac, *Les discours militaires*, 2nd ed. (Paris: 1622), 154–55.

[57] AAE, France, 820 fo. 200 early 1636 in Parrott, "The Administration of the French Army," 84.

[58] August 1640 letter from Richelieu to Castillon in Orest Ranum, *Richelieu and the Councillors of Louis XIII* (Oxford: 1963), 110.

then, to suggest that Le Tellier extended and regularized the best current practices rather than creating a new transportation system from whole cloth.

Le Tellier stipulated that bread was to be transported in caissons, about 6 feet by 3 feet long with a locked top, covered in waterproof waxed cloth. Each caisson was to be carried on a four-wheeled charrette drawn by three horses. Sixty charrettes would be sufficient to carry 25,000 rations per day.[59] André claims that regular army officers were put in charge of this train, and he adds this detail to support his argument that state agents replaced *munitionnaires* under Le Tellier. André may go astray by misinterpreting the language of the regulation, which apparently uses military ranks for those in charge of the train. As Nodot's treatise makes clear, captains of the *équipages* were civilians, not serving military officers, and were often private contractors. Van Creveld misconstrues André's description of the supply train to mean that it was a rolling reserve, which it was not.[60] The train was clearly designed to shuttle between the ovens and the army.

The *équipage* that Nodot describes in great detail at the close of the century varied only in particulars from that which Le Tellier prescribed in regulations. Late seventeenth-century caissons were larger, 8 feet 4 inches by 2 feet 6 inches, with a peaked cover, waterproof and locked.[61] Each caisson held 800 rations – a total of 1,200 pounds – and was carried on a charrette, a four-wheeled wagon driven by a single teamster. The method of transport by caissons seemed to be well suited to bread. In an example presented by Nodot, only eight loaves out of 16,000 were ruined in one run from ovens to army.[62]

The train was divided into *équipages* of twenty-five caissons and charrettes each, and as four horses now drew a charrette, the *équipage* contained 100 horses. A captain led each *équipage* and might own it and subcontract to the *munitionnaire*. He marked his red-painted caissons with the first initial of his name and numbered them from 1 to 25. The equipage for supply was organized in very much the same way as the horses and teamsters of the artillery train, also divided into units of 100 horses with a teamster for every four horses, commanded by a captain – a civilian operation again provided by contract.[63] In areas where wagons were impractical, *équipages* employed mules or donkeys bearing pack frames, and pack animals were divided into "brigades" of 100 or 50 with a captain in charge. A mule could carry 190 rations, according to Nodot and other contemporary sources.[64] This would mean it required about the same number of draft/pack animals to carry a given number of rations. The supply trains for French field armies varied. In 1690, the train

[59] André, *Le Tellier*, 452–53.
[60] Martin van Creveld, *Supplying War: Logistics from Wallenstein to Patton* (Cambridge: 1977), 19.
[61] Nodot, *Le munitionnaire*, 12–13.   [62] Nodot, *Le munitionnaire*, 359.
[63] Belhomme, *L'armée française en 1690*, 124, 129.
[64] Nodot, *Le munitionnaire*, 452; AN, G⁷1093, 5 May 1708.

for the Army of Germany numbered 1,600 horses, and that for the Army of Flanders included 1,200 horses; however, Moselle and Rousillon only had 600 horses each, while Piedmont counted 500 and Rousillon a mere 100, a single *équipage*.[65]

Supply involved a great deal of shuttling back and forth from magazines to ovens to field armies. While this was not the "five-march" system, which historian Perjès argues did not exist during the seventeenth century and van Creveld believes never existed at all, it did involve the continual movement of foodstuffs in convoy.[66] According to Nodot, the *munitionnaire* provided enough *équipages* to carry four times the daily ration. Du Praissac advocated only three times as many wagons as would be required to carry a single day's ration in 1622, and Gaya picked up that notion and repeated it much later, but Nodot's advice seems to have been the rule.[67] This fit the need for transport in accord with the life span of bread and economized on convoy escorts. The French, as well as other contemporary armies, usually distributed bread to the troops once every four days.[68] Because a full ration for the army took two or more days to bake, and perhaps another day or two to transport, a four-day's ration would push the life span of baked bread – about eight days in good weather, but less when it was hot and damp. This supply train or park occupied its own part of an army's camp: behind the main body of troops, along with the headquarters and the artillery park.[69] In order to keep the teamsters close by their horses and equipment, Nodot even recommended that the *parc des vivres* have its own chaplain, so that the men would not leave for mass.[70]

Even if the ovens were built in the army encampment, the *équipages* still had to cart flour in from the magazines, although this was an easier task than carting bread. The standard 200-pound bag of flour produced 180 bread rations of twenty-four ounces each, or 270 pounds of bread – a baking ratio of 3:4.[71] Transport of flour to the ovens could also be handled by local carters, as when flour and wood was brought to the ovens every two weeks circa 1690. Then the teamsters would be fed and the team owners paid for this temporary duty.[72] The use of local teams freed the train to haul bread from the ovens to the troops.

In the field, French armies ate bread prepared in brick field ovens established close to the army, within its encampment if possible. Such ovens were constructed with bricks found on site over a framework of curved iron rods,

[65] Belhomme, *L'armée française en 1690*, 152.

[66] G. Perjés, "Army Provisioning, Logistics and Strategy in the Second Half of the 17th Century," *Acta Historica Academiae Scientiarum Hungaricae*, 16, nr. 1–2 (1970), 27–29.

[67] Praissac, *Les discours militaires*, 155; Gaya, *Le nouvel art de la guerre*, 46–47.

[68] Perjés, "Army Provisioning," 28–29. Montecuccoli specified that "the troops get bread every four days."

[69] Gaya, *Le nouvel art de la guerre*, 56–58.   [70] Nodot, *Le munitionnaire*, 198–99.

[71] Nodot, *Le munitionnaire*, 4.   [72] Belhomme, *L'armée française en 1690*, 151.

or *cintres,* which were part of the *munitionnaire's* equipment.[73] This use of *cintres* greatly speeded construction, so a bank of ovens could be built and ready to fire in two and a half days.[74] *Munitionnaires* maintained a crew of masons to build ovens as the army moved. An army requiring 50,000 rations per day would need 20 ovens, each baking 500 rations a day.[75]

Early in the Dutch War, the French used portable iron ovens that could be set up in six hours, but these did not survive long.[76] Nodot explains that portable ovens were rejected because "they were very difficult to transport and it was not easy to fit them together again [*racommoder*] when the plates were disjointed or bent."[77] Plates cooled by pouring cold water on them must have often split or warped. Had the pace of warfare been significantly faster, the cumbrous, and expensive, iron ovens might have been worth the trouble, but such was not the case for the French.

Distribution of Bread Rations

The distribution of bread rations took place every four days in good weather and every two days during the hottest days of summer, because heat shortened the shelf life of bread.[78] The oldest bread was to be handed out first, for obvious reasons. Nodot cautions that if this bread "is a little suspect, give it to the cavalry, because . . . it is less careful [about its rations] than the infantry."[79] He comments more than once about this curious lack of concern among cavalry and advises that if rations are not sufficient, short the cavalry not the infantry, because the cavalry "waits [for food] more easily, always finding [a way] to subsist."[80] This can only be a reference to the mounted man's greater mobility and higher pay.

Ideally, distributions were to occur in the morning, with infantry showing up at break of day, cavalry at about 8 A.M. and dragoons about 10 A.M. Each regiment would be conducted to the *parc des vivres* by its major, aide-major, and *maréchal de logis,* who would present their review reports and agree to a set number of rations. The *commis général de parc* would supervise for the entrepreneur. Interestingly enough, Nodot recommended that the *commis* set his tent up in the center of the wagon park and keep his tent supplied with refreshments for the officers.[81] The soldiers would line up and collect their rations in cloth sacks while the entrepreneurs' men counted out the rations in a loud voice to avoid confusion and prevent any fraud by the troops.

---

[73] On oven construction, see Nodot, *Le munitionnaire,* 223, 304–14.
[74] Nodot, *Le munitionnaire,* 168.   [75] Nodot, *Le munitionnaire,* 139.
[76] Wolf, *Louis XIV,* 222–23.   [77] Nodot, *Le munitionnaire,* 223–24.
[78] On the details of bread distribution, see Nodot, *Le munitionnaire,* 157–60, 355–76.
[79] Nodot, *Le munitionnaire,* 364.   [80] Nodot, *Le munitionnaire,* 375.
[81] Nodot, *Le munitionnaire,* 356.

While common soldiers collected only one ration each, their commissioned and noncommissioned officers were entitled to multiples. By a regulation of 1656, the commanding general of an army would receive 100 rations and lieutenant-generals and *intendants* 50.[82] A series of regulations set the rations for regimental officers. During the personal reign of Louis XIV, officers received multiples of the single ration allowed an infantryman and, eventually, a trooper: Colonels drew 12 to 18 rations, captains 6, lieutenants 4, ensigns and cornets 3, and sergeants and *maréchaux de logis* 2.[83] These extra rations were required by the retinues of officers' valets, who could form as much as 10 or 20 percent of men associated with a regiment, although they could not be counted as soldiers.[84]

Rations that a unit was entitled to, but chose not to collect, would be bought back at a set rate by the *munitionnaire*. Officers, for example, might choose to buy good white bread for their tables rather than eat the coarser *pain de munition*. The buy-backs, or "*rachats*," turned out to be an important part of the *munitionnaire*'s accounts, since they were bought back at considerably less than they cost the *munitionnaire*, and he cleared the difference.[85]

Meat

Military authorities were well aware that men enduring the hard conditions of life in the ranks could not survive by bread alone. As Vauban wrote from the camp at Charleroi in 1693: "They cannot work two hours without resting . . . . In a word, one can do almost nothing since they are weakened by hunger, for they are reduced to *pain de munition* alone."[86] For soldiers to bear up to fatigue, they had to have meat in their diets.

Army meat rations varied far more according to regulation than did bread rations: Provisions varied over time and according to whether troops were on the march in the *étapes* system, in garrison or winter quarters, or on campaign. The *étapes* system was most generous, perhaps out of consideration for troops who endured those long marches while traveling from place to place. In addition, troopers got more than infantrymen on *étapes*, even at a time when mounted troops enjoyed no meat allowance at all when on campaign. The *étapes* regulations of 1636 prescribed one pound of meat for

[82] André, *Le Tellier*, 430–31.

[83] For example, see the *règlement* for *étapes* of 12 November 1665, article six, and Mallet, *Compts rendus*, 163–64.

[84] See Chapter 7 concerning valets. Quincy complained of "an infection of domestics mounted on the horses of their masters which form a quarter of the company." AG, A¹595, 1 January 1678, Quincy to Louvois, in Rousset, *Louvois*, 2:480.

[85] Concerning *rachats*, see Nodot, *Le munitionnaire*, 376–85.

[86] Vauban to Le Pelletier, 3 November 1693, in Albert Rochas d'Aiglun, *Vauban, sa famille et ses écrits*, 2 vols. (Paris: 1910), 2:404.

infantry per day but allowed cavalry two pounds, an amount repeated in a directive of 1693.[87]

For most of the *grand siècle,* the infantry received a daily meat ration on campaign, but cavalry did not. That basic ration stood at one half pound a day, except for Friday, in deference to Catholic practice. This meat was not free, and circa 1690, the state deducted its value from the soldiers' pay at the rate of 1 sol, 5 deniers the ration.[88] Before the Nine Years' War, meat was not a necessary part of the rations supplied to cavalry in the field. An interesting directive from Louvois during the brief war of 1683–84 stated that "The King does not want to give meat to the cavalry because a trooper who has 3 sols per day and bread is capable of buying it for himself, and one has only to make sure that the officer gives him these three sols exactly."[89] But if a trooper had no money, he had no meat. In 1677, an order at the camp of Ninoue announced that while the infantry had meat, the cavalry had no money; therefore, "many men will have need of food."[90]

During the last two great wars of Louis XIV, meat was added to the allotment for mounted troops, who in the War of the Spanish Succession, were supposed to receive 24 ounces of bread and one half pound of fresh meat daily in addition to their campaign pay.[91] In any case, meat was not normally provided in garrison and winter quarters, when a soldier provided his own out of his pay.

The most common contract supplier of meat was the *munitionnaire* who kept the army in bread, but other entrepreneurs provided meat on the hoof. A contract of 1672 was to provide men with two pounds of meat every three to four days, or roughly the half pound a day regulation ration.[92] In January 1689, the *intendant* La Goupillière contracted with a Frankfort supplier to

[87] Babeau, *La vie militaire,* 1:125, 127, 128, 128n. See, as well, Nord, C 2230, November 1678; and Letter of 14 August 1681 in Jacques Hardré, ed. *Letters of Louvois, University of North Carolina Studies in the Romance Languages and Literatures,* no. 10 (Chapel Hill: 1949), 167–68. Code Michau, 1629, article 272, in François André Isambert et al., eds. *Recueil général des anciennes lois françaises, depuis l'an 420, jusqu'a la Révolution de 1789,* vol. 16 (Paris: 1829), 293; SHAT, Bib., Col. des ord., vol. 32, #8. While Babeau doubted that this meat ration was ever really supplied, *étapes* tickets from Dijon state that rations were supplied exactly as ordered, including the pound of meat. Dijon, H 218 bis. During the early period, some cavalrymen were allowed three pounds, half in beef and half in mutton. Babeau, *La vie militaire,* 1:127n. Perhaps so much was there because this was a two-ration subsidy, as some cavalrymen were allowed. Three pounds per day is too much for a single person.

[88] Joseph Servan, *Recherches sur la force de l'armée française, depuis Henri IV jusqu'a la fin de 1806* (Paris: 1806), "Tableau de la valeur intrinséque de la solde, 1600–1805"; Belhomme, *L'armée française en 1690,* 153; Babeau, *La vie militaire,* 1:125.

[89] AG, A¹734, #59, letter from Louvois to Crequi, 16 April 1684 in Hardré, *Lettres,* 420.

[90] AG, A¹539, #2, 16 June 1677, order of Camp de Ninoue.

[91] See AG, A¹688, #98, letter from Louvois to Peletier, 24 August 1683 in Hardré, *Lettres,* 253; AG, A¹734, #59, letter from Louvois to Crequi, 16 April 1684 in Hardré, *Lettres,* 420; and the charts of campaign pay in Mallet, *Compts rendus,* 169–70.

[92] AG, A¹294, #29, 6 Aug. 1672.

purchase 6,650 sheep for the French army, and later that year, marshal Duras from Strasbourg ordered an entrepreneur to supply meat to his men.[93] The next year Louvois again contracted with entrepreneurs for meat, though this would not be for high-ranked officers because if they were to receive army meat, they would take all the best for themselves.[94] Cattle might cross significant distances to reach troops. In 1709, the government paid La Bourdonnaye to ship 1,500 head from Bordeaux to French forces in Spain.[95] But when money was tight, meat was probably the first item cut out of the soldier's diet, as Villars revealed in his description of hard times in the War of the Spanish Succession, when the king, "for lack of money, ceased to give the troops meat that he was accustomed to giving them."[96]

But entrepreneurs were not the only source of meat for the army. Armies may have found it difficult to depend on raids and requisitions for bread, but livestock remained a prime target for war parties. Its mobility saved the raiders even from having to secure transport; meat animals simply plodded along after the army and were butchered on the spot when needed. Interestingly enough, when parties did bring in meat on the hoof, it seems to have been awarded by priority to cavalry units.[97] This ability to secure its own meat in the field through the activity of war parties may further explain why cavalry did not receive a regular meat ration until relatively late.

Magazines and Convoys

Magazines were fundamental to keeping the large armies of the *grand siècle* in the field. The evolution of magazines did not begin with either Louvois or his father. As previously stated, stores of grain and forage had been amassed in the sixteenth century for winter quarters or even to support troops in the field. Potter's study of Picardy reveals that all major Picard towns boasted magazines in the first half of the sixteenth century and that *munitionnaires* contracted to keep them stocked.[98] Richelieu, too, set up magazines for the next campaign.[99] The fact that grain was collected in lieu of taxes or bought in large quantity for military use implies that it was stored in central sites, in, for want of a better word, de facto magazines. This evidence contradicts any claim, such as André seems to make, that Le Tellier originated the process of collection and storage. Without question, in the 1640s, Le Tellier went about the process of setting up magazines with great vigor, in part as a response to the failings of *munitionnaires*.[100] Constant war from 1635 to 1659 meant that the repeated creation of grain stores resembled the more permanent

---

[93] AG, A¹874 in Ronald Thomas Ferguson, "Blood and Fire: Contribution Policy of the French Armies in Germany (1668–1715)," Ph.D. dissertation, University of Minnesota, 1970, 105; AG, A¹875, 29 April 1689.
[94] Rousset, *Louvois*, 4:303.   [95] AN, G⁷1094, 11 June 1709.   [96] Villars, *Mémoires*, 3:49.
[97] Nord, C 2333, 17 April 1674; AG, A¹538, #446, 5 June 1677; AG, A¹539, #37, 18 June 1677.
[98] Potter, 196–98.   [99] Parrott, "The Administration of the French Army," 44.
[100] For Le Tellier's work with magazines, see André, *Le Tellier*, 455–68.

magazines of Louvois. With the return of peace, most of the magazines created by Le Tellier vanished with the return of peace, but he also created some permanent stores in key fortresses, such as Dunkirk, Arras, Brisach, and Pinerolo.[101] Already with Le Tellier, the *intendants* bore the responsibility of making sure that the magazines were stocked.

Louvois may not have founded the first great magazines, a feat that Rousset credits him with, but he certainly made a significant contribution.[102] If Le Tellier sketched the blueprint of a system of magazines, Louvois built it into the kind of structure that could support the weight of the massive armies that fought later.[103] The contemporary general Puységur ascribed the new dependence on magazines under Louis XIV to the increased size of armies, whose great proportions tied them to such storehouses.[104] Rousset credits Louvois with setting a standard that fortresses should at all times house enough grain for six-month's rations.[105] Beyond this, he also built up great general magazines on the frontier to feed field armies. The ministry charged *intendants* with stocking permanent magazines in fortresses and *commissaires* with inspecting them.[106]

The Dutch War saw the triumph of Louvois's magazine system. At the outset of the 1672 advance, he had accumulated enough grain for 200,000 rations a day for a full six months in seven magazines.[107] Such an impressive accumulation of grain was not a one-time affair. In preparation for the 1675 campaign, Louvois built up grain magazines. He ordered a total of 40,000 septiers of grain to be collected and stored at Maestricht and Liège, enough for seventy-five days at the stipulated rate of 80,000 rations per day.[108]

Sieges called for particularly prodigious accumulations of supplies. In preparation for the siege of Dunkirk, the French, with Jacquier in charge, planned to collect biscuits and enough flour to produce 400,000 rations of bread in 1657.[109] Later conflicts called for even greater efforts. For the siege of Mons in 1693, the attacking French army required a total of 360,000 rations per day from Namur, Philippeville, Dinant, and Givet, with the ovens established at Judoigne.[110]

It was often the duty of *munitionnaires* to fill up the magazines intended to support wartime campaigns; they generally went to work in the spring to

[101] André, *Le Tellier*, 468.

[102] Rousset, *Louvois*, 1:248–50, credits Louvois with the creation of magazines.

[103] Magazines founded by Le Tellier or Louvois followed the same rules as laid down through the *commissaires généraux des vivres*, drafted under Le Tellier. André, *Le Tellier et Louvois*, 375.

[104] Perjés, "Army Provisioning," 38.   [105] Rousset, *Louvois*, 1:249.

[106] André, *Le Tellier et Louvois*, 375.

[107] Louis XIV, *Oeuvres de Louis XIV*, Philippe Grimoard and Grouvelle, eds., 6 vols. (Paris: 1806), 3:117.

[108] AG, A¹433, 5 April 1675, Louvois to Morceau. I thank my student George Satterfield for putting me on to this document.

[109] Jules Mazarin, *Lettres du cardinal Mazarin*, eds. P. Chéruel and G. d'Avenel, vols. 6–9 (Paris: 1890–1906), 8:171. Mazarin to Turenne, 24 September 1657.

[110] Belhomme, *L'armée française en 1690*, 192–93.

accomplish this task.[111] Completely integrated with the system of magazines, *munitionnaires* even built up permanent stores in fortresses.[112] Stores collected by government agents or long-term purchases could also be turned over to *munitionnaires* charged with supporting a particular campaign, on condition that they purchase the grain from the government or later on replace it with new stores.[113] In this manner, existing magazines sped the work of the *munitionnaires*.

Intentionally left in the dark as to the exact details of the campaign, *munitionnaires* had little option but to spread their stocks in a series of magazines. Only at the last moment were they told the army's assembly point and line of advance.[114] The desire to disguise plans for the next campaign determined not only the need to multiply magazines along an entire front but also the sites chosen for them.[115] Of course, uncertainty concerning the enemy's plans also encouraged the creation of multiple magazines. Villars wrote that an army needed to scatter about in magazines half again as much flour as it would actually consume on campaign, "because, not knowing where the enemy will carry the war it is necessary to be able to move in a number of different directions."[116] As will be seen, the mountains of forage held in magazines had nearly as great an impact on campaigns as the grain there.

Magazines held more than grain and fodder. As early as 1667, Louis boasted that his magazines contained "all the things that one could imagine for war."[117] Secure fortress magazines provided the best places to store the weapons of war. At the close of the Nine Years' War, Metz contained 500 artillery pieces and small arms for 20,000 men.[118] The amount and variety of stores amassed for a major siege was staggering. For the attack on Mons, the French stocked 220,000 red-skinned Dutch cheeses in the citadel of Tournai.[119] This says nothing of the gabions, facines, shells, cannonballs, grenades, and so on that a siege required.[120]

To the extent that armies supplied themselves from stores diligently collected in the rear by *intendants* and *munitionnaires*, convoys became the essential links from magazines, to ovens, to field armies. Not surprisingly, instructions on how to form, move, and protect convoys fill treatises on

[111] Nodot, *Le munitionnaire*, comments on magazines repeatedly, e.g., 122.
[112] Rousset, *Louvois*, 1:249.
[113] Nodot, *Le munitionnaire*, 570. See, for example, the contract with Espines, 1694, in Nodot, *Le munitionnaire*, 531–50.
[114] Nodot, *Le munitionnaire*, 122.
[115] Louis sited his magazines in Picardie to threaten both England and Spain in order to confuse potential enemies in 1666. Louis, *Oeuvres*, 2:161–62.
[116] Letter of 1 June 1709 to Louis XIV in Villars, *Mémoires*, 3:46.
[117] Louis, *Mémoires*, 2:156.   [118] Corvisier, *Les Français et l'armée*, 218–19.
[119] Christopher Duffy, *The Fortress in the Age of Vauban and Frederick the Great, 1660–1789, Siege Warfare*, vol. 2 (London: 1985), 29.
[120] See, for example, AG, A¹209, #81, on amounts needed for siege of Luxembourg, 10 July 1667.

warfare written during the *grand siècle*.[121] Nodot lays out careful guidelines for escorts in plain and mountain terrain, prescribing cavalry for the first and infantry for the latter and declaring that the escort be placed in thirds at the front, middle, and rear of the convoy. Orders for and reports of convoys appear constantly in the correspondence at the Archives de guerre.[122] Concern to protect convoys reached strategic, or at least operational, proportions, as when Vauban urged that the French take Charleroi, in part because the need to supply escorts to protect convoys from raiding parties based on Charleroi was taking too many troops.[123]

Not only land routes but rivers proved immensely important for convoys, and thus river lines had to be protected.[124] Rivers proved particularly important supply lines when large quantities of food, siege supplies, and heavy artillery could be best moved by water. In order to ensure supplies on river routes, the army maintained companies of *galiots*, small armed gunboats, created in the 1670s, and companies of boatmen. These latter companies contained not only sailors but soldiers as well for protection against attacks from the banks, such as those mounted by snipers – *schnapphahns* – along the Rhine.[125] In September 1709, Villars's army was bound to the Escaut because Villars depended on river-borne convoys.[126] His experience was not unique.

FODDER

Not only men had to eat; horses too had to be fed. A seventeenth-century field army included a huge number of animals; a force of 60,000 soldiers probably required 20,000 horses for the cavalry and 20,000 for other purposes.[127] The mountain of fodder necessary to feed so many beasts far exceeded by weight and bulk the piles of bread amassed in the *parc des vivres*. The collection of fodder always proved burdensome and sometimes brought danger, but without fodder to fuel it, such a horse-drawn army stopped dead in its tracks.

The ration of forage stayed relatively constant. *Réglements* defined it in detail mainly for winter quarters or *étapes*, when it was composed of dry forage, although on campaign, horses ate green forage and oats. The 1651

---

[121] For information on convoys, see Nodot, *Le munitionnaire*, 60, 77–78; BN, f. fr. 6257, Villars, "Traité de la guerre de campagne."

[122] For example, see AG, A^{1}209, #38, 18 June 1667; AG, A^{1}433, many letters dating from May 1675; AG, A^{1}539, #285, 3 July 1677; AG, A^{1}539, #324, 7 July 1677; AG, A^{1}703, #113, 20 October 1683, in Hardré, 280; AG, A^{1}1215, #35, 17 August 1695, in Ferguson, "Blood and Fire," 145; AG, A^{1}2266, #141, état 23 April – 4 May 1710.

[123] Vauban to Le Pelletier, 29 June 1693, in Rochas d'Aiglun, *Vauban*, 2:390.

[124] For example, in 1667, Créqui left troops along the river to keep the Mozelle open for waterborne convoys. AG, A^{1}209, #16, 29 May 1667, Créqui to Louvois.

[125] Belhomme, *L'armée française en 1690*, 67–69.   [126] Villars, *Mémoires*, 3:63.

[127] Perjés, "Army Provisioning," 14.

winter-quarters regulation set a ration of forage at 20 pounds of hay and 10 of straw or 25 of hay; in addition, the horse was to receive 4 pecks of oats.[128] By 1665, this had altered somewhat to 20 pounds of hay and 4 pecks of oats.[129] By 1710, this was further differentiated for winter quarters into separate rations for infantry horses and cavalry horses. Infantry mounts received 12 pounds of hay and 8 of straw, or 16 of hay, plus 2 pecks of oats. Cavalry chargers got more: 15 pounds of hay and 5 of straw or 18 pounds of hay, plus 2 pecks of oats.[130] Some military authorities suggested stretching forage rations farther by mixing chopped straw with grain when it was late in the season and forage had to be hauled in from some distance.[131] If a trooper or officer had to buy his own forage, the price far exceeded that of his own rations. During the winter of 1688–89, the French figured forage as 20 sols per ration.[132] In the War of the Spanish Succession, officers could receive 16 sols per day to buy their own forage.[133]

Since officers were expected to have valets and extra horses, they received extra forage rations, just as they got extra measures of bread and meat. In 1651, a cavalry *mestre de camp* was to collect 12 rations of forage, a captain 6, a lieutenant 4, and a cornet 3.[134] About the same time, infantry officers enjoyed a less generous scale, with a *mestre de camp* at 8, a captain at 4, a lieutenant at 3, and an ensign at 2.[135] These rates stayed constant for the company-grade officers for the reign of Louis XIV.[136] The changes occurred for the field grades. In 1665, cavalry *mestres de camp* claimed 7 rations, while lieutenant colonels had 6; infantry colonels received 4. During the War of the Spanish Succession, cavalry *mestres de camp* got 12, while their lieutenant colonels got 10; infantry colonels then claimed 10 rations of forage, and their lieutenant colonels 7.

In special circumstances, *munitionnaires* might be hired to supply forage, as in 1708, when one contracted to provide 200 rations of fodder per day per squadron of cavalry and 100 per battalion of infantry in Rousillon.[137] But in general, and certainly for the large armies that fought in Flanders and along the Rhine, fodder had to be found in the fields. When on campaign, green grass rather than dried hay provided the bulk of the horse's diet. Carting green forage any great distance in the summer would have been prohibitive. Consider a hypothetical supply wagon pulled by four horses and carrying

---

[128] 4 November 1651 regulation for winter quarters in André, *Le Tellier*, 672.

[129] Articles 3–6, *règlement* for *étapes*, 12 November 1665.

[130] Rations statement, circa 1710, Mallet, *Compts rendus*, 165.

[131] Diderot et al., *Encyclopédie*, 15:582.

[132] AG, A¹829, 26 and 28 December 1688, in Ferguson, "Blood and Fire," 94.

[133] AG, A¹2265, #167.

[134] 4 November 1651 regulation for winter quarters in André, *Le Tellier*, 672–73.

[135] André, *Le Tellier*, 433.

[136] Compare articles 4–6, 12 November 1665, *règlement* on winter quarters and the extensive material on pay, *étapes*, and rations of the French army ca. 1710 in Mallet, *Compts rendus*, 165.

[137] AN, G⁷1093, vivres de Rousillon, 5 May 1708.

about 1,200 pounds. Since each of its four horses consumed about 50 pounds of green fodder each day, the team ate 200 pounds of green fodder per day.[138] Therefore, during a round trip three days up from a depot and three days back, the horses would require their entire load for themselves and have nothing to deliver. And this says nothing about the tendency of green fodder to rot unless it is properly dried. Dry fodder simplified the problem, since it weighed only about 20 pounds per horse per day; however, the hypothetical team would still consume 40 percent of its load.

These calculations do not take into consideration that European horses also required grain, usually oats, as well as roughage. Because some wagon space had to be devoted to grain, in reality, the wagons could carry even less green fodder than hypothesized here. For example, Nodot reported that each of the 100 horses in an *équipage* of twenty-five wagons consumed six pounds of oats per day, making for a daily total of 600 pounds – or one half a wagonload.[139]

The problems involved in carting fodder explain why it had to be burnt, rather than removed, to deny it to the enemy when the French withdrew from an area. In pulling back before enemy forces in 1688, Montclar ordered that Peyssonel "consume all the forage he can, . . . and burn the rest . . . . I shall take measures to have all the forage from the outskirts of the said city burned."[140]

An army simply had to harvest its own fodder most of the time, and the task of reaping it was great. If a force of 60,000 men had 40,000 horses, such a field force needed to cut and carry 1,000 tons daily. Most commonly, forage was bundled in cloth sheets, bound, and carried on horses' backs, rather than heaped into wagons.[141] If each horse sent on a forage party carried back 200 pounds of forage and forage parties went out every two days, then half the army's horses had to be sent out foraging. This task involved a great many men; clearly, a cavalryman spent far more time wielding a sickle than a sword. Perjés estimates at 4,000 to 10,000 the number of men necessary to mow forage for an army of 60,000 troops.[142] The contemporary Quincy mentioned a single party involving 15,000 men in 1710.[143] Such great forces required high-ranking officers in charge. As a rule, the lieutenant general of the day took charge of foraging, including assigning each unit a portion of the acreage that the army's *maréchal général de logis* surveyed in advance.[144]

---

[138] Perjès, "Army Provisioning," 16–17, gives the weight of green fodder as 25 kg and dry as 10 kg. Van Creveld, *Supplying War*, 24, allows a dry ration of 20 pounds and green forage as twice that.

[139] Nodot, *Le munitionnaire*, 30.   [140] AG, A¹829, 20 December 1688, Montclar to Louvois.

[141] Nodot, *Le munitionnaire*, 53–54 and 77–78. Contamine, *Histoire militaire*, vol. 1, plate 91, after page 466, is a fine illustration of men cutting and bundling forage, ca. 1700.

[142] Facts and figures on foraging come from Perjés, "Army Provisioning," 14–19, unless otherwise stated.

[143] Quincy, *Histoire militaire de Louis le Grand roi de France*, 7 vols. (La Haye: 1727), 6:381.

[144] Belhomme, *L'armée française en 1690*, 185–86.

Foraging entailed fighting, since large forces were often involved and the enemy did everything it could to interrupt and interfere.[145] The French, of course, did the same, as when Villars sent 2,000 cavalry against the enemy's forage party near Saint-Pol on 24 August 1710.[146] Such attacks on enemy forage parties were significant enough to be reported in the *Gazette*.[147]

The need to provide adequate fodder went a long way to set the rhythms of war in the *grand siècle*. Lack of grass in the fields compelled armies to withdraw to winter quarters every fall, and the growth of spring grass controlled the onset of the campaign season the next year. Administrators kept watch on the progress of the season and rated how well the pastures could support troops, as when Bellefonds reported to Louvois on 27 April 1684, "The grass is advanced enough to support 70 squadrons of 160 troopers each."[148]

Although, ultimately, horses had to be fed green forage during the campaign season, an ample stock of dry forage stored in magazines and supplied to armies early in the spring could allow the French to take the field weeks before their enemies, especially the Dutch, who had to wait for adequate grass in the fields.[149] As the Dutch Council of State commented: "The French habitually made considerable progress in the Spanish Netherlands in the winter and early spring, before we could subsist in the open field. This advantage is not just a question of superior forces, but proceeds from the practice of making magazines on the borders . . . . On our side, in that season, . . . we lack the fodder."[150] This French advantage was so prized that the advanced spring of 1676 worried Louvois: "It will be distressing if those who have no magazines can put themselves on campaign only a little while after me."[151]

Magazines did not always free the French from the constraints of weather and time. A hard winter, as in 1668, could still delay the opening of their campaign.[152] When the French could not build up stores due to natural conditions, lack of funds, or administrative shortcomings, they, too, became strictly subject to nature's timetable. Villars praised God that grass came two weeks earlier in 1703 to allow his army to move sooner, but in 1710, after the horrendous winter delayed spring, he complained, "Lacking magazines, we can only assemble our armies when the countryside can feed the horses."[153]

---

[145] See Perjés, "Army Provisioning," 18–19.   [146] Villars, *Mémoires*, 3:97.

[147] For example, see the issues of 24 August 1709, 271; and 12 October 1709, 291.

[148] Hardré, *Letters*, 492.   [149] Rousset, *Louvois*, 1:249.

[150] Duffy, *The Fortress in the Age of Vauban and Frederick the Great*, 11. Stephen Baxter says that the Dutch could not establish magazines because money dribbled in from the various provinces to the center too slowly to make advance preparations. Stephen Baxter, *William III and the Defense of European Liberty, 1650–1702* (New York: 1966), 114.

[151] AG, A^{1}483, Roi to Louvois, 2 April 1676, in Rousset, *Louvois*, 2:214.

[152] Rousset, *Louvois*, 1:144.

[153] AG, A^{1}1676, #44, in Ferguson, "Blood and Fire," 14–15; Villars, 15 March 1710, Jean Jacques Pelet and François Vault, eds. *Mémoires militaires relatifs à la succession d'Espagne*, 11 vols. (Paris: 1835–62), 10:241.

Fodder imposed other operational decisions in the field besides the start of spring campaigning. Armies could maintain a camp only as long as the forage lasted. When local sources were exhausted, the army must move, regardless of the operational situation. Louis, for example, instructed Villeroi in 1696 to maintain his camp of Malhelem as long as he could until "the lack of forage obliges you to change it."[154] Abundance or lack of forage could also influence decisions concerning siege warfare – which towns to attack or leave unmolested. Although Mazarin wanted to besiege Frieburg in 1644, the area around the fortress was too depleted to support a siege.[155] Mons could not be besieged effectively in 1684 owing to lack of forage in the area, and less desirable targets were chosen because they could support an army's horses.[156] Nearly a year before commencing a later siege of Mons in 1691, Louvois ordered *intendants* to buy secretly 900,000 rations of hay of fifteen pounds each.[157] In any lengthy siege, forage would ultimately have to be carted in from a distance, as local supplies gave out. Desire to exploit forage on enemy or neutral territory also compelled armies to campaign across the French border whenever possible.[158]

So forage magazines, although they did not contain an entire campaign's consumption, could be very important at key moments. Tasks of laying up dry fodder for winter quarters and stocking royal magazines fell primarily to *intendants*. Le Tellier relied on *intendants* for this duty as early as the 1640s, and it remained the task of provincial and army *intendants*.[159] Even in areas that French forces occupied outside their borders, *intendants* enlisted the aid of local authorities in amassing forage, as Robert did in 1667–68.[160] The magazines established under Le Tellier were not permanent, in the sense that they vanished with the peace, whereas his son established permanent magazines.[161] Oats could be shipped in from a distance with the same facility as wheat, but because of its bulk and weight, hay and straw were more closely tied to local sources, unless it could be shipped in by water. When building up stores, authorities might house these in local barns or "other covered and closed places" under the watch of guards residing near the stores and

---

[154] AG, A¹888, #68, 22 July 1696, Louis to Villeroi.

[155] Charles Derek Croxton, "Peacemaking in Early Modern Europe: Cardinal Mazarin and the Congress of Westphalia, 1643–1648," Ph.D. dissertation, University of Illinois at Urbana-Champaign, 1995, 155.

[156] Louvois to Chamlay, 12 June 1684, in Hardré, *Letters*, 366–67. See, as well, the similar problem at Luxembourg. Siege instructions to Créqui, 1 April 1684, in Hardré, *Letters*, 408–14; see also page 425.

[157] AG, A¹1043, 13 May 1790, Louvois to Bagnols and Chauvelin in Rousset, *Louvois*, 4:459.

[158] Forage for Villars's army in Alsace cost 10,000 livres a day, so his *intendant* urged him to move his forces into Germany as soon as possible. Villars to Chamillart, 13 May 1707, AG, A¹2027, #73, in Ferguson, "Blood and Fire," 229.

[159] André, *Le Tellier*, 455–68. See comments of Baxter concerning army *intendants* and forage, Douglas Baxter, *Servants of the Sword, French Military Intendants of the Army, 1630–1670* (Urbana: 1976), 107, 184–85, 190–91.

[160] Baxter, *Servants of the Sword*, 185–86.   [161] André, *Le Tellier*, 460.

responsible for maintaining them in good condition and distributing the forage rations as required.[162] Hay bought to support sieges could be left with the supplier until actually needed, as was the case with forage purchased to support the siege of Mons in 1691.[163]

ÉTAPES

When moving along the stipulated military roads, military units, from small detachments of recruits headed for their new units to entire regiments marching to the front or to winter quarters, lived by *étapes*, a system that determined the manner in which they were fed and housed. The term *étapes* derived from the medieval term for market or fair.[164] By the mid–fifteenth century, it had already taken on the meaning of a village in which foodstuffs were gathered to supply troops.[165] Both it and the term *routes* had become part of the vocabulary of French military ordinances in the mid-sixteenth century.[166] In addition, certain basic practices of *étapes*, such as stipulating that men could stay in each place no more than a single night, except for one day's rest each week, were already prescribed well before 1600.[167]

These facts disprove the often repeated assertion that Louis XIII created the French *étapes* system in his *règlement* of 14 August 1623. Historian of that system Bernard Kroener argues that the 1623 ordinance institutionalized existing practices, rather than originating them.[168] This ordinance defined four main *brisées*, meaning in this case paths, across France: from Picardy to Bayonne; from lower Brittany to Marseille; from mid-Languedoc to mid-Normandy; and from the extremity of Saintonge to the interior of Bresse.[169] These main lines split off into *brisées supplementaires*.[170] *Brisées* of Louis XIII became the military *routes* of Louis XIV. Kroener's study of the routes selected demonstrates that they followed river valleys where possible, which facilitated the transportation of necessary food and fodder.[171] Early in the

---

[162] André, *Le Tellier*, 457.   [163] Rousset, *Louvois*, 4:459.

[164] General Baron Bardin, *Dictionnaire de l'armée de terre ou recherches historiques sur l'art et les usages militaires des anciens et modernes*, 8 vols. (Paris: 1841), 4:2181.

[165] Kroener, *Les routes et les étapes*, 57.

[166] Kroener, *Les routes et les étapes*, 57, 58; Bardin, *Dictionnaire*, 4:2182; David Potter, *War and Government in the French Provinces: Picardy 1470–1560* (Cambridge: 1993), 196. Corvisier credits the 1549 ordinance of Francis I as the first *étapes* ordinance, which may be true, but it may also just have regularized or extended existing practices. Contamine, *Histoire militaire*, 1:344–45. Parker says that the French founded *étapes* for passage to Italy in 1551. Geoffrey Parker, *The Army of Flanders and the Spanish Road, 1567–1659: The Logistics of Spanish Victory and Defeat in the Low Countries Wars* (Cambridge: 1972), 88–89.

[167] See AG, MR 1881, #6, 12 February 1566 and AG, MR 1881, #14, 9 February 1584 for these stipulations.

[168] Kroener, *Les routes et les étapes*, 72–73.   [169] Diderot et al., *Encyclopédie*, 6:16.

[170] André, *Le Tellier*, 417–18.

[171] Studying lists and maps, Kroener determined that with the reorganization of 1666, of the 190 *étapes* villages in northeast France, 73 percent were on rivers, when only 34 percent of all villages in the area were so situated. Kroener, *Les routes et les étapes*, 167.

century, the roads chosen were only 10 to 46 feet wide, but an ordinance of 1669 declared that all major highways be cleared to 72 feet wide.[172]

Three days before entering a particular province or *généralité* by one of the prescribed routes, a commander on the road was to alert the governor, *intendant*, or major concerning the size of the approaching contingent and the date when it would arrive. Once first sketched out in 1623 and soon elaborated in succeeding ordinances, the *étapes* system showed surprising stability until 1718, at least on paper. The 1665 regulation, which defined *étapes* for the personal reign of Louis XIV, explicitly stated that it upheld regulations dating as far back as 1636.[173]

The 1629 Code Michau commanded that each province set up a system of military roads – that is, decide upon the actual roads that troops would employ and designate which towns would be organized as stops along the way at intervals of one day's march. Later ordinances repeatedly required that provincial authorities draft and update a series of maps of main and subsidiary military roads.[174] Those leading detachments were ordered to stick to these set routes and stay only at stipulated villages and towns on penalty of being deprived of rank in peacetime or executed in wartime. Their troops would be considered as "vagabonds and thieves."[175] Detachments marching along the *brisées* carried with them exact directions for the paths that they were to follow to their destination and the places at which they were to stop for the night; these directions went by the name *routes*. Large units might have a *commissaire à la conduite* with them to supervise the march; small detachments of recruits could be led by a sergeant or a lieutenant. The 1665 ordinance enjoined whoever was in charge "to follow exactly his march, from day to day, to the places written on his *route*, without lodging or staying anyplace else, and for a single night only in each place of *étape*, unless it is prescribed by his *route* to stay. And if the days of marching and those of resting are not marked on his *route*, he can, after eight days of marching, and not otherwise, rest in a place for one day only."[176] As the collection of *routes* preserved at Amiens and other surviving records demonstrate, under Louis XIV, soldiers on the road enjoyed very little, if any, latitude.

No later than the 1640s, regulations speak of the creation of magazines for the furnishing of *étapes*. The ordinance of 30 August 1643 commanded that

---

[172] Kroener, *Les routes et les étapes*, 62.

[173] The preamble of the *règlement* of 12 November 1665 states: "The King, being made to represent the regulations and ordinances concerning the providing and distribution of the *étapes*, police and discipline of soldiers marching to the field . . . of 27 March 1636, 4 October 1641, 26 February 1642, . . . 8 November 1644, and 30 September 1648, His Majesty has ordered and orders conforming to these, that which follows."

[174] André, *Le Tellier*, 418–20. See the detailed discussion of *étapes* maps in Kroener, *Les routes et les étapes*, particularly vol. 1, 68–72 and 166–70 and the maps in vol. 2.

[175] Code Michau, 1629, article 252, in Isambert et al., *Recueil général des anciennes lois*, 16:289.

[176] Article 11, 12 November 1665 ordinance.

such magazines be established at each designated *étape* town "for wheat and other things that can be preserved there."[177]

The 1623 regulation dealt only with the places at which soldiers would be quartered for the night, not with the job of feeding them. Of course, the three-day warning stipulated by the 1623 ordinance gave local officials time to collect foodstuffs and mill flour. By the end of the 1620s, however, royal command would determine the amount and cost of rations for troops marching by *étapes*. As already discussed concerning food rations, *étapes* rations were more generous than those provided to troops in garrison or on campaign. Probably this derives from the fact that troops on *étapes* marched all day long, as opposed to the greater repose of camp life. Cavalry also received rations when on *étapes*, even during periods when they normally had to purchase their food in garrison or on campaign.[178]

The Administration of Étapes *and Footing the Bill*

During the seventeenth century, at least four different methods were used to supply and pay for these rations consumed by troops on the military roads. First and most primitive, communities warned of the approach of troops would assemble food that would then be sold directly to the soldiers, who would purchase it from their pay. This was the practice for garrison troops and for detachments on the road in the late sixteenth and early seventeenth centuries, and it remained an option, intermittently practiced throughout the kingdom until 1665. In some areas, it even continued throughout the reign of Louis XIV, but then it was an exception, not the rule. Another method that did not survive as general practice after the Peace of the Pyrenees required communities to supply the food to soldiers entirely without charge, meaning that these communities were not reimbursed by the monarchy; consequently, *étapes* became a kind of tax. Two other methods employed before 1659 became the rule after that date – state reimbursement and contracting. In the one case, communities collected and distributed food and were then reimbursed by the province or monarchy. In the other case, an entrepreneur, known as an *étapier*, contracted with provinces or directly with the monarchy to supply rations at a set rate.

The first method, direct purchase by soldiers, had the advantage of requiring very little administration. The existing pay system became a supply system, as troops spent their wages to feed themselves. Some *étapes* ordinances prescribed payment out of pocket. Whereas the 1629 regulation provided that troops were to receive their food without charge, the ordinance of 1633 stipulated that soldiers were to pay: "We order that whatever will be taken

---

[177] SHAT, Bib., Col. des ord., vol. 16, #83. See, as well, the reference to magazines for *étapes* in the 4 October 1641 ordinance. Col. des ord., vol. 16, #28.

[178] See as examples, articles 3 and 6, 12 November 1665 ordinance on *étapes*, and the *étapes* table, circa 1710, in Mallet, *Comptes rendus*, 166.

by the said men of war for their food will be paid for at the time according to the price of the last three markets . . . ."[179] And even if the ordinance of 1636 went back to the provision of free food, one issued in 1637 ordered that troops pay for food on the march just as they did in garrison, but this seems to have been for limited purposes.[180] In any case, payment out of pocket was less common in the ordinances than some critics supposed.[181] No matter how attractive the simplicity of this system, it suffered inherent disadvantages, the most serious of which was an entirely practical one – for troops to buy their food en route, they had to be paid. Given the irregularities of pay, at least before 1659, such a system risked forcing soldiers to pillage. Briquet, who incorrectly thought that payment by soldiers was the rule and not the exception before the personal reign of Louis XIV, voiced another criticism in the eighteenth century. In explaining why Louis XIV decided to supply troops directly with food and not ask them to purchase it from their pay, Briquet argued that once troops had money in their pockets, they would try to keep it there by simply stealing food along their route of march. In fact, when the French dropped direct supply and went back to purchase by soldiers in 1718, similar problems occurred.[182]

Despite its inherent problems, supply by direct soldier purchase endured in certain areas late into the reign of Louis XIV. A survey of *intendants* in 1697–98 produced some surprising reports. "In all Hainault," stated the *intendant*, "the garrison troops and those in passage live by means of their pay."[183] His colleague in Artois wrote: "The *étape* is not established at all in Artois, the troops who pass through are lodged in barracks and live there by their pay."[184]

Since the presence of troops might drive up prices, ordinances such as those of 1628 and 1629 set prices for essential items.[185] This repeated the practice used in garrisons where troops regularly purchased their own rations. The most usual standard was to pay the amount established over that last three markets, as was the case in the ordinance of 14 February 1633.[186] Even Louis XIV addressed just this problem: "Foodstuffs go up in price naturally everywhere when a surplus of men capable of consuming them arrives."[187]

It was more common, even before 1665, for ordinances to stipulate that soldiers were to receive their rations gratis. This practice began as early as the great ordinance of 1629, which established as a general rule that food would

---

[179] Ordinance of 14 February 1633, SHAT, Bib., Col. des ord., vol. 14, #25.

[180] SHAT, Bib., Col. des ord., vol. 15, #18.

[181] Briquet, *Code militaire*, vol. 2 (Paris: 1741), 323–26, criticized the system for requiring the soldiers to pay, a criticism picked up soon by the article "Étapes" in Diderot et al., *Encyclopédie*, vol. 6, 16, and perpetuated in André, *Le Tellier*, 418.

[182] Briquet, *Code militaire*, 2:323–26. This article in Briquet was the basis for the article "Étapes" in Diderot's *Encyclopédie*, vol. 6, 16.

[183] Corvisier, *Les Français*, 259.   [184] Corvisier, *Les Français*, 259.

[185] Kroener, *Les routes et les étapes*, 73.   [186] SHAT, Bib., Col. des ord., vol. 14, #25.

[187] Louis, *Oeuvres*, 2:89–90.

be supplied to the troops "without the soldier having to pay anything for it."[188] While some provisions of this ordinance were altered in 1633, as mentioned earlier, that of 1636 restored the procedures of 1629.[189] But if soldiers received food free of charge to them, who actually gave the food to them, and who picked up the bill – the town, the *généralité*, the province, or the monarchy? At times it was clearly the locality that did the work and paid the tab. In 1636, the monarchy accounts for the fact that soldiers were not to be charged for food on the road by the fact that "the King having recognized that the payment that he has made for several years to all his troops for their subsistence and places of their route and passage, has been an excessive charge on his finance . . . ."[190]

But more generally, the task of rounding up foodstuffs fell to entrepreneurs, or *étapiers*, who performed much like *munitionnaires*, or in the absence of *étapiers*, the task went to local officials.[191] Under Louis XIII, communities were to put aside an amount of money sufficient to buy the necessary food for troops passing through.[192] The more usual writ of the regulations provided for reimbursement to localities that provided food to troops in passage.[193] Such considerable variety as to the source and method of payment typified by the regulations promulgated during the war with Spain that they leave an impression of expediency rather than rational system. One promises repayment "by means of a great fund of money that His Majesty is now distributing in each province," while another pledges that if localities supply and pay for the food, they will be compensated by deducting "a similar sum . . . from the *taille* and other impositions."[194]

André credits Le Tellier with a major shift in the regulation of 1643 and its successor; "He proposed . . . to put the provision of *étapes* at the charge

---

[188] Code Michau, 1629, article 272, in Isambert et al., *Recueil général des anciennes lois*, 16:293. See also the ordinance of 9 October 1629 in Jules Caillet, *De l'administration en France sous le ministère du Cardinal de Richelieu* (Paris: 1857), 370–71.

[189] Caillet, *De l'adminstration en France*, 371.

[190] Ordinance of 26 March 1636, SHAT, Bib., Col. des ord., vol. 14, #94.

[191] Regulations already refer to entrepreneurs supplying *étapes* as *étapiers* as early as 25 February 1642, and regularly thereafter. SHAT, Bib., Col. des ord., vol. 16, #44. This contradicts Kroener, *Les routes et les étapes*, 121, for whom the term *étapier* "is first found entering the official military terminology, however, towards the end of the century."

[192] Henri Thomas, *Droit romain des requisitions militaires et du logement des gens de guerre chez les Romains, sous la république et sous l'empire. Droit français des requisitions militaires et du logement des gens de guerre en France, depuis le Ve siècle jusqu'en 1789* (Paris: 1884), 177–78.

[193] AG, A¹ 62, ordinance of 26 March 1640. This refers back to 1636 for most provisions. So will the ordinance of 15 October 1640, SHAT, Bib., Col. des ord., vol. 15, #112.

[194] SHAT, Bib., Col. des ord., vol. 16, #28, 4 October 1641; SHAT, Bib., Col. des ord., tome 16, #79. For other examples of repayment arrangements, see AG, A¹62, #101, ordinance of 26 March 1640; SHAT, Bib., Col. des ord., vol. 16, #28; SHAT, Bib., Col. des ord., vol. 16, #130; SHAT, Bib., Col. des ord., vol. 18, #127; poster of 9 September 1652, Cotes d'Or, C 3673; Kroener, *Les routes et les étapes*, 109; and provisions of the 26 March 1636 ordinance, as repeated in 26 March 1640, in Patrick Landier, "Guerre, violences, et société en France, 1635–1659," doctorat de troisième cycle, dissertation, Université de Paris IV, 1978. 21.

of the state and no longer at the charge of the inhabitants."[195] For André, Le Tellier simplified the system and shifted power away from local authorities and placed it in the hands of the *intendants*.[196] But at best, this is true only to a degree; because earlier regulations already stressed the *généralité*, the role of the *intendant* could be seen as a product of preexisting reliance on this administrative district and thus predates Le Tellier. The ordinance of 1641, two years before Le Tellier came to office, already empowered the *intendant*, not local officials, to prepare the accounts of the *étapes*. And since localities ran the *étapes* if an *étapier* could not be found, Le Tellier did not really eliminate local officials, even into the 1650s.[197] Hence, again we see here more evolution than revolution under Le Tellier; regulations of 1623 and 1629 brought more important shifts than did Le Tellier. Once more, André tends to underestimate French military/administrative structures before Le Tellier and overestimate the immediate effect that Le Tellier had on the actual day-to-day operation of affairs, at least before 1659.

The basic statement of *étapes* for the personal reign of Louis XIV was the *règlement* of 12 November 1665, itself the culmination of nearly forty years of such ordinances. Its preamble specifically appeals to *étapes* ordinances of 1636, 1641, 1642, 1644, and 1648. This *règlement* required that detachments were, of course, to follow their *routes* exactly and give the standard three-day's notice to authorities that the soldiers would be coming. The list of the officials to be informed included governors, *intendants*, *trésoriers* of the *étapes*, and municipal leaders. Each time the unit crossed into a *généralité*, it had to stand for review early in the morning, so that heads could be counted to tally with the *route*. Upon arrival in a town, the unit would march, flags waving and drums beating, to a public space and form into line. There the bans would be read to the men, informing them of the penalties for infractions against regulations. After the men were counted, local officials would give officers slips of paper identifying which houses would quarter troops and how many men each would take. Officers would then assign particular quarters to particular men. Meanwhile the *étapier*, or his representative, or, failing these, local officials, would distribute the food to the hosts, who would then take it to their homes.[198] At their quarters, men would receive the *utensile*, defined as bed, pot, bowl, glass, and a place by the fire and the candle. Before leaving the next day, the troops assembled, and their hosts could lodge any complaints that they might have with the proper authorities.

The 1665 ordinance assumes *étapiers* and speaks of a *fond des étapes,* under

---

[195] André, *Le Tellier*, 418.   [196] André, *Le Tellier*, 418–19.

[197] The 2 October 1651 ordinance again urged officials to find an entrepreneur to furnish *étapes* either for entire *généralités* or the smaller elections, but if none could be found, private people were to supply *étapes* and be reimbursed through deductions from *taille*. SHAT, Bib., Col. des ord., vol. 18, #127.

[198] A later ordinance of 27 March 1668 stated that the *étapiers* were to give the food to the sergeant majors of infantry regiments or to company NCOs. SHAT, Bib., Col. des ord., vol. 22, #14.

the care of the Treasurers of France "who will have the care of furnishing the *étapes*."[199] At least by 1670, *étapes* showed up as a major budget item on royal financial *états*. Beginning at only 613,238 livres in the peaceful year of 1670, it peaked during the Dutch War at 6,165,782 livres in 1675 and reached 10,317,891 in 1695 during the Nine Years' War. An ordinance of 1718 stated that the amount spent on *étapes* during the War of the Spanish Succession climbed to 15 million livres in 1713.[200] But this did not mean that the state paid completely for *étapes* with tax levies, because expenses seem always to have been based on the *généralité*.[201]

Localities still bore heavy financial responsibilities under Louis XIV. Fodder was a case in point. The monarchy benefited from a set price for fodder in some provinces, and the province itself had to make up the difference between what the monarchy paid and what it really cost. As the *intendant* reported, around Lyon, "The king pays 5 sols for [a ration of] forage and the province gives 13."[202] Again, while officials may have preferred to deal with an *étapier*, this was not always possible. A printed order of 1676 in Burgundy complained that an *étapier général* could not be found, so the *intendant* passed the duties on to the provincial estates and the communities.[203] Apparently, this was a recurrent phenomenon in that province, because another printed poster of 1703 declared a reimbursement to communities who provided *étapes*.[204] Therefore, the old practice of dealing directly with towns in the *étapes* system survived right through the reign of Louis XIV, at least when entrepreneurs could not be found.

Contracts and reimbursements were based upon a certain amount of money per ration. In Provence during the Nine Years' War, the rate paid to an *étapier général* stood at 12 sols for an infantryman and 39 sols for a cavalryman and his horse.[205] In Burgundy, it varied during the War of the Spanish Succession from 8 sols per infantryman in 1703 to 10 sols early in 1710 and back to 8 sols by the close of the year.[206]

Promised payments were often late. Although this would be expected for the chaotic period before 1659, long delays for reimbursement continued after that date.[207] Given the relative slowness of seventeenth-century administration,

[199] Corvisier, *Louvois*, 112, describes as part of the regulation of 12 November 1665 a number of things that are not in it.

[200] The amounts listed come from two sources, Mallet, *Comptes rendus*, 353–55, 398–99, 130, and the ordinance of 15 April 1718, SHAT, Bib., Col. des ord., vol. 37, #16.

[201] See, for example, the 1668 ordinance, stating that *étapes* were to be paid for by arrangements with *receveurs généraux des finances* of the *généralités* of kingdom. 27 March 1668, SHAT, Bib., Col. des ord., vol. 22, #14. While the funds for *étapes* were recorded in central financial records, they probably never made it to a central treasury but stayed in the *généralités*.

[202] Corvisier, *Les Français*, 261.

[203] Printed sheet order, 27 August 1676, Côte d'Or, C 3675.

[204] Côte d'Or, C 169.   [205] Corvisier, *Les Français*, 262.

[206] Côte d'Or, C 169, 1703; and C 3676, 2 April 1710.

[207] See, for example, a 1652 order to pay for étapes of 1638 and 1641–47 Dijon, municipality, H 218. See also a list of payments ordered in 1642–43 but dated 28 May 1653. Côte d'Or,

it is not too much out of line that payments could be several years in coming. But it is less excusable that as late as 1680, officials from Autun were still requesting payment of the deficit that they had incurred for lodging and *étapes* in 1666–67, a shortfall of 18,000 livres.[208]

Since the number of troops passing through could be great, the amount of funds laid out by locals could be substantial. From Tours, hardly on the front lines, the *intendant* reported that during the Nine Years' War, 19,000 troops per year passed through that city.[209] During the same war, officials in Burgundy complained that their fund of 260,000 livres for reimbursement of *étapes* would not suffice because of the great passage of troops.[210]

Pillage, Cheating, and Abuse

The problems posed by the *étapes* system in practice far exceeded tardy payments. At the worst, troops on the road simply pillaged on their way with little respect for their *routes*, despite repeated orders to the contrary. Truly horrendous excesses occurred during the war with Spain before 1659. Ordinances from the 1640s and 1650s commanded local officials to arrest the leaders of soldiers not following their *routes*.[211] Of course, such orders did not spell out how town mayors were to separate officers from their armed and often battle-hardened troops. One directive of 1650 stipulated the assembly of the local men at the first sound of alarm bells [*la cloche et du tauxin*] to offer armed resistance, but this could be dangerous.[212]

Cheating on *routes* and billets was not unknown. By claiming that more troops were taken care of than actually were, extra money or rations could be obtained. *Étapiers* were guilty, but so were the common people who quartered soldiers in their homes.[213] Officers might refuse to assemble their men for review, presumably because they had fewer men than they claimed. Such was the case for six captains of the Champagne regiment who received fines of 150 livres at the close of the Dutch War for not undergoing such a review before the aldermen [*echevins*] of Sury.[214] Even sergeants offended; one sergeant Brunet even manufactured phony *routes*.[215]

C 3673. In 1659, the *parlement* sitting in Dijon requested the monarchy either to pay 20 sols per soldier, or at least allow this as a deduction on the *taille*. Dijon, municipal, H218.

[208] Côte d'Or, C 3675, 6 April 1680. See, as well, the case in which *élus* in Burgundy received orders in 1679 to pay for expenses incurred in 1675–77, meaning an arrears of as much as four years. 21 January 1679, Côte d'Or, C3675.

[209] Corvisier, *Les Français*, 247–48.   [210] 31 December 1696, Côte d'Or, C 3676.

[211] See the ordinance of 22 December 1641 in Landier, "Guerre, violences, et société," 19–20.

[212] See the order of 12 February 1650, Dijon, H217 bis. For the dangers of denying *logement*, consider the fate of Sanscoin described in the next chapter.

[213] For one complaint that an *étapier* was turning in *fausse routes*, see AG, A¹2265, #100, 8 February 1710. For an example of cheating by inhabitants, see Côtes d'Or, C 3675, 3 June 1687.

[214] AN, G⁷1774, #68. This document records a number of cases of fines against officers for this reason.

[215] AG, A¹1801, #522, 15 May 1704, Chamillart to Le Gendre.

More common after 1659 are the stack of complaints about minor insults, thefts, and fights.[216] These were enough to make life difficult or unacceptable in some towns. The inhabitants of Saint-Julien deserted their homes to avoid lodging troops.[217] In 1693, even Vauban testified that *étapes* around Cap had "depopulated the country."[218] So an *intendant* could speak of a town in his jurisdiction as "a little miserable town, weighed down by *étapes*."[219] It was no wonder that towns threatened with having their names added to the route protested.[220]

Complaints and abuses could hardly be avoided, and no doubt some communities were hard hit. But the question remains: Were *étapes* a universal disaster to the local community? There is reason to suppose that, while the system did not work perfectly, it functioned adequately and was not an inevitable disaster to French towns. Vauban opposed marching troops around unless absolutely necessary, owing to "an infinity of small pillages on the routes, that extremely inconvenience the country exposed to these passages."[221] Yet his proposals to correct abuses were surprisingly modest. He wanted movements restricted and small groups sent on the roads under proper command.[222]

LIVING OFF THE COUNTRY VERSUS SUPPLY BY MAGAZINES

Until relatively recently, historians have agreed that over the course of the *grand siècle*, armies became more and more bound to magazines by "umbilical cords" of supply. This conclusion stressed both the growing regularity and the increasing limitations of warfare in the seventeenth century. In 1977, Martin van Creveld, in *Supplying War*, challenged that orthodoxy by arguing that the armies of the late seventeenth and eighteenth centuries depended much less on magazines than usually believed and, to the contrary, lived off the country in the main.[223] The strategic, or at least operational, implications of his assertions not only attack stereotypes about the *grand siècle* but question common analyses of Napoleonic mobility that attribute it to Bonaparte cutting himself loose from the tyranny of supply from the rear, because van Creveld contends that this tyranny never existed. However, despite the value

---

[216] For controversies and combats between hosts and soldiers in and around Dijon, see Dijon, H 256 and Côte d'Or, C 3642, and C 3674.

[217] Côte d'Or, 15 February 1672, C 2897.

[218] 6 January 1693 from Nice, Vauban to LePelletier, Rochas, 2:364.

[219] Corvisier, *Les Français*, 274.

[220] See, for example, Côte d'Or, C3676, October 1703, an inquiry into replacing the town of Issueville with Gemeaux.

[221] Sébastien le Prestre de Vauban, *Oisivetés de M. de Vauban*, 3 vols. (Paris: 1842–46), 2:232.

[222] To limit abuses, he would give only ten men to a sergeant or fifteen men to a lieutenant. AG, MR 1828, piece 1.

[223] Martin van Creveld, *Supplying War: Logistics from Wallenstein to Patton* (Cambridge: 1977).

of his work in attracting attention to this understudied aspect of war, *Supplying War* is a flawed work.[224] Nowhere is it more misleading than in its denial of the essential role of magazines and orderly supply from the rear in early modern logistics. A brief discussion of some of the basic issues involved ought to make this clear.

The Complexities of Living off the Country

First, if the term *living off the country* simply means that soldiers traveled about without having to drag a supply train behind them, which seems to be van Creveld's notion, then this category of self-supply includes several very different methods. Some had nothing to do with supporting armies on the march by foraging parties who scoured the countryside to feed the army on a daily basis, the method of living off the country that most commonly comes to mind. Considering how important the concept of "living off the country" is to van Creveld, it is surprising that he did not explore it with much care.

There is no question that early modern armies exploited the matériel of areas that they occupied or passed through. As mentioned earlier in the discussion of fodder, its weight and bulk demanded that armies gather it on campaign. But granting the undeniable need to live off the country in terms of fodder for animals does not say anything about the need for an army to feed its human element with other kinds of supply. It is also true, as already mentioned, that troops might be paid and then simply required to purchase their food from local sources. Yet reliance upon pay gave rise to serious abuses when pay was late or insufficient or when the food supply fell short of meeting the needs of large numbers of soldiers concentrated in a small area.

A more regular form of extortion compelled towns, cities, and entire districts to support a passing or occupying army. This was an old system that crystallized during the Thirty Years' War as "contributions." Under the threat of force, civil authorities agreed to provide money and goods to the general of the threatening army or to officials of the ruler he served. Towns that refused to pay ran the risk of being sacked and burned. However, after the Thirty Years' War, contributions often shifted the burden of maintaining an army from regular taxes raised at home to war taxes imposed on the populations of occupied territory. As such, contributions might not affect the day-to-day operations of the logistic system. To the extent that contributions were used to stock permanent or improvised magazines, which then maintained the soldiers by more regular means – that is, by depots, army

---

[224] See criticisms in John A. Lynn, "The History of Logistics and *Supplying War*," in John A. Lynn, ed., *Feeding Mars: Logistics in Western Warfare from the Middle Ages to the Present* (Boulder, CO: 1993), 9–27. See, as well, Lynn, "Food, Funds, and Fortresses," 137–59, in the same volume.

ovens, and convoys – the raising of contributions really does not fit the category of "living off the country" as van Creveld defines it.

Moving by *étapes* freed troops from carrying their own supplies, but it required considerable administrative preparation. Such troops did not forage for food along their way, since they knew it would be waiting for them each evening at the end of their march. The most impressive march by any army during the War of the Spanish Succession, Marlborough's trek in 1704 from the Low Countries to the Danube, was supported by a form of the *étapes* system on the grand scale that harked back to the old Spanish Road. His troops arrived at prearranged stops and purchased food from local author-ities who had collected it in advance. The golden key to Marlborough's success was the cash that he brought with him in his strongboxes, a luxury extremely rare or even impossible for other armies of the period. By itself, this case offers poor proof that armies could have dispensed with supply lines and just foraged to maintain themselves on the march. There is little in common between Marlborough's march and that by Napoleon in 1805 along much of the same ground. Napoleon's soldiers foraged for the majority of their supplies; Marlborough's did not.

The form of self-supply that most usually comes to mind, foraging for supplies by entire field armies on campaign, did not typify French logistics in the second half of the *grand siècle*, since it posed many problems and dangers to French armies themselves. Turenne discussed living off the coun-try from his experience in Germany at midcentury. He argued that half of a force living by foraging had to be composed of cavalry, since it alone could forage effectively, and that a cavalryman could only seize enough for himself and one other man.[225] By his calculations, an army would have to be small and lopsidedly heavy in expensive cavalry to survive. Moreover, foraging could lead to pillage, or it could encourage desertion. Prior to 1659, French units established a grim record of excess against French and foreign popu-lations. After that date, French troops abused foreign populations on occa-sion, particularly when that abuse was part of a policy of intimidation and coercion, as during the invasion of Holland in 1672 or the devastation of the Palatinate in 1688–89; however, such foraging was not the standard manner of feeding troops in the field. Foraging for food was too wasteful of re-sources, unpredictable in results, and dangerous to discipline to become the primary means of supply. Reluctance to let armies forage had a great deal to do with fundamental and widely accepted assumptions about motivation and morale. Consequently, French armies did not live on the country in order to feed the troops.

Facts, Figures, and Food

Van Creveld asserts "In *no* instance . . . is there any question of a force on the move being supplied solely by convoys," and "magazines never contained,

---

[225] Louis Susane, *Histoire de la cavalerie française*, 3 vols. (Paris: 1874), 1:106.

nor could they contain, more than a fraction of the army's needs."[226] Such phrases are technically correct but create a misleading impression. In trying to demonstrate that armies lived off the country, van Creveld, by his handling of numbers, distorts the essentials of logistics. Part of the problem results from the way he measures supply, and part comes from the way in which he simplifies the task of preparing the most essential food item, bread.

He rightly points out that for field armies on campaign, the green fodder that kept the horses in the field had to be harvested locally because carting it great distances was prohibitive. Fodder could be found close by the army, and since it required no processing other than cutting it in the fields, it could be easily "produced" by troops on campaign. But any attempt to evaluate supply must distinguish between fodder for animals and food for men. By lumping supplies together and speaking of weights and percentages of the total, van Creveld does violence to this necessary distinction.

Weights can be deceiving. Assume an army of 60,000 soldiers; it would require 90,000 rations of bread daily, once the extra rations for officers and noncombatants are considered.[227] With a standard ration of 1½ pounds of bread per man per day, this hypothetical force would require 135,000 pounds, or 67.5 tons, of bread each day. The army's 40,000 horses, however, would require 1,000 tons of green fodder plus perhaps 120 tons of oats. By weight, then, food amounted to considerably less than 10 percent of the army's supply needs. Thus, van Creveld can rightly say that magazines only held a small percentage of the army's needs, since magazines provided so little forage. At one point he concludes "It is obvious that the need to obtain the ninety per cent of supplies that were not brought up from the rear must have done more to dictate the movement of armies than the ten percent that were . . . ."[228] The implication might be, why not just forget the 10 percent and dispense with supplies brought up from the rear? But the 10 percent minority of supply included the army's bread, and the 90 percent majority was overwhelmingly forage. By not considering the restraints of the 10 percent, an army would starve or dissolve.

Examine more closely the mathematics of foraging for bread by considering a scenario that van Creveld himself presents to prove his point that early modern armies could easily have supplied themselves on the march without being bound to magazines. An army of 60,000 requiring 90,000 bread rations per day is to march 100 miles at a rate of 10 miles per day.[229]

---

[226] Van Creveld, *Supplying War*, 25, 39. Van Creveld's emphasis.

[227] Puységur, a great authority of the day estimated that an army of 120,000 soldiers consumed 180,000 bread rations daily. Jacques-François de Chastenet de Puységur, *Art de la guerre par principes et par règles*, vols. 1 and 2 (Paris: 1749), 2:62 in Perjés, "Army Provisioning," 5.

[228] Van Creveld, *Supplying War*, 24.

[229] Van Creveld, *Supplying War*, 34. This use of an army of 60,000 requiring 90,000 rations and including 40,000 horses would seem to come from the discussion in Perjés, "Army Provisioning," a work cited in van Creveld's notes. It is probably Perjés who showed van Creveld the way to Puységur. It is a shame that van Creveld did not take Perjés whole, because Perjés comes to very different conclusions.

Such an army will require 600 tons of flour to feed itself on its ten-day march. Parties from the army will forage 5 miles to either side of the route of march, meaning that they can draw on 1,000 square miles. Van Creveld assumes a population of 45 per square mile and that the inhabitants have stored away six months' worth of flour and grain, yielding a total of 7,000 tons available to the army. He concludes that the army will have plenty of bread to eat.

But this is historical slight of hand. Consider the figures another way. Given that forage parties will roam 5 miles in each direction, they will cover an area 10 miles square – that is, 100 square miles – from which the army can draw each day. According to his calculations, this area squirreled away 700 tons of flour, and the army needs only 60 tons per day. But bread, not grain or flour, was the vital commodity. Grain might grow in the field, but it had to be cut, threshed, and ground into flour, and flour had to be baked before it became bread. With a population density of 45 people per square mile, there will be only 4,500 inhabitants in 100 square miles; therefore, the capacity of village mills and ovens in the area will only be sufficient to bake bread for approximately this number of consumers. Limited oven capacity explains why armies brought along their own ovens on campaign. Even if the local ovens burned night and day to double or triple their output, they would still produce only 10 to 15 percent of the bread required by the army. Within the parameters set by van Creveld himself, his army would not thrive but starve.

He cannot rescue himself by simply changing the scenario to add that the army could bring its own ovens along. The time consumed by setting up and breaking down field ovens meant that the only way to use them efficiently was to establish a bank of them and then supply an advancing force with convoys shuttling back and forth from the ovens. At this point, we are back to the limitations imposed by regular supply from the rear – exactly what van Creveld claims to avoid in his example.

To the extent that large armies required bread, they usually had to supply it via magazines and army ovens. Van Creveld's own example does not demonstrate his point but the rather different one that baking capacity limited movement as much as did the availability of grain.[230] A far more careful study of logistics by G. Perjés argues just this and concludes that seventeenth-century armies had to be supplied with bread from the rear.[231] Because *Supplying War* is a work of synthesis, we ought not to fault van Creveld for not having mastered all the campaigns or eras of warfare from original sources. Yet he remains open to criticism for overly selective use of the very works

---

[230] The importance of ovens and mills is highlighted by a French directive of 1636 designed to make it as difficult as possible for the attacking Spanish armies to continue their advance: "Tell all the generals to send out before them seven or eight companies of cavalry in a number of places with workers to break all the ovens and mills in an area stretching from their own fronts to as close as possible to the enemy" (in Landier, "Guerre, violences, et société," 86).

[231] Perjés, "Army Provisioning."

that he employs, a notable case in point being Perjés's important study, which if taken fully leads to very different conclusions than those reached by van Creveld.

During the late seventeenth and eighteenth centuries, the dependence on magazines and supply convoys on campaign was very real. Even such an exponent of mobility as Eugene of Savoy wrote in 1705: "Without a [supply] train . . . I am unable to advance further, especially when the army is going from one region to another, and the magazine located here or there is too far away, and it takes several days to establish a magazine in the new place, and to put the bakeries into operation. And meanwhile the army is in need of bread and if we cannot take bread with us, how should I help myself?"[232]

CONCLUSION

To feed the ever larger forces of the Bourbon monarchs, the French developed a logistic system with unprecedented capacity. In evolving this more effective system, military administration, particularly the central administration, did not undergo a radical transformation in personnel or practices, although it did develop substantially, most notably in establishing a series of permanent magazines and in extending the responsibilities and powers of the *intendants*. This more moderate change at the center was the case because logistics was handled primarily on the local, field-army level and because the impressive task of supplying food remained in the hands of private contractors. It would be tempting to credit logistic development to a single individual or to see it spring up through some sudden transformation. Such was not the case. While important development occurred, it grew incrementally out of older practices. Military administration, thus, followed the pattern of the *ancien régime*, where drastic and rapid change was seen as corrosive to the traditional nature of society and government, and where the future had to wear the garb of the past, often in several layers. In addition, while rational design played a part, it had to accommodate itself to financial necessity. In the matter of logistics, direct supply by the state gave way to supply by entrepreneurs, since those *munitionnaires* provided not only the necessities of war, but the credit without which the state's forces could not have taken the field. Once again, the ideal of absolutist control became the reality of private enterprise supervised by state inspection.

Whatever the administrative system, the technology of horse-drawn forces defined the logistics of food and fodder so that they imposed conflicting operational demands on the army of the *grand siècle*, demands that had to be balanced. On the one hand, an army benefited from maintaining contacts with its magazines in order to feed its men. Changes in camp complicated the matter, and rapid advances threatened the army with food shortages or

---

[232] Prince Eugene of Savoy, *Feldzüge des Prinzen Eugen von Savoyen*, 13 vols. (Vienna: 1876–86), vol. 8, supplement H, 305 in Perjés, "Army Provisioning," 29.

worst. On the other hand, since fodder had to be harvested in the area surrounding an army's encampment, and since an army soon exhausted the available green forage, armies had to strike camp and move periodically to ensure adequate supplies of fodder.

In any case, the army required more than food and fodder to maintain itself in the field; there were other essentials, the subjects of the next chapter.

5

Providing Other Essentials

THE expanding army of the *grand siècle* demanded more than food and fodder; the awesome giant had also to be paid, housed, clothed, and armed. Without these essentials, it could not or would not perform as ordered and expected; it might languish or turn angry. Either alternative was unacceptable. As in all other aspects of logistics and supply, growth of the army increased demands on administrators and entrepreneurs, yet they responded and the army survived, even when it did not thrive, as it exceeded 250,000 men and approached 400,000. Government met the needs of the Goliath it had created by adapting traditional practices and by instituting new ones. By and large, older ways had relied more on local resources and local agents, while now the state bit by bit took over the responsibility of providing for the troops, either through the action of its own agents or by more strictly regulating the entrepreneurs who actually supplied or served the army.

In this chapter, the focus changes to pay, *logement*, clothing, and small arms. Pay was an absolute necessity, since so much of what a soldier required he had to buy for himself either directly or through deductions from his wages. In addition, pay represented a bond, part of a contract between the soldier and the state. The soldier swore obediently to put his life at risk, and the state promised to provide for him, but when pay did not arrive, that bond lost its force. The housing of troops, *logement*, not only supplied necessary shelter; it brought the civilian and military communities together, since troops boarded in civilian houses. Clothing not only protected the soldier from the elements, it also came to represent a new psychology of uniform behavior, although the transition to uniforms in the seventeenth century did not come quickly. Arms, perhaps the most important items in defining the soldier, proved to be the most easily, or at least the most dependably, supplied of a soldier's needs. With all this, and food and fodder, the giant could live from day to day and contest the field at the king's command.

PAY

During the 1627–28 siege of La Rochelle, Louis XIII wrote that "for the accomplishing of these designs . . . it is necessary to maintain a good Army, well paid."[1] Pay was at the basis of successful campaigns; it also amounted to the largest single expense of maintaining the French army. This is not simply because of the cash actually put in the hands of the soldier, but because in addition to this, his food and clothing were also funded as deductions from his pay. With so much of the army's cost included in pay, the rates and mechanisms of pay were essential military questions.

Pay Rates

Official pay rates for French troops declined over the course of the *grand siècle*. That decline appears only slight when measured in monetary units, but when judged in terms of its purchasing power, the fall in military wages was far more substantial. It is less easy to explain this decrease than it is to observe its effect. Population abundance does not account for wage decline, because population, which increased during the first half of the century, fell somewhat after 1648. In general, wage rates were low in the seventeenth century, but military pay seemed to be even at the bottom of this scale. One thing seems certain though: Lower wages made it less costly to build the huge armies assembled by Louis XIV.

French records of the time count money in a system similar to the old English manner; 12 deniers equaled a sol, or sou, and 20 sols equaled a livre, the French pound. Occasionally, amounts were figured in écus, valued at 3 livres. Pay for the French infantry soldier doubled during the sixteenth century, beginning at 5 livres per month, or 3 sols 4 deniers per day, through the first quarter of the sixteenth century, and then rising steadily to 6 livres by the 1540s, 7 livres in the 1560s, 8 livres in the 1580s, and finally 10 livres per month, or 6 sols 8 deniers per day, in 1600.[2] The precise rate for infantry depended on the weapons they carried and the extent of their armor; in 1553, actual pay by regulation could run from 6 to 15 livres, pikemen with full

---

[1] Peter Mervault, *The Last Famous Siege of the City of Rochel together with the Edict of Nantes* (London: 1680), 26. I thank Brian Sandberg for this reference.

[2] Tabulations of pay rates for infantry and mounted forces can be found in Joseph Servan, *Recherches sur la force de l'armée française, depuis Henri IV jusqu'a la fin de 1806* (Paris: 1806), "Tableau de la valeur intrinséque de la solde, 1600–1805"; AG, MR 1972, #7, "État de ce qui revenait par année . . . 1340–1730"; manuscript tabulation in AG, Bib., A^lh 638, vol. 2; and the highly detailed material for the period ca. 1710 in Jean Roland de Mallet, *Compts Rendus de l'administration des finances du royaume de France* (London: 1789), 157–70. Other substantiation for the figures presented here come from the ordinance of 1553 in AG, MR 1881, #5; for 1707, AN, G^7 1780, #212. See as well Xavier Audouin, *Histoire de l'administration de la guerre*, 4 vols. (Paris: 1811), 2:249, 377; Louis André, *Michel Le Tellier et l'organisation de l'armée monarchique* (Paris: 1906), 271–328; and Camille Rousset, *Histoire de Louvois*, 4 vols. (Paris: 1862–64), 1:195–96.

armor receiving the best wages.[3] This basic rate of 10 livres remained constant through the first decades of the seventeenth century; during the long war with Spain, the rate for a soldier dropped to 6 sols per day and then fell further to 5 sols for a musketeer in 1660.[4] Pikemen continued to earn more than musketeers; during Louis's personal reign, pikemen received 5 sols 6 deniers per day at a time when musketeers' and fusiliers' rates stayed at 5 sols.[5]

Cavalry troopers always received higher pay than their foot-bound comrades. Cavalry wages also escalated during the sixteenth century, going from 7 livres 10 sols per month, or 5 sols per day, in 1500 to 60 livres per month, or 2 livres per day by 1600. By 1610, however, this decreased to 40 livres per month, or 1 livre, 6 sols, 8 deniers per day, where it remained through midcentury.[6] In the 1660s, this rate declined to 15 sols per day, against which 8 sols were withheld for forage and bread, giving the trooper an effective pay of 7 sols.[7] This rate of 7 sols per day held true for the rest of the 1600s, as the cost of fodder for the horse shifted directly to the state.[8] The War of the Spanish Succession saw the rate at 7 sols 4 deniers.[9] Dragoons earned less than cavalry but more than infantry. In the 1670s, dragoons received 11 sols per day, against which 5 were deducted for a yield of 6 sols. At the close of the *grand siècle*, they still earned 6 sols per day, the deductions for the care of the horse having been transferred.[10] At times, officers promised men a pay rate higher than the official one, apparently as an inducement to enlist, but this practice was condemned by law.[11]

---

[3] Ordinance of 23 December 1553 in AG, MR 1881, #5. During the Wars of Religion, a *halbredier* received 6 livres per month, an arquebusier 7, and a Swiss 9. Philippe Contamine, ed., *Histoire militaire de la France*, vol. 1 (Paris: 1992), 317.

[4] Contamine, *Histoire militaire*, 1:344, dates the drop to 6 sols as 1629, but Servan, *Recherches*, "Tableau de la valeur intrinséque de la solde, 1600–1805," lists pay as 6 sols 8 deniers as late as 1640, to fall to 6 sols by 1651. On 1660, see André, *Le Tellier*, 289. Pay rates given here for infantry and cavalry, ca. 1665, are also supported by a 1663 memoir written by d'Aurignac and published as Paul Azan, *Un tacticien du XVIIe siècle* (Paris: 1904), 100.

[5] Contamine, *Histoire militaire*, 1:404, for 1660; pay rates given in detail from the 6 February 1670 ordinance by Rousset, *Louvois*, 1:195–96; and Victor Belhomme, *L'armée française en 1690* (Paris: 1895), 26, shows the same for 1690. Servan, *Recherches*, "Tableau de la valeur intrinséque de la solde, 1600–1805," states that during wartime, 1668, 1689, and 1701, the infantry pay rate dipped to 4 sols 8.66 deniers.

[6] AG, Bib., A1h 638, vol. 2.   [7] Rousset, *Louvois*, 1:195.

[8] Servan, *Recherches*, "Tableau de la valeur intrinséque de la solde, 1600–1805," states that during wartime, 1689 and 1701, the cavalry pay rate dipped to 6 sols 10 deniers. This does not correspond to figures in Belhomme, *L'armée française en 1690*, 26, or in Mallet, *Compts rendus*, 157–70.

[9] Mallet, *Compts rendus*, 157–70.

[10] Rousset, *Louvois*, 1:195; and Mallet, *Compts rendus*, 157–70.

[11] Ordinances of 10 December 1686 and 20 June 1714 promised 30 livres and a discharge to any soldier denouncing another for receiving a pay higher than that allowed by law. Georges Girard, *Le service militaire en France à la fin du règne de Louis XIV: Racolage et milice, 1701–1715* (Paris: 1915), 49.

The rates quoted for all branches refer to regular French regiments at the rate for quartered troops. Guard units and foreign regiments had their own, higher, pay scales. In addition, the rates cited are full pay rates – that is, wages earned during peacetime and winter quarters; wages fell for most soldiers when they went on campaign. As a rule, troops in garrison during peacetime or in winter quarters paid for their food out of their pay, but troops on campaign in wartime received less cash, although their bread came directly from the state. Campaign pay during Louis's last two wars amounted to only 1 sol per day, plus rations for an infantryman, 2 sols for dragoons, and 3 sols for cavalry.

In fact, campaign and winter-quarters pay did not differ quite so much as first appears; it had more to do with bookkeeping for various deductions than with the amount that the soldier actually received. Consider the infantryman who received 1 sol per day on campaign. When he was in quarters at the end of the century, his captain withheld up to 2 sols per day for bread, 1 sol for the *masse* (a fund to buy new clothes), and a bit more for the Invalides. Moreover, at least after 1690, the soldier also was charged for the cost of half a pound of meat per day, which can be estimated at 1 sol 5 deniers.[12] With these subtractions from his 5-sols pay, the infantryman could expect to see no more than 1 sol per day in his hand over winter quarters – that is, the same amount he actually pocketed on campaign.

Within the context of official pay, regulations might redefine the actual pay received. The 1653 regulation for winter quarters, a time when infantrymen supposedly received pay of 6 sols per day, prescribed that infantry would actually get only 2 sols per day from the local population as *ustensile* (see later for details on *ustensile*), 2 sols per day as pay from the government, and 24 ounces of bread that could be valued at an additional 2 sols.[13] At times, real pay might exceed the regulation amount, as in 1666, when Louis XIV granted his troops in the low countries extra allowances of 1 sol for infantry and 3 sols for cavalry "because I knew that foodstuffs were more expensive there than elsewhere."[14] In 1704, troops garrisoned in Dijon also benefited from augmented pay, as the infantry got 8 sols per day.[15]

Full official pay earned by soldiers, troopers, and dragoons stood at about the rate of semi-skilled labor, but if you count only the amount actually given to troops by the paymaster, it was at the bottom of pay scales. The best estimate puts urban weavers' wages at 8 to 10 sols per day in the late seventeenth century. Country weavers made less at 5 to 6 sols per day, and spinners took in 3 sols 6 deniers or less. Skilled tradesmen earned far more.

---

[12] For bread, meat, and Invalides deductions, see Servan, *Recherches*, "Tableau de la valeur intrinséque de la solde, 1600–1805." This states that the bread deduction was at 1 sol 6 deniers by the regulation of 7 September 1660 and increased to 2 sols with the ordinance of 30 March 1684.

[13] *Règlement* for winter quarters, 4 November 1653, in André, *Le Tellier*, 667–82.

[14] Louis, *Mémoires*, 1:15, 244–45.   [15] Côte d'Or, C 3676, order of 14 March 1704.

Journeymen carpenters earned 17 sols a day in Nevers and 26 in Rouen.[16] It is interesting to note that civilians hired to stand watch in redoubts along fortified lines were paid substantially more than regular infantry. One set of documents shows that such civilians turned guards in Flanders received 15 sols per day in 1702 and 12 sols in 1703 and 1704.[17] This implies that civilians could not be tempted for the low wages that soldiers accepted. In fact, there is little reason to see the army as anything other than an employer of last resort, given the low wages. Only hard times seem to have driven men into the ranks when they had other opportunities, as during the famines of 1694 and 1709.

Some historians claim that the decrease in military real pay rates made possible the growth in the number of troops – here is a key issue.[18] Measured in terms of its purchasing power, how much did army pay rise or fall for enlisted men over the course of the *grand siècle*, 1610–1715? Servan compared the wage to the mark of silver, and judged by this standard, setting the base period as 1600–10, infantry pay declined 45 percent by 1660 and 57 percent by 1714.[19] It might be wiser to compare the wage with the price of wheat, a better index of value of money, and this is possible thanks to the Baulant series of wheat prices.[20] The average price for a sétier of wheat in Paris during the first five decades of the century, 1611–60, was 14.127 livres, while the average price during the personal reign of Louis XIV, 1661–1715, rose to 18.622. This represents a rise of 32 percent over the course of the *grand siècle*, a period when basic infantry pay went down from 10 livres to 7 livres 10 sols per month. Gauging the infantry soldier's purchasing power by the amount of wheat he could buy with that month's salary reveals a decline of 41 percent – a very sizable drop. Thus, measured in silver or pegged to a price index, the wages of common soldiers fell substantially over the course of the *grand siècle*, justifying the notion that diminished pay accompanied, and quite probably encouraged, the growth of the army. Indeed, the decline to 5 sols per day for infantry preceded the expansion in wartime forces for the Dutch War and the Nine Years' War.

Given their low pay, infantry took the opportunity to earn extra money by working on fortifications, as at Ypres in 1681, when soldiers earned 9 to

---

[16] Fernand Braudel and Ernest Labrousse, eds., *Histoire économique et sociale de la France*, vol. 2 (Paris: 1970), 668–70.

[17] AD, Nord, C 8645.

[18] David Kaiser, *Politics & War: European Conflict from Phillip II to Hitler* (Cambridge, MA: 1990), 146, writes: "Both Louis and his fellow European monarchs also seem to have been able to raise larger armies simply because the average soldier's wages were declining in the latter half of the seventeenth century." See the old claim that "the soldier, rich under Henri IV, was impoverished beyond the point of any other profession." Audouin, *Histoire de l'administration*, 2:248. See, as well, his comments on 2:377–78. André, *Le Tellier*, 290, makes a big point of denying a decline in pay, 1643–66, while Le Tellier was at the helm.

[19] Servan, *Recherches*, "Tableau de la valeur intrinséque de la solde, 1600–1805."

[20] Micheline Baulant, "Prix des grains à Paris de 1431 à 1788," *Annales, E. S. C.*, vol. 23 (1968).

10 sols per day for manual labor.[21] Soldiers benefiting from these higher wages had to surrender a sol a day, probably to compensate their comrades who had to stand guard while they labored.[22]

Noncommissioned officers received proportionately higher wages. Infantry sergeants were paid two or three times the amount given a private soldier; during the War of the Spanish Succession, when soldiers earned 5 sols per day, their sergeants earned 10. In cavalry, the situation was somewhat different. The *maréchal de logis*, today a noncommissioned officer, was considered an officer in the seventeenth century and paid at a rate three and a half times the wage of a trooper. A brigadier, a true noncommissioned officer, hardly made more than a trooper – by the end of the *grand siècle*, 8 sols per day as opposed to the trooper's 7 sols 4 deniers. Again, campaign pay was far lower, as during the War of the Spanish Succession, when an infantry sergeant's campaign pay dropped to 2 sols in addition to 2 rations of bread.[23]

Officers received a great deal more than did their men. Infantry captains pulled down 50 livres per month in 1500, 106 livres during the second half of the sixteenth century, and 125 livres during the first half of the seventeenth. This amounted to ten to fifteen times the wages of a soldier in the ranks. Lieutenants of infantry earned 50 livres when the captains earned 125 livres. Cavalry rates were higher, as one would expect. From 1550 to 1580, captains earned about 167 livres per month and lieutenants about 92. During the first half of the seventeenth century, the official rates stood at 412 livres 10 sols for captains and 262 livres 10 sols for lieutenant.[24] In the 1660s, pay rates for officers drastically declined. Infantry captains received 75 livres per month, while their counterparts in cavalry earned 180 livres. Infantry lieutenants got 45 livres and cavalry lieutenants 135. By the end of Louis's reign, officers made still less. Captains of infantry were paid 60 livres per month, while dragoon captains made 90 livres and cavalry captains 150. Lieutenants received 30 livres in the infantry, 50 livres in the dragoons, and 75 livres in the cavalry. To these sums must be added some special incentives to officers, such as pay supplements to captains who kept their companies full.

Just as with common soldiers, garrison pay for officers differed from their campaign pay. Rousset states that officers received 50 percent more wages on campaign than they did in garrison, according to regulations of the 1660s and 1670s. Thus, a captain earned 75 livres in garrison and 112 livres 10 deniers on campaign. Yet by the end of the reign, officers suffered a drop from garrison to campaign wages, just as did their men. During the Sun King's last war, an infantry captain made 2 livres, or 40 sols, per day in

---

[21] Henry Chotard, *Louis XIV, Louvois, Vauban et les Fortifications du nord de la France* (Paris: 1889), 179. In 1682, soldiers pulled from regiments were paid even more, 18 sols per day, or over three times their normal pay. Chotard, 45.

[22] AG, Bibl., Col. des ord., vol. 24, #92, 23 September 1680.

[23] Mallet, *Compts rendus*, charts, 163, 169–70.

[24] Wage chart in AG, Bib., A1h 638, vol. 2.

winter and only 6 sols per day on campaign. This contrast owes something to the fact that on campaign an infantry captain also drew six bread rations a day, costing 12 sols and four forage rations, which if they had to be bought cost as much as 12 to 20 sols per ration.[25]

Mechanisms of Pay

Regulations from the *grand siècle* prescribed strict guides for paying troops. Already in the sixteenth century, royal directives were quite complete on the subject. An ordinance of 12 August 1523 commanded that no payments would be made and no reviews held without the express command of the king or his agents and that *commissaires* and *contrôleurs* had to be present at such reviews.[26] Reviews and payment were inseparably linked. One directive, circa 1600, advised: Never hold a review without money "for sometimes the soldiers having been reviewed but not paid, seize the *commissaires* and *contrôleurs*."[27] Reviews not only counted the number of men in a company, verified the condition of their weapons and clothing, and paid the men present; they also provided the occasion at which troops took oaths of loyalty and obedience.[28] In 1629, the well-known but probably overrated Code Michau further regulated the pay process. The code prescribed that pay would be handed over in advance and that there would be a pay master in each regiment.[29] During the reign of Louis XIV, the military writer Gaya described the process; after the review by *commissaires*, the *trésoriers* would deliver the money as ordered by the army *intendant*, while an infantry guard would always stand over the treasury that would ordinarily remain in the headquarters section, the *quartier du roi*, in the encampment.[30]

Authorities calculated wages in *montres*, or "reviews," which was a unit of account; however, there was no set time of payment associated with a *montre*. The French experimented with ten *montres* in 1633, dropped the number to eight per year, each of forty-five days, by 1635, and then further reduced the figure to six of forty-five days in 1636, with the provinces to pick up the remaining two *montres*.[31] The amount presented to the troops was actually

---

[25] AD, Côte d'Or, C3676, order of 14 March 1704, states the figure as 12 sols for a ration. In the winter of 1688–89, forage cost 20 sols a ration in Germany, AG, A^{1}829, 26 and 28 December 1688, in Ronald Thomas Ferguson, "Blood and Fire: Contribution Policy of the French Armies in Germany (1668–1715)," Ph.D. dissertation, University of Minnesota, 1970, 94.

[26] AG, MR 1881, #1.   [27] AG, MR 1881, #17 (bis).

[28] See, for an example of oath taking at reviews circa 1600, MR 1881, #17.

[29] Code Michau, 1629, articles 222 and 239, in François André Isambert et al., eds., *Recueil général des anciennes lois françaises, depuis l'an 420, jusqu'à la Révolution de 1789*, vol. 16 (Paris: 1829), 285, 287.

[30] Louis de Gaya, *Le nouvel art de la guerre et la manière dont on la fait aujourd'huy en France* (Paris: 1692), 41.

[31] Richelieu, *Lettres, instructions diplomatiques, et papiers d'état*, d'Avenel, ed., 8 vols. (Paris: 1853–77), 4:523, Jan. 1634 in David Parrott, "The Administration of the French Army During the

paid in *prêts*, to be paid each nine or ten days, or essentially three *prêts* to the month.[32] The *prêts* also became something of a unit of account, so that the *règlement* for winter quarters of 12 October 1650 stated that troops were to be paid in eighteen *prêts* to be given in six payments – that is, one payment a month for each of the succeeding six months of winter quarters.[33] The *prêts* would remain the standard of payment for the rest of the *grand siècle*.

Specific *règlements* for winter quarters might alter the formal rules of payment in particular situations. The 1651 *règlement* broke the rule that combined payment and review. Companies took in the first three payments without passing reviews; captains would receive money on the basis of a full-strength company, forty men for infantry and thirty-six for cavalry, officers included. However, the fourth payment, to come on 1 March, would be made with a review; heads would be counted and money awarded according to the count. The fifth payment would come as the troops were to take the field in mid-April; by this point, the companies were to be at full strength.

When Le Tellier came to office, *trésoriers* of the *ordinaire* and *extraordinaire des guerres*, who handled the actual pay, took as their cut between 3 and 6 deniers per livre, or 1.25 to 2.5 percent.[34] The money did not always go through the treasurers. The ordinance of October 1650 cited previously stipulated that officials were to raise the money to pay the troops from the local population. These funds were then to be credited against their arrears in paying their *tailles* since 1647 or to be credited against future *tailles*.[35] The money then never reached Paris but was levied and spent on the spot. The 1653 *règlement* on winter quarters gave the same instructions to raise money for pay locally.[36] In 1703, Louis XIV instructed his marshal Villars to raise over 40 percent of the funds he needed to pay his army from contributions raised in Germany.[37]

Shortfalls and Shipment

The pay system suffered from a number of problems, ranging from fraud to lack of funds. Most commonly, captains tried to get additional cash allowances by padding their rolls with phony soldiers, *passe volants*, at reviews.

Ministry of Cardinal Richelieu," Ph.D. dissertation, Oxford University, 1985, 91; Contamine, *Histoire militaire*, 1:367.

[32] Code Michau, 1629, articles 223 and 239, in Isambert et al., eds., *Recueil général des anciennes lois françaises*, 16:285, 287. Nine days is the usual figure for the first half of the century. But the usual notion of three *prêts* to the month of thirty days also stipulated in regulations suggests that men were paid every ten days.

[33] 12 October 1650 *règlement* in SHAT, Bibl., Col. des ord., vol. 18, #84.

[34] André, *Le Tellier*, 303.

[35] SHAT, Bibl., Col. des ord., vol. 18, #84, 12 October 1650 *règlement*.

[36] "Ordinance portant interpretation et amplication du *règlement* du quartier d'hyver dernier, du 12 fevrier 1653," reproduced in entirety in André, *Le Tellier*, 683–90.

[37] AG, A¹1676, #41, 27 April 1703, Louis to Villars in Ferguson, "Blood and Fire," 11, 180, and 190.

While this problem existed throughout the century, it was far more prevalent before the personal reign of Louis XIV than once Louvois put his stamp on military administration. In any case, even at the worst, the abuse of *passe volants* did not pose the greatest challenge to army solvency; the real debilitating threat arose from the periodic collapse of an inefficient and overburdened fiscal system. The recent researches of David Parrott demonstrate how exhausted royal finances became once France entered the war in 1635. Several generations ago, Louis André pointed out that Le Tellier found military finances in a shambles when he came to office and that he would essentially have to wait for the return of peace before he could do much to clear up the problems.[38] In 1645, that great minister wrote: "And as for money, it is neither in His Majesty's power nor even less so in that of his Eminence [Mazarin] to find some where there is none."[39]

Complaints about pay that arrived in insufficient amounts, came late, or never got there at all fill volumes. In the spring of 1647, pay for Turenne's army was five or six months in arrears.[40] The next year, his army again ran short.[41] By July 1649, the French Army of Flanders had not received any wages since the campaign began; it was promised a *demi-montre* to see it through.[42] Problems continued after the Fronde as well; the pay for Turenne's forces again failed to arrive in 1657 and 1658.[43] While the flow of pay improved during the period 1661–1700, there were still important lapses; in the 1690s, Vauban complained that his engineer officers were not receiving their pay.[44] During the War of the Spanish Succession, the French suffered a financial collapse which approached that of the years before 1659, and as such, the reports about lack of pay and supplies became almost pathetic. The amount of money required was very great. Villars estimated the cash needed by his army as 531,000 livres per month.[45] A document from 1707 states that the entire army's requirement for pay amounted to 2,745,781 livres each month.[46] The government became increasingly unable to meet its bills. In 1706, Marshal Berwick feared that disorder would tear apart his army and begged for money "to pay this army that hasn't got a sol"; the same year in Hainault, the *prêts* of 13 February–3 March had not arrived. With the famine of 1709–10, the crisis became worse.

Even if the government had the funds, getting them to the army posed serious problems. These sums might be supplied to the front by letters for exchange, prearranged payments from financiers, or sent in cash by wagon.

---

[38] André, *Le Tellier*, 327.   [39] Letter of 22 August 1645 in André, *Le Tellier*, 273.
[40] Jean Bérenger, *Turenne* (Paris: 1987), 243.   [41] Bérenger, *Turenne*, 265.
[42] AG, A^{1}115, 13 Juillet 1649.   [43] Bérenger, *Turenne*, 333, 341.
[44] Reginald Blomfield, *Sebastien le Prestre de Vauban, 1633–1707* (New York: 1971), 96–97.
[45] AG, A^{1}1675, #143, 22 March 1703, "Dépense pour un mois de trente jours," memoir by Villars. Here he stated that he needed 661, 212 livres, 18 sols, 4 deniers per month, but that after deducting the cost of bread, 130,500 livres, from the soldiers' pay, he would finally need only the 530,713 livres.
[46] AN, G^{7}1780, piece 212.

Letters of exchange would have to be discounted when cashed. In 1706, there was what amounted to a 12 percent service charge for letters of exchange to Italy.[47] Letters of exchange depended on a healthy economy and on the king's credit, so the value of letters of exchange had plummeted by 1709, when one junior officer complained "We cannot get a sol; everything is in bills [of exchange], with which we cannot touch a sol." This anxious young officer stated that he had 1,800 livres in paper, but it was worthless.[48] He begged that his family send him hard currency so that he could take care of himself and his company. The use of government promissory notes to purchase equipment and to pay other military costs in the War of the Spanish Succession also involved heavy discounts; in 1706, suppliers demanded that captains pay 30 to 40 percent more if they were paying with notes.[49]

The government could also arrange to have financiers advance money at particular towns. In 1703, Louis XIV informed Villars that the marshal could get 300,000 livres payable at Augsburg, Munich, or Ulm for this army.[50] Once again, this depended on the credit of the government and upon the connections and credit of its financial officers. Sometimes officers and administrators personnally borrowed money to pay their troops. This occurred, for example, in 1644, when the *commissiare général* of the Army of Germany, the marquis de Tracy, borrowed money to pay the cavalry.[51]

There were times when only the literal shipment of cash could solve the problem, and such shipments were known as *voitures*. In 1640, Sublet de Noyers actually brought the money up himself; Richelieu asked the generals to send him an escort.[52] Mazarin dispatched a *voiture* of 300,000 livres in silver to troops in Germany in 1644.[53] Such major shipments continued to the end of the *grand siècle*. In 1706, the treasurers had to send 500,000 livres from Paris to Lyon in *voitures* and at the same time order 400,000 from Collioure to Barcelona.[54] Dangeau reports a shipment of 400,000 livres in newly minted money to Flanders in May 1709.[55]

[47] AN, G⁷1778, piece 245.

[48] Letter of 10 June 1709 in Georges Girard, ed., "Un soldat de Malplaquet: Lettres du capitaine de Saint-Mayme," *Carnet de Sabretache* (1922), 537.

[49] Contamine, *Histoire militaire*, 1:538.

[50] AG, A¹1676, #41, 27 April 1703, Louis to Villars in Ferguson, "Blood and Fire," 11, 180, and 190.

[51] Charles Derek Croxton, "Peacemaking in Early Modern Europe: Cardinal Mazarin and the Congress of Westphalia, 1643–1648," Ph.D. dissertation, University of Illinois at Urbana-Champaign, 1995, 150.

[52] Orest Ranum, *Richelieu and the Councillors of Louis XIII* (Oxford: 1963), 110 and fn. See as well AG, A¹115, #6, 13 July 1649, which concerned sending a *demi-montre* to the Army of Flanders.

[53] Jean Bérenger, *Turenne* (Paris: 1987), 195; AG, A¹115, #6 on, 13 July 1649.

[54] AN, G⁷1778, pieces 102 and 106.

[55] Philippe, marquis de Dangeau, *Journal du marquis de Dangeau*, Feuillet de Conches, ed., 19 vols. (Paris: 1854–60), 12:419.

Consequences of Lack of Pay

The consequences of lack of pay went beyond the privation of individual soldiers, troopers, and officers. Lack of pay tore the very fabric of the army, because discipline was clearly bound to suffer. A "Discours sur le règlement des trouppes," composed in 1637, spoke of the confusion and disorder that had slipped into the French army, concluding that "The essential cause of all these inconveniences is the lack of pay, the soldiers . . . believe with reason to be excused from the rigor of discipline and obedience."[56] Everhard van Reyd concluded brutally "One could not hang those one did not pay."[57] Is it any wonder that French ordinances concerning discipline began by detailing how troops were to be paid, since pay seemed the force that bound soldiers to obedience.[58]

Pushed to its extreme, lack of pay inspired mutiny. After defeating Spanish forces in 1635, an unpaid French army mutinied and sacked Tirlemont, massacring its inhabitants.[59] Perhaps the best known mutiny in the French army during that war with Spain occurred in 1647, when short of pay, elements of the Army of Germany under Turenne rebelled.[60] Lesser-known mutinies struck other field forces and garrisons, as that which affected the garrison of Câteau-Cambrésis in 1651.[61] The war with Spain was also filled with countless acts of mutiny on a small scale in which bodies of troops simply went on the rampage.

Although problems caused by the lack of pay afflicted the army worst during the long war with Spain, they were not restricted to that period. With the cruel winter of 1709–10, garrisons at Le Quesnoy, Arras, Mons, Saint-Omer, Tournai, Nassau, Valenciennes, and Cambrai mutinied.[62] Later, an *intendant* feared that units in his area might also become unruly owing to "the necessity in which the troops for whom the *prêt* is going to be lacking find themselves, which will cause disorders."[63] In short, as a 1712 memoir put

---

[56] Parrott, "Administration of the French Army," 114. See Le Tellier's comments on pay as well. Le Tellier to Molé, 13 April 1649, in André, *Le Tellier*, 274n.

[57] Everhard van Reyd in Tallett, *War and Society*, 123.

[58] By the 1690s, the ordinances always begin in this fashion. See Col. des ord., vol. 29, #8, #44, and #70 and vol. 31, #29.

[59] Contamine, *Histoire militaire*, 1:354. In 1637, Rohan's troops mutinied in the Valtelline when the state could not pay them, and in 1638, a French army refused to cross the Rhine into Germany unless it received at least some of its arrears. M.S. Anderson, *War and Society in Europe of the Old Regime, 1618–1789* (1988), 54; Contamine, *Histoire militaire*, 1:356.

[60] See Bérenger, *Turenne*, 241–51, for a short account of the mutiny.

[61] Jacques de Chastenet Puységur, *Les Mémoires de messire Jacques de Chastenet, chevalier, seigneur de Puységur, colonel du régiment de Piedmont, et lieutenant général des armées du Roy*, 2 vols. (Paris: 1690), 2:431–34.

[62] AG, A¹2149, 249–54, 256, 258. in Claude C. Sturgill, *Marshall Villars and the War of the Spanish Succession* (Lexington, KY: 1965), 82.

[63] AG, A¹2266, #316, Ormesson to Duplessis, 23 December 1710.

it, "the foundation of discipline is to pay well in order to be served well, otherwise license and impunity introduce themselves."[64]

LOGEMENT

The army of the *grand siècle* was no stranger to sleeping with a roof over its head within town walls. While wartime field armies camped out during the summer, they sheltered in towns and cities each winter for five or six months, seeking better protection against the weather than was provided by improvised huts or flimsy tents. War or peace, troops slept in town as they traveled by *étapes*. Beyond this, much of the army was always consigned to garrison duty, and during peacetime, the entire army could be considered to have been composed of garrison troops. Lodging within urban confines was a common existence for armies, and, if peacetime years are averaged in with those of conflict, it was probably the most common. The troops that wintered in town, slept there as they traveled by *étapes*, or garrisoned French fortresses obeyed different rules and received support by different systems than did units on campaign.

The material discussed in this section deals with *logement*, or the housing of troops, usually by quartering them on local civilians when these soldiers were not encamped in the field. Here the issue is quartering of troops on Bourbon subjects, not enemy populations and lands, which is dealt with in the next chapter. To some degree, the sources dictate a generic treatment of *logement*, since documents themselves often mix discussion of temporary and long-term quartering. Documents registering complaints against quartered soldiers, for example, rarely state exactly if the men had been quartered simply for a night or two of *étapes* or if the infraction had been committed during a stay of longer duration. And appeals for exemptions from lodging soldiers are blanket appeals to cover all situations.

In *logement*, army life transcended narrow military concerns. When quartered on the civilian population, soldiers rubbed shoulders with the people on a daily basis, and life within that community generated clashes as well as contacts. *Logement* defined an important and troublesome relationship between the army and the general population.

Living in Houses and Barracks

Troops lived differently in town from the way they did in the field. When encamped, soldiers lived side by side only with other soldiers or civilians who had opted to follow the army, and thus to accept its terms. Life followed regular rhythms, with rules and compliance enforced by officers and the army's own disciplinary agents, the provosts and their archers. As much as possible, all was orderly and controlled, with military officials guaranteeing

---

[64] AG, MR 1701, piece 15, 1712 memoir.

its regularity. But when an army or units of an army lodged with civilians, both regularity and control suffered.

The living conditions of quartered troops differed in a number of respects from those of men in the field. Obviously, by definition, soldiers lodged in towns and slept in fixed structures as opposed to camping in tents. Most commonly, troops were quartered in civilian houses, because special barracks were the exception in the seventeenth century.

Ordinances prescribed the construction of barracks, but such regulations expressed hopes more than they described reality. The *étapes* ordinance of 1623 detailed that barracks be built at the principle towns of the *étape* routes, but little was done.[65] The seventeenth century witnessed the construction of special housing for garrison troops, but not every fortress boasted such accommodations. When new fortresses were built, or old ones substantially enlarged, barracks were part of the project; certainly this was the case for Louis's first great fortress construction at Lille.[66] Expressing his desire for standardization and rationalism, Louis wanted all barracks in fortresses built on the same pattern. Vauban designed such a building in 1679, and a plate was made of the plan and copies sent to all fortresses.[67] But although Louvois and Vauban pushed for barracks after 1668, the 160 barracks built by Louis XIV were still insufficient.[68] And despite the ambitious plans framed during the period 1716–19, most of the army still lacked barracks in the mid–eighteenth century.[69]

Of course, when troops could be removed to their own separate buildings, the crown ensured greater control, and the townspeople enjoyed some defense from the abuses that soldiers were all too likely to commit. When Strasbourg fell to the French in 1681, the agreement with its new masters allowed the town to have barracks built at its own expense in order to keep troops from troubling public order.[70] The construction of barracks for the Gardes françaises began in Paris in 1692 and was complete by 1716.[71]

Even when special housing existed in the seventeenth century, it might accommodate only the permanent garrison companies, not regular line units temporarily quartered in a fortress. And certainly hardly any city provided enough barracks space to house the large numbers of troops stationed along the frontiers for winter quarters during wartime. Mons, which the French held during the Nine Years' War, was an exception to this rule, since by the 1690s, the town had beds for 12,000 troops.[72]

---

[65] Marcel Marion, *Dictionnaire des institutions de la France aux XVIIe et XVIIIe siècles* (Paris: 1923), 339.

[66] See 1668 contracts for barracks for troops in Lille. Lille, Affaires General, #719.

[67] P. Lazard, *Vauban*, 1633–1707 (Paris: 1934), 42–43.

[68] Contamine, *Histoire militaire*, 1:406.   [69] Corvisier, *L'armée française*, 2:848–50.

[70] André Corvisier, *Louvois* (Paris: 1983), 441.

[71] André Corvisier, *L'armée française de la fin du XVIIe siècle au ministère du Choiseul: Le soldat*, 2 vols. (Paris: 1964), 2:848.

[72] BN, f. fr. 22221, fol. 54, 22220, fol. 96; 22213, fol. 458; 22220, 59, 22210, fol. 108 in Corvisier, *Les Français et l'armée*, 230.

If towns lacked formal barracks, they might set aside particular buildings for the use of soldiers on a temporary or permanent basis. A 1641 regulation on *étapes* commanded "If the market building or other public structure of the town or city where the *étape* will be does not suffice, the said *commissaires* in charge of *étapes* will designate ten or twelve large shelters, such as barns or other similar places in the number that will be required to lodge a regiment of infantry of about 1,000 men."[73] Huxelles proposed to lodge thirty men each in deserted houses in Mainz during 1675.[74] An ordinance of 1696 stated that soldiers had to accept empty houses for their lodgings if they were available.[75] The reports sent in by *intendants* in 1697 displayed a number of methods for billeting troops in quarters. Furnes and Ypres continued to quarter men on the civilian population, while Menin, Rochefort, and, of course, Mons consigned them to barracks.[76]

In any case, the accommodations in homes or barracks could be quite "cozy." While common midcentury practice dictated that soldiers slept two to a bed, at Angers in 1649, soldiers slept four to a bed in cabarets.[77] By late century, three men to a bed was the rule in barracks, with sheets changed every twenty days in summer and once a month in winter.[78] This was tight, but so were the confines of eight-man tents.

Villages and Walled Towns

The kinds of towns chosen for *logement*, particularly long-term *logement*, varied. As early as the sixteenth century, the state restricted lodging to walled cities when possible.[79] This not only gave troops a better defensive position but allowed for better control of potentially troublesome troops who might wander and pillage if not closed in. Seventeenth-century ordinances often repeated this partiality for walled towns. One of 15 October 1640 commanded that not only would troops be quartered for the winter in *villes fermées* but that their routes to these forts would ensure that on the road they were also put up for the night in "walled places."[80] The key ordinance of 1651 repeated the insistence that troops be quartered within walls.

Circumstances did not always allow this, particularly when the financial

---

[73] SHAT, Bib., Col. des ord., vol. 16, #28, 4 October 1641 ordinance.

[74] AG, A¹875, 25 March 1675, d'Huxelles from Mayence.

[75] SHAT, Bib., Col. des ord., vol. 29, #8421 September 1696.

[76] Corvisier, *Les Français et l'armée*, 230.

[77] André, *Le Tellier*, 377; Albert Babeau, *La vie militaire sous l'ancien regime*, vol. 1 (Paris: 1890), 1:89.

[78] Corvisier, *Les Français et l'armée*, 230; Belhomme, *L'armée française en 1690*, 161.

[79] AG, MR 1881, 9 February 1584, companies to be lodged in "bonnes villes closes et grosses bourgades."

[80] AG. A¹62, #222, 15 October 1640. Patrick Landier, "Guerre, Violences, et Société en France, 1635–1659," doctorat de troisième cycle, dissertation, Université de Paris IV, 1978, 18, cites this as a 1641 ordinance.

frailty of the monarchy made it impossible, as when authorities dispersed troops to villages from 1655 through 1659, instead of to the walled towns envisioned in the regulation, to spread the burden of supporting the troops. A 1655 ordinance explained that the inhabitants of the villages that hosted soldiers were "obliged to advance the troops their food [*subsistence*] because it is not always possible to furnish their pay punctually from the state treasury."[81] Dispersal served as a form of credit, mobilizing local resources to support the troops while the crown promised to pay when it could. It was also common practice to require a locality to come up with the money to support troops in winter quarters, with the understanding that this amount would be deducted from *tailles* already owed by the community or from *tailles* slated to be collected in the future. An ordinance of 1653, for example, while generally confirming that of 1651, stipulated that troops were to be paid by the communities and that this be written off against back taxes owed since 1647.[82] Even when things were better, the notion of letting troops consume tax revenues on site applied. In 1666, Louis quartered troops on the Flanders frontier with the intention that they should live directly off of *taille* revenues.[83]

The 1655 decision to quarter troops in villages, especially the cavalry, not only relieved town economies, but it made fodder more available and protected the countryside.[84] Louis also dispersed his cavalrymen in 1666, spreading them out in neighboring communities that hosted perhaps no more than two cavalrymen each.[85] The desire to station infantry in large walled towns also fell victim to hard times in 1656, when foot soldiers were no longer to be exclusively quartered there.[86] Infantry as well as the cavalry went out to a multitude of villages, with only two men per parish at times. However, peace allowed a reversion to placing troops exclusively in walled towns in 1660.[87] After this return to the older practices, there was relatively little change in *logement* with Louvois.[88]

Of course, even large walled cities or fortresses could not hold entire armies, so they always dispersed to a large degree when they went into quarters. Some attempt was made to match the capacity of the towns to the number of troops detached there. In a 1657 reform, Le Tellier sent Terwil to inspect towns to see if they would be able to maintain soldiers.[89] Still, the pressures demanded that troops be reasonably well concentrated during winter

---

[81] AG, A¹147, #314, *règlement* of 20 November 1655, in Patrick Landier, "Guerre, violences, et société en France, 1635–1659," doctorat de troisième cycle, dissertation, Université de Paris IV, 1978, 24. Bérenger, *Turenne*, 328, credits Turenne with forcing this innovation on Mazarin and Fouquet.

[82] Ordinance of 12 February 1653, in André, *Le Tellier*, 689.

[83] Louis, *Mémoires*, 1:77.   [84] André, *Le Tellier*, 393.

[85] This was the case in 1666, when Louis dispersed his cavalry in villages, two by two, and forbade them to carry arms or gather in the houses of their hosts. Louis, *Mémoires*, 1:77. Oct. 1666.

[86] André, *Le Tellier*, 394–96.   [87] André, *Le Tellier*, 404.

[88] Corvisier, *Louvois*, 192.   [89] André, *Le Tellier*, 388.

quarters, and this meant that too many troops were stuffed into towns causing supply and disciplinary problems under Le Tellier.[90]

The young Louis declared that he wanted to lodge "my troops in such a way that they are no burden at all to the country where they are, and where they are ready to assemble in very little time."[91] But the presence of large numbers of troops was bound to overtax local resources. And the French could stuff a great many troops in bulging towns during winter quarters. On 25 October 1678, Vervien, a town of 6,500 souls, absorbed first twenty companies of infantry and eight of cavalry, totaling about 3,000 troops. Only six days later, another fifty-one companies arrived.[92]

When troops competed for lodging in the same town, disputes could arise over precedence, just as they did when camping in the field. This is one of the rationales behind the elaborate French system of ranking regiments by prestige and precedence. As early as 1595, a royal ordinance had to address precisely this matter of precedence in winter quarters.[93]

As previously noted, the simplest manner of feeding troops quartered in villages and towns was to pay them and let them purchase their food from normal local sources. Of course, this contrasted with the system of direct food supply in the field. By dispersing an army among major cities, troops imposed less of a burden on any single local economy; in fact, troops might even benefit it by pumping in extra sums.[94] With a modest number of troops in any one town, they could simply make use of the existing local networks of supply and food preparation.[95] When garrisons were enlarged during wartime and stretched local capacity, *munitionnaires* might be called upon to supply garrisons with their food.

Abuses and Exemptions

Soldiers quartered with a civilian family could be a mere inconvenience or could pose a real danger. Mazarin stated that "Three days of *logement* of soldiers is more of a problem for an individual than is paying the *taille*."[96] The worst abuses, by kind and frequency, occurred during the long war with Spain. The lesser run of misconduct by soldiers could be bad enough. If not kept in control, troops might abandon their assigned quarters in order to stay where they chose, as did the Gardes françaises in 1644.[97] They might

---

[90] André, *Le Tellier*, 383–84.   [91] Louis, *Mémoires*, 1:9.

[92] Myron P. Gutmann, *War and Rural Life in the Early Modern Low Countries* (Princeton: 1980), 37.

[93] SHAT, Bib., Col. des ord., vol. 12, #4. 21 February 1595.

[94] See *intendants'* comments in Corvisier, *Les Français et l'armée*, 276–79.

[95] Troops could be dispersed much more completely in peace time. For comments on the situation after 1659, see André, *Le Tellier*, 362–63.

[96] André Corvisier, *La France de Louis XIV, 1643–1715: Ordre intérieur et place en Europe* (Paris: 1979), 108.

[97] AG, A^{1}86, #88, 8 March 1644, report that *Gardes françaises* lodged outside of assigned quarters around Paris.

also try to demand money payments from their hosts.[98] To intimidate their hosts, either to extract goods and services or simply for the love of it, soldiers bullied them by petty actions of destruction, such as smashing glasses.[99] Blustering soldiers might also demand dinner and wine for their friends.[100] It is no great wonder that in 1675 the idea of having to lodge French troops horrified the women of Maestricht, "the thought alone of their approach made them tremble."[101] As late as 1697, Phélypeaux listed as cause of the depopulation in the generality of Paris "the *logements* and the frequent passage of soldiers through the towns and cities that are on their route."[102]

Owing to the inconvenience, expense, loss of privacy, and possible danger associated with boarding soldiers, the French prized exemptions from quartering. These were many and varied. Some entire provinces, such as Auvergne, enjoyed a full exemption from quartering troops during the winter. Languedoc received a promise of exemption from Louis XIV, but the monarch still compelled the province to quarter troops in 1674 and 1685.[103] Certain cities, such as Grenoble, also benefited from an exemption.[104] Provinces and cities could also purchase temporary exemptions. Always short of money during wartime, the monarchy greedily accepted such bargains. Champagne bought an exemption from lodging troops in 1651 by paying an additional tax.[105] The duchy of Burgundy paid the king of France to be free of all *logements* for a year in October 1656.[106] Towns might also purchase a legal, or illegal, exemption. In 1660, Boulogne purchased an exemption for 40,000 livres, a protection that rose in price to 43,950 livres by the 1690s.[107] The sale of temporary exemptions could turn into a kind of racket. Louis XIV tells of a case in which a captain of the Auvergne regiment took 300 livres from the inhabitants of Rethel to exempt them from a stay by his company. Louis broke the conniving officer; that is, the king stripped the guilty captain of his rank and banned him from the army.[108] Beyond provincial and town exemptions,

---

[98] AG, MR 1881, #6, 12 February 1566, declaration that infantrymen and cavalrymen are forcing people to buy them extra items; AG, A¹67, #68, 4 Febrauary 1641 in Landier, "Guerre, Violences, et Société," 20, hosts forced by soldiers to pay more money to soldiers; see, as well, AG, A¹138, #347, 1653; AG, A¹142, #271, 20 Avril 1654; SHAT, Bib., Col. des ord., vol. 19, #96, 25 April 1654, troops from Catalonia demanding money for *ustensile* and *subsistance*.

[99] Dijon, H 256, 24 March 1693.

[100] Nord, C 9741, and incident at Thuin, investigated by a commissaire des guerres, 18 February 1679, involving a man named Cigny who refused to let three soldiers come to eat where only two were lodged; an argument was followed by a fight; the soldiers ran away when armed townsmen arrived crying, "Kill, kill!"

[101] Jean Préchac, *L'héroine mousquetaire* (Paris: 1679), 63.

[102] Corvisier, *Les Français et l'armée,* 274.

[103] William Beik, *Absolutism and Society in Seventeenth-Century France* (Cambridge: 1985), 283–85.

[104] Corvisier, *Les Français et l'armée,* 230.

[105] AG, A¹125, #253, 14 January 1651 in Landier, "Guerre, Violences, et Société," 18.

[106] Côte d'Or, C 3674, 1 October 1656. This document promised a payment of 200,000 livres on 23 November 1656.

[107] Corvisier, *Les Français et l'armée,* 260.   [108] Louis, *Mémoires,* 1:248–49.

nobles of great status and prestige might secure privilege for their own lands. Turenne did so for his estates at Maringues, and in 1661, he won it for the viscounty of Turenne as well.[109]

Ordinances exempted entire classes of individuals. These included nobles, clergy, officers of sovereign courts, tax collectors, and so on.[110] The exemption for many offices stood as one of the benefits of purchasing positions for those with sufficient cash. Other more mundane functions also granted exemptions; service in the *maréchaussée* won this privilege, and enrolling in a garrison company might protect an individual from boarding soldiers.[111]

Municipalities also granted exemptions in special circumstances, and the debate back and forth as to who should lodge soldiers signaled a municipality's fairness. Dijon serves as an interesting case. Citizens openly complained when they felt that the authorities played favorites. A petition of the 1670s read: "There are many individuals who are in a better state to provide lodging for troops than the suppliants, yet those individuals nonetheless are exempt."[112] During the same period, a printed sheet posted on the Place des Cordeliers in Dijon complained that the army sent too great a number of soldiers to Dijon and then went on to name neighbors who had not quartered any troops in their homes, implying that they had won favors from the local authorities.[113] Perhaps in response to such complaints, the *intendant* Bouchu announced in 1678 "Lodgments will be assigned by the mayors . . . to begin with the first inhabitant until the last, without any exception, and in proportion of what each is taxed, in such a way that those of the said inhabitants who pay twenty livres of tailles will provide ten times as much *logement* as those who pay only forty sols."[114] But the charges of favoritism continued. Thirty years later, a man named Duplesy charged that "there is a woman at the port Guillaume who, by means of her cheating, has never lodged a soldier."[115] Older citizens repeatedly petitioned for exemptions. About 1700, a 72-year-old woman asked not to lodge officers anymore, since she lacked the strength to keep rooms clean enough for them, while a 92-year-old man requested a total exemption so he could "finish his last days in tranquillity."[116]

Abuses associated with *logement* explain the force behind the infamous *dragonnades*, in which troops were quartered on Huguenots in the early 1680s and then again in 1685 with little other purpose than to bully them into conversion. As a carrot to contrast with the stick, Louis promised a two-year exemption from quartering in 1681 for those Huguenots wise enough to see the error of their ways and convert to Catholicism. Louvois bragged that "This ordinance will cause a great many conversions in places of *étapes*."[117]

[109] Bérenger, *Turenne*, 77 and 337.   [110] Marion, *Dictionnaire*, 340.
[111] André, *Le Tellier*, 367.   [112] Dijon, H 218 bis.
[113] Dijon, H 218 bis, poster dated 26 December 1671.
[114] Dijon, H 218 bis, poster dated 16 April 1678.   [115] Dijon, H219, December 1702.
[116] See Dijon, H 219, for these and other examples of special exemptions granted because of age or infirmity.
[117] AG, A¹653, 18 March 1681, Louvois to Marillac in Rousset, *Louvois*, 3:444–45.

Yet with all this said, *logement* should not be seen as a universal disaster. *Intendants*' descriptions of the era at the end of the Nine Years' War speak of money as being available because troops were quartered in a given area. "Money is abundant in Flanders because the King consumes it for the payment of the troops."[118]

Winter Quarters

During wars, the armies that campaigned during the summer went to ground for the winter and dispersed to cities and villages. Up to 1642, French armies took up winter quarters all across France, with the exception of Brittany, apparently with the goal of spreading the burden.[119] Later, taxation equalized the costs, and the bulk of the troops remained quartered along the frontier. In any case, armies lost their combat integrity as they marched off to quarters. Cavalry units often moved into the interior to seek more abundant forage. The *munitionnaires*' supply trains disbanded entirely, awaiting reassembly for the next campaign.

Winter quarters began in November and ran through April. Each fall, usually in October, the crown issued a declaration concerning winter quarters, stating the principles that would govern the way the troops would be paid, fed, and quartered.[120] Historian Louis André ranked the regulation of 4 November 1651 as the most important of its kind during the seventeenth century, and it remained the basis for winter-quarters regulations until 1715.[121] The Sun King improved military practice more by insisting on strict execution of existing regulations than by innovation.

By this 1651 ordinance, troops were to go into quarters in walled towns. Troops would be paid for 150 days, infantry in fifteen *prêts* of ten days each. As discussed in the previous chapter, bread would be furnished to infantry privates, corporals, and sergeants, and forage would be supplied to cavalry troopers and all officers. Town officials, mayors and aldermen, were to assign lodgings to the men by giving the *maréchal de logis* of the regiments slips of paper, *billets*, listing how many officers and men could be put in each house. The ordinance also listed exemptions from *logements* (e.g., clergymen, gentlemen pursuing the profession of arms, royal officials, mayors, aldermen, and tax collectors). Captains were to see to the repair of weapons and to make sure that their companies had a full complement by spring. Officials of the central and local government, such as *intendants, commissaires des guerres,* and mayors, were to keep control and monitor the state of the units by carrying

---

[118] See several quotes in Corvisier, *Les Français et l'armée*, 276.

[119] Contamine, *Histoire militaire*, 1:372–73. See page 368 for a very interesting map of winter quarters in 1639, showing how armies were spread all over France.

[120] André Eugène Navareau, *Le logement et les ustensiles des gens de guerre de 1439–1789* (Poitiers: 1924), 39.

[121] "Règlement fait par le Roy pour le logement," 4 November 1651 in André, *Le Tellier*, 667–82. This regulation was, in fact, based on that of 1649. Navereau, *Le logement*, 58.

out a series of reviews, visits, and inspections and by maintaining meticulous records to be passed up the line to higher authorities. As earlier noted, the provisions of the 1651 ordinance were not always followed, particularly when authorities dispersed troops to villages from 1655 on.

The choice of good winter quarters was a major concern. Armies exhausted on campaign had the chance to restore themselves over the winter, provided that available food, fodder, and housing met the needs of the troops. Bad winter quarters could accomplish just the opposite. In 1630, Turenne's regiment, which numbered 500 men in summer and was reinforced to 700 in October, fell to 250 by the end of the winter.[122] Perhaps this experience convinced him of the importance of proper quarters for the rest of his long career. Insufficient rations raised the specters of sickness, desertion, and pillage. If all went well, however, men and horses regained their strength, equipment was repaired or replaced, and new recruits arrived to fill out the ranks in the spring. During wartime, army commanders prized winter quarters located in rich enemy territory because this allowed the army to live off enemy resources and spare the French treasury, but this will be the subject of the next chapter.

Since winter quarters made such demands on local communities, they sometimes resisted the imposition of troops. The French relied on Alsace so relentlessly for winter quarters in the 1640s that the incensed peasants attacked the troops. The crown even authorized this violence when troops strayed from their assigned quarters.[123] Resistance may have been precipitated by the brutal fashion in which the army seized quarters. A relative of Colbert once complained to him "Thus you see that winter quarters is established by actions of war as if one was *chez* the enemy."[124] Later, during the personal reign of Louis XIV, French peasants did not oppose winter quarters by acts of collective violence in the way that they had before.

The Ustensile

A quartered soldier could expect not only a roof over his head but certain essentials supplied by the host. These essentials went by the collective name of the *ustensile*. The history of the *ustensile* provides an interesting case of the evolution of winter quarters and taxation during the *grand siècle*. As the *ustensile* changed in amount and nature from the sixteenth to the eighteenth century, it also became a source of dispute between soldiers and civilians.

Regulations guaranteeing certain objects and services to quartered soldiers go back at least to the reign of Charles VII.[125] The list of promised items varied somewhat during the sixteenth and early seventeenth centuries. An

---

[122] Bérenger, *Turenne*, 87.   [123] Croxton, "Peacemaking in Early Modern Europe, 145.

[124] BN, Mélanges Colbert, 101, #136, 17 March 1658, Colbert de Terron to Jean-Baptiste Colbert.

[125] Reboul in Gabriel Hanoteau, ed. *Histoire de la nation française*, vol. 7, *Histoire militaire et navale*, pt. 1 (Paris: 1925), 264–65.

ordinance of 1545 listed wine, vinegar, salt, and firewood as part of the *ustensile* to be supplied without charge to the soldier.[126] When the 1617 assembly of notables complained that troops were demanding too much *ustensile* from townsmen, the assembly stipulated the following as legitimate: "table wear [*le couvert*], fire to warm themselves and cook their meat, a bed or pallet, and a candle for each man lodged." But soldiers frequently demanded more and "ransomed the poor people."[127] An ordinance of 1628, listed as *ustensile* salt, vinegar, wood, and candles; another of 1633 added table linen, bowl, and glass. Roughly speaking, the *ustensile* could be broken into two categories, the use of some items – a bed, bed linens, cookware, and tableware – and the outright donation of certain consumables – salt, vinegar, candles, and wood. The 1633 ordinance explicitly forbade commuting the *ustensile* to a money payment to soldiers, a prohibition common to many of the official pronouncements, since troops asked hosts to do this in an attempt to extort money in lieu of goods or services – anything to fill their empty purses.[128]

In the 1630s, the state levied an extra tax to cover the expenses of winter quarters. David Parrott has found that as early as the winter of 1637–38, the French substituted a tax, the *subsistances*, for the far more arbitrary practice of making the hosts in garrison towns bear all the costs.[129] For the next winter, an instruction of 24 July 1638 directed *intendants* to raise 9,600,000 livres to cover the costs of winter quarters. This amount was still higher by 1640.[130] The cost of the *ustensile* could be shared not only by taxing throughout the kingdom but also within the very city lodging troops through assessments on those who had no soldiers in their homes. This was the case in Verdun in 1654, when townsmen free of quartering were to pay into a fund that would provide 200 livres for each company of infantry and 600 livres for each one of cavalry.[131]

During the 1640s, much of the *ustensile* was transformed into a money payment, such as had been prohibited before, to be funded by a tax. Regulations like that of 18 October 1641 essentially split off those items that soldiers consumed from those that they merely used, and they offered money instead for the former. This was done in the name of equity, because the expense of boarding soldiers should not just fall on those who quartered them but should be borne by a broader community through the levying of taxes. As the regulation explained, "In order that the expense of the said wood and candles does not fall on the individuals who supply them, it will

[126] A 1530 ordinance stipulated that there would be no charge, and that of 1545 promised wine, vinegar, salt, and some wood. Navareau, *Le logement*, 167.

[127] Navareau, *Le logement*, 167.

[128] Ordinances of 13 November 1628 and 14 February 1633 in General Baron Bardin, *Dictionnaire de l'armée de terre ou recherches historiques sur l'art et les usages militaires des anciens et modernes*, 8 vols. (Paris: 1841), 8:5169.

[129] Parrott, "Administration of the French Army," 267–68.

[130] Côte d'Or, C 3673, 6 November 1638; Côte d'Or, C 3673, 12 October 1640.

[131] SHAT, Bib., Col. des ord., vol. 19, #127, Verdun agreement 24 December 1654.

be levied on all those liable to the *taille* in the entire *élection* in which the garrisons will be dependent."[132] The money raised could then be passed on to the soldiers to buy their own wood and candles. The 4 December 1649 ordinance spelled out what could and could not be expected: "His Majesty intends that because soldiers receive payment of the said *ustensile*, they can accept only a bed with its linens, table linens, pot and bowl, such as their hosts will have, but no wood, candle, salt, and vinegar nor any other staple whatsoever."[133] This directive was repeated in somewhat briefer form by the important 1651 ordinance, which also allowed only money payment for the *ustensile*.[134] In lieu of consumables, soldiers received a payment adjusted to branch and rank – for example, 2 sols per day for an enlisted infantryman and 60 sols for a cavalry captain in the 1651 regulation.[135] The 1653 and 1654 regulations incorporated language that became standard from that point on. Soldiers could only claim as *ustensile* the use of *"le couvert*, pot, and bowl, a place by the fire and in the candlelight at their host's dwelling according to that host's convenience, without any other items being supplied, not money, wood, candle nor anything else whatsoever under the pretext of *ustensile*."[136] There were several other *règlements* defining the *ustensile*, but the main outlines had been set by this point.[137] An integral aspect of winter quarters, the *ustensile* had evolved from a payment in kind by hosts into a money payment funded by impositions on entire areas.[138]

It underwent two more transformations as a tax in the seventeenth century. From 1692 on, hosts were to receive a payment of 1 sol per day "in order to compensate for the furnishing of the bed and the place by the fire and by the candle." Those who actually provided the service put in their claims for reimbursement at the end of the year.[139] This became a tax on the villages and *généralités* of those who actually lodged the men. This is an amount that Louis had discussed as early as 1666.[140] The ordinance of 25 September 1695 explained that the cost of *ustensile* had been so great the year before that while the king intended "during the coming winter to lodge the

---

[132] SHAT, Bib., Col. des ord., vol. 16, #31, 18 October 1641.

[133] Bardin, *Dictionnaire*, 8:5169; and 4 December 1649 ordinance in Marion, *Dictionnaire*, 549.

[134] 4 November 1651 *règlement* in André, *Le Tellier*, 670.

[135] Bardin, *Dictionnaire*, 8:5169; 4 November 1651 *règlement* in André, *Le Tellier*, 668–69.

[136] SHAT, Bib., Col. des ord., vol. 19, #65, ordinance of 1 February 1654. See, as well, the ordinances of 11 July 1653 (SHAT, Bib., Col. des ord., vol. 19, #39) and 28 November 1653 (SHAT, Bib., Col. des ord., vol. 19, #51).

[137] Navereau, *Le logement*, discusses the following ordinances that followed 1654: 12 November 1658, 27 July 1666, 1 November 1667, 20 October 1689, and 12 October 1701. However, there were others, those of 7 September 1666, for example.

[138] Bardin, *Dictionnaire*, 8:5169, says that the ordinance of 7 September 1666 abolished *ustensiles* in money and returned to *ustensiles* in kind; however, this seems in error. See SHAT, Bib., Col. des ord., vol. 23, #85, 10 October 1675.

[139] See, for example, announcements of reimbursements for 1702 and 1704 in Dijon, H 219. See Côte d'Or, C 367, for some individual *billets*.

[140] Louis, *Mémoires*, 1:247; Louis, *Oeuvres*, 2:90–91.

infantry in his frontier cities and fortresses, . . . the inhabitants of the interior cities will pay 100 sols per day during the 150 days of winter quarters for the ustensil of each of the companies of infantry."[141] The argument was that being saved the inconvenience of actually lodging troops, these towns should bear the burden by paying a tax.

A further analysis of this ordinance reveals another change in the *ustensile*. By Louis's last two great wars, the *ustensile* tax had become a way of augmenting the sums available to refurbish the arms and equipment of units in winter quarters. This represented a major shift from the origins of the *ustensile*. The monarchy, having created a tax, expanded its amount and function to finance the war effort. The 1695 ordinance requires 100 sols per day. This became a standard allowance for infantry companies, to be disbursed as follows: 6 sols for the lieutenant, 4 sols for the sous-lieutenant, 1 sols for the aide-major of the regiment, and 89 sols for the captain. This large amount for the captain was not simply an allowance to cover the personal costs of his lodgings but a contribution to what was required to ensure that his company was "complete, well armed and clothed, and to furnish tents."[142] Although this amount stayed at 100 sols for an infantry company through the 1690s and into the War of the Spanish Succession, by 1710, it had risen to 133 sols per day. Cavalry and dragoon companies received more than infantry, circa 1710. But their 30 livres, or 600 sols per day, was distributed very differently. Unlike the enlisted infantrymen, who received nothing directly, common troopers received 12 sols per day if they had served in the previous campaign or were to serve in the next one. The fact that cavalrymen received only 6 sols if they had not been or would not be on campaign shows again that the *ustensile* for the cavalry was also a device to prepare and refit companies.[143] Assessment of the *ustensile* tax rose to 12,741,000 livres in 1696, about 11 percent of total cost of maintaining the army.[144] The *ustensile* remained a means both of covering the expenses of *logement* and of assisting with the restoration of companies during the eighteenth century.[145]

CLOTHING

"It is not enough to have a lot of men. It is necessary that they be well formed, well dressed, and well armed."[146] With these words, Louvois expressed his concern that the numerous soldiers of Louis XIV were useless

[141] SHAT, Bib., Col. des ord., vol. 29, #51, ordinance of 25 September 1695. See earlier similar ordinances, SHAT, Bib., Col. des ord., vol. 27, #70, ordinance of 22 September 1691; SHAT, Bib., Col. des ord., vol. 28, #31, ordinance of 2 October 1692.

[142] SHAT, Bib., Col. des ord., vol. 29, #21, ordinance of 20 September 1694; and SHAT, Bib., Col. des ord., vol. 31, #57, ordinance of 12 October 1701.

[143] Chart of allowances by *ustensile* circa 1710 in Mallet, *Comptes rendus*, 167.

[144] AN, G⁷1774, #52, "Etat des troupes que le roy a eu sur pied, et leur depense."

[145] Lee Kennett, *The French Armies in the Seven Years' War* (Durham, NC: 1967), 93.

[146] Louvois in Corvisier, *Louvois*, 109.

without clothing and weapons. When it comes to discussing the clothing of French soldiers during the *grand siècle*, two questions dominate – adequacy and uniformity. First, were the troops dressed properly, by whom, and how? And second, were units dressed alike? One question is concerned with the physical nature of the soldier, the other with his psychology. On the whole, the second issue has attracted more interest than the first, although the first is more important.

The notion of dressing soldiers alike, not merely dressing them sufficiently, is rich in implications. Uniformity of dress implies uniformity of action – the soldier as disciplined automaton. John Keegan has recently argued that uniforms represented the soldier's loss of individuality and labeled him as a servant – as in the livery worn by domestics.[147] Keegan and others agree that uniforms fostered obedience and sharpened drill. To others, the appearance of identically clothed regiments marked the emergence of the modern army. To still others, troops dressed uniformly in the king's livery symbolized royal control of the army – that vital royal monopoly over the means of coercion so necessary for the rise of the modern state. Be this as it may, a discussion of soldiers' clothing quickly rises above a catalog of coats and shoes to one of attitudes.

In the seventeenth century, several factors encouraged the French to standardize the dress of their soldiers. On the one hand, and most practically, concerns for health dictated that the men be well clothed and well shod. This, of course, did not dictate a standard cut or color to soldier's outfits, but it did require that they all be supplied with a basic set of clothing, suitable to the weather and in conformity with efficiency and contemporary styles. On the other hand, convenience allowed that when a great number of items were being made, a single pattern was followed, producing uniform cut, and perhaps even color, for the sake of cost effectiveness. Stipulating the exact specifications of clothing items ensured against cheating by officers or contractors, who might otherwise turn a profit by using inferior fabric, shortening long coats, or forgetting collars, cuffs, and buttons. Lastly, and perhaps most persuasively, there was the matter of fashion and pride. Appearance was nothing to be sneered at, as one military handbook of the 1620s proclaimed: "200 well clothed soldiers look better than 400 badly attired men."[148] When it was clear that units simply looked better when dressed alike, an impression reinforced by the uniform dress of elite and foreign regiments, competitive vanity won over French colonels and captains to uniforms.[149] Given all these factors, it is most likely, as Rousset concluded, that the

---

[147] John Keegan, *A History of Warfare* (New York: 1993), 342.

[148] Mathieu de la Simonne, *Alphabet du soldat et vray eclaircissement militaire* (Paris: 1623), 110–11, in Babeau, *La vie militaire*, 1:95.

[149] For comments on the force of style and vanity among the French, see Jean-Baptiste Primi Visconti, *Mémoires de Primi Visconti sur la cour de Louis XIV*, ed. Jean-François Solnon (Paris: 1988), 18.

triumph of the uniform occurred first in fact and only later in regulations for the French.[150]

All the talk of uniforms should not, however, blind us to the fact that the primary functions of clothing were to guard the health of the soldier and to allow him to accomplish his job of marching and fighting. Ill-clothed troops could be a liability rather than an asset.

When Nani, the Venetian ambassador, described French troops during the minority of Louis XIV as being almost naked and in rags, this comes as little surprise.[151] The relative ineffectiveness of French military administration and the exhaustion of state finances made such conditions predictable. It is more surprising that such conditions did not disappear after 1659. The first war in Louis's personal reign, the War of Devolution, saw Turenne write, as winter set in: "Nothing is more necessary for them than clothing; many soldiers will perish there because of not having received it soon."[152] In some ways, French military administration overcame the challenges of the Dutch War better than it dealt with any other conflict during the seventeenth century, yet some of the correspondence of the period displayed real shortcomings in clothing supply. In 1673, a *commissaire des guerres* refused to review a company "which had 26 or 27 men as naked as a hand and the majority without shoes or socks."[153] While the situation generally improved with time, even in Louis's last war, clothing supply deteriorated so badly that many of the soldiers that Villars commanded at the hard-fought battle of Malplaquet stood in bare feet. So it is safe to say that the problem of manufacturing and supplying clothing to the French army was never entirely solved during the *grand siècle*, however Herculean the efforts.

Changing Styles and Costs

Military styles differed sharply during the century, and the lack of uniformity between men carrying different weapons multiplied the variety. At the start of the *grand siècle*, baggy breeches that fastened at the knee were standard for pikemen and musketeers. Pikemen sported as much armor as possible, including breast and back plates, thigh protection, and morion helmets. Musketeers were more likely to wear simply a loose coat and broad brimmed hat. Infantrymen, even officers, throughout the century wore stockings and shoes rather than boots, unless the officers were mounted. During the personal reign of Louis XIV, the most prominent piece of military clothing became the *justaucorps*, a coat reaching to the knees, decorated with a row of buttons down the front. The *justaucorps* usually lacked the turn-backs of the eighteenth century; however, it was often lined with a different color of cloth,

---

[150] Rousset, *Louvois*, 1:188.   [151] Nani in André, *Le Tellier*, 329.

[152] Turenne to Le Tellier, 22 December 1667, in Joseph Michaud and Jean Poujoulat, *Nouvelle collection des mémoires relatifs a l'histoire de France* (Paris: 1836), 3:512.

[153] Corvisier, *Louvois*, 110.

which showed on the large cuffs of the coat. Beneath it, soldiers wore a sleeveless vest along with shirt and knee breeches. A broad brimmed hat, often with the brim folded up in one fashion or another, protected his head. Armor disappeared for infantry. Cavalry troopers preserved their armor longer than did infantry, although they took off their helmets and breastplates eventually, except for the few heaviest units. Cavalry wore heavy tall boots and spurs, while dragoons wore shoes and gaiters to allow them to move more freely on foot. Cavalry were likely to adorn themselves more elegantly than infantry, which generally did not attain the prestige of the mounted troops.

From 1610 to 1715, the cost of soldiers' clothing rose sharply. In the early 1640s, Le Tellier was able to purchase a suit of clothing for an infantryman for from 10 livres 6 sols to 13 livres 7 sols.[154] In about 1650, the cost stood at 15 livres.[155] According to Victor Belhomme, the price of an infantryman's outfit climbed to 36 livres 10 sous, and by the War of the Spanish Succession, it had jumped considerably again.[156] Contracts for that period peg the price at between 44 and 57, while a cavalryman's clothing cost 111 livres.[157]

As mentioned in the section on pay, the monarchy authorized officers to deduct money from their men's pay packets to pay the ever higher clothing bills. This practice had precedents before the personal reign of Louis XIV. In 1645, Le Tellier explained to Harcourt, "I know that it would be very useful to resupply [habiller] the poorly clothed infantry soldiers; but as it is impossible to contract new expenses, it is necessary to try to make the commanders save from their pay what would be needed to cover their most pressing necessity."[158] However, such deductions only became the rule for the French army by royal ordinance in 1666. In May of that year, Le Tellier authorized officers in the Trois-Évêchés region "to retain 1 sol per day from the pay of each soldier in order to clothe him and furnish him with other necessities."[159] In December, he extended this deduction permanently to all the army. The new ordinance commanded that "captains and officers commanding companies of infantry and cavalry will retain 30 sols per month from the pay of each trooper or soldier, the said 30 sols will be employed by the said officer for clothing, shoes, and other necessities for the said troopers and soldiers and for the remount of the said cavalrymen."[160] To prevent captains from pocketing the money, *commissaires des guerres* were to supervise the accounts every three months. This authorization was periodically renewed.[161] In 1679, the deduction for clothing was split into two portions, 4 deniers going to the captain and 8 deniers to the *trésorier de l'extraordinaire des guerres*.[162]

---

[154] André, *Le Tellier*, 72n.   [155] André, *Le Tellier*, 334.

[156] Belhomme, *L'armée française en 1690*, 26.

[157] AN, G⁷1778, #303; AN, G⁷1092, 15 June 1708; AN, G⁷1779, #133–35, 7 June 1707.

[158] Letter of 8 December 1645 in André, *Le Tellier*, 331.

[159] SHAT, Bib., Col. des ord., vol. 21, #139, 24 May 1666 in André, *Le Tellier*, 340–41.

[160] SHAT, Bib., Col. des ord., vol. 21, #166, 5 December 1666 in André, *Le Tellier*, 341–42.

[161] SHAT, Bib., Col. des ord., vol. 24, #49, ordinance of 28 February 1679, art. 22, stated that captains could deduct 1 sol per day "for their remount, armament, and clothing."

[162] Contamine, *Histoire militaire*, 1:405.

Uniforms

No careful military historian would claim that French troops wore uniforms before the personal reign of Louis XIV, for the evidence points to the contrary. When large lots of clothing were distributed, the same batch was often broken up among many different units. Perhaps if a town supplied a single regiment with a refit of clothing, as in 1627–28, there might have been a moment of uniformity, simply because it was convenient to make similar outfits, but absolutely no policy set color, and it was only a matter of convenience to set the cut by means of sample coats, as in 1647. Instead of uniforms, regiments and entire armies declared their allegiance by wearing emblems or tokens stuck in the hatband or some other convenient place. For example, at the battle of faubourg Saint-Antoine in 1652, the army that Condé commanded wore straw, while the king's men wore paper. Such marks of loyalty could be quickly discarded if that loyalty became inconvenient. During the Wars of Religion of the sixteenth century, troops wore sashes of particular colors to advertise their party and their captain.[163] The wearing of a captain's colors was not uncommon; it dated back to the fifteenth century. By a directive of 9 February 1584, *gendarmes* and archers were to wear cloaks and *hocquetons* in their captain's colors, a fashion that carried over into the 1600s.[164] But this was not a complete uniform. Audouin claimed that the earliest true uniform in the French service was that worn by Concini's guard during the minority of Louis XIII, 1610–17.[165]

The first general order regulating the uniforms of an entire field army came in 1645, but it concerned the English New Model Army, not for the French, and it stipulated only that red would be the color for all regiments.[166] According to André, the first standardized uniforms for French units came in 1657, when Louis gave his bodyguard blue outfits.[167] But when Louis XIV took power, no directions for cut or color determined the dress of French line regiments.[168] The historian Daniel claimed that in 1661 several companies of the Gardes françaises wore gray or red uniforms; however, they followed little more than the whim of the captain.[169] Only in 1665 did at least the officers of this regiment adopt the blue *justaucorps*.[170]

At a review held at Breteuil in 1666, some regiments stood in uniform, which may have been a product of the generosity or vanity of their colonels, or these units might have been foreign, for in the line army of Louis XIV,

[163] Hanoteau, *Histoire de la nation française*, vol. 7, pt. 1, 263.

[164] Contamine, *Histoire militaire*, 1:224; AG, MR 1881, #14.

[165] Audouin, *Histoire de l'administration*, 2:157.

[166] J. W. Wijn, "Military Forces and Warfare, 1610–1648," in *New Cambridge Modern History*, vol. 4 (Cambridge: 1971), 215.

[167] André, *Le Tellier et Louvois*, 355.   [168] Rousset, *Louvois*, 1:185.

[169] Daniel in André, *Le Tellier*, 340.

[170] SHAT, Bib., Col. des ord., vol. 21, #101, 16 January 1665. This ordinance explicitly states only what officers were to wear; however, Rousset, 1:185–86, André, *Le Tellier et Louvois*, 355, and Corvisier, *Louvois*, 110, interpret this as meaning the men as well.

foreign regiments in French pay led the march toward uniformity.[171] Capitulations, or contracts, with such foreign units often stipulated that the men be dressed the same. Such was the case in the 1672 capitulation, which directed that the colonel, Ximenes, "will have all the sergeants and soldiers of the said regiment dressed in the same manner."[172]

Yet when Louvois concerned himself with native French regiments, there seemed no interest in enforcing uniform attire. Although a 1665 regulation enforced uniform clothing on the mounted troops of the *maison*, in his 1668 instructions to Martinet, the war minister cautioned that "It is not at all necessary to ask officers to have their clothing all the same nor made at the same time . . . ; but you must not allow, no matter what, that the soldiers be badly shod or badly dressed, nor that the arms not be in a state to serve, either by the caliber of their muskets or by their quality."[173] Nonetheless, certain standard histories inform their readers, incorrectly, that the infantry received uniforms in 1670 or shortly thereafter.[174]

The period of the Dutch War was important for the evolution of uniforms, but it did not complete its path during that conflict.[175] Many pieces of evidence demonstrate that, by and large, French soldiers were not in uniform early in the Dutch War. An *intendant* proposed selling the clothing of dead soldiers from the hospital to a company in the Regiment d'Orléans "which has need of them."[176] A commander of the chateau of Angers suggested that "soldiers would have more trouble in deserting if they were all dressed in the same manner, because one could recognize them everywhere

---

[171] André, *Le Tellier et Louvois*, 355.

[172] SHAT, Bib., Col. des ord., vol. 22, #174, 11 March 1672. See also the 1668 contract of the Royal Rousillion, a unit composed of men from Catalonia, Rousillon, Portugal, Spain, and Italy. AG, A¹219, #238, 15 October 1668. When Louvois reviewed the German regiment of Alsace in 1669, they were "all dressed in a single fashion," and at a review a few days later, other Germans in the Furstenburg regiment were "all dressed in blue, faced with yellow." AG, A¹241, 19 and 24 May 1669, in Rousset, *Louvois*, 1:186. Still, not every capitulation stipulated uniforms. See, for a Berne regiment, SHAT, Bib., Col. des ord., vol. 22, #143, 14 August 1671, and for one from Mulhaus, SHAT, Bib., Col. des ord., vol. 22, #143, 13 October 1671, neither of which do. Directions for raising troops in Savoy allow that men will be dressed "either in red or in blue, each to his own inclination." AG, A¹279, 22 October 1672, instruction to Servient.

[173] AG, A¹221, 20 December 1668, instructions to Martinet by Louvois in Rousset, 1:208.

[174] See, for example, Louis Dussieux, *L'Armée en France*, 3 vols. (Versailles: 1884), 2:182–83; even Corvisier, who should know better, states flatly: "During the Dutch war, each unit had its uniform, at least for the men in the ranks." Corvisier, *Louvois*, 191. He seems to retract this in his part of Contamine, *Histoire militaire*, 1:406.

[175] Pichat, in his history of the French army in 1674 states that only foreign regiments were to be dressed uniformly. H. Pichat, "Les armées de Louis XIV et 1674," *Revue d'histoire de l'armée*, 1910, 21.

[176] AG, A¹294, #312, 13 September 1672. Interestingly, from the 1690s, the clothes of a dead soldier would be returned to his captain, implying that the troops may have been in uniform, so the clothes would be appropriate only for a particular regiment. Records from 1691 to 1728 in Babeau, *La vie militaire*, 1:214.

more easily."[177] Would either request have been made if uniforms had been issued and soldiers of one regiment been required to dress identically? Quite to the contrary, in 1673, Louvois wrote to Luxembourg with exactly the opposite in mind, stressing that it was not necessary to dress the troops "in new clothes for this year, nor all in the same fashion."[178] Yet, apparently, steps were taken toward uniformity, for just as the commander at Angers predicted, it was possible to arrest deserters by spotting their uniforms. This happened to a deserter from the Royal Roussillon, when he was seen wearing items that the authority reported "I believe similar to those that had been given recruits of that regiment I had seen at Binche."[179]

The interwar period moved the process along. Correspondence concerning clothing in the early 1680s did not stress uniforms for the rank and file and only insisted on clothing of the same color for officers. In 1682, Louvois wrote concerning infantry that "His Majesty desires only that all the officers of the same regiment be dressed in the same color."[180] A 1683 directive to an inspector of cavalry went no further: "The intention of the king is that you inform the cavalry which is under your orders that His Majesty desires that between now and the next spring, the officers of each regiment be dressed uniformly."[181] But an ordinance of 1685 prescribed particular colors for regiments in French service: blue for the Gardes françaises and the royal regiments, red for the Swiss, and gray-white for regular French infantry.[182]

Regulations instructing authorities concerning raising the *milice* for the Nine Years' War explicitly stated that uniform dress was not an issue. While ordinances commanded that each *milicien* receive a hat, *justaucorps*, breeches, stockings, and good shoes, they carried the proviso that *miliciens* need not be bound "to any uniformity of clothing or color of coat, stockings, or hat."[183] Because *miliciens* fought in their own regiments during that war, it means that all these regiments explicitly had no uniform.

Yet this reluctance to impose uniforms on *miliciens* does not mean that uniforms were not becoming nearly universal for regular regiments in the Nine Years' War.[184] A regulation of 1690 prescribed uniforms for 116 regiments of French cavalry; 88 wore gray with red reverses, while 14 royal or princely regiments wore blue coats.[185] One surprising piece of evidence is that in this war, even the teamsters of the supply train seemed to have adopted

---

[177] AG, A¹279, #124, 9 October 1672.

[178] AG, A¹315, 8 April 1673, in Rousset, *Louvois*, 1:187.

[179] AG, A¹295, 3 October 1672, letter from Le Vacher.

[180] Louvois to d'Alauzier, 11 May 1682, in Rousset, *Louvois*, 3:294n.

[181] Rousset, *Louvois*, 3:295n.   [182] Contamine, *Histoire militaire*, 1:406.

[183] SHAT, Bib., Col. des ord., vol. 26, #18, 29 November 1688. A later regulation stipulated the fabric but not the cut or color of *milice* uniforms. SHAT, Bib., Col. des ord., vol. 26, #24, 3 January 1689.

[184] Certainly Belhomme believes that uniforms had become standard by 1690. Belhomme, *L'armée française en 1690*, 18–19.

[185] Louis Susane, *Histoire de la cavalerie française*, 3 vols. (Paris: 1874), 1:137–38.

standardized military attire. Nodot reported that since du Pille's efforts in 1689, teamsters were wearing uniforms supplied by the *munitionnaires*, with the cost being deducted from the teamsters' pay. Nodot explains this switch to uniform style: "Still another advantage is that all this uniform clothing makes a handsome sight, making all the wagon trains and brigades of mules look the same" with the exception that "the facings and cuffs of the brigades were of different colors."[186] There are also other insights. An ordinance of 1693 stipulated that officers must dress their valets different from their soldiers, implying that the soldiers wore recognizable clothing.[187] In addition, just as in the case of the unfortunate deserter from Royal Roussillion, deserters could again be spotted because of their uniforms. In a particularly bizarre case, a woman dressed as a male soldier in 1696 was arrested because she was wearing much of the uniform of the Regiment du Biez when she tried to enroll in another.[188] Although the army would seem to have adopted uniforms for regular regiments during the Nine Years' War, the first regulation detailing the fabric, color, and cut of uniforms in detail appeared in 1704.[189]

So the most reasonable position to take is that uniforms came into use gradually from the Dutch War to the end of the seventeenth century. In fact, by the close of this era, Vauban wanted not only uniforms, but standardized emblems of rank. He proposed red uniforms with a buff vest with fleurs de lis on the left breast indicating rank: blue for a private soldier, blue with silver borders for a sergeant, silver with gold border for a lieutenant, and gold for a captain.[190]

Clothing Manufacture

Clothing manufacture for the troops during the first half of the *grand siècle* relied on three sources. Colonels and captains responsible for outfitting their own men bought items singly or in lots. While this practice followed from regulations and the nature of the military system itself, the small scale of these purchases means that little record of them remains. However, documents bear witness to occasions when the monarchy supplied large quantities of clothing directly to the army. This seems to have been connected not with the initial outfitting of a unit but with resupply of men already suffering in the field. These items were produced either by entrepreneurs who contracted with the monarchy or by French cities upon which quotas were imposed by the monarchy as a kind of tax.

[186] François Nodot, *Le munitionnaire des armées de France* (Paris: 1697), 18, 19.

[187] 14 February 1693 ordinance in *Ordonnances militaires du roy de France reduites en practique, et appliquées au detail du service*, 2 vols. (Luxembourg: 1734–35), 1:203.

[188] AG, MR 1785, #6, 53–55. See John A. Lynn, "The Strange Case of the Maiden Soldier of Picardy," *MHQ, The Quarterly Journal of Military History*, spring 1990, 54–56.

[189] Regulation of 26 May 1704, Victor Belhomme, *Histoire de l'infanterie en France*, 5 vols. (Paris: 1893–1902), 2:396–97.

[190] Rochas d'Aiglun, *Vauban*, 1:288–89, and 294–95.

The practice of demanding clothing as tribute from French cities was employed repeatedly. The siege of La Rochelle, 1627–28, precipitated such demands, when Louis XIII required Paris to provide 2,500 complete outfits for the king's guards, while he assigned the task of clothing other regiments to other cities.[191] The monarchy turned to private contractors in the 1630s and into the 1640s, as indicated by correspondence, such as Sublet's order to buy 6,000 pairs of shoes for the army in Germany.[192] But as the treasury ran dry in 1647 and 1648, the royal government turned to the cities of the kingdom. Once again, letters went out to local authorities. In 1647, Paris was to supply 1,600 suits of clothing.[193]

At this time, Le Tellier sent a sample coat to the *intendants*, not to create a true uniform but to provide a pattern that would keep the clothing supplied within a general standard: "I send you a *pourpoint* or *justaucorps* that has been made here to serve as a model for all those that will be furnished by the principal towns of the kingdom."[194] This letter also stipulated that the clothing be made in three sizes, $\frac{1}{4}$ small, $\frac{1}{4}$ large, and the rest regular. Dependence on the towns to provide the king's army with clothes became so common that in 1649, the monarchy sent out form letters with blanks to be filled in for the town's name and the number of outfits it was to supply.[195] Such royal commands were not always obeyed; witness Le Tellier's complaints concerning Provins and Abbeville in 1650.[196] The imposition of quotas of clothing remained an alternate form of taxation on French towns until the end of the war with Spain.[197]

André believes that during the war with Spain, Le Tellier centralized the manufacture of uniforms in Paris in order that he could supervise the production of clothing. Thus, as time went on, he always demanded that Paris

---

[191] Letters of 25 October and 7 November 1627 addressed the officials of Paris. Jules Caillet, *De l'administration en France sous le ministère du Cardinal de Richelieu* (Paris: 1857), 366 and 367n; Thomas, *Droit romain des requistions militarires et du logement des gens de guerre*, 182–83. See also the 10 December ordinance ordering Paris to provide 2,500 habits, while similar demands were made of other "*villes de nostre royaume.*" SHAT, Bib., Col. des ord., vol. 13, #117. See François Duval Fontenay-Mareuil, *Mémoires*, in Joseph Michaud and Jean Poujoulat, eds., *Nouvelle collection des mémoires pour servir à l'histoire de France*, vol. 5 (Paris: 1837), 197, for a statement that each town had to supply one regiment.

[192] AN, K114^{A}, dos. 1, fol. 3 in Orest Ranum, *Richelieu and the Councillors of Louis XIII* (Oxford: 1963), 101. See, as well, the following: order issued 4 April 1630 to Allègre, general of the king's army in Italy, to deliver 5,075 habits to thirteen regiments of infantry in Susane, *Infanterie*, 1:185–86: Le Tellier's actions to contract with entrepreneurs to make clothes and shoes for the army in Italy in 1641, André, *Le Tellier*, 72–73; and SHAT, Bib., Col. des ord., vol. 17, #67, letter of king to Harcourt, 22 December 1645, to distribute 3,000 suits of clothing and 3,000 pairs of shoes to be distributed to each regiment in proportion to its numbers, just to go to those who needed them.

[193] André, *Le Tellier*, 334 and 336–37.

[194] Letter of 28 October 1647 in André, *Le Tellier*, 339.

[195] 15 December 1649, SHAT, Bib., Col. des ord., vol. 18, #55.

[196] 13 February 1650 letter from Le Tellier to Mazarin in André, *Le Tellier*, 337–38.

[197] See André, *Le Tellier*, 338n.

supply clothing, but he encouraged other cities just to give money.[198] This may explain André's conclusion that Le Tellier was first to work seriously on the issue of clothing.[199] What André means by this last claim is hard to tell; certainly Le Tellier was not the first to care that French soldiers be better clothed, and his reliance on French towns as a source of supply had its precedents long before Le Tellier came to office.

If requisition of clothing from major towns was the dominant manner in which the state supplied clothing directly to its troops during the war with Spain, the monarchy relied primarily upon contractors during the personal reign of Louis XIV. The excellent financial records preserved in the Archives Nationales for the period 1700–14 provide insights into the supply system in this last of Louis's great wars.[200] They demonstrate just how large the demands on contractors were – as many as 13,000 outfits of clothing or 18,000 pairs of shoes from a single entrepreneur.[201] The correspondence also shows that production was not centralized in Paris, since large quantities of clothing were produced in Lyon, Bordeaux, Toulouse, and elsewhere.[202] Lastly, much of the correspondence came in the form of petitions, *placets*, requesting payment, demonstrating that the government was usually in arrears.[203]

The demands sent by Gairaud to the government in Paris illustrate these points. Gairaud, a contractor from Lyon, petitioned the government in December 1704, requesting payment for 15,000 pairs of shoes for the armies in Spain and 3,000 for the army of duke de La Feuillade in Italy. He specifically wanted payment in money or in some form that could be quickly cashed out, not in assignations on future revenues that could take eight or nine months to be realized, such as had been paid to other contractors.[204]

---

[198] See André, *Le Tellier*, 339. See mention of a second shipment of clothing and a request to expedite the shipment of 1,000 pairs of shoes from Paris for Irish troops. Mazarin, *Lettres*, 6:79–80, Mazarin to Fouquet, 10 November 1653.

[199] André, *Le Tellier*, 330.

[200] AN, G^7 1774–1788 contains correspondence, memoirs, and accounts of the *trésoriers généraux* of the *extraordinaires des guerres* and other *trésoriers des guerres*, 1695–1715. For an extensive catalog of this series, see Claudine Fages, "Le service de la guerre sous Louis XIV de 1699–1715" (Paris: 1974). This hefty and immensely useful manuscript volume can be found in the Salle des inventaires at the AN. The most complete set of records concerns the year 1704 in G^7 1776 and G^7 1777.

[201] A detailed contract with Leleu and Lelarge stipulated the production of 12,449 outfits for 950,379 livres. 15 June 1708, AN, G^{7}1092. Giraud at Lyon contracted for 18,000 pairs of shoes. AN, G^{7}1776, #256–57.

[202] Justo van de Corbernt at Toulouse to be paid 100,000 écus for 6,500 habits for the army in Spain. AN, G^{7}1779, #133–35, 7 June 1707.

[203] As well as the examples that follow in the text, see Cournit and Genthon complaining that they were owed 266,122 livres 11 sols for the clothing of 6,000 *miliciens*, AN, G^{7}1779, #205, 20 May 1707; the petitions from the master shoemakers of Bordeaux demanding money owed for 1707–9 in AN, G^{7}1093 , and AN, G^{7}1094; Leleu and Lelarge billing 634,381 livres for clothing supplied on 7 October 1708 and submitting the same bill 29 January 1709, AN, G^{7}1093.

[204] AN, G^{7}1776, #256–57. See, as well, #331 and #419 on shoe transport and payment.

Gairaud followed this petition with another in January 1705, again asking to be paid and wanting to know if he should continue producing shoes, since nearly half of the shoes ordered had yet to be made, and, apparently, he had not been paid.[205]

Clothing contractors were businessmen with businessmen's concerns. When Astruc complained that he had been paid only 143,640 livres of the 443,640 livres owed for 10,000 outfits for the army in Italy, he reminded the minister of war that he needed the money "to maintain his credit." There was also a human side to Astruc's need for payment, since, "his manufacture [is] composed of 2,500 families, that he is obliged to support every day."[206]

Given the large amounts of clothing required by the army, it is not surprising that military needs had great influence on the cloth and leather trades. Reports from *intendants* at the close of the Nine Years' War testify to this impact. From Languedoc, the *intendant* stated that the wool trade increased greatly during times of war and that the best fabric produced in the area went into clothing for the troops.[207] Production at Chateauroux was "very much employed during the war. All that was made there was for the use of troopers and soldiers."[208]

Extravagant Dress by Officers

Considering the luxury and elegance of Louis's court, it comes as little surprise that officers displayed an expensive taste for extravagance in their own clothing, particularly in the matter of silver and gold lace trimming. A desire to stem such wasteful costs supplied some of the impetus behind clothing regulations. An ordinance of 1672 preached: "One of the things that contributes the most to the ruin of the king's officers is the luxury and the sumptuousness of their clothes." It forbade them to wear gold and silver on their own attire or on their saddle clothes.[209] When Louvois instructed the inspector Montbron to require that the officers of each cavalry regiment dress in a similar fashion, he insisted "that their dress be regulated in a manner that it will cause them the least possible expense."[210]

Concern for extravagance went beyond the officers. One reason to avoid dressing all the men in a more presentable or uniform manner was a need to hold down the officers' costs. A desire to keep them from spending too much for needless display comes out in Louvois's instructions vis-à-vis a trip that Louis took to inspect troops in the north of France: "The king does not desire that [the officers] hand out decorative ribbons or other things of this nature, nor even that they provide [new] clothing to their soldiers all at

---

[205] AN, G⁷1777, #137–38.　[206] AN, G⁷1778, #303, 1706.

[207] Corvisier, *Les Français*, 207.

[208] Memoire for Berry in Corvisier, *Les Français*, 207.

[209] SHAT, Bib., Col. des ord., vol. 22, #176, 25 March 1672.

[210] AG, A¹694,17 June 1683, Louvois to Montbron, in Rousset, *Louvois*, 3:295n.

once."[211] When proposals were made to adorn the clothing of sergeants and common soldiers with luxurious touches, Louvois fumed: "It is ridiculous to think of giving velvet facings [*parements*] to sergeants, as well as gloves and lace cravats."[212] He also ordered those officers who "believe they please His Majesty by putting gold or silver braid on the clothes of their sergeants and soldiers" to cease.[213]

THE SUPPLY OF WEAPONS: MUSKETS AND FUSILS

A soldier was not a soldier without the tools of war. French troops carried both edged weapons – swords and pikes in particular – and firearms, which included the musket, already a basic weapon at the start of the century, and the fusil, which became the standard firearm by 1700. This chapter discusses the supply of these basic arms rather than their technology and use. Even when pay never arrived or clothing fell into rags, weapons reached French troops. Of course, weapons were relatively durable and did not wear out with the rapidity of clothing, so troops once provided with them were in less need of resupply. But more to the point, weapons were absolutely essential to the business of war. The army at Malplaquet may have been bootless and hungry, but they had fusils and gunpowder.

Before the personal reign of Louis XIV, the army passed on the primary responsibility for the purchase of weapons to the captains. For example, in 1644, captains in the Army of Catalonia received 720 livres to enroll and equip thirty new infantry recruits.[214] This worked out to 24 livres for each recruit, a sum large enough to purchase weapons for the musketeers. At this time, a musket cost about 6 livres, although the price seems to have fluctuated from year to year and place to place.[215] Officers faced with the duty of arms supply did as they saw fit. When a young officer, Turenne even requested that his mother send him fifty pairs of pistols from Sedan, an arms manufacturing center, for his men.[216] Captains supplied weapons both to new troops

[211] Louvois in André, *Le Tellier et Louvois*, 354.

[212] Louvois to d'Alauzier, 23 November 1682, in Rousset, *Louvois*, 3:294.

[213] Louvois to d'Alauzier, 11 May 1682, in Rousset, *Louvois*, 3:294n.

[214] "Estat des troupes de l'armée de Catalogne," 12 December 1644, in André, *Le Tellier*, 351.

[215] SHAT, Bib., Col. des ord., vol. 16, #129, 29 March 1644, in André, *Le Tellier*, 346fn, quoted musket prices at 6 livres 10 sols; BN, f. fr. 4200, fol. 62v.–63, a letter of 10 April 1645, put the cost at only 6 livres; SHAT, Bib., Col. des ord., vol. 18, #12, 30 January 1649, in André, *Le Tellier*, 346, stated that muskets with bandoliers from Charleville, Mézières, and Liege cost more than 8 livres, but those from Holland cost over 10 livres. Mazarin claimed that he bought muskets with bandoliers for as little as 4 livres 10 sols. Mazarin in André, *Le Tellier*, 346. In 1672, a musket still cost 6 livres and the bandolier an additional 2 livres. Louis, *Oeuvres*, 3:118–19. By the 1680s, a musket could cost 9 livres and the more sophistocated fusil 14 livres. Corvisier, *Louvois*, 365.

[216] Bérenger, *Turenne*, 156.

and to veterans who needed replacement weapons, the cost of which was then deducted from their pay.[217]

Still, the state might intervene in the process of providing original equipment or resupply. In 1650, Le Tellier demanded 300 muskets from Abbeville, just as they were demanding clothes from large towns; in fact, Abbeville was also to supply 500 pairs of shoes.[218] The state could also purchase directly from manufacturers, as when Mazarin ordered the purchase of 4,000 muskets with bandoleers in Lyon, if they could be had for 5 livres each, and 1,000 pairs of pistols at 12 livres each.[219] When the state shipped arms to its troops, however, it apparently charged them to the captains' accounts, who then could be expected to pass the price on to their men.[220]

Captains clearly cut corners to save money, so a series of ordinances (1643–59) demanded compliance with the weapons' standards. Of all possible penalties, Le Tellier discovered that monetary fines worked best.[221] The 1670 instruction on inspections reiterated that if weapons did not meet inspection, it was the captain's job to replace them out of pocket.[222]

Once he was truly in control and peace had returned, Louis XIV tried to standardize French shoulder arms. A 16 November 1666 ordinance on weapons complained that most of the muskets in the magazines were of diverse calibers and often of too small a bore for the ammunition distributed to the troops; therefore, the ordinance forbade musket barrels to be of a smaller caliber than would accommodate balls weighing 0.8 ounce, or twenty to the pound. Interestingly enough, this ordinance controlled not only the captains, who would suffer penalties if they gave weapons of smaller caliber to their men, but it also fined workers who made weapons and merchants who sold them for 50 livres. Should these civilians continue to transgress after a first offense, they fell liable to corporal punishment.[223] Another directive of 1670 set barrel length at 3 feet 7 inches, from the touch hole to the muzzle.[224] The next year an ordinance confirmed the new caliber and ordered that all barrels be test fired, or proved, before being sold.[225]

Standardization took some time to take effect, as evidenced by the fact that magazines continued to store other calibers. A 1667 report from the magazine at Arras stated that it had two calibers of balls, twenty-four to the pound and thirty-three to the pound.[226] Still, in 1670, an ordinance instructed "*commissaires des guerres* to examine and to then refuse [weapons], if the arms

---

[217] André, *Le Tellier*, 351.

[218] Le Tellier to Mazarin, 13 February 1650, in André, *Le Tellier*, 338.

[219] 15 September 1653 letter from Mazarin to Colbert du Terron, in Mazarin, *Lettres*, 6:28–29.

[220] André, *Le Tellier*, 351–52.   [221] André, *Le Tellier*, 351–52.

[222] AG, MR 1881, #43, 6 February 1670 instruction.

[223] SHAT, Bib., Col. des ord., vol. 21, #164. André, *Le Tellier*, 350fn.

[224] 6 February 1670 ordinance in *Ordonnances militaires*, 1:172–73.

[225] 28 November 1667 ordinance in *Ordonnances militaires*, 1:172–73.

[226] AG, A¹209, #138, 18 August 1667 état. It also contained 9,808 grenades and 2,828 cannonballs.

of the said soldiers are of a length or caliber below regulation size . . . and replace them at the expense of the captain."[227]

There is a temptation to see the ordinances of 1666–70 as solving the problem and enforcing regularity, but problems persisted into the Dutch War, when one administrator complained of a company "being only peasants without swords and having only bad fusils of different lengths and of different calibers that the balls supplied will not serve."[228]

During the last two wars of Louis XIV, arms were supplied to the army by major administrators/entrepreneurs who paralleled the great *munitionnaires*. A shift in financing the purchase of arms came in 1688. Before that date, the *masse*, the 1-sol-per-day deduction from a soldier's pay, contributed to the cost of both his clothes and arms, but from 1688 on, it no longer paid for weaponry.[229] This increased the amount of money available for clothing, and it signaled that the state rather than the captain would take over direct supply of arms to the soldier, or at least to recruits. By this point, the king furnished arms, at his cost, to all recruits in field battalions – that is, those who actually went on campaign – and to garrison battalions involved in a siege.[230] Arsenals at Saint-Etienne and Charleville provided the bulk of small arms production; in the last decade of the seventeenth century, no less than 600,000 fusils were manufactured there.[231] Other arms workshops around France contributed, and foreign production was also enlisted. Powder consumption was also great, reaching 1,500,000 per year in the 1690s.[232] Again, the French tapped foreign production as well under Louis XIV; large amounts of powder and ball for French troops during the Dutch War had even been bought in Amsterdam in preparation for the conflict![233]

The fate of the arms entrepreneur could be an unhappy one, since the monarchy became steadily worse at paying its bills. The case of the administrator and entrepreneur Maximilien Titon during the War of the Spanish Succession reveals the problem. During the Nine Years' War, Titon managed the production of arms, including rifled carbines, for the king, and during the next war, he held the post of *directeur général du magazin royal de la Bastille*, in which he managed large-scale arms production in France.[234] He supplied great numbers of fusils to the army; between 1 December 1703 and 15 March 1704, winter quarters, he supplied 31,947 fusils and requested to purchase another 20,000 lock mechanisms from manufacturers in Liège and Luxembourg to produce more weapons.[235] By then he had been paid 1,745,000 livres.[236] But the government wanted him to make another 60,000 fusils, 30,000 bayonets, and 30,000 swords for which it promised to pay another

---

[227] AG, MR 1881, #43, 6 February 1670 instruction.

[228] AG, A¹295, #220, 26 October 1672.   [229] Contamine, *Histoire militaire*, 1:405.

[230] Belhomme, *L'armée française en 1690*, 17.   [231] Contamine, *Histoire militaire*, 1:411–12.

[232] Contamine, *Histoire militaire*, 1:411–12.

[233] Baxter, *William III*, 60; Corvisier, *Louvois*, 209.

[234] AG, A¹858, 14 October 1689, in Rousset, 3:332fn.

[235] AN, G⁷1776, #468, 17 March 1704.   [236] AN, G⁷1777, #258, 19 January 1704.

1,000,000 livres.[237] He claimed that he was delivering 8,500 fusils per month in 1704. Records show that Titon did receive at least 590,000 livres, from mid-January through mid-September 1704, but by December, he complained that he was owed 1,200,000 livres more, and that if he was not paid, everything would come to a halt.[238] Later letters begged repeatedly for payment. By July 1706, he claimed that he was owed 1,733,883 livres 15 sols, and that if he was not paid, he could not pay his own workers.[239] Production at Saint-Etienne was apparently most at risk, since the workers would either have to stop or to produce weapons of low quality: "the workers . . . will cease their work, and some of them already find themselves reduced to misery and to begging; all the manufacture will fall into great disorder."[240] Titon received some money in 1706, apparently three assignments totaling 1,038,000 livres, but in 1707, he was still appealing for 1,555,560 livres 16 sols for arms furnished in 1706.[241] Titon would go bankrupt at least once in his career.[242]

As the problems that beset Titon illustrate once again, the larger armies of the *grand siècle* simply exceeded the state's capacity to provide for them. A tension existed between military growth and supply; obviously, an army of 340,000 required more than did an army of 60,000. Ultimately, the demands for essential supplies and services became so staggering that to supply them adequately would have required resources greater than the state ever commanded. The need to mobilize necessary resources led the Bourbons to expand the power and staff of central administration, but financial necessity also forced French kings to preserve older practices that did not harmonize with efficiency, such as the sale of offices and the preservation of entrepreneurial rather than direct state supply. Military pressures pushed in opposite directions. And ultimately, to fill the gap between military need and state capacity, armies in the field requisitioned food, matériel, and money on the spot, with or without the blessing and supervision of royal authority. At times, this amounted to little more than pillage, and at times, it was carried out with the regularity of normal taxation. That is the subject of the next chapter.

---

[237] AN, G⁷1776, #474. The order also included 2,400 "armements de cavalerie," which were probably pistols.

[238] AN, G⁷1776, #216, accounts 30 August–20 September 1704; AN, G⁷1776, #245, 7 December 1704.

[239] AN, G⁷1778, #163, 27 July 1706; AG, G⁷1778, #179–87, July and August 1706. See, as well, his pleas a year earlier, AN, G⁷1777, #172, 30 July 1705.

[240] AG, G⁷1778, #194–95, 21 August 1706 and 5 September.

[241] AG, G⁷1779, #119.   [242] Contamine, *Histoire militaire*, 1:539.

❧

6

The Tax of Violence and Contributions

ON a June day in 1649, the Regiment de Conti stood before the gates of Thorigny, near Fontainebleau. After having asked for quarters and gained admittance, these French troops went on a twelve-day rampage. Witnesses testified how the soldiers "used extraordinary violence, having beaten and ransomed the inhabitants, pillaged and burned their furnishings . . . cut down their fruit trees . . . [and] eaten and scattered their flocks."[1] What could explain such barbarity? It did not stem solely from the depravity of the troops but erupted from something more basic: These soldiers – as with many of their peers – robbed and pillaged because the state that employed them lacked the resources to maintain them.

Indeed, in its large army, the Bourbon monarchy had created a monster that it could neither feed nor control; the growth of French armed forces simply outstripped government capacity. Greater forces demanded greater quantities of funds, food, and fodder, which the existing state apparatus scrambled to mobilize, but despite its efforts, the state proved incapable of satisfying the army's appetite, particularly during the first period of expansion, 1635–59. In order to make up the shortfall between what the battalions received directly from the government and what the troops needed to survive, the army turned on the civil populations around them. The result was violent abuse, strategic frustration, and fiscal collapse, which eventually compelled the French government to refashion itself so as to support its forces. Therefore, in a real sense, such agonies of war became the birth pangs of the modern state. While recent scholarship on state formation in early modern Europe has recognized this link between the pressures of war and emergence of absolutism, more needs to be said concerning the character and influence of the dangerous chasm that separated army need from state capacity.

---

[1] "Requête des habitans du bourg de Thorigny, selection de Sens," from an order of 10 February 1650 in Peter Jonathan Berger, "Military and Financial Government in France, 1648–1661," Ph.D. dissertation, University of Chicago, 1979, 94.

During the period of change and development, the army itself bridged the gap between demand and supply. Had it not, the Bourbons would have been unable to field such large forces. The army supplied itself through two distinct forms of violent requisition, the subjects of this chapter. First, military units large and small simply took what they wanted when the state did not provide it; in short, they turned to pillage, which the French called *mademoiselle picorée*. This brutal seizure of goods by Bourbon troops within the borders of France can best be labeled the "Tax of Violence," for reasons that will become apparent. This cruel practice proved costly, in military, political, and moral terms; therefore, Louis XIV and the marquis de Louvois took steps to suppress these excesses within France, and, to a large extent, outside France as well. Second, undisciplined and inefficient pillage, the fruits of which went directly to marauding soldiers, was replaced by a far more orderly and effective practice, the levying of "contributions" by the government itself. As opposed to the Tax of Violence, contributions were raised outside French borders, administered by civil agents, and benefited the royal war effort rather than particular units.

The ability of the monarchy to eliminate the Tax of Violence illustrates that the crown and its agents succeeded in improving military discipline, administration, and supply. These improvements were linked closely to increased royal authority, coupled with growing centralization and bureaucratization, in short with absolutism. Much of this book has stressed the evolutionary, rather than revolutionary, nature of change; nonetheless, two facts affirm the reality of fundamental innovations: the growth of the army and the elimination of the Tax of Violence. However, at the same time that the latter verifies substantial change, the need for contributions demonstrates that the monarchy had not been transformed enough to truly afford its gargantuan army. The exhaustion of the French state reflected by the decline in real troop strength during the War of the Spanish Succession testifies to the continued limitations on state power rather than to a full realization of monarchical absolutism.

TAX OF VIOLENCE

Taxes – the French absolutist state created, collected, and consumed them in greater quantity than its predecessors. Therein lay much of its strength. Taxes brought power because taxes bought soldiers. Yet regular taxation fell short of maintaining the huge new armies. Before 1659, it was supplemented by the violent confiscation of wealth, primarily within French borders, on an ad hoc basis – the Tax of Violence.

The prefaces of French military ordinances before 1659 speak grimly, but vaguely, of menacing infractions – "all sorts of ravages and disorders"[2] and

---

[2] SHAT, Bib., Col. des ord., vol. 18, 22 June 1652, #162.

"diverse disorders, excesses, and violences."[3] The frequency of official directives commanding soldiers "to demand nothing nor to mistreat their hosts" when they were quartered bears witness to the fact that soldiers were, indeed, extorting money and abusing people.[4] St. Vincent de Paul lamented in 1652 that "Everywhere the armies have passed, they have committed sacrileges, thefts and impieties."[5] Troops in the pay of the Bourbons were as rapacious as those who served Wallenstein.[6]

The brutal requisition that constituted the Tax of Violence becomes most obvious when one examines the way in which troops were housed and fed in the seventeenth century. When considering problems raised by quartering and *étapes*, it may be useful to segregate this violence into two categories, one that involved serious infractions of the rules but still remained within the broad outlines of the directives and another that cast all regulation and restraint aside.

Much of the lesser violence occurred while troops were on the march, when their need was great and there was less chance for supervision or punishment. When traveling from place to place, soldiers could become highwaymen. On *étapes*, soldiers might not follow the road prescribed, or they might refuse lodgings assigned to them and simply occupy those that pleased them.[7] Soldiers en route to a new station might cut grain on their way.[8] Although troops quartered on a household were entitled to a bed to sleep the night, a place to cook their meal, and candles to light the way, they often demanded more. Or they might demand money in lieu of services. All too often they simply extorted sums from their hosts.

Major cases of indiscipline and violence came completely outside the realm of the law, as French troops pillaged friendly towns as if they were foreign bastions. While campaigning against the Norman capital of Rouen, Harcourt's royal army based itself at Neubourg for twelve days "and caused the total ruin of the inhabitants . . . . [The army] burned more than 200 buildings besides losses of animals, wheat, and other grains such that the majority of the inhabitants were forced to abandon the area and are reduced to begging." Isolated villages were even more exposed to horrid pillage. In 1642, the

---

[3] SHAT, Bib., Col. des ord., vol. 19, 20 April 1655, #151.

[4] SHAT, Bib., Col. des ord., vol. 14, 1636, #99. See, for example, SHAT, Bib., Col. des ord., vol. 16, 12 January 1642, #38; SHAT, Bib., Col. des ord., vol. 18, 25 May 1651, #106; SHAT, Bib., Col. des ord., vol. 18, 22 June 1652, #162; SHAT, Bib., Col. des ord., vol. 19, 25 April 1654, #96; SHAT, Bib., Col. des ord., vol. 19, 6 November 1654, #125; SHAT, Bib., Col. des ord., vol. 20, 20 February 1657, #7. After 1660, these colorful, self-condemning ordinances no longer appear with such frequency.

[5] St. Vincent De Paul in Louis André, *Michel Le Tellier et l'organisation de l'armée monarchique* (Paris: 1906), 579–80.

[6] Patrick Landier, "Guerre, violences, et société en France, 1635–1659," doctorat de troisième cycle, dissertation, Université de Paris IV: 1978, argues that the French were probably less rapacious than other contemporary armies.

[7] See examples in Landier, "Guerre, violences, et société," 29 and 30.

[8] See SHAT, Bib., Col. des ord., vol. 18, 22 June 1652, #162.

lord of one such small community complained that local troops had "taken the inhabitants who remained there, put them in deep holes, and left them there to starve in order to make them pay ransom . . . ." Ransom of one kind or another was a disturbingly convenient way of extorting funds, while torture bludgeoned householders into revealing money stashed on their property.[9]

A more lurid case involved the larger town of Sancoins, in the Bourbonnais. In 1650, some 3,000 troops approached and without the proper authorization of *étapes* demanded entry. The townsmen denied the troops, but the soldiers convinced a few traitors to let them in at one gate. The troops then "lived as they pleased, raping, pillaging, and robbing." They "compelled the inhabitants to put together a sum of four thousand livres" and stole horses. They reserved a particular brutal treatment for the "women from whom they took away nursing children and locked these infants in rooms for twenty-four hours in order to force the women to become the soldiers' concubines or to buy their babies back with money rather than to see them die miserably."[10]

Violence bred violence; attack bred reprisal. The brutality of soldiers sparked resistance; mostly local, it would not appear in the great accounts of civil disruption. In his engravings, "Les misères et les maleurs de la guerre," Jacques Callot left a vivid record of the violence committed by and to soldiers during the first half of the seventeenth century. His most famous piece depicts the pillaging of a farmhouse, attended by torture, murder, and rape. But he follows this with a scene of peasants' revenge with the following caption "After the soldiers have committed much devastation, finally the peasants, whom they have treated as enemies, await them in a secluded place and by surprise . . . put them to death." Peasants smash skulls with grain flails and strip the dead of their clothes. In one of many recorded incidents, during 1644, inhabitants of seven Norman villages attacked and disarmed all the soldiers of a regiment that was to be quartered in Domfront.[11]

Such barbarous conduct exacted immense human and material costs. An ordinance of 1643 charged: "so desolate and ruined are the towns and villages of the countryside, that they are in large part deserted and abandoned: from

---

[9] Neubourg petition in Berger, "Military and Financial Government in France," 101; Mme. Elbeuf letter in Landier, "Guerre, violences, et société," 179.

[10] AG, $A^1$122, #401, 21 November 1650.

[11] AG, $A^1$86, 14 February 1644, #62 in Landier, "Guerre, violences, et société," 169. Twelve years later, villagers from Rocquigny, Largoye, and Mainbressy drove off companies of soldiers from Rocroi seeking loot in the countryside. AG, $A^1$146, #502, 20 July 1656. See Bernard Kroener, *Les routes et les étapes. Die bersorgung der französchichen Armeen in Nordostfrankreich (1635–1661)* (Munster: 1980), 136–37, 142–43, for other actions of French peasants and townspeople against troops. There is a tradition of peasants joining to attack troops. J. R. Hale, *War and Society in Renaissance Europe, 1450–1620* (Baltimore, MD: 1985), 191, tells how so many of Coligny's men were killed by peasants in 1569 that he sent troops back to punish the area. There are also cases in which peasants caught enemy soldiers and turned them over to military commanders for a *douceur*, a kind of tip. Fritz Redlich, *De praeda militari: Looting and Booty 1500–1815*, supplement 39, *Vieteljahrschrift für Sozial- und Wirtschaftsgeschichte* (Wiesbaden: 1956), 36–37.

which will follow general ruin if a good and certain establishment of *étapes* and food is not provided to [the troops] in passage."[12] A petition from the province of Burgundy, dated 1644, painted a most disturbing image of woe in the province which "suffered all the ruins that war can produce . . . by the passage and sojourn of several armies that have burned a great number of communities [and caused] the death of a fifth of the population . . . and the extreme poverty of the majority of those who survived."[13] These horrors accelerated during the rebellion of the Fronde, 1648–53, when the exhaustion of areas within France significantly lowered the tax revenues.[14] So dreadful were the extremes that the 1635–59 war caused population to fall from 20 million to 18 million.[15]

Necessity of the Tax of Violence

Contemporaries expressed little doubt as to the cause of violence directed by soldiers against the surrounding population: The force that drove them to brutal action was their own misery. Hungry, unpaid soldiers turned ugly. Their cruel behavior was rarely seen as gratuitous, and even the government, itself, saw reason behind it. An ordinance of 1651 provided a royal admission "that the disorders committed by my soldiers traveling to points of rendez-vous from my armies have resulted from the poor quality of the places of quartering and from the lack of *étapes* on their routes."[16] Mazarin wrote to Turenne in 1659: "I have received complaints from many areas along the frontier about the disorders and extraordinary violence committed by the troops. I know well that it is difficult to limit them and to try to subsist, since they have not been paid; but I ask you to take cares that they live with less license."[17] Perhaps the most authoritative, and one of the most damning, statements appeared in 1660. In the ordinance granting amnesty to French soldiers and civilians guilty of illegal acts during the preceding war, Louis XIV justified his sweeping pardon by arguing that "we know that, for the most part, the disorders committed by our soldiers have resulted only from the lack of their pay." It is not surprising that many of the seventeenth-

---

[12] SHAT, Bib., Col. des ord., vol. 16, #79, 15 July 1643. Problems with *étapes* is often singled out as a primary cause of misconduct. See, as well, van Houtte's comments, Hubert van Houtte, *Les Occupations etrangères en Belgique sous l'ancien régime*, 2 vols., *Recueil de Travaux Publiés par la faculté de Philosophie et Lettres de l'Université de Gand*, fasicule 62–63 (Ghent and Paris: 1930), 1:43.

[13] Côte-d'Or, C 3673, 4 January 1644.

[14] This is one of the primary theses of Berger, "Military and Financial Government in France."

[15] Philippe Contamine, ed., *Histoire militaire de la France*, vol. 1 (Paris: 1992), 382. It should be noted that Kroener, *Les routes et les étapes*, 105, 114, does not believe that the damage by troops, at least in the period 1635–38, was as claimed.

[16] SHAT, Bib., Col. des ord., vol. 18, #115, 15 July 1651.

[17] 8 November 1659 letter to Turenne, in Jules Mazarin, *Lettres du cardinal Mazarin*, eds. P. Chéruel and G. d'Avenel, vols. 6–9 (Paris: 1890–1906), 9:409.

century disciplinary ordinances began by stating how and when soldiers were to be paid.[18]

If violence in town and country resulted from shortfalls in supply and pay, that violence must be considered as a question of resource mobilization and administration rather than of discipline. Some historians have argued that an administrative revolution transformed the conduct of war before the personal reign of Louis XIV. However, recent inquiries question the nature and extent of administrative development before 1659. David Parrott charges that the Richelieu years did not greatly increase the efficiency of military administration and that scholars beguiled by royal ordinances miss the true catch-as-catch-can character of French military administration as revealed by ministerial correspondence.[19] As one-time *intendant* of the army and later *surintendant des finances*, Claude Bullion wrote in his 1637 memoir on *étapes*: "Up to now, [the king] has made handsome and good regulations that are not executed at all."[20]

However, it is necessary to go one step further. Abuse did not simply undermine the system; abuse *was* the system, or at least violent requisition constituted an essential element of the system. Extortion of money, goods, and even sex by soldiers did not exist outside the French method of maintaining troops in the field; instead, it was an integral and necessary aspect of the way in which the Bourbon monarchy tapped the resources required by its expanded army. Such brutal requisition may not have been orderly or efficient, and it may have put the French in a strategic straitjacket, but it was the only way that the French could maintain an army in the field when the regular flow of money and supplies to the army inevitably broke down.

French officials during the first half of the *grand siècle* accepted unauthorized seizure and extortion as necessary, even if it was regrettable. In other words, the Tax of Violence was, to a degree, policy. A letter written by the experienced military *intendant*, Charles Machault, to the secretary of state for war, Michel Le Tellier, in 1649 shows that he understood that insufficient pay would produce predictable results, and that those results, though lamentable, were a price that must be paid.[21] Machault argued that the regulation for winter quarters that he had just received from Le Tellier was "a complete impossibility" unless the minister doubled the allotted pay. The soldiers "are all naked," Machault insisted, and while "they will have nothing," they "will see their hosts drink and eat well." Machault reasoned "that it is better to institute laws and regulations that can be observed and to punish the infractions than to propose . . . austere ones that are not executed . . . ." These are

---

[18] SHAT, Bib., vol. 20, #134, November 1660. For some disciplinary ordinances see, vol. 29, #8, #44, and #70.

[19] David Parrott, "The Administration of the French Army During the Ministry of Cardinal Richelieu," Ph.D. dissertation, Oxford University: 1985.

[20] Bouillon, "Mémoire raisonné," BN, Chatre de Cangé, vol. 9, #367.

[21] AG, A[1]116, #482, 10 December 1649, Machault to Le Tellier. I would like to thank Professor Armine Mortimer for her assistance in interpreting this key document.

problems that Le Tellier already must have known "by reason and experience." Machault cautioned his master: "And if they do not have what they need, in my conscience, I could not [punish them] no matter what order I might receive." The *intendant* then mused that "It is only peace that can bring the remedies you seek for the pain and suffering of the people. As long as war lasts, soldiers are necessary, even with their vices and rapines."

Machault then offered an extended religious argument that men were flawed and that they might be forgiven their excesses if the state did not fulfill its obligations to them. Saint John the Baptist, he wrote, "did not fly into a rage against the soldiers nor did he scold them [for their deeds], except when they did evil [after] they had been paid"; and Jesus had "censured those who blamed the apostles for having gathered stalks of grain in the fields of others, since the need for food and clothing is so pressing." Finally he returned to the point that he would publish the orders if it pleased the king, but he would not accept personal responsibility for them.

As long as the king chose to raise and maintain armies above his means to pay and feed them, pillage was inevitable. As the *Mercure françois* put it in 1622, "One finds enough soldiers when one gives them the freedom to live off the land, and allowing them to pillage supports them without pay." A discussion of the royal council concerning the increase of forces in 1635 appealed to much the same logic: "By increasing his majesty's forces, which are already very large, it will be difficult for him to pay them on time . . . [but] they can be maintained without giving them much money if instead we give them more freedom than they have enjoyed before to live off the country." Louis expressed almost exactly the same sentiment in his memoirs for the year 1666: "Of late, some commanders are found who have made great armies subsist for a long time without giving them any pay other than the license of pillaging everywhere." Common soldiers easily calculated that pillage equaled pay. A report on the conduct of German troops who operated in Champagne during 1649 stated that "The Germans proclaimed loudly that they had been given Champagne as pay and prey."[22]

While heinous, the system produced results. To be a soldier was to carry a license: Pike and musket served as the final guarantees of pay and subsistence. In a sense, common soldiers acted as creditors behind the French state's investment in European mastery; the ultimate collateral behind this ambition was the capacity of soldiers to take for themselves, if need be. Without it, the French monarchy would have had to live within its means and reduce the numbers of its battalions.

In addition, officers felt compelled to tolerate the crimes committed by their own troops. If a military commander on campaign faced the dissolution of

---

[22] *Mercure françois* in Charles Tilly, *The Contentious French* (Cambridge, MA: 1986), 123; council of 28 April 1635 in Georges Pagès, *La Guerre de trente ans* (Paris: 1939), 225–26; Louis, memoirs for 1666, Louis XIV, *Mémoires de Louis XIV*, Charles Dreyss, ed., 2 vols. (Paris: 1860), 1:249; 1649 report in Landier, "Guerre, violences, et société," 155.

his unit because it could no longer subsist in the field from government supply and pay, it should come as no surprise that he allowed it to fill its needs through violent requisition. At least the unit would survive to be of military use rather than disappear through desertion.

The fact that officials regarded the Tax of Violence practically as a given should come as no surprise, since it was extorted during an era that considered brutal requisitions as standard. This was an age of "courses," raids by war parties used for several purposes, including plundering enemy territory to grab supplies for one's own army and deny them to the enemy. Even normal taxes were collected at gunpoint.[23] At times, regulations commanded soldiers to take what they needed from local friendly populations. The ordinance of 26 March 1636, much cited as an example of French administrative efficiency, ordered that when the king's troops were on the march, supplies "will be furnished to them in all the places of lodging on their route for free and without paying anything." The reason for this levy was that the king had realized "that the payments he has ordered made to his troops for subsistence and shelter on their route and passage have been an excessive charge on his finances for several years."[24]

In such an environment, the term *Tax of Violence* fits the treatment of the French population by their own troops better than does the generic word *pillage*, because soldiers acted in a predictable and accepted manner to seize resources necessary to support the army. What was the difference if armed force backed tax collectors who seized funds that went to support the army, or if troops simply took the money directly for themselves?

Rape: Mercenaries and Morality

Any argument that the violence committed by French soldiers in the first half of the seventeenth century flowed from the fact that they were ill-paid and ill-supplied must also account for the phenomenon of rape. At first glance, these attacks on women seem remote from the soldiers' need for material sustenance.

This complicated mix of lust, humiliation, and violent assault cannot be easily explained. The prevalence of rape partly resulted from the human tendency to go too far when a taboo is broken. Thus, when hungry soldiers crossed into the illicit realm of theft and torture, they also attacked women. This flowed from the contractual nature of military service. When the troops went unfed and unpaid, their contract was broken, and they were no longer bound by obedience and discipline. It comes as little surprise that they burnt

---

[23] See the discussion of *fusiliers des tailles* in the epilogue.
[24] SHAT, Bib., Col. des ord., vol. 14, #94, 26 March 1636. In fact, the 1636 ordinance simply returned to the system set out in the 1629 Code Michau, SHAT, Bib., Col. des ord., vol. 13, #129, January 1629.

as well as plundered and that they raped as well as stole. The fact that this became a group action further legitimated the individual's actions.

But more is involved. Soldiers both hated and envied civilians. Often of peasant origins themselves, men who had taken up arms regarded themselves as superior to the communities that they had left, while those communities saw soldiers as renegades. Soldiers exercised freedom and power; civilians enjoyed stability and possessions. Rape could very well have been a form of revenge. Certainly, military machismo compelled some men to enforce their masculinity just as they used their weapons. Yet it would also be wrong to see rape solely as a question of power; it also involved sex and money. For men whose notion of sexual intercourse could not have risen much higher than the mechanical and mercenary sex of camp prostitutes, sex must have been seen as little more than a commodity. For them, it was a necessity with a price on it, to be seized from women through violence the way that money was taken from men through torture.

A gruesome case of mass rape dating from 1652 offers another reason why rape was linked to the soldiers' material want. Troops under the command of the count d'Harcourt left tales of horror in southern France: "There was a gentleman of birth and position who watched . . . his wife, daughter, and sister violated without daring to say a word; in the lands of Besolles alone, seventy women and girls were raped . . . . The men of Condom, who had been taxed only 30,000 livres, paid 64,000 to exempt their women from violation, after which they were pillaged and lost fifteen hundred horses . . . . One young girl having been raped by eighty soldiers before being rescued, later was seen in a wood being pursued and finally trapped; she died at that very moment from fright."[25] Here soldiers raped with the frenzy of attacking sharks, yet even these troops held back to use the threat of rape as an effective tool of extortion. In another case, one company of the Regiment d'Enghien ran riot in Oger, near Reims, on April 14, 1649. They seized local women and threatened to dishonor them if not paid a ransom of 3,000 livres. The ransom was paid, the women released, but the troops still torched the town on their departure.[26]

The idea of demanding money on threat of rape carried more force than demanding money on threat of burning. Rape was an ultimate offense. It is worth noting that the French ordinance of November 1660, which pardoned all thefts, arsons, and other violence during the war that ended in 1659, specifically did not pardon rape.[27] A welcome aspect of the transition from the wilder form of extortion by marauding soldiers to the more refined extortion of contributions was the decline in rape – not that soldiers ceased

[25] Landier, "Guerre, violences, et société," 153–154.
[26] See, for example, the case of Regiment d'Enghien, 14 April 1649, in AN, E 236B fol. 195–96, 22 September 1649 in Berger, "Military and Financial Government in France," 108–9.
[27] SHAT, Bib., Col. des ord., vol. 20, #134, November 1660.

all sexual attacks in the late seventeenth century, but such offenses became far less common and were prosecuted more diligently.

Decline of the Tax of Violence

Acceptance of the Tax of Violence eventually turned to revulsion and then suppression. Early in the personal reign of Louis XIV, the practice all but passed from the scene. This does not mean that French troops never victimized Louis's own subjects. As late as 1693, Vauban complained that units on the march in the kingdom committed "an infinity of small pillages."[28] But such offenses involved more the presence of thieves in the ranks or the inevitable jostling between quartered soldiers and their hosts than systematic plundering of towns by units whose own misery legitimated such violent extortion. Both the incidence and intensity of abuses fell to such an extent that the problem changed in character to become merely a disciplinary one, rather than a practice essential to maintaining an army in the field.

The Peace of the Pyrenees, which ended France's longest and most exhausting struggle of the century, was bound to shift things for the better. With fighting at an end, the army demobilized to a paper strength of about 72,000, still large by prewar standards but smaller by half than wartime peaks.[29] Peace also allowed for military reforms to emerge – reforms that had amounted to little more than declarations of good intentions while the stress of war limited the government to a jumble of expedients.

But the return of peace did not immediately end the Tax of Violence; rather, it continued on to a lesser degree into the 1670s. Louis recognized the problem when he assumed power in 1661, complaining that "no troops . . . live without committing excesses."[30] Speaking of the mid-1660s, the finance minister, Colbert, attested to continuing problems: "All the troops live at their discretion in entering and leaving the place where they are lodged. The four generalities of Paris, Amiens, Châlons, and Soissons, have suffered more from quartering over the last six months than in the last six years of the war."[31]

A sampling of Parisian and provincial archives indicates that numerous excesses occurred through the early years of the Dutch War. Perhaps the continued abuses can be explained by the fact that soldiers who had conducted themselves in a rapacious manner before 1659 remained in the ranks.

---

[28] Sébastien le Prestre de Vauban, *Oisivetés de M. de Vauban*, 3 vols. (Paris: 1842–46), 2:232–33.

[29] AG, A^{1}198, 5 March 1666, letter from Louvois to Pradel, gives the figures as 61,000 men plus the Swiss and French Guards. Camille Rousset, *Histoire de Louvois*, 4 vols. (Paris: 1862–64), 1:97, estimates the guards at an additional 11,000 and gives the combined total as about 72,000.

[30] Louis XIV, *Mémoires*, 2:405.

[31] Jean-Baptiste Colbert, *Lettres, instructions et mémoires de Colbert*, Pierre Clément, ed., 8 vols. (Paris: 1862–82), 2:36.

Old habits died hard. It would take years to convince troops that the game had to be played by new rules. However, the late 1670s witnessed a notable decline in incidents of brutality against French subjects. A different standard of behavior had evolved.

Much of the credit for the decline of brutal extortion must go to Louis himself, who insisted that such "libertinage" must cease. Early in his reign, he wrote that "Any prince who cherishes his reputation . . . will not doubt that it is founded as much upon defending the goods of his subjects from pillage by his own troops as upon defending against pillage by his enemies."[32] Had he taken no steps to provide necessary food and pay and to punish troops who broke his ordinances, his pious words would have had no more effect than those of his father. However, Louis and his ministers carried out substantial administrative and disciplinary reform.

Louis inherited Le Tellier as his minister of war, showed the good sense to keep him, and had the good luck to be able to pass the office on to Le Tellier's son, whose very great, though crude, talents were committed to taming the army and making it the king's servant. An obvious sign of greater administrative action is the ever mounting pile of paperwork preserved at the war archives, as mentioned in Chapter 3. Record keeping in the provinces became equally impressive. The mountain of *route* slips preserved at Amiens and provincial ledgers such as those for Alsace testify to the concern for orderly and regular functioning.

Essential to the process was Louis's and his ministers' heightened control over army commanders. Louvois's imperious ways suited him for the task of forcing independent officers to become loyal subordinates. His leverage increased after 1675 because the death of Turenne and the retirement of Condé removed the only two marshals who could elbow him aside. After 1675, Louvois, his *intendants*, *commissaires*, and *commis* were unquestionably in charge. And they had no tolerance for the Tax of Violence.

Part of their response was more intense disciplinary action. The records make clear that agents of the crown exerted themselves in investigating and prosecuting violence and theft by soldiers or officers. Provincial and central archives overflow with records of inquiries and directives to punish the guilty and to compensate their victims. As the *intendant* Turgot declared, "I love discipline enough to spare nothing that can be done to maintain it."[33]

Correspondence demonstrates that abuses of the *étapes* and quartering ordinances were taken very seriously from the late 1670s until the end of Louis's reign. Comparatively minor infractions by soldiers, petty theft and minor violence, were pursued by the state with vigor. One exemplary case involves the regiment of Walloon Guards in January 1704.[34] During a march in the north, several small bands broke off from the main column to maraud.

[32] Louis XIV, *Oeuvres de Louis XIV*, Grimoard and Grouvelle, eds., 6 vols. (Paris: 1806), 2:92.
[33] AG, A^{1}2265, #234, letter of 3 March 1710.
[34] AG, A^{1}1801, #14, #16, #23; #33, #36, #76, #120, #125, and #140.

Report after report, involving depositions by officers and municipal administrators, leave a paper trail of inquiry, enforcement, and punishment. Not only were complaints registered and penalties demanded, but authorities detailed military police, *maréchaussées*, from Amboise and Loches to follow the regiment to make sure that similar infractions were not committed again.

The government ordered restitution to victims not only to punish the guilty and thus maintain discipline but also out of concern for the welfare of the king's subjects. Soldiers themselves might be called upon to pay compensation for their misdeeds, thus removing the incentive for pillage. Such restitution was not unheard of before 1659, but it was rare. In 1675, Louvois ordered that 6,000 livres be withheld from the pay of troops of the royal household who had abused homeowners and demanded more than the *étapes* allotted them. This practice long outlasted Louvois. In 1712, when troopers of the Regiment d'Estagnol committed violent acts against several people in Dijon, their major paid 350 livres from regimental funds in compensation.[35]

Under Louis XIV, it also became practice to punish officers not only for their own transgressions but for those committed by their men. Officers were rarely disciplined prior to 1659 and, in fact, stood by as men rampaged.[36] But in his memoirs for 1666, Louis boasted that, having learned that a captain of the Auvergne regiment had extorted money from the inhabitants of Rethel, "wanting to stop it and make it known with what severity I would punish similar exactions, I discharged [him] in the middle of a review."[37] In 1670, Louis turned his public wrath on an officer of his household troops who had abused a peasant.[38]

Louvois certainly believed in harsh punishments for officers. He wanted "to establish as a principle that a commander who did not make an effort to stop a disorder ought to be treated as if he had instigated it."[39] Louvois replied to the then general Luxembourg, who had shown some hesitancy to take action in 1672: "Punish an officer, and you will see all the disorder will cease."[40] And so it was done. That same year, the *intendant* Jean-Etienne Bouchu ordered officers of a company to pay for things taken when fifty-four of their men pillaged Issy l'Evesque.[41] When his troops pillaged in 1677, marshal Luxembourg not only hanged several soldiers on the spot but declared that he would "retain the value of what had been taken from the pay

---

[35] AG, A¹433, Louvois to Colbeuz, 11 May 1675; Archives municipales de Dijon, H 256, 20 November 1712.

[36] For example, in October 1638, officers of the Chanceau and La Force regiments were charged "for having committed pillage and theft on the peasants and villages." Jules Caillet, *De l'administration en France sous le ministère du Cardinal de Richelieu* (Paris: 1857), 374.

[37] Louis XIV, *Oeuvres*, 2:91.

[38] Paul Sonnino, *Louis XIV and the Origins of the Dutch War* (Cambridge: 1989), 111.

[39] Louvois in André Corvisier, *Louvois* (Paris: 1983), 180.

[40] AG, A¹277, #239, 30 August 1672, Louvois to Luxembourg.

[41] Côte-d'Or, C 2897, 20 March 1672.

of all officers of the army."[42] Marshal Villars continued the practice. When on campaign in 1707, he fined infantry captains one écu for each of their men found marauding; cavalry captains paid two écus.[43]

In one of the most unusual cases, officers who composed a disciplinary council prescribed a light penalty for an officer guilty of not stopping disorder and pillage. This so outraged Louvois that he ordered that the men who sat on the council be docked 2,000 livres from their own pay to be distributed to the churches in the area that had suffered. The captain in question was to be dishonorably discharged, or "broken."[44]

By such efforts, the Sun King and his servants curtailed the Tax of Violence early in his personal reign. They exerted control over the army, even with its expanded forces, yet they did not cut the Gordian knot of war finance. Thus, the end of the worst abuses did not signal that the state now mustered sufficient resources to maintain its armies in the field. In a sense, the Tax of Violence did not die but rather went through metamorphosis to emerge as contributions. The need for extorted resources persisted, and the ultimate pressure to pay remained violent; however, the victims were no longer French, and the practice was more regular, reflecting the values and abilities of absolutism.

CONTRIBUTIONS

The contributions that replaced the Tax of Violence evolved in Germany early in the Thirty Years' War, well before France openly entered the fray.[45] Circa 1600, the term *contribution* described a war tax levied within a given realm, with the consent of that area's estates. Thus, it was raised in a regular manner, by consent, and over a reasonably large area. *Brandschatzung*, or fire tax, served as the other ancestor of the later form of contribution. Local commanders extracted payments in kind or money, *Brandschatzung*, on abbeys, villages, or towns under threat of fire. This kind of extortion amounted to ransom for the property of the threatened locale. So the *Brandschatzung* was neither regular nor consensual, and it was not applicable to a large area, since it could be imposed on no more than could be burned in a single conflagration. Finally, the *Brandschatzung* filled the commander's purse, whereas the earlier contributions went to the prince's war chest.[46]

With Spinola, Mansfeld, and finally Wallenstein, contributions achieved

---

[42] AG, A¹547, 13 September 1677, Luxembourg to Louvois.

[43] Villars to Chamillart, 20 July 1707, in Ronald Thomas Ferguson, "Blood and Fire: Contribution Policy of the French Armies in Germany (1668–1715)," Ph.D. dissertation, University of Minnesota, 1970, 241.

[44] AG, A¹533, #506–7, 24 September 1677, Louvois to Luxembourg.

[45] For an excellent account of the evolution of contributions, see Fritz Redlich, "Contributions in the Thirty Years' War," *Economic History Review* 12 (1959–60), 247–54.

[46] Ferguson, "Blood and Fire," 2, defines *brandschatzung* as the same as contributions; here I think he missed the point a bit.

their new form by 1625. They were now funds imposed over a sizable area to be paid in a regular fashion, usually during an extended period of time. The local army commander set and apportioned the amount demanded and backed his demands with the threat of violence, essentially burning. Thus, an unholy marriage of the original contributions and *Brandschatzung* spawned the devil's child of *Kontributions*. While part might be paid in kind, Wallenstein's contributions were a money payment. By the late 1620s, the principle was established that through contributions "any population had to sustain whatever army was or could be quartered in its midst."[47] The Thirty Years' War in Germany was primarily funded through contributions.

Under Louis XIII, a particular commander, army, or garrison might levy contributions in German fashion, but under Louis XIV, civil officials administered contributions for the state's war effort. Funds poured directly into state coffers. In later stages, contributions operated very much like regular and reasonable war taxes, levied on non-French populations and backed by the threat of burning for those who obstinately refused to meet their obligations.

It is important to distinguish contributions not only from the Tax of Violence but also from courses, foraging, and destruction dictated by scorched-earth strategies. As defined here, the Tax of Violence was "levied" by French troops on subjects of the French king. Contributions, at least after 1659, were imposed on areas outside the Bourbon domains. Also, particular cases of the Tax of Violence affected no more than a village or town, and perhaps only a neighborhood, whereas contributions cast the net far more broadly. Courses were raids that fulfilled a number of capacities. War parties on courses might extort *Brandschatzung* or simply plunder friend or foe. Courses were regularly sent out into areas not laid under formal contributions and could net considerable one-time bounty.[48] They might also be part of a strategic plan or a means to punish villages late in their payment of contributions. In any case, courses were a device, not a policy.

Foraging to gather fodder, or sometimes food, for the army was part of military routine. Although forage parties occasionally got out of hand, acting little better than marauders, they were supposed to act in a disciplined fashion and take only what was necessary. Those whose fields had been foraged could make claim for repayment of the fodder, particularly if they were French.

The destruction associated with scorched-earth strategies also differed from contributions. For contributions to produce money, they must function like a sophisticated parasite and draw sustenance from the host, not kill it. On the other hand, scorched-earth strategies aimed precisely at destroying the resources of a region. While some goods and funds might be seized in the process, the goal was to deny an enemy the use of a territory by rendering

---

[47] Redlich, "Contributions in the Thirty Years' War," 249.
[48] See AG, A^{1}209, #114, 1 August 1667 letter from the comte de Grandpré in which he reports that "the two courses that I made will bring in a great quantity of money to the King."

it incapable of maintaining a hostile force. The devastation of the Palatinate by French forces in 1689 ranks as the most infamous case of this war practice.[49] True, as one part of a scorched-earth policy, the French might impose rapacious contributions to exhaust an area and thus deny its wealth to the enemy, but this was not normal practice. Even then, payment of contributions implied some protection, and this was preferable to utter destruction. In 1693, the residents of Mannheim begged to pay contributions to the French in order to avoid the destruction they suffered in 1688 and 1689, but the French refused, since they were determined to leave the Palatinate unfit to support enemy troops.[50]

French Use of Contributions to 1659

The French extracted contributions from outside Bourbon domains before 1659. David Parrott argues that the desire to invade Spanish-held Franche-Comté in 1636 derived from a desire to live off of foreign terrain through contributions.[51] But only with the shift in the fortunes of war in 1643 did the French occupy significant new territory to exploit for revenues. Le Tellier wanted these lands milked, not bled white, since he expected his king to annex many of them at the return of peace.[52] There was little desire to ruin what would soon be part of France. When the French occupied foreign terrain in Catalonia, they also demanded contributions from it.[53]

However, before 1659, French commanders probably imposed more contributions within Bourbon domains than they did across the borders. Repeatedly, the governors, or commanders, of French fortifications financed their garrisons by extracting contributions from nearby villages; in fact, this was a practice with a long history in France.[54] An order of 16 January 1637 complained that governors "order contributions on [the king's] people for the subsistence of soldiers" and went on to "deny to all governors . . . [the power] to order any tax or imposition whatsoever."[55] But the disorder and state poverty brought on by the Fronde caused the king's government to reverse its position and declare in 1650 that "His Majesty finds it good that

---

[49] On the Palatinate, see Kurt von Raumer, *Die Zerstörung der Pfalz von 1689* (Munich: 1930).

[50] AG, A^{1}1213, #61, 29 January 1693, La Grange to Barbézieux, in Ferguson, "Blood and Fire," 132–33.

[51] Parrott, "The Administration of the French Army," 47.

[52] Douglas Baxter, *Servants of the Sword, French Military Intendants of the Army, 1630–1670* (Urbana, IL: 1976), 108.

[53] See, for example, documents concerning contributions in Catalonia during 1649 in AG, A^{1}115, such as #51 and #86.

[54] Local villages in France paid "composition" to French garrisons in the sixteenth century to avoid raids. David Potter, *War and Government in the French Provinces: Picardy 1470–1560* (Cambridge: 1993), 225–30. The payment of "appatis," an earlier form of contribution to a captain to spare a particular population, dated from the middle of the fourteenth century and thrived in the fifteenth. Contamine, *Histoire militaire*, 1:191.

[55] AG, A^{1}42, #33, 16 January 1637.

each governor cause contributions to be levied."[56] By the time the war ended, Louis XIV saw the independence of these governors as a threat. In 1661, he wrote of the need "to moderate the excessive authority of the governors of frontier cities . . . who had made the same exactions on my subjects as on my enemies."[57]

The extortion of contributions by individual commanders without authorization could be best seen as just a variant of the Tax of Violence. In 1644, with French troops preying on French villages, the government was caught between the needs of its army and the protests of its subjects. To stop the troops from marauding, all the government could do was to advise that areas of Artois, Cambrésis, and Hainault pay contributions to buy off the courses.[58] A broadside issued on 5 October 1650 in Burgundy declared that since the soldiers have been paid, commanders are to make no more demands of villages northwest of Dijon, implying that levies had been made before.[59]

In contrast to contributions demanded by rogue commanders, during the war of the Fronde, the contending French armies raised regular contributions on French populations. The *conseil des finances* set the contributions for the hostile areas around Paris in 1649.[60] In civil war, it made perfectly good sense to submit French territory to contributions.

French Use and Administration of Contributions after 1659

The levying of contributions was too important a practice to perform a single role in the complicated play of war policy in the second half of the seventeenth century. There is no question that the primary function of contributions was to mobilize the resources of enemy, or neutral, territory to support the war effort of the French monarchy. As early as 1667, Louis made it expressly clear that conquered areas were to support his troops. "It is necessary to be able to make subsist a great number of troops and to profit from all the advantages that the enemy could take from the country" because the numbers of troops maintained during wartime were so great.[61] The demands at the close of his regime became more strident. The proud Sun King instructed Villars to draw contributions from Germany in 1703 so as to "husband as much as you can my finances which are too burdened by the immense expenses which I am obliged to bear."[62]

[56] Letter of 7 July 1650 in André, *Le Tellier*, 313.   [57] See Louis, *Mémoires*, 2:401–2.

[58] AG, A¹86, fol. 274, 15 November 1644 in Landier, "Guerre, violences, et société," 74.

[59] Côte d'Or, C 3673.   [60] Berger, "Military and Financial Government in France," 91.

[61] AG, A¹208, #22 and #31, September 1667, commissions to *intendants* Talon and Terruel.

[62] AG, A¹1676, #41, 27 April 1703, Louis to Villars in Ferguson, "Blood and Fire," 11, 180, and 190. For other appeals to raise money via contributions in 1703, see AG, A¹1675, #85, 24 February 1703, Louis to Villars in Ferguson, "Blood and Fire," 190, "You know . . . the immense expenses with which I am burdened, I hope that by your efforts they shall be considerably lightened for this winter, that you shall find [a] way to maintain my cavalry at the

In 1707, Chamillart, serving both as secretary of state for war and as controller general of finance, begged Villars's assistance. "Remember . . . that Germany is full of abundance and that I am in great distress, since for a long time it has not been possible to support at the cost of the kingdom an expense as great as that which the King is obliged to bear."[63] A month later, the same minister appealed again: "take me out of the sad situation in which I find myself concerning providing funds for the armies, the contributions can, it seems to me, spare the King the expense . . . you can easily draw all the money you will need from that."[64] According to Louis, the levying of contributions ranked as the "principal and sole object" of Villars's army in 1707.[65] Such appeals leave little doubt concerning the shortfall of state finances and the need to make up the difference as much as possible with contributions.

Before 1659, contributions often simply lined officers' pockets; such financial exactions were driven by greed, independent of state necessity. But the control over the practice exerted by the monarch and his agents after the Peace of the Pyrenees usually denied officers the chance to construct fortunes on a foundation of contributions, although there were exceptions.[66] Villars frankly admitted that in 1707 he skimmed off some of what he raised for himself "to fatten my calves," but Louis permitted this, since "he has done well by my finances too."[67] Villars was allowed personal gain as a reward for his victories and because he filled royal coffers as well.

While providing funds and goods to support the war, contributions could fit into other aspects of war policy.[68] Contributions could serve a policy of

expense of the enemy, and draw from him enough money in contributions to be used to pay part of my troops"; AG, A¹1675, #166, 27 March 1703, Chamillart to Villars in Ferguson, "Blood and Fire," 192, in which Chamillart reminded Villars that the enterprise in Germany would hardly cost the king anything as soon as Villars entered Germany; and AG, A¹1676, #106, Chamillart to Villars, in Ferguson, "Blood and Fire," 11fn, "With regard to contributions you know, as I, the necessity there is to levy them as far away as possible . . . that . . . shall considerably relieve the finances of the king for the payment of the army . . . ."

[63] AG, A¹2027, #98, 28 May 1707, Chamillart to Villars in Ferguson, "Blood and Fire," 10.

[64] AG, A¹2027, #105, 2 June 1707, Chamillart to Villars in Ferguson, "Blood and Fire," 10–11fn. For other appeals to raise money via contributions in 1707, see A¹2027, #97, 28 May 1707, in Ferguson, "Blood and Fire," 14fn, "subsist my army at the expense of enemy country . . . aid my finances whose state you know and the need they have of aid," and AG, A¹2027, #137, 13 June 1707, Chamillart to Villars in Ferguson, "Blood and Fire," 11, "I shall receive with gratitude several million if you are in a position to send it from Germany as Prince Eugene did from the Milanais to the Emperor."

[65] AG, A¹2027, #160, 23 June 1707, Louis to Villars in Ferguson, "Blood and Fire," 240.

[66] Ferguson, "Blood and Fire," 8, 12, wants to maintain this as a force behind the exploitation of contributions, but I believe he misses the point. His only example of someone who might have kept substantial amounts of money is Villars, but even here he expresses suspicion more than he demonstrates fraud. On page 12, Ferguson misreads evidence to see contributions as personal gain when the piece speaks of a state using contributions to punish its enemy.

[67] Villars in Babeau, *La vie militaire*, 2:138.

[68] Ferguson, "Blood and Fire," 70, gives seven goals for contributions: (1) war income, (2) campaign maintenance, (3) winter-quarters subsistence, (4) tool of impoverishment to create a zone of destruction, (5) revenge, (6) political leverage, and (7) support for a client prince.

destruction, designed to exhaust an area so as to make it impossible for the enemy to employ it as a base. Cases in point – the extraction of contributions in 1683–84 in the Spanish Netherlands and 1688–89 in the Palatinate aimed at stripping the area of resources that might be of value to the enemy.[69] Revenge or reprisal could also be a motive. Escalating exactions in the Low Countries often came as retaliation against Spanish actions. The French also levied financial demands in the hope of cowing Rhineland peasants and guerrillas (*schnapphahns*) into submission. Contributions aided wartime politics as well by pressuring enemies to make peace, or neutrals to aid the French. This clearly was an aim of the 1707 campaign into Germany, in which contributions were to serve both as a means to maintain the army and to intimidate the Germans into neutrality.[70]

Since allies shared in contributions exacted, contributions could win and keep a prince as a comrade in arms. Certainly, Maximilian of Bavaria drove a hard bargain in 1703, claiming two thirds of the contributions raised by the French in Germany.[71] French negotiators concluded that he would not have joined the French for any less. Dispute over contributions, as much as anything else, gave birth to the hostility between Villars and Maximilian, a hostility that cost Villars his command in Germany. Ferguson has argued that contradictions between conflicting goals of contribution policy doomed it to failure.[72] In the case of Villars's campaign of 1703, this argument rings true, since the French could not reap the financial advantages that they needed from contributions when Maximilian could skim off two thirds of the take as the price for his support.

First and foremost, after 1667, contributions became an integral part of the state's fiscal base for war, as they took on a greater degree of legal and administrative regularity. Contributions for major areas were set by formal agreements, *traités*, hammered out between local officials and French authorities. These *traités* laid out the financial obligations and promised protection to those who paid regularly, even offering compensation for possible damage caused by French troops after a *traité* was concluded. In the Spanish Netherlands, if an area received permission from Spanish authorities to contract a *traité* with the French because the Spanish could not defend it, that

He sees these goals as contradictory and insists that contributions might have worked had only one goal been pursued. Elsewhere he credits contributions with being first and foremost "part of an apparatus of power and majesty intended to impress the alien population with the force and success of the King's arms" (Ferguson, "Blood and Fire," 34).

[69] Van Houtte, *Les occupations étrangères*, 1:110; John A. Lynn, "A Brutal Necessity?: The Devastation of the Palatinate, 1688–1689," in *Civilians in the Path of War*, Mark Grimsley and Clifford Rogers, eds. (forthcoming).

[70] Ferguson, "Blood and Fire," 236.

[71] This split of contributions was laid down in article twelve, signed 17 June 1702, of the agreement between the Bourbon monarchy and the Elector of Bavaria. Sent to Villars as AG, A¹1675ᵗᵉʳ 24 March 1703. Ferguson, "Blood and Fire," 186.

[72] Ferguson, "Blood and Fire," 170.

area could usually deduct its payments to the French from its Spanish tax bill. During the Nine Years' War, in particular, localities often received just such permission to pay contributions.[73] Thus, contributions evolved into regular and structured impositions assessed on areas outside the king's domains and entered the law of war as recognized and legitimate. Practice set the minimum size of parties sent to exact contributions and defined *pays de contribution*, those areas that could be submitted to contributions.[74]

While major commanders, such as marshal Humières in 1676, might still be involved in negotiations with local officials, this duty most often fell to civil ambassadors of the Sun King. If a general did sit at the bargaining table, it was not to satisfy his own whims but to serve his royal master. Late in Louis's reign, marshal Villars enjoyed a special independence and took over the operation of contributions for his troops in Germany, although he was still served in raising contributions by civil administrators.

Regularization of contributions required a new set of personnel to assess and collect them. The primary administrator could be an army *intendant* or a special *intendant des contributions*.[75] The *intendant* received assistance either from *receveurs des contributions*, who in turn employed one or more clerks, or from agents of the *extraordinaire des guerres*. Once collected, contributions either went directly into the accounts of the local *intendants* as part of the *extraordinaire des guerres* or into the coffers of the treasurers of individual armies. The latter case prevailed when armies campaigned deep in enemy lands.[76]

French officials usually set the level of contributions in relation to prewar tax rolls, and such agreements were often on a town-by-town basis. In 1676, the community of Termonde agreed to pay the French "in proportion to their cost in the *transport de Flandres*," a local Flemish tax.[77] In the best of circumstances, the process of assessing contributions involved the consent of those burdened with the new payment, through some sort of bargaining with the *intendant*. In an exemplary case, Louis Robert, *intendant* of the conquered

[73] Van Houtte, *Les occupations étrangères*, 1:8.

[74] The best discussion of the evolution of contributions in law and fact during the period 1667–1748 is in Hubert van Houtte, *Les occupations étrangères en Belgique sous l'Ancien régime*. Van Houtte, 1:167, dates the origin of contribution *traités* with the War of Devolution. Geoffrey Parker, *The Army of Flanders and the Spanish Road, 1567–1659* (Cambridge: 1972), 142–43, describes an earlier regularization of contributions in the late sixteenth century, but this was not French practice and did not involve *traités*.

[75] See van Houtte, *Les occupations étrangères*, 2:8–10, for the commission to Talon as *intendant des contributions* in 1667. During the same year, Robert was also appointed as *intendant des contributions* when he was also the *intendant* for the army of marshal Aumont, Baxter, *Servants of the Sword*, 222.

[76] Concerning Villars's authority, see the Ferguson dissertation. See printed orders to pay to particular officials in Nord, C 2333, for their positions.

[77] Nord, C 2326, 20 April 1676, "Traité," concerning Termonde. Contributions levied on French territory by the Spanish in 1667 were set in relation to the taxes paid by those areas during 1665–66. Van Houtte, *Les occupations étrangères*, 1:158.

territories just east and south of Dunkirk, toured through the lands under his administration in October 1667 and then bargained with local authorities. The magistrates of Bergues gave him trouble in hammering out a compromise on the money and goods that they would pay to Louis XIV. After a great deal of tugging, he gained grudging compliance by January 1668. In 1672, the same Robert dealt with a more substantial adversary, the Estates of Guelder, to reach agreement on the contributions to be paid to the French army. By the mid-1670s, when such regular methods of negotiation and assessment had taken hold, the French notified towns to be tapped by printed forms, with blanks to be filled in.[78]

In addition to contributions, the French also sold other forms of protection in areas that they occupied or threatened – safeguards and passports. Contributions amounted to a war tax, backed by the threat of violence; safeguards guaranteed that French soldiers would not molest a particular property, village, or town as they passed or conducted their courses.[79] A safeguard could be bought by a community outside the reach of formal contributions but in range of raiding parties. However, areas that paid contributions might also purchase safeguards to ensure that they would not be molested by French troops.[80] Safeguards became so integrally related to contributions that some printed forms included fill-in spaces both for contributions demanded and for amounts to be paid for either "general safeguards" or "particular safeguards." The sale of such safeguards amounted to a significant source of income.[81] In 1711, when the Allies had advanced across the prewar borders, villages around Lille and Douai were required by the French to pay 500 livres in species for safeguards.[82] Passports allowing free travel within occupied areas or allowing those outside a French-controlled area to travel into one could also be purchased. Lieutenant generals had the right to issue these, but Louvois encouraged *intendants* to assume authority if possible.[83]

Notwithstanding their administrative propriety, contributions remained extortion, paid by a population that did not recognize the French king as their legitimate ruler and backed by the threat of immediate violence. Should

---

[78] For Robert's negotiations, see Baxter, *Servants of the Sword*, 183–86, and AG, A^{1}294, #229, letter of 30 August 1672 from Robert. For payment orders, see Nord, C 2333–34. During the same period, the Spanish set the level of contributions to be imposed on French subjects in relationship to French taxes. For example, in 1689, contributions were to equal half the value of taxes paid in 1687. Van Houtte, *Les occupations étrangères*, 1:157–61, 226–27.

[79] Redlich, *De Praeda*, 45, defines safeguards as protection from *Brandschatzung*.

[80] See van Houtte, *Les occupations étrangères*, 2:29–30 for a model safeguard of 1689. It promised both protection and reimbursement for damage that might be caused by French troops.

[81] Myron P. Gutmann, *War and Rural Life in the Early Modern Low Countries* (Princeton: 1980), 44–45.

[82] Lille, Af. gen. 281, dos. 9, treaty of contributions with Lille by the French, 14 October 1711. For the area outside the walls of Lille and Douai, 180,000 florins were to be paid. Each village was to pay 500 livres in species for safeguards.

[83] See letter of AG, A^{1}208, fol. 143, 7 November 1667, letter from Louvois to Chareul.

a town not pay, it was visited by French troops bound on destruction. "Executions," the burning of villages and towns that failed to pay contributions assigned them, revealed the brutal nature of this extortion. The printed orders to pay contributions often referred to this penalty, or of "all the rigors of war," hanging over a village's head, as in an order of 4 May 1689 demanding payment in forage "under penalty of being forced by military execution to the payment of double the said imposition."[84] Louvois could be callous, almost bloodthirsty. Commenting on Luxembourg's advance from Utrecht during the last days of December 1672 when his forces burned down 2,000 houses, Louvois boasted that in Swammerdam, "we grilled all the Dutch who were in it; we did not allow one to get out of the houses."[85] So it comes as little surprise that he urged executions of villages and towns delinquent in payments.[86] "I see with pleasure," he wrote in 1676, "that you have begun to burn the old city of Ghent, I beg you to continue . . . and to pillage and burn there until those people have fulfilled their treaty either in money or in notes, and not to cease until you are informed that they have actually done so."[87] Louvois does not bear full responsibility for his brutality, because he seems to have expressed something in Louis XIV himself. Certainly, Louvois's death in 1691 did not alter the French policy of executing villages. Louis XIV explained to Marshal Catinat shortly after that "It is terrible to be obliged to burn villages in order to bring people to pay the contribution, but since, neither by menace, nor by sweetness, can one oblige them to pay, it is necessary to continue to use these rigors."[88]

The French also took hostages to enforce the payments of contributions. This was regarded as a lesser form of coercion. Common peasants and the highborn spent time in French confinement. Among the nine hostages taken from Hailbron to Strasbourg in 1689 were two knights of the Teutonic order, taken to ensure the payment of 30,000 livres of contribution imposed on the order.[89] The single largest batch of hostages was probably the unfortunate Dutchmen shut up in Grave to ensure that Dutch towns put under contribution by the French in 1672–74 paid their obligations. When Louis's armies retreated in 1674, the avaricious French put a high priority on removing the hostages before the Dutch took Grave.

Not even peace could save the people from contributions. Laws and practices of war dictated that contributions still owed at the close of a war must be paid. After the end of the Dutch War, negotiations for the evacuations of

---

[84] Nord, C 2333.   [85] AG, A^{1}344, 7 January 1673.

[86] See, for example, his repeated demands to execute villages during the brief Spanish war 1683–84, reproduced in a very legible fashion in Jacques Hardré, ed. *Letters of Louvois*, University of North Carolina Studies in the Romance Languages and Literatures, no. 10 (Chapel Hill: 1949), 265, 273–74, 277, 302, 331, 335, 340–41, and 369.

[87] AG, A1484, 6 October 1676, Louvois to Chamilly in Ferguson, "Blood and Fire," 50.

[88] AG, A^{1}1041, #303, 21 July 1691, Louis to Catinat.

[89] AG, A^{1}875, 3 April 1689, from de la Grange. These hostages included members of the town Council, A1874, 1 January 1689, Tessé to Louvois, in Ferguson, "Blood and Fire," 113.

the Spanish Netherlands in 1679 guaranteed payment of contributions still owed the French at the cessation of hostilities and allowed French troops to perform executions if arrears were not paid within six weeks.[90] Article VII of the convention ending the War of the Reunions in 1684 with Spain required the payment of all outstanding contributions at the time of ratification, and Louis reserved the right to carry out executions against towns that remained in arrears.[91] Unique among the major peace treaties signed by Louis, the Treaty of Ryswick ending the Nine Years' War expressly forgave outstanding contributions to the French, although the Brandenburgers were to receive one third of the contributions pledged to them.[92] The Treaty of Utrecht between the Dutch and the French again stated that outstanding contributions must be paid, although no mention was made of executions.[93] Although, given the fact that the Allies held so much Spanish terrain late in the war, it was most probably the Dutch, rather than the French, who benefited by the payment of outstanding contributions in 1713–14.

Contributions in the Spanish Low Countries

The French assessed contributions wherever and whenever the military situation allowed, but they drew the largest sums from the Spanish Low Countries. Certainly, the French exploited other areas, such as western Germany, where they levied contributions in an irregular and spasmodic manner, but France's real "money cow" was the Low Countries. In these Spanish provinces, French contribution policy followed a particularly intriguing course.

The regularity of contributions ushered in by the War of Devolution kept them at a moderate level for a time. Early in the Dutch War, a form of reasonable restraint limited contributions to roughly equivalent levels. The French realized that heavy demands might precipitate enemy levies in return. In 1672, Louis decided to restrain impositions on Holland because they would expose French areas to enemy impositions. But as the war surged on, the rapacity of contributions and executions increased, particularly with marshal Humière's strike into the pays de Waes in 1676. This brought on an undeclared "rupture of contributions," a condition in which one foe decided that the other had broken the contribution understanding and so abandoned it himself. Mounting demands and harsh executions threatened to destroy the countryside along the embattled northeast frontier of France and the Spanish Netherlands.[94]

[90] J. Dumont, *Corps universel diplomatique*, vol. 7, pt. 1 (Hague: 1731), 396.

[91] Dumont, *Corps universel diplomatique*, vol. 7, pt. 2 , 81. See, as well, Louvois to Croissy, 20 August 1864, Hardré, *Letters*, 388, and 377, 388–89.

[92] Article XVII of the treaty, Dumont, *Corps universel diplomatique*, vol. 7, pt. 2, 410. See van Houtte, *Les occupations étrangère*, 1:171–72, 484–85.

[93] Article XXVII of the treaty, Dumont, *Corps universel diplomatique*, vol. 8, pt. 1 (Hague: 1731), 370.

[94] Concerning Holland, see AG, A^{1}294, #295 and #343. See van Houtte, *Les occupations étrangère*, 1:213–56, on rupture of contributions.

The escalation of contributions and violence climbed to such outrageous proportions that the French and the Spanish tried to limit them by treaty. There were precedents for treaties between contending states to limit violence visited on civilian communities by warring armies.[95] The idea for a conference seems to have originated with the French as early as January 1675. The commissioners of the rival kings met at Deinze, ten miles southeast of Ghent, in three rounds of talks between September 1676 and February 1678. Although the sessions produced no formal treaty, they resulted in an understanding to limit the level of contributions and the practice of executions. During the first negotiations, the commissioners agreed to apportion contributions according to the taxes paid by a particular region to its sovereign. After some hemming and hawing, they pegged 1669 as the base year. Furthermore, they forbade execution by fire, as long as people did not desert their villages. Instead, hostages would guarantee the payment of the reduced contributions.[96] A cynic might disregard the hopeful tone of Deinze and reply that it was merely a clever attempt on the part of the French to undermine their foes. The baron de Woerden, the French commissioner at Deinze, believed contributions to be more important to the Spanish war effort than they were to the French. He argued correctly that just holding the conference would prove advantageous regardless of its outcome, because "during the discussion, which will be rather long, they cannot raise contributions, [their] only financial resource."[97] In any case, the Deinze settlement broke down after the second suspension of the conference, and its impact on later wars is debatable.

Following the Dutch War, the short War of the Reunions brought new excesses. Van Houtte seems to skip over this brief but brutal clash, leading him to exaggerate the moderating influence of the negotiations at Deinze.[98] When full-scale war came again in April 1689, the French tried to return to

---

[95] See Potter, *War and Government*, 217, for an agreement between the French and the Spanish in 1544.

[96] Van Houtte deals with the Deinze conference both in his *Occupations* and in "Les conférences franco-espangnoles de Deynze," *Revue d'histoire moderne*, 2 (1927), 191–215. For extensive source materials on the Deinze conference, see van Houtte, *Occupations*, 2:157–202. For the 1675 date, see Nord, C 2333, poster of 24 April 1676. For examples of calculations of tax incomes as a basis for contributions, see Nord, C 2325 and Archives municipales de Lille, Af. etr. 279, dos. 3.

[97] AG, A^{1}513, #56, 12 September 1676, Woerden to Louvois. In fact, Woerden was correct. The receiver-general of the Spanish Netherlands, des Mottes, wrote governor-general Villahermosa during the Deinze negotiations to complain that unless he could collect contributions again, he would have to disband the Spanish army. Van Houtte, *Occupations*, 1:162.

[98] Van Houtte argued that the ban on executions by burning at Deinze endured, except during periods of rupture of contributions, and this marked a real advance. But van Houtte's interpretation can be criticized since (1) it disregards the horrors of 1683–84, and (2) a rupture immediately turned the Nine Years' War into one of brutal contributions. Really, improvement only comes with the War of the Spanish Succession, over twenty years after Deinze. Can we really credit this later amelioration to Dienze?

the more reasonable behavior discussed at Deinze, but exorbitant demands by the Dutch led to a declared rupture of contributions by December of that year.

During these two wars, reprisals for enemy demands and executions brought on even worse counterreprisals. In this brutal arithmetic, repeated orders condemned anywhere from two to fifty enemy villages or houses to be burned for every one village or house under Louis's protection. The most common multiplier was ten.[99] Louis and his ministers designed such reprisals to induce public opinion to put pressure on enemy officials. When, in 1684, Louvois ordered the count de Montal to burn twenty villages near Charleroi because the Spanish had burned two barns on the extremities of two French villages, the minister commanded the general to "throw around some broadsides that say that this is in reprisal for the burning of the two barns." Louvois charged Montal to leave not a single house standing in the twenty villages.[100]

According to the research of van Houtte, the worst period of excess ended in 1693, and the War of the Spanish Succession witnessed considerable moderation in the assessing and collection of contributions. However, before 1693, the French had already devised more effective means to protect their own resource base from the exactions of contributions. With reprisals and treaties ineffective in moderating hostile demands, the French took another tack: to wall out the enemy from the areas that Louis wished to reserve for his own benefit.

Engineers designed fortified trench lines and strings of outposts during the Nine Years' War and, especially, the War of the Spanish Succession. Although the use of entrenched lines or outposts to stop enemy parties did not originate in the 1680s, it attained a much grander scale at that time. At first these barriers were not designed to stop major armies from maneuvering, although they became more substantial with time and took on this function, particularly in the case of the Ne Plus Ultra Lines of 1711. The French began to build lines primarily as a means of barring enemy courses from pillaging and demanding contributions, and this continued to be an important rationale through the War of the Spanish Succession. The *intendant*'s memoir for Flemish Flanders, drawn up in 1697–98, praised lines between the Lys and the sea as so effective that "the inhabitants have not been bothered at all by enemy courses during the war." There was nothing particularly admirable about these efforts to protect subject villages. It was a question of fencing out the foxes so that the hens in the barnyard could continue to lay eggs in French baskets. The discussion of when and where to build defensive lines included analyses of how they would stop parties and the value in tax revenue

---

[99] For some execution orders, see AG, A^{1}722, #13–16; AG, A^{1}485, #215–20; letters from 1684 in Hardré, *Letters*, 290–91, 297, 327; and Nord, C 2333, 12 Nov 1690 poster.

[100] 18 February 1684 order to Montal, in Hardré, *Letters*, 343.

and contributions of the area they would shelter.[101] (See Chapter 16 for more on lines.)

Eventually the French tried to erect *legal*, as well as *physical*, barriers around their territory by buying off their enemies during the War of the Spanish Succession. In 1705, the French offered to pay the Allies 40,000 livres in contributions for Namur and the area between the Sambre and Meuse if the Allies agreed in the *traité* to ban their own parties from passing through the area that had bought protection. The contributing area would, thus, become an impenetrable buffer zone. Salions, the French negotiator, urged Louis to agree with haste, since if the Allies accepted the conditions, "The king will no longer be obliged to keep such large garrisons at Maubeuge, Philippsburg, and other places on Sambre. . . . The enemy, not being able to cross the region, will be unable to push their contributions any further than those borders they presently have."[102] The agreement of 1705 did not bring an end to raids, although its protection might have complemented the shorter French lines of 1706.

As the French were driven further out of Spanish territory, the 1708 lines of Cambrin relied not on paper guarantees but simply extended further entrenchments along the Sambre to Namur in order to place the threatened area behind real fortifications. In any case, enemy raids on French territory continued and forced the French to man lines of redoubts to contain them. The French contracted further contribution *traités* in 1709, 1710, and 1711 to limit destruction after the French could no longer defend their own border areas. The 1710 *traité* concluded at Douai paid the Dutch 800,000 livres to protect Artois and Picardy.[103]

Estimating the Income from Contributions

While the chaotic nature of the Tax of Violence defies any attempt to establish its cost, the more regular character of contributions allows some estimates. Surviving records usually ascribe a very low percentage of the *extraordinaire des guerres* to contributions. For example, a report comparing the size and cost of French troops, 1679–99, presented total receipts for 1692 of 112,523,000

---

[101] BN, f. fr. 22220, fol. 53. On rationale for the lines between Tournai and Courtrai, see Vauban to Peletier, 27 May 1696, in Albert Rochas d'Aiglun, *Vauban, sa famille et ses écrits*, 2 vols. (Paris: 1910), 2:443–44. On lines planned by revenue, see AG, A^{1}616, #21, 5 April 1678, Vauban letter; Nord, C 2242, undated but ca. 1700, discussion of lines of Waeste; and AG, MR 1047, #9, "Projet d'une ligne . . .", 6 April 1701. Lines also played a legal role because warring parties argued in *traités* that the "pays de contribution" ran from a belligerent army up to the first major barrier, a sizable river or entrenched line, that would hem in their war parties. On this point, see van Houtte, *Occupations*, 1:152–56.

[102] AG, A^{1}1837, #194, 21 August 1705, de Salions, "Remarques sur quelques articles du traité proposé." For other related documents, see AG, A^{1}1837, #11, 24, 100, 193. I owe this discovery to Mr. Christian Merrill, one of my graduate students, who discussed it in a 1991 paper on contributions. I have taken the liberty of using his translation of the documents.

[103] See André Corvisier, "Guerre et mentalités au XVIIe siècle," *XVII siècle*, 37 (1985), 230–31.

livres, with only 4,500,000 from contributions, confiscations, and passports, or 4 percent.[104] And a summary account drafted by the treasurers general of the *extraordinaire des guerres* in 1704, showing 97,050,545 livres of funds available from a variety of sources, lists only 4,871 livres from contributions and confiscations, or a mere 0.005 percent.[105] Considering that during most of that year the French maintained an army deep in Germany, where it was expected to subsist largely off contributions, this last figure seems absurdly low. Apparently, contributions did not normally make their way into the hands of the treasurers in Paris but stayed with the armies and *intendants* that raised them.[106]

However, while the treasurers left precious little evidence concerning more substantial levels of contributions, the archives contain some key information. A magnificently detailed and informative document lists 178 sources of special payments, including contributions, made during the last year of the Dutch War and into 1679. Perhaps these totals show up on central records, rather than on those of army treasurers and *intendants*, because the armies had been disbanded and the accounts shifted to Paris or because they were compiled in regard to treaty negotiations after the war. This document gives the most complete available survey of contribution payments. Still, even it is incomplete, since the accounting starts with item 107 and continues to 284. A separate list, now lost, must have dealt with the first 106 items. As it stands, the account shows 13,384,000 livres in receipts, of which 12,453,000 qualify as contributions and related impositions on foreign territories. Total military expenses posted for 1678 reached 67,901,000 livres, so the contributions shown in this key document amount to a hefty 18 percent, or nearly one fifth of what was posted.[107]

One provocative, and far more questionable, piece of information comes from the court diarist, the marquis de Dangeau. His entry for 23 August 1691 asserts that shortly after the death of Louvois, the two treasurers of the

---

[104] AN, G⁷ 1774, #52, "État des troupes que le Roy a eu sur pied, et leur dépense y compris celle des places."

[105] AN, G⁷ 1776, #294, 12 December 1704, "Compte du Roy estat abregé de recette et dépense."

[106] On instructions to pay troops directly with contributions rather than send them to Paris, see pieces in Ferguson, "Blood and Fire," 11fn, 190. The booty raised by contributions in the Palatinate, 1688–89, seems definitely to have been spent in place, judging from the detailed material in Ferguson.

[107] AN, G⁷ 1774, #68, "Receptes extraordinaires, déça 1679." Van Houtte, *Occupations*, 2:428–76, gives very impressive detailed accounts for contributions and damages, 1689–95, but they cover only the Spanish Netherlands. The "Receptes extraordinaires" could be read in different ways, but its correspondence to yearly levies listed in other sources convinces me that it is a good indicator of the annual take from contributions. For corroboration, see the following: contributions records in Nord, C 2325; AG, A¹700, 24 August 1683, letter to Peletier; and van Houtte, *Les occupations étrangères*, 2:428–76. Gross military budget figures used here come from Jean Roland de Mallet, *Comptes rendus de l'administration des finances du royaume de France* (London: 1789) and AN, KK 355, "Etat par abrégé des recettes et dépenses, 1662–1700."

extraordinaire des guerres held 18 million livres that Louvois had amassed by "contributions from Flanders and economies."[108] This was at a time when the total budget for the army ran 99,571,000 livres; therefore, the alleged cache of contributions comprised as much as 18 percent of the total.

Contributions take on even more weight when viewed from the perspective of armies in the field rather than from that of bureaucrats in Paris. Villars's 1703 campaign provides the best documented case of a field army that relied heavily on contributions. The acting *intendant* Baudouin reported to the war ministry that the treasurer of Villars's army brought with him only 450,000 livres and that, since his arrival, another 350,000 livres came in letters of exchange; to this sum, contributions added 460,000 livres, while hostages promised another 128,000 livres. According to these figures, cash impositions made by the army accounted for 42 percent of the army's funds. This was at a time when Villars estimated the rock-bottom cost of pay and bread for his army at 531,000 livres per month. Knowing this, Louis only promised Villars 300,000 livres per month, urging Villars to "act in such a way that this sum and that which you will raise in contributions will . . . meet the needs of my army." This correspondence reveals that Louis expected Villars to supply at least 43 percent of his financial needs through contributions.[109]

To the monetary exactions imposed by armies in the field must be added their demands for payments in kind, payments that do not show up on records of the cash paid in contributions. The greatest example of this is forage. Inside France, forage had to be purchased; outside, it could be seized. In 1688, La Grange reported to Louvois that by moving the winter quarters of just four cavalry regiments from Alsace to Württemberg and Baden, he expected to save 120,000 to 140,000 livres.[110] Van Houtte provides even more surprising evidence taken from the accounts of Spanish Flanders, 1689–94. He lists 10,351,400 livres of contributions and other financial impositions paid during this period, while showing that the total amount of forage, straw, and grain taken or destroyed by the French reached 12,227,600 livres.[111]

---

[108] Philippe, marquis de Dangeau, *Journal du marquis de Dangeau*, Feuillet de Conches, ed., 19 vols. (Paris: 1854–60), 3:387–88.

[109] AG, A¹1676, #183, 20 August 1703, letter from Baudouin; AG, A¹1675, #143, 22 March 1703, "Dépense pour un mois de trente jours," memoir by Villars; AG, A¹1676, #41, Louis to Villars, 27 April 1703, the text actually says 30,000 livres, but by checking surrounding correspondence, it is clear that this was a copyist's mistake and that 300,000 was the correct figure; Ferguson, "Blood and Fire," 180, gives the figure as 30,000. For another case, see the following documents concerning French troops in Italy, 1701–4: AN, G⁷1775, #54; AN, G⁷1775, #322; AN, G⁷1776, #466.

[110] AG, A¹827, #78, 12 November 1688, La Grange to Louvois.

[111] These figures are arrived at by subtracting the 2,156,740 florins for "grains, forrage, and straw" from van Houtte's table of contributions, *Occupations*, 2:442, and then adding it to "forage and camping" and "forage and straw" from his table of damages, 2:454. The totals probably overstate the value of animal forage alone but almost certainly by less than 25 percent. In any case, they give a vivid impression of just how much of a burden forage

Consequently, the value of forage in this major case approached or surpassed that of contributions.

Precise calculations of the total yield from contributions in the *grand siècle* are impossible to make. Yet a rough assessment can and ought to be attempted, particularly since estimates – whether by omission or commission – have already appeared. With regard to errors of omission, those who would study only the official figures miss contributions altogether, since they are not listed in the government's financial summaries, the *états au vrai*. At the other extreme, some historians have committed errors of commission by stating or implying that during the *grand siècle* armies on campaign simply lived off the country by extorting contributions.[112] There is no indication that French armies survived by plunder alone after Louis XIV assumed personal power.

This being said, it is possible to bracket contributions. To relegate them to approximately 10 percent of the material resources expended in war is too low, especially when impositions in kind are put into the equation with cash levies. To ascribe 50 percent of war finance to contributions is far too generous, although particular field armies at particular times probably relied on contributions for half or more of their operating funds. Contributions lay somewhere in between. At the height of a war effort, contributions probably accounted for something in the neighborhood of 25 percent of cost of land warfare. To be sure, this estimate derives more from a "feel" for the sources than from any rigorous computations.

Making War Feed War: Contributions and War Plans

The need to make war feed war through contributions drove strategy during the *grand siècle*. Of course, this need was not unique to the French; it was a general concern, one of great moment to the Bavarians, Swedes, and Imperialists as well. It is equally true that there was nothing new in trying to impose the costs of war upon the enemy, but the expansion of French military institutions added new urgency to this time-honored logic of war.

The return from contributions was far more modest before 1659, but even during the Thirty Years' War, the quest for contributions determined operations, particularly along the Rhine. The language of the time expressed this as a pursuit of winter quarters, but this can better be understood as a subset of contributions, because towns subject to quartering provided goods and services on threat of violence – that is, contributions by one name or another

requisitions could be. The original figures are in Flemish florins, which according to AN, G⁷890, "Recepte géneralle de finances de Flandre, 1689," were evaluated at 1.25 livres per florin.

[112] See Martin Van Creveld, *Supplying War* (Cambridge: 1977), ch. 1 and Ronald Martin, "The Army of Louis XIV," in Paul Sonnino, ed., *The Reign of Louis XIV* (Atlantic Highlands, NJ: 1990), 119.

– and because these towns controlled areas that were put under contributions.[113] Turenne's concern for quarters often seemed to overshadow all other matters on campaign. He described the late summer and autumn as critical, "the time which decides so many things in Germany, because then you can gain command of a tract of territory in which you have all winter to refresh and remake your army."[114] He even viewed battle as a means to obtaining quarters: "the fruit that one gets from [battles is] to gain a country in order to have quarters, and thus to augment one's army and diminish that of the enemy by the means which one takes from him, which with a little patience sends him to his ruin."[115] Others shared Turenne's concerns at the time; his own *commissaire général*, Tracy, insisted "My opinion will always be to leave the conquests [in Alsace] free and to go into the enemy's country if it is possible."[116]

Contributions played a much greater role in military finance during the personal reign of Louis XIV, so that the quest for this source of support set the course of warfare on virtually every front, compelling his forces beyond French borders and dictating campaigns. Louis echoed Tracy's conviction that commanders should live at enemy expense and thus spare his lands and treasury. He complained to Marshal de Lorge in 1691 that "I am upset to see my army where it is . . . you should cross the Rhine to use up the supplies and forage of Germany and to save Alsace."[117] The king instructed Villars that "your principal and sole object" for the 1707 campaign was "to establish a secure base" from which he could "draw sufficient contributions to allow my army to subsist at the expense of my enemies."[118]

As demonstrated in these pages, contributions became particularly lucrative in the Low Countries and thus particularly influential on military operations. Yet while royal coffers gained from milking the Spanish Netherlands before 1701, Louis's dependence on contributions exposed him to disaster in the War of the Spanish Succession. The addition of the Spanish Netherlands to the Bourbon dynasty and the fact that defeat banished French forces from that rich area prohibited Louis from rapaciously exploiting its wealth. The financial collapse of France during this war must, to a degree, be attributed to the failure of contributions. Given the great difficulty of examining French finances, this intriguing speculation will probably remain just that, although

---

[113] Derek Croxton in his analysis of the final phase of that conflict goes so far as to speak of a strategy of quartering. Charles Derek Croxton, "Peacemaking in Early Modern Europe: Cardinal Mazarin and the Congress of Westphalia, 1643–1648," Ph.D. dissertation, University of Illinois at Urbana-Champaign, 1995.

[114] Turenne in Christopher Duffy, *Siege Warfare: The Fortress in Early Modern History, 1494–1660* (London: 1979), 129.

[115] Turenne in Croxton, "Peacemaking in Early Modern Europe," 63.

[116] Tracy to Mazarin, 20 September 1644, in Croxton, "Peacemaking in Early Modern Europe," 165.

[117] Louis to marshal de Lorge, in John B. Wolf, *Louis XIV* (New York: 1962), 466–67.

[118] AG, A¹2027, #160, 23 June 1707, Louis to Villars.

future research might possibly reveal the precise role of contributions within the larger context of fiscal crisis.

Ultimately, contributions go a long way to explain why armies fought for cities and lands that statesmen knew could not be retained in the future peace. They were more than just bargaining chips at the conference table. Temporary conquests could be desirable simply because they supported the war itself, even if they did not add permanent acquisitions or provide diplomatic leverage.

THE TRANSITION TO CONTRIBUTIONS: STRATEGY, ETHICS, AND EFFICIENCY

The transition from the Tax of Violence to contributions as the primary method of requisition marked a major improvement in both the conduct of troops toward civilian populations and in the efficiency of resource mobilization for war. Obviously, French subjects benefited most from this transition, but its impact extended beyond them. Brutal abuse was inseparable from the Tax of Violence; it was, in fact, the method of collection. Contributions did not necessarily bring the same barbarities. Executions under contributions occurred when the regular method of collection failed, but while troops might inflict harsh consequences on communities that resisted contributions, those that paid suffered little more than the loss of their money. Payment of contributions explicitly bought protection against potential harm. The administrative regularity of this practice often made assessment and collection more analogous to taxation than to robbery. And it must be remembered that the imposition of contributions was in accord with international practice and law.

Within the history of French armed requisition, the decline of the Tax of Violence and the rise of contributions can be ascribed to three factors. First, a changed strategic situation allowed the French to mine the resources of foreign lands. Second, Louis and his government would not tolerate the Tax of Violence. Third, the expanded size of the army made indiscriminate pillage too costly a means of maintaining an armed force.

It may be attractive to explain the shift simply on the basis of France's improved strategic situation after 1659. Free from a serious Spanish threat, French armies took the initiative and fought as much as possible on enemy terrain. In addition, France was more at peace within her boundaries. As opposed to the series of internal rebellions that had forced her armies to campaign deep in France before 1659, the only sizable revolts after that date occurred in 1675 and 1702–4. Neither came close to approaching the severity of the Fronde. This meant that great armies were not fighting bitterly within the body of France. For contributions to be levied on populations outside Louis's domains, his armies had to occupy or to stand on the borders of enemy or neutral territory. And after 1659, that is precisely what French armies did. To some degree, the handiest victims of requisition were no longer Louis's subjects but those of his enemies.

This argument, however, must not be taken too far. French troops followed *étapes* routes and quartered on French territory during all of Louis's wars, even when the actual fighting occurred outside his domains. And during the last years of the War of the Spanish Succession, Marlborough's victories forced the largest French forces to pull out of the Spanish Netherlands and live on French soil. Therefore, French regiments constantly encountered a friendly population that they could have preyed upon, but did not.

It would seem that by the 1690s quartering troops actually enriched rather than impoverished localities. Instead of bemoaning the presence of troops, as had been the case before 1659, the *intendants'* memoirs of 1697–98, which were prepared for the education of the dauphin, claim that troops brought economic benefit. For example, "money is abundant in Flanders because the king spends it there to pay his troops." Or for Artois, "The sale of grain, the pay of troops, their consumption, and the work on fortifications are the usual sources that spread around money." *Intendant* Turgot predicted that Metz would be worse off in peace because the troops would no longer provide business for local artisans. Clearly, by the late seventeenth century, the Tax of Violence was over, and during the eighteenth century, the annual passage of troops along the highways of France became a positive gain to French communities.[119]

While strategy and geography undoubtedly played roles in bringing an end to the Tax of Violence, they do not provide a sufficient explanation of the transition to contributions. Louis XIV's subjects might have continued to suffer at the hands of the king's army had not Louis and his secretaries of state for war acted with such vigor to end the worst problems. Louis XIV abhorred the mistreatment of his own people by his troops, which he saw as anathema to the ethics of monarchy. He also desired discipline for its own sake. Perhaps the Sun King loved war too much, but he also measured his *gloire* by quieter victories that improved the well-being of his subjects. Louis XIV's statements of concern must be accepted at face value, since they accord with his deeds.

It is to his credit that Louis took steps to halt the Tax of Violence. Indeed, this success ranks as his greatest humane achievement. Earlier abuse of French subjects by French troops condemns the Bourbon monarchy and its great servants, cardinals Richelieu and Mazarin. Princes who proclaimed a paternal interest in the welfare of their people revealed their hypocrisy when they

---

[119] *Intendants'* comments in André Corvisier, *Les Français et l'armée sous Louis XIV* (Vincennes: 1975), 276–79. With a list of other reasons why the local economy depended on troops, Turgot added, "Repairs for the troops are the sole source of the maintenance and wealth of the artisans of these towns." For the eighteenth century, see Claude Sturgill, "Changing Garrisons: The French System of *Étapes*," *Canadian Journal of History*, XX, issue 2 (August 1985).

knowingly surrendered their subjects to pillage in order to pursue dynastic ambitions.

At base, however, it was a practical failure that created the avalanche of abuses that Louis regarded as an ethical collapse. There was nothing new about armies pillaging. Earlier forces had plundered, and, inevitably, such plunder led to excesses.[120] However, the army of the *grand siècle* was so large and so outstripped the state's ability to support it that it could not live by pillage without inflicting unacceptable cost to the surrounding communities and, ultimately, to itself. Abuses that might have been supportable and tolerable with an army of 60,000 became unbearable and unconscionable with an army of 150,000 or 400,000. The horrors of both the Thirty Years' War and the French war with Spain, 1635–59, revolted Europe. Louis could not condone such exploitation of his own subjects. He considered his decision as a personal and moral one, but it was also a recognition that great armies must be maintained in the field through more rational means.

Pillage was not only reprehensible; it was inefficient – likely to waste as much as it acquired. Troops on the rampage tended to take what they could use and destroy the rest, usually by fire. Their excesses drove inhabitants away, as in 1643 when pillage left French towns "deserted and abandoned," according to a royal ordinance.[121] The exit of the local population meant that it could no longer supply food to troops on the spot. As Villars confided to his king in 1703, "where there are no peasants there are no supplies."[122] The marshal repeated this conviction dramatically in an address to his troops at the opening of his successful 1707 German campaign: "My friends . . . . If you burn, if you make the people run away, you will die of hunger."[123]

The horrors and inefficiencies of pillage, born of the state's incapacity to maintain its gargantuan armies, pressed the search for more orderly means of resource mobilization during wartime. This quest resulted in government reform and in reliance on contributions. Army growth drove state formation because larger armies created crises that could only be eliminated by expanding, centralizing, and strengthening government. Clearly, for Louis, the Tax of Violence served as just such a crisis. The fact that he both increased his forces and banished the Tax of Violence demonstrates that French wartime administration made substantial strides under his regime, that the authority of the monarch and the power of his bureaucracy grew. The end of the Tax of Violence was also partly accomplished by the disappearance of the last

---

[120] For misconduct and pillage by French troops within France during the first half of the sixteenth century, see David Potter, *War and Government in the French Provinces: Picardy, 1470–1560* (Cambridge: 1993), 203, 210, 217. On pages 207–9, Potter provides tables of losses incurred during the war. Corvisier argues that the later Religious Wars cost France 2 million to 4 million in population. Contamine, *Histoire militaire*, 1:327.

[121] SHAT, Bib., Col. des ord., vol. 16, #79, 15 July 1643.

[122] AG, A¹1676, #118, 17 June 1703, in Ferguson, "Blood and Fire," 211.

[123] Claude Villars, *Mémoires du maréchal de Villars*, ed. marquis de Vogüé, 5 vols. (Paris, 1884–95), 2:229–30.

elements of the aggregate contract army. As Wijn notes, "From the very first days of its existence, the mercenary army was a two-edged sword. The homeland often had to suffer as severely as, if not more than, the enemy territory."[124] The new state commission army, even if it was larger, was also by nature more susceptible to discipline and control, even when it was not paid on time.

Yet, despite his substantial efforts, Louis never became independent of armed requisition. French need for contributions reveals that, although the government had increased its ability to support its army, the state still fell short of being able to shoulder the entire burden of war exclusively by internal revenues and credit. Dependence on contributions entailed its own hazards. They were an uncertain and unstable treasure, made possible by the proper strategic situation and guaranteed only by victory.

CONCLUSION

The goal here has been to establish the role of armed requisition in supporting the massive military expansion of the *grand siècle*. Faced with two possible scenarios – that administrative and fiscal reform made army growth possible or that military expansion forced governmental reform – the Tax of Violence and contributions argue strongly for the second. The Tax of Violence makes the more compelling case since it presents images, like the engravings of Jacques Callot, of a world gone wild. The hellish fate that French villages suffered at the hands of ill-supplied troops ostensibly raised to defend them demonstrates as nothing else that the monarchy first mustered regiments and only later bothered itself with supporting them. The necessity to gain control over such an army provided a powerful impetus to military and administrative change.

Contributions, by contrast, appeared more methodical, particularly in the Low Countries, and approached regular taxation so closely at times that one might forget that they were precarious and contrived, or that a horrible threat enforced payment. Like so much of absolutist practice, contributions put a rational face on what was at base a makeshift response founded on power and coercion. Although the Tax of Violence flourished, festered, and died before 1715, contributions were revived time and again over the course of the next century, surviving through the *ancien régime*. When statesmen and military planners talked of war feeding war, they thought in terms of contributions.

In the end, absolutism failed to match up to the mounting demands of international conflict, and the Bourbons never achieved the capacity to finance their wars through normal revenues. In seeking to meet expenses, the state turned to whatever expedients it could, borrowing at suicidal interest and

---

[124] J. W. Wijn, "Military Forces and Warfare, 1610–1648," in *New Cambridge Modern History*, vol. 4 (Cambridge: 1971), 206.

mortgaging its future tax revenues. The monarchy also asked its officers to spend their own money in support of their units, a subject discussed in the next chapter. Armed requisition was not the only means employed to meet the shortfall of the state, but it was the most notorious.

PART THREE

COMMAND

7

The Costs of Regimental Command

W HEN a French regiment marched into battle, its officers led from the front, braving the same dangers that their men faced. Casualty lists tabulated the costs of command in death and wounds. Families grieved, although there was much pride in their grief, for there was honor to be won on the field – honor to be won at any price. Like the king, this officer corps pursued *gloire*.

Regimental officers, from cadets to colonels, commanded and controlled the troops directly, and as such they were essential to the army of the *grand siècle*. Their story occupies this and the following chapter. The aristocratic origins and values of the officer corps were central characteristics of the state commission army, and the growing control of the monarchy over those officers constituted an important element of absolutism. Underlying all of this, however, was a question of finance. The aristocracy spoke of its sacrifices in war as a tax in blood, but another cost of command also defined the officer corps – a toll measured not in lives but in livres. The king not only drew upon the sons of the aristocracy; he also drew upon their wealth and credit through purchase and maintenance. Colonels, captains, and, in some circumstances, other regimental officers bought their posts, and once they secured a command, they continued to build upon that investment by contributing to the costs of maintaining their units. Only by understanding these monetary demands can one understand the composition of the officer corps and the tensions within it.

THE SEMI-ENTREPRENEURIAL SYSTEM

So much involving the French army in the seventeenth century hinged upon what can be called the "semi-entrepreneurial" character of its officer corps.[1]

---

[1] While I have described the purchase and maintenance systems and their impacts in print for twenty years, I owe the term combining them as the *semi-entrepreneurial* system to David

As was the case in other European armies, French captains and colonels purchased their commands and invested in their upkeep, and their outlays bought officers leverage vis-à-vis the state. Yet the Bourbon monarchy, gunshy of potential rebellion, did not allow its commanders the autonomy enjoyed by the fully entrepreneurial German commanders of the Thirty Years' War.[2]

The Bourbons confronted a dilemma as they sought to expand their forces on the one hand and assert state control over their army on the other. To achieve the first goal, the monarchy had to accept entrepreneurial practices that worked against its second goal. Because the monarchy could not pay the full bill for its growing army, the state had to mobilize other resources. In addition to the Tax of Violence and contributions, the state tapped a third fund of riches – the wealth and credit of its officers. In many cases, officers paid a substantial part of the cost entailed in creating the units that they would command, and commonly they had to bear some of the immediate expenses of keeping those units in the field, either outright or in the hope of future reimbursement. This practice can be labeled as the maintenance system. Unless captains and colonels literally owned their units, they could not be expected to contribute personal funds for the benefit of their companies and regiments. Therefore, the French preserved a purchase system that allowed officers to buy their commands and hold them as personal property. Hence, the officer corps remained entrepreneurial to the degree that colonels and captains owned and maintained their own commands.

Nonetheless, the monarchy could not turn over control of its army to its officers in the way that a completely entrepreneurial system would have required, since the government feared that independent entrepreneurs might become deaf to the royal will. So the monarch and his agents strove to assert their authority over the officer corps by separating ownership from control, conceding the former while insisting on the latter. It would always be an imperfect compromise. Royal authorities made progress toward increasing royal authority over the officer corps during the long war with Spain, although the chaotic conditions of that struggle provided officers more freedom than they enjoyed during the personal reign of Louis XIV. Royal control brought the financial abuses of officers to heel, lessening the profits implicit in ownership. Under the Sun King, the chances for officers to amass personal fortunes from exercise of command declined, and Louis's agents were quick to punish those who bent regulations to line their pockets. Obedience impinged upon independence.

From the point of view of captain or colonel, the French semi-

Parrott, "The Administration of the French Army During the Ministry of Cardinal Richelieu," Ph.D. dissertation, Oxford, 1985.

[2] On the German system of military entrepreneurship, see Fritz Redlich, *The German Military Enterprizer and His Work Force*, 2 vols., *Vierteljahrschrift für Sozial und Virtschaftsgeschichte*, vols. 47–48 (Weisbaden: 1964). Volume 1 deals with the heyday of the entrepreneur.

entrepreneurial system combined the worst of two worlds. As the century progressed, the autonomy enjoyed by officers decreased, while the demands on their personal fortunes remained great. The requirement that colonels and captains pay a substantial share of the costs of their units out of their own pockets amounted to an unofficial, but recognized, tax on the nobility.[3] Perhaps this system could only have operated as successfully as it did in France, where the nobility and those who aped them possessed a strong drive to achieve military command at almost any price for essentially cultural reasons.

After 1635, foreign colonels who contracted to raise regiments in Switzerland, Germany, or Italy for service with the Bourbon monarchy most closely approached the entrepreneurial model. They provided the same functions or nearly the same functions as did their predecessors who fought for the Valois. The contracts, or "capitulations," that they signed with the king's representatives stated the terms of service and payment in detail. Foreign contractors remained an important element in recruiting forces, since a substantial part of the Bourbon army was composed of their troops. Yet although these colonels may have enjoyed more autonomy than did their French counterparts, all units were still subjected to royal direction and inspection.

Concerning the French army during 1635–37, David Parrott writes, "In contrast to every other major European state, France rejected in principle the entrepreneurial system for the raising of troops."[4] His judgment is enlightening, but it is important to recognize that 1635 represented something of a watershed. While the French monarchy rejected fully entrepreneurial colonels and captains after that date, in the years before then, the aggregate contract armies of the sixteenth and early seventeenth centuries were based upon entrepreneurial units of foreign mercenaries and independent forces raised by French grandees. A case in point – the duke d'Epernon had created small armies from his own resources and put them to the king's use in 1617 and 1621–22, and Louis XIII had rewarded such efforts. But when Epernon offered to raise regiments in 1636 that would remain under his authority, Louis refused unless Epernon would give up his rights to them. Otherwise, the king concluded, "I am resolved rather not to create the said provincial regiments."[5] To accept Epernon's regiments as he had before would have limited the king's control over his own army, and Louis could not agree to this.

It is not that the French always simply rejected the entrepreneurial system, since they had a history of employing it, but that they evolved away from it, and the rest of Europe would soon follow. In fact, abandoning entrepreneurial

---

[3] See John A. Lynn, "The Pattern of French Military Reform, 1750–1795," in *Proceedings of the Consortium on Revolutionary Europe*, ed. Donald Horward (Gainesville, FL: 1978), for an early statement of the notion that commissioned service exacted a tax on the French aristocracy in the *ancien régime*, at least until 1762.

[4] Parrott, "The Administration of the French Army," 166.

[5] AAE, 821, fo. 251, August 1636, Louis XIII to Richelieu in Parrott, "The Administration of the French Army," 167–68.

captains was a necessary step in the creation of the state commission army. Even in Germany, the heyday of the military enterpriser had passed by 1650, and new German armies, such as that formed by Prussia, would be distinctly royal in character; they would be state commission armies. France created this new style of the army a generation earlier. The surprising thing is not that the French abandoned the fully entrepreneurial officer corps but that they so successfully preserved certain of its elements that benefited royal finances.

RANKS FROM CADET TO COLONEL

The ranks of regimental officers in the French army during the seventeenth century followed a progression similar to that of today. In the infantry, this hierarchy was defined by the ordinance of 28 July 1661.[6] A young man intent on an officer's career could serve an apprenticeship as a cadet or a volunteer. A cadet received an appointment and pay from the crown. Although formally part of a regular or cadet company, he exercised no command. In contrast, a volunteer held no regular position and received no wages. Without enlisting, he served as a common soldier in the company of a relative, at times his brother or father. When Louvois tried to channel the bulk of young officers through his cadet companies in the 1680s, he forbade companies to take on cadets or volunteers, but this practice returned after his death.

The ensign ranked as the lowest commissioned officer with command responsibility in the infantry, a position paralleled by the cornet in the cavalry. During wartime, each company contained an ensign or a cornet among its cadre. Cavalry companies also included a *maréchal de logis*, today considered an NCO but then rated as the lowest grade officer.[7] Above the infantry ensign stood the sous-lieutenant, a rank created only in 1657.[8] These lesser ranks tended to disappear at war's end. Only small numbers of ensigns and cornets remained during peacetime, when sous-lieutenants existed only in a few infantry regiments.[9]

[6] Louis André, *Michel Le Tellier et Louvois* (Paris: 1942), 322.
[7] He received twice the pay of a brigadier and 50 percent less than a cornette and did not disappear with peace. In reality, he seems more a top sergeant than an officer. Victor Belhomme, *L'armée française en 1690* (Paris: 1895), 88.
[8] André, *Le Tellier et Louvois*, 322–23.
[9] There seems to be some debate as to the survival of the ensigns, cornets, and sous-lieutenants in peacetime. Pichat states bluntly that ensigns and cornets always disappeared at the end of a war. H. Pichat, "Les armées de Louis XIV en 1674," *Revue d'histoire de l'armée*: 1910, 12–13. Rousset, who seems to be correct, claims that battalions retained two ensigns and cavalry squadrons retained two cornets. Camille Rousset, *L'histoire de Louvois*, 4 vols. (Paris: 1862–64), 1:213. His discussion of French rank in the seventeenth century is quite good, 1:213–17. Daniel wrote, "Ordinarily one eliminated the majority of sous-lieutenants at the end of a war, and one recreated them at the beginning of a new one." Daniel, *Histoire de la milice française* (1721), 2:61, in Albert Babeau, *La vie militaire sous l'ancien regime*, 2 vols. (Paris: 1890), 2:91. *Étapes routes* from Lille, Dijon, and Amiens bear out the existence of small numbers of ensigns and cornettes, as well as the disappearance of sous-lieutenants in regular infantry units during peacetime, except during the brief conflict 1683–84.

In regular cavalry regiments, the rank of sous-lieutenant seems not to have existed at any time, so the jump up from cornet was lieutenant. The smaller size of cavalry companies may explain the lack of a sous-lieutenant. The lieutenant of the company assisted his captain in command; therefore, in combat, the junior officer led part of the company. If no captain was present, as occurred in some cases, a lieutenant took charge of the entire company. In the mid-1670s, most French lieutenants were between twenty and thirty-five years of age.[10] Company-grade infantry officers circa 1690 carried sword and spontoon, a short ornamental pike, except for the lieutenants and sous-lieutenants of grenadiers, who carried fusils. All field-grade officers carried swords only.[11] An ordinance of 1710 required captains and subaltern officers, except for those of the French and Gardes suisses, to be supplied with fusil and bayonet.[12]

Captains led companies. In all but a few regiments, captains of line companies bought their commands and thus owned venal *charges*. Of course, there were exceptions to this rule, as there were to almost all rules in the seventeenth century. Louis outlawed purchase in certain units of the royal household. Grenadier companies, created during 1670–91, stood outside the purchase system; therefore, their commissions belonged to the king and could be awarded at his pleasure, opening the door to men promoted from the ranks – known as soldiers of fortune – and less well-to-do nobles. In cavalry regiments, senior captains led squadrons in addition to commanding their companies. And when no colonel or lieutenant colonel was present with an infantry battalion, a senior captain commanded the entire battalion as a "*capitaine commandant.*" This happened quite often, particularly when a battalion was not on campaign and senior officers took leave. Pichat argues that the average age for captains in the Dutch Wars varied from thirty-two to forty-five.[13]

Majors appeared during the seventeenth century. Unlike today, this rank was not a necessary way station in the journey from captain to colonel but rather a special administrative post for the battalion. In fact, the captain who moved up to major was supposed to divest himself of his company; but this was not always the case.[14] Normally, holding the position of major would be a sign that an officer was not on the fast track. A major could be assisted by

---

[10] Pichat, "Les armées de Louis XIV en 1674," 12–13.

[11] Belhomme, *L'armée française en 1690*, 13.

[12] Ordinance of 5 December 1710 in Babeau, *La vie militaire*, 2:256.

[13] Pichat, "Les armées de Louis XIV en 1674," 12–13.

[14] Rousset, *Louvois*, 1:216. Puységur bought and held concurrently commissions as both captain and major in Piedmont in 1632. Jacques de Chastenet de Puységur, *Les Mémoires de messire Jacques de Chastenet, chevalier, seigneur de Puységur, colonel du régiment de Piedmont, et lieutenant général des armées du Roy*, 2 vols. (Paris: 1690), 1:140–41. An examination of review reports turns up majors who had no company but also, on occasion, some who did, as in the case of major Gaillon of the Regiment de Vendome, quartered in Casal in 1684. AN, Z^{1C}414, April 1684 review of troops in Casal.

one or more aides-major, who were lieutenants or sergeants posted to this duty.[15]

In many a battalion, a lieutenant colonel was the highest-ranking officer present. Several common circumstances might dictate that a colonel could not exert direct command. He might be too young or incompetent, away on leave, fulfilling a temporary higher command, or his regiment might include more than one battalion, in which case, the colonel would directly command only the first. Neither the rank of major nor that of lieutenant colonel carried a price tag, and, like the major, the lieutenant colonel had also achieved the rank of captain, although, unlike the major, the lieutenant colonel kept his company when he assumed his new post.

Colonels commanded and, almost always, owned regiments, and they too owned their own companies. In fact, the colonel and the lieutenant colonel can be considered as the first and second captains of their regiment. The colonel's company, *la colonelle*, numbered as the first, and the lieutenant colonel's as the second company. The actual term *colonel* presents some confusion in the seventeenth century. Early in the century, colonels general commanded branches of the service: infantry, cavalry, Swiss regiments, and so on. In 1661, Louis eliminated the position of colonel general of infantry, when its occupant died; however, a colonel general remained at the head of cavalry. When a colonel general held office, regimental commanders below him officially bore the title of *mestre de camp*, rather than colonel. Then, technically, the lieutenant colonel represented the colonel general rather than the *mestre de camp*. At least by late century, even *mestres de camp* of cavalry regiments often were called *colonels* in such documents as reviews and routes, and lieutenant colonels sometimes appeared as *mestre de camp lieutenant*. To avoid confusion, here regimental chiefs will always be referred to as colonels, and their seconds-in-command as lieutenant colonels. Colonels differed greatly from lieutenant colonels in more than rank. Colonels were almost of necessity highborn and wealthy nobles, often who rose to the rank of colonel at a young age, whereas lieutenant colonels need not have such wealth. Babeau defines lieutenant colonels as "the soul and true head of the regiment" and as "older, of little wealth, from the lesser nobility, when not a son of the middle class."[16]

If an infantry colonel was present and capable, he exerted tactical command over only a single battalion; should his regiment contain more than one battalion, a lieutenant colonel led the second, and the others, if there were any, were put in the hands of *capitaines commandants*. Cavalry regiments contained three or four squadrons, but a squadron consisted of only

---

[15] Rousset, *Louvois*, 1:216–17, states that aide-majors were lieutenants, and this may have been most common. But records exist of captains as aide-majors. AG, A¹2265, March 1710, #239–42, reports on the military service of the La Farge family.

[16] Babeau, *La vie militaire*, 2:133. He also speculates that majors and lieutenant colonels were soldiers of fortune, 118.

a few companies and did not really exist as an independent command, in contrast to an infantry battalion. In battle, a cavalry regiment of three squadrons saw the colonel command the first, the lieutenant colonel the second, and the next senior captain the third.

The fact that two ranks, captain and colonel, were venal *charges* involving actual ownership of specific military units, while the other company and field-grade ranks did not, led to different career routes. The well-heeled officer might begin as a cadet or volunteer or might serve in certain units of the king's military household that regularly provided officers, and then buy a company command while still quite young. Men of birth and wealth might enter the service directly as captains, but it was usual to serve some kind of apprenticeship first. After a time as captain, the ambitious young man would then buy a colonelcy. At this point, further advancement could not be bought, although birth and wealth, as well as talent, played a role. The aspiring officer with less cash and influence might enter the army as a cadet, volunteer, ensign, or cornet and then rise to lieutenant. A poor lieutenant who did not possess the money to buy a company might rise no higher, although, since the grenadier company was not for sale, he might become a captain of grenadiers. Had a lieutenant funds sufficient to buy a company, though not a regiment, he might progress up the ranks again, to become major or finish his career as a lieutenant colonel. It is also possible that a deserving lieutenant colonel could rise to brigadier directly without ever holding the rank of colonel.

Alongside the regular company-grade officers stood those individuals holding "reformed" ranks – a practice designed to support officers who lost their commands but might soon be needed again. Officers remaining from units that were reformed, or disbanded, continually posed a problem for French monarchs. Early in the century, such individuals could just be sent home, with, of course, the thanks of the king, as was the case with all the officers of the Regiment de Saucourt in 1636.[17]

Le Tellier attempted to find places for reformed officers either in new regiments or to fill slots vacated in the regiments that they had served before.[18] In the 1650s, Louis chose "capable and experienced" reformed officers to receive six *demi-montres* per year (that is, half pay) to serve with pike or partisan in one of the thirty companies of the Gardes françaises.[19] Regulations issued in 1657 set down patterns for dealing with reformed officers. While the exact details varied, the goal remained to keep as many as possible in the service at reduced pay until openings could be found for them.

The demobilization of the army after 1659 brought a new problem, as the number of companies fell, in the infantry from 1800 to only 800.[20] What was

[17] AG, A¹27, fol. 105, 21 January 1636, in Parrott, "The Administration of the French Army," 185.
[18] Louis André, *Michel Le Tellier et l'organisation de l'armée monarchique* (Paris: 1906), 180–88.
[19] André, *Le Tellier*, 181.
[20] Louis XIV, *Oeuvres de Louis XIV*, Philippe Grimoard and Grouvelle, eds., 6 vols. (Paris: 1806), 1:205–6.

Louis to do with the great numbers of suddenly unemployed officers, particularly when France might be at war again soon? An ordinance of 1660 set down the exact status of reformed officers who chose to stay on in the army. *Capitaine-réformé* became a rank just below that of captain, as did *lieutenant-réformé* in regard to lieutenant. D'Aurigac commented that in 1663, "there are several captains and lieutenants *réformés* in a company."[21] Louis also decided to stockpile as many officers as possible in his *gardes du corps* and his musketeers and other household units, even creating a company of *chevaux légers* for his son the dauphin to fulfill this purpose.[22] Demobilization after the War of Devolution brought another attempt to keep experienced commanders. By billeting them in companies that would be maintained, Louis increased the proportion of officers to men.[23] This was just one reason why the French army tended to be a bit officer heavy. Immediately after the Dutch War, there were 326 captains and 980 lieutenants *réformés*, and this number rose to a total of 8,902 officers *réformés* in 1699.[24]

PURCHASE

The purchase system required an officer to buy his military post. Regulations established somewhat different rules for the king's household units, guard regiments, foreign units in French service, and French line regiments. In these last, only commissions as colonel and captain legally went up for sale, but other slots could also go on the block, contrary to regulations. Newly created French regiments were usually handed out to colonels without requiring the new commanders to pay for their commissions, although the new colonel had to contribute heavily to the expense of raising his unit. These colonels often sold the companies in their new regiments to aspiring captains, although this was not supposed to be done and was formally forbidden in 1705.[25] Captaincies in newly created companies of established regiments also did not carry a sale price. The fact that such commissions technically cost nothing allowed the king to disband them at the end of a war without any compensation to the displaced colonels and captains.[26] The resale of existing regiments and companies benefited their current commanders. It was always necessary to acquire the monarch's approval to raise a regiment in France, but Louis XIII exerted less control over officers' commissions than did his son.[27] Under Louis XIV, a would-be French officer had to gain the concurrence of the king or his ministers, the *agrément*, and Louis took pride

[21] Paul Azan, *Un tacticien du XVIIᵉ siècle* (Paris: 1904), 100.
[22] Louis XIV, *Oeuvres*, 1:205–6, 2:185–86.
[23] Louvois to Rochefort, 7 May 1668, in Rousset, *Louvois*, 1:161.   [24] AN, G⁷1774, #52.
[25] Georges Girard, *Le service militaire en France à la fin du règne de Louis XIV: Rocolage et milice, 1701–1715* (Paris: 1915), 17.
[26] Babeau, *La vie militaire*, 2:120. Belhomme, *L'armée française en 1690*, 50–51.
[27] Audouin, *Histoire de l'administration de la guerre*, vol. 2 (Paris: 1811), 170.

in controlling all promotions, even worrying himself about sous-lieutenants and lieutenants.

The drawbacks of a purchase system were many for both the officer and the army. Simply the cost of a unit might doom an able but poor officer to life as a perpetual lieutenant, but there was more to worry about than the initial purchase price alone, because an investment in a company or regiment carried inherent risks. Should an officer die in action, his commission did not automatically pass to his heirs, and the investment could be lost. The king might choose to award it to a surviving son, but he was not bound to do so. A bemused Primi Visconti wrote in the 1670s that while "the French ruin themselves vying with each other" to purchase military posts, "if an un-expected musket shot hits them, they lose their life and their money spent on the *charge*; thus their sons go to the workhouse [*l'hôpital*]."[28] More to the point, a majority of companies and many regiments were eliminated at the end of a great war, because the peacetime army was only about one third the size of a wartime force by the 1690s. Officers holding commissions in de-mobilized, or "reformed," companies and regiments received no compensa-tion beyond a possible appointment as an officer *réformé*. Therefore, in most cases, the individual who bought a commission had to accept the likelihood that he would lose his investment.

From the point of view of the government, purchase created severe prob-lems as well. The most obvious is that it could place incompetent men in command of regiments and companies, since wealth need not correspond to talent or experience. This was most apparent in the case of boy colonels. The need to seek the king's *agrément* put some limits on this problem, but it did not eliminate it. As Vauban complained in 1705, purchase placed "at the head of troops young men who have neither service nor experience."[29] But if purchase produced senior officers who were too young, it also resulted in junior officers who were too old, because poorer officers could not buy their way up the chain of command. So one sees a sixty-year-old captain who finally wished to retire by selling his company.[30] Although some held on in rank too long, others abandoned the army too soon, probably to protect their investment. This became such a problem that in 1654 the government declared that it would accept no more resignations from officers, since those buying their commissions were not equal to the sellers in experience and ability.[31] Venality could also make regimental officers difficult to control. While colonels and captains could be and were disciplined, the ultimate sanction, removal from command, meant seizing their property without com-pensation, something the monarchy was reluctant to do. Loyseau in 1610

---

[28] Primi Visconti, *Mémoires sur la cour de Louis XIV, 1673–1681*, Jean-François Solnon, ed. (Paris: 1988), 145.

[29] Vauban in P. Lazard, *Vauban, 1633–1707* (Paris: 1934), 487.

[30] *Mémoire historique de la vie d'un fantassin* (1711) in Babeau, *La vie militaire*, 2:184.

[31] Ordinance of 2 April 1654 in André, *LeTellier*, 202.

criticized venality of military office as "a great source of disorder in military discipline."[32]

Repeatedly, the government took steps to abolish, limit, or regulate venality, but with little effect. Article 190 of the 1629 Code Michau outlawed it; however, money continued to change hands.[33] Yet in 1638, 9,000 to 10,000 livres were paid for captaincies in Chamblay's regiment, and Bussy-Rambutin paid 36,000 livres to be a lieutenant in the *chevaux légers* of Henri de Bourbon.[34] With no more impact, Le Tellier abolished the purchase of commissions in elite household units in 1648.[35] Ordinances of 1649 and 1654 limited the sale of infantry commissions and banned resignations from officers who wished to give up their commissions simply in order to sell their posts.[36] But these, too, became dead letters. Later regulations of 1664 outlawed sale in the *gardes du corps*, except for captains.[37] Finally, during the Dutch War, Louvois forbade the sale of subaltern positions (that is, lieutenant and below) except for the royal household, the *gendarmerie*, and the regiments of guards.[38] These later regulations seemed to have stuck, but they did not eliminate purchase in the regular regiments.

If venality could not be abolished, prices might be controlled. In 1689, Louvois forbade paying more than 12,000 livres for a company or 22,500 livres for a regiment.[39] But over 230 actual sale prices recorded by the diarist Dangeau suggest that Louis's commands were often honored only in the breach. According to Dangeau, in the period from 1684 to 1701, dragoon regiments averaged 76,941 livres, cavalry regiments 55,694, and infantry regiments 38,750.[40] During the War of the Spanish Succession, average regimental

---

[32] Loyseau, *Cinq livres du droit des offices* (Chateaudun: 1610), 445, in Parrott, "The Administration of the French Army," 190.

[33] Louis André, *Michel Le Tellier et Louvois* (Paris: 1942), 315. Jacques de Chastenet de Puységur agreed to pay 15,000 livres for the position of major in Piedmont, one of the old regiments, in 1632. Puységur, *Mémoires*, 1:140–41, in Parrott, "The Administration of the French Army," 190. This was the father of the author of *Art de la guerre par principes et règles*. The going price for a captaincy in 1635 seems to have been 6,000 livres. AG, A¹26, fol. 58, 2 June 1635, in Parrott, "The Administration of the French Army," 190 n.

[34] AAE 830, fo. 51, 21 February 1638, in Parrott, "The Administration of the French Army," 190 n; Bussy-Rambutin, *Mémoires*, 1:117 in Parrott, "The Administration of the French Army," 190. A surprisingly high 70,000 livres was paid for a sous-lieutenancy of gendarmes in 1637. AG, A¹42, 13 March 1637, #73.

[35] André, *Le Tellier et Louvois*, 315.

[36] Babeau, *La vie militaire*, 2:121; André, *Le Tellier*, 202 fn.

[37] André Corvisier, *Louvois* (Paris: 1983), 103.

[38] See the letter of Louvois to Beringhem, 6 January 1673, AG, A¹301 in Rousset, *Louvois*, 1:213.

[39] Rousset, *Louvois*, 3:315. See, as well, Saint-Simon, *Mémoires*, A. de Boislisle, ed., 41 vols. (Paris: 1879–1928), 1:283 fn. Susane interprets Louis's order that all general officers sell their colonelcies as an attempt to keep prices down by making more regiments available for sale. Louis Susane, *Histoire de l'infanterie française*, 5 vols. (Paris: 1876) 1:211.

[40] My graduate student, Tod Woodman, compiled the figures from Philippe, marquis de Dangeau, *Journal du marquis de Dangeau*, ed. Feuillet de Conches, vols. 1–19 (Paris: 1854–60). Saint-Simon states that he exceeded the limit to pay 26,000 for a new cavalry regiment in 1693. Saint-Simon, *Mémoires*, 1:283.

prices increased still further, to 89,999 livres for dragoons, 81,292 for cavalry, and 43,500 for infantry.[41] Within these averages, costs varied widely; in 1704–5, dragoon regiments, for example, went for prices ranging from 70,000 to 129,000 livres.[42]

After the end of the War of the Spanish Succession in 1714, Louis again set maximum prices for regiments from 30,000 to 75,000 livres, depending on the regiment.[43] Other attempts to limit the purchase price of regiments were made in the eighteenth century.[44] But only in 1776 would the minister of war, Saint-Germain, phase out the system by lowering the value of a commission each time it changed hands. By 1789, a minority of commissions still had a price tag on the open market; thus, they reverted exclusively to the king.

With all its disadvantages, and considering the obvious government frustration with aspects of the purchase system, why did it survive? Why did it remain so basic to French military institutions until the late eighteenth century? To explain aristocratic willingness to support the system requires a discussion of the French culture of command, a subject addressed in the next chapter. On the other end, the government tolerated purchase because it guaranteed that only men capable of contributing financially to the maintenance of their troops would rise to command them.

MAINTENANCE

The French state preserved a semi-entrepreneurial system because it needed French officers to contribute their personal wealth and credit toward raising and sustaining the units that they commanded. The purchase system survived because it guaranteed the maintenance system. On the one hand, the

---

[41] Chagniot presents a table of prices of regiments, 1701–38, from contracts preserved in the archives; these prices, which seem to be the amounts approved by regulation, show that colonelcies were supposed to be sold at differing rates in the following different types of regiments: dragoon regiment, 80,000 to 110,000 livres; king's cavalry regiment, 90,000; permanent infantry regiment, 42,000 to 81,250; permanent cavalry regiment, 60,000 to 72,000; new infantry regiment, 10,000 to 24,000; new cavalry regiment, 22,500. Jean Chagniot, "De Rocroi à Rossbach," in Claude Croubois, ed., *L'officier français des origines à nos jours* (Saint-Jean-d'Angély: 1987), 41.

[42] Dangeau, *Journal*, 9:418, 450, 10:228, 261. In 1705, the parents of an officer desiring to purchase a dragoon regiment that cost 85,000 livres, sold land to cover the cost; in this case, his regiment almost literally became this officer's fief. Jean Chagniot, "Guerre et société au XVIIe siècle," *XVII siècle*, 37 (1985), 255. See another case of complicated finance to buy a regiment in 1705 in Philippe Contamine, *Histoire militaire de la France*, vol. 1 (Paris: 1992), 543.

[43] AN, AD VI, 33, 419, in André Corvisier, "Les généraux de Louis XIV et leur origine sociale," *XVIIe siècle*, no. 42–43 (1956), 39.

[44] An ordinance of 1762 set prices of infantry regiments at 20,000 to 40,000 livres; they had been running at 30,000 to 75,000 during the Seven Years' War. In the eighteenth century, a prestigious infantry regiment could cost 75,000 livres, with a cavalry command running as much as 100,000. Albert Latreille, *L'oeuvre militaire de la Révolution: L'Armée et la nation à la fin de l'ancien régime* (Paris: 1914), 87.

need to buy a regiment screened out those too poor to keep it in the field once they held command. On the other hand, only if officers felt that they owned a unit would they be willing to commit their private funds willingly. Perhaps even more than purchase, the maintenance system posed the greatest barrier to poor noble officers and offered the greatest opportunities to rich *annoblis* and *roturiers*.

The maintenance system placed the burden of paying many expenses incurred by companies and regiments directly upon the officers commanding them. In the most extreme, but still common, case, the monarchy required that new colonels raise their new units almost exclusively at their own expense. In a less obviously confiscatory manner, ordinances placed the responsibility for supplying necessary arms, equipment, clothing, and food upon the officers, who were then to receive reimbursement for legitimate outlays. The amount allowed by the government for a particular expense often fell short of the real cost, however, forcing the officer to pay the difference. And reimbursement might not come at all. The most subtle dimension of the maintenance system employed an officer's personal credit for the needs of the army. Even if just compensation were paid, it might be quite a while before the officer received it; in the meantime, the state essentially commandeered the officer's money without paying interest. To meet the demands placed upon him, moreover, the officer himself might have to borrow; this amounted to the state exploiting the credit of the officer without even covering the interest costs that he bore.

Army commanders might even force regimental officers to contribute funds toward that army's general use – a blatant use of the officers as a source of short-term credit. In 1706 or 1707, the duke d'Orléans and his *intendant* forced officers to pitch in to the coffers of the army in Piedmont. A letter from the major of the Regiment de la Reine complained that officers of his unit gave 8,820 livres to the treasurer of the army and that now these officers needed their money back, since they were "unable to reestablish their troops and their equipment" owing to their own lack of funds.[45]

Demands on regimental officers were consistent with those made on individuals in more elevated positions of power. It is shown in Chapter 9 that army *intendants* and generals found themselves compelled to shoulder the costs of entire armies in extreme situations. This principle transcended the military; ambassadors, for example, paid out huge sums to maintain themselves and uphold the honor of their king.[46]

Administratively, the maintenance system suited the personnel as well as financial limitations of the *ancien régime* monarchy. If the bureaucracy undertook directly to supply all goods and services required by its troops, the state

[45] AN, G⁷1779, #175 and #174, 26 March 1707, letter from the chevalier du Brueil, major of the Regiment de la Reine.

[46] See Camille Picavet, *La diplomatie française au temps de Louis XIV (1661–1715): institutions, moeurs et coutumes* (Paris: 1930).

would have had to have fielded a much larger number of agents than it already did. To sidestep any need for battalions of bureaucrats, the monarchy turned to the army itself by placing many administrative duties in the hands of regimental officers, stipulating exactly how these duties were to be carried out, and then sending round inspectors to check on adherence. Thus, tactical officers doubled as agents of supply and administration, saving the monarchy the expense of another layer of bureaucracy.

New Units at Officer Expense

Throughout the *grand siècle,* new companies and regiments were raised at the personal expense of their commanders – that is, their owners.[47] Louis XIV described with pride how in 1667, when word that there would be war in Flanders hit the court, captains begged him to be allowed to add recruits at their own expense, or even to raise entire companies.[48] Throughout his reign, Louis levied new regiments at the expense of young and well-heeled colonels, but this tendency hit full gallop only during his last two wars.[49] There always seemed to be enough willing candidates; in 1702, Louis XIV had seventy-two applicants for eighteen of the new regiments that he raised.[50] By this point, all the lucky colonel received for his men would be arms and *quartier d'assemblée* (that is, lodging and food) for the officers and recruits.[51] The rest was his responsibility.

The fact that Louis relied upon colonels to create new regiments militated for numerous small regiments. By multiplying regiments, Louis increased the number of colonels who would contribute their own wealth and credit to the maintenance of the army. In addition, small regiments would not overtax the means of their colonels as larger units might have. Creating a great number of small regiments also provided Louis with a way to satisfy rich young nobles who thirsted for command – at one stroke reducing tensions at court and increasing the nobles obligated to him. Rousset argues that Louvois fought to keep the number of regiments down, but after the minister's death, Louis XIV capitulated to the pressure to create more. In 1691, there were 88 regiments of French infantry, of which 72 were permanent; in 1714, there were 238 regiments of French infantry, of which 94 were permanent, while the rest carried the names of their colonels – that is, they were raised by and supported by their commanders.[52] Military critics attacked

---

[47] For early examples, see AAE 816, fol. 198, 31 December 1635, in Parrott "The Administration of the French Army," 194 fn.; AG, A¹28, fol. 413, 8 August 1636, in Parrott, "The Administration of the French Army," 194 n.; Mazarin, *Lettres,* 6:151. Mazarin to Besmaux, 17 April 1654.

[48] Louis XIV, *Mémoires,* 2:116 and 229.

[49] See discussion of this during the early years of the War of the Spanish Succession in Georges Girard, *Le service militaire en France: Racolage et milice, 1701–1715* (Paris: 1915), 15–19.

[50] Girard, *Racolage et milice,* 15.   [51] Corvisier, *L'armée française,* 1:159.

[52] Rousset, *Louvois,* 3:317–18.

the high number of regiments, arguing that larger units would be more efficient and make better use of scarce military skill and experience.[53]

Other problems beset the creation of regiments in this way. Officers who came with the 1702 expansion of the army showed a real lack of talent, or at least the disaster of 1704 was seen as evidence of their incapacity. Shortly after Blenheim, Chamlay suggested that another group of regiments be raised under the aegis of the very wellborn only, including the royal family and princes of the blood, who could attract good officers, and, it would be safe to assume, had sufficient means to do the job right.[54] In February 1706, Louis ordered the levy of new regiments at his own expense, probably in reaction against the procedures followed in 1702, but the king still chose the very sorts of colonels that Chamlay had suggested, men of great wealth and power, including his own sons.[55]

Bounties to Bread

Those who raised units from scratch were hit by heavy costs for everything from recruitment bounties to bread rations, but these expenses burdened officers in established units as well. Creating a company or regiment required paying recruitment bounties and buying clothes, equipment, and arms; if it was a cavalry unit, horses had to be added to the list of necessities. Even when the government footed the bill, its payments could fall short of matching the real costs. One complaint from 1633 insists that it was impossible to find good recruits at the state allowance of 3 livres 6 sols.[56] Here the officer is apparently referring to the need to lure recruits by paying a bounty. The shortfall between official allowances for recruitment bounties and the amount really needed to win over recruits drained the purses of officers well into the eighteenth century.[57] (See Chapter 11 for a discussion of bounties.) Circa 1690, a captain creating a new company received 20 livres to cover the cost of raising and arming each recruit, and by 1694, this amount had increased to 30 livres. This would not pay for everything; the recruit's sword and belt were expressly at the expense of the captain. The cost of the soldier's clothing

---

[53] See Feuquières, *Mémoires*, 1:180; also criticisms in AG, Arch. hist. 78, and AG, MR 1701, piece 3.

[54] Chamlay letter of 22 August 1704 in Girard, *Racolage et milice*, 18.

[55] Girard, *Racolage et milice*, 15; Sourches, *Mémoires*, 10:22–23.

[56] AAE 809, fol. 120, 12 July 1633, in Parrott, "The Administration of the French Army," 199n. David Parrott's research uncovered an "overwhelming number of complaints that officers had been forced to subsidize the levy to obtain reasonable troops" in the 1630s.

[57] For example, a century later, 1730 official instructions laid down a maximum enlistment bounty of 25 livres for the Gardes françaises, yet the actual bounty rose to 68 livres. Officers complained that they had to make up the difference out of pocket. André Corvisier, *L'armée française de la fin du XVIIe siècle au ministère du Choiseul: Le soldat*, 2 vols. (Paris: 1964), 1:324–25 and 328–29.

also came out of the captain's pocket, although he was permitted to reimburse himself from his soldiers' pay.[58]

Even in units already on the rolls, the monarchy shifted much of the real cost to their captains and colonels. Putting a unit back on its feet that had suffered on campaign could also drive officers to the poor house. New recruits had to be found and arms, equipment, and clothing repaired or replaced. Again, the state might or might not make good on the officers' outlays. In peacetime, the state only supplied arms to new recruits; it did not replace worn or damaged weapons. Vauban felt strongly about the expenses to captains of something as simple as marching to a new garrison. "These passages cause an infinity of desertions, use up the shoes and clothes of the soldiers and always create great expense for the captains who are ruined by them."[59] Items of apparel were key to loyalty and morale; Villars advised captains that to "make themselves loved by their soldiers, maintain them well with shoes and shirts."[60] If a simple march could bring about disastrous expenses, consider the costs in the wake of combat. If a unit undertook a costly assault, the loss of life and the damage to equipment could ruin an officer financially even if he survived the fighting. Desertion could also impoverish an officer, since even when the state compensated officers for new recruits, replacement of deserters came out of the captain's pocket.[61]

Although pay also might be late, officers would be expected to attend to their men's needs. This was particularly true during the first half of the century. In December 1636, officers of the Regiment Maugiron found themselves strapped with the need to provide 15,000 livres to pay the *prêt* for their men.[62] This need to fill in for the government failure to supply funds was made all the worse since the officers had not been paid either. Most of 15,000 Swiss in French service had not received a regular payment 1639–48, and officers used their private credit and booty to compensate the men.[63] Wage problems continued in crisis years, such as 1710, when the salaries of Villars's officers fell eighteen months in arrears.[64]

Lack of pay could mean lack of food as well, since soldiers were often required to buy their provisions. Should food not be available, the officer could be expected to supply it at his own expense and then hope the government would cover his costs. In 1635, this happened to La Rivière, who

---

[58] Belhomme, *L'armée française en 1690*, 14–15; Victor Belhomme, *Histoire de l'infanterie en France*, 5 vols. (Paris: 1893–1902), 2:397.

[59] Sébastien le Prestre de Vauban, *Oisivetés de M. de Vauban*, 3 vols. (Paris: 1842–46), 2:232–33.

[60] BN, f. fr. 6257, Claude Louis Hector Villars, "Traité de la guerre de campagne," BN, f. fr. 6257, 98–99.

[61] Babeau, *La vie militaire*, 2:123; Corvisier, "Les généraux," 40.

[62] AG, A¹31, #187, 29 December 1636. Much the same happened to officers of St. André, AG, A¹31, #106, 19 December 1636.

[63] Yves-Marie Bercé, "Guerre et État," *XVII siècle*, 37 (1985), 260.

[64] Claude C. Sturgill, *Marshal Villars and the War of the Spanish Succession* (Lexington, KY: 1965), 104.

petitioned the government for the repayment of 50,000 livres that he claimed to have disbursed for the subsistence of the garrison under his command.[65] In 1636, the captains of the Regiment de Bellefonds were obliged to buy bread for their troops.[66] A year later, the captains of the Regiment de Brézé also had to purchase and distribute food for their companies.[67] This problem did not end with the personal reign of Louis XIV. In 1693, the officers of the Regiment d'Aligny advanced 13,000 livres to feed their troops serving in Italy.[68]

The Need for Wealth and the Financial Distress of Officers

More than any other factor, the burdens imposed by the maintenance system dictated that officers be well-to-do. Throughout the seventeenth century, the king and his minister recognized the imperative that colonels and captains possess the means to maintain their units. When Richelieu explained the 1635 cavalry reorganization to La Valette, he defended it on the basis that regiments were created under "persons that [the king] believes to have the will and the means [*pouvoir*] to make them subsist."[69] In 1676, Louvois rejected the suggestion of Marshal Luxembourg that de Girouville be made colonel of the Regiment de Rambures, even though he was "a very good officer . . . because it would assuredly bring the loss of the regiment if the King failed to put at its head a man of quality capable of affording its expense." Therefore, he instead proposed the marquis de Nagis, who "had not yet much experience, but had 60,000 livres of *rente*."[70] In his memoirs, Louis XIV defended his appointment of rich court nobles to regimental command by insisting that "finding themselves able to sustain all the expenses necessary to make themselves respected in their corps they would be most capable of maintaining these units in the state they ought to be in."[71] His comments were echoed in the eighteenth century.[72]

---

[65] AAE 815, fol. 281, 30 September 1635, in Parrott, "The Administration of the French Army," 208n.

[66] AG, A^{1}31, fol. 190, 29 December 1636, in Parrott, "The Administration of the French Army," 208n.

[67] AG, A^{1}36, #229, 18 May 1637, and AG, A^{1}30, #1, 1 Oct 1636, in Parrott, "The Administration of the French Army," 208n.

[68] AG, A^{1}1237, 24 November 1693, letter from Catinat.

[69] 8 December 1635 letter in Louis Susane, *Histoire de la cavalerie française*, 3 vols. (Paris: 1874), 1:95.

[70] AG, A^{1}484, #199–200, 31 July 1676, Louvois to LeTellier.

[71] Louis XIV, *Oeuvres*, 2:15–16.

[72] Some eighty years later, in 1757, a dedicated soldier with fifteen years' experience as a colonel, the marquis de Mailly, wrote to the minister of war: "It is of the greatest importance to put at the head of companies only wealthy officers who can afford good recruits . . . and who can maintain their soldiers properly in linen, shoes, etc., and who will be in a state to remedy those accidents which happen only too frequently." Quoted in Tuetey, *Officiers*, 130. See, as well, Belle-Isle quotation in Babeau, *La vie militare*, 2:120, and Broglie in Latreille, *L'oeuvre militaire*, 365.

Captains as well needed to be well-heeled, and this marooned many capable men in the rank of lieutenant. In a letter of 1675, Vauban complained of this problem to Louvois: "I have a poor devil of a cousin, a lieutenant in the cavalry Regiment de Nonan, a good and old officer who would have been a captain a long time ago if he had the secret of turning bad companies into good ones without ruining himself."[73]

The fact was that command could bankrupt an officer without substantial resources. The trail of financial calamity attributable to military command stretched back into the reign of Louis XIII and lasted well into the eighteenth century.[74] The only redress that officers possessed was to petition the government for relief. Thus, a frustrated colonel pleaded to the minister of war in 1705: "I beg the liberty to explain to you that my regiment is entering on campaign without having participated in the ordinary graces that the king makes in such cases. The captains have exhausted themselves to rebuild their companies, and we are persecuted by the merchants who have given us tents, pots, and tools on credit." Therefore, he wanted to be included in whatever "graces," or payments, the king planned to make.[75] An appeal by a captain in the Artois regiment is almost embarrassing: "I have employed all that I have in the world to reestablish my company and have put thirty two men in it, one better than the other, who cost me 2,700 livres. It is all complete. I am now obliged to live on bread alone because it is necessary that I spend my wages on their clothes."[76] But such entreaties were not always received favorably. Characteristically, Louvois demonstrated little understanding. He counseled the equally hardhearted Martinet in 1669: "When officers allege that the deductions they can take from their soldiers' pay are so small that officers are hindered in maintaining their troops, do not listen to them."[77]

Although the administrative advances associated with Louvois may have improved the frequency of the payment of allowances and salaries, they also made command more demanding financially, since inspections made sure that units were kept up to snuff, an expensive procedure. There were possibilities to line one's pockets before 1659. When local commanders imposed their own contributions, for example, it was likely that much found its way into their pockets. With the state taking over administration of resource mobilization, and with the constant imposition of surveillance and inspection, officers lost both the possibility to make great sums and suffered even greater pressures to tap their own wealth and credit. The king certainly rewarded outstanding military acts when they were brought to his attention, and he granted his generals and marshals generous pensions and bounties,

---

[73] Letter of 19 September 1675 in Albert Rochas d'Aiglun, *Vauban, sa famille et ses écrits*, 2 vols. (Paris: 1910), 2:130.

[74] "The purchase of a military command could prove quite literally ruinous for the officer concerned." Parrott, "The Administration of the French Army."

[75] AG, A¹1831, #290, 19 June 1705, letter to Chamillart.

[76] AG, A¹1831, #332, 1 July 1705, letter from captain Compaign to Chamillart.

[77] AG, A¹252, 18 March 1669, Louvois to Martinet.

but heroes, generals, and marshals were few in number, and the officer corps numbered in the tens of thousands.

Eighteenth-century wars continued to drain the wealth of many officers.[78] Not until 1762 did the minister of war Choiseul issue an edict that effectively released captains from the responsibility of personally maintaining their companies. It was probably this move that allowed the French to phase out the purchase system through the 1776 edict announced by Saint-Germain.[79]

There is no question that maintenance strained the finances of many officers, but is there irrefutable evidence that it hurt the majority of officers? The anecdotal evidence presented here argues strongly that it did, but we lack a thorough statistical study to settle the matter.[80] This author is persuaded that the preponderance of evidence and logic establishes that on the whole officers lost rather than made money in military service. Besides individual tales of ruin and woe, the fact that Louis XIV thought it necessary to grant a three-year suspension of officers' debts at the close of the Nine Years' War strongly suggests that a systemic problem had hit the corps as a whole.[81] Incidentally, Jean Chagniot points out that this kind of respite did not really help in the long run, since creditors henceforth demanded that officers waive any future moratorium.[82] Most contemporary observations on the subject speak not of the enrichment but of the impoverishment of officers under Louis XIV.[83] As one couplet of the time went:

> You take away after five years
> Some debts and a little glory.[84]

While it would be valuable to establish the actual amount that officers contributed to their units, in a sense it is also important simply to know that the aristocracy saw itself as selfless in this regard. The perception of having sacrificed its fortunes for the good of the monarchy, gave the nobility a claim on preference and power, at least in its own eyes.

To the extent that officers contributed substantial sums to the upkeep of

---

[78] Marshal de Broglie pleaded the case of destitute officers dismissed at the close of the Seven Years' War by insisting that "all these captains bore considerable expense to keep up their companies during the war . . . ." Broglie in Latreille, *L'oeuvre militaire*, 349–50.

[79] This is the thesis of Lynn, "The Pattern of French Military Reform, 1750–1795."

[80] Louis Tuetey bases his case on an impressive assemblage of circumstantial and anecdotal evidence. An historian with more modern methods, Goubert, attributes the impoverishment of certain noble families of the Beauvaisis to military service. Goubert, *Beauvais et le Beauvaisis* (Paris: 1960), 218–20. However, Constant, who studies the Beauce, argues the opposite, since he finds that families with at least one person in service augmented their seigneuries, although this may simply be a statement that families who were on the way up financially invested in both land and the prestige of military command. Jean-Marie Constant dissertation in Chagniot, "Guerre et société," 255.

[81] Tuetey, *Les officiers*, 11.   [82] Chagniot, "Guerre et société," 254.

[83] For example, see Primi Visconti's 1678 comment that "they ruin themselves in war." Primi Visconti, *Mémoires*, 131.

[84] From Babeau, *La vie militaire*, 2:185n.

the army, maintenance became an undeclared but unavoidable tax on the nobility. While the exact amount of this burden will probably never be known, it was almost certainly substantial. It would seem, then, that when they donned the uniform, nobles paid more than just the tax in blood of which they so proudly boasted. Although it would be valuable to establish the actual amount that officers contributed to their units, in a sense it is also important simply to know that the aristocracy saw itself as selfless in this regard. The perception of having sacrificed its fortunes for the good of the monarchy, justified the nobility's claim on preference and power, at least in its own eyes.

How one views the financial impact of the maintenance system determines how one deals with the phenomenon of fraud by officers. If they paid a heavy price in the normal course of their duties, then cheating on *passe volants*, clothing allowances, and so forth may not have been evidence of boundless greed but instead simply a means to stave off financial collapse. As the contemporary military critic Saint Hilaire commented, "Colonels and the first officers of regiments can only maintain themselves by plundering and cheating."[85]

The Added Burden of Officer Extravagance

Whereas officers employed their own wealth and credit for the good of the army, and exhausted their fortunes in the process, they also added to their own financial difficulties by ostentatious spending. Men who could not afford the bill bought overly expensive clothing, equipment, and horses. Officers of means brought with them trains of servants and even performers, while their tables groaned with sumptuous meals in the midst of military camps. Officer extravagance in this age of display cannot be denied. It was an integral part of the semi-entrepreneurial system, or at least it was driven by the same culture that convinced officers to take on the burdens of a military command in the first place. On one level, military command was an obligation accepted by an individual because it composed a key element in the self-definition of the aristocracy, but on another level, it amounted to a form of conspicuous consumption designed to proclaim high status and claim deference and privilege.

Only through austere self-denial could an officer avoid major outlays for expenses for those expenses that announced his station in life. Clothing advertised wealth and status, and there was a tendency to overspend on decoration. Officers also might try to deck out their soldiers with unnecessary ribbons and lace, as previously noted. Other frills appeared. In 1683, an ordinance condemned companies of infantry with too many drums, fifes, and hautbois, "which are not only useless, but also cause an expense for the captains who maintain them." It limited companies to a single drum and a

---

[85] Saint Hilaire, *Traité de la guerre* (1712) in Babeau, *La vie militaire*, 2:156.

regiment to a single fife.[86] Even an average officer's entertainment could also be inordinately costly, gambling for example.

Costs of valets and horses also consumed officers' resources. Review reports on occasion count the number of valets, which could amount to as much as 15 percent of the fighting men of an infantry regiment.[87] Saint-Simon reports that in 1692, "to live honorably on his own, morning and night," he required thirty-five horses and mules and two gentlemen servants.[88] And this at no more than seventeen years of age. A year later, his household in the field included five stable boys and a valet in addition to his two gentlemen.[89] One captain of *chevaux légers* in 1683 had thirty horses and twenty-five valets.[90] Even a modest infantry officer such as captain Saint-Mayme felt that he required three horses.[91] A *règlement* of 1623 limited the train of a lieutenant or captain of *chevaux légers* to nine horses and eight men; by 1641, a lieutenant of cavalry could have eight horses, while a captain could have twelve.[92] And it was not just the exaggerated number but the ostentatious quality of the horses that emptied officers' pockets. In Villars's "Traité," he repeatedly attacked young dandies for spending too much on horses for the campaign. "A horse that costs 20 pistoles bears fatigue as well as one that costs 40 or 50."[93]

For commanders, the expense of hospitality could be enormous. The memoirs of d'Artagnan advised: "One of the most essential qualities of a colonel is to provide a good table. This will serve his officers marvelously, and they esteem him all the more by this than by all the rest."[94] Officers served lavish repasts; one regimental commander's table cost him 1,000 livres per day in 1635.[95] Culinary exorbitance continued as a phenomenon of the age. Sumptuary laws tried to limit the style of dinners served at officers' tables on campaign. In 1641, Louis XIII ordered that dinners at the tables of superior officers include only two courses.[96] Another ordinance of 1672 condemned officers for the "evil custom of serving in the armies meals more magnificent and sumptuous than they ordinarily serve at home" and limited

---

[86] SHAT, Bib., Col. des ord., vol. 24, #92, 18 January 1683.

[87] In July 1667, the officers of the Regiment de Piedmont, with twenty-four companies containing 1,158 soldiers and sergeants, dragged 178 valets in its wake. Thus, the valets amounted to 15 percent of the fighting men of the regiment. The Regiment de St. Vallier, also with twenty-four companies and 1,071 soldiers and sergeants, had 127 valets (12 percent). AG, $A^1$209, #105, 25 July 1667.

[88] Saint-Simon, *Mémoires*, 1:33.   [89] Saint-Simon, *Mémoires*, 1:249–50.

[90] Babeau, *La vie militaire*, 2:168.

[91] Georges Girard, ed., "Un soldat de Malplaquet: Lettres du capitaine de Saint-Mayme," *Carnet de Sabretache* (1922), letter of 29 August 1702, 514–15.

[92] Babeau, *La vie militaire*, 2:166n.

[93] BN, f. fr. 6257, Villars, "Traité," 86. A pistole equaled 13 livres.

[94] Memoirs of d'Artagnan in Babeau, *La vie militaire*, 2:175.

[95] Bernard Kroener, *Les routes et les étapes. Die bersorgung der franzoschichen Armeen in Nordostfrankreich (1635–1661)*, 2 vols. (Munster: 1980), 88.

[96] Ordinance of 23 April 1641 in Babeau, *La vie militaire*, 2:173.

the highest-ranking officers to dinners including no more than two courses of meat and one of fruit.[97]

The kind of expenses that a Saint-Simon viewed as necessary were regarded by others of a more practical turn of mind as needless burdens on individuals and on the army. When Louvois was confronted with the charge that officers were ruining themselves financially, he argued that it was because they wasted too much money on "foolish expenses."[98] Pressure to maintain a high profile not only heaped needless expenses on officers; it also overloaded the baggage train with useless freight. At the siege of Courtrai in 1646, although 1,800 horses were needed for the artillery train, only 1,000 to 1,200 were ordered, and of these, most were taken by officers to haul their personal baggage. Each *maréchal de camp* thought himself due a *charrette*, or two-wheeled cart. Le Tellier directed several ordinances against these abuses in the mid-1640s.[99] In 1707, Louis limited what his commanders could drag along; lieutenant generals could have three wagons and forty horses, and *maréchaux de camp* three wagons and thirty horses, but brigadiers and colonels would have to make do with one wagon and twenty horses.[100]

The problem seems to have gotten worse, rather than better, as the *grand siècle* progressed. One critical memoir of 1712 declared that "our fathers would be amused at this superfluous and unworthy luxury."[101] Vauban railed against excessive luxury in clothing and table. Officers already burdened with the expenses of maintaining a unit, absorbing half their income already, spent more on such display.[102] Villars insisted that the French must "banish luxury from the troops, and to put limits generally on all there is in relation to war, principally on the clothing of soldiers and the mounts of horsemen."[103] Poor men should not try to maintain their units in the same condition as was possible for rich officers, the marshal counseled.[104] Other thoughtful treatises condemned luxury in the field, but apparently to little avail.[105]

The reason why such expenses were assumed has less to do with sheer foppishness than with the need to maintain a certain exterior to command respect, a basic rationale behind the assumption of military command itself.

Fraud

Officers strained by the necessary costs and unnecessary extravagance of military life tried to make ends meet by any means possible, all too often through outright fraud, a subject much discussed but not necessarily well understood in the literature of military history. An appreciation of the financial

---

[97] SHAT, Bib., Col. des ord., vol. 22, #175, 24 March 1672.
[98] From the 1683 *Réponse au livre intitulé: la conduite de la France* in Corvisier, *Louvois*, 333.
[99] André, *Le Tellier*, 506–7.   [100] Babeau, *La vie militaire*, 2:170n.
[101] AG, MR 1701, piece 15, "Traité de la guerre," of 8 June 1712.
[102] Vauban in Rochas d'Aiglun, *Vauban*, 1:338–39.
[103] BN, f. fr. 6257, Villars, "Traité," 9–10.   [104] BN, f. fr. 6257, Villars, "Traité," 6–7.
[105] See AG, MR 1701, Piece 15, "Traité de la guerre," of 8 June 1712.

burdens imposed upon officers by the purchase system puts the financial and administrative abuses committed by those officers in a new light. Captains and colonels did not buy commissions with an eye to making a fortune. In extraordinary cases, French officers became rich in military service by achieving high enough rank that royal gratifications made them well off, but this was not the course for average officers. Still, if avarice did not drive the great majority of officers to enter the service, why did officers engage in fraud? The answer lies more in the need to stave off financial ruin, or at least to get by, than in the desire to achieve financial ease.

The early seventeenth century presented more possibilities to reap fraudulent gains than did the second half of the *grand siècle*. When he was still an *intendant* with the army in Italy, Le Tellier wrote to the secretary of state for war, Sublet de Noyers, in 1642, "There are no rogue's tricks that the commanders do not undertake to profit from the money that the king orders for them; they fear only punishment and have no honor at all."[106] Maybe, then, avarice carried a greater share of responsibility. Yet even early in the 1630s, gaining a military commission threatened the recipient with ruin.[107] Once Le Tellier and Louvois set their dogs on the hunt, there was far less gain in abuse, and the risks sharply rose. As early as 1666, Louis XIV inaugurated surprise inspections that "held the captains and the *commissaires* in a continual obligation to do their duty."[108]

Officers held an unfortunate reputation for petty larceny. Since money was the source of the problem, and since money flowed through a captain's hands on its way to his men, it is not surprising that some of it stuck to his palms. Puységur reported in 1617 that the commanding general himself, Guise, ordered that his men be paid directly "not wanting to give [the money] to the captains for fear that they would keep it for themselves."[109] In 1683, a minor rebellion broke out among troops whose officers had held back their wages.[110] Fearing a similar incident, Louvois advised his agent Lambert to monitor closely the distribution of a monetary reward to soldiers in order to assure that "the officers do not retain anything from it."[111] Officers were wont to deduct from pay to cover various expenses and had to be told to

---

[106] Letter of 1 December 1642 in André, *Le Tellier*, 78.

[107] Parrott concludes in his careful study "that military office holding represented an open-ended financial commitment, in which ultimate loss was probable, and overall profit almost inconceivable." Parrott, "The Administration of the French Army," 178–79.

[108] Louis XIV, *Mémoires*, 1:239–40.

[109] Jacques de Chastenet de Puységur, *Mémoires de messire Jacques de Chastenet, chevalier, seigneur de Puységur, colonel du régiment de Piedmont, et lieutenant général des armées du Roy*, 2 vols. (Paris: 1690), 1:3.

[110] Rousset, *Louvois*, 3:298–99.

[111] Louvois to Lambert, 19 November 1683, in Jacques Hardré, ed., *Letters of Louvois*, University of North Carolina Studies in the Romance Languages and Literatures, no. 10 (Chapel Hill: 1949), 306.

give their men all that was due them.[112] Under Louis XIII, officers even extorted money from their own men by threatening to throw them into prison or to charge them with desertion.[113]

The most discussed fraud by officers was the use of *passe volants*, phony soldiers who stood in the ranks on the day of a review so as to fool the official inspecting the troops into thinking that a unit was larger than it really was. Since the government allotted pay and allowances to a company based on the number of men present, a captain who convinced the government that he had more men than he did could pocket the money meant for the phantom soldiers. There were ready sources of instant soldiers in any camp. An officer's servants might stand in as soldiers, or peddlers might be willing to make a little money on the side as *passe volants*. Captains from different units might trade off soldiers to their mutual benefit. Since uniforms made their appearance slowly, and then only late in the century, it was relatively easy to switch men, as long as the other men in the ranks kept their silence.

Passe volants posed such a problem under Richelieu that he estimated that regiments ought to be figured at only half their official strength.[114] Robert Arnauld d'Andilly reported that in order to curb the practice during this period, he held reviews with a great space between companies "so that soldiers could not pass from one into another without being easily seen."[115] The problem continued into the reign of Louis XIV. Coligny-Saligny wrote to Le Tellier in 1664 that "It is true that there are many abuses in reviews; but it is an evil firmly established in the infantry, and the *commissaires* themselves are wrapped up in it, so ingenious are the officers in disguising valets and *passe volants*."[116] Of course, fraud was a good deal more possible if the supervising civil official collaborated with the offending military officer. In 1671, a captain in Dunkirk admitted that for six years he had paid off a *commissaire* with the wages of three phantom soldiers on his rolls.[117]

Harsh penalties for the *passe volants* did not seem to deter the problem until later in the century. Ordinances of 1653 and 1662 prescribed the death penalty for them, and the captain was to be broken. Later regulations were kinder, generally setting the penalty as a good whipping and branding with a fleur de lis on the face, although the death penalty was reestablished briefly

---

[112] See ordinance SHAT, Bib., Col. des ord., vol. 21, #144, 27 July 1666 and AG, A¹294, #268, 5 September 1672, Vacher from Charleroi to Louvois.

[113] Babeau, *La vie militaire*, 2:157

[114] See Richelieu, *Testament politique*, Louis André, ed. (Paris: 1947), 478. A letter of 6 May 1642 complained that officers, governors, and townspeople conspired to defraud the government through *passe volants*, so it was impossible to catch them. AG, A¹71, #14.

[115] Robert d'Arnauld d'Andilly, *Mémoires*, in Michaud & Poujoulat, eds., *Nouvelle collection*, vol. 23 (Paris: 1866), 415.

[116] AG, A¹190, fol. 385 v.–386 r., 1 November 1664, Coligny-Saligny to Le Tellier in André, *Le Tellier*, 257.

[117] Corvisier, *Louvois*, 187.

in 1667–68. The ordinance of 1676 raised the punishment to include mutilation, cutting the nose of the guilty. To add to the deterrent force of the law,
a reward was stipulated for a soldier who denounced *passe volants* in his unit.
The informer was to receive his discharge immediately and a bounty of 100
to 300 livres.[118]

Diligent enforcement was bound to take effect eventually. Reviews caught
culprits; a letter of 9 April 1662 reports the seizure of thirteen *passe volants* at
a review.[119] Surprise inspections were a useful weapon.[120] Four accounts
dating from 1672 illustrate that informants proved to be the most effective
weapon against *passe volants*.[121] At these reviews, a *commissaire* or other official began by reading the regulations banning *passe volants* and repeating the
penalties to be inflicted for the crime. Then he ordered any *passe volants*
present to leave the ranks; this apparently was their last chance to avoid
prosecution if discovered. In each of the four incidences, men from the unit
being inspected denounced the *passe volants*, publicly or with a whisper. The
informers ran the gamut from a common soldier to a lieutenant. In each
case, an inquiry followed the denunciation. The most common assertion of
the informant was that the phony soldiers were in fact officers' valets or
servants. In two cases, all the accused *passe volants* were found innocent, and
in the other cases, the punishments ranged from branding guilty domestics
to enrolling a sutler, making the phony soldier into a real one. In the one
of these four instances, documents record the fate of the informant. He
received a sum of money, a discharge from his regiment, and a transfer to
another. The fate of the informer was not always so pleasant. In 1673, a
captain arrested the sergeant who denounced a *passe volant* in his company;
however, the captain paid for his act by being dismissed from the service.[122]

The pursuit of *passe volants* drove down the incidence of the crime. A
revealing letter written during the Nine Years' War by the sous-lieutenant
Sarraméa indicates that by then regulations against *passe volants* had real
effect. He had intended to place his valet in review, but he found that would
have been a dangerous course, "there being an order of the King which
forbids dressing valets as soldiers, because they passed as soldiers and had the
king's bread."[123] Rousset argues that *passe volants* virtually disappeared by the
1680s, and Corvisier concurs.[124] Although this assertion probably overstates
the case, there is no question that reported incidents dropped off, even if the

---

[118] Rousset, *Louvois*, 1:197–98.

[119] BN, mélanges Colbert, vol. 108, #81, 9 April 1662, signed Colbert.

[120] See for example, AG, A^{1}190, fol. 385 v.–386 r., 1 November 1664, Coligny-Saligny to Le
Tellier in André, *Le Tellier*, 257.

[121] AG, A^{1}294, pieces 268 and 304 from September 1672 and AG, A^{1}295, pieces 35, 57, 243 from
October 1672.

[122] Corvisier, *Louvois*, 187.

[123] François Abbadie, ed., *Lettres d'un cadet de Gascogne, François de Sarraméa* (Paris: 1890), 9,
letter of 18 February 1695.

[124] Rousset, *Louvois*, 3:297; Contamine, *Histoire militaire*, 1:394.

problem did not entirely disappear. The suppression of *passe volants* was one of the more notable successes of French military administration under Louis XIV.

Officers practiced a wide repertoire of fraud beyond *passe volants*. Some tried to take advantage of the *étapes* system. Even well into the reign of Louis XIV, commanders claimed more soldiers than they really had or refused to stand for a review by the local officials who dealt out food and lodging.[125] In another fraudulent practice, officers might demand that the food due their units by *étapes* be commuted into a money payment.[126] In a related abuse, some officers claimed forage for cavalry companies that had been disbanded.[127]

Cheating captains could also protect their money by skimping on clothing. By supplying poor-quality clothes and shoes, officers could keep expenses down. Reviews were intended not only to count the men present but to survey the condition of clothes, equipment, and weapons. Le Vacher, a *commissaire* or *intendant*, found one company in such poor shape at a review, "without linen and without coats," that he felt bound to buy shoes and socks for them himself.[128]

Louvois believed that most infantry officers only let their men wear their new outfits for reviews and locked them away in between. Although he found it acceptable to protect new clothes and preserve old ones as long as possible, he instructed that this could be permitted "only on condition that the clothes the soldiers ordinarily wear shelter them adequately from the weather" and that they put up a good enough appearance not "to scandalize foreigners passing through the towns."[129] In 1682, the officers of the garrison of Casale gave their men shoes only for reviews.[130] Shoes seemed to be a particularly critical item. Louvois instructed Saint-Pouenges in 1690 to "Take guard that the shoes you will have distributed to the infantry be distributed by hand [to the men], for it often happens that the officers who make a profit from everything, have sold them."[131] Arms were also a potential source of profit for captains. A frustrated Le Tellier fired off a letter to Imbert insisting that fraud must be suppressed, "His Majesty not being resolved to

[125] One document, AN, G⁷1774, #68, which details fines in the forms of deductions from officers' pay in 1678–79, provides several cases of such abuses. For examples, see articles 161, 162, 167, 175, 176, 178, and 183 of this document. For example, ten captains of the Regiment de la Reigne were fined 100 livres for refusing to be reviewed by the *echevins* of Cateau-Cambresis, article 175, and a captain commandant of the first battalion of the Regiment of Orleans paid 215 livres for refusing a review and then demanding food for 151 men more than he commanded, article 78.

[126] AN, G⁷1774, #68. Article 179 fined fifteen officers of the Regiment of Hamilton 545 livres, 1 sols, and 8 deniers for having commuted *étapes* in the Lionnais into money.

[127] AN, G⁷1774, #68, articles 259–61.

[128] AG, A¹295, #22, 3 October 1672, letter from Le Vacher.

[129] 12 September 1680, Louvois to Alauzier, in Rousset, *Louvois*, 3:295–96. (Alauzier was an inspector, 3:301 fn.)

[130] 19 May 1682, Louvois to Alauzier, in Rouset, *Louvois*, 3:295n.

[131] AG, A¹965, 25 August 1690, Louvois to Saint-Pouenge.

pay for the armament of a soldier twice in order to allow the captain to turn a profit."[132]

To such lengths did the maintenance system push officers, and while some may have, indeed, had larceny in their blood, others did so simply to survive.

DISCIPLINARY ACTIONS
AGAINST OFFICER FRAUD

If officers needed to bend the rules to survive, one could expect a regretful and reluctant toleration of their abuses similar to that directed toward the Tax of Violence; however, there was a difference between the two phenomena – the Tax of Violence victimized the common people, whereas officer fraud often victimized the government. Eventually, an absolutist state could not claim control, insist on its rightful authority, and tolerate officer fraud.

For Mazarin, the repression of abuses and irregularities fell low on his list of priorities. The marquis de Bellefonds commiserated with Louvois in 1668: "Monsieur the Cardinal so strongly authorized these abuses that you will have need of an extreme application to put things back into order."[133] Such a comment indicates that for all of Le Tellier's efforts, he did not succeed in disciplining the officer corps. Louvois, as we have already seen, relentlessly pursued the job of keeping officers and administrators honestly at their tasks. Louvois, a bully by nature, pushed hard, within the limitations set by the semi-entrepreneurial system. Not only ministers of war varied in their attitudes toward officer conduct; field generals also differed. Marshal Luxembourg displayed a notoriously lax attitude toward his officers early in his career, although he became more demanding at the constant urging of Louvois and Louis XIV.[134] Villars, on the other hand, counseled commanders to oversee constantly the books of regimental commanders and to make them account for everything "down to a sol."[135]

The flux continued, but in the main, regulation and enforcement tightened over the course of the century. Louvois broke officers for fraud, if the crime was discovered. In 1673, a captain was denounced by a sergeant for filling out his company with a *passe volant*. In retaliation, the captain arrested the sergeant, and the major and governor of the fortress condoned this action. As punishment, all three officers were broken.[136] An officer could be cashiered for allowing his company to fall into bad shape, as befell one of Créqui's captains in 1675 – the assumption here being that the money allotted for the unit ended up in the officers' pockets.[137] Those enamored of the heavy-handed techniques of Louvois might see his administration as being the high point of compliance. Yet the evidence is not conclusive. The

[132] BN, 4200, fol. 62v–63, 10 April 1645, to Imbert.
[133] AG, A¹224, 8 January 1668, Bellefonds to Louvois.   [134] Rousset, *Louvois*, 1:395.
[135] BN, f. fr. 6257, Villars, "Traité," 89.   [136] Corvisier, *Louvois*, 187.
[137] AG, A¹433, 14 June 1675, Louis to Crequy. I thank George Satterfield for this reference.

bureaucracy did not loosen its grip or lessen its workload after 1691, so the death of Louvois did not necessarily precipitate a decline.

In reality, the most severe punishment usually inflicted on an officer was to deprive him of his command. Reformation, or disbanding, of an officer's unit was a penalty threatened under Louis XIII. However, Parrott argues that this was a hollow threat.[138] Le Tellier was not so averse to breaking officers. Breaking, stripping an officer of his command, and thus his property, and expelling him from the service, was tantamount to expelling him from his class and declaring him a nonperson. Breaking occurred in reasonably large numbers and with some regularity. At Le Tellier's insistence, Condé broke thirty captains at once in 1645.[139] Louis continued a harsh attitude during his personal reign, perhaps reinforced by Louvois's convictions, as a number of lists of broken officers testify. During the years 1686–93 alone, 448 officers were thus punished.[140]

Whatever the king might do, however, he could not utterly transform the officer corps. Purchase and maintenance bought for French officers a proprietary independence that produced fraud and ran counter to the Sun King's desire to master his own army. In addition, money and military effectiveness often pulled in different directions, and the costs of command gave money more leverage. Nevertheless, Louis made considerable progress in reshaping his officer corps. Severe government action not only moderated officer abuses, but the same policies and practices that punished officers for the fraud established a hierarchy of authority and obedience. Within limits set by the purchase and maintenance systems, Louis's efforts helped to create a more professional corps. Officers accepted the financial burdens of command and eventually submitted to greater monarchical authority because they so valued military service. These officers were not driven by coldly rational calculations; rather, they were expressing a culture of command, the subject of the next chapter.

---

[138] Parrott, "The Administration of the French Army," 212.

[139] Condé to Mazarin, from Verdun, 5 June 1645, in André, Le Tellier, 250.

[140] AG, MR 1787, pieces 1–4, cover breaking 1668–93. See piece 4 for the period 1686–93. Babeau comments that a great many lieutenants and captains were broken in 1680–92. Babeau, La vie militaire, 2:91.

8

The Culture of Command

PIKE and musket infantry of the *grand siècle* bore arms and fought in styles very different from those of today, but the contrasts between then and now are much more basic than obvious matters of weaponry and tactics. Among the fundamental differences, officers of the *grand siècle* represented a culture of command specific to their time and place. This culture was rooted in aristocratic concepts of masculine honor and grew into a set of values and practices characteristic of the French officer corps. This culture of command explains the willingness of officers to contribute their own wealth and credit to support their units, as set out in the previous chapter. The fact that seventeenth-century officers so eagerly sought command in spite of its potential of financial loss demonstrates that they measured things by standards very different from modern concepts of worth. The seventeenth-century culture of command assumed motivations, applied criteria of selection and promotion, and provided preparation specific to the *grand siècle*. As the century wore on, war ministers enforced higher standards of competence, demanded greater obedience, and imposed a clearer hierarchy upon the officer corps, but these efforts to create a more professional military met with only partial success. It proved impossible to eliminate all the abuses implicit in the culture of command. As a result, by the close of the *grand siècle*, the French officer straddled archaic values of aristocratic honor and independence, on one side, and new standards of professional competence and hierarchy, on the other.

MOTIVATIONS

Why did French officers pursue unit command as captain or colonel, when it carried with it substantial expense? The fundamental logic of the semi-entrepreneurial system decreed that officers paid dearly for the privilege of command. That privilege must have been regarded as very valuable for the aristocracy to part with its wealth in order to hold military rank. And that is just the point. The quest for that most esteemed of all seventeenth-century attributes, *gloire*, demanded that aristocrats, and those that aspired to such status, distinguish themselves as officers.

Hope of Reward and Risk of Ruin

One traditional way to explain the penchant for service has been to ascribe it to a desire for wealth, or at least for survival in a world that offered the aristocrat few career choices.[1] To what degree does this argument bear scrutiny? As previously discussed, it was possible for officers to profit from contributions. In Europe as a whole, such armed extortion promised the greatest riches for an officer of the seventeenth century, and French commanders did not shrink from assessing contributions beyond the needs of their units.[2] However, officers who gained from this practice usually held large independent commands, as did governors of the 1640s and 1650s who extorted from surrounding towns.[3] Moreover, opportunities to exploit this source of wealth shrank during Louis XIV's personal reign. Some leeway may still have been present, but only for the very powerful, as when marshal Villars fattened off contributions during the War of the Spanish Succession.[4] But the usual administrative procedures for raising contributions in areas occupied for any length of time cut commanders out of the process, except when their troops were required to punish recalcitrant villages. When Delacroix, brigadier and colonel of infantry, tried to pocket contributions that he assessed in Julich in 1702, he was forced to repay the sum to the crown – such was the fate of the sticky-fingered officer under Louis XIV.[5]

Officers might also garner less staggering, but still impressive, wealth as a consequence of outstanding service. Major commanders obtained gifts and lucrative positions as rewards for victories. Turenne received artillery pieces in 1649.[6] Vauban also got two artillery pieces, but far more important was the grant of the governorship of the citadel of Lille. The list of these rewards goes on, but they benefited only those already at the top.

More within the range of the regimental officers, gratuities and promotions granted by a grateful monarchy recognized and encouraged valor and noteworthy feats. Several forms of cash rewards were relatively common

---

[1] Ronald Thomas Ferguson, "Blood and Fire: Contribution Policy of the French Armies in Germany (1668–1715)," Ph.D. dissertation, University of Minnesota, 1970, 8.

[2] Fritz Redlich, *De praeda militari: Looting and Booty 1500–1815*, supplement 39, *Vieteljahrschrift für Sozial – und Wirtschaftsgeschichte* (Wiesbaden: 1956), 45.

[3] For example, the governor of Burgundy had to order that towns and localities were not to pay garrison commanders anything, because the Estates had set aside the money to pay the troops. Côte d'Or, C 3673, 5 October 1650.

[4] Montague Bernard, "The Growth of Laws and Usages of War," in *Oxford Essays, 1856* (London: 1856), 103; Villars in Albert Babeau, *La vie militaire sous l'ancien régime*, 2 vols. (Paris: 1890), 2:138.

[5] AN, G71777, #387, 6 June 1705.   [6] AG, A^{1}115, #60, 10 August 1649.

throughout the century. A captain de Lalande received a yearly pension of 600 livres in reward for a gallant action performed in 1637.[7] Louis XIV once bestowed gratuities to captains of the Regiment du Roi, because it looked and drilled so well on review in 1666.[8] The list of gratuities for 1691 shows 1,950,704 livres rewarded to over 1,000 officers.[9] The amounts ranged widely, from as little as 100 livres to as much as several thousand, but the average award on this list stood at about 500 livres – not enough to enrich an individual. When officers displayed bravery and resolve in such a manner that they caught the king's eye, virtue would be rewarded with promotion as well as money. Promotion must be seen as a monetary reward, since higher ranks carried higher salaries, or appointments.[10] For the run of the mill officer, the possibility of large rewards operated as a lottery in which all officers held tickets, but they represented only a remote chance. In fact, few regimental officers actually gained substantially from the crown's gratitude.

Although military command may not have promised wealth for most officers, neither did it lead all to financial suicide. The two ranks that bore the brunt of maintenance were colonels and captains. Whereas colonels laid out substantial sums, they were usually men of such wealth that they could afford the outlay without courting ruin. Captains, on the other hand, were far more numerous and generally from a lower rung than their colonels. Therefore, service correlated with real financial sacrifice most closely among captains.

If a man did not rise above lieutenant, he was not required to support his unit out of his pocket. A subaltern earned only subsistence wages, but at least he could pursue a carreer deemed honorable for younger sons of the aristocracy. Should a young man desire to put up a good show, he could court disaster. From winter quarters, sous-lieutenant François de Sarraméa begged money from his father because "I must go on campaign at my own expense, having only three sols [per day] from the king and needing no less than thirty to live with my valet."[11] Only an officer with a frugal nature could get by in the infantry. In the cavalry, it was more difficult to make ends meet, because service in a mounted regiment required the purchase of horses. Mme. de Sévigné referred to infantry as "the workhouse," because of its impoverished or ill-born officers.[12] When Matignon established his cadet company in

---

[7] AG, A¹42, #94, 11 April 1637.

[8] Louis XIV, *Mémoires de Louis XIV*, ed. Charles Dreyss, 2 vols. (Paris, 1860), 2:127–28.

[9] AN, G⁷893, fol. 276.

[10] Captain La Lande was awarded for the brave defense of a town in Montbelliard in 1637 with a captaincy in a more prestigious regiment and with a pension of 600 livres per year. AG, A¹42, #94, 11 April 1637. A sergeant Lafleur was promoted to lieutenant and received a gratuity of 500 livres in 1674. AG, A¹398, 12 June 1674, and A¹380, 27 June 1674 in Camille Rousset, *L'histoire de Louvois*, 4 vols. (Paris: 1862–64), 1:215–16.

[11] François Abbadie, ed., *Lettres d'un cadet de Gascogne, François de Sarraméa* (Paris: 1890), 8–9, letter of 18 February 1695.

[12] Marie Sévigné, *Lettres de madame de Sévigné*, ed. Gault-de-Saint-Germain, 12 vols. (Paris: 1823), 2:10, letter of 8 April 1671.

1702 as a form of relief for poor nobles, he thanked Chamillart for his support: "You have taken from misery an infinity of gentlemen of the most ancient nobility who would have remained in their villages all their lives to lead an unhappy existence, and you will give to the king good officers."[13] Vauban's "poor devil of a cousin" could not afford a company, but he survived as a lieutenant. Thus, financial ruin did not haunt junior officers who avoided unnecessary display, prodigious waste, or the responsibility of maintaining a unit.

Still, the semi-entrepreneurial system carried with it great risks for those who sought the honor and prestige of owning a military office, or *charge*. Expectation of monetary reward could not have prompted a reasonable man to accept such risk. Something else must explain why the French aristocracy pursued these positions as if they were irresistible.

An Environment of Glory and Honor

The engine that drove the semi-entrepreneurial system, which led officers to accept the maintenance of their units, was the desire for *gloire*. The word *gloire* translates best as "reputation," though "glory" gives the term the archaic flavor it deserves.

During the *grand siècle*, noblemen pursued glory with a consuming passion. For the Frondeur, Cardinal de Retz, "That which makes men truly great and raises them above the rest of the world is the love of *la belle gloire* . . . ."[14] Madame de Sévigné, an acute observer, regarded the desire for glory as a critical and worthwhile element in aristocratic education: "Since one constantly tells men that they are only worthy of esteem to the extent that they love glory, they devote all their thoughts to it; and this shapes all French bravery." She clearly identified *gloire* as a gendered concept, for she contrasted it with the less exciting expectations placed upon women: "As women are allowed to be weak, they take advantage of this privilege without scruple."[15] For her, *gloire* was definably masculine, and in the context of the army, this was essential to its nature.

To win glory, an aristocrat had to adhere to a code of honor. In terms of the culture of command, the pivotal quality in this aristocratic code was courage. But in this culture, appearance counted more than *essense*, so it was not enough to be brave; one must be *seen* as being brave by one's peers.[16] Thus, *gloire*, reputation, could only be won by demonstrating courage, and the danger of battle provided an opportunity to do so. A sense of honor

[13] AG, A¹1802, Matignon to Chamillart, 22 July 1704, in Louis Tuetey, *Les officiers de l'ancien régime. Nobles et roturiers* (Paris: 1908), 36.

[14] Cardinal de Retz in Gaston Zeller, "French Diplomacy and Foreign Policy in Their European Setting," *New Cambridge Modern History*, vol. 5 (Cambridge: 1961), 207.

[15] Sévigné, *Lettres de madame de Sévigné*, 7:394, letter of 23 October 1683.

[16] See the discussion of honor in Bertram Wyatt-Brown, *Honor and Violence in the Old South* (Oxford: 1986).

could be infused into an individual, but its origins and its power came from outside. It was a class standard, with ostracism the penalty for those who failed to live up to it. Within the definitions imposed by honor, to be an officer was to earn respect from the members of the aristocracy and to gain at least a modicum of glory.

The quest to attain glory by publicly fulfilling the demands of honor explains the undeniable taste for war on the part of the French aristocracy. A 1601 *Guide des courtesans* noted, "I hear our young nobility murmur against the peace which limits them from displaying [*mettre à jour*] what they have of good in their souls. They can appease their warrior ardors by taking themselves, with the leave of their prince, to some just war outside their country."[17] Louis XIV noted the enthusiasm of nobles to raise units to serve him during the first years of his personal reign. This enthusiasm did not flag during the Dutch War, when the raising of a new regiment could cause "great joy,"[18] and when it was "a marvel to see the quantity of people of high birth and others . . . who are eager to have employment [as officers]."[19] In 1693, Saint-Simon hurried to receive his first company, and to spend a good deal of money in a frenzied effort to put it back on its feet, because "I died of fear of not making the campaign that was about ready to open."[20]

The French repeatedly claimed a supposedly rare and special fighting spirit for their nobility. Vauban considered that French officers were "the best in the world" and that "all the nation loves war and takes up the profession of war every time that it finds in it some promise of elevation and of the ability to subsist with honor: [The nation] is of itself very courageous intelligent, proper to all that one wants, moved easily by honor, and in a word very proper to war."[21] Lisola, a Spaniard, described France as "always filled with an idle and seething [aristocratic] youth, ready to undertake anything, and who seek to exercise their valor regardless of the expense."[22]

A Menu of Incentives

A menu of other incentives aided the call of *gloire* in inspiring officers to serve their king. Some promised tangible benefits, such as the gratuities and promotions already discussed, but most were more subtle in their lure. And even in the case of financial rewards, although the money possessed value in itself, its worth in honor and glory multiplied its worth in gold.

---

[17] *Guide des courtisans* (1606), in Micheline Cuénin, *Le duel sous l'ancien régime* (Paris: 1982), 10.
[18] AG, A^{1}356, #29, 1 February 1673, Lebret to Louvois.
[19] Commissaire Lenfant to Louvois in Tuetey, *Les officiers*, 61.
[20] Saint-Simon, *Mémoires*, A de Boislisle, ed., 42 vols. (Paris: 1879–1930), 1:113.
[21] Vauban in Albert Rochas d'Aiglun, ed., *Vauban, sa famille et ses écrits*, 2 vols. (Paris: 1910), 1:269.
[22] Lisola, *Bouclier d'état* (1667) in Rousset, *Louvois*, 1:22–23.

Although the monarchy's system of symbolic rewards did not equal the elaborate series of medals and honors bestowed by modern armies, the Bourbons did recognize the power of honorific recognition. The most important such rewards were the military orders, the largest of which was the Order of Saint-Louis, founded in 1693 for Catholic officers with twenty-eight years of service. Since appointment to the order carried with it a pension of several hundred livres, it too had a monetary side. Earlier military orders, Saint-Lazare and Mont-Carmel, died out in the 1670s.[23]

Interestingly enough, while the monarchy offered the carrot of material and symbolic reward for service, there was little threat of the stick for those who refused to join the colors. The *intendant* Lafond, when seeking nobles to staff the new, low-prestige *milice* regiments, proposed limiting rich slackers' rights to bear arms and to tax the managers of their estates (since nobles enjoyed certain tax exemptions), but nothing seems to have come of this.[24] Later, he tried to compel wealthy nobles to accept commissions to command *milice* units in 1690, but Louvois called him off this hunt. "The King does not customarily make gentlemen serve by force."[25] Aristocratic honor and the sanction of opinion supplied enough incentive.

The possibility afforded by command to create or reinforce networks of clients also attracted men to the army. To gain clients, a patron had to bind others to him through the granting of favors. Since nobles valued military commissions highly, a colonel or captain who could bestow subordinate commissions possessed a valuable bounty. The potential to bolster clientage was even greater in a new, temporary, regiment than in an established one, since the new colonel held a *tabula rasa* unencumbered by existing holders of commissions. This may best explain why men eagerly sought to create new regiments at their own expense, since the money that they spent bought more than simply the command of a regiment doomed to be reformed at the end of the war. It became a means by which to forge or to increase a clientage that might last for life.

Military command also promised greater status for those newcomers troubled by the fragility of their claims to belong to the elite. Aspiring robe nobles and bourgeois *roturiers* believed that military service legitimated their upward climb. By taking up arms, they displayed their acceptance of sword standards of class and honor. Again, military command, though expensive, brought with it more than authority over a given number of soldiers; it granted prestige and legitimated the status of the officer.

As a luxury good, the expenses associated with military service often had little to do with practical value. Command and the costs that it entailed

[23] Babeau, *La vie militaire*, 2:113; Léon Mention, *L'Armée de l'ancien régime de Louis XIV à la Révolution* (Paris: 1900).

[24] AG, A^{1}837, #99, 28 November 1688, Lafond from Besançon to Louvois.

[25] AG, A^{1}981, 14 November 1690, Lafond to Louvois, and A^{1}981, 21 November 1690, Louvois to Lafond, in Tuetey, *Les officiers*, 72–73.

advertised the importance of the commander; they were a form of conspicuous consumption. The discussion of extravagant expenditures presented in the previous chapter demonstrates that officers spent a great deal of money to advertise their status, their glory. Attempts to maintain an elegant life style on campaign could be financially ruinous, but there was a sense that this was required of a man of station. In an entry for 1677, Primi Visconti singled out the duke de Lesdiguières as "the only one who by the quantity of his domestics, gentlemen, style of living, good table and liberalities of all sorts, did honor to the reputation of the French nobility, while the other lords, be it by poverty or by baseness of soul, did not distinguish themselves from the common and became, as the King wanted them to be, so many capuchins, capable only of obedience."[26] Contrary to Primi Visconti's claims, the sumptuous tables maintained by colonels, the extravagant display of highborn junior officers like Saint-Simon, and the flocks of valets who attended regiments, all attest to the fact that most officers hardly lived like monks.

Primi Visconti insisted that aristocratic society also promised sexual incentives to those who braved military service. Certainly, military behavior and military appearance involved sexual display, but Primi Visconti took the argument further; to him, war, not power, was the ultimate aphrodisiac. The man on the prowl needed military experience to win more intimate conquests. "The other princes, in order to have officers and soldiers are obliged to pay them a great deal; and here the King has subjects who ruin themselves vying to be in his service. It is the style, and whoever does not serve in the war is despised. The ladies do not want any other lovers; it is why many men of the robe leave the profession of the pen for that of the sword." Of Mme. de la Barre's attempts to interest the marquis de Montrevel, Primi Visconti said that she "gave to him all that she had in the hope of being the woman [*femme*] of a man of war, as is the fantasy of the ladies of Paris."[27] For more mature men, military office could promise a faithful wife. "The duke de Chaulnes said to me that the trouble that everyone imposes upon himself in order to obtain *charges* is caused by the fact that the women, in order to enjoy the advantages attached to these *charges*, remain faithful."[28]

Perhaps Primi Visconti's analysis verges on the frivolous, but one way or the other, he hit upon a truth. For the code of honor and glory to exert such leverage on aristocratic behavior, it had to be enforced by ladies as well as gentlemen. His observation that passion for soldiers ruled the women in the court and in Paris suggests just how much women embraced the aristocratic code of masculine honor.[29] They very well may have played as central a role in sending men off to war as they did in sending them off to the *pré*, or dueling ground.

---

[26] Jean-Baptiste Primi Visconti, *Mémoires sur la cour de Louis XIV, 1673–1681*, Jean-François Solnon, ed. (Paris: 1988), 104.

[27] Primi Visconti, *Mémoires*, 146, 85.   [28] Primi Visconti, *Mémoires*, 145.

[29] See Wyatt-Bown, *Honor and Violence*, 35, on "the mother as the moral arbiter of bravery."

DUELING: A MICROCOSM OF
THE CULTURE OF COMMAND

Long the subject of literature and scholarship, dueling provides a window into the culture of command that permeated the army of the *grand siècle*.[30] The same values that inspired men to pursue military careers despite the physical and financial risks implicit in that vocation drove them to the field of honor. Contemporaries recognized that dueling and military service drew upon the same aptitudes for honor and courage. When Vauban praised the French nobility as particularly apt for war, he cited their capacity for "taking offense easily over honor [*se piquant facilement d'honneur*]."[31] The penchant for quarrels that resulted in duels was seen as essential to the millitary character.[32] A strange either–or logic linked the duel and war, as when the 1645 *Catéchisme royal* put the following question in the young king's mouth: "If one forbids duels, how is it that the Nobility can give evidence of their courage?" This inquiry elicited the response, "In your armies, Sire."[33] A generation later, Primi Visconti testified to the same correspondence: "That bravery the French show among themselves in single combat, the King, by his edicts against duels, has made serve in war against his enemies."[34]

The duel evolved from the tradition of trial by battle, a matter of justice, and from the medieval joust, a matter of class honor and display. It retained both elements – seeking redress for a wrong suffered, and demonstrating the power, courage, and independence of an elite. For even if commoners fought duels, they did so only in imitation of the aristocracy. Dueling remained a rite of the nobility.

The modern practice of dueling developed in sixteenth-century Italy and, as did Renaissance art, arrived in France as a consequence of the Italian Wars. By 1600, dueling had developed into a subculture, involving codes of behavior, training by fencing masters, and stock ways to avoid the sanctions of law. The duel of the early seventeenth century enlisted seconds to fight alongside the principles, so duels became small skirmishes involving four, six, eight men, or more. The principal weapon of the duel, the rapier, was a refined weapon, rather too light for the battlefield, so beyond displaying status, it promised little utility except in fighting against a single, similarly armed opponent. Other weapons employed on the field of honor included

---

[30] Three recent works that discuss French dueling in the terms of modern scholarship are Cuénin, *Le duel*, François Billaçois, *Le duel dans la société française des XVIe–XVIIe siècles* (Paris: 1986), translated as *The Duel: Its Rise and Fall in Early Modern France* (New Haven, CT: 1990), and V. G. Kiernan, *The Duel in European History* (Oxford: 1988). Factual statements about the duel and laws concerning the duel are from these three works, when not stated otherwise.

[31] Vauban in Rochas d'Aiglun, *Vauban*, 1:269. See as well *Mémoire de M. d'Artagnan* in Babeau, *La vie militaire*, 2:10.

[32] André Corvisier, *Les Français et l'armée sous Louis XIV* (Vincennes: 1975), 62.

[33] *Catéchisme royal* by Pierre Fortin de la Hoguette in Cuénin, *Le duel*, 140.

[34] Primi Visconti, *Mémoires*, 146.

cutlasses and pistols. When combatants chose pistols, the results were likely to be particularly bloody. While most tests of honor matched men on foot, duels were also fought on horseback.

Dueling remained legal to some degree until 1626. Henri IV issued an edict in 1609 that still recognized the right to put disputes to the test of swords in certain restricted circumstances. Yet Henri's edict forbade dueling over the kinds of issues that usually brought men to the field, insults and women, and at least one unfortunate suffered execution for dueling during the early years of the reign of Louis XIII.[35] In any case, dueling peaked after his accession through the early years of the war with Spain.[36] In reaction, the king outlawed dueling altogether by his ordinance of 1626, and it never regained legal status. The penalties according to this ordinance included death, confiscation of goods, and loss of noble status. Although a famous case in 1627 led to the beheading of the young Montmorency-Boutteville, it is difficult to find another instance of the death penalty. However, it was common practice for authorities to hang a dead participant in public by his feet, to shame the duelist, and to deny his body burial in consecrated ground.[37] Mazarin continued to protest duels, but harsh laws failed to suppress the practice, as participants connived to disguise duels.[38] One fiction was to claim that no arrangement had been made but that the affair had been a "*rencontre*," a chance encounter that resulted in a fight.[39]

Dueling became a way for the French aristocracy to defy burgeoning absolutism. When authorities condemned one duelist for participating in a duel in 1625, 200 nobles escorted him into hiding as a form of protest. For the nobility, to duel was to assert aristocratic independence and to affirm an aristocratic concept of honor. A sword noble who submitted his dispute to the regular machine of justice surrendered his fate to the robe nobility who staffed the courts, an unthinkable action at a time when the sword still regarded the robe as bourgeois parvenus.[40]

The monarchy correctly regarded dueling as a form of rebellion, and as early as 1576, the king declared dueling to be a crime of *lèse majesté*. It comes as no surprise that Louis XIV, the archetypal absolute monarch, labored hard to curb dueling. He was aided in his crusade by a revulsion against dueling

---

[35] Legrain praised the young Louis XIII for executing a noble for dueling early in his reign. Baptiste Legrain, *Decade commençant l'histoire du Roy Louys XIII du nom, Roy de France et de Navarre* (Paris: 1618), 27–28, in Katherine B. Crawford, "Regency Government in Early Modern France: Gender Substitution and the Construction of Monarchical Authority," Ph.D. dissertation, University of Chicago, 1996.

[36] See the tables in Billacois, *Le duel*, 411.

[37] See the table listing punishments for dueling according to legislation and edicts, 1602–51, in Billacois, *Le duel*, 418–19.

[38] Mazarin to the archbishop, 16 September 1653, in Jules Mazarin, *Lettres du cardinal Mazarin*, eds. P. Chéruel and G. d'Avenel, vols. 6–9 (Paris: 1890–1906), 6:34–35.

[39] See the description of a *rencontre* in AG, A¹294, #311, 13 September 1672. See as well AG, A¹294, #12, 3 August 1672.

[40] See Bercé introduction to Cuénin, *Le duel*, 9–17.

that expressed itself in a religious and political movement set off by a declaration by men of the parish of Saint-Sulpice in 1651. They agreed to neither
issue nor accept calls to duel. In that year, the government issued a new edict
raising the penalties for dueling. By the early 1660s, Louis believed he had
made real progress in stemming such combat, priding himself on "the already advanced recovery from an evil so inveterate that there was a point
when it was necessary to despair of remedy."[41]

To a degree, he succeeded. He sought to have questions of honor submitted to the *Tribunal du point d'honneur*, founded in 1602 and composed of
marshals, it was charged with settling the kinds of disputes that led to duels.
Importantly, such arguments were to be dealt with by soldiers, not civilian
judges. Louis XIV's 1653 regulation was most advanced on this subject, meting
out punishments such as six months in prison for slapping someone, the
infamous *soufflet*. The next year, he addressed the duel in his coronation
sermon. His 1679 edict categorized killing in a duel as a common murder,
and in celebration of this edict, Louis commissioned a medal proclaiming
"The Duel Abolished."[42] But in reality, duels continued, although they lessened in intensity and in number for a time. Although some duels included
seconds in the action, this kind of gang combat went out of fashion, as
seconds simply regulated the combat between the primary adversaries.

Late in Louis's reign, the frequency of dueling seemed to have increased
again. The abbé Saint-Pierre estimated in 1715 that during the last thirty years
of Louis' reign, 10,000 duels were fought between officers. This number
included only those cases known by 500 commanders. In these duels, 400
officers fell dead on the field, and many others later died from their wounds.[43]
Despite this toll, in an edict of 1704, Louis continued to take credit for
extinguishing the evil.[44] To be sure, by comparison with the reign of Henri
IV, things had improved; Corvisier estimates that in the period 1598–1608,
some 8,000 gentlemen died in duels.[45]

Given the possibility of wounds or death, it is surprising how men rushed
into duels at the slightest provocation, or even with no provocation at all. In
one group duel of 1638 involving Bussy-Rambutin, his side brought only
four seconds while the other had five. A friend of Bussy-Rambutin then rode
over to the Pont-Neuf to find a fifth, and he recruited a musketeer.[46] The
musketeer had absolutely nothing at stake but joined this fray, with an apparently light heart. The question of dueling seemed not to hinge on the
gravity of the injury suffered by the wronged party but upon the necessity
to demonstrate one's courage. Thus, the musketeer would have risked seem-
ing a coward if he had not put his life on the line.

Despite the law, to deny a challenge to duel marked one as unworthy.

[41] Louis XIV, *Mémoires*, 2:377.   [42] Cuénin, *Le duel*, 219.
[43] Cuénin, *Le duel*, 233.   [44] Kiernan, *The Duel*, 96.
[45] Philippe Contamine, ed., *Histoire militaire de la France*, vol. 1 (Paris: 1992), 332–33.
[46] Cuénin, *Le duel*, 103–4.

Dueling gained an officer respect; as Henri IV claimed, dueling was "the only way by which young men believe that they can gain praise."[47] The abbé Saint-Pierre charged in 1715 that an officer who refused a challenge would "find himself forced by the other officers and by the commander himself to leave the regiment."

One counts for nothing that an officer would rather pass for a poltroon . . . than to commit a mortal sin and a capital crime in formal disobedience of the law and the will of the prince; one counts for nothing that he does not want to risk his safety and the loss of the good graces of his king; he does not fight, therefore he is a poltroon; he is a poltroon, therefore he must be driven away.[48]

The count de Forbin fought his first duel in 1672, which resulted in his disarming his foe. "I believed that my comrades from now on would be very circumspect in my regard and would fear having any dispute with me. This first test [*coup d'essai*] gave great pleasure to my uncle and to Marshal Vivonne." Instead of being punished for this sin against regulations, he was rewarded for his courage by being appointed to guard the flag.[49]

It is also noteworthy that while the best known duels pitted the rich and highborn against each other, dueling was primarily an affair of the lesser nobles. In a memoir of 1679, Marshal de La Feuillade protested that the strict penalties prescribed by the ordinances did not work. In particular, confiscation of property was moot since "out of a thousand who fight, there are but four who have lands."[50] Among the lesser duelists were also the young *annoblis*, who adopted dueling to demonstrate their acceptance of sword values and their own social success.[51]

The explanation for duels lay much more in the symbolic than in the real, for by their nature, duels were irrational. One historian claims that dueling survived because it advertised an aristocratic violence that cowed inferiors and thus ensured the social and economic order.[52] But more important than how the aristocracy was viewed from without was the way in which it defined itself. Ultimately, the aristocracy's fighting spirit was driven by the individual's drive to prove himself within the standards of his own class and thus win *gloire*. The nobility set standards that must be obeyed, or else the individual would lose caste. Duels were a human sacrifice to the god of peer opinion, and so was battle.

Just as in a duel, participation in battle gave an officer opportunity to display his courage by exposing himself to danger. As a theater for the drama of *gloire*, combat was its own reward on the *pré* or on the battlefield. There was no honor in hiding, and French officers led conspicuously from the front, and paid the price. Casualty rates were hideous among regimental officers. Of sixteen captains in the Regiment de la Ferté who took part in the

---

[47] Billaçois, *The Duel:*, 79. [48] Saint-Pierre in Cuénin, *Le duel*, 231.
[49] Forbin in Cuénin, *Le duel*, 200. [50] La Feuillade in Cuénin, *Le duel*, 218.
[51] Cuénin, *Le duel*, 227. [52] Kiernan, *The Duel*, 159.

combat at Altenheim in 1675, fifteen fell.[53] At the battle of Saint-Denis, in 1678, all but two of the captains in the first battalion of guards were wounded.[54] At the 1689 combat at Valcourt, the Regiment de Champagne lost its colonel, lieutenant colonel, major, seven captains, and eight lieutenants.[55] Leadership was a very dangerous business.

THE CRITERION OF
SELECTION AND PROMOTION

As best they could, officer selection and promotion reconciled this bloody culture of command with the financial demands of the semi-entrepreneurial system and the professional needs of the army. Four factors determined the course of an officer's career in the army of the *grand siècle*: birth, wealth, clientage, and merit. Observers agree on the inclusion of the first two factors – aristocratic status and wealth – although they do not agree as to which of the two rated more highly.[56] The fact is that both counted; privileged birth provided entrée at the lowest levels and proved virtually indispensable leverage at the top, yet the lack of funds to buy and maintain a company or a regiment marooned an officer in a lesser position, no matter how deeply his family roots burrowed down through layers of aristocracy. Clientage is less commonly mentioned as an influence over selection and promotion, but it should not be ignored. As mentioned earlier, the lure of acquiring power and honor by standing at the peak of a regimental pyramid drew men to purchase a colonelcy and then build a network of patronage among the company-grade officers. Demonstrated ability, or at least competence, also could propel a career, particularly if the individual passed tests of birth and wealth. Louis XIV and his ministers, never blind to talent, rewarded it when they could.

Any generalizations about selection and promotion in the army of the *grand siècle* need to be qualified by a recognition that things operated differently during the second half of the century than during the first. The nature of the problem makes it difficult to supply a precise description of the process before 1661, because practice differed from regulations, and particular commanders and regiments followed their own rules. In the 1660s, Louis took charge of his army and far more than before distributed military commissions as he saw fit, following his regulations. Before his personal reign, questions of promotion were often left to colonels general and to generals, who acted as authorities unto themselves. Afterward, Louis attended to promotions: "I also gave myself the care of distributing commissions [*charges*] down to the lowest, both in the infantry and the cavalry, which my predecessors had never done, it being left to the great officers, for whom this function

---

[53] Rousset, *Louvois*, 2:164.   [54] Rousset, *Louvois*, 2:519.   [55] Rousset, *Louvois*, 4:219–20.
[56] "The essential is money; birth is only secondary." Rousset, *Louvois*, 1:182. For Bérenger, "three elements worked together to set the pace of a career: birth, talent, and, in a subsidiary manner, money." Jean Bérenger, *Turenne* (Paris: 1987), 118.

remained an aspect of their authority [*dignité*]."[57] The greater regularity of practice, the presence of a single controlling hand for over fifty years, and the fact that authors such as Rousset, André, and Corvisier have concentrated on the second half of the century, almost necessarily compel a study of this phenomenon to concentrate on that period.

Birth and Wealth

Aristocratic birth qualified one for a commission, for society held that gentlemen were best suited to command. Moreover, a particularly prestigious noble lineage gave one advantages in reaching the higher ranks – colonel, general, and marshal. Military service was the aristocratic vocation par excellence. It not only occupied great numbers of nobles but justified the privileged position of the entire class; it was a matter of self-definition.

Since military service in the commissioned ranks connoted nobility, it was always possible to enter into the aristocracy through the army, although that doorway narrowed by the second half of the seventeenth century. During the sixteenth century, an officer whose father and grandfather had also been officers was "reputed" noble, meaning that the individual concerned gained aristocratic rights and privileges, but these did not become hereditary. Elements of this practice extended at least through the first decade of the 1600s in ordinances concerning tax exemptions based on military service and aristocratic status.[58] But this path of entry did not survive as a broad highway, and relatively few won patents of nobility in reward for military service.[59] In fact, 1664 saw the monarchy revoke letters of nobility that it had granted since 1634 based on service under arms, except for outstanding cases. Once again, in 1715, Louis annulled those given since 1689, even though he issued 1,000 blank patents of nobility during the Nine Years' War.[60] Still, some were ennobled for service, although not in large numbers.[61] A case in 1710 demonstrates the kind of claims made. Six brothers of the LaFarge family, born of a bourgeois father and an aristocratic mother, served in the army, two were killed in service, one reached major, with forty-two years of service. In total, the brothers could claim 144 years in the army. After this sacrifice, the family requested letters of nobility, and Louis demanded an inquiry.[62]

---

[57] Louis XIV, *Mémoires*, 2:119.

[58] See the discussion in Tuetey, *Les officiers*, chap. 7. See also Devyver, *Le sang épuré: Les préjugé de race chez les gentilshommes français de l'ancien régime* (Brussels: 1973), 68, and David Parrott, "The Administration of the French Army During the Ministry of Cardinal Richelieu," Ph.D. dissertation, Oxford: 1985, 175–77.

[59] Jean Chagniot, "Guerre et société au XVIIe siècle," *XVII siècle*, 37 (1985), 253–54.

[60] Babeau, *La vie militaire*, 2:84; Frank Tallett, *War and Society in Early Modern Europe* (London: 1992), 176.

[61] See letters of nobility granted as a reward for military service in Teutey, *Officiers*, 377–92. See also Babeau, *La vie militaire*, 2:84n.

[62] AG, A^{1}2265, #239–42.

Aristocrats dominated the officer corps, but scholars debate the degree to which the army monopolized the aristocracy. Corvisier calculates that circa 1690, one in two or one in three nobles of military age saw service in what he terms an "aristocratic mobilization without precedent."[63] In contrast, Constant carried out an extensive examination of the nobility in the Beauce and concluded that their participation in the army was lighter than in some other provinces, although it increased over time, and by the second half of the seventeenth century, participation reached 16.1 percent of all noblemen, or about one in six.[64] Yet in another study, he showed that in the Bourbonnais, 93 percent of the titled families and 64 percent of the nontitled families held military or court *charges*.[65]

Of course, to speak of noble representation in the officer corps in gross percentages should not disguise the fact that not all gentlemen were equal. In the seventeenth century, when the robe nobility was still relatively new, sword nobles felt themselves far superior to the robe. Sword nobles regarded the army as their exclusive domain, but sons of robe nobles still entered the army. Studying three generations of that famous robe family, the Colberts, Corvisier discovered that out of twenty-three adult sons, fourteen chose a military career, and that out of nine sons-in-law, five were officers.[66] Military service legitimated the new nobles' claim to privilege and status but also complicated tensions within the officer corps.

Moreover, as the army grew, *roturiers* served alongside the nobles. *Roturiers* were not entirely new to the commissioned grades. An edict of 24 July 1534 recognized the right of *roturiers* to become officers, and half of twenty-three Gascon captains of the Wars of Religion studied by Constant turned out to be non-nobles.[67] The *cahiers* of the third estate in 1614 wanted officer positions open to non-nobles and proposed that ten years service be seen as sufficient to qualify.[68] Under Louis XIV, certain ranks were reserved for officers of fortune – that is, men who had come up through the ranks. Such posts included

---

[63] André Corvisier, *Louvois* (Paris: 1983), 341–43. He estimates that there were 23,000 to 24,000 nobles in the army in 1690 and that there were 60,000 to 70,000 aristocratic males of military age. André Corvisier, "Guerre et mentalités au XVIIe siècle," *XVII siècle*, 37 (1985), 224, repeats the estimate of one third. In his *La France de Louis XIV, 1643–1715: Ordre intérieur et place en Europe* (Paris: 1979), 62, he stated that half of the nobility of military age were under arms.

[64] During 1500–60, the proportion of noblemen from this area who participated in military service stood at 4.45 percent; in 1560–1600, it rose to 5.98 percent, hit 8.78 percent in 1600–60, to top off at 16.1 percent in 1660–1700. These figures from Jean-Marie Constant's 1981 dissertation are discussed in both Contamine, *Histoire militaire*, 1:373, 439, and Chagniot, "Guerre et société," 252.

[65] Constant in Contamine, *Histoire militaire*, 1:373–74. In Anjou, only 19 percent of the titled families and 24 percent of the nontitled families did.

[66] Corvisier, "Guerre et mentalités," 224.

[67] Tuetey, *Les officiers*, 51; Contamine, *Histoire militaire*, 1:329.

[68] Corvisier, "Guerre et mentalités," 228.

grenadier officers and at least some majors and lieutenant colonels.[69] Many engineer officers were of *roturier* origins. The engineers who served Louvois were 64 percent nobles and 36 percent *roturiers*. Of the military engineers who worked for Colbert, 67 percent were *roturiers*.[70] But non-noble officers of fortune who came up from the ranks, and technical officers who performed duties thought less honorable by nobles of grand aspirations, constituted special groups; what struck the noble officers as threatening was the influx of *roturiers* receiving direct commissions in line regiments.

The *roturier* officer became necessary to the monarchy because he brought a new source of wealth to the army. While non-nobles played a role in command early in the personal reign of Louis, they became more common with the onset of the Nine Years' War.[71] Corvisier believes that until 1684 there were enough aristocrats to officer the army, but with the multiplication of regiments after that date, *roturier* officers became essential both because the supply of nobles willing and able to serve was insufficient and because the army required *roturier* wealth to supplement declining aristocratic fortunes in order to maintain the king's regiments.[72]

Although a statistical study of the social origins of field and company-grade officers in the seventeenth century is probably beyond the capacity of the sources, comments of the day make it clear that from the 1680s on, the influx of *roturier* officers was very real. It probably peaked during the War of the Spanish Succession, when the criticisms of *roturier* officers multiplied. Speaking of the hundred new regiments raised in 1702, de Guignard charged that "Among the men who have raised regiments, there are adventurers without name and without experience . . . ."[73] Bauffremont de Listenois snarled against officers who were "sons of butchers, merchants, and [*maltôtiers*]."[74] In 1713, Puységur praised the army before the outbreak of the Nine Years' War, saying that then "it was necessary to have birth and service to obtain a regiment" but that subsequently, "many" colonels could claim but "little birth." Puységur went on to assert that aristocrats rebelled at taking orders from "a son of a business man, who buys a regiment."[75]

The influx of *roturier* officers raises the issue of money, but the value of money did not necessarily undermine the importance of birth, as the highest-ranking nobles were also quite wealthy. Still, for regimental and company command, money was the sine qua non. Riches could take precedence over family history, since the affluent sometimes lacked noble pedigrees and the wellborn lacked funds.

---

[69] Babeau, *La vie militaire*, 2:87–88; Rousset, *Louvois*, 3:291.

[70] Contamine, *Histoire militaire*, 1:473.   [71] See AG, A^{1}2265, #239–42 and A^{1}362.

[72] André Corvisier, *Armies and Societies in Europe*, trans. Abigail T. Siddall (Bloomington, IN: 1979), 163.

[73] De Guignard in Louis Susane, *Histoire de l'infanterie française*, 5 vols. (Paris: 1876), 1:214.

[74] AG, A^{1}2219, 15 May 1710, Bauffremont de Listenois to Voysin, in Tuetey, *Les officiers*, 78–79.

[75] Puységur, "Mémoire sur la manière de fair la reforme des troupes," April 1713, in Tuetey, *Les officiers*, 78.

The lines of tension within the officer corps pulled in several directions: Sword resented robe; old noble resented *annobli*; aristocrat resented *roturier*; and poor resented rich. Extensive scholarship has documented these tensions during the eighteenth century. Although one might expect that in the 1700s, the greatest animosity smoldered between aristocrats and *roturiers*, this was not true. The deepest resentment arose between officers with talent and noble birth but little money and those rich newly ennobled individuals, the *annoblis*, who used their wealth to push to the top.[76]

No study of the officer corps in the seventeenth century rivals those on the eighteenth; however, a reading of the sources leads to several conclusions. Conflict between robe and sword was strident among seventeenth-century officers, almost certainly more so than it was after 1715. Before then, the robe was still a relatively new, and thus only partially legitimated, social category, and it was likely for the sword noble to see the robe as essentially bourgeois – thus, the emphasis on old families. It would seem that many quotations that state resentment against *roturiers* in fact show disdain for the robe and the *annoblis*. In fact, proud nobles showed a grudging respect toward *roturier* soldiers of fortune, who understood their station. Courtilz de Sandras reported that as a young officer in 1667, he was taught to respect officers of low birth: "It is necessary that a young man not imagine, under pretext of being of high birth [*qualité*], that he can lack respect towards a soldier of fortune."[77]

Complaints about the role of money in promotion occurred throughout the century. In 1614, Parisian nobles complained that venality introduced the wrong officers from the wrong class:

Your Majesty is very humbly begged to limit all venality in the future in both the offices of your household and in military positions, and in the future that they no longer be given to money but to recognized virtue and to the old nobility which owes its origin not to offices nor to money dishonorably acquired [*mal acquise*], but to valor, generosity, and blood shed by its predecessor in the service of the King.[78]

As the century progressed, fear grew that money would triumph over talent – and birth. In 1651, nobles of the Gatinais wanted to reserve places in *compagnies d'ordonnance* for aristocrats: "May it please Your Majesty to purge [these companies] again and forbid the sale of captains posts; these are a prize for your poor nobles, who not having the means to advance there for lack of money subside and are extinguished, the rich *roturiers* coming to

---

[76] See Emile G. Léonard, *L'Armée et ses problèmes au XVIIIe siècle* (Paris: 1958) and David Bien, "La réaction aristocratique avant 1789: l'exemple de l'armée," *Annales: économies sociétés, civilizations*, 29 (1974), 23–48, 505–34.

[77] Courtilz de Sandras in Jean Chagniot, "De Rocroi à Rossbach," in Claude Croubois, ed., *L'officier français des origines à nos jours* (Saint-Jean-d'Angély: 1987), 53.

[78] A 1614 *cahier* from Parisian nobility in Jean Chagniot "Du capitaine à l'officier, 1445–1635," in Croubois, *L'officier français*, 34.

suppress them."[79] Vauban hinted of such tensions on an army-wide scale in a memoir on the demobilization of French infantry, probably dating from the 1690s. He described colonels of new regiments as for "the most part young men who acquired this rank by money and not by service."[80]

There also emerges the unmistakable theme that became a given of eighteenth-century reform: the notion that nobles of limited means made the best officers. In another piece, Vauban defined his ideal officers as "young gentlemen of good morals, of good body and good spirit, especially the younger sons of families in which the fathers have but a small fortune for the young man to hope for. For rarely are those who are waiting for a great deal to come to them able to harden themselves to suffer all the troubles and fatigues of those who must make their fortune in war."[81] As different a pair as Turenne and Villars concurred.[82] To Villars, the poor noblemen were more inured to the hardships of campaigning than were their wealthier cousins, and when the going got tough, the poor officer would stay with the service, since he had nowhere else to go, whereas the rich officer could return to family, estates, and the court.[83] The military administrator Chamlay agreed, arguing that the best officers came from the lesser nobility who were "exhausted [*abîmer*] and ruined."[84]

Networks of Obligation: Patronage

In addition to class and wealth, a web of clientage also determined an officer's career. Much has been written on the importance of clientage in seventeenth-century France – how men of power and prestige buttressed their positions and enhanced their honor by binding men below them with ties of obligation and loyalty.[85] Military command offered valuable patronage to commanders who could employ it to create or reward clients. The more prestigious the command, as in the guards regiments, the stronger the patronage.[86]

On the regimental level, ties of family, region, and clientage mattered. An interesting case from the 1620s found the king deciding to give the Regiment de Ribeyac to the son of its deceased colonel, because "If I had given it to another the regiment would have entirely disbanded, since the captains are all from the area of the colonel and are all relatives and friends of the dead

---

[79] Chagniot, "Guerre et société," 250–51.   [80] AG, MR 1828, piece 21.

[81] Vauban in Rochas d'Aiglun, *Vauban*, 1:334.   [82] See Bérenger, *Turenne*, 378.

[83] BN, f. fr. 6257, Villars, "Traité," 9–10. This notion became even more strident in the eighteenth century; see Saxe's comment that "Truly the only good officers are the poor gentlemen who have nothing but their sword and their cape . . . ." Maurice de Saxe, *My Reveries on the Art of War*, in *Roots of Strategy*, ed. Thomas R. Phillip (Harrisburg, PA: 1955), 201.

[84] Memoir by Chamlay, 1711, in Babeau, *La vie militaire*, 2:81.

[85] See André Corvisier, "Clientèles et fidélités dans l'armée française aux 17e et 18e siècles," in Y. Durand, ed. *Hommage à Roland Mousnier. Clientèles et fidélités en Europes à l'époque moderne* (Paris: 1981), 213–36, on clientage in the army.

[86] Corvisier, "Clientèles et fidélités dans l'armée," 226–27.

man."[87] Turenne staffed his regiment in 1630 with Protestants, like himself, from his entourage in Sedan.[88]

On the highest level, Richelieu used his extensive patronage in the army to limit the ability of Louis XIII to make appointments. In the words of Bussy-Rambutin, "in the majority of graces, one counts the King as nothing."[89] Jacques de Chastenet de Puységur, commenting upon Richelieu's power, observed that "the Cardinal . . . wanted only persons who were his, and had promised him fidelity, to serve in the guards or as [fortress] governors."[90] The cardinal's control passed beyond the military units at court to those in the field; in fact, one letter charged that unless the most senior captain in a regiment was promoted to fill a vacancy at lieutenant colonel, it was assumed that the appointment was made under Richelieu's influence.[91]

When the opportunity presented itself, the monarchy itself used the reward of command as a way to bind powerful nobles to it. After annexing Franche-Comté, Louis created new regiments and gave them to families of the great nobles of his new domain.[92]

In the confusion and crisis before 1659, the possibilities for nobles to create clienteles were undoubtedly greater than would later be the case. When Le Tellier says that lieutenant generals and other officers acted like independent princes, or republics, he may be referring to the results of clientage.[93] Louis XIV's concern to eliminate the colonel general of infantry grew out of his wish to deny any individual the patronage that this position controlled during the first half of the century and his desire to seize this patronage for himself.

Louis's will to dominate did not eliminate the potential for colonels to nominate the officers in their units, although such nominees had to meet the king's standards. The Archbishop of Lyon believed that regiments could be more easily and effectively formed by "men of condition" who saw themselves as "little generals" and who "take their friends and relatives for captains." Such prominent men might otherwise not go to war.[94] If Louis had denied colonels this regimental patronage, he would have put off enthusiastic candidates willing to sink money into regimental command. Correspondence

[87] Letter from Louis XIII to Richelieu, 15 July 1628, in Pierre Grillon, *Papiers de Richelieu*, vol. 3 (Paris: 1979), 381.

[88] Bérenger, *Turenne*, 78.

[89] Bussy-Rambutin in Parrott, "The Administration of the French Army," 192.

[90] Jacques de Chastenet de Puységur, *Les Mémoires de messire Jacques de Chastenet, chevalier, seigneur de Puységur, colonel du régiment de Piedmont, et lieutenant général des armées du Roy*, 2 vols. (Paris: 1690), 1:246.

[91] AAE, 816, fol. 150, 22 November 1635, letter from Charost to Richelieu, in Parrott, "The Administration of the French Army," 192.

[92] Tuetey, *Les officiers*, 73. The use of patronage rewards to gain the loyalty of the nobility of a recently annexed province is well discussed in David Potter, *War and Government in the French Provinces: Picardy 1470–1560* (Cambridge: 1993).

[93] BN, f. fr., 4206, fol 362 r., 16 October 1650, LeTellier to Mazarin, in André, *LeTellier*, 117.

[94] AG, A^{1}362, 10 November 1673, Archbishop of Lyon to Louvois.

about creating several regiments in 1696 demonstrated that although Louis XIV demanded that regimental commanders submit the names of their candidates for officers in their new regiments, he generally approved the suggestions.[95] Interestingly, the royal government seemed to show more concern over sifting appointments for young officers at the lowest ranks than for their superiors. Royal control could be surprisingly firm; in January 1696, the secretary of war wrote a new colonel concerning his nominations for sous-lieutenants: "I have been ordered by the king not to send any commissions for anyone that I have not seen [to judge] if they have the qualities required; it is necessary, if you please, that you send [the candidates] here."[96] This was in sharp contrast to Louis XIII simply sending stacks of blank commissions to the likes of the duke d'Epernon, who formed private armies for him before 1635.[97] It seems reasonable to speculate that Epernon received control over patronage as partial compensation for his services.

Corvisier presents an interesting example of clientage in the Regiment de Vivarais, 1705–29. When Erard de Ray became colonel in 1705, he began recruiting new officers from lands around his estates in Rai-sur-Risle, no further than Orbec to the north and Saint-Paterne to the south, a span of roughly forty miles.[98] Ray stocked this old regiment with clients by bringing in sous-lieutenants and cadets who would then be promoted to fill vacancies at the higher ranks. This might be why Louis took the appointment of such low ranks so seriously, since he needed to screen officers at the start of their careers, precisely at the level at which a commander might try to pack a unit with loyal but unqualified young neophytes.

Captains as well as colonels bestowed positions upon their favorites. In 1673, Marshal Albert asked that captains expected to take on expensive cavalry companies be allowed to appoint subalterns who could "help them to make good companies, and in truth . . . it will not be possible for them to acquit themselves well without this little help and it is only on this condition that they have wanted to engage themselves."[99] Here the issue was one both of clientele and expense.

Networks also operated on the most elevated levels. Louis XIV's ministers and major commanders built up clienteles that benefited them. One important link connected Louvois and his client Vauban. Vauban then repeatedly tried to use his influence to find jobs for family, friends, and protégés.[100] It

---

[95] See, for example, AG, A^{1}1339, #40, 3 January 1696, letter from minister to Cézanne approving suggested names to fill the staff of his brother's regiment, and #189, 17 January 1696, letter from minister to Mouchy agreeing to appointments proposed by commanding officer.

[96] AG, A^{1}1339, #287, 24 January 1696, to Beuzeville; see as well in this volume #40, 3 January 1696; #47, 3 January 1696; #189, 17 January 1696; and #402, 30 January 1696.

[97] Guillaume Girard, *The History of the Life of the Duke of Espernon, the Great Favorite of France* (n.p.: 1670), 228, 380.

[98] Corvisier, "Clientèles et fidelités, 220–22.

[99] AG, A^{1}359, 31 March 1673, in Tuetey, *Les officiers*, 62 and quotation from AG, A^{1}360, #35, 7 April 1673.

[100] See, for example, letter in Rochas d'Aiglun, *Vauban*, 2:90.

will be argued that a reason why 1675 marked a watershed in French strategy is that in removing the aggressive Turenne and Condé, it removed not just major commanders and military advisors but also two strong patronage systems, and in so doing weakened an entire concept of offensive warfare. They were replaced by a new primary military advisor, Louvois, and his men, including Vauban, and with them a more defensive ideal.

Merit as a Moderator

Even if it emphasized class, money, and clientage, the culture of command was not blind to merit. Command and administration of military units were too demanding to allow general incompetance; ability mattered. As in the case of military forces today, merit could be defined as talent, seniority, or military education.

Vauban repeatedly appealed to the minister of war in the interests of deserving officers. In making the case for Latouche, he displayed hostility to promotions based on court favoritism. "Concerning his life, he has never seen the court nor set foot in Paris; he is, however, perhaps the man who carried out the best actions in the German wars . . . . He is a very determined soldier, he knows the country very well, and he is the best partisan in the kingdom."[101] Always a proponent of merit, Vauban wrote to Louvois in August 1674, "As the last combat has only opened too many vacant positions [*charges*], I beg you to reserve some companies and lieutenancies for those of our subalterns who merit them best."[102]

After Vauban, the marshal who seemed most adamant about merit was Villars. He insisted upon treating "in promotion the great lord the same as a soldier of fortune, up to a certain point."[103] When a Rohan, one of the exalted families of France, received promotion to brigadier over the more competent Colonel La Motte, Villars fumed, "I know that the names are different, but, in these great wars, I will say to you, as a good servant of the king very truly yours, that it is necessary to consider only merit."[104]

Promotion also came as a reward for *belles actions* in the field.[105] Should a worthy officer catch his commander's or, better yet, his king's eye, he could win a higher rank. It was the custom to send an officer who performed some noteworthy act to the king to announce a major victory, and the king in his joy would promote the bearer of good news.[106] Of course, the purchase system put limits on this kind of reward, since the king could not bestow

[101] Letter from Vauban to Louvois, 3 November 1671, in Rochas d'Aiglun, *Vauban*, 2:62.
[102] Letter from Vauban to Louvois, 23 August 1674, in Rochas d'Aiglun, *Vauban*, 2:115–16.
[103] BN, f. fr. 6257, Villars, "Traité," 2–3.
[104] AG, A^{1}2510, 23 April 1709, Villars to the minister of war in Tuetey, *Les officiers*, 86.
[105] For example, see the case of Captain Boisseleau who was made a permanent brigadier for services rendered in Ireland during 1690. Philippe, marquis de Dangeau, *Journal du marquis de Dangeau*, Feuillet de Conches, ed., 19 vols. (Paris: 1854–60), 3:234.
[106] Corvisier, "Les généraux," 32.

someone else's property as a prize, but only grant a commission that belonged to the crown.

In this aristocratic army, men were raised from the ranks, as already noted, and this represented a respect for merit above all. The 1629 Code Michau provided for promoting men from the ranks. "The Soldier, by his services, can mount to the *charges* and offices of companies, degree by degree, up to that of captain, and more if he renders himself worthy."[107] Thus, a Sergeant La Fleur carried off a brilliant raid in 1674 and was appointed a lieutenant and given a gratification of 500 livres as a reward.[108] Vauban put it bluntly; the service needed men of "good spirit and courage," and "It is necessary to take them where one finds them."[109]

There was some discussion of requiring time in a lower grade as a prerequisite for promotion. In his quest for military perfection, Vauban suggested a career pattern that would have a young man begin his military service as a cadet at age eighteen, reach sous-lieutenant at twenty-one, captain in his late twenties, and colonel no sooner than his mid-thirties.[110] Villars wanted to require seven years as lieutenant or captain before an aspirant could become a colonel.[111] Requisites for time in grade, however, did not find their way into regulations under Louis XIV. Such qualifications in practice remained rudimentary. Describing the early reign of Louis XIV, Rousset states that the minimum requirement to gain the king's *agrément* for the purchase of a company was two years of cadet service, even in household units.[112] Saint-Simon states in his memoirs that in the early 1690s, when he entered the service, there were three ways to qualify for the king's *agrément* to buy a regiment: one year as a musketeer, at the head of a cavalry company, or as a subaltern in the Regiment du Roi.[113] A year's service must have been considered more as a probationary period than as adequate training. All a young man could have mastered in so short a time was the appearance of command, but perhaps only this was considered absolutely essential.

EDUCATION AND TRAINING OF YOUNG OFFICERS

Improved military education for junior officers was a concession to merit and an attempt to inject more professional standards of competence into the culture of command. Proper preparation offered a way to raise the quality of officers without abandoning the aristocratic semi-entrepreneurial system. Because the system ran by its own necessary logic, once officers entered it,

---

[107] 1629 ordinance in Teutey, *Les officiers*, 56.
[108] AG, A¹398, #138, 12 June 1674, letter from Chamilly at Graves to Louvois; and AG, A¹380, #220–21, 27 June 1674, letters from Louvois to Chamilly.
[109] Vauban in Rochas d'Aiglun, *Vauban*, 1:325–26.
[110] Vauban in Rochas d'Aiglun, *Vauban*, 1:334–35.
[111] BN, f. fr. 6257, Villars, "Traité," introductory section.
[112] Rousset, *Louvois*, 1:213.   [113] Saint-Simon, *Mémoires*, 1:29.

the best method to improve the process was to feed better trained young men into it at the bottom. Still, the fact that merit only moderated, rather than determined, selection and promotion becomes particularly clear in the way that formal education for officers received little more than haphazard attention during most of the *grand siècle*.

Although Louis XIV and Louvois eventually showed great concern for officer education, the training of officers in the seventeenth century was not rigorously pursued. The most common type of training was a form of apprenticeship that put young men in subaltern positions to learn the basics of their craft. French practice varied according to wealth and class, and it was not professional by modern standards. Still, it probably functioned as well as most contemporary methods of officer preparation.[114]

In the first half of the seventeenth century, private military academies became fashionable, but this educational trend received only modest support from the monarchy.[115] Riding schools emerged in Italy before they were imitated as military academies in France during the reign of Henri IV.[116] Subjects taught there included horsemanship, fencing, dance, languages, and mathematics. Turenne entered one such private academy in 1626 at age fifteen. Direct state action in founding military academies remained more a dream than a reality. Noble representatives to the 1614 Estates General unsuccessfully requested that the crown create schools for the "poor nobility . . . in the capital city of each province" to instruct youth from ages eight to sixteen.[117] In 1626, an assembly of notables called for the creation of a military college, but little was done.[118] Richelieu and Mazarin showed some interest; the former provided scholarships for twenty youths to the short-lived *Académie royale des exercises de guerre* on the Rue du Temple. In 1636, Richelieu set out a *règlement* on what should be taught in this academy: "arms and letters being germane and inseparable, and both required for the establishment of great empires."[119] Condé attended it in 1637. Later, Bernardi directed the most renowned of the private academies under Louis XIV. Such schools had largely but not entirely disappeared by the Dutch War, and by 1691, only two survived.[120]

The first true military school in the modern sense was probably that

---

[114] See Fritz Redlich, *The German Military Enterprizer and his Workforce, 13th to 17th Centuries*, *Vieteljahrschrift fur Sozial – und Virtschaftsgeschite*, Beihelft XLVII (Wiesbaden: 1964), 1:162–65, on military education.

[115] On military academies see Babeau, *La vie militaire*, 2:29–33, 45–46; J. R. Hale, *War and Society in Renaissance Europe, 1450–1620* (Baltimore, MD: 1985), 143–45.

[116] The manège de Pluvinel, of grand renown, was founded in 1594; in 1606, the duke de Bouillon founded an academy at Sedan. Wallenstein supported similar institutions in the Germanies. Micheline Cuénin, *Le duel sous l'ancien régime* (Paris: 1982), 12.

[117] *Cahier* for the nobility of Orléanais, 1614, in Chagniot, "Du capitaine a l'officier, 1445–1635," in Croubois, *L'officier français*, 35.

[118] Mention, *L'Armée de l'ancien régime*, 70.

[119] *Règlement* de 1636, in Babeau, *La vie militaire*, 2:45.

[120] Corvisier, *Louvois*, 338; Babeau, *La vie militaire*, 2:33.

founded by Johan of Nassau in 1619 at Siegen, but it closed its doors in 1623, having only instructed a total of twenty students.[121] Louis XIV established no formal officer schools for his forces until 1669, when he founded a naval academy. Officers of artillery had always required special knowledge, mixing the skills of warrior, mathematician, and craftsman. Before Louis XIV, these skills had been gained by apprenticeship and individual study. However, Louis XIV provided his officers with formal training by founding the first French artillery school at Douai in 1679.[122] The principal artillery centers became Douai, Metz, and Strasbourg, where both officers and their men trained.[123] Louvois reported from Metz in 1680: "I have seen the firing of cannon and bombs by the company of sieur de Vigny, by the six new *compagnies de cannoniers* and by the officers of the artillery school."[124]

By late century, Louis XIV recognized the need to organize officer education better. Cadet companies formed by Louvois in 1682 and maintained into the Nine Years' War represent the most important attempt to regularize and improve training, but these companies only thrived for a decade. Notable officers, such as Vauban, Villars, and Feuquières, urged further strides forward, pointing the way to eighteenth-century reform.[125]

Military Apprenticeship

The most common method of military training for French officers in the seventeenth century remained apprenticeship. Young men learned their craft by working at it under the watchful eye of more experienced men. Early in the century, this could be accomplished by service overseas and later as a volunteer or a cadet in a French regiment or by service in one of the special units that the king designated for such purposes.

At the start of the *grand siècle*, French officers often left France to fight in the Dutch or the Swedish armies, when those two forces were the military colleges of Europe. Disregarding the complaints of the Spanish ambassador, Henri IV financed two French regiments to serve as Dutch forces in 1599 in order to give experience to a number of young officers.[126] Marshals Turenne and Guébriant, as well as the tactical innovator Pierre Arnauld d'Andilly, fought in Holland as infantry officers.[127] Once the French entered the war

[121] Geoffrey Parker, *The Military Revolution: Military Innovation and the Rise of the West, 1500–1800* (Cambridge: 1988), 163.

[122] Brunet, *Histoire générale*, 2:130; Surirey de Saint Rémy, *Mémoires d'artillerie* (Paris: 1745), 1:40, in John U. Nef, *War and Human Progress* (Cambridge, MA: 1950), 205; Corvisier, *Armies and Societies*, 107.

[123] Rousset, *Louvois*, 3:332.   [124] Rousset, *Louvois*, 3:333–34 fn.

[125] See, for example, BN, f. fr. 6257, Villars, "Traité," introductory section and elsewhere.

[126] Victor Belhomme, *Histoire de l'infanterie en France*, 5 vols. (Paris: 1893–1902), 1:311.

[127] Le Baoureur, *Histoire du maréchal de Gébriant*, 8, Babeau, *La vie militaire*, 2:13. Louis de Pontis, *Mémoires*, in *Collection complète des mémoires relatifs à l'histoire de France*, ed. M. Petitot, vols. 31–32 (Paris: 1824), 31:425–34.

against Spain in 1635, their nobles found enough to occupy themselves at home. The absolute numbers of French commanders who learned their trade abroad was probably not high; consequently, this was insufficient to train an entire officer corps. Yet the influence over tactical development of those who went abroad was probably great, since they helped to diffuse the most up-to-date military practices.

As the decades continued, young French aristocrats sought service as volunteers in native regiments. Although the volunteer performed the duties of a private soldier in a company, often one commanded by a relative, he never actually enlisted and thus received no pay and stood free of any obligations. This initiation to military service survived into the eighteenth century. Usually quite young, for obvious reasons, volunteers could be older; one was forty-nine.[128] A distinguished roll of officers began as volunteers: Pontis in the Regiment de Bonne, Feuquières in the Regiment du Roi, as well as Coligny, Henry de Campion, Puységur, and others.[129] While walking the rounds of his troops, Louis XIII once pointed out a soldier to the duke of Savoy: "See that soldier standing guard, his name is Bréauté; he is rich, worth 30,000 livres of *rente*."[130] The wealthy sentinel was simply learning his trade as a volunteer in the ranks. In fact, it should not be thought that volunteers lived the exact same rude life as men in the ranks. They were distinct from the normal recruit; as Pontis stated early in the century, volunteers "carried themselves almost as haughtily as did their officers."[131] A volunteer often received an education in the company, as Sirot received lessons in mathematics from a tutor hired by the captain, but there was no standard routine.[132] Although idiosyncratic as a form of service, being a volunteer was gauged as adequate preparation; five colonels commissioned in 1684, for example, claimed no other previous military experience but that of having served as volunteers.[133]

The role of cadet approximated that of volunteer, except that cadets formally enrolled as such and received pay. Before the 1680s, the practice was to place young men who had not reached their eighteenth birthday as cadets in companies of line regiments – normally not under the guidance of relatives.[134] So many young nobles desired placement as cadets that Louis limited their number to two per company.[135] In 1682, Louvois instituted formal cadet companies to train neophytes. By the early 1690s, when a number of these cadet companies existed, an aspirant to captain had to serve a year as a volunteer, a cadet, or in a household unit.[136]

[128] Babeau, *La vie militaire*, 2:18–19. [129] Babeau, *La vie militaire*, 2:12–13.
[130] Puységur, *Mémoires*, 1:71. [131] Pontis in Babeau, *La vie militaire*, 2:12.
[132] Babeau, *La vie militaire*, 2:18.
[133] Corvisier, *Louvois*, 335, and Mention, *L'Armée de l'ancien régime*, 102.
[134] Rousset, *Louvois*, 1:213.
[135] H. Pichat, "Les armées de Louis XIV en 1674," *Revue d'histoire de l'armée* (1910), 10.
[136] Corvisier, "Les généraux," 39; Saint-Simon had to serve a year as a musketeer before he could gain the king's agreement to buy a company. This was in 1691–93.

Service in exclusive, and expensive, household units or in the king's own regiment marked an individual for rapid rise. A year as a musketeer or a subaltern in the Regiment du Roi qualified an up-and-coming aristocrat to apply for the king's *agrément* to purchase a regiment.[137] Under Louis XIII, many well-placed young men began military careers in the king's guard; in 1629, Pontis's company, with a total of 250 men, included eighty young gentlemen.[138] This tradition continued with Louis XIV, who considered that his four companies of the *gardes du corps*, which he reorganized in 1664, along with the two companies of his musketeers, provided a superior training environment. Louis regarded such service as a way to prepare and to support future officers, proudly stating that "The majority of the officers were taken from the troops of my household where I kept them since the war."[139] His household provided him with a place in which he could "form them with my own hands."[140] "For a long time I have taken care to drill the troops of my household," wrote the young monarch, "and it was from there that I took almost all the officers of the new companies that I raised; in order that they would carry there the same discipline to which they were accustomed, and I filled their vacant places . . . with some young gentlemen that could not be instructed in a better school."[141]

Like his military household, his own infantry regiment, the Regiment du Roi, was something very special. He created it in 1663 as a model for the army, and its lieutenant colonel doubled as the inspector general for infantry. Of twenty-seven colonels commissioned in 1684, fifteen had attained the rank of captain in the Regiment du Roi.[142] Others left the regiment to serve elsewhere as lieutenants and captains.

Related to service in privileged guard units was service as a page to the king or a major personage, although one had to be well connected be a page to the king. In general, pages received military education and could aspire to a sous-lieutenancy. Villars made a point of launching his pages' careers. In 1714, he requested more young pages and promised that "I have them shown military exercises, and after they have been with me three or four years, I find them employment with the troops and equip them, giving them a horse."[143]

The Cadet Companies, 1682–96

The creation of cadet companies in 1682 was the most innovative and most promising French experiment in officer training during the century.[144] As the army and the art of war outstripped the capacity of the traditional apprentice system in peacetime to supply officers in sufficient numbers for wartime, the

---

[137] Saint-Simon, *Mémoires*, 1:29.   [138] Pontis in Babeau, *La vie militaire*, 2:13.
[139] Louis XIV, *Mémoires*, 2:116.   [140] Louis XIV, *Mémoires*, 2:118.
[141] Louis, *Mémoires*, 1:237.
[142] Corvisier, *Louvois*, 338 and Mention, *L'Armée de l'ancien régime*, 102.
[143] Letter of 6 Avril 1714, in Babeau, *La vie militaire*, 2:329.
[144] For details of cadet companies, see Rousset, *Louvois*, 3:301–14 and Corvisier, *Louvois*, 338–41.

king and his minister of war created companies of cadets to assemble the youths who had previously learned their trade as best they could in the regiments. In June 1682, Louvois ordered the provincial *intendants* to announce throughout the kingdom that two companies of cadets would be assembled in Metz and Tournai, to include gentlemen aged fourteen to twenty-five. An ordinance of 1 September barred regiments from taking in cadets as in the past, except for the colonel's company, which could keep three until further notice. In July 1683, even these were denied.

The response to this initiative went a bit awry. Louvois was dismayed that the first class contained men of low birth – surely, bourgeois parvenus pursuing an aristocratic life style.[145] The flood of cadets even included some illiterates. Late that year, Louvois addressed a letter to the captains of the two companies asking them to survey the origins of their cadets, since their first levy had included "all sorts of men." "The king does not want that one denies those who are of a low birth but if there are some of whom the birth is very obscure, it is without doubt that His Majesty will have them discharged."[146] The companies were supposed to serve the nobility.

The eventual response to the companies was so strong that in 1684 Louvois increased the number of companies to nine of 475 cadets each, commanded by a captain who was governor of the frontier fortress where the company was situated – Tournai, Cambrai, Valenciennes, Charlemont, Longwy, Metz, Strasbourg, Brisach, and Besançon. The course of instruction included a menu from the manual of arms to mathematics. They also took part in the duties of the fortress – standing guard, for example. Louvois inspected the companies himself, finding that the companies drilled quite well. Although cadets trained as infantry, authorities took note of those with the aptitude and finances required for cavalry command.

Grouping together such numbers of young, high-spirited gentlemen proved to be a disciplinary nightmare. Incidents in 1685 in the two companies at Charlemont and Besançon began with duels and ended with near mutiny. Trouble at Charlemont broke out when ten cadets released by force one of their comrades who had been condemned to prison, and it ended with the execution of two of their number.[147]

When war came in 1688, the companies reached a total strength of 7,000 but soon closed their doors to new aspirants.[148] With renewed combat, critics of the companies argued that the cadets would learn more in the field than in segregated training companies. Some denied the value of the entire institution; Saint-Hilaire concluded that "companies of cadets have produced

---

[145] Rousset argues that the cadet companies were an attempt "to assure to the young men of the lower nobility and bourgeoisie what the heirs of the great names already found in the two companies of the musketeers of the king." Rousset, *Louvois*, 3:302.

[146] AG, A¹681, 5 October 1682, and AG, A¹683, 27 December 1682, letters, in Corvisier, *Louvois*, 339.

[147] 16 June 1685 judgment of a *counseil de guerre* in Babeau, *La vie militaire*, 2:25.

[148] Corvisier, *Louvois*, 340.

nothing good."[149] Moreover, the companies were expensive. Louvois dismissed the criticism, but after his death, the companies ceased to take new cadets in 1692, and the last company was dissolved in the spring of 1696, as the few remaining cadets dispersed to regiments.[150]

The collapse of Louvois's attempt at formal officer education was disappointing for the army. It would not really be revived until the creation of the *Ecole royale militaire* in 1750. Yet there was at least one provincial attempt to copy the idea of cadet companies under Louis XIV, when Matignon, the lieutenant general of Normandy, established a body of cadets there. While Matignon created the company at his own initiative, it was recognized and supported by Versailles for much of the War of the Spanish Succession.[151]

Even after the demise of Louvois and the cadet companies, the king and his ministers kept an eye on the cadets with the regiments. Cadets proposed for commissions had to travel to Versailles to be interviewed by an agent of the military administration. When this practice was attacked as expensive and unnecessary, the minister of war reasserted its importance.[152] Colonels were not allowed to make their own choices among cadets without higher approval. When officers requested sous-lieutenancies for cadets in their regiments, the minister repeatedly insisted that the young men come to Versailles, since the king commanded him to commission no cadet unless "I have seen beforehand that he has the required qualities."[153]

With the return to the earlier, more haphazard, method of dispersed cadets, the provincial *intendants* played an even more central role in locating potential officers. In 1704, Chamillart urged *intendants* to find "young men of good will, in a condition to be officers, and of an age proper to bear the fatigues of war" to join the army in Bavaria.[154] In 1705, they were asked to find "the most proper to be officers" for service in Spain.[155] In 1709, Voysin asked the *intendant* of Évêchés to provide young nobles to fill slots as sous-lieutenants in the Regiment du Roi. Service in this showpiece regiment required a substantial outlay of 1,200 to 1,500 livres per year.[156] Apparently, the search was not successful, for letters of early 1710 from other *intendants* who had also been asked to find candidates report that they were unable to locate men of sufficient wealth.[157] This case was particularly interesting because it

---

[149] Babeau, *La vie militaire*, 2:25.

[150] Belhomme, *Histoire de l'infanterie*, 2:322. The company at Brisach was abolished in 1694, and its cadets transferred to Strasbourg, which was the last company remaining when it was disbanded in April 1696.

[151] See Teutey, *Officiers*, 35–37, on Matignon's company.

[152] Teutey, *Officiers*, 68–69.

[153] AG, A¹1339, #409, 30 January 1696, letter of minister to Despanet, captain in the Regiment de Rechau; and #287, 24 January 1696 Letter from minister to Beuzeville.

[154] Letter of 6 February 1704 in Tuetey, *Les officiers*, 80–81. See, as well, 81–82.

[155] Letter of 15 October 1705 in Tuetey, *Les officiers*, 84.

[156] 29 November 1709, letter from Orbesson to Saint-Contest, in Tuetey, *Les officiers*, 85.

[157] AG, A¹2266, #64, 26 January 1710, letter from Ormesson to Voysin, from Soissons; #347, 14 March 1710, letter from Harcourt in Champagne; this piece pled the "poverty of the nobility of Champagne."

also demonstrates that good officers with sufficient birth and wealth were becoming hard to find.

HONOR VS. PROFESSIONALISM

The perseverance of aristocratic honor in the face of bourgeois professionalism resulted in a series of problems, from underage officers, to swaggering violence against civilians, to chronic absenteeism. Such shortcomings were absolutely integral to the culture of command – the necessary price to pay for men imbued with French aristocratic honor. Although the king and his secretaries of state for war sought to impose more professional standards of competence on the officer corps, this culture limited their effectiveness. Still, with his irresistible force of personality, Louvois compelled greater obedience, and this in itself was an important erosion of earlier independence.

Young and Inexperienced Commanders

The interplay of birth, money, and clientage quickly propelled many well-placed but very young gentlemen into command positions. Such underage command could not be eliminated without a transformation of aristocratic values and of Bourbon finances. Turenne received his first regiment in 1625 at age fourteen, but the king ordered it disbanded only eighteen months after its creation.[158] When reestablished in 1630, it stayed on the army rolls; its colonel was now all of nineteen.[159] In 1634, at age thirteen or fourteen, Bussy-Rambutin received command of the first company of the regiment owned by his father. This meant that not only did the lad act as captain, he also commanded the regiment when his father was absent. In this case, his father sensibly vested real authority during his absence in a senior captain, but the point is that official regimental command rested in the hands of a boy barely entering puberty.[160]

Awarding command to adolescents continued under Louis XIV. In 1690, at age eighteen, and after he served as a captain for no more than a few months, the young count de Grignan became colonel of the cavalry regiment, succeeding his uncle. This boy-colonel, the grandson of Mme. de Sévigné, was the son of the governor of Provence. In 1702, a mere lad of thirteen begged to raise and lead one of Louis's new regiments, but fortunately the king refused.[161] Marshal de Saxe commented that during the first half of the eighteenth century, "A young man of birth regards it as an insult from the court if he is not given a regiment at the age of 18 or 20 years."[162]

Colonels rarely rose from the ranks of majors or lieutenant colonels.[163] Of

[158] Bérenger, *Turenne*, 65.   [159] Bérenger, *Turenne*, 72.   [160] Bussy-Rambutin, *Mémoires*, 6.

[161] Georges Girard, *Le service militaire en France à la fin du règne de Louis XIV: Racolage et milice, 1701–1715* (Paris: 1915), 16.

[162] Maurice Comte de Saxe, *Mes reveries ou mémoires sur l'art de la guerre* (The Hague: 1756), 21.

[163] Puységur bought posts as major and as captain in 1632. Puységur, *Mémoires*, 1:140–41.

twenty-seven new colonels created in 1684, none held either one of those two ranks. Twenty-two had been captains before their receiving regiments, and five had been volunteers and thus held no commission before becoming colonels.[164] Guignard was probably correct in condemning the colonels commissioned late in Louis's reign as men "without name."[165] In contrast, Guignard approved the 1684 colonels because they came from illustrious families. Not surprisingly, raising such young men to regimental command often grated on older company-grade officers "because they found themselves in the necessity of obeying children."[166] Guignard's prejudice may suggest that men of high birth did better, since their origins alone commanded respect.

A common contention among critics who wrote late in the reign of Louis XIV was that the French army had become so large that it could not find enough good officers. Even Vauban complained of "the near impossibility of being able to fill [the army] with major officers who possess the experience and knowledge necessary for their grade."[167] In other words, the army outgrew its capacity to find an adequate number of capable officers by traditional means. This helps to explain the concern for military education voiced from the 1680s to the French Revolution. Confined by demands of social privilege and the semi-entrepreneurial system, the French never really discovered a good way to provide officers in the seventeenth century. When Louis XIV suddenly needed 7,000 new officers in 1702, he was bound to commission great numbers of military debutantes, many of them young men with bulging pockets.[168]

Violence by Officers against Commoners

The aristocracy's code of honor assumed a strictly hierarchical society and disregarded the lower classes as unworthy. These attitudes appeared in special forms within the culture of command. For one thing, the belief that honor was exclusively aristocratic meant that officers expected little of their men, because low-born soldiers were capable of no more. Thus, tactics made increasingly limited demands upon the initiative or courage of the rank and file, who must be closely supervised in battle. More will be said of this in Chapter 14. In addition, because the elites viewed those below them as outside the polite demands of aristocratic codes, officers, often young "spirited" fellows, felt no need to treat common civilians with anything other than disregard or brutality. Officers were imperious members of a social elite accustomed to getting its way. As soldiers, they practiced the arts of violence

---

[164] Corvisier, *Louvois*, 335.   [165] Guignard in Susane, *Infanterie*, 1:214.

[166] Feuquières, *Mémoires*, 1:181.

[167] AG, Bibliothèque, Genie 11 (fol.), Vauban mémoires, a commentary on fortresses, ca. 1688–91.

[168] The number of 7,000 comes from Susanne, *Infanterie*, 1:214.

and at times crossed over the line between legitimate and illegitimate use of force. The state tried to eliminate violence against good, law-abiding citizens of villages and towns. A sampling of the archives suggests that complaints against physical abuse by officers was more common, or more commonly reported, late in the century than before. This may indicate a greater willingness on the part of administrators to pursue bullies than an actual increase in bullying.

Officers seemed to expect deference and turned to violence to punish those who refused to grant it. For example, four subaltern officers of artillery "full of wine" ran amok in Grenoble during 1694 and attacked passersby on a bridge; eventually, a crowd cornered them and killed two officers in the final fray.[169] A number of reported cases date from the War of the Spanish Succession. In February 1710, the *intendant* Turgot reported that a lieutenant Portail of the Regiment de la Sarre, then quartered at Moncales, caned a man for refusing to give him oats.[170] Again, the presence of *procès verbaux* in the archives indicates a willingness to pursue and punish such misconduct.

Absenteeism

Absenteeism by French officers grew out of the relationship between honor and military service. The individual desperately in need of displaying his courage in battle in order to legitimate himself may have felt only limited devotion to the soldierly profession per se, or at least to his troops. His company or regiment functioned as an arena and an audience for brave acts, but many of the fruits of these acts awaited him in civil society. Thus, French officers, having proven themselves, were only too willing to abandon their units whenever possible and return home or to court, where accolades awaited them.

Absenteeism pervaded the army. The Code Michau of 1629 set the time that officers had to be with their units in 1629; a colonel need be present only three months each year, a captain four, and lieutenants and ensigns eight months.[171] Thus, regular leaves for extended periods were a natural part of the operation of the French army. Colonels, for example, seem rarely to have been present with their regiments except on campaign.

Even in wartime, officers continued to spend a great deal of unauthorized time away from their men. A review held in July 1635 revealed that in La Force's army of about 10,000 troops, 140 officers were absent, 110 of them

---

[169] Babeau, *La vie militaire*, 2:256. For other examples of violent misconduct, see Babeau, *La vie militaire*, 2:242, 249; Côte-d'Or, C 2915, 7 November 1695 and AG MR 1785, piece #56, 26 April 1697.

[170] AG, A^{1}2265, #224–26, Turgot to Voysin, 12 February 1710. For other cases in 1710, see AG, A^{1}2266, #136, 137, 169–70, 180–81, 194, and 225–36.

[171] Code Michau, 1629, article 284, in François André Isambert et al., eds., *Recueil général des anciennes lois françaises, depuis l'an 420, jusqu'a la Révolution de 1789*, vol. 16 (Paris: 1829), 295–96.

without leave.[172] An 8 August 1636 ordinance threatened absent noble officers with loss of rank and class, and *roturiers* with condemnation to the galleys.[173] A rather surprising directive of 13 July 1649, from Le Tellier to his agent in the field, highlights the extent of absenteeism: "And because his Majesty has been informed that there are few officers in each troop he has deducted two thirds of the *états* and appointments of the absent officers and has given them to the other third.... His Majesty has also been informed that there are some entire cavalry regiments in which there is only one captain...."[174]

Absenteeism reached its zenith in winter quarters. Of course, this was a time of inactivity, when officers could be spared. Certain leaves were justified, since only on leave could an officer corral new men for his company. A regulation of 1643 decreed that one third of the captains must be present with their units during winter quarters, although the percentage permitted to leave was not always the same in succeeding years.[175] Ordinances of 1661 set this rule for all garrisons and established the method to select officers to go on leave.[176] During the war with Spain, officers were ordered back to their units; Le Tellier issued such orders nearly every spring. Officers sheltering in Paris received special attention, and laggards might find themselves thrown into the Bastille.[177]

While Louis XIV did not eliminate absenteeism, he did labor to control it. He discouraged absenteeism by declaring that an active officer who came to court would be degraded, since "It is prejudicial to the service of His Majesty that they abandon their duty to come and pursue appointments [*charges*]."[178] At the close of winter quarters in 1668, although hostilities were suspended at the time, the king ordered his minister of war to issue an ordinance demanding that all officers rejoin their troops on penalty of imprisonment in the Bastille. However, the king exempted "gallant colonels," who were allowed to stay away so as not "to give the ladies the occasion to cry over the separation."[179] Louvois pursued officers at court who should have been with their men. On a February day in 1689, he confronted a captain de Nogaret in the gardens of Versailles; Nogaret had opted to spend the winter in court rather than with his company:

LOUVOIS: Monsieur, your company is in very bad condition.
NOGARET: Monsieur, I did not know that.

---

[172] AAE, 819, fol. 64, 68, 28 July 1635 in Parrott, "The Administration of the French Army," 148.
[173] Contamine, *Histoire militaire*, 1:365.   [174] AG, A¹115, 13 July 1649.
[175] Article 11 of the regulation of 18 October 1643 in André, *Le Tellier*, 546.
[176] Ordinances of 4 April and 1 July 1661 in André, *Le Tellier*, 548.
[177] An ordinance of 4 March 1635 in Contamine, *Histoire militaire*, 1:365; see ordinances issued by Le Tellier 15 March 1643 and later, André, *Le Tellier*, 539–41.
[178] Ordinance of 31 October 1668 in Babeau, *La vie militaire*, 2:111–12.
[179] AG, A¹222, 21 April 1668, Le Tellier to Louvois.

L O U V O I S: It is your business to know. Have you seen it?
N O G A R E T: Monsieur, I will give the order.
L O U V O I S: You ought to have given it already. You must make up your mind, Monsieur, either declare yourself to be a courtier, or do your duty as an officer."[180]

One can only imagine the shame and fury felt by the wealthy young courtier when he was upbraided by the "bourgeois" but powerful Louvois.

During the Nine Years' War, ordinances of Louis XIV demanded that at least thirty officers stay in each regiment during winter quarters and that half of the infantry officers be present in garrisons.[181] But once again, reality did not come up to regulation. Documents from Amiens detail the number of officers actually serving with units on the march behind the front lines during the months of winter quarters. The number of officers present fell far below the full complement. When it passed through Amiens in December 1689, one infantry regiment of twenty-one companies was led by only fourteen lieutenants, backed by a few sergeants.[182] Regulations hardly sanctioned so many officers being away from their commands. In a case not quite so extreme, the Regiment de Beaujolais came to Amiens in January 1691, with its sixteen companies led by a lieutenant colonel, a major, seven captains, and eight lieutenants. Missing were the colonel, nine captains, eight lieutenants, and probably sixteen sous-lieutenants, or about two thirds of its full complement of officers.[183]

Absenteeism represented a particularly French culture of command. Slack devotion to the army witnessed by the officer's unwillingness to stay with his troops was not a general European phenomenon; the Prussian army, for example, insisted that an officer's place was with his regiment. French absenteeism was not limited to the *grand siècle*, but, in fact, characterized the army until the Revolution swept away the aristocratic officer corps and replaced it with bourgeois commanders who placed greater value on professionalism. Under the *ancien régime*, absenteeism reflected the officer's adherence to his own code of honor and symbolized his independence, as did his attitude toward dueling and his disregard of social inferiors.

Discipline and Punishment

It was impossible to eliminate completely abuses implicit in the culture of command, but the government attempted to weaken the strong sense of independence cherished by the officer corps. In the main, regulation and enforcement tightened over the course of the century. Those enamored of the heavy-handed techniques of Louvois might see his administration as being the high point of officer compliance, with a decline after his death. Yet the

---

[180] Letter of 4 February 1689, Mme. de Sévigné in Corvisier, *Louvois*, 332.
[181] Babeau, *La vie militaire*, 2:187.
[182] Amiens, EE 394, 8 December 1689 is a route for *étapes* concerning the Regiment de Davinde.
[183] Amiens, EE 396, January 1691.

evidence is not clear. In general, the bureaucracy did not loosen its grip or lessen its workload after 1691, and the threat of punishment directed against officers does not seem to have declined.

Among the menu of disciplinary actions threatening officers who transgressed against regulations, financial penalties played a particularly notable role. They helped to end one of the worst abuses of the *grand siècle*, the Tax of Violence. As explained in Chapter 6, if soldiers pillaged or extorted, the officers could be docked their pay and "appointments" to cover the loss. Deductions from pay and appointments became the most common punishment for offenses.[184] In a more extreme case from the War of the Spanish Succession, the effects of Captain de la Grange were sold to repay government allowances that he had been given to supply recruits with clothing and armament that they never received. This unfortunate officer also languished in prison for his misconduct.[185]

Execution, the ultimate punishment, was inflicted only rarely. Richelieu tried des Chapelles and Harcourt as governors who surrendered their fortresses without adequately resisting the enemy.[186] In 1673, Louis ordered that the governor of Naarden, Dupas, be executed for having surrendered his charge to the Dutch too easily. His harsh penalty was imposed "in order to make an example which will serve as a lesson to the other governors, and can warn foreigners that if Frenchmen commit such cowardly actions they will not be tolerated."[187]

The most severe punishment usually inflicted on an officer was to deprive him of his command. Reformation, or disbanding, of an officer's unit was a penalty threatened under Louis XIII, but Parrott argues that this was a hollow threat.[188] However, "breaking" occurred in reasonably large numbers and with some regularity. Breaking, or stripping an officer of his command, and thus his property, and expelling him from the service, was tantamount to expelling him from his class and declaring him a nonperson. With Le Tellier's insistence, Condé broke thirty captains at once in 1645.[189] A number of lists of broken officers testify to the continued use of this punishment.[190] During the years 1686–93 alone, 448 officers were broken.[191]

Absenteeism, fraud, and pillage could be punished by breaking. An ordinance of 15 July 1637 targeted absenteeism.[192] In a letter of 19 September 1645,

---

[184] See the deductions listed in AN, G¹1774, #68, *Receptes extraordinaires deça 1679.*

[185] AN, G⁷1777, #297 and 299, 14 and 28 January 1704. Grange's goods brought 205 livres 15 sols.

[186] Parrot, "The Administration of the French Army," 329.

[187] Louvois in Rousset, *Louvois,* 1:482. William III could also be harsh in such a case, ordering several officers who abandoned Niwerburg to be hanged in 1673. Rousset, *Louvois,* 1:412.

[188] Parrott, "The Administration of the French Army," 212.

[189] Condé to Mazarin, from Verdun, 5 June 1645, in Aumale, 4:645–46 in André, *Le Tellier,* 250.

[190] AG, MR 1787, pieces 1–4 cover breaking 1668–93.

[191] AG, MR 1787, piece 4 covers breaking 1686–93.

[192] Caillet, *Administration en France,* 374.

the king stated that the primary reason for breaking officers was "the absence of captains and the lack of assiduity that they have given in their *charges*."[193] Pillage could also bring down this ax. An order of October 1638 commanded that officers of the Regiment du Chancearu be broken at the head of La Force's army "for having committed pillages and thefts against the peasants and villagers."[194] Disobedience could also break an officer. Louvois told his severe inspector, Martinet, "You ought to make all the officers that command units understand that the intention is that they reestablish obedience without reply in regard to officers who are their subalterns and that the first who happens to disobey will be broken provided that I am informed of it."[195]

So Louvois insisted and intimidated. Unquestionably, his actions pushed the French officer corps in the direction of a modern professional force, but the movement, meeting resistance, could proceed just so far. For historians who see only the push, the French officer corps became a harbinger of the future; for those who see only the resistance, it remained a holdover from the past. A more complete truth can be found in the compromises and tensions of the middle course. No one, not even Louis XIV, could utterly transform the culture of command, which, in conjunction with the financial needs of the state, limited reform. Aristocratic values and the need to tap the wealth and credit of the officer corps, rather than an unimpeded search for talent, still determined officer selection, and Louvois's attempt at formal officer education foundered. In an age of *gloire*, the violent independence of the officer, reflected both by dueling and by absenteeism, could be moderated but not eliminated. As the next chapter suggests, the state probably enjoyed more success placing its generals in harness than in subduing the worst excesses of its regimental officers, for the fiscal imperatives and limitations of the state played less disastrous roles at the top of the military hierarchy.

[193] BN, f. fr. 4172, fol. 159, king (aged 7) to Harcourt, 19 September 1645.
[194] Order of council, 16 October 1638 in Caillet, 374.
[195] Louvois to Martinet, 13 March 1669, in Corvisier, *Louvois*, 188–89.

9

The High Command

SWORD in hand, the young duke d'Enghien, commanding the French army at Rocroi, spurred his horse once more. He had just led cavalry of his own right wing in a great arching attack, driving off Spanish horsemen and colliding with the now exposed flank of their reserve infantry. But on the other flank, La Ferté had disobeyed Enghien's orders and charged forward, only to be thrown back. Hearing of this and realizing that his army was in peril, the duke now led his own squadrons in a full circuit around the rear of the Spanish forces and smashed the cavalry that had just defeated La Ferté. This charge won victory for him that day. When his father died three years later in 1646 and Enghien succeeded to his father's title as prince de Condé, victory would proclaim him the Great Condé.

The Great Condé embodied much that was basic to those who exercised the highest levels of command during the *grand siècle*. At Rocroi, Condé displayed a style of leadership that combined the personal bravado of a knight with a sense of the battle as a whole. Wellborn – a prince of the blood – and ever aware of that birth, he fussed and quarreled over the deference due him and the awards owed him. His jealous sense of his own *gloire* rendered him not only proud but difficult, and soon rebellious. In 1649, he took up arms against the government of a young Louis XIV in the Fronde, largely out of a sense that his own worth had not been adequately recognized.

For Louis XIV, as a man, to avoid the political and military crises of his childhood, he must exert his authority over Condé and commanders like him; only by controlling his generals and his army could he truly control France. His relationship with the high command was, therefore, both a military and political fact of the first order.

Above the regimental officers in the French army stood the general officers, the high command. While these were two very different strata, those at the top of the French military hierarchy shared much with the officers below

them; the difference was one of degree. If regimental officers were aristocratic, general officers were more likely to come from the most powerful
families within the aristocracy. If regimental officers dueled to maintain their
reputation and sense of self, general officers quarreled endlessly over questions of precedence to ensure their personal *gloire*. To some degree, the high
command mirrored their subordinates, writ large. An understanding of the
high command during the *grand siècle* must comprehend the peculiarities of
French military hierarchy and how questions of social status, political reliability, and military competency defined it.

This chapter emphasizes French-born commanders. Foreign-born officers
also served in the high command but were a distinct minority. Between 1661
and 1715, only 11 percent of the 310 lieutenant generals who served Louis XIV
were not native to his domains.[1]

The most important military issue to be examined here is the balance
between the high command, the secretary of state for war, and the king
himself. As such, the story of the high command is one aspect of the relationship between the crown and the nobility. Throughout the first half of the
grand siècle, the high command jealously guarded and ambitiously asserted its
independence from the monarch, or at least from the king's ministers. This
independence climaxed during the Fronde but still remained a factor into the
Dutch War. Eventually, the death of Turenne, the retirement of Condé, and
the rise of Louvois gave Louis XIV leverage to control his general officers
as never before. As a result, the direction of strategy and even of operations
switched from the field to Versailles – the king commanded as the chief of
guerre de cabinet. Yet even as great an authority as Louis XIV could not rule
on the battlefield; his marshals and generals never became simply his ciphers.
They had to master the art of command in the *grand siècle*, the last focus of
this chapter.

DEFINING THE HIGH COMMAND

Over the course of the *grand siècle*, the highest levels of military command
included a range from independent noble leaders of private armies before
1635 to the far more obedient generals of Louis XIV's last two wars. As previously explained, army *intendants* performed many of the tasks today delegated to uniformed staff officers, but *intendants* did not actually command
troops; hence, they are not the subject here. Military hierarchy at the top,
while always complicated by questions of personal prestige and pretension,
took on a more regular shape and brought with it greater subordination as
the decades followed one another.

---

[1] André Corvisier, "Les généraux de Louis XIV et leur origine sociale," *XVIIe siècle* (1959), 41–
42.

Private Armies and Military Entrepreneurs

Armies that fought for Louis XIII were not always composed of the king's troops and led by generals dependent upon the monarch; in many cases, forces were led by the commanders who raised and financed their own armies, and thus enjoyed a large degree of autonomy. These can best be called "private armies," even if they were created in response to royal appeal or commission. Kings of France had long called upon their great lords to serve them in war, and often these lords came with their own forces. The right of arms claimed by the aristocracy gave those with sufficient wealth and power the authority to raise soldiers for their own purposes, which included both resisting and supporting the king. Such private armies and their commanders enjoyed their greatest hours during the sixteenth-century Wars of Religion. While they continued to take the field early in the *grand siècle*, by 1635, the old-style private armies had passed from the scene.

In the period between the accession of Louis XIII to the throne in 1610 and the defeat of Montmorency's rebellion in 1632, the monarchy relied upon wellborn and wealthy grandees to muster and finance armies for its use. The numbers of troops involved were far from trivial; from his personal resources, the prince de Joinville raised 5,800 infantry and cavalry in 1614–16, while at one point, Lesdiguières created six regiments in one year, totaling as many as 7,500 troops. Brian Sandberg argues that while French monarchs realized that private armies posed a danger as well as a convenience, they could provide forces cheaply and quickly, and so the monarchy turned to them out of necessity.[2] Grandees relied upon their personal influence and their clientele in their own home regions; the duke de Guise raised soldiers in Guise in 1617; Epernon mined Guienne for troops; Rohan found co-religionists in the Cévennes; and La Rochefoucauld mustered relatives and supporters from Poitou. The king dispatched Schomberg "to his Government of La Marche, with Orders to assemble his Tenants and Vassals."[3] However, when such resources did not supply enough manpower, the powerful might also hire mercenaries, as did Concini and Condé in 1615.[4]

Even though such forces were raised with the approval, or even at the express request, of the king, he granted the lord concerned a free hand in important matters. The commander could choose his own officers, for

---

[2] The material on private armies comes from the research of my graduate student, Brian Sandberg. I have employed both his conclusions and his references with his consent.

[3] François Eudes de Mezeray, *Histoire de la Mère et du Fils* (Amsterdam: 1730), 99; A. Lloyd Moote, *Louis XIII, The Just* (Berkeley: 1989), 249; Guichard Deageant de Saint-Martin, *Memoirs of Monsieur Deageant* (London: 1690), 141.

[4] Guillaume Girard, *The History of the Life of the Duke of Espernon, the Great Favorite of France* (London: 1670), 296; Louis XIII, *A Declaration made and Published by the King of France, Whereby the Princes, Dukes, and Barons Therin Named are all Proclaymed Traytors* (1620), 6; Sir John Throckmorton to V. l'Isle, *Report on the Manuscripts of the Right Honorable Viscount de l'Isle*, vol. 5, *Sidney Papers, 1611–1626*, ed. William A. Shaw and G. Dyfnallt Owen (London: 1962), 306–7.

example, without appeal to royal agents. In 1621, when Epernon formed an army to fight in Bearn, the king's orders arrived "without any assignation either of men, or money, wherewithal to begin the work, but a great cluster of commissions and dispatches only."[5] In such a situation, the loyalties of the officers ran directly to Epernon and only indirectly to the king, again making this very much a private force.

The duke d'Epernon, the colonel general of infantry, provides a particular case of a noble who repeatedly raised private armies. Simply to escort the king on a journey to Paris in 1615, Epernon created a force of 5,000 foot and 400 horse.[6] Responding to a royal proclamation of 1617, the duke mustered a private army in 1617.[7] When Louis asked him to disband it, Epernon did so, but knowing that he might soon raise troops again, he dismissed his troops "in such sort that most of the Commanders (most of them having relation to him) might be ready upon the least warning to re-unite in the same equipage as before."[8] In 1619, he complained that he had not been adequately compensated for the great costs he had assumed in raising troops for Louis: "Since your coming to the Crowne, having indebted my selfe above . . . 10,000 crowns for your service, for . . . which I pay interest at Paris, and having not since these two yeares received of your liberality any other gratification but the bare wages of a Colonel, at the rate of 10 moneths for a yeare."[9] Eventually, he would be repaid, in power if not in money, as Louis appointed Epernon governor of Guienne after he had recruited and commanded an army during the crisis of 1621–22.[10] At that time, when he was clearly trying to win the favor of his king, Epernon assembled forces in a mere six days for the Bearn campaign.[11] Again in 1630, as Imperial troops threatened Metz, Epernon, raising the necessary funds in Paris, mustered forces to serve the king.[12]

The practice of relying upon such private armies ended in the 1630s owing to the obvious fact that the same techniques that allowed nobles to raise troops for the king's purposes also allowed a rebellious aristocrat to create an army to oppose the king, as did Montmorency in 1632. The rebel forces of the Fronde were raised in the same manner as had been the private forces that once had supported the king, but these were not royal troops.[13] Their

---

[5] Girard, *History of the Life*, 228, 380.

[6] Berthold Zeller, *Louis XIII, Maire de Medicis, Chef du Conseil: États Généraux, Marriage du Roi, Le Prince de Condé* (Paris: 1898), 201; Jacques Humbert, *Le Maréchal de Créquy: Gendre de Lesdiguières (1573–1638)* (Paris: 1962), 69; Girard, *History of the Life*, 296.

[7] Louis XIII, *The French Kings Declaration against the Dukes of Vendosme and Mayenne* (London: 1617), 9. Girard, *History of the Life*, 302.

[8] Girard, *History of the Life*, 304.

[9] *Four Letters: One from the Duke of Bouillon to the French King* (Mylbourne: 1619), 7–8.

[10] Girard, *History of the Life*, 405.   [11] Girard, *History of the Life*, 380–81.

[12] Girard, *History of the Life*, 477.

[13] They were obviously rebels, though forces raised in 1650 styled themselves "The Army of the King, for the Deliverance of the Princes." Eveline Godley, *The Great Condé* (London: 1915), 299.

existence could only further resolve Louis XIV not to allow private armies in the future. Eventually, the rebel forces enjoyed Spanish backing and became something of a mercenary force serving Spain, albeit for its own purposes. In any case, substantial nonroyal French armies did not again march across France after 1653. Only the *émigré* forces assembled during the French Revolution would provide any kind of parallel, and their performance was more of a burlesque.

A partial exception to the demise of private armies may exist in the occasional creation of improvised forces by nobles who strove to put down local disturbances, and although these bands were often composed of no more than a few score, at times they were large. In 1658, La Tremoille assembled a force of 3,000 men in a day's time.[14] More modestly, the governor of Rennes employed a force of local nobles, numbering no more than 200, to restore order in Rennes in 1675, although in this case, the governor operated within his own legitimate authority.[15]

The only other great force that marched to the orders of the king, but was not really his own, was the army of Bernard of Saxe Weimar. Military entrepreneurship could be exercised on two distinctly different levels – that of the regimental officer and that of the army commander. The great innovation in the entrepreneurial system during the seventeenth century was the rise of the large-scale contractor, who offered an entire army to a prince – for a price. Wallenstein began this brief-lived practice by his 1625 contract with the emperor, but it died out by 1640.[16] Of the small number of men who played the part of "general contractor," the two greatest were Wallenstein and Bernard. The latter functioned as a regimental commander and army chief for the Swedes until their defeat at Nördlingen in 1634, after which his services and those of his entire army were purchased by Louis XIII in 1635. Bernard fought for France until his death in 1639, but he never threatened the power of Louis XIII in the way that Wallenstein challenged Emperor Ferdinand II. Bernard campaigned outside the borders of France and pursued no claims to Louis's authority. After Bernard died in 1639, the French hired his commanders and their units again en masse. Yet from this point on, it becomes legitimate to see this force as a French army, for although composed of foreign regiments, it was now led by French commanders, first Marshal Guébriant and then Marshal Turenne.

With the passing of private armies and the end of entrepreneurial forces, the Bourbon monarchy made a major step in military evolution. Privately raised and maintained armies represented a form of the aggregate contract

---

[14] Yves-Marie Bercé, *Histoire des Croquants: Etude des soulèvements populaires au XVII siècle dans le sud-ouest de la France*, 2 vols. (Paris: 1974), 1:120.

[15] Letter of 19 April 1675, Coëtlogon *fils* to Louvois, reproduced in Jean Lemoine, *La Révolte dite du Papier Timbré ou des Bonnets Rouges en Bretagne en 1675* (Paris: 1898), doc. 4. My graduate student, Roy McCullough, brought this case to my attention.

[16] Fritz Redlich, *The German Military Enterprizer and his Workforce, 13th to 17th Centuries, Vieteljahrschrift fur Sozial – und Virtschaftsgeschite*, Beihelft XLVII, 2 vols. (Wiesbaden: 1964), 1:227.

army, a military style left over from the sixteenth century, which now gave way to the state commission army, answerable only to royal authority. Constituting an important aspect of French military institutional change during the first half of the *grand siècle*, this evolution eroded not only the authority of private military commanders but also that of provincial governors as well, for often, as with Epernon, they were the same.

Territorial Command

Provincial governors and fortress governors exercised authority over geographical areas, and thus the troops in them, rather than over armies, at least after the 1630s. As such, it is fair to lump the two offices under the general category of territorial command. The office of provincial governors dated back to the Middle Ages; their authority included entire provinces and did not exactly coincide with the *généralités* administered by the *intendants*. During certain epochs of French history, governors had been dangerous rivals to royal power; at no time was this more the case than during the Wars of Religion. Their independence continued into the seventeenth century, as when Lesdiguières, governor of Dauphiné, intervened with troops on his own initiative in Italy in 1616. This autonomy included direct military command over troops in a governor's province, or troops he might raise there. Louis XIII relied on their independent commands. Faced with a rebellion in 1617, he issued a proclamation inviting "all Governors and Lieutenants General of our Provinces, Captaines, Chiefes, and Leaders of our Forces, to set upon them [the rebel Princes]."[17] But this kind of autonomous military command faded under Louis XIV. By the 1690s, a governor held certain authority over troops garrisoned in, passing through, or being raised in his province, but that authority was limited.[18] While all troops reported to the governor, he could neither inspect nor maneuver them. Yet the governor could shift garrisons of troops. Moreover, in emergencies, he could order regular troops to intervene, and he could call out the *milices* and the *ban*. Governors were chosen among princes, great nobles, marshals, and lieutenant generals – in short, men of prestige and/or military experience. They were figures at court or commanders attached to the army so did not reside permanently in their provinces. In the absence of a governor, the lieutenant general of the province assumed authority. The latter usually was a general officer in the army; however, the title of provincial lieutenant general was a separate rank referring to his regional post, not to the army.

Commanders of French fortresses also went by the title of governor. If the fortress qualified as a *grande place forte*, his authority extended to the citadel, town, and outlying posts, but if it was only a *place ordinaire*, his

---

[17] Louis XIII, *The French Kings Declaration*, 9.
[18] Victor Belhomme, *L'armée française en 1690* (Paris: 1895), 143–44.

power did not extend beyond the walls of the fortress.[19] By the 1690s, these governors came from the ranks of the king's lieutenant generals or *maréchaux de camp*, and as with provincial governors, fortress governors were often absentee, as in the case of the peripatetic Vauban, who was governor of Lille. A *grande place* boasted, in addition to its governor, a *commandant des troupes*, a *lieutenant du roi*, and a major, the last being the administrative officer of the fortress who was assisted by two or three aides. This staff was often composed of soldiers who for one reason or another were no longer suited to warfare on campaign; in fact, a post on a fortress staff could serve as a form of military retirement.[20]

During the first half of the *grand siècle*, fortress governors enjoyed a great deal of authority. They maintained their own troops by extracting contributions from surrounding areas, even in France. Although the government frowned on this practice, circa 1650, the monarchy finally had to accept it, since the state could not support garrisons from its own revenues. As forces raised and maintained by their own commanders, garrisons supposedly loyal to the king became little better than private armies. Louis XIV accused fortress governors of becoming "absolute in their fortresses, in the disposition of the contributions that they raised and in the liberty they took in creating their own garrison troops."[21] Accordingly, after 1659, Louis moved to reassert the royal authority and curtail the autonomy of fortress governors.

On the whole, just as in the case of those grandees who once raised their own private armies, the military independence of governors belonged to an earlier age. Territorial commanders continued to exist, but active military leadership really shifted to general officers commanding armies in the field.

Army Command

Louis XIV centralized actual wartime military command in the hands of the marshals and generals who answered directly to the king. At the same time that these general officers gained a monopoly of field command, they also accepted, or were forced to accept, higher standards of obedience to the will of the king, but this process of rationalization and subordination would take some time. At least into the 1670s, rules of hierarchy and responsibility were still in flux, and at times, it seemed that rules were made to be broken. Among other confusions, no absolute principles defined the precise nature of each rank and each command. Commenting on the first half of the seventeenth century, the historian Aumale stated that "These general officers had

---

[19] Belhomme, *L'armée française en 1690*, 144.

[20] See, for example, the case of a captain who wished to retire at age sixty and hoped to sell his company in order to buy the place of a major. Albert Babeau, *La vie militaire sous l'ancien regime: Les soldats*, 2 vols. (Paris: 1890), 2:184.

[21] Louis XIV, *Mémoires*, 2:401–2.

no fixed duties and not even a clearly defined grade."[22] Command could be fluid, improvised, and temporary.

This being said, the sphere of general officers was one in which the monarchy could eventually assert its will because the vulnerable issue of state finance was not involved. In contrast to so many offices of the *ancien régime*, high command remained free from venality. At this level, rank was not for sale; the highest grade with a price tag was that of colonel.

Among general officers, brigadiers occupied the lowest rung on the command ladder.[23] In one sense, a brigadier was not actually a general officer, since he continued in rank as colonel or lieutenant colonel while exercising authority as brigadier, which meant that if he owned a regiment, a brigadier retained that property. In contrast, Louis XIV commanded other general officers to sell their regiments.[24] In battle, they operated as subcommanders under the direction of a lieutenant general. Brigadiers arrived relatively late on the scene; the first appointment of a cavalry brigadier came in 1657, although this rank was not regularized until 1667. The first brigadier of infantry received his commission in 1668, and the dragoons followed in 1672. Promotion to brigadier became a necessary step on the ladder to higher rank; only princes of the blood and occasional foreigners could reach the most exalted ranks without serving for a time in this grade. In 1690, the French Army of Germany contained six brigadiers of infantry, one of *gendarmes*, eight of cavalry, and two of dragoons.[25]

The next step up the ladder, the *maréchaux de camp,* poses a particularly confusing problem for those trying to find equivalent modern ranks for traditional French grades.[26] First, this *maréchal de camp* should not be confused with the supreme rank of marshal of France. Second, most authorities translate *maréchal de camp* as major general, since it stood directly below the rank of lieutenant general; however, a *maréchal de camp* did not usually hold an independent command as does today's major general, who leads a division in the U.S. Army, for example. In fact, the rank was only honorific unless the *maréchal de camp* held a commission for duties with a particular army at a particular time. To make matters even more confused, about 1690, each field army contained an officer with staff and training duties who went by the title of major general of infantry, but he seems to have been more a

---

[22] Aumale in Godley, *The Great Condé,* 41.

[23] Concerning brigadiers, see Louis André, *Michel Le Tellier et l'organisation de l'armée monarchique* (Paris: 1906), 141–46; Louis André, *Michel Le Tellier et Louvois* (Paris: 1942), 318–19; Camille Rousset, *Histoire de Louvois,* 4 vols. (Paris: 1862–64), 1:231–32; Corvisier, *Louvois,* 183; André Corvisier, "Les généraux de Louis XIV et leur origine sociale," *XVIIe siècle,* nos. 42–43 (1956). François Sicard, *Histoire des institutions militaires des français,* 4 vols. (Paris: 1834), 1:251–54, seems to get the dates wrong. It is important to distinguish between this brigadier and the noncommissioned cavalry rank that went by the same name.

[24] Susane, *Infanterie,* 211.   [25] Belhomme, *L'armée française en 1690,* 170.

[26] Concerning *maréchaux de camp,* see Sicard, *Histoire des institutions militaires,* 1:247–51; Belhomme, *L'armée française en 1690,* 170; André, *Le Tellier,* 133–34; and Corvisier, "Les généraux."

supreme major than an actual general.[27] The rank of *maréchal de camp* dates from the sixteenth century. During the seventeenth century, a *maréchal de camp* acted as adjunct to a lieutenant general. Along with holding temporary commands under the authority of the lieutenant general, the *maréchal* also performed as chief of staff, supervising such mundane tasks as establishing camps, regulating routes of march, and providing convoy security. The creation of brigadiers eroded the troop command functions of the *maréchal de camp*, since these could be exercised by a brigadier. Not all aspirants to lieutenant general served as *maréchal de camp*. While *maréchaux de camp* were numerous during the minority of Louis XIV, by 1669 only five remained. Their numbers increased again later in the personal reign; in 1690, the Army of Germany alone contained eight.

A rank of *maréchal de bataille* also existed, but after 1647, it was restricted to a single individual. Technically, this officer had charge of arranging troops for battle. The last holder of this rare office was Fougerais, who came to it in 1662. After him, the office seems to have died out.[28] A similar office of *sergeant de bataille* withered away somewhat earlier, since its functions duplicated those of colonels and other general officers.[29]

Further up the hierarchy stood the lieutenant general, a rank that again brings some confusion because the term had two meanings. The first was the actual rank of lieutenant general, above a *maréchal de camp* and below a marshal. The second and less public usage, was the official title of an army commander, whether that individual bore the actual rank of lieutenant general or marshal. Thus, when Marshal Turenne received his command in December 1643, his commission awarded him "the power of lieutenant general of the Army of Germany."[30] This second sense of the term recognized an army commander as an officer who took the place of the king, who was literally the king's lieutenant.

The modern rank of lieutenant general per se appeared in 1621 among French forces, although it may have had more ancient antecedents.[31] A lieutenant general could command an entire field army as did the duke de Luxembourg in 1672–73; but independent command of large forces more usually fell to marshals or princes. More commonly, lieutenant generals exercised major subcommands under the direction of an army commander; a lieutenant general might lead the first or second line in battle or direct one wing or the other. In addition, lieutenant generals with an army rotated daily command; they were, so to speak, officers of the day for the entire army, and as such were in charge of a wide range of duties, including foraging. The rank of lieutenant general was, like that of *maréchal de camp*, honorific; unless the

---

[27] Belhomme, *L'armée française en 1690*, 170–71.   [28] See André, *Le Tellier*, 134–37.

[29] See André, *Le Tellier*, 138–41.   [30] BN, f. fr. 4169, fols. 163–65, in André, *Le Tellier*, 122.

[31] Concerning lieutenant generals, see Sicard, *Histoire des institutions militaires*, 1:239–46; Belhomme, *L'armée française en 1690*, 169; André, *Le Tellier*, 127–33; Corvisier, "Les généraux." Again, Sicard makes certain errors (e.g., stating that the lieutenant general was not created until 1638).

general had a specific royal commission allotting him a command, he in fact commanded nothing. In 1690, the Army of Germany contained ten lieutenant generals.

Maréchaux, or marshals, stood at the peak of the command structure; only princes of the blood and the king himself outranked a marshal on the field of battle. Since marshals enjoyed such exalted status, it is not surprising that their number remained small. According to André Corvisier, the period 1661–1715 brought 567 recorded promotions to *maréchal de camp*, 307 to lieutenant general, but only 36 to marshal.[32] As a rule, a marshal commanded an entire field army; however, more than one marshal could be present in the same army. In one case, that of Vauban, a marshal performed as a specialist simply in siege warfare rather than in field warfare. But his was a very special case, and Vauban's promotion to marshal in 1703 came at the very end of his career, primarily as a recognition of his past contributions. Alone among all French general officers, the marshals received their pay at all times, war or peace, active or inactive, and were addressed as *cousins du roi*.

On occasion, a marshal might technically serve under one of the royal princes, and in such cases, it is necessary to distinguish between actual and symbolic command. Members of the royal family, most notably the Sun King himself, went to the front. The king could hardly be called a symbolic commander, since he held the full authority of the state; however, if the king's brother, sons, or grandsons marched at the head of an army, they were there primarily to learn about war and to provide whatever morale boost their presence might bring with it. The brother of Louis XIII, Gaston d'Orléans, technically exerted command over rebel forces in Paris during the battle of faubourg Saint-Antoine but did not so much lead as simply react to circumstances and to the powerful personality of his daughter, who played a great role that day. Philippe d'Orléans, brother to Louis XIV, also journeyed to the front but had little vocation for war. Louis also sent first his son, the dauphin, and later his grandson, the duke of Burgundy, to lead forces. The dauphin summed up his actual authority in a letter written to his father in 1688: "All goes well between Vauban and myself, because I do whatever he wants."[33] When the dauphin appeared at the head of an army in 1690, not only was Marshal de Lorge at his right hand, but three advisors also arrived with the prince: Chamlay, Saint-Pouenges, and Béringhen.[34] This resulted in command by committee, an unhappy group torn by disagreements.

As already explained, even without the presence of the king's relatives, field command was split. The commanding general officer made strictly military and combat decisions, but administrative control rested in the hands

---

[32] Corvisier, "Les généraux," 29. His listings come from Pinard, *Chronologie historique militaire*, 8 vols. (Paris: 1760–66), a work that contains some 3,500 biographies of French officers.

[33] Philippe, marquis de Dangeau, *Journal du marquis de Dangeau*, Feuillet de Conches, ed., 19 vols. (Paris: 1854–60), 2:190–91, 17 October 1688.

[34] Rousset, *Louvois*, 4:390–93.

of an army *intendant* and his agents. This meant that much of what qualifies as staff duty performed by uniformed personnel in present-day armies was actually the responsibility of civilians during the *grand siècle*. This arrangement could run smoothly, but not always. That crusty veteran, Villars, objected to civilian interference: "The majority of times the *intendant* that one is given . . . can cause projects to abort on a hundred occasions. How many times has one seen the *intendant*, principally when the general is not in favor with the minister of war, be the instrument of the general's ruin by coming up short in the thousand things that depend on the *intendant*."[35] Clearly, Villars regarded the *intendant* as a rival, not as a partner. He suggested replacing the *intendant* by *commissaires ordonnateurs* responsible only to the commanding general.

In any case, since so much fell to the *intendant*, the general's personal staff had only limited duties, which Villars described as simply "to dispose marches and make camps."[36] A *maréchal de camp* normally operated as chief of staff, and a general staff in the nineteenth-century sense did not exist.

The Monarch

Lastly, the high command cannot be discussed without reference to the king and his ministers. A monarch set strategy, selected personnel, and exerted direct command over field armies when he took to the field – and kings did take to the field. If neither Louis XIII or Louis XIV played the role of the dashing cavalry captain as had Henri IV, the Louises were soldiers nonetheless. Louis XIII served with his troops around La Rochelle in 1627–28 and, overriding the objections of Richelieu, set strategy and led his troops during the Corbie year of 1636. Puységur, a noted seventeenth-century commentator, assessed the military abilities of Louis XIII: "It could be said that he is an able man, knowledgeable in that profession, a man who could pass for a master of it."[37]

Louis XIV regarded himself a soldier as well. From the age of twelve, Louis spent a great deal of time with his troops. During the Dutch War alone, he was in the field 647 days, the high point being 1673 when he was at the front 166 days. Only advancing years forced him to forgo such activity in 1693, at age fifty-five.[38] During the 1660s, he apprenticed to the greatest commander of the day, Turenne, for the young king could not have learned field command from Le Tellier or Louvois. Turenne exerted such authority that his biographer, Jean Bérenger, argues that he had essentially become the de facto minister of war. His influence over Louis peaked in 1667.[39] Louis

---

[35] BN, f. fr. 6257, Claude Louis Hector Villars, "Traité de la guerre de campagne," 27–28.
[36] BN, f. fr. 6257, Villars, "Traité," 37.
[37] Puységur in Charles Romain, *Louis XIII, un grand Roi malconnu* (Paris: 1934), 67.
[38] Philippe Contamine, ed., *Histoire militaire de la France*, vol. 1 (Paris: 1992), 384–85.
[39] Jean Bérenger, *Turenne* (Paris: 1987), 384.

never commanded a battle in the open field, though he came close to doing so at Heurtebise in 1676. There his advisors, including several marshals, counseled against it.[40] With the death of Turenne only the year before, and with memories of the regency and civil war still haunting men's minds, it seemed foolish to risk the life of the king. As the duke of Luxembourg commented shortly after the event, battles were not "the *métier* of kings."[41] This statement itself is telling; the monarch was no longer expected to play the role of warrior-king. But if battles were not Louis's *métier*, sieges certainly were. He was present for many of those directed by Vauban, who enjoyed a special credit with the king.

First ministers also significantly influenced the conduct of war. Richelieu had trained to be a soldier as a youth and seemed to feel at home in armor. Although his influence over Louis XIII was great, Louis did not abdicate his military judgment to the cardinal. And when the king felt strongly about a course of action, he overruled Richelieu, as the monarch did in 1636, opting to defend Paris rather than flee. Mazarin's position was both stronger and weaker than that of Richelieu. As first minister in a regency government, he had no independent monarch to contend with; Louis XIV, after all, was only age five in 1643. However, Mazarin was a foreigner and no soldier; moreover, from 1648 to 1653, the Fronde challenged his authority.

The king's role as head of the high command brought together two primary functions of the monarch. First, traditionally the monarch saw war as his particular milieu. Neither Louis XIII nor a mature Louis XIV deferred his authority or judgment to some other commander. Second, if nothing else, it was the king's responsibility alone to choose the men who would run both the government and the army. As Louis XIV counseled his son, "The principal function of the monarch is to assign each individual the post in which he can be useful to the public. We know well that we cannot do everything; but we ought to put things in order so that all may be well done, and that order depends principally on the choice of those whom we employ."[42] The king regarded his authority over policy and personnel as supreme and jealously guarded it.

THE STRUGGLE BETWEEN COMMAND INDEPENDENCE AND ROYAL AUTHORITY

For much of the seventeenth century, French monarchs and ministers fought to assert their authority over the independent French military commanders. If not opposed by an actively assertive monarchy, military and civil officials

---

[40] Concerning the debate over Heurtebise, the battle that never happened, see John B. Wolf, *Louis XIV* (New York: 1968), 249–53.

[41] AG, A^{1}499, #41, in Wolf, *Louis XIV*, 252.

[42] Louis XIV, *Mémoires de Louis XIV*, Charles Dreyss, ed., 2 vols. (Paris: 1860), 2:341.

tended to claim as private possessions the public powers delegated to them by the state and to entrench themselves in office. The struggles would seem amusing if they were not so deadly serious. Eventually, Louis XIV and Louvois effectively asserted royal authority and thus put a fundamentally modern stamp on the relationship between the state and the army high command, but that conflict lasted into the 1670s.

Disobedience among the high command during the *grand siècle* was more complicated and more basic than the modern case of a Guderian or a Patton who turned a blind eye to, or "stretched," an order because they saw a better way to achieve a military goal. Good generals must interpret directives to command effectively, since they know the immediate situation better than do leaders more removed from the scene. Napoleon expected his generals to act on their own initiative when situations altered. But during the *grand siècle*, a commander who disregarded his orders was as likely to be moved by a sense that he must challenge the authority or prestige of the individual who had issued those orders as by a conviction that the orders prescribed a wrong course of action. Lieutenant generals and marshals came largely from the upper reaches of the French aristocracy, a class jealous of its own privileges and whose more exalted members regarded themselves as partners in the royal authority. Such representatives of *les grands* often considered that they had as much right as anyone to decide what was best, particularly in war. Certainly they believed that they were superior to a war minister of low family, who had never led troops in battle. By acting independently, they asserted their rank or status as their *gloire* demanded.

The task of subduing haughty and potentially rebellious commanders to the royal will – and to the civil agents of that sovereignty – took time and energy. Richelieu tried. The terrorist tactics he used in his struggle to subdue *les grands* at court, including much-publicized executions, were expected to cow the military as well as civil society.[43] Mazarin also tried to reign in French commanders. He tolerated financial corruption, since his own hands were hardly clean, but he did what he could to limit the political power of his generals. Yet the pressures of war, the entrenched power of *les grands*, and, finally, the crisis of the Fronde frustrated these great first ministers. The challenge eventually fell to Louis XIV, who bridled his generals as had no French monarch before him. While a too hasty glance at the *grand siècle* might lead some to conclude that the problems of independent and contentious commanders ceased at the conclusion of the war with Spain, or at least with the coming of Louis's personal reign in 1661, the truth is that they remained a serious issue at least through the mid-1670s. Afterward, if Louis

---

[43] "The punishments of Marillac and of the duke de Montmorency have, in an instant, put to their duty *les grands* of this kingdom, and I dare to assure that those of offices and of soldiers maintain the entire armies in discipline." Richelieu, *Testament politique*, ed. Louis André (Paris: 1947), 389–90. See comments by David Parrott, "The Administration of the French Army During the Ministry of Cardinal Richelieu," Ph.D. dissertation, Oxford, 1985, 327.

did not often overtly employ his veto over his marshals often, he did not have to, because they had been trained to comply.[44]

Louis XIV had to contend with provincial governors, fortress governors, lieutenant generals, and marshals. Provincial governors posed an obvious threat because of the political dimensions of their authority. As mentioned earlier, in 1616 Lesdiguières responded to a Spanish attack on Piedmont by marching his troops off to the aid of the Piedmontese as he saw fit.[45] He had, as it were, declared war on his own. His might have been a special case, but it still demonstrated the potential of the office. During the Fronde, great nobles, such as Condé, used their power and patronage as governors to bring provinces into the rebel camp. It comes as little surprise that when Condé returned to grace after the Peace of the Pyrenees, he was stripped of certain governorships. Restricting the authority of provincial governors would not be so much a military act, however, as a political development that comprised part of Louis XIV's rapprochement with the great nobles after the Fronde.

During the confusion of the war with Spain, the more constant and perhaps the more dangerous threat came from fortress governors. Louis complained that "There is not a single governor who has not attributed to himself unlawful rights."[46] After the death of Mazarin, Louis did not wait long to take action against his governors. He boasted that "I began to moderate the excessive authority that the governors of frontier cities had possessed for a long time; they had so lost the respect that they owed to royal authority that they had imposed the same exactions on my subjects as upon my enemies."[47] And thus he "resolved to deny them both rights, and day by day to have troops that depended only on me enter all the important towns" and thus reassert "the royal authority."[48] Fundamental to Louis's efforts to impose compliance on his governors was his decision to limit their terms in 1662: "It was also this year, that continuing in the design to diminish the authority of the governors of fortresses and provinces, I resolved to appoint any vacant governorship for a period of only three years, reserving to myself alone the power to prolong this term by new provisions when I found it appropriate."[49] Then a circular of 1663 forbade fortress governors on the frontier to "cause troops to leave citadels or chateaux without the express order of the King."[50] Even in times of civil disturbance these governors could no longer act on their own authority. This represented quite a change from the freewheeling days before 1659.

[44] Wolf, *Louis XIV*, 531.   [45] Contamine, *Histoire militaire*, 1:339.
[46] Louis XIV, *Mémoires*, 2:405.   [47] Louis XIV, *Mémoires*, 2:401–2.
[48] Louis XIV, *Mémoires*, 2:402.
[49] Mémoire of 1662 in Louis XIV, *Oeuvres de Louis XIV*, Philippe Grimoard and Grouvelle, eds., 6 vols. (Paris: 1806), 1:197. André Corvisier, *Louvois* (Paris: 1983), 116.
[50] Letter of 22 July 1703, from the minister of war to Broglie explaining 1663 circular Languedoc in Jean-Joseph Vaissète, *Histoire générale du Languedoc*, 15 vols. (Toulouse: 1874–92), vol. 14, col. 1561–64.

While Louis's efforts did not end all his problems with fortress governors, when abuses came to his attention, he and Louvois struck them down. In 1673, the governor and major of the fortress of Belle-Isle took the side of a captain who arrested a sergeant for denouncing a *passe volant,* and thus compromising the captain. This could not be tolerated. Louvois commanded that the captain be broken and that the major be deprived of all wages for three months and the governor for one month.[51]

The lieutenant generals also vied for unhampered command over their troops. Louis André considered these officers the *"enfants terribles* of the French army."[52] In August 1650, frustrated by his inability to stir French generals into action, Le Tellier complained: "There is not a lieutenant general who does not . . . consider his army as his own domain."[53] Later that year, now drawing a parallel with a government without a king, Le Tellier lamented: "In a word, the army has become a republic composed of as many cantons or provinces as there are lieutenant generals."[54] They demanded not only authority but honor. Plessis-Bellière went so far as to refuse to lead troops in Catalonia during 1652 unless he were named a marshal.[55]

Marshals also asserted what they believed to be their prerogatives. During the 1640s, the Army of Germany, which eventually came under the command of Turenne, operated fairly independently of Paris authority.[56] In 1646, Turenne, three years a marshal, had no intention of following orders from court, since he believed his strategy was correct, and he only maintained the appearances of obedience.[57] It should be borne in mind that Turenne was not only a marshal but was also the son of a marshal and a member of the illustrious family la Tour d'Auvergne, which won the privilege of receiving the honors due a foreign prince at the French court. Both Turenne and Condé had rebelled against central authority during the Fronde. At different times, both led armies against Mazarin, all the time attesting their loyalty to the young Louis XIV. In fact, all five of Louis's greatest marshals, Turenne, Condé, Luxembourg, Vauban, and even Villars, were associated with the Fronde in some form or another.[58] After the end of the Fronde, Condé went so far as to serve as a Spanish general during 1653–59 rather than reconcile himself to Mazarin. The independence of French marshals and princes connoted rebellion, and Louis could hardly tolerate this.

---

[51] Corvisier, *Louvois,* 187.   [52] André, *Le Tellier,* 127.

[53] BN, f. fr. 4210, fols 43r, 44r–44v., 9 August 1650, Le Tellier to Mazarin, in André, *Le Tellier,* 116–17. It is not entirely clear which of the two meanings of the term *lieutenant general* Le Tellier meant here.

[54] BN, f. fr., 4206, fol 362 r., 16 October 1650, LeTellier to Mazarin, in André, *Le Tellier,* 117.

[55] André, *Le Tellier,* 128.   [56] Bérenger, *Turenne,* 194.   [57] Bérenger, *Turenne,* 232.

[58] Turenne had been a Frondeur in 1648–51; Condé was both a Frondeur and then a Spanish general in 1650–59; Luxembourg was a companion of Condé throughout Condé's rebellion; Vauban was a young protégé of Condé who fought in the Frondeur army until converted by Mazarin in 1653; and Villars, though born in 1653, was the son of a Frondeur.

The high birth of French general officers, especially during the first half of the *grand siècle*, and their cherished independence, produced one particularly seventeenth-century form of insubordination – the conflict over precedence among lieutenant generals and among marshals. Louis XIV was well aware of the rivalry between his commanders.

There is nothing that heats up spirits so powerfully as does jealousy of superiority. The pretensions of the commanders necessarily engages the men who are under their authority; each of the soldiers believes that it is a question of his own interest; all are animated with envy, and in a single camp there form two enemy armies, each forgetting in a moment the service of their prince and the safety of their county.[59]

Such rivalry might seem silly, except that it stymied active operations and caused needless losses. Vauban, always careful when it came to protecting the lives of French soldiers, was anything but amused: "The rivalry between general officers often makes them expose the soldiers inappropriately, demanding that these troops do more than is really possible and not caring if they cause a hundred men to die in order to advance four paces more than their comrades."[60]

Rivalry between commanders required that, when more than one officer of equally high rank was present in an army, they rotate command, as in 1635, when marshals Châtillon and Brézé feuded so relentlessly that this expedient of rotation, or *roulement*, was adopted.[61] When Le Tellier first took over as secretary of state for war, he continued the policies followed under Richelieu and awarded the command of armies to two, or even three, commanders. The rationale for such multiple commissions seemed to be more political than military, since men of power needed to be courted and supplicated by the grants of command.[62] Louis André states that with the declaration of the king's majority, in 1651, Le Tellier felt free to give command to a single general officer. Well he might, and this may have been the general rule, but cases of dual command still occurred into the 1670s.[63]

Roulement persisted for some time as the usual method of reconciliation. Mazarin directed Le Tellier that if more than one lieutenant general served with one army, they must rotate "by day as do the *maréchaux de camp*."[64] Here the term "lieutenant general" would seem to be the general sense of the king's lieutenant commanding an army. This system was particularly troublesome at the siege of Sainte-Menehould in 1653, an operation under the direction of three lieutenant generals, Castelnau-Mauvissière, Navailles, and Huxelles. The conflicts between them were so intense, each contravening the

---

[59] Louis XIV, *Mémoires*, 2:123–24, supplement to memoirs of 1666.
[60] Vauban in *Traité de l'attaque*, in Michel Parent and Jacques Verroust, *Vauban* (Paris: 1971), 106.
[61] Parrott, "The Administration of the French Army," 27.
[62] André, *Le Tellier*, 121–22.   [63] André, *Le Tellier*, 122.
[64] Mazarin to Le Tellier, 24 September 1650, in André, *Le Tellier*, 131.

other's orders, that Le Tellier could only stem it by placing Marshal du Plessis-Praslain over them all.[65]

Le Tellier wished to substitute seniority in grade for *roulement*. Directives of 1655 still instructed lieutenant generals to draw lots to determine the order in which they would rotate command; however, an important innovation came in 1656, when the king appointed the most senior among the lieutenant generals to function as supreme army commander when a commander in chief was absent.[66] Therefore, a single field army would always be directed by a single commander, even if the lieutenant generals continued to rotate in subsidiary commands, such as general of the day. Thus, Louis instructed Lieutenant General d'Estrades to take sole command of the army in Spain when the prince de Conti and the duke de Candalle were not present.[67]

Roulement for subsidiary commands enjoyed a long life. As late as 1674, when Condé commanded in the Netherlands, Louvois recognized that if Condé pulled all his forces together, multiple lieutenant generals would collide over limited commands. So Louvois decreed *roulement*, as usual, but Luxembourg, still a lieutenant general in 1674, objected vehemently in a letter of fifteen pages:

> However, here is what your lack of regard for me has reduced me to. I am supposed to remain in this army and rotate with Monsieur de Fourilles if I am not detached from it, seeing that Monsieur de Navailles will not rotate with anyone; or better I ought to command a small detached corps, which is not a very agreeable post . . . ; and in certain circumstances, I ought to join de Rochefort and act conjointly with him, a man who is nothing but a colonel when I am a lieutenant general. If I were in his place and he in mine, my modesty would make me loath to find myself on an equal footing with a man whom I have always obeyed.[68]

To his complaints, which went on and on, Louvois replied, "As long as one remains a lieutenant general, it is necessary to rotate with all those who attain the same rank."[69] Luxembourg responded to Louvois's relatively mild rebuke by appealing to the king. This brazenly awkward attempt to circumvent Louvois helps to explain the enmity that later rebounded against Luxembourg.

Feuds between marshals proved even more of an embarrassment than those between lieutenant generals. During the *grand siècle*, the kings of France were always served by many marshals. Their numbers varied – fourteen in 1630, eleven in 1638, fifteen in 1645, sixteen in 1651, fourteen in 1663, thirteen in 1665, eleven in 1674, ten in 1695, and nineteen in 1710.[70] The rise in the

---

[65] André, *Le Tellier*, 129–31.   [66] André, *Le Tellier*, 131.

[67] BN, f. fr. 4191, fols. 174–75, 24 May 1656, in André, *Le Tellier*, 131–32.

[68] AG, A¹399, 5 July 1674, in Rousset, *Louvois*, 2:31–32.

[69] AG, A¹369, 9 July 1674, in Rousset, *Louvois*, 2:33.

[70] See lists of marshals, Sicard, *Histoire des institutions militaires*, 1:187–90; and Daniel, *Histoire de la milice*, in André, *Le Tellier*, 122. Bérenger states that after the death of Lesdiguières in 1638, Louis XIII multiplied the number of marshals. Bérenger, *Turenne*, 193. But he is mistaken here: In 1630, fourteen marshals were alive; in 1638, there were eleven, and in 1645, there were fifteen. The numbers do not seem to have varied greatly.

number of marshals during Mazarin's administration was due to his using this rank as a political tool, as a reward or lure.[71] The number of marshals sank to its lowest point early in the Nine Years' War; in 1690, only six marshals remained alive. Multiple marshals implied conflicts between them. Princes of the blood also commanded armies without need of a marshal's baton; however, the only individual of consequence in this category was the prince de Condé, actively in command of royal French armies during 1643–50 and 1667–75.

Marshals could be fiercely independent. Gassion, who rose to the marshalate at age thirty-four in 1643, paid little if any attention to orders from court and ridiculed letters that he received from Mazarin.[72] When teamed with another marshal, Gassion feuded with his colleague, even to the point of drawing his sword, as he did against La Meilleraye at Gravelines in 1644. More than once, members of the royal family, including the queen and Gaston d'Orléans, had to intervene to reestablish a working relationship between Gassion and his fellow marshals. Gassion may have been the hardest case of aggressive assertion among the marshals, but his behavior was not unique. D'Erlach defended his prerogatives with such energy that he was close to impossible to work with. Mazarin had to caution Turenne to be careful in his dealings with the cantankerous d'Erlach in 1648 in order to assure any kind of harmony.[73]

Quarrels between rival marshals attempting to direct the same campaign compromised operations, since they could not agree on a course of action. Not surprisingly, Gassion engaged in a controversy of this kind in 1647. Even Turenne took part in such a dispute; the inability of that marshal and La Ferté to agree on a course of action in 1656 allowed Condé to relieve the siege of Valenciennes. When these two commanded again at Gravelines in 1658, Mazarin stayed at the front to mediate between them. Louis André concludes, "When two marshals were in the same army, disunion was inevitable: if an exception occurred, everyone cried miracle."[74]

Louis XIV tried to end the bickering between his marshals by raising Turenne to a preeminent position at a time when Turenne had established his superiority over the other marshals, demonstrated his loyalty to Louis XIV, and performed invaluable services to the crown. In 1660, Louis elevated Turenne to the title of *maréchal général des camps et armées du roi*, a dignity that Turenne held until his death in 1675.[75] As a weapon against the contentions of the other marshals, Turenne was a two-edged sword, since he saw himself as a rival of Louvois. The more prestige gained by Turenne, the more he could use that lofty position to snipe at the war minister, whom the marshal regarded as an upstart.[76]

---

[71] André, *Le Tellier*, 123.
[72] André, *Le Tellier*, 124–25, tells the surprising story of the difficult, though talented, Gassion.
[73] André, *Le Tellier*, 125.   [74] André, *Le Tellier*, 126.
[75] On the rank of marshal general, see André, *Le Tellier*, 119–20 and Bérenger, *Turenne*, 375.
[76] Turenne in Primi Visconti, *Mémoires sur la cour de Louis XIV, 1673–1681*, Jean-François Solnon, ed. (Paris: 1988), 63.

However, Turenne's elevation did not end the disputes between marshals. In 1672, three marshals refused to accept his authority over them.[77] Louis had set up a clear chain of command for leadership in the field at the start of the war; the king himself stood at the head, then his brother, next the prince de Condé, followed by Turenne. Marshals Bellefonds, Créqui, and Humières balked and were removed from command because of their obstinacy. Louis acted decisively, since, he believed, "it would be . . . too much of a limitation on the authority of a prince; he can divide his power as it please him, and . . . according to the needs of the state . . . not according to the pretensions of his officers."[78] When the three sought to be reinstated, Louis demanded that they appear with Turenne's army and serve for at least two weeks as mere lieutenant generals under Turenne. Bellefonds was the last to reconcile. Saint-Simon testified that while Turenne had been appointed marshal general to end disputes between the marshals, this solution only worked with the exile of Bellefonds, Humières, and Créqui.[79] In fact, not even the fate of these three ended the matter.

Bellefonds would again oppose the king's orders, in an act worthy of Gassion. When the widening scope of the Dutch War required that the French relinquish their conquests in the Dutch Netherlands, Louis ordered Bellefonds to withdraw. Instead of complying, Bellefonds argued that the king's advisors misunderstood the situation.[80] Louis showed great forbearance toward Bellefonds, always an outspoken man, but one of honor and dignity. Still, his opposition could not be permitted, and after Bellefonds submitted to the royal will and withdrew his forces, he retired to his estates. There is great irony in the fact that at the beginning of this affair, Bellefonds himself complained of unruly generals: "It is a hard thing that it is often necessary to change or alter projects because the commanders do not know how to get along among themselves."[81]

The death of Turenne on 27 July 1675 brought things to a head. Through Turenne, Louis and Louvois attempted to solve the problems caused by disputed precedence by appealing to the clear preeminence of a great and highborn marshal, but Louvois must have recognized for some time the need to adopt an institutional solution that did not rest solely upon the prestige of a great personality. On 31 July the king promulgated a new ordinance "giving command to the most senior of the officers of equal rank, and suppressing the old practice of *roulement*."[82] In a case when more than one marshal contended for command, the marshal who had first been promoted to the rank of lieutenant general would hold the command. This

[77] Concerning this crisis, see Rousset, *Louvois*, 1:348–52.

[78] AN, K 119, fol. 20, in Wolf, *Louis XIV*, 220.

[79] Saint-Simon, *Mémoires*. A. de Boislisle, ed. 42 vols. (Paris: 1879–1930), 1:132–33.

[80] Concerning the Bellefonds affair in 1674, see Rousset, *Louvois*, 2:6–17.

[81] AG, A^{1}396, 10 February 1674, Bellefonds to Louvois, in Rousset, *Louvois*, 2:7.

[82] Ordinance in Rousset, *Louvois*, 2:166. The ordinance is alternatively dated as 31 July or 1 August.

victory of seniority goes by the name of *ordre de tableau*, and it established time in grade as the deciding factor in promotions and disputed command.

To a large degree, the *ordre de tableau* simply extended the royal decision of 1656 that made seniority the criterion for deciding army command among contending lieutenant generals.[83] Such a decision was necessary because the marshalate had to be purged of the operational consequences of differences in social prestige. The *ordre* negated disputes over birth and status at a time when not all lieutenant generals and marshals came from the uppermost social strata, as they had earlier in the century.[84] For the good of the army, military rank had to act independently of social rank. The *ordre de tableau* replaced older standards based on birth with newer ones based on professional competence as defined by seniority.

The *ordre* was not universally greeted with approval. Those at the top of society saw it as a threat. The duke de Saint-Simon repeatedly condemned it. "Monsieur Louvois, in order to be completely the master, put into the king's head [the idea of] the *ordre de tableau* and promotions [by seniority], which made everyone equal, rendered work useless in all promotions, which rested only on seniority always with rare exceptions for those who Monsieur Louvois had reason to push."[85] For Saint-Simon, courtier and snob, the *ordre* left promotion "entirely in the hands of the king, or much more in those of his minister."[86]

The *ordre de tableau* was not the only means employed by the Sun King to bring his generals into orbit. More subtle was the king's control over lesser appointments, previously dependent on his generals. During the war with Spain, France's leading generals regarded such patronage as their right. When Mazarin installed his own man as governor of Ypres after Condé had taken the city and put forward his own friend as a candidate, a disgruntled Condé sniped, "I see that I am never to go through a campaign without some such mortification; and it is hard treatment to serve as I have served, and yet be unable to do my friends or myself any service."[87] Even after Louis XIV took the reigns of government in 1661, Turenne openly preferred this older system by which high officers could nominate their own clients to various posts, but Louis wanted all positions to be named by and dependent upon him.[88] He was well aware of the power that came from a large clientage. This, in fact, had been the rationale behind his abolition of the office of colonel general of infantry in 1661: "I did not think that a sovereign could give to an individual the right to carry out his own orders and to create for himself creatures in every corps which constituted the principal force of the

---

[83] Camille Rousset terms this "a revolution in command." Rousset, *Louvois*, 2:166. However, Louis André and André Corvisier point out that the *ordre de tableau* had evolved since the Le Tellier administration; it did not simply spring from Louvois. André, *Le Tellier et Louvois*, 319; Corvisier, *Louvois*, 184.

[84] See Wolf's argument on this point. Wolf, *Louis XIV*, 245.

[85] Saint-Simon, *Mémoires*, 13:341–42. [86] Saint-Simon, *Mémoires*, 12:53–54.

[87] Godley, *The Great Condé*, 206–7. [88] Bérenger, *Turenne*, 379.

state."[89] Louis's 1662 decision to limit the terms of all governors, and thus gain greater control over appointments, must be seen in the same light.

After Condé and Turenne left the stage, Louis used his power of appointment to ensure that never again would men with overwhelming personal power and prestige hold major commands. The duke de Saint-Simon, no fan of Louvois, blamed this exclusion on the hated minister: "Louvois exasperated by having to reckon with the first generals took care not to create others like them."[90] However, this policy so closely mirrors that of Louis toward his ministers, that it should be credited to the monarch, not simply his servant. Primi Visconti speculated that after the retirement of the Great Condé, Louis refused to appoint Condé's son to the command of an army simply because the Sun King did not want to share any glory with one so high.[91] Whether or not Saint-Simon and Primi Visconti were correct, it is important to note that such opinions circulated in court, so Louis's resolve to dominate was clear to all. Even a prince who did too well at the front might find himself sidelined, as did Louis's nephew, the future duke d'Orléans. The Sun King would not tolerate a potential rival for power among his generals any more than he would among his secretaries of state.

The unhappy fate suffered by the duke de Luxembourg shortly after the end of the Dutch War can be viewed as still one more demonstration of the lost power and independence of the high command. Marshal Luxembourg came from an honored family, the Montmorencys; he was a relation and protégé of Condé. Although a Frondeur, he posed no threat to Louis or Louvois after 1661. Soon after the start of Louis's personal reign, Luxembourg, a man of flexible principles, cozied up to Louvois. By the end of the Dutch War, Luxembourg was probably Louis's finest field commander, but his prominence may have compromised his safety. The enmity that began when Luxembourg tried to go behind Louvois's back in 1674 continued to fester. Sometime after peace returned, scandal rocked the court. Known as the affair of the poisons, it involved wellborn individuals with black magic, witches, and murder. Luxembourg was accused of complicity, and Louvois pushed the charges, for he bore the marshal nothing but ill will at the time. The unfortunate marshal spent fourteen months in prison, although he was eventually cleared of all charges. Whatever else Luxembourg learned from this experience, he could have no doubt as to the authority of the king and his ministers. When he returned to command, he worked marvels during the Nine Years' War; however, he deferred both to the king's authority and to his anxieties.[92] Luxembourg's biographer blames the marshal's downfall as simply a product of Louvois's callous ambition.[93] But Luxembourg, after the

---

[89] Louis, *Mémoires*, 2:401.   [90] Saint-Simon in Corvisier, *Louvois*, 200.

[91] Primi Visconti, *Mémoires*, 83.

[92] Luxembourg wrote long accounts of his rationale and actions to Louis; he learned as Turenne did not, or did not care to learn, that this was a way to placate the king.

[93] See Pierre marquis de Ségur, *Le Tapissier de Notre-Dame* (Paris: 1903).

falling out with Louvois during the Dutch War, had allied with the Colbert family, and this was an affront to Louvois. It smacked of political maneuvering by an officer who had once been counted among the Frondeurs. If nothing else, the unfortunate fate of Luxembourg after his triumphs during the Dutch War demonstrated that no marshal was beyond the law, or at least the reach of the minister of war. In a sense, Luxembourg played Fouquet to Louvois's Louis XIV.

THE TRIUMPH OF *GUERRE DE CABINET*

The death of Turenne and the retirement of Condé brought the triumph of *guerre de cabinet*, of war planning by the king and his ministers, particularly Louvois, at court.[94] There would be no need to placate the opinions and desires of these two military giants, and no new general could overshadow Louvois.

Even before Turenne's death, Louis and Louvois attempted to exert a stronger hand than Turenne liked. *Guerre de cabinet* had already appeared enough to infuriate the old marshal. Spanhiem even saw Louvois dominant by the start of the Dutch War: "Although the command of the armies of France was confided to noteworthy generals or to the prince de Condé or to marshal Turenne, they were ordinarily charged only with the cares of execution and restricted to conducting only those operations and steps set down in the orders of Louvois."[95] Perhaps Condé accepted direction better than did Turenne,[96] but the latter still followed his own judgment in direct opposition to Louvois. The marshal resisted orders and opinions transmitted to him by the war minister in 1672. "If you were here," he chided Louvois, "you would laugh at that idea."[97] Condé wrote to Louvois succinctly, "I strongly doubt that he will do what he has been ordered to do."[98] Turenne's refusal may well have been justified, but the point is that he felt no obligation to obey, or even to give a full explanation for his actions. Louvois had to request that when Turenne believed he could not do as instructed, "explain at length the reasons that hinder you."[99] When Turenne disregarded orders to withdraw from Alsace in 1674 and instead fought a brilliant winter campaign that drove out the invaders, history is tempted simply to praise his military judgment.[100]

Turenne's acts exemplified disobedience inspired by his arrogance in the face of directives from a minister that he despised. Primi Visconti recorded

---

[94] Corvisier, *Louvois*, 266.   [95] Spanheim in Bérenger, *Turenne*, 393.

[96] Wolf, *Louis XIV*, 239, says that both Condé and Turenne resisted taking orders from Louvois, but Bérenger, *Turenne*, 396, argues that while Turenne was against the new style of command, Condé accepted it.

[97] AG, A^{1}280, 14 November 1672, Turenne to Louvois, in Rousset, *Louvois*, 1:401.

[98] AG, A^{1}280, 16 November 1672, Condé to Louvois, in Rousset, *Louvois*, 1:400.

[99] AG, A^{1}280, 10 November 1672, Condé to Louvois, in Rousset, *Louvois*, 1:400.

[100] On this disobedience, see Bérenger, *Turenne*, 405; Rousset, 1:399.

this disdain: "[Turenne] complained that in Franconia, Louvois gave him the order not to attack at Wurzburg at a moment when he was sure of victory. The prince de Condé himself criticized Louvois, a young minister of thirty four, who wanted to play the role of general and to command, beyond the king, two old captains born, so to speak, sword in hand."[101] At another time, Turenne dismissed Louvois: "The king wanted to command on campaign, although he was not there, and thus Louvois played the part of the constable of France, and one day generals would be constrained to take his orders even though they were a hundred leagues from him . . . . [E]ven the Prince of Condé himself was disgusted when he saw the direction of armies in the hands of men who more merited the title of valet than that of captain . . . . [T]hat the king being resolved to garner for himself alone all the glory for *belles actions* . . . will leave to the generals only the shame of their defeats."[102]

With Turenne and Condé gone from the scene after 1675, the victory of *guerre de cabinet* brought not only a change in personnel and in the source of decisions but a change in the character of warfare. The primary military advisor and confidant of Louvois was not an aggressive field commander, but the cautious master of siege warfare, Vauban. Not surprisingly, the increased subordination of field commanders was accompanied by a shift away from an emphasis upon field armies in motion to one on static fortress lines.[103]

Reliance on fortresses and direction from the center, reinforced by the military success, 1675–88, encouraged an almost dismissive attitude toward the value of talented commanders. Chamlay, confidant of Louvois, and a future military advisor to Louis XIV, wrote the following revealing passage on the eve of the Nine Years' War.

The difference that exists between the present situation of the King's affairs and that of [the Dutch War], is that in those previous times, the fortune of His Majesty and of his kingdom was in the hands of men who, by being killed or by making a bad decision, could lose it in a moment, or at least compromise it in some way by the loss of a battle [from] which it had been difficult to reestablish. Whereas, presently, because of the great conquests that have been made, and because of the advantageous situation of the places that have been fortified, the King finds himself able to grant command of his armies to whomever it pleases him, without having anything to fear from the mediocre capacity of those to whom he confides it.[104]

There is some question that this near-famous statement may be a form of whistling in the dark, because at the start of the campaign in 1688, the French may well have felt that they had no first-rate field commander, since the mediocre Marshal Duras seems to have been judged their best and awarded the most important command. In any case, the sense of the passage is clear in proposing that great generalship was no longer required.

Louis's taste for *guerre de cabinet* fit well into his obsession with siege warfare. Not only did the quality of field generals matter less, but it was

---

[101] Primi Visconti, *Mémoires*, 24.   [102] Turenne in Primi Visconti, *Mémoires*, 63.
[103] Wolf, *Louis XIV*, 231.   [104] Chamlay, 27 October 1688, in Corvisier, *Louvois*, 459.

more appropriate in siege warfare that the king make the major decisions. Vauban explicitly defined as an *affaire de cabinet* the ultimate decisions as to which towns to besiege.[105]

The direction of French wars from the center reached the level of what would be called today, *micro-management*. During the siege of Aire in 1676, Louvois appeared in the field to supervise operations and to prevent conflict between the two marshals present.[106] In the orders for the campaigns of 1683 and 1684, transmitted by Louvois, the king included the most minute detail, stipulating which regiments were to march and exactly which routes were to be followed, including minor stops along the way.[107] After the death of Louvois, Louis took an even more direct hand in managing campaigns, particularly in the case of mediocre generals, such as Villeroi. In 1701, Louis chided his general for taking too much liberty with his instructions: "I ordered you to look for the enemies, to keep as close to them as you could, to give battle, but this order ought to be applied with prudence."[108] Louis gave his best marshals, such as Luxembourg and Villars, a longer leash, but he constricted even them. During the War of the Spanish Succession, Louis continually denied Villars the right to accept battle in 1710 and 1711.[109]

Louis's generals were never happy with such micro-management. Such very different commanders as Turenne and Villars expressed similar frustration. Turenne objected to Louvois directly: "Give me leave to tell you that detailed instructions sent from such a distance would not serve the King's interests, even if he were dealing with the most incapable man in France."[110] Villars agreed in his treatise on war: "I am persuaded that it would be to [the king's] interest to give [his generals] carte blanche after having explained perfectly to them his instructions. It is not necessary to pretend that a sovereign can command from his *cabinet*, and give his orders dealing with operations that are to be carried out during a campaign that changes every moment."[111] The difference is that Turenne disobeyed when he disapproved of directives sent by Louis or Louvois, while Villars complied, even though he might fume. The royal will had triumphed.

THE STATISTICAL DIMENSIONS OF THE HIGH COMMAND UNDER LOUIS XIV

André Corvisier provides an excellent social portrait of the generals who served Louis XIV from 1661 to 1715. Commenting on his sample as a whole,

---

[105] Sébastien le Prestre de Vauban, *De l'attaque et de la défense des places* (The Hague: 1737), 1.
[106] Rousset, *Louvois*, 2:233.
[107] Jacques Hardré, ed. *Letters of Louvois, University of North Carolina Studies in the Romance Languages and Literatures*, no. 10 (Chapel Hill: 1949), 284–85, 288–89, 299, 314, 351.
[108] AG, A^{1}1507, 11 September 1701, concerning Chiari.
[109] Claude C. Sturgill, *Marshal Villars and the War of the Spanish Succession* (Lexington, KY: 1965), 103.
[110] Turenne in Godley, *The Great Condé*, 559.
[111] BN, f. fr. 6257, Villars "Traité," 26–27.

Table 9.1. *Social origins of French general officers (in percents).*

Rank	Titled nobles	Untitled nobles	Non-nobles	Nobles of doubtful rank and foreign
Brigadiers serving 1700–15	50.0	33.0	8.5	8.5
Brigadiers promoted 1702–5	37.4	30.0		
Brigadiers promoted 1706–12	27.1	43.1		
Lieutenant generals serving 1700–15	65.7	13.9	6.5	13.9

Corvisier concludes "In the days of Louis XIV, the marshal's baton was found in the knapsack, if not of every soldier, at least in that of every young cadet."[112] He sees surprising equality among the general officers, and perhaps if one had expected to see all high rank concentrated in the hands of the most exalted nobility, this attitude is justified. But Corvisier's own evidence throws doubt upon his more extreme conclusions and illustrates the continued dominance of social prestige, or rather the emergence of a rough meritocracy. He also suggests that a reasonable degree of professionalism ruled among the general officers, and this conclusion is less open to question. Most generals reached high rank after many years learning their trade, so Saint-Simon's often repeated accusation that Louis's generals attained command with only limited experience beyond the company level is not true.

While Corvisier is correct that the door to the high command was not closed completely to officers of modest birth, social rank exerted a strong influence upon promotions, although not quite so strong as some have believed. For brigadiers of the era of the War of the Spanish Succession, Corvisier shows a preponderance of the titled, or generally more elevated, nobility, although the influx of new brigadiers shows a rise in the numbers of the lesser nobility, as the monarchy was forced to dig more deeply into the barrel.[113]

Corvisier's sample signals the higher social rank of lieutenant generals and contrasts the dominant role of titled nobles at that rank with their lower participation as brigadiers for the period 1700–15. In another piece of research, he examines a sample of 276 lieutenant generals who were born in France and who served during 1661–1715. From this sample, he extracts information on the social origins of 178 individuals.[114] The fact that data is lacking

---

[112] Corvisier, "Les généraux de Louis XIV," 26.

[113] Contamine, *Histoire militaire*, 1:542–43.

[114] Corvisier, "Les généraux de Louis XIV," 41–42. In the article itself, he says that he has information on the social origins of only 164 generals, but he then tabulates figures for 178 individuals. Here percentages are based on his total of 178; therefore, they differ from those he presents with his confusing mathematics. During this same period, thirty-four lieutenant generals were foreign born.

for nearly 100 lieutenant generals may skew his findings toward upper social strata, he admits, because it would seem likely that more of the generals about whom no social information can be found issued from obscure families. In any case, of the 178, eight (4.5 percent) were from bourgeois or robe families, thirteen (7.3 percent) from recently ennobled families, forty-three (24.2 percent) from families ennobled in the seventeenth and sixteenth centuries, forty-two (23.6 percent) from families ennobled in the fifteenth and fourteenth centuries, and seventy-two (40.4 percent) from families already in the nobility before 1300.

Understandably, marshals came from even more exclusive social origins. Of the thirty-two French-born marshals (1661–1715), only one (3.1 percent) was from a robe family; five (15.6 percent) were from families ennobled since 1500, twelve (37.5 percent) from families ennobled in the fifteenth and fourteenth centuries, and fourteen (43.8 percent) from families already in the nobility before 1300.[115]

Considering this social data as a whole, Corvisier concludes that "Venality of charges served the bourgeoisie only in the lower grades."[116] Sale of offices, touted as a means by which the wealthy non-nobles could purchase their way into the nobility and therefore defuse social tension, worked only to a point in the army. The high command was still largely a preserve of older, more prestigious clans.

Although the upper nobility as a whole dominated the high command, special families played a particular role in supplying generals. Before 1661, 225 families could have claimed two generals or brigadiers; ninety-eight of these families had no general under Louis XIV. During his reign, 127 families that already had a general or brigadier of infantry to their credit, produced at least one more general officer. This was matched by 128 new families. This number would decline during 1715–89, when only twenty-one new families figured in a total of 164.[117] Clans such as the Montmorencys and the Noailles demonstrated particularly military patterns. The Montmorencys alone boasted forty generals in the seventeenth and eighteenth centuries.

Therefore, Corvisier praises the system for an equality that it practiced only in unusual cases. In the sense that the petty nobility contributed some generals, Corvisier is correct, but the better families still dominated. And those of more humble origins did not compete on a level playing surface. Thus, when Villars argued that a good sovereign should "treat in promotion the Grand Seigneur the same as a soldier of fortune up to a certain point," he was speaking more of a future ideal than of the system as it was under Louis XIV; Villars recognized that equality of promotion such as he advocated would not be "to the taste of the courtier."[118]

---

[115] Corvisier, "Les généraux de Louis XIV," 42. During this period, four of Louis's marshals were foreign born.

[116] Corvisier, "Les généraux de Louis XIV," 43.

[117] Corvisier, "Les généraux de Louis XIV," 44–45.

[118] BN, f. fr. 6257, Villars, "Traité," 2–3.

Table 9.2. *Distribution of general officers by branch.*

Branch	Number of officers in 1710	Percent of total number of officers	Percent of maréchaux de camp	Percent of lieutenant generals	Percent of maréchaux
Infantry	15,898	75.5	39.0	34.8	17.3
Artillery	350	1.7	1.5	1.1	0.0
Cavalry	3,468	16.5	34.6	41.2	48.3
Dragoons	1,346	6.4	7.8	8.5	6.9
Total	21,062				

A look at the branch origins of the high command demonstrates an additional prestige associated with the cavalry. Those in that service were more likely to rise to the top, and since cavalry attracted officers with higher social standing and greater wealth, the rise of cavalry commanders supports the notion that social standing was still critical. The breakdown among officers between the major branches of infantry, artillery, cavalry, and dragoons in 1710 was as shown in Table 9.2.[119]

These statistics do not quite add up for the percentages that reached the ranks of the general officers, because Corvisier used figures that set apart engineer officers and the *maison militaire*. Considering the former, one finds that engineers supplied 1.5 percent of *maréchaux de camp*, 1.1 percent of lieutenant generals, and 3.4 percent of marshals – this last being Vauban. The much privileged *maison militaire* supplied 15.6 percent of *maréchaux de camp*, 13.3 percent of lieutenant generals, and 24.1 percent of marshals, although in 1690, the officers of the *maison militaire* numbered only 1,100, or 5.3 percent of all officers in 1690.

But the role obviously played by social prestige did not exclude professionalism, and Corvisier demonstrates that standards for promotion among general officers were more professional than often believed, at least when measured by the age of generals at the time of promotion and by years served in grade. Between 1661 and 1675, the average age at promotion of lieutenant generals was forty; this increased to forty-seven during 1675–1715.[120] Looking at all active generals, the average age was forty-six in 1674, while in 1708, it had risen to fifty-four.[121] It is important to distinguish the number of active generals from the total number of generals since many were inactive or retired. Out of ninety-five lieutenant generals on the army list in 1674, thirty-three exercised command, while the rest held the title in an honorific sense;

---

[119] Corvisier, "Les généraux de Louis XIV," 30, 51; and AG, MR 1701, #13, "Estat contenant le nombre des officiers, des soldats, des cavaliers, et des dragons dont les regimens étoint sur pied en 1710." The percentages supplied by Corvisier for officers as a whole differ because he uses Belhomme, *L'armée française en 1690*, whereas I use the archival source from 1710.

[120] Corvisier, "Les généraux de Louis XIV," 36.

[121] Corvisier, "Les généraux de Louis XIV," 37.

in 1689, with a total of sixty, thirty-three were employed, and of the 136 in 1708, sixty had commands.[122] In particular, it would appear that the rank of *maréchal de camp* was a "tomb-stone promotion," conferred on an individual at the end of his career without expectation that he would actually exercise that command.[123] Once an officer had reached brigadier, the wartime pace of promotion could be quite rapid. Of forty-four brigadiers appointed on 24 April 1688, twenty-five rose beyond that rank, while nineteen died in grade. Six reached *maréchal de camp* in 1689, after nine months in grade; thirteen made it in 1693, after nearly five years in grade; and six waited until 1702, more than fourteen years in grade. Of the original forty-four brigadiers, fourteen became lieutenant generals: one in 1693, seven in 1696, and six in 1702. Again, these promotions came only after a reasonable length of time. And finally, two joined the ranks of the marshals in 1709, twenty-one years after attaining high command.[124]

Therefore, young men received promotion to general only in unusual situations; Condé may have commanded a field army at age twenty-three, but he was a prince of the blood.[125] A more representative career pattern, although still accelerated, was that of Villars, another truly great French captain. At age nineteen, he saw his first campaign as a sous-lieutenant of cavalry, and at age twenty-one he rose to colonel, having caught the king's eye. But this favored soldier only reached brigadier at age thirty-six, at which post he so displayed his talent for command that he became a lieutenant general at thirty-eight. Villars finally became a marshal in 1702, at age forty-nine, and proved to be Louis's most effective army commander during the War of the Spanish Succession. Villar's career demonstrates three points: (1) a rapid rise to colonel for a young man with connections and money was not unusual; (2) entry into the ranks of the general officers still could take time; and (3) the *ordre de tableau* did not hinder the king from awarding unusual talent, or unusual influence, with unusually rapid promotion, as Villars jumped from brigadier to lieutenant general in only two years.

This last point is precisely the conclusion that Corvisier makes concerning the supposedly stultifying effect of the *ordre de tableau*: "However, the *ordre de tableau*, object of so much criticism, did not function before 1715 as a systematic manner to exclude choice in the employment of men."[126] There were promotions as a response to merit and influence.[127] In contrast, the

---

[122] Corvisier, "Les généraux de Louis XIV," 36.
[123] *Maréchal de camp* was the first rank at which the officer had to relinquish his regiment. Thus, an old officer would sell or hand down his colonelcy to a relative and retire with the courtesy rank of *maréchal de camp*. Corvisier, "Les généraux de Louis XIV," 36.
[124] Corvisier, "Les généraux de Louis XIV," 33.
[125] Corvisier also points out that some general officers retired young – Nassau-Sarrebruck at age thirty-two and the son of Humières at thirty-three. Corvisier, "Les généraux de Louis XIV," 36.
[126] Corvisier, "Les généraux de Louis XIV," 38.
[127] Corvisier, "Les généraux de Louis XIV," 32.

haughty Saint-Simon blamed the troubles of the War of the Spanish Succession on a system of promotion that he claimed selected generals who reached their rank "by their seniority without ever having risen beyond a subaltern position, . . . for the most part, never given the trouble to study or learn anything."[128] Here the spoiled courtier seems to have reflected his own prejudice rather than reality in the field.

Beyond social standing and professional qualifications, adherence to the Catholic religion became a final factor in selecting general officers midway into the personal reign of Louis XIV. Until the 1680s, a general's faith was a private affair. Turenne descended from an old Protestant line and maintained his beliefs until 1668, when at age sixty-seven, he appears to have undergone a genuine conversion to Catholicism. The Edict of Fontainebleau revoked the Edict of Nantes and thus ended official tolerance for Protestants in 1685. Louis XIV stripped Protestants of their power and privilege. One consequence was the 27 November 1685 ordinance stating that the king no longer wanted Protestants in his French regiments, although they could remain in foreign regiments, which retained their own chaplains. Most Huguenot officers converted under compulsion. Louis XIV himself proselytized when he tried to convince Marshal Schomberg to abjure. However, the old soldier refused, so Louis allowed him to retire and leave France. Schomberg's retirement did not last long; he soon joined the army of the Protestant prince of Orange, and he died fighting against Louis.

WEALTH AND HIGH COMMAND

Wealth was a great asset to a general officer for the same reason that riches were necessary for company or regimental command. This was not a uniquely French situation; Parma and Spinola had used their personal fortunes to sustain their Spanish armies.[129] The need for a French commander to tap his own wealth and credit was particularly strong for those who led private forces in the king's name, because they were expected to create and maintain entire armies with their own resources, although they might seek reimbursement later. The estates of Vivarais paid Montmorency 75,000 livres to compensate him for having supplied his own troops fighting rebels during the second decade of the seventeenth century, while the duke d'Epernon complained in 1619 that he spent 10,000 crowns in the king's service without being reimbursed.[130] Private outlays did not end with private armies. In 1635, La Rivière petitioned the government for the repayment of 50,000 livres that he claimed to have paid for the subsistence of the garrison under his

---

[128] Saint Simon in Corvisier, "Les généraux de Louis XIV," 24.

[129] Frank Tallett, *War and Society in Early Modern Europe* (London: 1992), 114.

[130] *Inventaire sommaire des Archives Départementales antérieurs a 1790. Ardèche. Archive Civiles*, vol. 1 (Paris: 1877), 140; *Four Letters: One From the Duke of Bouillon to the French King*, 7–8. Again, this information concerning private armies comes from Brian Sandberg.

command.[131] During 1635–36, Marshal Brézé had to employ his own resources to support his army wintering on Dutch soil.[132] In order to prepare his army for the siege of Philippsburg in 1644, Enghien ordered that money be borrowed in his own name.[133] Again in 1648, army commanders and army *intendants* provided for their troops out of pocket.[134] In general, before 1659, French commanders like Condé and Pléssis-Praslain often went unpaid and yet mobilized private resources to pay troops.[135] In 1657, Turenne reached such an extreme that he cut up his silver service to coin-sized portions of 14, 20, and 60 sols to pay his troops.[136] Turenne turned against Fouquet in 1658 because after Turenne had paid troops with his own money, he held the *surintendant* responsible for a poor state of public finance.[137] In 1659, the king even owed Le Tellier 300,000 livres for the maintenance of the troops.[138]

It is worth noting that major military administrators were also expected to contribute their wealth and credit as well. David Parrott asserts that the ministry simply assumed in the 1630s that *intendants* would make up shortfalls in the *épargne* with their own credit.[139] In 1644, the *commissaire général* of the Army of Germany, Tracy, borrowed money on his own credit to pay the cavalry.[140] In the 1690s, one finds an ex-treasurer of the Gardes suisses complaining that he had never been reimbursed for money he loaned to his accounts in 1666.[141]

It is only fair to comment that general officers could make their situation worse by the kind of extravagant display expected of commanders during the *grand siècle*. At the camp at Compèigne in 1698, Marshal Boufflers offered lavish hospitality, including a meal of thirty-five courses. The king had to tell his son not too reciprocate such ostentation.[142] In 1713, Broglie felt it necessary to have more than thirty officers at his table to eat.[143] Music might well accompany dinner; the Great Condé had twenty-four violins with him as he opened the trench before Lerida.[144]

---

[131] AAE 815, fol. 281, 30 September 1635, in Parrott, "The Administration of the French Army," 208n.

[132] Parrott, "The Administration of the French Army," 29.

[133] Godley, *The Great Condé*, 111.

[134] Bernard Kroener, *Les routes et les étapes. Die bersorgung der franzoschichen Armeen in Nordostfrankreich (1635–1661)* (Munster: 1980), 124. Also, see Parrott, "The Administration of the French Army," 306, on expenses assumed by army *intendants*.

[135] André, *Le Tellier*, 277. See, as well, Marillac's claim that he paid for his own army in 1630 and the fact that LaValette sold off his possessions to pay for the army. Parrott, "The Administration of the French Army," 335.

[136] Bérenger, *Turenne*, 333. He also used his own funds to pay his troops the next year. Bérenger, *Turenne*, 341.

[137] Bérenger, *Turenne*, 341.　[138] Corvisier, *Louvois*, 108.

[139] Parrott, "The Administration of the French Army," 306.

[140] Tracy to Mazarin, 11 July 1644, in Charles Derek Croxton, "Peacemaking in Early Modern Europe: Cardinal Mazarin and the Congress of Westphalia, 1643–1648," Ph.D. dissertation, University of Illinois at Urbana-Champaign, 1995.

[141] AN, G⁷1774, #4–8.　[142] Babeau, *La vie militaire*, 2:172.

[143] Babeau, *La vie militaire*, 2:175.　[144] Babeau, *La vie militaire*, 1:269.

The stories of personal outlays decreased during the personal reign of Louis XIV, but notable cases still occurred. During the generally successful Sicilian campaign of 1676, Marshal Vivonne had to borrow funds on his own credit and supply them to the *intendant* to feed his army.[145] Two factors changed the situation after 1661: first, the great improvement in military administration and the more regular financial situation of the monarchy, and second, the fact that armies grew to such proportions that the personal resources of a commander could not have been sufficient to keep his troops fed and paid.

It has already been argued that French regimental officers also probably lost money because of the responsibilities of their commissions; however, general officers had a much greater chance to gain from the king's liberality and thus found or restore their fortunes. Certainly, the king rewarded success. He made Vauban, who testified that "Fortune caused me to be born one of the poorest gentlemen in France," into a man of moderate wealth.[146] Generals received substantial pensions and gratuities in reward for their services.[147] In 1635, *maréchal de camp* Alès de Corbet got 3,000 livres in pension, which was the same as rent on 300 hectares of land.[148] Commanders felt justified in making requests for monetary rewards. Mortally wounded in battle, Lieutenant General Saint-Abre addressed an extraordinary appeal to his king to aid his six children: "I have lived all my life as a person of great means, but this has been only at the expense of the purses of my friends. I leave six children who all have the same sentiments; I hope that Your Majesty will have the goodness to not abandon them to the sorry state of my affairs."[149] In 1702, Vauban even asked for a house in Paris as a reward for his services.[150] Those generals who in the days before 1659 or in extraordinary cases later could appropriate contributions for their own use may well have prospered. Fortress governors fell into this category before Louis XIV brought them to heel. Villars also seems to have enjoyed an independence in matters of contributions that augmented his fortune, particularly in 1707.[151]

THE HIGH COMMAND AND "COMMAND"

While the personnel and control of the high command evolved over the course of the *grand siècle*, certain aspects of command in the field remained constant. As Louis discovered, despite Chamlay's opinions about the logic of

---

[145] In late May alone, he advanced 30,000 livres to the *intendant*. Rousset, *Louvois*, 2:429.

[146] Vauban letter to Louvois, 15 December 1671, in Albert Rochas d'Aiglun, *Vauban, sa famille et ses écrits*, 2 vols. (Paris: 1910), 2:65.

[147] Babeau, *La vie militaire*, 2:158.

[148] Jean Chagniot, "Guerre et société au XVIIe siècle," *XVII siècle*, 37 (1985), 255.

[149] Letter in Louis XIV, *Oeuvres*, 3:512, in Rousset, *Louvois*, 2:74.

[150] Babeau, *La vie militaire*, 2:159.

[151] Ferguson argues that Villars had no desire to be too specific about the contributions that he collected. Ferguson, "Blood and Fire," 28.

relying on mediocre generals, wars could not be fought without commanders of character, courage, and intelligence.

The modern military pundit, Martin van Creveld, describes the entire era from the fall of Troy to the French Revolution as the "Stone Age of Command." He argues that technological and intellectual limitations greatly circumscribed the role of commanders throughout those millennia. Van Creveld has a habit of dealing with the more remote past merely as prologue to what truly interests him, the modern military, and as such, he can be too dismissive of earlier change and variety. Yet who can deny the strangely medieval quality of Condé's conduct at Rocroi? The structures and style of command exercised on campaign during the *grand siècle*, even as Louis and Louvois tried to impose *guerre de cabinet*, did not evolve greatly.

In the modern context, command functions can be separated into two categories, those required to maintain the troops in the field and those concerned with directing the army as a combat force. Today, both of these functions belong to uniformed officers, but in the French army of the *grande siècle*, the first went to civil officials and the second to soldiers. *Intendants*, *commissaires*, and *munitionnaires* provided the essentials for a field army. Soldiers were involved, but only to support the civil administrators. Escorting convoys, foraging fodder, and raiding for contributions took on the appearance of a large military operation under the authority of the lieutenant general of the day; however, the rest did not come within the purview of the generals. Much of the work of a modern staff was not, strictly speaking, the affair of the high command in the seventeenth century. In fact, the staff surrounding an army commander was rather small, including several aides, clerks, and personal servants. The most important staff officer would be the *maréchal de camp*, who handled details of movement and encampment, and the lieutenant general of the day, who detailed parties and controlled foraging.

Command Style

Far more than today, military leadership bore an individual stamp and was seen as a personal test of martial virtues. Different commanders adopted different command styles. Basic to such style was a commander's level of familiarity with his troops. Turenne was very caring about his soldiers' needs, but while he shared their dangers, he was not particularly close to them. After all, he descended from princes. In contrast, Villars was noted for familiarity with common soldiers: "I passed part of the night with them; we drank a little brandy together; I told them stories."[152] Emile G. Léonard sees him as a new kind of general; certainly he did not rest on ceremony, although he belonged to a distinguished family.[153]

---

[152] Letter of 2 March 1703 from Villars to Chamillart, written at Kehl, Claude Louis Hector Villars, *Mémoires du maréchal de Villars*, ed. Vogüé, 5 vols. (Paris: 1884–95), 2:278.

[153] Emile G. Léonard, *L'armée et ses problèmes au XVIIIe siècle* (Paris: 1958), 82–83.

Sheer courage seemed to be a sine qua non of command, and as the products and paragons of a culture of command that emphasized *gloire*, generals provided examples of bravery to prove their courage and inspire their troops. Time and again, commanding officers led assaults. If a young duke d'Enghien led the attack that decided the day at Rocroi in 1643; an old Condé, so crippled by gout that he could not wear his boots, still rode at the head of his galloping squadrons at Seneffe in 1674. There, when Condé drew his sword to lead a cavalry charge, a young and exuberant Villars cried out "Now I have seen what I most longed to see! – the Great Condé, sword in hand!"[154] At Hornberg in 1703, the same Villars who had cheered Condé, led reluctant companies of grenadiers in an attack on the fortress, with his marshal's baton as his only weapon.[155] At Malplaquet in 1709, he again charged with this troops on foot and delivered sword blows.[156] Soldiers expected no less from a leader, and such bravado was not limited to generals in chief. At the battle of Sinzheim in 1674, where Turenne commanded a small army overwhelmingly composed of cavalry, during the first charge, every one of the French general officers were wounded or at least exchanged blows with the enemy. Two brigadiers were killed that day, and the lieutenant general commanding the right wing, Saint-Abre, died some days later from his wounds. His son perished in the same battle.[157] Of the 254 brigadiers in Corvisier's study of generals under Louis XIV, fifty-nine (23 percent) died of battle wounds.[158]

This style of leadership extended even to princes and kings. That stolid Dutchman, William III, was always in the thick of the fight, believing that he must physically lead the way.[159] Louis also believed that he must brave danger. Much was made of the fact that a soldier was killed in the trenches close to where Louis was observing at the siege of Mons in 1691 to demonstrate that the king had risked death himself.[160] Of course, in reality, Louis's generals did everything in their power to protect the precious life of their king.

Not all agreed that a general should risk personal combat. D'Aurignac wrote in 1663: "But especially the general ought not to fight or engage in a melée with the enemy, rather he should avoid it, because he would be the target of the first shots fired . . . ; and moreso, he has only two arms and one

---

[154] Villars in Godley, *The Great Condé*, 564.   [155] Sturgill, *Villars*, 39.

[156] André Corvisier, "Le moral des combattants, panique et enthousiasme, la bataille de Malplaquet," *Revue historique des armées*, 4, no. 3 (1977), 22.

[157] Rousset, *Louvois*, 2:74.

[158] André Corvisier, "Les généraux de Louis XIV et leur origine sociale," *Bulletin de la société d'histoire du XVIIe siècle* (1959), 31.

[159] Stephen Baxter, *William III and the Defense of European Liberty, 1650–1702* (New York: 1966), 94.

[160] A famous engraving memorialized this scene, with the fallen soldier lying not more than a yard away from Louis. A label by the soldier's feet reads: "Soldier killed by a cannon shot behind the King." Among other reproductions, this engraving appears as plate 93 in Contamine, *Histoire militaire*, vol. 1, between pages 466 and 467.

sword, no more than a simple soldier."[161] As sensible as this advice was, high-ranking officers still put themselves in harm's way, because even a suspicion of cowardice could prohibit an officer from command, and certainly from commanding respect.

Beyond familiarity and bravery, a general was supposed to have mastered battle tactics, but there was no official system of education or training for general officers besides the time spent on the job in lower ranks. Such a hard-bitten pragmatist as Villars might argue that a general officer should constantly study "his profession in his cabinet" when not in the field, but there was no requirement to do so.[162] Service under a lieutenant general or marshal who took real interest in bringing his protégés along probably provided the best training; Condé fell into this category, and his greatest legacy was the duke of Luxembourg.

The role of army commanders was focused on relatively few matters. The great decisions of the campaign fell to him, to be sure, but *intendants* dealt with administration, and subsidiary commanders routinely handled many of the day-to-day military matters. The French practice of rotating lieutenant generals in the post of general of the day spared the supreme army commander many lesser concerns. Military intelligence came under the purview of the commander in chief, and, of course, he took personal charge on those rare days when the army ranged for battle.

Primitive methods of transmitting messages on the battlefield greatly limited the actual control that an army commander could exert once fighting had begun. The commander's greatest role may well have been in bringing his men to the field, contributing to their morale, and arraying them in order of battle. On the battlefield, an army was subdivided into separate commands for each wing, line, and reserve. Riders linked subcommanders and commander in chief, but couriers could not supply instantaneous or even rapid communication. For a general to make his presence felt at the key part of the battlefield, he must be on the spot. Condé rode at the head of the cavalry on his own right wing at Rocroi. When Villars realized that a strong British threat compromised his left wing at Malplaquet, he rushed there and personally led troops, finally suffering such a serious wound that he had to be carried from the field. His opponent, Marlborough, was famous for being at the critical place at the critical time. If a general tried to command from the rear, he would have isolated himself both from exerting command control and from inspiring his troops.

Military Intelligence

Bravery reaching the level of bravado was not the only characteristic required of a general as a leader in the field. In contrast to the hot-headed courage

---

[161] Paul Azan, *Un tacticien du XVIIᵉ siècle* (Paris: 1904), 66.
[162] BN, f. fr. 6257, Villars, "Traité," 41, 43–44.

required to ride at the head of a cavalry charge, a successful general also had
to possess the cool-headed faculties required to consider military intelligence
carefully. Here the great captains of the age demonstrated finesse, even de-
viousness, proving themselves foxes as well as lions.

Military intelligence flowed from a number of different sources. War parties
scouted the theater of operations, making their own observations and questioning local inhabitants. In an age when soldiers need show little loyalty to
cause or king, prisoners told of the state of their army and its position.
Deserters did the same with even less inclination to hold back. Lastly, a wily
commander maintained his own network of spies.

Field armies and fortresses constantly dispatched war parties for a variety
of purposes. (See Chapter 15 for a more detailed discussion of partisan warfare.) In addition to whatever primary goal that a party pursued, it was
expected to gather intelligence. Handbooks of the time noted that not only
was strictly military information of value but also intelligence on the state
of crops, the density of population, and the wealth of towns.[163] Leaders of
parties regularly made it their business to question the peasants and villagers
encountered and to take enemy prisoners when possible, so that they could
be interrogated back in camp. For some parties, reconnaissance was their
primary mission, as when Gassion scouted the route to Rocroi in 1643,
assuring Condé that the Spanish had failed to block the defile through the
woods leading to the fortress.

Peasants, deserters, and prisoners provided valuable information. The local
population usually knew the kind of logistic information about crops and
forage that was essential to the maintenance of a seventeenth-century army,
but they also provided valuable military details. As Luxembourg reported in
1677, a peasant that came to the camp told the French where the Dutch
forces were encamped.[164] Deserters were sources of valuable information. At
Rocroi, a deserter warned Condé of the Spanish ambush in the woods to the
left of the French line and cautioned him that a force under Beck would soon
join the Spanish army opposing Condé.[165] Both pieces of information were
of great value. The *Gazette* frequently mentioned the intelligence gained
from deserters in 1709.[166]

Captured enemy soldiers were not usually reluctant to share their knowledge with their captors, and it was standard practice to interrogate them.[167]
After all, loyalty could run thin in this age when prisoners often enlisted in
the very army that captured them in order to escape confinement. Vauban
worried that the defense of French fortresses could be compromised by

[163] Jean-Léonor Grimarest, *Fonctions des généraux ou l'art de conduire une armée* (La Haye: 1710),
44, 45–48; Laon, I. de. Sieur d'Aigremont, *Practique et maximes de la guerre* (Paris: 1652),
227–43.

[164] AG, A¹539, #297, 5 July 1677, Luxembourg letter; Pellison, *Lettres historiques*, vol. 2 (Paris:
1729), 292.

[165] Godley, *The Great Condé*, 57.   [166] *Gazette*, 3 August 1709, 274.

[167] See Pellison, *Lettres*, 299.

prisoners: "When the enemy comes up to reconnoiter the fortress and the areas vulnerable to attack, the governor should take great care that no soldier deserts or lets himself be taken prisoner, so as to assure that no secrets reach the enemy."[168] In 1677, captured Spanish cavalrymen told the French the condition of their units.[169] When a French farmer and his men captured enemy raiders behind French lines in 1710, they brought the intruders to Guise, where authorities learned from one of the prisoners the name of the French curé, a traitor or spy with relatives in enemy territory, who had facilitated the raid.[170] The curé was arrested.

Spies operated on a number of levels during the *grand siècle*.[171] At the highest level, the secretaries of state for foreign affairs and for the army maintained networks of informants, but in this chapter, the concern is more for those agents who fed military intelligence directly to military authorities, particularly fortress governors, *intendants*, and field commanders. The governors' networks were probably the most restricted in scope, since they would tend to extend no further than did the area of the governor's territorial authority. Within their purview, governors dispatched individuals to discover enemy strength and movements. The governor of Germersheim, a French outpost in the Palatinate, used agents to keep watch on the Rhine to spot any operations that would threaten his fortress during 1703–4. At one point, he paid a man 15 louis to travel about the enemy camps to estimate the size of their forces. He also paid guides to direct French forces unfamiliar with the area. In six months, the governor spent 278 livres on some forty informants.[172] *Intendants*, both those in charge of border provinces affected by wars and those in charge of army administration, could be quite active in gathering military intelligence. Leblanc, as *intendant* of maritime Flanders and later as army *intendant* for the Army of Flanders during the War of the Spanish Succession, maintained a network of informants along the Flemish frontier, including merchants. He was able to judge such phenomena as the enemies' intentions for coming campaigns by the ways in which they marshaled supplies and forces. In September 1708, he took special note that forty-six English merchants had arrived in Ostende to supply the British army's needs. Leblanc fed information directly to the secretary of state for war and to Villars and Boufflers.

Military intelligence gathered by spies was essential to the effective conduct of campaigns by field commanders.[173] In addition to receiving intelligence from the highest echelons of government as well as from *intendants* and governors, field generals maintained their own spies. D'Aurignac counseled in

---

[168] Sébastien le Prestre de Vauban, *A Manual of Siegecraft and Fortification*, trans. G. A. Rothrock (Ann Arbor: 1968), 122.

[169] AG, A^{1}539, #161, 24 June 1677. [170] AG, A^{1}2266, #190, 1 July 1710, Ormesson letter.

[171] On spies, see Lucien Bély, *Espions et ambassadeurs au temps de Louis XIV* (Paris: 1990); in particular, pages 217–30 deal specifically with military spies.

[172] Bély, *Espions et ambassadeurs*, 222–23.

[173] Lucien Bély states that "the talent of the generals was measured by the use they made of their information." Bély, *Espions et ambassadeurs*, 219.

1663: "It is always necessary to be distrustful, and to not content oneself with only sending out war parties to learn the enemy's secrets [*langue*], but also to have good and faithful spies in the enemy's territory, in order to supply, each on his own, their ideas and their plans, and what they want to undertake."[174] Villars repeated this advice: "An essential thing for a general and even for anyone responsible for anything, is to have good spies and good guides in quantity."[175] Yet Saint-Simon blamed Villars's handling of spies for the fact that he was caught off guard when the British crossed the Schelde in 1711: "Villars, who took much from everywhere he could, but who paid his spies little and badly, was only warned late."[176] From time to time, the name of one of the agents paid by the French shows up in the military correspondence. A Monsieur Guiscard reported on enemy movements to the French during the Nine Years' War.[177]

The enemy employed spies as well, and the French labored to ferret them out, as occurred to the unfortunate curé mentioned earlier. Another spy arrested by the French in 1696 was also accused of stealing a silver vessel from Marshal de Lorge two years before.[178] Obviously, this culprit had been physically close to the marshal, possibly employed within the French camp.

There is something unhistorical about constantly examining sixteenth- and seventeenth-century military insitutions for the seeds of the modern army. Those institutions took shape during that epoch not to point the way to the future but to respond to the challenges of the time. Still, the history of the high command in the *grand siècle* recounts the change from a situation in which general officers still retained a strong sense of that warrior independence cherished by the great lords of a feudal era to a situation typified by a more modern relationship between the state and its army commanders. Against governors, generals, and marshals, kings and ministers struggled to assert royal authority. The *ordre de tableau* symbolized their victory. Professional criteria, modified by the king's will, determined command and promotion. This was not in itself the arrival of complete professionalism, since social position and personal influence still mattered; Louis was too much a traditionalist to break absolutely with the past. But the Sun King opened the door, altered the standards, and took command of his army; in short, he crossed the threshold to modernity. Louis as a mature monarch would brook no commander who shared Condé's rebellious nature, despite his talent for command. Because Louis did not depend on his generals to maintain their armies in the same way that he needed regimental commanders to support their troops, he could be more of the absolutist with his generals than with captains and colonels, and political factors made it imperative that he assert his regal authority.

---

[174] Azan, *Un tacticien du XVIIe siècle*, 39.   [175] Villars, "Traité," 44.
[176] Saint-Simon, *Mémoires*, 22:123–24.   [177] See AG, A^{1}1309, #51, 102, for example.
[178] AG, A^{1}1339, #32, 2 January 1696.

✤

PART FOUR

THE RANK AND FILE

IO

Army Composition

A QUAINT and crude engraving from late in the *grand siècle* portrays the soldiers of Louis XIV by ranks.[1] In forty images, blocked off one from the other in separate cells like a sheet of baseball cards before they have been cut, it pictures the ranks from marshal to fifer. The prejudices of the artist, or of the age, are revealed by the fact that fully half of the images are of cavalry, and only half of foot, though in reality, foot greatly outnumbered cavalry. Moreover, ten of the twenty images of foot soldiers are of officers, when officers, too, were a minority. Still, the childlike images display the human face of the army. The proportions and expressions of the soldiers make them seem more like boys than men, as if they were merely playing at war, and reminding us that the ranks were filled with the sons of flesh and blood, sons who are now reduced to dust or to cardboard figures.

The task of this chapter is to put a more scholarly cast on that engraving – to paint with words and numbers a portrait of the men, and women, who made up the rank and file of the French army during the *grand siècle*. The descriptions here represent the best of recent scholarship on the army and provide a more accurate picture than the old engraving. Still, in one respect, those images transmit a fuller sense of the truth, since they show both the pride and the vulnerability of their subjects. The nature of statistics robs fact of humanity.

The composition of the rank and file, particularly of the French regiments, has attracted much attention ever since the monumental *L'armée française de la fin du XVIIe siècle au ministère du Choiseul: Le soldat* was published by André Corvisier thirty years ago.[2] In deference to that notable scholar, the first set of questions addressed here follows his lines of inquiry concerning native French troops. Such items as rural versus urban background, regional origin, and social class appear on this list. However, there are other matters

---

[1] This engraving is reproduced as plates 83 and 84 in Philippe Contamine. ed., *Histoire militaire de la France*, vol. 1 (Paris: 1992), between pages 402 and 403.

[2] André Corvisier, *L'armée française de la fin du XVIIe siècle au ministère du Choiseul: Le soldat*, 2 vols. (Paris: 1964).

of composition that have broad implications in the context of this volume, and they follow. First, the changing balance between French and foreign regiments in service to the Bourbon monarchy says much about the evolution of army style and implies certain limitations as to generalizations concerning the character, identity, and motivation of the troops. Second, the diminishing but continuing presence of women with the army deserves interest in itself and demonstrates the growing professionalism and efficiency of the French army.

THE COMPOSITION OF FRENCH TROOPS

André Corvisier imposes certain terms of debate upon any study of the social profile of the early modern French army. He was the first to mine the *contrôles*, personnel records that the French army began to keep on the entire rank and file from 1716 on. The *contrôles* included such details as a soldier's name, age, height, birthplace, profession, and date and place of enlistment. Initial entries were then updated with details concerning promotion, discharge, desertion, or death. Scholars now employ the techniques that he used for the eighteenth century to explore periods before 1716 and after 1763. Without doubt, their findings tell us much about the composition of the army. However, to this date, one could argue that the data have illuminated the army more as a social institution than as a military institution. While this emphasis certainly mirrors current fashion in the study of history, it does not coincide with the thrust of this book. A study of army composition rightly begins with the work and categories of Corvisier, but it must ultimately go beyond them.

Age and Height

Let us begin with the more personal details of age and height. Matriculation records of the Invalides, 1670–91 – records that show the hand of Louvois – list details of a man's military career and why he was admitted to that old soldiers' home, along with his name, surname, *nom de guerre*, age, place of birth, height, and sometimes his profession.[3] On average, French soldiers enlisted during the Thirty Years' War at the age of twenty-four.[4] In his sample of 908 men who listed their age at enlistment, 221 (24.3 percent) signed on before they were twenty, while 555 (61.2 percent) enlisted at twenty to thirty, and 132 (14.5 percent) were thirty-one or more.[5]

Corvisier supplies some idea of soldiers' ages in the 1680s by reference to hospital records from the Hôtel-Dieu de Chartres during 1685–88. Then, the average age for soldiers from urban backgrounds stood at twenty-eight and

---

[3] André Corvisier, *Louvois* (Paris: 1983), 189.
[4] Robert Chaboche, "Les soldats français de la Guerre de Trente Ans, une tentative d'approche," *Revue d'histoire moderne et contemporaine*, 20 (1973), 23.
[5] Chaboche, "Les soldats français," 20.

that for soldiers from rural areas was twenty-eight years, eight months. Not surprisingly, NCOs were considerably older, with an average age of forty-four years, six months.[6] At this time, Louvois clearly believed that the best soldiers were in their late twenties. When he praised the French companies of cannoneers, he stated that he had never seen such good troops: "They are the best looking men in the world, among which the oldest is not yet 30, and I do not believe that the youngest is less than 25."[7]

Corvisier's detailed age breakdown of a sample of 3,204 French troops in 1716 demonstrates the age profile of the army late in the reign of Louis XIV. Considering the army as a whole, only 4.6 percent of the men were below the age of twenty, while 54.4 percent fell between the ages of twenty and thirty, with an additional 15.8 percent aged thirty-one to thirty-five. Thus, about 75 percent of the men in the ranks were young men aged thirty-five or less.[8] The relative rarity of men who enlisted before age twenty may be explained by the forced discharge of boys after the conclusion of the war, but that is pure speculation. It may be that better regulation and inspection made it more difficult for officers to fill their units with underage recruits.

These numbers, from the start of direct French involvement in the Thirty Year's War through the end of Louis XIV's reign, demonstrate that then, as today, war was a young man's job. This finding is unsurprising except in the context of claims that the French army was populated by mere boys. Perhaps Vauban's criticisms of troops in which teenagers were present in high numbers were all the more vehement because this sinned against the standards of the day.

In general, the monarchy did not set height requirements in the seventeenth century, except for the Gardes françaises; Corvisier's study shows that in 1716, French soldiers were reasonably tall for the time. The average height of his sample was 5 feet 3 inches in contemporary *pieds du roi*, which translates into modern English measure as about 5 feet 7 inches.[9] To put this in perspective, the average height of an American soldier in the Civil War was 5 feet 8½ inches, so the French soldier of the *grand siècle* was not unusually short.[10]

Social Composition

Questions of social and regional composition draw the most interest from historians who turn to the *contrôles*. Before their careful work, historians were

---

[6] Contamine, *Histoire militaire*, 1: 442.

[7] AG, A¹643–44, 27 August and 1 September 1680, Louvois to Louis, in Camille Rousset, *Histoire de Louvois*, 4 vols. (Paris: 1862–64), 3:333–34.

[8] Corvisier, *L'armée française*, 2:618–20.

[9] Corvisier, *L'armée française*, 2:640–41. The *pied du roi* equaled 0.3267 meters, or about 1 foot ³/4 inches in modern terms. Marcel Marion, *Dictionnaire des institutions de la France aux XVIIe et XVIIIe siècles* (Paris: 1923), 374.

[10] Robert A. Margo and Richard H. Steckel, "Heights of Native-Born Whites During the Antebellum Period," *Journal of Economic History*, 43, no. 1 (March 1983), 168.

likely to condemn the troops who fought for the Sun King as men "drawn from the bottom of the social heap."[11]

Under Louis XIII, there had been some attempt to bring nobles into the enlisted ranks of the French army. The Code Michau of 1629 expressed a desire to see nobles in the ranks; it wanted "the cavalry and infantry companies to fill with sons of the nobility . . . [so] that in each there would be at least a fourth."[12] Perhaps this was meant to mimic the Spanish practice of the aristocratic enlisted men, or *particulares*, who were said to stiffen the ranks and explain the excellent performance of their *tercios*.[13] Corvisier theorizes that of 20,000 nobles in the army in the early 1640s, half were enlisted men.[14] But the expansion of the army would eventually limit aristocrats to the commissioned ranks. One reads little of aristocratic rankers under Louis XIV, and by the eighteenth century, it was illegal for a noble to serve as a private soldier in a line regiment. Nobles were needed as officers.

Corvisier provides a statistical breakdown of the professional and social profile of French enlisted men at the end of Louis's reign in 1716. The sample of *contrôles* for 1716 that clearly stated profession before enlistment is fairly small, only 646 individuals, so Corvisier himself emphasizes the tentative nature of his findings.[15] Of these, twenty-four (3.7 percent) stated that they were noble; three (0.5 percent) stipulated that they were from what Corvisier terms the "non-noble notables," such as members of the liberal professions; and another sixty-four (9.9 percent) listed middle-class business pursuits of a less elevated nature, such as master craftsman. Of those who listed a profession, by far the most common were artisans, fully 494 (76.5 percent). Surprisingly, only thirty (4.6 percent) classified themselves as *laboureurs*, or better-off peasants. Perhaps paternal professions better measure the social origins of soldiers. Many more *contrôles*, 2,220, listed the profession of the father. Forty-six (2.1 percent) listed soldier fathers, of which nineteen were officers. Nobles accounted for twenty-four (1.1 percent), and non-noble notables amounted to 153 (6.9 percent). Other middle-class pursuits added up to 244 (11.0 percent). Paternal professions indicated the truly working-class nature of the rank and file. Artisans stood at 765 (34.5 percent), while laboureurs and peasants devoted to wine and garden culture amounted to 786 (35.9 percent). The poorer levels of the peasantry [*mainoeuvriers*] and assorted agricultural day laborers accounted for 159 (7.1 percent).

The outside world may have considered common soldiers to be the dregs of society, but Corvisier's sample suggests that they were the sons of solid

[11] John B. Wolf, *Louis XIV* (New York: 1968), 392.

[12] Code Michau, 1629, article 200, in François André Isambert et al., eds., *Recueil général des anciennes lois françaises, depuis l'an 420, jusqu'a la Révolution de 1789*, vol. 16 (Paris: 1829), 280.

[13] Geoffrey Parker, *The Army of Flanders and the Spanish Road, 1567–1659* (Cambridge: 1972), 40–41.

[14] André Corvisier, *La France de Louis XIV* (Paris: 1979), 62.

[15] Corvisier, *L'armée française*, table 1:500–1.

working-class and peasant families. This may suggest higher standards of performance in the ranks than might otherwise have been the case.

Rural/Urban Differences

Another key variable for those painting the social portrait of the army consists of the split between those soldiers who came from village, or rural, backgrounds as opposed to those who came from a town or urban milieu. Generations before Corvisier defined this split statistically, Babeau wrote: "It was noted also that the countryside furnished fewer recruits than did the towns."[16] Corvisier disproves this generalization in the literal sense but demonstrates that towns did supply relatively more recruits in proportion to their population.

Corvisier turns to a contemporary source to differentiate villages from towns. In his *Dictionnaire géographique, historiques et politique des Gaules et de la France*, published in 1762–70, Abbé d'Expilly listed towns and villages, and Corvisier bases his categorization on this list supplemented by Saugrain and by research of his own.[17] To qualify as a town or city, and thus an urban center, a community had to number at least 500 "fires," meaning it had a population of 2,000 to 2,500. Anything less fell into the category of village and constituted a rural community. Those who have extended Corvisier's work have accepted the same guidelines.

In Chaboche's sample of veterans from the Thirty Years' War, urban soldiers predominated. In his sample of 1,058 French soldiers who enlisted in the French army before 1648, 52 percent were urban and only 48 percent rural.[18] This imbalance in favor of urban enlistment would continue into the personal reign of Louis XIV, but not in such exaggerated form.

Looking at the Invalides records of 1715, Corvisier was able to glimpse the active army in the period prior to that date, since by the time men entered the Invalides, their military careers lay in the past. The composition of the Invalides in 1715 indicates army composition during the Nine Years' War and the War of the Spanish Succession, since the majority of *invalides* were over the age of fifty-five.[19] Among his sample of *invalides*, 60.9 came from rural villages and only 39.1 hailed from towns and cities.[20] This, as will be seen, mirrors that of active soldiers in 1716, suggesting that the breakdown of the army at the start of the reign of Louis XV persisted from the army late in the reign of Louis XIV.

For his study of the army in 1716, Corvisier used a sample of 21,893 soldiers whose *contrôles* stated place of birth. His breakdown of urban and rural

---

[16] Albert Babeau, *La vie militaire sous l'ancien régime*, 2 vols. (Paris: 1890), 1:38.

[17] See Corvisier, *L'armée française*, 1:387–89, for a discussion of sources and methods.

[18] Robert Chaboche, "Les soldats français de la Guerre de Trente Ans," 15.

[19] Corvisier, *L'armée française*, 2:799.   [20] Corvisier, *L'armée française*, 2:807.

Table 10.1. *Urban and rural composition of the army in 1716.*

Arm	Rank	Urban (%)	Rural (%)
Line infantry	Sergeants	41.33	58.67
	Corporals	33.91	66.09
	Privates	41.87	58.13
All infantry, including Gardes françaises	All enlisted ranks	40.25	59.75
Cavalry	Brigadiers (NCOs)	22.69	77.32
	Troopers	27.49	72.51
	All enlisted ranks	27.07	72.93
Dragoons	Brigadiers (NCOs)	42.85	57.15
	Dragoons	37.96	62.04
Army as a whole	All enlisted ranks	37.58	62.42

origins, based on Expilly's categories, is as shown in Table 10.1.[21] The most obvious contrast between the branches of the service is that cavalrymen were somewhat more likely to come from rural areas than were infantrymen. As a whole, the most striking fact is that in a country whose population was about 80 percent rural, the army was only 62 percent rural. Therefore, soldiers with urban backgrounds were significantly overrepresented, although they did not predominate under Louis XIV.

A look at Corvisier's figures for 1763 shows relative stability in the urban/rural split. Only modest change occurred; for example, the proportion of infantry from rural areas increased from about 60 percent to 66 percent.[22] This demonstrates that the army created by Louis XIV retained the pattern well into the eighteenth century.

Regional Composition

Findings on the regional composition of the French army reaffirm the notion that the army was not a representative sample of French society, but rather it drew more from some segments of the population than from others.

Chaboche's modest sample of 1,058 *invalides* suggests that the soldiers of the Thirty Years' War most commonly came from the provinces of the north, northeast, and northwest, and from Ile de France. Over half of this sample came from only five provinces: Picardy, Champagne, Burgundy, Normandy, and the Ile de France. The other half came from the remaining thirty-two provinces and districts that he mentions.[23]

Chaboche's profile of 7,252 French *invalides* admitted between 1670 and 1690 produces a somewhat different image.[24] The heaviest representation came from the old provinces of the northeast and Ile de France, areas that

---

[21] Corvisier, *L'armée française*, 1:406–7. The same figures, rounded off, appear in Contamine, *Histoire militaire*, 1:545.

[22] Corvisier, *L'armée française*, 1:406–7.

[23] Chaboche, "Les soldats français de la Guerre de Trente Ans," 15.

[24] Corvisier discussion of Chaboche's findings presented in Contamine, *Histoire militaire*, 1:444.

contributed at least one *invalide* for every 1,800 individuals in the provincial population. The next echelon of provincial representation was from the southeast, Dauphiné, and the center, Berry, Bourbonnais, and Nivernais, and the south, eastern Guyenne. These areas produced one *invalide* for every 1,800 to 2,000 in population. This distribution indicates a shift away from some areas that had contributed more soldiers in the earlier period; for example, Normandy was no longer among the provinces with the greatest contribution.

In his study of *invalides* alive in 1715, Corvisier reveals regional patterns which again differed a bit from earlier patterns but were markedly similar to those that would follow.[25] The most substantial contributions of soldiers, in relation to total population, came from the provinces of the north and east. The only provinces that contributed at a rate of one *invalide* or more per 1,300 population fell between Flanders and Picardy in the north down to Dauphiné in the south. The only exceptions were the frontier provinces of Rousillon and Foix on the Pyrenees.

Corvisier's examination of the active army in 1716 essentially repeats this pattern, as do his findings for 1763 and 1789.[26] French infantry regiments drew most of their men from the provinces of the north and the east, with a particularly high proportion coming from frontier provinces. In 1716, the provinces of Flanders and Picardy supplied 650 infantrymen and 143 cavalrymen per 100,000 inhabitants, whereas Orléanais furnished only 273 infantrymen and 29 cavalrymen per 100,000 inhabitants. Figured on the same basis, in 1763, Flanders and Picardy contributed 593 infantrymen and 135 cavalrymen as opposed to the 336 infantrymen and 39 cavalrymen of the Orleanais. By 1789, these numbers remained in similar proportions, 524 infantrymen and 188 cavalrymen from Flanders and Picardy, but only 223 infantrymen and 54 cavalrymen from Orleanais. In this respect, the army as created under Louis XIV remained the pattern until the Revolution.

There was a notable difference in the regional contributions of infantry and cavalry. Large numbers of infantrymen came from the band of provinces beginning with Flanders on the Channel and extending to Provence on the Mediterranean, but the heaviest contribution to cavalry regiments fell only in the provinces from the Channel to the Rhine. This pattern held for 1763 and 1789 as well.

On the whole, the conclusions of current statistical research are not very surprising. The army was not an exact cross section of French society, but one would not assume that a self-selecting, wholly or predominantly volunteer force would be. In addition, one learns the not-too-unexpected fact that either regiments were more effective in recruiting close to their garrisons than they were at a distance or that men in provinces constantly on the front lines of war found soldiering a more acceptable or normal career than men from provinces to whom war was a stranger. After thirty years of dealing with these figures, they have told us little about the army as a fighting instrument.

[25] Corvisier, *L'armée française*, 2:804–7.
[26] Corvisier, *L'armée française*, charts concerning regional composition 1716–89, 1:430–37.

FOREIGN REGIMENTS IN
FRENCH SERVICE

During the *grand siècle*, the French royal army evolved along several lines that as a whole constituted a fundamental shift in army style. Much of this volume deals precisely with that evolution from aggregate contract to state commission form, and in order to substantiate the argument, the changing significance of foreign troops within the French army deserves some comment here. During the sixteenth century, foreign mercenary units composed the backbone of French armies, or at least their infantry forces. To be sure, foreign regiments still constituted an important part of the armies that fought for Louis XIII and Louis XIV, but not in the same numbers nor the same kind of military formations. Instead, the army was composed primarily of national troops raised under the king's immediate control, and the foreign troops employed were created, equipped, and trained in an essentially French pattern.

Reliance upon Mercenary Units: The Numbers

The most obvious measurements of French reliance upon foreign mercenaries come down to figures – the total number of mercenaries who took French pay, and the percentage of Bourbon forces that these foreigners constituted. Given their importance to the force structure, it comes as a disappointment that foreign mercenaries have yet to receive the treatment that they deserve. No scholarly volume covers the full range and importance of the Bourbons' non-French defenders. The calculations presented here, therefore, must be pieced together from existing works and from a modest amount of new research, but they cannot completely fill this embarrassing gap in historical knowledge.

First, it is important to define the subject of this analysis. Before 1610, sources define foreign mercenary bands as a particular number of men (e.g., so many thousands of Swiss or Germans). After that date it is easier to discuss, not the numbers of foreign individuals, but the number of mercenary regiments that fought for the Bourbons. Without doubt, foreigners served as private soldiers in French regiments, and some French subjects enlisted in foreign regiments, but it would be impossible to count them given the record keeping of the time. In addition, the French counted as foreign not only regiments manned by soldiers from lands not subject to Bourbon rule, such as Switzerland, but certain units composed of men from the border provinces of France, such as the Royal Alsace Regiment and the Royal Roussillon Regiment. Units counted here as foreign are those that the king listed as such, even when that category seems to defy the map. It need only suffice to say that the monarchy's own categories underestimate the number of Bourbon subjects in the ranks.[27]

---

[27] In 1710, for example, the total of foreign infantry comes to 38,905, but subtracting the Royal Alsace and Royal Rousillon leaves only 34,720. AG, MR 1701, #13.

French reliance upon foreign mercenary regiments varied considerably over time and cannot be described in a simple manner. To put the *grand siècle* in perspective, it is necessary to begin a century earlier. During the Italian Wars, the French created their armies around a core of foreign infantry. Zeller wrote that the foot soldiers of François I were nearly all foreign.[28] This overstates the case, although unquestionably the reign of François I marked the high point of dependence on Swiss, German, and Italian infantry. His predecessors had not been as tied to non-French troops. During the sixteenth century, the proportion of foreigners was not only high in general; it was particularly great in front-line units. Native militias assisted by second-echelon French troops might man the walls of threatened towns, and mixed forces might garrison threatened provinces, but highly prized Swiss and Germans concentrated in the field armies.[29]

Before François I, during the campaigns of 1512 and 1513, the main French armies contained only 50 percent or less mercenary foot soldiers.[30] But in 1515, François's invading army numbered about 74 percent foreign infantry; at La Bicocca in 1522, this percentage was no less than 71 percent, and at Pavia, it rose again to about 73 percent.[31] François fought all of these campaigns in Italy, but the picture did not change that much when he faced enemies on French soil. The forces he mustered around Jalons, near Châlons, in 1544 to face off against the invading army of Charles V mustered as much as 76 percent Swiss, German, and Italian infantry.[32] During the reign of François I, cavalry had sunk to a nadir in number and importance. At La Bicocca, the combined French and Venetian armies contained 30,000 infantry but only 1,790 cavalry (5.6 percent), very few of whom were French.[33] At Jalons, the French army was composed of 10 to 15 percent cavalry, and it was predominantly or wholly French.[34]

After François I, the percent of mercenary units in French service declined, and the character of remaining mercenary forces changed. According to the best estimate, the main force that Henri II assembled for the Voyage d'Allemagne in 1552 was composed of 17,800 French infantry, 13,500 German mercenary infantry, and 6,350 French cavalry.[35] This puts the infantry at 43 percent foreign and the entire field army at about 36 percent foreign. Judging by the absence of Swiss, the French now favored German mercenaries. The shift to fewer mercenary infantry and more cavalry continued into the Wars of Religion. Solid archival information about the royal army during those

---

[28] Gaston Zeller, *La siège de Metz par Charles-Quint* (Nancy: 1943), 50.

[29] For forces that protected Picardy in the 1550s, see David Potter, *War and Government in the French Provinces: Picardy, 1470–1569* (Cambridge: 1994), 168–69.

[30] Ferdinand Lot, *Recherches sur les effectifs des armées françaises des Guerres d'Italie aux Guerres de Religion, 1494–1562* (Paris: 1962), 35, 38.

[31] Lot, *Recherches sur les effectifs*, 41, 47–48, 55–56.

[32] Discussion in Lot, *Recherches sur les effectifs*, 104.

[33] Lot, *Recherches sur les effectifs*, 47–48.   [34] Lot, *Recherches sur les effectifs*, 102–6.

[35] Lot, *Recherches sur les effectifs*, 129–30, 133. Lot makes an error in addition on page 130.

conflicts is sketchy, but James Wood has assembled detailed figures for main royal field armies during 1567–68.[36] The infantry contained 27 percent Swiss and Italian units, again showing a decline. The number of cavalry rose to 38 percent of the total forces, and of these horsemen, 47 percent were now prized German mercenary pistoleer cavalry. Combat forces contained a total of 36 percent foreign units. In the field, Henri IV continued to rely heavily on German cavalry. In his ill-conceived campaign against Parma, Henri's all-mounted force contained about 3,000 French cavalry, 3,000 German *reiters*, and 1,000 mounted arquebusiers, meaning that the proportion of foreign cavalry stood at 43 percent in 1591.[37] With the return of peace, the French cut their forces, eliminating expensive foreign units. The only foreign troops retained after 1600 were three companies of Gardes suisses, 600 men out of a total armed force of about 10,000, meaning that foreign units composed only 6 percent of the army.[38] However, by early 1610, Henry had added one large Swiss regiment to his forces, and the percentage of foreign troops had risen dramatically to 39 percent of his infantry, though all his cavalry was French.[39] In the plans for the aborted campaign of 1610, the main French army, to be commanded personally by Henri IV, was to have contained 20,000 French infantry, 8,000 Swiss, and 4,000 Germans or Walloons, making the infantry 38 percent foreign. This infantry was to be backed by 5,000 cavalry, apparently all French, making the entire force 32 percent foreign.[40]

The percentages of mercenary foreign regiments in the *grand siècle* decreased and increased according to no single trend. In general, foreign units concentrated among the infantry, while cavalry regiments remained overwhelmingly French. From 1610 until French entry into the Thirty Years' War in 1635, foreign regiments comprised about 10 percent of the infantry regiments maintained by Louis XIII.[41] For the rest of the 1630s, this proportion increased to an average of 14 percent. Richelieu believed that "It is almost impossible to successfully undertake great wars with Frenchmen alone. Foreigners are absolutely necessary to maintain the body of the army [*le corps des armées*]." He went on to state that foreigners composed half the Roman army "and that we have learned how dangerous it is to try to do otherwise."[42] Certainly the Bourbons did not again hire half of their soldiers from

---

[36] James B. Wood, "The Royal Army During the Early Wars of Religion, 1559–1576," in Mack P. Holt, ed., *Society & Institutions in Early Modern France* (Athens, GA: 1991), table, page 10.

[37] Charles Oman, *The Art of War in the Sixteenth Century* (London: 1937), 514.

[38] Joseph Servan, *Recherches sur la force de l'armée française, depuis Henri IV jusqu'a la fin de 1806* (Paris: 1806), 2–3. Regimental counts for the early seventeenth century come from Victor Belhomme, *Histoire de l'infanterie en France*, 5 vols. (Paris: 1893–1902), 1:312.

[39] Servan, *Recherches*, 8–9.

[40] Sully, *Mémoires des sages et royales oeconomies*, Petitot, ed., *Collection des Mémoires relatifs à l'histoire de France*, vol. 9 (Paris: 1821), 65–70.

[41] Regimental counts used for the *grand siècle* come from Belhomme, *Histoire de l'infanterie*, vols. 1 and 2, unless otherwise noted.

[42] Richelieu, *Testament politique*, Louis André, ed. (Paris: 1947), 394–95.

outside their borders, but the numbers did increase throughout the war with Spain. In the period 1640–48, the average stood at 18 percent, 21 percent during the Fronde, and 26 percent during the final phase of the war (1654–59). David Parrott estimates that the foreign contingent within the army as a whole in 1635–37 varied from between 10 percent and 30 percent.[43] Corvisier surmises that for the Thirty Years' War as a whole, 25 to 33 percent of the Bourbon army was composed of foreigners.[44] Corvisier explains the rise in the proportion of foreign infantry by the growing difficulty of recruiting Frenchmen over the course of the longest war fought by the French in the seventeenth century.[45] Chaboche's study of veterans, based on records at the Invalides, provides a gauge of the actual mix of foreigners in French service. By far the most common were the Swiss with 26.2 percent of the foreign contingent, followed by the Germans with 15.8 percent, the Lorrainers with 13.3 percent, and the Irish with 9.7 percent.[46]

The number of foreign infantry regiments declined sharply during the 1660s. By 1665–66, it had fallen to six regiments, or 12 percent, and during the entire first decade of Louis's personal reign, it averaged 15 percent. In contrast to this low figure, the Dutch War brought the high-water mark of foreign infantry in the army of the Sun King. Over the war as a whole, it averaged 32 percent. In 1674, twenty-six foreign regiments served Louis. Pichat states that this included 14,000 Swiss and 6,000 Scots, English, and Irish.[47] This fell to fifteen regiments, or 22 percent, in 1679. Here Belhomme tallies with archival evidence from a financial report on the number of troops maintained after the war. However, this source warns that simply counting the number of regiments does not equate with the number of troops, since foreign regiments were, in general, somewhat larger than French regiments at this point. A count of the theoretical numbers of French and foreign infantry regiments raises the proportion of the latter to 30 percent.[48] Since only 4 percent of Bourbon cavalry and dragoons served in foreign units, the proportion of men in foreign regiments of the army as a whole was only 27 percent. According to the same financial état, these percentages fell to the following levels by the end of 1684: 19 percent of infantry in foreign regiments; 2 percent of mounted troops in foreign units; and 16 percent of the entire army categorized as foreign.[49] The figure for the same year in Belhomme is 15 percent foreign infantry regiments.

With the return to war again in 1688, the number of foreign troops increased in absolute terms but in relative terms never equaled that attained during the Dutch War. While the number of foreign regiments in French service peaked at twenty-six during the Dutch War, Louis boasted forty-eight

[43] David Parrott, "The Administration of the French Army During the Ministry of Cardinal Richelieu," Ph.D. dissertation, Oxford University, 1985, 174–75.
[44] Corvisier, *Louvois*, 96.   [45] Contamine, *Histoire militaire*, 1:365.
[46] Robert Chaboche, "Les soldats français de la Guerre de Trente Ans," 17.
[47] Pichat, "Les armées de Louis XIV en 1674," *Revue d'histoire* 37, 109 (January 1910), 3.
[48] AN, G⁷1774, #52, 1679.   [49] AN, G⁷1774, #52, 1684.

foreign regiments at the height of the Nine Years' War. Nevertheless, the proportion of foreign troops within the army as a whole shrank significantly because the army had grown so substantially. In 1696, foreign infantry regiments constituted about 19 percent of the infantry by regiment. The average for the entire war stood at 21 percent. Comparing this to the percentage of troops in foreign regiments by head count again raises the percentages somewhat. In 1690, when the infantry was 21 percent by regimental count, it was 24 percent by head count.[50] In 1696, the regimental count yields a figure of 19 percent foreign infantry, while a head count yields 22 percent.[51]

War's end again brought demobilization, cutting back the army to 143 infantry regiments, of which thirty-five (24 percent) were foreign. The head count shows the proportion of foreign troops at 25 percent in the infantry and 19 percent overall.[52] The War of the Spanish Succession witnessed an increase in the absolute number of foreign regiments and in their proportion among all Louis's infantry regiments. Since the French opted in this war to multiply the number of regiments at the expense of regimental size, the numbers of regiments soared. In 1706, according to Belhomme a peak year, the French boasted 335 infantry regiments of which ninety-six were foreign, yielding a proportion of 29 percent. For the war as a whole, foreign foot regiments accounted for 25 percent of the total. An *état* for 1710 allows a surprising head count: Whereas Belhomme's regimental count puts the proportion of foreign infantry at 18 percent, the 1710 *état* would reduce this to 13 percent. And the *état* pegs the head count of troops in foreign regiments at only 14 percent of infantry and 12 percent of the army as a whole.[53] Compare this to the massive reliance on foreign troops under François I and Henri II.

Reliance upon Mercenary Units:
The Character of Mercenary Service

The transition in the role of foreign regiments was more than simply a matter of numbers. The mercenary hiring of the seventeenth century needs to be differentiated from that of the sixteenth in order to appreciate the evolution of the French army. Sixteenth-century hired bands arrived armed, trained, and ready to fight. In 1544, François I only contracted for 16,000 Swiss in mid-July, yet they provided the backbone of his army by September. They were purchased "off the shelf" and were just as easily put back there when the crisis ended. As can be imagined, this greatly simplified the administrative

---

[50] For the regimental and head count used here, see Victor Belhomme, *L'armée française en 1690* (Paris: 1895).

[51] The regimental count comes from Belhomme, *Histoire de l'infanterie française*, and the head count is based upon AN, G⁷1774, #52, 1696.

[52] Both the regimental and head counts come from AN, G⁷1774, #52, 1699.

[53] AG, MR 1701, #13.

complexity of creating an army, but it also produced soldiers who fought only if paid and who bore little loyalty to the French crown. In the sixteenth century, the dominant Swiss and German foot soldiers set a standard that the French might hope to copy or adapt, but certainly the foreigners did not mold themselves to any French pattern.

Mercenary regiments of the seventeenth century differed greatly from the bands of foreigners who fought in the Italian Wars or the Wars of Religion. As is explained in the next chapter, under Louis XIV, mercenary regiments were recruited of inexperienced men, not assembled from skilled professionals as before. Foreign recruits now also required arms and training like their French counterparts. Thus, the presence of mercenary units did not change the essential nature of the state commission army because the mercenaries copied the forms of the new state regiments, not the other way around.

François I looked upon Swiss and German infantry as superior troops that the French could not match; for him, they were not only convenient but indispensable. Although the Swiss retained some of their elite aura in the seventeenth century, Louis XIII and Louis XIV ceased to regard them as supermen. To be sure, during the long war with Spain, French infantry may still not have enjoyed as high a reputation as did foreign mercenaries, but French regiments could and did fight well.[54] As the kings and their ministers scrambled to assemble the greatest possible number of troops, however, foreign recruitment offered an additional source of manpower, a source that they could not afford to ignore. Whereas the contribution of non-French regiments waxed and waned over the course of the *grand siècle*, it probably exceeded that of the *milices provinciales* in the last two wars of Louis XIV.

The Pros and Cons of Hiring Foreign Regiments

If French kings had regarded some foreign infantry as innately superior to native troops during the sixteenth century, as the seventeenth century progressed, reliance upon foreign regiments had less to do with belief in their higher quality and more to do with the need to take advantage of every available source of manpower as the Bourbons assembled armies of unprecedented size. This primary rationale may have been buttressed by more subtle reasons. Chamlay wrote of the practice in 1711: "As politics, it is necessary to keep the foreign regiments, not so much as if one wanted them for the service for which they were taken, as in order to foster affection for us in some fashion among the nations from which the officers hail."[55] Perhaps this logic applied, although the present state of knowledge does not yet affirm Chamlay's conviction.

---

[54] See Charles Derek Croxton, "Peacemaking in Early Modern Europe: Cardinal Mazarin and the Congress of Westphalia, 1643–1648," Ph.D. dissertation, University of Illinois at Urbana-Champaign, 1995, 101, on the continued lower reputation of French infantry.

[55] Chamlay in Corvisier, *L'armée française*, 1:259.

Although foreign mercenary regiments may have been a valuable, or even necessary, source of manpower, they were not without their problems. They demanded their money up front, and should they not be paid, the threat of mutiny loomed. Richelieu, for all his desire to bolster the number of foreign troops in French service, had to complain: "The difficulty that I find myself in is the lack of money that it is necessary to give to the foreigners who want to be paid upon being levied at the place named."[56] Attempts to raise 12,000 German mercenaries under Feuquières in 1635 produced few troops because the cash failed to arrive in time to seal the contracts.[57] French colonels displayed a willingness to bear the costs of creating regiments out of their own pockets – not so, foreigners. The latter might also be unusually disobedient or rapacious. In 1647–48, as the Thirty Years' War ground to an end, and the French would not need to concentrate troops in Germany, Mazarin and Le Tellier tried to shift German mercenaries to the Low Countries, but they balked, and contentious negotiations followed. Le Tellier, at times, hid the destination of troops from them until the last moment.[58]

But much of the question of advantage or disadvantage comes down to price in this market of manpower. Just how expensive were foreign regiments in French service? The answer varies from period to period and from regiment to regiment. In estimating the cost of troops raised in 1610, Sully figured that he could maintain 20,000 French infantry for 5,040,000 livres per year, or 252 livres per man, and 8,000 Swiss and 4,000 lansquenets would cost 3,024,000, or 252 livres per man per year.[59] Thus, Sully argued that Frenchmen and foreign mercenaries cost exactly the same.

During the Thirty Years' War, there is reason to believe that at least German troops offered the advantage of economy. In the 1640s, Le Tellier felt that for French campaigns fought across the Rhine, "There will be a great saving for the king to raise as many Germans as possible, since not a single French soldier arrives in the army who does not cost more than thirty écus, taking into account the loss that occurs, even without counting those who desert [débandent], the number of which reaches almost two thirds."[60] This logic was compelling before 1648, but with the Treaties of Westphalia ending the war in Germany, it lost its force.

David Parrott's research on the 1630s demonstrates that prized German mercenaries theoretically cost no more than native French troops. The rates of pay stipulated in capitulations with German contractors equaled those set in regulations for French infantry, 12 livres per montre.[61] This, as he points out, is deceptive because whereas French troops could be made to wait for

[56] Richelieu, Les papiers de Richelieu, ed. P. Grillon, 5 vols. to date (Paris: 1975–), 5:511, 12 August 1630, in Parrott, "The Administration of the French Army," 172.
[57] AG, A¹24, #258, 7 May 1635, and A¹25, #35, 8 July 1635, in Parrott, "The Administration of the French Army," 173.
[58] Louis André, Michel Le Tellier et l'organisation de l'armée monarchique (Paris: 1906), 225.
[59] Sully, Mémoires des sages et royales oeconomies, 9:65–70.
[60] Letter from Le Tellier to Turenne, 17 September 1644, in André, Le Tellier, 217.
[61] Parrott, "The Administration of the French Army," 171–72,

their pay, foreign troops demanded it in full and on time. In addition, maintaining troops outside the borders of France was more expensive than maintaining men within France. It might be added that French officers would habitually foot part of the bill for maintaining their units, while foreign commanders could not be expected to be so generous. But this was not an exclusively French trait; when most of the Swiss in French service went unpaid during 1639–48, their officers used their private credit and booty to pay the men.[62]

While there is no complete study comparing the expense of foreign and French regiments in the service of the Bourbons, scattered documents support Parrott's conclusion that, in general, foreign regiments were promised the same basic pay as given French units during the French service during the war with Spain.[63] There also exist what appear to be exaggerated claims that mercenaries were vastly more expensive.[64]

It is possible that this relative equality lasted into the personal reign of Louis XIV. Regulations set infantry pay at 5 sous per day for Frenchmen, but that is also the rate stipulated for Louis's troops serving in Portugal and for certain foreign troops.[65] At least from the Dutch War on, Louis XIV paid a great deal more for most foreign regiments than he did for native units. Rousset ascribes Louvois's ability to raise so many foreign regiments at the start of the Dutch War to "the lure of an elevated pay."[66] In 1674, when the French musketeer still made only 5 sous per day, Duroque contracted to supply a regiment of Swiss in which the common soldier would receive 11 sous 6 deniers per day. Italians raised by Bellauny could claim an equally high rate.[67]

Pay rates varied quite widely in the last twenty years of the Sun King's reign. A detailed comparison of the costs of maintaining different regiments in the French army at the close of the Nine Years' War reveals native French regiments to have been the cheapest, German regiments somewhat more expensive, man for man, and Swiss 63 percent more expensive than French. Oddly enough, the most costly line regiment, man for man, was the Royal Italian, some 84 percent higher than the French units.[68] The notable variety in the cost of regiments, judging from a financial *état* of 1707, continued into

---

[62] Yves-Marie Bercé, "Guerre et État," *XVII siècle*, 37 (1985), 260.

[63] See capitulation of 26 November 1643 in André, *Le Tellier*, 222, and compare with AG, MR 1972, #140, on French pay rates.

[64] A 1649 address to *parlement* protesting the hiring of mercenaries stated that a Swiss mercenary cost six times what it cost to maintain one Frenchman. But the nobles who submitted this address were apparently demanding employment. Ruth Kleinman, *Anne of Austria* (Columbus, Ohio: 1985), 222–23.

[65] AG, A¹209, #228, 24 September 1667, Grauier from Lisbonne; AG, A¹210, #123, December 1667, capitulation with comte de Vandernack; AG, MR 1972, #140. The ordinance of 6 February 1670 set the pay rate for a musketeer at 5 sous per day. Rousset, *Louvois*, 1:195n.

[66] Rousset, *Louvois*, 1:328.

[67] AG, MR 1722, #1, 27 August 1674, articles of capitulation with Bellauny; MR 1722, #2, 4 April 1674, articles of capitulation with Duroque.

[68] AN, G⁷1774, "Etat des troupes que le Roy a eu sur pied, et leur dépense," 1699.

the War of the Spanish Succession. The daily pay of the common infantryman, after deductions for the *masse*, ran from 4.56 sols for a soldier in a
French regiment to 5.83 in the Royal Roussillon, and from 9.67 in Alsace or
other German regiments to 10.05 in Swiss regiments, over twice the rate paid
a Frenchman.[69] These figures justify Puységur's claim that "The highest pay
of all the nations goes to Germans and Swiss; a German or Swiss battalion
costs as much as two French ones."[70] Their remuneration and elite aura
meant that only Swiss men could join a Swiss unit; counterfeits were cast
out.[71] The money paid out to foreigners seemed to irritate Louvois, who
once complained to Louis, "You could pave the road from Paris to Basle in
gold with all the money that Your Majesty has paid the Swiss." An old Swiss
colonel within earshot fired back, "If one could see all the blood spilled by
the Swiss in the service of France, it would fill a canal as wide as that road
and flow all the way from Basle to Paris."[72] It may very well have been
Louvois's concern with the expense of foreign troops that inspired him to
create the *milices provinciales*, but even with that institution in place, Louis
could not do without foreign regiments. The premium paid for foreign troops
continued through the mid-eighteenth century. During the War of the Austrian Succession, French soldiers could be raised and equipped for 122 livres
11 deniers, while an Irishman, Scot, Italian, Corsican, or Walloon cost 160
livres to put in uniform, and a German ran 178 livres 11 sols and 1 denier.[73]

If the main point of Corvisier's laboriously collected figures on social and
regional composition is simply to demonstrate that the army was not a representative sample of French society, there seems a much easier way to get
to the same point. A substantial proportion of the army was composed of
foreign regiments. This obvious fact may say more than the differences between social classes or urban/rural breakdowns for French population as a
whole and those for the army. As a byproduct, the Bourbon monarchy could
not have depended on the national feeling of its troops if so many came from
outside the borders of France; clearly, other loyalties were expected and
required. But the presence of foreign troops and the conditions of their
service also reveal much about the character of the army and about the
eventual need to turn to conscription as a source of inexpensive manpower.

---

[69] AN, G⁷1780, #212, "Etat des régimens . . . pendant la campagne de 1707. Ensemble des sommes
qui reviennent par jour pour le prest . . . ."

[70] AG, MR 1777, #3, Puységur memoir of April 1713, in Corvisier, *L'armée française*, 1:260. This
pattern remained in the eighteenth century. Corvisier states that in 1741–48, a new French
soldier cost the treasury 112 livres 11 deniers, while an Irish, Scottish, Italian, Corsian, or
Walloon recruit cost 160 livres, and a German ran 178 livres 11 sols 1 denier.

[71] For example, see AG, A¹1339, #105, 11 January 1696, ordering that a Savoyard be expelled
from the Swiss Stoupe regiment.

[72] Folletête in Babeau, *La vie militaire*, 1:359.

[73] AG, A¹3631, #157, in Corvisier, *L'armée française*, 1:260.

WOMEN WITH THE ARMY

Women served with the army of the *grand siècle* in significant numbers. Unfortunately, they have seemed all but invisible to most military historians, and those who have paused to discuss women only complain of them as impediments to the mobility and discipline of the army. Yet duties performed by women were important to the maintenance of troops in the field. The work of women with the troops remained primarily that associated with gender roles in civilian life – food preparation, laundry chores, needlework, amateur nursing, and, of course, sex, although this last was not as dominant as might be supposed, particularly by the end of the century.[74] An important change in military life over the course of the century was the decline in the number of women that followed in the train of armies. It was part of the transformation of the army under the Sun King. However, the army could not afford to march without any women at all, since their work was essential to the appearance, comfort, discipline, and health of the soldiers.

The Number of Women with the Army

The presence of women in the army was part of a larger phenomenon of noncombatants who accompanied the troops. Armies in the early modern era always contained more than soldiers. Charles VIII calculated that he must feed 48,000 to 50,000 mouths a day to maintain an army of 20,000 combatants in the field.[75] Geoffrey Parker describes a body of 5,300 veteran Spanish soldiers who marched from the Netherlands in 1577 accompanied by 14,700 noncombatants.[76] Herbert Langer mentions a 40,000-man imperial army in Germany during the Thirty Years' War accompanied by 100,000 camp followers, many if not most of them women.[77]

The mass of noncombatants included a broad range of individuals. Many performed duties that would be assigned to uniformed soldiers today – for example, artillery teamsters, the *munitionnaire*'s personnel, and the administrative staffs attached to *intendants* and *commissaires*. Others qualified as valets or personal servants. The fact that officers received multiple rations did not indicate that they had particularly large appetites but that they brought other men along in their train. For example, a captain's allowance of six rations in the field implies that he had with him an additional five individuals. Coquault testified that during the Fronde, an army of 20,000 men had 10,000 "valets" alone.[78] Common soldiers also had servants, or *goujats*; this explains the two rations allowed infantry sergeants during the personal reign of Louis XIV. A

---

[74] Barton Hacker, "Women and Military Institutions in Early Modern Europe: A Reconnaissance," *Signs* 6, no. 4 (summer 1981), 643–71, provides a good discussion of the absolutely necessary tasks performed by women.
[75] Contamine, *Histoire militaire*, 1:232.   [76] Parker, *The Army of Flanders*, 87.
[77] Langer in Hacker, "Women and Military Institutions," 648.
[78] Babeau, *La vie militaire*, 1:198–99.

regulation of 1622 actually forbade common foot soldiers to have *goujats*, but they remained.[79] That touching printed illustration showing men of the army late in the reign of Louis includes a *goujat* dutifully trudging along carrying two muskets. Still others, such as peddlers or sutlers – *vivandiers* in the language of the day – provided essential services to the troops. To be sure, in the sixteenth and early seventeenth centuries, an army could also be followed by bands of ne'er-do-wells. A declaration of 1566 stated that "vagabonds and bad-living people" attached themselves to armies and "committed infinite evils."[80]

Women also tagged along with armies, to be with their men, to seek a livelihood, and to perform necessary support services for the soldiers. Describing German mercenaries of the seventeenth century, Wallhausen wrote: "When you recruit a regiment of German soldiers today, you do not only acquire 3,000 soldiers; along with these you will certainly find 4,000 women and children."[81] Babeau, in his classic study of French soldiers, states that so many woman marched with the French army in 1637 that they were thought to spread the plague.[82] An army during the first half of the seventeenth century included a great number of women and children.

Louis XIV drastically cut the number of women following his troops, but he could not eliminate them; they filled too many essential roles. Records from Dijon give some impression of the number of women actually attached to French regiments during the last two of Louis's wars. The municipal records recorded the number of individuals in a unit drawing rations and lodgings; consequently, by listing women, the local authorities recognized them as entitled to be provided for in the same way as the soldiers. The reports from Dijon show an average of fifteen women per infantry battalion, among those battalions that explicitly report women.[83] It is fair to note that some battalion reports list only that women were present, and a number of battalion reports from Dijon list no women at all, although this seems impossible. The number of fifteen here may be very close to the average for the army as refashioned by Louis XIV. A letter of 1772, a half-century after Louis's death, commented on the "fifteen or twenty women who are in the train of each unit."[84]

The decline in the number of noncombatants following armies during the late seventeenth century probably constitutes one of the most important military developments of the era and deserves a major study on its own. The

[79] Babeau, *La vie militaire*, 1:198–99.
[80] AG, MR 1881, #6. 12 February 1566 declaration.
[81] Johan von Wallhausen, *Kriegskunst zu Fuss* (Graz: 1971) (Orig. 1615), 7.
[82] Babeau, *La vie militaire*, 201.
[83] Dijon, H228, 232, 235, 241, 243, 244, 256. Another source of 1695 states that a French infantry company of thirty-five men had with them five women and demanded lodging for the women. Myron P. Gutmann, *War and Rural Life in the Early Modern Low Countries* (Princeton: 1980), 37.
[84] Letter of 30 January 1772 in Babeau, *La vie militaire*, 1:204.

most important part of this decrease was the banishment of so many women from the army. This action probably derived from the fact that the state provided more services to the soldiers, so crowds of camp followers were not necessary. Troops regularly supplied with bread did not need their wives to scour the countryside for food. Fewer women with the army meant that administrators could worry about fewer mouths to feed and commanders could march with less encumbrance and maintain better discipline. In addition, with women gone, the men of the army probably had to rely more on one another, and as a consequence, unit cohesion may have benefited. In any case, after Louis, Western armies would never look the same.

Women's Work and Marriage

The women who marched along with the troops fell into several categories and performed a variety of functions for the troops. The first function that comes to mind would be sexual, although this probably does not account for women's presence as much as do a range of more mundane duties. After the reforms of Louis XIV and his ministers, prostitutes were not welcome camp followers, or at least they plied their trade at great risk. Far more to the point were the soldiers' wives who performed the generally recognized tasks of needlework, laundry, and nursing. In earlier epochs, food preparation was also left to women, and they also might forage for their husbands who were confined to camp. As the number of women fell, however, mess groups composed of soldiers alone took up the slack by preparing their own food. Speaking of the early century, Sir James Turner described soldier's wives as "their husbands' mules" and noted that during the siege of Breda, 1624–25, "the married soldiers fared better, looked more vigorously, and were able to do more duty than the bachelors."[85]

By late in Louis's reign, when improved administration and supply allowed a decrease in the number of women with the army, those left in camp were supposed to be respectable individuals. In short, they were supposed to be the wives of soldiers in the regiment that they served. Perhaps paradoxically, this did not mean that military authorities encouraged marriage; in fact, the Sun King did just the opposite.

The debate over the relative merit or potential problems of married troops never ended. Marshal Fabert, who practiced his trade during the war with Spain, 1635–59, advised that when hiring foreign troops, it was best to have them bring their wives with them "in order that they will not desert to go rejoin them."[86] Many French troops in that war also married. An ordinance of 1667 provided some security for wives of troops of the Gardes françaises

---

[85] Sir James Turner, *Pallas Armata* (London: 1683) in Hacker, "Women and Military Institutions," 653–54.

[86] Fabert, *Mémoires* in Babeau, *La vie militaire*, 1:201.

who were left behind as the unit went off to fight.[87] However, regulations soon limited the ability of soldiers to marry and treated marriage almost as crime. Private soldiers had to receive permission to wed and would lose much by marrying in any case. Ordinances of 1685, 1686, and 1691 commanded that men who married were to lose their seniority, which would begin to accrue again only from the moment of the marriage.[88] Probably because authorities did not want their troops to become too attached to the local population, either because troops might have to act as a repressive force or to avoid desertion, regulations forbade soldiers to marry women from the towns in which the troops were garrisoned; this restriction applied to officers as well.[89] Even if the army did not promote marriage, it did provide spouses with some protection. A regulation of 1706 gave soldiers' wives and children the same right to lodging as provided for troops.[90]

Opponents of marriage contended that married men would be less likely to risk their lives and that women with a unit on campaign would simply get in the way, as well as complicate supply and lodging.[91] In the 1620s, Mathieu de la Simonne advised: "Let the captain do whatever he can to keep his men from marrying . . . because of the great impediments that [women] bring both on campaign and in garrison."[92] This remained a commonly held, though not universal, view. Montecuccoli believed that married men fought better.[93] Vauban held that the problems posed by too many women on campaign did not entirely rob marriage of its utility: "Despite the fact that married men are naturally less suited to war, I am not of the opinion that marriages ought to be totally prohibited. A married soldier deserts less than does another when he hopes to see his wife again." He referred to the situation of the Regiment de la Ferté in times past when it contained 700 to 800 married men who were able to rejoin their wives during winter quarters. This number of wives did not hamper the regiment, since "one took along on campaign only three or four women per company, who were a great convenience because of washing clothes."[94] The three or four wives that Vauban mentions were almost certainly married to sergeants. Sergeants in the army of the Sun King were more likely to be married than were enlisted men, and sergeant's wives commonly enjoyed the privilege of accompanying their husbands on

[87] A 13 May 1667 ordinance stated that wives of soldiers of Gardes françaises would be able to retain their lodgings when the regiment was on campaign, "even the wives of the sergeants and other veterans of the Regiment." BN, Reserves Cangé, vol. 30, fol. 268.

[88] Babeau, *La vie militaire*, 1:205; Contamine, *Histoire militaire*, 1:403; *Ordonnances militaires du roy de France*, 2 vols. (Luxembourg: 1734–35), 171–72.

[89] A 15 December 1681 ordinance forbade army chaplains to marry any soldier to any woman who lived in town where his regiment was in garrison, and a 1 February 1685 ordinance denied any officer the right to marry any woman who resided in or within ten leagues of his garrison without the express approval of an inspector. *Ordonnances militaires*, 171–72.

[90] Babeau, *La vie militaire*, 1:207.   [91] Contamine, *Histoire militaire*, 1:403.

[92] Mathieu de la Simonne, *L'Alphabet du soldat* (1623) in Babeau, *La vie militaire*, 1:203–4.

[93] Tallett, *War and Society*, 133.

[94] Albert Rochas d'Aiglun, *Vauban, sa famille et ses écrits*, 2 vols. (Paris: 1910), 1:340–41.

campaign.[95] This was so much the better for their husbands' pocketbooks, since women earned money as laundresses.

Pressures against marriage, plus the fact that the army refused to recruit married men, lowered the proportion of married men to only 15 percent of the enlisted ranks in the second half of the seventeenth century.[96] Not surprisingly, research by Chaboche indicates that marriage was more common among soldiers during the Thirty Years' War. Among *invalides* who served in that conflict, he found that of those who listed their family condition, 45.9 percent had been or were married.[97] But of the men admitted to the Invalides before 1691, only 21 percent were married, and of those admitted in 1715, a mere 16 percent had wives. These figures probably overstate the average, since veterans with many years of service and sergeants were more likely to gain the highly valued places at the Invalides. The same statistical sample reveals that those who did marry were most likely to choose women from their own regions – that is, a girl from home rather than someone they met while in the army. Of married men admitted in 1715, 68.8 percent had chosen women from their own regions.[98]

Vivandières

Women who attended the troops but who did not devote themselves to needlework and washing might serve as *vivandières*, or petty merchants who provided troops with some small amenities, including liquor and tobacco. (During the reign of Louis XIV, smoking came to be regarded as a necessity of life by soldiers.[99]) As with other camp followers, these peddlers, both men and women, were more numerous early in the century. So many marched with the army during the war with Spain that a law of 1653 cut down their numbers to four per regiment.[100] Authorities did not regard *vivandiers* and *vivandières* as a nuisance, but as a necessity of camp life; consequently, they were allotted specific places to set up their tents in camp.[101]

A series of letters at the ministry of war illuminates a few details of the life of one enterprising *vivandière*. Castres, her husband, a noncommissioned officer in the cavalry Regiment du Roi, petitioned authorities that since he was a soldier, his wife should be exempt from having to quarter soldiers at

---

[95] This seems to have remained the pattern through the eighteenth century. Interestingly, regulations for the British rifle corps in 1801 allowed for six wives to accompany each 100 men on campaign. They were to specialize in needlework and washing and were specifically referred to as sergeants' wives. Hacker, "Women and Military Institutions," 660–61.

[96] Contamine, *Histoire militaire*, 1:433.

[97] Chaboche, "Les soldats français de la Guerre de Trente Ans," 18.

[98] Contamine, *Histoire militaire*, 1:446. [99] Babeau, *La vie militaire*, 1:253.

[100] Law of 28 April 1653 in Babeau, *La vie militaire*, 1:200.

[101] See the "Ordre qui doit être observé afin que le camp de chaque bataillon soit alligné avec les proportions convenables," Archives de Guerre (AG), MR 1701, piece #7, which specifically allows for vivandières.

her home and business establishment in Guise.[102] The official inquiry reports: "This woman is a kind of *vivandière* who works at that profession during the campaign season, and in the winter she returns to Guise, in a house . . . [where] she now runs a cabaret." Mme. Castres obviously augmented the family income. Her husband appealed both to the law and to his thirty years of service and his wounds, but to no avail. The authorities decided that there were so many troops in Guise that Mme. Castre could not be exempt from quartering troops.

Prostitutes

Of course, the term *camp follower* connotes prostitution, and although not all camp followers plied that profession, it was a fact of military life. Military commentators described prostitution as both beneficial and dangerous. Writing in the late sixteenth century, the Spanish soldier Sancho de Londono defended prostitutes:

For, accepting the fact that well organized states allow such persons in order to avoid worse disorders, in no state is it as necessary to allow them as in this one of free, strong and vigorous men, who might otherwise commit crimes against the local people, molesting their daughters, sisters and wives.[103]

During the reign of Louis XIII, the French army tolerated prostitutes for much the same reasons. According to Simonne, "It is good for the local inhabitants, it is said, because their wives, daughters, and sisters will be more in security." Simonne reported that the number allowed was "4 per 100, although there are found old ordinances that brought the number to 8 per 100." These women received lodgings like soldiers, but in some out-of-the-way place, and they were subjected to inspection by army surgeons, infectious disease, particularly venereal disease, being such a problem.[104] This all seems relatively rational, but it was not always so. Prostitutes were still liable to prosecution and punishment. A document of 1644 stipulates that provosts were responsible for arresting and trying "filles de joie."[105] Prostitutes could also be whipped, or worse. At times, commanders tried to rid themselves of prostitutes in the most brutal manner. Strozzi is said to have ordered that 800 be thrown off a bridge, and all of these unfortunates drowned.[106]

Louis XIV, despite his own lust for women, adopted a more puritanical attitude toward prostitution in the army and tried to ban it. This was a trend of the age; Brandenburg prohibited whores from camps and garrisons by articles of war in 1656, and Fritz Redlich speaks of a policy of "restricting

---

[102] AG, A¹2266, #87–90, February and March 1710.

[103] Sancho de Londono (1589) in Hacker, "Women and Military Institutions," 651.

[104] Simonne, *L'Alphabet du soldat* (1623) in Babeau, *La vie militaire*, 1:200–1.

[105] SHAT, Bib., Col. des ord., vol. 16, #160, 1644, "Forme de la justice militaire de l'infanterie de France," in André, *Le Tellier*, 589.

[106] Brantome, *Couronnels françois, Oeuvres* in Babeau, *La vie militaire*, 1:201.

soldiers' copulations" by the end of the century.[107] In 1684, Louis banned prostitutes from a distance of two leagues from Versailles, where large numbers of troops were encamped, because soldiers were fighting over the women, and some men had been killed. Prostitutes caught within the restricted area were to be disfigured by having their ears and noses cut.[108] In 1687, Louis extended these provisions to the army as a whole. Women without gainful employment found in the company of soldiers within two leagues of a camp or garrison were to be whipped and disfigured. However, the historian André Corvisier comments that when war broke out again, the restrictions were relaxed: "There was no longer a question of depriving Mars of Venus."[109]

Women Soldiers

The most unusual way in which women served with the army was as soldiers. The issue of women fighting is a broader one than the consideration only of those women who joined regular military units. In siege warfare, women often played a part in defending their cities, from hauling earth for wall repairs to firing at the enemy. It was even possible that the governor of town could be female, as was case of the countess d'Entragues in Mâcon.[110] Moreover, on occasion, noble women from time to time would organize local defense in the countryside. One such impressive woman, the most famous "amazon" of the era of Louis XIII, was a local heroine from Lorraine. Barbe d'Ernecourt, Madame de Saint-Baslemont, led gentlemen, peasants, and local forces against the *cravates*, or bandits that plagued the countryside during the war between France and Spain, 1635–59. However, while she commanded her own band of fighting men, she never actually bore a commission from either the king of France or the duke of Lorraine.[111] Philis de la Tour du Pin de La Charce raised and led her vassals and peasants against troops of the duke of Savoy and in doing so bought time for Marshal Catinat during the Nine Years' War. Louis eventually gave her a brevet and pension as a colonel.[112]

Service in uniform was another matter, and by its nature difficult to document. The commissioned ranks would seem to have been essentially free of

---

[107] Fritz Redlich, *The German Military Enterprizer*, 1:208.

[108] SHAT, Bib., Col. des ord., vol. 25, #70, 31 October 1684, "Ordonnance du Roy pour faire condamner les Filles de mauvaise vie qui se trouveront avec les soldats, à deux lieues aux environs de Versailles, à avoir le nez et les oreilles coupées." See other ordinances against prostitution: SHAT, Bib., Col. des ord., vol. 25, #93, 1 March 1685; Col. des ord., vol. 25, #123, 20 May 1686; and Col. des ord. vol. 25, #149.

[109] Contamine, *Histoire militaire*, 1:403.

[110] André Corvisier, *Les Français et l'armée sous Louis XIV* (Vincennes: 1975), 90.

[111] See the fascinating volume by Micheline Cuénin, *La dernière des Amazones, Madame de Saint-Baslemont* (Nancy: 1992) and Charles Armand Romain (pseud. for Armand Charmain), *Les guerrières* (Paris: 1931), 91–93.

[112] Romain, *Les guerrières*, 94–95; Nicolas Edouard Delabarre-Duparcq, *Histoire militaire des femmes* (Brest: 1873), 202.

women. There is one famous case of a woman who became an officer of
regular troops. The Chevalier Balthazar, born Geneviève Prémoy in 1660,
eventually told her tale in *Histoire de la dragonne*, although there is reason to
believe that this tale of adventure cannot be taken as gospel. She had wanted
to dress as a man when only a youth and fled home to enlist in male attire.
She saw her first action at Condé in 1676, was promoted to cornet for bravery, and eventually reached the rank of lieutenant. Her service stretched into
the War of the Spanish Succession. When she fell wounded, she had to reveal
her sex, but instead of dismissing her, Louis presented her with a sword and
elevated her to the Order of Saint-Louis. After being discovered as a woman,
she wore a skirt as part of her uniform. Thus goes the tale.[113]

There is much more solid evidence for women serving as enlisted men.
The army was officially an exclusively male establishment; therefore, women
who wanted to serve in the ranks masqueraded as men. Popular notions
might portray these women as the lovers of soldiers they wished to follow
into the army. So, in fact, proclaims the song about Manon de Nivelle,
who wore the uniform of the Regiment de Provence in order to follow her
unfaithful lover, Sans-Quartier.[114] The reality was much more prosaic. Mas-
querading as a man and enlisting was one of the few avenues that a poor
woman could take to escape an unacceptable life. Dekker and Van de Pol
have studied this phenomenon in the Netherlands and conclude that the
young women involved came from the lower classes and "had a background
of rootlessness caused by the death of one or both parents, family quarrels,
or migration."[115]

At this time, the need for soldiers was so great and the technique of
recruitment so crude that women could pass into the army without much
trouble, providing they displayed some ingenuity. From the French Revolution on, when universal conscription eased the pressures on numbers and
medical inspections became more routine, women found it virtually impossible to follow the same escape route.

The nature of the situation, clandestine and illegal service, means that only
hit-or-miss evidence remains of this phenomenon. Still, enough is available
to make clear that women did serve in the ranks. One of the most compelling
cases is that of Marie Magdelaine Mouron, whose life emerges not from any
self-serving story or romantic song but from the records of a military inquiry
following her desertion in 1696.[116] Daughter of an armed guard for *gabelle*
tax collectors, and disliking her stepmother, this Picarde fled from home and
enlisted in the Royal Walloon Regiment in 1690. She then marched to

[113] Romain, *Les guerrières*, 97–104; Delabarre-Duparcq, *Histoire militaire des femmes*, 202–8.
[114] Babeau, *La vie militaire*, 1:263.
[115] Rudolf M. Dekker and Lotte van de Pol, *The Tradition of Female Tranvestism in Early Modern Europe*, trans. Judy Marcure and Lotte van de Pol (Houndsmill, Basingstoke: 1989), 99.
[116] AG, MR 1785, #53–55, 28 May 1696, *procès verbal* and accompanying documents concerning Marie Magdelaine Mouron. See a fuller account of her life in John A. Lynn, "The Strange Case of the Maiden Soldier of Picardy," *MHQ, The Quarterly Journal of Military History*, spring 1990, 54–56.

Provence, where she was forced to leave her regiment, but she soon enlisted again as a dragoon in the Regiment de Morsan. Eventually injured in a duel, she had to reveal her sex to receive treatment, but her army commander, Marshal de Noailles, took pity and sent her to a home for girls. Marie fled this environment as well, returned to Picardy, and there enlisted for a third time in the new Regiment du Biez, created in 1696. When her true identity was about to be revealed, she deserted that regiment and tried to enlist in a fourth, but this time she was apprehended as a deserter and her story recorded. It would appear that she was imprisoned, not for being a woman but for accepting recruitment bounties and then deserting.

Other cases reflect Marie's situation. Geneviève Grondar at age twenty-three served for ten months with the dragoon Regiment de Rannes.[117] Jeanne Bensa, who adopted the *nom de guerre* Joly-Coeur, campaigned with the Regiment de Bourbon. This young woman from Auvergne was raised as a Protestant by her brother and sister-in-law but converted to Catholicism, an act that so infuriated her sister-in-law that she beat Jeanne, who then stole some of her brother's clothes and fled. After working as a valet to two officers, she finally enlisted as a soldier in the Regiment de Bourbon. She served well in Italy but in 1704 became ill and was shipped back to the hospital at Antibes. There she told her story, apparently to secure her discharge. Her officers and comrades considered her a fine soldier and raised 40 livres for her. Finally, she received a royal gratuity of 40 écus as well.[118]

Madeleine Caulier was another poor girl who worked at an inn near Lille when Marlborough besieged that city in 1708. Her brother served in the garrison, and she was allowed to cross the lines to visit him. Learning this, French officers asked her to smuggle messages in to the commander of the garrison, Marshal Boufflers. This she did and in return requested the count d'Évreux to reward her by allowing her to masquerade as a man and enlist in a dragoon regiment. Her request granted, she fought well. She died at the battle of Denain in 1712, and only her dead body revealed her true identity.[119]

Other European armies also harbored females in the ranks. Oliver Goldsmith observed, "The late war with Spain, and even the present, hath produced instances of females enlisting both in the land and sea service, and behaving with remarkable bravery in the disguise of the other sex."[120] Dekker

---

[117] Georges Girard, *Le service militaire en France à la fin du règne de Louis XIV: Racolage et milice, 1701–1715* (Paris: 1915), 47.

[118] Girard, *Racolage et milice*, 47–48.

[119] Romain, *Les guerrières*, 104; Alfred Tranchant and Jules Ladimir, *Les femmes militaires de la France* (Paris: 1866), 317.

[120] Oliver Goldsmith, "Female Warriors," in *The Works of Oliver Goldsmith*, ed. J. W. M. Gibbs, 5 vols. (London: 1908), 1:317. He mentions Moll Davis, who fought as a dragoon in the War of the Spanish Succession and was admitted to the old soldiers' home at Chelsea. Daniel Defoe told the story of Mother Ross, a camp follower under Marlborough. She said, "Whenever my husband was ordered I always followed him, and he was sometimes of the party that went to search for and draw the enemy's mines; I was often engaged with their party underground." Mother Ross in David Chandler, *Marlborough as a Military Commander* (London: 1973), 250.

and Van de Pol present a number of Dutch cases, including the formidable Maria van Antwerpen, and the female dragoon Geertruid ter Brugge.[121]

There were also rare cases of women who did not follow the more usual social profile – women of better birth who served in the ranks. Christine de Meyrac, daughter of a baron, possessed a passion for the army, even as a little girl. This unusually tall girl eventually enlisted under the name of Saint-Aubin and served during the Dutch War.[122] Thérèse Gaumé, wife of a lieutenant in the Regiment de la Marche, dressed as a man to accompany the Regiment de Vaudemont in 1709.[123]

Such examples of women soldiers stand witness to many cases that went undiscovered or unreported. Incidental to this brief consideration is the propensity of women to seek service as dragoons, an odd choice but one that occurred time and again. In any case, women who actually handled weapons were a curiosity and an anomaly. The major presence of women with the troops was that of soldiers' wives playing very much the part of women, sanctioned with official recognition and burdened with serious duties.

The statistics and comments presented in this chapter give only a rough sketch of the men and women who marched with the army of the *grand siècle*. The numbers tell us enough to highlight important characteristics of the new state commission army, but not enough to flesh out the people who composed it. As so often happens to the many in history, their images have become obscured by our focus on the few – in this case, their officers and generals. Future historians may be able to correct this failing, or perhaps the records simply will not allow it. Then we must fall back to such pictures as those forty drawings of gallant though fragile figures with which this chapter began.

---

[121] Dekker and van der Pol, *The Tradition of Female Tranvestism*, 18, 73. In all, Dekker and Van de Pol discovered 119 cases of female cross-dressing in the Netherlands of the seventeenth and eighteenth centuries. The great majority of these women became sailors or soldiers.

[122] Romain, *Les guerrières*, 96–97.

[123] Girard, *Racolage et milice*, 47.

II

Recruitment

MARS lived on a diet of flesh and blood; massive armies consumed not only materiel but men. During the late winter and early spring, parties of recruits fit for service cluttered the highways of France as they trudged to the frontiers to replenish the ranks of hard-pressed regiments. Louis XIV cared not so much where these young men came from, only where they were going. In fact, they came from many sources, French and foreign, volunteer and conscript. The great monarch had to use every means at his disposal to collect his new soldiers; Mars was ever hungry.

During the *grand siècle*, the right to levy soldiers was a precious royal privilege. Royal decrees demanding that no military unit be created in France without the king's sanction dated back to the Middle Ages; in fact, Charles VII first declared this basic royal prerogative in an ordinance of 1439, and this assertion was repeatedly reasserted.[1] The Wars of Religion in the late sixteenth century pitted rival French armies against each other. Seen in the full context of the contending royal, League, and Protestant forces, those wars provided a deadly trial in which the great aristocratic houses asserted their own rights to raise and maintain troops, while the monarchy possessed no real monopoly over the institutions of violence. In 1583, Henri III issued the ordinance prohibiting the raising of military units without the king's approval, which remained in effect during the seventeenth century, but it was often breached. As the seventeenth century progressed, French kings and their agents strongly insisted that only the monarchy could legitimately authorize companies and regiments for their state commission armies. The last great surge of "unapproved" French units came with the Fronde, even as Mazarin and Le Tellier struggled to suppress such practices.[2] Finally, the

---

[1] David Parrott, "The Administration of the French Army During the Ministry of Cardinal Richelieu," Ph.D. dissertation, Oxford: 1985, 162–63 and notes.
[2] See, for example, ordinances against raising troops in Dauphiné, Provence, Languedoc, Limousin, la Manche, and Bordeaux without a royal commission. AG, A^{1}115, #16, 20 July

personal reign of Louis XIV gave de facto reality as well as de jure legality to the exclusive royal prerogative.[3]

To create and maintain his huge armies, Louis XIV required large numbers of recruits. André Corvisier estimates that during the War of the Spanish Succession alone, the French required 200,000 for augmenting or creating units, and another 455,000 for replacements, meaning that the French army needed 655,000 recruits, native and foreign.[4] The Sun King provided manpower for his armed forces through a variety of methods; these evolved over the course of the century in response to the military needs of the state and the growing authority of central authority. The basis of recruitment during the *grand siècle* remained the voluntary enlistment of French and foreign troops to follow the king's banners. Tradition also allowed the monarchy to summon the feudal *ban*, to levy commoners in extraordinary situations, and to demand that the peasantry supply labor for his army. Louvois eventually extended both the right to compel service from his population and the tradition of militia service in towns and provinces to create the *milice* in 1688, which provided a substantial number of the rank and file through a regular form of conscription.

REGULAR RECRUITMENT

The great bulk of the rank and file in the French army came from regular, voluntary enlistment. This basic form of recruitment remained the most productive throughout the century, although it had to be augmented at times by more compulsory methods. As in so many aspects of military institutions during the period, the system as defined by ordinance and regulation differed sharply from the system as it functioned in reality. Faced with wartime needs, state administrators often blinked at abuses, and voluntary enlistment often gave way to trickery and force. But although the system bent, it did not break or break down.

Defining the Terms of Engagement and the Recruit

Royal decrees and ordinances dealing with recruitment remained surprisingly vague throughout the *grand siècle*. It would seem that the monarchs and their ministers worried more about the financial details of recruitment than about defining a term of service or about setting minimum characteristics for recruits. The need for recruits left the door open to the widest latitude. Thus, while Le Tellier's regulation of 1643 stipulated the amount of

---

1649; #72, 21 August 1649, and #81, 2 September 1649. See, as well, the letter to M. de Pompadour against "levies against my will," AG, A[1]115, #74, August 1649.

[3] André Corvisier, *Les Français et l'armée sous Louis XIV* (Vincennes: 1975), 133.

[4] André Corvisier, *L'armée française de la fin du XVIIe siècle au ministère du Choiseul: Le soldat*, 2 vols. (Paris: 1964), 1:157.

money that the king would pay for new recruits, it set no firm standards for them.[5]

The French never adopted a fixed term of engagement for new recruits during the *grand siècle*, so from the royal perspective, enlistment remained theoretically for life.[6] Article 237 of the Code Michau in 1629 stipulated that a soldier enrolling must promise to serve for at least six months, but there was no promised release after that period.[7] Under Louis XIV, there were in practice a number of qualifications upon this open-ended commitment. First and foremost, the French demobilized at the end of every major war, a process that entailed the discharge of unwanted or excess soldiers. This process of *réforme* seems not to have actually released a great number of soldiers in 1659, but it did after all of the major wars of Louis XIV's personal reign. Beyond this, ordinances of 1666 and 1668 allowed that after four years of service, a soldier could request a discharge.[8] Yet such a request hardly guaranteed success, because regulations strictly limited the number of discharges that could be granted.

While it was not official practice, some officers promised a fixed, short term of service. Guaranteed short terms made potential recruits more willing to sign up and enabled officers to pay lower bounties to recruits, since the new soldiers were not obligating themselves to an open-ended commitment. Louvois condemned these limited contracts designed, as he said, "to raise soldiers more easily and more cheaply," so in 1682, he promulgated a regulation that set the minimum term of engagement at three years.[9] Only men who were reenlisting could sign on for less, although they had to agree to serve for at least one entire year.[10]

---

[5] "Règlement sur le sujet des recrues des troupes d'infanterie et de cavalerie," 20 December 1643, in Louis André, *Michel Le Tellier et l'organisation de l'armée monarchique* (Paris: 1906), 236–39.

[6] Georges Girard, *Le service militaire en France à la fin du règne de Louis XIV: Racolage et milice, 1701–1715* (Paris: 1915), 49. André Corvisier, "Le moral des combattants, panique et enthousiasme, la bataille de Malplaquet," *Revue historique des armées*, 1977, no. 3, 10, says that before 1686, engagements were for life, and after this, normally for six years; however, this may be a judgment extrapolated from his *L'armée française*, since there he concludes that in the eighteenth century, most soldiers spent about six years in the ranks. H. Pichat, "Les armées de Louis XIV en 1674," *Revue d'histoire de l'armée* (1910), 7, and Victor Belhomme, *L'armée française en 1690* (Paris: 1895), 16, write as if the term of enlistment was set at four years, but this was only a minimum.

[7] Code Michau, article 237, in François André Isambert et al., eds., *Recueil général des anciennes lois françaises, depuis l'an 420, jusqu'à la Révolution de 1789*, vol. 16 (Paris: 1829), 286.

[8] Philippe Contamine, ed., *Histoire militaire de la France*, vol. 1 (Paris: 1992), 396. These were ordinances of 1 October 1666 and 1 June 1668. Girard, *Racolage et milice*, 49n.

[9] See the ordinances of 1 August 1682, 18 December 1684, and 5 November 1685 in Girard, *Racolage et milice*, 50fn. These acts have been misinterpreted as setting the term of enlistment at three years for all recruits, but Girard makes the good point that this did not officially limit enrollment to three years but simply restrained an officer from allowing a soldier to commit himself to anything less. Richelieu had suggested a similar three-year minimum service years before. Richelieu, *Testament politique*, ed. Louis André (Paris: 1947), 473.

[10] Ordinance of 18 March 1684, in Girard, *Racolage et milice*, 50.

The pressures of Louis's last two great wars nullified nearly all provisions for discharge and limited terms of service. Ordinances of 1688 and 1689 canceled discharges during the Nine Years' War. Louis acted again to keep men in the ranks with an ordinance of 1701, which forbade discharges to any able-bodied soldier.[11] While André Corvisier points out that in 1709 the official terms of enlistment began to specify an obligation for the duration of the war – an innovation in recruiting that he identifies as a breakthrough – this would seem only to have accepted a *fait accompli* that was in place during wartime since 1688, or at least 1701.[12]

If the French were vague concerning terms of engagement, they were equally vague about the required age and height for recruits. The only rule seemed to be that men be judged fit for service.[13] Time and again, Louvois urged that boys not be sent away from the army: "When the soldiers of fifteen or sixteen years of age are well formed, you must leave them in the companies, because some years later they will be in a better state to serve than others who enter at an older age."[14] The 1680 recruitment ordinance stated only that new soldiers be "neither vagabonds [*gueux*], nor children, nor deformed."[15] Officers would be fined if they presented such men, but the lines were blurred. Louvois had no desire to lose "a young man of good promise."[16] As regards height, the only formal requirements appear to have been those imposed upon Gardes françaises, who had to be at least 5 feet 4 inches tall, which would translate into about 5 feet 8 inches in modern measurement.[17] Despite the vague quality of the regulations, men were discharged for being too short. In 1683, Louvois learned that eighty veterans had been thrown out because they lacked sufficient height and that another 200 were slated to meet the same fate. He shot back an order to the commanding general to keep the men, "since a soldier who has served eight or nine years is worth more than a big peasant recruit."[18] Two years later, Louvois informed his inspectors that "His Majesty does not want at all that one measure the soldiers, and it is not necessary to discharge a veteran soldier because he is too short."[19] Villars would have agreed with the minister

---

[11] See the ordinances of 20 September 1688, 15 October 1689, and 18 November 1701 in Girard, *Racolage et milice*, 51.

[12] Corvisier, "Le moral des combattants," 10.

[13] Girard, *Rocolage et milice*, 46. Girard cites an ordinance of 15 March 1686. Belhomme, *L'armée française en 1690*, 16, and Pichat, "L'armée de Louis XIV en 1674," 7, both insist that there was a minimum age of sixteen, but again without citing the ordinances involved.

[14] AG, A^{1}335, 23 June 1673, Louvois to Dufay.

[15] Ordinance of 23 December 1680 in Camille Rousset, *Histoire de Louvois*, 4 vols. (Paris: 1862–64), 3:296.

[16] AG, A^{1}741, 23 February 1685, Louvois to inspectors, in Rousset, *Louvois*, 3:297fn.

[17] Ordinance of 8 December 1691, in Girard, *Racolage et milice*, 46. Corvisier, *L'armée française*, 2:640–41. Belhomme, *L'armée française en 1690*, 16, states that there was a minimum height for recruits circa 1690 of 5 feet 7 inches in peacetime and 5 feet 6 inches for wartime, but he gives no sources for his firm conclusion.

[18] AG, A^{1}689, 27 January 1683, Louvois to Huxelles.

[19] AG, A^{1}741, 23 February 1685, Louvois to inspectors, in Rousset, *Louvois*, 3:297fn.

of war, for the great marshal had nothing against short soldiers and would have forgotten height restrictions as long as men were fit for service and marched well.[20] Yet it is clear that officers did apply rough standards, at least regiment by regiment. Recruitment posters might stipulate conditions, such as one which demanded that prospective recruits be at least eighteen years old and "above five feet in height."[21] Saint-Mayme, a simple captain during the War of the Spanish Succession, stated that he wanted nearly any men, "provided that they are 5 feet 1 inch . . . or even somewhat less provided that they are young."[22]

The Expense of Recruitment in the Semi-Entrepreneurial System

Recruitment was expensive; of course, part of this expense involved the equipping of new recruits, but it also entailed the paying of bounties to induce men to volunteer. Technically, the state was responsible for these costs, either paying the money up front or reimbursing officers for their expenses. When commanded to raise 300 new men per regiment in 1631, the army with which Turenne served sent an officer to court to collect the money in advance.[23] But, in reality, officers usually had to use their own financial resources to raise new recruits during wartime, when state finances were stretched to and beyond their limits. As previously discussed in Chapter 7, even if they did not take on the entire expense themselves, officers would commonly advance the funds on the expectation of repayment, thus giving the government free credit. Such was the semi-entrepreneurial nature of the regiments.

The costs of filling out regiments added up to great sums. A regulation of 1643 set the amount that the king would pay to recruit and arm an infantryman at 18 livres, or 24 livres for the armies of Italy or Catalonia, and 2,400 livres for a company of cavalry, which at the time numbered seventy men, making 34 livres per man.[24] At the start of the Dutch War, a lawyer, André de Goex, sought to raise a company of fifty soldiers in Savoy at 23 livres per man.[25] By the War of the Spanish Succession, the cost of raising a free

---

[20] BN, f. fr. 6257, Claude Louis Hector Villars, "Traité de la guerre de campagne," 92.

[21] 1702 poster for the fraudulent "Régiment de mousquetaires de Mgr le duc de Bourgoyne," in Girard, *Racolage et milice*, 77.

[22] Saint-Mayme in Georges Girard, ed., "Un soldat de Malplaquet: Lettres du capitaine de Saint-Mayme," *Carnet de Sabretache* (1922), 511.

[23] Turenne letter of 24 March 1631 in Jean Bérenger, *Turenne* (Paris: 1987), 87.

[24] André, *Le Tellier*, 237. For cavalry company size, see AG, Bib., A¹h 638, vol. II, table of pay rates, and Bernard Kroener, *Les routes et les étapes. Die bersorgung der franzoschichen Armeen in Nordostfrankreich (1635–1661)*, 2 vols. (Munster: 1980), 1:178. An officer at Thionville offered to create a company of forty cavalry for the sum of 7,500 livres, or 187 livres per man, but this seems to have been unusually high. AG, A¹210, #158, 18 December 1667, "Mémoire de M. le marquis de Créquy."

[25] Mugnier, *Un capitaine recruteur au XVIIe siècle* (1886), in Albert Babeau, *La vie militaire sous l'ancien régime*, 2 vols. (Paris: 1890), 1:42n. The cost of clothing and equipping a soldier for the *milice* in the 1690s could run anywhere from 40 to 75 livres. Léon Hennet, *Les milices et les troupes provinciales* (Paris: 1884), 29.

Table 11.1. *Bounties for the Gardes françaises.*

Date	Average bounty	Men enrolled
December 1691	26 livres 12 sols	2
January 1693	36 livres 6 sols	3
March 1694	6 livres 7 sols	7
December 1695	26 livres 4 sols	5
1696	41 livres	4

company of fifty fusiliers could run as much as 1,530 livres, or about 31 livres per man.[26] During the War of the Spanish Succession, the amount budgeted for recruits was considerable. For winter quarters in 1706–7, accounts listed 1,498,425 livres for infantry recruits and 1,181,000 livres for *remonte de la cavalerie*, which apparently included men as well as horses.[27]

Although ordinances attempted to set a limit for bounties, practice sanctioned whatever the market would allow, from a few livres to over a hundred.[28] Late in the reign of Louis XIV, Vauban advocated setting a universal recruitment bounty of 20 livres for a new infantryman with no previous service, but as with many of his projects, this remained unrealized.[29] As French forces expanded at the start of the Dutch War, one new middle-class officer of the Regiment de Champagne paid up to 3 pistoles (39 livres) to new recruits, and such high bounties gained him a "company that is very good."[30] Extreme circumstances, such as those imposed by famine in 1694–95 and 1709 could induce men to waive any bounty and enroll simply on the prospect of getting something to eat in the army.[31] In 1707, members of the orchestra of the Marseilles opera enrolled "because they were dying of hunger."[32] As Villars commented in 1709, "One could say, perhaps, that it is a good effect of a bad cause, and that the recruit levies are only as strong as they are because of the misery of the provinces."[33] Corvisier provides interesting detail on the ebb and flow of recruitment bounties in the Gardes françaises during the last two of Louis's great wars. The company belonging to Mennevillette paid recruits average bounties during the Nine Years' War, as shown in Table 11.1.[34] As bounties fell to their lowest, the number of men

[26] AN, G⁷1776, #332.
[27] AN, G⁷1778, #221, 24 October 1706, "Fonds pour les recrues du quartier d'hiver, 1706 et 1707." Mallet states that each company was allowed 317 livres for recruits, while cavalry companies received 700 livres for remounts every year; this would appear to refer to rates just after the War of Spanish Succession. Jean Roland de Mallet, *Comptes rendus de l'administration des finances du royaume de France* (London: 1789), 158.
[28] Girard, *Racolage et milice*, 49.   [29] AG, MR 1828, #21.
[30] AG, A¹362, 10 November 1673, letter from the archbishop of Lyons to Louvois, in Louis Tuetey, *Les officiers de l'ancien régime. Nobles et roturiers* (Paris: 1908), 63.
[31] Corvisier, *Les Français et l'armée*, 269, and André Corvisier, *Armies and Societies in Europe, 1494–1789*, trans. Abigail T. Siddall (Bloomington, IN: 1979), 69.
[32] Quincy in Corvisier, *L'armée française*, 1:317.
[33] Villars in Corvisier, *L'armée française*, 1:317.
[34] Corvisier, *L'armée française*, 1:317; Contamine, *Histoire militaire*, 1:434.

enrolled rose to its highest because starving individuals tried to escape the famine of 1694. An account of an incident by a Swiss officer in 1695 suggests that the going bounty was only 9 to 12 livres in the fall of that year, again low for a foreign regiment.[35]

Studying recruitment bounties in other companies of the Gardes françaises, Corvisier reports that they fell from 50 livres in 1706, to 30 livres in 1707, to 20 livres in 1710.[36] It is worth noting that bounties promised were not always paid, so when the young captain Saint-Mayme died in 1709, he still owed the price of engagement to some of his soldiers.[37] Not only did bounties fluctuate from year to year, but from season to season. For the Gardes françaises between 1701 and 1705, bounties bottomed out in September and peaked in December, at the start of the recruitment season and in May, at its close.[38]

Paying high bounties to the last men required to fill a company may have been well worth it to an officer, because officers often received extra gratuities for having brought their companies up to strength. In 1645, a captain could expect a reward of 600 livres if he produced a full company of seventy men or 300 livres if he had sixty men. However, the officer would lose 6 livres from his allowances for every man below the number of fifty-six.[39] An ordinance of 1671 decreed that captains who brought their companies up to the regulation strength of fifty would be paid for fifty-three men, as long as no valet of the captain was counted among the fifty.[40] At the start of the War of the Spanish Succession, in 1703, when infantry company strength was set at forty-five, a captain received three extra pays for having forty-five men, two for forty-two, and one for thirty-nine.[41] Circa 1690, there was also a reward for filling a company early; if a field company was complete by 1 February, its captain received a gratuity of 200 livres, but if it was not full

[35] Côte d'Or, C 2915, 28 October 1695.
[36] Corvisier, L'armée française, 1:323. See, as well, the bar graph on recruitment bounties for one company of the Gardes françaises, 1700–46, on page 318.
[37] Letter of 22 October 1709 from the commanding officer of Saint-Mayme's battalion to the brother of Saint-Mayme in Girard, "Un soldat de Malplaquet," 541.
[38] Corvisier, L'armée française, 1:320.
[39] Contamine, Histoire militaire, 1:365. A 1633 commitment to officers, still in effect when France went to war with Spain, promised captains that companies raised to 90 percent of their full strength of 100 would be paid as if the companies were complete, so the captain could pocket a reward of ten pays. AAE, France, 808, 12 October 1633, in Parrott, "The Administration of the French Army," 85. This arrangement is mentioned regarding captains of the Army of Germany in a letter from Richelieu to Servien, 18 June 1635, in Richelieu, Lettres, instructions diplomatiques, et papiers d'état, d'Avenel, ed., 8 vols. (Paris: 1853–77), 5:60.
[40] SHAT, Bib., Col. des ord., vol. 22, #135, ordinance of 1 April 1671. In 1684, when an infantry company was supposed to number fifty men, a captain who could produce forty soldiers received a gratification of two pays; with forty-five men he received three extra pays, and with a full fifty, he got four extra pays – that is, he received pay for fifty-four men if he had fifty and could thus pocket the four additional pays of 5 sols each for himself, legitimately. AG, Bib., A[1b] 638, vol. 2, 29.
[41] In 1705, this rose to seven pays for forty-five men, five for forty to forty-four, and three for thirty-seven to forty. Ordinances of 1 October 1703 and 1 March 1705 in Girard, Racolage et milice, 23.

by March 15, then 150 livres were withheld. Consequently, if replacements sent to the front did not fill up a battalion, its officers levied more at their own expense.[42]

Other pressures might encourage an officer to slack off on recruitment. In particular, the prospect of imminent peace made the expense of building a company back up to strength seem unnecessary. As an administrator complained after news spread that Louis XIV had appointed a peace negotiator early in 1710, "the majority of officers begin to relax in reestablishing their companies, neglecting to get recruits and to find horses for necessary remounts because of the fear of a *réforme* after the peace" – a *réforme* that would eliminate or reduce their companies.[43]

Seigneurial Recruitment

Regular French recruitment worked in different ways. All line troops were supposed to have volunteered for service, at least before the institution of the royal *milice* in 1688. Many of these volunteers were supplied by officers who sought new recruits from their own lands or districts, a practice known as *seigneurial recruitment*. Other recruits signed up with recruitment parties in towns and cities; in wartime, many of these recruits were tricked or cajoled into service as part of *racolage*, a term for recruiting that implied its rougher methods.

Volunteer recruitment was a responsibility of the captains above all. During the Richelieu ministry, *commissaires des guerres* bore the official responsibility for hiring troops who the *commissaires* were then to turn over to the captain, but in fact, the captains raised the troops themselves.[44] *Commissaires des guerres* always played a legitimating role in recruitment, because troops were not officially enrolled until presented to the *commissaires*. In order to avoid some of the fraud associated with recruitment, an ordinance of 1661 forbade officers to present their new recruits to fortress governors, but only to *commissaires des guerres* who would then carry out the official enrollment.[45] Provincial *intendants* also figured in the recruitment process, since they often negotiated with officers to raise units and authorized payments to the captains.[46]

Regiments preferred that captains bring in recruits via seigneurial recruitment, which took advantage of the officers' roles as *seigneurs*, or lords, on their own estates and districts.[47] Without regimental depots to send up replacements

---

[42] Belhomme, *L'armée française en 1690*, 17–18.

[43] AG, A¹2266, #77bis, 9 February 1710, letter to Ormesson. See, as well, A¹2265, #140, 12 February 1710, on the same subject.

[44] Parrott, "The Administration of the French Army," 187.

[45] Philippe Contamine, ed., *Histoire militaire de la France*, vol. 1 (Paris: 1992), 395–96.

[46] Douglas Baxter, *Servants of the Sword, French Military Intendants of the Army, 1630–1670* (Urbana: 1976), 5.

[47] Concerning the character of seigneurial recruitment, see Girard, *Racolage et milice*, 19–27 for the period of the War of the Spanish Succession and Corvisier, *L'armée française*, 1:165–78, for the period from 1700–62. A brief account can be found in Contamine, *Histoire militaire*, 1:441–42.

over the course of a campaign, regiments wore down until they entered winter quarters. When regiments entered winter quarters, the activity of campaigning ceased, and officers applied for leaves for the stated purpose of securing recruits for their companies. Officers departed for roughly half the year, or a semester, and so such a leave was known as a *semestre*. In the era of the Nine Years' War and the War of the Spanish Succession, roughly a third of the officers, generally including one from each company, received leaves to fill out those companies.[48] Circa 1690, officers who went on *semestres* had to return with two soldiers each or forfeit their pay for the leave.[49]

Officers planning to return to their homes on *semestre* would write to request that their relatives assist them in the task of rounding up recruits. Those left at home might know of peasant families with too many sons, or local men down on their luck and needing some form of subsistence. The young captain Saint-Mayme, when he learned that he would go on *semestre* in 1702, wrote home to request that his brother look for recruits: "If some man presents himself, you will please me if you engage him, even if he is not very tall."[50] To the extent that those relatives located recruits, the officer could regard his *semestre* as a vacation and simply send back the men that his family had collected. An officer on *semestre* need not even be burdened with the task of escorting his recruits back to the regiment, since this task could be left to other officers who willingly added a few more to their party as they passed near conducting their own *recrue* to winter quarters.[51]

Even when an officer did not enjoy a *semestre*, he might enlist his family in recruiting chores. The young Sarraméa asked his father to get him two recruits for 25 pistoles in 1697.[52] In a letter written in October 1707, Saint-Mayme regretted that he would get no *semestre* that year, but he still asked his brother "if by hazard you procure some man, you can give him to one of the groups of recruits who pass through Perigueux; several will pass by there for our regiment."[53] Not only male relatives, but mothers, wives, and sisters sought out likely recruits. Marshal Chamilly praised the sister of a captain in the Regiment du Dauphin: "There is not a trick that she does not know to enroll soldiers for him."[54]

Seigneurial recruitment could give companies, and even regiments, a regional caste. Even though regiments might bear provincial names, such as Picardie or Champagne, they lacked any special relationship with the provinces in question. However, recruitment patterns could draw an unusually large number of levies and replacements from particular localities. Bonds of clientage bound many regiments together, as colonels appointed friends,

---

[48] Belhomme, *L'armée française en 1690*, 17; Girard, *Racolage et milice*, 21.

[49] Belhomme, *L'armée française en 1690*, 17.

[50] Letter of 23 August 1702 from Saint-Mayme to his brother, the chevalier de Cablan, in Girard, "Un soldat de Malplaquet," 511.

[51] Girard, *Racolage et milice*, 27.

[52] François Abbadie, ed., *Lettres d'un cadet de Gascogne, François de Sarraméa* (Paris: 1890), 17.

[53] Letter of 14 October 1707 in Girard, "Un soldat de Malplaquet," 522.

[54] AG, A¹1897, #113, 10 May 1705, letter from marshal Chamilly, in Girard, *Racolage et milice*, 27.

relatives, and neighbors to command, and these officers tended to live in proximity and recruit in their own bailiwicks; thus, units came to have a regional character. During the 1630s, Turenne relied on fellow Protestants to lead his regiment and often drew soldiers from his own lands, using family connections.[55] Corvisier notes that in the early eighteenth century, soldiers in the colonel's company of the Regiment de Vivarais hailed mainly from the *généralités* of Alençon and Maine, both a long way from the Vivarais along the Rhône.[56]

While seigneurial recruitment shows relatively little evidence of fraud or violence, it had to be supplemented by bringing in certain recruits by officially sanctioned compulsion and by the more common regular activities of recruitment parties, *racoleurs*, on the prowl for willing, or not so willing, young men.

Forced Recruitment of Gens sans Aveu during the War with Spain, 1635–59

With the need for additional troops so great in the war with Spain, and the government in such poor financial shape, it periodically turned to compulsion to fill the ranks. Sometimes the army needed only temporary troops to aid at crisis moments; however, when it was necessary to garner new full-time recruits for the king's regiments, force played a role. For reasons not hard to understand, the burden of service was supposed to fall first on the least productive and the least desirable individuals, men defined as vagabonds and *gens sans aveu*, a range of disreputable characters, men without fixed residence or gainful employment, who made no contribution to the community. To the extent that such forced recruitment filled the ranks, the army would be populated by the dregs of society.

Le Tellier labored to improve and regularize such recruitment practices, apparently to minimize the disadvantages implicit in them. His ordinances of 1645 and 1647 describe the procedures that were supposed to be followed.[57] The *commissaires* in charge of the levy must inform local and provincial officials, including the *intendants* and governors. After gaining their approval and support, the *commissaire* was to have drums beaten in all the public places of the election and make public the royal ordinance so that all *gens sans aveu* would enlist. Bounties would be paid to the new recruits. Those who presented themselves were then conducted to particular towns of assembly where they would be formally enrolled in front of officials, apparently there to make certain that everything was above board. When 100 men were

[55] Bérenger, *Turenne*, 77–78, 133.

[56] André Corvisier, "Clientèles et fidélités dans l'armées française aux 17e et 18e siècles," in Y. Durand, ed., *Hommage à Roland Mousnier. Clientèles et fidélités en Europes à l'époque moderne* (Paris: 1981), 225.

[57] Ordinances of 27 June 1645 and 10 February 1647 in André, *Le Tellier*, 212–14.

assembled, they would be led off to the army. If no *gens sans aveu* appeared, the *commissaire* could impose a quota of men on each parish, a quota that could not be commuted into a money payment. Authorities could take volunteers first and then, if need be, name individuals.[58] This form of levy did not involve drawing lots, as would the later royal *milice*. It is to be wondered if the ordinances threatened the good citizens with quotas simply in order to encourage them to round up the local ne'er-do-wells relentlessly.

Paris provides examples of the compulsory recruitment of "low-lifes." When Mazarin needed 2,000 additional men for the siege of Cambrai in 1649, he wrote to Le Tellier demanding a levy in Paris. Vagabonds, *gens sans aveu*, and deserters were to present themselves to the provost of Paris. If they did so, they would then receive a bounty of 12 livres and go off to the army; if they did not, they risked being condemned to serve in the galleys.[59] Levies conducted in this manner – levies of what André terms "men without morality and without aptitude for military service" – ceased after 1652.[60]

Recruiting in the Prisons

Later recruiters also found men in the prisons, but there was no wholesale conversion of able-bodied prisoners to soldiers.[61] Refusing to regard enrollment as a punishment, Louis XIV resisted using convicts in the army. Pontchartrain explained the royal attitude in these words: "The obligation to serve the king has never been and will never be a punishment in itself; it will not be ordered and it will not be characterized in this manner. . . . It is for this reason that the obligation to serve in the troops should be regarded as a form of grace, when it is imposed on those who are condemned."[62] He did not want men with bad moral fiber in the ranks.

This meant that recruiters had to be selective. Those likely to desert were not taken. The favorite targets of recruiters were smugglers and debtors, men of vigorous make-up in the first instance and men who might have been victimized by circumstance in the second. Jailers could not simply open their cells. Creditors could refuse a debtor his liberty.[63] *Intendants* passed on the lists of those chosen, and, in the case of *faux-sauniers*, the *contrôleur général* had to agree, since he was the chief administrator of the salt tax. In one of the most unusual cases, in 1705, the secretary of state for war wanted to rebuild four dragoon regiments with *faux-saulniers* imprisoned at Rennes,

---

[58] Jacques Gébelin, *Histoire des milices provinciales (1688–1791): le tirage au sort sous l'ancien régime* (Paris: 1882), 19–20.

[59] Ordinances of 18, 25, and 26 June 1644 and 6 February 1647 in André, *Le Tellier*, 209n, and letter from Mazarin to Le Tellier, 3 July 1649, in André, *Le Tellier*, 209.

[60] André, *Le Tellier*, 215.

[61] See Girard, *Racolage et milice*, chapter 5, "L'enrolement dans les prisons."

[62] Letter of Pontchartrain, 13 June 1705, in Girard, *Racolage et milice*, 140.

[63] Girard, *Racolage et milice*, 141.

but he only netted nine men, aged twenty to forty.[64] Between 1708 and 1712, the *contrôleur général des finances* Desmaretz secured captured smugglers from the jails of Paris, Rouen, and Saumur as recruits for his son, a colonel.[65]

Only in the last years of fighting did the French actually call upon men who had been condemned to the galleys to march to the front. When the Army of Spain was unable to get sufficient recruits in 1712, the secretaries of war and the navy agreed to send it 1,500 convicts from the galleys of Marseilles.[66] Understandably, when these men marched to join the army, they were put under heavy guard.

Racolage and Its Abuses

The most common method of recruitment in wartime, *racolage*, relied neither upon personal contacts of officers in their home provinces nor upon compulsion organized by royal officials, but upon the labor and lure of recruiting parties dispatched to the towns and cities of France.[67] When a recruiting party arrived in a town, the officer in charge had first to secure permission from the local authorities, who might be highly reluctant to grant it. Once given the right to proceed, recruiters advertised their presence. Recruiters' drums must have been a common sound in the larger towns of France during wartime; local authorities could even provide the drummers. After a dramatic drum roll, the recruiter addressed those attracted by the racket, urging the young men to sign up; a second drum roll climaxed the performance. Trumpets might also blare out. By late in the reign of Louis XIV, posters came into play, as recruiters pasted up enticing accounts of the gallant company to be raised and the generous rewards for those brave enough to accept the challenge. In one such poster, decorated with a richly accoutered cavalier on a rearing horse, Captain Blanmont promised "all sorts of satisfactions" to the men who would come to the hotel of the Trinity on the rue St. Antoine to sign up in his company of Mounted Grenadiers of Monseigneur the duke of Brittany.[68] A decree from Limoges of 1700 nicely listed all the public techniques of recruiters, albeit in an attempt to ban them: "It is forbidden to make any levy of soldiers, and to this end it is forbidden to beat the drum, sound the trumpet or put up posters, without there being shown to us the commission of His Majesty, on threat of a 100 livres fine."[69]

---

[64] AG, A¹1901, #197, 198, 203, and 204, April and May 1705, in Girard, *Racolage et milice*, 146.

[65] Jean Chagniot, "De Rocroi à Rossbach," in Claude Croubois, ed., *L'officier français des origines à nos jours* (Saint-Jean-d'Angély: 1987), 44.

[66] Girard, *Racolage et milice*, 155–56.

[67] On *racolage* during the second half of the reign of Louis XIV, see Girard, *Racolage et milice*, 75–97, and Corvisier, *L'armée française*, 179–89. Unless otherwise noted, all details are from Girard.

[68] A 6 March 1705 poster used as frontispiece to Girard, *Racolage et milice*. See, as well, the recruiting poster from 1703 between pages 80 and 81.

[69] "Règlement de police de la ville de Limoges," 1700, in Girard, *Racolage et milice*, 75n.

Usually the recruiter set up shop in a cabaret, where the atmosphere of masculine camaraderie and the flowing wine lessened resistance. While the recruit could sign or mark a contract of enrollment to close the deal, he need not do even this to obligate himself; it was enough to drink the health of the king in the presence of the recruiter. So much for the formalities.

Racolage was open to many abuses, and military authorities did little to stop them, save for issuing pious words. Liquor played more of a role than simply solemnizing a contract. Many a recruiter got his prey drunk, before springing the trap. If the recruit finally accepted a drink bought with the king's money, he would shoulder a musket. A man who drank until he blacked out could be told that he had enrolled, and he would have no basis upon which to deny it.

Devious recruiters did not shrink from outright misrepresentation. The higher prestige of a cavalry unit might be dangled in front of some naïve young man, or he might be promised membership in some elite unit, when, in fact, he was enrolling in a simple infantry company. Such deceit was common, and unless the abuse was particularly heinous, the duped recruit received no more consideration from authorities than the fool who gets stung buying a faulty used car today. Let the buyer beware. One recruiter advertised by poster that he was recruiting for the Regiment of Musketeers of the duke of Burgundy, when those who committed themselves found themselves to be only privates in the company of Captain Duplessis in the Montboissier infantry regiment.[70] The marquis de Quincy, recruiting for an infantry regiment in 1709, put up posters for cavalry "not to fool [recruits], but to make them come to me," at which point he explained that they would really be signing up for infantry. He prided himself for such honesty.[71]

Some recruiters made extra money on the side by enrolling the sons of the well-to-do, caught in a weak moment, and then charging their parents considerable ransom to rescue their wayward children. A royal ordinance of 1701 spoke explicitly of officers enrolling "young men to serve who were not yet fit to bear arms, only in order to extract money from their parents who would want to reclaim them."[72] The unfortunates could be boys aged twelve or students. Universities forbade recruitment of their students in the university town or even outside the town walls, as at Douai in 1705.[73]

The courts might or might not take action concerning cases of enrollment fraud. If privileged parents appealed directly to the high authorities to secure the release of their sons, the government preferred substitutes to outright payment. In order to get his son back, a councilor of the Cours des Aides in Montauban received an order to replace his son "at least by three or four

[70] Girard, *Racolage et milice*, 77–78.
[71] Quincy in Chagniot, "De Rocroi à Rossbach," 44.
[72] Lille, Aff. gen. 288, dos. #2, 10 December 1701, printed ordinance.
[73] Girard, *Racolage et milice*, 93–94.

good soldiers."[74] Abuses of the recruitment system that the government did punish were more likely to involve officers' offenses against the king rather than against the common recruit. When recruiters pocketed the king's money, justice could be swift. In 1645, Condé broke thirty captains at a stroke for "misuse of recruitment money."[75] Moreover, laws on recruitment threatened fines for officers who brought in recruits incapable of service because of physical problems, because this too would be claiming the king's money on false pretenses.[76]

Methods used to gain recruits sometimes went beyond guile to naked force.[77] Whereas ordinances stipulated that enrollment must be voluntary, all too often this was not the case.[78] Complaints from the 1640s and 1650s make it clear that forced enrollment was then common. Often local magistrates or their armed agents, known as archers and exempts, became involved. In 1656, an ordinance complained:

Instead of beating the drum, several captains, lieutenants, and other officers, in order to carry out the levy of recruits for their companies more easily, conclude arrangements with exempts, archers, and other persons to bring them men. And, in order to carry out these agreements more easily, the said exempts, archers, or their agents take children, students, artisans, pickpockets, servants, and laborers, under the pretext of finding them positions in which they can work at their profession or of having them carry packages or other jobs, and put them in out of the way places, and keep them by force in particular houses. And, after having locked them up for some time, without allowing them to tell anyone of their detention, they make them leave during the night and hand them over to the said captains . . . .[79]

Recruiters not only grabbed men off the city streets; they invaded private homes and public buildings to kidnap male inhabitants and also seized travelers along the road.[80] A royal ordinance of 1701 condemned certain "levies which were made during the last wars" in which captains took men "by surprise or other ways forbidden by [the king's] ordinances" and then "took them by force to their companies."[81] Yet little changed. In 1705, soldiers of the Regi-

---

[74] AG, A¹1801, #329, 22 March 1704, Chamillart to Legendre in Girard, *Racolage et milice*, 93. Girard states that it was rare to require a single replacement, but two or four were usually demanded.

[75] André, *LeTellier*, 250 and 250n.

[76] The ordinance of 23 December 1680 detailed a fine of 20 livres for an officer who introduced an *invalide* into his company. Rousset, *Louvois*, 3:296.

[77] On enrollment by force, see the long chapter in Girard, *Racolage et milice*, 99–135.

[78] For example, see the ordinance of 8 February 1692, Girard, *Racolage et milice*, 45.

[79] SHAT, Bib., Col. des ord., vol. 19, #199, 20 March 1656, in André, *Le Tellier*, 235.

[80] During the Dutch War, Vauban complained of companies composed of "children and poor little miserable individuals who had been taken violently from their homes." Letter of 11 January 1675 from Vauban to Louvois in Albert Rochas d'Aiglun, *Vauban, sa famille et ses écrits*, 2 vols. (Paris: 1910), 2:121. The *intendant* Turgot in 1697–98 spoke of "the violence of enrollments," a violence that only peace could end. Turgot, BN, f. fr. 22210, fol. 70, in Corvisier, *Les Français et l'armée*, 268.

[81] Lille, Aff. gen. 288, dos. #2, 10 December 1701, printed ordinance.

ment d'Auxerrois broke into churches in the town of Troyes at vespers and snagged parishioners.[82] Such "recruiting" could also become a thin disguise for theft, either outright or by demanding ransoms for men seized.[83]

In general, it was more difficult to use violence in towns than in the country, but these difficulties did not stop recruiters. *Racoleurs* could turn to methods involving a bit more finesse. Perhaps a woman working in cahoots with the recruiter would ostensibly hire men to work for her, but when the young men arrived at their new job they found themselves seized as recruits.

Recruits forced to sign on had to be held before they could be shipped off to the front. They might be locked up in the home of a friend or relative of the recruiter. Soldiers might also employ royal jails, but this could be a problem, since the authorities might demand that the officers secure authorization from local officials, who were more concerned with protecting the local population than with filling the ranks of the army.[84] More secret lock-ups did not have this problem, and such cells were not hard to find. Cabarets frequented by recruiters generally provided a room or cellar where unwilling recruits could be hidden away under guard.[85] Part of the function of such imprisonment was to bring the recruit to at least grudging agreement, since service was supposed to be voluntary, and a signature was necessary to attest to the soldier's good will. Imprisonment thus became a kind of torture to coerce a change of attitude and get something in writing. Jailers could raise the pressure. As one complaint attested, the poor victim went "close to three days without seeing anyone, neither drinking nor eating."[86]

Such abuses sometimes drove peasants to flee at the approach of *racoleurs* or to avoid places where *racoleurs* preyed on country folk.[87] During the Dutch War, *intendants* reported that, owing to the threat of forced enrollments, markets were deserted and peasants feared leaving their homes.[88] During the Nine Years' War, the *intendant* of Orléans reported that "The markets are full of people who carry off men by force who are believed to be fit for service; this has happened so long at Brou, which is a large market, as well as at Chateaudun and at Vendôme, that the peasants of this area no longer come to market at all."[89] The frustrated *intendant* feared that commerce might grind to a halt.

Other peasants, tired of being victims, turned upon their tormentors, intimidating recruiters or setting recruits free. At the onset of the War of the

[82] Girard, *Racolage et milice*, 100–1.

[83] Girard, *Racolage et milice*, 102–3. [84] Girard, *Racolage et milice*, 106–7.

[85] This was know as a *four*, or oven. Girard, *Racolage et milice*, 107.

[86] AG, A¹1878, #291, 1705, complaint of sieur Cottin in Girard, *Racolage et milice*, 109. See pages 109–11 for other examples.

[87] Girard, *Racolage et milice*, 112. [88] André Corvisier, *Louvois* (Paris: 1983), 186.

[89] De Creil to the Contrôleur général, 11 February 1691, in A. M. de Boislisle, ed., *Correspondance des contrôleurs généraux des finances*, vol. 1 (Paris: 1874), 234. See, as well, the complaint registered that "the markets were no longer free" owing to the fear of recruiters during past wars: in Lille, Aff. gen. 288, dos. #2, 10 December 1701, printed ordinance.

Spanish Succession, one official warned secretary of state for war Chamillart that "Each of these officers believes that he can take soldiers with impunity everywhere," and "I believe that finally [the peasant] will throw himself on these violent recruiters."[90] A successful recruiter named Fitton felt such wrath in 1705, when he locked up nine recruits taken by force. The archpriest of Caixon led his parishioners, armed with everything from fusils to axes, to liberate the young men. This crowd besieged the house where the men were imprisoned, finally breaking in and beating the officer and his sergeant.[91] At Saint-Jean-d'Embournay, on a fair day in June of the same year, soldiers of a recruiting party arrived, the drum rolled, and the pitch began. The captain announced his intention to come away with twenty men, and his callous declaration ignited a violent rebellion in the village. A crowd beat up the drummer and then stoned the cabaret where the captain had set up shop. Five soldiers received serious wounds in this miniature siege.[92] Recruiters also ran great risks when they ventured out on the road to escort their prize to the front.

Louvois went through the motions of trying to keep men from being tricked or forced in enrolling. In January 1677, he wrote to La Reynie, head of the Paris police: "The intention of the king is not to tolerate the roguish acts which are committed in Paris in order to raise levies."[93] In 1678, Louvois again complained against violent enrollments.[94] He would express his dissatisfaction in the next war as well. An instruction from him to La Reynie, drafted in 1690, echoed Le Tellier's complaint of 1656:

The king, having been informed of the violences which are committed daily to secure enrollments in Paris, of those who kidnap men who pass in the streets, throwing them in carriages and carrying them to out of the way houses where, by means of beating them and frightening them, they are made to sign enlistment papers, His Majesty has commanded me to let you know that his intention is that you try to stop men who commit such enterprises and that you prosecute them in court, in order that an example be made that will in the future prevent such abuses from being committed any more.[95]

This was all fine and good, but at the same time, Louvois was not willing to accept soldiers' complaints that they had been forced to enlist: "It is a very poor excuse for a soldier, in order to justify desertion, to say that he had been enrolled by force; and, if one wanted to admit reasons of this nature, not a single soldier would remain in the king's troops, since there is not a one who does not believe that he has good reason to protest against his

[90] AG, A¹1611, #171, 23 December 1702, Sourdis to Chamillard, in Girard, *Racolage et milice*, 112.

[91] AG, A¹1986, #41–45, April–June 1706, in Girard, *Racolage et milice*, 115.

[92] AG, A¹1971, #60–70, December 1705–February 1706, in Girard, *Racolage et milice*, 121–24. See, as well, the case reported in AG, A¹2265, #174–76, 31 January 1710.

[93] AG, A¹517, 31 January 1677, in Rousset, *Louvois*, 2:478–79.

[94] AG, A¹574, 25 May 1678, Louvois to La Reynie, in Rousset, *Louvois*, 2:479n.

[95] AG, A¹916, 13 April 1690, Louvois to La Reynie, in Rousset, *Louvois*, 4:381n.

enrollment."[96] As Louvois commented in another letter: "A time when the king is short of men is not the moment to see if they are all properly enrolled."[97] Regarding enforcement of the regulations, Louvois wrote in 1673: "It is necessary to be a little less difficult at this time when men are rare."[98] There was little hope for a young man such as the fellow from Dijon who, in 1677, claimed that he had been enrolled by force and therefore refused to march to Châlons; he was arrested and imprisoned.[99] This condition apparently did not improve with time. At the close of the Nine Years' War, Vauban charged bluntly that "enrollments are still almost all fraudulent at the time that I speak."[100] Vauban complained of forced enlistments in 1706, stating that it would be more difficult now to conduct a siege than in years past, since the army "is filled with young men without experience and with recruits almost all of whom have been forced to serve and who have no discipline."[101]

Despite the official disregard evidenced by Louvois, officers were punished for abuses. The letters to La Reynie imply that culprits guilty of forced recruitment languished in Parisian jails. In 1694, an officer was imprisoned for one month for such offenses.[102] In 1704, Chamillart ordered two brothers, both officers with the Regiment de Charollais, who used violence against a miller whom they seized on the highway, to pay 200 livres, half of which was to be given to the miller, who was discharged. The same order broke another officer and incarcerated him for three months for similar offenses to set an example.[103] But struggle as they might to eliminate abuses, authorities such as the *intendant* Turgot realized that only the return of peace could end "the violence of the enrollments."[104]

Problems in Leading Recruits to the Front

Troubles for recruits and for recruiters did not end once the new soldiers had been signed up by fair means or foul, since the road to the front posed its own hazards. Recruits marched up to join their regiments in fairly small batches, supervised by an officer or even a sergeant. *Recrues*, or groups of recruits, coming through Amiens during the last two wars of Louis XIV most commonly included about fifteen men, led by an officer, but they could be larger.[105] Vauban, in fact, suggested that to limit abuses on the road, a

---

[96] AG, A¹530, 18 December 1677, Louvois to the *intendant* d'Oppède, in Rousset, *Louvois*, 2:479.

[97] Louvois in Corvisier, *Louvois*, 186.   [98] Louvois in Corvisier, *Louvois*, 186.

[99] Côte d'Or, C 2902, 12 March 1677.

[100] Vauban, memoir dating from shortly after the Peace of Ryswick, in Rochas d'Aiglun, *Vauban*, 1:271.

[101] Letter 16 January 1706, Vauban to Chamillart, in Rochas d'Aiglun, *Vauban*, 2:570.

[102] Babeau, *La vie militaire*, 1:55.

[103] AG, A¹1801, #460, 29 April 1704, Camillart to Legendre.

[104] Turgot, memoir of 1697–98, in Corvisier, *Les Français et l'armée*, 268.

[105] See the batches of *routes* held at Amiens in the series EE.

recrue led by a sergeant should number no more than ten, which could rise to fifteen if a lieutenant was in charge.[106] Most commonly, *recrues* seem to have been on the road in late winter and early spring. The month of March saw many *recrues* pass.[107] Orders concerning enrollment in the winter of 1710–11 directed recruiters to deliver their bounty by the end of February, and even if most had arrived by April, larger numbers were still on the road in May.[108] Officers might treat recruits on the road as little better than prisoners. La Rochelambert reported in 1709 that he saw *recrues* "led chained together like galley slaves."[109]

Officers in charge of *recrues* might engage in a new spectrum of abuses, both against the recruits themselves and against the king. Officers might refuse to dress the recruits in their charge properly, as in one case when authorities imprisoned the guilty captain.[110] Neglect could turn to abuse. In 1710, an officer beat a sick soldier, perhaps convinced that the man was malingering. Unable to stay with the party, the soldier remained in a village, where he died.[111] In both of the cases cited, authorities took action, or intended to take action, against the offenders. Perhaps those same administrators showed even more interest when the victim was not a young recruit but the king himself, or at least his treasury. One way an officer leading a *recrue* could turn thief was to sell recruits already bought and paid for to other officers in need of men. Vauban, usually a righteous critic of abuses, once appealed to the secretary of state for war, Chamillart, on behalf of a captain from the Regiment de Bresse, an officer with thirty years' service who had been broken and now languished in jail "for some minor offense rather common among men who are obliged to go recruiting," but the secretary turned down the request. "Reprehensible acts [*friponneries*] of the kind that he has committed in selling recruits who had been confided to him to take [to the army] are not pardonable."[112] In fact, it was fairly common for an officer or sergeant to try to lure individuals from a *recrue* to bolster the numbers of his own company.[113]

[106] AG, MR 1828, piece #21, memoir by Vauban.

[107] Amiens *routes* for recruits characteristically peaked in March. Amiens, series EE.

[108] AG, A¹2265, #158, 31 December 1710, and A¹2266, #326, 30 December 1710. Quincy states that circa April 1711, "The recrues of the king's troops had almost all arrived at their assigned units by that time, making the infantry of the army of Flanders more complete than it had ever been seen." Quincy, *Histoire militaire de Louis le Grand roi de France*, vol. 6 (La Haye: 1727), 491. Still one finds *routes* that show large numbers of recruits passing through Amiens in May 1710 and 1711. Amiens, EE 426–27, 431. In 1667, we see a particularly large *recrue* of 178 men arrive at its destination for the St. Vallier Regiment as late as mid-June. AG, A¹209, #46, 29 June 1667, Cartier from camp de Greuemaker.

[109] La Rochelambert , "Méditations militaires," in Babeau, *La vie militaire*, 1:74.

[110] AN, G⁷1777, #297, 299, June 1704.   [111] AG, A¹2266, #56, 358–61, 1710.

[112] Letters of 2 July 1705, from Vauban to Chamillart, and of 6 July 1702 from Chamillart to Vauban in Rochas d'Aiglun, *Vauban*, 2:558–59.

[113] See the case reported by Saint-Mayme of a sergeant in prison accused of having tried to debauch some soldiers from a *recrue* bound for Italy. Saint-Mayme letter of 2 March 1702 in Girard, "Un soldat de Malplaquet," 519.

Recruits could turn the table. In 1693, a lieutenant, his valet, and a ser-geant conducting six recruits to their regiment were attacked by their charges.[114] Another source of danger were relatives and friends of a recruit, who wanted to liberate the man in question. In May 1709, ten or twelve men armed with clubs and pitchforks jumped a *recrue* and its escort from the Regiment de Louvigny-Grammont at the village of Daumont. The father and uncle of one of the recruits led the gang. While the sergeant in charge confronted the attackers, his recruits, who claimed to have been enrolled by force, escaped out a back window.[115]

Such incidents illustrate that the "voluntary" nature of enlistment could be little more than a thin veneer over brutal practices. It is impossible to say how prevalent the abuses of *racolage* were, certainly they were common, but did men hoodwinked or beaten into service outnumber those who came willingly? French military morale would seem to argue against this, but the hard truth may never be known. What does come through the records, however, is the fact that force played a role because the demand for soldiers outstripped the supply of willing and easily available recruits in France. If compulsion supplied one method of increasing the number of men in the ranks, another was to look beyond the borders of France to hire foreign regiments for the kings's service.

RECRUITING FOREIGN REGIMENTS

Long before the *grand siècle*, French monarchs established a tradition of hiring mercenary regiments to fight their wars. Under François I and Henri II, the vast majority of infantry in French armies hailed from outside the lands that those kings ruled. Even though the French did not maintain in the seventeenth century the high percentages of foreign troops employed in the sixteenth, such recruitment was still significant in manpower procurement. In the French army, foreign recruitment essentially meant engaging entire units, but this took two different forms. In the sixteenth century, a monarch could hire a captain who would arrive with his off-the-shelf band of soldiers entirely outfitted and trained, instantly ready to fight and just as quickly sent home when the campaign was over. But under Louis XIV, foreigners were hired much more on the pattern of native French regiments; colonels re-ceived commissions and recruited individual soldiers whom they equipped, armed, and trained on a French model. These formations took time to raise and prepare for war; they were no longer off-the-shelf but rather regiments created by the king's commission, subject to his control, and maintained for long periods. In general, only foreigners, or those of his subjects that the king classed as foreigners, were to enter foreign regiments, while French regiments were to attract only Frenchmen. Yet in times of need, limited

---

[114] Babeau, *La vie militaire*, 74.
[115] AG, A¹2266, #8–10, February 1710, letters from Bignon de Blanz.

numbers of foreigners could enter French regiments. In 1703, Louis agreed to allow up to ten Germans per infantry company or up to six per dragoon company in Villars's hard-pressed army, but this was exceptional.[116]

In raising foreign troops, the Bourbons turned to a fully entrepreneurial system; that is, they contracted with foreign officers to raise regiments for French service on a strictly business basis. Elaborate contracts, called *capitulations*, stipulated the number of men to be recruited, when and where they were to be raised, wage scales, and how the entrepreneur and his officers were to receive money from the throne. Exemplary capitulations from 1643 and 1674 reveal surprising continuity.[117] The first stipulated that Moyerie was to enroll 2,000 Irishmen to form a single regiment of ten companies and pick his officers, as long as they were capable men.[118] Officers were to receive 12 livres for every man they presented in France, "the same sum that is always given." The troops were to disembark at Dieppe three months from the date of the capitulation; there the troops would be reviewed by a *commissaire* and take an oath to the French king. A rate of pay was set out for all ranks. Moynerie received the right of "ordinary justice that other colonels commanding troops of their nation are accustomed to having." The king was to supply the new Irish troops with arms upon their arrival in France. Lastly, conditions were spelled out for the dissolution of the regiment. The 1674 capitulation with Duroque authorized him to raise 1,500 troops in Vaux, Valery, Grisons, Val Telline, and the areas around them.[119] The king was to supply quarters for the recruits in towns under his dominion near the Swiss frontier. There they would be reviewed by the king's commissioners and receive arms from the royal magazines, but the money for said arms was to be deducted from the first year's pay. Each soldier was to receive a set rate of pay each month. Duroque should have the right "to exercise justice in the said regiment . . . with the same prerogatives as the Swiss regiments in the service of His Majesty enjoy." Should the regiment be disbanded, Duroque was to receive payment and the regiment a *route* to take care of its return home.

Recruiting troops on foreign soil required diplomatic agreements and involved certain restrictions designed to protect the position, or salve the conscience, of the rulers who allowed their subjects to fight for the Bourbons.

---

[116] AG, A¹1676, #107, 5 June 1703, Chamillart to Villars, in Ronald Thomas Ferguson, "Blood and Fire: Contribution Policy of the French Armies in Germany (1668–1715)," Ph.D. dissertation, University of Minnesota, 197, 207.

[117] For additional capitulations, see AG, A¹14, #49, 6 March 1633, capitulation for a Scottish regiment, in Patrick Landier, "Guerre, violences, et société en France, 1635–1659," doctorat de troisième cycle, Université de Paris IV: 1978, 61–62; AG, A¹42, #23, January 1637; AG, A¹210, #122, December 1667; AG, A¹210, #123, December 1667; AG, A¹219, #238, 15 October 1668; SHAT, Bib., Col. des ord., vol. 22, #143, 14 August 1671; and AG, MR 1722, #1, 27 August 1674.

[118] SHAT, Bib., Col. des ord., vol. 16, #105–6, 26 November 1643, in André, *Le Tellier*, 221–23.

[119] AG, MR 1722, #2, "Articles of capitulation," 4 April 1674.

The 1643 capitulation for the Irish troops discussed earlier required that recruits swear "to faithfully serve the king, offensively and defensively towards and against all, . . . except the king of Great Britain."[120] This kept enrollment in foreign service from crossing over to treason. The raising of 4,000 troops in England in 1667 required direct correspondence between Louis and Charles II to secure the latter's permission.[121] As already indicated, during the Dutch War, foreign units constituted a higher percentage of the French army than they did at any other time during the *grand siècle*. In preparation for the Dutch War, Louis XIV squeezed permission out of Charles-Emmanuel II to raise one Italian regiment in Piedmont; this rose to a total of four by the end of 1672.[122] The only concession granted to Charles Emmanuel was the proviso that these regiments could not be used against the emperor, since Charles held the post of the emperor's perpetual vicar in Italy. Louis next bullied Genoa into providing 1,200 troops, but this required a French threat to seize Genoese galleys.[123] In addition, at the start of the Dutch War, Louvois pushed the creation of two Irish, one Scottish, one English, one German, and one Spanish infantry regiment, as well as eight cavalry regiments.[124] The buildup in 1671–72 was impressive. Louvois dispatched his agent Stoppa to negotiate with the Swiss for 20,000 troops. Swiss Protestants went through something of a charade, claiming that religious sympathies limited their willingness to furnish the needed soldiers. Stoppa refused to take this seriously, writing, "A little money that the Dutch give them has caused all of this."[125] In any case, the able Stoppa got his men. By mid-1672, the French had contracted for an additional 10,000 to 12,000 English, German, Spanish, and Italian soldiers.[126]

During the Nine Years' War, Irish troops came to France in unprecedented numbers. This began in 1690 when Louis asked for 6,000 to 7,000 Irish recruits to compensate for the 4,000 to 5,000 troops that he dispatched to Ireland to support James's bid to regain his crown.[127] When James II met defeat and took refuge in France, the exiled king brought as many as 25,000 Irish troops into French service, a greater number than those sold to Louis XIII by Bernard. James's regiments, however, were not an army temporarily bought or rented but a collection of regiments in search of a permanent new home and master; they found both in France and Louis XIV.[128]

Once agreement was attained, or extorted, from foreign authorities and the capitulation signed by the contractor, the French ambassador normally paid mercenary colonels half the expenses of levying the troops in their

[120] SHAT, Bib., Col. des ord., vol. 61, #107, 26 November 1643, in André, *Le Tellier*, 222.
[121] AG, A^{1}209, #197, 15 September 1667, letter to Rouvigny in London.
[122] Rousset, *Louvois*, 1:330–32.
[123] AG, A^{1}315, 9 and 26 May 1673, Louvois to Gomont, in Rousset, *Louvois*, 1:329–30.
[124] Rousset, *Louvois*, 1:328.
[125] AG, A^{1}259, 22 September 1671, Stoppa to Louvois in Rousset, *Louvois*, 1:334.
[126] Louvois in Rousset, *Louvois*, 1:335.   [127] Rousset, *Louvois*, 4:204–5, 383.
[128] Louis Susane, *Histoire de l'infanterie française*, 5 vols. (Paris: 1876), 1:208.

native land, and the second half when the new regiment arrived in France.[129] Should the number of troops supplied come up short, the officers would have to repay French officials for excess allowances. This need to pay mercenaries up front posed serious problems for the French fisc.

As well as dealing with the usual regimental contractors, the French employed an entire army supplied by one of the century's most important military entrepreneurs, Bernard of Saxe Weimar. When Louis XIII entered the lists against Spain in 1635, he turned to the young Bernard, who at age thirty-one had already earned a strong reputation on the field of battle. In October, Bernard contracted to provide an army of 12,000 infantry and 6,000 cavalry for a sum of 4 million livres per year, to be paid in quarterly installments.[130] Salaries and armament were not stipulated in the contract, since Bernard was to handle all expenses out of the great sum he received from the French monarch. Interestingly, the treaty contained a clause that should offensive operations allow Bernard "to maintain his troops at the enemy's expense," he would "relieve His Majesty of the expense of the said 4,000,000 livres, in proportion." Actual payment was to be handled by a French treasurer with the army, who would be assisted in reviewing the troops periodically by French *commissaires* and *contrôleurs*. This contract was renewed in 1637. Bernard died suddenly of the plague in July 1639, and his officers made a new treaty with Louis XIII in October.[131] The payments fell to 600,000 livres every four months, with an additional payment of 300,000 per year "to be employed by the officers for the recruitment and re-establishment of their troops." While the officers that Bernard appointed retained their positions, supreme command shifted to the French marshal Guébriant, whose signature graced the treaty. Eventually, in 1643, the remnants of Bernard's forces came under the command of Turenne. The latter subsequently recruited more Germans en masse when the 1647 armistice with Bavaria put Bavarian troops out of work; rather than go without employment, they signed up with the French, their erstwhile enemies.[132] Bernard and his army constituted an isolated example during the *grand siècle*; only in this case did the French hire a "general contractor" to supply an entire army.

Recruitment of foreign troops for French service and regular domestic enrollment shared the voluntary principle – soldiers were supposed to join the colors of their own free wills. Yet it is clear, particularly in the case of *racolage* within Bourbon domains, that compulsion played an important, if veiled, role in regular recruitment. But beyond this surreptitious compulsion,

---

[129] André, *Le Tellier*, 219–20.

[130] Treaty of 27 October 1635 in J. Dumont, *Corps diplomatique du droit des gens*, 8 vols. (The Hague: 1732), vol. 6, pt. 1, 118–19, in Geoffrey Symcox, ed., *War, Diplomacy, and Imperialism, 1618–1763* (New York: 1973), 117–21, translation by Symcox.

[131] Treaties of 9 October 1639 in J. Dumont, *Corps diplomatique du droit des gens*, 8 vols. (The Hague: 1732), vol. 6, pt. 1, 185–86, in Symcox, *War, Diplomacy, and Imperialism*, 121–25, translation by Symcox.

[132] Bérenger, *Turenne*, 243.

the French monarchy also relied on a variety of openly obligatory forms of service to fill the ranks, even before the creation of the royal provincial militia in 1688.

FORMS OF COMPULSORY SERVICE

The French tradition of compulsory armed service dates back to the Middle Ages. In its most obvious and flamboyant form, feudal landholders had ridden off to do battle for their king. However, that monarch also claimed the right to call on town and provincial militias to fight, and even to require peasants and townsmen to supply labor to support his armies on campaign. In addition to these traditional forms of service, seventeenth-century French kings also compelled extraordinary levies to fill the ranks of the army at times of crisis, as when a Spanish invasion threatened to march all the way to Paris in 1636. All of these compulsory forms of service differed from duty in the king's regular army in two ways: first, men who enlisted into the ranks of the royal army did so voluntarily, at least in theory, and compulsory levies were there because of an open and official obligation; and second, men who enlisted in a regular fashion signed on for a long, perhaps permanent, commitment, whereas those called out by royal order served for limited periods defined either by tradition or by the nature of the crisis. Late in the *grand siècle*, Louvois extended and altered the tradition of compulsory service, creating the royal provincial militia, which supplied entire regiments to serve alongside the regular army during the Nine Years' War.

Feudal Service: The Ban and Arrière Ban

The armed forces of French kings from Charlemagne to Louis XIV counted among their cavalry a feudal array, but by the seventeenth century, military practice and state institutions had evolved to such a degree that the warriors who bore arms simply out of feudal obligation played but a small role, often more tragic or comic than heroic. At his discretion, the king could call out his *ban* and *arrière ban*. Technically speaking, the *ban* consisted of only those nobles with a direct feudal obligation to the king, whereas the *arrière ban* included their rear vassals as well – in other words, virtually the entire French nobility.[133] However, historians usually lump the two together when discussing them during the seventeenth century, most commonly just talking about an *arrière ban*.

French kings called out the *arrière ban* in 1635, 1674, and 1689, but never again after the Nine Years' War. From the time of Henri IV, the *arrière ban* was to equip itself not with armor and lance but as light cavalrymen, or *chevaux légers*. The last general regulations concerning the *ban* and *arrière ban*

---

[133] Marcel Marion, *Dictionnaire des institutions de la France aux XVIIe et XVIIIe siècles* (Paris: 1923, reprinted 1972), 34.

date from 1635 and 1639.[134] As Louis mustered his forces to take on Spain in 1635, an ordinance of 30 July demanded service of three months in the interior of kingdom and of forty days outside the frontiers from all who lived nobly. The results were not impressive. Louis XIII regarded the knights who obeyed the call as incapable of "the least fatigue." "When one wants to send them but three leagues from here, they all complain loudly that one wants to lose them and that they will go away. . . . Since yesterday we have lost eight to nine hundred noble horsemen, regardless of the harangues, promises, flattery, and menaces that I have made to them."[135]

Richelieu also lost his patience with the *arrière ban* since "the flightiness, cowardice, malice, or distaste of three or four individuals are capable of scattering it in a moment . . . if it does not fight as soon as it arrives. Just as it is prompt to come, it is prompt to go home and threatens to do so at every moment."[136] Owing to the facts that the *ban* was so rarely called, that capable young men were employed already as officers in the king's army, and that nobles could be excused by paying money, the *arrière ban* "was composed of hardly anyone but ruined petty nobles [*hoberaux*], and cut a sad figure with the armies."[137] In 1651, assemblies of the nobility objected to the *ban* and *arrière ban* because it threatened to become wholly fiscal, a kind of tax on the nobility.[138]

When called up in August 1674, it proved more of a problem than an asset. With Alsace threatened by invasion and Turenne hard pressed, Louis XIV summed half the available nobles within 100 leagues of the threatened province.[139] Between 5,000 and 6,000 assembled at Nancy, where Marshal Créqui took command of them. When they appeared in Turenne's camp in October, that great marshal could tolerate them for only a week, after which he sent them to the rear. The commander of the *arrière ban*, Marshal Créqui, next led them to Lorraine, where he gratefully received permission to disband them in November. A frazzled Créqui replied to the order to disband his "troops": "I ardently hope that the king will never again have any need to assemble his nobles, because it is a corps incapable of action and more proper to provoke disorders than to remedy accidents."[140] When Louis looked to his nobles again in 1675, it was not to summon them to the armies but to command them to pay a tax in lieu of serving.[141] The fact that the aristocracy proved to be inadequate soldiers did not mean that they had lost all coercive

---

[134] Gébelin, *Histoire des milices*, 29. 30 July 1635 and 17 January 1639.

[135] Letter from Louis XIV, October 1635 from Saint-Mihiel in Marion, *Dictionnaire*, 34.

[136] Richelieu, *Maximes*, in Contamine, *Histoire militaire*, 1:361.

[137] Gébelin, *Histoire des milices*, 30.   [138] Contamine, *Histoire militaire*, 1:373.

[139] On the ban in 1674, see Rousset, *Louvois*, 2:96–101. In 1674, nobles of the *arrière ban* were called up elsewhere than along the German frontier. When in June 1674 the Spanish menaced Bayonne, 10,000 *milice* and 500 of the *arrière ban* were summoned. Foucault, *Mémoires*, 24–28, in Gébelin, *Histoire des milices*, 22n.

[140] AG, A¹414, 22 November 1674, Créqui to Le Tellier, in Rousset, *Louvois*, 2:101.

[141] Gébelin, *Histoire des milices*, 30.

value, since they still could be used to oppose local uprisings, as occurred in Rennes in 1675.

In 1689, Louvois tried to make some use of the *arrière ban* once again, but this time not for service with the field armies. Instead, it turned its hand to internal tasks, such as coastal watch, and as such, it was called each year between 1689 and 1697.[142] These *bans* were in very poor shape, few in number, and poorly equipped.[143] Marshal d'Estrées complained of the nobles sent to patrol the coast of Brittany: "The *arrière ban* of Anjou especially is very miserable, and of seventy who are supposed to be here, there are not more than thirty-six in quarters . . . [Their help] is not worth the *étapes* that they consumed [to get here]."[144] Vauban complained in general about the quality of the *bans* called out to defend the coasts.[145] But at least it retained some of its fiscal value, for when it had assembled, the *intendants* decided who would serve and who would pay in lieu of service.[146] Louis gave up on the *ban* after the Nine Years' War.[147]

Milices *to 1688*

The *milice* formed under Louis XIV by Louvois in 1688 was not created ex nihilo. It grew out of two separate but related traditions, the urban and local *milices* and the right of the monarch to summon extraordinary levies for his wars. The commoners of France were no strangers to the use of arms. Even during the Middle Ages, they fought under their kings, and during the sixteenth and early seventeenth centuries, they participated in military organizations that both upheld and resisted royal power. A variety of *milices* defended towns and provinces, providing part-time soldiers for local tasks.[148] Local militia forces underwent a transition during the *grand siècle*, beginning the era as still considerable forces with strong local loyalties that threatened to turn rebellious, and ending it in a reduced condition as agents of royal authority. This transition had military and political implications; ultimately,

---

[142] Tuetey, *Les officiers*, 9.   [143] Tuetey, *Les officiers*, 9.

[144] AG, A¹1428, 1 July 1697, Estrées to Barbézieux, in Tuetey, *Les officiers*, 10.

[145] Vauban letter to Louis XIV, 15 July 1695, Rochas d'Aiglun, *Vauban*, 2:433.

[146] Roland Mousnier, *The Institutions of France under the Absolute Monarchy, 1598–1789*, 2 vols. (Chicago: 1979–84), 2:538.

[147] Marion, *Dictionnaire*, 34.

[148] Corvisier's concern with the ebb and flow of French military spirit attracts his attention toward the bourgeois and rural militias of France, not because of their military value but because they exposed populations to weapons and military practices. He concludes that *milices* were so widespread and that so many people were *miliciens* or had contact with *miliciens*, that 85 percent of the French "were not completely removed from military activities," whatever that means. Contamine, *Histoire militaire*, 1:373. His interest is not unique or even new. Over a century ago, Gébelin surmised: "The existence of the bourgeois *milices*, drilled, at least at intervals, in the handling of weapons, explains the warlike spirit that the population have, in certain cases, given proof of against invaders." Gébelin, *Histoire des milices*, 28.

local armed forces outside the direct control of the king were incompatible with absolutism.

Bourgeois Milices as a Danger to Royal Authority

Commoners often bore responsibility for their own defense; town, or bourgeois, *milices* provided immediate defense and, in the case of fortified towns, manned the walls. Under their medieval charters, towns built and maintained their own walls, maintained bourgeois *milices* to defend them, and owed contingents to the royal army in times of crisis.[149] Cities continued to fortify themselves at their own expense and provide *milice* for their defense through the sixteenth century and into the seventeenth century.[150]

Bourgeois *milices* were recruited and organized either by district of residence or by profession; that is, the men served in companies grouped together either from particular parishes or from particular craft guilds or corporations in the town.[151] In the towns, alongside the regular *milice*, which generally involved compulsory service by all qualified men, stood certain elite companies of volunteers.[152] Such elite companies, or *confréries*, were particularly common in north and northeast France. They went by the name of archers, arquebusiers, and the like, although they bore the modern arms of the day. Composed of more well-to-do elements in the town, *confréries* performed military and civic functions. *Conféries* drilled regularly, whereas the usual bourgeois *milice* assembled rarely.

The forces raised by bourgeois *milices* could be considerable. For defense, the small town of Blaye mustered only a small garrison, but this could be reinforced by 300 to 400 *arquebusiers* supplied by the town's inhabitants, in addition to several hundred peasants who came to shelter within the town walls. When Spanish raiders threatened Espelette and Itxassou, two towns along the Spanish border on 31 July 1635, these communities answered with a force of 1,600 to 1,700 musketeers and 800 pikemen, who assembled in less than half an hour at the sound of the *tocsin*, or alarm bell.[153] Such forces mobilized rapidly and at little expense to the monarchy.

During most of the century, the monarchy tolerated and employed bourgeois *milices*, but it also regarded them as potentially dangerous. As Gébelin commented, "[T]he bourgeois *milices* were an army all ready for insurrection."[154] It is no surprise that the bourgeois *milices* enjoyed their zenith during the Wars of Religion and the Fronde.[155] Even before the Fronde, bourgeois *milices* had been unreliable; on a number of occasions, they proved reluctant

---

[149] For a brief account of medieval compulsory service, see Gébelin, *Histoire des milices*, 2–14.

[150] Gébelin, *Histoire des milices*, 15.   [151] Gébelin, *Histoire des milices*, 26.

[152] Gébelin, *Histoire des milices*, 27–28.

[153] Yves-Marie Bercé, *Histoire des Croquants: Etude des soulèvements populaires au XVII siècle dans le sud-ouest de la France*, 2 vols. (Paris: 1974), 1:194. I thank Roy McCullough for pointing out this material to me.

[154] Gébelin, *Histoire des milices*, 28.   [155] Corvisier, *Les Français*, 140.

to put down troubles at Dijon, Caen, Lyon, Aix, Paris, Perigeux, Bordeaux, and Moulins.[156] When the revolt of the Nu-Pieds struck in 1639, bourgeois *milices* usually sided with town rebels, although they did march against rural insurgents.[157] The part played by some *milices* during the Fronde posed a serious threat to the monarchy. At the outbreak of the Fronde, the *milice* of Paris, numbering 133 companies with a total of 7,000 troops, went to the barricades in support of the rebels and against Mazarin.[158] In 1652, Condé rallied the *milice* of Paris to attack the royal forces outside the gates.[159] Given the political dangers of some local forces, the use of bourgeois *milices* declined during the second half of the *grand siècle*. Major fortifications would no longer be entrusted to them. Fortifications in the French interior fell into disrepair or were pulled down, and Louis XIV relied upon his frontier fortresses alone, garrisoning these with royal troops. Not all urban *milices* ceased to exist; certain of the open towns and great cities retained them in some form, but they lost their ability successfully to oppose the king in the personal reign of Louis XIV.

Local and Provincial Milices

Localities and provinces also enjoyed the privilege, and responsibility, of fielding militia units. Various provinces possessed their own *milices*, and in need, the king called upon them to contribute forces on a temporary basis. For example, it was an old privilege of the county of the Boulonnais to defend itself with troops that it raised itself, and it kept this privilege when incorporated into France. Louis XIV incorporated these local forces into French military organization. In 1670, he ordered that these *troupes boulonnaises* form six regiments of infantry and sixteen companies of cavalry, or 24,000 infantry and 960 cavalry, but it seems doubtful that such a force was ever raised.[160] In 1672, when the monarchy called the *troupes boulonnaises* for duty, there were only 2,000 infantry and 400 cavalry, who assembled for only six weeks, during which time they served as rear-echelon garrison troops. In 1690, this *milice* numbered about 4,700 men.[161] During conflicts, the troops provided security for Boulogne proper and watched the coasts of Flanders and Picardy.

---

[156] Boris Porchnev, *Les soulèvements populaires en France de 1623 à 1648* (Paris: 1963), 137, 143, 146, 164, 179, 195, 284; Jean H. Manéjol, *Henri IV et Louis XIII*, vol. 6, part 2, Ernest Lavisse (ed.), *Histoire de France* (Paris: 1905), 431; Bercé, *Histoire des Croquants*, 1:306–7. My graduate student, Roy McCullough, has undertaken interesting research on the use of armed forces used in civil control during the *grand siècle*. He has been kind enough to share his conclusions and his references with me.

[157] Madeline Foisil, *La révolte des Nu-Pieds et les révoltes Normandes de 1630* (Paris: 1970), 224.

[158] Contamine, *Histoire militaire*, 1:377.

[159] Eveline Godley, *The Great Condé: A Life of Louis II de Bourbon, Prince of Condé* (London: 1915), 371–72.

[160] On the Boulonnais *milices*, see Hennet, *Les milices*, 275–82.

[161] Belhomme, *L'armée française en 1690*, 117.

Perhaps those most commonly called upon to fight were the *milices* of Languedoc.[162] In 1637, they supplied 11,000 men; in 1639, they composed the bulk of the 22,000 summoned by Condé in Roussillon. They also contributed troops in 1642 and 1643. In 1674, Languedoc sent 10,000 men to fight under Schönberg in Roussillon, making up nearly all of his infantry. These troops remained for the entire campaign and then found themselves unwillingly incorporated. After 1676, the *milices* of Languedoc were not again called upon to serve with the armies of the king.

Local *milices* played a useful, though auxiliary, wartime role late in the *grand siècle*. *Milices* of Burgundy and Montauban also surveyed the Protestant population. Other local *milices* traditionally guarded their frontiers. Those of Bayonne, Navarre, and Roussillon watched the passes of the Pyrenees; those of Provence guarded the Alps. Belhomme estimated that during the Nine Years' War, some 67,000 Frenchmen served in local *milices*.[163] It should be borne in mind that by then, such *milice* performed ancillary duties only; these *miliciens* were part-timers who often rotated detachments, meaning that those on foot at any one time were only a fraction of the total number. These men rarely, if ever, appeared on lists of royal troops maintained by the state. In one such account where they do, an *état* of troops serving and paid in 1696, the records only list 15,000, which may indicate those actually present and under arms.[164]

Town and Provincial Forces as Instruments of Royal Authority

By the late seventeenth century, town and provincial militias, which had once posed a threat to royal power, had become loyal instruments of the king's will. Provinicial *milices* provided a bulwark against Protestant resistence after the revocation of the Edict of Nantes in 1685. From that date, regiments of Languedoc guarded against any potential religious rising.[165] They performed such duties again during the Nine Years' War, as did *milices* from Dauphiné and Montauban. In Languedoc, this watch-dog *milice* was composed, according to one *intendant*, of "all the men in the diocese who are the most fit to serve."[166] While recruited only among old Catholics, they were paid for by the newly converted. Such *milices* served only in the summer for three or four months.[167] Companies drilled only once a week and held an annual review. "The general review of these regiments that the commander of the province has performed every year under the eyes of the newly converted

[162] On the turnout by various provincial and local *milices*, see Gébelin, *Histoire des milices*, 21–27, and Hennet, *Les milices*, 275–96.

[163] Belhomme, *L'armée française en 1690*, 119.

[164] AN, G⁷1774, #52, "Etat des troupes que le Roy a eu sur pied," 1696.

[165] Corvisier, *Armies and Societies*, 32.

[166] Basville, *intendant* of Languedoc, memoir of 1697–98, in Corvisier, *Les Français et l'armée*, 139.

[167] Gébelin, *Histoire des milices*, 41–42.

has made them understand anything that they would try would only bring defeat and that we were in condition to repress them immediately."[168]

Circa 1690, the *milice* charged with surveillance over Protestants in Languedoc, Guienne, and Dauphiné totaled over 51,000 men.[169] Although this sounds like a substantial force, the condition of these "troops" hardly qualified them as a great military asset. A letter written by the *intendant* of Montauban on 7 January 1693 reveals the low quality of these *milices locales*:

> Beyond this, these regiments are without arms, without swords, without fusils . . . . Last summer when there was rumor of a descent on Bayonne, 2,000 men were commanded to be ready to march; you could not find among them 100 fusils that could fire. Their clothes are no better than their arms; the soldiers for the most part are almost naked, without socks or shoes. . . . The disorder and misery of these troops are known, and they are in the most extreme [*dernier*] misery.[170]

Even Basville, the *intendant* of Languedoc, who found the *milice* useful, conceded that "these troops have neither the leadership nor the discipline of regular troops." Still, "they are always better than a populace which assembles itself in tumult, without order, without ammunition, and without commanders."[171]

By the end of Louis's reign, the relationship between local forces and state power had changed fundamentally. The monarchy became so secure and its legitimacy so accepted that the king could once again appeal to local forces without danger of them turning against him. In 1675, an uprising in Mons was put down by the local bourgeois.[172] Faced with troubles in Rennes in April of that year, Coëllogen, the governor, and his son restored order by calling out town *milices* and assembling local nobles.[173] The suppression of the troubles in the Cévennes during 1702–4 further supports the notion that royal authority again relied upon local forces. When Protestants took to arms there, the *intendant* of Languedoc, Basville, and the governor, de Broglie, first called up local militia and mobilized nobles to oppose the threat; only later did regular troops become involved.[174]

The *milices* of Languedoc, Guyenne, and Dauphiné and the town-based forces raised in 1675 and 1702–4 provide interesting cases in which the repressive hand of royal authority was exerted not by a standing army but by local forces. This is not an isolated case. Contrary to the usual assumption that it

---

[168] Basville, *intendant* of Languedoc, memoir of 1697–98, in Corvisier, *Les Français et l'armée*, 139.

[169] Belhomme, *L'armée française en 1690*, 116–17.

[170] Letter from d'Herbigny, *intendant* at Montauban, in Boislisle, *Correspondance des contrôleurs généraux*, 1:310.

[171] Basville, *intendant* of Languedoc, memoir of 1697–98, in Corvisier, *Les Français et l'armée*, 139.

[172] Ernest Lavisse, *Louis XIV*, 2 vols. (Paris: 1978), 1:350.

[173] Letter of 19 April 1675, Coëllogen *fils* to Louvois, reproduced in Jean Lemoine, *La Révolte dite du Papier Timbré ou des Bonnets Rouges en Bretagne en 1675* (Paris: 1898), doc. IV.

[174] Antoine Court, *Histoire des troubles des Cévennes*, 2 vols. (Marseille: 1975), 1:62, 66.

was the standing army that provided the monarchy with the strong arm necessary to impose absolutism, it was more probably local forces that backed the king late in the *grand siècle*. However, these were not the old independent local *milices* that possessed the independence to oppose as well as to aid the monarch, but a more responsive kind of local levy. Much study remains to be done concerning the relationship between armed forces and the rise of the centralized bureaucratic monarchy, but it may well be that repression under absolutism relied far less upon the standing army than it did upon a new relationship with local forces in the provinces.

Milices Gardes-côtes

Another form of militia with medieval origins was the coast guards, or *gardes-côtes*, although it did not formally take this name until an ordinance of 1543.[175] Colbert reorganized the *milice* by an ordinance of August 1681. Although the *gardes-côtes* were land-bound infantry, they came under the jurisdiction of the secretary of state for the navy. By a regulation of 1696, parishes within two leagues of the sea were liable to service in the *gardes-côtes*. Parishes were grouped together in *capitaineries*. Parishes that supplied men to the *gardes-côtes* claimed an exemption from quartering and *étapes*. Men of the *gardes* were to keep in their homes a musket or fusil, a sword, and a half pound of gunpowder, and they drilled on Sunday. By the War of the Spanish Succession, service divided into the *compagnies détachés* and the *guet de mer*.[176] The first were chosen by lot among eligible men, aged eighteen to forty-five and standing 5 feet tall. These companies maintained a military organization and were supposed to march upon any threat posed by a landing party. Men not chosen for the *compagnies détachés* composed the *guet de mer* and maintained a sea watch. The potential numbers of men involved in the *gardes-côtes* was substantial, but again, they were part-time soldiers.[177] Although the *milices gardes-côtes* certainly represented a substantial organization, during the War of the Spanish Succession, they were of little military value.[178]

Extraordinary Levies: Levies of Soldiers

The French king retained the right to call on all his people, not just the nobility, to defend his realm. From the days of Philippe IV, the monarchy enforced this right to summon a general levy, a little-used right that it had always possessed.[179] The Hundred Years' War brought repeated calls for all fit men to arm themselves and defend their soil. Charles VII's creation of his

---

[175] See Hennet, *Les milices*, 297–338, for a brief sketch of the *milices gardes côtes*.
[176] Corvisier, *L'armée française*, 1:56–58.
[177] Hennet gives no numbers for the reign of Louis XIV, but Corvisier states that during the War of the Austrian Succession, the *compagnies détachés* numbered as many as 70,000, while the *guet* listed over 200,000. Corvisier, *L'armée française*, 1:57.
[178] Hennet, *Les milices*, 302.   [179] Gébelin, *Histoire des milices*, 9.

infantry reserve, the *francs-archers* in 1448, drew upon this same principle.[180] As men who remained resident at home but practiced at the military arts and rallied to the king's army when called, they were very much a militia in the normal sense of the word. A century later, François I fashioned his legions, assigning to them the same term of obligatory service due from the *arrière ban* – three months per year within France or forty days outside her border when called. The legions may have been François's attempt not to recreate either a Roman or a medieval past but to create modern off-the-shelf units that he could call upon in lieu of expensive mercenaries. Yet this sizable contingent – composed of seven legions of 6,000 men each – was not impressive as a fighting force. In the words of Vielleville, "The service of such men was completely useless."[181] Henri II tried to employ the legions as well, but they were discharged after the Peace of Câteau-Cambrésis.

Monarchs rarely summoned compulsory levies from 1559 to 1635. Under Henry IV, Sully called up 1,600 men to assist in taking back Amiens from the Spanish in 1597, but this seems to have been a unique case.[182] However, during the long war with Spain, 1635–59, the monarchy appealed again and again to extraordinary forced levies. The first came in 1636, a year of crisis as the Spanish advanced in Paris. In a series of ordinances, Louis XIII ordered all Parisian journeymen and apprentices out of their shops and into the armies.[183] An ordinance of 15 August commanded officials "to close down all the workshops of France and send off to the war all the chamberlains of the masters, journeymen and apprentices capable of bearing arms, except for one man in each boutique."[184] Lackeys also found themselves called to arms. Service was to last three months, and slackers faced being condemned to the galleys. Brittany received an order to supply one, two, or three men per village or town, or more if they could.[185] Instructions to generals at the front commanded them "to take all the men from the villages [at the front] and to use them to increase your troops as much as possible, giving them bread and promising them pay."[186] General levies occurred in 1643 and 1644 as well.

Partial call-ups were more common. For example, the 6 February 1647 ordinance decreed levies in Normandy, Poitou, Saintonge, Angoumois, and Aunis.[187] A case from Burgundy illustrates the specific nature of such partial

---

[180] Gébelin, *Histoire des milices*, 13–14. Gébelin observes that the francs archers were recruited and organized in a way very similar to the later royal provincial *milice*.

[181] Hennet, *Les milices*, 20. [182] Hennet, *Les milices*, 21.

[183] For the series of royal ordinances mobilizing the levies of 1636, see Gébelin, *Histoire des milices*, 17–20.

[184] Ordinance of 15 August 1636 in Babeau, *La vie militaire*, 1:33.

[185] Ordinance of 11 August 1636, in Gébelin, *Histoire des milices*, 18n.

[186] Instructions of 1636 in Landier, "Guerre, violences, et société," 86.

[187] Gébelin, *Histoire des milices*, 19n. For other use of small-scale compulsory levies during the period 1635–59, consider cases in 1636, 1637, 1642, 1649, 1650, 1654, and 1657. Gébelin, *Histoire des milices*, 22n–23n.

and local levies. The siege of Seure in March 1653 required 500 additional troops. In response to a royal order, authorities in Dijon ordered that mayors, aldermen, and syndics of all the towns "assemble in community bodies in the accustomed form and manner to choose and nominate [the assigned] number of men who are the most fit and capable of bearing arms and to serve the King at the said siege for a time of fifteen days only, to begin when they arrive at the army's camp."[188]

It is sometimes stated that compulsory levies of one form or another did not occur after 1659, but they continued in the personal reign of Louis XIV.[189] During the Dutch War, Louis XIV effectively conscripted local *milices* for temporary duty, as when 10,000 Languedoc *miliciens* received orders to fight in Rousillon in the summer of 1674.[190] This, too, was a response to a Spanish advance, just as was the great levy of 1636. Even after the creation of the royal *milice*, local *milice* could still be created and employed in emergencies, as in the uprising of the Cévennes in 1702. During the War of the Spanish Succession, when allied troops threatened to raid northern France, Marshal Besons raised four regiments of *miliciens*, aged eighteen to forty, in Picardy to stand guard along the Somme in an effort to stop enemy courses from crossing the river.[191]

During the Nine Years' War, Louis demanded that certain provinces and cities raise and maintain units for his army. Accordingly, the province of Brittany furnished the Dragoons of Brittany, commanded by the marquis du Cambout at a cost of 131,490 livres per year.[192] The monarchy also proclaimed at least one other special levy during the War of the Spanish Succession. On 10 December 1701, Versailles declared a levy intended to replace the men that had been drawn from *milice* battalions and sent to the Army of Italy. This ordinance did not literally conscript men; instead, it required merchant and artisan corporations to recruit volunteers by paying bounties varying from 60 to 100 livres. It was more of a levy of these corporations' wealth and effort than of men per se, since the corporations acted only as recruiters. Still, it once again expressed the king's ability to demand that his subjects take part in his wars.[193]

---

[188] Côte d'Or, C 3635, 13 March 1653.
[189] Gébelin states that the royal ordinances do not mention forced recruitment from 1659 to 1688. Gébelin, *Histoire des milices*, 21.
[190] Foucault in Gébelin, *Histoire des milices*, 22n. For other levies of *miliciens* in the Dutch War, see Gébelin, *Histoire des milices*, 22n–23n.
[191] Hennet, *Les milices*, 282–83.
[192] Limoges also maintained an infantry regiment, Tulle an infantry regiment, and Bordeaux a company of grenadiers. BN, f. fr. 22209, fol. 17, in Corvisier, *Les Français et l'armée*, 145.
[193] Hennet, *Les milices*, 38, 40, counts this levy as a *milice* levy, but Girard, *Racolage et milice*, 172–73, explains that it was in fact a *levée particulière*. The effort levy produced about 15,000 recruits.

Levies for Limited Duty

Beyond these forms of levies, the monarch could also summon his subjects for minor duties and for labor required by the army. The function of watching passes and river lines had long been a function of *milices*. From 1675 to 1679, local peasants manned the defensive line along the Meuse between Mézières and Stenay. At any one time, about 1,800 men stood on watch, rotating each week. They performed the same duty at the start of the Nine Years' War.[194] In 1705, the *intendant* at Lille ordered towns to send men "who they had the custom of furnishing" to redoubts along the Sambre.[195] Such peasants could be summoned for short periods without pay. In addition, special paid companies could serve along the lines; apparently, they were more reliable, and, of course, more expensive.[196] Most commonly, such peasant guards warned of and opposed enemy raiding parties, but they also might perform other duties, such as apprehending deserters.[197] Nor was the custom of requiring rural guards to patrol the road and guard river crossings limited to the French; the Spanish mobilized the villages of the Low Countries against the French.[198]

French *intendants* also exercised the royal prerogative of requisitioning local labor for military chores, particularly during sieges. Peasants who performed the spade work for the army were called *pioneers*. Digging siege lines, which often extended fifteen or twenty miles, consumed vast amounts of labor. To besiege Seure in 1653, the duke d'Epernon ordered Burgundy to raise 3,000 pioneers immediately.[199] During the Dutch War, Louis may have collected 20,000 peasant pioneers for the siege of Maestricht in 1673, while later in that conflict, 7,000 to 8,000 dug the lines for the sieges of Condé, Cambrai, and Ghent.[200] The numbers of such peasant pioneers could be substantial. Vauban argued that lines of circumvallation 4 to 5 leagues long

---

[194] Contamine, *Histoire militaire*, 1:397. In August 1691, peasants in the vicinity of Tournai who had to guard lines complained that this was a real hardship during the harvest season. About 600 peasants had been standing on the lines for two weeks. AG, A^{1}1061, #99, 25 August 1691.

[195] Nord, C 8645, printed, fill-in order of 17 March 1705. Even along the Rhine, local inhabitants were supposed to guard river passages against crossings by foreigners and Protestants during the War of the Spanish Succession. AG, A^{1}2265, #101, 8 February 1710.

[196] For examples of paid companies raised to watch lines, see Nord, C 8645, contract to pay for redoubt guards along the Meuse, 8 March 1703.

[197] Order of 16 July 1678 in Babeau, *La vie militaire*, 1:10.

[198] Hubert van Houtte, *Les Occupations etrangères en Belgique sous l'ancien régime*, 2 vols., *Recueil de Travaux Publiés par la faculté de Philosophie et Lettres de l'Université de Gand*, fasicule 62–63 (1930), 1:22.

[199] Côte d'Or, C 3635, 19 April 1653. Later that same year, he called out 1,000 men to raze Bellegard. Côte d'Or, C 3635, 9 June 1653.

[200] M. S. Anderson, *War and Society in Europe of the Old Regime, 1618–1789* (New York: 1988), 140. 8,000 at Condé in 1676. Rousset, *Louvois*, 2:216. 8,000 at Cambrai in 1677. AG, A^{1}532, 3 April 1677, Louvois to Courtin, in Rousset, *Louvois*, 2:291. 7,000 at Ghent in 1678. AG, A^{1}534, 1 March 1678, Louvois to Le Tellier, in Rousset, *Louvois*, 2:490.

required the labor of 15,000 to 18,000 peasants and 2,000 to 3,000 wagons.[201] At the siege of Mons in 1691, the French employed as many as 21,000 peasants.[202] Local labor could be summoned by nothing more dramatic than a printed form, with blanks for the name of the village and the number of pioneers to be supplied.[203] It should be remembered that although such work was not without risk, lines of circumvallation ran outside the range of enemy cannon, so that enemy fire did not menace the laborers. Approach trenches and parallels were another matter, and this work was reserved for soldiers.

Louis XIV also requisitioned peasant labor to construct his fortresses throughout his reign.[204] In January 1710, for example, orders went out to assemble 2,400 pioneers to improve the works at Maubeuge.[205] Such work might have to allow for the peasant's own needs. In August 1672, peasants working on the fortifications of Mazeik left to return to their harvest, and the frustrated commander had to request that Chamilly send him an additional 1,500 men.[206]

The king also could demand that his peasants, their animals, and their carts haul forage and other supplies. Peasants might receive pay for this duty, but it still amounted to requisitioned labor. During the war with Spain, peasants hauling forage for the army received 20 sols per day per horse.[207] The *intendant* of Hainaut reported:

Every time there are military works to be built or labor to be performed, be it by carts or by pioneers . . . , one ordinarily calls on [*commande*] the inhabitants of the villages.

When His Majesty has undertaken certain enterprises and principally during the year when he besieged and took Namur [1692], Hainault alone furnished 1,500 carts continually occupied either with the army or in carrying supplies to the places where the bread for the troops was cooked.[208]

ROYAL PROVINCIAL MILITIA

After considering the French monarchy's long tradition of compulsory levies and the existence of a variety of militia organizations, the royal provincial

---

[201] Sébastien le Prestre de Vauban, *De l'attaque et de la défense des places* (The Hague: 1737), 5.

[202] Frank Tallett, *War and Society in Early Modern Europe* (London: 1992), 152, and Anderson, *War and Society*, 140–41. The next year at Namur, Louis XIV boasted of 20,000 pioneers required for the extensive lines of circumvallation. "Relation de ce qui s'est passé au siège de Namur, in Louis XIV," *Oeuvres de Louis XIV*, Philippe Grimoard and Grouvelle, eds., 6 vols. (Paris: 1806), 4:359.

[203] For an example, see Nord, C 1609, October 1690, printed orders issued by the *intendant* Demadrys.

[204] André, *Le Tellier*, 527–28.

[205] See the use of pioneers to work on the fortifications of Maubeuge in 1710. AG, A¹2266, #62, 22 January 1710, letter to Dormesson. See as well #100, which states that they will be paid 4 sols per day for subsistence.

[206] AG, A¹294, #29, 6 August 1672.   [207] André, *Le Tellier*, 456–57.

[208] BN, f. fr. 22221, fol. 35 v°, in Corvisier, *Les Français et l'armée*, 188.

milice created under Louvois in 1688 seems simply one more step in a journey that began centuries before.[209] Louvois designed the *milice* to provide low-cost auxiliary troops to support the regular army. In a real sense, it was a child of the preexisting *milices*, and as such, it survived until 1697, when it disappeared, never to reappear in the same form. When Louis XIV turned to a *milice* again in the War of the Spanish Succession, the institution then created differed greatly from that of the Nine Years' War. The second reincarnation of the royal *milice* operated as a method of conscripting troops into line regiments, so in an odd way, it had more to do with compulsory levies of the war with Spain, 1635–59, than with the traditional *milices*. *Milices* underwent one more transformation under Louis XIV, when by 1708, money had become more valuable than men, and the *milice* was commuted into a money payment, becoming simply a financial expedient, an additional tax.

The royal *milice* has attracted much attention from scholars past and present for several reasons: *Milice* service became a serious popular grievance against the *ancien régime*; it prefigured the conscription of the Revolution and the nineteenth century; and it revealed popular *mentalités* concerning the military and war.[210] But for all the discussion of the *milices provinciales*, it is only fair to note that in neither of Louis's last two wars did it account for more than a fraction of his troops. In 1696, the *milice* supplied less than 10 percent of the manpower.[211] Because the *milices* raised between 1701 and 1712 were integrated into regular units, as opposed to standing in their own battalions as they had in the Nine Years' War, at present there is no way to calculate the total actually in the ranks at any one time. There is no conclusive evidence that the number of *miliciens* actually with the army in the later war was remarkably higher than it had been in the earlier conflict. For comparison, note that the initial levy in 1688 was for 25,000 and that in 1701 it stood at 33,000. It would probably be correct to argue that the *milice* constituted more than 10 percent of the total force of the army during the later war, but to credit it with as much as 25 percent of serving soldiers in any particular year seems overly generous, although, to be sure, any figure is essentially a guess. Corvisier concludes that the *milice* furnished 46 percent of the recruits raised from 1701 through 1712, but his method of calculation is highly suspect.[212] He counts as actually raised all the numbers decreed in ordinances, even though, considering the strong resistance to conscription, no one can

[209] Contrast this judgment with Rousset, *Louvois*, 3:320.
[210] The primary works on the *milice* are Gébelin, *Histoire des milices*; Maurice Sautai, *Les milices provinciales sous Louvois et Barbézieux, 1688–1697* (Paris: 1882); Hennet, *Les milices*; along with Girard, *Rocolage et milice*, and Corvisier, *L'armée française*.
[211] AN, G⁷1774, "Etat des troupes que le Roy a eu sur pied," 1696, lists a total of 415,237 troops serving that year, of which only 29,920 (7.2 percent) served in *milice* regiments outside their provinces. Even if one adds in the 15,000 listed for the *milice* of Languedoc and Dauphiné *who were not technically the milices provinciales* and who stayed at home sitting on the necks of the Protestants, the proportion would rise to only 10.8 percent.
[212] Corvisier, *L'armée française*, 1:249.

be sure that the quotas were ever attained. Moreover, given the high rates of desertion reported for *miliciens*, it can be debated how many of the men who began the march to the front reached the armies they were bound for and how many of those who made it to their regiments remained with them for long. His paper figures are extremely flimsy here. In any case, the mammoth armies of Louis's last two wars were not simply a product of recourse to the *milice*; rather, the *milice* served as one of several expedients employed in the search for as many troops as could be had.

The Royal Milice, 1688–97

The *milice provinciale* as envisioned by Louvois, moved toward conscription but in a manner consistent with French *milice* traditions. Whereas the new institution was unquestionably an innovation, it was one best described not as revolutionary but as evolutionary. This characterization of the *milices provinciales* as evolutionary bears out in several senses: The *milices provinciales* of the Nine Years' War developed out of earlier forms of compulsory service; these *milice* themselves then changed during that war; and they provided the precedent and experience from which the *milices* further evolved into a new form at the start of the War of the Spanish Succession. The *milice* of the Nine Years' War were part-time soldiers, serving in their own units based strictly on their native towns and regions, providing essentially auxiliary duties, and spending much of the year at home – characteristics shared with earlier forms of *milices*. But in the War of the Spanish Succession, *miliciens* merged into regular regiments and served under the same conditions as other royal soldiers, living, fighting, and dying at the front.

The ordinance of 29 November 1688 set the initial form of the new *milices provinciales*, and additional ordinances over the next few months supplied further details.[213] By this act, Louvois made the *milices* a general institution for the first time. The first call summoned 25,050 men, who were assembled into companies of fifty men and grouped into thirty provincial infantry regiments. An ordinance of 15 December modified the call-up to require that parishes furnish one recruit for every 2,000 livres paid in the annual *taille*. Recruits were to be unmarried, aged twenty to forty, and fit for service, but the law required no specific height. Marriage proved to be an effective shelter from service at first. The *intendant* of Caens complained in 1689 that "ever since the publication of the regulation, the curés occupy themselves continually with marrying the young men of this area where they are always trying

---

[213] In addition to the ordinance of 29 November 1688, other important instructions and ordinances were issued on 15 December 1688 and 3 January, 6 March, 16 March, 28 March, and 16 April 1689. See, as well, the ordinance of 26 February 1690. Useful and manageable accounts of the *milices provinciales* during the Nine Years' War can be found in Gébelin, *Histoire des milices*, 33–51, and Hennet, *Les milices*, 25–34. The account presented here is taken essentially from these works.

to elude the law."[214] In response, an ordinance of 26 February 1690 removed the exemption for newly married men.[215] Yet as late as 1697, Turgot, *intendant* of Metz, still commented that the *milice* encouraged marriage.[216]

Parishes chose whom they would send at an assembly held after mass on Sunday. Initially, a plurality of votes determined who would serve, but the democratic nature of the selection led to abuses, as friends and relatives acted to spare some from any service whatsoever.[217] For this reason, an ordinance of 23 December 1691 changed the selection process from voting to drawing lots; thus was born the practice of *tirage au sort*, at which the unlucky drew the infamous *billet noir*, or black slip. *Tirage au sort* remained basic to the *milices provinciales* from this point onward. Relatives drew lots for those who, though eligible, failed to attend the assembly. From the start, an individual named by a parish had to reside there. Should anything happen to him, from death to desertion, the parish bore the responsibility of replacing him. An ordinance of 1690 even declared that the family of a *milicien*, or militia man, who failed to report or who deserted bore the personal and financial responsibility to supply another recruit from the same parish.[218]

Parishes clothed and equipped their *miliciens* at first, but this practice imposed a hardship on poorer parishes. Each man was to carry fusil or musket and a sword and to be dressed in serviceable, but not necessarily uniform, clothing. The ordinance of 28 March 1689 relieved parishes of fitting out their own men and replaced it with a flat payment of 18 livres to be made each January, and a deduction of 8 deniers per day from the pay that each *milicien* received from the king. Parishes paid an additional 10 sols per year for linen and shoes, and officers deducted another 4 deniers per day for the same. Since the cost of clothing and equipping a single man ran anywhere from 40 to 75 livres, these payments represented a real break for the parishes.[219]

Neighboring parishes formed a company, and its officers resided in the same area, if at all possible. The officers, though nominated by the governor of the province or by his lieutenant general or lieutenant, were actually appointed by the king. Captains and colonels were to have prior service in command, and, if possible, so were lieutenants. These commissions were not up for purchase, unlike the regular army. At least one *intendant* tried to impose such commissions on local aristocrats whether they wanted to command *milice* or not.[220] Companies were to drill every Sunday when not

---

[214] AG, A¹ 902, 5 January 1689, letter from Courgues *intendant* of Caens to Louvois, in Sautai, *Les milices provinciales*, 30.

[215] See, for example, AD, Côte d'Or, C 3674, 7 January 1693. Printed form demanding that new men be raised for the *milices*, stipulated that all *garçons* and men married for two years would be eligible for the *tirage au sort*.

[216] Turgot, memoir of 1697–98, in Corvisier, *Les Français et l'armée*, 269.

[217] See ordinance of 23 December 1691 in Gébelin, *Histoire des milices*, 38.

[218] Ordinance of 26 February 1690, in Gébelin, *Histoire des milices*, 35n.

[219] Hennet, *Les milices*, 29.

[220] Letter from *intendant* de Lafond to Louvois, 14 November 1690, in Teutey, *Les officiers*, 72.

serving away from home. Authorities restricted a *milicien*'s movements; he could not be absent from his home for more than four days without permission. A deserter who abandoned his unit within France could suffer having his nose and ears cut, his cheeks branded, and then being condemned to the galleys. Desertion on foreign soil brought death.

The *milicien*'s rewards were few. When serving at home, he received 2 sols per day from his parish, and when he left home to serve the king, he got the king's standard pay for an infantryman, 5 sols per day, less deductions for bread and clothing. After his discharge, he could claim exemption from the *taille* for the first two years of his marriage if he married a woman from the same parish.

The original ordinance set the duration of service at two years, although this would change. Expecting a short conflict, Louvois had no qualms about this pledge, but when it came time to release the first class of *miliciens* in 1690, the fighting continued, and it would have been folly to ruin the *milice* regiments by sending all the veterans home. So the king went back on his pledge and announced a different system. A third of all *miliciens*, chosen by lot, were released in 1690, and another third in 1691. The rest were supposed to have returned home in 1692, but Louis refused to discharge them, and from that point onward *miliciens* had to serve until the return of peace.[221]

The number of *miliciens* increased when an ordinance of December 1692 raised company size from fifty to sixty men; the call went out in January 1693 for additional *miliciens*.[222] New regiments also appeared. By 1 August 1696, the *milice provinciale* numbered 531 companies in thirty-four regiments, or an official total of almost 32,000 enlisted men.[223] Corvisier argues that the number of *milice provinciale* increased from 25,000 at the start of the war to 60,000 at the high point, but this figure appears much too high, particularly when compared with documents from the 1690s.[224]

During the campaign season, regiments of *milices provinciales* served outside

[221] See the following ordinances: 10 May 1690, which set up the release by thirds, and those of 10 November 1692, 5 January 1693, 24 November 1693, 20 December 1694, 4 November 1695, and 25 October 1697, which repeatedly denied further discharges. Hennet, *Les milices*, 30–31.

[222] AD, Côte d'Or, C 3674, 7 January 1693, printed form.

[223] The numbers here come from Hennet, *Les milices*, 33. Gébelin, *Histoire des milices*, 39, mentions an *état* prepared at the end of 1692 that reported thirty-one regiments of *milice* with 512 companies and 25,600 men. For the campaign of 1693, the increased company size was to bring the total up to 30,720. AN, G⁷1774, "Etat des troupes que le Roy a eu sur pied," 1696, lists a total of 29,920 enlisted men in the *milices provinciales*. See Gébelin, *Histoire des milices*, 38–40, and Hennet, *Les milices*, 31–33, for additions to the original quotas. Compare the regiments of 1688–89, Hennet, *Les milices*, 31n, with those that stood in 1696, 33n; there was a certain amount of ebb and flow. One Paris regiment of *milice*, for example, was disbanded in 1695. *Intendant* of Paris, memoir of 1697–98, in Corvisier, *Les Français et l'armée*, 146.

[224] Contamine, *Histoire militaire*, 1:397. Corvisier's calculations here seem confused; certainly his figures do not accord with Gébelin, Hennet, Belhomme, or documents of the time. See AN, G⁷1774, #52.

their native provinces; distance hopefully would reduce desertion. This practice differentiated the *milices provinciales* from the local militias that stayed
close to home, including those of Languedoc and Dauphiné, who stood
guard against a Protestant rising. Yet, as a clever cost-cutting device, during
winter quarters the *milice* regiments returned to their villages, where the men
could live at home and be paid by their parishes, sparing the king's treasury.
Miliciens were not always welcome guests in their own regions, since they
sometimes practiced the violent ways that they had learned in the army. As
one frustrated official reported, "No matter how hard the winter, the soldiers of the *milice* that have been sent back to their own homes band together
in groups of 5, 6, 7, 8, etc., and raid and pillage the villages, killing chickens
and geese, grabbing the sheep, take drink, money, and commit a thousand
other malevolent acts of this nature."[225] In the spring, *milice* regiments reassembled and marched to their stations.

In general, *milice* regiments received second-echelon assignments. They
did not show up in the orders of battle for the primary armies of Flanders
or Germany but rather served as garrisons and guards. However, commanders of the less important armies fighting in Catalonia and in the Alps utilized
their *milice* regiments in the field. Of the twenty-five battalions in Catinat's
Army of the Alps, nine were *milices provinciales*. They, too, provided support
functions in the main, but *milice* regiments fought well and died at the battle
of Staffard in 1690.[226] They also engaged in the vicious wars against Protestant *barbets* in the mountains.

If most *milices* regiments were relegated to secondary roles, this stemmed
from a conviction that they were not very good. After all, *miliciens* served on
active duty only half of the year, merging into the civilian community during
winter quarters. Of course, some units were better than others; the Regiment d'Aligny from Dijon boasted 800 veterans out of 1,000 men.[227] It
served under marshal Catinat and suffered casualties at the battle of Staffard,
but the Regiment d'Aligny was the exception, not the rule.[228]

Perhaps the greatest problem with the *milice* was the unwilling nature of
the recruits, and at the bottom of this dissatisfaction lay the inequity of the
institution. The call imposed differing demands on the provinces; most frontier provinces were exempt, at least in the beginning. Only *roturiers* bore the
burden of *tirage au sort*, and because urban communities enjoyed considerable exemptions, the *milices provinciales* drew their recruits overwhelmingly
from the rural population. To identify, and insult, the *miliciens*, the line
troops dubbed them "peasants."[229] But even within the rural communities,

---

[225] Memoir of 1693 in Gébelin, *Histoire des milices*, 49.
[226] The four *milice* regiments suffered 202 casualties. Gébelin, *Historie des milices*, 47n.
[227] Rousset, *Louvois*, 3:chap. 5. Foucault in Gébelin, *Histoire des milices*, 47n.
[228] Gébelin, *Histoire des milices*, 50, states that there was often high mortality in the *milice*; for
    example, the Fontenay regiment lost two thirds of its soldiers, and Bournazel suffered a great
    deal, too.
[229] Gébelin, *Histoire des milices*, 40.

the *milice* drew primarily from the poorer families. As the *intendant* of Moulins commented, "It is the most poor and the most unfortunate that are chosen so as not to desolate and ruin agriculture."[230] Not surprisingly, peasants sought to avoid being chosen. As noted previously, initially marriage provided an escape route. Also, although it ran contrary to regulations, local families pooled their money to buy substitutes for those who drew the *billet noir*. "In other parishes where there were few young men, the fathers of sons who were named gave 20 and even 30 écus to young men of the parish who were willing to serve in their places."[231] In another case, "I have found that a parish paid, again in money, to send off its soldier, for one 60 livres, for another 75 livres, at least, and sometimes as much as 100 livres, and this money is paid by mutual consent by the young men, married or not, in order to spare themselves from going to war."[232] Sometimes substitutes did not even live in the parish that put them up.[233] *Intendants*, such as Miroménil at Tours, made efforts to stop the buying of substitutes or paying off of *milice* officers to substitute one man for another, but apparently with little impact.[234]

Dissatisfaction with *milice* service was not limited to the peasantry or to the administrators forced to carry out the royal ordinances. Vauban came to oppose the *milices*. He submitted a memoir to the king in 1696 criticizing recruitment in general and condemning the *milice* in particular: "The king can moreover considerably relieve his kingdom by regulating the levying of his troops in a fashion less onerous than that used now and by eliminating [*casser*] the *milices* that pillage everything [*pillotent tous*]."[235] Vauban also declared "that there are many officers of *milice* who have misbehaved and committed many disorders in the choice of levies, under the pretext of only wanting men who are well made and of proper height, which has caused the people infinite wrongs and vexations; but the necessity of repairing the troops and filling the ranks has obliged us to tolerate many malevolent acts and much corruption that would have been severely punished in another time."[236]

---

[230] Letter of Le Vayer, *intendant* of Moulins, 4 May 1695, in Boislisle, *Correspondence des contrôleurs généraux*, 1:389.

[231] Mémoire sur les dépenses de la milice dans la généralité de Paris, 17 August 1689, in Gébelin, *Histoire des milices*, 48n. See, as well, the letter of 26 June 1689 from de Creil, *intendant* of Orleans, in Boislisle, *Correspondence des contrôleurs généraux*, 1:187.

[232] Letter of Le Vayer, *intendant* of Moulins, 4 May 1695, in Boislisle, *Correspondence des contrôleurs généraux*, 1:389.

[233] Boislisle, *Correspondence des contrôleurs généraux*, 1:281. Miroménil stipulated that the *milicien* must come from the parish that sent him; apparently, this was often not the case.

[234] See letter of 21 March 1692 from Miroménil, in which he reported of his ordinance banning the buying of recruits or the paying off of officers to accept someone not chosen according to the laws on *tirage au sort*. Boislisle, *Correspondence des contrôleurs généraux*, 1:281.

[235] AG, Bib., Génie 11, 24 July 1696, Vauban, "Mémoire au Roi sur les sacrifices a faire pour la paix."

[236] Vauban, memoir dating from shortly after the Peace of Ryswick, in Rochas d'Aiglun, *Vauban*, 1:271.

The Royal Milice, *1701–14*

With the return of peace in 1697, Louis XIV discharged and dissolved his *milice provinciale*. When he resurrected the *milice* in 1701, it was not the same institution that came back to life.[237] No longer would *miliciens* form their own separate regiments. *Milice* regiments were simply not up to the quality of the regulars during the Nine Years' War, and incorporation into regular regiments promised to make far more effective troops out of the *miliciens*. *Miliciens* were full-time soldiers now, differing from the regulars only in the manner of recruitment.

The ordinance of 26 January 1701 demanded a levy of 33,345 *miliciens*, and as the years went by, different ordinances and instructions called up further levies of recruits until 1712. This tempts some historians to add up all the separate levies to calculate the *milice* contribution to the total force, but this is misleading. During the Nine Years' War, after their initial contribution, parishes were responsible for replacing men who ceased to serve for any reason whatsoever. This meant that as men died, deserted, or were invalided out, the parish automatically had to choose and send new men; it was necessary to order specific additional levies only in order to create new units or to augment the size of companies from fifty to sixty men. However, the new pattern of the *milice* in 1701 obligated villages to replace only men who had deserted. As the natural attrition of war thinned out earlier levies, the army required new ones. To an important degree, later levies were designed to fill the gaps in earlier ones; thus, they cannot simply be added together, since a process of subtraction was also involved in the equation. Consequently, it is impossible to ascertain how many *miliciens* were serving in the French army at any one time between 1701 and 1714.

The ordinance of 1701 returned to *tirage au sort* as the method of selecting *milice* recruits. Again, officials carried out the unwelcome drawing at an assembly right after Sunday mass. Qualifications for service varied somewhat from year to year. The ordinance of 1701 made men aged twenty-two to forty eligible for service; in 1702, this changed to twenty to thirty-five, and to eighteen to forty in 1703. Up to 1703, only bachelors risked the *tirage*, but soon it became obvious that this led once more to a rash of marriages. Bouville complained that all the men over twenty-two hurried to the altar "on the news of the levy 'of the *milice*."[238] Herbigny reported that "one

---

[237] When Corvisier insists that the War of the Spanish Succession had only the appearance of a seventeenth-century conflict and that, in fact, everything had changed, the case of the *milice provinciale* gives him some justification for what is otherwise an overly dramatic contrast. Contamine, *Histoire militaire*, 1:527. Girard also saw the new form of *milice provinciale* as a key: "From his time, to which we essentially owe our modern military organization, dates a first attempt to create a national army." Girard, *Racolage et milice*, 332. However, it is important to note that the War of the Spanish Succession was the first and only conflict in which all the contingents of *miliciens* were sent to the front to serve with the army. Girard, *Racolage et milice*, 178.

[238] Bouville, 30 April 1701 and 12 December 1702, AG, A^{1}1524, #336 and AG, A^{1}1605, #14 in Girard, *Racolage et milice*, 205.

cannot believe the number of marriages that have been performed since the levy of the *milice* last year." In December 1702, when it was time to raise the second levy of *miliciens* at the parish of Bois-Guillaume, only eight young men appeared for the *tirage au sort*. The rest had not run away; instead, 160 had taken wives after the first levy.[239] There was only one remedy to this dearth of bachelors; in 1703, men who were married for only three or four years entered the pool.[240]

Whereas no height limitation characterized the *milice* of the Nine Years' War, ordinances from 1701 on set a minimum height of 5 feet. This proved to be a problem for some areas of France, where men tended to be short, because some officers rejected men who failed the height standard, although in many cases, this seemed simply to hide other rationales for rejecting particular recruits.[241] At times, substitutions were allowed, and at times, they were banned, but in 1703, they were specifically forbidden. However, from 1708 through 1712, the law permitted, indeed encouraged, parishes to contribute money payments in lieu of sending men.

Parishes did not have to equip their own men this time around; everything would be charged to the *extraordinaire des guerres*. Now *miliciens* were to wear the king's uniform, and as his troops, they would receive the same pay as regular troops.[242] As additional compensation, they were to be exempt from the *taille* during service and for five years following their discharge.

The initial ordinance of 1701 created fifty-seven battalions of thirteen companies each, with forty-five men per company, to serve as second battalions for infantry regiments which up to that point had only one battalion each.[243] But soon *miliciens* were employed simply as replacements for whatever existing infantry regiments needed them. In order to make up for the losses suffered by the Army of Italy in 1701, authorities skimmed off 260 to 300 men from each of these *milice* second battalions and sent them south in the winter of 1701–2.[244] From 1702 on, new levies joined the army as replacements. In 1710, even cavalry units picked up replacements from the *milice*.[245] A shortage of officers may have decided authorities against trying to form whole new battalions of *milice* after 1701.[246] After 1701, *milice* levies were generally intended for specific armies rather than to some general replacement pool. The *milice* became a way of fleshing out hard-pressed forces unable to secure adequate

[239] AG, A¹1619, 23 December 1702, #190, letter of Herbigny, in Girard, *Racolage et milice*, 205–6.

[240] Gébelin, *Histoire des milices*, 52.   [241] Girard, *Racolage et milice*, 294–95.

[242] Concerning uniforms, see the circular of 6 February 1701 in Hennet, *Les milices*, 35.

[243] Hennet states that by the end of 1702, *miliciens* made up second or third battalions for seventy regiments. This goes beyond the January 1701 ordinance. Hennet, *Les milices*, 43.

[244] While Hennet, *Les milices*, 38, gives the number as 260, Girard, 169, gives it as 260 to 300. The monarchy proclaimed an additional levy on 10 December 1701 intended to replace the men sent to Italy. Hennet, 38 and 40, mistakenly counts this as a *milice* levy of 16,750; it was not. Instead of *milice*, it was a *levée particulière* by which the monarchy required merchant and artisan corporations to recruit volunteers by paying bounties varying from 60 to 100 livres. This effort levy produced about 15,000 recruits. Girard, *Racolage et milice*, 172–73.

[245] Hennet, *Les milices*, 44.   [246] Gébelin, *Histoire des milices*, 61.

Table 11.2. Milice *levies, 1701–7.*

Date of ordinance	Number of men	*Miliciens* destined to
26 January 1701	33,345	Roughly 15,000 were sent to Italy in January 1702.
2 November 1702	17,700	Army of Italy
30 October 1703	30,000	Diverse armies
30 October 1704	22,000	Armies of Italy and Spain
15 October 1705	27,000	Armies of Italy and Spain
20 November 1706	21,000	Armies of Italy and Spain
4 November 1707	10,100	Army of Spain

recruits in the normal manner. In general, the armies immediately on French borders could secure recruits more easily than could those posted further from France. Armies in Italy and Spain came up short, and the *milice* funneled men to them more than to others.[247] Table 11.2 lists the levies ordered and the destination of the new soldiers through 1707.[248] The levies shown in the table were clearly meant to produce large numbers of replacements in order to bring line units back up to strength, but this changed in 1708.

From 1708, hard times for the population made willing recruits more plentiful, since the army at least provided bread, and civil life threatened starvation. Moreover, the near collapse of royal finances made money a more valuable quantity than additional levies. As a consequence, during the period 1708–12, the *milice* mutated into a method of imposing a new tax on the French people. Starting in 1708, ordinances offered the possibility of substituting a payment of 100 or 75 livres for any man summoned up for the *milice*. Government policy went further than allowing parishes to commute the levy into a payment; authorities actively encouraged parishes to opt for payment. Secretary of state for war Voysin explained his priorities: "You will do very well to convince the communities to give money. It is precisely what is asked of them, because I encounter too many difficulties when they supply men, and money is necessary in order to give field regiments the means to restore themselves and to get their own recruits."[249]

When villages paid the 100 or 75 livres, the government clearly profited. From 1708–12, recruitment bounties for the regular army were far lower than this. In the Gardes françaises, a pricey regiment, recruitment bounties paid during winter quarters never reached 25 livres during the period when the money substitution was allowed, and they fell below 15 livres in 1710.[250] Owing to the hard times, some men enlisted simply to eat, and they took no bounty. Understandably, the troubles brought by the famine of 1709 made peasants more willing to except *tirage au sort*. In response, authorities issued

[247] Girard, *Racolage et milice*, 161.
[248] Figures here are taken from Girard, *Racolage et milice*, 200–1.
[249] Letter from Voysin to Baville, September 1709, in Girard, *Racolage et milice*, 275–76.
[250] Corvisier, *L'armée française*, 1:323. See, as well, the graph in Contamine, *Histoire militaire*, 1: 546.

Table 11.3. Milice *authorized to be substituted for money, 1708–12.*

Date of ordinance	Number of men	Livres per man
15 Nov. 1708	9,800	100
15 Sept. 1709	17,000	75
1 Aug. 1710	17,050	75
1 Aug. 1711	16,000	75
1 Aug. 1712	16,800	75
TOTAL	76,650	

secret instructions to put obstacles in the way of villages that wanted to supply men. Voysin advised, "If some villages want to give men, make it highly difficult to receive them . . . this is done in order to have the money in order to give cash to the officers."[251] So by 1708, the *milices provinciales* had become simply one more financial expedient. Table 11.3 lists the ordinances that allowed the substitution of money payment for service.[252] This transformation of the *milice* into a tax was only interrupted once because of the dire need of the Army of Flanders for replacements after the campaign of 1710. The ordinance of 20 January 1711 demanded 22,900 *miliciens* to march off to Villars's army, where they were intended to build up company size to fifty.[253] At this point, men were temporarily more valuable than livres.

The numbers demanded by the ordinances pose a challenge to the historian. Adding the January 1711 figure to those in Table 11.2 for 1701–7 yields a total of 184,045 men requested by the ordinances, or if one also totals the *milice* levies designed to be commuted into money payments, the sum rises to 260,695, which is the figure Corvisier employs. Yet exactly how many of them were raised, how many deserted before they reached the front, or how many left after they were incorporated into the army remains unknown. It is nothing short of impossible to state the number of *milice* with the army during any particular year, but it could never have approached the totals summoned by the ordinances.

The first call stated that service would last until the peace; or if war continued, after two years, one quarter of the levy would be discharged each year for four years. The ordinance of 1702 raised the required service to three years, and this term was repeated in succeeding ordinances. Just as during the Nine Years' War, royal ordinances extended service from year to year, and as a result, no levy of *milice* ever received a general discharge during the war; they remained in uniform until 1714.[254]

As during the previous war, the burden of the *milice* was not distributed

---

[251] Letter from Voysin to Bernage, 3 October 1709, in Girard, *Racolage et milice*, 277.
[252] Figures here are taken from Girard, *Racolage et milice*, 200–1.
[253] Girard, *Racolage et milice*, 201.
[254] See, for example the ordinances of 11 December 1706 and 6 December 1713, in Gébelin, *Histoire des milices*, 55n.

equally or fairly from one province to another or from one class to another. The secretary of state for war set the uneven quotas for different provinces and *généralités*, after which the *intendants* apportioned the demands within their *généralités*. As a province, Brittany received the highest demands over the course of the war, 22,000, and Rousillon the lowest, 585.[255] As another example of inequity, authorities in 1703 summoned 1,000 *miliciens* from Rouen and 600 from Caen, but the smaller Alençon had to supply 1,000 as well.[256] However, such gross numbers are not best for comparison. Instead, Corvisier measures the call for *miliciens* in all levies during 1701–12 against the populations of the areas from which they were demanded in order to arrive at a form of military-participation ratio – in this case, the number of *miliciens* required per 100,000 of population. The highest demands were those imposed on the *généralités* of Moulins (251/100,000) and Montauban (242/100,000), while the lowest was requested of Lyon (59/100,000) and Dijon (81/100,000).[257]

In addition to geographical differences, social and professional inequities marred the system. Nobles and significant officeholders enjoyed exemptions. To this list must be added masters and journeymen in artisan corporations, and most of the bourgeois. The exemptions covered such a great range that in 1705 an ordinance attempted to eliminate many of them and enumerate all the others in detail. However, the next year another edict reestablished the exemptions and went on to offer shelter to the holder of any office that cost 4,000 livres. This second ordinance allowed those with positions that cost less to pay the treasury an additional sum that would raise the cost to that amount, so it looks very much like one more financial expedient.[258]

In any case, the poorer segments of the population continued to view the *milices provinciales* with repugnance. But Louis XIV never fully realized how unpopular the institution had become. Saint-Simon suggests that in 1705 a conspiracy of silence isolated him from the truth.

The losses of men in Germany and in Italy caused the decision [to raise] a levy of 25,000 men of the *milice*, an act which brought great ruin and great desolation in the provinces. The king was deluded about the ardor of the people to join it; when going to mass at Marly he was shown some examples of two, four, or five carefully chosen fellows and he was told stories of their joy and of their enrollment. I have heard these stories several times, and the king tells them later while congratulating himself; whereas I, in my own lands and everywhere where it is talked about, know of the despair that this *milice* caused, even to the point that many mutilate themselves in order to be exempt from it. They proclaim in tears that they were being led to their deaths; and it was true that they were almost all sent to Italy, from where not a one ever returned. None of this was lost on anyone at court. One lowered one's eyes in hearing these lies and seeing the credulity of the king, and afterwards one said in a low voice what one thought of such ruinous flattery.[259]

[255] Girard, *Racolage et milice*, 200–1.   [256] Gébelin, *Histoire des milices*, 56.
[257] Corvisier, *L'armée française*, 1:198.   [258] Gébelin, *Histoire des milices*, 57.
[259] Saint-Simon, *Mémoires*. A. de Boislisle, ed., 42 vols. (Paris: 1879–1930), 13:169–70.

In contrast to the few willing *miliciens* that Louis saw, Duclos remembered, "I saw in my youth these forced recruits led in chains like criminals."[260] As an official from Poitou wrote, "The great majority of the soldiers march against their will; I have never seen men less inclined to war than these men of Poitou."[261]

Individuals did what they could to avoid the *tirage au sort*. Some men tried to bribe their way out of service; in 1701, a captain of Brie was convicted for having accepted 250 livres from the father of one unlucky young *milicien*.[262] As Saint-Simon observed, men mutilated themselves; some cut off fingers, and others used irritating plants to create sores.[263] Marriage ceased to provide exemption in 1703. The easiest form of avoidance was simply to flee. The mere announcement of a levy caused peasants to run away. As one report stated, "In the parishes which were supposed to furnish two soldiers, twenty peasants abandoned their land to avoid drawing lots."[264] When a *tirage* was held in 1702 at Nevers, of the 200 young men who were supposed to be present, only five showed up.[265] Chamillart reprimanded one *intendant* for publishing the notification of an upcoming levy too soon, because if the people knew too far in advance, "many young men will have time to absent themselves from their parishes before we can be ready to make them draw lots."[266] When possible, authorities could require relatives, or even children, to draw for those not present.[267] To force young men to show up, authorities even tried quartering soldiers on the families of recalcitrants, but nothing seemed to work.[268] Perhaps the oddest way of avoiding the *tirage au sort* involved jumping from the frying pan into the fire. Many individuals simply enlisted. The logic here was that it was better to serve with men and officers that you knew, that you could choose, rather than with strangers.[269]

Manifesting the unpopularity of the *milice* in another way, friends and relatives tried to liberate new recruits as they made the journey from their homes to the front. In 1701, when the *miliciens* formed their own battalions, recruits first assembled in companies of forty-five men and then joined their battalion at another town, from which the entire battalion marched to the army. But from 1702 on, *miliciens* did not constitute their own battalions, so they simply formed in groups, preferably of about fifty men, at a local town and traveled to the front under the supervision of officers and sergeants.[270] Municipal magistrates charged with taking men to the assembly town risked

[260] Duclos, *Mémoires secrètes*, 1:59, in Gébelin, *Histoire des milices*, 59.
[261] Girard, *Racolage et milice*, 235.   [262] Girard, *Racolage et milice*, 302.
[263] Girard, *Racolage et milice*, 236.
[264] Estates of Languedoc in 1719, in Gébelin, *Histoire des milices*, 58n.
[265] Girard, *Racolage et milice*, 238.
[266] AG, A¹1905, #294 and 295, November 1705, letter from Chamillart to de la Masssaye, in Girard, *Racolage et milice*, 228.
[267] Girard, *Racolage et milice*, 241.   [268] Girard, *Racolage et milice*, 244.
[269] Girard, *Racolage et milice*, 219. ·   [270] Girard, *Racolage et milice*, 304.

abuse, since *miliciens* resisted, even shooting the local officials.[271] When the government returned to the practice of levying men by *tirage au sort* in 1711, it encountered "the most violent action which has yet occurred in the levy of recruits."[272] A particularly nasty incident pitted a mob of 200 peasants, about thirty of them armed, against a *recrue* of seventeen men being transported by boat. The peasants negotiated with the civil authorities in charge, but finally the mob shouted "Kill! kill! we want all the recruits who are in that boat, otherwise no quarter!"[273] Those leading *recrues* of *milices* had to take precautions along the road. They locked recruits up at night when possible and secured armed escorts, which most commonly were composed of archers, armed marshals under the authority of provosts. The *maréchaussée* also assisted.[274] It was not just angry crowds or sympathetic civilians who threatened to take new *miliciens* away from their escorts. Officers from regular regiments out in search of recruits found *miliciens* a tempting target and lured them. This became such a serious problem that authorities promised soldiers who would denounce guilty officers a discharge and 100 to 300 livres as reward.[275] Not surprisingly, desertion posed a very serious problem for the *milices provinciales*.

Taking all of the foregoing into consideration, it comes as little surprise that *miliciens* often made poor soldiers; it seems probable that the selection process did not work to supply the best men. Marsin described the 7,700 *miliciens* sent to his army in Germany in 1703 as "only fit to fill the hospitals," and "the subaltern officers who have come at the same time are for the most part of the same quality, without experience, without equipment, and without money."[276]

Peace finally liberated the *miliciens* and spared the peasantry from the *tirage au sort*, at least for a time. The discharge of *miliciens* began in December 1713; those released kept their uniform and sword and received 18 livres. Further discharges followed in April 1714, and the remaining *miliciens* were free to leave their regiments in July 1714.[277]

The *milices provinciales* evolved continually between the onset of the Nine Years' War and the end of the War of the Spanish Succession. During both conflicts, the *milices* were treated as wartime expedients, as temporary institutions. But as circumstances required, *milices* would again play a role in 1719 against Spain. In 1726, the *milice* was finally reestablished to remain a permanent institution of the *ancien régime* army, although to be sure, the *milice* continued to evolve right up to the time of the Revolution.[278]

[271] Girard, *Racolage et milice*, 288.
[272] Letter from Legendre, 1711, in Girard, *Racolage et milice*, 289.
[273] Letter from Legendre, 1711, in Girard, *Racolage et milice*, 289.
[274] Girard, *Racolage et milice*, 306–9.   [275] Girard, *Racolage et milice*, 310–12.
[276] Marsin letter of 7 June 1704, in Gébelin, *Histoire des milices*, 60–61.
[277] Hennet, *Les milices*, 44.   [278] Gébelin, *Histoire des milices*, 2.

DISCHARGE

With all of the attention in this chapter on how men entered the army, it is only reasonable to comment on how they left the service. Many died in the ranks because of mortal wounds and, especially, disease, and others suffered wounds that either forced them out of the ranks or won them a pension as an *invalide*. But able-bodied men also received discharges in the course of affairs. The question of how many veterans returned to the civilian community after having served in the royal army deserves attention for a number of reasons, not the least of which is that these veterans may have carried with them into the general population a notion of service to the state and a firsthand sense of France, in contrast to the more natural parochialism of the civilian population. In the long run, this may have contributed to a nascent national consciousness.

The provisions for regular discharge were fairly stingy, and simply listing them leaves the impression that for the French army, once a soldier, always a soldier. However, such a negative analysis must also deal with the phenomenon of *réformes*, the demobilization of the army by wholesale downsizing or elimination of regiments at war's end. *Réforme*, as will be seen, and not discharge, was the real mechanism that produced the many able-bodied veterans during the *grand siècle*.

The formal passage from soldier to civilian in normal peacetime circumstances came rarely. At times, soldiers received discharges as both reward and protection; such was the case for soldiers who informed authorities concerning *passe volants* and dueling.[279] This reinforced the notion that, as the historian Georges Girard put it, discharge was "considered more as a favor than as a right."[280] In general, Louis XIV was reluctant to let experienced veterans leave the ranks if this meant the necessity to replace them with green recruits. Thus, the numbers allowed to leave the service by regulation remained small. In 1669, the number who could be discharged was limited to six men per company per year.[281] An ordinance of 15 November 1679 set a maximum of four *congés d'ancieneté*, or discharges based on length of service, each year; and this fell to only one in 1682.[282] The number stabilized at two per year by the ordinance of 2 October 1686, although men kept past the time that they were entitled to discharge received an extra sol per day in pay.[283] *Congés* that were granted came only during winter quarters, according to the ordinance

---

[279] See Rousset, *Louvois*, 1:197–98 on discharge as a reward for informing on officers who used *passe volants*. See Micheline Cuénin, *Le duel sous l'ancien régime* (Paris: 1982), 216 on 1676 and 1677 ordinances that rewarded soldier informants with a discharge and 150 livres.

[280] Girard, *Racolage et milice*, 50.

[281] Ordinances of 16 August 1669. Girard, *Racolage et Milice*, 49n.

[282] See the ordinances of 15 November 1679, and 1 August 1682. Girard, *Racolage et Milice*, 49n. This number rose back to three in 1730, Albert Babeau, *La vie militaire sous l'ancien regime*, 2 vols. (Paris: 1890), 1:312.

[283] Girard, *Racolage et milice*, 50.

of 5 November 1685, which remained in effect through the War of the Spanish Succession.[284]

Even this meager system of discharge was put on hold again and again. In 1684, the king decided that it would be best to keep the companies that he had raised over the past two years and to "give no discharges based on length of service."[285] When the Nine Years' War began, Louis suspended all discharges for *ancieneté* alone.[286] In 1701, Louis again forbade his officers to give any discharges "for whatever the cause and consideration might be." The tolerable exceptions would be for those "absolutely in no condition to serve because of extreme old age or incapacity, be it by wounds or some incurable sickness."[287] Wartime necessity put off promised releases of *miliciens* in both wars, as already recounted. The lack of a normal way out of the ranks may go a long way to explain desertion in the army of Louis XIV, since this appeared to be the only escape from duty, even after one had fulfilled one's obligation.

So far in the discussion, it would seem that few veterans ever left their regiments until they were turned out as *invalides*. But this was not the case, owing to the practice of *réforme*. Demobilization, at least from the Dutch War on, returned veterans to the civilian life. It can be debated whether the end of the war with Spain in 1659 brought any actual decrease in the number of French soldiers, as opposed to simply a decrease in the number of companies in the army. Mazarin stated that troops were not let go; however, when describing the process of increasing army size for the War of Devolution, Louis XIV made comments that implied that many veterans had been released about 1660.[288]

Louis significantly diminished his army after the War of Devolution, although he knew that his struggle with the Dutch and Spanish was far from over. By the high point of that war in 1668, Louis possessed an army of 134,000.[289] The return to peace again brought this down to an immediate post war figure of 70,000.[290] This would mean that nearly half the army

---

[284] Girard, *Racolage et milice*, 50.

[285] Louvois to Créqui, 18 January 1684, in Jacques Hardré, ed., *Letters of Louvois, University of North Carolina Studies in the Romance Languages and Literatures*, no. 10 (Chapel Hill: 1949), 401.

[286] This was ordered by ordinances of 20 September 1688 and 15 October 1689. Girard, *Racolage et milice*, 51.

[287] Ordinance of 18 November 1701 in Girard, *Racolage et milice*, 51.

[288] Jules Mazarin, *Lettres du cardinal Mazarin pendant son Ministère*, Chéruel and Avenel, eds., vols. 6–9 (Paris: 1890–1906), 9:378, letter of 19 October 1659. But in his memoirs for 1666, the king wrote, "Because finally, after seven years of peace, the majority of veterans being established in other professions, I had been obliged to take in many new men in all my troops." Louis XIV, *Mémoires*, 2:110.

[289] AG, BMG, Tiroirs de Louis XIV, pages 46–48, "Estat des trouppes d'infanterie que le Roy a sur pied en mars 1668"; pages 50–64, "Estat des trouppes de cavalerie que le Roy a sur pied en mars 1668."

[290] Paul Sonnino, *Louis XIV and the Origins of the Dutch War* (Cambridge: 1989), 127–28fn.

received discharges. The Treaty of Nymwegen ending the Dutch War brought a similar *réforme* from a paper wartime high of about 279,000 to roughly 147,000 men, officers not included, in 1679.[291] Once more, the army turned a great number of veterans out of their regiments. The largest discharge by *réforme* followed the Nine Years' War, when an army that topped 420,000 on paper in 1696 fell to a peacetime level of 154,000 in 1699. Such a large number of men would have to be dismissed at the end of the Nine Years' War that Vauban complained of the problems that would arise if they were released on the frontiers and left to their own devices to return home without funds for the trip: "It will create an infinite number of beggars, and considering the poverty of the peasants and their lack of charity towards soldiers, a great many will perish of hunger and cold during the winter before being able to return to their regions."[292] Between the months of February and December 1698, Louis eliminated 56 complete infantry regiments.[293] The *réforme* following the War of the Spanish Succession was not quite so great, because while the paper size of the army came close to equaling that during the Nine Years' War, in reality, the army was not as large during Louis's last war. However, more entire regiments were cut by this later *réforme*, as the French consigned over 150 infantry regiments to oblivion.[294] In cutting back to a peacetime army in 1713–14, Louis once again let many veterans become civilians.

The way in which the Bourbons raised manpower for their wars revealed a transition to the state commission army. Although many vestiges of the past remained, the old private armies and off-the-shelf units of the aggregate contract army disappeared. In their place, voluntary, individual enlistment – albeit often of reluctant recruits – dominated, to be augmented by limited conscription. There was no uniform method; men arrived at their posts by different routes. Some came from France, others from outside Bourbon domains. Some were driven by a sense of adventure, by an empty stomach, by a loyalty to their king, or by revenge. Some came only because they were forced to march to the front; embittered by resentment, they resigned themselves to service, or they deserted. How could such soldiers, from so many different origins and inspired by so many different motives, serve together for a common goal? No one can truly know the human mind and heart, but those who study war understand that this is a matter of great importance. It is the focus of the next chapter.

---

[291] AG, BMG, Tiroirs de Louis XIV, page 110, "Troupes que le Roy auvis sur pied le premier janvier 1678"; AN, $G^7$1774, piece 52.

[292] Vauban, 18 November 1687, in Babeau, *La vie militaire*, 1:311.

[293] Girard, *Racolage et milice*, 4.

[294] Sicard, *Histoire des institutions militaires*, 2:207, states that Louis XIV only kept 118 regiments after the War of the Spanish Succession. Subtracting this from the total generated by AG, MR 1701, #13, means that the French had to cut 158 regiments from the rolls.

12

Discipline and Desertion

THE "X" scratched beneath the transcript of the trial betrays the shaking
hand that drew it. Not only was the pen strange to the unfortunate,
illiterate infantryman, Pierre La Sire, but he could only regard his future with
a dread that must have made his hand tremble. Pierre deserted from the
company of the chevalier d'Huynes in the Regiment d'Antraynes, but he had
been caught and judged by a *conseil de guerre* on 21 April 1705. The *conseil*
sentenced Pierre to have his nose and ears cut, be branded on the cheek with
a fleur de lis, and sent to the galleys for the rest of his life.[1] This unfortunate
youth of twenty-one, without any profession, would now live out his life in
slavery, without hope. In all probability, he would not long survive. He had
fallen victim to the French disciplinary system because he had committed the
most important of disciplinary infractions by attempting to flee the army.
Now his quivering "X" verified his own testimony and certified his own
punishment.

Once a recruit entered the army, by whatever route, he fell under the jurisdiction of the military justice system; he must live according to military
discipline or suffer consequences that by modern standards were at least
severe and often brutal. Ultimately, military discipline was designed to compel proper behavior and thus ensure both order and performance. This chapter examines regulations regarding military conduct, institutions designed to
enforce obedience, and infractions against the disciplinary code.

Of the infractions elaborated here, none posed a greater threat to the
integrity of an army than did desertion. At least troops that resorted to
pillage, another cardinal military sin, remained with the colors, and if better
maintained would return to disciplined conduct. And in any case, the worst
pillage was over by the personal reign of Louis XIV. But soldiers who fled

---

[1] AG, A^{1}1831, #125, 27 April 1705. See, as well, *procès verbaux* on desertion, A^{1}1831, #20, 4 April
1704, and A^{1}1831, #28, 7 April 1705.

their units reduced its strength permanently, or at least until they were replaced. Desertion sapped an army's strength in a way more constant and
enervating than even battle; consequently, it attracted the attention of military theorists and practical soldiers alike. Its dangers were reflected in the
punishments inflicted on the guilty, on men like Pierre La Sire.

DISCIPLINE

Discipline is fundamental to the effectiveness of any armed force. Because
armies are complex organizations requiring coordinated and sometimes uniform behavior in the face of danger and chaos, their success depends upon
hierarchy and obedience, and discipline embodies both.

The character of discipline within the army of the *grand siècle* rested upon
assumptions basic to the culture of command within the army. That culture
posited a rigid social class structure and ascribed honor only to the aristocratic upper strata. By this logic, because common soldiers were men of low
class and, therefore, devoid of true honor, they could hardly be trusted to
comply voluntarily with high military standards. Such assumptions, though
based upon class prejudice, also reflected the reality that a great many soldiers within the army had been forced into the ranks against their will. Harsh
discipline and brutal punishment were essential to enforce compliance upon
individuals held in such low esteem. To be sure, some enlightened officers
came to know their troops better and to entertain higher opinions of them.
Observers did credit the common soldier with courage, although not in the
aristocratic mold. Moreover, as the century progressed, the monarchy tem-
pered coercion with appeals to the self-interest and even the loyalty of its
troops – aspects of motivation and morale that are discussed in the next
chapter. Nonetheless, the fundamental guarantor of obedience remained
coercion. Given the horrendous excesses committed by troops in the early
and mid–seventeenth century, it is no wonder that military commanders and
administrators constantly concerned themselves with coercive discipline.

On the whole, discipline improved over the course of the *grand siècle*, but
amelioration was not linear and even, and it involved more than the will of
the monarch and his ministers. Pontis in 1649 complained that discipline had
been much better under Louis XIII – that is, before 1643.[2] André concluded
from his study that discipline was better during 1643–45 than it was for the
next period, 1646–53, when it was at its worst, and that things improved after
the Fronde.[3] These evaluations imply that good conduct depended upon a
minimum level of material conditions, conditions that deteriorated very badly
during the 1640s. Unpaid and hungry troops obeyed not their officers but
their needs, as exemplified in the Tax of Violence. When conditions in the
field decayed in later wars, discipline again declined.

---

[2] Pontis in Louis André, *Michel Le Tellier et l'organisation de l'armée monarchique* (Paris: 1906), 595.
[3] André, *Le Tellier*, 573–74.

Military men recognized that without proper supply, disciplinary action was basically impossible and, in fact, probably unjustified. The English general, Monck, explained, "If a general ensures that his men are fed and clothed . . . if they are punctually paid . . . then your general can with justice punish them severely."[4] Such concerns did not end with the Peace of the Pyrenees. Speaking of food, the *munitionnaire* Nodot stated at the end of the seventeenth century that "[I]f an army lacks bread for several days, the soldier will be forced to leave his unit to go marauding."[5] Throughout the century, discipline was to an important degree a matter of logistics.

Mutinies were the converse of discipline, and, not surprisingly, they nearly always involved the failure to pay or feed troops. Important mutinies struck the French army, or troops in French pay, during the long war with Spain; this turmoil included outbreaks in 1644 at Brisach,[6] in 1647 with Turenne's Army of Germany,[7] in 1650 among cavalry of the army in Flanders,[8] and in 1651 at Câteau-Cambrésis.[9] At each point, pay was an issue. After 1659, actual mutiny was less common, but the threat remained on the minds of the king, his ministers, and his commanders. The year 1667 brought a minor rebellion over lack of pay.[10] When his troops mutinied against Marshal Créqui at Trier in 1675, they were at the end of a long siege and at the end of their tether, starving and desperate.[11] Famine produced tumult in the French army again in 1709. Garrisons at Le Quesnoy, Arras, Mons, Saint-Omer, Tournai, Nassau, Valenciennes, and Cambrai rebelled and turned violent against local officials.[12] This brief list by no means constitutes a full catalog.

Despite certain mutinies after 1661, the behavior of French troops markedly improved under Louis XIV, as, indeed, did the conduct of other European soldiers during this period. Desertion by individuals replaced mutiny by

---

[4] Monck in Frank Tallett, *War and Society in Early Modern Europe* (London: 1992), 272, n. 65. Richelieu counted at the top of his list to ensure "good discipline in the future" the need to provide "bread, six *montres*, and clothing." Richelieu, *Testament politique*, ed. Louis André (Paris: 1947), 475.

[5] François Nodot, *Le munitionnaire des armées de France* (Paris: 1697), 567. See, as well, AN, G⁷1778, 7 September 1706, letter from Marshal Berwick, and memoir of the late seventeenth or early eighteenth century, AG, MR 1701, #15.

[6] Patrick Landier, "Guerre, violences, et société en France, 1635–1659," doctorat de troisième cycle, Université de Paris IV: 1978, 213. In this mutiny, the troops shot their officers. See, as well, 1645 mutinies mentioned in Charles Derek Croxton, "Peacemaking in Early Modern Europe: Cardinal Mazarin and the Congress of Westphalia, 1643–1648," Ph.D. dissertation, University of Illinois at Urbana-Champaign, 1995, 220, 222.

[7] Jean Bérenger, *Turenne* (Paris: 1987), 245–51; for 1647, see BN, 4175, fol. 488–94, June 1647.

[8] AG, A¹120, 21 October 1650, Le Tellier to Bordeaux.

[9] Jacques de Chastenet de Puységur, *Mémoires de messire Jacques de Chastenet, chevalier, seigneur de Puységur, colonel du régiment de Piedmont, et lieutenant général des armées du Roy*, 2 vols. (Paris: 1690), 2:431–34.

[10] AG, A¹209, #46, 20 June 1667, Carlier.

[11] John B. Wolf, *Louis XIV* (New York: 1968), 245–46.

[12] Claude C. Sturgill, *Marshal Villars and the War of the Spanish Succession* (Lexington, KY: 1965), 82.

entire units as the prime threat to an army's integrity. There seems to be no question that the personal reign of Louis XIV brought troops to heel as never before, although the army's conduct in the early years of the Dutch War was hardly exemplary. Corvisier speculates that the apogee of French discipline came in the decade between the Dutch War and the Nine Years' War.[13] The stresses imposed by Louis's last two wars overtaxed supply and administration to the point that the highest standards could not be maintained after 1688.

It is impossible to account for the sterner French emphasis on discipline after 1661 without considering the intense concern of the king. Louis XIV raised order and discipline practically to the level of a fetish.[14] The great king wrote in his memoirs for 1666: "I was resolved to spare nothing to reestablish, at every point, discipline in the troops that served under my authority."[15] And he believed that his efforts produced the desired results: "I maintained a discipline so exact in my troops, that having sent them several times to my allies, in Italy, Hungary, and Holland, they never gave the least subject for complaint."[16] Louis XIV obviously did not discover discipline; its value had been stressed long before he asserted his authority. Turenne had written: "Obedience and discipline among the troops being without contradiction one of the first means of carrying victories, it is necessary to have [discipline] observed with the greatest exactitude."[17] But beyond its practical value, Louis's concern for discipline resonated with the rest of his character to such a degree that it arose as a natural and consuming conviction.

The king's emphasis on discipline did not always meet with praise. Saint-Simon dismissed it with scorn: "He ceaselessly concerned himself with the most petty matters concerning the troops [*les derniers sur les troupes*]: clothing, armament, evolutions, drill, and discipline, in a word, all sort of base details."[18] The haughty Saint-Simon, himself little more than a dilettante of a soldier who thought that the military art consisted of charging bravely, missed the point. Stories of glory at court might not involve such "base details," but they were the glue that held seventeenth-century armies together.

---

[13] Philippe Contamine, ed., *Histoire militaire de la France*, vol. 1 (Paris: 1992), 402.

[14] His biographer John B. Wolf insisted: "Indeed, the transformation into disciplined soldiers of the marauding bands that fought the earlier wars must in part be credited to Louis XIV. For him the discipline was almost an end in itself." Wolf, *Louis XIV*, 467. He also wrote: "This interest in discipline continues to be a most important theme in the military correspondence of Louis XIV from these early years until his death." John B. Wolf, *The Emergence of the Great Powers, 1685–1715* (New York: 1962), 196.

[15] Louis XIV, *Oeuvres de Louis XIV*, Grimoard and Grouvelle, eds., 6 vols. (Paris: 1806), 2:91–92 in André, *Le Tellier*, 605.

[16] Louis XIV, *Mémoires de Louis XIV*, Charles Dreyss, ed., 2 vols. (Paris: 1860), 1:244, memoirs for 1666.

[17] Turenne in Bérenger, *Turenne*, 510–11.

[18] Louis de Rouvroy, duc de Saint-Simon, *Mémoires*, ed. Gonzague Truc, 7 vols. (Paris: 1953–61), 4:952.

Personnel Charged with the Maintenance of Discipline

During the first half of the *grand siècle*, the maintenance of discipline would seem to have relied more on the actions of individual officers than it did during the personal reign of Louis XIV. A story dating from the early years of the war with Spain highlighted the rough-and-tumble nature of discipline. After Marshal Marillac had beaten a sentinel, the king suspended the marshal for six days as punishment, but the monarch also demoted the sentinel for not having killed the marshal rather than have suffered the disgrace of the beating.[19] It is hard to image Louis XIV responding in this same way; his sense of propriety and his desire for procedure would have precluded it.

The Sun King insisted upon far more regular disciplinary and judicial practices, although, as in so many other administrative matters, these practices were based on ordinances drafted by Le Tellier in earlier years. The king was the ultimate military commander and judicial authority in his realm, so he carried the main responsibility for discipline and the military justice system; however, he obviously had to delegate this authority. Under the direction of the secretary of state for war, *intendants* bore the primary obligation of these matters in the king's field armies. The most common formal title in commissions to military *intendants* was, after all, "intendant de la justice, police et finance." Eventually, the *intendant* oversaw the maintenance of discipline, the constitution of *conseils de guerre*, and the enforcement of the king's regulations and ordinances.

Within the army, provosts functioned as magistrates, with archers as their police officers. Before the reforms of Le Tellier, it would appear that the provost exercised much authority as judge as well as police official. A document of 1644 stated:

In all quarrels and differences arising between soldiers, in the towns and places of garrison and in their environs, the provost has jurisdiction [*en connaît*] – The provost is also judge of offenses committed by captains, officers of the regiment [and] their servants and lackeys being obliged to come to be heard before him.[20]

At least from the ministry of Le Tellier, military provosts served as officers of the court, just as did their civilian counterparts, and the military tribunal that a provost reported to was a *conseil de guerre*. An instruction of 1646 redefined the provosts' functions:

to cause our military regulations and ordinances to be exactly observed; . . . to provide information for trials and to report these to our *conseil de guerre* . . . ; to cause to be punished on the spot those who will be found by you flagrantly guilty of crimes for which the power is given to the said provosts by edicts and ordinances; to scour the country with your archers and provide security and free circulation on the roads; to cause soldiers, merchants, and all others to maintain the reasonable prices that will

---

[19] Puységur, *Mémoires*, 1:23–24.
[20] SHAT, Bib., Col. des ord., vol. 16, #160, 1644, "Forme de la justice militaire de l'infanterie de France," in André, *Le Tellier*, 589.

be set by the [military] *intendant* . . . for meat and foodstuffs in the said army; to keep the soldiers from breaking ranks [*débandement*]; to pursue deserters from our troops, to arrest them and cause them to be punished according to our ordinances and public declarations.[21]

As with so much of Le Tellier's fundamental military legislation, this definition of a provost's functions became the rule for the rest of the reign of Louis XIV.

The most important provost was the Grand Provost who commanded the Compagnie de la Connétablie, which directly served the marshals of France in their judicial role.[22] He commanded two lieutenants and sixty to 100 archers. Usually one of his lieutenants served as grand provost of the Army of Flanders, with forty to fifty archers under him; he bore general responsibility over the entire camp and the army on the march. In 1691, such a company included, along with the grand provost of the army, a *procureur du Roy* or prosecutor, a *greffier*, two exempts, a lieutenant, and forty archers.[23] Provincial grand provosts could also provide their services to armies. With forces in the field, the superior provost of the particular army could also go by the title *provost general*, as he is often termed in regulations.

Lesser provosts and archers also composed a portion of regimental staffs, but not every regiment boasted these police.[24] Under Le Tellier, only the oldest French infantry regiments and those with special privileges had a provost staff, or *prévôté*; late in the reign of Louis XIV, thirty battalions contained a *prévôté*.[25] Such a *prévôté* consisted of a provost, a lieutenant provost, a clerk [*greffier*], an executioner, and five archers. The regimental provost received a rate of pay and a ration allotment that placed him between a captain and a lieutenant of infantry, while his archers and *exécuteur* received the same rate of pay as common soldiers.[26] At this point, mounted regiments seem to have lacked *prévôtés* altogether. Since not every unit contained a *prévôté* and since the provost answered directly to the *conseil de guerre*, not simply to the colonel of the regiment, it had to be the case that on campaign, provosts and archers were not restricted to policing their own regiments but served the army they were with. The provosts assembled in a particular army fell under the jurisdiction of a provost general, or grand provost.[27] Foreign regiments in French service insisted on maintaining their own disciplinary codes and machinery; hence, this discussion is restricted to French regiments.

---

[21] Commission for a provost general circa 1646, in André, *Le Tellier*, 591.

[22] Victor Belhomme, *L'armée française en 1690* (Paris: 1895), 105–6.

[23] BN, f. fr. 4565, 3 June 1691.

[24] François Sicard, *Histoire des institutions militaires des Français*, 4 vols. (Paris: 1831), 2:211, is mistaken on this point.

[25] André, *Le Tellier*, 589. See Jean Roland de Mallet, *Comptes rendus de l'administration des finances du royaume de France* (London: 1789), 158, for a list of the thirty in 1710. This accords well with other records, such as the 1691 records in BN, f. fr. 4565–67.

[26] Mallet, *Comptes rendus*, 160.

[27] Douglas Baxter, *Servants of the Sword* (Champaign, IL: 1976), 67. He refers to the subsidiary provosts as *prévôts des bands*.

The archers of the Grand Provost in the Compagnie de la Connétablie also went by the name *maréchaussée*. Their name derived from the fact that they were responsible to the marshals and their *prévôts*. Provincial *maréchaussée* were under the authority of local *prévôts*. These provincial cavalry, considered as part of the army, provided security on the French highways, and when soldiers got out of hand on the march, the *maréchaussée*, ancestors of the *gendarmerie* of today, could be called upon to control disorder and shadow a troublesome unit.[28] The *maréchausée* grew in importance from the 1670s on and provided civil police functions in rural areas. In the second half of the seventeenth century, the terms *archers* and *maréchausée* seem to have been used almost interchangeably for provost troops with the armies, while the latter term had more relevance for provincial functions.

Despite the regularization of military law, the growing role of the *intendant*, and the other officials charged with enforcing military justice, field commanders still influenced the quality of discipline in their armies. Some developed reputations as rigid task masters, while others did not. Marshal Schomberg once hanged a dragoon who stole a sheep, and Chamilly hanged another for having taken a 2-sols loaf of bread from a peasant.[29] On the other hand, as a general, Luxembourg did not regard discipline as his highest priority during the Dutch War, an insouciance that maddened Louvois. Luxembourg's troops were prone to pillage, and he did not seem to insist that his officers pay their men promptly, an omission that raised the desertion rate. At one point, Louvois intervened to overturn the decision of a *conseil de guerre* in Luxembourg's army. This *conseil*, composed of *mestre de camp général* and some brigadiers of cavalry, failed to penalize a captain and two of his men for pillage.[30] Luxembourg tried to challenge the authority of Louvois during the Dutch War but failed and suffered disgrace following that conflict. It was a chastened man who, as marshal Luxembourg, commanded armies during the Nine Years' War. As evidence of his personal reformation, Luxembourg cracked down on misconduct by his troops, so that he could write in 1691: "You can count on the fact that there is no one who hates disorders more than I do."[31]

Conseils de guerre

Before Le Tellier came to power in 1643, individual officers sat in judgment over their own soldiers, and this practice continued to a large extent until the

[28] See the case of the *maréchausée* used to watch the Waloon guards in 1704. AG, A¹1801, #14, 16, 23, 33, 36, 120, 125, and 140.

[29] 1682 letter in Albert Babeau, *La vie militaire sous l'ancien regime*, vol. 1 *Les soldats*, and vol. 2 *Les officiers* (Paris: 1890), 1:287.

[30] AG, A¹533, 24 September 1677, Louvois to Luxembourg, in Camille Rousset, *Histoire de Louvois*, 4 vols. (Paris: 1862–64), 2:330–31.

[31] AG, A¹1047, 12 June 1691, Luxembourg to Louvois, in Rousset, *Louvois*, 4:476fn. See, as well, Luxembourg's letter AG, A¹942, 18 May 1690, Luxembourg to Louvois, in Rousset, *Louvois*, 4:398–99.

return of peace in 1659. But after the Peace of the Pyrenees, military administrators disapproved of such assertions of personal judicial authority by regimental officers. In 1664, when a captain decided to punish one of his soldiers
by having him lashed to a cannon and beaten by a Turk, a young and
scandalized Louvois fired back, "[W]hen it happens that a soldier commits
offenses that merit punishment, have him put before a *conseil de guerre* in
order to be judged as the case will require."[32] Captains and regimental commanders also wanted to form courts of their own and refused to subject
themselves to the authority of fortress governors or others.[33] But clearly, the
secretary of state for war now insisted that cases were to be tried formally,
according to regulation, by a military court, a *conseil de guerre*.

At least from the ministry of Le Tellier, *conseils de guerre* stood as the
highest forum of military justice in garrisons and in the field. While they
existed prior to Le Tellier, they functioned irregularly and displayed limited
effectiveness, as actual judgment and enforcement fell more to individual
officers and to the provosts. The rise in the position of *conseils de guerre*
reflected the increasing power of the military *intendant* as the primary judicial officer in the army, since a *conseil de guerre* was directly responsible to the
intendant.

It took some time for Le Tellier to define procedure and membership of
conseils de guerre. André found that the earliest ordinance stipulating membership and procedure for the *conseil de guerre* dated from 1646. While specific about certain details, it remained vague about others:

As to discipline and police, every two weeks a *conseil de guerre* will be held in each
army in order to maintain and observe exactly the regulations and to reform all the
abuses and offenses against them, to which the major officers, and especially the
maréchaux de camp, and the *intendant* will make their report [*dont . . . feront leur
rapport*], to which *conseil* the provost general will be called, both to account for the
order [*police*] [of the army] and to receive orders concerning what he will have to
do.[34]

Eventually, the army *intendant* took more responsibility for investigations,
eclipsing the provost general.

Conseils de guerres could also be held in garrisons as well as with field
armies. According to regulations set down by Le Tellier, governors of fortresses could arrest soldiers on the condition that the governor inform the
accused's captain within twenty-four hours. These authorities could also arrest
officers. Governors, lieutenant governors, or sergeant majors of fortresses
presided at trials, while officers of the garrison served as judges; captains
seem to have been most commonly involved. Seven constituted the minimum panel of judges, and if the garrison could not produce the required
number of judges, visitors came from neighboring garrisons. These provisions,

---

[32] AG, A¹183, 14 June 1664, Louvois to La Guette, in Rousset, *Louvois*, 1:80–81.
[33] André, *Le Tellier*, 595.
[34] SHAT, Bib., Col. des ord., vol. 17, #83, 4 May 1646, in André, *Le Tellier*, 592.

introduced and embellished in ordinances dated 1661–65 established the authority of the state in place of the authority of the captain or the regiment.[35] Circa 1690, a *conseil* ideally contained twelve senior officers.[36] At this late date, regimental *conseils* still persisted; these included the commanding officer and the twelve most senior officers, but a *commissaire des guerres* had to be present at all sessions as a representative of the king's military administration.[37]

These *conseils de guerre* judged cases between soldiers and those involving infractions against military ordinances. If a soldier ran afoul of civilian authority, however, he could be tried in a civilian court.

Penalties and Punishments

The list of offenses that carried penalties according to French military law ran a broad gamut from misdemeanors punishable by brief confinement or caning to a long list of capital offenses.[38] Forms of execution included the firing squad, hanging, burning, and breaking on the wheel. Soldiers also faced the living death of condemnation to the galleys for life. Lesser, but painful, punishments included running the gauntlet, riding the wooden horse, and whipping. Being drunk on guard duty, for example, would cost the drinker a painful hour a day on the wooden horse each day for a month. Some forms of punishment were meant not only to punish but to mark the guilty; cutting of the nose and ears and branding fell into this category.

Not surprisingly, the law operated on a double standard. Circa 1692, an enlisted man who resisted or drew his sword on an officer would have his hand cut off and then go before a firing squad.[39] However, a superior officer who struck and wounded a subordinate was to be pardoned "in that first impetuosity," according to a regulation of 1706.[40]

Ordinances prescribed death for murder, arson, marauding, rape, and most forms of theft. These were rough times, and such penalties were in line with civilian practice. In addition, various military offenses carried a death penalty; these included mutiny, sedition, carrying false *routes*, and wounding a provost or archer.

Penalties meted out varied with the times. *Passe volants*, those false soldiers used to pad a company's roster at reviews, suffered a particularly broad range. At the start of the war with Spain in 1635, they risked death.[41] This

[35] André, *Le Tellier* (Paris: 1906), 595–98. [36] Belhomme, *L'armée française en 1690*, 145.

[37] Belhomme, *L'armée française en 1690*, 145–46.

[38] See Adrien Pascal, *Histoire de l'armée*, vol. 2 (Paris: 1847), "Des délits militaires et des peines y attachées, conformément aux ordonnances antérieures à la Révolution," for a list of crimes and penalties. Most of these come from the codification of the military codes in 1727.

[39] Louis de Gaya, *Le nouvel art de la guerre et la manière dont on la fait aujourd'huy en France* (Paris: 1692), 218.

[40] Babeau, *La vie militaire*, 1:161.

[41] Jules Caillet, *De l'administration en France sous le ministère du Cardinal de Richelieu* (Paris: 1857), 365–66.

decreased to caning according to an ordinance of 1663 and then increased to whipping and branding in 1665.[42] Branding with the fleur de lis on the cheek served an obvious function here, removing the *passe volant* from the market without killing him. Capital punishment returned with the coming of war in 1667; however, Corvisier says that authorities were reluctant to enforce this penalty and preferred simply to enroll the man and thus make a real soldier out of a phony.[43] With peace, branding returned in 1668.[44] In 1676, the punishment again became more severe, for it included mutilation, cutting the culprit's nose.[45] The fate of *passe volants* reveals both the range of punishments for a single offense and the difference between what was prescribed by ordinance and what was actually done.

The French also punished units that had behaved disgracefully or illegally by executing soldiers drawn by lot from the offending unit. When cavalry and dragoons mutinied at Trier, forcing Marshal Créqui to surrender the fortress in 1675, the king ordered that one of every twenty men be chosen by lot and hanged.[46] Louis also sanctioned the action of the dauphin, who hanged men chosen by lot to stop disorder in 1694.[47] Lest this be thought a particularly French method of encouragement, it should be noted that William III also did the same thing when he ordered nine men chosen by lot to be hanged because of the cowardice of the Walenburg regiment.[48]

As in the case of decimation, punishment was always meant to be exemplary – that is, penalties were designed not only to punish the guilty but to instruct or "motivate" the rest. Troops were expected to embrace obedience and display courage out of a desire to avoid coercion if they could not be inspired by higher appeals.

DESERTION

Whatever punishments loomed, individual soldiers continued to disobey. The infractions that most threaten an army are those that most weaken it, so the military measures crimes by its own standards. Vauban condemned desertion as "the most pernicious defect that . . . ruins the troops, and that all the others are minor in this regard."[49] Desertion was an undeniable fact of military life during the early modern era, and it cut army strength more than did battle casualties. The army's response was less to attack the causes of the flight, although it did, than to punish the perpetrators that it caught. The

---

[42] Ordinance of 21 March 1663, in Rousset, *Louvois*, 1:198; ordinance of 25 July 1665, in Rousset, *Louvois*, 1:198.

[43] Ordinance of 15 July 1667, in Rousset, *Louvois*, 1:198; André Corvisier, *Louvois* (Paris: 1983), 187.

[44] Rousset, *Louvois*, 1:198.   [45] Rousset, *Louvois*, 1:198.

[46] AG, A^{1}434, 22 and 27 September 1675, in Rousset, *Louvois*, 2:179–80.

[47] Letter of 28 June 1694 to the dauphin in Louis XIV, *Oeuvres*, 4:423.

[48] Stephen Baxter, *William III and the Defense of European Liberty, 1650–1702* (New York: 1966), 143.

[49] Vauban in Albert Rochas d'Aiglun, *Vauban, sa famille et ses écrits*, 2 vols. (Paris: 1910), 1:271.

army's limited success in stemming desertion leads one to question the efficacy of coercion in the *grand siècle*, just as does the failure of horrid punishments to stop the Tax of Violence.

Given the limitations of seventeenth-century documents, it would be impossible to provide accurate statistics on desertion as a whole. Personnel records for enlisted men, *contrôles*, which were designed in part to combat desertion, were not kept until 1716. While contemporary sources do not allow an exact profile of desertion, they provide numerous examples of its corrosive power. The effect on individual units could be devastating. In the summer of 1630, Turenne raised a regiment of 500 men; the number fell to 400 in October and then was reinforced to 700. Yet by the end of winter quarters, it decreased to 250, a decline reflecting the work of sickness and desertion.[50] Desertion was particularly severe during the war with Spain. Richelieu wrote in a letter of 30 June 1635 that desertion shrank a reinforcement of 6,000 men dispatched to La Force to only 3,000 men by the time it arrived.[51] Between June 1635 and October of that year, the French army fell from 26,500 to less than 10,000, and desertion certainly played its part.[52]

Even with the improved military administration of Louis's personal reign, desertion continued, as demonstrated by military correspondence. Saint-Pouenges reported in 1677 that despite the fact that the army marched in good order, "17 dragoons deserted from the Regiment du Colonel Général this morning and took with them 25 horses."[53] Corvisier theorizes that desertion during the Nine Years' War did not reach the levels of the Thirty Years' War, and this seems a most reasonable conclusion especially after considering the relatively high numbers of men actually present per company in the later conflict.[54] An *état* of desertion from Marshal Catinat's army in Italy states that it lost a total of 280 men during 1697 and that of these, only ninety-nine had deserted.[55] However, desertion seems to have increased during the War of the Spanish Succession, although exact figures are again lacking.[56] The flow of desertion continued after this, the last of Louis's wars. In the eighteen months between 2 July 1716 and 31 December 1717, 11,499 cases were reported.[57] By midcentury, the desertion rate hovered at about 25 percent.

---

[50] Bérenger, *Turenne*, 87.

[51] AAE, France 814. fol. 210, letter of 30 June 1635 in David Parrott, "The Administration of the French Army During the Ministry of Cardinal Richelieu," Ph.D. dissertation, Oxford University, 1985, 32.

[52] Parrott, "The Administration of the French Army," 96. Geoffrey Parker, *The Military Revolution: Military Innovation and the Rise of the West, 1500–1800* (Cambridge: 1988), 58, implies this was all desertion, but this implication is really unfair, since the army had fought an entire campaign in that time.

[53] AG, A¹538, #282–83, 27 May 1677, St. Pouenge from Gesvryes.

[54] Contamine, *Histoire militaire*, 1:434.

[55] Etat des pertes de l'armée de Catinat in Babeau, *La vie militaire*, 1:328.

[56] See André Corvisier, *L'armée française de la fin du XVIIe siècle au ministère du Choiseul: Le soldat*, 2 vols. (Paris: 1964), 2:693–748, for a discussion of desertion in the eighteenth century.

[57] Extrait du quatrième registre des conseils de guerre, 1718, in Babeau, *La vie militaire*, 1:328.

As well as afflicting volunteers, desertion severely ate into the *milices provinciales* during the War of the Spanish Succession. When the army needed to replace its losses in Italy in 1701–2 and drew men out of *milice* battalions, volunteers came forward in abundance; this would appear to have been the case because these men planned to desert as they passed close to home. Of the 260 *milice* drawn from the second battalion of the Regiment de la Sarre, most deserted as they crossed their home country of Franche-Comté. Only sixty-three *miliciens* plus officers were left, although some deserters promised to rejoin their comrades at Salines.[58] In 1704, an officer complained to the *intendant* of Montauban that of 220 *milice* recruits sent from there to the front, 101 disappeared en route.[59] Gébelin claims that of the large levy raised early in 1711, the majority left their regiments and returned home.[60] Nothing seemed to stop desertion. As the secretary of state for war appealed to one of his agents: "It only remains for me to desire for the good of the service that by your exhortations you inspire in the new soldiers enough courage and firmness to resolve to join the regiment for which they are destined, for I know that desertion is great everywhere and it is a great evil that after so many efforts and infinite care, one can count on nothing for certain!"[61]

Desertion remained a problem throughout the *grand siècle*, but it did not always follow the same pattern. Although it may have been a group affair in the first half of the seventeenth century, Corvisier observes that after 1650, desertion did not involve groups of men but rather became the act of a single soldier or of two or three comrades. The only exception to this rule involved *milice* during the War of the Spanish Succession.[62]

Rationale for Desertion

Men fled their regiments for a number of reasons, from a reasonable need to escape intolerable conditions to a base desire to collect additional enlistment bounties. Cowardice seems not to have driven most men to desert. A memoir from the mid–eighteenth century explained desertion in terms that may have held true in the *grand siècle* as well. It commented that men almost never deserted at the start of a siege or on the eve of battle, but rather they fled when food was lacking, when the troops were worked to exhaustion with no good reason, or when the individual soldiers were overwhelmed with debt.

---

[58] Georges Girard, *Le service militaire en France à la fin du règne de Louis XIV: Racolage et milice, 1701–1715* (Paris: 1915), 170–71.

[59] Letter to Legendre, February 1704, in Girard, *Racolage et milice*, 298. Of the remaining recruits, seventeen were rated as bad, twenty-two mediocre, thirty-six passable, and only forty-two good.

[60] Jacques Gébelin, *Histoire des milices provinciales (1688–1791): le tirage au sort sous l'ancien régime* (Paris: 1882), 58.

[61] AG, A^{1}1901, #291, 11 February 1705, Camillart to Phélypeaux, in Girard, *Racolage et milice*, 325–26.

[62] André Corvisier, *Armies and Societies in Europe, 1494–1789* (Bloomington, IN: 1979), 179.

To the author of this memoir, deserters counted among the bravest of French troops.[63]

Mistreated men deserted. An ordinance of 1643 alleged that poor treatment by captains provoked desertion.[64] A generation later, Le Pelletier pointed out one such instance concerning a Swiss captain: "[T]his captain gives very little justice to his soldiers . . . the bad treatment that he gives them has obliged many to desert."[65] So worried was the king about the misconduct of his captains that in 1694 Louis XIV warned the dauphin, who went to the field as the titular head of an army, "Examine with care if the captains do not force [deserters] to leave."[66] Captains might, after all, benefit financially from desertion, because if it went unreported, the officers could pocket pay and allowances meant for men who were no longer there.

The suffering of common soldiers remained a major factor driving desertion in the War of Spanish Succession. As minister of war, Chamillart inquired if desertions from the Regiment de Lestrange had climbed so high because "of some injustice by the captains towards their soldiers."[67] In 1705, a *conseil de guerre* found Nicolas Dupont, an *étapier*, guilty of causing two soldiers to desert because they had received no food on *étapes*; Dupont had to supply the captain with two recruits to replace the lost men.[68] For reasons not stemming from personal conduct but related to the famine of 1709, Villars expressed a fear that the lack of pay and money would cause his army to dissolve, and so he appealed to the king. "M. Villars sent this courier to make it clear to the king the difficult state of the army that has not been furnished bread regularly and where there is very little money. Desertion begins and there is ever fear that the lack of money and food will make it increase greatly."[69] A month later Villars stated in a letter to the king that while he still lacked money, he did have bread, and that "desertion in our army is finished."[70] In 1710, Voysin promised to send pay to the Army of the Rhine that had been troubled by desertion, since "this little help can contribute to calming the cavalrymen and dragoons of the army again."[71]

Of course, a fundamental form of abuse was the very process of "voluntary" recruitment itself, which could be typified by force and chicanery. Yet the army would not accept such infractions as just cause for desertion; Louvois explicitly refused to consider them.[72] And, of course, the *miliciens'* resentment

---

[63] Memoir of 1765 in Babeau, *La vie militaire*, 1:327.

[64] AG, A^{1}88, #260, December. [65] AG, A^{1}295, #222, 26 October 1672.

[66] Letter of 28 June 1694, Louis XIV, *Oeuvres*, 4:424.

[67] AG, MR 1787, #101. [68] AG, A^{1}1831, #103, 24 April 1705.

[69] Philippe, marquis de Dangeau, *Journal du marquis de Dangeau*, ed. Feuillet de Conches, 19 vols. (Paris: 1854–60), 12:483, 30 July 1709. For Villars's personal comments on the lack of bread at this time, see Claude Louis Hector Villars, *Mémoires du maréchal de Villars*, ed. Vogüé, 5 vols. (Paris: 1884–95), 3:57–59.

[70] Dangeau, *Journal*, 13:19–20, 25 August 1709.

[71] AG, MR 1783, #218, 28 July 1710, Voysin to Belleisle.

[72] AG, A^{1}530, 18 December 1677, Louvois to the *intendant* d'Oppède, in Rousset, *Louvois*, 2:479.

against their forced enrollment goes a long way to explain their high rates of desertion.

Recruits may have also simply decided that military life was not for them after all. Many who signed up never stayed long enough to fight. A letter from 1637 complained that many soldiers who enlisted during winter quarters fled before their units began to leave for the campaigning season.[73] Thirty years later, a memoir by Marshal Créqui again noted high desertion rates among the new soldiers of the Regiment de Piémont and concluded that "desertion among so many recruits [*soldats de recrue*] is inevitable."[74]

Some soldiers left the service when told that they were going somewhere that they did not want to go. During the war with Spain, men might desert if sent to an undesirable area. French soldiers so disliked serving in Germany that "in order to get [1,000] actual men to Germany; it would be necessary to send at least 3,000."[75] German troops under Turenne mutinied when they believed that they would be transferred to Flanders.

For many deserters, the call of home and the needs of loved ones there demanded their presence. Vauban pleaded for a discharge to be granted a soldier accused of desertion in 1671: "He is an unfortunate man [*misérable*] who has five or six children who are dying of hunger and who seems to be a good [*fort honnête*] man to his friends."[76]

Not always spontaneous, desertion sometimes resulted from the actions of those bent on luring men away from the army. In 1641, the minister of war advised coaxing enemy soldiers away from their units with money.[77] During the Nine Years' War, Louis XIV felt it necessary to warn his soldiers of the ways in which foreign agents might try to tempt French troops to cross over, and the king did so by distributing a pamphlet among his regiments, *Relation curieuse d'un soldat déserteur*.[78] Letters from *intendants* in the field indicate that they received and distributed copies to the troops.[79]

It was not always the enemy who tried to steal men from a unit; sometimes officers in other regiments simply wanted to round our their own units. As previously mentioned, officers enticed men from *recrues*. In 1710, officers of the Regiment de Daubeterre cavalry complained that Spanish officers from the Dacosta Regiment had lured twenty troopers away. The Spaniards might have been allies then, but they encouraged desertion from a French unit.[80]

The last rationale for desertion evokes less pity than the others inspire. Described by the term *rouleurs* or *billardeurs*, many soldiers rolled from unit

[73] AG, A¹42, #126, 26 May 1637, printed order.
[74] AG, A¹209, #81, July 1667.
[75] BN, 4171, fo. 137, 9 March 1645, letter to Turenne in André, *Le Tellier*, 211.
[76] Vauban to Louvois, 17 October 1671, in Rochas d'Aiglun, *Vauban*, 2:57.
[77] Babeau, *La vie militaire*, 1:351.   [78] Babeau, *La vie militaire*, 1:330–31.
[79] Letter of 29 December 1689, from La Goupillière, and second letter from Lemarié in Babeau, *La vie militaire*, 1:331fn.
[80] AG, A¹2265, #57, 21 May 1710.

to unit simply to claim another recruitment bounty. A work published during the War of the Spanish Succession charged that 10,000 *billardeurs* switched units "because of the lure of a new piece of silver that they receive at each enlistment."[81] Corvisier estimates that *rouleurs* may have accounted for up to 10 percent of enlistments.[82]

Prevention and Punishment of Desertion

Commanders attempted to restrain desertion, although their efforts could do no more than reduce its toll. Different methods succeeded at different times. In garrison or winter quarters, certain steps could be taken to keep men with the flag. Late in the war with Spain, Turenne pressed Le Tellier to disperse the troops better in winter quarters, which succeeded in reducing desertion. This may have had as much to do with assuring them pay from local revenues as anything else.[83] In the field, commanders dispatched patrols to catch deserters on the roads, as did General Luxembourg, who reported in 1677: "For some days I have had parties continually around the camp on the roads to Mons, Namur, and Brussels in order to try to catch deserters."[84]

Louis XIV tried to control desertion into neighboring states by contracting treaties that provided for the mutual return of deserters who crossed the border. France concluded such arrangements with Savoy in 1689, the Duke of Lorraine in 1699, and the Dutch Netherlands in 1713.[85] A letter of 16 January 1702 discussed the costs of an agreement with Venice for the return of deserters.[86] Many French deserters accumulated in Italy, and Venice employed a great many French deserters in her wars against the Turks in the seventeenth century.[87]

The usual method of attempting to prevent desertion was the exemplary punishment of those who fled their regiments. During most of the *grand siècle*, desertion remained a capital crime. The Code Michau of 1629 stated that unless he had a discharge, an individual could not leave the flag, and the code decreed the death penalty for those who did.[88] A law of 8 August 1635 again penalized desertion by common soldiers with death, although the same

---

[81] AG, MR 1701, #15. Babeau, *La vie militaire*, 1:326 identifies this as Saint-Hilaire, *Traité de la guerre* (1712).

[82] Corvisier, *Armies and Societies*, 70–71.

[83] André, *Le Tellier*, 402–3; Bérenger, *Turenne*, 328.

[84] AG, A¹544, #538, 11 June 1677, letter from General Luxembourg. For other examples of this practice, see AG, A¹295, #25, 4 October 1672, letter from Gaffard, and AG, A¹538, #334–35, 30 May 1677.

[85] Babeau, *La vie militaire*, 1:332; AG, MR 1783, #37, "Estats des traités pour la restitution des deserteurs"; AG, MR 1783, #7, 16 January 1702, Chamillart to Catinat.

[86] AG, MR 1783, #7.

[87] J.-P. Filippini, "Le recrutement des soldats pour l'armée française à Livourne au XVIIe siècle et au XVIIIe siècle," *Revue historique de l'armée*, 2, no. 4 (1975), 8.

[88] Code Michau, 1629, article 302, François André Isambert et al., eds., *Recueil général des anciennes lois françaises, depuis l'an 420, jusqu'à la Révolution de 1789*, vol. 16 (Paris: 1829), 298.

law stipulated that noble deserters would simply lose their nobility, a form
of social death.[89]

In his memoirs for 1666, the young Louis XIV wrote that since desertion
was "in effect a very ruinous evil for the troops, I resolved to bring to it more
effective remedies than those which had been used up to that time."[90] Certainly he counted among these a more severe punishment of the culprits. Yet
even those close to the king came to question the effectiveness of the death
penalty. A "Mémoire contre la desertion des soldats" discussed this matter.[91]
The anonymous piece may be the work of Vauban, but that is unclear. The
memoir relates of the case of two men shot for desertion. The night after
their execution, ten men who had been chosen to shoot the two unfortunates ran away themselves. This, the author explains, led him to suggest to
Louvois in 1681 that the penalty be reduced to branding and the cutting of
nose and ears followed by condemnation to the galleys for life. In any case,
the law of 24 December 1684 adopted exactly this penalty for deserters, and
it would remain the penalty for desertion throughout the remainder of Louis's
reign.[92]

The lesser penalty did not mean that the royal government had grown
soft. At the same time that the law changed, Louvois urged his *intendants*
to crack down on deserters, since "one could not know how to devote too
much care to trying to stop deserters from the infantry in order to remedy
this ill by frequent examples."[93] Correspondence continually repeated the
notion that punishments would prevent desertion. Voysin argued just this
point to Belle-Isle in 1710: "It has been good to punish deserters severely in
order that these examples can restrain others."[94] Even Vauban conceded that
although rigorous punishment did not stop desertion, "it is certain that it
intimidates many, who without this would swell the number [of deserters]
even more."[95] Be this as it may, the horrors inflicted on convicted deserters,
even if universally applied, probably could not have stopped desertion.
Montesquieu certainly believed that severe punishment of deserters could
not be effective: "Men used to risking their lives twenty times for nothing
will never hesitate to risk their lives one time to recover their liberty when
they are seized by distaste for the service."[96]

There is something particularly tragic in reading the transcripts of the
conseils de guerre that condemned men for desertion. The case of Pierre La

[89] AG, MR 1783, #1, "Observations et notes sur la desertion depuis 1635." See, as well, a 1637
     printed order threatening deserters with death. AG, A^{1}42, #126, 26 May 1637, printed order.
[90] Louis, *Mémoires*, 1:240. See, as well, AG, A^{1}888, #27, 15 June 1696, Louis to Villeroi.
[91] AG, Archives historiques 79, #75–83.
[92] AG, MR 1783, #1, "Observations et notes sur la desertion depuis 1635."
[93] 20 May 1684, letter from Louvois to Chamlay, in Jacques Hardré, ed., *Letters of Louvois*,
     University of North Carolina Studies in the Romance Languages and Literatures, no. 10 (Chapel
     Hill: 1949), 354.
[94] AG, MR 1783, #218, 28 July 1710, Voysin to Belle-Isle.
[95] Vauban in Rochas d'Aiglun, *Vauban*, 1:271.
[96] Montesquieu in Babeau, *La vie militaire*, 1:337.

Sire that began this chapter was all too common. Like him, the men who deserted were often from unfortunate circumstances at the start. As several officers noted in the eighteenth century, men whose families possessed some property did not desert, since desertion would place these goods at risk.[97]

For all the suffering that it imposed, the new penalty does not appear to have stemmed desertion. From the promulgation of the 1684 ordinance until 1714, 16,500 convicted deserters made the sad march to Marseilles to serve in the king's galleys.[98] While a sizable number, it represents only a modest fraction of total desertion. As one *ancien régime* officer commented, "out of a hundred who desert, with difficulty one is captured."[99] Even when deserters were caught, a reluctance to punish might temper their treatment. While law decreed that a French deserter found under arms with the enemy should be executed, in practice, they were often simply enrolled back into the French army. Of the twelve deserters found among the prisoners taken at the battle of Staffard, eleven were put back into French units, while Catinat hanged only one as an example.[100]

Accusation of desertion did not guarantee punishment by a *conseil de guerre*. In some cases, officers charged men who were found innocent by a *conseil*, which then levied a fine on the officer for false accusation. This occurred in January 1705, when Captain de Raffetot was ordered to pay 286 livres 5 sols for having falsely accused Pierre Sauvestre of desertion.[101] By no means was this an isolated case, since a number of others mirrored it in 1704–5 alone.[102]

Harsh policies toward deserters were intermittently interrupted by amnesties that tried to solve the problem not by punishment but by welcoming back those who had successfully fled. While a full list of amnesties is not available, they left a trail revealed in military correspondence. A letter of 28 February 1689 from Louvois mentioned an amnesty for deserters that was in effect in Italy during the Nine Years' War.[103] General amnesties proclaimed during the War of the Spanish Succession included the following: 17 March 1701, 25 May 1704, 15 May 1706, 13 July 1706, 30 August 1706, 25 January 1709, 30 January 1709, 20 May 1710, 20 June 1710, and 22 June 1710.[104] This

---

[97] See a letter of 1731 and the comments of Minister of War St. Germain in Babeau, *La vie militaire*, 1:326.

[98] A. Zysberg, "Galley and Hard Labor Convicts in France (1550–1850)" in P. Spierenberge, ed., *The Emergence of Carceral Institutions: Prisons, Galleys, and Lunatic Asylums 1550–1900* (Rotterdam: 1984), 82–84 in Parker, *Military Revolution*, 58. Circa 1705, 48 percent of all galley slaves were French deserters. Contamine, *Histoire militaire*, 1:537.

[99] "Mémoire pur prévenir les désertions," in Babeau, *La vie militaire*, 1:336. Unfortunately, this is not dated. According to records on desertion for 1716–17, just after the death of Louis, of 11,499 cases denounced as deserters, only 360 were executed. Babeau, *La vie militaire*, 1:336.

[100] Catinat, *Mémoire et correspondance de Catinat*, 1:131, in Babeau, *La vie militaire*, 1:339–40.

[101] AN, G⁷1771, #254, 5 January 1704.

[102] See AN, G⁷1771, #261, 9 February 1704; AN, G⁷1776, #253, 11 October 1704; and several other cases for 1704–5, AN, G⁷1777, #320, 328, 370, 389.

[103] AG, MR 1783, #217, 28 February 1783.

[104] Girard, *Racolage et milice*, 67. Correspondence also mentions an amnesty in the late summer of 1703, in March 1704, and in August 1704; see AG, MR 1783, #7, 4 August 1703 letter.

last ordinance simply extended the deadline for the 20 May amnesty to 1 August for the armies of Flanders and Germany.[105] The May 1710 general amnesty permitted deserters to join any regiment they wanted, with the guarantee that their previous captains could not reclaim them.[106] An amnesty for deserters also followed the close of the War of the Spanish Succession; it was proclaimed on 2 July 1716.[107] The alternative to accepting this amnesty was to run the risk of a death penalty for desertion.[108]

The government also announced reprieves affecting *miliciens* in particular. In an attempt to lure back deserters, and those who had fled even before the *tirage* took place, the government issued a series of amnesties, beginning as early as 25 May 1701. Others were granted on 28 May 1703, 5 June 1706, and 10 October 1711 for both those who had deserted and those who had failed to show up for the *tirage*.[109] The amnesty of 1703 was contingent upon the deserter signing a regular enlistment with troops in the Army of Germany; that of 1706 required enlistment in the Army of Flanders.

Desertion was unquestionably a major problem for the French army of the *grand siècle*, but the meaning of this problem is much less clear than the fact of its existence. Modern studies of desertion stress the individual motives of the deserter rather than his act as a self-conscious statement of opposition to a regime or to a particular war. In the early modern era, desertion could clearly result from lack of pay or food, matters only distantly related to sentiment. So it remains unclear what the phenomenon of desertion says about motivation within the French army as a whole, although certainly for the deserter, his own sense of privation or injustice overrode any devotion to cause, country, or comrades that would have kept him in the ranks.

Severe punishment never ended desertion; therefore, it represented a failure of the disciplinary system, or at least desertion demonstrated the limits of discipline and coercion. If coercion alone could not keep men from fleeing the ranks, how could it ensure bravery on the field of battle? Other factors must be taken into consideration to understand morale and motivation among those who stayed in the ranks. Such factors include the growing dependence of the soldier upon the army and his sense of loyalty – the subjects of the next chapter.

---

[105] AG, A¹2265, #73, 9 July 1710.

[106] Quincy, marquis de, *Histoire militaire de Louis le Grand roi de France*, 7 vols. (La Haye: 1727), 6:333.

[107] *Ordonnances militaires du roy de France*, 2 vols. (Luxembourg: 1734–35), 2:1735.

[108] The 2 July 1716 ordinance punished desertion to the interior with death. André Corvisier, "La mort du soldat depuis la fin du Moyen Age," *Revue histoirque*, 254 (1975), 12.

[109] Amnesties of 12 March 1701, 25 May 1701, 28 May 1703, 1 February 1705, 5 June 1706, 10 October 1711 in Léon Hennet, *Les milices et les troupes provinciales* (Paris: 1884), 36, 42–43.

13

Elements of Morale and Motivation: Dependence and Loyalty

A T the battle of Malplaquet, the hard-pressed regiments of the French left wing fired volley after volley into the Imperial troops who advanced out of the woods against them. Sensing that this was the critical point of the fight, Marshal Villars rode off to these embattled troops, dismounted, drew his sword, and fought alongside his men. The brave and canny old marshal knew that his presence would bolster the courage of his soldiers. They stood, fought, and died. Malplaquet was the bloodiest battle of the wars of Louis XIV. Not for a century would more men become casualties in a single fight; 30,000 allied soldiers and 20,000 troops of the aging Sun King fell wounded or died that day, and the Bourbon regiments on the left contributed their blood to the terrible flood. Why did these soldiers, underfed and ragged, many without shoes, fight so resolutely that day? How can we know these men's minds, and their hearts?

The study of morale is necessarily an inexact science, even when one focuses on present-day troops and uses the research tools provided by modern social science and psychology. How much more difficult is the quest when the subjects are soldiers who fought 300 years ago – men we cannot interview and whose illiteracy barred them from setting down their thoughts on paper. Without solid records of their beliefs and opinions, the study of past morale can only be conducted around the edges. This chapter attempts to shed as much light as possible on morale and motivation by employing a variety of evidence that touches on these matters. Much of the material involves the kind of social history of the army so much in vogue, but the purpose here is not simply to offer a potpourri of the daily life of the soldier. The goal here is to gain some insight as to what sustained the army as a combat instrument.

Issues of morale and motivation deal with the attitudes and values of soldiers. Morale is a state of mind – satisfaction vs. dissatisfaction, confidence vs. defeatism, and so on – and as such, it is both cause and effect of the conditions of military life. The military historian and analyst S. L. A. Marshall refused to be any more specific than to state simply: "Morale is the thinking of an army."[1] And soldiers think about a great many things, from their next meal to the meaning of a war; consequently, an examination of morale must run a wide gamut of considerations. In contrast to the undercurrent of morale, motivation speaks explicitly of reasons for action – fear, hate, loyalty, and the like. Obviously, morale and motivation intertwine.

Modern theory is more explicit concerning motivation than it is concerning morale. Combat effectiveness theory offers the historian some guidance in a quest to understand the actions of soldiers from other eras. It posits three general categories of compliance, three sets of rationales that lead soldiers to obey orders and stay to their tasks, even in the face of discomfort, danger, and death.[2] The first is sheer force, or coercive compliance, the focus of the previous chapter on discipline. The second is material reward, or remunerative compliance. This certainly mattered in the seventeenth century, particularly in the first half, when plunder tempted men into service. The third is symbolic reward, or normative compliance, so called because it functions only if the soldier accepts the norms of his society, civil or military. These last two forms of compliance provide the substance for discussion in this chapter.

The motivation of the French officer is not difficult to fathom, because the culture of command supplied strong class norms driving the aristocrat to seek opportunities to demonstrate his courage and thus legitimate his place as a nobleman. On top of this, the officer professed a strong personal loyalty to his king, who personified the elevated status that the aristocrat himself claimed to share. Such logic explains officer motivation even before any other factors come into play, such as clientage.

It is quite another thing to try to probe the motivations of common soldiers. Louis XIV referred to them as "men of low condition"; they could hardly share aristocratic *mentalité*.[3] With little stake in the war, what, besides the threat of punishment, held the rank and file to their duty? In general, military commentators harbored few expectations of high-minded sentiments from the common soldier. Writing at the time of Louis XIII, du Praissac suggested the best way to employ French troops: "it is necessary to deprive the soldiers of any hope and means of escape, of fleeing from combat, and dispose them to fight courageously, proposing to them glory, booty, gain [*racompense*], and necessity."[4] This chapter makes the assumption that a dis-

---

[1] S. L. A. Marshall, *Men Against Fire* (1947; repr. Gloucester, MA: 1978), 158.

[2] For a short discussion of theories of combat motivation, see John A. Lynn, *Bayonets of the Republic: Motivation and Tactics in the Army of Revolutionary France, 1791–94* (Urbana, IL: 1984), chap. 2. On compliance theory in specific, see Steven D. Westbrook, "The Potential for Military Disintegration," *Combat Effectiveness: Cohesion, Stress, and the Volunteer Military*, ed. Sam C. Sarkesian (Beverly Hills, CA: 1980).

[3] Memoirs for 1666, Louis XIV, *Mémoires de Louis XIV*, Charles Dreyss, ed., 2 vols. (Paris: 1860), 1:248–49.

[4] Praissac, *Les discours militaires*, 2nd ed. (Paris: 1622).

missive statement reflects aristocratic prejudice more than a true understanding of the French common soldier.

Here morale and motivation are approached along two avenues, both of which are unashamedly inferential. The first argues that over the course of the *grand siècle*, the monarchy provided a growing array of services to the common soldier that improved conditions within the army and, as a consequence, probably improved morale. Furthermore, because better services seemed to express the monarchy's concern for its army, they encouraged the soldier to feel a growing sense of dependence upon and, as a consequence, attachment to the monarchy. Second, a set of loyalties built upon traditional foundations and upon the military unit itself provided powerful motivations. In particular, esprit de corps and small group cohesion inspired men to fight for their regiments and their comrades in order to command the respect of their fellow soldiers.

Some historians, most notably the renowned André Corvisier, have adopted a third approach, arguing that French soldiers displayed a form of patriotism under Louis XIV, particularly in 1709. This chapter argues (1) that evidence for such an assertion is meager at best, and (2) that claiming patriotism in 1709 may well reverse the actual relationship between military service and the emergence of national sentiment.

MOTIVATION AND MATERIAL REWARD

The theory of remunerative compliance and knowledge of the early modern army compel a consideration of material conditions and incentives. No study of morale should be so naïve as to forget that it rested upon material welfare in the army of the *grand siècle*, and leadership could not usually override the harmful effects of material want. When food and pay ran out, morale plummeted. The Tax of Violence can be viewed as evidence of morale fallen to such a low level that it resulted in rebellion. Other forms of mutiny could also arise from material want. Problems with troops at the end of sieges probably related to the lack of food and pay as much as anything. Even at the mythical height of French devotion to duty, 1709, the threat of hunger worked against the loyalty of the troops. Even as Villars praised his soldier's stoicism, Torcy worried, "Although the courage of the troops had been proven on all occasions, even the most unhappy, one doubted if they would resist in the absence of pay and of food."[5]

Beyond simple survival, the hope of plunder also motivated French soldiers, particularly before the personal reign of Louis XIV, when greater control and discipline left the ordinary soldier little opportunity for pillage in the old style. Commenting on the early decades of the century, Richelieu said, "Many

---

[5] Villars in John B. Wolf, *Louis XIV* (New York: 1968), 567; Torcy, *Mémoires du marquis de Torcy*, A. Petitôt and Monmerqué, *Collection des mémoires relatifs à l'histoire de France*, ser. 2, vols. 67 and 68 (Paris: 1828), 67:191.

seek more profit than peril in war."[6] And there were profits to be found. At the siege of Mantua in 1617, one soldier found 80,000 ducats of gold in the palace, but he gambled this fortune away and was hanged for his crime – not the theft but his wasteful use of it.[7] Many French troops that fought in Italy gathered such rich booty in 1622 that they deserted in order to take their fortunes home.[8] As one commentator observed in this period, however, "for every two soldiers who enriched themselves you will find fifty who gained only wounds or incurable diseases."[9]

Pillage exacted its greatest toll in France during the war with Spain, when troops in the pay of the French monarchy almost certainly turned to pillage as a source of compensation more than they did after 1659. Booty loomed so large a consideration and could become a source of such discord that commanders tried to regulate its handling and distribution. After men had been forced to hand over their stash, this booty was sold and the resultant sum distributed to the soldiers. A regulation of 1648 ruled that two thirds went to the cavalry and one third to the infantry.[10]

Louis XIV recognized the brutal greed of soldiers at the start of his personal reign: "[T]he spirit of libertinage is ordinarily one of the principal motives that makes men follow the military profession, and recently commanders have been found who have made great armies subsist for a long time without giving them any other pay than the license to pillage everywhere."[11] Louis may have taken steps to protect his subjects from pillage by his own troops, but his soldiers kept their rapacious ways outside of France. French partisans and war parties continued to claim a share of the contributions that they collected and the booty that they seized throughout Louis's reign. Pillage by French troops during the first years of the Dutch War raised specters of the Thirty Years' War. The horrors of the devastation of the Palatinate in 1688–89 hardly need to be described once again, although there were strategic rationales for that destruction.

Of course, one special category of booty was never eliminated; sexual booty constituted one of the most brutal forms of compensation that soldiers claimed. But again, this type of excess typified the first half of the century more than the second. When Louis XIII took Négropelisse, near Montauban, in 1622, the king ordered his men to give quarter to no man; when royal troops seized all the women, a captain who wished to save one had to hide her, and in an attempt to save what individuals he could, a

---

[6] Richelieu in Albert Babeau, *La vie militaire sous l'ancien régime*, 2 vols. (Paris: 1890), 1:279.

[7] Sirot, *Mémoires*, 1:169, 175 in Babeau, *La vie militaire*, 1:279–80.

[8] Babeau, *La vie militaire*, 1:278.

[9] Emeric Crucé, *Le nouveau cynée ou discours d'estat* (Paris: 1623), 13, in Fritz Redlich, *De praeda militari: Looting and Booty 1500–1815*, supplement 39, *Vierteljahrschrift für Sozial- und Wirtschaftsgeschichte* (Wiesbaden: 1956), 57.

[10] Regulation of 1648 in Babeau, *La vie militaire*, 1:280fn. See, as well, the regulation of 15 May 1638.

[11] Memoirs for 1666, in Louis XIV, *Mémoires*, 1:249.

gentleman-servant of the king bought forty women from soldiers.[12] The conduct of French troops toward women during the era of the Tax of Violence has already been documented. Unfortunately, but not surprisingly, it did not entirely cease with the personal reign of Louis XIV. When Catinat's army took Caours near Pinerolo in 1690, they pillaged and killed; the marshal himself took efforts to spare eighty women from his own soldiers.[13]

In sum, while it probably moderated under Louis XIV, a lust for plunder seems to have been a significant incentive among French troops throughout the *grand siècle*. Remunerative compliance remained a factor, yet under Louis, it was more restricted to specific categories of troops, partisans in particular, who enjoyed greater opportunities to take what they wanted.

DEPENDENCE

During the *grand siècle*, the bases of morale and motivation shifted, not enough to amount to a radical transformation of *mentalité* among the rank and file but surely and significantly. Discipline, with its reliance on punishment, represented not just control but incentive. For the early modern army, coercion kept to their duty men who showed little inclination to perform without the threat of punishment. But such coercive compliance never accounted fully for the behavior of troops. Throughout the sixteenth and well into the seventeenth century, the hope for material rewards also lured men into the ranks and supplied additional motivation. Late in the *grand siècle*, however, the realistic hope for plunder, for a windfall of riches gained by soldiering in the ranks, had declined. This was a product of improved administration and greater discipline that limited the chances for marauding. Moreover, at the same time that the common soldier lost much of the opportunity to scavenge for wealth, the rate of pay for French troops waned significantly. Remunerative compliance clearly declined in strength within the new state commission army.

Other, more subtle, bonds of dependence and loyalty took on increased importance at this point of military transition. The state compensated for the lessened expectations of wealth by providing a greater sense of well-being and security to the soldier and by encouraging him to identify with the army and the monarchy. Improved administration, new services, and new institutions designed to benefit the soldier enhanced the conditions of service, and better conditions of service strengthened morale. Moreover, to the extent that common soldiers came to see the army as their home and the monarch as the caring head of the family, they gained a new dimension of internal motivation to defend the monarchy. This was not yet nationalism, but it must have been an important step on the way toward forging a sense of loyalty to the state.

In several manners, the state now accepted the responsibility to care for

[12] Pontis in Babeau, *La vie militaire*, 1:278.   [13] Babeau, *La vie militaire*, 1:278–79.

its soldiers at a time when it did little for the average subject. Young and fit men in the ranks had good reason to look upon the monarchy as assurance that they would not be forgotten if they could no longer perform their duties. The army promised solace for the ill soldier, sustenance for the aged veteran, and release for the man held prisoner by the enemy. A number of innovations, particularly associated with Louis XIV, encouraged the soldier to rely upon the state for material and psychological support and thus to become dependent upon the monarchy. Rewards shifted from the unlikely hope for wealth to a more certain provision of life's necessities for those who served the state faithfully.

At a point in military evolution when the army changed from a temporary hireling to a long-term servant of the state, stronger links of dependence between the soldier and the state seem both necessary and natural. Soldiers of the aggregate contract army who came and went quickly formed no long-term attachment to the state, and the state undertook no long-term obligation to them. Such men could be discarded after they had served their purpose. Perhaps the most pathetic plate in Callot's "Les misères et malheurs de la guerre" shows battered and ragged men along the roadside – some beg, others lie exhausted, a priest offers the last rites to one dying man. These veterans, once blustering and bullying, are now reduced to pitiful relics. The verse below reads "How deplorable is the fate of the poor soldier. When the war is over his misfortune begins again." This is not the picture of the veteran of the Sun King, whose promised fate was symbolized by the architectural grandeur and solidity of the Invalides, with its tidy sleeping quarters, its large meal halls, its comforting infirmary, and its broad esplanade, perfect for a game of boules. The two contrasting images speak of a transformation in the monarchy's attitude toward its troops and imply a greater bond between the soldier and the state.

Hospitals

Military hospitals promised care and compassion to the soldier and therefore bound him to the army and his king. Of course, hospitals were not simply symbolic bonds; they were immensely practical as well, because they helped to preserve an army's combat strength by isolating the sick who might otherwise spread disease and by returning the cured to their regiments. As Richelieu put it, "Two thousand soldiers leaving a hospital cured and in a certain sense broken into their profession" were better than "six thousand new recruits."[14] Military pundits agreed that military hospitals were important to the maintenance of an army. Feuquières, whose military career spanned most of the personal reign of Louis XIV, wrote that an "army without good hospitals perishes easily, it being impossible that combat actions and sicknesses will

---

[14] Richelieu in Michael Duffy, ed., *The Military Revolution and the State* (Exeter: 1980), 41.

not fill them often and all too abundantly."[15] And Villars concluded that "badly run hospitals are a plague" and that in contradiction to contemporary medical science, "disorder in hospitals has killed more soldiers than infection of the air."[16] Louis XIV certainly agreed that the sick deserved special attention, since "contagion is the ruin of armies."[17] In 1667, he urged Turenne "to take great care to conserve my troops, principally the sick soldiers."[18] The concerns expressed here put little emphasis on the notion of the moral responsibility of the state to care for soldiers who fought in its name but instead stressed the practical value of controlling infection and restoring sick and wounded men to duty.

Yet another value of a proper hospital system surfaces in some writings. Mazarin commented: "I believe we must give priority to everything which is necessary for hospitals, besides the fact that charity requires it, there is nothing which produces a better effect in the armies than the sick and wounded being looked after."[19] A letter from the War of Devolution echoes similar sentiments concerning efforts made to prepare a hospital: "May the good order which will be maintained there contribute to encouraging the soldiers to serve well."[20] Thus, the practical administrator who wrote this letter expected the existence of a good hospital system to raise morale and motivation among the troops.

The institution of French army hospitals predates the *grand siècle*. Soldiers have required medical attention for as long as there have been wars. The Spanish established the first permanent military hospital in early modern Europe at Malines in 1585, and by 1637, it had 330 beds.[21] According to Audouin, Henri IV and Sully deserve credit for having founded the first French system of permanent and mobile hospitals and for drafting the first regulations on the subject. But be that as it may, financial difficulties under the regency of Marie de Medici killed off these institutions, and they only reappeared during the Italian campaigns of Louis XIII.[22] In any case, the modest size of the army before 1635 allowed the army to turn to existing civilian hospitals. Regulations of 1622 stipulated that a soldier who fell ill on the road could demand leave of his captain to go to the nearest town and receive attention there.[23]

[15] Feuquières in Louis André, *Michel Le Tellier et l'organisation de l'armée monarchique* (Paris: 1906), 475–76.

[16] BN, f. fr. 6257, Claude Louis Hector Villars, "Traité de la guerre de campagne," 45.

[17] Louis XIV, *Mémoires*, 2:250.   [18] Louis XIV, *Mémoires*, 2:188–89.

[19] Mazarin, in Cilleuls, "Le service de santé en campagne aux armées de l'ancien regime," *Revue historique de l'armée*, 1950, 7 in Duffy, *The Military Revolution*, 41.

[20] AG, A¹209, #7, 13 May 1667.

[21] Frank Tallett, *War and Society in Early Modern Europe* (London: 1992), 111–12. See Geoffrey Parker, *The Army of Flanders and the Spanish Road, 1567–1659: The Logistics of Spanish Victory and Defeat in the Low Countries Wars* (Cambridge: 1972), 167–68.

[22] Xavier Audouin, *Histoire de l'administration de la guerre*, 4 vols. (Paris: 1811), 2:63–64. Henri IV was a favorite of Audouin, so he may exaggerate the contribution of the first Bourbon king.

[23] *Règlement pour l'infanterie*, 1622, in Babeau, *La vie militaire*, 1:212.

As armies expanded under Richelieu, he created specifically military hospitals, the first of which was at Pinerolo.[24] Within the limits of the *grand siècle*, Richelieu deserves the credit for the attempt to initiate a complete medical service. The Code Michau of 1629 required that "in the train of the armies hospitals will be maintained" and provided that every regiment would contain a surgeon on staff and that each company of 200 men would also include a surgeon.[25] Later regulations continued to require the creation of hospitals to serve the armies. A 1635 ordinance stated that "It is necessary to have a well regulated hospital in each army."[26] Since some wounded did not want to go away to a hospital, Richelieu also instructed each army to have surgeons, apothecaries, Jesuits, and cooks to care for the sick who stayed with the army.[27] Thus, the Army of Italy in 1638 brought in its train one head cook with five assistants who were allotted five sheep per day to make bouillon for the sick.[28]

Early in the administration of Le Tellier, the army maintained major stationary military hospitals at Arras, Calais, Dunkirk, and Perpignan.[29] Le Tellier charged military *intendants* with the establishment and supervision of necessary facilities, particularly the mobile hospitals that accompanied armies on campaign.[30] However well intentioned the plans, a lack of money endemic to the period 1635–59, and particularly acute during the Fronde, limited their execution. In a letter of June 1650, Le Tellier explained that he could only send half of the funds normally given to the hospital for the Army of Flanders.[31] It comes as little surprise that Dubuisson-Aubenay would complain bitterly in the fall of that same year, "The disorder in our army is horrible; there is no hospital at all, and when a soldier is wounded, he is put in a barn where he is left to die like a dog."[32]

Louvois worked to establish permanent hospitals in each fortress and mobile hospitals, or *ambulances*, with armies in the field.[33] When Louis launched the War of Devolution, he took adequate measures to prepare the necessary hospitals. One administrator reported from Binche, "I do all that is possible for the sick and to the extent that they are returned to health, I give them means to rejoin their companies in whatever place they may be."[34]

[24] Audouin, *Histoire de l'administration*, 2:64.

[25] Code Michau, 1629, articles 226 and 232, in François André Isambert et al., eds., *Recueil général des anciennes lois françaises, depuis l'an 420, jusqu'à la Révolution de 1789*, vol. 16 (Paris: 1829), 285–86.

[26] SHAT, Bib., Col. des ord., vol. 14, #87.

[27] See ordinance of 1638 in Jules Caillet, *De l'adminstration en France sous le ministère du Cardinal de Richelieu* (Paris: 1857), 372–73.

[28] Babeau, *La vie militaire*, 1:213.

[29] Louis André, *Michel Le Tellier et Louvois* (Paris: 1942), 380.

[30] André, *Le Tellier et Louvois*, 379–82; André, *Le Tellier*, 475–87.

[31] Le Tellier to Mazarin, 19 June 1650, in André, *Le Tellier*, 471.

[32] Letter of 12 September 1650, in Dubuisson-Aubenay, *Mémoires*, 1:325 in André, *Le Tellier*, 470.

[33] Camille Rousset, *Histoire de Louvois*, 4 vols. (Paris: 1862–64), 1:250–51.

[34] AG, A^{1}210, #57, 29 November 1667, Destouches from Binche.

An ordinance of 1676 regulated the way in which hospitals in major fortresses were to be run.[35] The reports on hospitals improved significantly. Regarding those at Pinerolo and Casale in 1682, an official wrote: "That of Charity, in Paris, is not cleaner. The sick are better fed and better provided with everything that they need, as much for the body as for the soul."[36] Gaya, in a work that appeared in 1692, could speak in praise of the army mobile hospitals:

The hospital is a great help to the sick and the wounded; there they are as [well cared for] as in the hospitals of the best cities of the kingdom, through the care of the doctors, surgeons, apothecaries, and the *religieux* that have been established under the authority of a director.

It always follows the army until a proper and convenient place is found to establish it, [and] all the sick are brought to it; and one leaves at the camp only a detachment of the hospital to deal with the most pressing necessities . . . .[37]

Such glowing words should not blind observers to the often less than perfect conditions of the sick and wounded. An *intendant* who inspected the hospital at Strasbourg in 1689 reported: "The poor unfortunates die and will die, they are not otherwise relieved [of their suffering]; the majority being sick with flux of the blood, they infect one another, laying three to a bed."[38] And while each of the four French armies was supposed to have a field hospital in 1690, none did in order to save the funds; they only provided first-aid stations. Regulation was not always reality.[39]

The ordinance of 17 January 1708 often receives credit for creating the medical service, although, as mentioned previously, it was far from being the first to deal with the care of the sick and wounded.

The important services that our troops render us inducing us to see to their care when sick or wounded, we believe there to be no manner more advantageous than perpetually establishing in the train of our armies and in the hospitals of our fortresses, doctors for the officers and soldiers who are sick and wounded.[40]

The positions of military doctors and surgeons became venal offices. Fifty reorganized hospitals served the army, and their combined staff consisted of fifty *médicins-majors* and fifty *chirurgiens-majors*, plus twenty-two other superior doctors and surgeons charged with inspecting the hospitals and advising

[35] Philippe Contamine, ed., *Histoire militaire de la France*, vol. 1 (Paris: 1992), 407.

[36] Babeau, *La vie militaire*, 1:219.

[37] Louis de Gaya, *Le nouvel art de la guerre et la manière dont on la fait aujourd'huy en France* (Paris: 1692), 44–45.

[38] In Chabanès, *Chirurgiens et blessés à travers l'histoire* in R. Baillargeat, ed., *Les Invalides, trois siècles d'histoire* (Paris: 1975), 171. There was supposed to be a bed for every two in hospital, but often three were stuffed into a single bed. Victor Belhomme, *L'armée française en 1690* (Paris: 1895), 155.

[39] Belhomme, *L'armée française en 1690*, 156–57.

[40] Ordinance of 17 January 1708, in Chabanès, *Chirurgiens et blessés à travers l'histoire* in Baillargeat, *Les Invalides*, 171.

their doctors and surgeons.[41] The ordinance set staff, but it left the actual running of the hospitals to private entrepreneurs, subject to inspection. If Belhomme is correct, major military hospitals already enjoyed this kind of staffing well before the 1708 ordinance, so it probably just recognized existing practices.[42] Not until 1717 did *commissaires des guerres* take over the administration of military hospitals.[43]

Hospital staff received an allowance per soldier to provide for the care and food that each man required. At the Lille hospital in 1673, surgeons were to be paid 7 sols 6 deniers for each ill French soldier, and of this amount, the captain was to supply 4 sols, with the rest coming from the king.[44] From the 1690s, at Valenciennes, the caregivers received 11 sols 6 deniers per day for the sick and 6 sols per day for the convalescent. Clothes of a dead soldier would be returned to his captain.[45] The sum spent on hospitals could be substantial; in 1709, Louis sent at least 100,000 livres to care for the wounded from the battle of Malplaquet.[46]

In addition to hospital medical staff, individual surgeons still attended their regiments. In fact, regimental surgeons were the most numerous of all the professional staff. A glance at *étapes* reviews reveals that regiments normally included surgeons on their rolls. Reviews and *routes* from the particularly detailed sources for the Nine Years' War show that every first battalion of infantry regiments contained a surgeon major as part of the regimental staff; cavalry regiments were equally well staffed, and dragoon regiments rarely lacked a surgeon.[47] During the War of the Spanish Succession, an infantry surgeon and a chaplain received identical pay of 10 sols per day, at a time when an infantry lieutenant made 32 sols per day and a sergeant earned 11. A surgeon received an allowance of two bread rations per day, implying that he brought an assistant with him. In the cavalry, a surgeon earned 13 sols 10 deniers per day, at a time when a cavalry lieutenant made 50 sols per day and a brigadier, or sergeant, made 8.[48]

Along with strictly medical staff, the government provided religious

---

[41] Contamine, *Histoire militaire*, 1:539.
[42] See the description of hospitals in Belhomme, *L'armée française en 1690*, 154–57. He credits major military hospitals as having one doctor, one surgeon in chief, one *médicin major* for fevers, two to three chirurgiens majors, three to four chirurgiens aides major, a garçon-chirurgien for every ten wounded or fifteen sick, an apothecary, three to four garçons-apothecaires, and one or more chaplains.
[43] Baillargeat, *Les Invalides*, 171.
[44] Nord, C 2231, 25 January 1673. In the case of soldiers from Swiss units, the captain paid more and the king less.
[45] Records from 1691 to 1728 in Babeau, *La vie militaire*, 1:214.
[46] Philippe marquis de Dangeau, *Journal du marquis de Dangeau*, ed. Feuillet de Conches, 19 vols. (Paris: 1854–60), 13:46.
[47] Amiens, EE 403, 405; BN, f. fr. 4565–67. Of the eleven dragoon regiments listed in the latter source, eight had surgeons, just as was the case for *aumôniers*.
[48] Jean Roland de Mallet, *Comptes rendus de l'administration des finances du royaume de France* (London: 1789), 159–64.

personnel for the care of the ill. Richelieu seems to have preferred Jesuits for such duties.[49] In 1658, Mazarin specifically recommended certain measures for the wounded and sent Capuchins and Jesuits as well as surgeons to care for them.[50] Louis XIV apparently preferred to detail Recollets to the army; about 1670, they were, in Corvisier's words, "systematically" summoned to the army as hospital and regimental chaplains.[51] Feuquières commented on their presence: "For some time the army hospitals have been followed by a number of Recollets for administering to the spiritual needs [*pour l'admin-istration du spirituel*] of the sick and wounded; they are carried about at the king's expense, and have wagons for the ornaments of their chapel and their baggage."[52]

Chaplains had at least two roles in military hospitals. They offered religious care, including accepting confessions and administering last rites. Some chaplains claimed that dying soldiers bequeathed them money to say masses for their souls, but Louvois became suspicious and demanded that a *commissaire* or director be present at such confessions for claims to be considered valid.[53] Beyond performing their religious duties, chaplains also served as supervisors and on-site inspectors.[54] The chaplain seems to have overseen nursing. Routine care would seem to have been performed largely by women, but this should come as little surprise considering the belief, common at this time, that women were essential for nursing duties.[55] Reporting in detail on his work setting up a military hospital at Bergues in 1667, the *intendant* Robert discussed the staff at one location, commenting that "I have also established a chaplain with the suitable number of women and valets to assist him."[56] Another location in town was the convent of the "filles hospitalières," so it can be assumed that they also contributed to the task. At the garrison town of Valenciennes during the last two wars of Louis XIV, soldiers were cared for by nuns at the Hôtel Dieu.[57] The nineteenth-century historian Belhomme states that circa 1690, army hospitals maintained one nurse for every five wounded or ten sick.[58]

Stays in hospital could be quite long. A document from 1682 reported the number of days spent in hospital at Pinerolo by sick soldiers of the Piedmont

---

[49] See the ordinance of 1638 in Caillet, *De l'administration en France*, 372–73; it instructs armies to have Jesuits to help care for the sick and wounded.

[50] Letter of 12 June 1658 to Robertot, in Jules Mazarin, *Lettres du cardinal Mazarin*, eds. P. Chéruel and G. d'Avenel, vols. 6–9 (Paris: 1890–1906), 8:731. In several letters at this time, Mazarin expressed his concern for military hospitals.

[51] Contamine, *Histoire militaire*, 1:403.

[52] Feuquières, *Mémoires*, 1:164, in Babeau, *La vie militaire*, 1:224.

[53] Belhomme, *L'armée française en 1690*, 156.   [54] Belhomme, *L'armée française en 1690*, 155.

[55] See Barton Hacker, "Women and Military Institutions in Early Modern Europe: A Reconnaissance," *Signs* 6, no. 4 (summer 1981), 643–71, for contemporary opinion on the need for women to nurse the sick and wounded.

[56] AG, A^{1}209, #35, 10 June 1667, Robert at Furnes.

[57] Records from 1691 to 1728 in Babeau, *La vie militaire*, 1:214.

[58] Belhomme, *L'armée française en 1690*, 154–57.

regiment during what seems to have been an epidemic. In the company of Captain Bourht, twelve men spent time there before they were released; the longest period was twenty-five days, and the average stay was 5.5 days.[59] At Maintenon in the late 1680s, 483 men were hospitalized out of a military work force of 20,000 to 25,000, and of these, 14.7 percent died, half in the second or third week of hospitalization.[60]

In any case, a hospital stay constituted part of the military experience for a great many soldiers. Landier says that a quarter of the troops died each year of the war, 1635–59, and the killed and wounded totaled by Bodart for the years 1672–1713 topped 750,000.[61] Dupaquier argues that of every ten men who died, one fell in action, three died from wounds, and six died from disease.[62] Infectious disease was clearly the greatest threat; as one contemporary report observed, "A body of troops which camps cannot remain for long in the same place without an extreme infection occurring as a consequence of the dirtiness of the soldiers, the horses which die there and the beasts slaughtered there."[63] With death stalking soldiers in so many guises, the promise of hospital care must have provided a modicum of peace of mind.

Regimental surgeons and army hospitals reassured the soldier that his king and his generals cared about his well-being; however, the greatest improvements in health probably resulted from the more regular supply of food and clothing and, particularly, the greater control over the conditions of camp life. Wood cuts of sixteenth-century camps often show soldiers defecating where they would, unconsciously spreading disease. With the elimination of large numbers of women and children from army camps and the insistence that camps be set up in a regular and sensible manner, conditions improved. The French battalion camp circa 1680 marshaled the men's tents in neat rows, put kitchens behind the battalion, and removed latrines a full 160 paces in front of the battalions.[64]

Prisoners

Just as the French monarchy made an effort to care for men put *hors de combat* by wounds or disease, it also remembered those men taken prisoner by the enemy. The French soldier knew that should he be captured, he was

---

[59] AN, Z^{1c}414, days men spent in hospital by men that were released, August 1682.

[60] Contamine, *Histoire militaire*, 1:442.

[61] Landier and Bodart figures in Corvisier, *La France de Louis XIV*, 124, and André Corvisier, "La mort du soldat depuis la fin du Moyen Age," *Revue histoirque*, 254 (1975), 15.

[62] Dupaquier in André Corvisier, *La France de Louis XIV, 1643–1715: Ordre intérieur et place en Europe* (Paris: 1979), 124.

[63] Duffy, *The Military Revolution*, 32.

[64] For a detailed diagram of a French battalion camp in 1683, see Victor Belhomme, *Histoire de l'infanterie en France*, 5 vols. (Paris: 1893–1902), 2:236. For diagrams of the encampments for an infantry battalion and a cavalry squadron in the early eighteenth century, see Jacques-François de Chastenet de Puységur, *Art de la guerre par principes et par règles*, 2 vols. (Paris: 1748), 1:plates 9 and 11.

not lost. In fact, the changing fate of prisoners marks one of the important improvements in the practice of war during the *grand siècle*, and as the fate of prisoners became more reasonable, the military profession threatened its members with fewer horrors. Early in the century, prisoners might be killed, because they imposed a burden upon the army that had captured them and now had to guard and feed them. On one occasion during the reign of Louis XIII, the French massacred 800 prisoners because they were a hindrance to the army.[65] Over the course of the seventeenth century, prisoners more and more became the wards of the state, not to be forgotten or killed but ransomed or exchanged. Treaties detailing the exchange of prisoners became increasingly common during the first half of the century.[66] By the end of the period, Villars was indignant at the suggestion that he slaughter 7,000 prisoners in 1703.[67]

Once it was accepted that prisoners should not be killed, the question arose as to what to do with them. Grotius wrote in his *De jure belli ac pacis* (1623) that "From the instant that the victor allows his prisoner to keep his life, the victor has the right to impose any obligation whatsoever on the prisoner."[68] This would seem to open up a broad range of alternatives, but in fact, the options were restricted to holding them, ransoming them, or exchanging them. The handling of prisoners became a major chore involving transporting, feeding, and guarding thousands of potentially hostile men. When the French captured 6,000 Spanish prisoners at Rocroi and Lens in the 1640s, they were taken to Rouen and from there distributed throughout Normandy to be guarded by bourgeois *milice*.[69] In the 1650s, *commissaires des guerres* were charged with handling prisoners and dispersing them into appropriate prisons.[70]

Although immediate responsibility for feeding prisoners fell to the state that held them, the bill for their upkeep was to be paid by the state that the prisoners had served. Thus, the French king paid for the food for his men who were held by the enemy. A state could refuse to release prisoners until reimbursed for their care; the Peace of the Pyrenees stipulated just this in 1659.[71] A number of financial documents dealing with the War of the Spanish Succession go into detail on the transfer of funds to pay for the maintenance of prisoners held by Louis's enemies. During 1704, the bankers Hogguers advanced money for French and other prisoners held by the Dutch, and the

---

[65] Of these, 200 were hanged. Mazarin, *Lettres*, 1:316, in Babeau, *La vie militaire*, 1:289–90.

[66] See Fritz Redlich, *De praeda militari: Looting and Booty 1500–1815*, supplement 39, *Vieteljahrschrift für Sozial- und Wirtschaftsgeschichte* (Wiesbaden: 1956), 34–35.

[67] Babeau, *La vie militaire*, 1:290.

[68] Grotius in Contamine, *Histoire militaire*, 1:368.

[69] Contamine, *Histoire militaire*, 1:369; André Corvisier, "Guerre et mentalités au XVIIe siècle," *XVIIe siècle*, 37 (1985), 227.

[70] André, *Le Tellier*, 617n.

[71] See article III of the Peace of the Pyrenees. J. Dumont, *Corps universel diplomatique*, 8 vols. (Hague: 1726–31), 6:pt. 2:279.

Hogguers requested reimbursement of 59,650 livres in November.[72] Correspondence of the *extraordinaire des guerres* show that insufficient funds were
sent to an Amsterdam banker to care for French prisoners in the second half
of 1707. For some time, officers had not been paid, and the solders were
owed 300,000 livres by the French government.[73] This evidence underlines
that not only were prisoners to be fed by their own government; they were
also to be paid. As early as 1648, French prisoners of war were supposed to
receive 4 sols per day and a ration of bread and straw from their king.[74]

A prisoner could be recruited into the army that held him captive. During
the 1640s, the French Army of Germany enlisted enemy prisoners instead of
just keeping them under lock and key.[75] Such a practice eliminated useless
mouths and added men to French ranks – a double bounty. Not surprisingly,
during the Fronde, contending armies felt no compulsion against enlisting
Frenchmen from the opposing force.[76] This practice continued when possible. An *état* of prisoners taken at Oudenarde and Tournai in 1667 listed
twenty-six officers and 317 enlisted men, and of this number, eleven had been
recruited into French units.[77] Treaties eventually regulated such enlistments.
One section of a 1690 treaty with the Dutch on ransoming prisoners required that an army could sign up only those "who want to voluntarily enter
the service of the party that holds them prisoner."[78] In order to try to forestall troops held captive from enlisting in the enemy's forces, a law of 1668
tried to make it more likely that French soldiers would be repatriated. A
soldier not ransomed back by his captain after one month could sign on in
the company of any other French captain who would pay his ransom.[79]

The French monarchy concluded a series of treaties to regulate the exchange and ransom of prisoners of war. Such agreements date as early as
1639, when the French and Spanish signed an accord for exchanging prisoners, an accord that was repeated in later treaties of 1643, 1646, and 1648.
From 1645, the Spanish maintained a resident in France to look after the
interests of their troops held prisoner.[80] Such agreements, or cartels, for
exchanging prisoners involved straight exchanges for men of the same rank
and stipulated that the surplus would be ransomed at a given rate according
to rank. The cartel for the exchange of prisoners for 1643 set the ransom
at one-month's pay.[81] A *cartel d'échange* with Spain in 1675 set the values of

---

[72] AN, G⁷1776, #354, 15 November 1704. Other pieces on this matter are #355–57. See AN,
     G⁷1778, #209, 26 October 1706 concerning funds for prisoners held by the Empire.
[73] AN, G⁷1781, #48–76, *extraordinaire des guerres*, 1707.
[74] Babeau, *La vie militaire*, 1:295.   [75] Jean Bérenger, *Turenne* (Paris: 1987), 194.
[76] See, for example, enrollment of soldiers into Condé's forces in 1652. Eveline Godley, *The
     Great Condé: A Life of Louis II de Bourbon, Prince of Condé* (London: 1915), 365.
[77] AG, A¹209, #127.
[78] 29 December 1690, Dumont, *Corps universel diplomatique*, 7:pt. 2:277–82.
[79] Contamine, *Histoire militaire*, 1:396–97.
[80] 4 August 1639 treaty in Contamine, *Histoire militaire*, 1:368; Tallett, *War and Society*, 131.
[81] Contamine, *Histoire militaire*, 1:369.

prisoners as follows: a soldier, 7 livres 6 sols; a sergeant, 15 livres; a lieutenant, 35 livres; and a captain, 90 livres.[82] A marshal commanded 50,000 livres in a cartel with the Dutch the same year.[83] The standard for exchange could also set values in terms of an officer's worth in common soldiers, as was the case in a 1703 convention for prisoners, according to which a sergeant was worth two soldiers, a captain twelve, a colonel forty-eight, and a brigadier sixty-six.[84]

In such cartels, the king assumed the responsibility for captives and the right to ransom that once belonged to those who took prisoners. An ordinance of 1654 was quite specific: "it belongs to the king alone to dispose of the prisoners, be it freely, be it by exchange or by ransom and to tax them, at such a sum as seems good to him."[85] This does not mean that soldiers never struck their own bargains with men they captured. In 1692, a *grenadier à cheval* captured a rich Spaniard, who offered him a ransom of 100 pistoles (1,300 livres), but the enraged grenadier killed the Spaniard to revenge a fallen officer.[86]

Royal agents often expressed an urgency about exchange. In 1658, Mazarin sent money for ransom and exchange while pressing his agent to hurry: "I am dispatching a courier with the necessary money to pay the ransom for our prisoners; previously the enemy proposed the exchange with those that we have taken in Flanders, and I ask you to not lose a minute of time in getting them back, according to the agreement that has already been made."[87] The king meant to have his soldiers back and could pay for their release; it made no sense to prolong the process.

Understandably, treaties ending wars generally contained clauses for freeing prisoners, as did those ending the war with Spain in 1559 and the Nine Years' War in 1697.[88]

Invalides

Perhaps nothing expressed the monarchy's new concern for its private soldiers more than did its treatment of *invalides*, those aged or disabled veterans who became wards of the state. Because cured soldiers and returned prisoners reentered the ranks, maintaining hospitals and signing exchange treaties

---

[82] Contamine, *Histoire militaire*, 1:397. See other cartels: with Spain, dated 19 January 1669, Contamine, *Histoire militaire*, 1:397; with the Dutch, 21 May 1675, Dumont, *Corps universel diplomatique*, 7:pt 1:292–95; and with the Dutch, 29 December 1690, Dumont, *Corps universel diplomatique*, 7:pt. 2:277–82.

[83] Treaty of 31 May 1675 in Babeau, *La vie militaire*, 1:292fn.

[84] Convention of 4 November 1703 in Belhomme, *Histoire de l'infanterie en France*, 2:395–96.

[85] Ordinance in Contamine, *Histoire militaire*, 1:368.

[86] Babeau, *La vie militaire*, 1:302.   [87] Mazarin, *Lettres*, 9:53.

[88] See article III of the Peace of the Pyrenees for an example. Dumont, *Corps universel diplomatique*, 6:pt. 2:279. See Dumont, *Corps universel diplomatique*, 7:pt. 2:410 for one of the treaties of 1697.

could be explained on entirely practical grounds. But care for retired *invalides* promised no similar immediate reward for the effort extended. To be sure, contemporaries offered the more subtle argument that provision for old and infirm soldiers would make young and able men more willing to enlist, and this would obviously appeal to the monarchy's self-interest. But without denying the hard-minded benefits of Louis's policies, it would be incorrect to dismiss his expressions of personal commitment as nothing more than window dressing.[89] To disregard sincere royal concern may overlook a fundamental change in the nature of the military. The *grand siècle* replaced a temporary aggregate contract force with a permanent state commission army, so veterans could now be defined as faithful servants rather than as mere hirelings. The Sun King seemed genuinely to feel a sense of responsibility to men who had spent their lives in his service, and it would only add to his *gloire* to treat such men with compassion. He might also expect that by showing loyalty to his troops, he would inspire greater devotion in them.

Over the years, a great deal of scholarship has focused on *invalides* and in particular, on the *Hôtel des Invalides*, or the Invalides, the veterans' home established in Paris by Louis XIV in 1674.[90] The treatment of *invalides* stands out as the most extensive social welfare program maintained by the state, at a time when it did little for civilian poor and disabled. In addition, just as has been the case for the army *contrôles* after 1716, the records of the Invalides provide a rich source of social documentation on the army and society for the seventeenth century.[91] These factors have attracted the interest of social historians, who may or may not also have any curiosity regarding the army per se. The discussion of *invalides* and the Invalides here does not encompass the full richness of the literature devoted to them, for the focus of this volume is the army as an active fighting institution, and *invalides* were no longer really part of that army. From the perspective of this volume, the most important aspect of care for old and disabled veterans was the impact of that care on the morale and motivation of active troops.

The monarchy made desultory attempts to care for its veterans before the *grand siècle*, and it could be argued that the numbers of French veterans were not large enough before 1610 to call for much concern. During the first half of the sixteenth century, the king could oblige monasteries to accept military *invalides* as *oblats*, lay brothers.[92] The Concordat of Bologna put this practice

---

[89] Colin Jones, "The Welfare of the French Foot-Soldier," *History* 65, no. 214 (June 1980), argues that the motives for the better care for soldiers at this time were entirely practical. This is a debatable issue, but there need be no contradiction between practical value and moral commitment.

[90] See the nearly fifty pages of bibliography in Baillargeat, *Les Invalides*, 497–544, as a guide to this subject.

[91] For a readily available list of the documents concerning the Invalides, including the matriculation lists, see Baillargeat, *Les Invalides*, sources, 472–96.

[92] For brief treatments on the treatment of *invalides* before 1670, see Baillargeat, *Les Invalides*, 127–46; unless otherwise noted, the details in this section come from these pages.

on a firm footing in 1516. Of course, the life of a soldier was not the best preparation for life within a monastery, but at least the *invalides* would get the necessities of life. The Wars of Religion of the second half of the seventeenth century challenged this system. Many monasteries suffered such hard times that they could not take in veterans, a fact that concentrated veterans in the remaining institutions that could still accept them, and this aggravated the natural conflicts between soldiers and monks. And, of course, Protestant veterans lay outside the system altogether.

Religious houses chafed under the system and sought to avoid it. Some enjoyed exemptions going back to the Middle Ages. Others twisted the law and claimed that they had no room by accepting other oblates. An ordinance of 4 March 1578 commanded royal agents to verify the claims of such oblates, in the hopes of expelling many and thus clearing room for *invalides*. Soldiers themselves abused the system by selling the oblate positions that they had gained, and an edict of 1585 addressed this problem with the threat of fines.

Henri IV offered the *invalides*-oblates the choice between living in the cloister or receiving a pension and returning to their homes. But even more importantly, he took steps to establish an institution specifically for housing invalid soldiers and officers in Paris: He found this home in the *Charité chrétienne*, created under Henri III as a refuge for the poor and sick civilians, although it had already accepted some soldiers before. Henri transformed it into a residence exclusively for soldiers through royal acts of 1597 and 1600.[93] In 1603, the king granted some 240 men admitted to the house of the *Charité chrétienne* the right to wear a coat decorated with a white cross, emblazoned with a fleur de lis. The maintenance of the *Charité chrétienne* did not exclude the granting of pensions to *invalides*, a practice that only grew throughout Henri's reign.

The experiment with the house of the *Charité chrétienne* did not outlive Henri, and the old system of oblates returned. Louis XIII also offered pensions to *invalides*, which were fixed in 1624 at 100 livres per year, a grant reaffirmed in the Code Michau of 1629.[94] In 1633, Louis resolved to build a home for soldiers on the site of the chateau de Bicêtre; the funds to support it would come from taxes levied on religious houses. Construction began in 1634, but war and opposition by the clergy killed the project, and the buildings were never finished.

While different projects for the care of *invalides* were advanced during the ministry of Mazarin, little was done. The king continued to grant places as oblates, and pensions remained on the books, although the ever-present

---

[93] Some accounts state that the house of Charité chrétienne was a soldiers' home from its inception; Marcel Marion does in his *Dictionnaire des institutions de la France aux XVIIe et XVIIIe siècles* (Paris: 1923), 301. He also identifies another facility on rue de Lourcine in the faubourg Saint-Marcel, but that was the address of the maison de la Charité chrétienne.

[94] Code Michau, 1629, article 219, in Isambert, *Recueil général des anciennes lois françaises*, 283–84.

financial crisis made payment questionable. Indigent veterans became a problem for the authorities of Paris, where these *invalides* begged in the streets. To rid Paris of them, ordinances of 1644 sent them to frontier fortresses, where they were to be maintained as best they could.

Louis XIV finally launched a major effort after the War of Devolution. In 1668, he ordered an inquiry under Louvois to examine the support from religious houses. A law of 1670 raised veterans' pensions to 150 livres. More importantly, the same year funds collected from religious houses were to be consecrated to the building of a *Hôtel des Invalides*. According to the 1670 edict, all enlisted men with at least ten years of service, who could no longer remain in the ranks due to age or infirmity, would be accepted upon presentation of certificates from their colonels verifying their careers and incapacities. A temporary residence would be established awaiting construction of a grand establishment to house invalid soldiers and officers. Louvois found such a temporary house on the rue du Cherche-Midi in the faubourg St. Germain, and it began to receive its wards in 1670, the point at which the army began to keep registers of those admitted to the Invalides.

In 1674, the *Hôtel des Invalides* opened its doors. It housed normally about 3,000 veterans, although as many as 6,000 could be temporarily squeezed in during an emergency.[95] According to the matriculation registers, 27,172 men were admitted to the Invalides from October 1670 to March 1715.[96] Not all lived on the premises, since this list included those shipped out in detached companies. By 1710, admission standards had risen; an enlisted man required not ten but twenty years of uninterrupted service or wounds that rendered him absolutely incapable of any service.

Once admitted, enlisted men occupied rooms with four or six beds, and officers stayed in rooms with only two or three beds.[97] Married veterans could only sleep outside the Invalides two nights a week circa 1670 and three days around 1710. Enlisted men ate in one of four large dining halls at great long tables. Officers ate in smaller rooms with round tables that seated only twelve. Needless to say, the officers ate better than did the enlisted men. When men fell sick, they went to the 300-bed infirmary staffed by nuns of the Daughters of Charity. The *invalides* lived under military discipline, wore uniforms, and had to pass inspection. *Invalides* still able to bear arms made up guard companies, at first six, but eventually as many as twenty-five, and officers drilled these companies.

The creation of the Invalides recognized both a moral and a practical necessity. Both of these come through clearly in the edict that formally established the Invalides in April 1674:

---

[95] Isser Woloch, *The French Veteran* (Chapel Hill: 1979), 6.

[96] See Baillargeat, *Les Invalides*, 482–83, for a list of the registers. Also, a photograph of one page of a register appears on page 203, and excerpts from registers on pages 204–5.

[97] For details of life in the Invalides, see Baillargeat, *Les Invalides*, 199–226.

It is very reasonable that those who have freely exposed their lives and shed their blood for the defense and support of this monarchy, and who have so usefully contributed to winning the battles that we have carried over our enemies, to the taking of their fortresses, and to the defense of ours, and who by their vigorous resistance and their general efforts, have often reduced our enemies to ask for peace, enjoy the repose that they have assured to our other subjects, and spend the rest of their days in tranquillity . . . .

Also, since nothing is more likely to deter men who might have the will to bear arms from embracing that profession than to see the vile condition in which those who had done so would find themselves . . . [after they] had grown old or been crippled, if no one had cared for their subsistence, we have taken the resolution to provide for it.[98]

Thus, from the start, Louis both expressed his responsibility to veterans and recognized the implications for morale of founding the Invalides. It was viewed as an incentive for recruitment, and at this, it apparently succeeded. The Bishop of Nantes wrote to Pontchartrain, *contrôleur général des finances*, in 1691: "I know that the establishment of the Invalides in Paris has brought many men into the service who would never have entered out of apprehension that had they been crippled and unable to make a living, they would have found themselves reduced to demanding alms in order to live."[99] Soldiers soon expected that the government would take care of them. At the siege of Namur in 1692, a soldier who had just lost his arm said, "So, I am in no condition to work any longer; it is now up to the king to feed me."[100]

As the Sun King's armies swelled, so did the ranks of *invalides*, and soon the magnificent hôtel in Paris was too small to house them all. By ordinances of 1690, Louis created companies of *invalides* thought still able to serve in fortresses and sent 700 *invalides* to the frontiers.[101] Two thirds of French *invalides* eventually lived in such detached companies, far from the grandeur of Paris and the Invalides. At base, the problem was quite simple; an institution designed for a veteran population of 1670, before Louis's great wars, could not take care of the great number of *invalides* produced by Louis's burgeoning army and long conflicts. The notion of sending *invalides* to reside in frontier fortresses went back at least to the ordinance of 1644, banning them from Paris. The first battalion of 700 *invalides* marched to Montreuil in 1690. Eight new battalions went into garrison in fortresses of the northeast in 1695. By 1702, sixty-one companies of *invalides* lodged at the front, and this number was increased by seventeen in 1709 and an additional thirty in 1715.

[98] Edict of April 1674 in Rousset, *Louvois*, 1:254.
[99] Letter #990, September 1691, in *Correspondance des contrôleur généraux des finances*, A. M. Boislisle, ed., vol. 1 (Paris: 1874), 261.
[100] Racine, 3 June 1692, in Babeau, *La vie militaire*, 1:322.
[101] Ordinances of 16 February and 15 April 1690. For a discussion of the *compagnies détachés d'invalides*, see Baillargeat, *Les Invalides*, 147–60; unless otherwise noted, the details in this section come from these pages.

The creation of detached companies signaled no less concern for the fate of veterans, simply a recognition that they could not all be cared for in Paris. Louis's commitment to old and infirm soldiers remained a great example of his humanity. The Invalides also stood as a monument to a new relationship between the state and its soldiers, a monument that recognized the monarchy's responsibility toward soldiers and their dependence upon, their tie to, the monarch.

LOYALTIES

Trying to measure the loyalties felt by the rank and file during the *grand siècle* may be a fool's errand. An historian can make lists and guesses, trying to be as reasonable as possible, but that historian can appeal to very little direct evidence, because the largely illiterate common soldiers of the era left very little to go on.[102] Yet to overlook the question of loyalty altogether would be a greater sin than to forge on despite the relative lack of evidence. Hence, the following discussion is an admittedly speculative examination of the unprovable, but hopefully not entirely unknowable, allegiances and aversions that drove French soldiers.

The loyalties discussed here are traditional, on the one hand, and military, on the other. Traditional focuses of veneration include religion and the monarchy, subjects of strong and ancient devotion. Dependence examined in the previous section almost certainly augmented loyalty to the monarchy. Military bonds inspired men with fidelity to their regiments, expressed as esprit de corps, and to their comrades, expressed as primary group cohesion. An understanding of the ties of mutual responsibility and affection that bound soldier groups together is a recently discovered analytical tool that may tell us much about past military conduct.

Traditional Loyalties

Traditional loyalties appealed to an earlier age and clearly held sway among the aristocratic officer corps, but there is good reason to believe that they also inspired the rank and file. Religious feeling was more an underpinning of morale than an explicit motivation during the *grand siècle*, when confessional allegiance played only an occasional role in French wars. Devotion to the monarchy, while less fundamental, was also more accessible as a source of motivation on campaign.

It is unlikely that the role of religion and of priests in forming and maintaining morale in the army during the *grand siècle* will ever be completely understood at this distance, a separation that can be measured both in terms of time and *mentalité*. However, given the strength of religious sentiment, it cannot be dismissed.

---

[102] Babeau, *La vie militaire*, 1:260, estimates that about one third of French enlisted men were literate.

Early in the century, popular verses doubted the existence of piety among the troops.

> A pious solder, a rare bird and worth
> Being compared with a black swan[103]

Montaigne said of troops even during the Wars of Religion: "Let us confess the truth . . . that those who take up arms out of pure zeal for religion could hardly make up one complete company of *gens d'armes*."[104] Both quotes seem to confuse righteousness or complete devotion with lesser, but nonetheless sincere, religious convictions. The soldier guilty of pillage and murder might still believe in the assertions of the Catholic Church. The Mafia, they say, is filled with sincere Catholics. The threat of immediate death probably heightened hopes for a benevolent and forgiving God. If there were no atheists in twentieth-century foxholes, they were even less likely in seventeenth-century siege trenches.

Evidence abounds that religious issues commanded considerable attention among those in authority. The army punished crimes against religion. Louis XIV ordered five soldiers burned alive for pillaging a church in 1673.[105] Even profane language, something that might be assumed to go with soldiering, left a soldier open to pain and disfigurement. Ordinances from the sixteenth century penalized blasphemy only with time in the stocks or a fine; however, under Louis XIV, an irreverent mouth could be punished by piercing the tongue with a hot iron.[106]

Within France, the Protestant element in the population and in the army concerned Louis XIII and Louis XIV; both conducted religious wars in their kingdom, and the latter attempted to eradicate Protestantism from the ranks of his army. Until 1685, the monarchy tolerated Protestant soldiers, generals, and even entire regiments among its French troops. Corvisier speculates that perhaps 10 percent or more were Huguenots, although this may be too generous an estimate.[107] (Bourbon kings always allowed Protestants among its foreign regiments, and during the first half of Louis's personal reign, about a third of the soldiers in Swiss and German regiments were Protestant.[108]) Some attempt was made to ensure Protestants in French regiments

---

[103] Babeau, *La vie militaire*, 1:228.   [104] Montaigne in Tallett, *War and Society*, 103.

[105] 7 June 1673 *Gazette*, in Wolf, *Louis XIV*, p. 230.

[106] Ordinance of 23 December 1543, in AG, MR, 1881, #5; ordinance of 9 February 1584, in AG, MR 1881, #14. Gaya, *Le nouvel art de la guerre*, 218; Adrien Pascal, *Histoire de l'armée*, vol. 2 (Paris: 1847), "Des délits militaires et des peines y attachées, conformément aux ordinances antérieures à la Révolution." See the case of a privileged *garde du corps* who had his tongue pierced and then was hanged for having sung impious songs about God and the saints with two comrades in 1683. Babeau, *La vie militaire*, 2:220.

[107] Corvisier, *Louvois*, p. 417. Robert Chaboche, "Les soldats français de la Guerre de Trente Ans, une tentative d'approche," *Revue d'histoire moderne et contemporaine* 20 (1973), 19, states that in his sample of veterans of the Thirty Years' War, only twelve were noted as Protestant, while 730 were noted as Catholic in the registers of the Invalides.

[108] Corvisier, *Louvois*, 416.

the practice of their religion, as when Louvois instructed towns in Flanders in 1673: "The subjects of the towns of Flanders have nothing to complain about when it is only a question of troops following the practice of their religion. If the people insult a minister, one will punish them as disturbing the public peace."[109] Until 1685, the army may have been something of a haven of tolerance for Huguenots.

Following his revocation of the Edict of Nantes, Louis XIV issued the ordinance of 27 November 1685 proclaiming that he no longer welcomed Huguenots in his French regiments. To encourage Protestant soldiers to convert to the Catholic faith, Louis offered bounties: two pistoles for an infantryman, four for a sergeant, three for a trooper, and six for a *maréchal de logis*.[110] Nonetheless, the revocation hurt the army; Vauban estimated that 500 to 600 Huguenot officers and 10,000 to 12,000 of the best soldiers left their regiments.[111] However, the revocation may have contributed to the sense of unity among the French people, who were in the vast majority Catholic and approved of Louis's measures against Protestants. In fairness, it should be pointed out that Vauban, a font of common sense and humane attitudes, seems to have approved of the goal of religious unity, although he did not approve of persecution: "Never would anything have been better suited to the kingdom than this much desired uniformity of sentiment, if it had pleased God to bless the project."[112]

As far as common soldiers were concerned, Corvisier argues that once war began again, there was little concern over religious conformity in the army, although he does not document this conclusion.[113] At least in some cases, religion was a factor. In April 1689, Marshal Huxelles reported that "Sieur Sonnet de Boismenair, captain in the regiment of bombardiers who was of the [Protestant] religion, went over to the enemy three or four days ago."[114] Louis did not want Protestant officers, but they were present in the War of the Spanish Succession, enough so that in 1704, marshal Chamilly ordered that all officers "of the Religion" be immediately replaced by Catholics in his command.[115]

Throughout the century, the army attended to the religious needs of its men by providing chaplains, *aumôniers*. The Code Michau of 1629 listed a chaplain as part of the complement of every regiment.[116] In French regiments, Louis XIV left the matter of appointing chaplains to his colonels;

[109] Corvisier, *Louvois*, 417.   [110] Contamine, *Histoire militaire*, 1:403–4.

[111] Vauban, "Mémoire pour le rappel des Huguenots," December 1689 in Albert Rochas d'Aiglun, *Vauban, sa famille et ses écrits*, 2 vols. (Paris: 1910), 1:466.

[112] Vauban, memoir on the recall of Huguenots, presented to Louvois in December 1689, in Rousset, *Louvois*, 3:431–32.

[113] Corvisier, *Louvois*, 423. He claims that French Huguenots actually fled into the army to escape persecution, 356–57.

[114] AG, A^{1}875, 29 April 1689, from Huxelles.

[115] AG, A^{1}1801, #278, 8 March 1704, to Chamilly.

[116] Code Michau, 1629, article 226, in Isambert, *Recueil général des anciennes lois françaises*, 285.

they were only formally stipulated in foreign regiments.[117] The state assigned French chaplains a salary. In 1710, one drew 10 sols per day and two rations in an infantry regiment, or 1 livre 10 sols and two rations in a cavalry regiment. This meant that his pay equaled that of a cavalry cornette.[118] *Aumôniers* were attached to only the first battalion of infantry regiments that had more than one battalion, as was also the case for surgeons, majors, *maréchaux de logis*, and the *prévôté*, if the regiment had one. In a cavalry regiment, the chaplain was attached to the regiment itself rather than to any one of its squadrons. The French were not unique in their concern for chaplains, for in this period, only the Dutch did not provide them for their troops.[119]

Records show that even though the army lacked an official chaplain's corps, *aumôniers* virtually always accompanied units in the field. According to the particularly complete records for 1691 in Alsace every one of the first battalions of infantry regiments included a chaplain present; all but one of twenty-two cavalry regiments had *aumôniers*; and eight of eleven dragoon regiments also listed them.[120] The best information available stresses the preponderance of regular clergy among these military *aumôniers* – Jesuits and Capuchins early in the century, mostly Recollets by about 1670.[121]

How successful were these men charged with the spiritual well-being of the troops in promoting devotion and morale? Louvois believed them necessary for discipline.[122] Could the functions of *aumôniers* be seen in something of the same light as those performed by political officers such as the Representatives on Mission during the Revolution? Did they inspire, compel, or just forgive? Did these priests simply perform the duties they would have in a civilian community? At his death, the young officer Saint-Mayme left his *aumônier* 50 livres to distribute alms to the poor and to say masses, much as he would have given to his parish priest.[123]

Or did *aumôniers* adopt special standards and roles because they tended the army? About the standards there is little doubt. As one Jesuit wrote, "It is necessary to condescend to the dragoons. One cannot demand great moral regularities from these men, that would be ridiculous."[124] But it is reasonable to imagine that they aided in shaping motivation. By nature, they would be more concerned with the soldier's state of mind than would any other man on the regimental staff. Of course, their best efforts to raise the spirits might run amok, as when a chaplain tried to prepare his men for the trial of battle of Raucoux in 1746, a generation following the death of the Sun King. After

---

[117] Contamine, *Histoire militaire*, 1:403.   [118] Mallet, *Comptes rendus*, 161–62.
[119] Tallett, *War and Society*, 127.   [120] BN, f. fr. 4565–67.
[121] Babeau, *La vie militaire*, 224; Contamine, *Histoire militaire*, 1:403; André Corvisier, "Le moral des combattants, panique et enthousiasme, la bataille de Malplaquet," *Revue historique des armées: 1977*, no 3, 31.
[122] Corvisier, "La mort," 10.
[123] Georges Girard, ed., "Un soldat de Malplaquet: Lettres du capitaine de Saint-Mayme," *Carnet de Sabretache* (1922), 539.
[124] *Lettres françoise et germaniques*, 54 in Babeau, *La vie militaire*, 1:226.

he had gone on far too long, the lieutenant colonel broke in: "Soldiers! The priest [*M. l'abbé*] says to you that there is no salvation for cowards. *Vive le Roi!*"[125]

The questions are many, and at this point the answers few, but if the *ancien régime* possessed an ideology to fortify men against fear, it revolved around the love of God and the tenets of religion.

Whereas religion constituted a potential foundation for morale, loyalty to the king provided greater incentives for action. Corvisier sees expressions of loyalty to the sovereign as a code for nascent nationalism, saying that the French felt modern patriotic sentiments but simply expressed them in premodern language as devotion toward the king. But there is a great difference between early modern fidelity to a particular individual who possessed a semidivine character and modern identity with the abstract notion of an entire people. The king existed outside or apart from the nation and was the nexus of a web of personal loyalties involving clientage and paternalism. A foreigner could easily focus his loyalties on the person of the king of France without ever wanting to merge with the people of France. The call to patriotism would eventually produce a different kind of motivation and a different kind of army.

The major observers of the army during the *grand siècle* – historians such as Rousset, André, Babeau, and Corvisier – agree on the great loyalty felt among the troops of the French army to their king. In a contemporary stage play, the soldier proclaims "the king, that prince is the heart's best love."[126] Louis XIII may have mobilized this sentiment with a personal touch that his son lacked. Pontis claimed that he knew his bravest men down to the rank of sergeant and could address them by name.[127] Louis XIV would seem to have relied more on his grandeur, which had its effect simply by his presence with the troops. And Louis took great pains to be with his army until his advancing age made this impractical in the 1690s. When he could not be present, he dispatched members of the royal family. Both the dauphin and the duke of Burgundy went to the front in titular command of armies. In 1709, as Villars saw battle approaching, that keen judge of the soldier's heart requested that a prince of the blood join him in order to bolster morale. In this case, the court refused, although Villars, convinced of the importance of this gesture, continued to press the issue.[128]

The oaths taken by troops reinforced their bonds to the king. Normally, the focus of the oath would be the king alone; however, during the period when Louis XIV was a mere boy, it included the regent, as troops swore "to serve well and faithfully his Majesty and the Queen Regent his mother, towards all, and against all."[129]

[125] Babeau, *La vie militaire*, 1:227.
[126] Vadé, "Les Racoleurs," scene 16, in Babeau, *La vie militaire*, 1:236.
[127] Pontis in Babeau, *La vie militaire*, 1:17.   [128] Sturgill, *Marshal Villars*, 91.
[129] Oath prescribed by regulation, 18 November 1643, AG, MR 1881, #28.

Military Loyalties

Soldiers could be expected to be moved not only by loyalties common to society during their age but also by feelings more specific to the army. On a certain level, military life in one age resembles that of any other; it must be seen as a special existence, a unique subculture in addition to being a part of the broader culture of any particular age. When discussing early modern soldiers, J. R. Hale speaks of a "mental frontier between the man of war and the man of peace," and to a degree, the two populated very different worlds.[130] Within the confines of this distinct military existence, special bonds formed that constituted the fundamentals of identity and motivation – esprit de corps and primary-group cohesion – and the army as an institution and individual commanders also attempted to bolster morale and provide incentives.

ESPRIT DE CORPS

Esprit de corps provided a source of morale not specifically limited to the *ancien régime*. Men who invest themselves in a regiment or some other specific band, who come to define themselves by it, who suffer and die in it, take great pride in its accomplishments. Although the phenomenon may be in some ways universal, the expressions of esprit de corps did take on a decidedly *grand siècle* character, sometimes involving bitter disputes between regiments over precedence, their official ranking among the troops of the French army. On the one hand, this seemed as superficial as arguments between courtiers, but soldiers took the matter seriously. Precedence determined a regiment's place in camp, on the march and in the line of battle (senior regiments generally stood to the right). Laon commented: "The first line . . . is more honorable than the second line [*bataille*], and the *bataille* than the reserve [*arrière garde*], however, one puts the regiment of guards and the *gendarmes* [only] in the *bataille*."[131]

Such affairs of honor between regiments could hamper military effectiveness. In 1644, when the French took Gravelines, the Regiment de Navarre tried to enter before the Gardes françaises, which claimed precedence, and the contesting units practically came to blows in the breach.[132]

Interregimental conflict troubled Louis XIV, who condemned struggles between commanders and units.[133]

Arguments became such a problem that they could only be solved by regulations that explicitly stated the order of precedence. Two ordinances of 1 April 1654 set the tone, defining the *vieux* regiments – Picardie, Piémont, Champagne, Navarre, Normandie, and la Marine – and *petits vieux* as special, assigning their status, and then setting the precedence of other regiments

---

[130] J. R. Hale, *War and Society in Renaissance Europe, 1450–1620* (Baltimore, MD: 1985), 129.

[131] Sieur d'Aigremont Laon, *Practique et maximes de la guerre* (Paris: 1652), 65–66; Brent Nosworthy, *The Anatomy of Victory: Battle Tactics, 1689–1763* (New York: 1990), 81–82.

[132] André, *Le Tellier*, 195.

[133] Louis XIV, *Mémoires*, 2:123–24, supplement to memoirs of 1666.

"each by the day and date of the commission for its levy."[134] Later ordinances (1666 and 1670) reiterated and elaborated the decisions of 1654.[135]

The end of formal disputes over precedence did not end tensions between regiments that attracted the loyalties of their men. In one later incident, an Irish regiment clashed with a regiment of *fusiliers de la montagne*, and even the women of the Irish unit took part in the brawl, where one woman wounded a fusilier with a well-thrown rock.[136] In a combat that probably took place after 1715 at Maubeuge, fifty men of the Swiss Regiment Reinach fought a duel with fifty soldiers from the *chasseurs du Gevaudan*, and when the men were pried apart, it was found that two men had been killed and thirty-seven wounded.[137]

Individual soldiers also witnessed strong loyalty to their units in positive ways. The duke de Luynes wrote of a cornette's devotion to his company at the battle of Ramillies: "seeing that he was going to die, but not forgetting that he carried one of the company standards . . . he threw it as far as he could to those on the border of the marsh and cried 'Save the honor of the company.' "[138] An old sergeant tried to commit suicide when he learned that his regiment was to be disbanded, since he did not want to survive the disgrace of his regiment. Only the rapid intervention of an officer stopped the disheartened sergeant.[139] Another gravely wounded sergeant dismissed his wounds: "It is nothing; the regiment has shown itself well."[140]

SMALL-GROUP COHESION

The fact that soldiers bravely fought and died when they might have fled or surrendered can be rightly interpreted as evidence that they measured their conduct by something other than their own immediate self-interest. Modern research into combat motivation points to a basic and enduring explanation for such self-sacrifice: primary-group cohesion.[141] This theory stresses bonding between men who have face-to-face relationships in the highly charged atmosphere of combat. They come to rely upon each other for physical and psychological support. Soldiers treasure the respect of their comrades within the small group of their comrades – what military sociologists term the

---

[134] SHAT, Col. des ord., vol. 19, #80 in André, *Le Tellier*, 197. See André, *Le Tellier*, 188–205 on precedence, also Belhomme, *L'armée française en 1690*, 55–57, for a list of the different types of French regiments in 1690.

[135] See the ordinances of 19 and 28 February 1666 and 26 March 1670.

[136] AG, MR 1787, piece 50. [137] Babeau, *La vie militaire*, 1:236.

[138] Luynes in Jean Chagniot, "De Rocroi à Rossbach," in Claude Croubois, ed., *L'officier français des origines à nos jours* (Saint-Jean-d'Angély: 1987), 53.

[139] Babeau, *La vie militaire*, 1:191. [140] Babeau, *La vie militaire*, 1:192.

[141] On small- or primary-group cohesion, see Anthony Kellett, *Combat Motivation* (Boston: 1982) for a catalog of theories. For engaging treatments of the subject, see Marshall, *Men Against Fire*, and John Keegan, *The Face of Battle* (New York: 1976). For an attempt to apply the theory to the French army in the eighteenth century, see Lynn, *Bayonets of the Republic*.

primary group – and will go to great lengths to gain and retain it. In war, this can mean carrying one's burden as a soldier in the group: sharing duties, braving dangers, and coming to each other's aid. It was found with U.S. troops in World War II that even when patriotic motives wore thin under the strain of military life, primary-group ties remained strong.

Due to the scanty documentation concerning the opinions of enlisted men in the *grand siècle*, any discussion of primary-group cohesion is highly speculative. The best evidence for the importance of camaraderie in the army of the *grand siècle* is largely inferential. Such cohesion has been shown to be virtually omnipresent in modern militaries, and since it is not dependent upon present-day ideology but upon what can be best described as human nature, it seems reasonable to read it back into time. But even if an argument concerning the importance of small-group cohesion must be circumstantial, it may also be the best explanation of soldier's conduct, pending the unlikely revelation of direct testimony by common soldiers.

Exploration of primary-group cohesion would best start by trying to identify the group. During the second half of the eighteenth century, the *ordinaire*, or mess group, constituted the primary group. As defined by field regulations from 1758 to the end of the century, the *ordinaire* included fourteen to sixteen men who ate, camped, and fought together.[142] As much as possible, it was to be composed of men from the same squad, which in the infantry also numbered fourteen to sixteen men commanded by a corporal. Regulations on mounting guard demonstrate that infantry companies in the army of Louis XIV were also subdivided into squads. The key ordinance of 1661 directed "That each infantry company will be divided into three squads, which will mount guard one after the other, each on its day, in such a way that in three days each officer and soldier of the said company will be on guard, as it was done before the war."[143] A corporal would command each squad. The ordinance stipulated "as it was done before the war," thus implying that squad organization existed before 1635. Since infantry companies in French regiments usually varied from thirty to fifty-five men during Louis's personal reign, a squad would have run from ten to eighteen men, if the company was at full strength. This is consistent with the size of the later *ordinaire*.[144] Puységur, in diagramming a camp, shows each company with three squads, although he would have preferred only two squads in a company.[145]

---

[142] See Lynn, *Bayonets of the Republic*, chap. 7, concerning the *ordinaire* in the army during the Revolution.

[143] SHAT, Col. des ord., vol. 20, #157, 12 October 1661, art. 15, in André, *Le Tellier*, 560fn; *Ordonnances militaires*, 2 vols. (Luxembourg: 1734–35), 1:2.

[144] Actually, the nineteenth-century soldier-historian Victor Belhomme makes a great deal of the existence of the *ordinaire* in the army circa 1690: "Louvois . . . prescribed the adoption of the *ordinaire* by squads in all circumstances . . . . Each squad had its marmite and carried it everywhere, even to its post when it was on guard." Belhomme, *L'armée française en 1690*, 34–35. His lack of citations makes it difficult to discover the basis for his conclusion here.

[145] Puységur, *Art de la guerre*, 1:104 and plate 9.

According to studies of modern armies, the primary group is not simply a given number of men in a particular structure; it is also a repository and enforcer of group standards. There are hints that soldiers enforced their own standards of conduct during the *grand siècle*. According to Corvisier, soldiers at this time "often forced their officers to expel a man for 'low' behavior, perhaps for having mistreated a comrade or for having given a bad impression of the military valor of the corps."[146] Enforcement also had to do with shame and honor as defined by the primary group, since the desire for respect is one of the strongest impulses that drive the human race.[147] Villars counseled officers to work on their men's sense of shame when he commented on how to stop a rout. He wanted his officers to stay within earshot "and to call the men by their names."[148]

The declining number of women who accompanied the army is a fundamental reason to suppose that the primary group grew in importance under Louis XIV. As previously discussed, when large numbers of women and children followed the army, women filled many basic domestic roles, such as food preparation, and men probably ate with their wives and maintained something of a family existence in the field. Clearly, the pull of loyalties to the family would compete with the ties of the primary group. As a result of the reforms that separated the great majority of females from the regiment, men in the field lived more completely within the bands of comrades and relied more upon mess groups for functions once performed by the women.

During the wars of the French Revolution, the details of camp life tell us something about the *ordinaire*, as men of a particular *ordinaire* were supposed to sleep in the same tent or tents and share mess facilities. Camp life was also apparently very regular even in the first half of the seventeenth century, as evidenced by the fact that in 1646 in La Valette's camp, the companies each had a row of huts and a *rue*, or path.[149] Tents replaced huts, until by 1689 the army had eight-man tents for all enlisted ranks.[150] These tents compared well with the eight- or sixteen-man tents that held half an *ordinaire* or an entire one during the Revolution. Circa 1680, each company's tents stood in a row, with ten paces between companies; company kitchens

---

[146] André Corvisier, *Armies and Societies in Europe, 1494–1789*, trans. Abigail T. Siddall (Bloomington: 1979), 182.

[147] Montecuccoli may offer some insight on the fact that troops cared very much to retain the good opinion of other troops, although the case he refers to is not specifically about primary groups. "Troops who are known and familiar to each other are placed side by side . . . . This is because their proximity provides great strength in times of peril. One unit will generously bear the brunt of the struggle in order to rescue the other. For if it did not grasp the opportunity to earn merit vis-à-vis its neighbor, or if it were to abandon him through flight, the men would experience great remorse and shame." Montecuccoli in Tallett, *War and Society*, 49–50.

[148] BN, ff 6257, Villars, "Traité," 85.

[149] The rue was eight feet wide. Contamine, *Histoire militaire*, 1:367.

[150] Contamine, *Histoire militaire*, 1:407. Puységur, *Art de la guerre*, 1:plate 10, puts nine men in a tent. It is a very tight squeeze.

were to set up six paces behind the last tent.[151] Camp discipline and the sleeping arrangements bear further evidence of a new style of army in which women were a lesser presence and male bonds grew firmer.

As with so much else in the soldier's heart, the fraternity of the mess group can only be dimly viewed at this distance. Lack of firsthand testimony from enlisted men themselves makes it impossible to come to firm conclusions. However, modern parallels and common sense tell us that such camaraderie was potent. The use of *noms de guerre* suggests a world apart that was inhabited by soldiers who saw themselves as something different. When a man entered the ranks, he took on a new name, usually of a descriptive, humorous, or ironic twist: titles such as Sans-Regard, Belle-Rose, La Réjouissance.[152] It was as though in entering the military life, common soldiers had entered an entirely new society with new standards; primary-group cohesion played a major role in that new society.

THE CONSCIOUS MANIPULATION OF MORALE AND MOTIVATION

Within the specifically military context, officials and officers attempted to influence soldiers' motivation by bestowing rewards and by inspiring them through direct appeals to their pride or to shared camaraderie. Such methods have a long life within the confines of the military.

Recognizing the importance of material incentives, authorities often granted monetary rewards for distinguished service. Arnauld d'Andilly provided cash incentives in his model regiment during the 1620s. On one day, he awarded men on drill a total of 300 écus and also gave "bandoleers, swords, and other similar things."[153] Richelieu established a system of monetary rewards for bravery and outstanding conduct in the Code Michau.[154] Part of a system that Vauban proposed for recognizing talent and courage included small pensions for certain stipulated actions, such as killing two or three enemies in the same combat or seizing the flag of an enemy regiment.[155] Another memoir, possibly by Vauban as well, advocated rewards for enlisted men as a way of limiting desertion, although the author conceded that "not everyone is persuaded that common soldiers are delicate enough to be sensible to these kinds of honors."[156]

---

[151] For a discussion and detailed diagram of a French battalion camp in 1683, see Belhomme, *Histoire de l'infanterie*, 2:234–36. In his *L'armée française en 1690*, 178, Belhomme states that the kitchens were located twenty paces behind the company tents.

[152] On *noms de guerre*, see Babeau, *La vie militaire*, 1:139, and examples in Baillargeat, *Les Invalides*, 204.

[153] Arnauld d'Andilly, *Mémoires*, in Michaud and Poujoulat, eds., *Nouvelle collection des mémoires pour servir à l'histoire de France*, vol. 9 (Paris: 1838), 414–15.

[154] Code Michau, 1629, article 228, in Isambert, *Recueil général des anciennes lois françaises*, 285.

[155] Rochas d'Aiglun, *Vauban, sa famille et ses écrits*, 1:328–29.

[156] 19 December 1686 memoir on how to stop desertion, SHAT, Bib., Arch. hist., supplement 79.

To some extent, this was simply an extension of the system of offering gratuities to officers. Such payments were considered appropriate and normal, but some private soldiers regarded money as degrading. A soldier wounded in a reconnaissance refused 10 livres offered him by Vauban: "No, sir, that would soil my actions."[157] The grenadier who killed his Spanish captive in revenge, rather than accept a ransom, replied, "The grenadiers only put their hands on someone in order kill them."[158]

Promotion also served as a form of monetary reward, since material benefits came with a step up in rank, but promotion need not directly appeal to greed; it could be considered a higher form of incentive. The practice of promoting men from the ranks distinguished the French army throughout the *ancien régime*. Promotion for bravery alone was unusual, but it did occur. In 1674, a sergeant of the Regiment de Dampierre, while leading a party of twenty-one men, fought off 200 enemy. His conduct rated as so exceptional that it came to the attention of Louvois. After consideration, the king instructed that "His Majesty desires that [the sergeant] be made a lieutenant if there is one of these charges vacant in the Regiment de Dampierre."[159] Just as in the case of monetary rewards, Vauban wanted to make promotion of enlisted men into the commissioned ranks far more common and regular.[160] In fact, infantry battalions regularly provided advancement for poor men and commoners, because officer positions in grenadier companies were expressly not venal; therefore, the king could appoint whom he liked to them, and merit, not origin, mattered there.

Symbolic rewards, such as medals, hold an appeal for soldiers because they mark an individual as worthy of special respect, perhaps the most desired of all commodities. During the *grand siècle*, however, the French army lacked any system of awarding decorations to the rank and file. The cross of the Order of St. Louis, formed in 1693, was the closest thing to a medal, and it signified membership in an order restricted to veteran officers. Vauban proposed marks of distinction that would be worn by common soldiers on their uniforms.[161] But the monarchy adopted his ideas neither on uniforms nor on badges of merit.

The provision of specific recognition to individual soldiers came both as a reward and as an attempt to make one man's noteworthy action an example for all. Rewards in this second sense constituted an attempt to set high standards and to manipulate motivation. Officers used other means in addition to rewards to stir their men's hearts. Generals led from the front, by example and by their presence alone. This fact was not specific to the *ancien régime*; Napoleon mastered the art of inspiring and manipulating soldiers through his own actions, as did generals of the nineteenth and twentieth

---

[157] Babeau, *La vie militaire*, 1:302.   [158] Babeau, *La vie militaire*, 1:302.

[159] For an account of La Fleur's actions, see AG, A^{1}398, #138, 12 June 1674, letter from Chamilly; for Louvois's response, see AG, A^{1}380, #220–21, 27 June 1674, Louvois to the marquis de Chamilly.

[160] Rochas d'Aiglun, *Vauban*, 1:326.   [161] Rochas d'Aiglun, *Vauban*, 1:325–34.

centuries. Part of this manipulation lay not only in brave conduct but in caring for their men and in sharing an appropriate level of camaraderie with the troops. Pontis reported that a prince addressed a common sentinel as "my comrade."[162] Considering the base origins of soldiers, it may seem surprising to hear Turenne saying, "Love the soldier in order to understand him; understand him to lead him."[163] Turenne was noted for caring a great deal about his soldiers, but, it must be added, caring rather little for civilian populations that his troops might abuse.

Villars was probably the master of personal contact with the troops as a means of bolstering morale. For this reason, some see him as a precursor of modern generals, but this proceeds from the false assumption that only modern generals possessed the common touch when it was needed.[164] Nevertheless, after a series of generals who seemed blessed with little ability one way or the other, Villars stood out. As Mme. de Maintenon put it, "We finally have a general who has faith in the soldier, in the fate of France, and in himself."[165] Villars, never a reluctant man, bragged, "My presence encouraged the soldier, my familiarity made him gaily put up with the fatigues of the siege."[166] In his memoirs, Villars described how he ate and drank with the soldiers while encouraging them.[167] In his treatise on war, Villars summed up his opinion of the potential influence of the general on morale: "The soldier is a species of animal out of which one can make what one wants with nothing, . . . an audacious word, or a good word about them [*à leur égard*] decides their good or bad will."[168]

In the category of influences that could lift a soldier's heart, Villars insisted on the role of joy and amusement: "Two things are necessary to an army, money and joy, the latter is the slave of the former, but without joy one languishes and one finds that time drags." Diversions produced joy: "I want a general to devote attention to establishing games in his army, or something that can divert and occupy the soldiers, to spare nothing to inspire joy in the army."[169]

PATRIOTISM AND THE CRISIS OF 1709

In addition to the categories of loyalties in the foregoing discussion, some insist that patriotism also played a role for the common soldier late in the reign of the Sun King, but their insistence seems ill conceived. If love of country mattered so much, why was it so absent from the discussion of

[162] Pontis in Babeau, *La vie militaire*, 1:176.

[163] Turenne in Henri Lachouque, *Aux armes citoyens: Les soldats de la Révolution* (Paris: 1969), 19.

[164] See praise of Villars as a key figure in national revival in Emile G. Léonard, *L'Armée et ses problèmes aux XVIIIe siècle* (Paris: 1958).

[165] 4 March 1709, Léonard, *L'Armée et ses problèmes*, 83.

[166] Villars in Léonard, *L'Armée et ses problèmes*, 82–83.

[167] Letter of 2 March 1703 from Villars to Chamillart, written at Kehl, in Claude Louis Hector Villars, *Mémoires du maréchal de Villars*, ed. Vogüé, 5 vols. (Paris: 1884–95), 2:278.

[168] BN, f. fr. 6257, Villars, "Traité," 50.

[169] BN, f. fr. 6257, Villars, "Traité," 51. See also page 89.

leading contemporary observers and military writers? Individuals who expressed notable sympathy for the common soldier, such as Vauban and Villars, fail to discuss it, by and large. Even when authors approach this matter, their arguments seem vague. Hay de Chastenet spoke of defending "the laws and liberty of their country," but he still concluded that "Men should fight only for glory."[170] If patriotism was potent, the state should have attempted to foster or appeal to it, yet little was done along these lines. Historians have replied that this is simply a problem of words, that statements of loyalty to the king were nothing less than a code for patriotism. Yet this takes things too far; fidelity to the person of the monarch was a long way from patriotism.

In fact, there is good reason to doubt that patriotism ranked very high among the sentiments of French enlisted men during the *grand siècle*. For one thing, regionalism remained strong. As part of his contribution to the survey of the kingdom in 1697–98, the *intendant* from Provence described his charges in these less than glowing terms: "*Amour propre*, that of their compatriots and the high opinion of their region [*pays*] which few want to leave, makes them despise all that is foreign."[171] And here, "foreign" clearly means anything that is not Provençal. It is also revealing that the inhabitants of border areas exchanged their allegiances so easily. Van Houtte, in his extensive study of the Low Countries, states that in areas overrun by foreign armies in the late seventeenth century, there were "no traces of protest of a doctrinal character or any patriotic tendency."[172] Granted, he was mainly concerned with the Spanish Netherlands, but it still seems odd to see no patriotic sentiments witnessed on one side of the border but to expect deep national identification on the other. In fact, the relevant loyalty was to a sovereign, and this could be more easily adjusted. Certainly, the reluctance of French *miliciens* to fight for their country, and the need to lead them off under guard, often in chains, hardly indicates patriotic devotion to the national defense.

Still, some of the most prominent scholars, such as André Corvisier, continue the claims of patriotic motivation and offer the French response to the crisis of 1709 as their principal case in point.[173] They argue that it brought forth a great surge of patriotism, or proto-patriotism, insisting that 1709 bears comparison with 1792 as a true war of national defense. Repeated assertions that 1709 ushered in a great patriotic war demand that this notion be considered, if only to be rejected.

---

[170] Paul Hay de Chastenet, *Traité de la guerre* (Paris: 1668), 2, 5.

[171] André Corvisier, *Les Français et l'armée sous Louis XIV* (Vincennes: 1975), 62.

[172] Hubert van Houtte, *Les Occupations étrangères en Belgique sous l'ancien régime*, 2 vols., *Recueil de Travaux Publiés par la faculté de Philosophie et Lettres de l'Université de Gand*, fasicule 62–63 (1930), 1:335.

[173] André Corvisier asserts: "In effect the military power of the French people rested on their attachment to the king of France and the force of national sentiment. It is quite wrong that the historiography of the nineteenth century wanted to believe that [patriotism] awakened with the Revolution." Contamine, *Histoire militaire*, 1:305.

Much is made of the appeal made by Louis XIV to his subjects. Faced with unacceptable terms in 1709, Louis issued public declarations of his motives in order to explain why he felt compelled to continue the costly war. On the urging of Torcy, his foreign minister, Louis dispatched two letters dated 12 June, one to the Archbishop of Paris and the other to the provincial governors of France.[174] The letter to the governors was by far the more celebrated of the two. Louis explained that despite his willingness to accept nearly impossible conditions, the Allies offered only a two-months' truce in return. Furthermore, in their arrogance, the Allies expected Louis to drive Philippe, his grandson, from Spain.

> But although the tenderness for my peoples is no less strong than that I have for my own children . . . and [although] I have made all Europe see that I desire to let them enjoy peace, I am persuaded that they would themselves refuse to receive it on conditions so contrary to the justice and the honor of the French name. My intention is therefore that all those who for so many years have given me signs of their zeal by contributing their efforts, their goods, and their blood to undertake such a burdensome war should know that all that my enemies proposed to give in return for my offers . . . was a suspension of arms, . . . which . . . would procure for them advantages greater than what they could have expected from keeping their troops on campaign.[175]

This unprecedented letter received wide circulation within the kingdom; governors added cover letters and had it printed, and booksellers copied and sold it to enthusiastic buyers.[176]

However, the appeal's undeniable effect seems to have been concentrated at the top of society, not at its base. Saint-Simon said of it, "The success of it was every bit what had been hoped: it was a cry of indignation and vengeance, it was only proper to give all one's goods to support the war, and other such drastic measures to show one's zeal."[177] Mme. de Maintenon also commented that "All good Frenchmen have felt . . . the harshness of the peace conditions that are to be rejected."[178] On close examination, their much quoted testimony reflects only aristocratic sentiment. Yet with only such evidence from the elite, certain historians see this appeal as rivaling the declarations of 1792.[179]

Those who would claim that 1709 stands on a par with 1792 had best

---

[174] In fact, it is known that Torcy drafted the all-important letter to the provincial governors. Joseph Klaits, *Printed Propaganda Under Louis XIV* (Princeton: 1976), 214.

[175] Letter in Vault and Pelet, ed., *Mémoires militaires relatifs a la succession d'Espagne sous Louis XIV*, vol. 9 (Paris: 1855), 9:299–300.

[176] Klaits, *Printed Propaganda*, 217–18. The printer of the *Gazette de France* was one who printed and sold copies, as advertisements on the back of the *Gazette* for 6 and 13 July 1709 announced.

[177] Saint-Simon, *Mémoires*. A. de Boislisle, ed. 42 vols. (Paris: 1879–1930), 17:402–3.

[178] Letter from Mme. de Maintenon to the duc de Noailles, 30 June 1709, in Maintenon, *Lettres de madame de Maintenon* vol. 5 (Amsterdam: 1756), 123–24.

[179] See, for example, the claims of Wolf, *Louis XIV*, 564, and David Chandler, *Marlborough as a Military Commander*, 2nd ed., (London: 1979), 245.

compare Louis's appeal to the Legislative Assembly's declaration of "la patrie est en danger" on 11 July 1792:

Address to the French

Your constitution is based on principles of eternal Justice; a league of kings is formed in order to destroy it; their battalions advance; they are numerous . . . . Do you not feel a noble ardor inflame your courage! Will you suffer these foreign hordes to spread like a destructive torrent over your countryside, that they may ravage your harvest, that they may desolate our country by arson and murder, in a word, that they may weigh you down with chains stained with the blood of those you hold most dear . . . .
The National Assembly declares that the country is in danger . . . .[180]

The contrasts are greater than the parallels. Louis XIV appeals to "the French name" perhaps, but the relevant pronouns are always "I" and "my" as the king pleads his case. The other speaks of the *people's* political ideals, material welfare, and personal survival, in which the pronoun switches to "you" and "your" as it insists that the people's own interests are at stake.

Louis's propaganda effort seems to have precipitated little sacrifice for the defense of the realm. The only widespread act of self-denial that caught the public attention was the elite's donation of silver and gold plate to be melted down in order to coin new money for the war effort. Actually, this began before the publication of the letter to the governors. An order of council dated 8 June 1709 dealt with reimbursement of those who gave their silver to the mint.[181] However, this sacrifice of luxury gained momentum with the publication of the 12 June letter. Chamillart reported to Villars, "The people have not been less indignant than the soldiers at the conditions that the enemy wants to force the king to accept . . . . The majority of the lords of the country here have sent their plates and utensils to the mint and offered to the king all that he could take. His Majesty, to set the example, has sent there all his golden vessels, even the new ones."[182]

But this sacrifice was not as great as might at first be supposed. In regards to the donation of silver vessels, Noailles commented in his memoirs, "There remained few French, especially at court, who had the zeal and the courage of patriotism."[183] The actual take, though considerable, was certainly not enough to float the war effort. The *contrôleur général* composed a list of those who contributed precious metals to the Paris mint, including the value of

---

[180] Declaration of 11 July 1792 in Jean-Paul Bertaud, *Valmy: La démocratie en armes* (Paris: 1970), 7.

[181] Saint-Simon, *Mémoires*, 17:564. This ostentatious sacrifice was in fact initiated by the Duchesse de Gramont, who was out of favor at court and hoped to regain it by this act. Saint-Simon, *Mémoires*, 17:403–4.

[182] 9 June 1709 letter from Chamillart to Villars in Vault, 9:302. See, as well, Villars, *Mémoires*, 3:49.

[183] Duc de Noailles, *Mémoires du duc de Noailles*, 3 vols., in A. Petitôt and Monmerqué, *Collection des mémoires relatifs à l'histoire de France*, vols. 71–73 (Paris: 1828), 72:451.

their donations through the end of August 1709.[184] It contains the names of only seventy-six individuals, including the king. The total value of what was turned in was calculated at 1,489,343 livres, of which Louis contributed 296,953 – tidy sums, to be sure, but they must be put in context of war budgets that ran about 100 million livres per annum. What is more, the king announced his intention to return, at some future time, the value of the silver to those who donated plate. In addition, this sacrifice, limited as it was, was not unprecedented. Louis made a similar call for precious metal during the previous war, in December 1689, and this earlier effort gained 3 million livres, apparently more than that produced in 1709.[185]

How far beyond the silver donation went the public willingness to support the war? That is hard to say. Resolved to supply his army by any means necessary, Villars sent his troops to requisition grain in the late spring of 1709: "I have thus been forced to levy impositions in the towns of Flanders and in Artois, and I hope that they will assure us [food for] the month of June."[186] This precipitated popular protests, not support.[187] Giving evidence of reluctance to sacrifice for the war effort, the parish of Femy protested during the winter of 1709–10, when its lands were foraged by French cavalry: "it was forbidden for troops to touch the grain and forage of parishes of old France."[188]

Even more than the mobilization of material, the mobilization of manpower says much about the power of patriotism. Those who claim that 1709 was a great patriotic war see the War of the Spanish Succession as the greatest mobilization of manpower under Louis XIV. But as already discussed in Chapter 2, the army of 1709 was not the largest Louis raised; rather, it was considerably smaller than that created to fight the Nine Years' War, and in no way did it approach the number of men mobilized by revolutionary France in 1792–94. The belief that Louis's army was so large in 1709 is in part founded on the notion that it was swamped by enthusiastic volunteers.[189] As evidence of this idea, some refer to the fact that many recruits offered to sign up for reduced bounties or even without bounties. But this fact is best explained not by patriotism but by the famine that drove men into the army to find a crust of bread, just as was the case during the famine of 1694.

At base, then, there is scant evidence to suggest that the crisis of 1709–11

---

[184] AN, G⁷ 1435, dated end of August 1709, "Etat des vaisselles et matières d'or et d'argent apportés à la Monnoie des médailles pour être employée en nouvelle espèces à la Monnoie de Paris," attached as an appendix to Saint-Simon, *Mémoires*, 17:566–68.

[185] Rousset, *Louvois*, 4:377–79; Dangeau, *Journal*, 3:38, entry for 12 December 1689.

[186] Villars, *Mémoires*, 3:46. In a high-handed move, he broke into the warehouses of the *munitionnaires* to seize goods necessary for his army. Sturgill, *Marshal Villars*, 85.

[187] Sourches. *Mémoires du marquis de Sources*, vols. 11 (Paris: 1891), 325, 28 April 1709.

[188] AG, A¹2266, #56, 14 January 1710, letter from Ormesson.

[189] See statements concerning a wave of volunteers in Corvisier, *Armies and Societies*, 69, 133, 134; Chandler, *Marlborough as a Military Commander*, 245; and even the popular historian Nancy Mitford, *The Sun King* (London: 1966), 225.

brought a great war of patriotic defense. It remains a major clash of dynasties. It is worth noting that when the dust cleared, all that Louis had achieved at great cost was a crushing royal debt, essentially the *status quo ante* for French borders, and the throne of Spain for his grandson, Philippe d'Anjou.

THE ARMY AND THE EMERGENCE OF PATRIOTISM

Perhaps a desire to explain bravery propels Corvisier in a doubtful direction. There is no denying the suffering and heroism of French troops, but as suggested in this chapter, it may be explained more by traditional and military loyalties than by appeals to patriotism.

The problem of trying to force French soldiers into a patriotic mold in 1709, or at any time during the *grand siècle*, is that it distorts the army's relationship to the growth of national sentiment. More than benefiting from an existing legacy of patriotism, the army of the *grand siècle* was itself a creator of a national sentiment that it bequeathed to the France of later generations. Corvisier himself comes close to arguing this at times. When he discussed participation in that war, Corvisier had a second and better point than his emphasis on patriotic sentiment in the ranks. He claimed that the military experience itself served "to reinforce national cohesion."[190]

The fires of war drew together Frenchmen from all over the kingdom and welded them into one great institution . . . and one great people. This was more nation formation than state formation, and it may ultimately have been the greatest political contribution of the state commission army. Despite the fact that they sometimes bore provincial names, French regiments were not recruited from single areas, with the exception of the *milices* of the Nine Years' War. Instead, the army brought in soldiers from a variety of regional origins, so that it became a French melting pot. During Louis's last two wars, the monarchy maintained large armies that taught ordinary people that they had something in common with their fellows who lived hundreds of miles away in very different circumstances (i.e., that they were all French). Moreover, the change from home to the front, the moves from winter quarters to campaign, and the shifting of units from one front to another, all forced many common soldiers to travel broad sweeps of France that they never would have visited had they not been in uniform.

If the crisis of 1709 was not the great national defense of 1792–94, that later conflict owed its character to the fact that the Bourbon monarchy had been mobilizing the French people *en masse* for its wars since the seventeenth century. In the words of Fernand Braudel, "Along with the monarchy, the army thus became the most active tool in *la formation unitaire* of France."[191]

---

[190] Corvisier, *L'Armée française*, I:105.
[191] Ferdinand Braudel, *L'identité de la France, I: Espace et histoire* (Paris: 1986), 338.

✦

PART FIVE

THE PRACTICE OF WAR

14

Weapons and Tactics

CANNON fire deafened those near the guns with a noise more felt than heard. Its thundering voice rendered words useless, as the balls that spewed from the cannons' mouths overwhelmed the opposing ranks, smashing, severing, gutting. Men fell silent in death. After each piece roared, recoil drove the gun back, and crews sprang forward to ready the gun to speak again. Emblazoned on each cannon were the words, "Ultima Ratio Regis," the final argument of the king. In a perfect age, logic might settle disputes, but the seventeenth century was not such an age. And Louis's eloquence spoke with iron and fire.

So much of the conversation between states has come down to combat. It may not be a pleasant fact, but a fact it remains. And combat comes down to tactics. Tactics bore most historians; even those who express an interest in the institutional history of the army have limited tolerance for the details of combat. Why worry about the minutiae of the military art? After all, the peasant historian or the labor historian pays little attention to the way in which the plowman harnessed his horse or the way in which a printer set his type, for so much of those historians' questions have to do with the grievances, organization, and actions of their subjects on the social, economic, and political plane. Ultimately, the social historian is usually much more concerned about the way in which his or her subjects affected the world around them than in the way in which they did their work. However, the impact of a soldier upon the great social, economic, and political drama of war flowed directly from the details of his profession. Territories changed hands; political fates were made and unmade on the basis of his performance on the field – how he loaded and fired, how he rode in the charge, how handy he was at his cannon.

Combat defined the soldier in the most profound manner. It was unique. For the worker, his or her work might form a basic fact of his or her life, but by its very nature, peaceful labor rarely could be so encompassing as combat

was. Few civilian occupations so consumed and regulated a person's life.
And only for the soldier were danger and death such constant companions
at his task. How he stood in ranks, how he brought his weapon to bear, and
how he fired and reloaded spoke not only of his manual dexterity and professional skill but of his courage.

This chapter deals with the building blocks of combat – weaponry, unit
organization, and tactics. The tools of war provide the means and limitations
that affect every other aspect of combat. The marshaling of men in companies, battalions, squadrons, and regiments defined the playing pieces for the
deadly game, for war was not an affair of individuals but of groups. Armed
and organized, men could then apply the tactical doctrines and practices
commanded by their officers and sanctified by their era.

A close study of weapons and tactics reveals change, but, in common with
much of the institutional development during the *grand siècle*, this change
proceeded at a pace better described as evolutionary than revolutionary.
Although so much of current debate concerns various theories of a "Military
Revolution" that swept Europe at some point during the early modern
epoch, that is not the perspective of this discussion. French tactical change
was not as much a response to the adoption of any new weapon as it was the
product of a growing appreciation of firepower over cold steel, the *arme
blanche*. In the infantry, this drove the steady decline of the pike until it was
no longer useful and eventually was abandoned, or more properly shrank to
the bayonet, a vestigial pike. In this, as in so many things, the seventeenth
century worked out the technological implications of sixteenth-century innovations. Some authors have dismissed the late seventeenth and early eighteenth centuries as technologically and tactically unexciting; however, once
the entire *grand siècle* is recast as evolutionary, the Nine Years' War and the
War of the Spanish Succession do not appear as static, although, to be sure,
the French seem to have lost something of their tactical edge after 1700.

INFANTRY WEAPONS AND TACTICS

Infantry comprised the largest element of the French army; by the Nine
Years' War, foot soldiers made up fully four fifths of the army as a whole and
over two thirds of field forces.[1] Infantry provided not only the bulk but the
base for military action. In the omnipresent siege warfare of the age, they
carried out the attack, while cavalry simply isolated the fortress as best it
could. In field battles, which were more rare, cavalry played a conspicuous
role, but infantry still provided the foundation of combat, forming the main
battle lines from which the more mobile horsemen sallied forth. Any understanding of the French army of the *grand siècle* as a fighting force must begin
with its infantry.

Soldiers of the seventeenth century put a premium on heavy, or line,

[1] AN, G⁷1774, piece 52.

infantry, the fully equipped foot troops who manned the siege trenches and stood rigidly in the line of battle. Light infantry, which might skirmish as individuals and fight effectively over broken terrain during battle, were less common. They had played a greater role before 1659, and Turenne continued to employ skirmishers until his death, but in general, the importance of light infantry declined during the personal reign of Louis XIV, particularly in his last two wars.[2] So completely was light infantry eclipsed that the French had virtually to rediscover it in the eighteenth century. There were exceptions; partisan warfare always used infantry outside the confines of siege and battle. And in the mountainous terrain of the Pyrenees, the French repeatedly employed local light infantry, *miquelets*. Circa 1690, the French maintained eighteen companies of these troops, also known as *fusiliers de la montagne*.[3] *Miquelets* proved so effective that the *intendant* in the Cévennes even requested them to fight the Camisard rebels in 1702–4.[4]

Within the line infantry, *grenadiers* stood out as a particular elite. As the name implies, they were originally intended to hurl grenades at the enemy. The infantry grenade of the seventeenth century was a small hollow metal shell filled with gunpowder and fired with a wick. Such primitive grenades proved their value in siege warfare when troops sought shelter in trenches, which limited the value of musketry. Grenades were already in widespread use for siege warfare during the sixteenth century, and they continued to be employed in great numbers under Louis XIV.[5] In a 1666 list of ammunition that Le Tellier wanted amassed in magazines, he called for 140,000 two-pound grenades.[6] These bombs could also be potent against cavalry when pitched at the horses' feet, as d'Aurignac advocated in his treatise of 1663.[7] The grenade dictated that grenadiers carry particular arms and wear distinctive dress. They were among the first troops to receive flintlock weapons, and they also carried hatchets to be used against obstacles in siege warfare.[8] In order to throw a grenade, a grenadier had to sling his weapon across his back, which made wearing the usual broad brimmed headgear impossible, since the weapon would knock it off his head, so grenadiers donned caps, which eventually became the tall ornate affairs of the eighteenth century. Chosen for height and strength among the best soldiers, grenadiers claimed special status.

[2] Jean Colin, *L'infanterie au XVIIIe siècle: La tactique* (Paris: 1907), 20, 30.
[3] Victor Belhomme, *L'armée française en 1690* (Paris: 1895), 71–72.
[4] Jean-Joseph Vaissète, *Histoire génénale de Languedoc*, 15 vols. (Toulouse: 1874–92), 14:col. 1620. My thanks to my graduate student, Roy McCullough, for bringing this to my attention.
[5] Louis Susane, *Histoire de l'infanterie française*, vol. 1 (Paris: 1876), 200, dated the first use of hand grenades as the siege of Arles in 1536.
[6] List in Louis André, *Michel Le Tellier et l'organisation de l'armée monarchique* (Paris: 1906), 520.
[7] Paul Azan, *Un tacticien du XVIIe siècle* (Paris: 1904), 91. This is an edited version of a military treatise by d'Aurignac written in 1693.
[8] For a description of their equipment see the *Military Dictionary* of 1702 in David Chandler, *The Art of Warfare in the Age of Marlborough* (New York: 1976), 68.

A final category of line infantry, *fusiliers*, specialized in supporting and serving the artillery. They received their name from the fact that well before the normal line infantry, fusiliers carried the flintlock fusil in place of the matchlock musket, since their fusils proved handier and safer around barrels of gunpowder. So linked were fusiliers to the artillery, that they eventually merged with the gunners into the Regiment Royal Artillerie. Infantry or artillery fusiliers should be distinguished from armed bands of "fusiliers" used to support tax collectors in the period before the personal reign of Louis XIV; these latter units were not part of the army. (See the epilogue for a discussion of the *fusiliers des tailles*.)

Infantry Weaponry

To begin with the basics, the primary tools of war wielded by the French infantry were the pike and musket, later replaced by the fusil and bayonet. Common in the sixteenth century, pike and musket continued to evolve significantly in the seventeenth century. The fundamental tactical problem inherited by the infantry was the proper mating of shock and missile weapons, of pike and shot, to create the most effective military force. The fusil and bayonet would eventually eliminate this problem in the closing decades of the *grand siècle* by uniting both forms of weapons in a single instrument; however, their use did not profoundly alter tactics before 1715.[9] To these basic weapons, the soldier usually added a sword, which was particularly valuable in pike and musket days, since the pike was useless against an enemy at arm's length, and the musket was almost equally impotent after it had been fired. But the sword was secondary to the pike and musket or fusil and bayonet.

THE PIKE

The pike was the simplest of weapons, essentially a long spear. In the hands of Swiss infantry, the pike dominated continental battlefields in the late Middle Ages, and this primitive but effective weapon retained its value through the 1600s. Montecuccoli still considered it the "queen of the infantry."[10] The pike owed its deadly character to the length of the weapon and to the cohesiveness of the body of men who wielded it. Swiss pikes of the previous century towered a full eighteen feet, but over time, the pike lost some of its length. The fact that cavalry abandoned the lance for the pistol and sword allowed the infantry to shorten their own weapons. Circa 1666, the French pike was about fourteen feet in length and may have shrunk to less than that

---

[9] Jeremy Black incorrectly argues that the flintlock and bayonet combination rapidly transformed warfare at the end of the seventeenth century and the first decades of the eighteenth. See his *A Military Revolution? Military Change and European Society, 1550–1800* (Atlantic Highlands, NJ: 1991), and *European Warfare, 1660–1815* (New Haven, CT: 1994), 7, 38–41.

[10] Montecuccoli in Brent Nosworthy, *The Anatomy of Victory: Battle Tactics, 1689–1763* (New York: 1990).

during or after the Dutch War.[11] This weapon bristled with an iron point and was girded with metal strips down for a yard or so from the point to prevent swordsmen from hacking off its lethal tip. An iron cap on the butt protected the end.

Its great length allowed the pikes of men in rear ranks to protrude well in front of the formation, so that a solid block of infantry with pikes lowered threatened its enemy with a hedgehog of steel points. On the offensive, pikemen leveled their weapons, grasping them with both hands somewhere near the balance point, and lumbered toward the foe, moving at a measured pace in order to maintain cohesion and alignment. On the defensive, static infantry grounded their pikes – that is, the pikeman jammed the butt of his pike in the earth and leaned the weapon forward at its full length while supporting the pike with one hand and stepping on the butt to ensure that it did not budge. This was particularly useful against cavalry, since the ground, not the pikemen, would absorb the impetus of horse and rider.

The pike had been a great force on the attack in the sixteenth century, but it became more and more a defensive weapon in the seventeenth. Gustavus Adolphus briefly restored the pike to the offensive in the Swedish Army, but this aggressive use of the weapon seems to have died with him. However, the pike's ability to hold off cavalry was crucial to infantry, for musketeers were nearly helpless at resisting a shock attack without pikemen. Because of the weight and awkwardness of the weapon and of the armor sported by pikemen, they were chosen from among the tallest and strongest men of a battalion and received a higher rate of pay.

By the late seventeenth century, the pike seemed archaic and ineffectual to many. As the number of pikemen decreased, they could no longer defend their comrades from cavalry. Puységur reported that by the Dutch War, musketeers standing on the flanks of the shrinking core of pikemen were invariably run down in battle.[12] Vauban consistently opposed the continued use of the pike. In 1687, saying that he had fought against the weapon for decades, he claimed, "Of twenty occasions in which a battalion finds itself, it might cross pikes with an enemy perhaps only three times . . . . Yet in each one of those twenty cases a fire fight takes place in which the battalion would be a third or a fourth more effective if those carrying pikes had firearms instead."[13]

---

[11] Plate from Denis Diderot, *Encyclopédie*, reproduced as plate 12 in Philippe Contamine, ed., *Histoire militaire de la France*, vol. 1 (Paris: 1992). This shows a scale drawing of a "pique suivant l'ordonnance du 16 November 1666." As drawn, the pike is 14 feet 6 inches from the tip of the blade to the end of the butt. Jacques-François de Chastenet de Puységur, *Art de la guerre par règles et principes*, 2 vols. (Paris: 1748), 1:56, states that the pikes were 14 feet long. J. W. Wijn, "Military Forces and Warfare, 1610–1648," in *New Cambridge Modern History*, vol. 4 (Cambridge: 1971), 215, and Frank Tallett, *War and Society in Early Modern Europe* (London: 1992), 21, give the length of pikes in the seventeenth century as 13 feet.

[12] Puységur, *Art de la guerre*, 1:69–70.

[13] Vauban to Louvois, 21 December 1687, in Albert Rochas d'Aiglun, *Vauban, sa famille et ses écrits*, 2 vols. (Paris: 1910), 2:286.

At this time, even Louvois, though a tactical conservative, questioned if pikes were still worth carrying, since they "occupy [His Majesty's] best soldiers."[14] In battle, pikemen might change weapons on their own initiative. At Steinkirke, 3 August 1692, the majority of French pikemen discarded their weapons to pick up the fusils of fallen enemies.[15] It would, however, require another decade until the French army completely abandoned the pike in the winter of 1703–4.[16]

THE MUSKET AND THE FUSIL

At the start of the *grand siècle*, the musket was the basic firearm of the infantry. The term *musket* has become something of a generic term for any muzzle-loading weapon, but the word must be used with greater precision here. A musket was a smooth bore, muzzle-loading, shoulder arm. It fired by means of a matchlock, which ignited the powder with a lighted "match," a cord of flax or hemp soaked in a nitrate solution so that it would smolder, much like a modern cigarette. When the soldier had loaded his weapon, he clamped the glowing match to the end of a short cock. When he pulled the trigger, this cock snapped back thrusting the glowing match into a small pan of powder mounted on the barrel of the weapon. When this priming charge exploded, it flashed though a small hole bored into the chamber of the barrel and set off the main charge that then propelled the lead ball toward its mark. Although the musket ball could carry 250 yards or further, aimed fire was effective only to about eighty yards.[17] The complicated loading procedure limited the rate of fire to one shot per minute, and even then, the rate of misfire could be as high as 50 percent.[18]

The musket was not the only popular matchlock in use, but it was the heaviest, at least early in the century. About 1600, a lighter and older weapon, the arquebus or caliver, also saw service. Whereas the musket fired a ball of as much as two ounces, the standard arquebus shot a projectile weighing only one ounce, which also required a smaller powder charge.[19] Weighing

[14] Louvois to Chamlay, 8 September 1689, AG, A¹875, in Camille Rousset, *Histoire de Louvois*, 4 vols. (Paris: 1862–64), 3:330. "I ask you to inform yourself if it is true that the enemy troops have no pikes; for it is important, in that case, that His Majesty takes a position on pikes that occupy his best soldiers."

[15] Louis XIV to marshal Luxembourg, 12 August 1692, in Louis XIV, *Oeuvres de Louis XIV*, Philippe Grimoard and Grouvelle, eds., 6 vols. (Paris: 1806), 4:396–97.

[16] Puységur, *Art de la guerre*, 1:51, 57; Louis, *Oeuvres*, 4:396–97fn.

[17] Exact figures for musket accuracy are hard to find. The Prussians tested smoothbore flintlocks, which ballistically were the same as the earlier matchlocks, during the Napoleonic era and found that a smoothbore could hit a "large target" 75 percent of the time at eighty yards. At 120 yards, the smoothbore could hit a "small target" 50 percent of the time, but at 160 yards, accuracy fell to only 25 percent. Peter Paret, *Yorck and the Era of Prussian Reform, 1807–1815* (Princeton: 1966), 272–73.

[18] Chandler, *The Art of Warfare*, 76–77.

[19] Wijn, "Military Forces and Warfare," 215, gives the weight of a standard musket ball, 1610–48, as twelve to a pound, or 1.5 ounces.

from fifteen to twenty pounds, the heavier, longer, musket required a forked rest to support the barrel during firing; the arquebus, at about twelve pounds, did not. The arquebus per se disappeared from French service in the 1620s.[20]

Yet by midcentury, the French had opted for a lighter version of the musket than that wielded by their enemies; in fact, their musket approached the arquebus in some ways, weighing only about thirteen pounds by late century. As the musket became lighter, the forked rest became less essential and was finally discarded altogether.[21] The diversity of musket calibers by the end of the war with Spain had become a major problem, since some muskets were too small to accommodate the lead balls supplied to the troops. In an effort to standardize weapons, Louis XIV decreed ordinances during 1666–70 prescribing that French muskets should be of no less a caliber than the size of a lead ball twenty to a pound.[22] Although some believed that this weapon shot too small a projectile, the French retained this caliber throughout the rest of the *grand siècle*.[23] By ordinance, the barrel of these weapons had to measure at least 3 feet 7 inches from touch-hole to muzzle.[24] These prescriptions did not eliminate at a stroke the troublesome diversity of French weapons, which continued at least into the Dutch War.[25]

The fusil gradually replaced the musket from midcentury on. Instead of employing a lit match, a fusil relied upon flint striking steel to generate the spark needed to ignite the gun powder in the priming pan. When the soldier pulled the trigger, the flintlock mechanism drove forward the cock, or hammer, which held a piece of flint, which then struck a vertical iron plate, called a *frizzen*. This plate also acted as a cover over the priming pan. The impact of the flint striking the frizzen snapped it up, exposing the priming powder just as the sparks generated from the blow fell. There was no awkward match to handle, and once loaded, the weapon could be carried or slung, leaving the hands free for other tasks. For men detailed to throw grenades or manhandle artillery, this advantage was great. But the most important plus came simply from the elimination of the match, which might inadvertently set off grenades or powder kegs. To appreciate the complications imposed by loading,

[20] Contamine, *Histoire militaire*, 1:340.

[21] See the contemporary price list of clothing and equipment in Belhomme, *L'armée française en 1690*, 26, on which no forked rest is listed.

[22] SHAT, Bib., Col. des ord., vol. 21, #164, 16 November 1666 ordinance on weapons. This would mean that he would fire a ball slightly smaller than that.

[23] Early in the War of the Spanish Succession, some critics argued that the French caliber of twenty to twenty-two balls to a pound was too small to load properly. Victor Belhomme, *Histoire de l'infanterie en France*, 5 vols. (Paris: 1893–1902), 2:362.

[24] SHAT, Col. des ord., vol. 21, #164, 16 November 1666 ordinance on weapons. *Ordonnances militaires du roy de France reduites en practique*, 2 vols. (Luxembourg: 1734–35), 1:172–73.

[25] AG, A¹209, #138, 18 August 1667, état of munitions sent from Arras to army shows two calibers of balls, twenty-four per pound and thirty-three per pound; perhaps the smaller was for pistols. AG, A¹295, #220, 26 October 1672, complains of "the boulonnais compagnie, being only peasants without swords and having only bad fusils of different lengths and of different calibers that the balls supplied will not serve."

observe the illustrations of de Gheyn's drill manual of 1607, or its imitators. De Gheyn shows thirty-three steps to the loading and firing of a musket.[26] The musketeer had to detach the match from the musket after each firing, blow on it to keep it lit, and hold it and the body of the musket in his left hand, being careful to keep it out of contact with the gunpowder, as he primed and loaded with his right hand. The movements required all the precision of ballet in order to avoid disaster. None of this bother and worry attended the fusil, since its flint only generated sparks as it hit the frizzen; before that moment, it was benign. Also, imagine the fate of a musketeer who had put his weapon down to perform other tasks and suddenly needed to fire at a surprise enemy. Even if the musket was loaded, its match would not have been attached, and probably not even lit; the musket would be virtually useless.

In contrast, a fusilier could load in a third less movements, since he need not worry about the match.[27] He could prime and load his fusil, set it on half-cock safety, sling or stack the weapon, and still be instantly ready to fire the moment he seized the weapon, pulled back the hammer, and brought it to bear. No wonder that Feuquières stated that although the musket was mechanically simpler than the fusil, using the former was "infinitely more embarrassing."[28] Some historians argue that the rate of fire doubled because of the simpler loading procedure, but it would appear that French soldiers took about a minute to load either musket or fusil.[29] The slower French rate may have resulted from the fact that the French were late to adopt the use of paper cartridges. Most authorities agree that the number of misfires fell sharply, to only about one in three attempts.[30]

However, the French fusil suffered in comparison to its counterparts because it shot a smaller and lighter projectile, just as did the French musket. Whereas the English "William III" fusil had a bore of .85 inches, that of the contemporary French fusil measured only .68 inches.[31] The lighter projectile was less likely to render its target *hors de combat*.[32]

Before the Nine Years' War, Vauban opposed the matchlock and favored the fusil because it produced fewer misfires and because a glowing smoking match made surprise difficult and night action almost impossible, but even

---

[26] Jacob de Gheyn, *The Exercise of Armes*, ed. David J. Blackmore (London: 1986).

[27] Corvisier says the number of movements fell from thirty-six to twenty-three. Contamine, *Histoire militaire*, 1:409. Chandler writes that the reduction was from forty-four in 1690 to twenty-six for the fusil. *The Art of Warfare in the Age of Marlborough*, 76–77.

[28] Feuquières in André, *Le Tellier*, 354.

[29] Chandler, *The Art of Warfare in the Age of Marlborough*, 77.

[30] Chandler, *The Art of Warfare in the Age of Marlborough*, 77.

[31] See the table comparing infantry weapons in Chandler, *The Art of Warfare in the Age of Marlborough*, 137. Belhomme states that the French musket and fusil fired a ball weighing eighteen to the pound at this time. Given the other sources, this seems too heavy. Belhomme, *L'armée française en 1690*, 22.

[32] The contemporary Robert Parker believed so; see Chandler, *The Art of Warfare in the Age of Marlborough*, 77.

more dangerous was the fact that there were "a thousand fire accidents because of the match."[33] An awkward gesture with the match in the presence of black powder could prove injurious or fatal. Since a musketeer carried his measured charges of gunpowder in small flasks hanging from a bandolier across his chest, he was almost a walking bomb. Harford, an Englishman, wrote concerning the danger of bandoleers and careless matches: "When they take fire they commonly would wound and kill him who wears them and those near him; for likely, if one bandolier takes fire, all the rest do in the collar [portion of the musketeer *manche*]."[34]

It would seem that during the Nine Years' War, but certainly no later than the onset of the War of the Spanish Succession, the bandolier gave way to the leather cartridge box, *cartouche*, which contained charges of loose powder contained in tin tubes. Regulations of 1703 and 1704 required that the infantry carry cartridge boxes containing powder for ten rounds, plus another ten rounds worth of powder in a flask and a sack of lead balls.[35]

Eventually, the French adopted cartridges that were measured amounts of powder along with a ball wrapped together in paper. To load, the soldier tore the paper with his teeth, primed the pan, poured the rest down the barrel, and then rammed the ball down with the paper to wad it. The greatest advantage of the paper cartridge is that it speeded loading; using it and an iron ramrod, Prussian infantry could fire four to five rounds per minute by the mid–eighteenth century, and less able armies achieved rates of fire of two or three rounds per minute.[36] The French experimented with paper cartridges as early as 1677, but they only became regular issue in the 1730s.[37]

Slowly, the French integrated fusils into their armory. The first fusil was invented circa 1630 in Italy, and the French army contained units of fusiliers in the early 1640s, when both Cardinal Richelieu and Louis XIII had regiments of mounted fusiliers in their service.[38] For some time, Louis XIV favored the musket over the fusil and resisted its adoption by French infantry. Only in 1670 did he approve the inclusion of four fusiliers in every infantry company.[39] Permission to add fusiliers to the company probably did

---

[33] Vauban to Louvois, 21 December 1687, in Rochas d'Aiglun, *Vauban*, 2:286.

[34] Harford, *Military Discipline* (ca. 1680) in Nosworthy, *Anatomy of Victory*, 17.

[35] Belhomme, *L'armée française en 1690*, 21–22, says that circa 1690, the soldier carried only enough powder and ball for fifteen shots. Regulations of 8 March 1703 and 22 January 1704 in Belhomme, *Histoire de l'infanterie en France*, 2:396.

[36] Chandler, *The Art of Warfare*, 105.

[37] Contamine, *Histoire militaire*, 1:409; Chandler, *The Art of Warfare in the Age of Marlborough*, 77; Rousset, *Louvois*, 3:325–26fn. Quimby states that the paper cartridge was finally adopted by the French in 1744. Robert S. Quimby, *The Background of Napoleonic Warfare* (New York: 1957), 80. Earlier, in 1740, they replaced wooden ramrods, which bound and broke, with iron ramrods, in order to speed up loading. Colin, *L'infanterie au XVIIIe siècle*, 52.

[38] André, *Le Tellier*, 353. Caillet states that a regiment of *fusiliers à cheval* was created for Richelieu in 1640 and one for the king in 1643. Jules Caillet, *De l'adminstration en France sous le ministère du Cardinal de Richelieu* (Paris: 1857), 375.

[39] 6 February 1670 ordinance in Rousset, *Louvois*, 1:191.

not so much express royal approval of the newer firearm as demonstrate a desire to add grenadiers to the infantry. The four fusil-armed soldiers would be better able to throw bombs than would their musket-impeded comrades. When entire grenadier companies were added, these, too, were totally armed with fusils.

By the time fusils came into the French armory, they were of the same size and caliber as the lighter French muskets.[40] At least from this point on, no ballistic difference separated the musket from the fusil. Late in the century, that master of military science, Vauban, presented the following results: "According to a number of experiments [*experiences*], many times repeated, it is found that a soldier can easily fire 30 shots in a half hour without being too hurried, with fusil or musket, assuming the weapons are in good condition. He could fire more if he was not required to clean the weapon periodically." Vauban calculated the extreme range of musket and fusil at about 400 yards, but this seems generous. In any case, at long range, only 20 percent of the balls struck their mark.[41]

Part of French reluctance to adopt the fusil can be put down to the conservative nature of Louis XIV and his minister of war, Louvois. The Sun King was much involved in the minutia of weaponry, as was his father before him.[42] The proven matchlock probably seemed a safer choice than the new and more complicated flintlock. Also, the expense of converting the army from muskets to fusils would be considerable, particularly after the army reached its full size during the Nine Years' War. Therefore, the longer the French remained loyal to the musket, the more costly it would be to abandon it. Not only did a fusil cost considerably more than a musket – 14 livres as opposed to 9 – but the French would have to purchase hundreds of thousands at one time.[43] Consequently, as late as 1688, Louis and Louvois insisted that the French infantryman remain armed as he was before.[44] However, combat in the Nine Years' War shook French resolution. After the battle of Steinkirke, Louis requested that the victorious French commander,

---

[40] 6 February 1670 ordinance in Rousset, *Louvois*, 1:191.

[41] Rochas d'Aiglun, *Vauban*, 1:166. Colin agrees that by 1700, the rate of fire was one shot per minute; however, this improved dramatically to about three shots per minute by 1750. Colin, *L'infanterie au XVIIIe siècle*, 26, 52. Wijn, "Military Forces and Warfare," 215, gives musket range, 1610–48, as 200 to 270 yards with the heavier bullet of the time.

[42] Louis XIII played with the designs of weapons, as was noted in the *Gazette de Renaudot*, 6 August 1632: "The next day, the king presented cardinal Richelieu with matchlock and wheellock muskets of his own invention, in order to arm the guards that the king had given the cardinal."

[43] For costs of arms and equipment in 1690, see Belhomme, *L'armée française en 1690*, 25–26. Corvisier sees this cost factor as explaining the halting conversion. André Corvisier, *Louvois* (Paris: 1983), 364–65. Corvisier, 194, states that Rousset and André said that Louvois was hostile to the fusil; Corvisier argues that his resistance was not so strong. André, *Le Tellier*, 354, says that the "great inconvenience" and "notable losses" would attend a conversion to fusils.

[44] AG, A¹807, 23 August 1688, letter to inspectors in Rousset, *Louvois*, 3:329fn.

Marshal Luxembourg, advise the king as to whether "it would be most useful to the good of the service either to have the infantry entirely armed with fusils or to leave them as it is."[45] Soon regulations increased the number of fusils in infantry battalions. With the return of peace, the ordinance of 15 December 1699 prescribed the universal adoption of the fusil in place of musket.[46] The army seems to have retained some muskets until about 1704.[47]

The tardy pace of French conversion was not unique. The Dutch changed over earlier than most, in 1692, but they had a smaller force to rearm and more funds to do it.[48] However, consider the English. Although they re-armed the guards regiments with fusils in the 1680s, revolution and war made a shambles of the attempt by James II to reequip his entire army with the new weapons in 1688.[49] In fact, by 1697, two English soldiers still carried muskets for every three that bore fusils, and as late as 1704, there were probably still some matchlocks in use by English troops.[50] The culprit that slowed conversion in both the French and English cases was more likely financial necessity than military stupidity. When one realizes that colonels and captains would personally have to bear expense for rearmament, the slow conversion becomes even more understandable.

Reluctance to convert involved more than simply financial constraints, however. Although many historians simply assume the better performance of the fusil, the French experienced many problems with early fusils, perhaps because they opted for such a light version of it. For them, the fusil proved more fragile than the musket. Catinat opposed fusils; he claimed in 1686 that he had to recall his grenadiers after one half hour because so many fusils malfunctioned.[51] Louvois also complained, "One ought not to be astonished if the grenadiers' fusils break down, since they were not made to sustain a great fire because the officers want them very light."[52] Vauban's answer to

---

[45] Letter of 12 August 1692, Louis XIV, *Oeuvres*, 4:396. Also see John B. Wolf, *Louis XIV* (New York: 1968), 471, and Rousset, *Louvois*, 3:330–31.

[46] Colin, *L'infanterie au XVIIIe siècle*, 26.

[47] Puységur, *Art de la guerre*, 1:57.

[48] Chandler, *The Art of Warfare*, 79. Colin claims that the Germans had gone over to fusils for pikes at the outset of the Nine Years' War. Colin, *L'infanterie au XVIIIe siècle*, 26.

[49] War Office Records, *Royal Warrant – Armament*, 28 June 1683; War Office Records, *Royal Warrant – Armament*, 26 January 1684; MacKinnon, *Origins and Services of the Coldstream Guards*, 1:167; His Majesties Order for Regulation of the Musters (London: 1686–87), 3; H. R. Knight, *Historical Records of the Buffs*, 1:267. All references from John M. Stapleton, "Importing the Military Revolution: William III, the Glorious Revolution, and the Rise of the Standing Army in Britain, 1688–1712," Master's thesis, Ohio State University, 1994. Mr. Stapleton has been kind enough to share his thesis and his references with me.

[50] Chandler, *The Art of Warfare*, 79.

[51] Luxembourg also wanted to retain a high percentage of muskets. Belhomme, *L'armée française en 1690*, 25.

[52] Louvois to Créqui, 22 May 1684, in Jacques Hardré, ed., *Letters of Louvois, University of North Carolina Studies in the Romance Languages and Literatures*, no. 10 (Chapel Hill: 1949), 448. There was a good deal of correspondence about the breakdown of French infantry weapons in May 1684. Vauban reported that about one third of the soldiers at the siege of

this problem was not to give up, but to beef up, the fusil. He suggested a "reinforced fusil," with a longer barrel and firing a larger ball.[53] So adamant was he to win adherents for the fusil that in 1671 he even invented a weapon fitted with two mechanisms, a matchlock and a flintlock, to overcome conservative fears while giving the troops the advantages of a flintlock.[54] The perfected fusil was much superior to the matchlock, but in the French case, the fusil was plagued by its share of bugs at the start.

THE BAYONET

About the same time that the French finally set aside the musket for the fusil, they also put down the pike for the bayonet. The introduction of the bayonet eventually reshaped infantry tactics, perhaps even more than did the conversion to the fusil. Never before or since has an edged weapon had such an impact on firepower. By replacing formations that mixed musketeers and pikemen with formations composed entirely of infantrymen bearing fusils tipped with bayonets, the French increased the number of men equipped to fire on the enemy without losing the shock potential of a charge with cold steel.

A desire to give the musket some shock value for defense and offense by turning it into a short but stout spear produced the plug bayonet about 1640.[55] Belhomme claims that the first French army to employ such a bayonet was the Army of Flanders in 1642.[56] Puységur described plug bayonets of the 1670s as "straight, double-edged blades a foot long with tapering handles also a foot long."[57] The plug fit down the barrel of the musket, meaning that when the bayonet was in place, the weapon could not be loaded or fired – a great disadvantage. Even with this limitation, the bayonet had considerable utility, and the Dutch War witnessed the first French bayonet charges.[58]

Before 1670, Vauban already dreamed of a bayonet "which could be so well accommodated to the end of the fusil that the bayonet would transform the fusil into a halberd while allowing the weapon to be loaded and fired as if the bayonet was not even there."[59] It was not until the late 1680s that he

---

Luxembourg were disarmed by bad weapons. Letter of 22 May in Rochas d'Aiglun, *Vauban*, 2:237. See, as well, Louvois's response to Vauban on 24 May, "It is difficult to remedy the inconvenience caused by the break down of weapons that one wants light in order to serve on campaign." Hardré, *Letters of Louvois*, 448.

[53] Rochas d'Aiglun, *Vauban*, 1:290. Vauban's "fusil renforcé" would have a four-foot barrel and a ball weighing eighteen to the pound. Its full length with bayonet would have been 6 feet 9 inches long.

[54] Corvisier, *Louvois*, 365. Also see Rousset, *Louvois*, 1:192–93 and 3:328. There were two versions of the matchlock/flintlock – the first 1671 and a second in 1684; the last was to be adopted in 1688, but war came. Belhomme, *L'armée française en 1690*, 23–24.

[55] André, *Le Tellier*, 344.   [56] Belhomme, *Histoire de l'infanterie en France*, 1:392.

[57] Puységur in Chandler, *The Art of Warfare*, 83.

[58] AG, A¹531, 18 March 1677, Louvois to Courtin, in Rousset, *Louvois*, 2:288.

[59] Vauban memoir of about 1669, in Rochas d'Aiglun, *Vauban*, 2:288n.

solved this problem by attaching the blade of the bayonet onto a socket that fit snugly around, not in, the muzzle of the firearm and which locked into place by keying into a lug mounted on the barrel. In December 1687, the advocate of the fusil became the patron of the socket bayonet, "a soldier, with a single arm, would have two of the best weapons in the world, a good fusil and a spontoon, with which he could fire and load quickly without removing the bayonet."[60] This took Louvois aback: "The king heard [your proposal] with great attention. However, I request that you explain to me how you can imagine a bayonet on the end of a musket that does not at all hinder firing and loading it."[61] If he was at first skeptical, he soon became a convert. In 1689, he instructed the infantry inspectors: "The king judges it proper that all the infantry that go on campaign have bayonets to mount on the end of their muskets or fusils, that will be mounted in such a way that they in no way hinder firing or loading if it is necessary."[62] A circular of 11 November 1692 stated that "The king's infantry in field battalions [*bataillons de campagne*] will be supplied with socket bayonets to put on the end of their fusils or muskets on the day of battle, His Majesty desires that you tell all captains in order that they will give bayonets to those of their soldiers who do not have them."[63]

There was a certain irony in the French adoption of the bayonet. Although it became the great symbol of French confidence in the superiority of the *arme blanche* over firepower, Vauban, a military realist, invented the socket bayonet precisely to increase French firepower by rearming pikemen with firearms. When Louis XIV looked to the battle of Steinkirke as evidence of the superiority of fusils, he also saw it as a test of the bayonet. If his infantry were "entirely armed with fusils," bayonets would have to replace pikes for shock action.[64] In reality, the bayonet represented the triumph of the fusil, of a superior firearm, although it is remembered as an expression of French offensive *élan*. When the bayonet allowed the French to abandon the pike, no longer did some troops rest on their pikes while others fired salvoes, for every soldier was now a fusilier without sacrificing the ability to close with cold steel.

Infantry Companies, Battalions, and Regiments

Infantry troops were organized into companies, battalions, and regiments. From the 1670s at least through the Nine Years' War, the French differentiated between infantry units intended for field duty and those meant to be

---

[60] Vauban letter to Louvois, dated 21 December 1687 in Rochas d'Aiglun, *Vauban*, 2:287–88.

[61] AG, A^{1}789, 25 December 1687, in Rousset, *Louvois*, 3:328.

[62] AG, A^{1}861, 29 November 1689, Louvois to inspectors, in Rousset, *Louvois*, 3:330fn. Corvisier dates the order to equip all infantry with bayonets as 29 December 1689. Corvisier, *Louvois*, 365.

[63] Belhomme, *Histoire de l'infanterie*, 2:313.

[64] Letter of 12 August 1692, Louis XIV, *Oeuvres*, 4:396.

Table 14.1. *Strengths of French field infantry companies.*

Date	Size	Date	Size
1610	35	1671–78	50
1620	100	1684	50
1630	200	1688–92	50
1635	100	1692–96	55
1651	40	1697	50
1660	50	1699	35
1668	100	1701	45
1669	80	1710	50
1670	70		

employed for garrison duty only. The two types differed in armament, size, and organization.

For both field and garrison troops, the lowest administrative unit was the company, commanded by its captain, who bore much of the detail and expense of its maintenance. As Table 14.1 demonstrates, company size fluctuated quite a bit over the course of the *grand siècle*, particularly before the Dutch War.[65] Garrison companies could be smaller than field companies, as in 1684, for example, when the former included only forty enlisted men, while field companies had fifty; however, the garrison companies equaled the size of field companies early in the Nine Years' War, when both stood at fifty. Soldiers in garrison units carried only muskets and fusils, having no pikes, which would have been useless on fortress walls.[66] When grenadier companies were added to French battalions, these elite companies were often smaller than line companies; in 1679, they mustered only thirty-five soldiers and in 1684, forty.

Foreign and guard companies differed in size from line companies. German infantry in French employ during the war with Spain were supposed to muster companies of 200 men when French units were smaller; during Louis XIV's personal reign, German companies claimed 100 men in the ranks, generally twice the size of French units.[67] Swiss regiments in French service

[65] Figures for number of soldiers in French infantry companies are nicely collected in tableaux on infantry units in AG, MR 1972, piece 7, and AG, Bib., A^lh 638. Unfortunately, these two sources are not always in accord. For the years 1635–60, see Bernard Kroener, *Les routes et les étapes*, 177–78; however, beware his low figures for the start of the war. Georges Girard, *Le service militaire en France à la fin du règne de Louis XIV: Rocolage et milice, 1701–1715*, (Paris: 1915), 4–7, supplies company size figures for December 1699 and, using a "Mémoire des trouppes que le roy a sur pied," for January 1702. For other later key figures, see AN, G⁷1774, piece 52; SHAT, Bib., Col. des ord., vol. 28, #38; and AG, MR 1701. See, as well, the discussions of unit size by such standard authors as Belhomme, Sicard, and Susane.

[66] On garrison companies, see Belhomme, *L'armée française en 1690*, 9–14. For sizes in 1684, see AN, G⁷1774, #52.

[67] For the strengths of German companies in French service, see David Parrott, "The Administration of the French Army During the Ministry of Cardinal Richelieu," Ph.D. dissertation, Oxford, 1985, 88–89; AN, G⁷1774, #52; and AG, MR 1701.

usually boasted companies of 200 men.[68] During the same period, companies of the Gardes françaises began at 150 in the 1660s, fell to 104 in the 1670s and 1680s, and then rose to 124 in the Nine Years' War and 144 in the War of the Spanish Succession. The Gardes suisses rose from 120 at the start of Louis's personal reign and stabilized at 200 from the 1670s on.[69]

Companies were not subdivided as they are today. The confusing word *peloton*, or platoon, did not mean what it means in modern military language; it could even be larger than a company. There were smaller subdivisions within the company, however. By regulation of 21 October 1661, each company was to be divided into three squads, which rotated on guard.[70]

Whereas companies were largely administrative entities, the battalion, composed of several companies, constituted the true tactical unit in battle. During the war with Spain, the number of companies that comprised a battalion seems to have varied considerably.[71] Louis XIV achieved greater regularity; early in his personal reign, French line infantry battalions usually included twelve companies.[72]

Before long, grenadier companies were added to French battalions. In 1667, Martinet selected four men to be grenadiers in each company of the Regiment du Roi, and in 1670, this experiment seemed so promising that these grenadiers were united into their own company; this move was soon repeated in other French regiments.[73] The number of companies increased to sixteen by the close of the Dutch War, making the theoretical strength of a battalion 800 men, although such figures must be discounted.[74] After the war, the number of companies settled at fifteen or sixteen.[75] At the start of the Nine Years' War, line infantry battalions boasted sixteen companies, yielding a battalion size of 800 once again, but this fell to thirteen companies and 715 enlisted soldiers late in the war. The number of companies remained the same for the War of the Spanish Succession, although a smaller company size at the start of the war reduced the paper strength of a battalion to only 585, officers excluded.[76] Again, guard and foreign battalions differed from French

---

[68] Swiss companies numbered 200 men each in 1679, 160 in 1684, 200 in 1696, 200 in 1699, and 200 in 1710. See the very detailed company counts for 1679, 1684, 1696, and 1699 in AN, G⁷1774, #52 and for 1710 in MR 1701.

[69] François Sicard, *Histoire des institutions militaires des français*, 4 vols. (1834), 2:69–70; AN, G⁷1774, #52; and AG, MR 1701.

[70] *Ordonnances militaires*, vol. 1, 2.

[71] See the tables in Bernard Kroener, "Die Entwicklung der Truppenstärken in den französischen Armeen zwischen 1635 end 1661," in Konrad Repgen, ed., *Forschungen und Quellen zur Geschichte des Dreissigjährigen Krieges* (Munster: 1981), 194–213.

[72] Rousset, *Louvois*, 1:221. [73] Rousset, *Louvois*, 1:222.

[74] AG, Arch. hist. 78, feuille 166–67. Puységur, *Art de la guerre*, 1:56–57, give the number of companies as seventeen, one of which was a grenadier company, but he states that battalions were 800 men and therefore composed of only sixteen companies. See, as well, his numbers for the last two wars of Louis XIV.

[75] Contamine, *Histoire militaire*, 1:412; and AG, Arch. hist. 78, feuille 166–67.

[76] For the actual number of companies in a serving infantry regiment during the last two wars of Louis XIV, see the *étapes* documents in BN, f. fr., 4565–67 and Amiens, EE 403, 405. At

line regiments; for example, the Gardes suisses battalions had but three companies apiece, but with companies of 200, their battalions numbered 600.

Regiments included one or more battalions. Infantry regiments appeared
in the sixteenth century when the duke of Guise created the first three in
1560.[77] Two years later, the French infantry were ranged in eleven regiments.[78]
The first regiments were temporary affairs, but from 1574, some became
permanent, Henri III having kept the Gardes françaises, Picardie, Piémont,
and Champagne on a permanent footing with a theoretical complement of
twelve companies. By Sicard's count, Henri IV added seven more permanent
regiments by 1604, and Louis XIII added another nineteen during his reign;
but the monarchy never ceased to create short-lived regiments in abundance
during wartime.[79] By 1665, the list of permanent infantry regiments had
grown to forty-nine.[80] At the height of the Dutch War in 1677, Louis fielded
104 infantry French and foreign infantry regiments, a number that climbed
to 126 regular regiments and 35 of milice in 1691 and reached 213 regulars and
44 milice by 1696.[81] At the peak of the War of the Spanish Succession in
1706, Louis maintained the huge total of 335 French foreign infantry regiments.[82] To be sure, the multiplication of infantry regiments during wartime
always brought with it the elimination of dozens of temporary regiments at
the end of a conflict.

In a society so jealous of status and in an army so moved by regimental
loyalty, it comes as little surprise that regiments feuded over questions of
honor and precedence. Different regiments boasted different pedigrees; a
few could trace their roots back to the sixteenth century, while many existed
only for a particular war. Pride inspired older corps to look down on younger
units, just as nobles from ancient families despised parvenus. With his passion for order, Louis XIV resolved "to remove all the subjects of dispute that
had so often caused disorder in our troops . . . all the different pretensions
that each corps maintained with such intensity."[83] In order to forestall needless controversy, the monarchy officially set the precedence of regiments.
Louis André praises two ordinances of 1 April 1654 as decisive in establishing

their inception in 1688, the milice battalions had ten to twenty companies, half having fifteen
companies each. Jacques Gebelin, *Histoire des milices provinciales* (Paris: 1882), 37.

[77] F. Reboul, "Des croisades à la Révolution," in Gabriel Hanoteau, ed. *Histoire de la nation
française*, vol. 7, *Histoire militaire et navale*, vol. 1 (Paris: 1925), 261. Not all the standard works
agree; see Sicard, *Histoire des institutions militaires,* for a somewhat different version, 2:197.

[78] Reboul, "Des croisades à la Révolution," 262.

[79] Sicard, *Histoire des institutions militaires*, 2:197–200.

[80] AG, Arch. hist. 78, feuille 165. This apparently counts the guards regiments. A list of regiments for 1665–66 in Sicard, 2:202, shows forty-six regiments, exclusive of guards.

[81] Belhomme, *Histoire de l'infanterie*, 2:206–7, 296–97, 328–29.

[82] Belhomme, *Histoire de l'infanterie*, 2:422–23; AG, MR 1701, #13, states that in 1710, there were
235 French and forty-one foreign infantry regiments, at a time when Belhomme's numbers
were 290 and fifty-one, respectively, 2:466.

[83] Louis XIV, *Mémoires de Louis XIV pour l'instruction du dauphin*, Charles Dreyss, ed., 2 vols.
(Paris: 1860), 1:241.

rank among infantry regiments and claims that later ordinances of 1666 and 1670 simply restated and reshuffled the earlier directives.[84] At the top of the final hierarchy were the guard regiments, the Gardes françaises and the Gardes suisses. Then followed the old regiments, the *vieux corps*: Picardie, Piémont, Champagne, Navarre, Normandie, and the Regiment de la Marine. They were followed in honor by the six *petits vieux* regiments: Feuquières, Bourbonnais, Auvergne, Sault, Baubecourt, and the Regiment du Roi. The last enjoyed precedence not because of its lineage but because it was the king's private regiment. After the *vieux* and *petits vieux*, other regiments were ranked in the order of their creation. Despite this neat system, controversies still disturbed the army; for example, Piémont, Champagne, and Navarre continually quarreled over which of them really ranked second among the *vieux*.

Regiments varied greatly in size, depending on how many battalions they contained. During the Dutch War, the majority of French regiments included three battalions.[85] Later, the more prestigious regiments with acknowledged precedence in the army boasted much larger establishments, particularly at the start of the Nine Years' War. Then, the Gardes françaises contained six field battalions, while Picardie comprised 210 companies grouped in two field battalions and about fifteen garrison battalions, and Champagne, Piedmont, and Navarre each had two field battalions and about thirteen garrison battalions.[86] But financial necessity doomed the king to turn away from large regiments and create many small new regiments in order to tap the wealth of the new and ambitious colonels; this explains the huge surge in the number of regiments in his last two wars. In 1710, the Gardes françaises still had six battalions, but of the other French infantry regiments, only one had five battalions, one had four, and eleven had three; the rest had only two battalions or a single battalion (101 and 120 regiments, respectively).[87]

The Numbers of Muskets, Pikes, and Fusils in Infantry Companies

The composition of the battalion was not just a matter of how many men stood in how many companies; it was also a matter of the balance of pikemen, musketeers, fusiliers, and grenadiers in these units. While the pike had dominated early in the sixteenth century, the ever-rising number of firearms relegated pikemen to a secondary role and declining proportion of the battalion. At first, pikemen outnumbered musketeers; however, by the end of the 1500s, the proportion of firearms had risen, often equaling the number

---

[84] On questions of precedence and hierarchy between regiments of infantry and cavalry, see André, *Le Tellier*, 188–99, and Belhomme, *L'armée française en 1690*, 51–57, 103–4.

[85] Rousset, *Louvois*, 1:222.   [86] Belhomme, *L'armée française en 1690*, 6, 52–53.

[87] AG, MR 1701, #13. The Royal Artillery Regiment, with five battalions, and the Bombardiers Regiment, with two battalions, have been counted among the French infantry.

of pikes in a unit.[88] Billon, writing his military handbook in the 1620s, described battalions of 300 pikemen and 200 musketeers.[89] Up to midcentury, military handbooks advocated a 50/50 mix, and when Mazarin ordered weapons for troops in 1654 and 1658 he stipulated that half were to be pikes.[90] But at least some regiments circa 1635 mustered companies composed of 60 percent musketeers and 40 percent pikemen.[91] No later than 1651, ordinances stipulated that "Infantry captains will be obliged to have two thirds of their soldiers armed with muskets and one third with pikes," and regulation after regulation retained this ratio.[92] Local authorities declaring a levy of 500 men to serve at the siege of Seure in March 1653 stipulated that these soldiers were to be armed "two thirds with muskets and the other third with pikes."[93] The only firearms permitted were muskets; royal regulations demanded that fusils, though popular with the troops, were to be seized and broken.[94]

The split between musketeers and pikemen was complicated by the addition of grenadiers and fusiliers circa 1670. As noted earlier, in 1670 the Regiment du Roi added a full company of grenadiers; over time, other regiments followed suit, so the last to receive grenadier companies were the Swiss regiments in 1691. As a step in this direction, an ordinance of 6 February 1670 allowed four men in each line company to carry fusils; these must have been the prescribed grenadiers at first, because fusils were associated with grenadiers.[95] This explained why Louis allowed some fusils as early as 1670, even though he prohibited most infantrymen from carrying them until the

---

[88] For ratios of pikemen and musketeers in the sixteenth century, see Contamine, *Histoire militaire*, 1:251; Gaston Zeller, *Le siège de Metz par Charles-Quint* (Nancy: 1943), 54n; Nicholas Edouard Delabarre-Duparcq, *L'art militaire pendant les guerres de religion, 1562–1598* (Paris: 1864); Robert Arnauld d'Andilly, *Mémoires* in Michaud and Poujoulat, eds., *Nouvelle collection des mémoires pour servir à l'histoire de France*, vol. 9 (Paris: 1838), 408.

[89] Jean de Billon, *Les principes de l'art militaire* (Lyon: 1622), 255–56. Nicolas Edouard Delabarre-Duparcq, *Histoire sommaire d'infanterie* (Paris: 1853), 29–30, repeats a ratio of 2:3 probably based on Billon's handbook. Delabarre-Duparcq, *Histoire sommaire*, 32, used a diagram from Billon showing an archetypal battalion of 200 musketeers and 300 pikemen.

[90] Lostelnau, *Le maréchal de bataille* (Paris: 1647), 105–237, showed a battalion of 128 muskets and 128 pikes, pikes in the center. On page 245, he again describes a battalion as 50/50 pikes and muskets. For more on 50/50 pike/musket battalions, see Jules Mazarin, *Lettres du cardinal Mazarin*, eds. P. Chéruel and G. d'Avenel, vols. 6–9 (Paris: 1890–1906), 6:186, 22 June 1654, to Talon; Mazarin, *Lettres*, 8:725, 7 June 1658, to Guillolière.

[91] Belhomme, *Histoire de l'infanterie*, 1:360.

[92] Regulation of 4 November 1651, in André, *Le Tellier*, 679. SHAT, Bib., Col. des ord., vol. 19, #202, ordinance of 20 April 1656, insists that units have two thirds muskets and one third pikes, and that units without pikes should put them back in. See, as well, the regulation of 25 July 1665, art. 54, in Rousset, *Louvois*, 1:190–91. A 1668 capitulation for the Royal Roussillon regiment again set a ratio of two thirds muskets and one third pikes. AG, A¹219, #238, 15 October 1668.

[93] Côte d'Or, C 3635, 13 March 1653.

[94] André, *Le Tellier*, 355. For example, see the ordinances of 12 February 1653 in André, *Le Tellier*, 694, and SHAT, Col. des ord., vol. 19, #23, of 28 April 1653 and the regulation of 25 July 1665, art. 54, in Rousset, *Louvois*, 1:190–91.

[95] Ordinance in Rousset, *Louvois*, 1:191.

1690s.[96] However, even when grenadiers drew off in their own companies, line companies continued to contain a small number of men armed with fusils. Apparently, grenadier companies often combined to carry out separate actions, as when Louis ordered that during the passage of the Issel on 13 June 1672, "all the grenadiers companies of the army" would form the head of the attacking column.[97] On orders of battle, grenadier companies were usually listed separately from their regiments and battalions.[98] Grenadiers/fusiliers that stayed within line companies also were favored for duty in special detachments.[99]

The proportion of pikemen continued to decline over the remainder of the century. The experienced officer d'Aurignac, writing in 1663, already described companies in which only a quarter of the infantry carried pikes.[100] Regulations that appeared immediately before the Dutch War set the number of pikemen to this level. One issued in 1670 put the proportion at two pikemen to five musketeers, and the 22 June 1671 regulation cut it to 1:3.[101] These regulations not only set the proportion of muskets and pikes, but they also continued the war against the use of fusils by any infantrymen except the picked grenadiers. As the 1670 ordinance complained, "there are almost no pikemen in the companies, and most soldiers give themselves the right to carry fusils."[102]

With the Nine Years' War, the number of pikemen slipped again. Just before the war began, Louvois considered replacing pikes with *chevaux de frise* for defense against cavalry, but the pikes remained.[103] A campaign company of fifty enlisted men in 1690 included only ten pikemen; in addition, it had six fusiliers. The ratio of pikemen had fallen to 1:4 in campaign

---

[96] Susane, *Histoire de l'infanterie*, 1:200, maintains that grenadiers received fusils in 1671, but this seems to be a year late. The 25 February 1675 ordinance restated that each infantry company would include four men armed with fusils. Rousset, *Louvois*, 3:193.

[97] Louis, *Oeuvres*, 2:200. Also, at the siege of Kehl, July 1678, all grenadiers were united in one unit for the storm. Rousset, *Louvois*, 2:548.

[98] See AG, A^{1}875, 3 April 1689, "Contrôle des troupes qui doivent passer le Rhin le 6e avril 1689."

[99] AG, A^{1}337, #11, 4 January 1673. Commissaire le Camar at Lille complained that no fusils had been given to the new companies, which proved to be very embarrassing when detachments had to be sent out. He inquired if captains should be obliged to have four fusiliers in each company.

[100] Azan, *Un tacticien du XVIIe siècle*, 82.

[101] Based on a seventy-man company, the 6 February 1670 ordinance decreed that there must be twenty pikemen, while the 22 June 1671 ordinance with a fifty-man company, reduced the number of pikemen to twelve. Rousset, *Louvois*, 1:191n. Puységur says that the infantry companies of the Dutch War had thirty-two muskets, four fusils, and twelve pikes. Puységur, *Art de la guerre*, 1:56. A provincial document from 1675 also set company strength as fifty, including twelve pikemen. AD, Nord, C 2235, 10 August 1675.

[102] 6 February 1670 ordinance in Rousset, *Louvois*, 1:191.

[103] See correspondence of 12 December 1687 in Rochas d'Aiglun, *Vauban*, 2:281. Louvois, learning that the emperor's army had no pikemen, but used *chevaux de frise*, wondered if the French ought to do the same. Vauban replied in the negative.

companies, and garrison companies included no pikemen at all.[104] *Milice* battalions, intended primarily for garrison service, also carried no pikes.[105] Soon the experience of Steinkirke, mentioned previously, inspired Louis to increase the number of fusiliers by the end of 1692. A company of French infantry now numbering fifty-five men would include ten pikemen, twenty-one musketeers, twenty-one fusiliers, two sergeants, and a drummer, a structure that dropped the ratio of pikemen slightly to 1:4.5.[106] With the return of peace, the decree of 1699 stipulated that the fusil replace the musket entirely in French ranks, but the final demise of the musket did not immediately bring with it the end of the pike. Some regiments still show a ratio of 1:4 coming into the War of the Spanish Succession.[107] In 1702, Villeroi received permission to reduce the numbers of, or entirely eliminate, pikemen from his Army of Italy, and during the 1702–3 winter quarters, the Army of Italy cast off its pikes.[108] The fusil and bayonet had triumphed, eliminating the need to balance musket and pike in a line company.

Battalion Formations and Tactics

As the capacities of weapons and the balance of arms within battalions changed during the *grand siècle*, so did the way in which battalions marshaled for battle. Battalion formations stretched out into progressively thinner and longer patterns. With pikemen usually concentrated in the center of the battalion, and the number of pikemen decreasing, their capacity to protect musketeers effectively on the extended flanks declined. The need to group men together according to the weapons they carried, and the fact that foot soldiers of the same company brought three different weapons to the field, required that infantry companies break up into their constituent parts to form for battle, and in this sense, they ceased to exist when the battalion closed for combat. This fact complicated formations, deployments, and tactics, as will be seen.

During the Italian Wars (1494–1559), the French relied primarily upon their mercenary Swiss and German infantry, which fought in massive pike squares, as did the Spanish tercios arrayed against them. Michael Roberts ascribed the turn away from such massive formations and the adoption of

---

[104] Belhomme, *L'armée française en 1690*, 11.

[105] Speaking of the difficulty of arming all the *milice* with fusils, one royal decree stated that "there are always thirty soldiers armed with muskets and the surplus remains as before, armed with fusils." SHAT, Bib., Col. des ord., vol. 26, #80, 19 December 1689.

[106] SHAT, Bib., Col. des ord., vol. 28, #38, 1 December 1692. The change was made since "fusiliers are very necessary in the companies." The twenty-one fusiliers included two sergeants, three corporals, and five anspessades who were armed with the new weapon, so only thirteen privates carried fusils. Belhomme, *Histoire de l'infanterie*, 2:313.

[107] Review reports from Lille, dated 1701, state that the companies of the Alsace regiment contained fusiliers and pikemen, while the 2nd battalion of the Hessy regiment contained about one fifth pikemen. Lille, 11, 113. Susane, *Histoire de l'infanterie*, 1:202, claimed that fittingly the Swiss were last to abandon pikes in the winter of 1702–4.

[108] Belhomme, *Histoire de l'infanterie*, 2:359, 380.

more effective linear battalions of much smaller size to the reforms of Maurice of Nassau and Gustavus Adolphus, and this he labeled as a Military Revolution, thus beginning the extensive historiographical debate on the phenomenon of military change in early modern Europe.[109] Whatever the value of Roberts's thesis for countries other than France, the French followed an evolutionary course different from that he described.[110]

In the Wars of Religion, necessity forced commanders to experiment with different tactical combinations.[111] Without the resources of royal taxation, and lacking the crown's permanent Swiss and French units, French Protestants faced particularly serious problems in organizing and fighting with their infantry. Partisan warfare, or *petite guerre*, which called for small units acting independently, familiarized the French foot troops with fighting as isolated companies. These companies maintained their integrity in battle, so regiments formed for combat as a single line of small company squares in which soldiers stood only ten or twelve ranks deep. These company squares were separated by intervals equal to the front of one square, but the intervals could be closed when cavalry threatened.[112] Large squares that marshaled together as many as 3,000 to 5,000 troops might occasionally be formed in defense against cavalry, but French infantry usually stood in regimental formations totaling no more than 1,000 men.[113]

Even as the French adopted small units and abandoned large squares, there were those, François de la Noue for example, who still argued in favor of more massive units of 2,000 men.[114] Thus, the debate continued, and military handbooks encouraged controversy. The late sixteenth century witnessed a flood of such handbooks, which displayed a variety of ornate formations in defiance of simplicity and common sense.[115] Arrowheads, windmills, and other fanciful and impractical battle orders were proposed. But this handbook literature should not blind us to reality.

Under Henri IV, the battalion became the standard combat unit for French

---

[109] Michael Roberts, *The Military Revolution, 1560–1660* (Belfast: 1956).

[110] See John A. Lynn, "Tactical Evolution in the French Army, 1560–1660," *French Historical Studies*, fall 1985, 176–91.

[111] The best general summaries of the art of war from 1500 to 1648 are the classic Charles Oman, *The Art of War in the Sixteenth Century* (London: 1937), and the more recent chapters by J. R. Hale and J. W. Wign in *The New Cambridge Modern History*, vols. 2–4. A nineteenth-century work, Delabarre-Duparcq, *L'art militaire pendant les guerres de réligion, 1562–1598* provides a first-rate treatment of this subject.

[112] Delabarre-Duparcq, *Histoire sommaire*, 29.

[113] Oman, *The Art of War*, 446; Nicolas Edouard Delabarre-Duparcq, *Histoire de l'art de la guerre depuis l'usage de la poudre*, 2 vols. (Paris: 1860–64), 2:95.

[114] Delabarre-Duparcq, *L'art militaire*, 63.

[115] The Bibliothèque Nationale in Paris contains a fine collection of military handbooks from the sixteenth and seventeenth centuries. On this side of the Atlantic, perhaps the best collection of such works is held by the Newberry Library in Chicago; for a list of these works, see John A. Lynn and George Satterfield, *A Guide to Sources in Early Modern European Military History in Midwestern Research Libraries*, 2d. ed. (Urbana, IL: 1994). Both collections were essential in preparing this chapter.

infantry. Because French tactical units were already relatively small and formed in an essentially linear order, the most obvious traits that separated battle arrays before Henri IV from the battalion formations that he employed were (1) in earlier formations, companies rated as distinct tactical elements, and (2) these companies were separated from each other by intervals. Now the intervals disappeared, and a French battalion massed in a single body, with all pikemen gathered together in the center, flanked on either side by musketeers. Henri's battalions were also designed to support each other in line or in a checkerboard formation, in the fashion associated with the Dutch. This alteration of French tactics, which so resembles the work of prince Maurice, occurred at roughly the same time as, or even predated, the Dutch reforms.[116] In sum, the French appear to have independently evolved battalions of a size, composition, and disposition similar to the Dutch before the reforms of Maurice strongly influenced French practices. Consequently, the imitation of Dutch formations could hardly have brought a "Military Revolution" in Roberts's sense.

Nonetheless, there is no question that the French turned to the Dutch, and later to the Swedes, to improve their own battalion formations and tactics. Maurice enjoyed a European reputation as a soldier-scholar, a brilliant innovator, and a talented general. His skill in all elements of warfare made the Netherlands "the military college of Europe."[117] French commanders of note served in Dutch armies to gain better knowledge of the most advanced military practices of the day. The great Marshal Turenne, for one, a nephew of Maurice, began his military career under the guidance of Maurice and the prince's brother, Frederick Henry.[118] The work of Maurice probably was all the more impressive to the French because it reinforced their own tactical development and offered refinements and improvements readily adaptable to French methods.

Louis XIII encouraged technical military reforms in the French army. Even if he possessed neither the dash of a cavalry leader like his father, Henri IV, nor the penchant for military administration and siege craft typical of his son, Louis XIV, Louis XIII still took a lively interest in tactics and training. A noted seventeenth-century commentator assessed the king's military abilities highly: "It could be said that he is an able man, knowledgeable in that profession, a man who could pass for a master of it."[119]

---

[116] J. R. Hale, "Armies, Navies, and the Art of War," *The New Cambridge Modern History*, ed. G. R. Elton, vol. 2 (Cambridge: 1958), 194; Delabarre-Duparcq, *Histoire de l'art de la guerre*, 2:117–20; and Idem, *Histoire sommaire*, 30. In fact, Henri IV's units were somewhat smaller than those used under Louis XIII. F. Reboul, "Des croisades à la Révolution," 368. At La Rochelle in 1627–28, the French used fifteen battalions of about 1,200 men each; see F. de vaux de Foletier, *Le Siège de La Rochelle* (Paris: 1931), 238.

[117] J. W. Wijn, "Military Forces and Warfare," 203.

[118] Jules Roy, *Turenne, sa vie et les institutions militaires de son temps*, 2nd ed. (Paris: 1896), 56–62; Jean Bérenger, *Turenne* (Paris: 1987), 65–69.

[119] Jacques de Chastenet de Puységur in Charles Romain, *Louis XIII, un grand Roi malconnu* (Paris: 1934), 67. For a general evaluation of Louis XIII as a soldier, see Romain, 67–78, and Maxime Weygand, *Histoire de l'armée française* (Paris: 1938), 133.

A new generation of military handbooks appeared that made Louis's task easier. Du Praissac's *Discours militaires* (1614) already showed some influence of Maurice, but it did not demonstrate Dutch battalions and still regarded huge squares of as many as 4,096 men as valuable tactical formations.[120] Louis de Montgomery, sieur de Courbouson's *Milice française* (1615) described "exercices hollandoises," but he limited the actual use of the Dutch system largely to words of command, and once again, great squares predominated.[121]

Judging by its advanced system and its numerous editions (at least six are recorded between 1617 and 1641), the most important manual was a work by Jean de Billon, which bore the illustrative title, *Les Principes de l'art militaire . . . qui sont observée en Hollande par le Prince Maurice.*[122] Here Billon presented battalions of a size consistent with French evolution, marshaled in formations proven by the Dutch. While Billon also described large battalions and provided the obligatory square root table for forming great squares, his archetypal battalion contained only 500 soldiers standing in a rectangle fifty men across and ten deep, with 300 pikemen massed in the center files and musketeers in two bodies of 100 men each on the wings.[123] The intervals between the soldiers varied according to circumstances. For drill, he allowed 6 feet between ranks and files. Three-foot intervals separated men during the approach in combat; and actual attack distance shrank to half of that, 1.5 feet. Since he estimated that a soldier was physically 2 feet wide and 1.5 feet thick, his battalion in firing order combat stood roughly 69 feet deep on a front of 394 feet. (See Figure 14.1.) Because only ten files of musketeers flanked the pikemen to the left and right, the pikemen could provide some protection to the musketeers without any major shift when the battalion had reduced its intervals for close combat. However, Billon suggested alternating files of musketeers and pikemen in action against cavalry.

It is important to note that even in close combat, Billon would not eliminate the distances between files and ranks entirely. In contrast to mid–eighteenth-century practice, in which men could advance or stand firm elbow to

---

[120] Praissac, *Les questions militaires* (1614), 210–15, really talks of mass infantry formations, even supplying the traditional square root table allowing a sergeant major to set up his men in a massive square of as many as 4,096 men. Even in the later edition, Praissac, *Les discours militaires*, 2d ed. (Paris: 1622), 202, he still supplies the square root table and does not have Dutch formations in his description of forming battalions.

[121] Louis de Montgomery Courbouson, sieur de, *La milice française* (Paris: 1615), 1615, again supplied square root tables.

[122] The generally reliable Delabarre-Duparcq in his *Histoire sommaire*, 32, considered that it typified French tactical practice. It has been argued that Henri duc de Rohan's *Parfait capitaine* was the most popular military book of the century; see Henry Guerlac, "Vauban: The Impact of Science on War," in *Makers of Modern Strategy*, ed. E. M. Earle (Princeton: 1941), 32.

[123] Jean de Billon, *Les principes de l'art militaire* (Rouen: 1641). Delabarre-Duparcq, *Histoire de l'art de la guerre*, 2:117–20, argues that under Henri IV, infantry went down from ten to eight ranks, and that French order before Swiss reforms was represented by Billon, but if this is so, the French still stood in ten ranks in the 1620s.

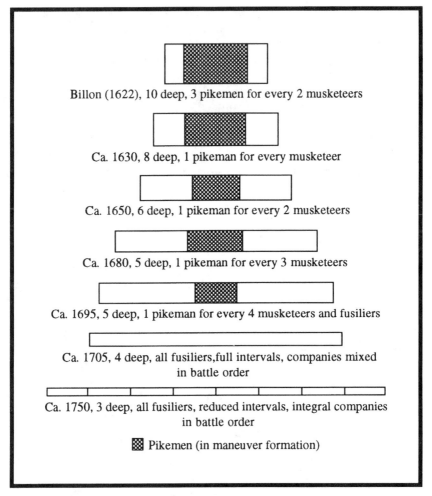

Figure 14.1. The evolution of infantry battalion formations, 1600–1750.

elbow, placing musketeers that close to each other in an age of matchlocks would have endangered them; a lighted match demanded respect, and distance, around gunpowder. In fact, Billon's recommended intervals for close combat are comparatively small. Spaces of at least two feet, or a "petite pas," would be typical even through the War of the Spanish Succession. Circa 1620, still greater intervals between files were required if a battalion intended to maintain a constant fire against an enemy, because in that circumstance, the musketeers required room to carry out the countermarch. The standard firing technique at this time, a countermarch required each musketeer at the head of a file to fire, then walk to the back of the file and begin to reload as the next man stepped forward, presented, and fired. Eventually, a soldier who had fired would work his way back to the front of the file to fire again in a form of human conveyer belt. Vauban argued that countermarching required a distance of six feet between files.[124] This would mean that if a battalion closed ranks for close combat, it could no longer employ the basic firing maneuver. The complicated and dangerous loading procedure not only determined distances between men; it also influenced the depth of a formation, or at least the number of musketeers in a file, because that depth was to a degree a function of the time required to reload. The slower the men loaded, the thicker the battalion would have to be to ensure that it could keep up a constant fire. If men required a minute to load, and if the commander wanted to fire a volley every six seconds, he would have to stack his musketeers ten deep for the countermarch.[125]

Just as French officers served under Maurice in the first years of the seventeenth century, so others learned their trade under Gustavus Adolphus in the 1630s. For example, Claude de Le Touf, baron de Sirot, who later commanded the reserve at Rocroi, soldiered through 1632 and 1633 with the victorious Swedes.[126] Once the French entered the war openly as enemies of the Habsburgs and allies of Gustavus, this contact with Swedish methods brought further adjustments in French tactics.

In accord with Swedish practice of marshaling their battalions in six rather than the Dutch ten ranks, the French thinned out their battalions during the war with Spain, at least by the 1650s. A 1638 directive for the guards declared that "battalions will be formed six deep."[127] One authority credits Turenne with cutting the depth to six ranks about 1640, following Swedish practice, and with decreasing the number of pikemen to one third of the battalion.[128] As shown earlier, the winter-quarters ordinance of 1651 stipulated companies composed of two thirds musketeers and one third pikemen. *Practique et maximes de la guerre* by Laon, which followed on the heels of this ordinance, prescribed battalions of 600 to 800 men, "put six deep for good troops, and eight deep for the less skilled."[129]

As formations thinned and the number of pikemen decreased, their role

---

[124] Rochas d'Aiglun, *Vauban*, 1:169.

[125] Nosworthy, *Anatomy of Victory*, 14, posits a fire rate of one shot each six seconds.

[126] Claude de Le Touf, Baron de Sirot, *Mémoires*, 2 vols. (Paris: 1683), 1:139–40, 193–225, 2:40.

[127] Belhomme, *Histoire d'infanterie*, 1:377.

[128] Delabarre-Duparcq, *Histoire sommaire*, 32; idem, *Histoire de l'art de la guerre*, 2:207–8. A reduction in the number of pikemen actually ran counter to the intentions of Gustavus Adolphus, who had increased both the number and offensive power of pikemen. Bérenger argues that Turenne still stacked his infantry in ten ranks as late as the Dutch War. Bérenger, *Turenne*, 518–19.

[129] I. de sieur d'Aigremont Laon, *Practique et maximes de la guerre* (Paris: 1652), 65. Lostelneau's *Le maréchal de bataille* appeared in 1647, and while he allowed battalions to stand six or ten deep, Lostelneau preferred a battalion marshaled in eight ranks, eighty files across, composed half of pikes and half of musketeers. The maximum battalion size that Lostelneau would accept was 1,000. Lostelnau, *Le maréchal de bataille*, 3, 105–237, 245–46, 385–439. Puységur, *Art de la guerre*, 1:58 and plate 1, states that in the minority of Louis XIV, infantry stood eight ranks deep.

of protecting the musketeers in the battalion became more difficult. A battalion of 600 men, two thirds of whom were musketeers, standing six ranks deep, would put over thirty files of musketeers to either flank of the central body of pikemen. Since the pikemen by this time carried weapons about fourteen feet long, they could offer immediate physical shelter to only a minority of the musketeers. One solution to the problem was "fraising the battalion" – that is, spreading out the pikemen in a rank or ranks along the entire length of the battalion. However, the French strictly prohibited "fraising" after 1650 because it limited the mobility of a battalion.[130]

Through the first decades of the personal reign of Louis XIV, it remained standard practice to form battalions in lines of six ranks. D'Aurignac almost certainly reflected practice late in the war with Spain when he wrote in 1663 that the normal formation was six men deep.[131] Lamont, writing a few years later, preferred six-deep formations, but allowed for three-, four-, or five-deep lines if a battalion was short on men.[132] In 1672, Allain Mallet also showed his infantry stacked in six ranks, although he conservatively described battalions that were 50/50 pikes and muskets. Interestingly, in Mallet's work, the intervals between ranks and files increased over those advocated by Billon fifty years earlier. Under cannon fire, they would be six paces to allow greater alleys for the cannonballs to pass through a unit. Intervals for reviews, and probably drill, were reduced to three paces, while the gaps allowed in combat depended on the foe, 1.5 paces against infantry and a *"petit pas"* against cavalry.[133]

By the Dutch War, French formations had thinned even further, at least in practice. Gaya, writing toward the end of the Dutch War, discussed battalions standing five or six deep.[134] The experienced soldier and military author, Puységur, explained this variety in depth during the wartime era. Battalions began the campaign season standing six deep when they had a full complement of men, but with losses diminishing the number of men, "towards the end of the campaigns the ranks were reduced to five." Apparently for the same reason, "During the last year of the war . . . one formed line only five deep."[135]

About this time, official tactical directives appeared that had a greater

---

[130] See Nosworthy, *Anatomy of Victory*, 33, on fraising. Bérenger, *Turenne*, 518, claims that "Turenne had the pikemen of the first two ranks of the battalion kneel, and behind them the musketeers remained protected against the charges of the enemy cavalry." However, this does not seem to jibe with tactical handbooks and directives, for it assumes that pikemen stood across the entire front of the battalion two ranks deep, which no source that I have encountered describes. Puységur, *Art de la guerre*, 1:70, praises the idea of fraising but says that it was neither used nor "spoken of in all the drill regulations."

[131] Azan, *Un tacticien du XVIIe siècle*, 56.

[132] Lamont, *Les fonctions de tous les officiers de l'infanterie*, vol. 2 (La Haye: 1693), 85. The original edition was printed in Paris in 1668.

[133] Allain Mallet, *Les travaux de Mars* (Amsterdam: 1672), 14–16.

[134] Louis de Gaya, *L'art de la guerre et la manière dont on la fait a présent* (Paris: 1677), 154.

[135] Puységur, *Art de la guerre*, 1:56.

immediate impact on French practice than did the tactical handbooks produced by individual authors. An order from Turenne, dated 1674, prescribed ranks open at two paces distance for rapid movement, but closed down to one pace when infantry approached the enemy. At thirty paces distance, musketeers would present to fire. Grenadier companies were to stand to the right of their battalions.[136] Gaya also described battle instructions that he claimed were employed by Turenne. Infantry battalions marched with pikes in the center and muskets on the wings, with a single file of sergeants occupying both extreme flanks. Officers stood to the front sides and back of the formation. Battalions advanced at the "petit pas" until they reached half musket range from the enemy, at which point, flags went to the center of the battalion and the ranks closed to *point d'épée* – that is, the ranks closed until a rank touched the sword points of the men in front of them, somewhat less than a pace.[137]

A fascinating directive, "Order that the King wants his infantry to observe on the day of combat," dates from a period between the late 1670s to the late 1680s.[138] Battalions were normally to form in five ranks, with the pikemen gathered in the center files. The right flank of the battalion was to be guarded by the grenadier company and the left by fifty fusiliers. When the unit went into combat, one quarter of the pikemen marched to the left flank of the battalion while another one quarter of the pikemen moved off to the right flank, leaving only one half the pikemen in the center of the battalion. The flanking units of pikemen would themselves be flanked by two files of musketeers and one of sergeants. The musketeers on the wings closed on the center to fill the gaps left by the flanking bodies of pikemen. Looking at a full-strength battalion of fifteen line companies of fifty men each and a grenadier company of forty men arrayed according to this directive, one would see a unit five ranks deep and 150 files across. Those files would be ordered as follows from left to right: ten of fusiliers, one of sergeants, two of musketeers, nine of pikemen, forty-five of musketeers, eighteen of pikemen, another forty-five of musketeers, nine of pikemen, two of musketeers, one of sergeants, and eight of grenadiers. According to this order for combat, as units approached to a distance of 100 paces from the enemy, pikemen presented their weapons, and musketeers brought their muskets to bear. Ranks closed to two paces distance. The order cautioned commanders to advance slowly, so as not to leave the pikes in the center behind.

An instruction of 15 May 1693 prescribed an almost identical combat formation.[139] It differed in only two respects: First, the central bodies composed of musketeers in the earlier order now included fusiliers as well, since

---

[136] AG, Arch. hist. 78, fol. 79–82, "Ordre de M. de Turenne pour la disposition des bataillons dans un jour de combat," 26 August 1674.

[137] Louis de Gaya, *Le nouvel art de la guerre et la manière dont on la fait aujourd'huy en France* (Paris: 1692), 201–3.

[138] AG, Arch. hist. 78, fol. 67.

[139] Instruction of 15 May 1793 in Belhomme, *Histoire de l'infanterie*, 2:317–20.

there were more fusiliers in a company by that point, and second, the flanking bodies of pikemen stood on the extreme ends of the battalion so that only two files of fusiliers on the left and of grenadiers on the right flanked them. Considered in addition to the earlier order, the 1693 instruction suggests that this was probably the standard combat formation for the French from the 1680s until the elimination of pikes.

These directives demonstrate how a central body of pikemen was to protect an entire battalion in which the pikemen only accounted for about one quarter of the unit strength. By shifting to the right and left, the pikemen stood in three bodies that supported both flanks and the center. On the defensive, there may have been other ways for pikemen to cover musketeers by forming ranks that ran the entire length of the battalion, a return to fraising the battalion, but neither royal instruction commanded such a practice.[140]

However, it is unclear if these ornate instructions were followed. Puységur, who served in Louis's armies from 1677 through 1735, complained that while the pike was meant solely for protection against cavalry, it could not accomplish its job. Pikemen always remained massed in the center of the battalion, and from that position, they could not protect the flanking bodies of musketeers. So no matter how solid the pikemen, if a cavalry charge reached the infantry line, it could rout the musketeers and swirl about to take the pikemen from the rear. Thus, by the time pikes were replaced, they had been virtually useless for some time.[141]

In any case, the shifting of pikemen, fusiliers, and musketeers demonstrates how individual line companies broke down into their constituent elements to form the battalion. A company's pikemen marched off to the center, or at the flanks, in order to combine with other pikemen. Fusiliers moved off to the left in a separate body, while musketeers might be in one of four groups. Meanwhile, a company's sergeants, rather than staying with their own men, moved off to the flanks and back of the battalion. It is even unclear whether or not the musketeers of a single company stood together or simply mixed in with the other musketeers of the same battalion, and likewise for pikemen and fusiliers. The only company that maintained its integrity in this scheme was the elite grenadier company off on the right of the battalion. The need to reposition soldiers into their proper places for battle necessitated relatively large intervals between the ranks, because men moved along these corridors. With such a battle order, the need to drill as a battalion was crucial, since the companies could not adequately practice on their own what would be required of the men in combat.

Gaya stated that before 1683, the French followed a standard weapons'

---

[140] Both H. Pichat, "Les armées de Louis XIV en 1674," *Revue d'histoire de l'armée*: 1910, 23, and Bérenger, *Turenne*, 518, describe fraising in the Dutch War, but this does not seem to jibe with tactical handbooks and directives.

[141] See discussion in Puységur, *Art de la guerre*, 1:69–70.

drill for infantry and certain common evolutions or maneuvers.[142] The battalion formed for drill with its companies lined up with their musketeers and pikemen arrayed in five or six ranks. The pikes within each company always stood to the left of the musketeers. On command, the musketeers marched off to the wings and the pikemen gathered to the center. Thirteen feet, or two halberd lengths, separated the ranks, while the files opened to a distance of one pace. A file of sergeants stood at each extreme flank of the battalion, while a rank of other sergeants formed behind the battalion; thus, it was bordered on three sides by its NCOs. Once the battalion was formed, the musketeers went through a series of thirty-seven movements, very much the same as those illustrated in the Dutch manuals of the early seventeenth century. The musketeers having finished, the pikemen went through their routine of thirty-five movements and poses.

Whatever the type of drill used before 1683, that year the king issued a new regulation entitled, "Drill that the King orders for all his infantry, French and foreign."[143] It would appear to be the first officially prescribed general drill regulation issued directly by the French monarchy. It was quite modest and short; in fact, it was a drill regulation in the most literal sense of the word, instructing officers exactly how they were to conduct a drill, not on how they were to fight. Here this regulation differed sharply from the "Order that the King wants his infantry to observe on the day of combat." It may be that these two documents were planned to be used together, but this is mere surmise. The rationale for a standardized formal drill would seem to be that such a drill allowed infantry inspectors to view and judge units more fairly, since they all would perform the same movements. Still, since the drill standardized movements and formations, it also defined the basis for combat, the fundamental tactical order of French infantry.

According to Gaya, battalions stood in the same formation to perform the 1683 drill as they had for the earlier drill. The 1683 drill differed, however, from earlier practice in that the battalion drilled as a whole, not first as a body of musketeers and later as one of pikemen. On given commands, musketeers and pikemen moved together in set patterns of a set number of beats. This must have made this drill much more like battle maneuvers, in which the actions of the musketeers matched those of the pikemen. To this extent, the 1683 drill was a step toward the notion of drill not as simply a mastery of the manual of arms but of actual battle practice.

[142] The earlier unofficial drill appears in Gaya, *Le nouvel art de la guerre*, 156–75. Earlier editions of Gaya contain only the earlier drill. See, for example, his *L'art de la guerre et la manière dont on la fait a présent* (1677), and the English translation, *The Art of War* (London: 1678). Since he uses the same description and diagram to demonstrate the way in which the battalion formed for drill (1692 edition, 150–55), this seems to have remained a constant from the Dutch war through the Nine Years' War.

[143] SHAT, Bib., Col. des ord., vol. 25, #1, January 1683. The 1683 regulation appears in Gaya, *Le nouvel art de la guerre* (1692), 156–75. Pichat, "Les armées de Louis XIV en 1674," 22, dates this regulation as 19 April 1683.

The very large distance between ranks in the drill allowed the men to handle their weapons (and to be closely observed while doing so), to march, and to deploy for battle. As already mentioned, the complicated and dangerous process of loading and firing a musket originally demanded a good deal of space between the ranks.[144] Of course, as this weapon gave way to the fusil, the large distances between ranks could have been suppressed, but interestingly, they were not. Puységur continued to assume a twelve-foot distance between ranks even during the War of the Spanish Succession.[145] Two factors pressed for the maintenance of such large intervals. First, the French did not march in step, so reduced intervals would have made movement awkward, as men risked literally stepping on each others' heels. In fact, the first French drill regulation to stipulate marching in step did not come until 1754, making the French distinctly backward in this regard.[146] Second, large intervals were required to shift pikemen, fusiliers, and musketeers sideways. In any case, battalions shrank the distances between ranks at the last minute before combat, sometimes down to *point d'épée*.

During the Nine Years' War and the War of the Spanish Succession, French infantry battalions continued to evolve into more and more linear formations. A 1693 ordinance officially reduced the number of ranks to five, with four paces distance between ranks, although this seems to have done no more than recognize standard practice.[147] In an instruction of 1690, Catinat set the normal distance at two paces in an assault, but since the attack distance was usually only half the normal distance, this would accord well with the 1693 ordinance, as well as according with existing French combat practice.[148]

From this point on, regulations continued to prescribe five ranks but practice often reduced this even further. Puységur reports that during the Nine Years' War, losses again forced battalions to reduce their depth: "towards the end of the campaigns, the majority put themselves only in four ranks."[149] The War of the Spanish Succession continued to witness the thinning of battalion formations. Sturgill's study argues that at Malplaquet, the French infantry fought in four-rank lines.[150] And in his unpublished treatise

---

[144] On this necessity for space, see, as well, Colin, *L'infanterie au XVIIIe siècle*, 23.

[145] For example, Puységur, *Art de la guerre*, 1:54.

[146] Colin, *L'infanterie au XVIIIe siècle*, 32. The French regulation of 1753 only required that men step off on the same foot; that of 1754 stated that during maneuvers, the troops had to hit the ground with the same foot at the same time. Roberts incorrectly ascribes a cadenced step to Martinet. Roberts, *The Military Revolution*, 20.

[147] Colin, *L'infanterie au XVIIIe siècle*, 23fn.

[148] Colin, *L'infanterie au XVIIIe siècle*, 24. Pichat argues that in the Dutch War, French troops would advance, close intervals between files to elbow to elbow, and then give fire with the first three ranks. Pichat, "Les armées de Louis XIV en 1674," 23. Belhomme, *L'armée française en 1690*, 40, also argues that the distance between files disappeared in the attack.

[149] Puységur, *Art de la guerre*, 1:57.

[150] Claude C. Sturgill, *Marshall Villars and the War of the Spanish Succession* (Lexington, KY: 1965), 95.

on the art of war, Villars spoke of only four ranks.[151] Describing practice in the War of the Spanish Succession, Puységur testified that "On entering on campaign, the largest part of the infantry stood in line in four ranks, the rest in three. [But] towards the end of the campaign, there were always very few in four ranks."[152] If this often quoted authority is correct, as a practical matter, the French ended the *grand siècle* with most of their infantry marshaled in only three ranks for battle.

The regulation that prescribed drill for the era of the War of the Spanish Succession appeared on 2 March 1703.[153] It originally included pikemen in its instructions, but since these were abolished later that same year, the regulation was soon modified in practice.[154] The ordinance set the line depth at five ranks, although this would seldom seem to have been the actual depth of French battalions by then.[155] The modified regulation decreed that the ranks were to stand two halberd lengths apart, the length of the halberd again being set at 6.5 feet. The grenadier battalion was to stand to the right of the battalion, and a picked body of forty fusiliers drawn from the twelve line companies would guard the left flank, so this, in fact, resembles the combat order issued by Louis XIV twenty years earlier. A file of sergeants would stand at both extreme flanks of the body of the battalion, separating the twelve line companies from the two elite bodies on the flanks. The rest of the sergeants would form rank three paces behind the battalion. The battalion would be formed of its companies standing in their "natural order"; there was no more need to subdivide the companies to form up the battalion, except for the three or four picked fusiliers extracted from each company to form the body of fusiliers covering the left flank. Battalions defiled from line to column by advancing the battalion six paces forward and then commencing a simultaneous quarter wheel to the right or left by all the *demi-manche* and stepping off in the new direction. A battalion could go from column to line by (1) advancing perpendicular to the new line, (2) turning the column to a line parallel to the desired line, and then (3) wheeling each rank of each division to the right and advancing into position in succession, as it reached its appointed part of the line.[156] Such maneuvers were very time consuming, but more direct and more rapid movements were prohibited by the considerable intervals between ranks and the lack of a cadenced step. In addition,

[151] BN, f. fr. 6257, Claude Louis Hector Villars, "Traité de la guerre de campagne," 93.
[152] Puységur, *Art de la guerre,* 1:57.
[153] SHAT, Bib., Col. des ord., vol. 32, #46, ordinance of 2 March 1703.
[154] The modified version is printed in its entirety in *Ordonnances militaires,* 1:206–34. While the publication date is 1734, the privilege to print shown in the first volume is dated 1707, which effectively dates the first volume and, thus, the version of the regulation.
[155] See the diagram of a battalion according to the 1703 regulation in Chandler, *The Art of Warfare,* 99.
[156] See the discussions of early eighteenth-century deployments in Colin, *L'infanterie au XVIIIe siècle,* and Quimby, *The Background of Napoleonic Warfare.*

all movements were made from a fixed pivot, so they were doomed to be slow.[157]

It should be noted that linear order as exemplified by French regulations not only attempted to maximize the number of weapons that could be brought to bear on the enemy; it also allowed officers and sergeants to direct and control their men. At a time when the culture of command denigrated the rank and file, formations arrayed troops so they could be easily seen, supervised, and, if need be, coerced. Linear order was not simply a matter of technology, but one of psychology as well. Drill augmented this control, and more is said concerning that aspect of drill in the next chapter.

Even though the final regulation of the *grand siècle* eventually encompassed the disappearance of pikemen, it remained essentially conservative because it did not take advantage of the new tactical possibilities promised by the conversion of all the infantry to fusils and bayonets. Large intervals between ranks, once required to shift men within the battalion but no longer so necessary, were maintained, as were intervals between files, which once protected musketeers from their comrades' matches but which were unnecessary with fusils. In a throwback to times of muskets and pikes, the battalion was to maneuver and defile by *demi-manche*. The two *manches* were originally the two flanking bodies of musketeers to either side of the core body of pikemen. As the ratio of pikemen to musketeers had dropped to 1:4 by the 1690s, a half *"manche"* of musketeers became equal to the number of pikemen, so maneuver by *demi-manche* neatly divided a battalion into five equal "divisions," the contemporary term for any subunit of the battalion. Maneuver by *demi-manche* meant that company integrity was not maintained; once this was required by the mixed armament in each company, but this was no longer the case. Had company integrity been respected, the group cohesion of companies could have been better exploited in combat, and company drill would have become a direct building block of battalion drill, a fact that could have improved performance since infantry could be exercised more effectively and frequently in company than in battalion. In fact, tactical maneuver as decreed by the regulation of 1703 remained a product of the old pike days and remained so until the 1750s – evidence of conservative, one might even say backward, military practice.

Figure 14.1 illustrates just how gradual was the character of French tactical change, as reflected in the way battalions stood for battle over the course of the *grand siècle*.

This discussion of royal regulations and ordinances should not create the false impression that absolute regularity reigned in the army of Louis XIV. Inspectors might have witnessed similar weapons drills shaped by royal decrees, but there remained a great deal of variety between battalions when it came to battlefield practices. Therefore, a detailed description of tactical usage

---

[157] Colin, *L'infanterie au XVIIIe siècle*, 24. Such a slow process of setting up made it difficult to impose battle on an enemy who might choose to retire.

here would either be too long or misleading. The French would not really possess uniform regulations that set out the complete menu of the manual of arms, deployment, and maneuver until the 1750s. As late as 1727, as one French officer complained, it was impossible "to make several regiments drill together, there being not one who does it in a uniform manner," and each colonel followed his own tastes.[158]

Firing Orders: Musketry and the Arme Blanche

Nothing illustrates better the conservative nature of French tactics by the end of the *grand siècle* than the way in which the French retained outdated forms of volley fire. At the start of the seventeenth century, musketeers stood in heavy formations many ranks deep, as discussed previously, and at such a depth that not all men could fire their weapons at the same time. The Dutch solved this problem in the 1590s with the invention of the countermarch, which guaranteed that there was always a man at the front ready to discharge his weapon.[159]

By the 1630s, French infantry used at least two basic patterns of firing. The first required an entire rank to volley; then, if the battalion was stationary, that rank would perform a countermarch to the rear and reload while the next rank stepped forward. In assault, the rank would stand firm as the next rank advanced to fire, and, therefore, the battalion moved forward. In retreat, the rank having fired would countermarch through the battalion where it would stand firm, as other ranks fired and retired past it until it was uncovered by the retreat; then it raised its weapons, fired once again, and repeated the process. The other form of firing required one or more files to advance, form line, fire, and then return to their original positions.[160] This second form of firing may only have been used when the battalion was in a sheltered position, and its files moved forward and were clear to shoot.[161]

By the 1680s, the basic French manner of volley fire was a different form of fire by ranks. When a battalion stood firm, the first four ranks would kneel, and the fifth rank would remain standing, fire on command, and begin to reload. Then the fourth rank would stand and fire, repeated by the other ranks until the first rank had fired, when the first four ranks would again kneel, clearing the way for the fifth rank to fire.[162] Apparently, the first volley was delivered by more than one rank, so it was particularly devastating. This could be accomplished if one rank stooped to fire while the other shot over

---

[158] Butler, *Choiseul* (1980), 1:278 in M. S. Anderson, *War and Society in Europe of the Old Regime, 1618–1789* (1988), 105–6.

[159] Geoffrey Parker, *The Military Revolution: Military Innovation and the Rise of the West, 1500–1800* (Cambridge: 1988), 19. He says it was first proposed by William of Nassau in a letter of 8 December 1594.

[160] Contamine, *Histoire militaire*, 1:340.   [161] Nosworthy, *Anatomy of Victory*, 49.

[162] Gaya, *Le nouvel art de la guerre*, 179–182. Advancing and retiring fire by ranks were also retained.

it.[163] David Chandler stresses the point that even during the War of the Spanish Succession, all files still dressed exactly forward – that is, with one soldier standing precisely behind the man in front of him, which precluded men in rear ranks from firing between gaps in the forward ranks, thus making salvos difficult.[164] The origin of the French style of fire by ranks is somewhat obscure, but Turner, writing in 1683, credits it to Martinet, who he says developed it in the 1670s.[165] Other armies admiringly copied the French fire by ranks. The English in particular patterned their tactics on it. The 1686 *Abridgement of Military Discipline*, which was published with the approval of James II, adopted it. Austrians and Russians also used a similar fire order.[166]

If the French set the pattern before the Nine Years' War, the Dutch soon replaced them in the lead. Their method was known as *platoon firing*, and it was soon adopted by the English when the Glorious Revolution brought the Dutch William III to the English throne. In platoon firing, a battalion was divided into eighteen platoons, which were then grouped into three "firings." The firings included platoons distributed along the whole length of the battalion, so that no sector would be denuded of fire. Intervals closed to only a foot between ranks, and the first rank kneeled while the second two ranks stood, one firing through intervals in the other. On command, all three ranks of the platoons in a given firing blazed away at the enemy, although sometimes the kneeling first rank was reserved for a fourth firing.[167] The advantages of platoon firing were several. First, it put out a higher volume of fire per salvo than an equal number of men in fire by ranks in five ranks. Second, it allowed greater control of the men because they acted as a unit in any one segment of the line. Third, fire could be better directed because the men were not bobbing up and down. Fourth, platoon fire seemed to afford a greater morale effect than fire by rank, perhaps because more weapons were fired in any one salvo.

In a classic confrontation at Malplaquet, two Irish regiments, one in French service and the other with Marlborough, confronted each other on the battlefield and opened fire, each by its own method. Captain Robert Parker of the Royal Irish Regiment gave this description:

We continued marching slowly on, til we came to an opening in the wood. It was a small plain, on the opposite side of which we perceived a battalion of the enemy drawn up, a skirt of the wood being in the rear of them. Upon this Colonel Kane, who was then at the head of the Regiment, having drawn us up, and formed our platoons, advanced gently toward them, with the six platoons of our first firing made ready. When we had advanced within a hundred paces of them, they gave us a fire of one of their ranks; whereupon we halted, and returned them the fire of our six

---

[163] Nosworthy, *Anatomy of Victory*, 60.   [164] Chandler, *The Art of Warfare*, 115.

[165] Turner, *Pallas Aramta* (1683), cited by Nosworthy, *Anatomy of Victory*, 50.

[166] Chandler, *The Art of Warfare*, 115–16; Nosworthy, *Anatomy of Victory*, 52–54.

[167] For descriptions of platoon firing, see Chandler, *The Art of Warfare*, 116–21, and Nosworthy, *Anatomy of Victory*, 57–60.

platoons at once; and immediately made ready the six platoons of our second fire, and advanced upon them again. They then gave us the fire of another rank, and we returned them a second fire, which made them shrink; however they gave us the fire of a third rank after a scattering manner, and then retired into the wood in great disorder; on which we sent our third fire after them, and saw them no more.[168]

Parker ascribed his regiment's victory not only to platoon fire but to the heavier weight of English musket balls that were of a larger caliber. Other armies copied Dutch and English practice; at a battle in Alsace, reported in the *Gazette* on 26 August 1709, German troops also formed in three ranks, with the first rank kneeling, and fired on attacking French troops.[169]

During the War of the Spanish Succession, the French later imitated with their own style of platoon fire, with the first rank kneeling, but it never equaled Dutch or English practice. In 1705, Villeroi ordered the new French form of firing and provided powder for his men to practice it.[170] This method, which required only a twelfth of the battalion fire at any one command, became an official procedure of volley fire for the entire army in the winter of 1707.[171] It may be that the French lagged behind in firing practices because their preferred tactic on open ground was the attack without firing at all.[172]

The French preferred cold steel in the charge *à prest*, which put a premium on speed in closing with the enemy rather than halting to fire. The notion that infantry should hold its fire to the last minute was common throughout the century. In one case, defending troops held fire against a French assault until the attackers were only fifteen paces distant.[173] Grimarest argued that the battalions should present their bayonets when they reached forty to fifty paces from the enemy, and he recommended firing last.[174] Some French went one step further and advocated that attacking troops not fire at all. One colonel of a foreign regiment in French service, Greder, outlawed any musketry in the attack, ordering his men to shoulder their muskets during the charge and forbidding them even to light their matches.[175] Until the invention of the socket bayonet, bayonet assaults automatically implied that the musketeers and fusiliers could not fire their weapons. The earliest French bayonet attack occurred no later than 1677 at the siege of Valenciennes, where, after an enemy cavalry charge, "The Musketeers, having put their bayonets in their fusils, marched at them and with grenades and bayonets, chased them back in the town."[176] In another use of the plug bayonet,

---

[168] Parker in Chandler, *The Art of Warfare*, 120.
[169] *Gazette de France*, 14 September 1709, 259.
[170] Chandler, *The Art of Warfare*, 116–21. [171] Nosworthy, *Anatomy of Victory*, 60.
[172] This is Nosworthy's interpretation of the French conservatism on firing systems, *Anatomy of Victory*, 6.
[173] *Gazette de France*, 14 September 1709, 259.
[174] Jean-Léonor Grimarest, *Fonctions des généraux ou l'art de conduire une armée* (La Haye: 1710), 78–81.
[175] Nosworthy, *Anatomy of Victory*, 100.
[176] AG, A¹531, 18 March 1677, Louvois to Courtin, in Rousset, *Louvois*, 2:288.

dragoons beat back enemy forces at a river crossing near the same town in 1684.[177] But even with the introduction of the socket bayonet, attackers still held their fire. At the battle of Marsaglia, 3 October 1693, Catinat ordered a charge "with bayonets on the ends of their fusils and without firing a shot."[178]

As they have so often in their history, the French pictured themselves as particularly apt in the assault with cold steel. A belief in a special French talent in combat *a l'arme blanche* probably goes back as far as Merovingian times. The cult of the bayonet peaked late in the eighteenth century and again, with tragic consequences, just prior to World War I.[179] Much of the language later assumed by advocates of the bayonet was already current in the seventeenth century. Writing in 1652, Laon expressed the belief that "French infantry is more suited to the attack than to the defense."[180] The French never seemed to tire of contrasting their own energy in the assault versus their enemies' stolid nature, particularly when Germans were involved. "The [German] infantry is constant enough when standing fast, but it is not lively in the attack and cannot carry off a *coup de main*."[181] Chamlay agreed in the superiority of the French infantry on the offensive, stating in 1690 that "During the last war, the enemy infantry ordinarily did not hold against the vigor of ours."[182] The same confidence typified opinion in the War of the Spanish Succession, when another memoir said of the enemy, "it was difficult for them to resist the valor of our nation in the first shock [of the attack]."[183] No less a figure than Marshal Villars praised "the air of audacity so natural to the French."[184] He affirmed, "In my opinion, the best method for the French infantry . . . is to charge with the bayonet on the end of the fusil."[185] Unlike in other eras, however, the seventeenth-century attack was meant to be carried out with little sound. Tactical directives again and again insisted that men in the ranks maintain a strict silence, all the better to hear the officers' commands.[186]

Their offensive predilection did not mean that the French always went on the attack. In fact, during the major battles fought in Flanders during the War of the Spanish Succession, the French assumed the defense. And at Malplaquet, French troops on the right flank, who had badly mauled the

---

[177] See the 21 May 1684 letter from Louvois to Schomberg in Hardré, *Letters of Louvois*, 355.

[178] Rousset, *Louvois*, 4:524. Bayonet attacks also took place at Staffarde in 1689 and at Fleurus in 1690. Rousset, *Louvois*, 4:366, 408.

[179] Regarding the cult of the bayonet during the French Revolution, see John A. Lynn, *The Bayonets of the Republic: A Study of Motivation and Tactics in the Armies of Revolutionary France, 1791–1794* (Urbana, IL: 1984), 185–93; and John A. Lynn, "French Opinion and the Military Resurrection of the Pike," *Military Affairs* (February 1977).

[180] Laon, *Practique et maximes de la guerre*, 70.   [181] SHAT, Bib., Arch. hist. 78, fol. 83.

[182] AG, A¹974, 2 June 1690, Chamlay to Louvois, in Rousset, *Louvois*, 3:325fn.

[183] SHAT, Bib., Arch. hist. 78, fol. 143, dated 1713.

[184] Claude Louis Hector Villars, *Mémoires du maréchal de Villars*, ed. Vogüé, 5 vols. (Paris: 1884–95), 3:82.

[185] BN, f. fr. 6257, Villars, "Traité," 83.

[186] For simply one such insistence on silence, see Azan, 65.

attacking Dutch, showed no inclination to switch over to the offensive themselves, albeit the French had by that point suffered serious casualties themselves and probably were exhausted.

As it turns out, firearms and not bayonets caused the greatest amount of wounds on the battlefield. At Malplaquet, for example, the best evidence indicates that two thirds of the wounds received by French troops came from the enemy's fusils, while only about 2 percent were inflicted by bayonets.[187] Of the men wounded by gunfire, 60 percent had been struck in the left side, the side facing the enemy as a soldier stood in line to fire himself.[188] Looking at a larger sample of veterans admitted to the Invalides in 1715, Corvisier arrived at the following breakdown of wounds: 71.4 percent from fire arms, 15.8 percent from swords, 10.0 percent from artillery, and only 2.8 percent from the bayonet.[189] Perhaps the figures for bayonet wounds are so small because bayonets may either have killed more effectively, and thus allowed less soldiers to survive to be admitted, or produced wounds that were more survivable without permanent maiming. It is also possible that bayonet charges proved their worth by driving defenders from their positions before the troops actually collided.

On the attack, cavalry, far more than infantry, proved decisive in the assault during the *grand siècle*. Of course, infantry had to believe in its own capacity to resist the mounted arm. Puységur wrote reassuringly that "if infantry understands its force, cavalry can never break it."[190] He might even have been correct; however, this was not the guiding principle of French battle tactics, which relied so much on cavalry for the crucial stroke.

CAVALRY WEAPONS AND TACTICS

Cavalry enjoyed great prestige and remained a potent offensive force in battle throughout the *grand siècle*. D'Aurignac, a student of Turenne who presented a military treatise to the king in 1663, wrote: "It is the cavalry that ordinarily wins battles."[191] Despite its tactical success, or perhaps because of it, French cavalry underwent only modest change in its armament, formations, and tactics, although it made a major advance in changing from a company to a regimental organization during the *grand siècle*.

Types of Cavalry and their Weapons

The army of the *grand siècle* employed a variety of cavalry types that shared the considerable mobility of the horse but exploited it in different manners and with different weapons. When Charles VIII invaded Italy in 1495, his

---

[187] André Corvisier, "Le moral des combattants, panique et enthousiasme, la bataille de Malplaquet," *Revue historique des armées*, 4, no. 3 (1977), 24.

[188] Contamine, *Histoire militaire*, 1:549.   [189] Contamine, *Histoire militaire*, 1:443.

[190] Nosworthy, *Anatomy of Victory*, 35.   [191] D'Aurignac in Bérenger, *Turenne*, 519.

cavalry had primarily been composed of armored lancers of the *compagnies d'ordonnance*.[192] As late as 1580, La Noue's cavalry company still numbered fifty lancers along with fifty pistoleers and twenty arquebusiers.[193] However, regular use of the lance by French cavalry had very nearly ceased by Coutras (1587) and the weapon had almost disappeared by Ivry (1590) and both the French and the Dutch abandoned it altogether in the next decade.[194]

The king's *gendarmes* considered themselves the true descendants of the *compagnies d'ordonnance* in the seventeenth century. The *gendarmes* retained a strictly company organization, never being grouped into regiments, and they counted among the king's military household under Louis XIV.[195] Unlike the normal cavalry, whose enlisted men were poor commoners, the troopers of the *gendarmerie* were aristocrats and bourgeois "living nobly" – that is, adopting the life style of aristocrats and thus engaged in "honorable" pursuits.[196] The *gendarmerie* provided a haven for nobles too poor to purchase a company. The royal household contained four particularly privileged companies classed as *gendarmes*, but the battle cavalry known as *gendarmes* consisted of sixteen other companies by late 1690, numbering sixty men each, exclusive of officers. They had shed their armor by then. In fact, the French had begun to set aside cavalry armor much earlier in the seventeenth century. So unpopular had it become by 1638 that in that year, Louis XIII had to order aristocratic officers to wear their armor or risk losing their noble rank.[197] Louis XIV issued a similar command in 1675, demanding all cavalry officers to wear *cuirasses*, but the law was widely disobeyed.[198] The only entire regiment still wearing any armor, reduced to a *cuirasse*, was the Royal Cuirassiers.[199]

During the *grand siècle*, line cavalry bore the title of *cavalerie légère*, although they were hardly "light cavalry" in the literal sense of the word; they only earned this description in comparison with the heavy armored lancers that they had replaced. By the seventeenth century, *cavalerie légère*, by far the most numerous French horsemen, constituted the regular battle cavalry, and in the eighteenth century, it dropped the *légère* from its title. The *cavalerie légère* carried the sword as their primary weapon.[200] This weapon was straight bladed, designed for thrusting more than slashing. After the Dutch War,

---

[192] Oman, *The Art of War in the Sixteenth Century*, 41.

[193] Delabarre-Duparcq, *L'art militaire*, 41. By the 1579 organization, cavalry alternated between pistol or lance as weapon. Before la Noue's company had sevety lancers, it counted fifty lancers, fifty pistoleers, and twenty arquebusiers.

[194] Oman, *The Art of War in the Sixteenth Century*, 463.

[195] See, for example, the lists of troops maintained in 1679, 1684, 1696, and 1699 AN, G⁷1774, #52.

[196] On the gendarmerie, see Sicard, *Histoire des institutions militaires*, 2:424–31, and Belhomme, *L'armée française en 1690*, 81–83.

[197] Caillet, *De l'administration en France*, 374–75.

[198] Ordinance of 5 March 1675, in Rousset, *Louvois*, 1:220.

[199] Louis Susane, *Histoire de la cavalerie française*, 3 vols. (Paris: 1874), 1:136.

[200] As late as the 1620s, Billon, *Les principes de l'art militaire*, 325, recommended lances for the lead company of cavalry.

Louvois instructed French cavalry to replace its swords with sabers, a curved weapon, better suited to slashing than thrusting.[201]

Cavalrymen also carried some sort of firearm, most commonly a brace of pistols, that fit neatly into a pair of holsters resting on the horse's withers. These pistols operated by a wheel-lock mechanism early in the *grand siècle*. This lock spun a serrated wheel against a piece of iron pyrite or flint to generate sparks that lit powder in the pan. Because of the clockwork mechanism that spun the wheel, wheel locks were expensive and delicate. Still, a matchlock would have been worse than useless on a cavalry pistol, since a rider occupied with controlling his horse could not have constantly fiddled with the match as an infantryman was required to do. Once the flintlock came into general use, it replaced the wheel lock. The pistol became the primary weapon for some cavalry, particularly for German *reiters* or pistoleers, who appeared as mercenary horse in French forces; however, the native French were less enamored of it.

Other firearms employed by horsemen included arquebuses, muskets, musketoons, fusils, and carbines. Such shoulder weapons were not carried by every cavalryman but by specialists. Henri IV had special units of arquebusiers and carabiniers on horseback.[202] These weapons were shorter and lighter than the standard musket. In 1622, Louis XIII took carbines away from his personal company of horse and replaced them with muskets.[203] By his death, the French possessed regiments of mounted musketeers and fusiliers, and to this was added in 1635 a new kind of cavalry, dragoons, who fought as mounted infantry, using the horse's mobility to arrive *en scène* quickly, but fighting on foot.[204] At first, dragoons carried a type of blunderbuss called a *dragon* – hence, their name – but later they carried muskets and finally fusils, which better fitted the needs of the dragoon.[205]

Regular cavalry could also integrate shoulder weapons into its tactics. Early in the personal reign of Louis XIV, d'Aurignac described squadrons in which eight to ten men in each company of cavalry carried a musketoon, a blunderbuss with seven to eight balls, intended to let off a devastating initial volley in cavalry actions.[206] In 1679, Louis XIV designated two picked shots in each cavalry company to carry rifled carbines.[207] Rifled shoulder weapons appeared relatively early in the history of firearms. If rifling gave weapons superior range and accuracy, it also made them much more expensive. In addition, rifles were more difficult to load, because the bullet had to be pounded into the rifling all the way down the barrel, and because the rifling frequently fouled, requiring scouring. All these reasons restricted rifling from becoming the standard in French firearms until the mid–nineteenth century.

[201] AG, A¹618, 22 February 1679, in Rousset, *Louvois*, 3:331.
[202] Xavier Audouin, *Histoire de l'administration de la guerre*, 4 vols. (Paris: 1811), 2:91.
[203] Caillet, *De l'adminstration en France*, 375.   [204] Caillet, *De l'adminstration en France*, 375.
[205] Rousset, *Louvois*, 1:224–25.   [206] Azan, *Un tacticien du XVIIe siècle*, 90.
[207] Rousset, *Louvois*, 3:331–32.

Still, for hunting and for special military purposes, rifles were available by the late sixteenth century.[208] The French army received significant numbers of rifles in the 1680s.[209] The carabiniers were, so to speak, the grenadiers of the cavalry; they proved so successful that they soon composed entire companies and, finally, their own regiment.[210] Infantry rarely carried rifled carbines.[211]

The last type of horseman to join the ranks of the French cavalry were hussars, a form of mounted unit composed of Hungarian light cavalry who forged their methods of combat fighting against the Turks. Hussars were true light cavalry, used best for raiding and scouting. They rode smaller horses, carried somewhat lighter weapons and curved sabers, and wore costumes typical of their origins. Proposals for *cavalerie hongroise* came in 1635, and by 1637, at least five companies of such exotic horsemen showed up on French rolls, but they disappeared with the Peace of the Pyrenees.[212] The first genuine French hussar regiment was raised in 1692 from Imperial deserters, and by 1710, the French counted three regiments of these often outlandish cavalry, regarded by some more as thieves on horseback than as true cavalrymen.[213]

Organization of Cavalry Regiments, Squadrons, and Companies

The basic administrative unit of cavalry, as with infantry, was the company, which, just as in the case of infantry, varied in size during the seventeenth century. French companies of *cavalerie légère* included 100 troopers in 1610, fell to 60 in 1620, climbed to 100 in 1630, and declined to 70 from 1640 through the end of the war with Spain.[214] Companies were reduced in size to 50 by an ordinance of 7 September 1659, and the great majority stayed at that level in the War of Devolution.[215] The companies retained after the War of Devolution rose to 100 troopers each. Company size fell to 50 in 1670, as

---

[208] For example, the Chicago Art Institute arms and armor collection includes rifled shoulder weapons dating from 1594 and the mid–seventeenth century.

[209] The arms manufacturer Titon was making rifled carbines for the cavalry about 1689. AG, A¹858, 14 October 1689, in Rousset, *Louvois*, 3:332fn.

[210] Rousset, *Louvois*, 3:331–32. Susane, *Histoire de la cavalerie*, 1:148–49. The arms manufacturer, Titon, made rifled carbines for the cavalry about 1689. AG, A¹858, 14 October 1689, in Rousset, *Louvois*, 3:332fn.

[211] In the fighting around Turin, 1690, Louvois supplied the best infantry shots with rifled carbines. Rousset, *Louvois*, 4:336.

[212] Caillet, *De l'administration en France*, 376.

[213] AN, G⁷1780, #212, *état* of French troops in 1707; AG, MR 1701, #13, *état* of French troops in 1710. Chandler, *The Art of Warfare in the Age of Marlborough*, 38, counts four hussar regiments in 1701, but that would seem to be in error. See "Mémoire des trouppes que le roy a sur pied," in Girard, *Racolage et milice*, 7.

[214] AG, Bib., A1h 638, vol. II.

[215] This account of the strength of cavalry companies, 1659–72, is derived basically from Susane, *Histoire de la cavalerie*, 1:115, 118, 119–22.

the old companies were split in two to form a small squadron, followed in 1671 by a confusing move that first saw the two companies increased to 100 troopers each and then split into three companies of 60 to 70 each to form an entire squadron. During the Dutch War, company size stabilized at 50 once more, where it stayed until reduced to 30 in 1679.[216] These companies rose to 45 a few years later in 1684.[217] From this point on, the size of regular *cavalerie légère* companies steadily declined, to 40 at the start of the Nine Years' War, to 35 later in that conflict, to 30 enlisted men by early 1699, and then down to 20 men by an ordinance of December 1699.[218] The outbreak of the War of the Spanish Succession drove up company size again to 30 by early 1702 and then to 35 at the height of the conflict.[219]

Special mounted units followed somewhat different paths. In 1679, dragoon companies counted 40 dragoons each and retained that number until they decreased to match the regular cavalry figure of 35 by 1696.[220] In 1689, Chamlay proposed adding one entire company of carabiniers to each cavalry regiment. After consideration, 107 companies were created by the ordinance of 25 October 1690. These companies contained 30 men each at the height of both the last two wars of Louis XIV. On campaign, the carabiniers from each field army massed in their own brigade.[221] Hussar companies counted 50 hussars each in 1710.[222]

French cavalry regiments were born in the *grand siècle*, for, unlike the infantry, cavalry regiments could not trace their origins back before 1635. In the early seventeenth century, companies existed as independent, or "free," units, unattached to any larger entity. A regulation of 1634 reorganized French cavalry into ninety-one squadrons of cavalry and seven of carabiniers.[223] By an ordinance of 16 May 1635, Louis XIII, at the insistence of Richelieu, established twelve regiments of cavalry and one of carabiniers; then on 27 May, he created six regiments of dragoons. At this point, French regiments

---

[216] AG, Arch. hist. 78, feiulle 165; and Sicard, *Histoire des institutions militaires*, 2:433; and AN, G⁷1774, #52. Rousset, *Louvois*, 1:221, states that Louvois regularized this organization into companies of fifty troopers each in 1668. D'Aurignac in 1663 describes a cavalry company as 100 enlisted men. Azan, *Un tacticien du XVIIᵉ siècle*, 100.

[217] AN, G⁷1774, #52.

[218] Belhomme, *L'Armée française en 1690*, 86; AN, G⁷1774, #52, for February 1699; Girard, *Racolage et milice*, 4, for December 1699.

[219] AG, Arch. hist. 78, feiulle 165; "Mémoire des trouppes que le roy a sur pied," in Girard, *Racolage et milice*, 7, for January 1702; and AG, MR 1701, piece 13, for 1710. Actual review reports of the cavalry regiments Dauphiné, Grignan, and Royal Cravate from Lille show cavalry companies at twenty at the start of 1701, rising to about thirty later that year, and climbing again to thirty-five in the spring of 1702. Lille, 11,113.

[220] AG, Arch. hist. 78, feiulle 165; AN, G⁷1774, #52.

[221] Rousset, *Louvois*, 3:331–32. For company size and brigades in the War of the Spanish Succession, see AG, MR 1701, #13.

[222] AG, MR 1701.

[223] This account of the regimental development, 1634–78, is derived basically from Susane, *Histoire de la cavalerie*, 1:88–91, 95, 105, 113, 115–16, 119–20, 122, 125.

were composed of two squadrons, each of two companies. During the war that ended in 1659, the number of cavalry regiments in French service fluctuated from sixty to 170, and 112 were still in being as the war ended. In the few years immediately following the war, the king at first disbanded all but one or two companies of each regiment, and then abandoned regiments almost entirely, until he retained but four complete regiments and some sixty companies belonging to the colonels (*mestres de camp*) of previous regiments that might serve as the nuclei of new ones. All the carabiniers of the war with Spain were disbanded in 1661. Louis rebuilt his regiments for the War of the Devolution until they finally numbered ninety-five, but following the war, he again reduced all but a few of those he retained to single companies. In a 1670–71 buildup that finally created a force of permanent regiments, each of these companies became the basis for an entire squadron, as mentioned earlier. When the Dutch War broke out, each of these squadrons became the core of a regiment once more, most of which contained two squadrons of three companies each. Susane, the historian of cavalry, considers the creation of the squadrons and regiments in 1671–72 as the true origin of the permanent regiments, rather than seeing them as stemming from the 1635 ordinance. By January 1678, the French army counted ninety-nine regiments of *cavalerie légère*.

At their inception, these truly permanent regiments were composed of squadrons of three companies each, and regiments included two, three, or four squadrons; however, the number of companies in a squadron increased to four by the Nine Years' War and remained at that level for the rest of the reign of Louis XIV.[224] Regular French cavalry and dragoon regiments contained two or three squadrons.[225] Rather than the company or regiment, the squadron served as the tactical unit of cavalry in battle. In many ways, it paralleled the battalion, except that whereas the battalion enjoyed a degree of administrative independence, the squadron did not.

Specialist cavalry assembled in their own regiments. Dragoon regiments appeared alongside cavalry units on army lists at an early date. A *milice de dragons*, suppressed after 1628, reappeared in 1635, and soon after this, cardinal Richelieu created an entire regiment of dragoons for his service.[226] In addition, many cavalry regiments included a company of *mousquetaires à cheval*, another term for dragoons before 1669.[227] Although dragoons also were disbanded after the Peace of the Pyrenees, there were two regiments of them by 1668.[228] At the start of the Dutch War, there was still only this pair of regiments, but dragoons so proved their worth that commanders requested more.[229] By the last year of the war, the number of regiments rose

---

[224] See Belhomme, *L'armée française en 1690*, 86; AN, G71774, #52, for 1696, and AG, MR 1701, #13, for 1710. Susane, *Histoire de la cavalerie*, 1:133, is incorrect.

[225] See, for example AG, MR 1701, #13.

[226] Caillet, *De l'adminstration en France*, 375–76. This regiment included 1,200 dragoons.

[227] Caillet, *De l'adminstration en France*, 375.   [228] Susane, *Histoire de la cavalerie*, 1:119.

[229] In 1677, Luxembourg complained about the lack of dragoons, which he used for convoy escorts, and he had only one regiment. AG, A¹539, 7 July 1677.

to fourteen, at a time when the *cavalerie légère* claimed ninety regiments.[230] By 1690, Louis XIV increased the number of dragoon regiments to thirty-three.[231] The carabiniers were so popular that in 1693, Louis united the companies that were attached to regular cavalry regiments into a huge regiment of their own that included five brigades, each of ten squadrons.[232]

After the Nine Years' War, the number of cavalry regiments stood at seventy-four of *cavalerie légère*, fourteen of dragoons, and one of carabiniers.[233] In 1710, Louis had 105 French regiments of *cavalerie légère*, the regiment of carabiniers, four foreign cavalry regiments, three regiments of hussars, and thirty-four regiments of dragoons, but at the conclusion of the war, this was cut to fifty-eight regiments of cavalry and fifteen of dragoons.[234]

As is obvious from the preceding discussion, most regiments created for war did not enjoy a long life. Throughout the *grand siècle*, the number of regiments that appeared only to disappear, either by outright extinction or by absorption into a permanent unit, was very great. Between 1635 and 1715, this was the fate of 420 mounted regiments![235] Certain specialist and elite cavalry regiments enjoyed brief existences during the *grand siècle*. Companies of mounted musketeers, fusiliers, carabiniers, and hussars came and went during the first half of the century.[236] However, the cavalry regiments kept on the permanent list under Louis XIV included only *cavalerie légère*, dragoons, carabiniers, and the units of the royal household, which included the companies of *gendarmes*.

Cavalry Formations and Tactics

Michael Roberts argues that by the early seventeenth century, European cavalry abandoned the natural advantages that momentum bestowed upon mounted troops.[237] Instead of turning the tide of battle by charging the enemy with sword or lance, horsemen wasted their potential by drawing their pistols to dicker with the enemy in such unfortunate maneuvers as the caracole. To perform the caracole, a body of cavalry several ranks deep approached the enemy. The first rank fired its pistols, wheeled about, and rode to the rear of the formation to reload; the succeeding ranks fired and wheeled in a mounted countermarch. By the time the last rank had fired, the first would be ready to discharge its weapons once again. The intention was to

---

[230] Rousset, *Louvois*, 1:225, 221. [231] Belhomme, *L'armée française en 1690*, 100.

[232] Susane, *Histoire de la cavalerie*, 1:149. [233] AN, G⁷1774, #52.

[234] AG, MR 1701, #13; Susane, *Histoire de la cavalerie*, 1:151. Sicard accepts Daniel's statement that in 1715, there were only twenty-four cavalry regiments and thirty-five dragoon regiments. This seems a serious error, since this turns the figures on their heads. Sicard, *Histoire des institutions militaires*, 2:435.

[235] Sicard, *Histoire des institutions militaires*, 2:436.

[236] For Bérenger, some of this type of cavalry simply metamorphosed into dragoons. Bérenger, *Turenne*, 520.

[237] Again, Roberts's analysis cannot be accepted without challenge. See Geoffrey Parker, "The 'Military Revolution' 1560–1660 – A Myth?" *Journal of Modern History*, 48 (June 1976), 199, on Spanish cavalry.

blow a hole in the enemy square, but when used against infantry, the caracole almost invariably cost the attacking cavalry more than the defending infantry, because infantry muskets outclassed cavalry pistols in range and power. Roberts awards Gustavus considerable credit for "the emancipation of cavalry from the caracole." By restoring cavalry to its traditional role of charging sword in hand, the great Swede gave his armies a tool for decision on the battlefield that his enemies lacked.

When considered in terms of French experience, Roberts's generalizations concerning cavalry bear up under scrutiny somewhat better than do his characterizations of infantry tactics, but they still place too little emphasis on the independent development of tactics within France itself.[238] French cavalry began the sixteenth century fighting in an essentially medieval style. The *gendarmes* of the *companies d'ordonnance* still charged with the lance in a thin, extended line, *en haie*. A number of factors, including the shortage of proper horses and the loss of traditional military skills among young gentlemen, but primarily the difficulties of defeating unshaken infantry squares with lance-armed cavalry, led the French to adopt the weapons, armor, and tactics of the German *reiters* by the mid–sixteenth century.

The Wars of Religion manifested the triumph and the later decline of *reiter* tactics among the French. Under Charles IX and Henri III the caracole predominated. To apply this tactic, the French abandoned their traditional formation *en haie* and marshaled troopers in dense formations twelve or even sixteen ranks deep.[239] Pistols, carbines, and blunderbusses served the horsemen who, after the firefight, closed for the melée with sword in hand. Considering the French taste for edged weapons, *l'arme blanche*, it is surprising to see them relying on the pistol as they did. But it comes as no surprise that the French did not rest easy with this tactical formula.

The emphasis on firearms as opposed to cold steel certainly did not have to await Gustavus to find its critics. The tactical debate was well underway by the end of the sixteenth century, as works of the Huguenot la Noue and the royalist Tavannes attest.[240] Temperament and professional conviction prevented Henri IV from accepting the sterile caracole. He reshaped French cavalry formations and tactics, reducing the depth of squadrons to six ranks, and even to five. At Coutras (1587) and Ivry (1590), his cavalry used their firearms for an initial shot but then charged home with the sword at the gallop. In accord with the counsel of la Noue, Henri demonstrated that in shock attack, the six-rank formation was superior to cavalry drawn up *en haie*

[238] On French cavalry tactics in the sixteenth century, see Reboul, "Des croisades à la Révolution," 294–96; Oman, *Art of War in the Sixteenth Century*, 462–65; Delabarre-Duparcq, *Histoire de l'art de la guerre*, 155–56, 165–66; and idem, *L'Art militaire*, 37–45.

[239] Oman, *Art of War in the Sixteenth Century*, 402, argues that the French still charged *en haie* during the Religious wars.

[240] See François de la Noue, *Discours politiques et militaires* (Basle: 1587) and Gaspard de Saulx, Seigneur de Tavannes, *La vie de Gaspard de Saulx, Seigneur de Tavannes* in *Collection complète des mémoires relatifs à l'histoire de France*, ed. M. Petitot, vols. 23–25 (Paris: 1822).

as the royalists were at Coutras.[241] To bolster his cavalry, Henri also interspersed companies of musketeers between his squadrons, a tactic that continued into the Thirty Years' War.[242] This practice was dropped about midcentury.[243]

Thus, by 1600, the French were already moving toward the style of attack advocated by Gustavus a quarter-century later.[244] What influence Gustavus exerted upon French cavalry was restricted to significant but not radical adjustments, such as the Swedish practice of forming cavalry in three ranks and of discharging pistols at a greater distance from the enemy than Frenchmen were accustomed to doing, but this hardly constituted a revolutionary change in their techniques.

Throughout the reign of Louis XIV, native French cavalry adopted a depth of three ranks, as the Swedes had done before them.[245] The formation in three ranks remained standard for French cavalry for the remainder of the century, although Puységur comments concerning the War of the Spanish Succession that "on entering the campaign, they were not all in three ranks, because all were not complete, towards the middle many were in two ranks, and towards the end, few were in three ranks."[246] A directive for combat, apparently dated about the same time as the order for infantry combat, that is from the late 1670s to the late 1680s, stipulated a three rank formation and advised putting the best men in the squadron in the first rank.[247] Not only were the best troopers concentrated at the front of the squadron but also on its flanks, where the twenty troopers posted to both the extreme right and the left flanks were known as "commanded" men, and were chosen not only to anchor the squadron but also for special tasks.[248] Intervals between ranks

---

[241] La Noue was critical of caracole tactics, La Noue, *Discours militaire*, 444–45, in Oman, *The Art of War in the Sixteenth Century*, 42. La Noue favored cavalry six to seven deep. La Noue, *Discours militaire*, 415–16. The best men should be in the first two or three ranks, with recruits or men with inferior horses or armor in the rear ranks. Oman, *The Art of War in the Sixteenth Century*, 464.

[242] Susane, *Histoire de la cavalerie*, 1:75–76, says that at the end of the sixteenth century, the French cavalry formed on three ranks at least, often five or six deep, and that often cavalry companies of about eighty troopers were placed between infantry battalions.

[243] Colin, *L'infanterie au XVIIIe siècle*, 19.

[244] Reboul, "Des croisades à la Révolution," 372.

[245] On cavalry organization and tactics in the seventeenth century, see Nosworthy, *Anatomy of Victory*, 121–40; Chandler, *Art of War in the Age of Marlborough*, 27–61; Reboul, "Des croisades à la Révolution," 368–72, 439–41; Delabarre-Duparcq, *Histoire de l'art de la guerre*, 211–12; and Susane, *Histoire de la cavalerie*. For recommendations that the cavalry form on three ranks see Laon, *Practique et maximes de la guerre*, 64–65; Mallet, *Les travaux de Mars*, 14–16; Gaya, *Le nouvel art de la guerre*, 109–10; Birac, *Les fonctions du capitaine de cavalerie*, vol. 1 (La Haye: 1693), 100; BN, f. fr. 6257, Villars, "Traité," 88; Puységur, *Art de la guerre*, 1:53.

[246] Puységur, *Art de la guerre*, 1:52, 58. Belhomme, *L'armée française en 1690*, 93, states the same for the Nine Years' War.

[247] AG, Arch. hist. 78, fol. 71–72. "Disposition de la cavalerie reglée par Sa Majesté pour un jour de combat."

[248] Nosworthy, *Anatomy of Victory*, 95.

and files varied; several military handbooks of the late seventeenth century prescribe a distance between ranks of two horse lengths.[249] For combat, the squadron tightened; d'Aurignac recommended closing the files knee to knee and the ranks to only a foot in the charge.[250]

Cavalry evolutions and deployments were relatively few in number. As Gaya put it, the main drill for cavalry consisted only of forming a squadron and defiling from it.[251] French cavalry commonly marched by fours or twos on the road but always formed squadron in three ranks for fighting, so the movements were relatively simple.[252] It was the charge itself that most concerned cavalrymen and military writers. In general, cavalry had to balance order with momentum; the slower the pace, the better the squadron could maintain its formation, but the faster the pace, the greater the shock of the charge. The French compromised by advancing at the trot in order to maintain cohesion and to avoid exhausting the horses; then they spurred into a gallop for no more than the last fifty yards. Once they accelerated, there could be little chance to maintain exact order and distances. The disciplined charge at the gallop, knee to knee, was a Prussian invention of the 1740s that was beyond the capabilities of seventeenth-century cavalry.

Puységur states that until the Dutch War, French cavalry still employed a form of the caracole using a musketoon, and recently some historians have echoed this claim.[253] According to this point of view, French cavalry employed the caracole before they were liberated from it by Turenne and Condé, although some French troops still engaged in this sterile tactic up to the Dutch War. From the 1670s into the 1690s, the French got it right, abandoning firepower and resorting exclusively to the charge with sword alone. However, sometime in the 1690s, the French reverted to firing at an enemy before they charged, a tactic that cost French horsemen momentum and lost them the superiority that they had enjoyed on the battlefield since the 1640s. Thus, just as infantry stuck to outmoded fire tactics, the cavalry too took a wrong turn that contributed to defeat in the War of the Spanish Succession. Were this analysis correct, it might explain a great deal, but it seems to be flawed, or at least it must be questioned.

As already stated, native French cavalry seemed to have abandoned the caracole in the sixteenth century, not the seventeenth. If Turenne suppressed the caracole among his troops, it is important to recognize who those troops

---

[249] See Gaya, Le nouvel art de la guerre, 109–10; Mallet, Travaux de Mars (1684), 102; Birac, Les fonctions du capitaine de cavalerie, 100. Belhomme, L'armée française en 1690, 93, gives the interval for drill as three paces.

[250] Azan, Un tacticien du XVII' siècle, 65. Pichat, "Les armées de Louis XIV en 1674," 26, gives a combat formation with three feet between ranks and two between files, but for the charge, this also reduced to a foot between ranks and "boot to boot" between files.

[251] Gaya, Le nouvel art de la guerre, 109–110.

[252] Birac, Les fonctions du capitaine de cavalerie, 100.

[253] Puységur, Art de la guerre, 1:120–21. It should be noted that Puységur reports very conservative practices before the 1670s, even arguing that Condé and Turenne marshalled their infantry eight ranks deep, which does not seem that probable. 1:58 and plate 1. Nosworthy, Anatomy of Victory, 38 and 127, repeats Puységur's claim concerning the caracole.

were – Germans.[254] Turenne gained his first great command when he took over the remnants of the army assembled by Bernard of Saxe-Weimar, and this force contained German pistoleers who might be expected to still practice the caracole. So, while Puységur is an important source, his statement regarding the longevity of the caracole needs to be regarded with some skepticism.

D'Aurignac, a student of Turenne, and a writer who probably presents one version of contemporary practice at the close of France's long war with Spain, wanted cavalry in the charge to close with pistols at the gallop "and to not shoot until pistols cross, and especially not to discharge their weapons before the enemy fires theirs."[255] A charge such as this can in no way be described as a caracole. In fact, the intervals allowed between files within the squadron by midcentury would never have permitted a countermarch. D'Aurignac would also have the first rank armed in part with musketoons that would be fired at thirty to forty paces, just before breaking into the final run.[256] The greatest problem here would be that the squadron had to halt to give fire.

Tactical historians debate the degree to which French cavalry reverted to using their pistols in the last two wars of Louis XIV.[257] Although there is plenty of evidence of French cavalry firing during the War of the Spanish Succession, Villars, the greatest French commander of that war, clearly favored the charge with the sword alone; in fact, he did not even want his dragoons to fire from horseback but rather to fight with the sword.[258] In all probability, different regiments followed different practices as suited their commanders. It would be foolish to expect uniformity during the *grand siècle*. The safest generalization is that pistol fire always, or nearly always, played some role in the cavalry charge *à la française* during most of the century, but that it was fired preparatory to going at the enemy with the sword. Incidentally, shots might be aimed not at the adversary but at his horse, in order to dismount him.[259]

An entirely separate issue may cloud the debate concerning the firepower of French squadrons. As mentioned earlier, French cavalry adopted the rifled carbine from 1679 on. The function of the carabiniers was to keep the enemy skirmishers at a distance until the cavalry was ready to close; thus, carabiniers would spare French cavalry from harassing fire. Villars advised putting

[254] See Susane, *Histoire de la cavalerie*, 1:94, for a list of the "Weimarian" regiments.

[255] Azan, *Un tacticien du XVIIe siècle*, 65.   [256] Azan, *Un tacticien du XVIIe siècle*, 90.

[257] Nosworthy and Chandler argue that French cavalry relied only on their swords from the Dutch War into the Nine Years' War and then reverted to fire. However, the historian Belhomme exactly reverses this, saying that directives of 1690 altered French practice in the opposite direction. Before then, the French came to within thirty paces of the enemy, fired their pistols, and drew their swords to close at a gallop, but 1690 instructions ordered the men not to fire but to simply gallop at the enemy sword in hand for the last fifty yards. Belhomme, *L'armée française en 1690*, 93.

[258] BN, f. fr. 6257, Villars, "Traité," 60–61, 82.

[259] Micheline Cuénin, *Le duel sous l'ancien régime* (Paris: 1982), 124, tells of a 1643 duel on horseback, which reflected on battle practice.

carabiniers on the flanks of the squadron "in order to fire on the enemy at a distance."[260] The addition of carabiniers within the cavalry regiments may well have been an attempt to gain the firepower advantages provided by interspersed bodies of musketeers, without suffering the limitations on mobility that they imposed. The carbine was above all a skirmishing weapon, not a tool of the caracole or the charge.

ARTILLERY WEAPONS AND TACTICS

Artillery increased in importance over the course of the *grand siècle* due to its value on the battlefield and its prominence in siege warfare, which certainly became the more common form of conflict during this period. As the century progressed, artillery equipment and personnel evolved; cannon differentiated between those designed for positional warfare and those meant for the open field. Fusiliers were created to serve and protect the guns as artillery specialists; their regiment eventually became the Regiment Royal Artillerie and was joined by another regiment of bombardiers – that is, mortar specialists. At the start of the century, artillery began as a separate arm under the supervision of the grand master of artillery, but as time passed, artillery fell more and more under the jurisdiction of the secretary of state for war.[261]

Cannon to 1659

Any discussion of artillery must begin with the weapons themselves. The French army of the *grand siècle* employed primarily two types of artillery pieces: cannon and mortars. Although howitzers were available, the French made little use of them. For siege warfare, perriers, stone-throwing pieces, also played a part heaving anti-personnel loads in high trajectory.

The cannon, by far the most numerous piece, fired solid round shot and various packaged rounds, which included grapeshot, a cluster of smaller balls, and canister, a container of musket balls that gave a cannon the destructive potential of a huge shotgun at short ranges. Solid shot was, however, the primary projectile of the cannon, and calibers were rated by the weight of shot that they could fire. According to the ordinance of 1686, such projectiles were propelled by gunpowder that was composed of 75 parts saltpeter, 12.5 parts sulfur, and 12.5 parts charcoal. It was the same powder used for small arms.[262] The power of solid shot could be amazing; a 24-pound cannonball could penetrate thirty-five feet of packed earth at 150 yards.[263] This was deadly force both in siege warfare and in battle.

It would not be excessive to say that cannon set the parameters for warfare in the early modern era, particularly since they defined both the attack and

---

[260] BN, f. fr. 6257, Villars, "Traité," 82,
[261] Louis André, *Michel Le Tellier et Louvois* (Paris: 1942), 384–85.
[262] Chandler, *The Art of Warfare*, 185.   [263] Chandler, *The Art of Warfare*, 183.

defense of fortresses. Some would go even further and argue that artillery also played a political role, because the great expense of artillery gave a political/military advantage to monarchs over their independent nobility, since monarchs could best afford them.[264] Any discussion of the Military Revolution, either in the mode of Michael Roberts or Geoffrey Parker, must deal with these great machines of war. When Michael Roberts turned to discuss artillery as a component of the Military Revolution, he chose to concentrate only on cannon for the open field, and thus he emphasized the development of small mobile pieces by Gustavus Adolphus, who he claims "revolutionized" missile support "by the use of a light three-pounder gun" and by "decisive improvements in the mobility of field artillery."[265] Since this chapter has measured the extent to which Roberts and other theorists of a Military Revolution have done justice to the French case with regard to infantry and artillery, it is only right and fitting that it do so for artillery as well.

The chief factor that limited the use of cannon in the early modern era, particularly on the battlefield, was their weight. In the 1620s, the barrel alone of a 34-pounder weighed 5,600 pounds, and the cannon on its carriage required twenty horses to pull it and a crew of thirty-five to serve it.[266] Artillery trains possessed neither their own draft animals nor their own teamsters; instead, armies hired civilian drivers and their teams to haul cannon. On the day of battle, these civilian contractors would drag the heavy pieces into position and then withdraw out of harm's way. Once in place, the cumbrous cannon could not be shifted to keep pace with the movement of the action.

Roberts credits Gustavus with developing light pieces that could be manhandled to support advancing infantry. Without abandoning the larger calibers, Gustavus multiplied the numbers of 3-pounders and attached one such light cannon to each infantry battalion. In France, these close support weapons went by the name "regimental guns." A survey of calibers reveals that the French had a long tradition of smaller pieces and that although these were certainly heavier than the Swedish, the use of small-caliber cannon on the battlefield was nothing new to the French.

At the beginning of the reign of François I, the French possessed a bewildering variety of at least seventeen calibers; he later cut the official number to eight. Henri II further reduced the system to the "six calibers of France," which included guns firing projectiles of 33 pounds 4 ounces, 15 pounds 2 ounces, 7 pounds 2 ounces, 2 pounds, 1 pound 1 ounce, and 14 ounces.[267]

---

[264] For a recent statement of this argument, see Bruce D. Porter, *War and the Rise of the State* (New York: 1994), 31.

[265] Roberts, "Military Revolution," 8.

[266] These figures come from the very interesting and very detailed tables supplied by Praissac, *Les discours militaires*, 112–30. I have called his 33⅓-pounder a 34-pounder and his 15¼-pounder a 16-pounder for convenience.

[267] On the matériel and organization of the French artillery during the sixteenth and early seventeenth centuries, see Reboul, "Des croisades à la Révolution," 274–79, 296–97, 372–73, 441–43; Jean Brunet, *Histoire générale de l'artillerie française*, 2 vols. (Paris: 1842): and Louis Susane, *Histoire de l'artillerie française* (Paris: 1874).

Admittedly, attempts to standardize military practices in the sixteenth and even the seventeenth century were just that – attempts.[268] Although the confusion of reality did not yield easily to the rationality of system, it is important that efforts were made to standardize and simplify. Not too surprisingly, the turmoil of the Wars of Religion witnessed a breakdown of Henri II's system. With the return of peace, Henri IV and his able minister Maxmillien de Béthune, duke de Sully, labored to standardize artillery matériel. As grand master of artillery, Sully restricted French pieces to calibers of only 34, 24, 16, 12, 8, and 4 pounds.[269] Writing in 1622, du Praissac also regarded six calibers as standard, but his list did not correlate exactly with Sully's system.[270] In fact, they were even lighter, being much closer to Henri II's six calibers than to those associated with Sully. On close examination, then, it is plain that the French had a long tradition of small caliber pieces, stretching back to the falcons of Charles VIII.[271]

As for the deployment of light cannon, admiration for Swedish victories and contact with the great Gustavus Adolphus and his able lieutenants led the French to imitate the Swedish use of regimental guns. French regimental pieces proliferated after 1635. As early as 1636, the French used small regimental pieces to good advantage in resisting the Spanish at the Somme. At the high point of this enthusiasm for regimental guns, French troops employed five types of 4-pounders and several varieties of 3-pounders.[272] However, the historian of artillery, Brunet, called this emphasis on regimental pieces "a matter of style" that caused the French to neglect their artillery parks, the central assemblage of cannon directly under the general's control.[273] The vogue for regimental pieces enjoyed a short life. From about 1643 on, regimental pieces disappeared, to the relief of major artillery officers who wished them returned to the parks. At the same time, the French reestablished Sully's system of guns – though light cannon clearly predominated – so that 4- and 8-pounders made up the majority of guns in the artillery parks of Condé and Turenne.[274] One is forced to reach the conclusion that Roberts's claim that Gustavus introduced the wide use of light cannon and won Europe over to the use of regimental guns seems at best an overstatement of the case for France.

Viewed with the hindsight of military history, there were good reasons

---

[268] It is important to recognize the bewildering confusion of reality. AG, A^{1}210, 7 December 1667, #88 list of artillery pieces in Perpignan, seventy-three pieces in thirteen calibers from twenty-eight pounds to fourteen ounces, in André, *Le Tellier*, 518. In 1666, for example, 38-, 28-, 26-, 24-, 14-, 9-, 8-, 6-, and 5-pounders were found at the fortress of Pignerol. André, *Le Tellier*, 518.

[269] Reboul, "Des croisades à la Révolution," 372.

[270] Du Praissac's cannon ran 33⅓ pounds, 15¼ pounds, 7½ pounds, 3½ pounds, 1½ pounds, and ¾ pounds. Praissac, *Les discours militaires*, 112–30.

[271] Reboul, "Des croisades à la Révolution," 372, makes precisely this point.

[272] Brunet, *Histoire générale*, 2:57.   [273] Brunet, *Histoire générale*, 2:65.

[274] Brunet, *Histoire générale*, 2:87–88.

why Gustavus's system of light regimental guns would not become a French standard. Two conflicting pressures drove artillery development, presenting seventeenth-century artillerists with a serious dilemma. Battlefield tactics required lighter, more mobile pieces, but the growing importance of fortification and siege warfare demanded cannon capable of firing heavy shot great distances. Artillery thus split into two categories: field and siege. As siege warfare came to predominate in the second half of the century, there were real advantages to constructing even field artillery with barrels long enough and chambers thick enough to be used effectively in siege warfare. Thus, the extremely light and short-barreled cannon popularized by the Swedes possessed certain inherent limitations, and it is little wonder that the French returned to more substantial pieces by midcentury. To this extent, the impact of Swedish practice on seventeenth-century artillery was doomed to be short-lived.

French Artillery Systems under Louis XIV

The French responded to the problems imposed by the great weight and limited mobility of artillery pieces in a way that demonstrates both the promises and limitations of technological innovation in early modern warfare. Immediately after the Dutch War, the French tested and then introduced an entirely new artillery system, the cannon *"de nouvelle invention"* to stand alongside the older guns *"de vielle invention."*

By midcentury, the French had settled essentially on Sully's system of six calibers; 12- and 24-pounders considered "Spanish," while 33-, 16-, 8-, and 4-pounders were thought of as "French."[275] But this apparently rational system encompassed much more variety, and much less uniformity, than might at first be obvious. For one thing, cannon of a given caliber could be had in three forms. Those whose bores had been cast at maximum thickness to take a full charge of powder, equated at the full weight of the ball, were "doubly fortified." But there were lighter weights as well, the "legitimate" that could take four fifths of a charge and the "bastard" that could only accommodate two thirds of a charge. But the variety did not end here. In fact, cannon supposed to employ shot of the same weight were of different-sized bore; thus, shot made to fit a 33-pounder cast at Saint-Gervais would not fit a 33-pounder cast at Charleville.[276]

Whatever their caliber or type, cannon *de vielle invention* were quite heavy. First, they were cast with chamber walls thick enough to accommodate powder charges of two thirds the projectile's weight, or more. Second, the guns were not only heavy-walled but long, ranging from 11 feet 1 inch to 10 feet 7 inches

---

[275] Chandler, *The Art of Warfare in the Age of Marlborough*, 176–93.

[276] Chandler, *The Art of Warfare in the Age of Marlborough*, 177, gives this example. According to Belhomme, the major French artillery foundries circa 1690 were at Strasbourg, Auxonne, Douai, Tournai, Metz, and Perpignan. Belhomme, *L'armée française en 1690*, 121–22.

over the entire range of calibers. Their length resulted from a self-conscious decision to make every cannon long enough to fire through gun embrasures on fortress walls or in siege works. A barrel that was too short could damage the embrasure with its muzzle blast. Casting every piece long meant that fortress pieces were interchangeable with field pieces; only their carriages differed. It is informative that when d'Aurignac spoke of the "six calibers of the king" in 1663, he described them in terms of their use in fortress defense, so even the light pieces fit in "for service both in the *chemin couvert* as well as in works outside the main fortress."[277]

Cannon *de nouvelle invention* resulted from discoveries attributed to Antonio Gonzalès, who first tried to market his system in Spain and, after meeting failure there, brought it to France in 1679.[278] By reshaping the powder chamber into a spherical form with a larger diameter than the bore, it was found that one could achieve acceptable results with powder charges only one third the weight of the projectile. This minor miracle was made possible by the shape of the chamber and by igniting the charge at the top rather than at the back of the older cylindrical chambers. In the new design, the powder charge burned more rapidly because as the powder burned, it exposed a larger surface area of the remaining powder to ignition. With less powder, the walls of the bore, if not the chamber, could be thinner and thus lighter. Also, the new pieces were designed specifically for field use and therefore much shorter. Excluding the casabel, the knob that projected at the rear of the barrel, a 24-pounder of the old system extended 10 feet 2 inches, whereas a 24-pounder of the new system was only 6 feet long.[279] With much less metal, the new pieces were much lighter; excluding the carriage, the old 16-pounder weighed in at 4,100 French pounds, or livres, and the new came in at 2,220; the respective weights for a 4-pounder were 1,300 livres and 600 livres.[280] Mobility was further enhanced by changes in the carriage and the addition of an *avant train* for it.

---

[277] Azan, *Un tacticien du XVIIᵉ siècle*, 93.

[278] For accounts of cannon *de nouvelle invention*, see Ernest Picard and Louis Jouan, *L'artillerie française au XVIIIe siècle* (Paris: 1906), 44–47; Howard Rosen, "The Système Gribeauval: A Study of Technological Development and Institutional Change in Eighteenth-Century France," Ph.D. dissertation, University of Chicago, 1981, 128–33; and Chandler, *The Art of Warfare in the Age of Marlborough*, 176–93.

[279] Chandler, *The Art of Warfare in the Age of Marlborough*, 178, gives the contrasting dimensions as 10 feet 10 inches and 6 feet 3 inches. My dimensions come from Denis Diderot et al., *Encyclopédie*, 17 vols. text, 12 vols. plates (Paris: 1751–65), vol. 1 plates, plates V and VI in Art militaire, fortification. These plates allow a close comparison that demonstrates how the metal was tapered differently in the cannon *de nouvelle invention* to allow for the force of the charge but still employ thin walls along the bore. N.B.: All measurements of length and weight are given here in the French system of the *ancien régime*.

[280] The livre, or French pound, was slightly heavier than the modern English pound. The livre weighed 489.506 grams, while the pound comes in at 453.592. Therefore, the old livre equals 1.079 pounds. See Marcel Marion, *Dictionnaire des institutions de la France aux XVIIe et XVIIIe siècles* (Paris: 1923), 373–76, for weights and measures of the *ancien régime*.

Such pieces promised many advantages, but Louvois was attracted by the potential economies resulting from the use of less gunpowder. That is, the war minister saw the new artillery in financial rather than tactical terms. Louvois sent Captain Gonzalès to Douai to conduct tests in 1680. There the new guns caught the interest of Lieutenant General François de la Frézelière, a brilliant artillery officer who became the greatest proponent of Gonzalès's system. In 1681, models of the lighter guns were sent to all French foundries to serve as templates for production.

Cannon *de nouvelle invention* would seem to have promised a great breakthrough in artillery matériel, but they also suffered from three drawbacks that finally led the French to reject them in the eighteenth century. On the one hand, the spherical chamber, being of greater diameter than the bore, was hard to swab out between rounds, so burning residue left in it had a nasty habit of setting off the next charge rammed home. This "produced bad accidents to the cannoneers servicing the pieces, particularly when they were obliged to fire rapidly."[281] On the other hand, *nouvelle* cannon went off with such violence that they jerked back sharply, which in turn damaged gun carriages, battered embrasures, and hampered accuracy.

The second problem may have resulted from both the way in which the powder was ignited and the light weight of the barrels. The touch-hole in guns *de nouvelle invention* ignited the powder at the top of the spherical chamber. This may have set off a vertical reverberation in the gun that made it jump.[282] (The old method lit the powder at the back of the chamber.) Also, a barrel of reduced weight simply provided less mass to dampen the kinetic effects of the explosion. These factors eventually caused the French "to abandon the use of these pieces, despite their particular advantages; and one even recast the majority of them found in arsenals and in fortresses."[283] The new system was formally abolished in 1720.[284]

It is interesting to compare the ultimate failure of the cannon *de nouvelle invention* with the success of the Gribeauval system adopted in the 1770s. The guns themselves were of essentially the same weight, although the Gribeauval guns boasted more precise manufacture and improved powder chambers; therefore, cannon *de nouvelle invention* might have made possible the same kind of mobility afforded by Gribeauval pieces.[285] Yet this potential failed to

---

[281] The three criticisms stated here come from Diderot, *Encyclopédie*, 2:613. Two of these criticisms are echoed in Picard and Jouan, *L'artillerie française*, 45–46.

[282] This idea was proposed to me by John F. Guilmartin, Jr., historian of early modern warfare and military technology at Ohio State University.

[283] Diderot, *Encyclopédie*, 2:613.

[284] Picard and Jouan, *L'artillerie française*, 46, states that only Frézelière employed these guns and that the French abandoned them at his death.

[285] See comparative weights in Diderot, *Encyclopédie*, vol. 2, 608; Picard and Jouan, *L'artillerie française*, 44–47; Howard Rosen, "The Système Gribeauval: A Study of Technological Development and Institutional Change in Eighteenth-Century France," Ph.D. dissertation, University of Chicago, 1981, 130; Picard and Jouan, *L'artillerie française*, 45; Matti Lauerma,

materialize. To be sure, Gribeauval guns enjoyed certain advantages of design and employment. Problems in laying Gribeauval pieces between rounds may have been less because they made use of elevation screws instead of the wedges of the *nouvelle invention*, wedges that were displaced by the more violent recoil of the lighter pieces. Also in the case of the earlier pieces, guns were still hauled by private contractors who brought a minimum number of horses on campaign and who withdrew from harm's way as soon as they had placed the cannon on the battlefield, leaving the guns to be manhandled by their crews and thus putting a great limit on mobility.

But it would appear that the key difference between the two lighter artillery systems was that pieces *de nouvelle invention* did not fit easily with the seventeenth- and early eighteenth-century predilection for siege warfare. Fired through an embrasure, the new pieces damaged the openings both with their muzzle blast and by striking the sides of the embrasures as they recoiled; this latter problem also damaged the guns and their carriages. Given the choice, it is not hard to understand why a gunner would prefer the more stable and safer old, and heavier, designs to the lighter pieces when mobility on the battlefield was not an overriding factor. It is possible that the politics of gun production also hampered the adoption of cannon *de nouvelle invention*, because the regional lieutenants general of artillery saw the new guns as a challenge to their authority to produce the guns that they desired.[286] Judged by weight reduction alone, the cannon *de nouvelle invention* equaled the innovations of Gribeauval, and because the former came a century earlier, their improvement was perhaps even more dramatic because so unprecedented. That the cannon *de nouvelle invention* failed to revolutionize tactics speaks to the point that military technology must fit into a broader conception of warfare to be truly effective.

The old and new systems did not encompass the full variety of the cannon in Louis's arsenal. Because artillery pieces could enjoy long lives, pieces of earlier ages and different systems were still in use late in the seventeenth century, at least on fortress walls.[287] And because the French captured and employed cannon from their enemies, they put still other calibers into use at times.

Contemporary authorities differed somewhat on the range of this varied artillery. Du Praissac, in his 1622 treatise, lists the point-blank range for a 16-pounder as no more than 800 paces. He also remarks that such a piece could fire ten times each hour, or a total of 120 rounds per day.[288] Writing in the 1690s, Saint-Remy also credits a 16-pounder with a point-blank range of 800

L'artillerie de campagne française pendant les guerres de la Révolution (Helsinki: 1956), 10, 16; Chandler, *The Art of Warfare in the Age of Marlborough*, 178.

[286] Rosen argues that the lieutenant generals resisted efforts to standardize artillery as political threats. Rosen, "The Système Gribeauval," 132.

[287] For example, AG, A¹209, 15 June 1667, #42, an inventory of pieces at Furnes included one 31-pounder and three 61-pounders.

[288] Praissac, 112–30.

paces, the same as a 24-pounder.[289] Vauban, who studied such matters with scientific rigor, based his calculations in siege craft on "the very greatest range of the cannon . . . that is to say 1,000 or 1,200 *toises* of range," or an absolute maximum of about 2,500 yards, since a *toise* equals 2.14 yards.[290] This range was neither aimed nor effective but was simply the greatest distance that a cannonball might fly through the air and then skip along the ground with the potential of doing damage. Other tests demonstrated that a 24-pounder with a powder charge only one third the shot weight could send a ball about 2,000 yards at eight degrees elevation, probably the maximum elevation for a piece on a normal carriage, so this accords more or less with Vauban's figures.[291]

Mortars and Bombardment

By contrast to the cannon, a weapon of field battle and siege, the mortar was a weapon of the siege alone. It launched a hollow iron bomb filled with powder and fired by a fuse that either the gunner lit or that lit automatically when the mortar fired. French siege mortars ran from six to eighteen inches in bore.[292] An eighteen-inch mortar bomb contained forty-eight pounds of powder. The mortar itself looked rather like an inverted pot and sat on a wheel-less carriage set upon the ground. It threw its deadly package at a very high trajectory to sail over walls and other obstacles. In 1675, Blondel published *Art de jetter les bombes*, a work that set firing tables for mortars. According to him, a twelve-inch mortar at an elevation of forty-five degrees could fire its projectile 940 yards with a propellant charge of 2.5 pounds of gunpowder.[293] When its shell exploded, it spewed shrapnel about and set fire to buildings in the town.

Bombardment via mortars enjoyed a deadly vogue during the 1680s. Louvois and Louis became fascinated with mortars as terror weapons. Bombardment could bully or punish an adversary without risking loss to French

---

[289] Saint-Remy in Chandler, *Art of War in the Age of Marlborough*, 180. According to David Chandler, most artillery experts agreed that maximum effective range was no more than 500 *toises*, or just over 1,000 yards. Chandler, *Art of War in the Age of Marlborough*, 192–93.

[290] Rochas d'Aiglun, *Vauban*, 1:181. De Saxe testified that at the battle of Fontenoy, "a battery situated 800–900 *toises*" from the Dutch was able to stop their "offensive movement." De Saxe in Chandler, *Art of War in the Age of Marlborough*, 193.

[291] Chandler, *Art of War in the Age of Marlborough*, 192–93. He also presents figures that the same cannon could fire 3,340 yards at fifteen degrees, and 4,600 yards at forty-five degrees.

[292] Contamine, *Histoire militaire*, 1:410–11. Saint-Remy listed four main calibers of mortars in the late seventeenth century: 18, 12½, 8⅓, and 6¼ inches. Chandler, *Art of War in the Age of Marlborough*, 252.

[293] Chandler, *Art of War in the Age of Marlborough*, 252–53. In 1680, Rousset reported from the artillery center of Metz that "The sieur de Vigny and his bombardiers threw bombs more than 700 *toises* from the battery and *bales à feu* nearly 600 *toises*." Rousset, *Louvois*, 3:333–34fn.

troops, who would not have to storm a city to destroy it.[294] At Mons in 1683, Louvois wanted 2,500 to 3,000 bombs thrown into the city by mortars.[295] The bombardment of Genoa the next year revealed the brutality of Louvois.[296] The taste for bombardment became something of a blood lust for Louvois and Louis, but it did not go unopposed among the high command. In 1691, Marshal Luxembourg and Vauban opposed the proposed bombardment of Brussels on a number of grounds. Vauban argued strongly:

[T]he bombardments of Oudenarde, of Luxembourg and even of Liège acquired not a single inch of territory for the king, and, quite the opposite, they consumed a great deal of ammunition uselessly and fatigued the troops greatly and weakened them .... [I]t seems to me also that it is a very bad way of reconciling the heart of the people in a time when the spirits of that country are better disposed to the King than ever before.[297]

Number of Artillery Pieces with the Armies

Throughout the early modern era, French field armies dragged along an impressive number of artillery pieces, but the number of guns per thousand troops remained surprisingly stable. At Marignano in 1515, François I is believed to have had seventy-two guns for his army of 30,000, or 2.4 guns for every thousand men. Twenty-eight years later at Ceresole, twenty cannon added firepower to the 13,000 French troops who fought that day, this being about 1.5 guns per thousand. One account of Henri II's Voyage d'Allemagne in 1552 credits his army with thirty-four pieces for an army of 37,000 to 41,000 men, or .83 to .91 guns per thousand. The Wars of Religion saw a decline in the use of artillery, probably owing to the limited resources available to all parties. For example, at Dreux, the Protestants had five guns for 11,500 troops, dropping the ratio to .43 guns per thousand troops. The seventeenth century saw a return to the intensive investment in artillery that had typified the French before the Wars of Religion. At Rocroi in 1643, the future Great Condé had twenty cannon for 21,000 men, or .95 per thousand troops.

The wars of Louis XIV generally continued to see artillery ratios on this level. In 1674, at Enzheim, Turenne had thirty guns for 22,000 troops (1.36 per thousand), and at Neerwinden in 1693, Luxembourg brought seventy-one guns to the field for an army of 80,000 (.89 per thousand), and Villars counted sixty guns for a force of 80,000 at Malplaquet in 1709 (.75 per

---

[294] In advocating bombing Ath in 1683, Louvois argued that bombardment would spare the troops from "what could imperil them." 26 November 1683 letter from Louvois to Humières in Hardré, *Letters of Louvois*, 315.

[295] 20 October 1683 in Hardré, *Letters of Louvois*, 277. See the other letters from Louvois urging bombardments of Bruge, Oudenard, Ath, and Mons in 1683, Hardré, *Letters of Louvois*, 313–17.

[296] Rousset, *Louvois*, 3:274–76.

[297] 17 July 1691 letter from Vauban to Louvois in Rochas d'Aiglun, *Vauban*, 2:327. See letters in Rousset, *Louvois*, 4:476–77, as well.

thousand).[298] Saint-Remy advised a train of fifty artillery pieces for an army of 50,000 men, and de Saxe in 1733 advised essentially the same, fifty guns for 46,000 men.[299] As a whole, Louis may have had 13,000 cannon in the Nine Years' War and 14,000 in War of the Spanish Succession.[300]

The pieces with an army were organized in its artillery train. These were temporary entities tailored to the particular size and mission of the force. A French train was generally led by a colonel who had a staff that generally paralleled that of a regiment, including its own *prévôté*, surgeon, and chaplain. Saint-Remy suggested an ideal train for a French army of 50,000, which was subdivided into five brigades. It included four 24-pounders, six 12-pounders, twenty 8-pounders, twenty 4-pounders, a pontoon train of twenty boats, 220 wagons, 1,225 horses, and about 1,000 men.[301] Belhomme lists the actual artillery trains for French forces in 1690, contemporary with Saint-Remy. The Army of Flanders had a park of forty pieces and that of Germany thirty pieces.[302]

When an army undertook a siege, the royal siege park joined it. In 1690, Louis XIV's siege train included ten 33-pounders, thirty-six 24-pounders, four 16-pounders, and eight 12-pounders, along with two 18-inch mortars, twenty-four 12-inch mortars, twelve 8-inch mortars, and eight perriers, stone-throwing artillery.[303] It and its considerable supply of ammunition, including a million pounds of gunpowder, were assembled at Douai, Valenciennes, and Tournai. It would eventually see service before Mons in the spring of 1691. So massive was a siege train both in the size of the guns and in their sheer number that it was advantageous to move it by water if possible.

Organization of Artillery Troops

Artillery organization had several levels. First, the artillery officers and staff of provincial artillery fell under the grand master of artillery throughout the *grand siècle*; it was known as the *Corps royal*. Manning provincial fortifications, its duties were restricted to siege warfare. The officer corps of the artillery with the field armies was also originally under the authority of the grand master of artillery, but it eventually came within the purview of the minister of war and military command.

Louis André argues that when Le Tellier came to office in 1643, artillery administration and organization were in very nearly the same state that it had

---

[298] Figures for the numbers of cannon employed have been taken from Contamine, *Histoire militaire*, 241–42; Chandler, *Art of War in the Age of Marlborough*, 150; Frederick Lewis Taylor, *The Art of War in Italy, 1494–1529* (Cambridge: 1921), 92; Reboul, "Des croisades à la Révolution," 299; Delabarre-Duparcq, *L'Art militaire*, 22–24.

[299] Chandler, *The Art of Warfare*, 146, 171.   [300] Chandler, *The Art of Warfare*, 148.

[301] Chandler, *The Art of Warfare*, 170–71.   [302] Belhomme, *L'armée française en 1690*, 135.

[303] Belhomme, *L'armée française en 1690*, 136. Marlborough's great siege train of 1708 included eighty cannon, twenty mortars, and 3,000 wagons with 16,000 horses. Chandler, *The Art of Warfare*, 144.

been a century before.[304] The hostility of governors and the disarray of French finances made administration difficult and improvement next to impossible.[305] The political and financial improvements of Louis XIV's personal reign exerted a favorable impact on artillery. Brunet, the historian of artillery, argued that artillery benefited even more than did the other arms.[306] Because the state of artillery depended both on the transfer of effective authority from governors to the monarch, and on the financial ability of the state to pour money into expensive artillery matériel, this comes as little surprise.

However, for a long time, the artillery remained in the odd situation of boasting a corps of officers without any enlisted men. The men actually handling the guns were a mixture of professional officers, hired civilian specialists, and borrowed infantrymen.[307] When Le Tellier sent artillery personnel to the Army of Italy in 1653, this group numbered thirty-nine, of which only twelve were "cannoneers."[308] The actual train of horses, drivers, and wagons was supplied by contract, much like the *équipages des vivres*.[309] This kind of staff remained the pattern during Louis's personal reign. A list of military personnel serving the artillery train of the 20,000 man army under Condé's command in 1674 included only 106 men, some administrators, and some skilled tradesmen who maintained the equipment; only seventeen were cannoneers.[310]

The men who served the guns and supported the batteries eventually formed the Regiment Royal Artillerie. In the field, the cannon were drawn by civilian drivers and their teams, supplied to the army by contract. Through most of the seventeenth century, artillery officers had few troops to manhandle guns in the field, so they commandeered infantrymen to do the heavy work, but during the 1670s, the French created specialist artillery troops. Louvois first formed a company of cannoneers, drawn from infantry companies, and two of fusiliers, composed of "workers," to serve the artillery in 1671. Each company numbered about 100 men.[311] In 1672, the force of fusiliers grew into its own regiment with two entire battalions of thirteen companies each. For reasons relating to the character of the weapons involved, these battalions included no musketeers or pikemen. The Fusiliers du Roi, listed as an infantry formation, performed many of the traditional duties of infantry, but it had no regular place in the line of battle. Instead, the fusiliers provided much of the muscle power required to man batteries, and they stood alongside the guns to defend them. The colonel of the Fusiliers was the grand master of artillery.[312] Vauban spoke of this regiment with great

---

[304] André, *Le Tellier*, 499. Audouin insisted that artillery was not well administered under Richelieu. Audouin, *Histoire de l'administration*, 2:169.

[305] André, *Le Tellier*, 503.   [306] Brunet, *Histoire générale*, 2:113.   [307] Rousset, *Louvois*, 1:235.

[308] BN, f, fr. 4187, fol. 164 in André, *Le Tellier*, 508.   [309] André, *Le Tellier*, 507–8.

[310] AG, A¹379, 2 January 1674, "Etat de l'équipage d'artillerie pour l'armée de Monsieur le Prince," in Rousset, *Louvois*, 1:235–36.

[311] AG, A¹255, 21 April 1671, Louvois to Louis, in Rousset, *Louvois*, 1:238.

[312] Rousset, *Louvois*, 1:238–39.

pride, calling it "the most handsome regiment in the world, from its last soldier to its first officer."[313] In 1693, the Fusiliers du Roi became the Regiment Royal Artillerie, which by 1710 included five battalions, totaling 3,700 men and 236 officers. The regiment contained fourteen companies of cannoneers, fifty-two of fusiliers, and four of workers.[314]

Just as the artillery regiment served the cannon, a regiment came to serve the mortars as well. Two companies of bombardiers were formed in 1676.[315] In 1684, with the concern of the king and his war minister for mortars, the two companies of bombardiers grew to a full regiment of twelve companies with the grand master of artillery as its colonel.[316] In 1695, it became the Regiment des Bombardiers du Roi.[317] By 1710, it mustered two battalions with 1,450 enlisted men and ninety officers grouped into twenty-eight companies.[318]

How eloquently spoke the cannon of France. The argument of force literally shaped France during the *grand siècle* because it determined the borders of Bourbon lands. Success on the battlefield and in sieges expanded Bourbon domains, but defeat could shrink them. Some assert that French reverses during the last of Louis's wars can at least in part be explained by the fact that the French tactically lagged behind their enemies. At one point, the French – who had learned so much from their own experience and from the Dutch and the Swedes – became the military teachers of Europe. Their administration, weaponry, and drill set the style in the age of Le Tellier, Louvois, Turenne, Condé, and Luxembourg. French advances in weapons and tactics had been more evolutionary than revolutionary, but they were improvements nonetheless. Yet if Bourbon troops enjoyed real advantages in the 1670s, had they been outclassed tactically at the close of Louis's reign? This seems unclear. Certainly, French infantry tactics were conservative and lagged behind those of the Dutch and English, but that did not stop shoeless French infantrymen from decimating their tactically superior Dutch foes at Malplaquet. French cavalry were eventually beaten back at the same battle, but it was a near thing, and the French were outnumbered. The excellent cannon of both new and old systems provided the French with as fine and innovative an arsenal of field pieces as could be found in Europe, but at Malplaquet, the French brought only sixty guns to the field, while their opponents boasted 100.

France, which had mustered such a huge army for the Nine Years' War, could not equal it after 1701. Could exhaustion explain the poorer showing of French forces against Marlborough? Were French cavalry outclassed because they stopped to fire, or were financially strapped officers unable to

[313] AG, A¹255, 11 May 1676, Vauban to Louvois, in Rousset, *Louvois*, 1:238–39.
[314] AG, MR 1701, #13.   [315] AG, A¹485, 21 November 1676, in Rousset, *Louvois*, 1:239.
[316] Rousset, *Louvois*, 3:334.   [317] Brunet, *Histoire générale*, 2:129. Rousset, *Louvois*, 3:333–34.
[318] AG, MR 1701, #13.

supply their troopers with horses of sufficient quality to carry the charge? What part was played by Louis's inability, until late in the war, to find commanders who could stand comparison with Marlborough and Eugene? Such questions may remain unanswered, but they are worth asking nonetheless. Perhaps some light can be shed by looking beyond the details of weaponry and unit tactics and examining training and battlefield practice, as is done in the next chapter.

15

Learning and Practicing
the Art of Field Warfare

GOOD order makes us look assured, and it seems enough to look brave, because most often our enemies do not wait for us to approach near enough for us to have to show if we are in fact brave."[1] For Louis XIV, good order equated with victory; the secret was to appear unshakable. He was not alone in this opinion. For generals and military thinkers, battle, particularly infantry combat, had become a test of wills, and the winner seemed to be the force not that inflicted the greatest physical casualties on the other side, but the force that absorbed the worst that the enemy could inflict yet still maintain order. Marshal Catinat, a practical soldier, in describing an assault, insisted that "One prepares the soldier to not fire and to realize that it is necessary to suffer the enemy's fire, expecting that the enemy who fires is assuredly beaten when one receives his entire fire."[2] This emphasis on taking losses stoically was far from the assertive, and more primitive, warrior ethos to attack the enemy and do damage. The surprising truth is that seventeenth-century Europe developed a battle culture based less upon fury than upon forbearance.[3]

The triumph of firepower brought the triumph of suffering. Cannon could destroy at great range, and little could be done about it, save to cross the valley of death to seize the guns. Any long-range weapon compels an army to take losses before it can close with the enemy. Roman forces confronting the Parthians and medieval troops who faced English longbowmen had to deal with something of the same problem. But no earlier weapon equaled the range of artillery or could inflict such hideous damage. Muskets were closer to bows in range and in some other characteristics as well. Similar to the

---

[1] Louis XIV, *Mémoires de Louis XIV pour l'instruction du dauphin*, ed. Charles Dreyss, 2 vols. (Paris: 1860), 2:112–13.

[2] Catinat in Jean Colin, *L'infanterie au XVIIIe siècle: La tactique* (Paris: 1907), 25.

[3] This notion of a battle culture of forbearance in combat first came to mind in conversations with my graduate student William Reger.

longbow, the musket was above all a defensive weapon, more capable of stopping an enemy assault than in overpowering an enemy by offensive action. Yet while longbowmen very rarely fought other longbowmen, musketeers and fusiliers regularly confronted forces armed with the same weapon. And even on the offensive, the musket was brought to bear. The losses could be staggering when forces stood off at close range to pour volley after volley into each other. However, as Louis noted, one side usually broke, ending the duel. As firepower became the norm, the use of armor died out; even the illusion of protection disappeared.

Consider the almost universal dictum to hold fire until the last moment, to not fire "until you see the whites of their eyes." In a memoir dedicated to his young king in 1663, the experienced soldier d'Aurignac advised generals that above all, they must "command both cavalry and infantry when approaching the enemy to fire only after the enemy had fired first." His instructions were conventional. Vauban put it succinctly: "Usually, in man to man combat the advantage lies with those who fire last."[4] To be sure, there was good reason in an age of inaccurate and slow-loading weapons to hold fire until close enough to make it tell, and at close quarters, he who fired first disarmed himself. All this is true. But to do so, the soldier must endure, must hold back natural fear and the instinct to do something, anything, in the face of danger. D'Aurignac's soldier must exert self-control, or at least his officers must impose control upon him. Even in the charge, the infantryman was forbidden to speak. Silence, order, control.

The ability to perform with forbearance in the face of such danger and chaos was far from natural; it had to be learned. Some of this had to do with weapons handling, but much had to do with attitude. Training was based on obedience and restraint. It was not enough to master the tools of war; the soldier himself must be mastered. In later ages, officers would come to trust in the initiative of their troops, but during the *grand siècle*, such confidence was forestalled by a culture of command that assumed a low level of honor and motivation among the rank and file. So self-control had to give way to control by officers. Actions must be automatic and obedience complete, and both must be drilled into recruits. Drill was the key, and it was an invention of the century – what Michael Roberts terms "the revolution in drill."[5]

In a recent volume, the distinguished American military historian Russell Weigley defined the entire period 1631–1815 as "The Age of Battles," a period in which soldiers believed that battle promised decisive results.[6] The notion of battle as forbearance does not really fit this picture. Within the French battle culture that came to dominate the second half of the *grand siècle*, battle

[4] Sébastien le Prestre de Vauban, *A Manual of Siegecraft and Fortification*, trans. G. A. Rothrock (Ann Arbor: 1968), 123.

[5] Michael Roberts, *The Military Revolution, 1560–1660* (Belfast: 1956), 10.

[6] Russell F. Weigley, *The Age of Battles: The Quest for Decisive Warfare from Brietenfeld to Waterloo* (Bloomington, IN: 1991).

was expected to be costly, and it was. At the same time, these battles of attrition also failed to produce war-ending decisions; in fact, the great losses suffered in combat simply magnified the crushing expense of conflict that was such a dominant theme in the *grand siècle*.[7] Within the givens of this battle culture, then, field combat might not seem the best alternative, particularly since the presence of numerous fortified towns and the dependence on cumbersome logistics made it difficult to turn victories won on the field into decisive military or political results. The same king who counseled that good order was enough to gain victory also came to distrust the promise of battle.

DRILL AND TRAINING

The intricacies of the linear tactics of the *grand siècle* demanded a high level of skill on the part of the soldiers who employed them and required habits of obedience and discipline. Such skills and such attitudes could only be gained and maintained through constant practice. If historians only look at the tactical details discussed in the preceding chapter, they will miss something fundamental about the art of war during the *grand siècle*. The preceding chapter argued that French developments in weaponry, organization, unit size, and tactical formations were evolutionary and that native French currents played a preeminent role, although this gradual process was significantly modified by the adoption of Dutch and Swedish styles and refinements early in the *grand siècle*. Yet to deny the radical impact of some aspects of Dutch and Swedish technical innovation is not to argue that it fell short of being revolutionary in every detail. Quite the contrary, viewed from the French perspective, the Dutch creation of drill especially rates as an absolutely crucial innovation with profound implications both on the battlefield and beyond it.

Drill developed by Maurice and further extended by Gustavus enabled maneuver and a rate of fire unknown before.[8] This promise of tactical effectiveness lured French officers to the Netherlands and northern Germany, where they learned the great stress that the Dutch and Swedes placed on drill. Apprenticing at his trade in the Netherlands in 1631, an impatient young Turenne wrote: "We are still at the same place and do nothing. All we do is drill the majority of the troops each morning."[9]

Under the direction of Maurice of Nassau, Dutch infantry learned to

---

[7] Keegan believes that battle was intrinsically indecisive because of equilibrium of weapons, but this seems an ill-considered argument, for there was relative equality of weaponry even at the most decisive battles, such as Blenheim. John Keegan, *A History of Warfare* (New York: 1993), 345.

[8] In his provocative "Middle-class Society and the Rise of Military Professionalism: The Dutch Army, 1589–1609," *Armed Forces and Society* 1 (1975), 419–42, M. D. Feld states that Maurice must share credit for drill innovations with his cousin, Louis of Nassau.

[9] Jean Bérenger, *Turenne* (Paris: 1987), 90.

maneuver precisely under fire. Although the square Spanish formations of the sixteenth century could present a strong face to all four directions, they had done so at the cost of wasting manpower, for relatively few weapons could be brought to bear to the front. Formations were thus solid but inefficient. Linear tactics, such as those employed by the Dutch, made the most of manpower by facing all weapons to the front in relatively thin formations. However, a threat to the flank or rear posed a serious problem. Linear formations claimed greater efficiency, then, but were more vulnerable if taken off guard. The best way to overcome this intrinsic disadvantage was to train troops to maneuver under fire, so that they could face front to flank or rear, whenever they were threatened, without losing cohesion. Dutch drill rendered such maneuvers reliable and rapid.

During the seventeenth century, the level of skill expected of an infantryman seems to have been higher than that demanded of cavalry. Chamlay wrote that "five or six years were necessary to create a regiment of infantry and it required only a year to make a good cavalry regiment."[10] This is the reverse of late eighteenth-century opinion – that it took much longer to create a cavalry regiment. There seems to be little question that the tactical sophistication of infantry was far above cavalry, which seems to have done little more than to form squadron and charge. In addition, the greater complexity of infantry drill stemmed from the problem of effectively combining pikes with firearms, a problem that did not exist a century later. Louis XIV may have echoed Chamlay's estimate when that monarch stated that while his cavalry was adequate in 1667, after many years of peace, his infantry fell short because it was composed of new men.[11]

Under the leadership of Maurice and Louis of Nassau, the Dutch regulated and improved the use of the pike and the loading and firing of the arquebus and the musket. Maurice broke down the handling of weapons into a series of steps and trained troops to perform these in strict sequence, with thirty-two steps for the pike and forty-two each for the arquebus and the musket. The military historian John Keegan sees formalized loading by these steps as a safety measure to avoid accidents; musketeers would be less likely to set each other alight if their movements were more studied and controlled.[12] As an aid to instruction, Johan II of Nassau, another cousin of Maurice, commissioned an illustrated manual that presented this system of positions and steps in engravings and descriptions. When this *Wapenhandlinghe van Roers, Musquetten ende Spiessen*, by Jacob de Gheyn, appeared in 1607, it became a cornerstone of military tactical reform and went through many editions and translations.[13] A French edition, published in Amsterdam,

---

[10] Chamlay in Bérenger, *Turenne*, 384–85.   [11] Louis, *Mémoires*, 2:170.

[12] Keegan, *A History of Warfare*, 342.

[13] For discussions of this crucial book, see Feld, "Middle-Class Society and the Rise of Military Professionalism," 423–25. Recent reproductions of de Gheyn have been published by McGraw-Hill in 1971 and Greenhill Books in 1986.

appeared in 1608. As mentioned in the last chapter, Maurice also introduced a finely choreographed countermarch for his musketeers.[14] The French seem not to have developed a native tradition of military drill, and they in fact adopted it in imitation of the Dutch.

The Kings' Efforts

Louis XIII, a king extremely interested in military detail, occupied the French throne when the French began to borrow elements of Dutch and Swedish military reforms. In 1624, he sent the young lieutenant de Pontis to observe the drill and discipline practiced by the *mestre de camp* Pierre Arnauld d'Andilly, who had fought in Holland, and to render a confidential report.[15] De Pontis stayed with Arnauld at Fort-Louis for six months. But he was not the only one, for "young gentlemen were drawn from all points of the compass to Fort-Louis to learn their profession there."[16] The discipline there was reputed to be especially strict, on the Roman style. In this process of self-education and adaptation, model regiments, notably the Regiment de Champagne, under Arnauld d'Andilly, and the Regiment de Rambures, under Fabert, played a major role.[17] The king regarded reviews as means to maintain discipline and attended them as a matter of course. In 1629, for example, he watched a drill by four battalions prior to their departure for Italy.[18] Military literature also influenced French practice, as military handbooks of the first quarter of the seventeenth century referred to Dutch methods and formations, as did Billon's *Instructions militaires*.

It seems that the first French ordinance demanding that troops drill appeared under Louis XIII and Richelieu. Article 286 of the Code Michau set the pattern of required drill in 1629; other regulations of the *grand siècle* built upon this foundation. This article read simply: "In order to instruct . . . the soldiers, drill will be done at least one time a week in garrisons, at which the sergeant majors will be in control."[19] Later ordinances repeated this

---

[14] On the countermarch, see William H. McNeill, *The Pursuit of Power* (Chicago: 1982), 129; Feld's characterization of the countermarch as a technique of continuous production, in "Middle-Class Society and the Rise of Military Professionalism," 425; and, most importantly, Geoffrey Parker, *The Military Revolution: Military Innovation and the Rise of the West, 1500–1800* (Cambridge: 1988), 19, 23.

[15] Louis de Pontis, *Mémoires*, in M. Petitot, ed., *Collection complète des mémoires relatifs à l'histoire de France*, vols. 31–32 (Paris, 1824), 31:425–34.

[16] Robert Arnauld d'Andilly, *Mémoires*, in Michaud and Poujoulat, eds., *Nouvelle collection des mémoires pour servir à l'histoire de France*, vol. 9 (Paris: 1838), 416.

[17] F. Reboul, "Des croisades à la Révolution," in Gabriel Hanoteau, ed., *Histoire de la nation française*, vol. 7, *Histoire militaire et navale*, vol. 1 (Paris: 1925), 133.

[18] Jean de Gagnières, comte de Souvigny, *Mémoires du Comte de Souvigny, Lieutenant Général des Armées du Roi*, vol. 1 (Paris: 1906), 220–21. I thank my graduate student Brian Sandberg for this reference.

[19] François André Isambert et al., eds., *Recueil général des anciennes lois françaises, depuis l'an 420, jusqu'a la Révolution de 1789*, vol. 16 (Paris: 1829), 296.

requirement; the ordinance of 4 November 1651, which set the tone for winter-quarters directives, insisted on it.[20]

One news item, carried in the *Gazette de Renaudot* in 1639 suggests that Louis even established a drill school for infantry.

The king continually directs his concern to the cultivation of arms, His Majesty has authorized a Royal Academy of Military Drill [*Académie royale des exercices de guerre*] for his infantry, where all the *mestres de camp* and captains of infantry can send their newly levied soldiers to be instructed there in the manual of arms and in what these drills depend, without being obliged to pay anything for this instruction.[21]

The fate of this initiative seems unknown. Had it been instituted, which seems unlikely, it could not have lasted for long. André's extensive research on the ministry of Le Tellier uncovered no mention of it. The undeniable importance of this royal authorization is that it again demonstrates the French willingness to innovate and adapt in drill and training.

Louis XIV would not be a soldier-king in the exact mold of Louis XIII; the father had been more of a field commander, whereas the son became more of a military administrator. But no French monarch surpassed Louis XIV's intense interest in drill. He was convinced that "many more battles are won by good march order and by good bearing [*contenance*] than by sword blows and musketry . . . . This habit of marching well and of keeping order can only be acquired by drill."[22] Here again, he repeated the theme that the maintenance of disciplined order, rather than bloody combat, wins battles.

He personally commanded his troops and attended exercises when possible. Louis confessed that "I often employed my leisure hours in having drilled before me a body of troops, sometimes one, sometimes another, and sometimes several together."[23] However, this was not just idiosyncrasy gone wild; he also had good reason, since he hoped to set an example. "I continue to carefully drill the troops which are close to my person in order that, by my example, the other individual military chiefs will learn to take the same care with those that are under their command."[24] Because he wanted his troops to realize quickly that "I would see exactly in what manner they served me," Louis also announced that "I would hold a review each month of all the troops that I could conveniently assemble."[25] Without apology, he advised his heir that "this application to drill the troops is one of the things in which I council you to imitate me the most."[26]

Louis expended part of his effort on model military units, such as had

[20] Ordinance of 4 November 1651, art. 25, in André, *Le Tellier*, 680.
[21] *Gazette de Renaudot*, 31 December 1639, 852, in Jules Caillet, *De l'administration en France sous le ministre du Cardinal de Richelieu* (Paris: 1857), 376–77.
[22] Louis XIV, *Mémoires*, 2:112–13.   [23] Louis XIV, *Mémoires*, 2:125.
[24] Louis XIV, *Mémoires*, 1:237n.
[25] Louis XIV, *Oeuvres de Louis XIV*, Philippe Grimoard and Grouvelle, eds., 6 vols. (Paris: 1806), 2:77–78.
[26] Louis XIV, *Oeuvres*, 2:113–14.

existed under his father. The troops of his military household stood closest to him and, understandably, received much of his effort. Since many of the best-born young nobles, with the brightest military futures, filled these billets, Louis treated household units as something of a military school.[27] The most important body of model troops in the regular army was his cherished Regiment du Roi, created in 1663 for display, experiment, and training. Louis himself served as its colonel, and Jean Martinet as its lieutenant colonel. This was the same Martinet who later became the inspector general of infantry. The king lavished special attention on his own regiment, requiring its troops to drill for him whenever possible. As with those in the royal military household, officers who learned their trade in the Regiment du Roi enjoyed special advantages in competition for new posts as captains and colonels of other regiments.

Regular Drill during the Personal Reign of Louis XIV

With the end of the war with Spain in 1659, Louis's concern for drill increased. By then, it was well accepted that troops required constant practice in order to master the complexities of battlefield tactics. Louis grew up in an era of constant warfare, a time during which combat itself taught harsh lessons. But when peace returned, it dulled the sharp edge of military ability. Understandably, Louis regarded drill as a way to teach and retain lessons that war had previously taught.

Soon after his personal reign began, he worried that his troops were not as capable as they had once been. The king advised Coligny in 1664 that "If there are soldiers who are no longer able in handling their arms, they ought to become so again soon through frequent drill."[28] When war approached in 1667, he advocated drill because "the oldest soldiers of my troops have almost forgotten their trade" and the newly levied companies "having never seen war, assuredly would have found themselves very much surprised by it if, by continual drill, I had not tried to make them see in advance some image of the combat in which they would probably find themselves some day."[29] New troops especially concerned him in 1667: "My cavalry was really very good, but the infantry, which would be the most useful in sieges, was almost all new."[30]

Early in his personal reign, Louis attempted to make up for these deficits through a series of ordinances and directives that set the pattern for the remainder of the *grand siècle*. An ordinance of 1661 increased the training burden: "In order to maintain the said infantry troops in military order and discipline, to teach the soldiers the handling of their weapons and evolutions, and to instruct them in the form and manner of fighting, the sergeants-major of the towns and fortresses will cause general drills to be conducted for the

[27] Louis XIV, *Mémoires*, 1:237. [28] Louis XIV, *Oeuvres*, 5:206, letter of 15 August 1664.
[29] Louis XIV, *Mémoires*, 2:110–11. [30] Louis XIV, *Mémoires*, 2:170.

infantry troops who are in garrison one time each month; and the chiefs and officers of the said troops will have the soldiers of their companies who are not on guard perform [drill] at least two times each week; and those soldiers who neglect to instruct themselves and do not drill well will be broken."[31] Similar orders appeared in 1663 and 1665.[32] In 1668, the king issued orders that governors were to drill their garrisons every Sunday. Cavalry officers were to drill their men each week; twice each month, all the cavalry of a garrison were to perform general evolutions and fire salvos, to accustom their horses to fire.[33]

The most common infantry drill was that conducted within the company. The responsibility for drill often fell to the lowest-ranking officer of the company. Belhomme states that soldiers actually drilled by *ordinaire*, commanded by the head of each *ordinaire*, under the supervision of sergeants.[34] Villars testified to the importance of sergeants in training recruits circa 1700.[35] Not all sergeants were competent, however. One authority complained in 1672 that among the newly raised companies, some sergeants were "incapable because of their inadequacy, brutality, and drunkenness."[36] Certain picked men with experience, *anspessades*, received extra pay and bore special responsibility for training, along with the corporals.[37] This form of training could only have emphasized weapons handling – that is, mastering the complicated list of positions and commands required to maneuver the pike or to load and fire musket or fusil. Companies did not maneuver as units, since they broke down into their constituent elements within the battalion.

Drill also required that soldiers actually fire their weapons from time to time, although this was an expensive type of training. Regulations specified that despite the expense, troops were to fire their weapons. The 1668 order mentioned previously also demanded that at the weekly drills, the soldiers each fire three shots.[38] An ordinance of May 1682 decreed that governors were to supply enough powder to their troops to allow the soldiers to each fire three shots twice a month.[39] This ordinance apparently remained in effect

---

[31] SHAT, Col. des ord., vol. 20, #157, Ordinance of 12 October 1661, art. 19, in André, *Le Tellier*, 557fn.

[32] See SHAT, Col. des ord., vol. 21, #41, 12 August 1663, art. 49, and vol. 21, #112, 25 July 1665, art. 49 in Louis André, *Michel Le Tellier et Louvois* (Paris: 1942), 399–400.

[33] AG, A¹216, 9 July 1668, in Camille Rousset, *Histoire de Louvois*, 4 vols. (Paris: 1862–64), 1:209–10fn.

[34] Victor Belhomme, *L'armée française en 1690* (Paris: 1895), 35.

[35] BN, f. fr. 6257, Claude Louis Hector Villars, "Traité de la guerre de campagne," 102.

[36] AG, A¹294, #4, August 1672.

[37] Albert Babeau, *La vie militaire sous l'ancien regime*, 2 vols. (Paris: 1890), 1:185. Bérenger argues that because the NCO staff was not up to the task, veterans played a big role in teaching the newcomers. Bérenger, *Turenne*, 510.

[38] AG, A¹216, 9 July 1668, in Rousset, *Louvois*, 1:209–10fn.

[39] Ordinance of 21 May 1682 in *Ordonnances militaires du roy de France*, 2 vols. (Luxembourg: 1734–35), 1:164–65. The powder was figured at 1 livre for twenty-four shots. An order from 1696 ordered officials to provide each field battalion in garrison in Cambrai with powder "in

for the rest of Louis XIV's reign.[40] His advisor Chamlay urged increased musket practice to ready the troops for war in 1690:

[S]ince there are many new soldiers in the infantry, it would be good to drill them at firing often; at the same time, it would do good for the old soldiers who, because of the duration of the peace, have lost the habit of firing. One will consume a little powder in this practice; but one will employ it usefully, in order to be able to make as great a fire as the enemy, who surpass us in this drill in which they are instructed every day.[41]

In 1705, when Villeroi wanted his troops to practice the French method of platoon fire, he distributed fifty pounds of powder to each battalion so it could conduct two firing practices.[42] Of course, the best of intentions could be stymied by supply shortages. In 1692, Barbézieux ordered Tallard to discourage firing practice because "powder is a rather rare material in these times."[43]

Since only powder is mentioned in the ordinances and other documents, it may mean that the troops practiced firing without musket balls. If so, the exercise constituted firing practice, not target practice. However, it may be that only the powder was regarded as lost, since balls could be recovered and recast. Although the average smoothbore musket or fusil was hardly a sharpshooter's weapon, men were expected to aim. One of the reasons Louvois insisted that the musketeers support their weapons on their shoulders and not their chests or stomachs, as some did, was because the men could not sight their weapons unless they were at their shoulders. He wanted the troops to be skilled enough "that it be easy for those who know how to fire well to send the ball to the place where they want it to hit."[44] Louis wanted his officers to know how to shoot and favored sharpshooting competitions between them. Because some officers did not know how to shoot fusils, they were to be supplied with them, and inspectors were instructed, "when you hold your reviews, encourage them to fire at the target from time to time." Officers were to compete for prize money raised from the competitors.[45] Puységur also urged that men be taught "never to fire without an order,

order to have the soldiers fire this winter." AG, A¹1339, #131, 1696, order to Montbron at Cambrai.

[40] Its longevity is indicated by its inclusion in *Ordonnances militaires*, meant as a practical collection of current military ordinances at the time of its permit, 1707.

[41] AG, A¹974, 2 June 1690, Chamlay to Louvois, in Rousset, *Louvois*, 3:325fn.

[42] Brent Nosworthy, *The Anatomy of Victory: Battle Tactics, 1689–1763* (New York: 1990), 60.

[43] AG, A¹1156, #115, 8 March 1692, Barbézieux to Tallard in Ronald Thomas Ferguson, "Blood and Fire: Contribution Policy of the French Armies in Germany (1668–1715)," Ph.D. dissertation, University of Minnesota, 1970, 168.

[44] AG, A¹800, 5 January 1688, Louvois to inspectors, in Rousset, *Louvois*, 3:325fn.

[45] AG, A¹806, 15 July 1688, Louvois to inspectors, in Rousset, *Louvois*, 3:325fn. This runs counter to Vauban's opinion that officers should carry fusils, because as hunters, they were probably better shots than their men. Albert Rochas d'Aiglun, *Vauban, sa famille et ses écrits*, 2 vols. (Paris: 1910), 1:291–92.

and never to do so without aiming, thus avoiding the waste of fire to no purpose."[46]

Winter quarters figured large in training, because during this period, soldiers in temporary garrisons had the time and energy to devote to drill. In addition, recruits arrived in the months between campaigns and had to be taught their craft. The regulations and ordinances mentioned previously dealt specifically with winter quarters and garrison life. During the war with Spain, military instruction took place primarily in winter quarters and at the start of the campaign. The value of winter quarters to the training process was so great that when peace returned in 1659, Turenne argued for still keeping the troops concentrated in winter quarters to supervise their training.[47]

During wartime, training had a special urgency. Troops seem to have commenced the required drills immediately upon entering quarters. In October 1672, Boistel reported from Dunkirk that there were "agents in the fortresses of this area [department] to ensure that the drill of the troops will be performed."[48] In order to ready the army to take the field early in 1691 for the siege of Mons, an October 1690 ordinance promised a reward of 200 livres to every captain whose company was at full strength and trained by the end of February 1691.[49]

It is also possible, perhaps even probable, that in wartime, new individuals and new units were placed in garrison rather than in the field during the campaign season in order to allow them to train. A large share of the French army garrisoned fortresses while the field armies faced the enemy. Were it possible to follow individual regiments in the same way that records allow a century later, it might be demonstrated that a stint in garrison allowed troops to refit and retrain. It is true that battalions that began the Nine Years' War as garrison regiments were turned into field regiments in 1691.[50] In 1702, reinforcements first went through garrison battalions to receive their basic training.[51]

Training did not end in winter quarters and garrisons. Troops drilled at quieter moments when on campaign, as in encampments. In addition, the French occupied peacetime summers with training camps and great military reviews, which allowed large bodies of troops to maneuver together. At a camp near Bouquenon on the Sarre, established in the summer of 1683, Louis visited to see his troops. The infantry drilled within their companies from 5 to 10 A.M. and then maneuvered by battalion or brigade 4 to 7 P.M.; once a week, the entire assemblage of twenty-four battalions of infantry

[46] Puységur, Jacques-François de Chastenet de, *Art de la guerre par principes et par règles*, 2 vols. (Paris: 1748), 1:67.
[47] Bérenger, *Turenne*, 510.   [48] AG, A^{1}295, #55, 6 October 1672, Boistel from Dunkirk.
[49] Rousset, *Louvois*, 4:460.
[50] In 1684, *batallions de garnison* became *régiments de garnison*; then, by the ordinance of 19 September 1691, they became field regiments with provincial names. Louis Susane, *Histoire de l'infanterie française*, 5 vols. (Paris: 1876), 1:204.
[51] Philippe Contamine, ed., *Histoire militaire de la France*, vol. 1 (Paris: 1992), 538.

maneuvered as a whole.[52] Such camps also practiced the troops in the difficult business of living on campaign and sharpened the military administration in the very complicated job of maintaining a large force in the field.[53] In addition to sound military rationale, these camps sometimes also filled the frivolous agenda of amusing the court.

In 1666, Louis held reviews for 9,000 to 11,000 troops at Breteuil and 72,000 troops at Mouchy.[54] These assemblies functioned both to train troops and to move them up toward the frontiers for the impending War of Devolution. In 1667, the king assembled troops for another review "to accustom our men to camp well and in order to have a pretext to make tents."[55] In 1669 and 1670, Louis held camps at Saint-Sébastien for both military and political reasons, as part of his campaign to bully the Dutch.[56] After the return of peace following the Dutch War, the French cavalry held camps for maneuver and training each summer.[57] In 1683, the cavalry met on the Saône. A small army of 14,000 to 15,000 men, including infantry, also assembled the same year at Bouquenon (1683). In later years, the cavalry would assemble on the Sarre with the old infantry regiments. Another, later camp was held at Stenay, where Boufflers brought together fourteen dragoon regiments. Concerning the effect of these camps, one historical memoir concluded that they "contributed a great deal to the good state in which the troops found themselves when the war of 1688 began."[58]

During the few years between the Nine Years' War and the War of the Spanish Succession, the most famous camp was held at Compiègne in 1698.[59] An official report of the camp outlined its purpose and size: "In 1698, the King, wanting to teach [the art of] war to monseigneur the duke of Burgundy, gave orders to assemble an army near Compiègne composed of 53 battalions and of 152 squadrons with 40 cannons, 6 mortars, and 8 pontoons."[60] The camp lasted two weeks and involved not only drills but a mock battle, an attack on entrenchments, and convoy escorts.

---

[52] Belhomme, *Histoire de l'infanterie*, 2:236–38.

[53] See the rationale supplied by AG, MR 1701, piece 15. "Traité de la guerre ou il est parlé des moyens de rediger les trouppes et y restablir l'ancienne, et bonne discipline," par M. de St. Hilaire, 8 June 1712.

[54] Regarding the camps at Breteuil and Mouchy, see Louis, *Mémoires*, 2:127–28; André, *Le Tellier*, 9, 558; Rousset, *Louvois*, 1:95–97; and Bérenger, *Turenne*, 385.

[55] Louis, *Mémoire*, 2:164.

[56] On these camps, see Rousset, *Louvois*, 1:298 and Paul Sonnino, *Louis XIV and the Origins of the Dutch War* (Cambridge: 1989), 101. Over the summer of 1671, the cavalry united and drilled on the Sarre.

[57] Concerning the training camps of the 1680s, see AG, Arch. hist. 78, fol. 186; Rousset, *Louvois*, 3:332; and Reboul, "Des croisades à la Révolution," 445. On the 1683 camp at Talmay in August 1683, see Cote d'Or, C 3675. On that held at Bouquenon, see Corvisier, *Louvois*, 352.

[58] AG, Arch. hist. 78, fol. 186, undated historical memoir.

[59] For documents on the camp de Compiègne, see AG, MR 1817, pieces #3 & 4; AG, A²c 346, piece #3. These accounts include maps and diagrams. See, as well, Rousset, *Louvois*, 4:545–46.

[60] AG, Library, A²c 346, piece #3.

By the close of Louis's personal reign the army clearly recognized the need to practice its warlike tasks in peacetime, so the annual training camp was now seen as essential. It comes as little surprise that a military savant, in proposing ways in which to reestablish the army as the War of the Spanish Succession approached its end, suggested that the French "hold camps every year on one of the frontiers."[61]

In wartime and peacetime, the inspectors general played a vital role in training French troops, for they provided a mechanism to ensure standard and uniform drill. In 1667, the office of inspector general for infantry was created and filled by Jean Martinet, whose name has become a byword for rigorous discipline and drill.[62] In 1668, Fourilles was named to the new post of inspector general of cavalry. From the start, inspectors were charged with evaluating the ability of units to drill properly and with enforcing measures to make sure that they did. An order setting out the tasks for Martinet in 1668 stipulated that he was "to go visit all the garrisons of the conquered fortresses of Artois, in order to inform [His Majesty] of the state of the troops, if they drill well or badly . . . ."[63] A second order issued soon after the first commanded him to set up a network of officers in each garrison under his authority "to report to you every week what each officer [of the garrison] is doing both to instruct the soldiers and to reestablish his company in the manner that you have ordered . . . [and] to make the soldiers perform musket drill, movements to the right, to the left and forward, in order to teach them in detail to march well. This, joined to the Sunday drill in all garrisons, will surely make the soldiers skillful in a little time."[64] By the Nine Years' War, inspectors visited twice each year, in the spring and again in the fall.[65]

Essence and Implications of Drill

The innovative drill discussed here combined training with discipline in a new manner. In a certain sense, training and discipline were not integrally linked to each other until the seventeenth century. Monarchs and commanders of the fifteenth and sixteenth centuries viewed training as important, and when the need arose, great effort might be expended to teach troops a new system of warfare. A good example is the training camp established by Louis XI (1461–83) at Pont-de-l'Arche, where French infantry bands received instruction from Swiss mercenaries.[66] Yet training was regarded as a one-shot affair. It went no further than teaching weapons-handling and combat technique, and once troops had mastered their weapons and learned how to

---

[61] AG, MR 1701, piece 15. "Traité de la guerre ou il est parlé des moyens de rediger les trouppes et y restablir l'ancienne, et bonne discipline," par M. de St. Hilaire, 8 June 1712.
[62] Corvisier, *Louvois*, 187–89.
[63] AG, A¹219, 27 October 1668 order to inspector Martinet in Rousset, *Louvois*, 1:207.
[64] AG, A¹221, 20 December 1668, order to inspector Martinet in Rousset, *Louvois*, 1:208–9.
[65] Belhomme, *L'armée française en 1690*, 146.
[66] Susane, *Histoire de l'infanterie française*, 1:54–55.

stand for battle, their training was considered complete.[67] Few argued that there was any need for constant practice.

At the same time, discipline was seen as a question of control and restraint. Most contemporary references to discipline, or the lack of it, stressed the need to limit pillage and to ensure the good conduct of troops quartered on the civilian population. Surprisingly little was said concerning the need for obedience in battle; it seems that discipline was not an important combat issue. But in the seventeenth century, although the earlier use of the term survived, it also took on this second meaning.

Dutch drill united training with discipline in the name of maximizing the battlefield assets of maneuver and firepower by minutely regulating the actions of the troops. To achieve this end, troops required constant practice responding to commands under the watchful supervision of their sergeants and officers. Drill ingrained habits of obedience that affected the soldiers' attitudes and conduct while they heightened the officers' control. The latter constrained the soldier's individualism as a whole; with the coming of uniforms, soldiers even took on a common appearance. It was not enough to simply practice the practical, mechanical movements of musket loading or pike handling; these actions had to become so automatic and obedience so complete that troops performed their duties regardless of danger, that they suffered and endured without losing their effectiveness or resolution on the battlefield.

Discipline and control learned in battle could also possess implications off the battlefield. The superior control of troops that resulted from drill facilitated the tremendous growth of the French army after 1610, because unless soldiers could be kept under close and effective supervision, larger armies could be more of a detriment than a benefit to the state that supported them. In addition, the fact that troops must be well trained to fight effectively, combined with the fact that training required constant drill, provided some of the rationale for maintaining a standing army instead of demobilizing entirely at the close of each war. There is no question that the maintenance of large forces in peacetime was a defining characteristic of the state commission army, and it may have had fundamental political importance in announcing royal authority. Beyond this, it is important to note that the army constituted the first large body of the population that the state could control. The state regulated soldiers' lives as the more autocratic states would later try to regulate the lives of their civilians as well.[68] In more ways than one, drill became a metaphor for society.

---

[67] See Susane, *Histoire de l'infanterie française*, 1:174–75, on the minimal nature of training and drill. See, as well, McNeill, *The Pursuit of Power*, 128.

[68] See Feld, "Middle-class Society and the Rise of Military Professionalism," and McNeill, *Pursuit of Power*, 130–35, for some particularly thought-provoking comments on the importance of drill beyond the tactical field. See Michel Foucault, *Discipline and Punishment*, trans. Alan Sheridan (New York, 1979), 152–56, 187–88 on the social implications of drill and discipline as well.

THE ARMY ON CAMPAIGN
AND IN BATTLE

Field armies on campaign practiced the art of war based upon weaponry and organization, fashioned in unit tactics, and taught by drill; however, such armies united many individual units and thus involved a level of military practice above the material discussed previously. This section examines the composition, balance between arms, and battle formations of field armies, as well as details concerning forces on the march and in camp.

Size and Composition of Field Armies, Orders of Battle

Individual French armies in the field possessed a profile which, while related to that of the army as a whole, was quite distinct. Unlike earlier discussions of army size in this volume, this section concerns only the number of troops present for battle at a particular place on a particular day. Whereas the size of the entire army was an administrative and strategic fact, the size of a field army in battle was a tactical fact. And here, tactics are paramount.

Over the course of the wars fought during 1635–1714, the size of French forces in battle jumped over 250 percent.[69] During the long war with Spain, the average French army stood at 14,700 men; the median did not exceed 12,000. The largest battle force assembled by the French took the field in the first year of the war at Avein, where the French marshaled 34,000 against 16,000 Spanish and won. However, the size of that force and the ease of the victory were not typical of war. The battle of Avein came at a rare moment when, with relatively full coffers, Louis XIII and Richelieu mobilized what was perhaps the largest field army that the French would assemble in that war. Another forty years would pass before the French put forth so large an array in combat.

During the Dutch War, the average size of armies in battle rose to 24,500, which is 67 percent above the same figure for the war with Spain. The median force stood at 22,000. The Great Condé commanded the largest French force committed to battle in the Dutch War – the 50,000 who fought at Seneffe in August 1674. With the Nine Years' War, field forces swelled again by 60 percent to reach an average strength of 39,125, with a median level of about 33,000. At Neerwinden in 1693, Marshal Luxembourg led 80,000 men in victory over William III of England. By then, the maximum size of field armies in battle probably exceeded levels that a single general could effectively control. Turenne argued that "An army larger than 50,000 men is

[69] Battle size data from Gaston Bodart, *Militär-historisches Kriegs-Lexikon* (Vienna and Liepzig: 1908). While any source can be questioned point by point, what was required here was a consistent and reasonably complete source. For this survey, I counted the seventy-two battles listed in the *Kriegs-Lexikon* that involved French forces acting alone or with allies in which the French or French/allied army exceeded 6,000 men.

awkward to the general who commands it, to the soldiers who compose it, and to the *munitionnaires* who supply it."[70]

The War of the Spanish Succession did not bring a further growth in battlefield forces. Historians have long told their readers that the marshal Villars led 80,000 to 90,000 underfed but valiant French troops at the battle of Malplaquet in 1709. Even if we accept this figure – and the considerable gap between official and real company size during that conflict makes such a total unlikely – the French only mustered an army of such proportions at Malplaquet and Oudenarde.[71] They were involved in a number of other combats at which far smaller forces stood to their guns. On average, only 29,700 French alone or French and allied troops took part in any individual battle, and the median force mustered only 22,000. This represents a decline of 24 percent from levels reached during the Nine Years' War, again suggesting that the earlier conflict was Louis XIV's greatest war. In fact, the average and median levels are closer to those for the Dutch War than the Nine Years' War.

There was a direct and surprisingly close correlation between the size of the French army as a whole and the size of individual field armies during the *grand siècle*. If the aforementioned average battle sizes are calculated as percentages of the discounted maximum strength of the French army for particular conflicts, the relative size of campaign armies varied only slightly: 11.8 percent for the war with Spain (1635–59); 9.7 percent for the Dutch War; 11.5 percent for the Nine Years' War; and 11.6 percent for the War of the Spanish Succession.

The Balance between Cavalry and Infantry

The balance between cavalry and infantry within field armies shifted to the benefit of the mounted army from 1610 to 1715. By 1640, cavalry made up a sizable proportion of field armies during the *grand siècle* and played important tactical roles in battle and on campaign. Its mobility helped to spare cavalry from the most exacting standards of endurance and forbearance required of infantry.

In analyzing the tactical value of cavalry, it might be tempting to view the seventeenth century as simply the midpoint in a steady and irreversible slope of decline, slipping from a high point in the Middle Ages down to the nadir of irrelevancy and elimination in the early twentieth century. Tempting, but wrong. Chasing after the decline of cavalry is a bit like tracing the rise of the bourgeoisie. The ebb and flow of cavalry's importance and numbers present

---

[70] Turenne in Xavier Audouin, *Histoire de l'administration de la guerre*, 4 vols. (Paris: 1811), 2:244.

[71] Claude Sturgill in his *Marshall Villars and the War of the Spanish Succession* (Lexington, KY: 1965) ridicules the notion that the French had 90,000 men at Malplaquet. In Contamine, *Histoire militaire*, 1:540, Corvisier discounts the size of French forces at Malplaquet to 65,000, although he still claims 80,000 for Oudenarde.

an uneven and intricate pattern. Both Michael Roberts and Geoffrey Parker described a decline in the value and number of horsemen from the late Middle Ages to the early seventeenth century, followed by a resurgence in the Thirty Years War.[72] Cavalry lost its battlefield preeminence at the hands of the pike square and the caracole.

The French case does not replicate Roberts and Parker's description exactly, but it follows a similar pattern. Roughly 50 percent of the men that Charles VIII commanded in 1495 were cavalry.[73] Yet contemporary sources peg the army that Henri II assembled for his Voyage d'Allemagne in 1552 at 32,000 to 36,000 infantry and 3,100 to 5,600 cavalry, or only 10 to 18 percent horsemen.[74] Late in the Wars of Religion, main battle forces most commonly counted about 20 percent cavalry, judging by Coutras (1587), Arques (1589), and Ivry (1590).[75] Cavalry did not totally disappear, but its numbers flagged and continued to diminish for another generation. According to Sully, the forces that Henri IV planned to raise and lead against the Spanish in 1610 numbered 54,600, including only 6,600 cavalry, or only 12 percent.[76] When his son mobilized to fight the same enemy in 1635, the French monarchy strove to raise even larger forces, 144,400 men, but only 12,400, or 9 percent, were cavalry.[77] The lesson seems clear: The early seventeenth century represented something of a low for French cavalry. But it was not to last long.

As a general rule, from 1635 to 1715, cavalry made up about one third of field armies.[78] Although the first great battle of the war with Spain, the battle of Avein, saw the French take the field with only 18 percent cavalry, soon the proportion of cavalry rose to an average of 35 percent cavalry.[79] At the Dunes in 1658, Turenne's victorious force of 15,000 contained a mounted force of 6,000, or 40 percent. During the Dutch War, to fight the three great battles of 1674 – Sinsheim, Seneffe, and Enzheim – the triumphant French mustered armies that averaged 47 percent mounted troops. Armies had about 30 percent horsemen during the Nine Years' War, and this figure shrank only slightly to 27 percent during the War of the Spanish Succession, when the French were pressed to exhaustion. These percentages assume that units were at full strength. In fact, because cavalry companies were more likely to

---

[72] Roberts, *Military Revolution*, 4–6; Parker, *Military Revolution*, 69–70.
[73] Contamine, *Histoire militaire*, 1:240.   [74] Contamine, *Histoire militaire*, 1:241–42.
[75] Charles Oman, *The Art of Warfare in the Sixteenth Century* (London: 1937), 471, 484, 488, 495–96. J. R. Hale, "Armies, Navies, and the Art of War," *The New Cambridge Modern History*, vol. 3 (Cambridge: 1968), 191, seems to have overestimated the average for cavalry at this time at about 1:3, or 25 percent.
[76] Sully, *Mémoires de Maximilien de Béthune, duc de Sully*, vol. 3 (London: 1747), 390.
[77] Jules Mazarin, *Lettres du cardinal Mazarin*, eds. P. Chéruel and G. d'Avenel, vols. 6–9 (Paris: 1890–1906), 4:688–89, 5:3–6, in Parker, *Military Revolution*, 69.
[78] Chandler calculates that during the Thirty Years' War, cavalry composed 35 percent of French field armies, a figure that declined somewhat to 30 percent for the period 1648–1715. Chandler, *The Art of Warfare*, 30.
[79] Again the figures generated here are based on Bodart, *Militär-historisches Kriegs-Lexikon*.

be full than were infantry companies, the percentage of cavalry is probably understated by official tallies.

The greater cost of cavalry did not forestall its expansion during the *grand siècle*. Horsemen were certainly more expensive than foot soldiers. In 1632, the *surintendant des finances*, Bullion, figured that a cavalryman cost the state 445 livres per annum but that an infantryman cost only 203 livres.[80] Nearly a century later, Santa-Cruz said that a state had to spend as much to maintain 1,000 troopers on horseback as it did to maintain 2,500 soldiers on foot.[81] Both estimates portray cavalry as twice as expensive as infantry. It is clear, however, that the tremendous army growth of the seventeenth century was accompanied by expansion in the absolute numbers and percentages of cavalry with field forces. Official figures for the army in 1696 list 67,334 horse, a figure in the range of the size of the *entire* French army at any time during the sixteenth century.

Rather than being restricted by war finance, the proportion of cavalry in French field forces was magnified by the importance of horsemen in combat. Although mounted charges might seem archaic in hindsight, a closer look at key battles leaves no doubt as to the decisive nature of mounted assaults. Condé won Rocroi with a sweeping attack by his squadrons on the right wing. Neerwinden became a French victory when the French cavalry pierced the center of the Anglo-Dutch defenses. Marlborough won at Blenheim and drove back the French at Malplaquet with climactic cavalry assaults. Neither military conservatism nor the unmistakable aristocratic preference for cavalry account for this reliance on mounted troops. The fact is that well-timed cavalry attacks worked. Certainly, cavalry did not enjoy such a vogue as to eliminate infantry; nor did a mounted charge seal the fate at every battle. But to claim that infantry rendered cavalry obsolete at any time during the *grand siècle* is to misread the military record. D'Aurignac, a student of Turenne, expressed not just his own opinion but a military fact when he wrote in 1663: "It is cavalry that usually wins battles."[82]

Although the subject here is battle tactics, it ought to be noted that a large cavalry contingent also played vital roles in logistics and partisan warfare. Mounted detachments performed the important task of foraging for supplies to maintain an army in the field, particularly in Germany, where the French were not supplied or financed as required and were expected to seize on campaign much of what they needed. For this reason, it will be recalled, Turenne argued that fully half an army must be cavalry, and, in fact, he would seem to have achieved this percentage.[83]

[80] Richard Bonney, *The King's Debts* (Oxford: 1981), 173, n. 3.

[81] Chandler, *The Art of Warfare*, 29.

[82] Bérenger, *Turenne*, 519. The historian David Chandler argues that "Throughout the War of the League of Augsburg [the Nine Years' War], indeed, there seems to have been no stopping the French cavalry." Chandler, *The Art of Warfare*, 53.

[83] Louis Susane, *Histoire de la cavalerie française*, 3 vols. (Paris: 1874), 1:106. As much as half of his army of 10,000 men in Germany during the 1640s was composed of cavalry. Charles

The appreciation of cavalry in open field battle revolves once again around the nature of combat and the battle culture of the period. During the Thirty Years' War, French infantry suffered from a reputation as being below average in quality and performance, while their cavalry rated high.[84] Later, Louvois placed his faith in infantry, but Louis XIV was convinced that victory in the field depended on cavalry.[85] So adamant was Louis that he instructed marshal Luxembourg: "[M]ake use of my cavalry rather than engaging yourself in an infantry battle, which causes the loss of a lot of men but which never decides anything."[86] It may be that the considerable losses suffered at Senef, losses suffered to little effect, soured Louis on "infantry battle."[87] The collision of infantry, with both sides likely to be exposed to their enemy's fire for considerable time before resolving the fight, was bound to cause casualties. There the issue was bravery under fire, which meant the ability to take losses but maintain unit cohesion and effectiveness. Cavalry could not escape long-range enemy fire, particularly that of artillery, but their tactics were based on closing at high speed usually against other horsemen who fired very little or not at all. The decisive moment, the crossing of swords, could come before units had taken many casualties – thus, the economy of relying upon a "cavalry battle" if possible.

Battle vs. Maneuver or Siege

The choices recognized as alternatives by operational and strategic planners during the *grand siècle* were more varied than usually described. Yet, for the sake of brevity, they can be divided between two classic alternatives: (1) seeking the destruction of the enemy's main forces so as to disarm him, or (2) trying to defend or seize territory without necessarily destroying the enemy's army in combat. The first alternative led to battle, hopefully on the most favorable terms. The second produced two kinds of campaigns, either one based on taking and defending fixed fortifications or one designed to drive off the enemy by maneuvering one's own field forces in such a way as to make his position untenable. Although any generalization runs the risk of oversimplification, it may be said that French armies were more willing to engage in open field combat during the first half of the *grand siècle*. Later, Louis XIV was more hesitant to risk his fortunes on costly battles, so he relied more on maneuver and positional warfare – that is, the construction, defense, and attack of fortifications. When forces clashed in this period, the

---

Derek Croxton, "Peacemaking in Early Modern Europe: Cardinal Mazarin and the Congress of Westphalia, 1643–1648," Ph.D. dissertation, University of Illinois at Urbana-Champaign, 1995, 101.

[84] Croxton, "Peacemaking in Early Modern Europe," 101.   [85] Rousset, *Louvois*, 4:509–10.

[86] Louis XIV to Luxembourg, 5, 10, 12 August 1691, in Rousset, *Louvois*, 4:510.

[87] Rousset, *Louvois*, 2:50.

classic encounter was the siege. What battles still took place between field armies usually covered or contested sieges.

Basic statistics illustrate this turn away from battles and toward sieges in French wars. A sample of battles and sieges indicates that the latter were decidedly less common than battles in the period 1635–59, with only .81 sieges occurring for every battle. However, sieges were 2.23 times more common than battles during 1701–14.[88] Although no clear boundary divided these two eras, a good case can be made for splitting things at 1675. Turenne and Condé typified the older school. An aggressive field commander, Turenne preached, "In the end the army must fight."[89] He once advised the young Condé to "Make few sieges, and fight plenty of battles; when you are master of the countryside the villages will give us the towns."[90] Condé himself was even more likely to rush at the enemy if given the opportunity.[91] But these two warrior gods disappeared in 1675, one by death and the other by retirement. At the same time, Dutch resistance stalled Louis XIV's expansionist ambitions, and he began to think more in terms of defending what he had won than of adding more domains. In this task, fortresses became his primary weapon, and Louvois and Vauban his principal advisors.

Louis's demonstrable distaste for battle may have also come from his horror at the long casualty rolls produced by the indecisive battle of Seneffe in 1674.[92] How could such a price be paid and nothing gained? That same year, Vauban advised Louvois that "I believe that our enemies ought to seek combat and we to avoid it, since, avoiding combat is the sure means to beat them."[93] But by the late 1670s, siege warfare seemed to eclipse the contest of arms in the open field. As the contemporary Behr complained, "Field battles are in comparison scarcely a topic of conversation . . . . Indeed at the present time the whole art of war seems to come down to shrewd attacks and artful fortifications."[94] Consequently, the military commentator Gaya observed that "battles are not as frequent as in the past."[95] Marlborough may have said that

---

[88] Battle count from Bodart, *Militär-historisches Kriegs-Lexikon*, and siege count from John A. Lynn, "The *trace italienne* and the Growth of Armies: The French Case," *Journal of Military History*, July 1991, 324–30.

[89] Turenne in John B. Wolf, *Louis XIV* (New York: 1968), 79.

[90] Turenne, in David Chandler, *Marlborough as a Military Commander* (London: 1973), 63.

[91] Condé's audacity was legend. Chamlay compared the two saying: "M. le Prince is the first man in the world for a single day, and M. de Turenne for a campaign: the one is more suitable for gloriously finishing a battle, and the other for successfully concluding a war." Chamlay in Ronald Martin, "The Marquis de Chamlay, Friend and Confidential Advisor to Louis XIV: The Early Years, 1650–1691," Ph.D. dissertation, University of California at Santa Barbara, 1972, 63.

[92] Rousset, *Louvois*, 2:50.

[93] AG, A^{1}371, 12 August 1674, Vauban to Louvois, in Rousset, 2:55–56.

[94] Behr quotation from 1677 in Christopher Duffy, *The Fortress in the Age of Vauban and Frederick the Great, 1660–1789, Siege Warfare*, vol. 2 (London: 1985), 13–14.

[95] Louis de Gaya, *Le nouvel art de la guerre et la manière dont on la fait aujourd'huy en France* (Paris: 1692), 93.

winning a battle was "of far greater advantage to the common cause than the taking of twenty towns," yet during the War of the Spanish Succession, he fought only four major battles, while he conducted twenty-six sieges.[96]

Battle Formation

Throughout the *grand siècle*, armies arrayed for battle followed a single basic plan. The bulk of the battalions and squadrons stood in two main lines, one behind the other. A reserve stationed itself to the rear of both lines. Early in the century, large gaps separated battalions in the infantry lines, but as the decades passed, the intervals shrank, although they never entirely disappeared before 1715.[97] With these as the basic themes, a number of variations fit the changing circumstances and styles.

During the long war with Spain, the French adopted the Dutch and Swedish styles. Each of the two battle lines were composed of infantry at the center, flanked by cavalry. The first line went by the confusing name *avant garde* but was in fact the primary battle force. The second bore the title *bataille*. The units of the *bataille* were placed opposite gaps in the *avant garde*, in checkerboard fashion, allowing units of one line to advance or retire through the gaps in the other.[98] Often on the cavalry wings, companies of infantry occupied the gaps between squadrons.[99] The *avant garde* was generally larger than the *bataille*, and while the reserve, or *arrière garde*, varied in size, it was always considerably smaller that the first two lines. At Rocroi, the first two lines held a total of fifteen battalions and twenty-seven squadrons, but the reserve consisted of only three battalions and five squadrons.[100]

Writing in the early 1650s, Laon provided his own version of the contemporary formula.[101] Laon believed in putting almost all of the infantry in the first two lines, leaving the reserve as more of a cavalry force. The two lines would take the usual checkerboard form. "The squadrons and battalions of the *bataille* put themselves across from the intervals between those in the *avant garde*, so that the troops of the *bataille* can pass between those of the

---

[96] Chandler, *Marlborough as a Military Commander*, 62, appendices list battles and sieges, 334–38.

[97] Nosworthy, *Anatomy of Victory*, 25, 83, emphasizes this difference between the gapped line and what he calls a *truly linear order*, a line without major intervals between units, which was common after 1715.

[98] For French handbook discussions of the checkerboard formation, see Lostelnau, *Le maréchal de bataille* (Paris: 1647), 385–439, and I. de. Sieur d'Aigremont Laon, *Practique et maximes de la guerre* (Paris: 1652), 64–74.

[99] Nicolas Edouard Delabarre-Duparcq, *Histoire de l'art de la guerre depuis l'usage de la poudre*, 2 vols. (Paris: 1864), 2:165–66.

[100] Reboul, "Des croisades à la Révolution," 397–98. At Rethel (1650), the *avant garde* contained six battalions and twenty-nine squadrons, the *bataille* consisted of five battalions and twenty-one squadrons, and the reserve held only two battalions and fifteen squadrons. AG, A²C 346, piece #45.

[101] Laon, *Practique et maximes de la guerre*, 64–74.

avant garde to go at the enemy, and that those of the *avant garde* if broken can pass in the intervals of the *bataille* without being thrown back into the troops themselves." He advised that the two lines be close enough to one another that the *bataille* could come to the aid of the *avant garde* before it was broken. He stationed the units in each line according to seniority, the most senior troop on the right flank, next on the left flank, then alternating to the middle, "which is always the least place."

During much of the personal reign of Louis XIV, military manuals and actual practice continued to follow the pattern that Laon described; however, the gaps between battalions decreased. La Valière, read from mid- to late century, and Gaya, publishing first in 1677, both perpetuated the two-line battle order, intervals between units, units in the second line placed over the intervals between units in the first, and small independent reserve.[102] The space between lines remained constant, since it was determined by the range of infantry weapons. Writing in 1663, d'Aurignac wanted 300 paces between the first and second lines and 600 paces between the second and third lines, while Puységur who wrote after the death of Louis XIV still advised the same distances. As d'Aurignac explained, "The distance of 300 paces is in order that shots that escape will not wound the second line" – that is, that the second line will remain out of range of the enemy, because shots passing through front-line units or through the intervals between units would not reach the second line.[103] If possible, commanders strengthened their flanks by abutting them on woods, hills, or broken ground.[104]

The cavalry was more likely than the infantry to maintain full intervals between their squadrons because of the technique of the charge. On the day of battle, squadrons usually marshaled abreast on the flanks of the line of battle. It was practice to form separate brigades of the carabinier companies.[105] D'Aurignac recommended placing bodies of musketeers between squadrons in 1663, and as late as Enzheim, 4 October 1674, Turenne employed this practice, but by then it seems to have been more a hangover from the Thirty Years' War than a wave of the future.[106] Since cavalry combat often devolved into a series of charges and withdrawals, the gaps between squadrons provided valuable corridors for cavalry riding back through the line to reform. During the cavalry combat that occurred the day before the battle of Fleurus in 1690, seventeen French squadrons encountered a huge body of enemy

---

[102] La Valière, *Practique et maximes de la guerre,* which appeared first in 1667 and in later editions of 1671, 1673, and 1675, literally copied Laon word for word in its first part. Louis de Gaya, *L'art de la guerre et la manière dont on la fait a présent* (1677) was immediately translated into English and continued in updated editions to at least 1692.

[103] Azan, *Un tacticien du XVIIe siècle,* 56; Jacques de Chastenet de Puységur, *Les mémoires de Jacques de Chastenet de Puységur avec des instructions militaires,* 2 vols. (Paris: 1690), 2:609.

[104] See, for example, d'Aurignac on this point. Azan, *Un tacticien du XVIIe siècle,* 73.

[105] Louis de Gaya, *Le nouvel art de la guerre et la manière dont on la fait aujourd'huy en France* (Paris: 1692), 111, recommends this on the day of battle.

[106] Azan, *Un tacticien du XVIIe siècle,* 82; Rousset, *Louvois,* 2:86.

horsemen. The French formed in a checkerboard formation in two lines with gaps between the squadrons. Each line charged repeatedly, afterward retiring through the gaps in the other line to reform.[107] At Neerwinden in 1693, Saint-Simon with the third squadron of Royal-Roussillon, made five charges in succession; after the third, he changed horses.[108] The problems of keeping order in a cavalry unit when another friendly cavalry unit retreated into or past it was a matter of serious concern. Villars instructed that when a retreating body of horsemen came toward a squadron, that squadron should close up head to tail and if need be fire pistol shots to cause the fleeing cavalry to veer off.[109]

The size and position of artillery batteries varied according to situations. In general, commanders prized high ground from which artillery could command a large part of the battlefield. Battery size generally varied between four and twenty guns; Saint-Hilaire at Enzheim put thirty-two cannon in four batteries, and the battery on the right side of the French line at Malplaquet mounted twenty guns.[110]

Typically, a lieutenant general commanded each of the seven subdivisions of a field army – that is, the two cavalry wings of the *avant garde*, its infantry core, each cavalry wing of the *bataille*, its infantry, and the reserve.[111] As dragoons became more numerous late in the century, they tended to take up stations in the second line or reserve.[112] By late in the seventeenth century, French field armies were further organized in brigades, temporary organizations formed for a particular campaign. Circa 1690, infantry brigades contained four to six battalions and cavalry brigades eight to twelve squadrons. These brigades then became the building blocks of the lines of battle; for example, the Army of Germany put three infantry brigades in each of its two main lines.[113] In 1694, in the dauphin's army, infantry formed brigades of four to ten battalions; and the cavalry, brigades of eight to sixteen squadrons.[114]

Orders of battle for the Nine Years' War suggest that although the same basic pattern survived, the reserve became successively smaller and was almost exclusively composed of cavalry or cavalry and dragoons. In addition, a second reserve of cavalry appears. The order of battle for the Army of Flanders for 25 July 1689 lists a first line of fourteen battalions and thirty-nine squadrons, a second line of ten battalions and thirty-four squadrons, and a reserve of only eleven squadrons.[115] Luxembourg's army in August 1691 was organized as a first line of twenty-nine battalions and sixty-eight squadrons,

[107] Rousset, *Louvois*, 4:403–4.

[108] Saint-Simon, *Mémoires*, A. de Boislisle, ed., 42 vols. (Paris: 1879–1930), 1:249–50.

[109] BN, f. fr. 6257, Villars, "Traité," 88.   [110] Chandler, *The Art of Warfare*, 205.

[111] Rousset, *Louvois*, 1:233–34.

[112] As an example, see AG, A¹538, #122–27, order of battle of the army of the king in Catalonia, with Noailles commanding, May 1677.

[113] Belhomme, *L'armée française en 1690*, 176–77.   [114] Nord, C 2238, 1694.

[115] AG, MR 22. See, as well, the order of battle for the same army in October. AG, MR 22.

a second of twenty-four battalions and fifty-two squadrons, a reserve of fifteen squadrons, and a *"corps de cavalerie"* of another thirty-three squadrons.[116] In 1694, the army under the nominal command of the dauphin included a reserve of thirty squadrons and a second reserve of twenty-four squadrons of dragoon and three of cavalry.[117]

Battle formation continued to evolve subtly but significantly toward the end of Louis's reign. Intervals between battalions narrowed even further, because as firepower became increasingly important, it became essential to bring as many fusils to bear against the enemy as possible.[118] Commanders decreased the gaps between battalions to concentrate more weapons in a given space. This does not mean that intervals completely disappeared, though the old checkerboard order of battle no longer made sense, since it depended on intervals at least as large as the front of a battalion. Villars, who favored decreasing intervals between battalions in both the first and second lines, still wrote to "Take care that the second line be in range to support the first, in such a manner that if the latter is obliged to retreat [*plier*], it can do so by [passing through] the intervals of the second, and put itself in line without confusion."[119] Villars also advised keeping a suitable reserve, matched to the terrain and circumstances of battle.[120] He also wanted the wind at his back so that the smoke from the cannon and the ever greater number of fusils blew into the enemy's face.[121] In any case, the victory of the fusil and bayonet over musket and pike did not radically alter the linear style of battle that the French had practiced since early in the *grand siècle*. Just as in the minutiae of tactics, conservatism impeded innovation.

To deploy into a line of battle from a marching column was a lengthy and complicated affair. Armies approached the field in one or more columns; during the Thirty Years' War, the use of several small columns predominated, as it would later, but d'Aurignac in 1663 describes a deployment from a single column advancing perpendicular to the line of battle.[122] However, as the army approached, it needed eventually to march in column parallel to the line of battle so that individual units could then simply wheel into position. An approach left to right was preferred, because it made wheeling into position easier. Several factors, including the thickness of battalion formations, made it impossible for every unit in the army to swing simultaneously into

---

[116] Order of battle for 9 August 1691, AG, A²C 81¹. See, as well, two other orders of battle for that year in the same source.

[117] Nord, C2238, 1694, order of battle for the army commanded by the dauphin.

[118] Robert S. Quimby, *The Background of Napoleonic Warfare* (New York: 1957), 12.

[119] BN, f. fr. 6257, Villars, "Traité," 57. It may be tempting to read this quotation as indicating gaps only in the second line, as occurred in the mid–eighteenth century. However, the plates presented after page 156 of his "Traité" make it clear that Villars placed gaps in both lines and the same number of battalions in the second line as in the first.

[120] BN, f. fr. 6257, Villars, "Traité," 59.   [121] BN, f. fr. 6257, Villars, "Traité," 57.

[122] Nosworthy, *Anatomy of Victory*, 65; Azan, *Un tacticien du XVIIe siècle*, 49, 53, 55.

line at a given signal, so units deployed individually in sequence, which consumed a good deal of time.[123] Puységur reported that there was little uniformity to these battalion deployments even late in the *grand siècle*.[124]

Combat often began with an artillery exchange or cavalry action. The logic of opening with a barrage is obvious, since cannon could usually hit the enemy before any other weapons could be brought to bear. Cannon fire practically became the formal announcement of battle. At Heurtebise, the one time Louis personally commanded an army prepared to fight a battle in the open field – a battle that finally never materialized – the king fired three cannon shots to declare that he was ready to fight, and the enemy responded.[125] Still, many fights, such as those at Rocroi and Seneffe, began with a clash of cavalry, because the mobility of horsemen usually allowed them to close before the infantry could. Yet at some point, most combats became battles of attrition between rival infantry who approached to within firing range and blasted away at each other. After infantry was either decimated or badly shaken by fire, it was vulnerable to an advance by opposing infantry or to a cavalry charge.

On the March and in Camp

When on the move, French armies adapted their marching formations to the situation. D'Aurignac, who represented French practice at the close of the war with Spain, marshaled his columns differently, depending on where the enemy was, so that an army on the march could stop and face the enemy in order of battle. Each regiment's baggage marched in same order as its regiment, and a *capitaine generale du charroi* commanded the whole train.[126] In his much later treatise on war, Villars showed a great variety of marching orders, with cavalry in the van, now on one flank, now on both flanks, as infantry and artillery made up the main column.[127] Advance and rear guards were usually composed of cavalry, for the obvious reason that their mobility allowed them to patrol and respond more effectively.[128] Belhomme states that armies usually marched in three columns circa 1690, with the artillery and baggage on the road in the center, flanked with infantry and cavalry. As much as possible, peasant pioneers prepared the way for the troops.[129] Since armies marched in the order they fought, disorder on the march would hamper forming up for combat in an emergency.

Marching columns carried with them pontoons for building bridges. Armies favored copper pontoons over wooden ones because the former were

---

[123] Nosworthy, *Anatomy of Victory*, 70.   [124] Puységur in Nosworthy, *Anatomy of Victory*, 72.
[125] Rousset, *Louvois*, 2:222.   [126] Azan, *Un tacticien du XVIIe siècle*, e.g., 35, 45.
[127] BN, f. fr. 6257, Villars, "Traité," plates after page 156.
[128] See, for example, Bernard Kroener, *Les routes et les étapes. Die bersorgung der franzoschichen Armeen in Nordostfrankreich (1635–1661)*, 2 vols. (Munster: 1980), 90.
[129] Belhomme, *L'armée française en 1690*, 186.

lighter, but apparently they did not appear before the Dutch War.[130] Floating bridges could be quite long and involve numerous pontoons; the one at Philippsburg in 1667 required thirty.[131] A French bridge *équipage* of the Nine Years' War contained twenty pontoons, and the Army of Flanders had three *équipages*.[132] Bouffler's order of battle for 1701 included not only seventy cannon but forty pontoons.[133] Guarding one's bridging train was almost as important a matter of honor as protecting one's artillery train. These were prized trophies of victory, and being allowed to keep them in surrender was comparable to the honor of being allowed to march away under arms.[134] So essential were pontoons to the functioning of an army in the field that when Louis wanted to teach his grandson the art of war at the camp of Compiègne, he included eight pontoons among the equipment assembled for the maneuvers.[135]

En route, troops awoke at daybreak, broke camp, and marched through midmorning.[136] Villars directed that when marching in the presence of the enemy, an army make many short halts to "put the troops back in order."[137] The march was over no later than early afternoon. About 1663, d'Aurignac insisted that "It is necessary to arrive early in camp, in order to have the time to send men to forage and to build huts [*huter*] for the troops, without which they would perish."[138] When eight–man tents eventually replaced huts – by 1689, all the army had them – it still took time to pitch them, although they must have been a great convenience compared to huts.[139]

In the field, an army camped in order of battle, generally in two lines.[140] Just as in the line of battle, the main lines camped 300 paces apart.[141] As mentioned earlier, soldiers lived in huts early in the century and in tents later. Armies in camp followed a rather elaborate routine, awaking by drumbeat beginning with the guard regiments and passing to the other units. Louis,

---

[130] Frederick II, *Frederick the Great on the Art of War*, ed. Jay Luvaas (New York: 1966), 71. See Chandler, *The Art of Warfare*, 223, for a diagram of a contemporary pontoon bridge.

[131] AG, A¹210, #232, 28 December 1667, cost 9,908 livres.

[132] Belhomme, *L'armée française en 1690*, 137.   [133] Nord, C 2238.

[134] At the siege of Grave in 1674, Chamilly gave up the city after resistance and took twenty-two artillery pieces and an entire "bridge train made of copper." AG, A¹382, 2 November 1674, Le Tellier to Turenne, in Rousset, *Louvois*, 2:67. Similarly, when Dufay surrendered Philippsbourg after a heroic resistance, he was allowed to leave with eight artillery pieces and four copper pontoons. Rousset, *Louvois*, 2:265–66.

[135] BMG, A²ᶜ 346, piece #3.

[136] Pellison describes march order, get up at daybreak, march to 9 or 10 A.M. Pellison, *Lettres historiques*, vol. 2 (Paris: 1729), 29. I thank my graduate student George Satterfield for this reference.

[137] BN, f. fr. 6257, Villars, "Traité," 66.   [138] Azan, *Un tacticien du XVIIᵉ siècle*, 56.

[139] Contamine, *Histoire militaire*, 1:407.

[140] On camping in two lines, see Azan, *Un tacticien du XVIIᵉ siècle*, 30–36; Gaya, *Le nouvel art de la guerre*, 56–58; and BN, f. fr. 6257, Villars, "Traité," 38, where he prescribes two lines with reserve in the third line. D'Aurignac also describes troops camping in one long line. Azan, *Un tacticien du XVIIᵉ siècle*, 27–30.

[141] Belhomme, *L'armée française en 1690*, 177.

himself, took such interest in these details that he drafted regulations covering this topic.[142] As would be expected, each regiment had its place. Cavalry
regiments received twice the room of infantry regiments, for the cavalry
camped next to their horses. Three special areas occupied the rear of the
encamped army: the artillery park on the left, the *vivres* park in the center,
and the *quartier du roi*, or headquarters, on the right.[143]

PARTISAN WARFARE

It would be a mistake to devote a discussion of combat exclusively to the
conduct of great battles or sieges, because much of the fighting between foes
took place in lesser engagements, fights between small bodies of troops,
between opposing war parties. It has become something of a stereotype to
condemn the armies of the second half of the seventeenth century for avoiding battles. This criticism claims first that sieges paralyzed strategists, and
second that field armies sank into inactivity. In response, it can be argued
that avoidance of battle may have made good strategic sense when battles
were seen as such costly contests of attrition, as defined by the battle culture
of the time. Moreover, armies in the field were anything but inactive. With
or without those great clashes of arms that the Napoleonic-minded historians demand, the armies of the *grand siècle* constantly engaged in hostile
operations on the lower level known as *petite guerre*, which is translated here
not as "little war," which seems to degrade the activity, but as "partisan
warfare" or the warfare of parties, a term which lends it the greater importance that it deserves.[144] The principles of forbearance and control were not
as prominent in partisan warfare; consequently, it differed not only in the
level of intensity but in *mentalité*. Perhaps the most challenging skills of the
soldier lay not in the formal tactics of battle but in the more flexible and
individual tactics of partisan warfare. This is the least understood of the
aspects of warfare during the *ancien régime* and demands attention, which it
is only beginning to receive.

Functions of Parties

War parties performed a variety of functions vital to seventeenth-century
warfare; some applied directly to the daily operations of an army in the field,
while others had more to do with fueling the war effort by procuring supplies

---

[142] For the details of camp and march as crafted by Louis himself, see his regulations of the
1670s in Louis XIV, *Oeuvres*, 3:134–51 and 4:51–66.

[143] Gaya, *Le nouvel art de la guerre*, 56–58.

[144] André Corvisier has recently written that the War of the Spanish Succession was a war of
partisans. True, but why limit that statement to this war? In fact, warfare always had an
important partisan element throughout the *grand siècle*. Contamine, *Histoire militaire*, 1:540.

and money through courses and contributions.[145] Under the first category, parties foraged for fodder, protected friendly convoys and attacked enemy convoys, scouted and gathered intelligence, provided security from enemy parties, sealed roads leading to besieged fortresses, or, alternatively, tried to break through to bring aid to beleaguered garrisons. Under the second category, parties performed most of the nasty duties associated with contributions. They imposed demands, took hostages, executed reluctant villages, and gathered in the take. Parties also raided for livestock, particularly cattle, and penetrated deep into enemy territory on raids, or "courses," to seize whatever they could lay their hands on. Lastly, when a scorched-earth strategy ruled, they ravaged the countryside to deny its resources to the enemy.

Because the amount of green fodder consumed by an army was so great, forage parties continually ventured out to cut, bundle, and carry feed for their horses. In a good-sized army, forage parties could be quite large; an army of 60,000 could regularly require forage parties of 4,000 to 10,000 troops, and larger ones are on record.[146] Forage activities with a field army were the province of the lieutenant general of the day, and they were such huge operations that putting an officer of such exalted rank in charge was altogether appropriate. A royal regulation for cavalry in 1672 was adamant that forage parties not leave camp in advance of their armed escorts.[147] Essential to an army's existence, foraging parties provided a legitimate target for enemy action. Such actions could be on a small scale, as when a commander reported in 1677 that "yesterday some small parties that I had sent to cover our foragers fought two enemy parties and took ten to twelve cavalrymen prisoner."[148] But clashes involving forage parties could also reach the level of a small battle. In 1711, a French attack on an enemy forage party even netted the lieutenant general commanding it.[149]

Parties not only guaranteed the supply of fodder to horses; they also protected shipments of food to men. Both infantry and cavalry guarded convoys of bread, flour, and other essentials.[150] Conflicts over convoys were

---

[145] Contemporary military handbooks have a good deal to say about *petite guerre* and parties. For example, Laon, *Practique et maximes de la guerre*, 98, comments on parties; and Jean-Léonor Grimarest, *Fonctions des généraux ou l'art de conduire une armée* (La Haye: 1710), 45–48, provides a list of duties for parties.

[146] Facts and figures on foraging come from G. Perjés, "Army Provisioning, Logistics and Strategy in the Second Half of the 17th Century," *Acta Historica Academiae Scientiarum Hungaricae* 16, nr. 1–2 (1970), 14–19, unless otherwise stated. Quincy mentions one involving 15,000 men on 3 October 1710. Quincy, *Histoire militaire de Louis le Grand roi de France*, 7 vols. (La Haye: 1727), 6:381.

[147] Règlement du Roi pour la cavalerie, 1672, in Louis XIV, *Oeuvres*, 3:145–46.

[148] AG, A¹538, #441, 5 June 1677.

[149] Claude Louis Hector Villars, *Mémoires du maréchal de Villars*, ed. Vogüé, 5 vols. (Paris: 1884–95), 3:131.

[150] See Nodot for details of convoy guard in different terrain, etc. François Nodot, *Le munitionnaire des armées de France* (Paris: 1697).

not small affairs, one of the young Condé's first combats at age eighteen was a clash between a French convoy escort and an attacking party. This minor battle involved 3,000 cavalry on both sides, and marshal La Meilleraye commanded the French horsemen personally.[151] So important was guarding convoys that when Louis XIV organized the camp at Compiègne in 1698 for the military education of his grandson, the duke of Burgundy, one of the exercises performed by the assembled troops was the escorting of a convoy.[152] Authorities worried constantly about the need to protect convoys, because they made such good targets and because what they carried was so vital.[153] The French too raided their foes' convoys for the same reasons that French shipments came under attack.

Parties also gathered intelligence either as their main purpose or as a byproduct of another mission. This might involve the observation of enemy camps and columns; however, the presence of enemy parties could make such a direct approach dangerous. A well-commanded army maintained outposts and patrols designed to keep enemy parties at a distance. The commentator Grimarest advised parties "to master the countryside and to keep those of the enemy at a distance from [French] armies and fortresses."[154] A classic method of gaining intelligence was the interrogation of enemy prisoners or local inhabitants, as when a French party overran an enemy party, taking eight prisoners who told the French that the enemy main body numbered 8,000, a fact that the French then confirmed by questioning a local townsman.[155] Reports of such interrogations occasionally appear in the correspondence with the war minister.[156] Any war party might uncover valuable military information, so Grimarest advised an officer commanding a party to always seek news of the enemy – information that included both explicitly military items and reports on the state of forage and livestock in the countryside.[157]

One less obvious but important advantage of dispatching parties was to wear down an opponent. The task of protecting against every possible threat of attack by hostile parties was understandably greater than the amount of effort it took to mount enough raids to keep such a threat credible. A report from the era of the Dutch War informed the war ministry that all was fairly

---

[151] Eveline Godley, *The Great Condé: A Life of Louis II de Bourbon, Prince of Condé* (London: 1915), 25.

[152] AG, MR 1817, pieces 3 & 4.

[153] Concern with covering convoys against parties sent from Ath, to Humières, 20 October 1683, Jacques Hardré, ed., *Letters of Louvois*, University of North Carolina Studies in the Romance Languages and Literatures, no. 10 (Chapel Hill: 1949), 280. See, as well, Vauban's concern for the need to guard convoys against parties coming from Charleroi in 1693. Letter of 29 June 1693, from Vauban to Le Peletier, in Rochas d'Aiglun, *Vauban*, 2:390.

[154] Grimarest, *Fonctions des généraux*, 45–48.

[155] AG, A^{1}538, #280–81, 26 May 1677. See AG, A^{1}538, #441, 5 June 1677, for another case of prisoner-taking with intelligence value.

[156] See, for example, two records of interrogations, A^{1}2266, #164, 165–7, May 1710.

[157] Grimarest, *Fonctions des généraux*, 44.

quiet on the front "except the happy success of our parties that extraordinarily fatigue the enemy army."[158] During the Nine Years' War, Vauban complained that the parties venturing out from Charleroi required that every nearby convoy have its escorts, that the French send out parties of their own, and that all this activity was exhausting 15,000 to 16,000 troops that could better be used elsewhere.[159]

Siege warfare charged parties with new tasks, both offensive and defensive. When investing a fortress, the attacking army dispatched parties to seal off the roads so that additional supplies and troops could not enter. Defenders trusted parties to break through the siege lines to the beleaguered garrison, bringing in needed supplies and fresh soldiers. This led the besieging army to detail other parties to ward off these attempts at relief, as when Louvois ordered Montal to have small parties fall on Spanish parties that attempted to break the ring around the fortress of Luxembourg in 1684.[160]

The war party was also the primary tool of contributions; here the function was not so much the immediate support of troops in the field as it was the acquisition of the resources that fueled the war effort itself. Much of the story of contributions is a story of war parties. The records of their accomplishments fill innumerable letters in the volumes of military correspondence. Such parties played into both the more regular pattern of contributions in the Netherlands and the more sporadic pattern imposed on German lands across the Rhine. An unquestionably vicious aspect of enforcing contributions was the brutal business of burning and hostage taking, as discussed in Chapter 6.

Closely related to contributions were raiding courses. Both types of partisan activity were designed to net money and foodstuffs for the military; however, it is useful to separate the system of contributions, which could involve long-term payments in a fairly regular manner, from spasmodic or unique raids, which struck deep in enemy territory and seized one-time-only hauls of booty. In 1689, the marquis de Feuquières led an extraordinary raid 500 miles through Germany; he briefly took Wurzburg, Nurenburg, Ulm, Augsburg, and Pforzheim and netted 4 million livres of contributions and loot.[161] Villars sent parties across the Schelde in 1710; they returned with 20,000 *écus* and horses.[162]

An important task undertaken by war parties was to counter the enemy's partisans. Parties were forever fighting troops sent to thwart them or laying ambushes for their foes. Lines and posts were established to shelter areas from raids and contributions. As Duras explained, "it is not easy to cause parties to pass from Bonn beyond the Rhine, because the enemies occupy

[158] AG, A^{1}539, #153, 23 June 1677. See, as well, AG, A^{1}539, #303, 5 July 1677, on the role of parties draining enemy forces of their strength along the Mozelle.
[159] Letter of 29 June 1693, from Vauban to Le Peletier, in Rochas d'Aiglun, *Vauban*, 2:390.
[160] Louvois to Montal, 7 May 1684, Hardré, *Letters*, 349.
[161] Chandler, *The Art of Warfare*, 52.   [162] Villars, *Mémoires*, 3:96.

diverse posts . . . and among others Sibourg where they have a rather large body in range to fall at any moment on our parties."[163] Again, posts were related to controlling or extending contributions, a fact that Villars pointed out to Louis.[164] Anti-party parties could operate from strings of posts, as in Louvois's order to raise four companies of cavalry in Artois that could be "lodged in bodies of fifteen to twenty in places when he believes that they will be well posted to cut off the little parties that will enter the country."[165] Fortresses themselves could be judged viable solely or mainly for their value in resisting enemy raids, as was the case in the debate over keeping La Fère.[166] Forces meant to thwart parties could muster many troops. In 1667, a French course of 300 troopers ran into and fought a party of 1,800 cavalry under none less than the prince of Liège.[167] A decade later, Créqui moved up several regiments to contain a course led by the duke of Lorraine.[168] Casualties could be heavy in such clashes. A French party of fifty men met and defeated a hostile band in 1677 at the cost of two French killed and six wounded, while the hapless foes suffered thirteen or fourteen killed.[169]

In addition to their roles in direct support of field armies or in contributions and courses, parties also performed less well-known or discussed roles. In 1677, Luxembourg sent out parties on the main roads leading from his camp in order to snag deserters.[170] In 1710, parties of troops even acted to suppress the illicit salt trade.[171]

The Partisans and Their Opponents

Partisan warfare involved a considerable variety of fighting forces. Regular line regiments detached parties. The mobility of cavalry gave them an advantage; but infantry also marched off on courses or rode double with cavalry.[172] Handbooks intended for cavalry officers made a point of discussing the conduct of partisan warfare. Regular troops from a field army often undertook "little war" tasks that maintained that army on campaign, such as foraging and convoy escort, or attacks on enemy forage parties and convoys.

Beyond the intermittent use of regular troops for this irregular warfare,

---

[163] AG, A¹875, 3 April 1689, letter from Duras.

[164] AG, A¹1676, #150, 13 July 1703, Villars to Louis XIV. See also AG, A¹295, #222, 26 Oct. 1672, letter from Le Pelletier; Louis XIV, *Oeuvres*, 3:456–57; AG, A¹2266, #228, 8 August 1710, to Ormesson.

[165] Louvois to Montbrun, 22 December 1676, in Hubert van Houtte, *Les Occupations etrangères en Belgique sous l'ancien régime*, 2 vols. (Ghent and Paris: 1930), 2:191.

[166] Gaston Zeller, *L'organization défensive des frontières du nord et de l'est au XVIIe siècle* (Paris: 1928), 62–64; AG, A¹340, #287, 22 December 1673, Vauban to Louvois, in Rochas d'Aiglun, *Vauban*, 2:98.

[167] AG, A¹209, #122, 8 August 1667, letter from Vaubrun.

[168] AG, A¹538, 1 May 1677, letter from Créqui.   [169] AG, A¹538, #446–47, 5 June 1677.

[170] A¹538, #544, 11 June 1677, Luxembourg.   [171] A¹2266, 1710, #13, 16–20, 43–44, 93, 171.

[172] Feuquières wrote of one raid: "I made good speed with 800 cavalry and 500 infantry on their cruppers." Feuquières in Chandler, *The Art of Warfare*, 52.

certain specialists did little else; they earned the title "partisan." During the Dutch War, the king put bodies of partisans in frontier fortresses, paying and feeding them as if they were regulars.[173] This practice was revived in 1694.[174] They might qualify as a free company – that is, an individual company unattached to any particular regiment. Several partisan leaders of such irregular troops won a certain fame – men like Chevalier, La Croix, and Ecrevisse.[175] Partisan warfare demanded a high level of skill with a command of the tactics and tricks of the trade. A successful leader must know the country, master the local language. He must be able to stage an ambush and avoid being trapped in one himself. It was safest to march at night, avoiding the main roads and villages. The choice of guides in unfamiliar country was critical.[176] Innumerable little ruses aided the partisan; Grimmelshausen even mentioned reversing the shoes of ones' horses and putting horseshoes on cows to mislead pursuers.[177] It comes as little surprise that Huxelles complained that raids were depleting his army, because he had to send only his best men on them.[178]

Because professional partisans claimed a percentage of what they brought in, there was something of the buccaneer about them. Although leaders attempted to reign in the worst excesses of their men, parties were prone to abuse those who lay in their paths. Grimarest advised that an officer must allow a little brigand behavior, "because without this, and without these unjust delights [douceurs], the soldier does not like [to go on] the party at all."[179] In any case, Louis XIV refused to tolerate excesses when news of them came to his attention.[180] The French also tried to regulate the conduct of parties, even going so far as to stipulate when and how often parties might demand "refreshment" from villagers; life service on the galleys threatened those who failed to abide by this stipulation.[181] However, there is little reason to suppose that the French were able to keep their raiders to the letter of the law.

---

[173] André Corvisier, *Louvois* (Paris: 1983), 202.

[174] Belhomme, *L'armée française en 1690*, 70.

[175] See A¹1339, 3 January 1696, for a letter from the partisan Chevalier; regarding La Croix and Ecrevisse in 1709, see Quincy, *Histoire militaire*, 6:146.

[176] For suggestions concerning the principles of partisan warfare, see Grimarest, *Fonctions des généraux*, 43–45; Laon, *Practique et maximes de la guerre*, 227–43; Sandraz de Courtilly, *La conduite de Mars* (La Haye: 1685), 206.

[177] Grimmelshausen, *Simplicius Simplicissimus*, trans. George Schulz-Behrend (Indianapolis: 1965), 132–33.

[178] AG, A¹829, 11 December 1688, Huxelles to Louvois.

[179] Grimarest, *Fonctions des généraux*, 42–43.

[180] In 1673, he ordered that five soldiers who had pillaged a church be burned alive. *Gazette*, 7 June 1673, in Wolf, *Louis XIV*, 230.

[181] Nord, C 2333, 26 May 1677, regulation on the conduct of parties to go out for contributions says that men were only entitled to two refreshments per day on French or Spanish territory, and these at least two lieus from each other, to cost only 4 patans per man. Those who did not obey were to go to the galleys.

Partisans often acted so much like brigands that military and civil law carefully had to draw a line between the two. Regulations of 1677 stipulated that a party must contain at least fifteen horsemen; otherwise, it would be considered as simply a band of marauders.[182] This minimum size was confirmed in an ordinance of 1 April 1707, stipulating that parties could not be smaller than fifteen men, led by a subaltern officer.[183] Should infantry make up the party, it had to number at least twenty soldiers; "otherwise they are considered as thieves and brigands; and these are called '*partis bleus*.'"[184] This requirement rose to twenty-five cavalry, dragoons, or infantry late in the War of the Spanish Succession; it was feared that smaller parties might more easily slip into French territory.[185] War parties of about fifty men seem to have been relatively common; however, far more could ride out as the situation required; reports mention parties of 300, 350, 600, 1,500, and even 3,000.[186]

But partisan warfare involved more than regulars and professionals; the fact that this style of warfare was directed at common people put ordinary peasants and townsmen in the thick of it. All too often, it is assumed that civilians stood by and let soldiers do all the fighting, but in the seventeenth century, they did not. Common folk operated as individuals, in groups acting on their own initiative, and as local militia or guards created in response to directives issued by the authorities. French officials sought to counteract enemy war parties by mobilizing the populace. As a consequence of an earlier order not to pay contributions to the enemy, in 1673, d'Aigremont, the lieutenant governor of Lille, issued the following directive:

We order that all inhabitants of the cities, towns, villages, and hamlets of this government, from ages 18 to 60, including valets and domestics of ecclesiastics and nobles, none excepted, are to take arms and assemble and perform *guet* and guard with a full third of the inhabitants day and night; and the others are to relieve them and thus to continue each in his district, . . . to keep a sentinel in the bell tower to discover the enemy, to sound the tocsin, to chase them, and to inform the governors.[187]

During the War of the Spanish Succession, when enemy parties threatened to raid the interior of France, Louis XIV called upon his own people to guard river crossings and otherwise hamper the movement of hostile parties.[188] Peasants also guarded their own parishes from the ravages of enemy parties.[189]

---

[182] Nord, C 2333, 26 May 1677.   [183] *Ordonnances militaires*, vol. 1 (1734), p. 57.

[184] Grimarest, *Fonctions des généraux*, 41.   [185] Contamine, *Histoire militaire*, 1:541.

[186] AG, A^{1}209, #15, 28 May 1667, #97, 16 July 1667, #122, 8 August 1667; AG, A^{1}538, #439–40, 441–42, 446–47, all 5 June 1677; AG, A^{1}829, 26 December 1688, Puysieulx to Louvois; AG, A^{1}2027, #127, 11 June 1707; AG, A^{1}2266, #266–72, 7 November 1710, Ormesson report; and Quincy, *Histoire militaire*, 6:364.

[187] Nord, C 2333, 16 November 1673.

[188] AG, A^{1}2265, #101, 8 February 1710. Later, it was reported that the locals offered to guard the crossing of the Rhone near Ecluse themselves. AG, A^{1}2265, #133, 30 September 1710.

[189] AG, A^{1}2266, 6 October 1710, Harcourt writing from Châlons, said that "the peasants have always performed guard duty in the parishes."

The monarchy even provided ball and powder to villages of Rousillon that wished to defend themselves.[190] In turn, the enemies of the French also organized their own citizens to resist French raiders, perhaps with greater effect. In the Spanish Netherlands, rural guards patrolled the roads in peacetime to suppress vagabonds. In peacetime, there were only twelve per village, but all able-bodied men were mobilized during wartime.[191] Spanish authorities directed their people to attack convoys or operate as snipers, *francs tireurs*.[192] During the struggle of 1635–59, Spanish authorities promised compensation to peasants who resisted contributions.[193] Early in the Dutch War, the council of Liège ordered their subjects "to arm themselves against all those who molest them without making a distinction between nations."[194] Some peasant resistors became particularly famous, or infamous. French parties and convoys suffered at the hands of German *schnapphahns* – literally, "highwaymen," but in this case, partisans who emerged from the local peasantry to snipe at the French. In 1689, "their numbers were swelled by the peasants of the Palatinate who desert every day."[195] Chamlay complained about these *schnapphahns* "who fire from all the woods and at all the passages. It is absolutely necessary to bring these people back to reason by taking them [prisoner] and by burning their villages."[196] The French detested the *schnapphahns* not only because they were particularly dangerous but also because they did not take prisoners.[197] To the south, the Spanish employed *miquelets* in the rough and mountainous terrain that guarded their frontier along the Pyrenees.[198] Just as did their German cousins, *miquelets* fell on isolated detachments; 100 attacked a French forage party of only twenty men in 1677.[199] It would appear that the French used this term both for legitimate enemy light infantry and for armed peasants; the French would raise their own *miquelets* as well to fight the Spanish. Other effective peasant resistance to French parties occurred in the Franche-Comté in 1674 and Sicily in 1677.[200] At times, the enemy might stiffen local resistance by sending regulars to fight alongside peasants.[201]

---

[190] AG, A¹1989, 28 April 1706. I would like to thank Dr. David Stewart for providing me with this reference.

[191] See van Houtte, *Les Occupations etrangères en Belgique*, 1:19, concerning the rural guard.

[192] Van Houtte, *Les Occupations etrangères en Belgique*, 1:3.

[193] Van Houtte, *Les Occupations etrangères en Belgique*, 1:153–4. On resistance, see 1:76.

[194] Notification by placard, AG, A¹295, #57, 6 October 1672, report by Charuel.

[195] AG, A¹875, 3 April 1689, Goupillières says that the islands along the Rhine are full of them. See, as well, his letter AG, A¹875, 31 March 1689.

[196] Chamlay to Louvois, 22 July 1689, in Rousset, *Louvois*, 4:227–28.

[197] Rousset, *Louvois*, 4:394.

[198] For references to *miquelets* in 1675, see Rousset, *Louvois*, 2:195–96. Two years later, a party of 100 fell on a French forage party of twenty. AG, A¹538, #243–44, 22 May 1677, Camus from Perpigan.

[199] AG, A¹ 538, #243–44, 22 May 1677, Camus from Perpigan.

[200] Rousset, *Louvois*, 2:22, 30 April 1674 letter from Condé to the king. Insurgent villages and peasants defeated the French at La Mole in December 1677 in Sicily. Rousset, *Louvois*, 2:462.

[201] AG, A¹875, 5 March 1689, Chamilly to Louvain.

Resistance bred reaction. In 1672, Luxembourg punished villagers who fired on French parties by burning their houses.[202] In 1674, Turenne also dispatched soldiers to burn villages in reprisal for murders and mutilations by the local population.[203] Huxelles believed the peasantry to be such a threat in 1689 that he tried to disarm them; however, he had to admit, "I believe that it is difficult to take arms away in such a manner that there do not remain enough [for the peasants] to put themselves in the woods and disturb those who pass as soon as the leaves come out."[204]

During the *grand siècle*, the French at first built upon their own tactical tradition by selectively borrowing from others and then came to set the standards for all of Europe.[205] One aspect of their preeminent influence was in forming a European battle culture of forbearance during the *grand siècle*. This culture was not uniquely French; it was at base a reflection of European technology and society. But as Louis XIV's regiments became the paradigm army on the continent, the French provided the model of forbearance for Europe. The nation of the *furia francese* now preached drill, discipline, and control. The implications of this military style were great. A concept of endurance in the face of danger, rather than one of assertive action, may have been the most important advantage that Europeans took with them when they went overseas to confront warrior cultures. It was not enough to bring firearms, for these could quickly be adopted by foreign peoples; one must also bring a superior way of employing those weapons in battle, or even a way of thinking about those weapons. But if this battle culture brought victory overseas, where Europeans fought other peoples who did not share their concept of war, in Europe this view of battle as attrition came to defeat battle itself, and other forms of combat came to take its place. Paramount among them was siege warfare, the subject of the next chapter.

[202] A¹278, 16–17 November 1672, Luxembourg to Louvois in Rousset, *Louvois*, 1:393.
[203] Van Houtte, *Les Occupations etrangères*, 1:120–21.
[204] AG, A¹875, 9 March 1689, Huxelles from Mayence.
[205] The French led the way on prescribing regular periods of drill and on training camps according to Chandler, *The Art of Warfare*, 107.

✠

16

Positional Warfare

NO nation has worshipped the offensive spirit more than has France, and this idolatry has brought her both victory and defeat. The triumph of the attack columns that overwhelmed her enemies during the wars of the French Revolution cannot hide the tragedy of the bayonet charges that spilled rivers of French blood to no advantage in World War I. "*Marchons, marchons, qu'un sang impure abreuve nos sillons!*"* But for all the sacrifices that France has made at the altar of the offensive, she has not worshipped it alone. There are other altars that have received her offerings – more of gold than of flesh – shrines built of brick and stone, of steel and concrete: her fortresses. The France that built the Maginot Line in the twentieth century constructed the *pré carré* in the seventeenth. If in the *grand siècle*, Turenne preached the glory of attacking the enemy in the open field, Vauban advocated the more dependable rewards of positional warfare.

Ultimately, Vauban spoke more directly to the character and goals of Louis XIV, and positional warfare took precedence over field warfare. The term *positional warfare*, as employed in this chapter, encompasses the construction, defense, and attack of fortifications, be they fortresses or entrenched lines; by the close of the *grand siècle,* it was the most common form of military operation. Although the French were no strangers to sieges under Louis XIII, warfare of maneuver played a more important role during his reign than it would under his son's. Louis XIV displayed an overriding taste for positional warfare. In part this preference reflected a personality that abhorred violation of his lands and desired control. And in part this preference stood as a reasonable alternative in a battle culture that defined combat in the field as costly and uncertain.

Louis XIV, the Sun King, appears in historical accounts as an aggressive

---

* "March on! March on! May [the enemy's] impure blood water our furrows!" There is obvious irony to this applied to World War I.

proponent of his own glory, who admitted, "I loved war too much."[1] But this "love" amounted to a willingness to resort to war for reasons that had as much to do with fear as bravado. Louis grew up in an atmosphere of territorial and political insecurity. During a century and a half of conflict, Hapsburg power had usually overmatched the French. Louis's grandfather and father had both fought off invasions by the Spanish, who marched down from the southern Netherlands again early in Louis's reign. The rebellion of the Fronde, which struck when the boy-king was only ten years old, threatened the monarchy and merged into the duel with Spain. He may have pursued glory through conquest when he first commanded the reins of power, but after the Dutch War, Louis was more intensely concerned with protecting his domains than with extending his possessions. What gains he did pursue through diplomacy or force were often intended to secure a better defensive line, for Louis came to dread any threat to his territory. Fortresses both protected his lands and symbolized his claims. In a marvelously striking metaphor, the historian George Livet wrote of Louis: "He marked France [with fortresses] like a peasant sets out boundary stones on his land."[2]

Positional warfare appealed to Louis on other levels as well. He was drawn by the details of life, government, and war. He was, as summed up by John Rule, "le roi bureaucrat," and positional warfare, particularly great sieges conducted according to Vauban's dictums, were affairs of meticulous detail. In addition, positional warfare appealed to his passion for control. When Chamlay said that the fate of France no longer depended on the quality of her generals in 1688, he meant that it now rested solely on what the king could control; it was a prescription for *guerre de cabinet*. Bowing to the king's authority, Vauban stated that "The decision concerning sieges is an *affaire de cabinet*."[3]

Of course, Louis's interest in fortification was not unique. Seventeenth-century conflict was shaped by positional warfare. Behr exemplified this trend in 1677 when he wrote: "Field battles are in comparison scarcely a topic of conversation . . . . Indeed at the present time the whole art of war seems to come down to shrewd attacks and artful fortifications."[4] The French underwent a dramatic shift to positional warfare, so that by the War of the Spanish Succession, the French were well over twice as likely to engage in a siege as to undertake a field action.[5]

---

[1] Louis is reputed to have said these words on his deathbed to the boy who would succeed him as Louis XV. John B. Wolf, *Louis XIV* (New York: 1968), 618.

[2] Georges Livet, *L'Equilibre européen de la fin du XVe à la fin du XVIIIe siècle* (Paris: 1976), 94.

[3] Sébastien le Prestre de Vauban, *De l'attaque et de la défense des places* (The Hague: 1737), 1.

[4] Behr in Christopher Duffy, *The Fortress in the Age of Vauban and Frederick the Great, 1660–1789* (London: 1985), 13–14.

[5] Sieges were 2.23 times more common than battles during 1701–14. Data base on battles compiled from Gaston Bodart, *Militär-historishes Kriegs-Lexikon, 1618–1905* (Vienna and Leipzig: 1908); data base on sieges presented in John A. Lynn, "The *trace italienne* and the Growth of Armies: the French Case," *Journal of Military History*, July 1991, 324–30.

Louis XIV's emphasis on positional warfare not only grew out of his personality and policy but out of the somber expectations of field battle. He and his generals, at least after the disappearance of Turenne and Condé, saw battle as unpredictable and costly, whereas sieges both rendered warfare more predictable and limited losses. Vauban offered positional warfare as an alternative to the bloody uncertainties of field warfare: "Today it may be said that only siegecraft offers the means of conquering and holding territory."[6] Vauban repeatedly emphasized reducing casualties through careful technique. Perhaps sieges were as much an affair of attrition as were battles, but their cost was measured more in material than in men.

The French not only led in their reliance upon sieges; they also led Europe in improving fortress design and in developing the techniques of siege warfare. If they lost the edge in the field, they did not in the trenches. Of course, the central figure here was the great Vauban.

FUNCTIONS OF FORTRESSES AND FORTIFIED LINES

During the *grand siècle*, positional warfare played a wider variety of roles in war than might at first be apparent. Most fundamentally, and most obviously, fortifications defended territory, yet fortresses also served offensive, logistic, and internal control functions as well.

Fortresses stood like stone-faced sentinels guarding the lands of their master. Siting and constructing fortifications was a science of denial. The massive walls, deep ditches, and brooding artillery of modern fortifications, all marshaled in rational and deadly order, defied attackers, threatening them with brutal repulse. Although determined foes could overcome a fortress, they triumphed only by great investment of manpower, matériel, and time. Even a victorious attacker emerged beaten and bloody.

It might be tempting to try to avoid the great cost of a formal siege by marching around a fortress that blocked an army's path. However, it was unwise for an invader to bypass a fortress, since its garrison could cause mischief entirely out of proportion to its numbers. The garrison could sweep out of the fortress and strike at the attacker's lines of communication and fight with his foraging parties and raiders, jeopardizing his ability to requisition forage, food, and funds. So dangerous would this threat be that an advancing enemy would at least have to mask the fortress, and this would take far more troops than the garrison itself maintained, thus sapping the attacker's troop strength. In a sense, then, fortresses were what the modern military terms *force-multipliers* because they allowed a relatively small number of soldiers to occupy in one way or another a much larger number of enemy troops. Because the defensive potential of a fortress arose from its garrison

---

[6] Sébastien le Prestre de Vauban, *A Manual of Siegecraft and Fortification*, trans. G. A. Rothrock (Ann Arbor: 1968), 21.

as well as its geometry, a string of fortresses, even though not physically linked to one another, could render Louis's kingdom, in the words of Vauban, "impenetrable to the enemy."[7] When an enemy could not advance into French-controlled territory, he could not exploit its resources for the maintenance of his army, and as a result, that area was reserved as an exclusive preserve for French exploitation.

Implied in a fortress's ability to bar a path to the enemy was its promise to open that path to friendly forces. Particularly during the first half of the seventeenth century, diplomatic and military language spoke of fortresses as "gates" into the enemy's territory. Vauban linked the defensive and offensive potential of fortifications in an essay that listed as the first value of fortresses: "to close the entries of our country to the enemy and to open for us those into his country."[8] This offensive potential multiplied the value of fortifications, which in many cases were literally bridgeheads across river barriers, as Strasbourg was on the Rhine. Richelieu wanted that fortress "to acquire 'une entrée' into Germany."[9] One concerned German observer fretted over the French seizure of Strasbourg in 1681: "everyone says that it is one wheel of the chariot on which [the French] can enter the Empire, and that the gate to Alsace is now closed [to German attackers]."[10]

By dominating major routes, fortresses made logistics easier for friends and more difficult for foes. Supply lines were essential, particularly by the late seventeenth century. Rivers proved highly advantageous for moving food and equipment, and fortresses were particularly well designed to dominate rivers and river crossings. Turgot, *intendant* in Lorraine, described one role literally flowing out of the other: "[Fortresses] occupy almost all the passages and posts advantageous for blocking access and hold . . . the rivers, in such a way that to enter enemy territory we have only to go down river, and this with much less effort than is required of the enemy since they must go up river."[11] Thus, the French tried to command the Rhine bridges and to control the water courses that penetrated France along its eastern and northern frontiers.

Fortresses not only guarded routes of supply; they also served as the storehouses for those supplies. Louis XIV's fortresses sheltered his magazines, which gave the French considerable advantage in the conduct of warfare, at least through 1691. The amounts of food and fodder stored in magazines could be impressive. In 1672, Turenne listed 251,000 *septiers* of

---

[7] Vauban concerning the fortifications of Provence, in Reginald Blomfield, *Sébastien le Prestre de Vauban, 1633–1707* (New York: 1971), 127.

[8] AG, Bibl. Génie, ii, fol., Vauban, "Mémoire sur l'utilité des places fortes," dated 1689.

[9] Richelieu to Louis XIII, 1629, in John C. Rule, ed., *Louis XIV and the Craft of Kingship* (Columbus: OH: 1969), 7.

[10] Letter written from Wurtzbourg on 14 October 1681 to Baron de Montclar, in Camille Rousset, *Histoire de Louvois*, 4 vols. (Paris: 1862–64), 3:50.

[11] BN, f. fr. 22210, fol. 107, Turgot's report, in André Corvisier, *Les Français et l'armée sous Louis XIV d'après les mémoires des intendants, 1697–1698* (Vincennes: 1975), 115.

wheat stored in Kaiserwerth, Dorstein, Liège, Charleroi, Mezière, and Ath, an amount he estimated as enough for 100,000 rations per day for about a year, or 200,000 rations for the six-month campaign season.[12] At the same time, the French had six months' worth of grain stored in the front-line magazines at Pinerolo, Brisach, Metz, Nancy, Thionville, Rocroi, Dunkirk, La Bassée, Courtrai, Lille, and Le Quesnoy.[13] Fortresses also provided a safe place to store arms; in 1697, Metz held 500 pieces of artillery plus small arms for 20,000 men.[14] Their well-stocked and well-sited magazines allowed the French both to take the field earlier in the year than could other armies and also to change lines of operation with greater ease. The French particularly benefited from being able to feed their horses from stored fodder and thus take the field before the spring grass was substantial enough to let horses graze off the land.

Since seventeenth-century armies also sought to supply themselves directly from the areas that they occupied or marched through, the offensive potential of fortifications as gates into enemy territory promised great logistic rewards. It was of tremendous importance for armies to campaign and to set up winter quarters on enemy lands in order to make war feed war. No wonder that in 1702, Chamlay lamented the loss of fortresses on the far side of the Rhine, "which enabled [the King's] armies to cross to the other bank and subsist on German territory."[15]

Fortresses also served as bases from which to impose contributions on the enemy and from which to launch courses against his territory. Fortresses exerted control over the areas surrounding them. In these zones, garrisons could exact contributions for their support. Fortresses also provided bases for raiding parties that constantly plundered regions in search of food and forage. At one time or another, Heilbron, Mannheim, and Mons, to name only a few, served as central fortresses from which French troops carried out the brutal business of assessing and collecting contributions. During the War of the Spanish Succession, Louis regarded Landau as so essential to controlling Lower Alsace for contributions that his armies battled over its possession through four sieges. Smaller posts, often fortified, were also chosen for their use in launching contribution raids.

Of course, enemy fortresses threatened to impose contributions or dispatch raids against French-held territory. In 1687, Louvois feared that because of enemy forces in Philippsburg, "Lower Alsace remains their prey,

---

[12] Louis XIV, *Oeuvres*, eds. Grimoard and Grouvelle, 6 vols. (Paris: 1806), 3:116–17, "Premier état du maréchal de Turenne, vivres et munitions pour la Meuse et le Rhin."

[13] André Corvisier, *Louvois* (Paris: 1983), 191. In 1675, an army of 80,000 men was to be supported for two months solely by food grain stored in Maestricht and Liège. AG, A¹433, 5 April and 14 May 1675, letters from Louvois to Estrades and Moreau. I thank my graduate student George Satterfield for pointing the way to this material.

[14] BN, f. fr. 22210, fol. 117–18, Turgot's report, in Corvisier, *Les Français*, 219.

[15] Jean Jacques Pelet and François Vault, eds., *Mémoires militaires relatifs à la succession d'Espagne*, 11 vols. (Paris: 1835–62), 3:756.

and they can always . . . entirely exhaust [*manger*] that country."[16] Similarly, Vauban pleaded for a French attack on the enemy stronghold of Charleroi in 1693, since it served as a safe harbor for bands of land-pirates who struck at French territory: "This single fortress . . . obliges us to maintain guards at eighteen or twenty small fortresses. . . . It causes the ruin of a territory equivalent to a good province . . . and obliges the King . . . to maintain in his fortresses 15,000 or 16,000 more men who will be lost annually in convoys and escorts."[17]

Conversely, fortresses and fortified lines were designed to shield areas from enemy raids. In 1672, Vauban argued for maintaining the fortress of La Fère precisely to limit the possibility of courses, even though by other criteria, La Fère should have been razed.[18] A Vauban memoir of 1689 argued for holding Ypres and a companion fortress in the southern Netherlands, since "these two places if they are ours bar enemy contributions from the sea to the Lys and limit the penetration of their courses."[19] During the War of the Spanish Succession, the French constructed four complete systems of lines to cover the Spanish Netherlands from the Meuse to the sea. These lines of trenches, redoubts, and towers made use of rivers and canals where possible. Unlike the trench lines of World War I, most such entrenchments were not meant primarily to stop field armies but rather to shelter the rich hinterland from enemy courses and to reserve them for the levying of contributions to support French forces.

Lastly, fortresses, or the citadels that dominated cities, proved useful to control potentially rebellious subjects, inhabitants of newly acquired lands, and populations of territories occupied in war. Richelieu believed in the use of fortifications "to curb mutinous towns."[20] Louis XIV defended his decision to construct a citadel in newly conquered Lille in 1667, "a heavily populated city which it was troublesome to secure without this precaution."[21] Vauban promoted maintaining Saint-Omer in good condition because it was

---

[16] Letter from Louvois to Vauban, 25 August 1687, in Rochas d'Aiglun, *Vauban, sa famille et ses écrits*, 2 vols. (Paris: 1910), 2:280.

[17] Letter of 29 June 1693, from Vauban to Le Peletier, in Rochas d'Aiglun, *Vauban*, 2:390. In 1644, the enemy fortress of Frankenthal forced the French to tie down such large forces in nearby garrisons that the French lacked the troops to take Frankenthal itself. Charles Derek Croxton, "Peacemaking in Early Modern Europe: Cardinal Mazarin and the Congress of Westphalia, 1643–1648," Ph.D. dissertation, University of Illinois at Urbana-Champaign, 1995, 167–68. In 1678, Vauban had urged taking Luxembourg for very much the same reasons that he pleaded in the case of Charleroi; see 1678 memoir in Rochas d'Aiglun, *Vauban*, 1:190–91.

[18] AG, A¹340, #287, 22 December 1673.

[19] AG, Bibl. Génie, 11 fol., Vauban, "Mémoire sur l'utilité des places fortes," dated 1689.

[20] Richelieu, *Lettres, instructions diplomatiques, et papiers d'état*, d'Avenel, ed., 8 vols. (Paris: 1853–77), 3:180. Vauban argued for maintaining the fortress of La Fère because "it is a secure fortress against all disorders of state from wherever they may come, whether from within or without." AG, A¹340, #287, 22 December 1673 letter from Vauban to Louvois.

[21] Louis XIV, *Mémoires de Louis XIV pour l'instruction du dauphin*, Charles Dreyss, ed., 2 vols. (Paris: 1860), 2:190.

in an area, "which is still not well de-Spanified [*désespagnolisé*]."[22] In a memorandum, he defined one of the purposes of fortifications as "to maintain newly conquered peoples in obedience."[23] Of course, the existence of some fortresses could pose a danger because the townspeople might seize them and resist the monarchy's forces; this helps to explain why the king decided to destroy the walls of Paris in 1670.[24] Bordeaux lost its exterior walls and had to accept a citadel as the reward for its rebellion in 1675. However, the fact that fortresses could be used to keep watch over a rebellious population should not lead to the conclusion that Bourbon France was a garrison state, for few fortresses dotted the interior. In fact, French fortresses were concentrated on the frontiers, sea coasts, and on three key rivers, the Loire, Rhône, and Seine.[25] The fact is that the destruction of fortress walls was more of a political act than was the construction of new strongholds.

FORTRESS DESIGN AND CONSTRUCTION

The Artillery Fortress and the Trace Italienne

Offense and defense have danced a deadly *pas de deux* throughout history. The primitive offensive weapons of knight and archer yielded priority to the high stone walls of the medieval castle; the defense triumphed. But the arrival *en scène* of effective artillery in the fifteenth century stripped the castle of its dominating role, since even early cannon could topple the thin vertical walls of medieval strongholds. A new style of fortification was needed to deal with the deadly effect of gunpowder.

During the last decades of the fifteenth century and the first of the sixteenth, Italians engineered defensive works that could both withstand bombardment by artillery and use gunfire effectively in their own defense – what can be called the "artillery fortress." One key to the new design was the bastion. While medieval square and round towers provided flanking positions to fire down on attackers before the main walls, they left "dead zones" in which attacking forces could shelter from defending fire at the base of such towers. The bastion, an arrowhead-shaped artillery tower, eliminated dead zones and allowed cannon and hand guns to sweep ground in front of the walls. (See Figure 16.1.) The first bastion design dates from the 1480s, but it was the French invasion of 1494 and the wars that it precipitated that drove the adoption and improvement of the bastion. The bastioned trace, or fortress plan, is so rooted in Italy that it became known as the *trace italienne*.

---

[22] AG, A¹III5, 19 August 1688 letter from Vauban in Zeller, *L'organization défensive*, 100.
[23] AG, Bibl. Génie, 11, fol., Vauban, "Mémoire sur l'utilité des places fortes." J. R. Hale, *War and Society in Renaissance Europe, 1450–1620* (Baltimore, MD: 1985), 250, wrote "The most obvious symbol of coercion was the citadel."
[24] Philippe Contamine, ed., *Histoire militaire de la France*, vol. 1 (Paris: 1992), 422.
[25] Contamine, *Histoire militaire*, 1:467, 482. See maps 28 and 31 for the positions of French fortifications during the *grand siècle*.

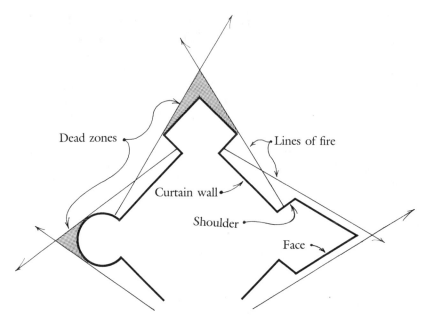

Figure 16.1. Dead zones created by round and square towers.

The first bastions, offspring of medieval towers, were rather small and built entirely of masonry. They projected at intervals from the walls rather in the fashion of their ancestors. By the seventeenth century, bastions had evolved into large, flattened structures built of earth faced with stone or of earth alone.

Geoffrey Parker insists that the spread of the *trace italienne* revolutionized warfare, rendering positional defense possible against the new cannon. Remember, a trace is a ground plan or outline – an aerial view of the fortification, as it were – that stresses the bastion. Fascinatingly intricate, indeed beautiful, the *trace italienne* as brought to its zenith by Vauban would seem to be a dominant piece of military technology. While the bastioned trace was unquestionably a crucial development in fortress architecture, one can become seduced by it. In examining these Italian designs, most historians, like Parker, have concentrated on the development of the bastion, but more fundamental to the new pattern of positional warfare were the walls themselves and the cannon that stood atop them. In fact, the bastion composed only part of the new artillery fortress. To be effective in the new gunpowder environment of early modern warfare, fortifications had to: (1) protect the fortress from storm by infantry; (2) absorb bombardment without toppling or crumbling; (3) shelter the defenders from attacking fire; and (4) subject the attackers to effective cannon fire. The bastioned trace was absolutely essential only to the first of these requirements, resisting close-in attack by enemy infantry.

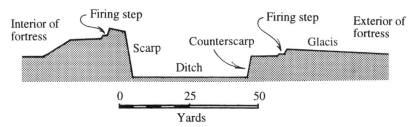

Figure 16.2. Cross-section of the wall of an artillery fortress.

To prevent infantry from storming the fortress, either in a sudden *coup de main* or in a final *coup de grace* of a formal siege, engineers designed a new style of wall, surrounded by ditches, unless the terrain provided better obstacles. (See Figure 16.2 concerning the wall cross-section.) Height remained the best barrier to infantry, but the height of a medieval wall made it vulnerable, since it was usually too thin to resist the battering of artillery. By greatly thickening the wall and making it protrude less above ground level, military architects rendered it artillery resistant. Its function as a high barrier to infantrymen was preserved by surrounding it with a ditch. Thus, in a sense, architects preserved the high wall by simply sinking it into the ground. The defenders atop the wall sheltered behind thick earthen ramparts, stout enough to protect them from cannonballs. Just over the outside wall of the ditch, the counter scarp, further firing steps gave infantry forward positions from which to defend the fortress, and beyond these, the ground sloped away in a glacis that provided infantry and artillery on the wall with the best possible field of fire against attacking infantry.

The fact that defenders now stood behind ramparts of earth as much as fifteen feet thick meant that they were masked from the ditch directly below them, and they could not shoot down into it without exposing themselves to enemy fire. Consequently, some firing platform had to project from the walls to flank the ditch. This brings us back to the bastion. By the seventeenth century, it was a direct geometric necessity of the thicker walls of the now artillery-resistant walls. Bastions allowed defenders to sweep the ditch between them with flanking fire, while the arrowhead design of these structures themselves allowed gunfire from neighboring bastions to sweep the ditches before the faces of threatened bastions. Without the bastions, the ditch would have provided shelter for the attackers. Consequently, the essential function of the seventeenth-century bastion was close-in defense of the ditch. The placement and angles of the bastions allowed musket and cannon fire to rake the ditch, thus allowing short-range defense with modern gunpowder weapons.

The massive earth-backed walls of the modern fortress provided excellent, stable positions for defensive artillery to answer the attacker's guns and drive off his infantry. The most effective defense of the artillery fortress was the fire of its cannon. Far more than the bastion, the characteristics of artillery determined the patterns of siege warfare. Most importantly, siege operations began at such great distances from fortresses because of the range of artillery, not because of the projections of bastions. The cannon, not the angled bastion, was the most potent aspect of the new fortifications. In a sense, as long as the modern wall cross-sections were applied, a fortress could have been a simple square and still have been just as effective at resisting and dueling with the enemy guns. Only when attacking troops came within one hundred yards would the square fortress become more vulnerable than one in the *trace italienne*. The *trace italienne* was a necessary aspect of the modern artillery fortress, but it was not a sufficient explanation of its power.

Perhaps bastions have captured historians' attention because the early Italian bastions not only provided covering fire to sweep the ditch, but they also functioned as artillery towers. Therefore, they expressed all vital aspects of the artillery fortress at its inception. But the functions must be separated. The primary function of the bastion, that for which only it served, was to sweep the ditch with musket and cannon fire. Guns devoted to long-range fire against besieging artillery after the commencement of a siege might best be mounted on the curtain wall between bastions, not on the bastions themselves. In fact, as Vauban advised, once the point of attack of the enemy siege was clear, the defenders shifted their cannon to the threatened side to concentrate their fire on the attackers.[26] The shoulders of the bastions, where cannon were sited to sweep the ditch, was probably the worst place to station cannon meant to make a besieging army keep its distance.

The Evolution of the Artillery Fortress in France to 1660

Fortifications adapted to artillery in ways that varied from minor modification to complete replacement. Older city walls could be converted into reasonably effective artillery fortresses short of adopting the *trace italienne*. The easiest, and cheapest, response to the wall-smashing force of cannonballs was simply to lower the medieval towers, whose height now became a liability, and back the old walls with thick earthen ramparts. But this was only a temporary solution. To reduce vulnerability, the entire works had to be sunk into the ground, but if the medieval fortifications included a moat, wet or dry, this necessary element was already included. Another way to incorporate medieval walls was to add bastions to medieval walls or build a series of modern bastions beyond the medieval walls, as was done at Tournai and Douai.[27] In the latter case, the old walls became a second line of defense

---

[26] Vauban, *A Manual of Siegecraft*, 123.

[27] On Tournai, see photo of fortress model, P. Lazard, *Vauban, 1633–1707* (Paris: 1934), in figure 9. Concerning Douai, see the plans in Michel Roche, *Histoire de Douai* (Westhoek: 1985), 69, 123, and 134. With the addition of only two bastions, its medieval walls stayed as they had been in the fourteenth century, except that they were backfilled with earth.

against infantry. The most radical modification would be to replace the medieval walls with an entirely new circle of walls in the *trace italienne*, made either of earth throughout or in a more permanent style of earth faced with stone or brick. There was no exact timetable for this evolution. Some cities in France, like Saint-Omer, did not replace their medieval walls with more modern patterns until the late seventeenth century.[28]

The process of transition to *trace italienne* fortifications in France began with François I. This renaissance king brought engineers from Italy to become the primary engineers for the French. François introduced the engineer and architect Girolamo Marini to France in 1534, and within a decade, no less than 100 Italian engineers were working in France under his direction.[29] By François's death, most of the fortified towns in northeast France had been or were being refashioned. This did not necessarily mean that they had been transformed à la *trace italienne*, however. During the famous siege of Saint-Quentin in 1557, the town, though devoid of bastions, possessed medieval walls, lowered and buttressed from behind with a thick earthen rampart and protected in front by a wet ditch.[30] Artillery stood on broad platforms on the ramparts. As Henri II concentrated on the frontier of Champagne, more fortifications were remodeled or transformed there. The Wars of Religion, as they did in so many ways, slowed or halted military improvements. Henri IV constructed fortifications directed against Spain, spending 35 million livres during 1600–10.[31]

The French also developed their own engineers, so at least by the reign of Henry IV, the long dominance of Italian engineers ended. Henri did not seem to employ Italians, replacing them with native Frenchmen such as Espinai de Saint-Luc and Claude de Chastillon. At any rate, by this point, the Dutch had come to rival the Italians as leaders in the science of fortifications, most notably in the person of Simon Stevins (1548–1620). By royal order, Jean Errard de Bar le Duc published in 1594 the first important French book on fortifications, *La fortification demonstrée et reduicte en art*. This began a flow of works on fortification by French authors, including Jacques Perret in 1594, De Ville in 1628, Fabre in 1629, Blaise de Pagan in 1640, and Fournier in 1647. Despite numerous books on the subject, the half-century 1610–60 was not particularly notable in the actual work of fortification. The reign of Louis XIII brought decline and decay in French fortification, owing to the lack of a stable financial support for engineers and gunners.[32] Louis XIII continued to build works, but the pace slowed when Richelieu came to power, and particularly with the start of war in 1635, but by then, France was

---

[28] See illustrations showing medieval walls in 1668 and bastioned walls in 1685 in Alain Derville, *Histoire de Saint-Omer* (Lille: 1981), 151.
[29] Christopher Duffy, *Siege Warfare: The Fortress in Early Modern History, 1494–1660* (London: 1979), 45.
[30] See woodcut reproduced in Robert Fossier, *Histoire de Picardie* (Toulouse: 1974).
[31] Contamine, *Histoire militaire*, 1:463.   [32] Duffy, *Siege Warfare 1494–1660*, 116.

well girded with fortresses.[33] As the war with Spain drew to a close, Louis-Nicolas Chevalier de Clerville claimed the palm as the most important practicing military engineer in France; perhaps his major enduring claim to fame was that he supervised the apprenticeship of the great Vauban.

Vauban, the Soldier and the Engineer

Vauban's career encompasses the story of fortifications during the personal reign of Louis XIV. Vauban achieved excellence and success, yet greatness never sat easy on his modest shoulders. Certainly, he was not born to it. This man who rose to become the valued advisor and comrade in arms to Louis XIV was but the son of a minor and recently ennobled Burgundian family.[34] The noted diarist Saint-Simon, who raised snobbery to an art form, dismissed Vauban's noble origins as "nothing so short, so new, so low, or so thin."[35] But even haughty Saint-Simon praised Vauban as "the most honest man, and the most virtuous, perhaps, of his century."[36] Neither was money a key to his success; Vauban himself admitted that "Fortune caused me to be born one of the poorest gentlemen in France . . . ."[37] The answer for his rise was talent and the times.

While his family's background was in law and commerce, his father, Urbain, fought as a soldier. The family owed a certain allegiance to the Condés, so it comes as little surprise that when the seventeen-year-old Sébastien entered military service in 1651, he did so as a cadet in the personal regiment of the prince de Condé. When a relative presented the lad to the Great Condé, the prince is reputed to have said to those assembled there, "Remember, monsieurs, this young man will go far."[38] At that time, the prince had taken up arms against Louis XIV in the Fronde, which ended in 1653, but before it did, Vauban left the rebel forces and joined the king's army as a young officer with some interest and skill in siege warfare.

Vauban took part in the siege of the rebel stronghold Sainte-Menehould. After its fall, he aided in the repair of the defensive works. In 1655, he received the post of *ingénieur ordinaire du roi*. During this era, there was no regular education and training for young military engineers; rather, they apprenticed with some master of the art, and Vauban worked under the guidance of Clerville. He learned well, and after a decade and a half of

---

[33] Contamine, *Histoire militaire*, 1:463. Anne Blanchard believes that Louis XIII deserves more credit than normally given in regard to fortifications. See the map of fortresses, ca. 1635, Contamine, *Histoire militaire*, 1:467.

[34] The best biography of Vauban remains Lazard, *Vauban*. I have relied upon Lazard for the basic facts of the story.

[35] Louis de Rouvroy, duc de Saint-Simon, *Mémoires*, ed. A. de Boislisle, 42 vols. (Paris: 1879–1930), 12:357.

[36] Saint-Simon, *Mémoires*, 11:27.

[37] Vauban letter to Louvois, 15 December 1671, in Rochas d'Aiglun, *Vauban*, 2:65.

[38] Condé in Lazard, *Vauban*, 65.

service, he surpassed his pedantic and somewhat dull teacher. Following the French conquest of Lille in 1667, Louis hastened to refortify this crucial town, and he requested proposals from both Clerville and Vauban; the latter's plan was clearly superior. This triumph established the younger man's dominance as the premier military engineer in France, a preeminence that he would relinquish only through death in 1707.

His career reached heights never scaled by any previous engineer. He became *commissaire général des fortifications* in 1678 and the key individual in fortress administration throughout France. Before Vauban, no engineer officer had risen above the rank of captain, but he became a brigadier in 1674, *maréchal de camp* in 1676, and lieutenant general in 1688. In 1703, Louis XIV elevated his premier engineer to the highest French military rank, marshal, albeit in the twilight of his life.

Vauban's military career was extraordinarily busy. His nonstop duties were only interrupted by wounds and illness. He drew up plans for about 160 forts, in whole or in part; like a pharaoh, he erected his own monuments, many of which stand to astound the visitor. He directed forty-eight sieges, during which he took considerable personal risk. During the siege of Lille in 1667, for example, he was struck by an enemy musket ball in the left cheek, a scar that shows clearly in his portraits. More than once he was ordered not to go into trenches, since his life was too valuable, but this does not appear to have deterred him. He also undertook a seemingly endless series of inspections, a task that wore him out in traveling and made him an infrequent visitor to his own home. He once jested that while troops could be brought to an inspector, fortifications demanded that he visit them; "there is not a single watch-tower in all the king's fortresses which will move so much as an inch at my command."[39]

His other accomplishments included an able and productive pen, although he never published a single work for public consumption during his lifetime. His most important military works were two treatises on siegecraft, but he also wrote manuscripts on everything from pig breeding to taxes. Although a reformer at heart, he was a discreet reformer who wished to operate from the top down, so his memoranda circulated privately.

Vauban built his outstanding career on a foundation of engineering innovation, siege methodology, and strategic vision during an age of positional warfare, but that edifice might well have never risen had it not been for the unusual symbiosis between the great engineer and his masters, Louis XIV and Louvois. By the mid-1670s, Louis XIV saw strategy in terms of defensible frontiers buttressed by fortifications, so his obsession demanded the services of a master of positional warfare. Vauban vibrated a resonant cord in Louis himself. In birth and temperament, Vauban conformed with the profile of the archetypal government servant under Louis XIV. Louis had a

---

[39] Letter of 10 May 1696 from Vauban to Le Peletier de Souzy in Rochas d'Aiglun, *Vauban*, 2:442–43.

taste for experts, and Vauban was the kind of highly skilled, but modest, expert that he preferred. Even his age was right, only five years senior to the king. Vauban attained his peak as an engineer at a period when France enjoyed the wealth, population, and stability to pursue grandeur. Louis XIV knew and admired Vauban. The king commanded at nineteen sieges directed by Vauban, though the monarch fought in not a single battle in the open field. During sieges, Louis instructed officers who outranked Vauban to follow the bidding of this premier engineer. Yet so deep-seated was Louis's preoccupation with the defense of his borders that if Louis had not enjoyed the services of Vauban, Louis probably would have elevated some other engineer, though it is hard to believe that he could have found another as outstanding.

Louvois was the third individual in this triumvirate. Vauban began his career as a client of Mazarin and Colbert, but he passed over to the rival Le Telliers about 1667, and he would remain in Louvois's camp until the death of the minister. Historians have argued that Louvois saved Vauban from a Colbert-inspired scandal about this time, but that seems to be a misreading of the evidence.[40] Vauban's loyalty to Louvois was unrelated to any such alleged rescue. Once within the orbit of the secretary of state for war, Vauban's career benefited from Louvois's support. Engineers who attempted to appeal over Vauban's head were firmly put back into their place. Vauban and Louvois maintained a voluminous and extremely frank correspondence that bears witness to a high level of mutual respect. When Louvois died, Vauban had amassed such credit with the king that the engineer no longer required a personal sponsor and operated as his own man.[41]

Much has been made of Vauban as an expression of his age. He symbolized, so the line goes, science or Cartesian rationalism applied to war.[42] He was elected to honorary membership in the French Academy of Sciences in 1699, and the scientific popularizer Fontennelle delivered a funeral oration for him that is still read today. Also, there is no question that his prescriptions for siege warfare bestowed upon it a regularity applauded by those who loved system for its own sake. But a glance at his design of fortifications makes it clear that for Vauban reason did not take precedence over reality. He insisted, "The art of fortification does not consist of rules and systems, but uniquely in good sense and experience."[43] In fact, Vauban held it absolutely essential to adapt to terrain; he once criticized the fortifications of Mannheim 1688: "I do not understand these people at all, for they have fortified Mannheim as one would fortify at pleasure on a piece of paper,

---

[40] See the new and careful analysis in Ben Scott Trotter, "Marshal Vauban and the Administration of Fortifications under Louis XIV (to 1691)," Ph.D. dissertation, Ohio State University, 1993, chaps. 8–10.

[41] Trotter, "Marshal Vauban," argues that after 1691, Vauban needed no patron.

[42] See Henry Guerlac, "Vauban: The Impact of Science on War," in Edward Meade Earle, ed., *Makers of Modern Strategy* (Princeton: 1941).

[43] Vauban's words reported by his secretary Thomassin, in Lazard, *Vauban*, 373.

without having any regard for the Neckar or Rhine Rivers, of which they have not taken any advantage, so to speak."[44] If anything, Vauban rejected adherence to geometry for its own sake. Certainly, Louis and Louvois turned to Vauban not because he expressed an age of reason but because he brought to its highest state a form of warfare – positional warfare – that was particularly crucial because of the character of military technology, the form of military institutions, and the capacity of the state to pursue warfare. Louis and Louvois encouraged and financed Vauban's projects and sieges because they won victories, because he was a master of military architecture and siege warfare. He was effective; that was enough.

The Three Systems of Vauban

Arguably the greatest military engineer in Western history, Vauban refused to lecture dogmatically on fortress design to his contemporaries. He was refreshingly modest about his talents and accomplishments, once calling himself "only half an engineer."[45] He also refused to write a treatise on the design of fortifications, since he saw his contributions here as not particularly original. Ironically, the designs of this engineer who mocked system are conventionally discussed as three systems. It remains convenient to do so only as long as it is understood that the three systems are, at most, useful categories, not rigid plans.

The first system represented little that was new with Vauban; rather, it artfully and effectively combined elements of fortification common by mid-century. Bastions conformed to dictates set down by Blaise de Pagan in his 1640 publication, *Les fortifications de Comte de Pagan*. Whereas some engineers had seen the curtain wall as the heart of the trace, Vauban followed Pagan in emphasizing the bastions, which operated as mutually supporting strong points simply connected by the curtain. Effective musket range determined the placement of bastions, which stood roughly sixty *toises*, or about 125 yards, apart so that musket fire could spray the ditch. Beyond the bastions and curtain, Vauban employed the standard menu of outworks at the disposal of the military engineer – tenailles, demi-lunes, ravelins, hornworks, crownworks, and so forth – in all their variants. (See Figure 16.3.) This first system appeared initially at Lille in 1668, which he called his "oldest daughter." Here his genius lay in application, not in innovation.

The second system was truly original, though he continued to see it as simply a perfection of existing designs. The crucial creation of this system was the *tour bastionnée*, or bastion-shaped tower, and the detached bastion. To understand the origins and function of the *tour bastionnée*, it must be remembered that Vauban designed for all terrain, including mountainous sites, where the fortress could be commanded from surrounding heights. In

[44] Vauban letter of 18 November 1688 in Lazard, *Vauban*, 220.
[45] Vauban in Duffy, *The Fortress in the Age of Vauban*, 78.

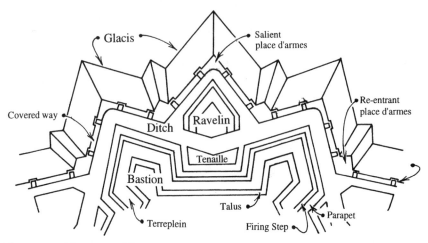

Figure 16.3. Elements of fortifications.

such cases, he needed to protect the rampart and gun positions from fire from above. He did so by covering them with wood or stone galleries and placing the guns in casemates. To this experience must be added his siege-war innovation of using high-angle cannon fire to clear enemy ramparts, his *tir à ricochet*, which implied that the open batteries of the first system must now be shielded even on flat terrain. The *tour bastionnée*, with its casemated artillery, was the answer.

With the primary artillery now concentrated in a small tower instead of along the open flanks of the bastion, the bastion could be detached from the main wall with no threat of losing the artillery on it should the bastion fall. In detaching the bulk of the bastion, Vauban considered the manner in which most fortresses were attacked. Because an assault on the curtain wall risked the crossfire of two bastions, and because the curtain was usually shielded by the thickest set of outworks, bastions themselves became the preferred target of attack. Once an attacker breached the bastion rampart, he compromised the entire inner *enceinte*, or wall, because the bastion's ramparts were contiguous with the curtain. By separating the bastion from the curtain wall with a ditch, a breach of the bastion did not endanger the fortress as much. Vauban described this aspect of the second system with the rather painful analogy "pull out the nose in order to throw it in the face of its enemy."[46] His second system was first employed in his plans for Besançon, Belfort, and Landau in 1687.

Vauban only employed his third system on a single fortress, Neuf Brisach, designed in 1698. This plan retained the *tour bastionnée* and detached bastion of the second system but added a recess in the curtain. It is as though he

---

[46] Vauban in Michel Parent and Jacques Verroust, *Vauban* (Paris: 1971), 99.

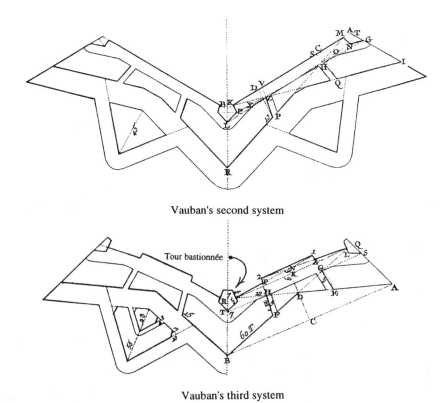

Vauban's second system

Vauban's third system

Figure 16.4. The second and third systems of Vauban. (From Diderot, *Encyclopédie.*)

turned the curtain into a shallow bastion with two small shoulders into which he placed casemates for artillery. In essence, it added more gun positions to cover the ditch and the faces of the *tours bastionnées.* He was unable to apply this design to other fortifications because it came so late in his career and because the expense was so great.

The Pré Carré

With unvarnished realism, Vauban condemned war: "War has interest for its father, and ambition for its mother, and for close relatives all the passions that lead us to evil."[47] Still, princes must be proficient in it or risk ruin. Across the frontiers, he saw predatory foes surrounding a beleaguered France: "all interest themselves in her ruin or at least in the diminution of her power."[48]

[47] Vauban in Lazard, *Vauban,* 486.
[48] Vauban in Alfred Rebelliau, *Vauban* (Paris: 1962), 141–42.

The war he foresaw for France was defensive, and while regrettable, it remained unavoidable.

In this hostile environment, Vauban advocated a fortified frontier that he labeled a *pré carré*, a term susceptible to two interpretations. On the one hand, the term meant a dueling field; on the other hand, it implied that the frontiers would be straightened out, or squared off, to make them more defensible. In a famous letter of January 1673, Vauban proposed the *pré carré* to Louvois:

> Seriously, Sir, the King must think some about creating a *pré carré*. I do not like this pell-mell confusion of fortresses of ours and the enemy's. You are obliged to maintain three for one; your men are plagued by it; your expenses are increased and your forces are much diminished .... That is why, be it by treaties, be it by a good war, if you believe what I say, Monseigneur, always preach squaring things off, not the circle, but the *pré*.[49]

This soon became his standard for strategic and operational advice. In September 1675, when Vauban urged the taking of Condé, Bouchain, Valenciennes, and Cambrai, he wrote to Louvois that "their seizure would assure your conquests, and create the *pré carré* so much desired ...."[50]

His most elaborate plan dealt with the highly vulnerable frontier with the Spanish Netherlands, the border most dependent on masonry to establish a defensible line in depth. There he achieved a defensive frontier, which he described as "two lines of fortresses" formed "in imitation of an army's order of battle."[51] Not meant for flexible defense, he intended these barriers as enemy-tight seals designed to preserve the sacred land of France.

In pursuit of his goal, Vauban proposed to Louvois and Louis which fortresses ought to be taken in war, and which could be regarded as expendable. To shorten the frontier and ensure its integrity, some valuable works in enemy hands should be seized. Thus, the *pré carré* became a goal of warfare, a direction for strategy. For instance, Vauban advised taking Condé, between Mons and Valenciennes, because it would save useless garrisons "and create a *pré carré* in Flanders, that twenty years of war could not tear up."[52] In addition, the *pré carré* meant building some new works. Along the vital stretch of frontier from Sedan to Dunkirk, eight fortresses received entirely new walls or new citadels, and twenty-three were significantly renovated.[53] The greatest of all these projects was at Lille. But, again, it was not a question of building more, but better or better placed, fortifications.

Treaties earned his praise or condemnation depending on whether they helped to produce a defensible frontier. The good Treaty of Nymwegen, which ended the Dutch War in 1678, awarded the French valuable towns and

---

[49] AG A¹337, #III, 20 January 1673, Vauban to Louvois.

[50] Vauban to Louvois, 21 September 1675, in Lazard, *Vauban*, 161.

[51] Vauban, "Mémoire des places frontières de Flandres," November 1678 in Rochas d'Aiglun, *Vauban*, 1:189.

[52] Vauban in Blomfield, *Vauban*, 74.   [53] Contamine, *Histoire militaire*, 1:482, map.

forts that strengthened and rationalized their border. The subsequent policy of forcible "reunions," by which Louis XIV appealed to dubious claims in order to "reunite" certain key towns with France, won Luxembourg and Strasbourg, both of which Vauban regarded as vital. The Truce of Regensberg, which recognized these last gains in 1684, came closest to realizing Vauban's goal.

By the 1690s, Vauban opposed French expansion: "It does not suit the ambition of [the King] to possess an inch of land in Italy, or beyond the Rhine or the Pyrenees."[54] But Vauban's lack of territorial ambition does not mean that his *pré carré* was, or should have been, viewed as benign by those who saw France as an enemy. Louis's and Vauban's notion of absolute security put potential enemies at risk. Bridgeheads that Louis held on the Rhine in order to deny the enemy the opportunity to attack France provided him with the avenues to attack them. His fortresses not only covered his frontiers; they projected French power.[55] Because his security must by nature compromise theirs, it was reasonable for those suspicious of the French to read Louis's intentions as offensive.

Demolition of Fortresses during the Grand Siècle

To create a rational *pré carré*, not only must the French seize or build new fortresses; they had to inactivate others. In fact, fortress demolition had occupied the Bourbons since Henri IV. It was practically a necessary handmaiden of fortress construction. Old medieval castles and fortified houses of the Wars of Religion became a problem for the first Bourbon monarch, since they housed nests of brigands. In 1593, Henri wanted Sully to draw up a plan distinguishing "those places that are absolutely necessary for defense" from those that could be safely demolished when "the governorships fall vacant."[56] Henri IV promulgated an ordinance demanding their destruction, but it was only partially observed. The 1617 Assembly of Notables also made their demolition a major demand.

This was followed by Richelieu's 31 July 1626 ordinance pronouncing the destruction of all internal fortifications – that is, all fortifications and fortresses that did not protect the frontiers of France. This ordinance resulted from political as well as military motives. Destruction would rob rebellious nobles of dangerous strongholds, and the decree could be read as a message to *les grands* that the monarch was now in charge, even of their ancestral homes. After the fall of La Rochelle, Richelieu advocated a program of demolition to the King: "It is necessary to raze all the fortresses that are not on

---

[54] Vauban in Rebelliau, *Vauban*, 170.
[55] My graduate student, George Satterfield, first attached the modern strategic term *power projection* to Louis's fortresses.
[56] David Buissaret, *Sully and the Growth of Centralized Government in France, 1598–1610* (London: 1968), 175, in Duffy, *Siege Warfare*, 115.

the frontiers, do not bar the passage of rivers or do not serve to curb mutinous towns."[57] An *intendant* reported in 1697 that no fortresses stood in Auvergne because they "were demolished and razed by order of the late king in 1634 on the occasion of a trip that monsieur the cardinal Richelieu made in the province which caused him to adopt this plan in fear of some revolution."[58] Again for political reasons, once Lorraine fell under French occupation, authorities pursued a rigorous enforcement of the 1626 ordinance, with a commission to settle on demolitions. Fifty fortifications were razed.[59] Such destructive efforts were, however, far from complete, and many lesser fortifications remained. Vauban reported that at the end of the seventeenth-century, there still existed "old chateaus or little citadels remaining from the times of the Wars of Religion."[60]

Demolition promised the added benefit of freeing troops from garrison duty so they could join the field armies. As a 1629 edict explained, demolition would "save us the costs of the garrisons which are maintained to no purpose [*entretenues sans besoin*]."[61] In 1644, Turenne worried "that in putting the infantry necessary in the fortresses there will not remain any for the campaign."[62]

Under Louis XIV, the crown pursued far more demolition than construction of fortifications.[63] During his reign, strategic imperatives weighed more heavy than did political concerns, although the latter never disappeared. The greatest fortification decision of the seventeenth century was not to fortify Paris but rather to defend it on the frontiers. Paris had added four more bastions to its walls in 1633, but the work had dragged. In 1670, the monarch decided to raze the remaining fortifications of Paris.[64] Vauban later drew up a plan for refortifying Paris, but the cost in money and manpower would have been staggering. The garrison alone would have required 30,000 troops and 10,000 armed citizens.[65] Paris remained without defenses until the nineteenth century.

The need to eliminate fortresses obsessed Vauban. By this policy, he argued, the French would both cut their military expenses, by saving on upkeep, and add considerably to their field armies, by liberating garrison forces. In 1675, Vauban urged elimination of forts to save manpower: "It seems to me that the King has too many advanced places; if he had fewer, five or six that I

[57] Richelieu *advis* to Louis XIII, 13 January 1629, in Richelieu, *Lettres, instructions diplomatiques, et papiers d'état*, d'Avenel, ed., 8 vols. (Paris: 1853–77), 3:180.
[58] AN, f. fr. 22219, fol. 116, in Corvisier, *Les Français*, 125.
[59] Zeller, *L'organization défensive*, 38.
[60] AG, Bibl. Genie 11, "Places fortes" commentary by Vauban.
[61] Contamine, *Histoire militaire*, 1:458.
[62] Turenne letter of 3 September 1644 in Croxton, "Peacemaking in Early Modern Europe," 164.
[63] Zeller, *L'organization défensive*, 38.
[64] Geoffrey Parker, *The Military Revolution: Military Innovation and the Rise of the West, 1500–1800* (Cambridge: 1988), 43.
[65] Lazard, *Vauban*, 414–20; Blomfield, *Vauban*, 114–15.

know well, he would be stronger by 12,000 to 14,000 men and the enemy weaker by at least 6,000 to 7,000."[66] Three years later, he calculated that "ten fortresses less ought to be worth 30,000 men more to the King."[67] In 1694, he urged the demolition of twenty-three fortresses, and the consequent freeing of eighty-two battalions and thirty-four squadrons.[68] The amount of troops dedicated to garrisons was not trivial. Circa 1666, about 25,000 French troops garrisoned the frontier, but this number had increased to 116,370 at the height of the Dutch War.[69] Vauban claimed that in the Nine Years' War, French garrisons required 166,000 troops, a number that climbed to 173,000 infantry and cavalry early in the War of the Spanish Succession.[70] The only way to put some of these men back into the field was to eliminate their fortresses.

Fortifications could not simply be abandoned; they had to be razed. An unoccupied fortress simply invited the enemy to seize it, with the attendant disaster to French security. A royal order of 1649 to destroy the fortress of Islers explained that it must be destroyed because, while it was "useless to my service in its present state," the monarch feared enemies "coming to seize it."[71] Not to staff a fortress on the frontier was to offer a defensive position to the enemy, who could take the works with a small force that, once ensconced there, could do infinitely more damage than its modest numbers might imply. They could interdict communications and subject an area to contributions from the relative safety of the fortifications. Unmanned or weakly held forts located in the interior might be seized by rebels, giving them a bastion to resist royal authorities.

PRACTICE OF SIEGE WARFARE

The conduct of sieges had become a specialized form of warfare in the gunpowder age long before Vauban arrived *en scène*, yet there is no denying that he raised it to a new level. Well before 1600, European armies developed new methods to attack artillery fortresses; in this new orthodoxy, the shovel

---

[66] Vauban to Louvois, 4 October 1675, Rochas d'Aiglun, *Vauban*, 2:131–32. Condé and Luxembourg urged destruction of fortresses early in the Dutch War. See AG, A^{1}301, 7 January 1673, letter to Condé, in Zeller, *L'organization défensive*, 52–53, and AG, A^{1}336, 15 September 1673, Luxembourg to Louvois.

[67] Vauban, "Mémoire des places frontières de Flandres," November 1678, in Rochas d'Aiglun, *Vauban*, 1:190.

[68] Vauban, "Places dont le Roi pourrait se défaire en faveur d'un traité de paix sans faire tort à l'état ni affaiblir sa frontière," January 1694, in Rochas d'Aiglun, *Vauban*, 1:205.

[69] AG, A^{1}198, 5 March 1666, letter from Louvois to Pradel; SHAT, Bib., Tiroirs de Louis XIV, *état* of 1 January 1678.

[70] SHAT, Bib., Gen. 11 (fol.), Vauban, "Les places fortifiées du Royaume avec les garnisons necessaires à leur garde ordinaire en temps de guerre." This document is without date, but marginal notes, apparently by an archivist, analyze the date of the document by the fortresses mentioned; SHAT, Bib., Génie 11 (fol.), Vauban memoirs, "Etat général des places forts du royaume," dated November 1705.

[71] AG, A^{1}115, 19 October 1649.

triumphed over the sword. Fortifications were taken not so much by impetu-
ous storm as by methodical digging. The siege began as troops of the attacking force invested the fortress, surrounding it and cutting off aid and supply.
Investments were often carried out at night to heighten surprise and limit
losses. From the 1570s on, besieging forces surrounded their prey with two
complete rings of entrenchments: one facing inward toward the besieged
works, the lines of contravallation; and the other facing outward to protect
the attackers from attack by a relief army, the lines of circumvallation. Experiments with lines of circumvallation and contravallation date from 1522
and 1524. At Mons in 1572, Alva made the first systematic and complete use
of such siege lines, and from that point on, they became essential. A complete circumvallation of a fortress commonly ran fifteen or twenty miles.

From the contravallation, approach trenches zigzagged a course toward
the glacis. The angular paths of the saps denied the enemy a clean shot up
the trenches. To guarantee their protection, the approach trenches took on
a sharper and sharper angle vis à vis their targets as they inched forward. (See
Figure 16.5.) In order to resist sorties from inside the works, besiegers constructed small redoubts along the approaches. The Dutch built fairly elaborate redoubts; a contemporary described their lines before Grave in 1602 as:

more befitting a great Sultan of Turkey than a small state which owes its survival to
the disorder that exists among its enemies, to some small economies, and to a little
help from its friends. The works which Prince Maurice has made before this place are
truly gigantic. Every redoubt, no matter how small, has its own wet ditch and draw-
bridge, and the continuous line is so huge and vast that it takes nearly five hours to
make the circuit.”[72]

During the first half of the seventeenth century, the Dutch and Spanish
honed their skills in the attack of fortified places, while the French style of
assault amounted to little more than an ill-prepared storming of the work
targeted for attack. The French seemed incapable of employing contemporary European siege techniques. Tallement des Reaux commented in 1621,
“[O]ne was so ignorant, that at the siege of Saint-Jean-d'Anglely no one
knew how to make trenches.”[73] The bloody frontal assault, known as an
attack “à la française,” survived into the reign of young Louis XIV. Enghien's
siege of Courtrai in 1646 witnessed such a costly attack.[74]

Vauban's Contributions to Siegecraft

With Vauban, the practice of besieging a fortress became more sophisticated,
rational, and predictable. He devoted to the attack of fortresses the same

---

[72] Contemporary report in Duffy, *Siege Warfare*, 93.
[73] Tallement des Reaux in Jules Caillet, *De l'adminstration en France sous le ministère du Cardinal
de Richelieu* (Paris: 1857), 361.
[74] Nicolas Edouard Delabarre-Duparcq, *Histoire de l'art de la guerre depuis l'usage de la poudre*,
2 vols. (Paris: 1864), 2:165–66.

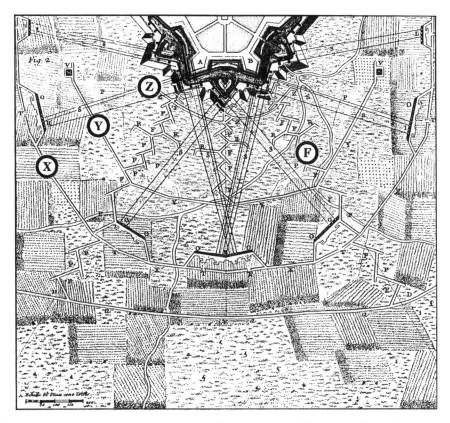

X = 1st parallel; Y = 2nd parallel; Z = 3rd parallel; F = approach trenches

Figure 16.5. Parallels as used by Vauban. (From Diderot, *Encyclopédie.*)

mastery and care that he put into his designs for bastions and curtains; however, there is one intriguing contrast. Although Vauban shunned "system" in fortifications, he insisted upon it in the laying of sieges. He did so because a steady methodical approach proved effective, and because he passionately believed that it saved lives. Vauban changed the traditional technique of assault in ways that strengthened, rather than challenged, the methodical nature of siegecraft. This generalization holds for all three of his most important innovations: parallels, *tir à ricochet*, and *cavaliers de tranchée*.

At the important siege of Maestricht in 1673, he first introduced his system of parallels, trenches dug parallel to the area of the enemy fortress to be assaulted.[75] Parallels did not extend all around a fortress as did the circumvallation. Vauban calculated the extreme range at which a cannonball might do some harm as 1,000 to 1,200 *toises*, so the lines of circumvallation had to

[75] Rousset, *Louvois*, 1:460.

lie 1,500 to 1,800 *toises*, or 3,210 to 3,852 yards from the fortress.[76] However, the range at which cannon on fortress walls might do harm to troops was much greater than the maximum range at which guns could reliably damage those same walls. Vauban believed this range to be approximately 500 *toises* and set his first parallel and its batteries well within it, at about 300 *toises*.[77] From there, sappers drove forward toward the enemy and dug a second parallel, again complete with artillery batteries, which he advised should be 120 to 145 *toises* from their target.[78] At the classic siege of Ath in 1697, Vauban placed the second parallel at about 250 yards. The third parallel, with breaching batteries, was sited at the base of the glacis, only 15 to 20 *toises* from the wall.[79] Parallels with refused flanks, and often buttressed with redoubts on each end, served as admirable defensive positions for the attackers. By stretching the attack laterally, instead of driving at a single point as before, the parallels caused confusion and forced the defender to spread his efforts. They additionally provided more room to assemble parties, and better protection, than did the older practice of driving toward the enemy simply with zigzag saps on a line perpendicular to the enemy defenses. Parallels could also economize labor because they could replace lines of contravallation, as was the case at the siege of Ath.

Vauban invented *tir à ricochet* to drive defenders from the covered way and the rampart, including their artillery positions. Cannon usually battered walls, but their flat trajectory sent balls sailing over the heads of troops sheltered behind parapets. Vauban reduced the charges in cannon so that they would lob their balls over the parapet to bound along covered ways and ramparts. This required that he site guns to fire along, parallel to, these normally sheltered positions, instead of battering them with perpendicular fire. Gunners actually disliked this technique because their cannon boomed less ferociously and inflicted less obvious damage. He experimented with *tir à ricochet* as early as 1674 and at Philippsburg in 1688. The first full-scale use of this technique came during the siege of Ath in 1697.[80] Montalembert, nearly a century later, praised the siege of Ath as "the highest state of perfection to which the art of attacking fortresses has ever been brought."[81]

The third of his notable innovations, the *cavalier de tranchée*, was a raised

---

[76] Vauban, *De l'attaque et de la défense des places*, 33; Vauban in Rochas d'Aiglun, *Vauban*, 181. Denis Diderot et al., *Encyclopédie*, 17 vols. text, 12 vols. plates (Paris: 1751–65), 3:464, cites the figure of 1,200 *toises* as maximum range at ten to twelve degrees elevation. The recent translation by George Rothrock, Vauban, *A Manual of Siegecraft*, is very misleading on this point. He states that the attackers' camp must be established no closer than 300 *toises* and no further than 500 *toises*; this must be a mistake in translation.

[77] Vauban, *De l'attaque et de la défense des places*, 51, 53; Sébastien le Prestre de Vauban, *Oeuvres de M. de Vauban*, 3 vols. (Amsterdam and Liepzig: 1771), 1:plate V.

[78] Vauban, *De l'attaque et de la défense des places*, 53.

[79] Vauban, *De l'attaque et de la défense des places*, 53.

[80] Duffy, *The Fortress in the Age of Vauban*, 30.

[81] Montalembert, *La fortifications perpendicular*, vol. 1 (Paris: 1776), 8, in Duffy, *The Fortress in the Age of Vauban*, 31.

firing platform for infantry erected only thirty or so yards from the covered way. (See Figure 16.6.) Such cavaliers allowed besieging troops to enfilade the covered way, much as did *tir à ricochet*. Vauban viewed the *cavaliers de tranchée* as an effective means "which has saved us many casualties," since he argued that the besieger generally lost three quarters of his casualties just in getting to and taking the covered way, and any improvement in this process was most likely to spare the attacker.[82] *Cavaliers de tranchée* made their appearance at the siege of Luxembourg in 1684.

It can be argued that parallels, *tir à ricochet*, and *cavaliers de tranchée* were developments not entirely original. There is good evidence that Vauban introduced parallels in imitation of the Turks, who used them first in their siege of Candia in 1667–69, since an engineer serving with him had been at that siege.[83] A form of *cavalier de tranchée* appeared in sixteenth-century siegecraft, and students of engineering argue that Vauban adapted his from Turkish raised firing platforms. Nonetheless, Vauban altered, extended, and systematized what he found. It is the last term, *systematized*, that most clearly indicates Vauban's contribution. More than any single element, it is the style and method of siege warfare that bore his stamp. He found the art of the attack in a jumble of general approach and specific technique and put it in order.

He wrote two works on the attack of fortifications. Vauban penned the first, and shorter, treatise sometime between 1667 and 1672, but it was not published until 1740; the second treatise, a much longer work, was written for the duke of Burgundy, probably after 1697, and was published in 1737.[84] He meticulously set procedures and timetables for siegework. If Vauban's methods were applied intelligently, a fortress was almost always doomed from the moment the first spade broke the ground. He was so bold as to promise in his first treatise: "I guarantee an infallible success without a day's extra delay if you will defer to my opinion and follow faithfully the rules I lay down."[85] At the siege of Ath, where he used his *tir à ricochet* to great effect, he took the fort in only two weeks with a loss of but fifty-three dead and 106 wounded against a garrison of 3,850. Speaking of Maestricht in 1673, the count d'Aligny wrote: "The first days of open trench did not cost much; M. de Vauban, in this siege as in so many others, saved many men by his knowledge."[86] This is a man who believed that "the saving of one hundred of his subjects, ought to be a more important consideration to the King than the loss of a thousand of his enemies."[87]

---

[82] Vauban in Rochas d'Aiglun, *Vauban*, 2:229–30, in Duffy, *The Fortress in the Age of Vauban*, 27.

[83] Vauban told Pellison "that he had imitated the Turks in their works before Candia." Paul Pellisson-Fontainier, *Lettres historiques de Monsieur Pellisson*, 3 vols. (Paris: 1729), 3:270.

[84] Vauban, *A Manual of Siegecraft*, x. Rothrock's translation is of the earlier and shorter of these works.

[85] Vauban, *A Manual of Siegecraft*, 65.

[86] *Mémoires inedits du comte d'Aligny*, in Rousset, *Louvois*, 1:461.

[87] Vauban in Blomfield, *Vauban*, 96.

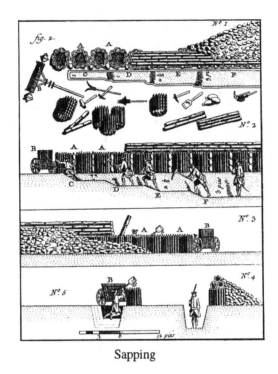

Sapping

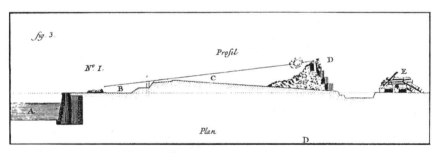

Cavalier de tranchée

Figure 16.6. Elements of siege warfare. (From Diderot, *Encyclopédie.*)

In contrast with his contributions to the attack in siege warfare, he contributed little to the defense – except, of course, for his designs of fortifications themselves. Although he wrote a treatise on the defense of forts, it was a hurried and relatively unimportant work compared to his work on the attack. He never actually conducted a defense personally; he was always on the other side of the entrenchments. His draftsman, Thomassin, commented, "Like many other people I often heard him say that his one remaining wish was to find himself under siege, for he had worked out an infallible method of defending a fortress. His friends often questioned him on this matter, but he died without giving a word of his secret away."[88] The amount of stores necessary for a major siege was staggering.[89] Vauban calculated that 20,000 men would be required to besiege even a fortress of modest dimensions, while larger forces undertook major sieges.[90] Attacking armies consumed mountains of food, ammunition, and siege stores. Saint-Rémy calculated that an army involved in a major siege would require 3,300,000 rations for the troops involved and 730,000 forage rations for the horses in a forty-day period. Such a theoretical force would also require 40,000 twenty-four–pound shot and an equal number of grenades, in addition to 944,000 pounds of gunpowder.[91] For the siege of Mons in 1691, the French stockpiled 900,000 rations of hay and 220,000 red-skinned cheeses.[92] This says nothing of the mountains of fascines and gabions and myriad shovels and spades necessary for the work. Fascines could be requisitioned and were. For the siege of Aire in 1676, French officials demanded fascines to be produced by commandeered local labor and carted to the siege camp.[93] Defenders too had to amass supplies to hold out. A garrison of 3,600 men in a six-bastion fortress with sixty cannon would require about 340,000 pounds of gunpowder and over 820,000 pounds of grain to withstand a forty-eight–day siege.[94]

Sieges conducted by Vauban's principles required so many troops and were so costly in material and money that the French rarely conducted more than one at a time. Consider the War of the Spanish Succession, a conflict with numerous sieges. For the French, this conflict involved four European land theaters: the Low Countries and certain areas of the lower Rhine that were strategically tied to the Low Countries; the Alsace-Lorraine frontier and that part of Germany and Luxembourg that faced it; the land south of Switzerland extending to the Mediterranean, that is, Provence, the frontier with Italy, and northern Italy; and Spain. Only twice did French forces in a single theater of the war undertake two sieges at the same time. In 1704, a small French army of 12,000 under La Feuillade besieged Susa, from 31 May to 8 June.[95] The main French force of 26,000 under Vendôme began its

---

[88] Thomassin in Lazard, *Vauban*, 340.

[89] AG, A¹209, #49, 21 June 1667, Carlier lists the amount of supplies necessary for the expedition to Limbourg.

[90] Vauban, *De l'attaque et de la défense des places*, 33.

[91] St. Rémy's figures are based on a force of 60,000 men, which is much larger than the 32,000 that he felt would be adequate for a normal siege. David Chandler, *The Art of Warfare in the Age of Marlborough* (New York: 1976), 241.

[92] Duffy, *The Fortress in the Age of Vauban*, 29. In preparation for a potential siege of Strasbourg in 1678, the French amassed 400,000 pounds of powder, 30,000 grenades, and 60,000 cannonballs. Corvisier, *Louvois*, 206. To besiege Barcelona in 1714, the Spanish king requested that nearly 20,000 cannonballs and 30,000 mortar shells be shipped to him from France. AN, F⁷1094, 14 August 1713, request from the King of Spain.

[93] Nord, C 2333, printed fill-in order of 22 July 1676.

[94] Chandler, *The Art of Warfare*, 241.   [95] Bodart, *Militär-historishes Kriegs-Lexikon*, 136.

attack on Vercelli, which proved a much tougher nut to crack, on June 5.[96] In 1712, Villars's victory at Denain set the tide of success firmly in a French direction. Villars detached 28,000 men under Saint-Frémont to besiege Le Quesnoy, from 8 September to 4 October, but before that siege had run its full course, Villars began the siege of Bouchain on 1 October with 20,000.[97] In both of these cases, the second siege began only during the final three days of the previous siege. It also seemed beyond the resources of Louis XIV to conduct simultaneous sieges on multiple fronts. Only once, involving a total of three sieges, did the French pursue different sieges in different theaters of war at the same time. In 1704–5, the siege of Gibraltar (21 October 1704 to 30 April 1705) overlapped the sieges of Verrua (14 October 1704 to 9 April 1705) and Mirandola (19 April to 10 May 1705). Vauban's techniques undoubtedly saved lives, but they were prodigal with other resources. That seems to have been the extent of overlapping sieges for the French, though three instances of similar overlap can be cited for the Allies.

More common were sequential sieges by the same army. Each of the two brief overlaps within single theaters made up part of a series of French successes. In the first case, Vendôme, after taking Vercelli (5 June to 24 July 1704), went on to take Ivrée (30 August to 30 September 1704), and Verrua (14 October 1704 to 9 April 1705). In the second case, French forces under Villars enjoyed the momentum of victory in the Low Countries during 1712, taking Marchiennes (25–30 July), Douai (14 August to 8 September), Le Quesnoy (9 August to 4 October), and, finally, Bouchain (1 to 19 October).

The regularity of sieges lent them an air of inevitability that gave some the notion that the fall of a fortress was so unavoidable that resistance seemed a waste. This could give rise to certain rules concerning surrender. It was, for example, considered honorable to capitulate after an attacker had advanced to the glacis, breached the wall, and made a first assault. But sometimes the niceties of surrender could sink to the level of farce. In 1679, the governor of Homburg offered to surrender his city on 17 September if the French fired ten to twelve rounds at his fortress and he answered with three shots in the air.[98] Still, such a story can be misleading. Earlier in the *grand siècle*, Richelieu tried des Chapelles and Harcourt as governors who surrendered their fortresses.[99] In 1635, Jacques de Coucy was decapitated for surrendering Dunkirk to the English, and Damsy also lost his head for cowardice in a poor defense of Lens in 1642.[100] And even in 1673, Louis ordered that the governor of Naarden, Dupas, be executed for surrendering his charge to the Dutch without adequate resistance. This harsh punishment was "in order to make an example which will serve as a lesson to the other governors, and can warn

[96] Bodart, *Militär-historishes Kriegs-Lexikon*, 137.
[97] Bodart, *Militär-historishes Kriegs-Lexikon*, 169.
[98] AG, A¹632, #221–22, 19 September 1679, Louvois to Louis XIV.
[99] David Parrott, "The Administration of the French Army During the Ministry of Cardinal Richelieu," Ph.D. dissertation, Oxford University, 1985, 329.
[100] Albert Babeau, *La vie militaire sous l'ancien regime*, 2 vols. (Paris: 1890), 2:253.

foreigners that if Frenchmen commit such cowardly actions they will not be tolerated."[101] And in 1705, it was forbidden to surrender a fortress without a considerable breach in the walls.[102]

The formal and technical aspects of siege warfare might make it seem the exclusive occupation of professional soldiers, but sieges also involved huge numbers of civilians, whose greatest concern could only have been survival. Attackers compelled the local peasantry to dig the initial line of circumvallation. Within the besieged fortress, the goods and labor of the townspeople were drafted into the defense at the pleasure of the military commander. As Louvois instructed his garrison commanders in 1675, "From the moment that a town is besieged, it is necessary to make use of all there is in the townsmen's homes for the subsistence of the garrison."[103] Citizen militias backed garrisons; work details employed even women and children. And should a town fall to storm, the nearly inevitable pillage and rape devastated the civilian population.

Time, Frustration, and the Opposition to Vauban

Vauban towered above all others as a practitioner of positional warfare, but he was challenged late in his career not by anyone attempting to unseat him as the master of the formal siege, but by those who wished to find some substitute for the time-consuming formal siege itself.

Vauban's methods virtually guaranteed success with the proper investment of money, matériel, and time. Money and matériel devoted to a siege could be replaced, but time was forever lost. Formal siege techniques moved methodically toward the inevitable. Vauban calculated that by following his techniques, a well-defended fortress could be taken in about forty-five days.[104] In reality, major sieges usually consumed four to eight weeks. Lille (1667) fell in fifty-one days, Maestricht (1673) in twenty-five, Luxembourg (1684) in thirty-seven, and Namur (1692) in thirty-six. The average duration of a major siege increased from thirty-two days in 1672–84 to forty-three days 1702–4.[105] The time required to subdue a fortress does not encompass the entire length of a siege, however. Siege preparations preceded the attack, and after victory was won, the victor had to return the fortress to a "state of defense." This meant that the siege trenches must be filled in, lest the enemy turn the tables and the besiegers become besieged. Walls and outworks had to be repaired at least to the point that they would once again pose an obstacle to an

---

[101] Louvois in Rousset, *Louvois*, 1:482. William III could also be harsh in such a case, ordering several officers who abandoned Niwerburg to be hanged in 1673. Rousset, *Louvois*, 1:412.

[102] Babeau, *La vie militaire*, 2:253.

[103] AG, A^{1}452, 4 January 1675 letter from Louvois in Rousset, 2:254.

[104] Vauban, *A Manual of Siegecraft*, 140–41, gives the figure as forty-three days for a good fortress and then adds extra days if the fortress boasts additional defenses. Chandler sets Vauban's prediction at forty-eight days. Chandler, *The Art of Warfare*, 246.

[105] All figures are taken from Lynn, "The *trace italienne* and the Growth of Armies," 324–30.

attacker. This process could on occasion take nearly as long as the actual siege, and it was always a considerable chore if the enemy had put up a reasonable resistance.[106]

Because sieges took so long, the capture of one or two major fortresses could consume an entire campaign season. And in a theater where fortresses lay thick on the ground, the capture of a fortress could usually only dent an enemy's zone of control and prepare the way for next year's sieges. This obviously frustrated armies and prolonged conflicts, condemning the French to wars of attrition. Also, as long as an army defeated in battle could easily reach a sheltering fortress line, it could not be utterly destroyed in the field by the loss of a battle. This logic argues strongly that the character of positional warfare tended to render both sieges and battles relatively indecisive.

To be fair, it should be noted that although great sieges were laborious and lengthy, many fortresses and towns fell quickly, either because they were not prepared for a long siege or because holding out seemed less attractive when the besieged entertained little hope of relief.[107] Instances of fortresses and towns falling in rapid succession occurred throughout the *grand siècle*: After Philippsburg fell to the French in 1644, Worms and Mainz capitulated without a fight.[108] In 1667, out of twelve towns that the French took, five towns fell with no opposition, six were invested and taken in five days or less, and only one, Lille, required a serious siege.[109] The Allies took four towns in 1702 when Ruremonde held out for only four days, Stevenswert for eight, and Liège for nine.

Despite such exceptions, however, the costly, time-consuming, and generally indecisive character of siege warfare frustrated those who wished to reach a more rapid decision in warfare. Menno van Coehoorn, the Dutch engineer, seemed to offer an alternative. Coehoorn employed classic siege technique up to a point, but he gained a reputation for bringing sieges to an early and successful conclusion by storming the enemy works. His style was effective, but for it to work, the attacking commander had to possess Coehoorn's outstanding genius and *coup d'oeuil*. Coehoorn recognized the crucial moment and identified the vulnerable spot for the violent assaults that

---

[106] Jamel Ostwald analyzes allied sieges in Flanders during the War of the Spanish Succession by stages: investment to opening the trenches, opening the trenches to capitulation, and capitulation to the point when the besieging army could leave the area. At the siege of Menin (1706), the second stage lasted for eighteen days and the third for seventeen; comparable figures for Ath the same year were twelve and eleven days. Ostwald's emphasis on this period of reconstruction is, to my knowledge, original, and it is a very important point. Jamel Ostwald, "The Failure of 'Strategy of Annihilation': Battle and Fortresses in the War of the Spanish Succession," M.A. thesis, Ohio State University, 1995, 99–101, Table 5.

[107] Commenting on the Thirty Years' War, Derek Croxton observes that "Sieges were difficult against a determined enemy, but the enemy was most determined when there was hope of an army coming to relieve him." Croxton, "Peacemaking in Early Modern Europe," 161.

[108] Croxton discusses the rapid fall of under-garrisoned fortresses during 1644 and 1645. Croxton, "Peacemaking in Early Modern Europe," 73, 108, 109.

[109] Rousset, *Louvois*, 1:111.

climaxed his siege operations, but few could equal his talent. On the other hand, Vauban's methodical system guaranteed success to any reasonably competent commander. Thus, the techniques of Vauban were capable of wide application, while Coehoorn's methods were too personal to achieve success without incurring considerable casualties. Nonetheless, they were attractive, especially to field commanders who were impatient or thought too much of their own *gloire*.

Vauban recognized that his time-consuming methods frustrated the natural impetuosity of French commanders. He once lamented that a distaste for digging in and seeking cover was "an original sin of which the French will never be cured."[110] In response, he insisted that casualties were "always a result of excessive haste; we do not take half the precautions demanded by such an enterprise, and consequently instead of gaining a day we lose two – at the cost of our best troops who perish miserably on such occasions."[111] Commenting on Coehoorn's storming of Namur in 1695, Vauban dismissed it "as one of the most utterly foolish acts that has ever been committed in the attack of a fortress."[112] When French officers wanted to emulate Coehoorn's aggressive techniques at the siege of Charleroi, an exasperated Vauban chided them with the words, "Let us burn gunpowder and spill less blood."[113] And Vauban's technique could be very stingy with that precious liquid.

Vauban conducted his last great siege in 1703, after which the old engineer was put out to pasture. When Vauban volunteered for the siege of Turin in 1706, he was politely refused. He became so vocal in his disapproval of the techniques used there that the minister of war wrote to La Feuillade commanding there: "Vauban announces to his friends and the world at large that he is willing to have his throat cut, if you ever succeed in taking Turin by keeping up the attack on the point you have chosen."[114] Needless to say, Vauban's throat remained intact. More damning than the incapacity of La Feuillade was the callousness of Villars when he had learned to disregard Vauban's methods. In 1703, Villars pushed forward a siege of Kehl against the advice of Vauban, who argued for a thirty-nine–day formal siege. Villars took the town in only twelve days.[115] In 1713, when engineers objected that Villars must delay the assault on Freiburg because not enough brush had been cut to fill in the ditch, he replied that the bodies of the men in the first line would accomplish this task.[116] Something profound had changed from Vauban's principles.

Vauban also did not approve mortar bombardment of the interior of towns, and he argued against it as early as 1683.[117] This practice was a terrible

---

[110] Vauban in Blomfield, *Vauban*, 73.   [111] Ibid.
[112] Vauban in Blomfield, *Vauban*, 137.   [113] Vauban in Lazard, *Vauban*, 257.
[114] Chamillart to La Feuillade, 6 July 1706, in Duffy, *The Fortress in the Age of Vauban*, 54.
[115] Duffy, *The Fortress in the Age of Vauban*, 45.
[116] Claude C. Sturgill, *Marshall Villars and the War of the Spanish Succession* (Lexington, KY: 1965), 134.
[117] AG, A^{1}704, 2 December 1683, Vauban to Louvois.

"waste of time, and consumes ammunition to little use, for such things contribute nothing to success of the siege, and the repairs always cost a great deal after taking the fortress."[118] In 1691, Luxembourg and Vauban opposed Louvois's plan to bombard Brussels.[119] But on the question of bombardment, Vauban lost ground even during the lifetime of Louvois, who liked to employ this tactic. The use of bombardment had come to stay. Villars sited the guns to fire directly into the town for intimidation at Freiburg.[120] Again, Vauban's humane directive was cast aside.

Several factors may account for the unfortunate decline in Vauban's influence. Ministers of war after Vauban may have seen his influence as corrosive to their own. Vauban was, after all, one of Louvois's creatures, and after Louvois's death, Vauban was more rival than aid to the administrators at the top. But perhaps Vauban's concerns were born of another age. He wished to save lives when the numbers of troops were smaller. When armies swelled to such great size during the first years of the Nine Years' War, field commanders might be more willing to trade lives for time.

Relief Armies and Armies of Observation

A final aspect of siege warfare deserving of discussion was the use of relief armies and armies of observation. Relief armies tried to raise sieges by defeating or drawing off attacking forces, and armies of observation covered the troops engaged in siege works to fend off relief forces. During the sixteenth and early seventeenth centuries, relief and observation forces were not the constant companions of sieges. But later in the seventeenth century, particularly at its end, huge numbers of troops were devoted to these purposes. At Mons in 1691, while 46,000 French troops occupied the siege lines, an equal amount covered the siege, while 38,000 tried to relieve the garrison.[121] A later siege of Mons in 1709 turned the tables, and while 20,000 allied troops surrounded the town, a covering force of 90,000 fought at Malplaquet against Villars with a relief force of 80,000.[122]

The great size of relief and observation forces might prove that siege warfare against the *trace italienne* drove up army size, just as Parker claims that it did. After all, these armies were accessories to sieges – part of the practice of positional warfare. Since these forces spectacularly increased, and since their activities related to the taking or defending of fortresses, can their growth be ascribed to the technology of the *trace italienne* fortresses that so concerned them? Or, at the very least, can their growth be attributed to the

---

[118] Vauban, *Oeuvres*, 1:186.   [119] Rousset, *Louvois*, 4:476–77.   [120] Sturgill, *Villars*, 134.
[121] Bodart, *Militär-historishes Kriegs-Lexikon*, 137; Lazard, *Vauban*, 225–26; and Corvisier, *Louvois*, 468.
[122] David Chandler, *Marlborough as a Military Commander* (London: 1973), 338–39; Bodart, *Militär-historishes Kriegs-Lexikon*, 161; and R. Ernest Dupuy and Trevor N. Dupuy, *The Encyclopedia of Military History* (New York: 1970), 623.

techniques of siege warfare? The answer to both these questions is "no." Relief and observation forces were not involved in the actual defense or attack of fortresses; by definition, they stood miles, often tens of miles, from the actual siege. Since they occupied neither the besieged fortress nor the trenches that threatened it, such armies could have been dictated neither by the narrowly technical characteristics of the *trace italienne* nor by the Vaubanesque style of attack.

Larger relief and observation forces were more a result of army expansion than its cause. To argue otherwise puts the cart before the horse. Consider the logic behind armies of observation. At a time when armies on campaign hovered around 20,000, roughly the number also required for a successful siege, an army attacking a fortress could depend upon its own numbers to deal with a relief force. Turenne, when engaged in the siege of Dunkirk in 1658 with 21,000 men, turned to face a Spanish relief army of 14,000. Leaving troops to hold the siege lines, Turenne mustered 15,000 to 16,000 for battle and triumphed.[123] He needed no army of observation. But as entire armies grew and field forces mushroomed, mainly in the Nine Years' War and the War of the Spanish Succession, a siege force required an army of observation to protect it. When the Allies besieged Landrecies in 1712, 20,000 men sufficed to hold the lines and pursue the siege against the French garrison of 5,000. But because Villars could march to the relief of Landrecies with 90,000, prince Eugene braced to resist him with 60,000 troops.[124] Siege forces required armies of observation because great field forces had been mobilized.

Usually, an army in the field had little choice but to become involved in an ongoing siege. As objects of value, important enough to be worth the considerable expense and effort of formal sieges, fortresses were also worth the time of field forces. In addition, an army besieging a fortress posed a threat not only to the fortress but to the enemy's field forces as well, since it could turn away from the siege at any time, and certainly would once the siege was over. A relief army was not only laboring to save a fortress but also to confront the enemy's forces. Lastly, siege armies could be vulnerable since they were often smaller than field armies from the 1690s on; therefore, the siege army as a thing of value itself had to be protected by an army of observation. So sieges attracted conflicting field armies, drew them close, and made battle between them likely.

With relief armies maneuvering against armies of observation, many, if not most, major battles of Louis XIV's later wars were associated with the attack on fortified towns and fortresses. The battle of Schellenberg allowed Marlborough to take Donauwerth in 1704. The French risked the battle of

---

[123] Jean Bérenger, *Turenne* (Paris: 1987), 335; Dupuy, *Encyclopedia of Military History*, 561; and Bodart, *Militär-historishes Kriegs-Lexikon*, 84, who gives the size of the Spanish relief force as 12,000.

[124] Bodart, *Militär-historishes Kriegs-Lexikon*, 168.

Ramillies to prevent Marlborough from seizing Namur in 1706, and in the same year, the Battle of Turin lifted the long and fruitless siege of that city by the French. Marlborough and Eugene attacked the French at the Battle of Oudenarde to rescue that town from siege in 1708. And the greatest battle of the period, Malplaquet, resulted from Villars's attempt to forestall an allied siege of Mons in 1709.

In sum, there is no contradiction in denying that siege warfare created larger armies while maintaining that larger armies became harnessed to siege warfare in the late seventeenth century. The fact that great battles were generally associated with great sieges was not a product of the technology of defensive artillery or the *trace italienne* but, instead, stemmed from a strategic and logistical fixation on land. Territory was the object of, and the key to, the ruler's will. But perhaps even more fundamental was the fact that command over territory brought with it the ability to tap that area's resources. Since the ultimate challenge of seventeenth-century warfare was simply to sustain an army, and since local funds, food, and fodder were essential to this task, logistics absolutely demanded territorial control. The larger the field army, the more it needed the resources that only territorial possession and control ensured. Holding towns and fortresses was the sine qua non of exploiting enemy lands, and, for that matter, of defending your own resource base. It was not the necessities of positional warfare that called great armies into existence but rather the creation of greater armies that increased the importance of positional warfare. As states raised the stakes of war and put more chips on the table, they changed the rules of the game.

POSTS AND LINES

The strings of redoubts and entrenched lines constructed to shield French-controlled territory during the *grand siècle* comprise a category of defensive works not given enough emphasis by most historians. Such fortifications were essential to the prosecution of war given the fiscal and logistic dimensions of warfare at the time, because outposts and lines protected friendly or occupied territory from enemy raiders and therefore reserved the people and resources of these areas for the support of the French war effort. Although lines constructed late in the War of the Spanish Succession may have been designed to stop the enemy's main forces, such was the exception. Their primary duty was to shelter resource areas. Vauban thought well of lines late in his career. Recognizing that it was hard to hold them against a large army, since the attacker could choose his time and place, Vauban still believed that "In all other cases, one maintains lines easily with ordinary guards, with good order, against all sorts of [raiding] parties."[125]

---

[125] Vauban letter of 21 July 1693 in Lazard, *Vauban*, 28.

Strings of Redoubts, 1610–1714

The French made use of strings of outposts before the personal reign of Louis XIV. In 1643, Mazarin decided to construct thirty-eight redoubts at fords on the Meuse river in order to protect the population along the river from Spanish contributions and *courses*. The engineer Le Rasle reported the next year that twenty-five towers should be constructed, each twenty feet high and eighteen wide, with a door cut fourteen feet from the ground, so that the only way to enter the tower would be with a ladder.[126] Three years later, at least twelve of these redoubts were constructed at the urging of marshal Fabert. Designed by Chastillon, each was to contain a garrison of ten men. This line was later revived and extended to the banks of the Chiers river during the Dutch War.[127]

The practice of setting up outposts need not necessarily mean construction of new fortifications. During the 1640s, towns utilized their own defenses, such as fortified churches and cemeteries as redoubts.[128] Rivers almost invariably constituted vital elements in outpost lines; therefore, merely guarding or cutting bridges could be useful.[129] When enemy raiders struck Picardy in 1676, burning eighty-four villages and levying contributions, Vauban urged the following response: "give 1,200 or 1,500 cavalry to baron de Quincy.... Occupy the post of Haspres and all the bell towers which can give us a good view [*nous peuvent donner de la decouverte*] with some advantage; reestablish the redoubt of Arleux; break all the bridges and crossings on the Sinsée up to Bouchain."[130] Here the Sinsée provided the primary defense, with Haspres extending the defensive barrier some eight kilometers overland. The actual fighting was to fall to regular cavalry assigned to protect the area around Cambrai while the countryside stood on guard.

One report gives a detailed accounting of a double line of outposts, including seventy detachments in posts along the Semoy, from its junction with the Meuse to Arlon, and twenty-four posts along the Chiers and Crusnes rivers from Volmerange to Torgny.[131] Posts were garrisoned either by local peasants, who were paid for their duty, or by small detachments of troops. Those posts staffed by locals held from four to twenty-two men, with the average post manned by only seven along the Semoy and fourteen along the Chiers and Crusnes. Troop detachments ran higher, with as many as seventy-five soldiers.

The frontier enclosed by the Sambre and Meuse rivers was a perpetual worry, and the French sought security in posts. An order of July 1702

---

[126] AN, KK 1069, fol. 88, letter from Rasle, February 1644.
[127] Zeller, *L'organization défensive*, 43–44.   [128] Zeller, *L'organization défensive*, 44n.
[129] Notations concerning cut bridges are common; see one such case when bridges across the Oise and the Thon were broken at Etreaupont early in the Dutch War. AN, f. fr. 22219, fol. 48 v., report by *intendant* 1697, in Corvisier, *Les Français*, 185.
[130] Vauban letter to Louvois, 30 May 1676, in Rochas d'Aiglun, *Vauban*, 2:137.
[131] AG, MR 1047, piece 3, "Etat des postes et redoutes sur la rivière Semoy," 28 March 1697.

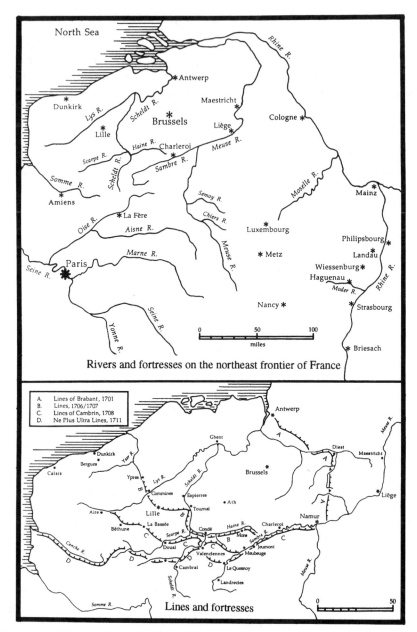

Figure 16.7. The northeast frontier of France in the *Grand siècle*. (Lines and fortress map based on the map in Christopher Duffy, *The Fortress in the Age of Vauban and Frederick the Great, 1660–1789*, 34.)

commanded that steps be taken "to prevent any enemy party from being able . . . to establish contributions there." Fortress commanders from Maubeuge to Mezières were to establish guards along the rivers and in the villages.[132] In November of that year, Louis XIV ordered "that the redoubts which had been constructed along the Sambre and Meuse during the last war be reestablished . . . to prevent enemy parties from passing." The cost of these garrisons was an obligation of the local communities, who were to pay special levies for the purpose.[133]

Although emphasis centered on continuous lines during the War of the Spanish Succession, allied victories by 1710 renewed the interest in outpost lines. Protecting the line of the Semoy again concerned government officials. Voysin ordered Harcourt to replace 300 paid peasants holding posts by 300 regular troops, to be raised on the spot and formed into six companies.[134] Officials lavished attention on the gap between the Somme and Oise; it must have been something of a highway for enemy courses. At first, the government promised little help, arguing that the peasants of the area "are almost all people used to war [*aguerris*]" and could be organized to repel raiders.[135] Later, the king judged it better "to establish posts between the Oise and the Somme than to make a line between the two rivers which would cost considerable sums." The chateau at Bohain, with 100 infantry and 100 cavalry, was to be the linchpin of this string of posts.[136] Ormession at Soissons, who was to carry out such orders, replied that some measures would also be taken on the Aisne, though it was more remote from the frontier.[137]

Lines, 1672–97

Continuous lines can be said to have descended from outposts. Yet French planners may also have been influenced by discussions of ancient lines in the works of classical military treatises, but that link would be hard to establish. In any case, strategists had more modern precedents, including similar lines built by the Dutch in 1605.[138]

French defensive lines appeared first in the Dutch War, became more prevalent during the Nine Years' War, and rose to paramount importance in

---

[132] Nord, C 8645, 31 July 1702.

[133] Nord, C 8645, 3 November 1702, affiche issued by Charles Maignart, the *intendant* in the area, with fill-in blanks ordering such and such a town to pay a particular sum "on pain of execution." C 8645 contains several reports on these redoubts, including money raised by communities.

[134] AG, A¹2266, #336, Voysin to Harcourt, 16 February 1710. See, as well, #348, 23 March 1710.

[135] AG, A¹2266, #189, Voysin to Ormesson, 23 June 1710.

[136] AG, A¹2266, #299, Voysin to Ormesson, 3 December 1710. See, as well, #263, 266, 272, 318–21, and 324 for further details on the line and the chateau of Bohain.

[137] AG, A¹2266, #184, Ormesson to Voysin, 20 June 1710.

[138] See "The Great Wall of the Dutch Republic" in Parker, *The Military Revolution*, 39.

the War of the Spanish Succession.[139] Such lines used rivers and canals as wet-ditch barriers whenever possible, buttressing these barriers with redoubts and where necessary running between water courses with entrenchments embodying a high state of military engineering. In a sense, the lines simply advanced one step beyond the strings of outposts along rivers that had been employed as early as the 1640s. Yet this evolution brought with it a basic change in the method of staffing defensive works. Lines seem always to have been garrisoned by regular troops. On the other hand, locally hired paid guards often held outposts.[140] Peasant levies imposed upon villages near the outposts might also supply guards; however, peasants resented such duty, particularly during harvest.[141]

Elaborate lines ran between water barriers. Extant contemporary plans of the lines show state-of-the-art works. One, dating from 1703, details a small section of a defensive line around Hesdin; the complex works employed a hornwork at one bridge, a redoubt at a second, and two further redoubts built into the entrenched line, which was covered by a wet ditch.[142]

Lines came quickly in the Dutch War, when the Dutch dug a twenty-six–mile-long line along the Issel in 1672.[143] The French followed suit a year later, laying out entrenchments from the sea to the Lys.[144] The first, or eastern, section ran from the sea to Commines, incorporating the fortresses of La Kenocque and Ypres, as well as several canals.[145] In 1678, Vauban, under direction by Louvois, proposed entrenchments between Ypres to Commines, after Ypres had fallen to the French in March of that year. He expressed great confidence: "It is almost impossible that the enemy parties could carry out their designs beyond these entrenchments."[146]

In 1683, with the brief war between Spain and France, Louvois ordered

---

[139] For a good short discussion of lines, see Zeller, *L'organization défensive*, 107–17.

[140] In 1703, for example, major Davignan received 1,250 livres to pay for guards in outposts along the Sambre. Nord, C 8645, 8 March 1703 contract for guards.

[141] See, for example, a printed fill-in order of 17 March 1705 ordering such and such a town to send to the redoubt at such and such a place on the Sambre a specific number of men. Nord, 8645. Regarding peasant resistance, see letter of 25 August 1691 about 600 resentful peasants sent for guard duty, AG, A^{1}1060, #99.

[142] Nord, C 2238, report on 27 June 1703 attack on lines around Hesdin.

[143] Stephen Baxter, *William III and the Defense of European Liberty, 1650–1702* (New York: 1966), 64.

[144] There seems to be some confusion as to when the French built their lines during the Dutch War; Lazard, *Vauban*, 282, credits the first construction in 1672, while Zeller argues "the first lines worth of the name" came only at the end of the war; in any case, they were not extensive and covered only a space between the Lys and the sea. Zeller, *L'organization défensive*, 109.

[145] Lazard, *Vauban*, 282–83, states that this line was at least begun in 1672. Lazard seems to have erred here, since Ypres, which he counts as part of the line, did not fall into French hands until 1678.

[146] AG, A^{1}616, #21, 5 April 1678, letter from Vauban to Louvois.

lines reestablished between the Lys and Ypres, now a French fortress, to fend off Spanish courses. The correspondence first mentions lines to cover the country between Bergues and the Lys; later Louvois stated that lines stretched from Ypres to Tournai, further than they had during the Dutch War.[147] During the first months of the Nine Years' War, Louis ordered that the lines protecting Flanders be reestablished.[148] These were the old lines of 1678 and 1683, running from the sea to Commines and then to Espierres on the Schelde, following the previous paths with only minor modifications.[149] With the French seizure of Mons, new lines linked it with Jeumont, on the Sambre, by following the stream La Trouille.[150] Louis's strategy was already profoundly defensive. In 1695, when Villeroi proposed an offensive, Louis replied that the safest plan was simply to hold the lines. "If in holding the lines, one loses a great many troops, one can hope that the enemy will lose considerably more . . . . One must defend my country foot by foot."[151] When Villeroi protested, Louis again denied his offensive plan but praised him for "having work done on the entrenchments to prevent the enemy from penetrating my land if they cross the Iser."[152]

The *intendant's* memoir for Flemish Flanders, drawn up by the engineer Caligny, 1697–98, credits lines between the Lys and the sea as so effective that "the inhabitants have not been bothered at all by enemy courses during the war."[153] It also describes these lines in some detail, how they connected fortresses and how they aided in fighting off enemy parties with small forces from the forts' garrisons.[154] Vauban believed that these lines guaranteed the lands they sheltered: "[When] these lines [are] guarded by only a very small corps, no party, large or small, would dare to pass them; it would take an army to do so." However, he objected to "the negligence or rather the feebleness with which one guards them when the army is on campaign."[155] Raiders did cross the lines, but Vauban refused to reject the concept of lines because of this fact. "The example of the poor success of the lines of Flanders is not very convincing for me, because I know without any doubt that it is not their fault if the enemy has carried out *courses* on our lands owing to the lack of order and the poor guard which has been kept in the lines."[156]

---

[147] See Louvois letters dated, 24 October 1683, 4 November 1683, 13 November 1683, and 11 May 1684 in Jacques Hardré, ed., *Letters of Louvois, University of North Carolina Studies in the Romance Languages and Literatures* (Chapel Hill: 1949), 286, 296, 302, and 352.

[148] Zeller, *L'organization défensive*, 111.

[149] Duffy, *The Fortress in the Age of Vauban*, 35, argues that the 1694 "Lines of Clare" from the sea to the Schelde were the first continuous trench lines, but this seems in error.

[150] Zeller, *L'organization défensive*, 112.

[151] AG, A¹1309, #81, 23 June 1695, letter from Louis to Villeroi, in Wolf, *Louis XIV*, 481.

[152] AG, A¹1309, #131, 27 June 1695 letter from Louis to Villeroi.

[153] BN, f. fr. 22220, fol. 53.

[154] Ibid.   [155] Vauban to Le Peletier, 27 May 1696, in Rochas d'Aiglun, *Vauban*, 2:443–44.

[156] Letter of 18 June 1698, in Lazard, *Vauban*, 283.

Use of Lines in the War of the Spanish Succession

For the French, the defensive ruled supreme during the War of the Spanish Succession, so it is little wonder that entrenched lines played such a great role in this conflict.[157] French and Spanish constructed the lines of Brabant beginning at Antwerp and stretching for 130 miles past Diest to the Meuse, just below Namur.[158] This was an unprecedented project. The intention of the first lines of the War of the Spanish Succession was to continue the tradition of halting enemy raids. Documents concerning the siting and construction of this line make it clear that it was meant to stop enemy raids, not enemy armies.[159] Boufflers praised the lines of Brabant to Louis in a letter of April 1701: "The whole of the people of the countryside, as well as the local officials, look upon these lines as their salvation."[160]

While lines provided the most complete coverage in the Southern Netherlands, the fashion for entrenchments spread much further. The Allies built lines of their own; Louis of Baden created the lines of Stollhoffen in 1701.[161] French forces under Villeroi dug the lines of the Moder in 1704, running from the Rhine to the Vosges and based on Hagenau, and the next year, the Allies erected a line on the Lauter.[162] Villeroi in 1706 built the lines of Wissembourg on the same site.

Meanwhile, as the Allies forced the French back in the Spanish Netherlands, they relied on three more lines. In 1706–7, lines ran up from Ypres to Lille to Condé and then along the Haine to the Sambre; however, the loss of Lille in 1708 compromised this position. The French next dug in from Aire to Douai to Valenciennes to Maubeuge in 1708; such were the lines of Cambrin. Yet the losses of Douai, Béthune, Saint-Venant, and Aire in 1710 eviscerated this position, too.

The French built their last great lines in 1711, christening them defiantly, the Ne Plus Ultra Lines. By this point, lines were meant to do more than stymie raiding parties; the fortifications were intended to resist entire armies. Chistopher Duffy, therefore, draws a parallel between the Ne Plus Ultra lines and the trenches of World War I.[163] Whatever the intention, these lines also failed to contain Marlborough, who crossed them at Arleux in a magnificent maneuver in 1711.

---

[157] Duffy, *The Fortress in the Age of Vauban*, 34, provides a useful map of the series of French lines in the Spanish Netherlands.

[158] Duffy, *The Fortress in the Age of Vauban*, 35.

[159] AG, MR 1047, pieces 9–11 discuss aspects of this first line of the War of the Spanish Succession.

[160] Boufflers to Louis XIV, 27 April 1701 in Pelet Vault, ed., *Mémoires militaires relatifs à la Succession d'Espagne sous Louis XIV*, 11 vols. (Paris: 1835–62), 1:66, in Duffy, *The Fortress in the Age of Vauban*, 36.

[161] Zeller, *L'organization défensive*, 113.   [162] Zeller, *L'organization défensive*, 113.

[163] Duffy, *The Fortress in the Age of Vauban*, 36.

Lines and Resource Mobilization

But the attempt to stop invasion must not obscure the primary use of lines during Louis's last three wars; they were designed to control the mobilization of resources for war. To see lines only as a detail of fortification misses the point; the need for lines evolved out of attempts to stop enemy courses and contributions.

Before the Nine Years' War, Louis tried to deter his foes from raiding French preserves primarily by ordering retaliations against enemy villages. Unfortunately, the enemy reciprocated. These dueling contributions and reprisals clearly got out of hand, so by the close of the Dutch War, Louis tried to make a treaty with the Spanish at Deinze to limit the amount of contributions demanded of local populations.[164] But negotiations broke down. Deterrence and negotiation having failed, prudence demanded the construction of lines as the main method of forestalling enemy raids, although reprisals remained part of French practice after 1678. The construction of such lines was determined by the value of the territory that they shielded, wealth that could be exploited to supply French armed forces.[165] Therefore, strategic and operational decisions to hold certain areas and to build defensive works derived from logistical considerations.

Vauban proposed many reasons for field entrenchments; among them was "in order to deny entry into our territories [pays] to the enemy and limit him from putting them under contribution."[166] A memoir discussing the lines of the Moder in 1704 listed as its first goal "to conserve Alsace from the payment of contribution and to limit the enemy from penetrating with an army."[167] When discussing abandoning lines along the Lauter in 1711, the author of a memoir noted: "If the plan to abandon the lines of the Moder is carried out, it is to be feared that Franche-Comté will have to pay contributions."[168] Selection of when and where to build defensive lines included analysis of how they would stop parties and the value in tax revenue and contributions of the area that they would shelter.[169] One typical piece, which proposed moving the 1701 line forward, stressed the amount that the area thus covered "paid for contributions, forage, cattle, and other impositions" from April 1689 to October 1697.[170]

---

[164] Documents on this peace conference can be found in Nord, C 2333. See Hubert van Houtte, "Les conferences franco-espangnoles de Deynze," *Revue d'histoire moderne*, Vol. 2 (1927), 191–215.

[165] See discussion of lines to cover Alsace in AG, MR 1066, nos. 13–16, and lines to cover north of Spanish Netherlands in AG, MR 1047, pieces 9 and 10.

[166] Vauban in Rochas d'Aiglun, *Vauban*, 1:165.   [167] AG, MR 1066, #14.

[168] AG, MR 1066, #16 "Mémoire sur la prop. de retablir les anciennes lignes de la R. de Lauter," Strasbourg, 30 April 1711.

[169] See AG, A^{1}616, #21, 5 April 1678, Vauban letter; Nord, C 2242, undated but ca. 1700, discussion of lines of Waeste.

[170] AG, MR 1047, #9, Projet d'une ligne, 6 April 1701.

ADMINISTRATION,
CONSTRUCTION, AND EXPENSE

The administration of fortifications evolved during the *grand siècle* in a way that mirrored other aspects of bureaucratic development; it did not follow a steady, obvious path, but eventually a more rational and effective system took shape under Louis XIV.[171] Henri IV and Sully put together a workable system from the bits and pieces that they inherited from the late Middle Ages and the sixteenth century. As *surintendant des fortifications*, Sully was predominant, and a key ordinance of 1604 exerted royal control and imposed some uniformity; however, in the confusion that followed Henri's death, provincial governors usurped the authority of the *surintendant*.[172] Under Richelieu and Mazarin, provincial and army *intendants* supplanted the governors and became the primary agents of royal administrative authority over fortifications, such as it was. These *intendants* answered directly to the four secretaries of state.

Each secretary of state had a set of provinces that he administered in addition to special responsibilities for the state concerns that vested themselves in a particular secretary, such as war, the navy, foreign affairs, the Huguenots, the royal household, and so on. Therefore, although the army came under the jurisdiction of the secretary of state for war, the 1626 ordinance also gave him control over Lyonnais, Dauphiné, Provence, Saintonge, La Marche, Angoumois, Limousin, and Poitou. This list of provinces varied a bit over time; by 1661, the secretary of state for war had lost Provence but picked up Roussillon.[173] Part of territorial responsibility involved control over the fortresses within that territory; hence, the secretary of state for war controlled only those fortresses within this list of provinces. After 1661, Colbert used his dominance over finances to erode this system extensively and thus gain de facto control over the fortifications under three of the secretaries of state, leaving only Le Tellier with his old authority intact. This was a power grab by Colbert, not a rational attempt to restructure fortress administration. At this point, it is correct to speak of only two jurisdictions over fortifications instead of four.

In 1661–62, the king created a new office, *commissaire général des fortifications*, and awarded it to Clerville. Clerville, who was supposed to work with Colbert and Le Tellier, was a client of Colbert and not welcomed by the Le Telliers, who gave him very little to do. In contrast to the Le Telliers, Colbert also employed venal *intendants des fortifications* and *directeurs*, while the Le

---

[171] The best work on fortress administration is the recent dissertation by Ben Trotter, "Marshal Vauban and the Administration of Fortifications under Louis XIV." The material on administration presented in the next several paragraphs has all been borrowed from Trotter's fine work.

[172] Contamine, *Histoire militaire*, 1:460.

[173] Roland Mousnier, *The Institutions of France under the Absolute Monarchy, 1598–1789*, 2 vols. (Chicago: 1979–84), 2:143–44; Trotter, "Marshal Vauban," 51.

Telliers worked directly through the more able provincial *intendants*. Colbert's control of fortifications began to slip in 1667, when responsibility for all of the fortresses in new conquered territories were given to the secretary of state for war. At this time, too, Vauban passed over into the service of Louvois, and the great engineer's abilities added to Louvois's leverage. Early in the Dutch War, it became apparent that Colbert's fortresses were not as well cared for or as well run as those managed by Louvois. Colbert simply had too much to do, but he tried to do it all, using Clerville simply as a trouble-shooter. Louvois, on the other hand, delegated his authority to Vauban, who could devote undivided attention to fortifications. Due to the insistence of the king, by the end of 1674, Vauban had become inspector and planner for Colbert's fortresses as well as Louvois's, even though he technically worked for Louvois. This role became more obvious when Vauban inherited Clerville's title of *commissaire général* at the latter's death in 1677. Although the administration of fortifications remained under two rival authorities, Vauban lent it a unity that it might otherwise not have had.

When Colbert died in 1683, his control of fortresses passed to his son, Seignelay, but when he died in 1690, the administration of fortifications merged into a single office under Louvois. It was a brief victory for Louvois, because he died the next year. Although many of his responsibilities went to his own son, Barbézieux, the king withheld control over fortifications and vested it in a revived post of *surintendant général des fortifications*, filled by the able Michel Le Peletier de Souzy, who operated as a separate authority, independent of the secretary of state for war. Le Peletier had direct access to the king, who met with him regularly each week.[174]

In addition to administrators, who handled financial and other bureaucratic matters, the French required a series of senior military engineers to supply technical expertise. Le Rasle, a captain in the Regiment de Champagne and governor of Rethel, rated as the most celebrated engineer under Mazarin.[175] Mazarin relied on the strictly technical ability of Rasle and also used him as an advisor.[176] Eventually, the chief military engineer held the office of *commissaire général des fortifications*, a post first occupied by Clerville and then passed to Vauban in 1678, although he had performed the duties of the office for some years before that date.

The design and the supervision of construction of the increasingly important fortresses, as well as the technical conduct of sieges, fell to the military engineers, but this duty carried little prestige. Grimarest expressed the reluctance of well-placed young men toward such a technical service, saying that

---

[174] Dangeau reported that Louis met with Le Peletier each Sunday afternoon. Philippe, marquis de Dangeau, *Journal du marquis de Dangeau*, ed. Feuillet de Conches, 19 vols. (Paris: 1854–60), 4:353.

[175] Louis André, *Michel Le Tellier et l'organisation de l'armée monarchique* (Paris: 1906), 532–33.

[176] AG, A¹81, #115, 18 January 1644, commission ordering Le Rasle to undertake an inspection trip to survey the condition of French fortifications.

it was not "much to the taste of the officer."[177] After all, the culture of command valued a commission because it provided the opportunity for dramatic displays of bravery in battle, but the work of the engineer seemed remote from such theatrics.

Step by step, engineers emerged as a separate corps within the army. Before the 1670s, engineers remained infantry officers, and in addition to their infantry commissions, they received brevets as engineers. They did not rise rapidly. The great Vauban, at forty-one and already a confidant to the king and the minister of war, was a mere captain in the Regiment de Picardie in 1674. Only then was he elevated to brigadier. Vauban proposed that the engineers be put on a more regular basis, and Louvois adopted his proposals; by the late 1670s, a corps of engineers emerged, even though it still constituted part of the infantry. These engineers were grouped into brigades after 1669.[178] The first formal *état* of engineers listed about 190 military engineers in 1683.[179] Some 350 engineers joined the service during 1661–91, and 250 to 275 served at any one time, with 60 percent in the department of war and 40 percent in the Colberts' department of the navy. Roughly a third of the engineers who worked for the Le Telliers were *roturier* in origin, while those who worked for the Colberts were two thirds *roturier*.[180] In 1693, Le Peletier reorganized the engineers into "directions," and by 1696, the nineteen directions counted a total of 274 engineers; a total of 393 new engineers joined the army from 1661 to 1715.[181]

The engineers performed a relatively thankless task with only modest rewards, but the demands upon them stayed high. Danger stalked the military engineer in the trenches before a besieged fortress. So many died that Vauban called his engineers the "martyrs of the infantry."[182] Yet if siege warfare presented the most danger, the construction of fortifications called for the greatest skill. As Vauban insisted, "there is not an officer with a little good sense who I cannot render capable of conducting a trench . . . in three sieges . . . ; but a good builder is made only in fifteen or twenty years of application."[183] For military engineering "is a profession beyond our capacities [*forces*]; it embraces too many things for a single man."[184]

Vauban insisted that "It is necessary that merit and capacity alone bring men positions [*emplois*]."[185] Yet despite the premium that he placed on ability and the fact that competence in engineering required education, the education of engineers was surprisingly haphazard. For most of the century, a young officer who displayed interest or talent was simply apprenticed to an

---

[177] Jean-Léonor Grimarest, *Fonctions des généraux ou l'art de conduire une armée* (La Haye: 1710), 41.
[178] Contamine, *Histoire militaire*, 1:471.   [179] Lazard, *Vauban*, 40–41.
[180] Contamine, *Histoire militaire*, 1:472–73.
[181] Lazard, *Vauban*, 47; Contamine, *Histoire militaire*, 1:474.
[182] AG, A^{1}832, #5, 2 November 1688, letter from Vauban to Louvois.
[183] Vauban in Rochas d'Aiglun, *Vauban*, 379.
[184] Vauban in Rochas d'Aiglun, *Vauban*, 380.   [185] Vauban in Blomfield, *Vauban*, 81.

established engineer. Vauban learned from Clerville and then received the commission of *ingénieur ordinaire du roi* after sitting an examination of sorts. Not until 1687 did Seignelay begin the first effort at state education of engineers when he instructed the abbé Gallois to teach five or six young men in the fundamentals of their chosen profession.[186] Engineers were not to receive a more formal education until the eighteenth century. After 1697, Le Peletier refused to admit new engineers who had not passed an examination by Vauban.[187]

Military engineering was a difficult and demanding profession, yet field commanders insisted on overseeing and second guessing their engineers. Villars argued that it was the lieutenant general's duty to observe and correct the work of his engineers rather than simply to delegate the authority to these technicians.[188]

Vauban wanted the engineers to be supported by specialist troops for the conduct of sieges. He secured the creation of two companies of miners, the first in 1673 and the second in 1679.[189] He wanted a regiment of sappers, or a company of sappers to be added to every regiment of infantry, but neither suggestion bore fruit.[190] In fact, volunteers from regular infantry companies continued to supply the trained personnel for the dangerous job of sapping trenches toward besieged works.

The construction of fortresses required a great deal of labor, which was performed by contractors, skilled craftsmen, day-laborers, and soldiers who were granted special pay for the back-breaking work.[191] Still, soldiers were cheaper than private labor, receiving only about 75 percent of what entrepreneurs charged.[192] The numbers of men engaged in fortress construction soared. In 1671, Vauban commanded 30,000 workers, including soldiers, at Dunkirk, where the soldiers worked in three four-hour shifts beginning at 4 A.M.[193] The use of soldier-labor in large public-works projects had now become commonplace. In 1685, 9,000 to 10,000 troops were at work building an aqueduct to Versailles, and at the palace, Swiss soldiers dug the *piece d'eau* that bears their name.[194] Things had come a long way from the days of the Thirty Years' War, when mercenaries shunned taking part in construction of field works.[195]

Fortifications could be built entirely of earth or with permanent facings of stone or masonry. Construction in earth alone lowered cost and accelerated

---

[186] Lazard, *Vauban*, 42.   [187] Lazard, *Vauban*, 47; Contamine, *Histoire militaire*, 1:474.
[188] BN, f. fr. 6257, Claude Louis Hector Villars, "Traité de la guerre de campagne."
[189] Rousset, *Louvois*, 3:334–35.   [190] Rouseet, *Louvois*, 1:247.
[191] See AG, A¹294, #82, 13 August 1672, *état* of workers and pay engaged in works on Ath; for example, they are listed by occupation. Soldiers working on the fortress of Ypres in 1681 received 9 to 10 sols per day, twice their normal salary. Henry Chotard, *Louis XIV, Louvois, Vauban et les Fortifications du nord de la France* (Paris: 1889), 179.
[192] In 1682, soldiers made only 18 sols, and entrepreneurs received 23. Chotard, *Louis XIV, Louvois, Vauban*, 45.
[193] Michel, *Vauban*, 141–52.   [194] Corvisier, *Louvois*, 391.
[195] Herbert Langer, *The Thirty Years' War* (Poole, Dorset: 1978), 89.

progress, but such fortifications decayed severely over time, whereas stone-
and masonry-faced walls did not. Still, in war, limited time, money, and
manpower could leave little choice but earthen construction. As one *intendant*
wrote in 1697: "The works that the king had built are only of earth and it
has not been possible during the war to make them of masonry."[196] The
amount of labor required to build a modern work was astounding, particularly by contemporary standards. In constructing the works surrounding
Longwy, workmen had to move 640,000 cubic meters of earth and set
120,000 cubic meters of masonry.[197] In 1669, Vauban insisted that 20,000
large facing stones be laid each day at Lille.[198]

Money expended on fortress construction boggled the minds of contemporaries. The French budget for fortifications registered Louis's rising interest in defensive masonry. During the first sixty years of the seventeenth
century, the French invested relatively little in fortresses. From 1643 to 1660,
the average yearly outlay inscribed on French accounts was 347,000 livres.[199]
This figure increased markedly in the 1660s; the average during 1663–67
reached 1,374,000 livres. The great spurt in building, and thus the great
surge in costs, came only after 1667 and lasted until the late 1680s. During
1669–72, the amount allocated to fortifications in the *états au vrai* averaged
3,600,000 livres, but it fell once war began to only 1,591,000 in 1673. Between 1679 and 1688, the budget for fortification peaked, averaging 6,775,000
livres, with a high of 11,993,000 in 1688. Never again would construction
outlays reach this level. These were substantial sums, but they do not represent the full expense, since towns contributed to the costs of their walls. In
the late 1690s, Lille paid 37,500 livres annually for the maintenance of its
walls and an additional 75,000 for new works; Douai paid 40,000 for fortifications and Tournai 25,000 to 30,000.[200] The cost of individual projects
was considerable. Vauban's 1678 plan for Dunkirk cost 3 million livres, and
his Neuf Brisach, built from the ground up after the Nine Years' War, cost
4,048,875 livres.[201]

Siege works could also consume a great deal of labor and material. Soldiers and local peasants found themselves called upon to dig siege lines,
including the extensive works of the Nine Years' War and the War of the
Spanish Succession.[202] Besieging armies commandeered civilian laborers in
the thousands to construct lines of circumvallation.[203] However, if lines were

---

[196] BN, f. fr. 22221, fol. 25, v. 36, in Corvisier, *Les Français*, 113.

[197] Duffy, *The Fortress in the Age of Vauban*, 6.   [198] Chotard, *Louis XIV, Louvois, Vauban*, 71.

[199] AN, KK 355. These budgetary figures are collected in Jean Roland de Mallet, *Comptes rendus de l'administration des finances du royaume de France* (London, 1789).

[200] BN, f. fr. 22220, fol. 34, 20, 76, 87, 100, 114 in Corvisier, *Les Français*, 258.

[201] Blomfield, *Vauban*, 82, 141.

[202] See Nord, C 1609, for examples of printed fill-in orders commandeering labor.

[203] For examples of documents concerning the requisition and massing of civilian laborers, see
the commissions to Talon and Terreul as *intendants*, AG, A¹208, #22 and #31, September
1667; and A¹434, 4 July 1675, Louvois to Sousy.

the work of civilians, approach trenches and parallels were constructed by soldiers only, for that was work under fire. Soldiers also received extra pay for working on the trenches during a siege. Those who built the dike at the siege of La Rochelle received a token for each measure of stone they hauled; this gave them a tidy sum of 20 sols per day to augment their regular salary.

Modern military observers are prone to condemn positional warfare as decadent and unimaginative. Yet during an age in which the defensive strength of walls matched the offensive power of cannon, positional warfare was the key to territory. And the quest to control territory commanded seventeenth-century struggles; land was a political goal for rulers and a logistic necessity for their armies. The essence of military institutions required that armies in the field mobilize what resources they could, and positional warfare was indispensable to this imperative.

In another sense, positional warfare matched French policy needs best. Louis XIV finally strove to protect his own lands more than to conquer new ones, and positional warfare was the ultimate tool of consolidation rather than conquest. A policy with moderate goals achieved moderate but enduring results. Those who decry the sterility of French warfare under Louis XIV and praise the dynamic techniques of Napoleon had best ponder one point. Napoleon, god of war as he was, added nothing to the permanent lands of France; his style of conquest produced dramatic short-term results, but they dissolved, for his methods of war were linked, probably necessarily so, to a program of aggrandizement unacceptable to Europe. In contrast, just in the course of Louis XIV's personal reign, France added and retained Franche-Comté, parts of Artois, Flanders, and Hainault, plus a long list of cities, including Strasbourg. If the net is cast wider, for all of Louis's reign, Alsace and Roussillon must be added to the gains. Louis retained these lands because his goals were reasonable enough when weighed by the standards of the time to be sanctified by European opinion and diplomacy. Positional warfare so corresponded with contemporary attitudes toward war and diplomacy that it was ultimately effective.

Epilogue: Insights on State Formation

THE last major French military action of the *grand siècle* concluded in
September 1714; typically, it was a siege at which French and Spanish
troops commanded by Berwick took Barcelona and ended the War of the
Spanish Succession. This last war of Louis XIV tried the aging monarch
sorely. French armies predominant from the 1640s now suffered repeated
defeats of humiliating proportions: Blenheim, Ramillies, Turin, Oudenarde.
In 1709, Louis had been close to capitulating; his armies wore tatters and
lived off crumbs; famine stalked his country, and his policies lay in ruins. But
Villars rescued French honor and confidence at the battle of Malplaquet,
even if he abandoned the field. Although Marlborough would gain new
successes over the next two years, they would not be as before, and in 1711
he disappeared, a victim of failed policy and court politics. During 1712–14,
the French were rewarded with victory when Villars bested Eugene's troops
at Denain and won back town after town in the Netherlands and along the
Rhine. In Spain, the last years of the war brought triumph as well; in the fall
of 1710, Vendôme won at Briheuga and Villaviciosa, restricting the Allies to
Barcelona. By the close of 1714, a Bourbon prince sat securely on the Spanish
throne, and Louis had achieved his goal, albeit at great cost to France. His
army once again served him well.

Giant of the Grand Siècle has explored the character of that army. This
epilogue does not summarize the findings presented in the preceding chapters; instead of retracing steps already traveled, these pages suggest where the
road ahead might lead. Arguments and particulars presented up to now have
concentrated on the army per se, but they can serve not only as a destination
for military specialists but also as a point of embarkation for those with
different interests. The quest that may yield the greatest rewards for this
second audience employs the details uncovered here to discover more about
the phenomena of absolutism and state formation in Europe, the fourth
context of this volume announced in Chapter 1. Within this context, *Giant
of the Grand Siècle* contributes to the scholarly discussion not so much by

solving existing riddles as by challenging current assumptions and indicating new lines of inquiry.

In examining the role of warfare upon the state in early modern Europe, it is essential to distinguish between (1) the way in which war and its demands encouraged centralization, fostered bureaucratization, and concentrated power and (2) the specific place of the army in this process. Obviously, a history of the army per se, such as this one, will have much more to say about the latter than the former.

Scholars acknowledge a link between war and the growth of the state; however, belief that the two are joined does not define the causal nature of the relationship. Social scientists seem more willing to argue that war created, or helped to create, a more powerful state, while historians are more likely to see a stronger state as enabling wars and military institutions to increase in scale.

Samuel Huntington wrote: "War was a great stimulus to state building." Charles Tilly put it even more bluntly: "War made the state, and the state made war."[1] At present, Tilly leads the charge for seeing war, or coercion as he categorizes it generally, as the basis of the state; for him, the state is little more than the accumulation and concentration of coercion.[2] He is quite specific that changes in warfare preceded and caused changes in government, and that the "framework of an army" provided the form of the French state.[3] In their recent book on war and the state, Rasler and Thompson agree that the principal Western powers were the products of war making.[4] Porter insists that "modernity derived from the pressures of war."[5] If for some, war and the tools of war drove state formation, for others, changes within the polity allowed the expansion of war and armies; certainly Jeremy Black argues the latter.[6] For the historian I. A. A. Thompson, "war was less a stimulant than a test of the state," in the sense that warfare actually eroded royal control because of the confusion and compromise that were associated with mobilizing a state for war.[7]

War demands manpower, materiel, and money on a massive scale, and the need to mobilize these resources explains why and how conflict forces the state to accrue power. For Tilly, "state structure appeared chiefly as a

---

[1] Karen A. Rasler and William R. Thompson, *War and State Making: The Shaping of the Global Powers* (Boston: 1989), 2. Charles Tilly, "Reflections on the History of European State-Making," in Charles Tilly, ed., *The Formation of National States in Western Europe* (Princeton: 1975), 42.

[2] Charles Tilly, *Coercion, Capital, and the European States, A.D. 990–1990* (Oxford: 1990).

[3] Charles Tilly, *The Contentious French* (Cambridge, MA: 1986), 128.

[4] Rasler and Thompson, *War and State Making*, xv.

[5] Bruce D. Porter, *War and the Rise of the State* (New York: 1994), 101.

[6] Jeremy Black, *A Military Revolution? Military Change and European Society, 1550–1800* (Atlantic Heights, NJ: 1991).

[7] I. A. A. Thompson, *War and Government in Habsburg Spain, 1560–1620* (London: 1976), 287.

by-product of rulers' efforts to acquire the means of war."[8] He observes that "the more costly the activity, all other things being equal, the greater was the organizational residue."[9] Nothing left an "organizational residue" as thick and as tenacious as did the ultimate expense, war. Some theorists stress not only war as a phenomenon that increased the powers of the state but also as a factor that influenced the way in which the state was governed. For Brian Downing, the way in which states mobilized resources for war determined the fate of representative institutions in Europe.[10] Those states that had to mobilize extensive resources within their own borders in order to fight great land wars became more autocratic, or absolutist. So for him, the basic variable was the cost of the war effort, not the nature and structure of the military institutions. Arguments that point to warfare and resource mobilization as driving forces behind absolutism are particularly telling since the seventeenth century witnessed an intensity of warfare not really matched until the twentieth century. By Levy's count, of the ten greatest wars of the last 500 years – measured by battle deaths, not monetary cost – four occurred during 1610–1715, and three directly involved France.[11]

THE ARMY AND STATE FORMATION

When the discussion shifts specifically to armies and state formation, the first subject that demands attention is army growth. The links between army size and state formation seem obvious, since the larger the army, the greater its demands upon the state, and this feeds directly into arguments concerning resource mobilization. If some historians and social scientists assert that the change was forced upon the state by the demands of the army and made possible by its coercive potential, others hold that through administrative reform and an accommodation with elites, Louis gained the authority needed to carry out military expansion. Although they reach different conclusions, these scholars share the same assumption that the expansion of the royal army must have gone hand in hand with an equally great transformation of the French government, either as effect or cause. But this assumption is flawed, because the real paradox, and weakness, of French absolutism and its great army was that the changes in the institutions of central government never really matched the magnitude of army expansion.

This apparent contradiction resulted from the fact that the administration of the army was not concentrated only in the central government and the department of war. As this volume demonstrates, the French mobilized and controlled the resources required by their huge army at four different levels:

---

[8] Tilly, *Coercion, Capital, and the European States*, 14.

[9] Charles Tilly, "War Making and State Making as Organized Crime," in Peter B. Evans, D. Rueschemeyer, and Theda Skocpol, eds., *Bringing the State Back In* (Cambridge: 1985), 81.

[10] Brian M. Downing, *The Military Revolution and Political Change in Early Modern Europe* (Princeton: 1992).

[11] Jack S. Levy, *War in the Modern Great Power System, 1495–1975* (Lexington, KY: 1983).

the central government, provincial institutions, field armies, and, lastly, the regiments. Certainly, the monarchy levied taxes, contracted debts, and funneled these resources to the army through the bureaucracies of the secretary of state for war and the *contrôleur général des finances*. This is important, and this is where most scholars end their discussion. However, other personnel and institutions collected and dispensed resources on the regional level. The ubiquitous provincial *intendants* operated as the king's agents, but provincial estates, governors, and private contractors all played important roles as well. One way in which the king exploited the wealth of France was to delegate the responsibility for funding certain military costs to localities, and evidence of their labors and expenses may never have made their way into Parisian archives. Localities shouldered some or all of the costs for fortifications, garrisons, winter quarters, *étapes*, and matériel. Provinces even paid the wages for the royal provincial militia for half of each year during 1688–97 and maintained other kinds of militia year-round.

During wartime, when great field armies formed, they supplied many of their own needs through the efforts of administrators attached directly to those field armies. Army *intendants* come to mind, but also the *commissaires*, *contrôleurs*, *receveurs*, and *trésoriers* with the troops. *Munitionnaires* organized and maintained army food supplies, filling many functions that today would fall under the aegis of the state. Through contributions and courses, armies seized substantial amounts of the money and foodstuffs that maintained them on campaign, to say nothing of the more mundane but essential matter of foraging for fodder. Regimental colonels and their captains also bore many administrative responsibilities that kept their units in the field. So much fell upon these officers that in a sense, the military administration expanded automatically every time the army added new regiments and companies. And it needs to be stressed that not only did these officers carry out bureaucratic and logistic tasks; they regularly drew upon their own wealth and credit to pay costs in whole or in part.

Any study that would claim to document the links between army growth and state formation must take into consideration the multi-tiered way in which the army was maintained, and to date, none has. Since the monarchy tried to accomplish as much as it could through a technique of regulation and inspection, as opposed to centralizing all services directly in the hands of government agents, it minimized the multiplication of bureaucratic staff and left a great deal of authority outside of Paris. A bureaucratic and financial revolution that exactly matched the magnitude of army expansion could be avoided because the burdens and powers could be distributed in a variety of ways. This does not mean that government did not change to keep pace with its army, but it may mean that *central* bureaucracy could alter much less than would seem warranted, and that to appreciate the full impact of the army on *government*, that term must be defined more widely. Ultimately, the partial nature of state transformation, while it allowed military expansion in the short run without necessitating radical change, may have doomed the state to long-term exhaustion by the end of Louis's reign and eventually contributed to the onset of revolution seventy-five years later. Thus, perhaps the theoreticians are correct in the sense that a revolutionary change in army size should have brought with it an equally dramatic revolution in government, but the problem remains that it seems not to have done so during the *grand siècle*.

If the army's impact on the state was less, or at least less obvious, than might at first be supposed, there is no doubt that the growing powers of the monarchy affected the military. Seen from the perspective of the army, the now much-debated term *absolutism* still makes sense in describing a new level of control exerted by the monarch. Historians who reject the term because Louis XIV did not transform French society may be looking in the wrong place for absolutism. Louis did not set out to restructure everything within his domains; how could he launch an assault on all of the most fundamental traditions of French society when the monarchy looked to those very traditions for its own rationale? Seek absolutism not in the concerns of the modern social, economic, or cultural critic, but in the concerns of an early modern monarch – control over his government, foreign policy, and army. Absolutism is not to be found in peasant cottages or in countinghouses but in the bivouacs and barracks. There Louis so increased his leverage and so eroded that of his rivals that he deserves the title of absolute monarch.

THE STANDING ARMY

The exact role of a standing army as a coercive force in state formation is also not nearly as self-evident as theoreticians suppose it to be. Their basic line of argument is that standing armies imposed the will of the ruler upon his subjects and gave the monarch the power to extract necessary resources and to overawe or repress resistance. Thus, the creation of a standing army allowed a ruler to create a military/absolutist government. William McNeill asserts with confidence that "[Louis XIV's] standing army was initially designed to assure the king's superiority over any and every challenge to his authority within France, and only secondarily intended for foreign adventure."[12] And Tilly is equally sure that, in his words, "standing armies provided the largest single incentive to extraction and the largest single means of state coercion over the long run of European state-making."[13] Perhaps Tilly is correct "over the long run," but the focus here is seventeenth-century France, and the creation and use of a standing army is more complex in this case.

A standing army must be differentiated from the generic term *army*. The term *standing* implies that the army existed in peacetime; that is the real innovation. Long before the seventeenth century, states assembled large fighting forces to wage their wars. The Valois created a modest permanent peacetime

[12] William McNeill, *Pursuit of Power* (Chicago: 1982), 125.
[13] Tilly, "Reflections on the History of European State-Making," 73.

army composed of cavalry in *compagnies d'ordonnance* and garrison infantry. However, this was an extremely small force of not much over 10,000 men, and it remained so most of the time until the reign of Louis XIV. However, at the close of the war with Spain in 1659, he kept 70,000 troops on foot, a figure that then doubled over the next twenty years. Here is the true standing army of absolutism; the question is, for what was it used?

One would expect the answer that this army fought against civil rebellion and oppressed the French population, but did it? The greatest civil disturbances of the seventeenth century occurred before the personal reign of Louis XIV. Louis XIII and Richelieu conducted their campaigns against the Huguenots in the 1620s as full-scale wars with an army mobilized to take La Rochelle and then campaign against Rohan's Protestant forces. The tax revolts that shook France between 1635 and 1659 were, by definition, wartime rebellions, and the troops used against them cannot be termed a *standing army*, but simply units created for war and diverted to fight the rebels. The same can be said for the Fronde, when defeating the Frondeurs and their Spanish allies became the primary task of the royal army. The most notable rebellions that troubled Louis's personal reign struck in 1675 and 1702–4, and again the regular troops used to put down these risings were drawn from field armies mustered to fight interstate wars. There is no doubt that the peacetime army did fight against some internal risings – for example, that of the Boulonnais in 1662 – but these were decidedly minor affairs. On the whole, the standing army spent precious little time beating the king's subjects into submission.

And a glance at where the peacetime army was posted demonstrates that it was not deployed to control the bulk of France during the personal reign of Louis XIV. To be sure, certain garrisons served political authority. Richelieu saw citadels as tools to overawe potentially rebellious populations, and soon after the Peace of the Pyrenees, Louis XIV undermined independent fortress governors by replacing their troops with his own.[14] However, under the Sun King, the standing army generally occupied fortresses along the frontiers and seacoasts of France; troops were not dispersed throughout the interior to police Bourbon domains. In areas just recently added along the borders, some fortresses and their garrisons were maintained to ensure loyalty "until the newly conquered peoples become completely accustomed to our domination."[15] Immanuel Wallerstein insists that France was split into core and peripheral zones that pulled against one another for economic and political reasons, so that a strong government with a strong army was necessary to unite the whole through force.[16] Wallerstein might take some comfort, then,

[14] Louis XIV, *Mémoires*, 2:402.
[15] Vauban 1682 memoir in Gaston Zeller, *L'organization défensive des frontières du nord et de l'est au XVIIe siècle* (Paris: 1928), 99–100.
[16] Immanuel Wallerstein, "France: A Special Case? A World-Systems Perspective," in E. D. Genovese and L. Hochberg, eds., *Geographic Perspectives in History* (New York: 1969).

in the idea that the standing army garrisoned the frontiers, those areas far-thest from the core. But to say that the army stood on the border in order to control a restless populace seems farfetched. Foreign threat and territorial security, not internal political repression, remained the primary factors deter-mining troop placement.

A more subtle case could be made that a standing army enhanced royal power by freeing the monarch from a dependence on the private forces of major aristocrats. As pointed out earlier, in the era before 1635, the king, hampered by financial limitations, called upon grandees to raise private armies which the king, then, could use for his own purposes. A great noble who could raise an army to curry favor with the king, however, also had the power to raise an army to resist him. Ultimately, the danger for the king was too great, and the monarch needed to eliminate his reliance upon such pri-vate forces by maintaining troops of his own at all times.[17]

The standing army also replaced potentially troublesome urban militias once needed to defend fortresses. Defense of city walls had long depended primarily or in part on bourgeois *milices*. They offered advantages similar to the private armies of the grandees – they were inexpensive and could be quickly mobilized. In addition, town forces were devoted to the defense of their city out of self-interest. But urban militias and private garrisons also had some real disadvantages, since they might choose to defend their walls against the royal army in times of revolt.[18] This was certainly the case during the Fronde, when cities, including Paris itself, took the side of the Frondeurs. The logic of power thus demanded that the king replace town militias with his own troops. Even with the destruction of internal fortifications no longer necessary for the defense of the realm, frontier fortifications created the need for a large standing army to hold them securely against the threat of enemy attack. Vauban's great fortress lines and Louis's concept of defensible fron-tiers, not a fear of civil revolt, determined the size of the standing army.

If the argument concerning urban militias holds true, it overturns an accepted explanation for the creation of standing armies. Instead of being the *means* to increased royal power, the standing army appears as the *result* of Bourbon triumphs. Louis XIV maintained large peacetime forces as a con-sequence of victories won by French wartime forces against various revolts, most notably the Fronde. Humbled cities lost their ability to raise and maintain independent forces, since the monarch could not allow the existence of mili-tias that might turn against royal authority. To fill the void created by his triumph over local military forces and independent governors, Louis created a standing army to provide for the defense of his realm. Cities had to be

---

[17] I owe this argument to Brian Sandberg.

[18] Louis XIII complained that rebel dukes of Vendôme and Mayenne "have made levies of Souldiers, and quartered them in those Townes and places, the guard wherof wee have committed to their trust." Louis XIII, *The French Kings Declaration against the Dukes of Vendosme and Mayenne* (London: 1617), 6. My thanks to Brian Sandberg for bringing this material to my attention.

garrisoned, or they could quickly fall to the enemy in the opening moves of war, and current military thought required garrisons of a given size. There is an interesting phrase in Turenne's commission giving him the right to command "in peace as well as in war a great number of troops, both infantry and cavalry, which will always be in good condition to act to keep our people in the obedience and respect they owe, to insure the peace and tranquillity that we have won."[19] The last words, "to insure the peace and tranquillity that we have won," imply a standing army as a result of past royal triumph, which is primarily what it was.

Coercion and Extraction: Military and Paramilitary Forces

One of the ways in which standing armies were supposed to have aided state formation was by their capacity to coerce resources, primarily taxes, from populations, but closer examination suggests that scholars have too often jumped to hasty conclusions about the role of royal military units in tax collection. Samuel Finer speaks of an "extraction-coercion cycle," in which armies compelled reluctant subjects to hand over money to the state, which it then spent to increase its forces so as to extort even more.[20] Tilly and others have also stressed the ability of an army to enforce the demands of the state upon its own inhabitants. The historical record confirms that in seventeenth-century France, tax collectors employed bands of men armed and organized in a military fashion, but there is good reason to doubt that such "troops" were elements of the royal army. If they were not, then the standing army did not supply the muscle that compelled payment to the absolutist state. *Fusiliers des tailles* provide an interesting case in point.[21]

These fusiliers composed company-sized units of fifty to 100 men, commanded by captains, lieutenants, and ensigns. They enforced collection of the *taille* at gunpoint, often being quartered on recalcitrant villagers. The first such company seems to have been that formed in Angoumois in 1636.[22] However, *fusiliers des tailles* were neither created nor maintained in the same

---

[19] Commission in Frank Tallett, *War and Society in Early Modern Europe* (London: 1992), 191.

[20] Samuel E. Finer, "State- and Nation-Building in Europe: The Role of the Military," in Tilly, *The Formation of National States in Europe* (Princeton: 1975).

[21] For a useful account of the *fusiliers des tailles,* see Yves-Marie Bercé, *Histoire des Croquants: Etude des soulèvements populaires au XVII siècle dans le sud-ouest de la France,* 2 vols. (Paris: 1974), I:105–12.

[22] Bercé discusses this company and says that in addition to it, Villemontée, the *intendant,* had four companies of regular infantry to collect taxes, but the citation for this comes from the summer of 1637, when Villemontée conducted a military action against rebellious towns that had gone so far as to kill three *commis* of the tax collectors. So regular troops probably played no part in the normal collection of revenues. See the letter of 8 June 1637 from Villemontée in Henri Renaud, ed., "Correspondance relative aux provinces d'Aunis, Saintonge, Angoumois et Poitou entre l'intendant François de Villemontée, le chancelier Séguier, le commandeur de La Porte, Jean de Lauson et autres, 1633–1648," *Archives historiques de la Saintonge et de l'Aunis* 7 (1880), 316–18. I must thank Douglas Baxter for pointing out this letter to me.

manner as royal soldiers. Although they served under the control of the *intendant*, fusiliers were recruited and paid by financial entrepreneurs, or *traitants*, who had contracted to collect the *taille*. One wonders how real the *intendant*'s supervision really was, when, for example, the company raised in 1636 was disbanded in 1643 because it had become a source of "oppressions, violence, and thefts."[23] Fusiliers received high pay and operated outside the constraints of the military hierarchy.

The creation of such companies spread across France from 1640 to 1644. Apparently, they could also be called *carabiniers*.[24] Their elimination constituted an important part of the demands against the royal fiscal regime at the start of the Fronde. As one pamphlet of 1648 protested, the *taille* was "in part raised by the means of companies of fusiliers who are so many unchained devils . . . ."[25] They disappeared during the Fronde, only to reappear in 1656. After the war with Spain, the government cut down their numbers and tried to repress the use of fusiliers in tax collection, probably as much because of the high expense incurred in using armed men as because of the excesses they committed.[26] Even then, fusiliers remained in some *généralités*, including Limoges, Bordeaux, and Montauban. *Fusiliers des tailles* survived late in the reign of Louis XIV for, as one *intendant* of Limousin insisted, "The use of fusiliers is the most mild [*doux*] and the most suitable to be exercised."[27]

If agents of the monarchy resorted to coercion to extract revenues from a reluctant population, this did not automatically involve the army in the process. As local forces obedient not to army officers but to tax collectors and financed outside the *extraordinaires des guerres*, *fusiliers des tailles* can no more be counted as soldiers than can night watchmen or policemen today. Fusiliers served the fiscal administration just as did the guards hired by the tax farmers who collected the *gabelle*, or salt tax. Such forces survived into the eighteenth century; in 1768, the "veritable private army" maintained by the farmers-general to protect their goods and enforce their monopolies included 19,500 men organized in a military fashion in companies of 200 men each.[28] The institution of *fusiliers des tailles* suggests that violence in the

---

[23] Condemnation by Villemontée, *intendant* of the pays d'Ouest, in Bercé, *Histoire des Croquants*, 1:109.

[24] Jean de Lauson used a company of "carabiniers" to collect taxes in the Perigord in 1644. Although the source is not specific, it would seem likely that these were not regular troops. Francis Loirette, "Un intendant de Guyenne avant la Fronde: Jean de Lauson (1641–1648)," *Bulletin philologique et historique, Comité des travaux historiques et scientifiques. Section de philologie et d'histoire* (1957), 454. I must thank Douglas Baxter for this reference.

[25] "La requeste des trois Estats présentée à messieurs du Parlement," in Patrick Landier, "Guerre, violences, et société en France, 1635–1659," doctorat de troisième cycle, dissertation, Université de Paris IV, 1978, 146.

[26] Charles Godart, *Les pouvoirs des intendants sous Louis XIV, particulièrement dans les pays d'élections de 1661 à 1715* (Paris: 1901 reprint Geneva: 1974), 245–46, 250.

[27] *Intendant* writing in 1689 in Bercé, *Histoire des Croquants*, 1:112.

[28] Roland Mousnier, *The Institutions of France under the Absolute Monarchy, 1598–1789*, 2 vols. (Chicago: 1979–84), 2:457–58.

service of the fiscal administration had little to do with the army on a day-to-day basis. Historians need to know more about armed forces outside the army – what might be called *paramilitary* bands that acted on the local level. The key to absolutism may have more to do with such paramilitary bands than with the army proper.

The role of soldiers in repressing outright revolts, as opposed to tax collection or police control, is more apparent, although even here, the forces that imposed the king's will were not always composed solely of regular troops. Tax revolts, the most common form of contemporary popular rising, occurred with the greatest frequency in the 1630s, when Aix, Languedoc, Saintonge, Angoumois, and Normandy all experienced open rebellions. The greatest rebellion against the royal fisc, although it was other things as well, was the Fronde, which escalated into a full-scale civil war with dreadful human costs. The personal reign of Louis XIV saw fewer of these troubles, although the last major tax revolt hit Brittany in 1675. Rebellions by great princes also challenged royal authority before Louis's personal reign. The Fronde was the greatest of these, but they also plagued the period from 1610 to 1632. When open rebellion flared, troops either put down the revolts or punished the populations after overt resistance to royal authority had subsided. Consequently, there is little question that the army, but primarily the wartime army, occasionally lived up to the expectations of modern theorists who cast it as an agent of extraction, and this was not the limit of its use for internal control.

Obviously, civil wars won by the monarchy tended to strengthen its authority, and it is important to note that during the *grand siècle*, the monarchy eventually won all of the civil wars, great and small, that troubled France. To be sure, there were setbacks, as occurred in the first brushes with the Huguenots and early in the Fronde, but the army always managed to enforce the royal will in the end. Victories in civil wars, 1610–59, made possible the relative domestic peace of the personal reign; it was not a peace of exhaustion and compromise such as that which concluded Louis XIV's great external wars, but a peace of victory within.

Louis XIV not only demanded that his subjects finance his wars and recognize his authority; he also desired religious unity in his absolutist state, and he called upon the army to enforce this policy as well. The infamous *dragonnades* of the 1680s saw troops, usually dragoons, quartered on Huguenot families to convince them of the errors of their faith and of the benefits that conversion to Catholicism might bring. Of course, the open civil wars fought by Protestants in the 1620s and in the first decade of the eighteenth century brought royal troops into the field to fight against the Huguenots in military campaigns.

The tax revolt of 1675 and the religious rebellion of 1702–4 demonstrate, as did the use of *fusiliers des tailles* before, the role of paramilitary forces. It is true that the monarchy diminished the size of, and often eliminated, local forces, such as bourgeois *milices*, during the first half of the *grand siècle*, but at least by the 1680s, Louis created new paramilitary forces for internal control, notably those *milice* of Languedoc designed to watch over the potentially dangerous Protestant community after the revocation of the Edict of Nantes. And when officials in Bordeaux and Brittany in 1675 and Languedoc in 1702 employed forces to put down rebellion, they first called upon local aristocratic levies and upon hurriedly raised citizen militias, not upon regulars.[29] In fact, the governor in Brittany in 1675 asked that the royal army send fewer troops than promised to deal with the local rebellion.[30] Against the Camisards, Marshal Montrevel ordered the creation of 130 companies, totaling 7,800 men, of bourgeois *milice* to garrison posts.[31] Could an essential element in the king's repressive forces be a new relationship with local forces which now served the monarchy's interests whereas they had once opposed them, or at least possessed the potential to resist? If so, something more profound than simply the existence of permanent regiments was involved in guaranteeing that there would be bayonets behind the throne.

Violence, Intimidation, and Legitimacy

One of the questionable assumptions underlying the current discussion of state formation is the belief that overt violence by royal troops was a constant element in the creation and maintenance of the absolutist state. This epilogue has already challenged the idea that a standing army was the sole repressive arm of absolutism and suggested that forces commonly employed for both extraction and control were not military at all, but certain paramilitary bodies responsive to local authority or even to *traitants*. Taking the argument even further, perhaps overt violence, though important in the process of state formation, was not the usual, primary, or preferred means of gaining and guaranteeing absolutist authority.

Below the level of overt violence lies intimidation, which still implies the threat of force but not does not require its use. Since actual violence creates

---

[29] The use of a combination of local and military forces was not unique to the major revolts. In 1709, after peasants had pillaged a convoy of grain wagons around Montbrison, the local *prévôt* of the *maréchaussée* took his company of *maréchaussée* plus "around thirty inhabitants of Bourg-Argental, twenty dragoons, and some gentlemen" to deal with the culprits. Henri Hours, "Émeutes et émotions populaires dans les campagnes du Lyonnais au XVIIIe siècle," *Cahiers d'histoire* 9 (1964), 138. In the eighteenth century, *maréchaussée* and urban militias worked together. Ian Cameron, *Crime and Repression in the Auvergne and the Guyenne, 1720–1790* (Cambridge: 1981). My thanks to Roy McCullough for these references.

[30] Letters of Louvois to the de Chaulnes, 8 May 1675, and de Chaulnes to Louvois, 15 May 1675, in Jean Lemoine, *La Révolte dite du Papier Timbré ou des Bonnets Rouges en Bretagne en 1675* (Paris: 1898), docs. XIII and XVII. My thanks to my student Roy McCullough for these references.

[31] Victor Belhomme, *Histoire de l'infanterie en France*, 5 vols. (Paris: 1893–1902), 2:379–80. Montrevel gave an order of 10 February 1703 to form bourgeois companies of sixty men each to garrison certain posts. There would be forty in the *généralité* of Montauban, forty in Languedoc, and fifty in the Rouergue.

victims and, thus, hatred that may inspire future resistance, intimidation can be far superior, since it can control with much less sense of victimization. With time, the absence of outright violence and resistance may create an atmosphere of legitimacy, lessening the need even for intimidation. This certainly seems to have occurred under Louis XIV. The relative internal peace with its sense of order and security that flowered during his personal reign, the impression of a strong monarchy that Louis fostered through real administration and through symbolic display, and the fact that he occupied the throne for so long, all strengthened assumptions of legitimacy, which made the kind of violence practiced against and by Louis XIII, Richelieu, and Mazarin unnecessary or at least far less common.

But such observations do not eliminate the army from a repressive role; they simply caution against too mechanical a definition of the relationship between force and authority. Royal troops and the institutions that supported them exerted undeniable, but less obvious, influence over the course of royal absolutism. Perhaps military violence was more essential in suppressing or channeling certain forms of resistance than others. For example, it may have been more necessary literally to defeat the aristocracy in battle during the first half of the century because that elite saw itself as a military class, and thus clung to the notion that it could by right take up arms to assert its interests. Royal victory in the revolts of 1610–32 and in the Fronde, then, may have been a key element to future consolidation.

At the same time that the army overpowered aristocratic rebellion, the military also gave the monarchy leverage over the aristocracy by offering the lure of commissions within the royal forces. The culture of command demanded that young noble males seek opportunities to demonstrate their courage, the essential attribute of aristocratic masculinity. Noblemen displayed their enthusiasm for military service by competing for commissions and by contributing a great deal of their own wealth and credit to the maintenance of their own units in ways that make little sense to the modern mind. In fact, the taste for war, like the mania for dueling, evinced attitudes specific to the age. As Corvisier concludes, "War is the normal climate in which society developed during the seventeenth century. It reinforced through social cleavage the superiority of the aristocratic element that cultivated the chivalric virtues, the cult of honor, the poetry of the sword, and magnanimous generosity."[32]

War and military expansion provided the quid pro quo for greater authority in the hands of the monarch. This is an old argument with a good deal of force to it; it only goes astray if it is stretched to the point of asserting that the king expanded his army precisely to appease noble officers, for there is little evidence of that. Louis was an aristocrat himself and desirous of personal glory, as were his nobles, and this alone explains why he rushed into war early in his regime. But once committed to the maintenance of large

[32] Philippe Contamine, ed., *Histoire militaire de la France*, vol. 1 (Paris: 1992), 331.

military forces, he benefited from the leverage that they gave him over his aristocracy, and war became a tool of domestic policy. Tilly stresses the need for bargaining between rulers and their subjects in the process of state formation, and the army provided a bargaining ploy to win support for royal policy among the elite.

In contrast to this logic, William Beik offers a Marxist interpretation of absolutism as a consensus between the aristocracy and the monarchy, in which the former exploited the authority of the latter, including the power to tax, to serve its own class interests and to augment its wealth. However, if the examinations of the costs and culture of command presented here are correct, then the monarchy promoted consensus not by capitulating to the aristocracy but by harnessing that class to the royal program of military expansion, a program that appropriated noble wealth in exchange for honor. In this manner, the monarchy could call upon feudal values to take a major evolutionary step toward the modern state. Here, as in other particulars, the new state commission army may have been both a means toward achieving absolute monarchy and its defining characteristic.

Military institutions may also have neutralized those outside the dictates of aristocratic honor, the lower levels of society, without resorting to outright repression. Here the key was intimidation. Certainly, much of military pomp was designed to impress civilians with the army's might. There seems little other reason for all the flag waving and drum beating prescribed by regulations when troops entered towns along their routes. Military display was probably the most that rural populations saw of the royal ceremony that mattered so much during the reign of the Sun King. Frequent changes of garrison paraded the king's armed might along the roads of France and, in addition, ensured that regiments not become too attached to civilian populations around them. Marriage restrictions also isolated garrison regiments from the locals; neither enlisted men nor officers were allowed to marry women from the towns that the men garrisoned. Regiments were intended not only to be impressive but to be remote. The standing army may have been more the creation of a triumphant monarchy than the means of that triumph, but once created, the standing army advertised the power of the Bourbons by its intimidating, and eventually reassuring, presence.

In a different manner, the institution of the royal provincial militia demonstrated the omnipotence and reach of the royal government in the latter half of Louis's personal reign. Conscription through *tirage au sort* brought royal administrators bearing what was often life-or-death power into remote areas of France. The army did not hold every town and village in its grasp, but through the *milice*, the military imposed itself on civilian communities across the length and breadth of France. The *tirage au sort* was a potent and constant form of intimidation carried out by the state in the name of the military. To be sure, conscription left in its wake profound resentment among the peasantry, but it also confirmed the authority of the absolute monarchy.

The army's most valuable contribution to state formation may not have

been through the use of violence against subject populations, but through
the elimination of the need to use overt force because larger military institutions either intimidated or won over potential opposition to royal authority. At a certain point, and it would appear that this point was reached in the
late seventeenth century, the task of effective day-to-day control and repression could be returned to local paramilitary forces and, as they developed, to
police because assumptions of legitimacy had taken deep enough root.

The military past may have strengthened the state's legitimacy in another
manner as well. It is possible that memories of war and rebellion provided
the most compelling arguments for acquiescence to the royal absolutism of
Louis XIV, who could avoid similar catastrophes through the exercise of his
power. During the quarter century of struggle, 1635–59, France suffered the
kind of discord, destruction, and death associated with the Thirty Years' War
in Germany. Spanish and French troops victimized Bourbon subjects for
many of the same reasons that applied across the Rhine, as unpaid and unfed
soldiers ravaged the countryside in hopes of sustenance and booty. Much in
the same way that memory of the exploitation of Brandenburg during the
Thirty Years' War eased the Great Elector's task of gaining concessions from
the Landtag, so the memory of war and the Fronde aided Louis XIV in his
policies of consolidation. A stronger monarchy and larger armed forces promised to, and did, protect France from similar ravages in the future. To this
extent, the state commission army could have been a tool for building a
consensus that extended well beyond the elites. If so, the giant of the *grand
siècle* was not simply the iron fist beneath the richly embroidered glove of
absolutism. But more research alone can test the truth of these speculations
concerning state formation.

It is only fitting that this volume should close with an appeal for more study.
The preface warned that the search for evidence and explanation would often
result only in identifying questions that have yet to be answered. And, indeed, the effort to gain understanding here has frequently led to challenge or
doubt. Perhaps there is no surprise in this – such is the nature of knowledge.
The importance of the subject and the questions asked here will, hopefully,
lead others to take up the inquiry despite the fact that the latest fashions in
contemporary scholarship reject military history, even the "new" military history that was thought to hold such promise. Today historians regard other
aspects of the past as highly significant and little examined, an attitude guaranteeing that young and eager minds will accept the challenge to investigate
them. On the other hand, the self-defined avant-garde rejects the history of
war and military institutions as inconsequential, derivative, and overworked.
But it is none of these. To the extent that this volume has identified gaps
in our knowledge with significant consequences for major issues, it advocates
that scholars accept the field as legitimate and explore its many unknowns.
Ought something so central remain so hidden; ought the giant to remain
invisible?

A year after French victory at Barcelona, Louis died, as if he were worn down not only by age, but by his battles – a final casualty of war. With his passing, the *grand siècle* ended as well. Versailles would fill with new voices and its splendor awe new visitors. But the stone trophies of arms on the garden front would still dominate the paths below. The work of his armies would not vanish like the old king.

Bibliography

ARCHIVAL SOURCES

The Archives Nationales, referred to here as AN, holds the main general collections of documents on the French past. Of notable service to this study was the G^7 series of financial records.

The home of the French war archives is the Service Historique de l'Armée de Terre, or SHAT, in the Château de Vincennes just east of Paris. There the Archives de Guerre, referred to here as AG, houses the primary collections of documents. The essential source is the A^1 series, containing the military correspondence of the *ancien régime*. In addition, the MR series contains miscellaneous memoirs and documents. Over the last two decades, other historical libraries have joined the Archives de Guerre at Vincennes. The library of SHAT, referred to here as SHAT, Bib., and documents once housed in the Bibliothèque du Ministère de Guerre, referred to here as BMG, share new quarters in one of the two stately seventeenth-century pavilions at Vincennes. That library also holds valuable document collections, such as the collection of military ordinances. That set of seventy-seven volumes, Collection des ordonnances militaires depuis 1112 jusqu'à 1801, is referred to in this volume as Col. des ord. The archives and library of the engineer corps, cited here as Bibl. Génie, are also located on the grounds of the Château de Vincennes.

A great many documents can be found in the Bibliothèque Nationale manuscript collection, referred to here as BN. Notable collections include the fonds français (f. fr.) and the Collection Chatre de Cangé (Chatre de Cangé).

References to the foreign affairs archives, the Archives des Affaires Étrangères, referred to here as AAE, have been taken from other historical studies, notably those by Parrott, Bonney, and Croxton, who have mined those archives to great use.

Local archives used in the preparation of this study include the following:

Archives municipales d'Amiens, housed in the municipal library, referred to here as Amiens;
Archives du département du Côte d'Or, referred to here as Côte d'Or;
Archives municipales de Dijon, referred to here as Dijon;
Archives municipales de Lilles, referred to here as Lille;
Archives du département du Nord, referred to here as Nord.

PUBLISHED WORKS

Abbadie, François, ed. *Lettres d'un cadet de Gascogne, François de Sarraméa* (Paris: 1890).

Adams, Simon. "Tactics or Politics? 'The Military Revolution' and the Hapsburg Hegemony, 1525–1648," in *Tools of War*, John A. Lynn, ed. (Ubana, IL: 1990), 28–52. This article is reprinted in Cliff Rogers, ed., *The Military Revolution Debate: Readings on the Military Transformation of Early Modern Europe* (Boulder, CO: 1995).

Anderson, M. S. *War and Society in Europe of the Old Regime, 1618–1789* (New York: 1988).

André, Louis. *Michel Le Tellier et l'organisation de l'armée monarchique* (Paris: 1906. Reprint Geneva: 1980).

André, Louis. *Michel Le Tellier et Louvois* (Paris: 1942).

André, Louis, Emile Bourgeois, et al., eds. *Recueil des instructions données aux ambassadeurs et ministres de France depuis les traités de Westphalie jusqu'à la Révolution française*, 30 vols. (1884–1983).

Archard, C. "Le recrutement de la milice royale à Pézenas 1689 à 1789," *Recrutement, mentalités, sociétés* (Montpellier: 1974), 45–56.

L'armée à Nancy, 1633–1966 (Nancy: 1967).

Arnauld d'Andilly, Robert. *Mémoires* in Petitot, ed., *Collection des mémoires relatifs à l'histoire de France*, ser. 2, vols. 33–34 (Paris: 1824).

Arnauld d'Andilly, Robert. *Mémoires* in Joseph Michaud and Jean Poujoulat, eds., *Nouvelle collection des mémoires pour servir à l'histoire de France*, vol. 23 (Paris: 1866).

Audouin, Xavier. *Histoire de l'administration de la guerre*, 4 vols. (Paris: 1811).

Azan, Paul. *Un tacticien du XVIIe siècle* (Paris: 1904).

Babeau, Albert. *La vie militaire sous l'ancien régime*, vol. 1 *Les soldats*, and vol. 2 *Les officiers* (Paris: 1890).

Babelm, Jean Pierre. *Henri IV* (1982).

Baillargeat, R. ed. *Les Invalides, trois siècles d'histoire* (Paris: 1975).

Bardin, General Baron. *Dictionnaire de l'armée de terre ou recherches historiques sur l'art et les usages militaires des anciens et modernes*, 8 vols. (Paris: 1841).

Baulant, Micheline. "Etudes: Prix des grains à Paris de 1431 à 1788," *Annales, E.S.C.*, vol. 23 (1968), 520–40.

Baxter, Douglas. *Servants of the Sword, French Military Intendants of the Army, 1630–1670* (Urbana, IL: 1976).

Baxter, Stephen. *William III and the Defense of European Liberty, 1650–1702* (New York: 1966).

Beaumont, Edouard de. *L'Epée et les femmes* (Paris: 1881).

Beaurain, Chevalier Jean de. *Histoire militaire du duc de Luxembourg*, 2 vols. (La Haye: 1776).

Beik, William. *Absolutism and Society in Seventeenth-Century France* (Cambridge: 1985).

Belhomme, Victor. *L'armée française en 1690* (Paris: 1895).

Belhomme, Victor. *Histoire de l'infanterie en France*, 5 vols. (Paris: 1893–1902).

Bély, Lucien, et al. *Guerre et paix dans l'Europe du XVIIe siècle*, 2 vols., *Regards sur l'histoire*, vols. 77–78 (Paris: 1991).

Bercé, Yves-Marie. "Guerre et État," *XVII siècle*, 37 (1985), 257–66.

Bercé, Yves-Marie. *Histoire des Croquants: Etude des soulèvements populaires au XVII siècle dans le sud-ouest de la France*, 2 vols. (Paris: 1974).

Bérenger, Jean. *Turenne* (Paris: 1987).

Berger, Peter Jonathan. "Military and Financial Government in France, 1648–1661," Ph.D. dissertation, University of Chicago, 1979.

Bernard, Montague. "The Growth of Laws and Usages of War," in *Oxford Essays contributed by Members of the University* (London: 1856), 88–136.

Bertaud, Jean-Paul. *La Révolution armée* (Paris: 1979).

Bertaud, Jean-Paul. *Valmy: La démocratie en armes* (Paris: 1970).

Bien, David. "La réaction aristocratique avant 1789: l'exemple de l'armée," *Annales: économies sociétés, civilizations*, 29 (1974), 23–48, 505–34.

Billaçois, François. *Le duel dans la société française des XVIe–XVIIe siècles* (Paris: 1986); translated as *The Duel: Its Rise and Fall in Early Modern France*, trans. Trista Selous (New Haven, CT: 1990).

Billon, Jean de. *Les principes de l'art militaire* (Lyon: 1622).

Billon, Jean de. *Les principes de l'art militaire* (Rouen: 1641).

Birac, sieur de. *Les fonctions du capitaine de cavalerie*, vol. 1 (La Haye: 1693).

Biron, Armand Gontaut. *Maximes et instructions de l'art de la guerre* (Paris: 1611).

Black, Jeremy. *European Warfare, 1660–1815* (New Haven, CT: 1994).

Black, Jeremy. *A Military Revolution? Military Change and European Society, 1550–1800* (Atlantic Highlands, NJ: 1991).

Black, Jeremy, ed. *The Origins of War in Early Modern Europe* (Edinburgh: 1987).

Blancpain, Marc. *Monsieur le prince* (Paris: 1986).

Blomfield, Reginald. *Sebastien le Prestre de Vauban, 1633–1707* (New York: 1971).

Bodart, Gaston. *The Losses of Men in Modern Wars* (Oxford: 1916).

Bodart, Gaston. *Militär-historishes Kriegs-Lexikon, 1618–1905* (Vienna and Leipzig: 1908).

Boislisle, A. M., ed. *Corresponance des contrôleurs généraux des finances avec les intendants des provinces*, vol. 1, 1683–99 (Paris: 1874).

Bonney, Richard. *The King's Debts* (Oxford: 1981).

Bosher, J. H. *French Finances, 1770–1795* (Cambridge: 1970).

Bourelly, Jules. *Le maréchal Fabert (1599–1662)* (Paris: 1881).

Boutaric, Edgard. *Institutions militaires de la France avant les armees permanentes* (Paris: 1863).

Boyer, Jean-Claude. "Les représentations guerrières et l'évolution des arts plastiques en France au XVIIe siècle," *XVII siècle*, 37 (1985), 291–305.

Braudel, Fernand. *L'identité de la France, I: Espace et histoire* (Paris: 1986).

Braudel, Fernand, and Ernest Labrousse, eds. *Histoire économique et sociale de la France*, vol. 2 (Paris: 1970).

Briquet, Pierre de. *Code militaire*, 8 vols. (Paris: 1761).

Brunet, Jean. *Histoire général de l'artillerie*, 2 vols. (Paris: 1842).

Buissaret, David. "Organization défensive des frontières au temps d'Henri IV," *Revue hist. de l'armée*, no. 4 (1964).

Buissaret, David. *Sully and the Growth of Centralized Government in France, 1598–1610* (London: 1968).

Cabié, E. *Guerres de religion dans le sud-ouest de la France* (Paris: 1906).

Caillet, Jules. *De l'adminstration en France sous le ministère du Cardinal de Richelieu* (Paris: 1857).

Cameron, Iain. *Crime and Repression in the Auvergne and the Guyenne, 1720–1790* (Cambridge: 1981).

Canal, Séverin. "Essai sur Auguste-Robert de Pomereu, intendant d'armée en Bretagane, 1675–1676," *Annales de Bretagne*, 24 (1908–9), 497–513.

Canne, Gaston de, ed. *Documents sur la ligue en Bretagne: Correspondence du duc de Mercoeur et des Ligueurs breton avec l'Espagne*, vol. 1 (Vannes: 1899).

Capelle, Guy. *Histoire de Condé et ses fortifications* (Beuvrage: 1978).

Caron, Narcisse-Léonard. *Michel Le Tellier: Son administration comme intendant d'armée en Piémont, 1640–43* (Paris: 1880).

Carrias, Eugène. *La Pensée militarire française* (Paris: 1960).

Carrot, Georges. *Histoire de la police française: Des origines à nos jours* (Paris: 1992).

Ceriziers, René de. *L'année françoise ou la première campagne de Louis XIV*, 4 vols. (1655–58).

Ceyssens, Jean. "Deux documents concernant les guerres de Louis XIV dans notre pays," *Leodium*, 5 (1906).

Chaboche, R. "Le recrutement des sergents et caporaux de l'armée française au XVIIe siècle," *Recrutement, mentalité, société* (Montpellier: 1974), 25–43.

Chaboche, R. "Les soldats français de la guerre de Trente Ans: Une tentative d'approache," *Revue d'histoire moderne et contemporaine*, XX (1973), 10–24.

Chagniot, Jean. "Du capitaine à l'officier, 1445–1635," and "De Rocroi à Rossbach," in Claude Croubois, ed., *L'officier français des origines à nos jours* (Saint-Jean-d'Angély: 1987), 9–66.

Chagniot, Jean. "Guerre et société au XVIIe siècle," *XVII siècle*, 37 (1985), 249–56.

Chambord, Marcel. "La grande guerre de manoeuvre (1702–1704): III Partie: Le mercenariat national," *L'armée la nation* (November 1960).

Chamillart, Michel. *Correspondance et papiers inédits*, 2 vols. (Paris: 1885).

Chandler, David. "Armies and Navies: Art of War on Land," in *New Cambridge Modern History*, vol. 6 (Cambridge: 1970), 741–62.

Chandler, David. *The Art of Warfare in the Age of Marlborough* (New York: 1976).

Chandler, David. *Marlborough as a Military Commander* (London: 1973).

Chastenet, Paul Hay de. *Traité de la guerre* (Paris: 1668).

Chotard, Henry. *Louis XIV, Louvois, Vauban et les Fortifications du nord de la France* (Paris: 1889).

Childs, John. *Armies and Warfare in Europe, 1648–1789* (Manchester: 1982).

Church, William F. "Louis XIV and Reason of State," in John C. Rule, *Louis XIV and the Craft of Kingship* (Columbus, OH: 1969), 362–406.

Clark, G. N. *War and Society in the Seventeenth Century* (Cambridge: 1958).

Cobb, Richard C. *Les Armées revolutionaires* (Paris: 1963).

Colbert, Jean-Baptiste. *Lettres, instructions, et mémoires de Colbert*, Pierre Clément, ed., 8 vols. (Paris: 1862–82).

Colin, Jean. *L'infanterie au XVIIIe siècle: La tactique* (Paris: 1907).

Colomban. *L'art militaire français, pour l'infanterie* (Paris: 1696).

Condé, Louis Bourbon, prince de. *Lettres de Louis Bourbon, prince de Condé, au maréchal de Gramont, 1641–1678* (Paris: 1895).

Condé, Louis Bourbon, prince de. *Lettres de Louis Bourbon, prince de Condé, au prince son père, 1635–1636* (Paris: 1806).

Contamine, Philippe. *Guerre, état et société à la fin du Moyen Age. Etudes sur les armées des rois de France, 1337–1494* (Paris and The Hague: 1972).

Contamine, Philippe, ed. *Histoire militaire de la France*, vol. 1, series editor André Corvisier (Paris: 1992).

Contamine, Philippe. *War in the Middle Ages*, trans. Michael Jones (Oxford: 1984).

Corvisier, André. *L'armée française de la fin du XVIIe siècle au ministère du Choiseul: Le soldat*, 2 vols. (Paris: 1964).

Corvisier, André. *Armies and Societies in Europe, 1494–1789*, trans. Abigail T. Siddall (Bloomington: 1979).

Corvisier, André. "La captivité militaire au XVIIe siècle, le sort des prisonniers de guerre espagnole en France (1635–48)," *Actes du 94e congrès national des Société savantes* (Paris: 1969).

Corvisier, André. "Clientèles et fidélités dans l'armées française aux 17e et 18e siècles, in Y. Durand, ed. *Hommage à Roland Mousnier. Clientèles et fidélités en Europes à l'époque moderne* (Paris: 1981), 213–36.

Corvisier, André. *Les Français et l'armée sous Louis XIV* (Vincennes: 1975).

Corvisier, André. *La France de Louis XIV, 1643–1715: Ordre intérieur et place en Europe* (Paris: 1979).

Corvisier, André. "Les généraux de Louis XIV et leur origine sociale," *XVIIe siècle* (1959), 23–53.

Corvisier, André. "Guerre et mentalités au XVIIe siécle," *XVII siècle*, 38 (1985), 219–31.

Corvisier, André. *Louvois* (Paris: 1983).

Corvisier, André, "Le moral des combattants, panique et enthousiasme, la bataille de Malplaquet," *Revue historique des armées*, 4, no. 3 (1977), 7–32.

Corvisier, André, "La mort du soldat depuis la fin du Moyen Age," *Revue histoirque*, 254 (1975), 3–30.

Corvisier, André. "Quelques aspects sociaux des milices bourgeoises au XVIIIe siècle," in *Villes de l'Europe Mediterraneenne et de l'Europe occidentale du Moyen Age au XIXe siècle* (Saint-Brieuc).

Courbouson, Louis de Montgomery, sieur de. *La milice française* (Paris: 1615).

Cournet, Jean-Gabriel. *Les voleurs, les vagabonds et l'armée* (Toulouse: 1905).

Court, Antoine. *Histoire des troubles des Cévennes*, 3 vols. (Villefranche: 1760) reprinted in 2 vols. by Lafitte Reprints (Marseille: 1975).

Courtilz de Sandras, Gatien, sieur de. *La conduite de Mars* (La Haye: 1685).

Crawford, Katherine B. "Regency Government in Early Modern France: Gender Substitution and the Construction of Monarchical Authority," Ph.D. dissertation, University of Chicago, 1996.

Croquez, Albert. *L'intendance de la flandre wallonne sous Louis XIV (1667–1708)* (Lille: 1912).

Croxton, Charles Derek. "Peacemaking in Early Modern Europe: Cardinal Mazarin and the Congress of Westphalia, 1643–1648," Ph.D. dissertation, University of Illinois at Urbana-Champaign, 1995.

Cuénin, Micheline. *La derniére des Amazones, Madame de Saint-Baslemont* (Nancy: 1992).

Cuénin, Micheline. *Le duel sous l'ancien régime* (Paris: 1982).

Dangeau, Philippe, marquis de. *Journal du marquis de Dangeau*, Feuillet de Conches, ed. 19 vols. (Paris: 1854–60).

Daniel, Gabriel. *Histoire de la milice françoise* (Paris: 1721).

Deageant de Saint-Martin, Guichard. *Memoirs of Monsieur Deageant* (London: 1690).

Dekker, Rudolf M., and Lotte van de Pol. *The Tradition of Female Tranvestism in Early Modern Europe*, trans. Judy Marcure and Lotte van de Pol (Houndmills, Basingstoke, Hampshire: 1989).

Delabarre-Duparcq, Nicolas Edouard de. *L'art militaire pendant les guerres de religion, 1562–1598* (Paris: 1864).

Delabarre-Duparcq, Nicolas Edouard de. *Histoire de l'art de la guerre depuis l'usage de la poudre*, 2 vols. (Paris: 1860–64).

Delabarre-Duparcq, Nicolas Edouard de. *Histoire militaire des femmmes* (Brest: 1873).

Delabarre-Duparcq, Nicolas Edouard de. *Histoire sommaire d'infanterie* (Paris: 1853).

Delarue, M. "L'Education politique à l'armée du Rhin, 1793–1794," mémoire de maitrise, Université de Paris-Nanterre: 1967–68.

Delmas, Jean, ed. *Histoire militaire de la France*, vol. 2, series editor André Corvisier (Paris: 1992).

Dent, Julian. *Crisis in Finance* (New York: 1973).

Derode, V. *Histoire de Lille* (Lille: 1848).

Derville, Alain. *Histoire de Saint-Omer* (Lille: 1981).

Les devoirs de l'homme de guerre, vol. 3 (La Haye: 1693).

Dickson, P. G. M., and John Sterling. "War Finance, 1689–1714," in *New Cambridge Modern History*, vol. 4 (Cambridge: 1970), 284–315.

Diderot, Denis, et al. *Encyclopédie*. 17 vols. text, 12 vols. plates (Paris: 1751–65).

Dollar, Jacques. *Vauban à Luxembourg* (Luxembourg: 1983).

Doucet, R. *Les institutions de la France au XIVe siècle*, 2 vols. (Paris: 1948).

Downing, Brian M. *The Military Revolution and Political Change: Origins of Democracy and Autocracy in Early Modern Europe* (Princeton: 1992).

Drune. "Henri IV, chef de guerre," *Revue historique de l'armée*, 17, no. 4 (December 1961).

Duffy, Christopher. *Fire and Stone: The Science of Fortress Warfare, 1660–1860* (Newton Abbot: 1975).

Duffy, Christopher. *The Fortress in the Age of Vauban and Frederick the Great, 1660–1789, Siege Warfare*, vol. 2 (London: 1985).

Duffy, Christopher. *Frederick the Great, A Military Life* (London: 1985).

Duffy, Christopher. *Siege Warfare: The Fortress in Early Modern History, 1494–1660* (London: 1979).

Duffy, Michael, ed. *The Military Revolution and the State* (Exeter: 1980).

Dumont, J. *Corps universel diplomatique*, vol. 6 (Hague: 1728), vol. 7, pt. 1–2, vol. 8, pt. 1–2 (Hague: 1731).

Dupâquier, Jacques, ed. *Histoire de la population française*, vol. 2, *De la Renaissance à 1789* (Paris: 1988), section 2, "Le peuplement," by Jacques Dupâquier, 51–98.

Du Praissac. *Les discours militaires* (Paris: 1624).

Du Praissac. *Les discours militaires*, 2 ed. (Paris: 1622).

Du Praissac. *Les questions militaires* (1617).

Dupuy, R. Ernest, and Trevor N. Dupuy. *The Encyclopedia of Military History* (New York: 1970).

Dussieux, Louis. *L'Armée en France*, 3 vols. (Versailles: 1884).

Dussieux, Louis. *Les grands généraux de Louis XIV* (Paris: 1887).

Ekberg, C. J. *The Failure of Louis XIV's Dutch War* (Chapel Hill: 1979).

Estienne, Jeanne. *Le bel Amiens* (Amiens: 1967).

Fages, Claudine. "Le service de la guerre sous Louis XIV de 1699–1715" (Paris: 1974).

Favitski de Probobyz, A. *Répetoire bibliographique de la literature militaire* (Paris: 1935).

Feld, M. D. "Middle-class society and the Rise of Military Professionalism: The Dutch Army, 1589–1609," *Armed Forces and Society*, 1 (1975), 419–42.

Fénelon. *Oeuvres de Fénelon*. Aimé-Martin, ed. vol. 3 (Paris: 1843).

Ferguson, Ronald Thomas. "Blood and Fire: Contribution Policy of the French Armies in Germany (1668–1715)," Ph.D. dissertation, University of Minnesota, 1970.

Ferrier-Caverivière, Nicole. "La guerre dans la littérature française depuis le traité des Pyrénées jusqu'à la mort de Louis XIV," *XVII siècle*, 37 (1985), 233–47.

Feuquières, marquis de. *Mémoires du marquis de Feuquières* (Londres: 1736).

Filippini, J.-P. "Le recrutement des soldats pour l'armée française à Livourne au XVIIe siècle et au XVIIIe siècle," *Revue historique de l'armée*, 2, no. 4 (1975), 7–28.

Finer, Samuel E. "State- and Nation-Building in Europe: The Role of the Military," in Charles Tilly, ed., *The Formation of National States in Europe* (Princeton: 1975), 84–163.

Foisil, Madeline. *La révolte des Nu-Pieds et les révoltes Normandes de 1630* (Paris: 1970).

Foletier, F. de vaux de. *Le Siège de La Rochelle* (Paris: 1931).

Fontenay-Mareuil, François Duval. *Mémoires*, in Joseph Michaud and Jean Poujoulat, eds. *Nouvelle collection des mémoires pour servir à l'histoire de France*, vol. 5 (Paris: 1837).

Foucault, Michel. *Discipline and Punishment*, trans. Alan Sheridan (New York: 1979).

Fossier, Robert. *Histoire de Picardie* (Toulouse: 1974).

France, Army. *L'art militaire français pour l'infanterie contenant l'exercise et le maniement des armes tant des officiers que es soldats* (Paris: 1696).

France, Army. *The French Army Way of Exercizing Infantry* (London: 1672).

Frémont, Paul. *Les payeurs d'armées (1293–1870)* (Paris: 1906).

Gaya, Louis de. *L'art de la guerre et la manière dont on la fait a présent* (Paris: 1677).

Gaya, Louis de. *The Art of War* (London: 1678).

Gaya, Louis de. *Le nouvel art de la guerre et la manière dont on la fait aujourd'huy en France* (Paris: 1692).

Gazette de France.

Gébelin, Jacques. *Histoire des milices provinciales (1688–1791): le tirage au sort sous l'ancien régime* (Paris: 1882).

Gérôme. *Essai historique sur la tactique de l'infanterie*, 2 ed. (Paris: 1903).

Gheyn, Jacob de. *The Exercise of Armes*, David J. Blackmore, ed. (London: 1986).

Giloteaux, Pauline. *Histoire de Landrecies des origines à nos jours* (Le Quesnoy: 1962).

Girard, Georges. "Bibliographie et sources de l'histoire des institutions militaires de l'ancien régime: état de question," *Bulletin de la société d'histoire moderne*, ser. 4, no. 23 (December 1923–January 1924), 419–28.

Girard, Georges. "Le logement des gens de guerre à Montpellier à la fin du XVIIe siècle," *Carnet de sabretache* (1921), 369–403.

Girard, Georges. *Le service militaire en France à la fin du règne de Louis XIV: Racolage et milice, 1701–1715* (Paris: 1915).

Girard, Georges, ed. "Un soldat de Malplaquet: Lettres du capitaine de Saint-Mayme," *Carnet de Sabretache* (1922), 497–541.

Girard, Guillaume. *The History of the Life of the Duke of Espernon, the Great Favorite of France* (London: 1670).

Godart, Charles. *Les pouvoirs des intendants sous Louis XIV, particulièrement dans les pays d'élections de 1661 à 1715* (Paris: 1901. Reprint Geneva: 1974).

Godeau, Antoine. *Catéchisme royale* (Paris: 1650).

Godechot, Jacques. *Les institutions de France sous la République et l'Empire* (Paris: 1968).

Godley, Eveline. *The Great Condé: A Life of Louis II de Bourbon, Prince of Condé* (London: 1915).

Goubert, Pierre. *L'ancien régime*, vol. 2, *Les pouvoirs* (Paris: 1973).

Goubert, Pierre. *Beauvais et le Beauvaisis de 1600–1730* (Paris: 1930).

Goubert, Pierre. *Louis XIV et vingt million des français* (Paris: 1966).

Grand-Carteret, John. *La femme en culotte* (Paris: 1899).

Griffet, Henri. *Recueil de lettres pour servir a l'histoire militaire du règne de Louis XIV*, 8 vols. (1760–64).

Grillon, Pierre. *Papiers de Richelieu*, vol. 3 (Paris: 1979).

Grimarest, Jean-Léonor. *Fonctions des généraux ou l'art de conduire une armée* (La Haye: 1710).

Grimmelshausen. *Simplicius Simplicissimus*, trans. George Schulz-Behrend (Indianapolis: 1965).

Grotius. *De jure belli ac pacis* in *Classics of International Law* (Oxford: 1925).

Guerlac, Henry. "Vauban: The Impact of Science on War," in Edward Meade Earle, ed., *Makers of Modern Strategy* (Princeton: 1941), 26–48.

Guignard, Pierre-Claude de. *L'ecole de Mars ou mémoires instructifs sur toutes les parties qui composent le corps militaire en France* (Paris: 1725).

Gutmann, Myron P. "Putting Crisis in Perspective: The Impact of War on the Civilian Populations in the XVIIth Century," *Annales de demographie historique* (1977), 101–28.

Gutmann, Myron P. *War and Rural Life in the Early Modern Low Countries* (Princeton: 1980).

Hacker, Barton. "Women and Military Institutions in Early Modern Europe: A Reconnaissance," *Signs*, 6, no. 4 (summer 1981), 643–71.

Hale, J. R. "Armies, Navies, and the Art of War," in *New Cambridge Modern History*, vol. 2 (Cambridge: 1958), 481–509.

Hale, J. R. "Armies, Navies, and the Art of War," in *New Cambridge Modern History*, vol. 3 (Cambridge: 1968), 171–208.

Hale, J. R. "The Early Development of the Bastion: An Italian Chronology, c. 1450–c. 1534," in J. R. Hale, J. R. L. Highfield, and B. Smalley, eds., *Europe in the Late Middle Ages* (London: 1965), 644–94.

Hale, J. R. *Renaissance Fortification: Art or Engineering* (London: 1977).

Hale, J. R. *War and Society in Renaissance Europe, 1450–1620* (Baltimore, MD: 1985).

Hall, Bert S., and Kelly R. DeVries. "The 'Military Revolution' Revisited," *Technology and Culture* (July: 1990), 500–7.

Hanoteau, Gabriel, ed. *Histoire de la nation française*, vol. 7, *Histoire militaire et navale*, pt. 1 (Paris: 1925).

Hanoteau, Jean, and Emile Bonnot. *Bibliographie des historiques des regiments françaises* (Paris: 1913).

Hardré, Jacques, ed. *Letters of Louvois, University of North Carolina Studies in the Romance Languages and Literatures*, no. 10 (Chapel Hill: 1949).

Hatton, Ragnhild. *Europe in the Age of Louis XIV* (New York: 1969).

Hatton, Ragnhild. "Louis XIV and his Fellow Monarchs," in John C. Rule, ed., *Louis XIV and the Craft of Kingship* (Columbus, OH: 1969), 155–95.

Hatton, Ragnhild, ed. *Louis XIV and Europe* (Columbus, OH: 1976).

Hennet, Léon. *Les milices et les troupes provinciales* (Paris: 1884).

"Histoire de l'armement française," special issue, *Revue Historique de l'armée* (June 1964).

Histoire de la fortification dans le pays de Thionville (Thionville: 1970).

Houdaille, J. "Les miliciens du poitevins et charentais en 1705," *Population*, numéro spécial (November 1975).

Hours, Henri. "Émeutes et émotions populaires dans les campagnes du Lyonnais au XVIIIe siècle," *Cahiers d'histoire*, 9 (1964).

Houtte, Hubert van. "Les conferences franco-espangnoles de Deynze," *Revue d'Histoire Moderne*, 2 (1927), 191–215.

Houtte, Hubert van. *Les Occupations etrangères en Belgique sous l'ancien régime*, 2 vols., *Recueil de Travaux Publiés par la faculté de Philosophie et Lettres de l'Université de Gand*, fasicule 62–63 (Ghent and Paris: 1930).

Hubscher, Ronald. *Histoire d'Amiens* (Toulouse: 1906).

Humbert. *La campagne d'Huxell, 1628* (1958).

Humbert, Jacques. *Une grande entreprise oubliée: les français en Savoie sous Louis XIII* (Paris: 1960).

Inventaire sommaire des Archives Départementales antérieurs a 1790. Ardèche. Archive Civiles, vol. 1 (Paris: 1877).

Isambert, François André et al., eds. *Recueil général des anciennes lois françaises, depuis l'an 420, jusqu'a la Révolution de 1789*, vol. 16 (Paris: 1829).

Jones, Colin. "The Welfare of the French Foot-Soldier," *History*, 65, no. 214 (June 1980), 193–213.

Jouan, Louis, and Ernest Picard. *L'artillerie française au XVIIIe siècle* (Paris: 1906).

Kaiser, David. *Politics & War: European Conflict from Phillip II to Hitler* (Cambridge, MA: 1990).

Kastner, Georges. *Les chants de l'armée française* (Paris: 1855).

Keegan, John. *The Face of Battle* (New York: 1976).

Keegan, John. *A History of Warfare* (New York: 1993).

Kellett, Anthony. *Combat Motivation* (Boston: 1982).

Kennett, Lee. *The French Armies in the Seven Years' War* (Durham, NC: 1967).

Kiernan, V. G. *The Duel in European History* (Oxford: 1988).

Kiernan, V. G. "Foreign Mercenaries and Absolute Monarchy" in Trevor Aston, ed., *Crisis in Europe, 1560–1660: Essays from Past and Present* (Garden City, NY: 1965), 117–40.

King, James E. *Science and Rationalism in the Government of Louis XIV* (Baltimore: 1949).

Klaits, Joseph. *Printed Propaganda Under Louis XIV* (Princeton: 1976).

Kleinman, Ruth. *Anne of Austria* (Columbus, OH: 1985).

Klein-Rebour, F. "Les femmes soldats à travers les ages," *Revue historique de l'armée*, 16 (1960), 3–20.

Knecht, Robert. *Richelieu* (Harlow, Essex: 1991).

Kroener, Bernard. "Die Entwicklung der Truppenstärken in den französischen Armeen zwischen 1635 end 1661," in Konrad Repgen, ed., *Forschungen und Quellen zur Geschichte des Dreissigjährigen Krieges* (Munster: 1981), 163–220.

Kroener, Bernard. *Les routes et les étapes. Die bersorgung der franzoschichen Armeen in Nordostfrankreich (1635–1661)*, 2 vols. (Munster: 1980).

Labrousse, Ernest, et al. *Histoire économique et sociale de la France*, vol. 2 (Paris: 1970).

Lachouque, Henri. *Aux armes citoyens: Les soldats de la Révolution* (Paris: 1969).

Lambin, Jean-Michel. *Quand le Nord devenait français* (Paris: 1980).

Lamont. *Les fonctions de tous les officiers de l'infanterie* (Paris: 1668).

Lamont. *Les fonctions de tous les officiers de l'infanterie*, vol. 2 (La Haye: 1693).

Landier, Patrick. "Guerre, violences, et société en France, 1635–1659," doctorat de troisième cycle, dissertation, Université de Paris IV, 1978.

Langer, Herbert. *The Thirty Years' War* (Poole, Dorset: 1978).

La Noue, François de. *Discours politiques et militaires* (Basle: 1587).

Laon, I. de Sieur d'Aigremont. *Practique et maximes de la guerre* (Paris: 1652).

La Valière. *Practique et maximes de la guerre* (1673).

La Valière. *Practique et maximes de la guerre . . . avec l'exercise general et militaire de l'infanterie du sieur d'Aigremont*, vol. 4 (La Haye: 1693).

Latreille, Albert. *L'oeuvre militaire de la Révolution: L'Armée et la nation à la fin de l'ancien régime: Les derniers ministres de la guerre de la monarchie* (Paris: 1914).

Lauerma, Matti, *L'artillerie de campagne française pendant les guerres de la Révolution* (Helsinki: 1956).

Lavisse, Ernest. *Louis XIV*, 2 vols. (Paris: 1978).

Lavisse, Ernest, and A. de Saint-Léger, A. Rébelliau, P. Sagnac. *Histoire de la France depuis les origines jusqu'à la Révolution*. E. Lavisse, ed. vol. 8, pt. 1 (Paris: 1908).

Lazard, P. *Vauban, 1633–1707* (Paris: 1934).

Lecat, Lucien. *Deux siècles d'histoire en Picardie* (Amiens: 1982).

Lecat, Lucien. *Histoire d'Abbeville* (Abbeville: 1972).

Le Moigne, François-Yves. *Histoire de Metz* (Toulouse: 1986).

Lemoine, Jean. *La Révolte dite du Papier Timbré ou des Bonnets Rouges en Bretagne en 1675* (Paris: 1898).

Lemonnier, Henry. *Histoire de France*. Ernest Lavisse, ed. vol. 5, part 1, *Les guerres d'Italie, 1492–1547* (Paris: 1903).

Lemonnier, Henry. *La lutte contre la maison d'Autriche: La France sous Henri II, Histoire de France*. E. Lavisse, ed. vol. 5, pt. 2 (Paris: 1904).

Léonard, Emile G. *L'Armée et ses problèmes au XVIIIe siècle* (Paris: 1958)

Lescan, André. "Les manoeuvres de Catinat et Berwick autour de L'Oisans, 1690–1710," *Revue historique de l'armée*, no. 3 (1968).

Levy, Jack S. *War in the Modern Great Power System, 1495–1975* (Lexington, KY: 1983).

Livet, Georges. *L'Equilibre européen de la fin du XVe à la fin du XVIIIe siècle* (Paris: 1976).

Livet, Georges. "International Relations and the Role of France, 1648–60," *New Cambridge Modern History*, vol. 4 (Cambridge: 1971), 411–34.

Loirette, Francis. "Un intendant de Guyenne avant la Fronde: Jean de Lauson (1641–1648)," *Bulletin philologique et historique, Comité des travaux historiques et scientifiques. Section de philologie et d'histoire* (1957), 433–61.

Lossky, Andrew. "France in the System of Europe in the Seventeenth Century," *Proceedings of the Western Society for French History* 1 (Flagstaff, AZ: 1974), 32–48.

Lossky, Andrew. "International Relations in Europe," in *The New Cambridge Modern History*, vol. 6 (London: 1970), 154–92.

Lossky, Andrew. *Louis XIV and the French Monarchy* (New Brunswick, NJ: 1994).

Lossky, Andrew. "Some Problems of Tracing the Intellectual Development of Louis XIV," in John Rule, ed., *Louis XIV and the Craft of Kingship* (Columbus, OH: 1969), 317–44.

Lostelnau, de. *Le maréchal de bataille* (Paris: 1647).

Lot, Ferdinand. *Recherches sur les effectifs des armées françaises des Guerres d'Italie aux Guerres de Religion, 1494–1562* (Paris: 1962).

Lottin, Alain. *Les grandes batailles du nord* (Paris: 1984).

Lottin, Alain. *Histoire de Boulogne-sur-mer* (Lille: 1983).

Louis XIII. *A Declaration made and published by the King of France, Whereby the Princes, Dukes, and Barons Therin named are all proclaymed Traytors* (1620).

Louis XIII. *The French Kings Declaration against the Dukes of Vendosme and Mayenne,* (London: 1617).

Louis XIV. *Mémoires de Louis XIV pour l'instruction du dauphin*. Charles Dreyss, ed. 2 vols. (Paris: 1860).

Louis XIV. *Oeuvres de Louis XIV*. Philippe Grimoard and Philippe Grouvelle, eds. 6 vols. (Paris: 1806).

Louvois, François-Michel Le Tellier, marquis de. *Testament politique* (Cologne: 1695).

Lynn, John A. *Bayonets of the Republic: Motivation and Tactics in the Army of Revolutionary France, 1791–94* (Boulder, CO: 1996, orig. ed. pub. 1984).

Lynn, John A. "The Evolution of Army Style in the Modern West, 800–2000," *International History Review*, 18, no. 3 (August 1996), 505–45.

Lynn, John A. "Food, Funds, and Fortresses: Resource Mobilization and Positional Warfare in the Wars of Louis XIV," in John A. Lynn, ed., *Feeding Mars: Logistics in Western Warfare from the Middle Ages to the Present* (Boulder, CO: 1993), 137–160.

Lynn, John A. "The Growth of the French Army during the Seventeenth Century," *Armed Forces and Society*, summer 1980, 568–85.

Lynn, John A. "The Pattern of Army Growth, 1445–1945," in John A. Lynn, ed., *Tools of War* (Urbana, IL: 1990), 1–27.

Lynn, John A. "The Publications of the *Section historique*, 1899–1915," *Military Affairs* (April 1973), 56–59.

Lynn, John A. "Recalculating French Army Growth During the *Grand siècle*, 1610–1715," *French Historical Studies*, vol. 18, no. 4 (Fall: 1994), 881–906. This article is reprinted in somewhat expanded form in Cliff Rogers, ed., *The Military Revolution Debate: Readings on the Military Transformation of Early Modern Europe* (Boulder, CO: 1995), 117–47.

Lynn, John A. "Soldiers on the Rampage," *MHQ, the Quarterly Journal of Military History*, winter 1991, 92–101.

Lynn, John A. "The Strange Case of the Maiden Soldier of Picardy," *MHQ, The Quarterly Journal of Military History*, spring 1990, 54–56.

Lynn, John A. "Tactical Evolution in the French Army, 1560–1660," *French Historical Studies*, fall 1985, 176–91.

Lynn, John A., ed. *Tools of War* (Urbana, IL: 1990).

Lynn, John A. "The *trace italienne* and the Growth of Armies: The French Case," *Journal of Military History* (July 1991), 297–330. This article is reprinted in Cliff Rogers, ed., *The Military Revolution Debate: Readings on the Military Transformation of Early Modern Europe* (Boulder, CO: 1995).

Lynn, John A., and George Satterfield. *A Guide to Sources in Early Modern European Military History in Midwestern Research Libraries*, 2d ed. (Urbana, IL: 1994).

Maintenon. *Lettres de madame de Maintenon*, vol. 5 (Amsterdam: 1756).

Mallet, Allain. *Les travaux de Mars* (Amsterdam: 1672).

Mallet, Allain. *Les travaux de Mars* (Paris: 1684).

Mallet, Jean Roland de. *Comptes rendus de l'administration des finances du royaume de France* (London: 1789).

Manéjol, Jean H. *Histoire de France*, ed. Ernest Lavisse, vol. 6, part 2, *Henri IV et Louis XIII* (Paris: 1905).

Manucy, Albert. *Artillery Through the Ages* (1949).

Margo, Robert A., and Richard H. Steckel. "Heights of Native-Born Whites During the Antebellum Period," *Journal of Economic History*, 43, no. 1 (March 1983), 167–74.

Marion, Marcel. *Dictionnaire des institutions de la France aux XVIIe et XVIIIe siècles* (Paris: 1923. Reprint Paris: 1972).

Marshall, S. L. A. *Men Against Fire* (1947; repr. Gloucester, MA: 1978).

Martin, Henri. *The Age of Louis XIV*, vol. 2 (Boston: 1865).

Martin, Ronald. "The Army of Louis XIV," in Paul Sonnino, ed., *The Reign of Louis XIV* (Atlantic Highlands, NJ: 1990), 111–26.

Martin, Ronald. "The Marquis de Chamlay, Friend and Confidential Advisor to Louis XIV: The Early Years, 1650–1691," Ph.D. dissertation, University of California at Santa Barbara, 1972.

Masse, Claude François, and Claude-Félix. *Les ingénieurs géographes* (La Rochelle: 1979).

Massiac, lieutenant de. *Mémoires de ce qi s'est passé de plus considerable pendant le guerre depuis l'an 1688 jusqu'en 1698* (Paris: 1698).

Mazarin, Jules. *Lettres du cardinal Mazarin*. P. Chéruel and G. d'Avenel, eds. vols. 6–9 (Paris: 1890–1906).

McNeill, William H. *The Pursuit of Power* (Chicago: 1982).

Mears, John. "The Emergence of the Standing Professional Army in Seventeenth Century Europe," *Social Science Quarterly* (June 1969), 106–15.

Melegari, Vezio. *The Great Military Sieges* (New York: 1972).

Mention, Léon. *L'Armée de l'ancien régime de Louis XIV à la Révolution* (Paris: 1900).

Mercur, James. *Attack of Fortified Places* (New York: 1894).

Mesnard, Jean. "Conclusion," *XVII siècle*, 37 (1985), 307–15.

Meyer, Jean. " 'De la guerre' au XVIIe siècle," *XVII siècle*, 37 (1985), 267–90.

Mezeray, François Eudes de. *Histoire de la mère et du fils* (Amsterdam: 1730).

Michaux, Monique. "De quelques ouvrages anciens en fait d'art militaire," *Revue historiques de l'armée* (May 1959).

Michel, Georges. *Histoire de Vauban* (Paris: 1879).

Mignet, F. A. M. *Négotiation relatives à la succession d'Espagne sous Louis XIV*, 4 vols. (Paris: 1835–42).

Miller, John, ed. *Absolutism in Seventeenth-Century Europe* (Houndmills, Basingstoke, Hampshire: 1990).

Mitford, Nancy. *The Sun King* (London: 1966).

Montalembert, Marc René. *La fortification perpendiculare*, vol. 1 (Paris: 1776).

Montecuccoli, Raimondo. *Mémoires de Montecuculi* or *Principes de l'art militaire en général* (Paris: 1712).

Montecuccoli, Raimondo. *Sulle Battaglie*, trans. in Thomas M. Barker, *The Military Intellectual and Battle: Raimondo Montecuccoli and the Thirty Years' War* (New York: 1975).

Moote, A. Lloyd. *Louis XIII, The Just* (Berkeley: 1989).

Moreau de Brasey. *Journal de la campagne de Piémont, sous le commandement de M. de Catinat, année 1690* (Paris: 1691).

Mousnier, Roland. *Colloque Turenne*.

Mousnier, Roland. "The Fronde," in *Preconditions of Revolution in Early Modern Europe*. Robert Forster and Jack Greene, eds. (Baltimore: 1970), 131–60.

Mousnier, Roland. *The Institutions of France under the Absolute Monarchy, 1598–1789*, 2 vols. (Chicago: 1979–84).

Mulard, Nelly. *Calais et les secrets de l'histoire* (1968).

Navareau, André Eugène. *Le logement et les ustensiles des gens de guerre de 1439–1789* (Poitiers: 1924).

Nef, John U. *War and Human Progress* (Cambridge, MA: 1950).

Noailles, Adrien Maurice. *Mémoire politiques et militaires pour servire à l'histoire de Louis XIV et Louis XV*, 6 vols. (Paris: 1777).

Noailles, duc de. *Mémoires du duc de Noailles*, 3 vols. in A. Petitôt and Monmerqué, eds. *Collection des mémoires relatifs à l'histoire de France*, vols. 71–73 (Paris: 1828).

Nodot, François. *Le munitionnaire des armées de France* (Paris: 1697).

Nosworthy, Brent. *The Anatomy of Victory: Battle Tactics, 1689–1763* (New York: 1990).

Oman, Charles. *The Art of War in the Sixteenth Century* (London: 1937).

Ordonnances militaires du roy de France reduites en practique, et appliquées au detail du service. Ouvrage très utile à tous les gens de guerre. Il contient l'explication des fonctions militaires, & un abregé des XV tomes d'ordonnances du roi, disposée selon l'ordre des matières, 2 vols. (Luxembourg: 1734–35).

Orrery, Roger, earl of. *A Treatise on the Art of War* (London: 1677).

Ostwald, Jamel. "The Failure of 'Strategy of Annihilation': Battle and Fortresses in the War of the Spanish Succession," M.A. thesis, Ohio State University, 1995.

Pagan, comte de. *Les fortifications du comte de Pagan* (Paris: 1645).

Pagès, Georges. *La Guerre de trente ans* (Paris: 1939).

Palmer, R. R. *Twelve Who Ruled* (Princeton: 1970).

Parent, Michel et Jacques Verroust. *Vauban* (Paris: 1971).

Paret, Peter. *Yorck and the Era of Prussian Reform, 1807–1815* (Princeton: 1966)

Paret, Peter, Gordon A. Craig, and Felix Gilbert, eds. *Makers of Modern Strategy: From Machiavelli to the Nuclear Age* (Princeton: 1986).

Parker, Geoffrey. *The Army of Flanders and the Spanish Road, 1567–1659: The Logistics of Spanish Victory and Defeat in the Low Countries Wars* (Cambridge: 1972).

Parker, Geoffrey. "The 'Military Revolution' 1560–1660 – A Myth?" *Journal of Modern History*, 48 (June 1976), 195–214. This article is reprinted in Cliff Rogers, ed., *The Military Revolution Debate: Readings on the Military Transformation of Early Modern Europe* (Boulder, CO: 1995), 37–54.

Parker, Geoffrey. *The Military Revolution: Military Innovation and the Rise of the West, 1500–1800* (Cambridge: 1988).

Parrott, David. "The Administration of the French Army During the Ministry of Cardinal Richelieu," Ph.D. dissertation, Oxford University, 1985.

Parrott, David. "Strategy and Tactics in the Thirty Years' War: The 'Military Revolution,'" *Militärgeschichtliche Mitteilungen*, XVIII, 2 (1985), 7–25. This article is reprinted in Cliff Rogers, ed., *The Military Revolution Debate: Readings on the Military Transformation of Early Modern Europe* (Boulder, CO: 1995).

Pascal, Adrien. *Histoire de l'Armée*, vol. 2 (Paris: 1847).

Paul, Pierre. *Denain* (Paris: 1963).

Pellisson-Fontainier, Paul. *Lettres historiques de monsieur Pellisson*, 3 vols. (Paris: 1729).

Pepper, Simon, and Nicholas Adams. *Firearms and Fortifications* (Chicago: 1986).

Perjés, G. "Army Provisioning, Logistics and Strategy in the Second Half of the 17th Century," *Acta Historica Academiae Scientiarum Hungaricae*, 16, nr. 1–2 (1970), 1–52.

Pernot, Michel. *Les guerres de réligion, 1559–1598* (Paris: 1987).

Pérouse, G. *Les communes et les institutions de l'ancienne Savoie* (Chambérry: 1911).

Picard, Ernest, and Louis Jouan. *L'artillerie française au XVIIIe siècle* (Paris: 1906).

Picavet, Camille-Georges. *Les dernières années de Turenne 1660–1675* (Paris: 1914).

Picavet, Camille-Georges. *La diplomatie française au temps de Louis XIV (1661–1715): institutions, moeurs et coutumes* (Paris: 1930).

Picavet, Camille-Georges. *Documents biographiques sur Turenne 1611–1675* (Paris: 1914).

Pichat, H. "Les armées de Louis XIV en 1674," *Revue d'histoire de l'armée* (1910), 1–28.

Pichon, J. *Les femmes soldats* (Limoges: 1898).

Pinard. *Chronologie historique militaire* (1760–66).

Pohler, Johan. *Bibliotheca-historico-militaris*, 4 vols. (Leipzig: 1887–99).

Pontis, Louis de. *Mémoires*, in M. Petitot, ed., *Collection complète des mémoires relatifs à l'histoire de France*, vols. 31–32 (Paris: 1824).

Pontis, Louis de (by Thomas du Fossé). *Mémoires*, in Joseph Michaud and Jean Poujoulat, eds., *Nouvelle collection des mémoires pour servir à l'histoire de France*, vol. 20 (Paris: 1866).

Porchnev, Boris. *Les Soulèvements Populaires en France de 1623 a 1648* (Paris: 1963).

Porter, Bruce D. *War and the Rise of the State* (New York: 1994).

Potter, David. *War and Government in the French Provinces: Picardy 1470–1560* (Cambridge: 1993).

Préchac, Jean. *L'héroine mousquetaire* (Paris: 1679).

Prémoy, Geneviève. *Histoire de la dragone, contenant les actions militaires et les aventures de Genevieve Prémoy sous nom du chevalier Balthazar* (Brussels: 1721).

Primi Visconti, Jean-Baptiste. *Mémoires sur la cour de Louis XIV, 1673–1681*, Jean-François Solnon, ed. (Paris: 1988).

Prinsterer, Guillaume Groen van, ed. *Archives ou correspondance inédite de la maison d'Orange Nassau*, series 3, vol. 3 (Leyden: 1909).

Puységur, Jacques de Chastenet de. *Mémoires de messire Jacques de Chastenet, chevalier, seigneur de Puységur, colonel du régiment de Piedmont, et lieutenant général des armées du Roy*, 2 vols. (Paris: 1690).

Puységur, Jacques-François de Chastenet de. *Art de la guerre par principes et par règles*, 2 vols. (Paris: 1748).

Quimby, Robert S. *The Background of Napoleonic Warfare* (New York: 1957).

Quincy, marquis de. *Histoire militaire de Louis le Grand roi de France*, 7 vols. (La Haye: 1727).

Ranum, Orest. *Richelieu and the Councillors of Louis XIII* (Oxford: 1963).

Rasler, Karen A., and William R. Thompson. *War and State Making: The Shaping of the Global Powers* (Boston: 1989).

Raumer, Kurt von. *Die Zerstorung der Pfalz von 1689* (Munich: 1930).

Rebelliau, Alfred. *Vauban* (Paris: 1962).

Reboul, F. "Des croisades à la Révolution," in Gabriel Hanoteau, ed., *Histoire de la nation française*, vol. 7, *Histoire militaire et navale*, pt. 1 (Paris: 1925), 105–576.

Reboul, F. *La vie au dix-huitième siècle: L'armée* (Paris: 1931).

Redlich, Fritz. "Contributions in the Thirty Years' War," *Economic History Review*, series 2, 12 (1959–60), 247–54.

Redlich, Fritz. *The German Military Enterprizer and his Workforce, 13th to 17th Centuries, Vieteljahrschrift fur sozial- und Virtschaftsgeschite*, Beihelft XLVII, 2 vols. (Wiesbaden: 1964).

Redlich, Fritz. *De praeda militari: Looting and Booty 1500–1815*, supplement 39, *Vieteljahrschrift für Sozial- und Wirtschaftsgeschichte* (Wiesbaden: 1956).

Renaud, Henri, ed. "Correspondance relative aux provinces d'Aunis, Saintonge, Angoumois et Poitou entre l'intendant François de Villemontée, le chancelier Séguier, le commandeur de La Porte, Jean de Lauson et autres, 1633–1648," *Archives historiques de la Saintonge et de l'Aunis*, 7 (1880), 285–350.

Richelieu, Armand Jean du Plessis, cardinal and duc de. *Lettres, instructions diplomatiques et piers d'état du cardinal de Richelieu*. Avenel, ed., 8 vols. (Paris: 1853–77).

Richelieu, Armand Jean du Plessis, cardinal and duc de. *Testament politique*. Louis André, ed. (Paris: 1947).

Roberts, Michael. *Gustavus Adolphus*, 2 vols. (London: 1958).

Roberts, Michael. *The Military Revolution, 1560–1660* (Belfast: 1956).

Rochas d'Aiglun, Albert. *Vauban, sa famille et ses écrits*, 2 vols. (Paris: 1910).

Roche, Michel. *Histoire de Douai* (Westhoek: 1985).

Rochfoucauld. *Maximes*, 5 ed. (1678).

Rocolle, Pierre. *2000 ans de fortifications française*, 2 vols. (Paris: 1973).

Rogers, Cliff, ed. *The Military Revolution Debate: Readings on the Military Transformation of Early Modern Europe* (Boulder, CO: 1995).

Rogers, H. C. B. *The Mounted Troops of the British Army, 1066–1945* (London: 1959).

Roget, A. *L'invasion de la France et le siège de Saint Diger, 1544* (Paris: 1910).

Rohan, duc de. *Le parfait capitaine* (Paris: 1636).

Rohan, duc de. *A Treatise of the Interest of the Princes and States of Christendom* (Paris: 1640).

Romain, Charles Armand (pseud. for Armand Charmain). *Les guerrières* (Paris: 1931).

Romain, Charles Armand (pseud. for Armand Charmain). *Louis XIII, un grand roi malconnu* (Paris: 1934).

Rosen, Howard. "The Systeme Gribeauval: A Study of Technological Development and Institutional Change in Eighteenth-Century France," Ph.D. dissertation, University of Chicago, 1981.

Rouche, Michel. *Histoire de Douai* (Westhoek: 1985).

Rousset, Camille. *Histoire de Louvois*, 4 vols. (Paris: 1862–64).

Roux, Antoine de, and Nicolas Faucherre. *Les plans relief des places du roy* (Paris: 1989).

Roy, Jules J. F. *Histoire du grand Condé* (1879).

Roy, Jules J. F. *Turenne, sa vie it les institutions militaires de son temps* (Paris: 1884).

Rozet, A. *L'invasion de la France et le siege de Saint Diger, 1544* (Paris: 1910).

Rule, John C. "Colbert de Torcy, an Emergent Bureaucracy, and the Formulation of French Foreign Policy: 1698–1715," in Ragnhild Hatton, ed., *Louis XIV and Europe* (Columbus, OH: 1976), 261–88.

Rule, John C., ed. *Louis XIV and the Craft of Kingship* (Columbus, OH: 1969).

Saint-Remy, Pierre Surirez de. *Mémoires d'artillerie*, 2 vols. (Paris: 1697).

Saint-Simon, Louis de Rouvroy, duc de. *Mémoires*. A. de Boislisle, ed., 42 vols. (Paris: 1879–1930).

Saint-Simon, Louis de Rouvroy, duc de. *Mémoires*. Gonzague Truc, ed., 7 vols. (Paris: 1953–61).

Saxe, Maurice Comte de. *Mes reveries ou mémoires sur l'art de la guerre* (The Hague: 1756).

Saxe, Maurice de. *My Reveries on the Art of War*, in Thomas R. Phillip, ed., *Roots of Strategy* (Harrisburg, PA: 1940).

Schmidt, Charles. "Le rôle et les attributions d'un intendant des finances aux armées, Sublet de Noyers, de 1632 à 1636," *Revue moderne et contemporaine*, 2 (1900–1), 156–75.

Ségur, Pierre, marquis de. *Le maréchal de Luxembourg et le prince d'orange, 1668–1678* (Paris: 1902).

Ségur, Pierre, marquis de. *Le tapisseur de Notre Dame, 1678–1695* (Paris: 1903).

Servan, Joseph, and Philippe Grimoard. *Recherches sur la force de l'armée française, depuis Henri IV jusqu'à la fin de 1806* (Paris: 1806).

Sévigné, Marie. *Lettres de madame de Sévigné*. Gault-de-Saint-Germain, ed., 12 vols. (Paris: 1823).

Sicard, François. *Histoire de l'armée et de tous les regiments avec des tableau synoptiques réprésentant l'organization de l'armée aux diverses époques*, 5 vols. (Paris: 1847–58).

Sicard, François. *Histoire des institutions militaires des français*, 4 vols. (Paris: 1834).

Sidney, Sir Philip. *Sidney Papers, 1611–1626*, vol. 5 of *Report on the Manuscripts of the Right Honourable Viscount de l'Isle*. William Shaw and G. Dyfnallt Owen, eds. (1962).

Silberner, Edmond. *La guerre dans la pensée économique du XVI au XVIII siècle* (Paris: 1939).

Sirot, Claude de Le Touf, baron de. *Mémoires*, 2 vols. (Paris: 1683).

Sonnino, Paul. *Louis XIV and the Origins of the Dutch War* (Cambridge: 1989).

Sonnino, Paul. "The Origins of Louis XIV's Wars," in Jeremy Black, ed., *The Origins of War in Early Modern Europe* (Edinburgh: 1987), 112–31.

Sourches. *Mémoires du marquis de Sources*, vols. 11–12 (Paris: 1891–92).

Souvigny, Jean de Gagnières, comte de. *Mémoires du Comte de Souvigny, Lieutenant Général des Armées du Roi*, vol. 1 (Paris: 1906).

Stapleton, John M. "Importing the Military Revolution: William III, the Glorious Revolution, and the Rise of the Standing Army in Britain, 1688–1712," Master's thesis, Ohio State University, 1994.

Steriens, Philip H. *Artillery Through the Ages* (New York: 1965).

Stoye, J. W. "Armies and Navies: Soldiers and Civilians," in *New Cambridge Modern History*, vol. 6 (Cambridge: 1970), 762–90.

Sturgill, Claude C. "Changing Garrisons: The French System of Etapes," *Canadian Journal of History*, 20, #2 (August 1985), 193–201.

Sturgill, Claude C. *Les commissaires des guerres et l'administration de l'armée française, 1715–1730* (Vincennes: 1985).

Sturgill, Claude C. *Marshal Villars and the War of the Spanish Succession* (Lexington, KY: 1965).

Sully. *Memoirs*, trans. Charlotte Lennox, 5 vols. (Philadelphia: 1817).

Sully. *Mémoires de Maximillien de Béthune duc de Sully*, 3 vols. (London: 1747).

Sully. *Mémoires des sages et royales oeconomies*. Petitot, ed. *Collection des Mémoires relatifs à l'histoire de France*, vols. 8 and 9 (Paris: 1821).

Susane, Louis. *Histoire de la cavalerie française*, 3 vols. (Paris: 1874).

Susane, Louis. *Histoire de l'infanterie française*, 5 vols. (Paris: 1876).

Symcox, Geoffrey. "Louis XIV and the Outbreak of the Nine Years' War," in Ragnhild Hatton, ed., *Louis XIV and Europe* (Columbus, OH: 1976), 179–212.

Tallett, Frank. "Church, State, War and Finance in Early-Modern France," *Renaissance and Modern Studies*, 36 (1993), 15–35.

Tallett, Frank. *War and Society in Early Modern Europe* (London: 1992).

Talon, Omer. *Mémoires*, in Michaud and Poujalat (Paris: 1839).

Tapié, Victor. "Louis XIV's Methods in Foreign Policy," in Ragnhild Hatton, ed., *Louis XIV and Europe* (Columbus, OH: 1976), 3–15.

Tavannes, Gaspard de Saulx, Seigneur de. *La vie de Gaspard de Saulx, Seigneur de Tavannes* in *Collection complète des mémoires relatifs à l'histoire de France*. M. Petitot, ed., vols. 23–25 (Paris: 1822).

Tessé. *Mémoires et lettres du marechal Tessé*, 2 vols. (Paris: 1806).

Thomas, Henri. *Droit romain des requisitions militarires et du logement des gens de guerre chez les Romains, sous la république et sous l'empire. Droit français des requisitions militaires et du logement des gens de guerre en France, depuis le Ve siècle jusqu'en 1789* (Paris: 1884).

Thompson, I. A. A. *War and government in Habsburg Spain, 1560–1620* (London: 1976).

Tilly, Charles. *Coercion, Capital, and the European States, AD 990–1990* (Oxford: 1990).

Tilly, Charles. *The Contentious French* (Cambridge, MA: 1986).

Tilly, Charles, ed. *The Formation of National States in Western Europe* (Princeton: 1975).

Torcy. *Mémoires du marquis de Torcy*, in A. Petitôt and Monmerqué, *Collection des mémoires relatifs à l'histoire de France*, ser. 2, vols. 67 and 68 (Paris: 1828).

Tranchant, Alfred and Jules Ladimir. *Les femmes militaires de la France* (Paris: 1866).

Trenard, Louis. *Histoire de Cambrai* (Lille: 1982).

Trotter, Ben Scott. "Marshal Vauban and the Administration of Fortifications under Louis XIV (to 1691)," Ph.D. dissertation, Ohio State University, 1993.

Tuetey, Louis. *Les officiers de l'ancien régime. Nobles et roturiers* (Paris: 1908).

Turenne. *Mémoires de Turenne* (Paris: 1872).

Turenne et l'art militaire (Paris: 1975).

Vaissète, Jean-Joseph. *Histoire générale du Languedoc*, 15 vols. (Toulouse: 1874–92).

Van Creveld, Martin. *Command in War* (Cambridge. MA: 1985).

Van Creveld, Martin. *Supplying War: Logistics from Wallenstein to Patton* (Cambridge: 1977).

Van Creveld, Martin. *Technology and War* (New York: 1989).

Vauban, Sébastien le Prestre de. *De l'attaque et de la défense des places* (The Hague: 1737).

Vauban, Sébastien le Prestre de. *A Manual of Siegecraft and Fortification*, trans. G.A. Rothrock (Ann Arbor: 1968).

Vauban, Sébastien le Prestre de. *Mémoire sur les camps retranchés* (1696).

Vauban, Sébastien le Prestre de. *Oeuvres de M. de Vauban*, 3 vols. (Amsterdam and Liepzig: 1771).

Vauban, Sébastien le Prestre de. *Oisivetés de M. de Vauban*, 3 vols. (Paris: 1842–46).

Vault, Francois, and Jean Pelet, eds. *Mémoires militaires relatifs à la succession d'Espagne*, 11 vols (Paris: 1835–62).

Vaux de Folletier, F. de. *Le siège de la Rochelle* (Paris: 1931).

Verley, André. *Boulogne-sur-mer à travers les ages*, 3 vols. (Paris: 1978).

Villars, Claude Louis Hector. *Mémoires du maréchal de Villars*. Vogüé, ed., 5 vols. (Paris: 1884–95).

Wallerstein, Immanuel. "France: A Special Case? A World-Systems Perspective," in E. D. Genovese and L. Hochberg, eds., *Geographic Perspectives in History* (New York: 1969), 144–57.

Weigley, Russell F. *The Age of Battles: The Quest for Decisive Warfare from Breitenfeld to Waterloo* (Bloomington, IN: 1991).

Westbrook, Steven D. "The Potential for Military Disintegration," *Combat Effectiveness: Cohesion, Stress, and the Volunteer Military*. Sam C. Sarkesian, ed. (Beverly Hills, CA: 1980), 244–78.

Weygand, Maxime. *Histoire de l'armée française* (Paris: 1938).

Wijn, J. W. "Military Forces and Warfare, 1610–1648," in *New Cambridge Modern History*, vol. 4 (Cambridge: 1971), 202–25.

Williams, H. Noel. *Henri II* (New York: 1910).

Wolf, John B. *The Emergence of the Great Powers, 1685–1715* (New York: 1962).

Wolf, John B. *Louis XIV* (New York: 1968).

Woloch, Isser. *The French Veteran* (Chapel Hill: 1979).

Wood, James B. "The Royal Army During the Early Wars of Religion, 1559–1576," in Mack P. Holt, ed., *Society & Institutions in Early Modern France* (Athens, GA: 1991), 1–35.

Wright, John W. "Sieges and Customs of War at the Opening of the Eighteenth Century," *American Historical Review*, 39 (1934), 643–44.

Wyatt-Brown, Bertram. *Honor and Violence in the Old South* (Oxford: 1986).

Zeller, Berthold. *Louis XIII, Marie de Médicis, Chef du Conseil: États Généraux. Marriage du Roi. Le Prince de Condé, 1614–1616* (Paris: 1898).

Zeller, Gaston. *Aspects de la Politique francaise sous l'ancien régime* (Paris: 1964).

Zeller, Gaston. "French Diplomacy and Foreign Policy in their European Setting," in *New Cambridge Modern History*, vol. 5 (London: 1970), 198–221.

Zeller, Gaston. *Les institutions de la France au XIVe siècle* (Paris: 1948).

Zeller, Gaston. "La monarchie d'ancien régime et les frontières naturelles," *Revue d'histoire moderne*, 8 (1933), 305–33.

Zeller, Gaston. *L'organization défensive des frontières du nord et de l'est au XVIIe siècle* (Paris: 1928).

Zeller, Gaston. *La siège de Metz par Chalres-Quint* (Nancy: 1943).

Zeller, Gaston. *Les temps modernes*, vol. 1 *De Christophe Colombe à Cromwell* and vol. 2, *De Louis XIV a 1789*, in Renouvin, Pierre, ed., *Histoire des relations internationales* (Paris: 1953).

Index